THE WORLD'S BEST

The Ultimate Book
For The International Traveler

Edited by
Kathleen Peddicord

Agora Inc.
824 E. Baltimore St.
Baltimore, MD 21202

THE WORLD'S BEST

Publisher: William Bonner
Editor: Kathleen Peddicord
Editorial Assistant: Siri Lise Holland
Art Director: Alex Nosevich
Research Assistants: Stephanie Dawley, Ann Perrelli, Chris Hawley, and Donna Robinson
Proofreaders: Ken Danz and Chapin Clark

Contributing Writers: Eddy Starr Ancinas, Karen Arrigoni, David Biemesderfer, Sylvia Ann Blishak, Victor Block, Thomas Booth, Peggy Cannam, Janie Smith Choice, Audrey Smith Fields, Cynthia Foster, Robert C. Gray, Pam Grout, Steenie Harvey, Frank Korn, Kostadin Kostadinov, Cecil Kuhne, Joseph Leach, Jane Lears, Marcia Levin, Paul Lewis, Raphael Lewis, Chris Lizza, Patt Moratti, Michael Moynihan, Mark Mussari, Marlene Nadle, Jane Parker, Lora Price, Mary Reed, A.M. Reynolds, Ellen Roblou, Thomas Rothwell, Bill Shafer, Bill Strubbe, Lin Sutherland, Warren Trabant, Penny Visman, Patricia Welch, and Ken Wilcox

Special thanks to Christoph Amberger, Amanda Blake, Steenie Harvey, Deeba Jaffries, Kostadin Kostadinov, Jane Lears, Marcia Levin, Vivian Lewis, and James Ward

Cover Illustration: *Allies Day, May 1917,* 1917, by Childe Hassam (1859-1935). Courtesy of the National Gallery of Art, Washington, D.C.

ISBN # 0-945332-33-5

Manufactured in the United States of America

Fifth Edition

Table of Contents

Section 1: The World's Best Destinations
Austria 1
Britain 13
France 43
Germany 73
Greece 101
Ireland 117
Isle of Man 127
Italy 131
Portugal 163
Scandinavia 175
Spain 193
Switzerland 219
Eastern Europe 231
Commonwealth of Independent States 249
China 253
Hong Kong and Macau 273
Japan 281
India 297
Southeast Asia 315
Africa 327
North Africa 347
Israel 369
Australia 383
New Zealand 399
The United States 411
Canada 463
Mexico 487
Brazil 507
Latin America 521
The Caribbean 535

Section 2: The World's Top Retirement Havens 549
Section 3: The World's Best Employment Opportunities 553
Section 4: The World's Best Education Opportunities 557
Section 5: The World's Best Real Estate Buys 559
Section 6: The 1992 Quality of Life Index 563
Section 7: Currency Exchange Chart 569
Index 571

Introduction

> Who that is busy to measure and compare
> The hevyn and erth an the worlde large
> Descrybynge the clymatis and folke of every place
> He is a fole and hath a grevous charge.
> —*Alexander Barclay,* The Ship of Folys, *1509*

Consider for a moment how much bigger the world is today than it was in 1986, when we published the first edition of *The World's Best*. How many more people there are. How many more places open to foreign travelers. How many more opportunities.

The original *World's Best* was 207 pages. The book you are now reading is more than 600 pages. And still I would caution that this new and expanded *World's Best* is far from comprehensive. We have tried to include bests in every corner of the globe...in Burma and Buenos Aires...in Nepal and Nova Scotia...in Washington, D.C. and Wales...but we realize that we have but skimmed the surface.

To create this new edition, we called upon our regular correspondents all over the world...more than 40 of them...and asked that they send us their personal world's bests— their picks for the world's best art museum, sunset, surfing, scuba diving, opera house, ski resort, canyon, champagne, castle, nightclub, island, garden, market, train ride, travel bargains, restaurants, cafés, and neighborhoods. To their lists we added our own superlatives, our choices for the biggest, the oldest, the smallest, the cheapest, the grandest, the prettiest, the tallest, the coziest, the most remarkable...

Thus, our *World's Best* is neither comprehensive nor objective. It has been compiled and edited within the limitations of our many biases and personal preferences.

What we have attempted to do is to draw forth for you a small sampling of the incredible wealth the world has to offer. We believe it is the best guide to the world's best you will find.

Of course, we hope you will agree.

Kathleen Peddicord
July 1992

P.S. Details, details.

Prices throughout the book are given in both the local currency and in U.S. dollars. The U.S. dollar price is given only as a guideline; it will be outdated by the time you read it. The same holds for the Currency Exchange Chart included at the end of the book. This is meant to give you an idea of the current exchange rates *as we go to press*. Remember, exchange rates fluctuate daily.

Furthermore, even local currency prices should be taken with a little grain of salt. Hotels and restaurants typically raise their prices every season. And inflation in some countries rages wildly.

One final note: In the interest of readability, we have spelled and punctuated non-English words according to American rules as nearly as possible.

The Best of Austria

Austria is Switzerland, speaking pure German and with history added.

—*J.E. Morpugo, 1963*

Austria—the land of Mozart, Strauss, Schubert, and Mahler—is the music capital of Europe. Instead of Muzak, classical music is played in elevators and offices. School children learn to play musical instruments at an early age. And Austria's yearly classical music festivals draw music lovers from around the globe.

Vienna alone supports four major symphony orchestras, two opera houses, and a host of theaters.

The world's best music festivals

The world's biggest and most famous music festival is the **Salzburg Festival**. Other important Austrian melomaniac delights include the **Haydn Festival** in Vienna and the **International Chamber Music Festival**. Tickets to the festivals are cheapest if you buy them in Austria. *Tickets for Events in Austria,* an information sheet, is available from the **Austrian National Tourist Office**, *500 Fifth Ave., New York, NY 10110; (212)944-6880.*

The best of Vienna

Vienna, the capital of the Hapsburg empire for 600 years, is one of the loveliest cities in the world. Magnificent palaces, theaters, and ballrooms from its days of glory remain throughout the city. The best way to explore Vienna is on foot, and the place to begin is the **Ringstrasse**, affectionately known as the Ring. One of the most beautiful avenues in the world, the Ring circles Vienna's old quarter. Most of Vienna's major sights line this shaded, treelined boulevard created by Emperor Franz Josef in December 1857.

You can walk the most picturesque section of the Ring in 45 minutes. (You can walk the entire Ring in two hours.) Begin at the 600-year-old Vienna University, near the Schottentor (Scottish Gate), and work your way around the Ring past the Stadtstheater, Europe's leading German-language theater; the neo-Gothic *Rathaus*; the Greek-style Parliament building; the Hofburg Palace; the Natural History Museum; and the Art History Museum. Then continue past the great opera house, the Imperial Hotel, and the town parks (as well as the airline bus terminal).

Vienna's number-one attraction

The most important sight in Vienna is the **Hofburg Palace** (known as the Hofburg),

1

once the winter residence of the Hapsburgs. Built in the 13th century, it has been embellished with every architectural style up to the modern day. More a city than a palace, it is now filled with government offices and museums.

The great entranceway to the Hofburg, the **Michaelertor**, is on the Michaelerplatz flanked by two grand fountains. On the left as you enter are the Imperial Apartments, where you can see the exercise equipment of Emperor Franz Josef's beautiful, reclusive wife Sisi, who was obsessed with her figure (more than 100 years before it was fashionable to be so).

Beyond the courtyard to the left is the gateway to the **Schweizerhof**, the original nucleus of the Hofburg. The 13th-century Schweizerhof was named for the Swiss Guards who watched over the ruler. The **Hofburgkapelle** (the chapel), where Mozart and Schubert played, is in the courtyard of the Schweizerhof. Today, the Vienna Boys' Choir sings here on Sundays during the summer and on holidays.

The Hofburg also contains the **Imperial Treasury**, where you can see the ancient Imperial Crown, encrusted with gems and dating back to A.D. 962; objects said to be made of unicorn horn; the elaborate cradle designed for Napoleon's son; and an agate bowl once thought to be the Holy Grail.

In the Augustinerkirche of the Hofburg is the **Chapel of St. George**. The crypt of the chapel contains 56 urns holding the hearts of the Hapsburgs. However, the chapel is not just a place of death. Maria Theresa and Francis of Lorraine were married here, as was Napoleon, by proxy, to Marie Louise.

The world's best horsemanship

The 400-year-old **Spanish Riding School**, located in the Hofburg, trains the noble white stallions that descend from the Spanish horses imported to Austria by Emperor Maximilian II in the 16th century. The horses dance to Viennese music, guided by expert riders wearing the traditional gold-buttoned brown uniform and gold-braided black hat.

Performances are held at the school most Sunday mornings at 10:45 a.m. and occasional Wednesday nights at 7 p.m. from March to June and September to December. It's difficult to get tickets; write six months in advance to the **Spanische Reitschule,** *Hofburg, A-1010 Vienna, Austria; tel. (43-1)533-9031.*

Gothic architecture at its best

The most important Gothic structure in Austria is the early 12th-century **St. Stephen's Cathedral.** Most of the Gothic touches were added in the 14th and 15th centuries. Climb the 345 steps to the top of the 450-foot church spire for a view of Vienna.

Inside, the black marble baroque altar is carved with illustrations of St. Stephen being stoned to death. The pulpit, designed by Anton Pilgram between 1510 and 1515, is carved with the heads of the early fathers of the church (Augustine, Gregory, Jerome, and Ambrose), as well as animals symbolizing the sins. Pilgram's own face peers out from the stairs.

Another masterpiece is contained in the theater: the tomb of Frederick III, created by Nikolaus of Leyden from 1467 to 1513. It is covered with carvings representing good and evil and topped with a marble statue of the emperor in his coronation robes.

Beneath the cathedral in the catacombs are the internal organs of 56 Hapsburgs minus the hearts, which are in the Church of the Augustin Friars. The bodies are in the Imperial Burial Vault at the Church of the Capuchin Friars. (The reason behind separating the body parts was if one church burned down, not all the Hapsburg remains would be lost.) You also can see the foundations of the original basilica, which burned in 1258.

Maria Theresa's favorite palace

Schönbrunn Palace, west of town, was the summer home of the Hapsburgs from

1695, when it was built, to 1918, when the last Hapsburg emperor, Charles I, abdicated. Maria Theresa ruled Austria from here while raising 16 children (Marie Antoinette was one of them) and fighting a war for her right to the throne. She redesigned the palace, and today it is much as she left it.

Often compared to Versailles, the Schönbrunn has 1,441 rooms (45 can be visited) and a vast baroque garden. The rococo palace theater, once the stage for Max Reinhardt's famous acting school, still houses a drama school. See the collection of royal carriages; the room where Napoleon stayed; the Millions Room, a highly ornate rococo room with gold-framed mirrors and Indian paintings; and the Great Gallery, with its frescoed ceilings. The Schönbrunn is also home to the oldest zoo in Europe, designed in 1752 by Jadot. It is probably the only baroque-style zoo in the world.

The favorite park of the Viennese

Prater Park, across the Danube River, is famous for its Ferris wheel, the Riesenrad. (The best view in Vienna is from the top.) The park was the royal hunting ground until 1766, when Emperor Joseph II opened it to the public.

The three-mile-long Hauptallee leads through the center of this garden-filled park. Lined with chestnut trees, this road is a great place to bike ride. Avoid the Krieau section, where thieves lurk.

Austria's greatest museum

If you see only one museum in Vienna, make it the **Kunsthistorisches Museum** (Art History Museum), which is across the Ringstrasse from the Hofburg. The greatest museum in Austria, it houses the paintings, sculptures, jewels, and bibelots collected by the Hapsburgs from 1500 to 1918.

The Kunsthistorisches Museum looks more like a palace than a museum, with its columned windows, enormous doors, broad central staircase, heraldic patterns, painted ceilings, and high cupola. Spread through seven buildings, it can be confusing, and the easiest way to see it is to ramble. Be sure to see the works of Pieter Brueghel the Elder in Gallery X, Dürer's works in Room 15, Giuseppe Arcimboldi's surreal works in Room 19, the Titians in Gallery I, the Tintorettos in Gallery II, the Raphaels in Gallery III, and Vermeer's works in Gallery VIII.

Vienna's other top museums

The **Österreichische Galerie** (Austrian Gallery), *Prinz Eugenstrasse 27*, contains modern, baroque, and church art. Located in the baroque Belvedere Palace, which was built by Hildebrandt between 1714 and 1723, the gallery is divided into three parts. Modern artworks are kept in the Upper Belvedere. Look for the works of Gustav Klimt (1862-1918), many of which are embellished with gold. The Lower Belvedere, where the beloved Prince Eugene (who protected his country from the Turks) once lived, is now the Museum of Austrian Baroque. The Orangerie houses the Museum of Medieval Austrian Art.

The **Graphische Sammlung Albertina** (Albertina Graphic Arts Collection), near Augustinerbastel, has the greatest collection of drawings by old masters in the world. The etchings of Dürer are the biggest attractions. Also here are works by Rubens, Fragonard, and other masters. (Reproductions are usually on display, for conservation reasons.)

The **Naturhistorisches Museum** (Natural History Museum), across the street, houses the world's oldest-known sculpture, the *Willendorf Venus*, created in Moravia about 2900 B.C. You'll find this ancient fertility figure in Room 11. The 5-inch limestone carving of a plump woman represents the mother goddess.

The **Akademie der Bildenen Kunste** (Academy of Fine Arts), near Getreidemarkt, is the respected art school that rejected the young Adolf Hitler after he failed the entrance exams. Some say this rejection fueled Hitler's anti-semitism. (He claimed Jewish professors kept him out.) Established in 1692, the academy houses the impressive triptych *The Last Judgment* by Hieronymus Bosch.

Neue Hofburg, a wing of the Hofburg, has a collection of Roman sculptures from the ancient city of Ephesus, which were found on the western coast of Turkey. The museum also houses musical instruments, including the pianos of Beethoven, Schubert, and Mahler.

The world's best boys' choir

The world-famous **Vienna Boys' Choir** performs every Sunday and religious holiday Jan. 1 through late June and mid-September through Dec. 31 in the Imperial Chapel of the Hofburg. High Mass begins at 9:15 a.m. The choir sings from the loft of the church and can be heard (although usually not seen) from all seats. Tickets ordered in advance cost from 50 to 217 Austrian schillings ($4.50 to $19.50). Order tickets (well in advance) from **Verwaltung der Hofmusikkapelle**, *Hofburg Schweizerhof, A-1010 Vienna, Austria; tel. (43-1)533-9927.* Tickets sometimes can be obtained at the last minute from local ticket agents. Get to the chapel early if you want a seat.

Austria's finest musical experience— and Europe's most beautiful opera house

The finest musical experience in Austria is a night at the **Staatsoper**, *Opernring 2; tel. (43-1)514-440.* This opera house is considered the most beautiful in Europe. The Vienna State Opera, one of the world's finest opera companies, is accompanied by the Vienna Philharmonic, one of the world's finest orchestras.

If you plan to attend the Vienna Opera in June, September, October, or May, order your tickets two to three months in advance from **Bundestheaterverband**, *Goethegasse 1,* or call the ticket information office at the tourist board, *tel. (43-1)515-33135.* Don't send money; you pay for the tickets when you arrive in Vienna. Take your passport and a copy of your confirmation letter when you pick them up. Do so no earlier than four days and no later than one day before each performance.

If you haven't ordered tickets in advance, go to the ticket office a few minutes before 9 a.m. to see what is available for the next four days. A bulletin board lists the performances. The cheapest tickets are sold at the ticket booth an hour before the performance.

Café culture at its coziest

The Viennese have gotten the café down to an art. Cafés have been a way of life in Vienna since the Turks retreated in 1683, leaving their sacks of coffee beans outside the walls of the city. People spend hours in cafés sipping coffee and talking or reading newspapers. (Cafés usually supply an assortment of international newspapers.)

Café Hawelka, *Dorotheergasse 6; tel. (43-1)512-8230,* is a dark café with black chairs, coatracks, seats upholstered in red and brown stripes, and heavy curtains. It draws students, old people, artists, and businessmen. Caricatures and drawings paper the walls of this café, once frequented by Trotsky and his contemporaries. Orson Welles came here to soak up atmosphere and prepare for his role in the film *The Third Man.* English and American newspapers are available. Try friendly Frau Hawelka's freshly baked *Buchteln* (a sort of doughnut) with a pear brandy.

Café Central, *Herrengasse 14; tel. (43-1)53-33-763,* is another cozy place that was an intellectual hangout at the turn of the century. It is decorated with frescoes, marble columns, and fountains and is in an enclosed courtyard. It serves the best *Topfenstrudel* in Vienna.

Café Schwarzenberg, *Kärntner Ring 17; tel. (43-1)512-73-93,* is a 120-year-old café with oak-paneled walls, mirrors, and a white tile ceiling. The pianist draws crowds. Café Schwarzenberg stays open until 6 a.m. during the Christmas season.

Vienna's best restaurants

Gottfried, *Untere Viaduktgasse 45, Maxgasse 3, A-1010; tel. (43-1)713-82-56*, awarded a Michelin star, specializes in fish and *Rohe Rinderfiletscheiben mit Rührei und Schalottenrahm* (raw beef with scrambled eggs and shallot-flavored whipped cream). Meals are 300 to 700 Austrian schillings ($27 to $62) per person. Make reservations in advance. The restaurant is closed Saturday and Sunday at lunch.

At **Hauswirth**, *Otto-Bauer-Gasse 20, A-1060; tel. (43-1)587-1261*, try the *Roulade von der Bachforelle* (baked trout), *Kalbsbriesrose mit Gänseleber im Blätterteig* (sweetbreads and goose liver in puff pastry), or *Rehrückenfilet in der Semmelhülle auf Wacholdersauce* (venison filet in juniper sauce). Meals are 300 to 600 Austrian schillings ($27 to $53). Reservations are required. The restaurant is closed on Sundays and on bank holidays.

Sacherstube, the Hotel Sacher's restaurant, *Philharmonikerstrasse 4; tel. (43-1)51-45-60*, is a pleasant surprise to those who assume that hotel restaurants are just so-so. The food is good, and the ambiance is inviting. Sacherstube is a favorite among operagoers who come to dine here after a show. Save room for the sinfully rich chocolate *Sachertorte* for dessert. Meals are 900 to 1,000 Austrian schillings ($80 to $90). Wear a tie and make reservations.

Zu den Drei Husaren, *Weihburggasse 4; tel. (43-1)51-21-092*, is the essence of old Vienna, serving superb hors d'oeuvres and desserts. Opened by three veteran hussars of Kaiser Franz Josef more than 50 years ago, the restaurant is decorated with stag horns, antique busts, Gobelin tapestries, and old portraits. It serves imaginative specialties, such as zucchini-garnished *Lammrücken in Strudelteig* (saddle of lamb in strudel pastry). Save room for the *Preiselbeeren* omelette with praline sabayon, the dessert to end all desserts. The restaurant's guest book, filled with the names of dignitaries, celebrities, and royalty, reads like a Who's Who. Dinners are 900 to 1,000 Austrian schillings ($80 to $90). Reservations are necessary.

The world's best pastries

Vienna's *Konditoreien* (pastry shops/cafés) produce the world's most delectable pastries—seductive arrays of tempting cakes, dripping with icing and whipped cream. Imagine a horseshoe-shaped *Kipferl* with shredded almonds or a *Schifferl*, shaped like a small boat, with tiny strawberries as passengers. Sweets lovers can be spotted on any afternoon lingering in *Konditoreien* over savory confections and a cup of coffee or tea.

Vienna's *Konditoreien* are as colorful and varied as the pastries they serve. **Demel's**, from its exalted position on the Kohlmarkt, calls itself *K.K. Hofzuckerbäckerei* (imperial and royal sugar baker). **Gerstner**, with its enviable position overlooking the Kaerntnerstrasse, also claims royal recognition: Emperor Franz Josef prophetically remarked more than 100 years ago, "Gerstner will have a great future." Another landmark, famous for its dainty china and delicious cakes, is **Heiner's**, with *Konditoreien* on both the Kaerntnerstrasse and the Wollzeile.

The best Viennese night life

The **U4**, *Schönbrunnerstrasse 222; tel. (43-1)85-83-07*, is our favorite nightclub in Vienna. Named because it is downstairs from an elevated subway stop on the U4 line, it is popular with a mature, sophisticated clientele.

Queen Anne, *Johannesgasse 12; tel. (43-1)512-0203*, is the most popular disco in town.

The best place to go for jazz is **Jazzland**, *I Franz-Josefs-Kai 29; tel. (43-1)533-25-75*, which has a smoky, funky atmosphere. Famous bands sometimes play here.

Popular among young professionals is the **Reiss Bar**, *Marco d'Aviano Gasse; tel. (43-1)512-7198*, near the Kärntnerstrasse. A wide selection of champagnes is served in this art-retro spot, where executives hobnob.

Griechenbeisl, *Fleischmarkt 11; tel. (43-1)533-1941,* claims to be the oldest tavern in Vienna, dating back to 1500. It has good local food and live music in the evenings. You can get Austrian wines and Pilsner beer on tap.

Vienna's best hotel

The **Imperial**, *Kärntner Ring 16, A-1015; tel. (43-1)501-100,* is a deluxe hotel located in a former palace. Built in 1869 for the duke of Württemberg, it was turned into a hotel in 1874. Wagner lived here for two months during the productions of his operas around the corner. Elizabeth Taylor stayed here with her three dogs and two cats, her mother, and her servants. Other noted guests have included Ormandy, Nureyev, Fonteyn, Domingo, and Carreras. During World War II, the Nazis used the Imperial as a guesthouse, and Hitler stayed here several times. When the war was over, the hotel served as the Russian headquarters.

Rooms at the Imperial are furnished with antiques and have wall safes. The magnificent central staircase of red, yellow, and black marble is supported by reclining gods and goddesses. Gobelin tapestries and portraits of Emperor Franz Josef and Empress Elizabeth hang on the walls. The hotel has a staff of 252 employees for the 160 rooms. Rooms are from 4,500 to 5,100 Austrian schillings ($411 to $457).

Three top-rung hotels

The **Bristol**, *Kärntner Ring 1; tel. (43-1)51-51-60,* is a luxurious, traditional hotel across the street from the opera house. It has large, beautifully furnished bedrooms and one of the best hotel bars in Europe. The Bristol's restaurant, the **Korso**, received a star from Michelin for its terrific food. A double room is 3,420 Austrian to 4,320 Austrian schillings ($306 to $387).

The **Sacher**, *Philharmonikerstrasse 4; tel. (43-1)51-45-60,* is a first-class place with lovely rooms that are furnished with antiques. Musicians and music lovers stay at this hotel, which is next door to the opera house. The concierge is said to be able to get tickets to almost any of Vienna's musical events—for a handsome fee, of course. A double room is 1,600 to 4,600 Austrian schillings ($143 to $412). Credit cards are not accepted.

The **Hotel im Palais Schwarzenberg**, *Schwarzenbergplatz 9; tel. (43-1)78-45-15,* is in a converted 17th-century baroque palace in a quiet location. Its restaurant has a Michelin star. Once a palace, it has ceiling frescoes and elaborate chandeliers and is furnished with antiques. Surrounded by a 37-acre park in the center of Vienna, the hotel has very good service. A double room is 3,750 to 4,800 Austrian schillings ($335 to $430).

The most romantic hotel in Austria

Less than an hour from Vienna, the **Schloss Dürnstein**, *A-3601 Dürnstein, Danube; tel. (43-2711)212,* presides over a wide curve of the Danube River. Located deep in the wine district of Wachau, this magnificent castle is surrounded by distinctive vine-clad hills, age-old ruins, and timeless picturesque villages with one-lane streets. According to legend, it was here that the imprisoned King Richard the Lionhearted was reunited with his faithful minstrel, who had sung his way across Europe searching for his master.

Also intriguing is the wine cellar (which can accommodate 8,000 "buckets" of wine), the arch-crossed cobbled courtyard, and the 33 chandeliered chambers fronting the Danube. A double room is 2,650 Austrian schillings ($237) a night.

Bargain hotels

Amadeus, *Wildpretmarkt 5, A-1010; tel. (43-1)63-87-38,* is a consistently good, centrally located hotel with private baths and telephones. It is closed Dec. 22 to Jan 6. A double room is 1,580 to 1,800 Austrian schillings ($141 to $161).

Kaiserin Elisabeth, *Weihburggasse 3; tel. (43-1)51-52-60,* is a charming hotel in a 14th-century building that is centrally located. A double room with a bathroom is 1,500 to 1,900 Austrian schillings ($135 to $170), including breakfast.

The baroque **Römischer Kaiser**, *Annagasse 16; (43-1)512-77-51*, was built in 1684 as the private palace of the imperial chancellor. It has been a hotel since the turn of the century. A double room with a bathroom is 1,800 to 2,600 Austrian schillings ($161 to $233), including breakfast.

The most tragic site: Mayerling

A chapel in **Mayerling**, in the middle of the Vienna woods, marks the spot where Crown Prince Rudolf, son of Emperor Franz Josef, and his mistress Baroness Mary Vetsera committed double suicide. The emperor had refused to allow Prince Rudolf to end his unhappy marriage.

Heurigen, or little wine bars, are located in Grinzing and other villages in the woods. A sprig of pine above the door of one of these bars means the new wine, less than a year old, is ready to be drunk.

Innsbruck: the prettiest Alpine city

Innsbruck, the capital of Tyrol, is one of the most beautiful cities in the world and one of the biggest ski centers in Europe. The towering Alps can be seen from nearly every street corner. The **Nordkette**, a steep Alpine headwall, is the closest and most dramatic of the mountains that surround the city. **Maria-Theresien-Strasse**, the main street, has an especially inspiring view of the mountains.

Miles of free cross-country ski tracks can be found outside Innsbruck, as well as Olympic legacies, including the Olympic bobsled run (which tourists can ride), a ski jump, and a large ice-skating and hockey arena.

Gothic architecture (the pointed, arched, and vaulted style prevalent in Europe from the 13th to 15th centuries) can be seen throughout 800-year-old Innsbruck. Much of it was built by order of Empress Maria Theresa and Emperor Maximilian I. Gothic arcades, forerunners of modern malls because they kept shoppers out of the weather, can be found off Herzog Friedrichstrasse.

Innsbruck's treasures

The **Goldenes Dachl** (Golden Roof) is the symbol of Innsbruck. The ornate Gothic balcony, built in 1500 by Maximilian I to commemorate his wedding, was used by the royal couple to watch armor-clad knights jousting below. The regal balcony has sculpted crests and heroic wall paintings. A roof made of 2,657 gold-plated tiles tops the balcony.

Next to the Golden Roof is the **Goldener Adler** (Golden Eagle Inn), the oldest hostelry in the city. Andreas Hofer, the leader of the Tyrolean uprising against Napoleon, gathered his small and poorly armed troop of volunteers here. His troops, despite their poverty, managed to defeat the well-equipped French and Bavarian armies in three battles.

Hofkirche (the court church), on the Renweg, is known as the Tyrolean Westminster Abbey. It was commissioned by Emperor Ferdinand I as a cenotaph dedicated to his grandfather Maximilian I (who is buried at Wiener Neustadt). Built from 1553 to 1563, it contains a white marble tomb with a monumental bronze statue of the kneeling Maximilian on top. Standing vigil are 28 enormous bronze statues of royal figures. It also contains the tomb of Andreas Hofer.

Across the Inn River is the **Hungerburgbahn** (a funicular) that will carry you to the peaks with the best views of Innsbruck. It crosses the Inn and ascends the mountainside to Hungerburg, a lofty section of the city. An aerial tram continues from here to Seegrube and Hafelaker, affording breathtaking overlooks on the Nordkette.

Downhill from here is the **Alpine Zoo**, which contains species already extinct in the Eastern Alps, as well as rare animals and birds seen only by hunters in the high mountains. Wildcats, wolves, bears, bison, otters, beavers, griffons, vultures, owls, and eagles are kept in surroundings as similar as possible to their natural habitats. The zoo is open every day from 9 a.m. to 6 p.m. You can get here from Innsbruck via Bus Z.

The best way to explore the mountains

Club Innsbruck arranges daily hikes and ski trips in the mountains outside Innsbruck. You don't have to be a member; you get a Club Innsbruck card when you register at a hotel in town for at least three nights. Sign up for Club Innsbruck's programs at information centers or your hotel before 4 p.m. the day before you plan to participate.

From June to September, the club offers daily guided hiking tours, with a free loan of hiking boots and a rucksack. Bus transportation to the starting point of each day's tour and back from the end point is free, as are the services of experienced, licensed guides.

During the winter, the club provides free ski buses to the five main ski areas surrounding Innsbruck and a daily cross-country ski bus. Winter hiking trips with guides are scheduled Mondays through Fridays. If you would rather hike on your own, buy the map called *Innsbruck und Umgebung*. Many of the best trails start at Hungerburg. The blue trails can be followed in good walking shoes, but don't try the red ones without sturdy climbing boots.

The best summer skiing

For a real thrill, try summer skiing on the **Stubai Glacier**, 25 miles from Innsbruck. You can get there via Post Bus or bus line ST from Stubaitalbannhof. A round-trip ticket is 130 Austrian schillings ($12). A day's skiing is 275 Austrian schillings ($24).

Innsbruck's best inn

The 600-year-old **Goldener Adler**, *Herzog-Friedrichstrasse 6; tel. (43-512)586-350*, in the heart of Old Town, is the best inn in Innsbruck. Request a room with antique trappings. A double room is 400 to 1,360 Austrian schillings ($36 to $125), including breakfast.

The best of Salzburg

Mozart's birthplace, dominated by a 12th-century fortress called the Hohensalzburg, is a baroque city surrounded by mountains. The Salzach River divides **Salzburg** into two worlds. On the left bank are narrow streets and ancient buildings that date back to the 13th to 15th centuries. The right bank is a modern city in the shadows of the Kapuzinerberg Mountain.

The Salzburg Music Festival

The best time to visit this musical town is during the **Salzburg Festival**, held from late July to August. Advance ticket sales usually end by January.

For information on the Salzburg Festival or other festivals in Salzburg, contact **Austrian National Music Festivals**, *20th Floor, 500 Fifth Ave., New York, NY 10110; (212)944-6880*, or the **Ticket Office of the Salzburg Festival**, *Festspielhaus, A-5010 Salzburg, Austria*. The Salzburg Festival office has tickets available until the beginning of April, or you can reserve them through a travel agent in the United States.

The old quarter

The best place to begin your exploration of Salzburg is the **old quarter**. In the shadows of the castle, it is a maze of winding old streets with little shops, medieval wrought-iron signs, and fountains. Explore on foot—cars are banned here.

The main thoroughfare, Getreidegasse, leads into **Judengasse**, once the Jewish ghetto. Today, it is a picturesque neighborhood with five- and six-story houses. Continue on to the **Alter Markt** (Market Square), where flower stalls scent the air and a 16th-century fountain splashes.

Salzburg's top sights

Mozart was born at *Getreidegasse 9* in 1756, and he lived here for his first 16 years. Early editions of his works (he began composing when he was 5) and models of sets of his most famous operas are on display at the house, which is open every day. (The house where Mozart lived from 1773 to 1787, on the other side of the river at *Makatplatz 8*, is open during the summer only.)

The **Dom** (cathedral), with its two towers, marble facade, and massive bronze doors, is also in the old quarter. Look for its blue terra-cotta dome. Consecrated in 1628, the early baroque structure was modeled on St. Peter's in Rome.

Across from the cathedral is the **Residenz**, a series of buildings that once comprised the palace of the prince-archbishops. On the first floor are 15 staterooms decorated with frescoes and paintings. A gallery of European paintings from the 16th through 19th centuries on the second floor contains works by Rembrandt, Rubens, and Breughel.

The **Glockenspiel**, in front of the Residenz, is a 35-bell carillon constructed in the 18th century. The bells are played every day at 6 and 11 a.m. and 7 p.m.

The magnificent **Mirabell Palace**, with its elaborate formal gardens, is on the other side of the river. Built in 1606 by Archbishop Wolf Dietrich for his mistress (and the mother of his 12 children), it is known for its grand ceremonial staircase, which is decorated with marble angels, and its Marble Hall. The gardens are filled with statues, pools, and flowers of every shade and variety. Candlelight chamber music concerts are held here.

Guarding Salzburg from a great rock 400 feet above the city is the **Hohensalzburg**, a fortress built between 1077 and 1681. This stronghold of the bishops of Salzburg is filled with Gothic wood carving, coffered ceilings, and intricate ironwork. To get to the fortress, which offers the best view of the city, walk or take the funicular from Festungsgasse, near St. Peter's Churchyard. Tours of the castle are scheduled every 15 minutes.

Outside Salzburg is the 17th-century **Hellbrunn Palace**, built by the archbishop and prankster Markus Sittikus. Hidden nozzles in the benches, walls, sculptures, floors, and ceilings were used by the archbishop to spray unwary guests. The palace is open to the public every day from April through October.

The best eating in Salzburg

The two best restaurants in the Salzburg area are **Weisses Kreuz**, *Bierjodlgasse 6; tel. (43-662)845641,* and **Eschlböck-Plomberg**, five miles northeast of Salzburg in Mondsee, *tel. (43-662)31660.* Weisses Kreuz offers garden dining. It is closed for two weeks in February and every Tuesday. Meals are about 200 Austrian schillings ($19) per person.

Eschlböck-Plomberg, which is located on a beach, also serves meals on the terrace. It is closed Mondays during the winter. Meals are 200 to 300 Austrian schillings ($19 to $30) per person.

Stiftskeller Sankt Peter, *1 Sankt Peters Bezirk; tel. (43-662)841268,* near the cathedral, is a 16th-century wine cellar that serves wines from its own vineyards. Divided into eight rooms, it also serves traditional Austrian dishes at reasonable prices.

Salzburg's best affordable hotels

Hotel Schöne Aussicht, *Heuberg 3, Salzburg 5023; tel. (43-662)6406-080,* is a chalet hotel on a hill with a view of Salzburg and the Alps. It has a pool, tennis courts, a sunny terrace, and a cozy, beamed bar. Some of the rooms have balconies. Service is friendly, and fresh flowers decorate the rooms. However, the walk from the bus stop is up three steep hills, so it's best to have a car if you stay here. A double room is 800 to 1,100 Austrian schillings ($76 to $104).

The **Hotel Kaserbräu**, *Kaigasse 33, Salzburg 5020; tel. (43-662)842445,* is a small hotel in the shadows of the Hohensalzburg. The building dates back to 1342, and some of the rooms have been furnished in baroque style. Others are furnished in pinewood. A double room is 1,090 to 1,500 Austrian schillings ($97 to $135).

The **Hotel Elefant**, *Sigmund-Haffner-Gasse 4, Salzburg 5020; tel. (43-662)843397,* is a medieval town house in the historic heart of Salzburg. The tall, narrow building is on a quiet pedestrian street five minutes from the opera house. The public rooms have inlaid furniture and old paintings. The floors on the first floor are marble, and the rooms are decorated with antiques. The upper floors are less elegant; some of the rooms are small and plain. About half have private baths. A double room is 1,050 to 1,450 Austrian schillings ($94 to $130) a night.

Salzburg's castle hotels

Gastschloss Mönchstein, *Mönchsberg 26, A5020 Salzburg; tel. (43-662)8485550,* parts of which date to 1358, is a many-tiered, ivy-covered castle on a mountaintop above Salzburg. Once a guesthouse for archbishops, it became a retreat for scholars from the University of Salzburg in 1654. Today, it is a hotel. You can take an elevator to the castle from the streets below. Half the rooms have private bathrooms. The hotel is open May through January.

Schloss Haunsperg, *tel. (43-6245)2662,* is a 14th-century castle hotel just south of Salzburg. The spacious rooms are furnished with antiques, and guests can use the tennis courts on the grounds. The castle is near the Autobahn that runs south from Salzburg past the airport; exit at Hallein and follow the signs to Oberalm and the castle. A double room is 1,350 to 1,500 Austrian schillings ($121 to $134).

The best hotel outside Salzburg

Just east of Salzburg is the **Simony Hotel**, *Hallstatt; tel. (43-6134)231,* where you can get a true feel for old Austria. The rooms look out over the lake, and the cuisine at the hotel restaurant is marvelous. A double room is only 270 Austrian schillings ($25) a night.

The world's best salt mines

The salt mine at **Hallein**, 10 miles south of Salzburg, is a bit like a roller coaster. To get around inside the tunnels, you slide down a series of long wooden chutes at 40 miles per hour. To visit, you must put on a special uniform, which consists of baggy white overalls with a white hood and a leather backside.

The mine contains sketches of the 1,000-year-old body of a man found in 1666 perfectly preserved in salt. And at midlevel is a salt lake, which, during the off-season, you can raft across to see a cathedrallike cavern 270 feet long and 150 feet wide.

Europe's best tobogganing

Don't leave Austria before you visit the Lake District, an area about 30 minutes east of Salzburg. In the winter, Austria's 200 lakes are covered with ice skaters, and the surrounding mountains with skiers. In the summer, these lakes are filled with sailboats. (Motorboats are not allowed.)

The area around **Wolfgangsee** is especially popular. You can't really explore the Lake District without a car. If you don't have a rental car, join a tour. If you're lucky, your guide will introduce you to the little-known sport of mountain tobogganning. To participate, you pick up a metal, saucerlike toboggan and then take a chair lift to the top of the mountain, carrying the toboggan with you. At the top, place the toboggan on the metal track that curves its way down to the bottom, sit cross-legged on the toboggan, and push off. It is like riding a roller coaster, only better because you can go as fast or slow as you want. (A stick in the front acts as a brake.) It takes about five minutes to get to the bottom; the ride costs $5.

After the trip down the mountain, drive to **St. Gilgen,** a small resort town near Lake Wolfgang. It is a favorite spot among the people of Salzburg, who come here for weekend getaways. St. Gilgen is a small place with only a few restaurants and small shops—but that is as it should be. The charm of this lakeside village would be lost if someone built condominiums here.

If planning to spend time at Wolfgansee, find a room in one of the inns situated on the side of the mountain overlooking the lake. Ask when you arrive in the area; a local should be able to point the way to a good one.

Europe's highest waterfall

The **Krimml Waterfall** (the highest in Europe) splashes down 1,250 feet through the mountains 30 miles east of Innsbruck. You know when the fall is close; it fills the valley with mist.

The highest Austrian village

The highest village in Austria, **Obergurgl** (6,320 feet), is where Professor Auguste Piccard landed his famous hot-air balloon in the 1930s. Nearby is a little ski settlement called Hochgurgl, where you can catch a chair lift to a year-round ski area.

Austria's strangest tradition

The little mountain town of **Landeck** has a fascinating tradition. Each year at Christmas, young men from the town climb to the top of the rocky crags that loom above Landeck. Here, they light huge bonfires that can be seen for miles. Then they set fire to circles of wood dipped in tar and roll them down the hill. The blazing circles are quite a sight against the black night sky. Finally, the daredevils ski downhill, racing the fiery disks at breakneck speed!

Austria's best skiing

The **Arlberg** region of Austria is the best place in the world for skiing. It offers a combination of features not duplicated anywhere else: a high altitude, which guarantees good snow; slopes for skiers of all levels of experience; interconnected villages that range from quaint to crowded to exclusive; serious ski instruction; and a cheery dose of *Gemütlichkeit,* or coziness. Some of the villages are large, such as Lech or St. Anton; others, including Zürs, are small and exclusive.

Kitzbühel, the prettiest ski town

A treasure of a ski village is **Kitzbühel,** a friendly, uncrowded town with slopes for skiers of all experience and enough activity to keep even snow haters happy. This is the place to go to avoid irritating crowds and the ridiculously high prices often found in the Alps. It has well-groomed slopes, a casino, and plenty of night life.

Kitzbühel is worth visiting even if you don't ski. An ancient walled town, it has crooked, narrow streets and Tyrolean architecture, with gabled stone-and-stucco houses that date back to the Middle Ages.

The skiable part of the Kitzbühel Alps reaches as high as 7,750 feet. The greatest vertical drop here is 4,150 feet. These heights may seem small compared with those at other Alpine resorts; however, the smooth pastures of these mountains require less snow for good skiing than the rockier slopes of other ski areas. And the weather is milder than in other areas. Kitzbühel's 60 ski lifts and trails provide an overwhelming choice of trails, all accessible by a single ski pass called the Kitzbühel Ski Circus.

The best place to stay in Kitzbühel is **Schloss Lebenberg,** *Lebenbergstrasse 17, A6370 Kitzbühel; tel. (43-5356)4301.* Situated on a hill overlooking the valley and the mountains, the castle was built in 1540 by the dukes of Lebenberg. The hotel's 11 guest rooms are all furnished with antiques. Rooms in the newly added chalet wing have private baths.

11

Other modern additions include health facilities, a heated pool, a sauna, and tennis courts. A double room is 795 to 1,750 Austrian schillings ($71 to $156) per person.

The best ski school

St. Anton is the best place to go for ski instruction, thanks to tradition and the city's 300 instructors. This is the cradle of modern skiing, where Hannes Schneider began teaching the now-accepted Arlberg School ski technique. The runs from the top of the Galzig and the Valuga (9,216 feet) are superb—as are the views.

St. Anton is also a good place to go for night life. The Hotel Hospiz has a fine restaurant. And the Krazy Känguruh is a hopping nightclub.

Zürs, the most exclusive resort

Zürs, a first-class ski resort where tour groups are discouraged, is for skiing purists who also like fine living. The city has one ski instructor for every 10 beds, and most of the instructors give only private lessons. And in Zürs it's common for the ski instructor to come to the hotel to pick up his class.

All the hotels in Zürs are first-class or better. The **Zorserhof**, *Zürs am Arlberg, Austria; tel. (43-5583)25130,* is an expensive five-star deluxe establishment that regularly attracts celebrities, such as King Hussein of Jordan. It may be the best ski hotel in Austria. A double room is 2,470 to 2,700 Austrian schillings ($224 to $245).

The Best of Britain

> The way to ensure summer in England is to have it framed and glazed in a comfortable room.
> —*Horace Walpole, 1774*

Britain is a land of perfectionism. Shirts must be made with precision. Suits are of good English wool. Tea must be made just so. And politeness is practically law.

The land itself is a place of wonders—mighty castles, charming villages with thatched cottages, ancient cathedrals, pre-historic stone circles, misty lakes, and dramatic shorelines.

Although hundreds of regions throughout Britain demand a visit, the number-one destination is London. Here, many of the world's most famous playwrights and artists blossomed; history's most bloody and fascinating tales unfolded; and the outcome of World War II was sealed. We begin our look at the best of Britain, then, in this remarkable city.

London, the most memorable city

"What has made London the most poignantly memorable city of the world is its continuing ability to recognize the human condition," writer Richard Condon once said. "From Battersea to Woolwich, across the 32 boroughs of the city, humans reign in perpetual celebration of one of the most complex multilayered communities on the planet....Quirky, steeped in the past but actively and civilly pursuing the present, London—and Londoners—continue to honor all that is human. And 1,250 years after its founding, visitors are still drawn to the city's idiosyncrasies—all those facets that endure and enrich life."

The top sights in London

The most famous sight in London, **Big Ben**, is usually misidentified. Many people believe, incorrectly, that Big Ben is the clock in the Parliament tower; it is actually the 13 1/2-ton bell.

The home of **Parliament**, beneath Big Ben, is surprisingly young, built a mere 100 years ago on the site of the old Royal Palace of Westminster. This huge complex of Victorian buildings covers eight acres and includes 1,100 rooms. The guided tour is definitely worth your time.

Westminster Hall, built from 1394 to 1402, is part of the original palace. The entrance is in Victoria Tower, and today you don't have to be a traitor to get in. Admission is free, but donations are accepted for restorations.

English kings and queens begin and end their careers at Westminster Abbey, where royal coronations and burials have been held since the time of William the Conqueror. **Poets' Corner** in the south transept contains the tombs of Geoffrey Chaucer, Charles Dickens, Robert Browning, and Thomas Hardy.

The **Tate Gallery** has a collection of works by British painters, including Turner, Blake, Hogarth, and Constable. It also contains works by French Impressionists Manet, Monet, Cézanne, and Degas, as well as sculptures by Rodin, Picasso, and Henry Moore. The gallery is on Millbank Street, near the Pimlico underground station.

Whitehall, where fiery King Henry VIII once had his palace, is now an efficient, modern-day government center that runs between the Thames River and St. James' Park. **Number 10 Downing Street,** where the prime minister lives, is part of Whitehall. The War Rooms at 70 Whitehall served as Churchill's subterranean headquarters during World War II. The rooms are open to the public 10 a.m. until 5 p.m.; call *(44-71)930-6961* for details and to arrange a visit.

The **Banqueting House** in Whitehall, where Charles I was beheaded, is used today for less violent government receptions. Designed by Inigo Jones and completed in 1622, it is decorated with nine allegorical ceiling paintings by Rubens. A bust of Charles I on the staircase marks the position of the window the king walked through to get to the scaffolding where he was beheaded.

Surrounded by four regal lions, the mighty **Nelson Column** rises from the heart of Trafalgar Square, a monument to Admiral Nelson. (Nelson died in battle with the French off Cape Trafalgar. Here, he spurred his men on to victory with the inspiring words "England expects every man to do his duty.")

Concerts are held Sundays at noon in the templelike **St.-Martin-in-the-Fields** (1721-1726), also on the square. Nearby is the **National Gallery,** with works by Vermeer, Turner, Botticelli, Michelangelo, Holbein, El Greco, and Delacroix. Take a look at the gallery's controversial annex, added only a few years ago.

Europe's largest medieval fortress

The **Tower of London,** the largest medieval fortress in Europe, has witnessed foul deeds and splendid spectacles. Inside the fortress, on Tower Green, innumerable heads rolled, including those of Anne Boleyn, Lady Jane Grey, Sir Walter Raleigh, and the Earl of Essex, Queen Elizabeth I's rejected lover. In the Bloody Tower, as it is known, Richard III supposedly murdered 13-year-old King Edward V and the king's little brother.

The **Crown Jewels** are kept in the Tower of London. The Cullinan diamond here is the largest ever found. It was sent to London from the Transvaal in a brown paper package via third-class mail.

London's oldest church

Any visit to the Tower of London should include a visit to the **Chapel of St. John.** The chapel was built in 1080, making it the oldest church in London.

The most famous sea clipper

At the waterfront in Greenwich, the *Cutty Sark,* the most famous sea clipper ever built, rests in its own dry dock. Built in 1869, it was one of the few sailing ships to survive despite the dawn of the steam age. Rescued from oblivion and restored, the *Cutty Sark* now houses an interesting collection of figureheads and full-scale cabin replicas. The clipper is open Monday through Saturday 10:30 a.m. until 6 p.m. and Sunday 2:30 p.m. until 6 p.m.

London's best post office

The **Trafalgar Square Post Office,** *24-28 William IV St., WC2; tel. (44-71)930-9580,* is London's best—and it's also open the latest. It is open until 8 p.m. Monday through Saturday and Sunday until 5 p.m.

The worst place to tell secrets

St. Paul's, an ornate cathedral built in 1633 by Inigo Jones, has a **Whispering Gallery** where you can hear a word whispered on the other side of the dome as loudly as if the person speaking were right next to you. Of course, it's no secret that Prince Charles and Lady Diana were married here.

The best changing of the guard

The best changing of the guard in London isn't at Buckingham Palace, as you might expect. It is in the middle of **Whitehall,** where the red-suited Horse Guards are stationed. The changing of the guard here is as picturesque as at Buckingham Palace and a good deal less crowded. (Tourists visit Buckingham Palace by the millions.)

The best repartee

The best entertainment in London is a session of the **House of Commons,** on Parliament Square, where insults are exchanged with wild abandon. Florence Horsbrugh, once minister of education, suffered the following insult: "I do not know what the Right Honorable Lady, the Minister of Education, is grinning at. This is the face that sank a thousand scholarships." And Winston Churchill, when accused of being drunk by a female political foe, replied, "And you, Madam, are ugly. But tomorrow I shall be sober!"

You can observe these verbal battles from the gallery. The 156 seats are filled on a first-come, first-served basis. Join the queue and wait for a spot Monday through Thursday after 4:15 p.m. or Friday after 10 a.m. at the St. Stephens entrance. (Incidentally, admission to the **House of Lords** is at this same spot. Lines form after 2:30 p.m. Monday through Wednesday, after 3 p.m. Thursday, and after 11 a.m. Friday.)

London's strangest sight

Cleopatra's Needle is the most surprising monument in London. This Egyptian obelisk dates back to 1500 B.C. Set in the shadow of Waterloo Bridge on the edge of the Thames embankment, it bears the carvings of two of Egypt's greatest rulers: pharaohs Thothmes III and Ramses II. Offered to England in the 19th century by the ruler of Egypt, the obelisk actually had nothing to do with Cleopatra—it was transported down the Nile into the Mediterranean aboard a boat called *Cleopatra.*

When the Needle reached the Bay of Biscay on Oct. 14, 1877, it fell overboard during a storm. Six men volunteered to recover the monument and drowned trying to save it. (Their names are inscribed on the south face of the base.) Several days later, the monument was rescued by a freighter that lugged it to London.

London's liveliest corner

Piccadilly Circus is as crazy and colorful as its name. Crowded with people and filled with brightly colored billboards, the square is centered around a small statue of Eros and known as a pickup spot and a favorite haunt of pickpockets. But don't worry about the criminal elements—Piccadilly is also crowded with ordinary citizens and tourists and perfectly safe.

Piccadilly is also where you'll find the **Royal Academy of Fine Arts,** the **Ritz,** and **St. James' Church,** which offers concerts during the summer.

The artiest neighborhoods

Covent Garden, where Professor Higgins met Eliza Doolittle in *My Fair Lady,* has become the city's favorite hangout for yuppies. It's home to the **London Transport Museum**, the **Theatre Museum**, the **Theatre Royal** and **Royal Opera House**, and a **crafts market**. The area is used as an impromptu stage for clowns, mimes, musicians, and other entertainers, who perform and then pass the hat.

Bloomsbury was once the home of the literary and intellectual "Bloomsbury Group," which included Virginia Woolf, John Maynard Keynes, and E.M. Forster. This charming area offers the British Museum, the Courtland Institute Galleries, and Pollock's Toy Museum.

Chelsea, the literary enclave where Thomas Carlyle, Oscar Wilde, and Bertrand Russell once lived, today is home to blue-haired punkers. The main drag, King's Road, is populated by roller skaters and high-fashion strollers.

Seedy **Soho** is home to London's red-light district, but it's also lined with little restaurants and shops. Like Piccadilly, its criminal element is pretty harmless, because there are always so many people around. The square, which is home to nightclubs and London's biggest cinemas, is being renovated.

Soho's **Berwick Street** has a great produce market. **Leicester Square** was the home of painters Hogarth and Reynolds. **Hampstead** is a writers' and artists' quarter on a hill overlooking the city. Here you can rummage in antique stores and bookshops before enjoying afternoon tea in an area café. Visit **Keats' home** on Wentworth Place and **Freud's** home at 20 Maresfield Gardens.

London's most romantic park

The most romantic park in central London is off Guilford Street in Bloomsbury. But it has a strange restriction—no adult, a sign by the gates announces, may enter unless accompanied by a child. **Coram's Fields** is six acres of playground on the site of the Foundling Hospital for abandoned children, set up by Captain Thomas Coram more than 250 years ago.

The best place to rant and rave

Amateur orators spout forth at **Speakers Corner** in Hyde Park every Sunday. If you feel the urge to speak from a soapbox, this is the place. If you'd rather just listen, be prepared. You never know what you might hear—anarchists, religious zealots, racists, communists, or vegetarians!

Hyde Park is worth a visit even if you aren't interested in all the ranting and raving. On a pretty day, you can go boating in the park or just take a long stroll.

The world's best waxworks

Madame Tussaud's, *Marylebone Road, London NW1; tel. (44-71)935-6861,* is just about as touristy as you can get in London, but if you like waxworks, these are the best in the world. Madame Tussaud began her museum in Paris in the late 18th century, but revolutionary events drove her to London in 1802. The Chamber of Horrors is still the most interesting section of all, but rock stars, politicians, sports personalities, and royalty are certainly equally well-presented.

The best place to see blue hair

Blue-haired, mohawked punk rockers are on the endangered species list, even in London. But you can still find them—near Oxford Street on King's Road.

The world's best theater

London is the world's theater capital. Most of the major theaters are in the West End, a short walk from Trafalgar Square, in Covent Garden, or in Leicester Square. Notable exceptions are the National Theatre complex on the South Bank, next to the Royal Festival Hall, and the splendid Barbican Centre for the Arts, permanent London home of the Royal Shakespeare Company. Numerous fringe theater groups perform all over London.

You can get half-price tickets to major shows at the **Leicester Square Ticket Booth** (right in Leicester Square). Tickets are available for same-day West End shows only, and you'll rarely find tickets for recent hits. Nevertheless, the selection usually is pretty good. What's available is posted on the boards next to the booth. The line is usually long, and the tickets go fast, so keep an eye on the boards for changes as you wait.

On matinee days (Tuesday, Wednesday, Thursday, and Saturday), two queues form at the Leicester Square Ticket Booth—one for matinees, one for evening tickets. So be sure you're in the right line.

You also can get discounted tickets by going to the theater lobby right before the performance—although you may find yourself running from theater to theater. Last-minute tickets are sometimes also available for sold-out shows, although not at discounted prices. Tickets are always discounted for students with international student identification cards and senior citizens.

The best fringe theater

London's so-called fringe theaters are far removed from the neon lights and star-studded marquees of the fashionable West End. Yet, these small (each seats less than 100 people), out-of-the-way theaters offer some of the city's most inspired, innovative, and imaginative theatrical performances.

One of the best-known fringe theaters in London, and for good reason, is the **Albany Empire**, *Douglas Way, Deptford; tel. (44-81)691-3333*. It offers two plays simultaneously year-round.

The three best ways to spend a Sunday afternoon

Where should a bargain hunter in London head on a Sunday afternoon? **The Bayswater Road Art Exhibition.** From modern art to detailed still lifes, baroque to Romantic, portraits to landscapes, watercolors to oils, copper etchings to pastels—it's all at Bayswater, one of the largest open-air art exhibitions in the world. The exhibits stretch for eight-tenths of a mile, beginning at Clarendon Place and continuing until Queensway, and they are open every Sunday, rain or shine, 8 a.m. until 5 p.m. The Queensway and Lancaster Gate Underground stations bring you right to the heart of the area.

The second best place to spend a Sunday afternoon is **Camden Lock**, London's largest, gaudiest, and most unpredictably varied flea market. It's cheap and friendly—and for dedicated "people watchers," it offers a never ending flow of exotic youth. To get there, take the Northern Line to Camden Town or Chalk Farm.

And the third best way to spend a Sunday is to take a tour of **Little Venice.** You come upon it unexpectedly—it's just a short walk from the Warwick Avenue tube station to the little bridge over the canal. Here Regent's Canal meets the Grand Union Canal, forming a wider stretch of water flowing around a tree-covered island named for Robert Browning, who once lived nearby. Sycamore trees line the banks of the canals, and the Nash-designed houses, with their distinctive white stucco facades and lawns and gardens sweeping down to the water's edge, boast an 18th-century elegance.

One of the best outfits offering tours to Little Venice is **Jason's Trip**, *Opp. No. 60 Blomfield Road; tel. (44-71)286-3428*. The boat departs from Little Venice to Camden Town at 10:30 a.m., 12:30 p.m., 2:30 p.m., and 4:30 p.m. The cost is £4.50 ($8.50) round trip, £3.50 ($6.60) one way. Advance arrangements can be made for lunch. Another good tour company is the **Waterbus Company**, which departs hourly from the intersection where Grand Union Canal and Regent's Canal cross. The Waterbus Company lands at the zoo; it offers a reduced ticket price—and none of the waiting lines found at the main gate. Both tours pass Browning's Island, Regents Park, the zoo, the Maida Hill tunnel, and Camden Locks.

London's best flea market

Petticoat Lane Flea Market, held Sundays on Middlesex Street, is chock-full of bargains. The lively outdoor market has antiques as well as inexpensive new goods (especially clothing and appliances), bric-a-brac, and used items. The real bargains are found before 8 a.m. Take the underground to Liverpool Street and then walk up Bishop's Gate to Middlesex Street. (You won't find Petticoat Lane on the map; it's a nickname for Middlesex Street.)

The most entertaining flea market

One of the largest and most entertaining flea markets in Europe is held every Sunday on **Portobello Road**. To get there, take the underground to Notting Hill Gate and then walk down Pembrook Road to Portobello Road. On Saturdays, the road is lined with street performers and part-time vendors selling everything from punk-rock buttons to antiques. Fine hats and shoes that once bedecked Britain's elite can be found here at paupers' prices. If you aren't interested in buying, just watch the people. Be careful, though—this West Indian neighborhood can be seedy.

Antique hunting at its best

Since it opened in the late 1960s, **Antiquarius**, *134-141 King's Road, London SW3; tel. (44-71)351-5353,* has been one of the best places in London to shop for antiques. More than 200 stalls offer a breathtaking array of items from the Georgian, Victorian, Edwardian, and art nouveau periods, including jewelry, china, glass, books, prints, and antique clocks. This is a wonderful place to get lost for an afternoon.

Camden Passage is another great place for antiques—it has more than 100 shops. Decorative and Victorian antiques are of especially good quality in this corner of London, so don't expect knockdown prices. Take the underground to the Angel Islington and then walk up Islington High Street. An early morning flea market is held here Wednesday and Saturday.

Serious antique hunters flock to the **New Caledonian Market** (Bermondsey) at the London Bridge underground station. This huge market has quality silver, china, jewelry, memorabilia, and objets d'art. It is open Friday 5 a.m. until 1 p.m. Arrive early for the best buys.

The best antiquarian bookdealer

A Mr. Maggs still owns **Maggs Brothers**, *50 Berkeley Square, London W1; tel. (44-71)493-7160.* This bookdealer specializes in illuminated manuscripts, first editions, and autographed letters of English authors. Many priceless works are in stock, and the bibliophile (with clean hands) is welcome to stop in and see the treasures. For instance, you can inspect one of the original privately printed editions of T.E. Lawrence's (Lawrence of Arabia's) *Seven Pillars of Wisdom.* The lover of fine books will find no worthier shrine.

The best brass rubbing center

The best place for brass rubbing in London is the **London Brass Rubbing Centre** itself, *St. Martin-in-the-Fields, Trafalgar Square, London WC2N 4JJ; tel. (44-71)437-6023.* Located in a magnificent 18th-century church, famous for its lunchtime concerts of chamber and choral music, this is one of the few places in London where you can still make your own brass rub bings. The center is open Monday through Saturday 10 a.m. until 6 p.m. and Sunday noon until 6 p.m.

The world's best maze

Hampton Court Palace, *East Molesey, Surrey; tel. (44-81)977-8441,* contains England's oldest and most popular maze. The labyrinth is bounded by high hedges and reinforced with railings to prevent cheating. Arrive by boat from Westminster Pier or by train from the Waterloo station in London (a distance of 10 miles). The palace, which dates from the early 1500s, is open daily 9:30 a.m. until 6 p.m. Tuesday through Sunday and 10:15 a.m. until 6 p.m. on Monday. (The last entry is at 5:15 p.m.)

The best place to go fly a kite

The **Kite Store**, *48 Neal St., London W2; tel. (44-71)836-1666*, was the first shop of its kind in Europe, and it now stocks more than 200 kinds of kites, as well as boomerangs and frisbees. Once you've purchased your kite, the best place to fly it is on Hampstead Heath, which offers a tremendous view of the city below.

The world's largest toy store

Hamley's, *196 Regent St., London W1; tel. (44-71)734-3161*, proudly proclaims itself to be the world's largest toy store. And who would argue? The six enormous floors are packed to the gills with every imaginable kind of diversion for both children and adults.

The oldest cheese store

Paxton & Whitfield, *93 Jermyn St., London SW1; tel. (44-71)930-0250*, is the oldest and best cheese store in London; it came to Jermyn Street in 1797. With more than 300 European cheeses (including 40 to 50 British varieties), Paxton & Whitfield assuredly will have the kind you are looking for. The cheeses are stocked not according to price but according to tradition. There's absolutely no risk of buying an off-brand wheel of Brie, for instance. The counters are also stacked with preserves, pickles, and fine wines.

The best stuffed shirts

The stuffed shirts of the world know the best shirt shopping is along **Jermyn Street** in London. Here, traditional shirts are made of Sea Island cotton or two-fold poplin. The collars are perfectly shaped and stitched, as are the cuffs. The buttons are mother-of-pearl. The cut is generous, and the shirttails are long.

Hildich & Key, *87 Jermyn St.*, produces the finest and most expensive shirts in London. Made of soft cotton, they have hand-sewn buttonholes, removable collar stays, and double cuffs. A bright striped shirt here is £79 ($150). Less expensive shirts made of poplin are £49 ($92).

Turnbull & Asser, *71 and 72 Jermyn St.*, has shirts with collars roomy enough for T&A's generous ties. And the cut of the shirts makes them extra comfortable. A Turnbull & Asser shirt is £55 ($104).

The finest linens in the world

Despite its tiny interior, the **Irish Linen Company**, *35-36 Burlington Arcade, London W1; tel. (44-71)493-8949*, has a beautiful selection of some of the finest handworked linens you can find anywhere. Price-conscious shoppers will be most interested in the decorative tablecloths and napkins.

London's best tailor

Stovel & Mason, *32 Old Burlington St.; tel. (44-71)734-4855*, is a London tailor who offers Savile Row quality at more moderate prices. A hand-tailored suit here is £700 ($1,325). (Always have suspenders or brace buttons attached to the inside of your pants, and insist on 13-inch-deep pockets and jacket cuffs that unbutton.)

London's finest shoemakers

The three best shoemakers in London are **Lobbs**, *9 St. James Place, London SW1* (the waiting list is six months long); **Wildsmith**, *Prince's Arcade, Piccadilly*, which makes the best old-fashioned shoes in London; and **Tricker's**, *67 Jermyn St.*

The best brollies

Swaine & Adney in Piccadilly makes umbrellas by hand. The very best brolly (a favorite in the House of Lords) is a Brigg.

The city's best lace market

Nottingham holds the best lace market at Sneinton. The market is open Monday, Wednesday, Friday, and Saturday 10 a.m. until 4 p.m. To learn about the history of lace or to see demonstrations about how lace is made, visit **Lace Hall**, *High Pavement*, or **Severn's Building**, *Council Road*. Both are open daily 10 a.m. until 5 p.m. Admission to Lace Hall costs £1.95 ($3.70) for adults, £1 ($1.90) for children. Admission to Severn's Building, which is located in a 15th-century building, is free.

The best ways to explore London

If you can afford it, the ritziest way to explore London is by taxi. Government-accredited tour guide-cabbies will lead you on detailed tours of London for a mere £85 ($150) a day. Stanley Roth, one of these 60 knowledgeable guides, includes historical, literary, and just plain funny anecdotes in his personalized tours. To reach Mr. Roth (or guides like him), contact the **London Visitor and Convention Bureau**, *tel. (44-71)730-3450*, which keeps a list of "blue badge guides," as they are called. Booking agents that can set you up with guides include **The Driver Guides Association**, *tel. (44-71)839-2498*; **Take-A-Guide**, *(800)825-4946* or *(44-81)960-0459*; and **British Tours**, *tel. (44-71)629-5267*.

Walking is the best way to see the city if you don't have money to blow on a private guide. And on foot, you can see London in greater detail and mingle with the British. You can make your own way through the city using a guidebook and a map, or you can join one of London's many walking tours. One of the best is offered by **Citisights of London**, *London Walk, London SW3; tel. (44-71)600-3699*, which offers history and archeology walks of Roman, Saxon, and medieval London. The two-hour tours are led by professional archeologists.

London Walks, *87 Messina Ave., London NW6 4LG; tel. (44-71)624-3978*, takes you in the footsteps of Jack the Ripper, Shakespeare, Dickens, Virginia Woolf, and other notables.

If your feet get tired, rest a while on a double-decker bus or London's famous subway, known as the tube or the underground. The underground is the world's oldest and most extensive rapid transit system, with more than 250 stations and 750 miles of track.

Fares are set according to the length of your ride. On buses, you can pay the conductor, but you must buy an underground ticket before you get on the train. And make sure you don't throw your ticket away—you'll need it to leave the station at the end of your journey. Fares are steep. It can cost as much as £1.10 ($2) to go completely across town. Passes save you money in the long run.

A **London Travelcard** ticket allows you unlimited travel on the London bus and tube systems. It is available from travel agents, at any subway station, and at the London Regional Transport Travel Information Center. One-day cards cost £3.40 ($6.50) for five travel zones, £2.90 ($5.50) for four zones, and £10.90 ($20.60) for seven days.

Tour buses depart Victoria Station and Piccadilly Circus daily at 9:30 and 11:30 a.m. and 2:30 p.m. The rates are £8 ($15) for adults, £4 ($7.50) for children.

London double-decker bus tours also are available, *tel. (44-71)222-1234*. The open-topped buses depart Piccadilly Circus, Victoria Station, and Marble Arch daily 9 a.m. until 4 p.m. The tours last about two hours and 20 minutes and cost £8 for adults, £4 for children under 16. A free map is included. Reservations aren't necessary.

The best places to take tea

In a city known for its tea, a few places stand scones and Devonshire cream above the rest. The most elegant place to enjoy a pot of hot tea with scones is the **Dorchester Hotel** on Park Lane.

The coziest place for tea is **Brown's**, a Victorian hotel on Dover Street. Rudyard Kipling once stayed here. Men must wear a tie to take tea at Brown's after 4 p.m. (And they should take a moment to glance into the men's room before they leave; the scale is an extremely rare antique.)

Another good place to take tea is the department store **Fortnum and Mason**, *181 Piccadilly, London W1*. If the fashionable Fountain Room is too crowded, go upstairs to the more discreet St. James Restaurant—few people know about it.

A quiet, modest place to have tea, especially if you are shopping, is **Liberty's** on Regent Street. Of the two restaurants here, the one upstairs is the prettiest.

The best restaurant in London

The **Grill Room** at the **Connaught Hotel**, *16 Carlos Place, London W1Y 6AL; tel. (44-71)499-7070*, is the best restaurant in London. This elegant establishment serves traditional French and English food to cabinet ministers and art dealers. As an hors d'oeuvre, try the mouth-watering *croustade d'oeufs de caille Maintenon* (quails' egg yolks in a pastry boat). Also try the seafood with shrimp and lobster in a wine sauce. Order coffee following your dinner—it comes with sugar-glazed grapes and strawberries dipped in chocolate.

The best service in London

The **Terrace Restaurant** at the **Dorchester Hotel**, *53 Park Lane, London W1; tel. (44-71)629-8888*, has one staff member for every two guests. This marble-columned, elegantly lit institution serves exquisite nouvelle cuisine, served in a series of leisurely courses.

The best roast beef in London

At **Simpson's in the Strand**, *100 Strand; tel. (44-71)836-9112*, a maître d'hôtel dressed in tails ushers diners into the paneled dining room. Six 30-pound four-rib loins are roasted simultaneously. Roast beef and saddles of mutton are wheeled directly to guests' tables and carved there. The cattle are chosen by Simpson's agents at auctions in Scotland. The Duke of Wellington and Margaret Thatcher are said to prefer Simpson's.

The best kosher eateries

One of the best ethnic restaurants in London is **Reuben's**, *20 Baker St;, tel. (44-71)935-5945*, a kosher eatery. Reuben's serves food in the Anglo-Continental style, although it does offer a wide variety of traditional foods as well.

Another good kosher eatery is **Bloom's**, *90 White Chapel High St.; tel. (44-71)247-6001*.

The best Indian food

Bombay Brasserie, *140 Gloucester Road*, next to **Bailey's Hotel**, *Courtfield Close; tel. (44-71)370-4040*, is the best of the upscale Indian restaurants in London. Especially good are the Goan fish curry, the aromatic chicken dishes, and the bean curries.

A more economical choice is the **Diwana Delicatessen**, *114 Drummond St., NW1; tel. (44-71)387-5556*. This restaurant is open daily noon until 10 p.m. but is closed Mondays.

The best Southeast Asian restaurant

The small, comfortable room at **Nam Long**, *40 Frith St., London W1; tel. (44-71)439-1835*, features Vietnamese specialties. Although the decor is unremarkable from the outside, inside the elegant wallpaper and tile floor convey a feeling of well-being. The food is well-prepared, and the sizzling dishes are served in containers set in varnished wood. The service is attentive.

London's best night life

One of the trendiest of London's now-very-trendy wine bars is the **Ebury Wine Bar**, *139 Ebury St., Belgravia*. (If you're unfamiliar with the term, *wine bars* are bars that serve good wine by the glass.)

If you'd prefer something rowdier, **Brahms and Liszt,** *19 Russell St.,* is the best place for a rip-roaring good time. (*Liszt* is Cockney slang for *pissed,* meaning drunk.)

The funniest place in London
The Comedy Store, *28a Leicester Square, London W1; tel. (44-71)839-6642,* offers the best stand-up comedy in London on weekends and a mixture of jazz, soul, and funk during the week.

London's best pub
London's heart is in its pubs. They are located on nearly every street corner and are an integral part of British life. Each has its own inimitable character.

Choosing London's best pub is a big task—everyone has his own favorite. Our favorite is the **Anchor Tavern,** *34 Park St., Southwark; tel. (44-71)407-1577,* on the south side of the Thames. This cozy riverside pub was once frequented by writer Samuel Johnson, as well as smugglers, rivermen, and wardens from the nearby Clink Prison. (The slang word for prison comes from the Clink.)

The Anchor Tavern originally was built near the site of Shakespeare's Globe Theater; it was rebuilt about 170 years ago. The low-beamed rooms are many and varied.

Legend has it that a special brew known as Russian Imperial Stout was prepared at the pub for the empress of Russia. Besides beer, try the roast forerib of beef or the steak and mushroom pudding. The Anchor is open noon until 2 p.m. and 7 until 10 p.m. It is closed Sunday evenings.

The Flask, *77 Highgate West, Hampstead; tel. (44-81)340-7260,* is our second choice for a best pub in London. (You couldn't expect us to pick just one.) The Flask is tremendously popular among Londoners, primarily because of its friendly atmosphere.

The oldest pub in the world
The **George and Vulture** is the oldest pub in the world. The original, called the George, was built in the 12th century. Sir Richard Wittington, the "thrice-round mayor of London," visited here in the 1500s, just as Chaucer (and Chaucer's father) had done earlier. Daniel Defoe, Jonathan Swift, and Charles Dickens were also customers.

The Pickwick Club meets at the George and Vulture quarterly, and members quote from the many Dickens passages about the place. The fictional Mr. Pickwick, when asked where he spent his leisure time, replied that he was "at present suspended at the George and Vulture." A framed check written by Dickens to the proprietor hangs on the wall.

Other historic pubs
Ye Olde Cheshire Cheese was opened in 1538 and rebuilt in 1667 after the Great Fire of London. The Cheese was a favorite of Goldsmith and Johnson and was mentioned by Dickens in *A Tale of Two Cities.* It is one of London's few remaining 17th-century chophouses.

The Cheese has sawdust on the floors (changed twice daily), and the tables are boxed in, with a bench for three diners on each side. An open fire cheers the original bar in winter, which, until recently, was reserved for men only. Try the savory baked cheese and Guinness on toast, the steak and kidney pie, and the Yorkshire pudding.

One of the oldest riverfront pubs, the **Prospect of Whitby** was popular with painters Whistler and Turner. While drinking here, Hanging Judge Jeffreys watched his sentences being carried out at nearby Execution Dock.

The Trafalgar is located on the Thames at the place where time begins—Greenwich mean time, that is. The Greenwich observatory and a maritime museum are also located here. The food is good but expensive. The view is superb—and free. Take a ferry from Tower Bridge to Greenwich.

The best hotels in London

The **Connaught Hotel**, *16 Carlos Place, London W1Y 6AL; tel. (44-71)499-7070*, is the best in town, with old-fashioned elegance and perfect service. The exterior of the Connaught is elegant, with a gracefully curving facade. Flowers brighten the porch. The interior is cozy, with wood paneling, Oriental rugs, and upholstered chairs.

A magnificent staircase with dark wood banisters leads to bedrooms on the upper floors. The spacious rooms have cheery wallpaper, brass beds, and antique desks. And the bathrooms are luxurious, with grand tubs, fine soaps, thick towels, and a cord to ring for the maid. Breakfast, including fresh orange juice, is brought to your room on a cloth-covered table and served on fine china. Write to request a room on the Carlos Place side. Book dinner reservations six weeks in advance. A double room is £194 to £210 ($367 to $397).

Claridge's, *Brook Street, London W1A 2JQ; tel. (44-71)629-8860*, in the heart of Mayfair, is a close second to the Connaught. It boasts a Hungarian Quartet that has been playing in the lobby for most of this century. Liveried attendants greet you at the door, and dress-maids are available to help you choose what you'd like to wear for the evening. Rooms have fireplaces, bells to ring for the maid or valet, and royal-sized bathtubs. The hotel recently underwent a facelift and now has new carpeting, paint, and air conditioning and a health club. A double room is £285 ($540).

Hyde Park, *Knightsbridge, London SW1X 7RJ; tel. (44-71)235-5000*, is the third best hotel in London. It is an enormous place that aspires to modern efficiency but doesn't quite succeed. But it does have a magnificent entrance hall, with marble floors and walls, an enormous mirror, and chandeliers. And the bedrooms are comfortable, with large beds and French doors that open onto balconies. A double room is £225 to £250 ($425 to $475).

The **Beaufort**, *33 Beaufort Gardens, London SW3; tel. (44-71)584-5252*, is an early Victorian house converted to an elegant guest residence in 1985. Each room is decorated in a different style, but all have telephones and color televisions. It's like staying in someone's home—but enjoying the amenities of a luxury hotel, including fluffy robes, wooden and silk hangers, a dish of chocolates, a personal decanter of brandy, and a Sony Walkman. A double room is £160 to £220 ($302 to $416).

Last, but not least, is **Brown's**, *19-22 Dover St., London W1A 4SW; tel. (44-71)493-6020*. The building dates back to 1660; it opened for business as Brown's in 1837. Teddy Roosevelt was married at Brown's, Kipling wrote here, and Queen Victoria visited Queen Wilhelmina here. From 1924 to 1935, it was the official court of the king of Greece. Oak paneling, 19th-century prints, antiques, and stained glass add atmosphere to the 12 connecting buildings that make up Brown's. A double room is £200 ($378).

The best hotels for the money

11 Cadogan Gardens, *Sloane Square, London SW3 2RJ; tel. (44-71)730-3426*, near the intersection of Sloane Square and Draycott Place, is so popular that you must book a room months in advance. Bookings from travel agents are not accepted. This Victorian hotel is filled with mahogany and silver. A butler serves breakfast and tea. A double room is £132 to £172 ($249 to $325) a night.

Ebury Court, *26 Ebury Street, London SW1; tel. (44-71)730-8147*, is quaint, with white woodwork and chintz curtains. It has a steady British and American clientele. A double room is £95 to £125 ($179 to $236) a night, including breakfast.

The **Cranley Place Hotel**, *1 Cranley Place, South Kensington, London SW7; tel. (44-71)589-7944*, is in a Regency-style house near Harrods. Bedrooms are decorated Laura Ashley-style and furnished with antiques. Breakfast can be taken in the dining room or in your hotel room. A double room with a private bath is £80 to £100 ($151 to $189) a night.

The **Wilbraham**, *1 Wilbraham Place, Sloane Street, London SW1; tel. (44-71)730-8296*, feels more like a country inn than a London hotel. It is in a converted Victorian house in Belgravia, near Sloane Square Station. A double room is £70 to £85 ($132 to $160).

Inverness Court, *1 Inverness Terrace, London W2; tel. (44-71)229-1444,* was built for Lily Langtry by Edward VII and truly stands out from countless others in the neighborhood. For a truly royal experience, rent the Langtry Suite, which comes with a four-poster bed and a decadent sunken bath. A double room starts at £70 ($132).

The most luxurious apartment

If you are planning an extended stay in London, and you really want to go in style, **St. James's Court**, *Buckingham Gate, London SW1; tel. (44-71)834-6655,* is the place to stay—it offers sheer, unadulterated luxury. Every conceivable service is offered—concierge, maid, laundry, and 24-hour room service—plus an excellent health club and two restaurants. The individually and stylishly decorated apartments are housed in a group of late Victorian mansion blocks overlooking a beautiful quadrangle. One-bed apartments are £1,800 ($3,406) per week, two-bed apartments are £2,700 ($5,110) per week, and three-bed apartments are £3,000 ($5,677) per week.

London's most affordable accommodation

University residence halls are the least expensive (and least discovered) form of accommodation in London. The rooms are well-equipped and conveniently located—and you don't have to be a student to take advantage of them. The greatest selection of rooms is available during university vacations, but you can book rooms at other times of the year as well. A double room typically costs £16 ($30) to £25 ($47) a night. Contact each respective university for specific rates.

The best side trips from London

Most travelers to Britain see little more than London. Yet it's outside London that you see the real England. The easiest way to get to the sights outside London is by rail or bus (or coach, as the British say). London has eight main train stations, each dealing with a different region—so make sure you are leaving from the right station. Each has an information office.

Buses are the least expensive way to take side trips. London has two main bus services: **National Express** and the **Green Line**. The main station for National Express is **Victoria Coach Station** (NOT Victoria Train Station, which is nearby), *Buckingham Palace Road, London SW1; tel. (44-71)730-0202.* The main station for the Green Line is **Eccleston Bridge**, just down the street; *tel. (44-81)668-7261.* If you are in a hurry, take a National Express bus. The Green Line makes more stops and is slower. However, the Green Line does have some express buses (called Rapid Buses).

Cambridge—the prettiest town

Cambridge is the prettiest of England's two rival university towns. A serene place, Cambridge was originally a Roman crossing over the River Cam. At the time of the Domesday Book (1086), Cambridge was a small trading village. Scholars gathered here in 1209 after being ousted from Oxford by irate townspeople. They opened a series of colleges that eventually became the university. The lovely old city (in Britain, any town with a cathedral is called a city) did not always see eye to eye with the university—riots were staged in 1381. The phrase "town and gown" indicates some of the old animosity.

The most impressive Gothic structure

The magnificent architecture of Cambridge and the beautiful surrounding countryside are good reasons to spend several days here. **King's College Chapel** is one of the most impressive Gothic structures in England. Be sure to see "Evensong" on Sunday, sung by a boys' choir at the chapel.

Oxford—the oldest university

Oxford University, with its 34 colleges and thousands of students, draws visitors from around the world. The college's 100 acres include lawns, gardens, water walks, and a private deer park where the famous Magdalen deer can be spotted. **New College**, built in the late 14th century, is one of the most inviting colleges on campus, with its medieval cloisters and peaceful gardens. A section of the old city walls can be found here.

While the university was founded in the 12th century, the town itself dates back to A.D. 912. The hero of many Dorothy Sayers mystery stories, Lord Peter Whimsey, studied at Oxford.

The oldest museum in Britain

The oldest public museum in Britain, the **Ashmolean,** is in Oxford. It has a great collection, including works by French Impressionists and Renaissance artists Raphael and Michelangelo. It also contains historical curios, such as the lantern Guy Fawkes carried when he tried to blow up Parliament in 1605.

The best inn

The **Bear Inn,** *Park Street, Woodstock; tel. (44-993)811-511,* is the best place to stay in Oxford. This establishment is seven centuries old and has oak beams and low ceilings. Rooms on the upper stories have sloping floors, and the steps are uneven. A double room is £100 ($190).

The Bear Inn is an important part of Oxford tradition—students meet here to sing university songs and to hold parties. The famous collection of neckties hanging on one wall here includes more than 4,200 ties donated by customers since 1951. Each bears the owner's signature. The collection includes ties from members of rowing clubs, cricket teams, student societies, the police, and the military. The ties are displayed according to nationality.

British silks at their best

A visit to Gloucestershire, just west of Oxford, is a real treat. **Beckford Silk,** *Beckford GL20 7AD; tel. (44-386)881-507,* is a silk mill where you can watch hand-screen printing of fabrics and talk to the printers about their skills.

Just a stone's throw away in the little village of Kemerton, another talented craftsperson also works in silk: **Tilly M,** *Stables Cottage, Kemerton GL20 7AY; tel. (44-386)892-83,* an artist who's eager to chat with visitors about her designs.

The best cheeses—and the craziest sport

In addition to its silks, Gloucestershire is also world-famous for its cheeses and for its cheese-rolling rituals. Originally, these rituals were associated with the rites of Midsummer. At one time, they were common throughout Gloucestershire and Wiltshire; now they are kept up only in Cooper's Hill and Randwick.

In Randwick, three cheeses play a role in two celebrations. At 10:30 a.m. on the first Sunday in May, the cheeses are taken to the village church, St. Johns', for a short service. From there, they are rolled three times around the church, and then one of them is cut up and distributed among the congregation.

The other two cheeses reappear the following Saturday, known as Wap, or Mayor's, Day (May 11). Displayed on litters, they occupy a place of honor in a colorful procession that also includes a Wap Queen, a band, and the Wap Mayor, accompanied by his sword-bearer and a sheriff.

The entire procession makes its way to the Mayor's Pool, where the Wap Queen officially welcomes the Mayor, who is then ceremoniously thrown into the water. After the dunking, the crowd accompanies the Mayor and the Queen to the hill near the village school, where the cheeses are rolled down the slope to open the Wap Fair.

Cheese-rolling at Cooper's Hill involves a much steeper slope. The ceremonies here take place on Spring Bank Holiday (May 27). Races are staged at half-hour intervals, beginning at 6 p.m. For each race, six to 10 runners line up at the top of the hill, set their cheeses (usually 7-pound Double Gloucesters) rolling downhill, and then take off after them in hot pursuit. The cheeses have been known to pick up such speed on their way down the hill that they have bounced right over the roof of the house at the bottom. The winner of the race keeps his cheese.

The best ecclesiastical maze

Grey's Court, near Henley-on-Thames in Oxfordshire, has the best example of an ecclesiastical maze in all England. Based on an ancient pagan design, it is formed by brick paths running through turf. At its center are two crosses—one Roman, one Byzantine. Made to celebrate the enthronement of the present Archbishop of Canterbury in 1982, the maze is said to represent the path of life and to symbolize pilgrimage.

The best racetrack in England

Known as the "horse racing capital of the world," Newmarket is renowned not only for its racetrack—with some of the best flat racing to be found anywhere—but also for the many training establishments and stud farms close by. This delightful small town just 60 miles and about two hours from London is a must for anyone interested in horses and racing.

Newmarket has two courses: the Rowley Mile and the July Course. The three major race meetings are in spring (April/May), summer (July/August), and autumn (late September/October), with the most famous events being the One Thousand and Two Thousand Guineas (late April), the Cambridgeshire (early October), and the Caesarewich (mid-October).

This little Suffolk town is also home to the National Horse Racing Museum, *99 High St.; tel. (44-638)667-333*, which presents exhibits that bring to life the social history of racing and includes pictures and sculptures by such masters of the genre as Stubbs and Munnings. The museum has five galleries, a coffee bar, a restaurant, and a gift shop and shows videos of famous races.

The best antique shopping outside London

Strangers usually visit Hungerford for one reason—to browse and to buy in the many antique shops. Here the collector can concentrate on the business at hand, undistracted by any other major attractions. The **Hungerford Arcade** on High Street has more than 80 stalls to investigate. There's some pretty junky stuff there, but treasures can still be found. For quality antique kitchenware, try **Below Stairs**, across the road from the Arcade. Over the Kennet and Avon Canal, where High Street turns into Bridge Street, is a whole cluster of shops sheltered beneath ancient red-tiled roofs. On the left is **Styles**, with a fine collection of quality silver and Edwardian to Georgian wine labels.

A bit farther on is **Pandora's Box**, where Joan Gleave stocks mainly Victoriana and specializes in Staffordshire pottery figures. The latter were often made to commemorate historic events (note the delightful group from the Crimean War) or a famous personality (generals and royalty were favorites).

On Charnham Street is **Bow House Antiques**, where upstairs Mrs. Herrington has a nursery of toys, dolls, teddy bears, and some bewitching dollhouse furniture. On the same street is an old cottage called **The Collector's Shop**, which has a wide variety of stock from different dealers that is well worth rummaging through.

The world's only rocking horse workshop

In the small Shropshire village of Wem, about 150 miles from London, is a workshop that makes nothing but rocking horses, *tel. (44-939)232-335*. These beautiful, large-eyed creatures were a popular feature of many Edwardian and Victorian nurseries. David and Noreen Kiss have made a profession out of restoring old horses from the 18th and 19th centuries, and the barn in their garden has become the world center for these wooden chargers of old. The rocking horses are made in a variety of woods, and visitors can view the entire process of reviving the rockers; everything is on display, from a basic block of timber to the full-colored model horse on its curving runners.

The oldest inhabited manor house in England

New Hall, *Walmley Road, Sutton Coldfield, West Midlands B76 8QX; tel. (44-21)378-2442*, isn't new. It's a 12th-century manor house, destined to become a more than worthy rival to the rather soulless conference hotels in nearby Birmingham— and a pleasant relief from the hotels in London. There are 65 rooms in the house, all with private baths. A double room starts at £110 ($208).

Britain's most charming village

The village of **Shanklin**, on the Isle of Wight off the southern coast of England, is charming—just what you'd imagine a British village should be. Thatched-roof cottages, many of them restaurants, pubs, and gift shops, line the streets. St. Blasius, the old parish church, dates in part from the 14th century. Climb down into the Shanklin Chine, a narrow ravine with a waterfall.

The Isle of Wight is accessible from Portsmouth or Southampton on the mainland by hydrofoil or ferry.

The largest inhabited castle in the world

Windsor Castle, still used by royalty after 850 years (construction of the castle was begun by William the Conqueror in the 11th century), is the largest inhabited castle in the world. Many of Britain's kings and queens are buried in **St. George's Chapel** here.

Located on the River Thames, Windsor is a picturesque Victorian town. Across the river from Windsor is **Eton College**, the most exclusive boys' school in Britain. Founded in 1440, it has educated many of the nation's leaders.

Canterbury: Chaucer's favorite

St. Augustine established Christianity in Canterbury in A.D. 597, and in 1197 the martyr Thomas à Becket was murdered in the cathedral here. Canterbury has been a settlement since the Iron Age. Visit **Canterbury Cathedral**, the mother church for the Anglican faith and a center for pilgrimages (including the one Chaucer wrote about). The structure was begun in 1070 and completed in 1503.

The world's most famous cliffs

The white cliffs of **Dover** are world-famous for their brilliant white color and their sheer drop into the sea. The best view of the cliffs is from the ferry that crosses the English Channel on its way to France.

Dover has recently become home to the White Cliffs Experience, England's Visitor Attraction of the Year. The exhibit outlines thousands of years of British history, from the Roman invasion of Britain in 55 B.C. to the air raids during World War II. It's located at Market Square and is adjacent to the Dover Museum. You can visit daily from 10:30 a.m. until 4:30 p.m.; admission is £4 ($7.50).

England's most romantic bed-and-breakfast

Hope End, *Ledbury, Hereford and Worcester HR8 1JQ; tel. (44-531)3613*, is one of the most inviting bed-and-breakfasts in England. Located in the coach house and stables of the house where Elizabeth Barrett Browning lived for 23 years (her house was demolished in 1873), it is cozy and serves delicious meals. You can ramble the "gentle land" where Browning's "steps in jocund childhood played." Forty acres of wooded valley and park surround the inn.

To get to Hope End, take a train from Paddington Station in London. Get off in Ledbury and take a taxi to the inn. There are only seven rooms, so make reservations. Hope End is closed Nov. 30 through February. A double room is £95 to £135 ($180 to $255).

The most picturesque region: the southwest peninsula

The southwest peninsula—Devon and Cornwall—is for people who like to breathe tangy sea breezes, explore fishing villages, walk harbor walls, swim in the sea, and wallow in England's maritime history. The southern coast faces the English Channel, which affords a mild climate with gentle waves softly lapping the secluded bays and ancient smugglers' coves. The northern coast of the peninsula faces the full force of the Atlantic.

All along the peninsula are little villages that appear to tumble down the hillsides. Inland are the granite moors. Dartmoor, Exmoor, and Bodmin are designated National Trust areas, protected from development.

Cornwall—the least changed region

Cornwall is one of the last genuinely unchanged counties of England. The motorway doesn't go here, but the meandering route from London is pretty. Cornwall is nearly 300 miles from London. (The train journey takes about five hours.)

This region, the one-time hideout of smugglers and pirates, is also the location of Tintagel, the legendary home of King Arthur. The tiny village of Camelford is supposedly the original Camelot. You can partake in a medieval banquet in the Great Hall at Tintagel, surrounded by the colors and banners of the Knights of the Round Table.

The best outdoor theater

Penzance, a colorful old South Cornish town of pirates and smugglers, is nearly 300 miles from London. In the summer, open-air opera, including the apt Gilbert and Sullivan work the *Pirates of Penzance*, is performed at the **Minack Theater** at Portcurno.

(The Minack Theater is carved out of a cliff. The audience watches the performance in the open air looking out over the Atlantic. Take along a warm sweater and a blanket.)

The prettiest Cornish town

St. Mawes, on the southern coast of Cornwall, is one of the prettiest towns in Britain. Located at the mouth of Percuil Creek, it is known for its fine sailing and its castle, which was built by King Henry VIII from 1540 to 1543. The castle is shaped like a clover leaf for good luck.

Cornwall's best hotels

The best seaside hotel in Cornwall is the **Falmouth Hotel**, *Castle Beach, Falmouth, Cornwall TR11 4NZ; tel. (44-326)312-671.* Overlooking Pendennis Point and Pendennis Castle, it was opened in 1865 and has accommodated Edward VII and stage stars Anna Neagle and Herbert Wilcox. A double room is £47 ($89), including breakast.

Allhays Country House, *Talland Bay, Looe, Cornwall PL 132 JB; tel. (44-503)72434*, is one of the best bed-and-breakfasts in the region. A double room is £26 to £36 ($49 to $68).

Truro Farm, *Park Farm, St. Clements, Truro, Cornwall; tel. (44-872)72532*, is a rambling stone house constructed in a jumble of periods from the 16th through the 18th centuries. Rooms have lovely antiques ranging from Georgian to Victorian.

A footpath leads to the village of Malpas, from which you can take boat trips downriver to Falmouth. This house is a particularly good bargain—a double room is £15 ($28), half price for children younger than 10.

The best moor: Dartmoor

In the heart of Devon is the 365-square-mile **Dartmoor National Park**, *tel. (44-626)832-093*, which embodies the county's mystery and beauty. Dartmoor is the setting of *The Hound of the Baskervilles*, as well as the location of the notorious Dartmoor Prison. Its desolate moors are relieved by cozy villages and rolling hills.

Wild ponies canter through Dartmoor's fields of wild flowers. Thatched cottages dot the landscape, and towns here—Widecombe-in-the-Moor, Ashburton, Okehampton, and Chagford—are all within walking distance of the moors. Try to be in the area during a village fair or stock show. You will think time has stood still.

If you want to explore the wilds of Dartmoor National Park, pick up an ordinance map of the park, don your waterproof boots, and set out.

After hiking all day, stop in at **Barton's** in Chagford, where you can enjoy an authentic Devonshire tea, complete with scones, strawberry preserves, and thick Devonshire cream.

The best stone rows

Dartmoor has the country's best example of stone **rowsyard**—high rocks set in a line. The rocks are sometimes covered with circular designs. Look carefully—they are often hidden by heather. The rows lead to round barrows or cairns (burial mounds).

The best Bronze Age village

Grimspound in Manaton is one of the best examples of a fortified Bronze Age village on the moor. It is also the largest, with 24 hut circles in a 150-yard enclosure. The protecting wall was originally 10 feet high and had three entrances. The hut circles had cooking holes, stone platforms, and flat center stones that supported the roof poles.

The most luxurious hotel in Devon

The most luxurious place to stay in Dartmoor National Park is **Gidleigh Park**, *Chagford, Devon TQ1 38HH; tel. (44-64743)2367.* This peaceful country manor has blazing fires, chintz-covered furniture, and oak-paneled walls. The hotel has 12 rooms and an exceptional restaurant and is surrounded by 30 acres.

Gidleigh Park is rather expensive—£135 to £250 ($255 to $473) a night for two. But it's worth the price. Make reservations in the United States through **David B. Mitchell & Company Inc.**, *(800)743-8033.*

The coziest bed-and-breakfast by the moor

Burrator House, *Sheepstor, near Yelverton, Devon PL20 6PF; tel. (44-822)853121,* is a Georgian house on 20 acres. It is on the B3212 Road and has a trout pool, a miniature waterfall, a swimming pool, and a Victorian snooker table. (Snooker is a form of pool.) A double room is £30 to £45 ($56 to $85) per person; a family room with its own bath is £40 ($75).

The best of the Cotswolds

The "Heart of England" lies just an hour and a half (by train) west and slightly north of London. Here, a softly rolling ribbon of hills enfolds rustic villages of another, more romantic age. This region, known as the **Cotswolds**, was the prosperous hub of the wool trade in the 13th through 16th centuries, and you can still glimpse an occasional flock of sheep. Towns and villages nestling in these hills are made up of houses built of the local stone, with steep slate roofs.

The most charming village

Tetbury is the most charming village in the Cotswolds, an old market town with hilly streets that weave and curve around the Old Market House, built in 1655. Early in the morning, bottles of milk with cream on top sit outside the doors of the town's quaint houses.

Tetbury has a beautiful church, **St. Mary the Virgin**, some antique shops—and little else. The town is surrounded by royalty—the Prince and Princess of Wales, Princess Anne, and Prince and Princess Michael of Kent all have homes within a few miles.

Shakespeare's favorite

Stratford-upon-Avon, Shakespeare's home town, sits at the northeast tip of the Cotswolds. Despite its commercialized, touristy flavor, Stratford is pretty, with authentic Tudor buildings on practically every street.

You're cheating yourself if you don't make it to one of the Royal Shakespeare Company's productions. Also worth a stop is the Dirty Duck Pub, where actors hang out between shows. It is across from the theater, right up from the McDonald's.

Stratford-upon-Avon Brass Rubbing Centre, *The Summer House, Avon Bank Gardens, Stratford-upon-Avon, Warwickshire; tel. (44-789)297671*, is the best brass rubbing center in the area. It traces the history of commemorative brasses from the 12th through 17th centuries.

The best of Cheltenham

Cheltenham, the tourist base of the Cotswolds, is a melange of old and new. Georgian terraced houses with flower-draped, wrought-iron balconies stand beside gray cubelike office buildings and utilitarian storefront strips.

The nicest strip is the **Promenade**, a treelined avenue with ornate Georgian buildings. Visit the Cheltenham Racecourse, one of England's finest steeplechase courses.

The best castle in the Cotswolds

Six miles up the A46 from Cheltenham is **Sudeley Castle** in Winchcombe. Catherine Parr, the sixth wife of Henry VIII and the only one to survive him, lived and is buried here. (Henry's fourth wife, Anne of Cleves, also survived him, but their marriage was annulled.)

The best places to stay

Two hotels that make ideal bases for touring the Cotswolds are the Close at Tetbury and the Hotel de la Bere, just outside Cheltenham. The Close was once the home of a 16th-century wool merchant. The Hotel de la Bere is a sprawling, grandiose 16th-century building. For reservations, contact **Ray Morrow Associates**, *4228 Hermitage Road, Virginia Beach, VA 23455; (800)243-9420*.

The best way to get there

One of the best things about the Cotswolds is the region's proximity to London. The capital is less than two hours away by the M4 or M40 motorway.

The best place in England to take a bath

England's most magnificent spa is, appropriately, **Bath**. According to legend, the mineral springs at Bath were first discovered by King Bladud (the father of King Lear), who had been banished into the countryside because of his leprosy. He became a swineherd, and his pigs led him to the springs, which cured him of the disease.

Visit the Roman Baths and the Pump Room, where you can drink the bubbling hot mineral water from the fountain. The Great Bath is exposed to the sky. Next door is a museum displaying Roman and prehistoric relics. Stroll along the Royal Crescent, a sweep of 30 Georgian houses joined by one facade and fronted with Ionic columns.

England's best-preserved town

Chester, on the west coast in Cheshire County, is one of the few English towns still encircled by a medieval wall. The thick wall doubles as an attractive promenade lined with shops. Within the walls are Tudor half-timbered houses.

Founded in A.D. 60, Chester was the headquarters of the Roman XX Legion, and many Roman relics remain.

Residents of this friendly town invite overseas visitors to spend an afternoon in their homes for tea and conversation. The program is called **Chester at Home**. For information, call Mr. and Mrs. Read, *tel. (44-51)339-6615*. Locals also offer free tours to visitors.

The most inspiring region: Yorkshire

Yorkshire has inspired a number of English writers, including James Herriot and the Bronte family. Herbert Read, the poet and art critic, was a more recent Yorkshire literary light.

James Herriot Country, as Yorkshire County is known, is a patchwork of undulating pastures dotted with sheep and lined with ancient stone walls, desolate moors, rugged coastlines, and medieval towns.

The best of the Brontes

The Brontes lived in **Haworth**, a romantic town perched precariously on a hillside, commanding superb views from its cobblestoned streets. From 11 a.m. until 5:30 p.m. April through September, you can visit the parsonage that was their home; it closes at 4:30 p.m. October through March.

The most colorful place to dine or stay in Haworth is the **Black Bull House**, *Main Street, Haworth; tel. (44-5356)42249*, where Branwell Bronte obtained his supplies of opium.

The best view of the area

At **Thirsk**, a charming market town in Yorkshire, a natural ridge provides a superb hang-gliding site. Visitors are welcome to take glider rides, enjoying bird's-eye views of the area. For more information, contact the **Yorkshire Gliding Club**, *Sutton Bank, Thirsk, Yorkshire Y07 2EY; tel. (44-845)597-237*.

The best guidebook

The guidebook that offers the most insight into this region is James Herriot's *Yorkshire*. The animal lover and writer knows the region inside out—and his love of the area is evident in his writing.

The coziest place to stay

The **Black Swan Hotel**, *Market Place, Helmsley, North Yorkshire; tel. (44-439)70466*, is an old coaching inn on the edge of North York Moors National Park. It serves full English breakfasts, traditional teas, and traditional Sunday lunches. Try the venison, the Barnsley chops, and the puddings. A double room is £59 to £74 ($110 to $140) per person.

The most historic city: York

In A.D. 867, the Danish Vikings vanquished York, and many of the area's street names, such as Micklegate, Bootham, and Walmgate, date from this period. After the Vikings, the Normans took possession. The city's architecture bears witness to their influence. During the sixth century, the legendary King Arthur is said to have captured York, and in the seventh century the Saxons moved in. They built a small wooden church, the original **York Minster**. (A *minster* is a church that was once a monastery.) Until the 14th century, York was strategically and economically more important than London and was the nation's capital.

In the early 1970s, it was discovered that the foundations of the York Minster were on the move. Draining and underpinning were urgently required. During the work, which began in 1976, evidence of a massive Roman military fortress and a Roman drainage system were discovered. The drains were in such good condition that they could be used for the necessary drainage without repair! Quite impressive for something built in A.D. 71.

During the excavations, one of the workmen on the site insisted that he saw the ghosts of an entire battalion of Roman soldiers marching before him. The British workman was visibly shaken. "One of the strangest things," he said, "was that they were only visible from the knees up. You couldn't see their legs." Further excavations revealed an ancient Roman road at just about the level the soldiers' feet would have been.

Work continues in the south transept of the church, repairing damage caused by a fire started by a bolt of lightning on July 31, 1984. Some say it was divine retribution after disparaging remarks were made by the Bishop of Durham from the minster pulpit about the Trinity. The Queen and Prince Charles have donated ancient oak trees from their estates to help rebuild the roof sections of the transept.

The best city walk

A footpath along the top of the walls that surround York provides a pleasant three-mile saunter on a warm summer evening. You can circle the entire city on the walls, coming down the stone steps at intervals to see the sights. Modern traffic runs between these steps and their ancient gatehouses. The York Minster is visible from the walls at all times. It is a delightful contrast to the black-and-white Tudor buildings that surround it.

The best sightseeing tip

Don't take a car into York. Sights are within easy walking distance of one another, public transportation is available, and parking is a nightmare not to be contemplated.

The most esteemed chocolate maker

Just southwest of Yorkshire is a renowned chocolate maker known as **Thorntons,** *Thornton Park, Somercotes, Derbyshire DE55 4XJ; tel. (44-773)608-822.* Founded in 1925, Thorntons was initially famous for its distinctive toffee, but it is now equally renowned for its chocolates. Try to visit at Easter, when you can buy a chocolate egg and then wait while it's personalized with your name in icing. You can also shop for confections made of almonds, apricots, vine fruits, and the like, all of which may be carried away in one of Thornton's edible lacy-weave chocolate baskets.

The Brits' favorite holiday place

If it came to a choice between London and the Lake District, any Briton would choose the **Lake District**. An area of outstanding natural beauty, it covers the northwestern corner of England, just south of the Scottish border. It is easily accessible via the M6 Motorway, approximately a five-hour drive from London.

The Lake District is rich in literary connections. Wordsworth was born here and was visited often by Shelley and Coleridge. Robert Southey lived in Keswick for more than 40 years. And John Ruskin's name pops up everywhere, from Ruskin House Pottery in Ambleside to the cross commemorating him in the churchyard at Coniston. This is also the country of Beatrix Potter, the much-loved author of delightful children's stories. Charles Lamb vacationed in Keswick.

The best way to see the Lake District

The best way to see the Lake District is leisurely. You'll absorb more of the atmosphere by sitting beside one lake for a few hours than by racing around the largest lakes and main towns and villages. The tiny roads that weave between and over the hills will defeat anyone in a hurry. Also keep in mind that wandering sheep have the right of way here, and you'll often have to leave your car to open and close sheep gates that cross the road.

Head first for Brockhole, a country house halfway between Windermere and Ambleside on the main road. The house is an information center and has a pleasant tearoom.

The best-kept secret in the Lake District

If you want to escape the crowds of tourists shuttling around the Lake District, head for the **Wasdale Head Inn**, *near Gosforth, Cumbria CA20 1EX; tel. (44-9467)26229*. This remote, secluded pub is a haven of peace set in one of Lakeland's most beautiful, unspoiled valleys. The views of Great Gable, Sca Fell, and other massive peaks are an inspiration, and nearby Wastwater is perhaps the most dramatic of the lakes. Walkers, rock climbers, and anyone interested in the great outdoors find this traditional mountain inn a real delight. And a visit to Wasdale Head will put you in good company, for Wordsworth, Coleridge, and Dickens are known to have frequented the area, and British novelist Nicholas Monsaratt bought his first glass of beer ever in the inn. A double room starts at £68 ($128).

The two most spectacular lakes

Ullswater, which is surrounded by hills and highlands rising from the water's edge, is the most spectacular of the lakes. Wordsworth immortalized the daffodils he saw here and described Ullswater as "perhaps...the happiest combination of beauty and grandeur, which any of the Lakes affords."

The best place to stay on the banks of Ullswater is the **Sharrow Bay Hotel**, *Penrith, Cumbria CA10 2LZ; tel. (44-7684)86301*. Proprietor Francis Coulson goes to great lengths to please his guests. A roaring fire warms the lounge, and rooms are equipped with backgammon and Scrabble boards. The views are tremendous. A double room is £118 to £140 ($223 to $264), including breakfast.

Mr. Coulson despises cuisine *minceur* and believes in cream with everything, so the food is sinfully delicious. Try the cream of watercress soup and, for dessert, the kiwifruit pavlova and cream profiteroles with chocolate sauce.

The most beautiful stone circle

Just two miles east of Keswick is **Castlerigg Stone Circle**, the most beautifully situated stone circle in England. And unlike the famous Stonehenge, it is not inundated with tourists.

You can work out a number of astronomical details from this circle, which is 100 feet in diameter with 38 stones in its outer ring (almost all standing in their original positions) and 10 more within.

From Castlerigg, you can see the north Lakeland hills. Three miles away is a hill called Threlkeld Knott, over which the sun rises during an equinox.

Wordsworth's favorite spot

Tiny **Grasmere** village is more famous for its delightful position, nestled as it is beneath Helm Crag and Nab Scar northwest of Lake Windermere, than for its amenities. Wordsworth called it "the loveliest spot that man hath ever found." He made his first home nearby at Dove Cottage. Open to the public, Dove Cottage is tiny and charming, with a museum next door. Historian Philip Crowl says, "The management of this site is a model of graciousness combined with efficiency. Few stately homes, for all their large staffs and high entrance fees, do as well." Even the garden is a delight.

Britain's most regal beach resort

The seaside town of **Brighton** became popular with aristocrats in the mid-18th century. (It later lost standing and became a big favorite of P.G. Wodehouse's Jeeves, the butler, who liked to fish here.) Brighton was originally a tiny fishing village that is mentioned in the Domesday Book.

The best walks in Brighton are along Old Steine, which is the center of activity; out to the Palace Pier, a Victorian structure that juts nearly a third of a mile into the English Channel; and along the Marine Parade, an attractive promenade with 19th-century terraces.

The biggest attraction in town is the restored **Royal Pavilion**, a pseudo-Oriental structure built by the Prince Regent, George, Prince of Wales (later King George IV) from 1787 to 1822. The pavilion graphically demonstrates the excesses and extravagances of the Regency period.

If you tire of the sun—or rain—the most inviting places for tea are the lounge of the Metropole and the veranda of the Grand Hotel (rebuilt after the Irish Republican Army bombed it in 1984 in an attempt on the life of Margaret Thatcher).

Wheeler's Sheridan and English's are Brighton's most elegant restaurants.

The world's best gardens

English gardens are known worldwide for their colorful, wild abandon. Gardening is something the British do well. And the rainy weather and mild winters, particularly in the south, provide a congenial environment for cultivating trees and plants.

Today, you don't have to be wealthy to enjoy the immense gardens of England's royal estates. Apart from financial considerations, most owners today believe that it's right to share their historic homes and gardens with the rest of us.

The most beautiful garden

Of all the gardens in England, the most beautiful is **Sissinghurst Castle Garden**, two miles northeast of Cranbrook. Created by writer Vita Sackville-West (who wrote a gardening column for the *Daily Telegraph* for years) and her husband, diplomat Sir Harold Nicolson, Sissinghurst is a series of walled gardens located between the surviving parts of an Elizabethan mansion.

The prettiest is the white garden, planted with only white flowers. Also lovely are the rose garden, with old-fashioned English roses (old-fashioned roses predate hybrids, which are what most gardens grow today), the herb garden, the yew walk, the moat walk, and the orchard. The gardens are open April through Oct. 15, Tuesday through Friday, 1 until 6:30 p.m.

The most splendid Temple gardens

The 350 acres of **Stowe**, in Buckinghamshire, are set around the great Palladian house of the Temple family, whose punning motto *Templa quam dilecta* (how splendid are the temples!) is equally splendidly realized in the grottos, columns, bridges, arches, and monuments amid the woodlands and undulating, grassy landscape. In the Augustan era of Georgian England, these classical temples were intended to evoke ancient Rome.

The Temples had dissipated their great fortune by the end of Victoria's reign and soon thereafter had to sell their Buckinghamshire estate. Today it has become one of Britain's foremost schools.

The names of the designers give the clue to Stowe's greatness: Vanbrugh, Kent, and Gibbs, three of the foremost architects of the 18th century, worked on these gardens. Lancelot "Capability" Brown, the man who developed the natural look and advocated informal planning of gardens, was the Temples' head gardener from 1741. Under his visionary eye, the garden was transformed into a spectacular, classical landscape.

The best guides to English gardens

Historic Houses, Castles, and Gardens is an indispensable catalog of more than 1,400 historic properties and gardens in England that are open to the public. Included is a brief history of each, its hours, entry fees, what you'll see, and how to get to the property. The price is £6.95 ($13); order from **ABC Historic Publications**, *World Timetable Centre,*

Church Street, Dunstable, Bedfordshire; tel. (44-582)600-111.

National Gardens Scheme lists private gardens open to the public alphabetically by county. The Scheme is a charitable trust begun in 1927 as a memorial to Queen Alexandra. It now comprises more than 1,600 gardens. Proceeds are administered by the Queen's Nursing Institute. You can order the list from the **National Gardens Scheme Charitable Trust**, *57 Lower Belgrave St., London SW1 W0LR; tel. (44-71)730-0359.*

England's best palaces

Castle Howard, in the rugged north, is the most beautiful of England's castles. This 18th-century home 15 miles north of York was the film site for Evelyn Waugh's *Brideshead Revisited,* the renowned British television series.

Actually a palace, Castle Howard was designed in 1699 for Charles Howard, third Earl of Carlisle, and is aglow with paintings by Rubens, Gainsborough, and Reynolds. Some of the furniture is by Sheraton and Chippendale, and the costume galleries have displays dating from the 18th century. The grounds are extensive, with lakes, fountains, and a beautiful Temple of the Four Winds. A replica of an 18th-century rose garden has old-fashioned roses that are no longer available commercially.

Blenheim Palace, in Oxfordshire, is a close second. Near the old town of Woodstock, it was the home of the 11th Duke of Marlborough and the birthplace of Sir Winston Churchill. The gardens and park were designed by Queen Anne's gardener, Henry Wise, and later added to by Capability Brown, an 18th-century landscape gardener who created Blenheim Lake. If you weren't told it was landscaped, you'd think it was all natural. Blenheim is open mid-March through October.

The best English cathedral

Salisbury Cathedral, the only English cathedral built of a single type of stone, can be seen for miles. Set in a grassy plain, the 13th-century structure has the tallest spire in England, rising 404 feet. The best way to see this immense cathedral is to take the 90-minute guided tour, which gives you a look at parts of the cathedral not generally open to the public. The tour is held at 11 a.m. and 2:30 p.m. year-round and at 6:30 p.m. during the summer.

The cloisters and **Chapter House** that adjoin the cathedral are also worth seeing. The walls of the Chapter House are decorated with bas reliefs of the Old Testament. Enjoy the open lawns of the Cathedral Close. (Novelist Henry Fielding once lived in one of the houses on the close.)

The best of Wales

Wales, that poetic land to the west of England, is renowned for its mighty castles. Dozens can be visited. They perch on rocky cliffs, cling to the mountains, hide in the moors, and rise up from the sea.

Many of the finest Welsh castles were constructed by King Edward I in the 13th century. The best known and grandest Welsh castle is **Caernarfon** in the north, birthplace of Edward II, the first Prince of Wales. Enclosed by 13th-century town walls, it is a masterpiece of medieval architecture. Prince Charles was dubbed Prince of Wales here by his mother when he turned 18. Nearby is the Roman fort **Segontium**, founded in A.D. 78.

The two best hotels in the town of Caernarfon are the Royal, a historic coach house, and Black Boy Inn, which dates back to the 14th century.

Cardiff Castle, in the Welsh capital, is the second-best castle in Wales. Built in the 11th century on the site of an old Roman camp, it was reconstructed in 1865 and given an ornate Victorian exterior. Inside, it is romantic and extravagant, especially the Arab Room and the Chaucer Room. The roof garden is colorful.

Parts of the original Roman fort on which the castle was built still exist. And you still can see the Norman keep in the northwest corner.

Last but not least is **Harlech**, an enormous castle that watches over a tiny village. Actually, you should put it first on your itinerary. Because it's not as well preserved as Caernarfon, it's spared the crowds of tourists.

Built by Edward I in 1283, the castle was the last to yield to the Yorkists in 1468 during the War of the Roses. It is set high on a cliff and protected by a massive double doorway. One of the best views of Snowdonia Mountain is from the top of the castle wall. Nearby is the most gorgeous beach on the Welsh coast.

The best fortification in Wales

Offa's Dyke, the eighth-century earthwork created by King Offa to keep out the marauding Welsh, marks the English/Welsh border. The 1,200-year-old earthwork can best be seen from the cliffs near Llanymynech in Shropshire, six miles from Oswestry. (Llanymynech's other claim to fame is the Lion Hotel, which is half in England and half in Wales.)

If you have time, one of the best ways to see Wales is to follow the 176-mile **Offa's Dyke Path** from Prestatyn, on the northern Welsh Coast, to Sedbury Cliff, Chepstow. It leads from sea to sea through the Black Mountains, the Clun Forest, and the Vale of Clwyd. The prettiest part of the path is over the bare central uplands of Clun Forest, where the remains of the Dyke are best preserved.

Another highlight is the beautiful ruin **Tintern Abbey**, the site of Wordsworth's poem by the same name. Nearby, the devil supposedly tempted the monks. The gabled ends of the 13th-century abbey church rise out of a green meadow. The slate roof of the church was destroyed after Henry VIII dissolved the monasteries in 1537. For more information, contact **Offa's Dyke Association**, *West Street, Knighton, Powys; tel. (44-547)528-753.*

The best book browsing in Britain

Hay-on-Wye is a charming little border town with typically narrow streets and a surprising number of bookstores, the result of one man's passion for things literary. His book collection overflowed from his own huge bookstore, with shelves from cellar to attic, into the town's movie theater and dozens of smaller bookstores throughout the town. It is a monument to British eccentricity and well worth a browse.

The best Welsh national park

Pembrokeshire Coast National Park is 150 breathtaking miles of immense rocky cliffs that drop into the sea, remote bays, inviting inlets, caves, coves, strangely shaped rock formations, and tranquil islands. Many of the rocks along this coastline are made of lava from volcanos that erupted 600 million years ago. A marked footpath follows the coastline, passing more than 50 Iron Age fortresses, a number of Celtic churches, and Norman castles at Pembroke, Carew, Haverfordwest, Cardigan, Manorbier, and Tenby.

Visit the seaside towns nearby. Llandudno and Aberystwyth are lively, elegant resorts. Tenby and Aberaeron are quieter places with harbors and whitewashed houses. Baby yourself at the Rock Park spa in the 19th-century spa town of Llandrindod Wells.

For more information, contact the **Pembrokeshire Coast National Park Development Office**, *County Offices, Haverfordwest, Dyfed SA61 1QZ; tel. (44-437)764-591.*

The highest peak in England or Wales

Mount Snowdon, in Snowdonia National Park, is the highest peak in England or Wales, at 3,560 feet. It is also the steepest and most barren mountain. A narrow-gauge railway climbs to the top. Snowdonia offers 1,000 square miles of rugged mountains and moors, lakes, and rolling green hills. The park can be visited via the Snowdon Sherpa bus service, which runs every half-hour, Monday through Thursday, July 15 through Sept. 1. You can catch the bus in Caernarfon.

Hiking here is spectacular, but it can be dangerous. Follow an ordinance survey map. Be sure to wear sturdy boots and bring a sweater and rain gear. For information on hiking trails and accommodation, contact the **Snowdonia Park Information Office,** *Penrhyndeudrach, Gwynedd LL48 6LS; tel. (44-766)770274.*

The best walled town in Wales

Tenby, a 14th-century walled town, has two sandy beaches (the best is North Beach) and a lovely harbor. The town's narrow streets lead to Castle Hill, a spit of land edged by cliffs that drop to the beach. St. Catherine's Island, which has an abandoned fort, can be seen from Castle Hill.

The nicest place to stay is the **Imperial Hotel,** which uses the town wall as one of its walls. For information, stop at the Croft, above North Beach.

The largest weekly market

Welshpool is the first town over the English border—160 miles northeast of London. Visit Welshpool on a Monday to see the largest weekly market in Wales. Farmers have been bringing their sheep and cattle here for more than 500 years.

The best Welsh beach resort

Aberystwyth is a popular beach resort with a lively seafront promenade, pastel-colored Victorian houses, black-and-white Welsh houses, and the ruins of a castle. It is also home to the oldest university in Wales (a neo-Gothic building opened in 1877) and the center of the revival of Welsh culture. You can hear traditional Welsh music at the **Cooper's Arms,** *Northgate Street.* Stop in at the National Library of Wales, which houses most of the surviving Welsh medieval manuscripts.

The best island in Wales

Holyhead, off the coast of Aberystwyth, is the prettiest island in Wales, complete with palm trees, pastel-colored houses overlooking tranquil bays full of fishing boats and yachts, and a spate of fine restaurants.

The best of Scotland

Scotland's capital, **Edinburgh,** lost its rank as Scotland's largest city to archrival Glasgow in the 19th century. The result has been to make Edinburgh the more attractive tourist destination (except for Victoriana buffs, who prefer Glasgow).

Edinburgh's **Royal Mile,** which runs along the spine of a hill from Holyrood to Edinburgh Castle, is the most beautiful section of the city. Parts of the stretch date back to the Middle Ages. Few cities in the British Isles have so well preserved a medieval quarter. The Royal Mile has survived because of the 18th-century New Town in the plains below. New Town was built to house the surplus population and to avoid demolition of the old sections.

Follow the Royal Mile beginning at the castle end. It's downhill in this direction. The castle is mostly a shrine to British militarism, complete with red-kneed and kilted Scottish guards at the entrance (the regiment changes daily) and a military museum with historic mementos of these regiments and the parade grounds where they march.

The palace, or lodging, in the castle is where Mary Queen of Scots gave birth to James I of England (also known as James VI of Scotland). The lodging was heavily restored in the last century.

The oldest building in Edinburgh, built in 1076, is the miniscule whitewashed church inside the castle walls called the **Chapel of St. Margaret.** Margaret, queen of Scotland, was canonized for her holy life. (Her immediate predecessor as queen was Lady Macbeth, so she had a hard job of it.) Margaret helped Anglicize the Scots, starting with her husband, King Malcolm III.

The main street running below the castle features historic houses associated with the city's luminaries: John Knox, Robert Burns, Walter Scott, Robert Louis Stevenson. It also provides a fascinating glimpse of historic Scottish life: old shops and breweries, an old printing press, a Presbyterian cathedral, a school, a sugar refinery, and a bakery.

One of the most interesting sites along the route is the tollbooth, which was the prison setting for Sir Walter Scott's *The Heart of Midlothian*. Another is Golfers' Land, the property purchased by a 17th-century golf champion with his winnings. John Patersone, a shoemaker, began his golfing career as a caddie and later became the partner of James II.

At the bottom of the main road, just one mile from the castle, is **Holyrood**, a converted abbey that was home to Scottish kings. Its style was heavily influenced by the French style Charles II learned about in exile. Charles II also commissioned a series of paintings of his ancestors that graces the picture gallery. Dutch artist Jakob de Witt knew how to please his royal patron. He made all 111 forebearers of Charles II look terribly like Charles II.

Holyrood is closely associated with Mary Queen of Scots, who lived and held court here from 1561 to 1567. She married Henry, Lord Darnley in 1565 in the Chapel Royal. You can see the room where she received John Knox (who fulminated against "a monstrous regiment of women") and the room where her secretary, David Riccio, was dragged from her presence and murdered (probably by one of her husbands).

The finest hotel in Edinburgh is the **Caledonian**, *Princes Street, Edinburgh EH1 2AB; tel. (44-31)225-2433*. This grand hotel has magnificent views of the castle. Recently refurbished, the Caledonian, with 212 rooms, three dining rooms, and three bars, is a favorite among celebrities. A double room is £165 ($312).

If you're unsure where to stay, contact the **Tourist Accommodation Service**, *Waverley Market, 3 Princes St., Edinburgh EH2 2OP; tel. (44-31)557-2727*, which can help you find a room.

The world's best tenement

The best tenement in the world is **Gladstone's Land** in Edinburgh, although until 1934 it was just another grossly overcrowded slum dwelling. Restoration of the house, now a museum on Landmarket along the Royal Mile, has returned the place to what the Gladstones originally set out to erect in 1617. At that time, the tenement was simply a plot of ground on the main street, on which the Gladstones erected a six-story walk-up building with shops on the ground floor.

Britain's best festival: the Edinburgh International

Millions of visitors visit Edinburgh each summer for the **Edinburgh International Festival**, which draws prominent musicians and theater groups from around the world. Tickets are £11 to £40 ($20 to $70). **Edwards and Edwards**, *1 Times Square Plaza, New York, NY 10036; (212)944-0290*, sells tickets in the United States.

While known as one of the world's leading musical and theater festivals, the Edinburgh International Festival has a little-known sideshow. Edinburgh also provides a stage for some of the best avant-garde productions in the English language. The **Fringe**, as part of the festival is called, boasts more than 1,000 events and 9,000 performances, including theater, comedy, musicals, cabaret, revues, opera, mime, dance, children's shows, folk, jazz, rock/blues, poetry, and multimedia presentations.

Scotland's best art collections

A medieval city surrounding a 13th-century cathedral, **Glasgow** houses three remarkable art collections:

The **Burrell Collection** is housed in a beautiful building with glass walls through which you can see the landscape of Pollok Park. The collection includes Oriental ceramics, French tapestries, and medieval stained glass.

The **Kelvingrove** contains masterpieces by Lippi, Rubens, and Constable. Its pride, however, is its collection of Impressionist paintings. Works by Monet, Pissarro, Matisse, Dégas, and van Gogh grace the walls.

The **Hunterian Museum** has paintings by Rembrandt, Stubbs, Chardin, and Whistler.

When you tire of art, take tea at the **Willow Tea Room**. Or dine at the **Ubiquitous Chip**, *12 Ashton Lane*, off Byres Road.

The **Central**, *Gordon Street; tel. (44-41)221-9680*, is the most comfortable and old-fashioned hotel in Glasgow. A double room is £33 to £56 ($62 to $105). For more information on accommodation in the city, contact the **Greater Glasgow Tourist Board**, *Georges Square, Glasgow G1 2ER; tel. (44-41)204-4400*.

The best Scottish castle

Stirling Castle in Fife, where Mary Queen of Scots was crowned in 1543, offers views of the Grampian Mountains from its cannonades. For centuries it was Scotland's only defense against English invaders. Once the palace of Stuart kings, Stirling is embellished with bacchanalian figurines. King Robert Bruce (known simply as The Bruce) and Sir William Wallace held the castle against the English for years. In 1305, however, Wallace was betrayed to the English and hanged, drawn, and quartered in London.

For atmosphere, no hotel in Stirling beats the **Golden Lion**, *8 King St.; (44-786)75351*, which has hosted Robert Burns, members of the royal family, and movie stars. A double room is £60 ($113).

The world's best golf course

The **Old Course** in St. Andrews, Scotland, is the most venerable (and the oldest) golf course in the world. It dates back to the 15th century and has been the site of 24 British Opens. It is a difficult course, with sandy greens and an ever-changing wind, but golfers love to face its constant challenges.

The Old Course, like most Scottish greens, is a links course, which means it is made up of tough seaside dunes covered with only a little grass. You may want to get a few tips on playing links courses before you give it a try.

Contact the **Links Management Committee of St. Andrews**, *Bilmore Cottage, St. Andrews, Fife, KY16 9JA Scotland; tel. (44-334)75757*, eight weeks before your visit to apply to play on the Old Course. (It is most difficult to get a tee time in July and August.) If you can't get permission to play on the Old Course, try one of its younger counterparts in St. Andrews: New Course, Eden, or the Jubilee.

An angler's dream

The area around Loch Lomond, Stirling, the Trossachs, and the Firth of Clyde, in the heart of Scotland, offers some of the best fishing you'll find anywhere in the world. And the best spot in this region to drop your line is the western end of Loch Tay at Killin. If you are interested in fishing, this place is perfect. Contact the **Central Scotland Anglers Association**, *53 Fernieside Crescent, Edinburgh EH12 9DQ; tel. (44-31)664-4685*, or the **Scottish Anglers National Association**, *5 Kramond Glebe Road, Kramond, Lothian EH4 6ND*, for more information about the area.

The best skiing in Scotland

Where should you go for the best skiing in Scotland? The Cairngorm mountain range, which rises 4,084 feet and offers the most developed facilities in the country. It has the greatest range of downhill runs, as well as 17 lifts and tows. Runs vary from long, easy slopes to the black-graded West Wall, for experts only.

The most dramatic region: the Highlands

The desolate beauty of the **Highlands** should not blind you to its violent past. Over the centuries, the Gaelic Highlanders have suffered terrible defeats to the English, fought bloody battles among themselves, and been driven from their homes by wealthy landowners. During the Highland Clearances in the 18th century, crofters were driven from their homes by landowners who wanted to raise sheep. Those who refused to go had their houses and goods burned.

Peaceful today, the Highlands are known for their secluded glens, craggy peaks, and sparkling lochs. The country is virtually unspoiled. Route A82 leads from Glasgow into the Highlands, curving along the west bank of Loch Lomond. When the famed lake turns into a stream, you are in the Highlands. The country is wild, steep, and unfenced.

The bloodiest place in the Highlands

One of the most ruggedly beautiful places in the Highlands is **Glencoe**, the misty valley that was the scene of a brutal massacre on Feb. 13, 1692. Here, the Macdonald clan, which had fought for James II, was butchered by the Campbell clan, soldiers of William of Orange. The Macdonalds were stabbed to death in their beds at dawn. Their homes were burned and their cattle stolen. Nothing remains of the human inhabitants of the Glen of Weeping, as it's known today. The only residents are golden eagles and red deer.

The most beautiful Highland drives

The **Road to the Isles**, A830, follows the spectacular Atlantic coast. One of the most beautiful passes en route is **Glenfinnan**, where in 1745 Bonnie Prince Charlie, the 25-year-old son of the exiled Stuart Pretender, launched his campaign to reclaim the British crown. The statue of a Jacobite Highlander tops Glenfinnan Monument on the shore where the prince raised the Stuart standard.

The tiny town of **Arisaig** is also steeped in history. Bonnie Prince Charlie landed here to begin his uprising. He hid in a cave in the region. The rocky coast is a short walk away. While here, stay in **Arisaig House**, *Beasdale, Arisaig PH39 4NR; tel. (44-6875)622*, an outstanding hotel with a walled rose garden. Prices are moderate.

On the route to Mallaig from Arisaig is an unpaved track leading to a remote and beautiful hamlet called **Bracora**. The road follows Loch Morar, Scotland's deepest lake, which is 1,017 feet.

Inverary: the prettiest Highland town

Make **Inverary**, on the peaceful shores of Loch Fyne, one of your stops in the Highlands. Meaning "at the mouth of the Aray River," Inverary has been inhabited by the Campbells of Argyll for 500 years. Its white-walled buildings are reflected in the water. Services are still held in Gaelic at the town's church, the **Episcopal Church of All Saints**, *the Avenue*, which has the world's second-heaviest ring of 10 bells, which chime every day.

Nearby **Inverary Castle**, home to the Duke and Duchess of Argyll, is open to the public. The Armory Hall, which is 95 feet high, has an impressive display of antique weapons. The family portraits were done by such famous painters as Reynolds and Raeburn. A tour of the castle takes about an hour and is a good introduction to Highland history. For information, call *(44-499)2203*.

Britain's highest mountain

Ben Nevis, at 4,406 feet, is the highest peak in Great Britain. Near Inverness in the Highlands, it guards Glen Nevis. The view from the summit (where the ruins of an observatory remain) seems endless. A precipice on the northeast side drops more than 1,450 feet. Combine a trip to Inverness and Ben Nevis with a look at nearby Loch Ness, home of the most famous monster in the world.

The best place to stay near Inverness is **Culloden House Hotel**, *tel. (44-463)790461*, an 18th-century palace near Culloden Moor where the final Scottish uprising was defeated in 1746. This hotel has spacious rooms, ornate trim, and beautiful antiques. A double room is £95 to £135 ($179 to $255), including a full Highland breakfast.

The best Highland hotel

Inverlochy Castle, *Fort William, Inverness Shire, PH33 6SN, Scotland; tel. (44-397)702177*, near Glencoe and Ben Nevis, is the best hotel in the Highlands. Reservations can be made in the United States through **David B. Mitchell & Company**, *70 Old Kings Highway N., Darien, CT 06820; (800)422-1323*. Rooms are £200 ($380).

The Hebrides: the best escape from civilization

If you are "a mere lover of naked nature," you'll be drawn to the Scottish islands as Dr. Samuel Johnson was in 1775. The **Hebrides** are the best place in Britain to escape civilization.

The most spectacular isle—Skye

The most spectacular island in the Hebrides is the Misty Isle, as **Skye** is known. Sir Walter Scott described the Misty Isle in *The Lord of the Isles*: "The vapour which enveloped the mountain ridges obliged us by assuming a thousand shapes, varying its veils in all sorts of forms, but sometimes clearing off altogether."

Wild still and distant from population centers, Skye is so far north that in June the sun never really sets. From 11 p.m. until 1 a.m., a period of duskiness falls, but there's never real darkness.

Canadians, Americans, Australians, and New Zealanders of Scottish descent often look to the isle of Skye with nostalgia. Boatloads of Skyemen were shipped, often unwillingly, to these new lands during the Highland Clearances. Traces of their habitations can be seen all over Skye—foundations of walls, weeds growing over rubble, the outlines of houses, the stones of a hearth.

A trip through Skye's jagged, cloud-enshrouded Cullins and down primitive roads to Glen Brittle leads to excellent hiking country. The Cullins are beautiful seen from across Portree Bay or from Tarskavaig, across the waters of Loch Slapin. The grandest view is from the summit of Bidean Druim nan Ramh or Sgurr a'Mhadaidh.

The easiest (and most embarrassing) defeat

According to British history books, John Paul Jones was turned away from the isle of Skye by a funeral procession he mistook for an army. The American Navy captain appeared on the coast of Skye in 1779 in the *Bon Homme Richard* (named for Benjamin Franklin's *Poor Richard's Almanack*). He had been harrying the shipping lanes in British waters. The appearance of his gunboat caused a flurry at Dunvegan Castle, because General MacLeod was away on military service in America. But when Jones saw the funeral party bearing the body of Donald MacLeod, he thought it was the MacLeod army in full battle array. He turned and fled. (You might take this tale with a grain of salt. American history books would probably report the incident differently.)

The favorite holiday isle

The favorite holiday isle among the British is **Arran**. Fluffy Arran sheep graze on green hillsides crossed by miles of hiking trails, especially on Goatfell, the "mountain of the winds." **Brodick Castle**, once the home of the dukes of Hamilton, can be seen in Lochranza. Now a ruin, it was once the hunting lodge of Robert the Bruce, king of the Scots.

Upon arrival in Brodick, check in at Mrs. Henderson's guesthouse in time for her to serve up a true Scottish breakfast—an amazing spread of juice, oatmeal, farm-fresh eggs, bacon, broiled tomatoes, pancakes, oatcakes, toast, and coffee or tea.

The most important sight on Arran is **Holy Island**, containing the cave of St. Molaise and runic inscriptions. It lies off Lamlash Bay.

The Queen of the Hebrides

From Kennecraig, on Kintyre, a day tour crosses to the **Isle of Islay**, known as the

Queen of the Hebrides. The island's fertile soil is carpeted with bright emerald fields dotted with sleek cows and ubiquitous sheep. Good roads wind over the moors past salmon-filled lochs and farmhouses snuggled amid tidy flower and vegetable gardens. Wild cliffs tower above secluded sandy bays.

Near Port Charlotte are the graves of U.S. troops who lost their lives when the *Tuscania* and *Otranto* were torpedoed in 1918.

The most thrilling three-island hop

For a thrilling three-island hop, take the tour from Oban to **Mull, Staffa,** and **Iona.** Bus rides on Mull are exciting enough, with single-track roads, but the trip to Staffa takes you through 6-foot troughs. Huge foaming waves dash against dark columnar rocks on the island's coast. **Fingal's Cave,** a rocky formation beaten by waves, inspired Mendelssohn to compose the *Hebrides Overture* after his visit here in 1829. On calmer days, it is possible to disembark and explore the vast cavern.

The most sacred island

The sacred island of **Iona,** burial place of Scottish kings, is renowned as the location where Christianity was introduced to Scotland by St. Columba in A.D. 563. Abbey ruins, a reconstructed cathedral, and rugged ninth-century crosses stand silently on the buffeted shore.

The best Scottish standing stones

The islands of **Harris** and **Lewis** are famous for their Harris tweeds, but most travelers have never heard of the islands' well-preserved standing stones. Yet the prehistoric **Standing Stones of Callanish** on Lewis Island are more complete than Stonehenge in southern England and just as impressive. The best part, of course, is that they're free of Stonehenge's crowds.

The best way to explore the isles

The **Scottish Rail Pass** can be purchased at any main rail station in Scotland; it offers unlimited travel for 15 days for £88 ($166), seven days for £64 ($121). The **Highlands and Islands Travelpass** can be purchased at any British rail station, or at **Hi-Line,** *Station Road, Dingwall, Ross-shire, Scotland I-V15 9GE; tel. (44-3)496-3434.* A seven-day pass costs £80 ($151), a 14-day pass £120 ($227).

Scotland's best-known battle sites

The **Scottish Lowlands** were the site of Scotland's two best-known battles: **Stirling Bridge,** where William Wallace drove back the English forces in 1297, and **Bannockburn,** where Robert the Bruce was victorious against the English in 1314.

The most Nordic region

The **Orkney Islands,** north of mainland Scotland, belonged to the Norse from the ninth through the 16th centuries. Eventually, they became part of Scotland. The shops here sell Nordic sweaters rather than kilts. Lush and fertile, the islands, populated by birds of all species, are popular among bird watchers. The pace of life is slow, and in the summer the days are long.

The world's best Scotch whiskies

The *New York Times Magazine* recommends Macallan and Glenfarclas-Glenlivet as the best single-malt Scotch whiskies for their "sherrylike aroma" and "intense flavor," respectively. Among blends, the *New York Times Magazine* prefers sipping Usquaebach (Gaelic whiskey) for its "peatlike aroma and hot finish." Chivas Royal Salute is hailed for its "round, elegant flavor."

The Best of France

They once said, or rather told us, every man has two countries; his own and France. That might be amended now to: every man has three countries—his own, France, and the poorhouse.
—*Ernest Hemingway, 1934*

If you asked a Frenchman to name the world's most civilized country, he would surely name his homeland. Few in the world would argue. And if you asked a Frenchman to describe himself and his countrymen, he surely would assert that a Frenchman is a wine expert; a gourmet; well-versed in art, history, and literature; dressed in the latest fashion; possessing of impeccable manners; and the world's best lover. Again, few would argue.

The best cuisine, wine, and cheeses in the world come from France. High fashion begins in Paris. And the world's greatest artists and writers are drawn to the land of the Gauls.

The greatest city in the world: Paris

Paris is not only the heart of France but also one of the world's most fascinating cities. Four-star restaurants, cozy cafés, wide boulevards, colorful outdoor markets, and fascinating museums, theaters, parks, squares, monuments, and churches are found in every section of this capital city. The best way to visit Paris is to stroll—past 17th-century houses, butcher shops with whole pigs hanging in the windows, ancient churches, high-fashion boutiques, street performers, art galleries, Africans selling wooden carvings, and Gypsy beggars. The streets are filled with the smells of roasting coffee, expensive perfume, Gauloise cigarettes, crêpes, roasting chestnuts, fresh bread, diesel fuel, and the damp breeze coming from the Seine.

When you get tired, stop in a café for a comforting cup of coffee and a chance to watch the people go by. You can sit for hours. Or buy a pastry at one of the hundreds of pâtisseries in Paris. Your heart will soar as you bite into a flaky, creamy, or fruit-filled delight.

Paris' most famous sight

The **Eiffel Tower** is the most famous (and unarguably most touristy) Paris landmark. The view from the top is remarkable—if you don't mind waiting in an endless line to get there. Built for the Universal Exposition of 1889, it faced demolition in 1909 but was saved when the French army discovered it could serve as a radio tower.

Since its creation, the Eiffel Tower has been the site of 400 suicide leaps. If you want to prove that you climbed the Eiffel Tower's 1,710 steps (you can cheat and take the elevator), mail a letter from the mailbox at the top. Letters mailed here are canceled with a special Eiffel Tower postmark. Lights added a few years ago make the Eiffel Tower dazzle at night.

The city's most beautiful church

Notre Dame Cathedral is gorgeous, especially at sunset, when the splendid stained-glass rose window glows. Druids once worshiped on this site, and the Romans had a temple here before the Christians built Notre Dame in 1163. One of the finest examples of Gothic architecture, the cathedral was used for the coronation of Napoleon. (Napoleon scandalized the world by seizing the crown from Pope Pius VII and crowning himself.)

Beneath the church are the foundations of third-century Roman structures. Take a look at the side portals of the cathedral. According to legend, they were carved by the devil after he bought the soul of the ironsmith Biscornet. (The devil was unable to decorate the central portal, because that is the one the Host was carried through in procession.)

The world's best museum

The **Louvre** is the greatest museum in the world. Begun in the 12th century as a palace, it has been a museum since the 18th century. A controversial glass pyramid (three stories high) by I.M. Pei now covers the new underground entrance in the main court that faces the Jardin des Tuileries. Parking arrangements, shops, cafés, and restaurants are underground.

In 1190, the Louvre was one of Philippe Auguste's fortresses. Charles V made it an official residence, and Catherine de Medici had the long gallery built. It was extended under Henry IV and Louis XIII, and the quadrangle was completed under Louis XIV. Today, the museum is divided into six extensive sections: paintings and drawings, Greek and Roman antiquities, Egyptian antiquities, Oriental antiquities, *objets d'art*, and sculpture.

The *Venus de Milo* and the *Mona Lisa* are just two of the 208,500 works of art in the Louvre. The number of masterpieces is overwhelming. So are the crowds, especially on weekends and during the summer. The best way to avoid the masses is to steer clear of the European paintings. Instead, view the collection of ancient art, located in the Cour Carrée. Gigantic statues loom above you, the air is cool, and sounds echo off the walls like long-lost voices of Greek and Egyptian gods.

Paris' biggest attraction

Although it is less famous than the Eiffel Tower, the **Centre Beaubourg**, *rue St. Martin, 4th,* is the biggest attraction in Paris. More than 25,000 visitors are drawn to this art center each day—twice as many as visit the Eiffel Tower and almost equal to the number who frequent Disneyland. The multicolored modern structure built of steel tubes, concrete, and glass houses the Musée National d'Art Moderne, which displays works by Picasso, Braque, Chagall, Leger, Brancusi, and Calder.

Officially called the Centre National d'Art et de Culture Georges Pompidou, but unofficially known as the Pompidou or the Beaubourg, this arts center also has a 40,000-volume (reference) library, a theater, a restaurant, and temporary exhibits. The library averages 11,000 visitors a day and up to 19,000 a day on weekends. Only 2,000 people are admitted at a time. Outside, street performers breathe fire, perform pantomime, and play guitars.

The world's most beautiful cemetery

Père Lachaise Cemetery, on the northeastern edge of Paris, is the most beautiful cemetery in the world. Located in a wooded park, it is so enormous that the walkways have names and maps are given out at the entrance. The tombstones are monumental and elaborate. Balzac, Sarah Bernhardt, Chopin, Colette, Corot, Delacroix, Abélard and Héloise, Molière, La Fontaine, Edith Piaf, and Oscar Wilde are among the greats buried here. The most visited grave is that of rock star Jim Morrison.

Four favorite sights in Paris

Sacré-Coeur, a glowing white Byzantine-style church on a hill in Montmartre, can be seen from almost anywhere in Paris. On summer evenings, a cool breeze wafts across the hill. The church was begun in 1876 to celebrate the end of the Franco-Prussian War. It was completed in 1910. Its interior is decorated with mosaics and stained glass. Nearby is a hokey but entertaining pseudo artist's quarter.

La Sainte Chapelle, located in the Palais de Justice on the boulevard du Palais, was built by St. Louis to contain the Crown of Thorns, which he purchased from the Venetians in 1238. (The Crown of Thorns was moved to Notre Dame during the French Revolution.) The Gothic chapel has 15 brilliantly colored stained-glass windows and a graceful 247-foot spire. The stained-glass windows are the oldest in Paris and among the most vivid.

The **Conciergerie**, around Sainte Chapelle, is where Marie Antoinette spent her last days before facing the guillotine. It is also where 1,200 less-famous prisoners were held. This fascinating place has dark, dank dungeons. The conciergerie was built by Philip the Fair in the 14th century and contains three Gothic halls in addition to the prisons.

St.-Germain-des-Prés is the oldest church in Paris, begun in A.D. 558 "in the fields" outside the walls of Paris. The steeple and tower date from 1014, when the monastery was rebuilt after attacks by the Vikings. Enlarged in the 12th century, it was once self-sufficient, housing its own bakers, butchers, law courts, and defense force. All that exist of this today, aside from the church, are street names referring to parts of the ancient abbey. The abbey precincts now form a quarter of small hotels, antique shops, bookstores, publishing houses, and l'Ecole des Beaux-Arts.

The seven best museums in Paris

Musée des Arts de la Mode, *109 rue de Rivoli, 1st,* is the most entertaining museum in Paris. The city that has set fashion for 300 years is an appropriate setting for this institution, which displays the clothing of 19th-century chambermaids as well as 20th-century celebrities.

Musée Carnavalet, *23 rue de Sevigné, 3rd,* is the most Parisian of Paris' museums. Located in a Renaissance mansion in the Marais district, Carnavelet covers the turbulent history of the city and its people from the 16th to the 19th centuries.

Musée Marmottan, *2 rue Louis Boilly, 16th,* has the most significant collection of Monet paintings in Europe. Most of the works were painted at Monet's Normandy home in Giverny. This small, private museum near the Bois de Boulogne is hidden away in what appears a mundane residence. Inside, it boasts 65 paintings by Monet, the Wildenstein collection of medieval illuminated manuscripts, and Renaissance and Empire works. It is open on Tuesdays, when other museums are closed.

Musée d'Orsay, located in the renovated Orsay train station, is the newest in Paris. This museum of the 19th century houses many Impressionist paintings once displayed at the Jeu de Paume. The enormous vaulted glass ceiling gives a 19th-century industrial atmosphere. The exhibits include 1,500 sculptures, 2,300 paintings, 1,100 *objets d'art,* and 13,000 photographs, works by Dégas, Manet, and Rousseau.

The **Picasso Museum**, *5 rue de Thorigny,* in the Marais, is the best place to study Picasso. It contains an intelligent selection of the artist's life's work and provides a complete, carefully documented and illustrated biography. The collection charts Picasso's artistic development through the rooms of a magnificent 17th-century mansion, the Hôtel Salé.

Musée Rodin, *77 rue de Varenne, 7th,* is where the best of Rodin's work is kept. This one-man museum is housed in an imposing 18th-century residence, the Hôtel Biron, where Rodin worked and lived toward the end of his life. He presented his art as payment for rent.

Musée de Thermes (Roman baths) and the **Hôtel de Cluny,** *6 place Paul-Painlevé, 5th,* is the most beautiful museum in Paris. A combination of second-century Gallo-Roman remains and an 18th-century mansion, it is set back from the busy corner of the St. Michel and St. Germain boulevards on the Left Bank.

The Cluny, a Gothic house, once the Paris residence of the wealthy abbots of Cluny, houses one of the world's best collections of medieval art, including the exquisite unicorn tapestries. The lion represents chivalric nobility, the unicorn represents bourgeois nobility, and the lady may represent the Le Viste family from Lyons. The Roman baths were used in the third century as a vast public bathhouse.

The best way to see Paris

The best way to really see Paris is by bicycle. And the two best bicycle rental companies are **Paris Vélo,** *2 rue du Fer à Moulin, 5th; tel. (33-1)43-37-59-22,* and **Paris by Cycle,** *99 rue de la Jonquière, 17th; tel. (33-1)42-63-36-63.* Bicyclists should refer to the Michelin maps known as Paris Map #10 and Paris and Its Suburbs Map #196. Both are available from **Michelin,** *P.O. Box 3305, Spartanburg, SC 29304; (803)599-0850.* The cost is $5.95 each.

The three most colorful quarters

The greatest pleasures in Paris are its neighborhoods, which most tourists scarcely notice as they rush from sight to sight. Take time to wander through the streets of Paris. Absorb the smells, sounds, sights. Our favorites for wandering are the Marais, the Latin Quarter, and Montmartre.

The Marais

The **Marais** is vaguely bounded by the rue Beaubourg to the west, the boulevard Beaumarchais to the east, the Seine to the south, and the rues Réaumur and Bretagne to the north. Within its confines are scores of fine old town houses, many built with paved forecourts and walled gardens. You'll also find several museums; the National Archives; a half-dozen churches; the Jewish Quarter with its little bakeries, delis, and shops; and the Place des Vosges. Tour the Marais during the week, when it is possible to enter most of the buildings. Begin your walk at the St. Paul metro station.

The Marais (which means *marshland*) was shunned until the 13th century, when the Knights Templars (a military-religious order) built its headquarters on the rue St. Antoine, a raised highway since Roman times. In the mid-14th century, Charles V built a palace in the area today bounded by the rues St. Antoine, St. Paul, and Petite-Muse. (Some say it was originally Pute-y-Muse, or *whore's muse.*)

Place des Vosges was given its current shape in 1605, when Henri IV developed a royal square on the site of the former palace. Uniform houses were built, red-brick buildings trimmed with white stone and slate roofs.

After the court moved to Versailles, the quarter began to lose its chic inhabitants, and its popularity. By the end of the French Revolution, it was virtually abandoned. The Marais remained in a declining state until 1962, when the government named the area a historic district. Since then, the Marais gradually has been restored to grandeur.

Don't miss the **Victor Hugo House,** *6 place des Vosges;* the **Palais Soubise,** *60 rue des Francs-Bourgeois,* which contains the National Archives; the **Historical Museum of France;** and the **Hôtel de Rohan,** which contains a Gobelins tapestry and the fresco *Horses of Apollo* by Robert le Lorrain on a wall of its former stable.

Montmartre

Renoir was among the many 19th-century artists who lived in **Montmartre** and loved it. When traveling in Italy in 1881 he wrote, "I feel a little lost when away from

Montmartre. I am longing for my familiar surroundings and think that even the ugliest girl is preferable to the most beautiful Italian." Renoir painted *La Balançoire* sitting in a large garden, actually an abandoned park, behind the house on rue Cortot.

Traces of the artists who loved the quarter can be found throughout Montmartre. A restaurant called Mère Catherine's, looking out on the Place du Tertre, is little changed since it appeared in a painting by Utrillo. The Bonne Franquette on the corner of rues St. Rustique and des Saules once had a tea garden where van Gogh painted *La Ginguette*. If you walk down rue des Saules—something few tourists do—you'll pass a tiny vineyard and come to a bar-cabaret called Le Lapin Agile. Here artists and writers, such as Picasso and Vlaminck, kicked up their heels.

The wrought-iron gate at 11 ave. Junot marks the home of Utrillo's mother, the beautiful Suzanne Valadon. A painter herself and a model for Renoir, she appears among a group of voluptuous nudes in the painting *Les Grandes Baigneuses*.

The Moulin de la Galette, a windmill in Montmartre, has been painted almost as often as the Moulin Rouge. Renoir's painting of the Moulin is well-loved. Corot painted the mill also, and van Gogh painted it twice. The windmill survives in an altered state—it has been restored as an architectural feature above the roofs of a new development of apartments along avenue Junot and rue Lepic.

Picasso created cubism in his studio above the *bateau-lavoir* (laundry) that once existed next to Place Emile Goudeau. This tiny space, with a bench and a fountain, is on the downward slope toward the rue des Abbesses.

The most pleasant spot in Montmartre is the vineyard at the corner of rues St. Vincent and des Saules, near the Montmartre Museum. The vines still produce a wine called *picolo*. Every autumn, usually the first Sunday in October, when all the grapes are in, a *fête des vendanges* (harvest festival) is held at the vineyard. The more than 300 liters of wine produced are sold, and the proceeds are given to the old age home on the *butte* (hill).

Le Quartier Latin

The **Latin Quarter**, surrounding the boulevards St. Germain and St. Michel, is a bustling student quarter with twisting little streets, buskers and street vendors, restaurants, bookstores, and throngs of people.

The Roman conquerors of ancient Gaul settled here, on the Left Bank of the Seine, 50 years before the birth of Christ. They constructed thermal baths, an arena, and a theater. What is now rue St. Jacques was the Roman road to the south.

The **University of Paris** gave the area its ambiance after the departure of the Romans. One of the oldest universities in the Western world, it was established at the beginning of the 12th century. (Its rivals were Bologna, Salerno, Oxford, Cambridge, and Leipzig.) The university was started by Pierre Abèlard, who left the cloisters of Notre Dame to give lessons away from the bishop's influence. He took with him the best students and, at the foot of the Montagne Ste. Geneviève, began new courses taught by liberal masters. Rich benefactors founded colleges to house the students and classrooms. Everyone spoke only Latin; hence, the area was named the Latin Quarter.

In 1792, following the revolution, the University of Paris was discontinued. It wasn't until 1806 that the Emperor Napoleon re-established the university. It exists today pretty much as it was set up then, which is one reason its students riot and strike.

The best bus lines for sightseeing

One of the easiest ways to sightsee in Paris is by bus. And the best buses for sightseeing purposes are 24, 29, 30, 32, 38, 42, 47, 52, 58, 63, 69, 72, 73, 75, 82, 84, and 87. Use the buses for sightseeing during the off-hours, after 10 a.m. and before 5:30 p.m. In summer, when it remains light later, do your sightseeing from 7:30 p.m. until the buses stop running.

Remember, with your Carte Orange you can get off the bus, visit a museum, walk

47

through a neighborhood, have lunch or coffee, and then get back on and finish your tour without paying any additional charges.

For information on the city's bus system, ask at the metro ticket windows.

The oddest corner of Paris

A place of pilgrimage is hidden in the 7th arrondissement at 140 rue du Bac, next to the department store Bon Marché. Most of the inhabitants of Paris, including those who live in the neighborhood, do not know where the high, wooden door leads. But a million and a half pilgrims visit a simple chapel at the back of the court every year. It commemorates Catherine Laboure, a 24-year-old novice of the order of the Sisters of St. Vincent-de-Paul.

In November 1830, Catherine swore she had a vision. In it, she was told to cast a medal in the image of what she had seen. She was told that those who carried the medal in faith would be blessed.

The demand for the Miraculous Medal is so great that a slot machine has been installed in the chapel. When three 5-franc pieces are put in the slot, the machine discharges a medal.

An odd twist to the story behind the medal: When the body of Sister Laboure was exhumed in 1933, it was miraculously intact. Her eyes were still blue. Her limbs were supple, as if she were sleeping. Dressed in the famous white habit of the Sisters of Charity, the body of the saint can be seen today in the rue du Bac chapel.

The most famous gallows

Paris bus number 75 takes you to an intriguing street called **la rue de la Grange-aux-Belles**. At number 53 stood the 13th-century **Gibet de Montfaucon**, one of the king's gallows. Its 16-yard arms served two purposes: to hang those condemned and to exhibit corpses (often beheaded) as examples. In 1954, while excavating for a garage at number 53, two beams believed to be from the gallows were found.

The most beautiful bridge

The **Pont Alexandre III** is the most beautiful bridge in Paris. It crosses the Seine near the Jardin des Tuileries and the Petit and Grand Palais. The view from the bridge is as beautiful as the bridge itself.

The world's finest feathers: haute couture

Paris is not only the city of fashion but also the city of haute couture. Everyone is fashion-conscious here, from 8-year-old school girls to white-haired grandmothers. To make a splash, you must have an outfit specially made and custom-tailored.

Many of the world's finest *couturiers* are found in Paris. (A *couturier*, as opposed to a mere dress designer, is one who presents collections of individually made clothes twice a year.) The world's celebrities come to them looking for flair and unique style.

The top couturiers in Paris include the following:
➤ **Chanel**, *31 rue Cambon, 1st; tel. (33-1)42-86-28-00, and 42 ave. Montaigne, 8th; tel. (33-1)47-20-84-45*
➤ **Christian Dior**, *30 ave. Montaigne, 8th; tel. (33-1)40-73-54-44*
➤ **Givenchy**, *3 ave. George V, 8th; tel. (33-1)47-23-81-36*
➤ **Jean Patou**, *7 rue St. Florentin, 8th; tel. (33-1)44-77-33-00*
➤ **Yves St. Laurent**, *5 ave. Marceau, 16th; tel. (33-1)47-23-72-71*
➤ **Philippe Venet**, *62 rue Francois I, 8th; tel. (33-1)42-25-33-63*

The best sweater bargains

You can get some great sweater bargains in Paris at **Irlande**, *58 rue Montmartre, 2nd*. One-ply Scottish cashmeres are FFr1,280 ($246), and two-ply sweaters are FFr1,680

($323) for all models. Cashmere scarves are only FFr389($75). Soft Irish wool pullovers without pattern cost FFr395($76), and the Aran Island patterned sweaters are only FFr589 ($113).

The largest collection of secondhand scarves

The best collection of secondhand designer scarves can be found in a tiny shop in the picturesque but hard-to-find Passage Molière that runs between rues Quincampoix and St.-Martin in the 4th arrondissement, midway between the Pompidou Centre and the Forum des Halles. Thick silk scarves, mostly large squares, with hand-sewn edges, each a veritable work of art, sell for an average price of FFr800 ($153). Steep—unless you compare that price with what you'd pay for a Hermès or Dior scarf, new, which costs more than double that.

The best cures for homesickness

If you feel lonely in Paris and want to hear people speaking English, pop into **Shakespeare & Co.**, an English-language bookstore across the river from Notre Dame Cathedral.Writers frequent the bookstore. Poetry readings are held on Monday nights.

Also, the American Library in Paris is the oldest and largest English-language library in Europe, with more than 100,000 books and a collection of 350 periodicals. In 1928, Stephen Vincent Benét wrote *John Brown's Body* in the reading room. The library was also used by Gertrude Stein, Louis Bromfield, and Thornton Wilder. It has been an arena for debates by such formidable figures as John Kenneth Galbraith, Raymond Aron, and Charles Frankel. It survived and grew through the Great Depression, the Occupation during World War II, the Liberation of Paris in 1944, the street riots of 1968, and the energy crisis of the mid-1970s.

During the past 10 years, the American Library had a resurgence, developing a program that the trustees believe will be more responsive to the needs of the international community in Paris. Aging and fragile periodicals are being replaced by microfilm, and certain operations are being computerized.

The best flea market

For nearly 100 years, **Le Marché aux Puces** (flea market) has been operating from Saturday to Monday in the village of St. Ouen, just outside Paris' 18th arrondissement. The largest flea market in Europe, it is a maze of little booths selling everything imaginable, from fine and expensive antiques to cheap, secondhand clothing. To get there, take the metro to Porte de Champerret; take bus 85 Gare de Luxembourg-St. Denis; or take the metro to Porte de Clignancourt.

The best time to browse (if you can manage to wake up early enough) is between 5 a.m. and 7:30 a.m. The buyers at this hour are professionals looking for really good buys. They move fast, checking every item with an experienced eye and then buying without hesitation. Large amounts of cash are exchanged, and the goods are shipped to warehouses.

From 7:30 a.m. until 7 p.m., *le marché* is open officially for the 200,000 visitors it receives each week.

Le Marché aux Puces began in 1890, when sanitation laws first required that used clothing and bedding likely to contain vermin not be sold in the city. The ragpickers moved out to a muddy meadow appropriately called The Plain of the Ill-Seated. They were licensed to sell only to dealers and required to clean all materials before offering them for sale.

Over the years, however, the market became fashionable and began drawing large crowds. Today, seven markets make up a huge complex. There is less junk and more antiques (both good and fake).

Le Jules Vallès, a covered market, is the best place to look for collectors' items—toys, postcards, medals, dolls, and old newspapers and magazines. **Le Marché Malik** stocks old

49

clothes. The newest markets, **Le Marché Serpette** and **Le Marché Cambo,** specialize in art deco and period furniture, respectively.

Be careful with your money when you're shopping at Le Marché aux Puces, which is full of pickpockets.

The last of the open markets
For the true flavor of Paris, visit one of the city's 12 covered markets. If you enjoy food, you will appreciate the displays of seasonal fresh fruits and vegetables, meats, and cheeses; the stacked mushrooms and melons; and the fall and winter displays of furred and feathered game—hare, deer, boar, wild duck, pigeon, partridge, pheasant, and quail.

The best remaining covered markets of Paris include the following:
> **Beauvau St. Antoine,** *between rues d'Aligre and de Cotte, 12th*
> **La Chapelle,** *rue de l'Olive, 18th (open until midnight on Fridays and Saturdays)*
> **Enfants Rouge,** *39 rue de Bretagne, 3rd*
> **St. Didier,** *corner of rues Mesnil and St. Didier, 16th*
> **St. Quentin,** *85 bis blvd. Magenta, 10th*
> **Ternes,** *rues Lebon, Faraday, and Torricelli, 17th*

The freshest food
The open-air street markets sell Paris' freshest produce and meats and have the largest selection of cheeses. The supermarkets in Paris just don't compare in price or quality.

The best way to lunch in Paris is to stop at one of the open-air markets and buy a fresh baguette, a chunk of cheese or paté, a few pieces of fruit, and a bottle of wine. Take your bundle to the little Parc du Vert Galant on the Ile de la Cité and have a picnic. Sit on the tip of the island and watch the river flow by on either side.

There are 55 open-air street markets. Each sets up and is ready for business by 7:30 a.m., folding and disappearing at 1:30 p.m. two or three times a week. (The street markets are never set up on Mondays.)

Our favorite open-air market is on **rue de Seine,** near St. Germain-des-Prés. Small but well-rounded, its booths have fresh fruits and vegetables piled high in colorful pyramids.

The city's other outstanding open-air markets include the following:
> **Boulevard de Charonne,** *between rue de Charonne and rue Alexandre-Dumas, 11th;* Wednesdays and Saturdays
> **Carmes,** *place Maubert, 5th;* Tuesdays, Thursdays, and Saturdays
> **Père Lachaise,** *blvd. de Menilmontant, between rue des Panoyaux and rue Tlemcen, 11th;* Fridays and Sundays
> **Port-Royal,** *along the wall of l'Hôpital Val-de-Grâce, blvd. Port-Royal, 5th;* Tuesday, Thursdays, and Saturdays
> **Raspail,** *along the center island of blvd. Raspail between rue du Cherche-Midi and rue de Rennes, 6th;* Tuesdays and Fridays
> **Woodrow Wilson,** *ave. Woodrow Wilson 16, between Place d'Alma and Place d'Iéna;* Tuesdays, Thursdays, and Saturdays

The world's best pastry shops
The best pastries in the world are made in France, where layers of cake, as light as feathers, are molded together with airy, sweet buttercream and topped with curls of fine chocolate. Pastries in France are too beautiful (and too fattening) to eat but too delicious not to.

Within France, the most tempting *pâtisseries,* or pastry shops, are in Paris, where they adorn every corner. There are 2,300 of them!

One of the best known and most honored *pâtisseries* is **Dalloyau,** which specializes in *marrons glacés* (candied chestnuts), *mogador* (layers of chocolate cake, chocolate mousse, and raspberry confiture), and sherbet cakes. Dalloyau shops can be found at *99 rue Faubourg St. Honoré, 2 place Edmund Rostand, 69 rue de la Convention,* and *16 rue Linois.*

The king of pastry is **Gaston Lenôtre**, who runs Lenôtre shops throughout Paris. His 350 pastry chefs and cooks use at lest 12 tons of butter and 300,000 fresh eggs each month. Lenôtre also has the best chocolates in Paris. His shops are at *44 rue du Bac, 5 rue du Havre, 44 rue d'Auteuil,* and *49 ave. Victor Hugo.*

The best ice cream in Paris

The most delicious ice cream in Paris is sold at **Berthillon**, *31 rue St. Louis-en-l'Ile.* The list of rich, homemade flavors is long; so are the lines.

The loveliest gardens in Paris

The **Jardin du Luxembourg,** in the heart of the Left Bank, is an oasis for all ages. Children romp in the park's elaborate playground, watch Punch-and-Judy shows in the outdoor theater, and sail their boats in the fountains. Adults stroll through the formal gardens and read in the sun. During the summer, palm trees line the pebble paths. In winter, they are stored in the Château de Medicis, which also houses the French Senate.

The most elaborate fountain is the **Medicis Fountain,** at the end of a long pool. Scores of statues decorate the lawns. The best are those in the Delacroix group by Dalou. Find yourself a bench and relax. But, unless you are younger than 6, don't touch the grass.

The formal **Tuileries Gardens,** which lead from the Louvre to the Orangerie, are also magnificent. Colorful flowers are planted in careful formations. A pleasant day can be spent rambling through the park, from one museum to the next, stopping for a picnic in between.

The best woodland escape

Every large city needs its escape valve—even Paris. The **Bois de Boulogne** is where Parisians let off steam. You can lie on the grass in this immense wooded park (a no-no almost everywhere else in Paris). And you can hike for hours around its 2,500 acres. The Bois de Boulogne offers horseback riding, biking, rowing, and a zoo. Don't stay here after dark, however, unless you want to experience Paris' seamy side. When the sun sets, streetwalkers and transvestites work the area.

The deepest tour of Paris

The creepiest but perhaps most fascinating tour of Paris takes you beneath its streets. Eighty-two feet underground is a series of endlessly branching tunnels—156 miles of them in all. They are corridors left over from when the limestone used in building the city was quarried. In 1785, these tunnels were turned into ossuaries for bones removed from graveyards. The bones of most of the victims of The Terror were transferred here.

The southern part of the city around Montparnasse and the northern part of the city beneath Montmartre are honeycombed with the old tunnels. It's possible to go from one end of Paris to the other by way of these passages, called *les catacombes* by Parisians.

The section of the catacombs directly under the Place Denfert-Rochereau is open to the public. The entrance is on the southwest side of the square. Escorted tours of the catacombs (which are not for the fainthearted) are arranged on the first and third Saturdays of each month at 2 p.m. and every Saturday during the summer. (Bring a flashlight.)

The best toilets

Wandering in a strange city often raises unpleasant problems. Where do you go when nature calls? In Paris, this can be a puzzling question. The malodorous *pissoirs* (public urinals) along the street are frequented primarily by smelly old bums. They aren't recommended. Many cafés still have old-fashioned Turkish toilets, which consist of holes with footprints on either side. Also unpleasant. The problem is being ameliorated, however.

More than 400 *sanisettes* have been installed throughout the city. Each consists of a block of white cement ridged on the exterior to discourage the posting of bills and graffiti. The interior is heated, expertly ventilated, and wired for Muzak. Washbasins, perfumed toilet paper, and hooks for hanging clothing or handbags are provided. All this for a mere 1-franc piece. Caution: Don't linger more than 20 minutes. After 20 minutes, the assumption is that you need help, and a siren sounds automatically.

The best restaurant toilets (and telephone facilities)

If you want to avoid the public *sanisettes* of Paris, the best restaurant toilets are at the Brasserie Bofinger and Le Café Costes, with Chez Francis a close runner-up. **Bofinger,** *3 rue de la Bastille, 4th,* offers art deco style as well as comfort. You'll find beautiful tile work, brass faucets, and generous double sinks mounted on an antique cabinet. On the wall, framed in blue tile, a topless figure tells an allegorical story. A light lavender odor prevails. A telephone, well apart, is in a roomy booth.

Close on the heels of Bofinger is **Le Café Costes,** *Place des Innocents, 1st.* Quite different from Bofinger's, this toilet is like Le Café above it—starkly simple, with glass and mirrors everywhere. There are no faucets and no soap; hands are washed in running water turned on by a foot pedal.

At **Chez Francis,** *7 Place d'Alma, 8th,* the toilets are found at the foot of a magnificent rose marble staircase. Fresh flowers, isolated telephones in glass cabins, built-in sinks, and mirrors afford lots of taste and style.

The best cafés in Paris

Cafés are an institution in Paris. Parisians use them as living rooms. (Apartments in Paris are usually tiny.) All that is required is the purchase of one cup of coffee. During the summer, tables are set outdoors. Customers soak in the sun while they watch passers-by. In the winter, cafés smell like good coffee and Gauloise cigarettes.

In the 19th century, cafés were gathering spots for artists. Modigliani, the flamboyant Italian painter, frequented the **Café de la Rotonde** on the boulevard Montparnasse, just around the corner from his atelier on the rue de la Grande Chaumière. He and writer Beatrice Hastings often lingered in the café smoking hashish and drinking absinthe (a potent alcohol now illegal in France). He eventually died on the steps here. The Café de la Rotonde still thrives, cheerful despite its history. You can see its red awnings.

Le Dôme in Montparnasse is decorated with old photos of bygone customers: Picasso, Bonnard, Dufy, Gauguin, and Modigliani.

Paris cafés continue to draw celebrities. Many famous faces can be seen at **La Coupole** on the boulevard Montparnasse. This café was a favorite of Gauguin and his Javanese mistress.

Three of the most famous cafés in Paris are across the street from St. Germain-des-Prés Church on the boulevard St. Germain: **Café de Flore, Les Deux Magots,** and **Brassérie Lipp.** All three of these cafés have attracted artists, writers, and celebrities for decades. Their notoriety, however, has made them crowded and expensive. Lipp, which is also a restaurant, has art deco decor and attracts the artistic elite. (British wine dealer Steven Spurrier is a regular.) Les Deux Magots is filled with tourists, but it is a good place to people-watch. The lively Flore was Picasso's favorite.

The hottest night life

You'll find plenty to do in Paris, regardless of the size of your purse. You can stroll free through the Latin Quarter or Beaubourg, where lively circles of spectators watch street performers. A beer in one of the little cafés won't cost much, and you can sit for hours watching the crowd. Or you can go all out and have dinner in a fine restaurant and then dance until the wee hours of the morning in a *boîte de nuit.*

The coolest clubs

Castel's, *15 rue Princesse, 6th; tel. (33-1)43-26-90-22,* is where the jet set hobnobs. Guests are screened at the door, and only the most prestigious or fashionable are permitted to enter. You might need a bit of help to get into this private club, but it's not impossible, especially if you are staying at a first-class hotel and ask the concierge to make the reservation for you. Some of the most famous people in the world can be spotted in this club, which is made up of a series of little rooms on different levels.

Les Bains-Douches, *7 rue du Bourg l'Abbé, 3rd; tel. (33-1)48-87-01-80,* is a super-chic club that attracts the trendiest. Located in an old public bathhouse, it has a small pool. Celebrities can be seen here from time to time.

The jazziest joints

You can hear excellent jazz at **Le Petit Journal,** *71 blvd. St. Michel, 5th; tel. (33-1)43-26-28-59.* It has been around for years and features such musicians as Stephane Grappelli, Memphis Slim, and Claude Bolling. Most credit cards are accepted.

New Morning, *7-9 rue des Petites Ecuries, 10th; tel. (33-1)45-23-51-41,* is another hot jazz club. Live jazz groups from all over Europe and America perform here.

Le Slow Club, *130 rue de Rivoli, 1st; tel. (33-1)42-33-84-30,* has good New Orleans-style jazz. It is an old-timer in Paris. Standards from the 1930s and 1940s are played by such musicians as Claude Luter and the Haricots Rouges.

The coziest cave

Paris has a concept missing in most other cities—the *cave* (pronounced *kahv*). These cozy little wine cellars often have good music and always have good wine. They are ultra-Parisian. The **Caveau de la Huchette,** *5 rue de la Huchette; tel. (33-1)43-26-65-05,* is one of the best. It has jazz bands and a warm atmosphere.

The best cabarets

Parisian cabarets can be good fun. In many you have the choice of a dinner show or drinks and the show. The best of the cabarets is the **Crazy Horse,** *12 ave. George V, 8th; tel. (33-1)47-23-32-32.* The late show is more fun. It's the best of its genre—a sophisticated and professional performance that never fails to please. A minimum of two drinks is required, a matter of about FFr600 ($115).

Cultural bests

Classical music and ballet can be found at numerous theaters. The best performances are at the **Paris Opéra** and the **Opéra de la Bastille.** but you also can hear good music in the famous concert halls, including Salle Gaveau, Salle Pleyel, Théâtre des Champs-Elysées, and Palais de Chaillot. Up-to-date information is available in *Pariscope,* which you'll find at any newsstand.

The cheapest fun

Churches in the Latin Quarter and Marais offer free concerts. Listen for music wafting out of St. Severin or St. Julien le Pauvre around 8 p.m. The Centre Pompidou also puts on free programs: one night a ballet company, another evening a short play. Street entertainers attract crowds on the plaza outside the building. St. Merry offers concerts Saturday nights and Sunday afternoons. Contribute at the entrance.

The seediest night life

Tawdry Place Pigalle, on the edge of Montmartre, is beginning to show signs of a renaissance. It was here that Paris acquired its reputation as "Gay Paree" at the turn of the century, when artistic and literary cafés dominated the scene. (Le Chat Noir was made famous by Toulouse Lautrec's posters.)

Today, Pigalle is better known for drug traffic, prostitution, and tattoo parlors. But new faces are appearing on stage, new customers in the audience. One place that has shown enough improvement to warrant a recommendation is the **La Nouvelle Eve**, 25 *rue Fontaine, 9th; tel. (33-1)45-26-68-18*. It is open Friday nights starting at 11 p.m., and the entry fee is about FFr120 ($23). This is the meeting place once a week for Paris' answer to preppies—the BCBG (*les bon chic, bon genre*).

If you'd rather wallow in the seedy side of Pigalle, the area has quite a few strip joints. **French Lovers**, *62 rue Pigalle, 9th; tel. (33-1)42-85-32-69*, has live sex shows, pure and simple. It is open every day from 2 p.m. until midnight except Sundays. The entry fee is FFr300 ($57).

The best restaurant in Paris

La Tour d'Argent, *15 Quai de la Tournelle, 5th; tel. (33-1)43-54-23-31*, has pleased the palate of many a dignitary. Henry III learned to eat with a fork here.

Notre Dame is the backdrop of La Tour, which opened 400 years ago. A 120,000-bottle wine cellar graces this time-honored institution, where 150 employees serve 95 people.

Until the beginning of this century, the place was modest, with sawdust on its wooden floors. Frederic Delair brought it to fame in 1890, when he began numbering the *canard pressé*, the famous duck specialty of the house. Each duck was engraved with a social security number. Since then, about 600,000 ducks have been served. The duck is still delicious, the best dish on the menu. But anything à la carte is good. If the *maître d'hôtel* feels you are ordering something you aren't familiar with, he will explain the dish very carefully and recommend gently that you try something else.

First-class restaurants

Le Carré des Feuillants, *14 rue de Castiglione, 1st; tel. (33-1)42-86-82-82*, serves the cuisine of southwest France with a generous dash of creativity. Chef Alain Dutournier's delicacies include ravioli stuffed with foie gras and truffles.

Ramponneau, *21 ave. Marceau, 16th; tel. (33-1)47-20-59-51*, has 1920s charm. The tables are well apart, the tree-shaded terrace is delightful, the wines are excellent, and the service is perfect. The place is always full, but not with tourists.

Robouchon (formerly Jamin), *32 rue de Longchamps, 16th; (33-1)47-27-12-27*, is a superb restaurant, the reputation of which is due to the finesse of chef Joel Robouchon. Enjoy the truffles, foie gras, and seafood.

Mercure Galant, *15 rue des Petits-Champs, 1st; tel. (33-1)42-97-53-85*, is a place where everything is good and the service matches the food.

Chez Pauline, *5 rue Villedo, 1st; tel. (33-1)42-96-20-70*, was handed down from father to son, and it has consistently remained first-class. It is one of the few restaurants in France where you can have a soup called Billy By that is made with cream and mussels.

L'Epi d'Or, *25 rue Jean-Jacques Rousseau, 1st; tel. (33-1)42-36-38-12*, is a relatively unknown restaurant but is very fine.

L'Oulette, *38 rue des Tournelles, 4th; tel. (33-1)42-71-43-33*, was rejuvenated by a young couple—not only the decoration but the food as well.

The best pasta

Pasta et Vino, *59 rue Dauphine, 6th*, has without a doubt the best pasta in Paris—and, unfortunately, the worst wine.

The fishiest restaurant

Charlot Ier, *128 bis blvd. de Clichy, 18th; tel. (33-1)45-22-47-08*, is closed from July 14 to Aug. 23. It's the best, but by no means the cheapest, place for good fresh fish in the city.

The best meals for the money

Ambassade d'Auvergne, *22 rue du Grenier St. Lazare, 3rd; tel. (33-1)42-72-31-22,* serves the most delicious Auvergnat food in town. Don't miss the *aligot* (mashed potatoes with mountain cheese).

Chez l'Ami Louis, *32 rue du Vertbois, 3rd; tel. (33-1)48-87-77-48,* has fine fare—if you can put up with the disgusting atmosphere. The chef is (literally) a dirty old man and can be quite insulting.

Chez Georges, *273 blvd. Péreire, 17th; tel. (33-1)45-74-31-00,* is a good place for traditional French meat dishes: *gigot* with *flageolets, pot au feu, navarin, boeuf mode, blanquette de veau,* and *petit salé.* Closed in August.

Chez Pierrot, *18 rue Etienne Marcel, 2nd; tel. (33-1)45-08-17-64,* is a traditional restaurant with good food. In 1971, when Les Halles was torn down, a small restaurant disappeared. One of the waiters, Pierrot, retained the old phone number and opened this new place nearby. It captures the flavor of the old food halls and the streets that once surrounded them.

Dominique, *19 rue Bréa, 6th; tel. (33-1)43-27-08-80,* is one of the few really great Russian restaurants left in Paris. You can sit at the counter, eat blinis with caviar or smoked salmon with cream, and wash it all down with ice-cold vodka.

Le Babylone, *13 rue de Babylone, 7th,* is one of the best lunch buys in town. Each day's menu includes one of the following standard dishes: *petit salé, roti de porc, blanquette, boeuf bourguignon, boeuf mode,* or *boeuf gros sel.*

Le Foux, *2 rue Clement, 6th; tel. (33-1)43-25-77-66,* received a Pomme d'Or (Golden Apple) award from William Chamberlayne, the noted travel writer. The food is Lyonnaise/Niçoise, and the ambiance is warm and pleasant. On Saturdays stop here for a typical bistro lunch. Le Foux is located in the center of the book-publishing district, St. Germain-des-Prés. Occasionally, the French president drops in.

The best food and atmosphere for the lowest price

When you want a French waiter, a French menu with French dishes on it, and a Gallic ambiance—at the lowest prices—try a *soupe populaire.* These uniquely Parisienne institutions offer cut-price meals and plenty of atmosphere. Two of the best in Paris are the courtyard **Restaurant Chartier** and **Le Drouot,** both located off the Grands Boulevards, at the intersections of rue du Montmartre and rue de Richelieu respectively. Neither takes reservations, and business hours are from 11 a.m. until 3 p.m. (Chartier) and 6 p.m. until 9:30 p.m. (Drouot).

The most efficient restaurant

Le Train Bleu, *Gare de Lyon, 12th; tel. (33-1)43-43-09-06,* is the splendidly decorated upstairs dining room of the Gare de Lyon. The Gare de Lyon was the station built by the Rothschilds in the Victorian era to take on passengers for the south, and the restaurant murals show romantic vistas of their eventual destination. The food is Victorian, too—hearty southern fare graced by one of the city's best-priced wine lists (strong on the Burgundies from the Lyons area, of course). Recommended dishes include broiled *poulet de Bresse,* vegetable terrine, and *quenelles de brochet with sauce Nantua* (forcemeat rolls made with pike and covered with a crayfish sauce).

Since this is a railroad station, the service is fast and efficient—perfect for catching the opening curtain at the new Opéra de la Bastille nearby. The restaurant also stays open into the wee hours for those interested in dining after the show.

The best hotels in Paris

The **Ritz,** *15 place Vendôme, 1st; tel. (33-1)42-60-38-30,* is the ritziest place in town. Elegant and catering always to the comforts of its clients, the Ritz attracts such celebrities as Bill Blass. Hemingway once said, "When in Paris, the only reason not to stay at the Ritz is if you can't afford it." Indeed, you may not be able to afford it. The deluxe rooms are terribly expensive. They feature Persian and Chinese carpets, large brass beds, down pillows, and fireplaces. The cost of all this is FFr2,550 to FFr7,050 ($490-$1,355) a night. The Imperial Suite is an imperial $5,000 a day! This is where Fiat's owner (Gianni Agnelli) and *New York Times* Publisher Punch Sulzberger stay in Paris.

Plaza-Athénée, *25 ave. Montaigne, 8th; tel. (33-1)47-23-78-33*, is a close second. Although it isn't as opulent as the Ritz, it is more appealing. Redecorated in 1984, it has an ambiance of the 1930s that is more attractive (and less expensive) than the other super-deluxe establishments in Paris. It attracts the likes of Audrey Hepburn. The couches are in silk, and surfaces are marble. You can stroll in the lovely courtyard. Rooms are FFr2,780 ($534) a night.

Hôtel de Crillon, *10 place de la Concorde, 8th; tel. (33-1)42-65-24-24*, is less famous than the Ritz and the Plaza-Athénée but more private and peaceful. This grand 18th-century palace across the street from the American Embassy was built for Louis XV. Tapestries, columns, and marble baths give it a feeling of luxury. While rooms on the place de la Concorde side have the best views, they are also the noisiest. Rooms begin at FFr3,150 ($605) a night.

Hôtel George V, *31 ave. George V, 8th; tel. (33-1)47-23-54-00*, is an elegant art deco hotel. It has a lovely courtyard, and rooms have their own balconies with good views. The hotel has a great bar with a bartender who knows how to mix a good martini. Rooms begin at FFr3,250 ($625) a night.

The best hotels for the price

Hôtel d'Angleterre, *44 rue Jacob, 6th; tel. (33-1)42-60-34-72*, is an inexpensive hotel near St. Germain-des-Prés. The hotel garden is pretty, and the salon has a grand piano. A double room is FFr700 to FFr950 ($134-$182) a night. Reserve in advance. Credit cards are not accepted.

Hôtel des Deux Iles, *59 rue St. Louis-en-l'Ile, 4th; tel. (33-1)43-26-13-35*, is in a 17th-century building on the other island from the one on which Notre Dame is located. The entrance hall is filled with greenery and flowers, and the popular bar has a fireplace. Rooms are small and start at FFr690 ($132) a night. Reserve at least a month in advance. Credit cards are not accepted.

Esmeralda, *4 rue St. Julien le Pauvre, 5th; tel. (33-1)43-54-19-20*, is popular with the theater crowd. Rooms are cozy with views of Notre Dame and the little park of St. Julien-le-Pauvre. Guests can use the sauna. A double room is FFr450 ($86). Reserve at least two weeks in advance. Credit cards are not accepted.

L'Hôtel, *13 rue des Beaux Arts; tel. (33-1)43-25-2722*, is filled with fresh flowers and antiques. The walls are covered with fabric, and the baths are marble. A winding staircase, marble columns, and stone floors make the entrance rather grand. Oscar Wilde died in one of the rooms. A double room is FFr900 to FFr2,100 ($173 to $403) a night. Reserve several months in advance.

The **Royal Alma**, *35 rue Jean-Goujon, 8th*, near the place d'Alma and across the street from the Seine, is pleasant. This small, modern hotel has bedrooms with private bathrooms. Prices are reasonable, about FFr1,250 ($240), considering the quiet, elegant neighborhood. Free parking.

The world's best subway

The Paris subway, or metro, will take you anywhere you want to go in Paris quickly, efficiently, and cheaply. Every metro station has a map explaining the system, which is easy to understand. Trains are labeled with their destinations.

A single metro ticket will take you anywhere in the city with as many transfers as you wish. You must use a second ticket on buses if you go beyond two sections of the city, and you must use an additional ticket each time you transfer from one bus to another.

A single ticket (good for the metro or buses) costs FFr4.50 (90 cents) when purchased separately and FFr2.75 (50 cents) when purchased in a *carnet* of 10. (*Carnets* are available at metro stations and *tabac* stores.) The RER (Réseau Express Régional, or Regional Express System) goes north, south, east, and west to suburbs outside Paris. You can catch them at metro stations in Paris.

The world's most beautiful château

The one side trip from Paris that you must make time for is to **Versailles**, the most magnificent of all French châteaux. Louis XIV created this enormous and elaborate palace and its formal gardens, which cover 250 acres. A river was diverted to feed the gardens' 600 fountains. The king moved the court here to get away from the depressing throngs of Paris. During his reign, Versailles housed 6,000 people.

Be sure to see the Hall of Mirrors, the royal apartments, and the chapel. Le Grand Trianon and le Petit Trianon were smaller retreats for the royal family. Le Hameau was Marie Antoinette's little farm, where she played at being a shepherdess when she tired of the rigors of palace life.

Versailles' greatest rival

The second-best château in France is **Vaux-le-Vicomte**, an hour south of Paris. At the entrance are two enormous stone gods. Beyond the iron gates are pavilions, gardens, terraces, cascades, statuary, and a forest. Across the moat and at the top of two grand staircases is the château itself, which has five floors and 80 rooms, 27 open to the public.

Nicholas Fouquet, superintendent of France's treasury and protegé of Cardinal Mazarin, dreamed up the château. He bought 12,000 acres and commissioned three artists to design the building, which was completed in 1661. Le Vau is responsible for the architecture, Le Brun for the paintings, and Le Nôtre for the gardens.

To celebrate the completion of the château, Fouquet made the mistake of inviting Louis XIV to a feast there. Three weeks after the visit, the king had Fouquet arrested for embezzlement and imprisoned for life.

The most beautiful cathedral in France

Chartres has the most beautiful cathedral in France—and one of the finest in the world. It once drew thousands of pilgrims, who came to worship at the shrine of the Virgin. Located about 50 miles southwest of Paris, it is known for its stained-glass windows, which date from the 12th and 13th centuries. The present cathedral is the sixth built on the site.

The best French champagne

Champagne may be made legally only in the province of that name, northeast of Paris. Inferior bubbly cannot be called champagne in Europe (by law). Within Champagne province, the best champagnes are found near the cathedral town of **Rheims.**

It's great fun to explore the quaint villages and rolling countryside of Rheims, sampling champagne en route. The champagne cellars are often in subterranean caves up to 13 miles long. Two of the best are **Epernay**, about 13 miles south of Rheims on N51, and **Montagne de Rheims**, near the city.

The finest church in the world

The great Gothic cathedral at **Amiens**, north of Paris, was designated the finest religious edifice in the world by UNESCO. Built in 1220, this cathedral is 470 feet long. The nave is 141 feet high, the spire 360 feet high. Four-sided reliefs on the lower half of the west front portray the virtues and vices and illustrate fables. The 16th-century choir stalls are richly carved, and the rose window glows softly. For more information, contact the **Comité Régionale de Tourisme de Picardie**, *9 rue Allart, BP 0342, 80000 Amiens; tel. (33-22)92-21-20.*

Europe's most expensive theme park

The heralded **EuroDisney**, which opened in April 1992, is complete with roller coasters, castles, and miniature replicas of areas around the world. It is the mirror image of the other Disneys, except for the prices—you have to pay big bucks in this fantasy land. A set of Mickey Mouse ears is FFr25 ($5). A hot dog, a Coke, and a brownie will set you back FFr48 ($9). And the park charges a hefty FFr225 ($40) entrance fee for adults, FFr150 ($28) for children under 12.

Lyons: the gastronomic capital

Although Parisians may disagree, Lyonnais are sure their city is the gastronomic capital of the world.

Sampling the fare

The best restaurant in the city of great dining is **Vettard**, *7 place Bellecour; tel.(33-7)842-07-59*. It is a favorite of former French Prime Minister Raymond Barre and other French VIPs. The house specialty is *quenelle de brochet financière* (a pike dumpling), which is incredibly light and airy. Also delicious is the sea bass in olive oil and sherry wine vinegar. The wine list includes the best regional wines at very reasonable prices. The belle epoque decor is pleasant, and the service is friendly. Vettard is closed Sundays and in August.

World-famous chef **Paul Bocuse's restaurant**, too, is excellent. It is located seven miles outside Lyons, *69660 Collonges-au-Mont-d'Or; tel. (33-7)822-01-40*. Try the superb Bresse chicken and the Elysées soup, served in a flaky pastry cover. Closed in August.

Henry, *27 rue de la Martinière, 69001; tel. (33-7)828-26-08*, has a solid reputation. It serves traditional food with inventive touches. Try the warm *salade de homard aux pousses d'épinards et au beurre de truffles* (lobster salad with spinach and truffles) and the *gâteau de ris de veau à la crème de graine de moutard* (sweetbread in a creamy mustard sauce). The service here is remarkably friendly. The restaurant is closed for lunch on Saturdays; all day Mondays; and from July 15 through Aug. 15.

Léon de Lyons, *1 rue Pléney, 69001; tel. (33-7)828-11-33*, serves the best Lyonnais specialties. If you are adventurous, try the *Lyonnaiseries en salade* (calf's foot, lamb's trotters, cervelas sausage, brawn, blood pudding, and lentil salad). Chef Lancombe's own inventions are also delicious. Try his *pigeonneau cuit en croûte de sel* (squab cooked in salt). The restaurant is closed Sundays and Mondays for lunch and Dec. 22 through Jan. 4. VISA and MasterCard are accepted.

L'Industrie, *95 cours du Docteur-Long, 69003; tel. (33-7)853-27-05*, is a tiny seven-table restaurant. Owner André Perez visits with customers to discuss the cuisine and to explain recipes. The chef is a stickler for high-quality ingredients. L'Industrie is closed on weekends and in mid-August. Make reservations well in advance.

The best chocolates

Before you leave Lyons, purchase some of the world's best chocolates at **Maurice Bernachon**, *42 cours Franklin-Roosevelt, 69006*. Some are sprinkled with gold leaf.

The most heroic past

During World War II, Lyons was the center of the French Resistance. (It was also the site of the recent trial of Nazi Klaus Barbie.) Resistance groups hid operational headquarters and clandestine printing presses in the city's complex of covered passages, or *traboules*.

The silkiest city

The city's third claim to fame (aside from being the second-largest business center in France) is its silk industry. Developed in the 17th century, the silk industry in Lyons continued to expand until recent years. The city produces beautiful materials, many involving processes that are mastered nowhere else.

Before you leave the city, explore its silk shops. A good place to buy silk ties, scarves, and shirts is **La Maison des Canuts**, *10 rue d'Ivry.* **Minouche Picot**, *11 Quai André Lassagne,* has women's silk clothing. The greatest choice, however, is available at the **Centre Commercial de la Part-Dieu**, *rue de Bonnel,* an enormous 220-store shopping center.

Lyons' finest hotel

La Cour des Loges, *2468 rue du Boeuf; tel. (33-7)842-75-75,* is a Renaissance palace in the old part of Lyons that was recently renovated and turned into a modern hotel. It is decorated in an interesting blend of medieval, Renaissance, and modern decor. The interior courtyard, circular stairways, beamed ceilings, and terraced gardens add charm. Double rooms are FFr1,150 to FFr1,600 ($220 to $307).

The fastest way to Lyons

These days, getting from Paris to Lyons is a cinch. A railroad line has been built between the two cities enabling operation of very fast trains called **Trains à Grande Vitesse**, or TGV. They run every hour from Paris' Gare de Lyons (where else?). If you want to combine the train journey with a meal other than breakfast, choose the first-class option, because the food in second-class will make you think you are not in France.

Peak experiences: the Alps

The Alps are the most beautiful mountains in the world. Like the Rockies, they are snow-capped and dramatically jagged. But unlike their American counterparts, their valleys and slopes are bedecked with picturesque villages. From the peaks, you can look miles down into valleys where tiny church spires are surrounded by gingerbread houses. Stone shepherds' huts offer shelter in the trees. And luxurious hotels pamper tired hikers and skiers.

While the Alps are famous for their tremendous ski slopes, you don't have to be a skier to enjoy them. They are gorgeous year-round. Wild flowers cover the mountains in the spring and summer, and during the fall the leaves turn bright yellow. Hikers, campers, fishermen, and hunters ramble the Alpine peaks long after the ski slopes have closed for the summer.

The mightiest Alp

The mightiest Alp is **Mont Blanc**, Europe's highest peak, which rises 15,772 feet into the sky. A good place to stay while you enjoy the snow-topped mountain is **Chamonix**, a convenient train ride from Paris. From this posh and expensive ski resort radiate many hiking trails and cable car rides.

The best ride is from the *téléphérique* to the Aiguille du Midi, which costs FFr125 ($20) round trip. You'll hover thousands of feet above rocky drops and seas of ice. Try to take the ride in the morning, when the view is clearest. Wear warm clothes, because it's chilly at the top! If you'd rather hike through the mountains, you can follow the miles of signposted trails. For more information, contact the **Compagnie des Guides**, *Maison de la Montagne, 190 place de l'Eglise; tel. (33-50)53-00-88.*

The most popular ski resort

Chamonix, *place d'Eglise; tel. (33-50)53-00-24,* is the most popular ski resort in the French Alps. The deep-powder snow and the variety of runs in the 13,000-foot mountain range attract experts from all over the world. The 12.4-mile glacier run down the Vallée Blanche is one of the most exciting in the world.

For those who find skiing too tame, Chamonix also offers one of the newest thrills: parapente, which involves parachuting off steep vertical cliffs high in the mountains. You also can hang-glide in the mountains for about FFr300 ($58) a ride.

The most inviting lakes

Of course, the Alps have more to offer than Mont Blanc. Lakes Geneva, Annecy, and Bourget are bordered by charming resorts and invite sailing, water skiing, and fishing.

Lake Annecy is especially attractive. It hasn't yet been discovered by hordes of tourists, and its water is still pure. The town of Annecy, on the lake, is dominated by a 12th-century castle and lined with canals. The 16th-century Palais de l'Isle is surrounded by a picturesque old quarter. And the town's monastery is known for its relics of St. Francis de Sales.

When visiting Lake Annecy, stay in Talloires, a village on the lake. The **Hotel de l'Abbaye,** *tel. (33-50)60-77-33,* is located in a converted 11th-century Benedictine abbey. L'Abbaye has dominated the village for 1,000 years and has a breathtaking view of the lake. About FFr1,025 ($200) a night. Closed from Dec. 14 through Jan. 16.

The prettiest ski resort

Les Contamines-Monjoies, *tel. (33-50)47-01-58,* is one of the prettiest ski towns in the Alps—and one of the least known. This small ski area set in a high wooded valley is not far from Chamonix. It has 62 miles of slopes beginning at about 8,000 feet and served by 25 lifts. Facilities also include 15 miles of cross-country ski trails. Lift passes are FFr120 ($23) per day. Bus service to Chamonix and other nearby resorts is available for an additional FFr114 ($22).

The best place to stay is **Le Gai Soleil,** *tel. (33-50)47-02-94,* just outside town in a small farmhouse. The building itself dates back to 1823. Prices for two range from FFr2,280 to FFr2,790 ($438 to $537) per week.

The most spectacular drive

The most spectacular drive through the Alps, the **Route des Grandes Alpes** (D902), can be made only during the summer (from the end of June to the end of September). By October, the route is covered with snow. Begin at Bourg St. Maurice in the Savoie region and head through the Val d'Isère. You will be on the highest mountain highway in Europe. The highest point is the Iseran Pass, 9,084 feet high. Savor the view of the Tarentaise mountain range and the glacier-covered peaks of Albaron and Charbonel. You also will pass the deepest gorges in France.

Brittany: the most beautiful coastline

Brittany (Bretagne), in the west, has 600 miles of the most ruggedly beautiful coastline in France. Along it are sheltered coves, fishing villages, wide deserted beaches, dramatic cliffs, smart resorts, and lush farmland. The stone-built villages are rich in history.

The Quiberon Peninsula's rocks, caves, and reefs make its coast the most dramatic in the province. Walk the Côte Sauvage (Wild Coast) from one end to the other, stopping at the strange rock formations: Grottes du Taureau (Bull's Cave), la Fenêtre (Window), and La Vieille (Old Woman). East and south of the coast are wide beaches and fishing ports.

Brittany's greatest sight

St. Malo, a fortified island-city in Brittany that dates back to the 12th century, was bombed during World War II but has been restored. Visit the castle (the best view of St. Malo is from its ramparts) and the Quic-en-Groigne waxworks museum.

The best hotel in St. Malo is the **Central,** *Grande-Rue 6; tel. (33-99)40-87-70,* in the heart of Old Town.

The oldest culture

Natives of Brittany consider their region a separate country. Its original inhabitants, who left prehistoric megaliths, were overrun by the Gauls, the Celts, and finally the Romans. Brittany didn't become French until 1532. The Breton language and folklore are more like those of Celtic Wales than France.

Carnac is dotted with strange prehistoric megaliths—standing stones that are believed to have been erected by the Druids, but which actually are even older. Especially eerie are the Alignements de Menec two miles outside Carnac on D196. More than 1,000 gigantic rocks are set in perfectly straight, miles-long rows.

The **Gulf of Morbihan** is dotted with islands with prehistoric megaliths that stand against the sky. **Locmariaquer,** an island village, has some of the most important megaliths in Brittany. Another islet contains the Tumulus of Gavrinis, thought to be the tomb of a Celtic king.

The best seafood

Brittany has the most delicious seafood in France—sole, crabs, shrimp, oysters, and smoked salmon. Try a bottle of muscadet, the dry white wine of Brittany, or the potent hard cider.

One of the best places in the region for seafood is **Lorand-Barre,** *Damour, Ponts-Neufs; tel. (33-96)32-78-71.* This rustic Breton restaurant eight miles from St. Brieuc has fabulous grilled lobster and dessert crepes.

Normandy—the Riviera's coldest rival

Normandy's world-famous resorts—Deauville, Trouville, and Cabourg—are the Riviera's colder rivals. These elegant towns along the Cherbourg Peninsula are warmed by the Gulf Stream in summer. And they are far less crowded than their southern counterparts.

Deauville has great shopping (including branches of the leading Paris jewelers and designers), elegant hotels and restaurants, and a casino. A boardwalk runs the length of the beach.

A peaceful contrast is **Honfleur,** a small fishing harbor. At sunset, fishermen bring in the day's catch. A pleasant and comfortable place to stay is **Lechat,** *15 place St. Cathérine; tel. (33-31)89-23-85,* in the heart of the old district.

The most beautiful beach town

The most beautiful beach in France is **Etretat,** in Normandy. Two magnificent white cliffs loom above the wide, rocky beach. While the beach is gorgeous, it is not particularly comfortable. But because of this, it is seldom crowded.

The Hotel Dormy House has a breathtaking view from the top of the cliff.

Incomparable Mont St. Michel

Mont St. Michel is an eighth-century abbey that sits atop cliffs rising from a flat island, said to have been built at the command of the Archangel Michael, who appeared on the spot. Guides will show you an indentation in the rock that is supposedly the archangel's footprint. The abbey contains the silver shrine of the archangel, who is supposed to have fought the devil hand to hand on a nearby hill. View the Escalier de Dentelle (Lacework Stairway), the Gothic buildings, and the cloister.

Mére Poulard, *Grand' Rue, tel. (33-33)60-14-01,* has an outdoor terrace where you can dine during the tourist season and a stone fireplace where you can huddle in winter. Try the dessert omelette. A double room with a bathroom is FFr700 ($135).

Where saints are made

Rouen, the Norman town where Joan of Arc was burned at the stake, is a medieval treasure. The Maid, as Joan was known, was executed in 1431 at the Place du Vieux-Marché. Of the town's 100 churches, the most beautiful is the cathedral, built in the 11th and 12th centuries. Residents live in 15th-century houses lining narrow old streets. Note the Norman architecture—wide oak beams and sharp roofs.

The most dramatic landing in history

Hundreds of American World War II veterans visit the sight of the D-Day landing each year. The drama of the Normandy landings can be imagined at Arromanches, Utah, and Omaha beaches. The American Military Cemetery is about 1.5 miles beyond Omaha Beach (Colleville-sur-Mer).

Bayeux was the first town liberated after D-Day. The 11th-century cathedral is worth visiting to see the Bayeux tapestry. This shows in elaborate detail the events of the Battle of Hastings in England, during which William the Conqueror won his name. (The tapestry is misnamed; it is actually an embroidery.)

Disneyland come true—the Loire

The **Loire Valley**, southwest of Paris, puts Disneyland to shame. Known as Château Country, the region is filled with turreted castles, where royalty once amused itself. The valley's mild climate, rolling green hills, and lush pastureland attracted French nobility centuries ago. Their early châteaux were fortresses designed to ward off invaders. In later years, they became ornate palaces. Today, these châteaux are enjoyed by visitors from around the world. Don't expect to see the 120 castles, 20 abbeys, and 100 churches all at once.

The most beautiful Loire château

Chenonceaux is considered the most beautiful château in the Loire Valley. Straddling the Cher River, it was embellished by eight women over a period of 450 years and has been dubbed "The Castle Women Built." It is approached by a promenade of tall trees. The interior is furnished with tapestries, statues, and portraits.

The château was built between 1513 and 1521 under the supervision of Catherine Briconnet, a wealthy 21-year-old heiress. After Catherine's death, Chenonceaux became the property of Henri II, who presented the castle to his mistress, Diane de Poitiers. She planted fine gardens and had a five-arch bridge built to the far bank of the Cher, where she liked to go hunting.

When King Henri died, his wife, Catherine de Medici, forced her rival out of Chenonceaux. The queen then added her own touches, including a 197-foot gallery filled with fine paintings. Catherine had elaborate, erotic parties at Chenonceaux. One party she gave for the Duke of Anjou included regattas, fireworks, and satyrs chasing wood nymphs in the background. The most beautiful noblewomen in France waited on guests—topless!

The largest Loire château

Chambord is the largest of the Loire châteaux. Designed by Leonardo da Vinci for King François I as a pleasure palace, it is set in a 13,600-acre game reserve and surrounded by a 20-mile wall, the longest in France. The 440-room hunting lodge is laced with spires, pinnacles, gables, turrets, towers, and 365 chimneys. The palace has 74 stairways, including a double staircase constructed of twin spirals. One person can ascend while another is descending without meeting.

The most violent château

The **Château d'Amboise** has a violent history. In 1560, 1,000 Huguenots involved in a plot to abduct Francis II and his queen, Mary Stuart (later Mary Queen of Scots), were hanged in the castle courtyard.

Charles VII, who was born here, imported Italian architects, sculptors, decorators, and gardeners to embellish the château. He died from injuries received when he bumped his head on one of the castle's low stone doorways. Leonardo da Vinci spent his last years at Amboise and was buried in the adjoining Gothic chapel.

The most regal castle

Blois was the residence of kings for four centuries. Louis XII, François I, Louis XIII, and Henri III lived here and left their respective marks on the architecture. The powerful Duc de Guise, who had plotted to overthrow the king, was assassinated here in Henri III's bedroom in 1588. Catherine de Medici's study has 237 secret panels. The Louis XII wing is now a museum with 16th-century frescoes, furniture, paintings, and sculpture.

Where to sleep like a king

While you are in the Loire Valley, you can live like a king. The region is filled with lovely château-hotels that are beautiful but not expensive.

The **Domaine de Beauvois**, *37230 Luynes; tel. (33-47)55-50-11*, dates from the 15th century. Rooms have beamed ceilings and antique furnishings. The dining area is in the tower. Modern amenities include a heated pool, tennis courts, boating facilities, and an elevator. You can fish and hunt in the region. Rooms start at FFr850 ($163).

Château de Pray, *tel. (33-47)57-23-67*, is a lovely old château with moderate prices located two miles northeast of Amboise. Dine on the terrace in the summer. **Château de Chissay**, *Chissay-en-Touraine; tel. (33-54)32-32-01*, has hosted Charles VII, Louis XI, and General DeGaulle. The 15th-century château-hotel has a restaurant, a tearoom, and an art gallery. Minimum three-day stays are requested. It is located in the heart of the Loire castle region on RN76. Rooms are FFr420 to FFr1,365 ($80-$262) a night.

The best of the Bordeaux wine region

The region around **Bordeaux** is known for its great red wines—Margaux, Mouton-Rothschild, and Haut-Brion. Bordeaux itself is a river port with fine 18th-century architecture. But a half-hour drive from the city brings you to the heart of wine country. Nearly 100 châteaux in the Médoc region offer wine. They vary from small mansions to splendid castles. All are surrounded by acres of vines.

The best wine stores in Bordeaux are **Badie**, *place Tourny*; **La Vinothèque**, *cours du XXX Juillet*; and **Vignes et Vins de France**, *4 rue des Bahutiers*. The Maison du Vin offers maps of the wine regions and lists châteaux that receive visitors.

The prettiest wine town

St. Emilion is one of the most picturesque villages in France. The medieval town is perched on a plateau looking over the valley of the Dordogne. In the 12th century, pilgrims stopped here on their way to the shrine of St. James of Compostela in Spain. While you are in St. Emilion, visit the seventh-century hermitage, which was hollowed out of rock.

Nearby is the entrance to a chapel with a strange underground shrine. It, too, was carved out of rock 900 years ago. A subterranean passage leads to catacombs containing skeletons in ancient tombs. (You must have a guide to visit the shrine.)

At the **Syndicat d'Initiative**, *place des Crénaux*, you can get a list of wine châteaux nearby. The Château Ausone produces the St. Emilion's vintage, among others.

The best way to explore

From the center of Bordeaux City, follow the signs for Soulac. About two miles beyond the turnoff for the Paris Autoroute, the road branches to the right toward Pauillac. Head to the right, and you will be on D2e—the vineyard road.

Near Cantenac is the entrance to the **Château Prieuré-Lechine**, *tel. (33-56)88-36-*

28. This American-owned 16th-century wine cellar is the oldest in the Médoc. Wines can be bought and tasted with the permission of the cellar master.

Nearly a mile beyond Cantenac is the well-known **Château Margaux,** *tel. (33-56)88-70-28.* The Empire-style château has garden ponds filled with swans. A guide will take you through by prior appointment.

Château Beychevelle, *tel. (33-56)59-23-00,* near St. Julien, is the main attraction along the wine route. Tour the cellars and the gardens.

The most exotic of the Médoc châteaux is the 19th-century **Château Cos d'Estournal,** *tel. (33-56)44-11-37,* which has pagoda towers and massive carved-wood doors.

Burgundy—the most bountiful

Burgundy (Bourgogne) is the most bountiful region in France. The food is sumptuous, the wine rich, and the forests filled with game. The landscape is dotted with tiny Romanesque churches, old abbeys, canals, and sleepy towns. The area is known for its medieval churches.

Bourgogne is for those who prefer to pamper themselves while slowly savoring the atmosphere, the wine, and the food. Follow the wine route through the region, sampling the vintages. Treat yourself to Burgundy's legendary casseroles, *coq au vin,* or *boeuf bourguignon,* accompanied by a bottle of local red.

Beaune is the wine capital of the region. Typical of Burgundy, Beaune has narrow cobblestoned streets and old houses with little gardens. It also has tour buses, tourists, and expensive gift shops.

Known for its fine wines, Beaune is also the center for excursions northward to vineyards and châteaux. Ancient cellars in town include Cave du Bourgogne, Maison Patriarche Père et Fils (a working cellar), and Maison Calvet. Nearby are the wineries around Aloxe-Corton or Nuits St. Georges. The famous Pommard vineyards are just south of the town.

To explore the greatest wine country, drive from Beaune north to Dijon on the Ouche.

Beaune's best sight

Before leaving Beaune to explore the surrounding countryside, visit the **Hospice.** Founded in 1443 by Nicholas Rolin, chancellor of Burgundy and Flanders, it used to be a working hospital. It is divided into two sections, the **Hôtel-Dieu** and the **Hospice de la Charité.** The Hôtel-Dieu is the greater attraction, with its Burgundian-Flemish architecture and its art collection. Outside, it is somber, with a stone facade and a steep, multicolored tiled roof. Inside, it is a museum. You must pay for a tour—individual visits are not allowed.

The **Grand' Salle,** or Paupers' Room, in the hospice displays original 15th-century furnishings, including 28 red-canopied beds used by patients 400 years ago. The masterpiece of the museum is *The Last Judgement,* by Roger van der Weyden, in a side annex.

The hospice also owns vineyards all over Bourgogne. Each year on the third weekend in November, the hospice sells the wine at auction and uses the money for charity. Prominent wine growers from around the world attend. (If you plan to be in Beaune that weekend, make sure you have a reservation.)

Burgundy's best restaurant

L'Espérance, *St. Père, 89450 Vézelay; tel. (33-86)33-20-45,* is a classic, three-star restaurant in an 18th-century stone house. Chef Meneau creates a delicious *fricassée de champignons des bois* from wild mushrooms. For dessert have warm raspberries poured over vanilla ice cream. *Parfait.* Closed from Jan. 4 to Feb. 12.

The world's best lodge

The best lodge in the world to join is the **Chevaliers du Tastevin,** which inducts new members twice a year in the Clos de Vougeot, the manor house in the midst of the Burgundy vineyards. Only wine produced from those vinyards can bear the prestigious Burgundy label.

The ceremonies begin with the entrance of the halberdiers (uniformed men carrying medieval weapons), who are followed by the counsels of the order in their scarlet and gold robes. Each new member, or postulant-knight, is welcomed by a witty poem recited by the grand master in French. He is then dubbed a knight by being struck three times on the shoulder with a grapewood stick "in the name of Noah, the father of the vine; Bacchus, the God of wine; and St. Vincent, the patron of vintners."

The ceremony is followed by a dinner of six courses, each accompanied by a selected vintage—for example, meat pies with 1985 Aligoté from the Hautes-Côtes de Nuits; turbot with 1983 Puligny-Montrachet; wine-cooked eggs with 1982 Savigny-lès-Beaune; mustard chicken with 1981 Beaune Grèves; local cheeses with 1980 Latricières-Chambertin; or pear ice cream and petits fours with coffee and Marc or Prunelle from Burgundy. You may smoke only at the end of the meal.

The three best hotels

Along the wine route is the **Château d'Igé**, *tel. (33-85)33-33-99*, a hotel in a re-modeled 12th-century château near Cluny. Fortified towers, ancient exposed stonework, and a spiral stairway of hewn stone give the hotel a medieval atmosphere. Constructed by the counts of Macon in the 12th century, the castle has six hotel rooms and serves gourmet French cuisine. Rooms are FFr480 to FFr695 ($92 to $133).

Another charming old hotel is the **Hostellerie de la Poste**, *13 Place Vauban, 89200 Avallon; tel. (33-86)34-06-12*, located off Route Nationale 6 halfway between Chablis and Dijon in Avallon. Napoleon stopped at this inn. Established in 1707, it has one of the best restaurants in France, located in old converted stables and on a cobblestoned terrace. Most of the 30 rooms have baths. The hotel is closed from December to March 11.

The **Hôtel de la Poste**, *5 blvd. Clemenceau; tel. (33-80)22-08-11*, on the site of the former ramparts, is the most popular in **Beaune**. A charming old place with a garden courtyard, it also has the best restaurant in town. (Try the crayfish in cream sauce or the roast quail.) Rooms are FFr600 ($115). The hotel is closed from late November to March.

Alsace—the most German region

Alsatians describe themselves as *entre deux portes*, or between two gates—France and Germany. This French *département* that stretches between the Vosges Mountains and the Rhine River has been passed between France and Germany five times, and, as a result, its culture is an interesting blend of French and German. Try the local dishes: onion pie, *choucrôute* (sauerkraut), and *charcuterie*, accompanied by a glass of the wine or beer of the region. *Kugelhupf*, a yeast-based cake, is the traditional dessert.

Strasbourg: the prettiest old town

Strasbourg, the ancient capital of the province, has a centuries-old center enclosed by the branches of the Ill River and guarded by the Strasbourg Cathedral. Built on Roman foundations, the pink Gothic cathedral was begun in 1176 and completed in the 15th century.

Ancient half-timbered buildings line the cathedral square and surrounding streets. One of the most striking is the **Maison Kammerzell**, a restaurant in a 15th-century house with elaborately carved wood trim. Wander along the rue du Bain aux Plantes to La Petite France. Four massive square towers, remnants of 14th-century ramparts, stand over the covered bridges that cross the Ill.

Alsace at its best

Farther up the river in **Colmar**, where Charlemagne once had his summer villa, are houses with carved-wood gables, balustrades, towers, and balconies. Visit the Customs House and the Musée d'Unterlinden, located in a 13th-century convent and cloister.

Small farming villages dot the Rhine plain as it reaches west to the Vosges. Betschdorf, just north of the Haguenau Forest, is where potters make the region's distinctive blue and gray stoneware.

The best white wines

Regional wines of Alsace, unlike those of the rest of France, are labeled by grape varieties rather than by the name of the village or château. Because they don't understand this German labeling system, the French mistrust Alsatian wines. As a result, vintage Guebwiller Gewurtztraminer is the best wine bargain in France, available for FFr20 ($4) a bottle.

Along the Alsatian **Route du Vin** (Wine Road), stretching 90 miles from Marlenheim to Thann, are centuries-old towns surrounded by vineyards. **Eguisheim** is a 16th-century town with half-timbered houses with low doorways. Three medieval towers guarded the town until the 15th century. Stop at the Caveau d'Eguisheim (dated 1603) for lunch.

Riquewihr is a pretty Alsatian town that clings to a vine-covered hill, within a circle of 16th-century walls. Cars may not enter its cobblestoned streets.

The best views in the Vosges

A last line of defense over the centuries, the **Vosges Mountains** are dotted with the ruins of fortresses and with convents and churches. Château de Fleckenstein is carved into a rocky hill high above the German border.

Also in the Vosges, in the Saverne Forest, is the **Rocher de Dabo**. Atop this narrow pinnacle is a small chapel dedicated to Alsace's 11th-century pope, Leo IX. From here the view is terrific.

Dordogne—the least spoiled area

This *département* in the heart of France is rural, traditional, and relatively unspoiled. But tourists are beginning to discover the area. **Dordogne** is known for its prehistoric cave drawings and gourmet cuisine. Deep green valleys and river gorges break up the landscape. In the Dronne Valley, walled castles top nearly every hill.

The best country cuisine

The **Perigord**, a historic province contained within Dordogne, is famous for its cuisine. This is a place to linger over long meals. The area's foie gras, *confit d'oie*, and truffles are famous. But the game and fish are equally delicious. Try the crayfish and the morels. Wash your meal down with a full-bodied Bergerac.

The world's finest porcelain

Limoges, the largest city in the region, is famous for its fine porcelain. Cross its Roman bridges, stroll the little streets in the old section, and visit the ancient cathedral of St. Etienne. Notice the old half-timbered houses by the river. They have open spaces between the roof and the top floor, held up by wide beams. In the old days, residents dried their wash and kept their food provisions in this airy space below the roof.

Tour the porcelain factories or enamel workshops. You can get lists of factories and workshops from the **Tourist Information Office**, *boulevard Fleurus; tel. (33-55)34-46-87*, and from the **Regional Tourist Committee**, *8 Cours Bugeaud*.

The most disturbing sight

Northwest of Limoges are the charred remains of **Oradour-sur-Glane**, where 650 men, women, and children were murdered by the Nazis during World War II in reprisal for having sheltered Resistance fighters in their village.

The prettiest town in Dordogne

One of the most charming villages in France is **Brantôme**. Bordered on two sides by the Dronne River, it has an 18th-century Benedictine abbey (now the town hall) and a good museum, the Desmoulin. Stroll along the canals past the old houses and then visit the Monks' Garden.

The superb **Restaurant Chabrol**, *rue Gambetta; tel. (33-5)305-70-15*, makes a trip to Brantôme worthwhile. Try the *magret et saumon fumés maison* (smoked duck and salmon) or the *pigeonneau Rossini* (squab with foie gras).

The most spectacular town in France

Dordogne boasts medieval castles and walled cities dating back to Richard the Lion-Hearted. The most spectacular of the towns is **Rocamadour**, built into the face of a steep cliff. Narrow, cobblestoned streets climb the cliff to its summit, where the Basilica of St. Sauveur is perched along with several shrines. Pilgrims on their knees have climbed the Great Staircase to the shrine since the Middle Ages. See the Black Madonna in Notre Dame chapel.

The **Château de Roumegouse**, located between Rocamadour and Gramat off N140; *tel. (33-65)33-63-81*, is a hotel with views of Rocamadour and a wooded park. It is expensive—rooms are FFr490 to FFr900 ($94-$173) a night.

Medieval musts

East of Le Bugue is the **Château Beynac-et-Cazenac**, a well-preserved fortress atop a cliff. The castle was destroyed and rebuilt twice: in 1189 by Sir Mercadier in the name of Richard the Lion-Hearted and in 1214 by Simon de Montfort during the Crusade against Albigensian heretics. From the ramparts of the castle, another great fortress, the Château de Castelnaud, can be seen. The restored castle was once a headquarters for Simon de Montfort.

The village of St. Cirq-La Popie, set in a gorgeous valley, sits beneath the ruins of a 1,000-year-old castle. The town's name commemorates St. Cirq, a saint who lived here in the third century, and Sieur La Popie, lord of the castle. St. Cirq is known for its woodcraft, although the art has largely disappeared.

More than 80 walled cities still stand from Perigord to the Pyrenées, including Monpazier, Domme, Lalinde, Villereal, Beaumont, and Ste. Foy-la Grande.

Europe's favorite summer playground

The French Riviera, known as the **Côte d'Azur**, is Europe's favorite summer play-ground. It is hot, crowded, expensive, and oh-so-trendy. Avoid St. Tropez in July and August, when it is jam-packed. Visit in September and October, after the summer season and before winter. Prices drop, the weather is mild and sunny, and the beaches are yours.

The coast is 72 miles long, with 25 miles of long beaches of pebble or sand, from Marseilles to Menton. From Nice to the Italian border, beaches are of gravel or rock. Between Cannes and St. Raphaël, the rocks of Corniche are breathtakingly beautiful. But the best beaches are along the coast from St. Raphaël to Hyères: Cabasson, Le Lavandou, St. Clair, Cavalière, Tahiti, Pampelone, and Salins.

The most famous Riviera town is **St. Tropez**. Its three best-known beaches are Le Plage de Pampelone, which is spectacular; Le Plage de Tahiti, where the very rich sunbathe; and Le Plage des Slins, where the clothes get skimpy.

The nicest town

Nice is a lovely town with old houses and wide views. Although its beach is rocky, you still can take a pleasant walk along the sea—on the Promenade des Anglais. The casino is elegant. Visit the Terra Amata paleontological museum near the old harbor, located on the spot where the remains of a mammoth-hunters' camp 400,000 years old were discovered.

Le Chantecler, *37 Promenade des Anglais; tel. (33-93)88-39-51,* in the Hôtel Negresco, serves the excellent inventions of chef Jacques Maximin. The **Hôtel Negresco** is more an institution than a hotel. It has been revived with splendid authentic antiques and decorated in the styles of the 16th and 18th centuries.

The best casino
In Cannes, the glamorous **Palm Beach Casino** is a big attraction—except when the French police have closed it. The beaches are sandy, and luxury yachts line the marina. The Promenade of the Croisette is lined with jet-set hotels. And the splendid new Palace of Festivals houses a theater, a casino, a nightclub, boutiques, and a convention center. It is the site of the famous film festival.

St. Yves, *49 blvd. d'Alsace; tel. (33-93)38-65-29,* in Cannes is a charming old hotel in a villa surrounded by palm trees. Rooms are FFr290 to FFr340 ($55 to $65) a night.

The best drive
The drive along the **Grande Corniche,** the high road along the crests of the mountains, is spectacular. At times you will see the high snow-covered peaks of the Alps. At other places, you will see the sea. On the way down, visit Roquebrune, where a château was hewn from the rock.

The Corniche is where the Monte Carlo Grand Prix car races are held and where the spectacular chase in *Casino Royale* was filmed.

The most romantic town
Antibes, the center of the perfume market, has lovely beaches, a quaint old port, and a colorful fruit and flower market.

Hôtel du Cap-Eden Roc, *boulevard Kennedy; tel. (33-93)61-39-01,* was once a favorite of Scott and Zelda Fitzgerald. It's romantic and glamorous and has great views. Rooms are from FFr2,300 ($442).

For a magnificent dinner, take a boat from Antibes to La Napoule and dine at **L'Oasis,** *rue Jean-Honoré-Carle; tel. (33-93)49-95-52.* Chef Louis Outhier creates unforgettable desserts.

A princely resort
Monaco, a separate though tiny nation on the Riviera, attracts the world's royalty. The little kingdom set above the sea looks like the setting for a fairy tale. But it's far from innocent, with its casinos, decadent hotels, and beaches where the world's best bodies sun topless.

Monaco's capital, Monte Carlo, has some of the most glamorous hotels, restaurants, and casinos in Europe. The magnificent **Hôtel de Paris,** *Place du Casino; tel. (33-93)50-80-80,* attracts jet-setters, gamblers, yachtsmen, and the Grand Prix crowd. It has lovely views of the Mediterranean, a private beach, and a nice pool. Double rooms are FFr2,100 ($403).

The hotel's greatest feature, however, is its restaurant, **Louis XV.** One of Europe's finest new chefs, 31-year-old Alain Ducasse, is the mastermind behind the marvelous meals served here. (Try the cream of shrimp soup, the crayfish salad, and the strawberries.) The restaurant's wine cellar contains nearly 280,000 bottles. Gold and ivory frescoes decorate the walls.

The hottest nightclub on the Riviera is **No Rock,** *11 rue du Portier, 9800 Monte Carlo; tel. (33-93)25-09-25.* Princess Stephanie can be spotted here. The atmosphere is cozy yet exciting, with a piano bar, romantic nooks, and a disco. Drinks are bought by the bottle. The club is open from 11 p.m. until morning.

Provence, the sweetest region
The Mediterranean region of **Provence** is a sweet land, literally and figuratively. Its air

is scented by the lavender, basil, rosemary, thyme, and sage that grow in its rocky fields. And old traditions and a simple way of life survive here. This is the land of Marcel Pagnol, the beloved French writer, who wrote about his boyhood adventures in these rocky hills, olive groves, and stone houses.

Provence looks like an Impressionistic painting. Villages climb the white rocks; the pines are a dark green, the soil red, and the olive groves green; and lavender grows in the fields.

Framed by the sea, the Alps, the Rhone and Durance rivers, and the Italian border, Provence stretches from the medieval town of Aigues-Mortes in the west, beyond Marseille to Cassis in the east. It includes the lower Rhone Valley; the flat, windy marshes of the Camargue; and the foothills of the Alps.

The most typical town

Arles, the most characteristically Provençal town, is also the most Roman town. It has an ancient Roman arena and theater. Around the Place du Forum are buildings that date back to the Roman era. Be sure to see the Roman sarcophagi and mosaics at the Museum of Pagan Art in the former Church of St. Anne.

Of the medieval monuments, **St. Trophîme** is the most famous, boasting carved details from the Old and New Testaments.

If you happen to be in Arles on a Saturday, visit the outdoor market on boulevard des Lices. Regional produce, lavender, crafts, and homemade sausages are sold.

Le Vaccarès, a restaurant once frequented by Vincent van Gogh, is the most agreeable place to lunch. It looks over the Place du Forum.

Jules César, *boulevard des Lices,* is a beautifully run hotel with a fine restaurant, Lou Marquest. The charming **Hôtel d'Arlatan,** *26 rue du Sauvage; tel. (33-90)93-56-66,* is located in the 15th-century ancestral home of the counts of Arlatan. The courtyard is tranquil with its palm trees and shade. Double rooms are FFr620 ($119).

The Vatican's only rival

Avignon, the seat of the papacy from 1309 to 1403, is famed for its **Palais des Papes.** For a time, Avignon was a center of Christianity and medieval civilization. Later it was the home of a schismatic pope, put in power by the ambitious kings of France.

The Papal Palace is a massive, handsome building. Tours in English are offered twice daily. Examine the Gobelin tapestries in the banquet hall, the kitchen tower, the frescoed tower of St. John, the papal bedroom, and the stag room, lined with hunting scenes.

Avignon's Place de l'Horloge, between the rue de la Republique and the place du Palais, is lively, filled with restaurants, cafés, and street musicians. The Auberge de France is the best restaurant. The Petit Palais, on the square, is filled with 14th- and 15th-century paintings and sculpture, including an early Botticelli.

For the best view of the city, climb to the Rocher des Dômes, just above the Papal Palace. You'll see clearly the **Pont d'Avignon** of the French folk song. (It's real name is the Pont St. Benezet.) The ruined bridge goes only partway across the river.

Our favorite hotel is **Hôtel d'Europe,** *12 place Crillon, 84000 Avignon; tel. (33-90)82-66-92.* Located in a 16th-century aristocrat's house, it hosted Napoleon in 1799. Rooms are furnished with antiques, and the atmosphere is peaceful. The restaurant serves classic cuisine, as well as the best croissants in France. You can eat outside beside a fountain in the courtyard. Rooms are FFr550 to FFr1,250 ($105-$240) for a double.

The oldest houses in France

The road to the golden-hued city of Gordes leads through flat vineyards and steep hills to the **Village des Bories.** This collection of prehistoric stone buildings, or *bories,* dates back to 3000 B.C. The huts were used by shepherds until the 18th century. They have been restored to look as they did 4,000 years ago and are filled with old cooking implements and tools.

The wildest region

Camargue, a marshy area where wild horses and bulls live, is the wildest region in France. Horseback riding is a big attraction in Camargue, which has many horse ranches.

Hotels in Camargue are often built in the style of the traditional low white farmhouse, or *mas*. Two of these hostelries are **Mas de la Fouque**, *tel. (33-90)97-81-02,* and **Mas du Clarousset**, *tel. (33-90)97-81-66.* Mas de la Fouque is a little more than two miles from Stes. Maries de la Mer on the road to Aigues-Mortes. This beautiful *mas* has a shallow lake that attracts flamingos. Rooms start at FFr1,850 ($355) for two people per night. It is open from the end of March to November. Mas du Clarousset, also in Stes. Maries de la Mer, has fireplaces, terra-cotta tiles, and flowers everywhere. Rooms start at FFr1,200 ($230) a night.

Stes. Maries de la Mer, the informal capital of Camargue, is a 20-minute drive from Arles. It is host to Gypsy pilgrims every year. They come by the thousands from all over Europe May 24 and 25 to visit the town's 12th-century church. In a corner of the crypt is the statue of St. Sara, patron saint of the Gypsies, cloaked in purple velvet.

The best-preserved fortified town

Aigues-Mortes, surrounded by marshes, is one of the few perfect surviving examples of a fortified medieval town. The walled city dates back to the 13th century, when Louis IX, later known as St. Louis, sailed off for the Seventh Crusade to the Holy Land.

The best Roman ruins in France

North of this ancient town is **Nîmes**, which has the most splendid Roman arena in the country. Well-preserved, it is used for bullfights. Nimes' Roman temple, known as the Maison Carée, is also perfectly preserved.

The most fragrant town

The sweetest-smelling town in Provence is **Grasse**, 10 miles from Cannes. It is the perfume capital of the world. Violet, lavender, jasmine, lily, rose, jonquil, and mimosa grow here. Once the favorite resort of Queen Victoria, Grasse is a picturesque old village with winding cobblestoned streets and weathered houses.

Each year the perfumeries in Grasse process more than 700 tons of roses, 600 tons of orange blossoms, and 800 tons of jasmine. **La Parfumérie Fragonard** (named after the painter and engraver born here in 1732) and **La Parfumérie Gallimard** are open daily. English-speaking guides explain how the perfume is made. Villa Fragonard houses paintings by Fragonard.

The most Spanish region: Roussillon

West of the Riviera, stretching the length of the Golfe du Lion, from the Pyrénées to the Rhône Delta, is the **Roussillon** region. Medieval walled cities, the peaks of the Pyrénées, Mediterranean resorts, and quaint villages mark this varied region. Also known as French Catalonia, Roussillon has a Spanish air. It belonged to Spain until 1659, and the people are Catalan, as are the people of Barcelona. The red and yellow Catalan flag flies over the region's capital, **Perpignan**. Some Catalans would like to see the region become autonomous.

The least-spoiled coast

Traditional fishing villages still can be found along the western end of the Mediterranean coast. **Collioure** is the most charming fishing port. Matisse painted here. **Sète**, the birthplace of Paul Valéry and Georges Brassens, also retains its original appeal.

The largest walled city

Carcassonne, Europe's largest medieval walled city, is west of Narbonne. A mighty circle of towers and battlements surrounds the hilltop town. Parts of the walls were built by the Romans. In the fifth century, the Visigoths enlarged the fortress. Charlemagne laid siege to the city for five years in the ninth century. And in the 13th century it fell to Crusaders; Simon de Montfort took it over. St. Louis strengthened the fortress. It was rebuilt in the 19th century by Violet-le-Duc to conform to Victorian ideas of how a walled city should look.

The best place to stay in Carcassonne is the **Hôtel de la Cité,** *Place d'Eglise; tel. (33-68)25-03-34,* located in a former Episcopal palace built into the old walls near the Basilica of St. Nazaire. Some rooms have canopy beds, and the dining hall is beautiful. The hotel is open from April through October; a double room is FFr850 ($163) a night.

The most exotic region: Basque Country

The southwest of France and the northwest of Spain combine to form an exotic region known as **Basque Country.** The Basques have a common language, culture, and history identifiable as neither French nor Spanish.

The Spanish Basques, in particular, have agitated for autonomy. A separatist movement exists in France as well, but it is milder. The Basque language is related to no other; it is not Indo-European. Some believe that the cavemen spoke Basque.

The mountainous region is known for its cuisine. The most prized dish is seasonal—the wild dove that migrates from northern Europe to Spain in October.

The most typical town

St. Jean-Pied-de-Port, near the Spanish border, is the most typically Basque town in the region. It was fortified in the time of Louis XIV, and its narrow cobblestoned streets are guarded by a tall citadel. Sheep graze in the moat. The typical Basque houses are stone, sturdy, half-timbered, and whitewashed with red or green trim and chaletlike stucco.

The church's clock tower tolls the hour twice, following local custom. A stone bridge crosses the Nive River to the tower. The *fronton,* or ball court, is always filled with *pelota* players. And flat, round tombstones from pre-Christian times can be seen in the graveyards. *Pelota,* or jai alai, is the Basque ball game, played with a hard ball and a racquet. It is very fast.

High fashion and fine surfing

Biarritz, a seaside resort on the Bay of Biscay, has one of the longest beaches in France and offers the best surfing on the French coast. Stroll along the promenade from the Hôtel du Palais to the Côte des Basques. Visit the Rocher de la Vierge for a good view of the ocean. The lower promenade, along the boulevard du Prince de Galles, leads past the foaming breakers that give the coast its name—Côte d'Argent, the Silver Coast. The lighthouse on the summit of Cap St. Martin has a splendid view.

Biarritz was made famous by the Empress Eugénie (the wife of Napoleon III), who attracted fashionable clientele to the resort. Queen Victoria and Edward VII, among others, slept in Eugénie's villa, now the Hôtel du Palais.

The Best of Germany

Germany, the diseased world's bathhouse.
—*Mark Twain*

We believe Germany is the best all-around travel destination in Europe. As balanced as a fine cuckoo clock, it has something for everyone. Its old cities have museums, concert halls, and gourmet restaurants. Romantic little villages nestle beneath the snow-capped Alps. Its North Sea beaches are edged by 30-foot sand dunes and beautified with goose-pimpled, bronzed (and sometimes nude) bodies. The avant-garde lives side by side with folk culture: New wave is popular, but so is oompah music; in the South, leather skirts are seen as often as dirndls.

Berlin: the most exciting city

Berlin has an exciting, devil-may-care atmosphere. Sidewalk cafés, little shops, parks, and offices exist side by side with the remains of the graffiti-covered Berlin Wall. Berlin is changing a great deal as East meets West, and today it is one of the most exciting cities to visit in the world. (Although the city telephone codes are still separate for East and West, Germany will have only one code soon, a sign that the two halves of the city are finally as one.)

Berlin is a lively city. Its slogan is *"Berlin weil's Spass macht"* (Berlin because it's fun). Berlin is a fashion center, known for its chic, quality clothing. It has 5,000 restaurants, cafés, and bars situated along its Kurfürstendamm (the local Champs-Elysées, known as the Ku'damm). Unlike bars and restaurants in other German cities, these stay open all night.

What used to be West Berlin is more modern than its sister. There are lakes, rivers, and forest covering 35% of the city's area. Western Berlin is ablaze with neon and gleaming with chrome and glass architecture. Germany beyond the Berlin Wall was always rich in culture and perfectly preserved historical treasures, however, and now these treasures are easily accessible to visitors. This eastern part of Berlin will slowly catch up with its twin sister, but the remains of its Communist history are still evident in these early stages of unification.

The best view of Berlin

The **Fernsehturm**, the television tower between Alexanderplatz and Marx-Engels-Platz, offers the best view of Berlin—especially of what used to be East Berlin. Rising

73

1,209 feet, the slender spire is Europe's second-tallest tower. You can have a meal or a cup of coffee in the revolving sphere that tops the tower at 655 feet. The tower is open every day. You can spot it from almost any section of town.

Berlin's best museums

The **House at Checkpoint Charlie** displays many of the ingenious, homemade contraptions used by East Berliners in their attempts to cross the Berlin Wall when it stood as a barrier between East and West. The museum is located in a dilapidated tenement building at Friedrichstrasse 44, near the gate between East and West Berlin in the American sector. Displays include a miniature submarine created with a motor taken from a motor scooter; a low-slung sportscar that zoomed beneath the horizontal barrier at Checkpoint Charlie; a homemade ski lift that carried an East Berliner, his wife, and their son to freedom; a homemade bulletproof truck that crashed through the wall; and photos of a 476-foot tunnel that 57 people crawled through to the West.

Museumsinsel (Museum Island), formerly in East Berlin, surrounded by the Spree River and the Spree Canal, is one of the world's largest and most magnificent museum complexes. It includes the Pergamon, Bode, and Altes museums, as well as the the National Gallery, the Berlin Cathedral, and several ruins.

The magnificent **Pergamon** is the most important of the complex's museums. Everything here is on a giant scale. The huge **Ishtar Gate** was transported centuries ago stone by stone from ancient Babylon.

The museum has an extensive collection of ancient art, including artifacts from 200 B.C. Far Eastern, Near Eastern, and Islamic Art also also featured. The beautiful **Pergamon Altar** is one of the Seven Wonders of the Ancient World. Originally part of a temple complex to Zeus, it was brought from Turkey and reconstructed here.

The neoclassical **Altes Museum** houses contemporary paintings and 135,000 prints by 15th- to 18th-century masters, including Botticelli's illustrations of Dante's *Divine Comedy*.

The **National Gallery** has a comprehensive collection of 19th- and 20th-century art from the Soviet Union and other East bloc countries. The **Bode Museum** has an outstanding collection of Egyptian, early Christian, and Byzantine art.

The museum complex shares the island with Berlin's **Lutheran Cathedral**, built from 1894 to 1905 and recently restored; the **French (Huguenot) Cathedral**; and ruins of the former main synagogue, which was destroyed by Nazi vandals and by bombings during World War II. Designed by the architect Knoblauch and built from 1859 to 1866, it is a curious combination of Western and Moorish influences.

Berlin's most important sights

Only 100 of the original 347 buildings along the Kurfürstendamm survived World War II. Most notable is **Kaiser-Wilhelm-Gedächtniskirche**. The ruins of the church were left standing as a permanent reminder of the horrors of war. (On a lighter note, the chapel and bell tower, adjacent to the church, are known by Berliners as the lipstick case and the powder box.)

Across the square is the **Europa Center**, much bigger than New York's Rockefeller Center, encompassing five acres of office buildings, shops, restaurants, an ice-skating rink, saunas, and a swimming pool.

The **New National Gallery**, *Potsdamer Strasse 50*, houses modern European paintings, including some by German Expressionists. This starkly modern building houses changing exhibitions. Its collection includes works by Manet, Renoir, and Monet, as well as Munch, Klee, and Picasso. The gallery is open Tuesdays through Sundays, 9 a.m. until 5 p.m. Admission is free.

The **Deutsche Staatsoper** (the opera house, located in what used to be East Berlin), *Unter den Linden 7; tel. (37-2)205-4556*, seats 1,500 people and hosts some of the finest opera performances in the world. It was built in 1743 but burned down 100 years later. The rebuilt facade is modeled on the original.

Hegel, Max Planck, and Einstein taught at **Humboldt University**, *Unter den Linden 6*. And Marx and Engels studied here. The largest university in what used to be East Germany, it was built in the mid-18th century. The palace of Emperor William I, built in 1836, is now part of the university. The emperor spent the last 50 years of his life here. The **Alte Bibliothek** (Old Library) also is part of the university. Formerly the Prussian State Library, it is set back from Unter den Linden, on Bebelplatz. The Nazis burned books here in 1933.

Zeughaus, *Unter den Linden 2*, is a baroque structure housing the Museum of German History. It is worth visiting to see a Marxist view of history. The museum is closed Fridays.

Just south of the *rathaus* is the ornate **Saint Nicholas Church**, the oldest in the city, begun in 1230. You have a splendid view of the city from the tower.

Marienkirche (St. Mary's Church), *Karl-Liebknecht-Strasse*, Berlin's second-oldest church, near Museumsinsel on Karl-Liebknecht-Strasse, was built in 1240.

The world's largest Rembrandt collection

Gemäldegalerie, *Arnimallee 23/27*, displays the world's largest Rembrandt collection. The Picture Gallery, which seems to go on forever, also displays works by Dürer, Giotto, Fra Angelico, Ghirlandaio, Titian, Holbein, Rubens, Van Dyck, Hals, and Vermeer.

The Gemäldegalerie is one of several museums that make up the immense Dahlem museum complex, which includes sculpture, prints, the Ethnographical Museum, the Museum of Far Eastern, Islamic, and Indian Art, and the Botanical Museum. You could spend days here. The Dahlem museums are open Tuesdays through Fridays, 9 a.m. until 5 p.m., and Saturdays and Sundays, 10 a.m. until 5 p.m. Admission is free.

Berlin's most famous work of art

The **Egyptian Museum**, *Schlossstrasse 70*, is the home of the most famous piece of art in Berlin—the painted limestone bust of beautiful Queen Nefertiti, created more than 3,300 years ago.

Germany's best park

When you tire of museums, go to the **Tiergarten**, Germany's most inviting park. Originally the royal hunting preserve, it is now one of the world's largest urban parks, dotted with lakes and ponds. At its western edge is Berlin's famous zoo, which has more species than any other zoo in the world. At its eastern edge is the Reichstag, Germany's former Parliament building, which burned down in 1933 but was rebuilt after the war. It is used for political meetings—the German Parliament now meets in Bonn. The Brandenburg Gate at the eastern end of the Tiergarten marks the former border between West and East Berlin.

Berlin's best castle

Schloss Charlottenburg, *Luisenplatz*, is the best example of royal Prussian architecture in Berlin. Begun in 1695, the palace took 100 years to build. The Schloss was destroyed during World War II, but it has been restored. You can tour the castle, which is surrounded by lovely grounds and a lake, Tuesdays through Sundays, 9 a.m. until 5 p.m. (The tours are given only in German.)

Charlottenburg houses a great porcelain collection, the museum of arts and crafts, and sumptuously decorated royal apartments, including the splendid white-and-gold rococo gallery. The **Charlottenburg Mausoleum** contains the tombs of King Friedrich Wilhelm III and Queen Luise.

Counterculture bests

For a taste of Berlin's counterculture, visit **Kreuzberg**, Berlin's answer to New York's East Village. Art galleries, bookstores, used-clothing shops, high-fashion boutiques, and small theaters thrive in this area. Restaurants offering every imaginable cuisine line the streets. The Berlin Wall, which is covered with colorful graffiti, is the eastern boundary of the neighborhood. A sign here reminds you that you are at the site of Gestapo torture chambers.

The heart of the Kreuzberg is the **Mehringhof complex**, a former factory at *Gneisenaustrasse 2*. It is used by about 30 counterculture organizations, including theater troupes, jazz bands, political groups, a health cooperative, and a bookstore.

The most avant-garde of the art world

The most far-out modern art is on display at the **Akademie der Künste** (Academy of Art), *Hanseatenweg 10*, in the Hansa Quarter. Exhibitions on *le dernier cri* in art from all over the world are displayed here. In the evenings, lectures, performances of experimental music, and theater are staged in the Akademie's studio. It is open every day during the summer from 10 a.m. until 7 p.m. Admission to the downstairs section is free; admission upstairs, where exhibitions are larger, is DM4 ($2.50).

The most decadent shopping

Stop in at **Kaufhaus des Westens**, known locally as KaDeWe, Berlin's version of Harrods in London. Located near the Ku'damm, it has an enormous selection of clothing, as well as 450 kinds of bread, 1,000 types of sausage, and 1,000 different cheeses.

The best bargains

A much less expensive place to shop is Berlin's flea market, **Die Nolle**, open every day except Tuesday 11 a.m. until 7 p.m. It is situated in 16 old subway trains at Nollendorfplatz, a 10-minute walk from Wittenbergplatz, the square near KaDeWe. Old sewing machines, furniture, and antique dolls are some of the best buys. Stop at the little restaurant here, where a *Boulette* (hamburger without a bun) sells for DM3 ($2). You may also hear live jazz in the streets.

The wildest night life

The **Metropol**, *Nollendorfplatz 5*, in a former theater building, is the largest disco in Germany. It draws 3,000 Berliners a night. By the end of the night, dancers are in an elated frenzy.

The **Riverboat**, *Hohenzollerndamm 177*, is another energetic night spot, where frenetic jazz is played. The building itself is a maze of halls and booths. The Riverboat is closed Sundays and Mondays.

If you are looking for an older crowd (the Metropol and the Riverboat draw young groups), try the **Café Keese**, *Bismarckstrasse 108*. This is a large dance hall where women must ask men to dance and it is against house rules for a man to refuse. Men can ask women to dance only once an hour. No admission is charged, and drink prices are reasonable.

All age groups can be seen chugging beer in 3-liter steins at the **Wirthaus zum Löwen**, *Hardenbergstrasse*. The dancing here is lively, too. No entrance fee is charged on weekdays.

Jazz concerts are held in the sculpture garden of the **New National Galerie**, *tel. (49-30)2666*, during the summer.

The Berlin Philharmonic is wonderful. Performances are at the **Philharmonie**, *Matthäikirchstrasse 1; tel. (49-30)261-4383*.

Top restaurants

Rockendorf's, *Düsterhauptstrasse 1; tel. (49-30)402-3099*, is the best restaurant in Berlin. Off the beaten track in the suburb of Waidmannslust, it is an old-fashioned establishment that serves continental dishes and has a good wine selection. It is closed Sundays and Mondays and July 5 through Aug. 3. Reservations are preferred. Dinner is DM156 to DM210 ($104 to $140).

Another little-known restaurant with German atmosphere is the **Blockhaus Nikolskoe,** *Nikolskoer Weg; tel. (49-30)805-2914.* Set in the forest high above the Havel River, it was built log-cabin-style in 1819 by Prussian King Friedrich Wilhelm III for his daughter Charlotte and her husband, Grand Duke Nicholas (later Russian Czar Nicholas I). Continental cuisine is served. Dinners are DM11 to DM38 ($7 to $26). The Blockhaus is closed Thursdays and after 8 p.m. in winter. Ask directions when you make reservations, because the place can be difficult to find.

Conti Fischstuben, *Bayreuthstrasse 42; tel. (49-30)219-021,* is the best seafood restaurant in Germany. This small restaurant in the Hotel Ambassador is closed Sundays and four weeks in July or August. Dinner starts at DM32 ($22).

I-Punkt, *tel. (49-30)261-6968,* has a panoramic view of Berlin from its location on the 20th floor of the Europa-Center complex. At night, the city lights are spectacular. The international menu is good. Dinners are DM32 to DM48 ($22 to $32).

Ermeler Haus, *Am Märkischen Ufer 10-12,* a continental restaurant in a 16th-century mansion, serves good food in a romantic ambiance. Reservations are suggested.

Hecker's Deele, *Grolmanstrasse 36; tel. (49-30)88-901,* serves Czech beers on tap. It's a favorite among locals.

The **Bristol Kempinski Hotel Grill,** *Kurfürstendamm 27; tel. (49-30)884-340*, serves high-quality food for slightly higher prices.

The best hotel

The best place to stay in Berlin is the **Bristol-Hotel Kempinski,** *Kurfürstendamm 27, 1000 Berlin 15; tel. (49-30)884-340.* The sprawling, old-fashioned hotel has been newly renovated and now boasts a sauna. A double room is DM460 to DM510 ($307 to $340).

Close seconds

The **Hotel Ambassador,** *Bayreutherstrasse 42; tel. (49-30)219-020,* has a heated swimming pool and serves enormous buffet breakfasts. The views from the rooftop are impressive. A double room is DM310 to DM350 ($207 to $233).

For a taste of the elegance that existed in Germany at the turn of the century, stay at the **Schloss Hotel Gerhus,** *Brahmstrasse 4-10; tel. (49-30)826-2081.* Formerly known as the Pannwitz Palast, it was built in 1912-1914 to house the art and china collections of the personal attorney of Kaiser Wilhelm II. The immense ceilings are hung with elaborate chandeliers. Antiques and larger-than-life mirrors give the rooms a stately air. Surrounded by a large park, the Gerhus is in the Grunewald, five minutes from the Kurfürstendamm. A double room is DM110 to DM385 a night ($73 to $257).

Hotel Belvedere, *Seebergsteig 4, Grunewald, Berlin 33; tel. (49-30)826-1077,* is next to a forest and near the Havel. A big, turn-of-the-century villa with gardens, it is peaceful and has antique-furnished bedrooms. Rooms have televisions and telephones. Some have private bathrooms. A double room is DM75 to DM115 ($50 to $77).

Palast, *Karl-Liebknecht-Strasse 5; tel. (37-2)23-82-8,* is another luxury hotel with first-class service. The rooms are attractive and have views of the city. The hotel restaurant is good. A double room starts at DM340 ($227).

The best hotel in what used to be East Berlin is the **Metropol,** *Friedrichstrasse 150-153; tel. (37-2)23875,* a modern high-rise hotel built by a Swedish firm (perhaps the reason it features saunas). Rooms are luxurious and the service good. A double room starts at DM330 ($220).

The best of Frankfurt

Frankfurt is the logical center for touring Germany. Frankfurt-am-Main Airport is the largest and busiest of Germany's international airports. (All major trains go beyond Frankfurt's main railroad station to the airport, allowing incoming tourists to make train connections to all parts of Germany—or Europe for that matter.)

A modern, industrial city and Germany's banking and finance center, Frankfurt has a charming old section with good beer halls. The *Altstadt* (Old Town) is ringed by the *Innenstadt* (Inner Town), which developed in the 14th century.

Frankfurt's top five sights

Stroll through the *Altstadt* past the **Römer** (town hall), which is made up of a group of eight 15th-century Gothic buildings on Römerberg Square. The Römer is covered with carved decoration and has beautiful courtyards. It houses the ornate Imperial Hall, where coronation banquets were held, and it is hung with portraits of the emperors from Charlemagne to Francis I.

Near the Römer is the red sandstone **Dom** (Cathedral) **of St. Bartholomäus.** The 13th-century cathedral was badly damaged during World War II but has been restored. Here Holy Roman emperors were crowned. And a short distance away, at Grosser Hirschgraben 23, is the restored house (now a museum) where the poet Goethe was born in 1749.

On the other side of the Main River is the **Sachsenhausen Quarter,** once a fishing village, where pleasant cafés, popular cider bars, and lively taverns line the streets. A riverside promenade called the Schaumainkai borders the Main in Sachsenhausen. The view of the *Altstadt* from the promenade is beautiful, especially in the evening.

The **Städel,** a museum on the Schaumainkai, houses European paintings from the 14th century to the present day, including Rembrandt's *Blinding of Samson.*

Frankfurt's zoo, *Tiergarten Rhönstrasse,* is one of the best in the world. More than 5,000 exotic animals are allowed to roam freely. Rather than fences, ditches and pools of water are used to keep animals confined in large, open areas. One of the best exhibits is the Nocturnal Animals House.

Palmengarten, which is bounded on two sides by Miquelallee, is one of the best and largest botanical gardens in the world.

Frankfurt's best restaurants

Weinhaus Brückenkeller, *Schützenstrasse 6; tel. (49-69)28-42-38,* is one of the best restaurants in Germany. The old vaulted cellar is furnished with precious antiques. It is closed on Sundays and bank holidays. Only dinner is served, and reservations are required. Dinner is about DM28 to DM48 ($19 to $32) for a four-course meal.

Restaurant Français, *Bethmannstrasse 33; tel. (49-69)21-502,* located in the Steigenberger-Hotel Frankfurter Hof, was awarded one of Michelin's coveted stars for its delectable fare. Its reputation is well-known, so reservations are essential. Dinner is DM98 ($66). The restaurant opens at 7 p.m. It is closed on Sundays, bank holidays, and for four weeks in July and August.

Restaurants with the most atmosphere

German specialties are served at the reasonably priced **Dippegucker,** *Eschenheimer Anlage 40; tel. (49-69)55-19-65.* This *Weinstube* (wine bar) has wood paneling and beams, stained-glass windows, a tiled floor, and tables set in alcoves. The wine of the month is usually a bargain. Try the shrimp served with green sauce on toasted rye bread. Dinner is about DM9 to DM28 ($6 to $19) per person without wine.

Another restaurant offering a lot of atmosphere is the **Gutsschänke Neuhof,** *6072 Dreieich-Götzenhain; tel. (49-6102)3214,* a 500-year-old building outside Frankfurt. The low, half-timbered building is surrounded by birches, weeping willows, and carpetlike lawns. The interior is rustic, with a fireplace. The mouth-watering specialty is venison served in its own juices. Try the house wine, made by the owner with grapes from his own vineyards. Dinner is DM38 ($26) per person, not including wine.

The two finest hotels

Steigenberger-Hotel Frankfurter Hof, *Kaiserplatz 17; tel. (49-69)21-502*, is the doyen of Frankfurt's hotels, having welcomed visitors since 1876. Central and comfortably old-fashioned, it has two pleasant bars, three good restaurants, and an outdoor café. Rooms have polished wood furnishings and modern facilities. A double room is DM360 to DM 540 ($240 to $360).

Hessischer Hof, *Friedrich-Ebert-Anlage 40; tel. (49-69)7-54-00*, receives four stars from Michelin for its deluxe accommodation. The hotel restaurant is excellent, too. A double room is DM427 to DM490 ($285 to $327).

Frankfurt's best undiscovered hotels

If you don't mind staying across the Main in Sachsenhausen, we recommend the **Hübler**, *Grosse Rittergasse 9, Sachsenhausen; tel. (49-69)616-038*. This small, family-run hotel has a swimming pool and costs half as much as city hotels; a double room is DM140 ($94), including breakfast.

The **National**, *Baselerstrasse 50; tel. (49-69)23-48-41*, is a homey, comfortable hotel with quiet charm and reasonably priced rooms (plus all profits from the hotel go to an orphanage). Newcomers are often discouraged by the drab exterior of the National—but regulars love its cozy interior. Rooms are furnished with antiques, and many have views of the neighboring park. Service is friendly. A double room is DM306 ($204), including breakfast.

About seven miles outside Frankfurt is an elegant castle hotel called the **Schlosshotel Kronberg**, *Hainstrasse 25, 6242 Kronberg im Taunus; tel. (49-6173)70-101*. Built in 1888 as the residence of Kaiser Wilhelm II's mother, it became a gathering place for European royalty. After World War I, French Occupation officials took possession of the castle. After World War II, American Occupation forces used it as a club for high officers and civilians. Today, the palace is a hotel with 19th-century furnishings. The cuisine is excellent; guests can use the 250-acre golf course. A double room starts at 170 marks ($113).

The best night life

Frankfurt, surprisingly for a German town, is not a big beer-drinking city. The preferred drinks are hard cider (known as *Appelwein, Äppelwoi, Ebbelwoi,* and *Ebbelwei*) and wine (because Frankfurt is so close to the wine-growing Franconia region). Try the cider, which is delicious—but be aware that it carries a much stronger punch than its sweet taste suggests.

Frankfurt is filled with Weinstuben. The **Volkswirt**, *Kleine Hochstrasse 9; tel. (49-69)283-419*, is popular among young professionals. It has the greatest wine selection in town. **Peter Dunker**, *Bergerstrasse 265*, is a wine bar beneath a half-timbered building. The wine list is long, and the prices are low. **Operncafé**, *Opernplatz 10; tel. (49-69)285-260*, is a trendy place where good-looking young people ogle one another before and after concerts.

Jazz is big in Frankfurt. **Der Jazzkeller**, *Kleine Bockenheimer Strasse 18a; tel. (49-69)288-537*, features top performers. And good jazz concerts are staged Sunday mornings in the courtyard of the **Historisches Museum**, *Saalgasse 19; tel. (49-69)212-7599*.

Heidelberg, the most romantic town

Heidelberg is the hub of German Romanticism. Schumann began his career as a Romantic composer in this pretty town, and Goethe fell in love here. Heidelberg is also the oldest university town in Germany and the site of scenes from the movie and opera *The Student Prince*.

The best place to ramble in Heidelberg is the **Haupstrasse**, which is lined with coffeehouses and little shops. Have a drink in one of the cafés beneath the *rathaus*. Or meander along **Philosopher's Walk**, where Goethe and Hegel wandered. From the path you'll have a bird's-eye view of the city and Heidelberg Castle.

Don't leave town without visiting the **Electoral Palatinate Museum**, where the 500,000-year-old jawbone of Heidelberg Man is kept.

The most beautiful sight

Above town is **Heidelberg Castle**, a magnificent red structure with octagonal towers and ruined belfries. It was the residence of the Wittelsbach family from the 12th through 19th centuries (the Wittelsbachs being a powerful German family that ruled Bavaria and the Rhenish Palatinate). From the castle, you have a panoramic view of the city's red roofs, the spire of the Heiliggeist Kirche, and the Neckar River.

The castle's most awe-inspiring feature is the **Grosses Fass** (Great Vat), a 58,000-gallon wine vat. Local legend has it that a dwarf named Perkeo once drank its contents. The castle also houses Germany's **Pharmaceutical Museum**, which displays a unicorn's horn (so they say) and bizarre body parts.

Weinstube Schloss Heidelberg, the restaurant in the middle of the castle courtyard, has marvelous food. The ceiling is ornately paneled, and the tables are natural wood. The restaurant is closed Tuesdays. Dinner for two is DM43 to DM76 ($29 to $51).

Heidelberg's best hotels

While **Der Europäische Hof**, *Friedrich-Ebert-Anlage 1; tel. (49-6221)2-71-01*, is the most elegant hotel in Heidelberg, it is also the most expensive. Luxurious and traditional, it charges DM370 to DM400 ($247 to $267) per night.

We prefer **Zum Ritter Sankt Georg**, *Hauptstrasse 178, 6900 Heidelberg; tel. (49-6221)202-03*. A cozy establishment in one of Heidelberg's few Renaissance buildings (built in 1592), it has reasonable prices and good service. A double room is DM220 to DM295 ($147 to $197). The least expensive rooms don't have private bathrooms. The restaurant, which serves good regional dishes, is also recommended.

Hamburg: the most worldly city

Hamburg, an international port, is Germany's most worldly city, known for the steamy sex shows and wild discos along the Reeperbahn in Sankt Pauli. However, Hamburg also has a more peaceful section. The lakes at its center are bordered by wide green avenues, opulent shops, and hotels. The old section is laced with waterways and has a town hall built on 8,000 piles over marshy ground.

It is difficult to get a handle on the many sides of Hamburg. The best place to take in Hamburg at a glance is the tower of the baroque Michaelis Kirche. The view of the river, the old section, and Sankt Pauli is panoramic.

The most historic quarter

The most historic section of Hamburg is along **Deichstrasse**, near the docks. Many of the 17th-century houses are now restaurants. While in the area, visit the **Museum of Hamburg History**, the best place to research your European ancestry. (See page 81.)

Germany's best fish market

The best fish market in Germany is held on Sunday mornings in Hamburg. This raucous but fun affair is located by the docks in Altona and begins at 5 a.m.

The largest warehouse complex in the world

You can take a boat tour through the canals of Hamburg's **Warehouse City**, the largest warehouse complex in the world, with buildings dating from the 1800s. Look for the statue of the pirate Klaus Stoertebeker on the Magdeburg docks, where he and 71 of his mates were beheaded in 1401.

The best place to dig up your European roots

Hamburg's Historic Emigration Office is located in the **Museum of Hamburg History,** which has displays relating to Hamburg's history as a harbor town and exhibits dedicated to the emigrants who left for America via Hamburg. If you visit the office in person, you can receive information on your ancestors within one or two hours.

A ship's roster can provide your ancestor's family name and surname (which may have changed upon arrival in the United States; ask your grandparents for the original name); a list of all family members traveling together; the place of your ancestor's birth; his marital status, profession, age, and sex; the name of the ship; and the date the ship left Hamburg.

To complete the research, the emigration office needs the name of your ancestor and the year he left Hamburg. The fee for the service is $30 for each year researched, even if the search is unsuccessful. The office is open Tuesdays through Saturdays, 10 a.m. until 1 p.m. and 2 until 5 p.m. For more information, contact the **Historic Emigration Office,** *Museum für Hamburgische Geschichte, Holstenwall 24, 2000 Hamburg 36; tel. (49-40)300-500-50.*

Germany's sexiest strip

Hamburg's **Reeperbahn** in the Sankt Pauli district west of Hamburg is world-famous for its sex shows and wild discos. It's worth a visit, but be careful! This is the territory of criminals, prostitutes, and pimps.

The best strip show is at **Colibri,** *Grosse Freiheit 34.* Live music is played (unlike in many of the bars), and the strippers are young and good-looking. Beer with peppermint schnapps is sold for a reasonable price. (You can't get beer without the liqueur.)

Moonlight has the raunchiest shows, with sexual acts of all varieties. **Salambo** is salacious. **Erotica,** which has no entry fee, is easiest on the pocket (but films are shown rather than live shows).

Hamburg's finest dining

The best restaurant in Hamburg is the **Landhaus Scherrer,** *Elbchaussee 130, Altona; tel. (49-40)880-13-25.* North German cuisine is served at tables overlooking the Elbe. Prices are humble—129 marks to 165 marks ($86 to $110), despite the restaurant's Michelin star. And a la carte prices are even lower—22 marks to 42 marks ($15 to $28). A three-course lunch is 60 marks ($40).

Schümanns Austernkeller, *Zundseinstiez 34; tel. (49-40)34-53-28,* is another good bet. An elegant Belle Epoque restaurant, it has been in the same family for years. The decor is sumptuous, and the service is first-class. Try the seafood platter (Seezungen-platte), which is delicious. Dinner for one is about 100 marks ($67).

The **Fischerhaus,** *Fischmarkt 14; tel. (49-40)31-40-53,* in Sankt Pauli, serves inexpensive but wonderful seafood. The atmosphere is plain, but the fish isn't. Dinner for two is 40 marks to 65 marks ($27 to $44).

Hamburg's best hotel

The best hotel in Hamburg—in all Germany for that matter—is **Vier Jahreszeiten,** *Neuer Jungfernstieg 9-14; tel. (49-40)349-40 or (800)223-6800 in the United States.* This elegant establishment on Lake Alster has a grand white facade rising eight stories and decorated with window boxes. Inside, you will find antique furniture, wood paneling, marble floors, brass trim, and modern facilities. All rooms have telephones, color televisions, and private bathrooms with bath, shower, bidet, bathrobes, thermometers, and toiletries.

Founded in 1897, this family-run hotel has an especially comfortable lobby, with leather armchairs, Oriental rugs, wood paneling, and a huge fireplace. Just off the lobby is a lounge with a large stone fireplace, tapestries, and views of the lake. A staff of 450 caters to the requests of guests staying in the 175 rooms. While you are here, you can have your suits mended or altered by the in-house Italian tailor.

The hotel restaurant, **Haerlin**, also is excellent. Vegetables, fruit, flowers, and poultry come straight to the restaurant from the hotel's farm on the outskirts of town. Choose a fine German wine from the hotel's 65,000-bottle cellar.

A double room is DM465 to DM545 ($310 to $364).

Charm for less than a fortune

Hotel Abtei, *Abteistrasse 14; tel. (49-40)442-905*, is a small hotel on a shady street in a quiet residential section of Hamburg. Rooms are spacious, bright, and clean. Breakfast is delicious. A double room is DM180 to DM230 ($120 to $154).

Hotel Atlantic Kempinski, *An der Alster 72; tel. (49-40)28-8001*, is a first-class hotel. convenient to the center of town with a view of Lake Alster. A double room is DM420 to DM460 ($280 to $307).

Hotel Prem, *An der Alster 810, Hamburg 1; tel. (49-40)24-17-26*, is a small, elegant hotel also on Lake Alster. The rooms are large, airy, and filled with flowers. Some look out over the lake, others the gardens. Rooms facing the street are noisy. A double room starts at 220 marks ($147).

Bremen, the most beautiful city

Bremen is Germany's most beautiful city and its oldest port. It became a bishop's seat 1,200 years ago and in 1358 joined Hamburg and Lübeck as a leading member of the Hanseatic League, an association of independent merchant towns. Bremen prides itself on its historical buildings. The oldest (some are 800 years old) are grouped around the Markplatz. The Gothic city hall was built in 1405 to 1410.

The oldest building in Bremen

The massive, twin-towered **cathedral**, built in the 11th century, is the oldest building in Bremen. Its other claim to fame is the mummy in its cellar. According to legend, the body of a roofer, who fell to his death in 1450, was put in the cellar for safekeeping but forgotten. When the body was discovered many years later, it had been perfectly preserved by the cellar's dry air.

Outside the cathedral stands the famous bronze **Statue of Roland**, a famous knight of Charlemagne.

Germany's best banquet hall

Grosse Halle in the city hall is one of the largest and most elegant banquet halls in Germany. A large mural, the *Judgment of Solomon*, hangs on the wall. A richly carved spiral staircase ascends to the upper stories.

Germany's oldest inn

Der Ratskeller, west of the town hall, is one of the oldest and most traditional of Germany's inns. It is known for its huge selection of more than 500 German wines, including a 1653 Rüdesheimer.

The oldest quarter

Schnoor Viertel, Bermen's oldest district and a former fishermen's area, has artists' workshops and colorful restaurants and inns. Many of the half-timbered, gabled houses in the quarter are 400 to 500 years old.

The best fish dishes

When you are ready for dinner, stop in at **Grashoff's Bistro**, *Contrescarpe 80; tel. (49-421)14740*. This little restaurant doesn't look like much, but it serves some of the best fish dishes in the region. The haddock in mustard sauce is especially good. Expect to pay DM49 to DM125 ($33 to $84) for dinner without wine. The bistro is closed Sundays. Reservations are recommended.

The best ship museum in the world

Just north of Bremen in Bremerhaven (the most important fishing port in Europe) is one of the best ship museums in the world, the **Schiffahrtsmuseum**, *Columbusstrasse*, in the old section. The *Seute Deern* (*Sweet Girl*), a Hanseatic tall ship wrecked in 1380, is especially impressive.

Bremen's best hotels

Park Hotel, *Bürgerpark; tel. (49-421)3408555*, is Bremen's most prestigious hotel. It has spacious public rooms, a garden terrace, rooms with balconies overlooking a pond, and a fine restaurant. A double room is DM400 ($267), including breakfast.

The **Marriot**, *Hillmannplatz 20; tel. (49-421)17670*, is the most convenient hotel in Bremen, just a five-minute walk from the pedestrian area. It is picturesque, located opposite a windmill. A double room is DM320 ($214).

Cologne: best carnival, best churches

If you like churches, you'll believe yourself at the gates of heaven when you reach **Cologne** (Köln). The number of churches marking the city's skyline is remarkable (13 in all). What's more, many of these churches are among the most beautiful in Germany. While some were damaged during World War II, most have been restored to their former beauty and are open to the public.

It's probably a good thing Cologne has so many churches, considering that it also is the site of Germany's wildest carnival season. If you like a good bacchanalia, visit Cologne the week before Ash Wednesday. Carnival begins with Weiberfastnacht, the Women's Carnival, held on the Alter Markt. Women choose their dancing partners and dance from morning to midnight. (This custom is said to have its origins in 16th-century pre-Lenten orgies.)

Cologne's beautiful churches

Cologne's famous Gothic **cathedral** is a gigantic structure that can be seen from almost any point in the city. Begun in 1248 and completed in 1880, it houses several great works of art, including the 12th-century *Shrine of the Three Magi*, a masterpiece of the goldsmith's art created to house holy relics.

Hlg. Maria im Kapitol was the church most severely damaged during World War II, but it has been well-restored. Its extraordinary, carved wooden doors, with 26 reliefs illustrating the life of Christ, date back to 1050. There's also a 12th-century sculpture of the Virgin on display.

Hlg. Pantaleon, a twin-towered structure with a 10th-century nave and cloister, is the oldest remaining Romanesque church in Germany.

Hlg. Aposteln is the finest example of Rhineland Romanesque architecture. Built between 1192 and 1230, it has a squat nave with ribbed vaults, a trefoil choir, and a tower.

The oldest church in Cologne is **St. Gereon**, *Gereonsdriech 2*. Its walls, crypts, and pillars are from the fourth century.

When you tire of touring churches, visit **Rhine Park**. During the summer, dances and concerts are held here. Concerts begin at 4 p.m.; dancing begins at 8 p.m.

The prettiest part of Cologne is the old section, near the Rhine, where 12th- and 13th-century buildings remain.

Cologne's best restaurant

Seafood dishes and the best German wines are served at **Weinhaus im Walfisch**,

Salzgasse 13; tel. (49-221)21-95-75, situated in a 350-year-old building. Weinhaus is closed Sundays. Reservations are recommended.

The coziest hotel
The **Hotel Bristol**, *Kaiser-Wilhelm-Ring 48; tel. (49-221)12-01-95*, is a cozy, family-run hotel near the cathedral. Rooms on the lower floors can be noisy. Bedrooms have intricately carved wooden furniture and modern bathrooms. Some rooms have canopy beds. A double room starts at DM195 ($130), including breakfast.

Aachen: a history buff's favorite
Aachen (*Aix-la-Chapelle* in French) is the most historically interesting town in Germany. Located near the Belgian and Dutch borders, Aachen's hot, curative mineral springs were used by the Romans, and remains of their baths and temples can be seen near the cathedral.

Holy Roman Emperor Charlemagne made Aachen a stronghold in A.D. 794. His empire united the people of what later became France and Germany. He died in Aachen on Jan. 28, 814 and is buried in the town's cathedral. The cathedral also contains parts of the clothing of Jesus, the Virgin Mary, and John the Baptist.

Aachen has seen the crowning of 32 kings. During World War II, most of the town was destroyed, but the important historic buildings have been restored.

Aachen's best dining, playing, and sleeping
The **Schloss Friesenrath**, *Pannekoogweg 46, Aachen-Friesenrath; tel. (49-2408)50-48*, is an elegant restaurant in Aachen's castle. The setting and furnishings are authentic.

After dinner, gamblers (and curious non-gamblers) frequent **Spielcasino Aachen**, *Monheimsallee 44*, where you can play roulette, baccarat, and blackjack. The casino is open 3 p.m. until 2 a.m. daily; it stays open until 3 a.m. Fridays and Saturdays.

The **Steigenberger Hotel Quellenhof**, *Monheimsallee 52; tel. (49-241)15-20-81*, is the best hotel in Aachen. It has well-appointed rooms, an indoor thermal swimming pool, and a sauna. A double room is 313 marks ($209), including breakfast.

A fairy-tale lover's favorite: the Black Forest
If you loved the movie *The Princess Bride* and you know all Grimm's fairy tales by heart, the best place in Germany for you to visit is the **Black Forest**. This region has dense pine forests, quaint villages, and lone thatched cottages. Surely, Hansel and Gretel got lost here.

The best drives through this fairy-tale land are along the **Black Forest Crest Road** and **Route 500**, which winds for about 120 miles on its way to Hinterzarten. At an altitude of 3,500 feet and higher, the road rides the summit of a series of steep mountains. Sunlight seeps through the firs in white shafts of light.

The road passes gingerbread villages and serene lakes, eventually coming to an open-air museum just north of Gutach. The museum is a restored town with low-ceilinged houses built into hillsides.

Stop in **Triberg**, where an immense clock sounds the hour every hour and an automatic organ plays the *William Tell Overture.* A figure representing Death rings a bell on one side and an angel rings on the other. The 12 Apostles rotate past a wooden Jesus who raises His arms in blessing.

Another pretty drive is along the shores of **Bodensee** (Lake Constance), which leads past little fishing villages. Near Bodman you'll see Neolithic, Celtic, and Roman ruins. In Unteruhldingen, you'll pass reconstructed thatched dwellings on stilts over the water. Mammoth tusks are on display at the local museum in Überlingen, an ancient walled town on the lake.

Cuckoo favorites

The woods around **Triberg** are known as the home of cuckoo birds, who cuckoo like crazy all day. Known as *cuculus canorus* among scientists, the bird is shy and rarely seen (or heard) elsewhere.

If you fail to spot a real cuckoo in the woods, stop in the **Heimat Museum** in Triberg, which houses the largest collection of cuckoo clocks in the world. Also visit Triberg's **Uhrenmuseum,** which houses an alarm clock made in 1690.

The oldest castle in Germany

Meersburg, an almost vertical village pitched high above a ravine, lies in the shadows of the oldest castle in Germany. Locals claim it was built by Dagobert in A.D. 630. Some of the walls do date back to A.D. 1000, but most of the building is from the 16th century. The entire castle was restored in 1877. The chapel and the courtyard are especially worth seeing.

Across from the old castle is the ancient residence of the bishops of Constance. Stand on the terrace and enjoy the view.

Meersburg has a marvelous hotel—the stately **Hotel Bad Schachen,** which looks out over Bodensee toward Lindau. Its grand dining room serves delicious meals.

The forest's highest peak

The highest peak in the forest is the **Feldberg.** Take a chair lift to the top. The village of Feldberg at the foot of the mountain was the birthplace of German skiing and is one of the oldest winter resorts in Germany.

Baden-Baden: the world's most famous spa

Baden-Baden, the world's most famous spa, was founded by Roman legionnaires. Located south of Heidelberg in the Black Forest, it is known for its curative waters. The magnificent 19th-century spa (*Kurhaus*) was built directly over the ruins of the ancient Roman baths.

The casino, where Dostoyevsky lost all his money, has attracted royalty for centuries. Massive old hotels line the Oos River.

The best time to visit (if you can stand the crowds) is the last week in August, **Baden-Baden Week,** when horse races, balls, and receptions are held.

Baden-Baden's best hotels

Brenner's Park-Hotel, *Schillerstrasse 6; tel. (49-7221)3530,* is the best hotel in Baden-Baden, and one of the best in Europe. This Edwardian hotel is a traditional part of any visit to the spa. It has large, graceful public rooms, excellent service, an indoor heated pool, a sauna, and a solarium. Take the waters, see the sights via horse and buggy, and have tea while listening to a string quartet. The hotel has views of the park and the river. A double room is DM250 to DM890 ($167 to $593).

If you'd rather not empty your pockets at the rather expensive Brenner's Park-Hotel, the **Hotel Badischer Hof,** *Langestrasse 47, 7570 Baden-Baden; tel. (49-7221)22827,* is a good, family-run alternative. A double room is DM290 to DM380 ($194 to $254).

The coziest shelter in the forest

One of the loveliest hotels in the Black Forest is the **Park-Hotel Wehrle,** *Haupstrasse, Triberg 7740; tel. (49-7722)86020.* It has a swimming pool, a sauna, and an excellent restaurant known for its trout dishes. A double room is DM230 ($154), including breakfast.

The **Bühler-Höhe Hotel,** *Schwarzwaldhochstrasse 1, 7582 Bühlertal; tel. (49-7226)55100,* is a great place to absorb the atmosphere of the forest. It is hidden behind a thick canopy of evergreens and covered with ivy. Originally a hunting lodge, it is now a fitness center.

Bacchus' bests

Germany's 11 **wine-growing districts**, which stretch from the middle Rhine at Bonn south to the Bodensee, produce the lightest white wines in the world. These regions are filled with classic scenery—castle ruins, grand cathedrals, gabled houses, elegant spas, and enchanting little villages.

The world's best Rieslings

The **Rheingau region** on the right bank of the Rhine is the aristocrat of Germany's wine-producing areas. This small region, extending from Hocheim in the east to Lorch in the west, is known for the Riesling grape. Sample the wines at the local wineries for a taste of the best white wines in the world. This is also the place to buy good German wine cheaply. In addition to wine, the Rheingau is also known for its wealth of monuments, monasteries, and wine cellars, some of which date back to the time of Charlemagne.

A good place to sample the local Rieslings is the crowded but exciting town of **Rüdesheim.** The Drösselgasse, a narrow, cobblestoned alley, is lined with wine taverns and restaurants. Order a *Römer* (a wine goblet with a green pedestal) of the local wine and watch the crowds. Rüdesheim is the site of rousing wine festivals in May and August. One of Germany's best wine museums is in Brömser Castle at the west end of town.

A fine restaurant that features wine tasting is located in the Waldhotel Jagdschloss Niederwald, three miles from Rüdesheim. Delicious game dishes are served in season. This castle hotel, *tel. (49-6722)1004,* is impressive, set on a hill high above the Rhine. It is closed in the winter. A double room here is DM260 ($174), including breakfast.

The best German reds

Stuttgart is the perfect base for touring the Württemberg area, which follows the Neckar River south of Baden-Baden. Red wines, such as Trollinger and Limberger, can be sampled throughout Württemberg. (They are rarely exported, so this could be your only chance to enjoy them.)

Following your wine tasting, visit the old Renaissance palace or the Staatsgalerie (National Gallery) in Stuttgart, the Roman baths and castle ruins in Weinsberg, or the Palace Gardens of Ludwigsburg.

The best place to sample local Württemberg wines is the **Wirtshaus zum Götzenturm,** *Allerheiligenstrasse 1,* in the medieval walled town of Heilbronn. The owner of this restaurant also runs the Beichtstuhl, a wine cellar around the corner. Both places are closed Sundays, Mondays after lunch, and in August.

The wine cellar of the Holy Roman Empire

The elegant wines of the **Rheinpfalz region,** northwest of Württemberg, have been famous since the days of Holy Roman Emperor Charlemagne, when this area was known as the Wine Cellar of the Holy Roman Empire. The picturesque Deutsche Weinstrasse (German Wine Road) runs its length.

Detour if you can to nearby **Speyer** (Spier), where the town's museum houses the oldest bottle of wine in the world, dating from the third century. The best place to sample the local wine is **Café Hindenburg,** *Maximilianstrasse 91.*

The oldest wine region

Fine wines are produced northwest of Rheinpfalz in the **Moselle Valley,** which has the oldest vineyards in Germany and the steepest vineyards in the world. The Moselle's vines are ancient. The Romans used the *Neumagen* wine ship in the Trier Museum to bring vines to Germany.

Markers along the Rhine describe the wines produced here: Piesporter, Wehlen, Bernkasteller, and Graach. The finest Moselle wines are Bernkasteler Doktor and Wehlener Sonnenuhr.

The most beautiful wine region

The **Ahr Valley**, Germany's northernmost wine region, is the most beautiful. Between Altenahr and Bad Neuenahr, the river forces its way in a rapid, winding course between rugged slate crags. Vineyards climb steep slopes in the shadows of castle ruins. Wine villages are sandwiched by the hills.

Wine has been made here since ancient Roman times, and today the area produces Germany's best reds and bubbling whites. Try the local wines at the **Weinstube Sankt Peter** in Walporzheim or at the lively **Lochmühle** at Mayschloss. Hikers can follow the 30-kilometer Red Wine Trail through vineyards from Lohrsdorf to Altenahr.

The best rosés

Between Heidelberg and the Badensee is the **Baden region,** famous for its sweet whites and Schillerwein rosés. A giant cask holding 52,000 gallons of the region's wine is located in Heidelberg. You can try the local wines at **Perkeo,** *Hauptstrasse 75,* a large beer and wine house in Heidelberg. A more scenic place to sample the wines is on the terrace of the **Weinstube im Schloss Heidelberg,** a restaurant in a castle outside Heidelberg.

How to become an expert wine taster

To better understand the wines within each region, enroll in a seven-day English-speaking seminar offered by the German Wine Academy, which is located in Kloster Eberbach, a former 12th-century monastery near Wiesbaden. Each seminar includes lectures by experts, tastings, and visits to wine-growing regions, vineyards, and cellars. The cost is DM1,690 to DM2,790 ($1,127 to $1,860), per person, including room, board, transportation to Germany, and program fees. For information, contact the **German Wine Academy,** *c/o Reisebüro, A. Bartholomae GmbH, Wilhelmstrasse 8, D-6200 Wiesbaden,* or the **German Wine Information Bureau,** *79 Madison Ave., New York, NY 10016; (212)213-0909.*

The most charming castle hotels on the Rhine

The Rhineland is a fairy-tale region, home to more than 30 medieval castles. And the best way to soak up the atmosphere here is to stay in one of these Rhine castles that has been turned into a hotel.

The **Rheinfels,** which is the largest of the Rhine castles, has also become one of the best castle hotels in Germany, the **Schlosshotel auf Burg Rheinfels,** *Schlossberg 47, 5401 Sankt Goar; tel. (49-6741)8020.* An immense maze of courtyards and towers, the castle was built in 1245. The view of the Rhine Valley from the Rheinfels is panoramic; the castle is perched on a high bluff over the river. If you listen carefully from the terrace, you might hear singing from the nearby Lorelei. The treacherous and craggy 450-foot rock is where ghostly maidens are said to lure sailors to their deaths with their singing. (For more on the Lorelei, see below.) Some say this is also where the treasure of the Nibelungs (the Burgundian tribe of Wagner's operas *The Ring*) is hidden. Terraces, a fireplace, a chapel, walking paths, a heated indoor pool, and a sauna are some of the hotel's other charms. The dining room serves delicious venison. A double room is 180 marks to 225 marks ($120 to $150).

The **Klostergut Jakobsberg,** *5407 Boppard/Rhein; tel. (49-6742)30-61,* a monastery turned hotel, is also near the Lorelei. Built in 1157 by Kaiser Friedrich I, it is situated on a bluff overlooking the Rhine. The monastery was owned by the archbishops of Trier. In 1640, it became the property of the Jesuits, who used it as a university center until the French Revolution. The monastery was later taken over by the Prussians. Today it is a hotel with modern amenities, a good restaurant, and an indoor pool. A double room is 226 marks to 268 marks ($151 to $179).

The **Hotel Burg Reichenstein,** *6531 Trechtingshausen/Rhein; tel. (49-6721)6117,* has a magnificent view of the Rhine. Its 13th-century Gothic arches and rough stonework remain. Robber-knights once watched the river from the castle's towers. Inside the castle is a museum displaying medieval weapons and armor. A double room is DM120 ($80).

Germany's oldest city

Trier is the oldest city in Germany, founded by the Celts 1,300 years before Rome. Roman relics in Trier include the Porta Nigra, which was the northern gateway to the Roman Empire, Roman baths, and an amphitheater that can hold 30,000 spectators. The 11th-century cathedral contains what is believed to be a piece of Jesus' clothing. Pilgrims from all over the world come to see the tomb of Saint Matthias at Sankt Matthias Abbey. (Saint Matthias was the only apostle buried north of the Alps.) Sankt Maxim Abbey has a register of all the witches in the area during the 16th century—the list includes more than 6,000 names! More recently, Karl Marx was born in Trier. His house is now a museum.

Trier's **Petrisberg Hotel**, *Sickingenstrasse 11; tel. (49-651)4-11-81,* is a family-run bed-and-breakfast that has a pleasant atmosphere and serves big breakfasts. Try to get a room in the front of the hotel, where you'll enjoy a balcony and a fine view of the city. A Roman amphitheater is nearby, and town is a 20-minute walk away. A double room is DM140 ($94), including breakfast.

Worms: the strangest history

The city of **Worms** has a strange name and an even stranger history. It was named for a legendary giant worm with fangs and webbed feet that lived in the Rhine and demanded human sacrifices.

Worms was the fifth-century capital of the legendary Nibelungs. The tribe left the area, according to legend, after the wicked Hagen slew their hero, Siegfried, and threw their treasure into the river. A huge statue of Hagen commemorates the story. The town was destroyed in A.D. 436 by Attila the Hun.

In the center of the town's old section is the tall, spired Cathedral of Saints Peter and Paul, built in the 11th and 12th centuries. Worms has a huge statue of Martin Luther; the oldest synagogue in Germany, built in the 11th century and restored in 1961; and the oldest and largest Jewish cemetery in Europe. Tombstones date from the 11th century. The synagogue and the cemetery are among the few remaining traces of pre-World War II German Jewry.

The most disappointing sight in Germany

Lorelei, subject of myth, poem, and song, turns out to be something other than a beautiful river nymph whose golden tresses led sailors to their deaths. If you follow the Rhine between Mainz and Cologne through the sharp valley cut by the river between wine-laden hills topped by great castles and picturesque villages, you eventually come to Sankt Goarshausen, south of the only intact castle (Marksburg) on the route. Here, 82 miles south of Cologne and 29 miles from Mainz on the right bank of the Rhine, is the Lorelei, which is nothing but a huge rock overhanging a hairpin bend in the river. What the sailors took for a mermaid was the play of light on the peak—which is not to say that they did not risk drowning as their boats maneuvered the narrow passage between the rocks in an effort to get close to the mermaid. On either side are other peaks named by superstitious sailors: Burg Katz (Cat's Castle) and Teufelsstein (Devil's Stone).

Germany's best beaches

Most travelers visit Germany to see its deep forests and medieval villages. But few realize that Germany also boasts beautiful beaches. The **East Frisian Islands**, which fringe the North Sea coastline, have long, sandy beaches guarded by dunes and frequented by nude sunbathers. The islands also have fishing villages, seal-covered rocks, and an ancient language and culture. Five of the seven islands are closed to cars—you can drive only on Borkum and Norderney.

Borkum, the largest island, has particularly salty air because of the heavy surf along the beaches. **Sylt** is the most beautiful island, dotted with traditional fishing villages and dolmens erected by prehistoric man. The islanders' thatched-roof houses are sharply pitched to ward off the cold winds of the North Sea. Spectacular 30-foot dunes are covered with purple heather. But the beaches can be brisk—sunbathers rent wicker protectors or build small walls of sand to protect themselves from the wind. And the water is bracing. The area between Borkum and Sylt is home to herds of seals numbering in the hundreds.

The small islands of **Juist** and **Memmert,** between Ems and Weser, attract hundreds of birds and bird watchers. **Westerland** has a casino. **Amrum** has high sand dunes—the sites of ancient pagan sacrifices. And most of the islands have resorts with seawater swimming pools (which are a good deal warmer than the sea itself).

For more information on the East Frisian Islands, contact **Fremdenverkehrsverband Nordsee Niedersachsen-Bremen,** *Ostfriesische 19-20, Postfach 1820, D-2900 Oldenburg; tel. (49-441)1-45-35,* or visit the tourist office in the railroad station in Oldenburg.

The Harz: the most bewitching region

According to legend, witches live in Germany's northernmost mountains, the **Harz.** They are said to fly on Walpurgis Night, the last night of April. Residents of the area celebrate Walpurgis Night with more abandon than Germans elsewhere, dressing as devils, witches, and demons. Try to time your visit to the area so that you too can participate in the revelry.

If you can't manage to make it to the Harz for Walpurgis Night, don't despair. The region is bewitching year-round.The mountains are covered with evergreen forests, inhabited by deer, and brightened by waterfalls, ravines, and rocky streams. One of Germany's highest peaks is the Wurmberg near Braunlage in the Harz. Take a cable car to see the top.

The Harz was made famous by the celebrated German poet Heinrich Heine (1797-1856) in *Die Harzreise (The Harz Journey),* a cycle of poems and prose set to music by Schubert.

Bavarian bests

Bavaria, which was independent until 1918 (Munich was its capital), is the largest and most visited section of Germany. This southeastern region is touristy, but with good reason—Bavaria is beautiful. You can avoid the masses by exploring Bavaria off-season, in the spring or fall. The Alps stretch along the region's southern border with Austria, offering wooded slopes, flower-filled meadows, lakes, and castles. The mountain-encircled Königsee is a gorgeous deep-blue lake surrounded by sheer alpine cliffs.

Munich: the most fun-loving city

Munich is Germany's party town. Every season provides an excuse for a party—and in Munich, there are nine seasons: spring, summer, winter, fall, bock beer time, the opera festival, beer garden days, carnival, and Oktoberfest.

Munich's best party

If you like a good party and crowds, visit Munich during **Oktoberfest** at the end of September. But make sure you have a hotel reservation; the city never has enough rooms for all the revelers. If you can't find a hotel, contact the **Munich Tourist Office (Fremdenverkehrsamt),** *Sendlingerstrasse 1, 8000 Munich 2; tel. (49-89)23911.* The staff may be able to help you find a homestay.

The first Oktoberfest was in 1810, when 40,000 royal merrymakers celebrated King

Ludwig's wedding reception. Since then it has been celebrated every year beginning three Saturdays before the first Sunday in October and continuing for 16 days. Festivities start with a parade through the streets of Munich to the Theresienwiese (a meadow named after King Ludwig's bride). Here, after horse-drawn beer wagons arrive, the mayor taps the first of more than 700,000 kegs. Thousands quaff Bavarian brew and enjoy brass-band music.

Enormous beer tents, sponsored by Germany's 13 major breweries, are the hub of activity. Stein-serving waitresses in folk costumes weave among wooden tables. Midway rides and sideshows add to the carnival atmosphere.

On the second day of Oktoberfest, from 10:30 a.m. until noon, groups in national costumes parade. After this, it's back to the beer gardens, which remain open from noon until 10:30 p.m. Spend the afternoon drinking and feasting on *Weisswürste* (white sausage made out of veal and pork). By nightfall, you'll be ready to join the rousing, if slightly slurred, renditions of *"In München steht ein Hofbräuhaus."*

Munich's heart
The historic center of the town is around the **Marienplatz**, a huge pedestrian mall surrounded by the new (19th-century) and old (15th-century) city halls. The ringing of the **Glockenspiel** from the new city hall spire is a daily ritual at 11 a.m. Life-size figures enact a knights' tournament, the dance of the coopers, and a medieval royal wedding ceremony.

The highest points in Munich
Although Munich lost many of its old buildings in World War II bombing raids, almost all have been restored. **Frauenkirche**, with its two onion-domed spires, and the 960-foot **Olympic tower** are the most prominent landmarks on Munich's skyline. Take an elevator to the top of the Olympic tower for a breathtaking view of the city.

The world's largest science museum
The **Deutsches Museum**, which takes up an entire island in the middle of Munich's Isar River, is the world's largest science and technology museum. It's great fun for people who love gadgets. Most of the displays involve participation (pushing buttons, turning cranks). Exhibits trace the development of technology and include a turn-of-the-century transformer, antique cars, and glass-blowing demonstrations. You can avoid the crowds by visiting during the week and arriving at 9 a.m., when the museum opens. Almost all the display information placards are now in English as well as German.

The best collection of Dürer and Rubens
Alte Pinakothek (the old art gallery), *Barerstrasse 27,* has the most complete collection of Dürer and Rubens paintings in the world, as well as works by many other famous artists of the 15th to 18th centuries, including Rembrandt, Van Dyck, and El Greco. The museum is free on Sundays but closed Mondays.

Munich's three top sights
Neue Pinakothek (the new art gallery), which was destroyed during World War II, was rebuilt in postwar years and today is Munich's best modern art gallery. Its natural lighting sets off the paintings well. Sloping ramps lead past artworks hung in chronological order. The collection of works by 18th- and 19th-century masters is especially good—it includes works by Manet, Monet, Dégas, Cézanne, Van Gogh, Gauguin, Klimt, and Goya. The museum is closed Mondays.

The **Schatzkammer** (Treasure House), *3 Max-Joseph-Platz,* holds the splendid treasures of Bavarian royalty: jeweled crowns and crosses, goblets, medals, swords, dishes, and jewelry. Perhaps the most beautiful object is in the third room: a statue of St. George slaying the dragon, which was made in 1590 and inlaid with precious stones.

Residenzmuseum shares a building with the Schatzkammer. Once the palace of the

Wittelsbach kings, it contains rooms from the Renaissance, baroque, and rococo periods. Damaged during World War II, it has been restored. The Ancestors Gallery houses portraits of all the Bavarian kings.

Munich's most inviting park
When you tire of the historic and cultural sights, take a walk through the **Englischer Garten**. The park was designed by an American Tory named Benjamin Thompson, who was forced to leave America during the Revolutionary War after he was found spying for the British. Thompson hailed from Rumford (now Concord), New Hampshire, and was known as Count Rumford. He became an adviser to the Bavarian King and in 1795 transformed what had been a royal hunting ground into Germany's first public park.

The park has woods, brooks, and a Chinese tower turned beer garden that is a fun place to drink huge steins of beer, eat Bavarian pretzels and Wiener schnitzel, and meet people. There's an area set aside in the park for nude sunbathing. Take an ice-cold dip in the Isar River to end your day.

Munich's oldest church
Alte Peterskirche (Peter's Church), just off the Marienplatz near the *rathaus*, is often overlooked, although it is the oldest parish church in Munich. Begun in 1050 and finished in 1294, it contains few of its original furnishings. However, it does still house a macabre relic—a gilded and bejeweled skeleton of the martyr St. Munditia (the patron saint of lonely women). Fake eyes look out of her skull, gems glitter where her teeth should be, and a jeweled coronet balances on her head of fake hair! If you don't mind climbing the 277 steps to the top, you'll have a great view of the Alps from the Alte Peter's 300-foot tower.

The world's best Kandinsky collection
Städtische Galerie im Lenbachhaus (Municipal Gallery), *Luisenstrasse 33*, has the most comprehensive collection in the world of the works of abstract painter Vassily Kandinsky. It also displays works by other Munich artists, including some early Paul Klee paintings. The gallery is in an imitation Italian villa with a small garden. Works by Kandinsky and Klee are housed in the older part of the villa, once the home and studio of Germany's most famous 19th-century portrait painter, Franz Lenbach. His works and collections also are on display. The museum is open every day except Monday, 10 a.m. until 6 p.m.

Peerless puppets
The **Munich Municipal Museum**, *Sankt-Jakob-Platz 1*, has one of the most extensive displays of puppets and puppet works in the world. It traces the history of puppetry through time and countries and houses the famous Moriska-Tänzer statuettes, all dancing with bizarre expressions on their faces. (They were created in 1480 by Erasmus Grasser for the dance hall of the old *rathaus*.) After seeing the exhibits, you can try your hand at puppeteering in the theater.

Other sights in the museum include a beer-brewing exhibit, a musical instrument collection, and displays of children's furniture from times past. The museum is open every day except Monday, 9 a.m. until 4:30 p.m., and Sunday, 10 a.m. until 6 p.m. (Admission is free on Sunday.)

The best place to buy folk fashions
Loden-Frey, *Maffeistrasse 7; tel. (49-89)236-930*, in Munich's *Fussgängerzone* (pedestrian precinct), is the best place to buy German folk-style clothing in traditional fabrics. This family-run establishment has been in business since 1842. It was bombed during World War II but later rebuilt in South German style at its old address.

Climb the store's circular stairway to the third floor, where you can shop for dirndls, hunting and walking wear, sports clothes, and evening wear, all in the traditional style. The staff will welcome you with a Bavarian greeting, *"Grüss Gott,"* and then help you find just what you're looking for in Loden or *Tracht* (traditional costume) for men, women, or children.

You can write the store for a copy of its catalog, issued twice yearly.

Munich's best bargains
An enormous flea market is held every Friday and Saturday along **Marsstrasse**, just outside Munich. Disney memorabilia, especially Mickey Mouse T-shirts, is especially popular. (The Germans are crazy about Mickey.) If you tire of perusing old junk, stop for a stein in the beer hall here.

Used cars (BMWs, Volkswagens, and Mercedes) are sold by their owners (not dealers) for a good price along **Leopoldstrasse**. They are cheaper than in the United States. One enterprising young American bought a car along Leopoldstrasse, had it inspected and repaired, and then shipped it back to the United States, where he sold it for a nice profit.

The most magnificent sight
Schloss Nymphenburg, outside Munich, is a magnificent 17th-century palace set in a 500-acre park filled with fountains, statues, lakes, waterfalls, and formal gardens. Portraits of the 24 most beautiful women in Europe 200 years ago, commissioned by King Ludwig, hang in the south pavilion.

Also on the palace grounds is the **Marstallmuseum**, one of the finest coach museums in all Europe. Housed here are Ludwig II's ornate carriages and sleds, laden with gold and sculptured cherubs, curlicues, lions, and roses. And don't miss the rococo Amalienburg, built from 1734 to 1739 as a hunting lodge for Electress Amalia. Although its intended use was humble enough, the lodge includes a hall of silver-framed mirrors.

When your feet give out, stop for lunch in the junglelike palm house, where you can get *Bockwurst mit Senf und Brot* (sausage and mustard on bread) for DM6 ($4) and a beer for DM3.50 ($2.50).

To get to the Nymphenburg, take subway 1 from the Hauptbahnhof, get off at Rotkreuzplatz, and change to streetcar 12. This sounds complicated, but the total travel time is only 15 minutes.

The darkest side
Munich has its dark side. Outside the city is the **Dachau Concentration Camp**, now a memorial to those who died in the camp during World War II. More than 200,000 people, mainly Jews, were labeled undesirable by the Nazis and imprisoned here between 1933 and 1945. The camp is virtually intact. Several barracks can be seen, as well as the morgue, the crematorium, and the Brausebad (where prisoners were gassed to death). Documentary films of the Holocaust are shown, and photo displays are on view.

To get to Dachau, take the S-Bahn 2 (marked Petershausen) from the Munich Hauptbahnhof. Trains leave every 20 minutes except Saturday, when they run every two hours. Then take bus 722 from the railroad station to the camp.

Munich's best restaurants
The best restaurant in Munich is **Die Aubergine**, *Maximiliansplatz 5; tel. (49-89)598-171.* The first German restaurant to receive a three-star Michelin rating, Die Aubergine serves French-influenced German nouvelle cuisine based on traditional favorites. Try the venison served with wild berries in season or the lobster fricassée. Die Aubergine is closed Sundays, Mondays, and bank holidays. Make reservations well ahead, because the restaurant is small.

Altes Hackerhaus, *Sendlingerstrasse 75; tel. (49-89)260-5026,* is the best place for Bavarian specialties. (If you have the nerve, try the pig knuckles.)

Franziskaner und Fuchsenstuben, *Perusastrasse 5; tel. (49-89)231-8120,* serves delicious sausage and *Leberkäs',* a kind of meat loaf that is made of ground beef, liver, and bacon and eaten with sweet mustard.

Traditional Bavarian food is served at **Nürnberger Bratwurstglöckl,** *Frauenplatz 9; tel. (49-89)22-03-85* or *(49-89)29-52-64,* near the Dom. The decor here is charming, featuring large prints, arms, and carved woodwork.

The best restaurant in Germany

Weichandhof, *Betzenweg 81; tel. (49-89)811-1621,* in Obermenzing, just outside Munich, is one of the most charming restaurants in Germany. Bavarian and international foods are served in the converted farmhouse. The restaurant is cozy in cold weather, with an open fireplace and a wood stove. During the summer, tables are moved outside under the apple trees. Venison is served in season. Try the Bavarian classic, *Schweinebraten mit Kartoffelknödeln* (roast pork with cracklings and potato dumplings). To get to Weichandhof, take bus 73 from Pasig Station to Blutenburg and walk from there. The restaurant is located on the Munich-Stuttgart highway.

The hottest night life

Schwabing, Munich's student district, has more than 200 restaurants and cafés, as well as myriad nightclubs and bars. It is the best place to wander if you're looking for a lively night out. Sidewalk artists sell their goods and working girls strut their stuff, along Boulevard Leopold.

The **Park Café,** at the end of Ludwigstrasse near the Residenz, is a '50s-style lounge that has some of the best new music in Munich. It is *the* place to go.

P-Eins is a small but good disco near the National Museum.

Steamy jazz is played at **Domicile,** *Leopoldstrasse 19;* **Musicland,** *Siegestrasse 19;* and **J.A.M.,** *Rosenheimerstrasse 4,* in downtown Munich. On Sundays, steamy jam sessions are held 11 a.m. until 3 p.m. at the **Unterfahrt,** *Kirchenstrasse 96; tel. (49-89)448-2794,* which opens at 8 p.m. every day except Monday.

Germany's best beer cellars

Munich is famous for its beer cellars—informal halls where lots of beer is downed at long, friendly tables. The city has 12 historic *Bierkeller,* which serve huge steins of beer and Bavarian specialties. Sit anywhere these are friendly meeting places. Often oompah bands play and patrons sing.

The most famous beer hall is the **Hofbräuhaus,** *Platzl 9; tel. (49-89)221-676.* Although it is touristy, the Hofbräuhaus has such a friendly atmosphere that it's worth a visit. Beer, which is drunk from 1 liter blue-glazed jugs, is served on the ground floor, which is a great vaulted hall, and in the outside beer garden. Upstairs is an enormous banquet hall.

Across the street is the **Platzl,** which has a floor show with Bavarian skits. The **Mathäser Bierstadt,** *Bayerstrasse 5,* is an enormous area with a cavernous beer hall. More locals than tourists drink here. The **Donisl,** *Weinstrasse 1,* is the oldest of Munich's beer halls, popular since 1715. The **Augustinerkeller,** *Neuhauserstrasse,* is one of the oldest and nicest of the beer cellars. The restaurant attached to it, the **Augustiner,** is also good—everything is fresh, tasty, and authentic. Two pleasant outdoor beer halls are the **Chinesischer Turm** and the **Aumeister,** both in the English Gardens.

Munich's best hotel

The **Hotel Vier Jahreszeiten Kempinski,** *Maximilianstrasse 17; tel. (49-89)23-03-90,* is the best hotel in Munich. A deluxe, traditional hotel with yellow stucco external walls and blue awnings, the Vier Jahreszeiten exudes Bavarian hospitality. Modern amenities include an indoor pool and sauna. The hotel's Walterspiel restaurant is excellent. Munich's bigwigs lunch here. A double room is DM465 toDM 510 ($310 to $340).

The world's best gingerbread

North of Munich is **Nuremberg**, the gingerbread capital of the world. The best time to visit is Christmas, when the local bakers take advantage of the Christmas market to show off their matchless skills in this art.

Alpine peaks

The **Alps** stretch along Germany's southern border from the Bodensee in the west to the Watzmann Peak near Berchtesgaden in the east. This mountain range rose from the sea about 80 million years ago. You can find fossils of sea creatures among the peaks. The beautiful lakes in the Voralpenland are remnants of the Ice Age.

Germany's highest peak

The **Zugspitze**, Germany's highest peak (9,840 feet), overlooks Garmisch-Partenkirchen and is part of the Wettersteingebirge, an ancient formation of hard rock. You can take a cable car or train from Garmisch to the summit. Even when clouded over (about 35% of the time), the view is spectacular. You can see the peaks of other mountains rising above the blanket of clouds. Get a beer at the top, or just breathe in the intoxicatingly thin mountain air.

The best skiing

Garmisch-Partenkirchen, the most popular resort in the German Alps, offers Germany's best skiing. The powdery peaks are accessible via an assortment of lifts. Trails are geared toward every level of skier. A pretty town with gaily painted alpine houses, Garmisch has aprés-ski entertainment, a casino, and concerts. Proximity to the American Army base, however, is causing the town to lose some of its Germanic charm. Nearby are Ludwig II's Linderhof Castle and the domed Benedictine abbey of Ettal.

The best place to stay is the **Schneefernerhaus**, *tel. (49-8821)58011,* a miracle of engineering perched at 8,692 feet atop the Zugspitze. The view is absolutely incredible, but the hotel is basic and inexpensive.

The best alpine hikes

The German Alps are crisscrossed by 9,000 hiking trails. They are well-used by the Germans, who consider *das Wandern* (walking, rambling, exploring the world) a way of life.

The most beautiful walking trail in the Alps is along Bodensee between the towns of Friedrichshafen and Lindau. The snow-capped Alps are reflected in the waters of the lake. The walk is not difficult and can be done in tennis shoes. The entire length takes about two days (longer if you stop in some of the towns along the way). For a map of the trail, stop in at the tourist office in Friedrichshafen or Lindau.

The trail from the town of Füssen to Neuschwanstein Castle is also beautiful. Füssen is a picturesque village in the shadows of the turreted castle. The trail leads past several lakes and into the shadows of the Austrian and German Alps. The walk isn't difficult.

Our third-favorite hike begins at a path leading from the Olympic Ski Stadium in Garmisch-Partenkirchen to the Graseckbahn cable car, which carries you to the Forsthaus Graseck. At the peak is an inviting little restaurant with panoramic views. From the terrace, you can pick up another trail along the spectacular Partnachklamm, a very narrow and deep gorge filled with torrents of water. You'll be thankful for the guardrails along the path, which is narrow and sometimes slippery.

Hitler's favorite hideout

The **Kehlsteinhaus** (also known as Eagle's Nest), perched on a rocky crag above the town of Berchtesgaden, was Hitler's favorite hideout. No wonder—the view from the hideaway-turned-restaurant is exhilarating. Anyone could develop delusions of grandeur here. Alpine peaks rise above cottony clouds at this level. The snow at their summits glistens in the sun. Below, a thick carpet of dark green pines stretches toward the valley.

The road to Eagle's Nest is so steep and dangerous that cars are not allowed to use it; you must take a special bus from the Obersalzberg-Hintereck parking lot. You can dine in the restaurant from mid-May through mid-October.

The world's best passion play

Every 10 years, the world's most moving passion play is performed in the shadows of the Alps in the little artisan town of **Oberammergau.** From May through September in years ending in zero, local amateur actors put aside their daily professions and devote themselves entirely to the play. Written in the 17th century, it enacts Christ's suffering between the Last Supper and his death. Because the text is so old, many consider it anti-semitic. It blames the Jews for Christ's crucifixion. Villagers have performed the play every 10 years since the 17th century, when they vowed they would perform the passion if the black plague ceased. It did, and they have.

The picturesque **Passionsspielhaus** (Passion Play Theater) can be visited any time of year. The immense open-air stage holds 700 actors, and the theater's wooden benches hold 5,200 people. You can see the elaborate costumes used during the passion play when you visit. Performances begin at 8:30 a.m. and finish at 6 p.m., with a two-hour break for lunch.

The best hotel in Oberammergau is the **Alois Lang.** This quiet place has rooms with private bathrooms and three good dining rooms.

Bavaria's looniest king

Mad King Ludwig, who ruled Bavaria from 1864 to 1886, built the most fanciful and beautiful buildings in Germany, despite (or perhaps because of) his insanity. But his magnificent creations were extremely costly, and his extravagance nearly bankrupted Bavaria. An important patron of the arts, Ludwig was a great fan of Wagner. He built the Bayreuth Opera House for the composer and lived in a fantasy world based on Wagner's operas.

Ludwig's death by drowning has raised many questions over the years. Some say his madness drove him to suicide, others say it was a fatal accident, and still others hold it was murder. Whatever the case, Ludwig died shortly after having been declared insane.

Germany's most beautiful castle

Ludwig created Germany's most beautiful castle: **Neuschwanstein.** The turreted white castle reaches high into the sky from its perch on a cliff above a valley. Walt Disney liked it so much that he copied it for his Disneyland and Disney World. It looks enchanted, with its mountain backdrop. Inside, the walls are decorated with murals of German heroic sagas. In Ludwig's bedroom, stars in the dark blue ceiling light up to look like the night sky. Ludwig lived at Neuschwanstein for 102 days before he drowned in the waters of nearby Lake Starnberg at age 40.

Germany's smallest castle

The smallest castle in Germany also was the product of Mad King Ludwig's imagination. **Linderhof Castle,** near Garmisch-Partenkirchen, is an ornate, one-man palace designed as Ludwig's personal residence. The mad king preferred to be alone and went to great lengths to maintain his privacy. He had the dining room built directly above the kitchen and installed a dining table that could be lowered into the kitchen, set by the cooks, and lifted back up to the dining room. Thus, he could be waited on at dinner without having to see the servants. Ludwig lived the longest at this castle.

Up the hill from the castle, Ludwig created a grotto. Entered by way of a hinged boulder, the artificial cave is the recreation of Venus Mountain from Wagner's *Tannhäuser*. Inside the grotto is an artificial lake with a waterfall and Ludwig's boat.

The world's best violins

The world's most perfect violins are crafted in **Mittenwald**, a pretty Bavarian town sporting buildings decorated with brightly colored frescoes. The craft has been passed down through generations of local artisans, who make the instruments to order for famous musicians. The meadows, mountains, and village houses around Mittenwald are so typically Alpine that they were used as location sites for the filming of *The Sound of Music*.

The most scenic drives through Germany

Germany is known for its beautiful scenic drives. The longest is the Alpen-Ostsee, stretching from the Baltic Sea island of Fehmarn to the Bavarian village of Berchtesgaden. The most unusual is the Windmill Road in the marshy area of Minden/Lübeck. The roads overlap in many of the most picturesque places. For instance, the Romantic and the Alpine roads both lead to Mad Ludwig's castle Neuschwanstein.

The Romantic Road

The **Romantic Road** runs from Würzburg in the north to Füssen in the south. The road, which follows a medieval trade route, is about 200 miles long and passes vineyards, ruined castles, and wooded hills.

Begin by heading east from Heidelberg along the Neckar River on the Castle Road (Route 37). At Nedkarelz, turn left on Route 27 and go through Mosbach. Take Route 292 to Bad Mergentheim. Stop in Weikersheim to visit the town's castle, which has a marvelous Hunting Hall and baroque gardens.

The best-preserved walled town

From Weikersheim, continue along the Romantic Road to **Rothenburg ob-der-Tauber**, the best-preserved medieval town in Germany, with gabled houses topped by steep Gothic roofs. You can walk around the city atop its huge encircling fortress walls. Climb the tower of the *rathaus* for a superb view of the town's fortifications, which are shaped like a wine goblet. Visit the Medieval Crime Museum and stroll the Burggarten, the lovely public gardens.

Don't miss the clock on the 15th-century **Ratstrinkstube** (City Counselors' Tavern). Its mechanical figures re-enact the heroic feat of Burgomaster Nusch, who saved the town from plundering by Imperial forces in 1631. According to legend, Nusch offered the commander of the army a cup of the best local wine, after which the commander agreed to spare the town if someone could down six pints (three liters) of the wine at once. Nusch obliged. You can watch the astonishment on General Tilly's face as Nusch downs the draught seven times a day—when the clock strikes 11 a.m., noon, 1 p.m., 2 p.m., 3 p.m., 9 p.m., and 10 p.m.

There are two restaurants with inviting medieval atmospheres in the marketplace. **Baumeisterhaus** is in a 16th-century patrician residence surrounded by a garden that serves German food at reasonable prices. **Ratsstube** is a tavern-restaurant that offers good regional dishes, including sausage with sauerkraut. Dinner is inexpensive, about DM34 ($23) for two.

The best hotel in Rothenburg is the **Eisenhut**, *Herrengasse 3; tel. (49-9861)7050*. This historic inn is actually several medieval patrician houses that have been joined together. It has a much-admired restaurant with a paneled, galleried dining hall and a garden terrace by the Tauber River. Try the trout specialties in season. A double room is DM260 to DM350 ($174 to $234) a night.

The best of Augsburg

Another gem of a town along the Romantic Road is **Augsburg**, founded by the Romans in 15 B.C. Once a medieval metropolis, it has mansions, palaces, Gothic churches, towers, and ramparts. Don't miss the **Fuggerei,** founded in 1519 by the Fugger family (bankers for the Hapsburgs) as a refuge for the old and needy. A town within a town, the Fuggerei has its own church, gabled houses, and courtyards. The needy still live here on the original terms—an annual rent of 2 marks ($1.50) and a daily prayer for the soul of the founder!

Augsburg's cathedral has 11th-century bronze doors, an altar by Holbein the Elder, and the oldest stained-glass windows in Germany (from the 12th century). Climb the Perlach tower of the *rathaus* for a view of the Alps. A yellow flag flies if they are visible.

The best way to go

You can drive the Romantic Road yourself, which gives you the freedom to come and go as you please, or you can take a convenient Europa Bus tour. A two-day trip is 220 marks ($147) per person, including breakfast and accommodation; a three-day trip is 386 marks ($258) per person. The bus company can arrange hotels for you along the route. Make reservations (far in advance) by contacting **Europa Bus,** *German Rail, 747 Third Ave., 33rd Floor, New York, NY 10017; (212)308-3100.*

The German Alpine Road

The **Deutsche Alpenstrasse** (German Alpine Road) leads from Bodensee through the Bavarian Alps. It passes Germany's highest peak, the Zugspitze; the limestone massifs of the Alpine National Park; the ski resorts of Garmisch-Partenkirchen; Berchtesgadener Land, where the mighty Watzmann Mountain drops down suddenly to the deep-blue Konigsee; Mittenwald; and the castles of Hohenschwangau and Neuschwanstein, where Mad King Ludwig lived out his fantasies. The natural scenery along the route is consistently awe-inspiring.

The best place to stay along this route is the **Posthotel Partenkirchen,** *Ludwigstrasse 49; tel. (49-8821)5-10-67,* in Partenkirchen near Garmisch. This 15th-century family-run hotel overflows with Bavarian atmosphere. The exterior of the three-story building is covered with paintings. Inside are oil portraits, dark wood furniture, beamed ceilings, and wood paneling. Many of the rooms have balconies, and a roof garden affords a view of the Zugspitze. A double room starts at 142 marks ($95).

The Road of the Nibelungs

The **Nibelungenstrasse** (Road of the Nibelungs) is a favorite among devotees of the Siegfried sagas. (Wagner used these tales for his *Ring* operas.) The route, which goes from Worms to Wertheim, passes through the Odenwald, an inhospitable forest region in the time of the Nibelungs. Today, the hilly, wooded region is much more welcoming, with a series of health spas (Amorbach, Bad König, Beerfelden, Erbach, and Michelstadt). The **Bergstrasse-Odenwald Nature Park** is a good place to stop and appreciate the rocky forest. The park is covered by an extensive network of footpaths.

The Fairy-Tale Trail

The **Fairy-Tale Trail** leads from Bremen through Hamelin to Steinau, the home of the brothers Grimm. The road leads 360 miles south, through medieval towns and past castles, palaces, and seemingly enchanted forests. It takes you to the 13th-century castle of Neustadt, where Rapunzel was locked in a tower by a witch; the town of Schwalmstadt, where Little Red Riding Hood lived; and Kassel, where the brothers Grimm collected their first book of fairy tales in 1812.

The most magical place to stay en route is Sleeping Beauty's castle (or one of them) in Sababurg. Built in 1334 to protect pilgrims heading for Gottsbüren, the castle has two massive towers. The hotel is closed January through March. To make reservations, contact **Hotel Sababurg**, *3520 Hofgeismar-Sababurg; tel. (49-5678)10-52.*

Dresden: the finest porcelain

Dresden and nearby **Meissen** are known for their fine porcelain. But Dresden is also becoming known for the beauty of its now-restored buildings. During World War II, the city was fire-bombed by the Allies, and 80% of it burned to the ground. It has been beautifully reconstructed. Linden trees line the banks of the Elbe River, and the city boasts some of the best museums in Germany.

Stroll along **Prager Strasse**, once one of Dresden's most fashionable streets. It is lined with apartments and shops and embellished with fountains and benches. This street connects the new section of Dresden with the old section.

Frauenkirche (Church of our Lady), *Am Neumarkt,* has been left in ruins purposely as a memorial to the city's bombing.

Dresden's best

Located along the Elbe River, **Zwinger Palace**, and the portrait gallery it contains, is Dresden's drawing card. Carefully restored following the bombings of World War II, it retains much of its original structure, including a majestic courtyard where fountains play in the summer. Built as a fortress in the 18th century, it houses Raphael's *Sistine Madonna,* as well as a dozen Rembrandts, 16 Reubens, and several Tintorettos. The bells in its carillon tower are made of Dresden china.

A music lover's favorite

Dresden's second jewel is the **Semper Opera**, *Thaterplatz,* where Wagner and von Weber conducted and Richard Strauss' operas premiered. The opera house was designed by architect Gottfried Semper and completed in 1850. After 1945, it was restored based on original drawings. The building was immortalized in a painting by the 18th-century artist Canaletto.

Dresden's best art museum

The 16th-century glass-domed **Albertinum**, *Georg-Treu-Platz 1,* contains the state collection of 19th- and 20th-century paintings, including many works by French Impressionists. The museum's **Grünes Gewölbe** (Green Vault) displays works of goldsmiths and jewelers from the 15th through 18th centuries. The collection once belonged to the kings of Saxony, whose capital was Dresden. The museum is closed Thursdays.

The best restaurants

Oberlausitzer Topp'l, *Strasse der Befreiung 14; tel. (37-51)5-5605,* serves the hearty fare of the Lusatia area, home of the Sorbs, a Slavic people of Eastern Germany numbering 100,000 and speaking a language related to Polish. (Lusatia is a rural area along the Spree River.) The dark beers served here are excellent. Reservations are suggested.

Meissener Weinkeller, *Strasse der Befreiung 1B; tel (37-51)55814,* on the Elbe, offers a comprehensive list of wines from eastern Germany and inexpensive meals. The view from the terrace is lovely. Reservations are suggested.

The best hotels

The **Astoria**, *Ernst Thälmann-Platz; tel. (37-51)47-15-17,* is a small, comfortable hotel in the heart of the city. The service is friendly, and the prices are good—DM80 to DM230 ($54 to $154) a night. Not every room has a shower or bath.

Königstein, *Prager Strasse; tel (37-51)4856669,* a hotel on the main shopping street in Dresden, is pleasant but not luxurious. All rooms have private baths. A double room starts at DM170 ($114).

Germany's most beautiful palace

Potsdam (where the 1945 Potsdam Agreement was signed by Truman, Stalin, and Churchill, allowing Soviet forces to remain in control of what was then East Germany) is home to Germany's most beautiful rococo palace. **Sanssouci** (literally, *free from care*) was built by Frederick the Great in imitation of the French Versailles in 1745. He built it not as a memento to his own power but as an escape from the pressures of his job. You must wear felt-soled slippers when you visit, to protect the beautiful floors. Voltaire, the French philosopher admired by Frederick, lived here for a time. Paintings by Rubens, Van Dyck, and Caravaggio hang in the palace galleries.

Interhotel Potsdam, *Lange Brücke; tel. (37-33)4631,* is one of the most prestigious hotels in in this area. It has a sauna, shops, dancing, entertainment, a restaurant, and a bar. A double room in this large, high-rise hotel is 240 marks to 270 marks ($160 to $180) a night.

Buchenwald—the blackest memory

Just north of Weimar is the infamous **Buchenwald Concentration Camp**, where 56,000 people died in World War II. The camp and its museum of torture and extermination devices are chilling. Even in spring the site is so cold and bleak that you cannot imagine surviving a winter in the scanty barracks. Outside the camp is a memorial to the victims.

The world's best asparagus

Every spring, Germans go stalk-raving mad, gorging themselves on the country's *Weisser Spargel*, or white asparagus.

The German asparagus, introduced 2,000 years ago by the Romans, is plump and ivory white with delicate purple tips. It is prized among epicures, who come from around the world every April, May, and June to the world's asparagus mecca.

Asparagus is especially big business in Finthen, near Mainz, where all 5,000 inhabitants are engaged in the cultivation of the white vegetable; in Lampertheim, between Worms and Mannheim, where every housewife grows the prized vegetable in her back yard; in Schrobenhausen, the center of the only area in southern Bavaria where asparagus is grown; and in Tettnang and Schwetzingen, known together as the asparagus capital of Germany.

The Best of Greece

Hail, Nature's utmost boast! unrivalled Greece...
Clear sunny climates, by the breezy main,
Ionian or Aegean, temper'd kind;
Light, airy soils; a country rich and gay;
Broke into hills with balmy odours crown'd,
And, bright with purple harvest, joyous vales;
Mountains and streams, where verse spontaneous flow'd;
Whence deem'd by wondering men the seat of gods,
And still the mountains and the streams of song;
All that boon Nature could luxuriant pour
Of high materials, and my restless arts
Frame into finish'd life.
—*James Thomson*, Liberty, *1734-1736*

Greece is a breathtaking country of mountains and islands and sea. Its special light gives a clarity to the blue sky above and the colors below—colors that include a profusion of wild flowers in early spring. When you visit Greece, forget the packaged tours. This is a do-it-yourself country that should be experienced outdoors. Camp out under Greece's stars to best experience the country. If you decide to stay in a hotel, call ahead; many of them are seasonal. Travel light and be prepared to follow the impulse of the moment. You'll find anything you need along the way, at throwaway prices.

Athens: the birthplace of modern civilization

Athens—the birthplace of Western democracy, poetry, drama, art, and philosophy—is no longer at the center of the world it nurtured. A decaying, polluted city, it has a Third World flavor. Nonetheless, Athens merits more than a quick visit. It has the world's largest and most remarkable collections of ancient ruins, including the ancient Parthenon and one of the world's finest archeological museums. And beyond these archeological wonders is an exciting night life and a unique lifestyle, part European, part Middle Eastern.

The Acropolis: the heart of ancient Athens

You shouldn't miss the **Acropolis** and the ancient city. You couldn't miss the Acropolis even if you tried—it stands in full view on a hill above Athens, adding a majestic dignity and beauty to what otherwise would be a shabby city.

101

Buildings in Athens are subject to a height limit so that the **Parthenon,** the most important structure of the Acropolis, remains visible from most points in the area. Dedicated to the goddess Athena, the Acropolis was the religious center of the ancient capital. It was reconstructed in the fifth century B.C. by Pericles.

Acro means *top,* and *polis* means *city.* Together they mean the highest point, or citadel, of the city—which also means a stiff climb. Wear walking shoes. It is best to visit the Acropolis at dawn or in the late afternoon, because of the play of light. In summer, midday temperatures are too intense.

To the right of the entrance to the Acropolis is the **Temple of Athena Nike,** built to commemorate the victory of the Athenians over the Persians. At the top of the hill is the beautiful Parthenon, temple of the goddess Athena. Also on the hill is the **Acropolis Museum,** which houses some of the Acropolis' statuary pieces (some older than the Parthenon) to protect them from the city's pollution. The Acropolis is open from 8 a.m. until 4:30 p.m. Tuesdays through Fridays, from 10 a.m. until 4:30 p.m. Mondays, and from 8:30 a.m. until 2:30 p.m. Saturdays and Sundays. The entrance fee is 1,500 drachmas ($8) for adults and 750 drachmas ($4) for students.

Just beneath the Acropolis on the southern slopes are two ancient amphitheaters. The **Theater of Dionysos,** where the first Greek tragedies were performed, dates back to the sixth century B.C. The **Odeion of Herodes Atticus,** which dates to A.D. 161, is the site for performances of theater, opera, ballet, and music during the Athens Festival held between July and September each year. The amphitheaters are open from 8:30 a.m. until 3 p.m. daily. The entrance fee is 400 drachmas ($2) for adults and 200 drachmas ($1) for students.

The ancient **agora,** or marketplace, is on the eastern slopes of the Acropolis hill, on the north end of the Plaka. Now a major archeological excavation site, this was the downtown area of the ancient city and the main crossroads for routes to other major towns, such as Piraeus. Here you will find the **Stoa of Attalus,** a trading center built in 20 B.C.; the **Roman Forum,** begun during Julius Caesar's reign; the **Kerameikos,** the ancient city cemetery; and **Hadrian's Library,** built in the second century. A museum, *148 Ermou St.; tel. (30-1)346-35-52,* houses artifacts found during excavations. The museum is open fromTuesdays to Sundays from 8:30 a.m. until 3 p.m. The entrance fee is 400 drachmas ($2) for adults and 200 drachmas ($1) for students.

The oldest section of Athens

When evening begins to fall, head for the **Plaka,** where hanging lights twinkle in the dark and you'll hear the sounds of *bouzouki* music. Have supper at an outdoor table along one of the narrow streets. Although most of Greece is crime-free, this area of Athens is the one place where you may encounter it.

The Plaka is the oldest part of Athens. The earliest Athenians lived on the hill of the Acropolis. Later the top of the hill was reserved for worship and civic functions, and the citizens moved down from the summit to dwell on the slopes surrounding it, the Plaka. It wasn't until the Turks left Greece in the 1800s that the city began to expand beyond the Plaka.

The world's finest sculptures

The **National Archeological Museum,** *44 Patission St.,* has the finest collection of sculptures in the world. Treasures include giant figures of Greek gods and men, a world-renowned collection of Greek vases, pieces of ancient Cycladic art, and magnificent frescoes from the Minoan sites of Knossos on Cyprus and Akrotiri on Santorini. The gold Mycaenean death mask here is reputed to be that of Agamemnon, the ancient Greek king of the *Iliad.* The museum is open from 11 a.m. until 5 p.m. Mondays, from 8 a.m. until 5 p.m. Tuesdays to Fridays, and from 8:30 a.m. until 3 p.m. on Saturdays and Sundays.

Athens' main square

Syntagma Square (Constitution Square), the heart of the business district, is Athens' main square. A favorite pastime of both visitors and native Athenians is to sit at one of the square's outdoor café tables and watch pedestrians walk by. The 3,000 chairs in the square are arranged so that they all face the sidewalk for a better view. Have a coffee, beer, or ouzo and Greek *meze* (snacks) while you watch.

The grand dame of the city's hotels, the **Grande Bretagne,** is on the north side. Watching the wealthy, famous, and sometimes outlandish-looking people step from limousines and taxicabs to be ushered into the elegant old hotel by fancy-dressed doormen is part of the fun of a long sit in the square.

Many of Athens' most important sights and monuments border Syntagma Square. The **National Parliament Building** faces the square on the east side. The changing of the palace guards takes place here every hour on the hour each day. On Sundays at 11 a.m., the ritual of the *evzone,* when the guards dress in kilts, white tights, and turned-up shoes, is accompanied by a regimental brass band.

The **Benaki Museum,** *1 Koumbari St., off Syntagma Square,* to the left of the Parliament Building, is an old private house crammed with clothes, furniture, and photos dating from Byzantine times to the present. The museum is open from 8:30 a.m. until 2 p.m.; it is closed Tuesdays. Admission is 400 drachmas ($2) for adults and 200 drachmas ($1) for students.

The **Byzantine Museum,** *22 Vasilissis Sofia,* in a villa not far from the Benaki, is the best place to see Greek icons. Two rooms are replicas of Byzantine basilicas of the fifth and 11th centuries. The museum is open from 8 a.m. until 7 p.m. Tuesdays to Fridays and from 8:30 a.m. until 3 p.m. Saturdays and Sundays; it is closed Mondays. Admission is 400 drachmas ($2) for adults and 200 drachmas ($1) for students (free for Greeks).

The **Arch of Hadrian,** located near the square in the direction of the Acropolis, was erected by the Romans in A.D. 132 to mark the boundary of the ancient city. One side of the arch bears the inscription "This is Athens, ancient city of Theseus." The other side of the arch says, "This is the city of Hadrian and not of Theseus."

The largest Greek temple

The **Temple of Olympian Zeus** stands directly behind Hadrian's Arch. Also built by Hadrian during the third century (on foundations laid 700 years earlier by the Greeks), this is the largest temple in Greece. It is open from 8:30 a.m. until 3 p.m. Tuesdays to Sundays; it is closed Mondays. The entrance fee is 200 drachmas ($1) for adults and 100 drachmas (50 cents) for students.

The trendiest neighborhood

Kolonaki Square, a 10-minute hike up the hill from Syntagma Square, is trendy, with boutiques and Greek outlets of expensive international shops, such as Laura Ashley. Rub elbows with young Athenian professionals, the occasional Greek movie star, and stylishly dressed teen-agers who stake out the tables of little sidewalk cafés.

The best view of Athens

Lykabettos, a hill northeast of the Acropolis and behind the fashionable homes of Kolonaki, has a spectacular view of Athens, the Acropolis, Pireaus, and the Saronic Gulf. Take a funicular ride 910 feet to the top (board at the end of Ploutarhou), where you'll find a small church and a café. The trip back down through the wooded slopes to Kolonaki is more romantic on foot.

Athens' best shopping

The Plaka, where you can buy any kind of handicraft made in Greece, is the best place for shopping. However, if you're heading out to the islands, where goods are cheaper, wait.

Monastiraki, better known as the Athens flea market, is a special part of the Plaka. It runs from Monastiraki Square to Ifestou Street and includes shops offering both antiques and old junk. The best time to visit is Sunday morning.

Kolonaki has posh boutiques, modern art galleries, expensive antique shops, and good dress designers.

Omonia Square is where the locals shop. The Greek-style department stores here offer better prices than in Kolonaki. Goods are sensible rather than stylish.

Pandrossou, the Street of Shoes, also has shops selling brassware, peasant costumes, Greek dolls, and good imitation antiques. (You can't take real ones out of the country.)

The **National Archeological Museum** sells copies and castings of Greek museum pieces.

The **National Organization of Hellenic Handicrafts,** *9 Mitropoleos; tel. (30-1)322-1017;* the **YMCA,** *28 Omirou St.; tel. (30-1)362-6970;* the **YWCA,** *11 Amerikas St.; (30-1)362-4294;* the **Ethniki Pronia Institute,** *24 Zoukourestiou St.;* the **Ikotechnia** of the Greek Lyceum, *6 Ypatias;* and the **Ergastirion Aporon Gynekon,** *46 Vassilissis Sophias Ave.,* all sell popular arts and crafts.

The best food and drink in Athens

The best guide to eating, drinking, and current events in Athens is the English-language *Athenian* magazine, which not only lists every restaurant and bar in the city but also critiques them.

The old **Xynos Taverna,** *4 Agg. Geronda; tel. (30-1)322-1065,* serves Greek wine from the barrel and features guitar music. Dinner costs about 3,000 drachmas ($16).

Five Brothers, *Aiolou Street,* off the square behind Hadrian's Library, is inexpensive.

For late-night reveling, try the **Erotokritos,** *16 Lyssiou St.,* which presents musicians in national costume.

Athens' most elegant (and among its most expensive) restaurants are **G.B. Corner,** *Syntagma Square,* at the Grande Bretagne Hotel; *tel. (30-1)323-0251;* the **Balthazar,** *27 Tsoha; tel. (30-1)644-1215;* and the **Dyonissos,** *43 Roberto Galli; tel. (30-1)923-3182,* a first-class restaurant across from the Acropolis.

The best fish restaurants are in Pireaus and along the coast from Glyfada to Sounion. The fish restaurants with the most atmosphere (but also the most expensive prices) are located in the yacht harbor known as Mikrolimano. In Glyfada, try the **Psaropoulos,** *2 Kalamou St.; tel. (30-1)894-5667,* which has a view of the yacht marina.

Athens' *ouzeries* are a dying tradition. Take the time to visit one, where you can sample Greek hors d'oeuvres and the national Greek licorice drink in the company of Greek intellectuals. Stop in at tea time or late in the evening.

The most famous *ouzerie* is the **Orfanides,** *7 Panepistimiou,* in the same block as the Grande Bretagne Hotel. **Apotsos,** *10 Panepistimiou Ave.,* is the oldest *ouzerie* in Athens; it opened in 1900.

Mezodopolieon are restaurants that serve only appetizers, which the Greeks call *mezes.* **Savories,** in the arcade at *10 Panepistimiou,* off Syntagma Square, is a good place to sample a selection. The **Salamandra,** *3 Mantzarou and Solonos streets,* has *bouzouki* music at night. One of the most famous and unusual *mezodopolieon* is the **Vasilena,** *72 Aitolikou, Piraeus; tel. (30-1)461-2457.* At this seemingly ancient restaurant located in an old grocery store, you pay a set price and are served about 20 varieties of *mezes.*

Bouzoukia concentrate more on music than food. Most of these Greek-style nightclubs are located in an area along the seafront between Athens and Piraeus known as Tzitzines. Ask your hotel which clubs are in at the moment. It usually depends on the artists playing.

The best places to sleep

The **Grande Bretagne,** *Syntagma Square; tel. (30-1)323-0251* or *(800)223-6800 in* *the United States,* is located at the heart of things and, as mentioned above, is touted as one of the world's greatest hotels. Although it's crumbling a little around the edges now, the old hotel retains an air of 1920s splendor. It has been welcoming guests since 1862. Rooms are spacious, and those in the front have balconies looking out at the Acropolis. The public rooms have baroque furnishings. This hotel is a favorite among celebrities. Rooms are 37,000 to 55,301 drachmas ($200 to $300).

Meridien, *2 Vas. Georgiou, Constitution Square; tel. (30-1)3255-301,* is a good second if the Grande Bretagne is booked up. Because it is newer, its physical amenities are more modern. Rooms are 35,000 drachmas ($191).

St. George Lycabettus, *2 Kleomenous; tel. (30-1)7290-710,* is less expensive and has more atmosphere. Its hilltop location gives it views of the city and the sea. It's not quite as convenient as hotels in the heart of things on Syntagma Square, and the rooms are only adequate, not particularly praiseworthy. But a swimming pool adds a point to its scorecard. Rooms are 21,030 to 29,720 drachmas ($115 to $162).

For atmosphere, stay in the Plaka. Hotels here are among the least expensive in the city. One charming one is **Hotel Phaedra,** *Andrianou Street, Lisicratous, Herefondos 16; tel. (30-1)323-8461,* in a quiet part of the old section. Double rooms are about 3,500 drachmas ($20). Another is **Diomia,** *5 Diomias; tel. (30-1)323-8034,* where a double room is from 8,930 to 11,210 drachmas ($48 to $61).

The best side trip from Athens

Cape Sounion, which is about 40 miles from downtown Athens, is crowned with the magnificent, white-columned, wind-swept **Temple of Poseidon,** standing alone on the point of the cape and looking out over the sea. From here, you can see all the way to Piraeus.

The solitary temple is most beautiful at sunset, when its white luster turns pink against the green pine trees and blue sea beneath it. Take your bathing suit—two fairly unpolluted beaches are nearby: Vouliagmeni and Varkiza. The temple is open from 9 a.m. to sunset Mondays to Saturdays and from 10 a.m. to sunset on Sundays. The entrance fee is 300 drachmas ($1.60) for adults and 150 drachmas (60 cents) for students.

If you want to get the full benefit of sunrise and sunset at this impressive site, spend the night at the **Aegean Hotel,** *tel. (30-292)39-200.* The hotel is right on the beach, and double rooms are 8,000 drachmas ($43).

The best of the Byzantine

The Greeks claim the sixth-century **Dafni Monastery,** five miles west of Athens, is their most important surviving Byzantine monument, famous for its mosaics. It is closed Mondays. The nearby **Kaesariani Monastery** was built in the 11th century near the ruins of a temple to Aphrodite.

Each year from June 29 to Sept. 29 the Greeks hold a wine festival at the Dafni Monastery. (The entrance fee is 300 drachmas, or $1.50.) You can sample Greek wines free and participate in dancing, singing, and contests.

The best of northern Greece

Northern Greece is the home of the country's tallest mountains, including the magical Mount Olympus; of the Macedonia of Alexander the Great; and of Thessaloniki, the only other city in this essentially rural nation. The farther north you go, the thicker the woods and the more Balkan the atmosphere.

Mount Athos: a misogynist's best

The large Greek Orthodox complex perched on the rocky cliffs of **Mount Athos,** at the end of the Chalkidiki Peninsula overlooking the Aegean, is one of the major wonders of the Christian world. The only self-governing monastic state in Europe, it is made up of about 20 monasteries, many of them individual walled towns.

Only adult males are allowed to visit this impressive Byzantine fortress-state. All others are considered temptations. Admission rules, issued by Emperor Constantine Monomachos of Byzantium in 1060, forbid women, children, and female animals within the complex. To this day, ships with women on board may not come within 500 meters of the shores around Mount Athos.

Even a man must obtain a permit to enter the complex. He must get a letter of recommendation from a diplomatic or consular officer of his own country and then apply for a permit from the **Greek Ministry of Foreign Affairs**, *Directorate of Churches, 3 Academia St., Athens; tel. (30-1)362-6894*, or the **Ministry of Northern Greece**, *the Directorate of Civil Affairs, Platia Diikitiriou, Thessaloniki; tel. (30-31)270-092.*

Mount Olympus: home of the gods

Mount Olympus is the home of the gods of Greek legend. It's easy to see why this huge, impressive mountain looming above in the clouds, which cut off its tip, captured the imagination of the ancient Greeks.

With an altitude of 9,620 feet, Olympus invites skiers in winter (through May) and mountain climbers and hikers in summer. Hotels in the area include the **Markessa,** *5 Dionisiou St.; tel. (30-352)818-31,* halfway between the mountain and the Aegean; the **Olympios-Zeus,** on the beach at the foot of the mountain; and three government-run **Xenias,** a chain of small hotels with views of both the mountain and the sea. All are moderately priced.

The best Greek cave

The **Petralona Cave** on the Halkidi Peninsula is 30 miles from Thessaloniki. A Neanderthal skull was found here in 1960, and the site appears to have been inhabited a half-million years ago.

The world's best fur bargains

Kastoria, in western Macedonia, is the center of the Greek fur industry and offers some of the best fur bargains in the world. Craftsmen here have been expertly sewing together the scraps from fur cutters around the world since the 15th century. You can get a coat for as little as a million drachmas ($3,000).

The best buy on handwoven rugs

Trikala is a small village in the mountains of northern Greece. This is where the famous shaggy Greek *flokati* rugs originated, thanks to the local sheep population and the crystal-clear mountain streams that are necessary for the manufacturing process. Villagers have been handweaving the rugs, now considered an art form, for 700 years. They hang them on their walls to keep out winter cold and damp.

The rugs available in Trikala are less expensive than those you'll find elsewhere. Stay away from the dyed ones.

The best of central Greece

Most of Greece's highest mountains are in the center of the country, where all points are within a few hours of Athens.

Mount Parnassus: the best skiing

About an hour and a half from Athens stands **Mount Parnassus** (8,059 feet), where Greece's most serious skiers spend their winters. For overnight stays, book **Hotel Anemolia;** *tel. (30-267)316-40,* in Arahova, which is high up on the mountain; a hotel in Delphi; or a government ski hut. Doubles are 15,900 drachmas ($86) on the weekends and 6,500 ($36) on the weekdays.

Delphi: the most sacred sight

Just a short drive down from the ski area of Mount Parnassus is one of Greece's most important and impressive ancient sacred sites, **Delphi**, where Apollo was worshiped, Greek games were held, and the famous oracle was consulted about matters of great significance by pilgrims from throughout the ancient world. Both the ruins and their setting on the steep side of Mount Parnassus are magnificent.

The **Vouzous Hotel**, *tel. (30-265)82233*, built into the side of a mountain, is the best place to stay in Delphi. Its rooms have spectacular, if dizzying, views of the Gulf of Corinth. A double room with breakfast is 17,000 drachmas ($93). The terrace at the **Taverna Vakhos**, *31 Apoollonos St.*, which serves great food, overlooks mountains and the Gulf of Corinth.

Meteora: the best monastery

More accessible than Mount Athos is the monastic complex of **Meteora**, perched on the summits of some precipitous rocks above the valley of the Pineios River, about five miles from Kalambaka. The monasteries here were built in the 14th century. In all, 33 monasteries and cells still stand, but only four are now occupied. In these are housed rare manuscripts, icons, miniatures, and ecclesiastical objects of Byzantine art.

The Peloponnese: the most beautiful island

The **Peloponnese** is a lovely, wild place covered with wild flowers in spring. You will never feel you've wandered long enough among its mountains, rolling plateaus, and numerous ruins. More major archeological sites are located in the Peloponnese than anywhere else in Greece.

Among the must-see ruins are the city of **Corinth**, known for its luxury and decadence during Roman times; **Mycenae**, the main attraction, site of some of the best archeological finds in the world, including the tombs of Agamemnon and Clytemnestra; **Nafplion**, a pretty town that is the site of a Venetian fortress; **Epidaurus**, where Greek plays are performed in an ancient theater every summer; and **Olympia**, site of the ancient games.

Five miles from the site of ancient **Sparta**, where only a few stones are left, is the pretty Byzantine town of Mistra, once known as the Florence of the East. Its steep, winding streets are full of churches, old mansions, and fragrant flowers and also sport a citadel and a monastery.

The best music and drama festival

The **Summer Festival of Music and Drama** at Epidaurus is one of the world's most exciting performing-arts events. The ancient theater holds 14,000 people, and its famous acoustics system enables each of them to hear the tiniest whisper from the stage.

The best hotel in the Peloponnese

The **Xenia Palace**, *Akronasplia; tel. (30-752)289-81*, situated inside the walls of the old Venetian fort in Nafplion, is the best of the government-run hotels. Situated on the bay, it has gorgeous views all the way to Mycenae. A double room is 25,600 drachmas ($140).

The best eating in the Peloponnese

The fish *tavernas* along the waterfront in **Nafplion** are recommended as much for their views as for their fresh fish and wine served straight from the barrel.

Roadside stands between Corinth and Nafplion sell the Blood of Hercules, the rich red wine famous here.

The Cyclades—the most visited Greek Islands

The **Cyclades Islands** are the most visited of Greece's island groups. They offer dramatic beauty and a civilization within a civilization. The Cycladic culture was a subculture of the ancient Mediterranean civilization led first by the Minoans and then by the Mycenaeans.

About 17 of the islands are suitable for vacationers. The most famous members of the group are Mykonos, Santorini, and Delos. Others often visited by tourists are Tinos, a destination for pilgrims of the Greek Orthodox faith; Los, with a dramatic setting and a town built on the side of a mountain; and lovely Paros, where you can get away from it all. The island of Kithnos has one of the best government-run **Xenia** hotels, *tel. (30-281)31-217*, situated in a renovated building dated 1840, near spas recommended for rheumatism and gynecological disorders.

Mykonos: the island for the jet set

Mykonos, a favorite spot among the jet set, has a reputation for being both wild and flashy and quaint and romantic. It is more open, vivacious, and relaxed than other Greek spots, with a philosophy of live and let live. It is a place where people are allowed and encouraged to do their own things, and where lovers of all persuasions are tolerated—and hardly even noticed. The Greek community itself is more tightly knit and warmer here than perhaps anywhere else in Greece.

Like the other islands in the chain, Mykonos is dry, with few trees, but beautiful in a dramatic way. Its whitewashed windmills are its trademark. Mykonians are almost compulsive about the spotlessness of their white houses and cobblestones, which offset nicely the beautiful colors of the potted flowers growing everywhere.

Mykonos' little houses, inns, hotels, and restaurants are hidden in a maze of tiny winding streets. It takes about a week to decipher the layout of the alleyways. Legend has it that the citizens of Mykonos purposely designed their streets in a random pattern to confound pirates.

Mykonos' beaches, by the way, particularly Paridis, Superparadis (predominantly gay), and Ilia, are covered with nude sunbathers.

The best clothes shopping

Mykonos' alleyways are filled with quaint boutiques and handicraft shops offering some of the finest-quality clothing in the country. This is the best place in Greece to buy hand-knit sweaters, from heavy fishermen's knits to stylish mohair and cotton creations.

Many shops in Mykonos, an enclave for artists, offer special designs and one-of-a-kind fashion experiments. Fur stores here offer good bargains, too.

The island's best photographs

A Greek-American photographer, Bo Patrick, sells lovely artistic photographs, as well as his book called *Whitewash and Pink Feathers*, a story about Mykonos for children. *Whitewash* refers to the locals' habit of whitewashing their houses and the cobblestoned lines on their sidewalks each Friday. The paint is actually not whitewash but something called *asbesti*, used to kill insects. *Pink feathers* refers to Petros the Pelican, a living character of local fame you'll see standing by the small fishing boats tied up on the waterfront. Bo's shop is in Little Venice, the quaintest part of town.

Wining and dining in Mykonos

Niko's, just off the harbor and opposite Ta Kiouria, is the best restaurant in Mykonos, with good prices and fresh fish. It is the favorite among local fishermen, who dock their tiny boats a few yards away in the harbor every evening.

Little Venice is the most charming area to eat in, with outdoor *tavernas* on the water's edge looking out on a gorgeous view.

The hottest night life

The **Mykonos Disco Bar** is the place to see Greek dancing. Get here about midnight. There is a cover charge of 800 drachmas ($4.40), including one drink.

Staying in Mykonos

Although the town is full of quaint little alleyway inns, some of the better places to stay in Mykonos are situated on the hillside overlooking the town. Even though staying at the top of the hill means a steep five- to 10-minute climb home, the view is worth it—as are the lower prices. The stepped paths up the hill pass windmills, flowers, and sometimes a goat or two.

The best of the in-town hotels include the **Leto**, *tel. (30-289)22207 or (30-289)22918*, right on the harbor (9,000 to 18,000 drachmas, or $49 to $98, for a double), and **Kouneni**, *tel. (30-289)22301*, with a lovely little secret garden (7,000 drachmas, or $38, for a double, including breakfast).

Hotel Aphroditi, *tel. (30-289)71367*, located on remote Kalafati Beach, is a beautiful place to hide away. Rooms are like bungalows, built in levels stepped up the hill along cobblestoned alleyways behind the main building. Each has a balcony. In the beflowered central patio is a large warm saltwater swimming pool, just a few yards from the white sandy beach across the driveway. The Aphrodite has a small disco, a nice restaurant, and a couple of private little *tavernas* at the end of the beach. Double rooms are 7,826 to 13,104 drachmas ($43 to $72).

The **Hotel Paralos Beach**, *tel. (30-289)23437*, has easy access to Delos Beach, and the *taverna* is excellent.

Delos: Apollo's birthplace

An excursion you must take from Mykonos is to the tiny island of **Delos**, now an archeological park. The god Apollo was born on this sacred island. You can visit this beautiful and eerie island via tour boat from Mykonos, a half-hour away. In spring, wild flowers grow among the impressive ruins.

Government boats at the Mykonos harbor offer tours to Delos Tuesdays through Sundays. They depart at 8:30 a.m. and return at 1 p.m.. The 30-minute ride costs 740 drachmas ($4). Bigger, more stable boats depart at 10 a.m. and return at 2 p.m. The cost is 1,200 drachmas ($6.50), round trip. You can also hire excursion boats at the Delian ruins for 3,000 drachmas ($16.50). Once on Delos, you'll be charged a few drachmas to enter the park. The island has no refreshment facilities, so take a canteen.

Climb the centuries-old stone steps up the small mountain in the center of the island for a memorable view of what was once the center of the Mediterranean world.

Santorini: the best sunsets

Santorini is a volcanic island. Its towns of Oia (on the northeastern tip) and Thira (the capital—also known as Fira) are situated way up in the clouds, looking down on a dramatic harbor shaped like a huge cauldron. In the evening, people gather along the mountain to watch the magnificent colors of Santorini's sunset.

Ferries pull in at one of two jetties. If you are lucky, your ferry will pull in at the one just below town, giving you the opportunity to be transported to the center of town by donkey.

Akrotiri, at the southeastern tip of the island, is one of Greece's most perfect excavations of a Bronze Age town, thought by many to be the legendary lost Atlantis.

Other things to see on Santorini include churches in Thira; Oia, known for its antiques; the beaches of Kamari, Monolithos, and Perissa (black sand) on the southwest coast; the island's castles; and the active Nea Kaimeni volcano on the small island in the harbor. (Tour boats are available to take you there.)

Buses are the least expensive way to tour the island. You also can rent a car or a moped and go it on your own. Santorini has great out-of-the-way country restaurants and isolated beaches.

The best beds on Santorini

Hotel rooms are a little hard to come by in Thira—if you insist on a room overlooking the harbor. If you do find one, you'll pay dearly for it. The **Atlantis**, *26 Amalias Ave.; tel. (30-286)22232*, is the nicest hotel, but it is expensive—23,000 drachmas ($126) a night. The **Hotel Villa Renos**, in downtown Thira, is located on a cliff overlooking the sea; each room has a private balcony. A double room is 19,000 drachmas ($103).

The most unusual place to stay on the island—and one of the most unusual in all Greece—is the government-renovated traditional settlement at Oia. Fifteen old Greek houses, complete with kitchens, patios, and gardens, are for rent. Oia, like Thira, is perched high on the cliffs overlooking both sides of the island. Rates are 1,330 drachmas ($7) per bed per night. The largest house has three double beds and three singles. The smallest has one double and one single. Contact the **Hellenic Hotel Reservation Office**, *tel. (30-1)3237-193*. The office is open 8:30 a.m. until 2:30 p.m.

The best of the Dodecanese Islands

Situated near the Turkish coast, the **Dodecanese Islands** have a more Turkish atmosphere than other Greek islands, because they recently were ruled by Turkey. Rhodes was a major trade hub of the ancient world. Patmos is considered one of the most beautiful. Kalymnos offers both a busy harbor town and quiet countryside.

The best island for golfers and gamblers

Rhodes is a favorite among European tourists. It has a more sophisticated atmosphere than other Greek playgrounds. The city is located in and around the walls of the medieval **Fortress of the Knights of St. John.** There are two districts: the New Town (north and west) and the Old Town below it, which is encircled by the medieval fortress walls. Wandering among the shops and restaurants inside the fortress is like visiting Disneyland. Its amusements include an evening sound-and-light show best seen from a boat off the harbor, costumed Greek dances at the summer wine festival, painting and handicraft exhibits, and an aquarium and a small zoo.

The **Rhodes Casino**, in the Grand Hotel, *tel. (30-241)28109*, open from 7 p.m. to 2 a.m., Mount Vasiliavias' 18-hole golf course and casino, is located at Afandou. And the archeological site of Lindos is about an hour's drive from town.

Rhodes' most tempting shops

Rhodes is a free port with numerous shops selling Greek handicrafts and high-fashion European goodies. Gucci, Yves St. Laurent, and other top European designers have shops here. Exquisitely crafted modern gold jewelry is available.

Rhodes' hottest night life

Kontiki, *Limin Mandrakiou; tel. (30-241)22-477*, is a houseboat nightclub with a close-up view of the harbor.

The best places to stay

Luxury hotels with huge swimming pools are common on Rhodes: The **Grand**, *1 Akti Maou; tel. (30-241)26284*, has double rooms for 14,500 drachmas ($79), and the **Rodos Palace Hotel**, *Trianton Avenue., tel. (30-241)26222*, is located just four kilometers from town. Facilities at the Rodos include three pools, a shopping arcade, a disco, tennis, golf, and a variety of water sports. Rooms are 27,000 to 31,000 drachmas ($148 to $170), including breakfast and one other meal.

Patmos: the holiest island

St. John the Divine is said to have written the last book of the New Testament in a mountain cave on **Patmos**. A huge 11th-century monastery atop the rocks marks the spot.

The best of the Sporades Islands

These islands, covered with pine and olive trees, are among Greece's most beautiful. Reached by plane or boat from the mainland port of Vollos, Skiathos is the major destination. Only three other of the islands receive attention from tourists: Skopelos, Ilonissos, and Skyros, all quieter versions of Skiathos.

Skiathos: the best beaches

Skiathos has the best sand beaches (most beaches in Greece are pebbly), and its Old Town section is charming. Not as tourist-trodden as the other, better-developed islands, such as Corfu, Rhodes, and Mykonos, Skiathos is said to be the Greeks' favorite island. Its large British expatriate community colors its cultural atmosphere. A few of the resident artists are British. English pubs are sprinkled among the alleyways of Old Town.

Vacation amenities include water-skiing, windsurfing, and boating; yet those who want to get away from it all will find a sense of privacy. Small boats gather on the town waterfront each morning to offer tourists excursions to nearby islands, beaches, and the Kastro, a castle ruin on the other side. The best organized trip is to an uninhabited island across from the town, which has a beautiful beach with flowers growing in the sand and a myriad of butterflies.

The best places to stay

The **Skiathos Palace**, on Koukounaries beach, *tel. (30-427)22242*, is the most luxurious hotel on the island—but it's a bit too perfect and not very Greek.

The government-run **Xenia**, also on Koukounaries, *tel. (30-427)22042*, has more charm if you want to stay on the beach. You'll find more atmosphere at a room in town or in a villa along one of the beach roads. Tourist agents can find you a room in just about any price range.

Savoring Skiathos' cuisine

Skiathos' seafood restaurants offer some of Greece's best meals, prepared with more European subtlety than elsewhere. You can't go wrong at any of the outdoor *tavernas* along the harbor in town. For the best lunch, go where the local fishermen eat—it's a plain establishment, right in the middle of the row of *tavernas* at the bottom of the hill.

Skopelos: the least discovered

Skopelos is an unspoiled Greek gem smothered in plum trees, where traditional Greek costumes are still the everyday dress. The lack of tourists and their trappings make this island especially inviting.

The most Turkish islands: the northeast Aegean

Less visited than others, these seven, which include Lesbos, Samos, and Chios, are the most Turkish of Greece's islands.

Lesbos: the prettiest in the group

The large, tree-covered island of **Lesbos** is as pretty an island as you're likely to encounter. It has a Genovese castle in the northern town of Molyvosa and a petrified forest. The ancient castle above the lovely harbor town of Mytilani is the site of summer concerts performed by international artists each summer. The island's sardines, wine, and locally made ouzo are excellent. The best place to stay is the government-run **Xenia**, *tel. (30-251)22713*, with its pool that looks out toward Turkey. Double rooms are 3,720 drachmas ($20).

Samos: the best red wine

Dominated by 5,000-foot Mount Kerketeos, **Samos** has been famous for centuries for its dark red wine. It was considered by the ancients to be the birthplace of Hera, Zeus' wife. The human immortals Pythagoras and Epicurus were born here. The island is popular among Germans and Scandinavians.

Chios: the most inviting

This island's main attraction is a government-run guest settlement, a renovated 14th-century Genoan village. On a small island off Chios is another guest settlement, built in an old church cloister, that is both cheap and charming. Reserve with the **Hellenic Hotel Reservation Office,** *tel. (30-1)3237-193.*

Corfu: the most beautiful island in Greece

Northern **Corfu** is said to be the most beautiful island of Greece—which is saying something. (Corfu has recently gotten some bad press, however, because of trash left by hordes of tourists each summer.) Covered with lemon, orange, cyprus, fig, and olive groves, it is a lush place. Many of the island's beautiful villas belong to British expatriates. The main port, Kekira, is a town of Venetian elegance, more Italian than Greek. Corfu offers shops, hotels, restaurants, and night life.

The southern and western coasts of Corfu have the most striking scenery. Eight miles south of the port is the impressive **Achilleion Palace,** once a summer residence of Kaiser Wilhelm II of Germany and now a gambling casino. The jet set hangs out in **Paleokastritsa,** on the west coast. The north coast is the most touristy area, with several resort towns. **Kassiopi** is one of the least spoiled and most reasonable places to stay.

The best shopping on Corfu

One of Greece's best shopping sites is on Corfu. The island's specialties are woolen items, woodwork, jewelry, and embroidery. The island also has an artists' colony that produces paintings and sculptures. The best shopping is in **Hora,** in the center of town.

Corfu's best hotel

Cavalieri Corfu, *4 Kapodistriou St., tel. (30-661)39041,* an elegant Venetian mansion, was King George II's summer residence in the 1920s. It is expensive but not the highest-priced place on the island. A double room is 11,000 drachmas ($60), including breakfast.

The best home away from home

There are so many Americans, Canadians, and British visiting and working at the **Pink Palace,** *Agios Gordios; tel. (30-661)531034,* you will feel like you never left home. The Palace has the wildest disco on the island, and water-skiing, parasailing, and cliff-diving excursions are all available. Rooms cost 3,200 drachmas ($17). And when you arrive, you are treated to a shot of ouzo.

The best eats on Corfu

Corfu food is a combination of Greek and Italian. The island's wine is said to be among the nation's best. (Try the Hyma, a local unbottled wine.)

Paliokastritza is a world-renowned eating spot. After lunch, swim in this beautiful cove where Odysseus is said to have washed ashore.

Crete: the most Middle Eastern of the islands

Crete, the most Middle Eastern of Greece's islands, is like a small county with its own lifestyle and culture. A huge island of more than 5,000 square miles, it really warrants a separate trip. Unless you are planning an extended stay, do not try to visit Crete and the rest of Greece on the same trip.

Crete has some of the world's most impressive ruins. Rent a car to see the island. Camping is also recommended here.

The most important sight

The major attraction of Greece and one of the most important archeological sites of the Mediterranean world is the ancient capital of Minoan civilization, **Knossos**. If you're only in port for a day, you can sign up for tours to Knossos in Iraklion. However, the public bus, which leaves from Venizelou Square, is more economical.

The tourist belt

To the east of Iraklion is the tourist belt of Crete, with beaches and hotels. The most popular area is near **Elounda**. Nearby is the ancient city of Hersonissos; Gournia, a completely preserved Minoan town; and Zakros, another Minoan palace.

The least developed coasts

The southern and western coasts of Crete are the least developed. The interior is virtually unspoiled. Phaistos Palace is inland from the central-southern coast. Gortys, an old Roman town, is nearby, and Agia Triada, another Minoan site, is on the coast to the west. Limnes, a picturesque fishing village, and Matala, which has ancient cave tombs overlooking a beach, are modern-day resort areas near the ruins.

Europe's most beautiful gorge

The natural wonder of the island is the **Samarian Gorge**, located in central-western Crete. It is the largest—and many think the most beautiful—gorge in Europe and a popular jaunt for hikers. Buses leave from Hania early in the morning and drop hikers off at the top. The walk down takes about five hours. The gorge exits onto a beach, where you can stop for a swim.

Hania, the capital

Hania, the capital of Crete, has a picturesque Venetian harbor and narrow streets. Although not particularly beautiful, it has a special charm. Visit the Venetian quarter.

Accommodation is easy to find and reasonable. Among the best hotels is an old mansion called **Hotel Doma**, *124 Venizelos St.; tel. (30-821)217723*. Once the British Consulate, it opens every year in March.

The best hotel

The **Elounda Beach Hotel**, *tel. (30-821)414123*, one of the world's best hotels, was designed by one of Greece's great architects, Spiro Kokotas. It is on a beautiful beach, set off by lots of flowers. The adjoining Elounda Mare has bungalows with private swimming pools. Terrific service, food, and amenities make this resort outstanding. It is pricey.

The best travel tips

Unless you come in July or August, when bookings are tight, wait until you arrive in Greece to arrange your itinerary. The local prices for tours, cruises, transportation, and hotels are much better than those of the agents at home.

The first thing to do when you arrive in Athens is visit the **Greek National Tourist Organization** (EOT in Greek), *Dieftynsi, Ekmetalefseos, 2 Amerikis St., Athens 10564*. The office is open from 8 a.m. to 9 p.m. Mondays through Fridays. Here you can pick up free publications describing sites throughout the country. You also can pick up ferry and train schedules and get directions.

Europe's cheapest cruises

You can spend several thousand dollars to sail the Greek islands for a week or two on a passenger liner. Or you can spend just a few dollars to do the same thing on a ferry. Greek ferries are incredibly inexpensive. A six-hour ride from Athens to Mykonos, for example, is only 150 drachmas ($1) deck-class. In addition, with ferries you have the flexibility to stay in a port as long as you choose—and the opportunity to participate firsthand in Greek life.

Connections among the islands are numerous, and part of the adventure of ferry travel is finding out when you arrive on an island what the next possible connections are. (Inquiring about ferry, bus, train, or plane connections should be the first thing you do when you arrive at any Greek destination—they may not be daily.)

When you disembark, you'll be met by people wanting to rent you rooms. Most will have photo albums showing their accommodations. These rooms are much cheaper than hotels (although they usually don't have private baths). If the pier where you disembark is not in the middle of a fishing village, buses and taxis or donkeys will be waiting to get you where you want to go.

For information on ferry schedules, call the **Piraeus Port Authority**, *tel. (30-1)451-1313,* or the **Volos Port Authority**, *tel. (30-421)20-115.*

The best way to see the country

Renting a car is the best way to see the country, especially in the Peloponnese. Rental cars are available from **Avis**, *tel. (30-1)322-4951;* **Hertz**, *tel. (30-1)994-2850;* **Budget**, *tel. (30-1)92-14771;* and **Thrifty**, *tel. (30-1)922-1211.* Daily rates, including insurance and taxes, are about 10,500 drachmas ($57). Weekly rates are about 83,500 drachmas ($456).

Should you have car trouble while driving through Greece, the **Automobile and Touring Club of Greece** (ELPA in Greek) provides free assistance to tourists. For emergency medical service on the mainland, dial *104.*

The best way to fly

Domestic air service in Greece is dirt cheap. **Olympic Airways**, *6 Ophonos St; tel. (30-1)961-6161,* provides the only domestic service in the country, offering numerous flights among the islands and to mainland destinations. Reserve as far in advance as possible—it's not easy to book on a whim.

A one-way flight from Athens to almost any of the islands costs about 12,300 drachmas ($67). All domestic flights in Athens go through the domestic airport—not the international airport. Be sure to specify to your taxi driver which airport you want. On most islands, bus service between the village office of Olympic and the airport is available (for a minimal charge, sometimes free).

The worst way to travel

Although train travel in Greece is cheap, it is painfully slow. One line runs from Athens to encircle the Peloponnese, with offshoots to Kalamata and Kiparissia; another runs from Athens to Thessaloniki and onward to a dead end at the Turkey-Bulgaria border. First- and second-class season tickets allowing unlimited travel for a specified time are available at reduced rates. Round-trip tickets are 20% cheaper than one-way tickets.

Sailing: the best way to travel

Renting your own boat is the best way to explore the islands. You can rent either a bareboat vessel or a crewed luxury yacht with sail or motor. Prices range from 11,970 drachmas to 931,000 drachmas ($54 to $6,000) per person per day, including fuel and other supplies. Hiring a skipper costs an additional 4,655 drachmas ($25). A cash deposit of 53,200 drachmas to 119,700 drachmas ($290 to $654), depending on the size of the boat, is required before you can board.

To charter a bareboat, the charterer and at least one member of the crew must have a certificate or a letter of recommendation from a recognized sailing club.

To rent a boat, contact the **Yacht Brokers and Experts Association,** *Felelinon 7, Athens; tel. (30-1)325-3556.*

How to get the best deal on a hotel

The only time it makes sense to make hotel reservations from home is if you'll be arriving in Greece in July or August. To reserve hotel rooms directly, contact the **Hellenic Chamber of Commerce,** *24 Stadiou; tel. (30-1)323-7193,* open from 8:30 a.m. to 2:30 p.m.

Your best bet, however, is to wait until you arrive and stop by the hotel reservation desk at the airport.

If you have the time and energy, shop around. Offer about 200 drachmas less than the going rate. The Greeks always say their bottom price is a hundred or two more than yours. You can get rooms on the islands for as little as 1,995 drachmas ($11) in the spring and fall. Prices rise by about 30% in July and August.

The Greek government has begun a program of restoring traditional Greek homes around the country, especially in Oia (on Snatorini) and Mesta (on Chios), for tourist rental. These offer the most unique accommodation you'll find.

EOT-run campsites are located in some of the most picturesque parts of the mainland. One is at the foot of the legendary Mount Olympus. Charges for using the campsites are 240 drachmas to 400 drachmas ($1.50 to $2.50) for adults and 120 drachmas to 220 drachmas (50 cents to $1.50) for children over 10. Children under 10 can stay free. You have to pay additional fees for vehicles and electricity. If you're traveling without a tent, you can rent a hut with two to four beds for 1,500 drachmas to 2,000 drachmas ($8 to $11).

The Best of Ireland

Of all the people in the world, the Irish are the happiest, according to the Happiness Index developed by two London-based market research firms. The good-natured Irish are a joy to spend time with. So make sure you visit the people of Ireland as well as the Irish countryside. Don't miss the most pleasant occupation in Ireland: sitting in a pub, sipping a Guinness or a Harp, and chatting.

The best way to tour Ireland's emerald countryside, charming villages, and ancient ruins is to circle around its coast, traveling from Dublin to Wicklow, Wexford, Waterford, Cork, Killarney, and finally Limerick. Venture inland to Kilkenny. Then go beyond the pale to the region the English never conquered: the Burren, Galway, Mayo, and Sligo.

The best ways to explore Dublin

The most pleasant way to visit Dublin is to follow the lines of an old song: "Have coffee in Dublin at 11 and walk in Stephen's Green, and you'll be in heaven." Actually, have tea. Coffee in Ireland is usually instant and weak, but the tea is always good. Go to **Bewley's**, either on Grafton or Westmoreland, for a nice hot cup. Later, spend time shopping along bustling Grafton, Anne, and Duke streets. Look for lace curtains, tailored tweed suits, and Irish knit sweaters.

The most efficient way to explore Dublin if you are in a hurry is via the **Dublin Trail**. Well posted, it leads past the city's major sights. A map of the trail is available at the **Dublin Tourist Office**, *14 O'Connell St.; tel. (353-1)376-387.*

Another good way to explore Dublin is to follow in the footsteps of **James Joyce**. The house where Joyce was born, *41 Brighton Square W.,* in the agreeable suburb of Rathgar, is marked with a plaque. **Mulligan's,** *Poolbeg Street,* a pub Joyce frequented in his student days, has a special aura, especially in the back parlor, where Joyce often sat and wrote. Joyce once lived at **Martello Tower and Museum,** at Sandycove, as did his characters in *Ulysses.*

Also look for the homes of other famous Dubliners: Shelley lived at 1 Grafton St.; Sheridan lived at 79 Grafton St., and George Bernard Shaw was born at 33 Synge St.

Dublin's greatest treasure

The jewel in Dublin's crown is *The Book of Kells*. More than 1,000 years old, it is the most intricate illuminated manuscript in the Western world.

The manuscript is kept at **Trinity College.** After entering the college through its arched front entrance, look back at Merrion Square among the tall red-brick houses dominating the skyline, the pristine remains of Georgian Dublin. From there, head for the campus. In the fourth quadrangle on the right is the library. Among the celebrated ghosts that reportedly still haunt Trinity College are those of William Congreve, Oliver Goldsmith, Jonathan Swift, and Oscar Wilde.

The greatest furniture, antiques, etc.

Althoughly slightly more expensive than your average furniture store, **Paul Cooke's Shop,** *79-85 Francis St., Dublin,* offers the best selection of period furniture, architectural antiques, and Georgian marble chimneypieces in Ireland. A Kilkenny chimneypiece inlaid with fossils is I£17,500 ($30,000), for example, and a chimneypiece inlaid with rare and semiprecious Blue John stone is I£65,000 ($112,000).

Ireland's best stout

The **Guinness Brewery** at St. James' Gate on the banks of the Liffey in Dublin produces Ireland's rich and frothy national drink, the brown stout found on tap in every pub. Tours, conducted from 10 a.m. to 3 p.m. Monday through Friday, end in the tasting room. (You get one free sample.) This English-owned concern is the largest brewery in Europe.

The oldest pub in Ireland

The **Brazen Head,** *Bridge Street, Dublin,* is the oldest pub in Ireland, dating back to the 12th century. It is five minutes away from the antique shops on Francis Street, and it's a perfect break from your shopping. The Guinness here is superb; the brewery is only a stone's throw away, and the smell of hops stays with you for hours after you've moved on.

The pubs with the most atmosphere

Dublin boasts more than 600 pubs, but if you want atmosphere, head to the **Palace Bar,** *Fleet Street,* or the **Long Hall,** *South Great Georges Street.* Both have authentic stained-glass partitions, wood paneling, and collections of Victorian prints.

Dublin's best sights

Dublin Castle, restored after a bombing, has handsome state apartments that are open to the public. Castle upon castle has been built on this site. The earliest construction was Celtic. The Vikings later improved upon this; then, in the 13th century, King John of England built a fortress on the site. The British ruled Ireland from this stronghold for 400 years.

The **Records Tower** is the only part of the castle that dates back to the original 13th-century fortress. The **Bedford Tower,** which houses the Heraldic Museum, built in the 15th century, was once used as the state prison. If you are of Irish ancestry, you can trace your family tree in the Genealogical Office.

The **General Post Office,** *O'Connell Street,* was the scene of the 1916 Easter uprising, the major step along Ireland's road to independence. You can read the declaration of Irish independence on the walls. After they proclaimed the free Republic here, the Irish Volunteers were bombed by a British gunboat docked in the River Liffey. Those who surrendered were hanged.

The **Kilmainham Jail Historical Museum,** open only on Sunday afternoons, is another monument to the centuries of struggle against the British. It held political prisoners from 1796 to 1924.

The **National Museum,** *Kildare Street,* has a collection of Irish antiquities from the Stone Age through the War for Independence. It is open daily; admission is free.

The **National Gallery,** *Leinster Lawn,* has a fine collection of old masters, including works by Rembrandt; it also houses the National Portrait Gallery. It is open daily; admission is free.

The creepiest experience

Centuries-old bodies lie perfectly preserved in the dry crypt of **St. Michan's Church** on Church Street. The 17th-century church was built on the site of a 10th-century Viking church. Perhaps because of its dryness, the crypt has remarkable preservation qualities. You can actually touch an 8-foot Crusader. It is said to be good luck to shake the hand of one of the corpses here. The crypt is open weekdays and Saturday mornings.

Dublin's best park

Phoenix Park in Dublin is the largest public park in Western Europe and the largest enclosed city park in the world. The official residence of the Irish president is here, as well as the residence of the American ambassador. The 1,760-acre park includes a racetrack, a soccer field, sports grounds, flower gardens, a herd of fallow deer, a lake, and a monument to Wellington.

Dublin's most picturesque bridge

Peer into the Liffey from the wrought-iron Halfpenny Bridge, named after the toll once charged for crossing the river. Its southern end brings you through Merchant's Quay into the cobblestoned alleyways of Temple Bar. This is Dublin's "left bank," teeming with secondhand book shops, bars, and alternative cafes. It's popular with students.

The best escape from Dublin

If, by some amazing chance, the weather is hot while you are in Dublin, visit the famous seaside resort called **Bray.** It is about 15 miles south of Dublin City, adjacent to the town of Dun Laoghaire (pronounced Dunleara) in County Dublin.

Dublin's best night life

The best night spots in Dublin are the pubs, with their evenings of Guinness, ballads, and poetry. Busiest from 9 p.m. onwards, most pubs open at 11 a.m. and close at 11 p.m. in winter; in summer, they stay open until 11:30 p.m., just about the time the sun sets.

The oldest pub in Dublin is the **Brazen Head**, which was first licensed in 1666. The low ceilings give this pub an old and cozy air. You'll find it in a courtyard off Usher Quay.

The **Abbey Tavern**, *Abbey Street, Howth; tel. (353-1)322-006*, has good seafood to accompany the entertainment. Reserve ahead—it's a popular place.

Slattery's Pub, *Capel Street; tel. (353-1)727-971*, features traditional Irish music nightly and from 12:30 until 2 p.m. on Sunday.

At the **Culturalann na hEireann**, *32 Belgrave Square; tel. (353-1)2800-295*, in Monkstown, you'll hear some of Ireland's finest fiddlers, accordionists, and pipers.

On Wednesdays, you can hear light rock at the **Baggot Inn**, *Baggot Street; tel. (353-1)761-430.*

The world's best pub crawl

Every summer, the infamous "Dublin literary pub crawl" staggers off at 7 p.m. every Monday through Thursday. First pints are downed at **The Bailey** on Duke Street, where the owners still display Michael Collins' revolver. Also on Duke Street, try **Davy Byrne's** pub, where Leopold Bloom fictionally dined on Gorgonzola and Burgundy.

The best Dublin Market

For local color head for the **Moore Street Market**, off O'Connell Street. Although you won't meet Molly Malone with her wheelbarrow, you will be able to shop for everything from socks to strawberries, sold out of battered old prams. The language is just as colorful as the people.

The best seafood restaurant

King Sitric, *East Pier, Howth; tel. (353-1)325235*, offers the best seafood in or around Dublin. It is a popular, small restaurant overlooking the harbor at Howth, well worth the 30-minute drive out of the city.

Dublin's finest hotels

The **Shelbourne Hotel**, which graces St. Stephen's Green, is the grand Victorian hotel where the Irish Constitution was drafted. Inside the hotel's turreted red-brick facade are ultramodern rooms with seaweed salt baths (an unusual luxury that is supposed to be good for your health). William Thackeray stayed here.

Don't miss the sumptuous afternoon tea at the Shelbourne, which is served in a restored art nouveau tearoom. A harpist plays while you enjoy sandwiches, scones, cakes, cookies, and India or China tea.

A double room starts at I£97.50 ($145) per person, including tax. To book a room, contact **Trusthouse Forte Hotels Inc.**, *5700 Broadmoor, Suite 500, Mission, KS 66202; (800)225-5843.*

The **Jurys Dublin Hotel**, *Ballsbridge 4, Dublin; tel. (353-1)605000*, is also a good hotel in Dublin, although not as grand as the Shelbourne. It offers a particularly pleasant atmosphere and a good location, with the city's center five minutes away. A double room starts at I£57 ($97) per person.

Ireland's greenest county

County Wicklow, which is known as the Garden of Ireland, is the greenest of Ireland's counties. A good base for exploring both Wicklow and neighboring county Wexford is **Wexford** town, a small Viking-founded seaside town with narrow streets. Henry II repented at the nearby abbey for the assassination of Thomas à Becket. Oliver Cromwell massacred the townspeople in 1649 in an anti-Catholic rage. The town features a statue of John Barry, father of the U.S. Navy, who was born nearby. John F. Kennedy laid a wreath here. (You can visit the John F. Kennedy Park near the Kennedy family homestead at Dunganstown.)

The **Crown Bar**, an establishment on Monck Street in Wexford, has been in the Kelly family for 100 years. It is a cozy place for a drink or a light meal. Stay at **Killiane Castle**, *off Rosslare Harbour Road, Drinagh*, and enjoy its 230 acres. A room in this guesthouse is inexpensive, about I£30 ($51) a night. Wexford, Ireland is 83 miles from Dublin through the Wicklow Mountains.

Enniskerry, one of Ireland's prettiest villages, is also part of County Wicklow. Located in a wooded hollow and surrounded by hills, the village is famous for Powerscourt, one of Ireland's great estates. The ruins of a Georgian mansion are surrounded by 14,000 acres of grounds, including the 400-foot Powerscourt Waterfall.

Wicklow's other highlight is **Glendalough**, a deep valley in the Wicklow Mountains. In the sixth century, St. Kevin took refuge in this peaceful glen between two lakes. However, his refuge didn't remain secret. His disciples followed him and founded a monastery and a famous center of learning here. View the remains of a medieval round tower, as well as buildings from the ninth through 13th centuries. This is a good region for hikers; nature trails head through the valley.

Waterford: the world's best crystal

Waterford, a fine old harbor city and an important shipping port, is best known for producing some of the finest hand-cut crystal in the world. The Waterford Crystal Plant, which you can tour, is about two miles from the city center on the right-hand side of N25, the main road between Waterford and Cork. Craftsmen make about 90,000 pieces of crystal a week; 70% goes to the United States.

Shops selling the products include **Kelly's Ltd.**, *75 The Quay;* **Shaw's**, *53 Barronstrand St.;* and **Joseph Know**, *4 Barronstrand St.* Often you can get better buys in the United States, once you've figured in the high costs of shipping. But these shops are good places to look for rare patterns that are unavailable at home.

Cork: the best Irish market

County Cork's capital, **Cork**, houses the fascinating **English Market**, a vast covered arcade on Prince's Street that was built in 1788. Here you can soak up a bit of local color and enjoy the unmistakable Cork accent.

The famous **President's Restaurant**, *Longueville House, Mallow; tel. (353-22)4-7156*, on a 500-acre estate, is nearby. Homegrown produce is served at this superb restaurant. Reservations are required. (Avoid this trip in August, when a mass exodus takes place from Cork City to Mallow.)

The best-named newspaper

Cork boasts the world's best-named newspaper: The *Cork Examiner.* We assume its wine reviews are extensive.

Cork's biggest ding-dong

Be sure to climb the pepperpot steeple of **Shandon Church** and ring its bells. Using numbered cards, you can even regale the "rebel" city with your own eight-belled version of *Waltzing Matilda*.

Cork's best country restaurant

For country house ambiance (including a heated swimming pool), try **Ballymaloe House**, *Shanagarry; tel. (353-21)652-531*. Bed and breakfast is I£52 ($88) per person. Twenty miles from Cork City and only two from the coast, the Ballymaloe is run by Ivan and Myrtle Allen. Produce for the award-winning restaurant comes from the home farm; other members of the Allen family run the Ballymaloe Cookery School, arguably the most presitigious in Ireland.

The blarniest sight

Outside Cork City is **Blarney Castle**, where kissing the **Blarney Stone** is said to give the gift of eloquence. Doing so is practically an acrobatic feat. You must lie on your back over a sheer drop and stretch to kiss the stone.

According to one legend, the Blarney Stone was first kissed by a man with a lisp after he had rescued a witch from death. As a reward for saving her life, the witch told him to kiss the stone. He did so, and his lisp disappeared. Another legend says that the lord of Blarney Castle, McCarthy, flabbergasted Queen Elizabeth with his eloquent excuses for having attacked England. She finally dropped the charges against him, calling his excuses "blarney."

The yacht crowd's favorite

Kinsale is an international yachting center overflowing with gourmet restaurants. The *Lusitania* was torpedoed off its coast by a German submarine in 1915. This was also the site of the 1602 Battle of Kinsale, during which the northern chieftains were defeated by the English, establishing English domination of Ireland. The heavy, woolen Kinsale cloak is a popular purchase.

Ennis—the best base for exploring

The town of **Ennis** in County Clare is the best base for exploring the west of Ireland, from which so many Americans stem. The old market town (population 20,000) has escaped relatively unscathed from the tourist flow, even though Shannon Airport is close by.

The main street in Ennis boasts antique shops selling genuine (if pricey) antiques. But the town's gem is its monastery—the most evocative in Ireland. This roofless, weed-covered ruin's tottering Gothic walls exactly fit Shakespeare's phrase, "bare, ruined choirs."

Bunratty House, built in 1846, is worth a visit. (Skip the fake feast in its cellar.) The house gives you an idea of how Irish nobility lived. The folk park behind the elegant house shows how lesser Irishmen survived.

The **Old Ground**, *O'Connell Street; tel. (353-65)28127*, is the most charming place to stay in Ennis. Rooms are well-equipped with such comforts as direct-dial telephones and modern plumbing. A double room is I£60 ($103), including a full Irish breakfast.

The restaurant at the Old Ground is splendid and serves Irish specialties, including Dublin Bay prawns (shrimp), mutton chops with kidneys, and apple pie.

Ireland's most spectacular cliffs

The **Cliffs of Moher**, a few miles north of Ennis, are the most spectacular in Ireland, perhaps in all Europe. The 700-foot black cliffs face the constant onslaught of the Atlantic.

The most beautiful drives

County Kerry is known for the spectacular **Ring of Kerry**, a 110-mile drive that hugs the coast of the Inveragh Peninsula. Highlights of the drive include **Rossbeigh Beach**, near Glenbeigh on the north coast, which offers the best view of Drung Hill; **Glencar**, near Caragh Lake, a good place to hike; cells carved from solid rock by monks escaping the Vikings at **Skellig Rocks**; **Ballaghisheen Pass**, which takes you through scenic mountains; and the peaceful beaches that line the southern half of the ring. You can make the drive in a day.

Wild and Gaelic **Dingle Peninsula** is another beautiful drive in County Kerry. Begin the drive in the town of Dingle, on the ocean. Surrounded by hills, this fishing town is protected by an ancient wall. From Dingle, take the road to **Ventry**, which has an inviting beach. Outside Ventry are beehive huts built by monks of early Irish monasteries. **Slea Head**, at the tip of the peninsula, has a lovely view of the seven Blasket Islands. And the beach at Slea Head has water warm enough for swimming, thanks to the Gulf Stream.

Northeast of Slea Head is **Gallerus Oratory**, an unmortared stone building from the ninth century. After 1,000 years, it is still watertight. From the **Conair Pass**, you can see the lakes and Brandon, Tralee, and Dingle bays. **Sybil Head** has high green-sodded cliffs topped by thatched cottages and washed by the Atlantic below.

While in Kerry stay at the **Ballyseede Castle Hotel**, *tel. (353-66)25799*. Acres of greenery surround this 15th-century castle. A double room starts at I£35 ($60) per person. Reservations are required.

Or stay at the ideally situated **Parknasilla-Great Southern**, *County Kerry; tel. (353-64)45122*. It offers outstanding atmosphere, great service, beautiful room decor, and extensive facilities, including swimming, tennis, golf, and horseback riding, all on 300 acres of beautiful grounds. The hotel overlooks Kenmare Bay. A double room starts at I£48 ($82) per person.

Ireland's loveliest lakes

The town of **Killarney** offers a dreamlike setting of lush green hills and deep blue lakes. Spend time enjoying the town, but concentrate on the surrounding Lower, Middle, and Upper lakes. At their banks, ferns and mosses grow in the shade of oak, birch, holly, and ash trees. Much of this lake district lies within the 11,000-acre Bourne Vincent Memorial Park.

You can do your sightseeing in a horse-drawn jaunting car. Visit Muckross House, a 19th-century manor in the park that is now used as a folk museum. Hike or ride a pony through the mountains and around the lakes.

The kitschiest castle

Bunratty Castle, near Limerick, is one of the kitschiest sights in Ireland. While it does house Lord Gort's superb collection of medieval furniture, tapestries, paintings, and glass, most visitors come for the castle's corny medieval banquet. Guests eat without silverware as they did in the old days, and mead (fermented honey) is served by colleens in low-cut medieval gowns. You sing *Danny Boy* and all the other cliché St. Patrick's Day songs. If you're interested in reservations, contact **Shannon Castle Tours**, *Shannon Airport, County Clare; tel. (353-61)6-1788.*

The Aran Islands—time's greatest foe

The **Aran Islands** are fascinating, if barely habitable. Gaelic language and traditions survive on these three islands 35 miles from the mainland. The islanders maintain their traditional dress—women wear red skirts and moccasins called *pampooties,* the men vests and peaked caps. They grow potatoes in a mixture of sand and seaweed and fish in wicker-framed, hide-covered *curraughs,* or boats.

Dun Aengus, an Iron Age fortress built on a cliff on the island of **Inishmore**, has 18-foot-thick walls. The prettiest islands are the two smallest, **Inishmaan**, which is known for its traditional music and dancing, and **Inisheer.** In good weather, boat service is available regularly to most of the islands. The closest point on the mainland is Doolin, where you can catch a boat to Inisheer. Steamers run daily from Galway to Kilronan on Inishmore.

The best horseback riding

The **Connemara Trail**, which winds its way along the coast of Ireland's County Galway, passes through rugged mountains and along deserted beaches. Beginning near the sea in Barna, the trail goes from village to village and mountain to mountain, leading you eventually to the Atlantic Ocean on the beaches near Clifden.

One of the best trail-riding expeditions is led by William Leahy. A six-day/six-night trail holiday costs I£705 ($1,216) in the spring and fall, I£745 ($1,285) in July and August. For more information, contact William Leahy, **Aille Cross Equitation Centre**, *Aille Cross, Loughrea, County Galway, Ireland; tel. (353-91)41216.*

Biggest horse fair, smallest ponies

Held annually in County Galway, the **Great Fair of Ballinasloe** is Ireland's oldest and biggest horse fair. For the first week of October, Ballinasloe's Fair Green heaves with horse flesh. Many deals are done with a spit and a handshake.

Ireland's smallest ponies are found in the wilderness of Connemara. With their sweet faces and shaggy coats, Connemara ponies are tiny. Clifden, the colorwashed capital of this mountainous region, hosts the annual Connemara pony show during the third week in August.

The most delicious oysters

For some of the best oysters in all Ireland, visit **Paddy Burke's Oyster Tavern**, *Clarinbridge; tel. (353-91)962-26.* Oysters are sold by the dozen (for I£9.50, or $16), or you can sit down for a good meal. To preserve the taste of the sea, you should hold the shell horizontally. With nothing more than perhaps a squeeze of lemon for flavoring, squash the oyster with your tongue, savor its flavor, and then gulp the liquid from the shell.

Yeats' favorite land

The dramatic countryside of **Sligo** is where the poet William Butler Yeats spent his

123

childhood summers. He asked to be buried in Drumcliffe Churchyard, five miles north of Sligo proper. At the summit of the nearby Glen of Knocknarea is said to be the grave of the legendary Queen Maeve from the *Queen of the Immortal Faeries.* Six miles east as the crow flies, shimmering Lough Gill is the site and source of Yeats' best-known poem, *The Lake Isle of Innisfree.* Sixty years ago, Sligo was the center of the Irish literary revival.

The area around Sligo claims one of the largest concentrations of prehistoric graves and monuments in Western Europe. Most are neither fenced off nor mentioned in tourist brochures. You must find them by word-of-mouth.

"A pearl, a gem, a jewel in the crown of Mother Ireland"

Well, that's how **Hargadons** on Sligo town's O'Connell Street modestly describes itself. Even the atmosphere in this peculiar drinking den is intoxicating. Needless to say, it serves memorable Guinness. But there's more to Hargadons than fine brew—just look around; you'll see a potbellied stove, huge glittering mirrors, open turf fires, and customers who can talk the hind leg off any proverbial donkey. Don't miss it.

Donegal: the best tweed

"You'll wear out two suit linings," the Irish brag, "before you'll wear out a Donegal tweed." The county of **Donegal** in northwest Ireland sells some of the best tweed in the world. **Magee's Tweed Shop** in Donegal town is a good place to begin your search.

Also try the peninsula just west of Donegal town. Take the road to Glencolumbkille and stop in **Mount Charles** (pronounced Charless) at the Tweed Shop. Owen Gillespie and his sister Mary, proprietors of the shop, are both knowledgeable about tweed and tailoring. Their parents owned the shop before them. Spend some time here looking through the selection of herringbone, houndstooth, and Harris tweeds. If you buy any tweed during your visit, be sure it is labeled "Genuine Donegal Hand-Woven Tweed. Pure New Wool."

The price and quality of tweed fluctuates throughout Ireland—but it usually runs about I£15 ($26) per 60-inch-wide yard. A man's suit takes about 4 yards; a jacket 2 1/2.

The toughest pilgrimage

In the bare blue hills of County Donegal, the Lough Deng pilgrimage is a trip to purgatory. Every year, from June 1 through Aug. 15, pilgrims spend three days on Station Island, site of St. Patrick's Purgatory, depriving themselves of food, sleep, and all physical comforts. It costs a mere I£13 ($23) for the boat trip and all-inclusive stay, but make sure you know what you're letting yourself in for. The penitential exercises include dragging your bare feet over the jagged remains of monastic cells. It is an excruciating experience.

Ireland's most beautiful ruin

In the northern midlands of Ireland, south of Athlone in County Offaly, is the haunting ruin of **Clonmacnoise**, a flourishing monastic settlement more than 1,000 years ago. Still here are ruins of an abbey founded in A.D. 541 by St. Kieran, the Seven Churches of Clonmacnoise, a castle, a bishop's palace, and two round towers where townspeople watched for invading Vikings in search of Celtic gold. Celtic crosses from the time when Ireland was the Island of Saints and Scholars also stand here still.

The boggiest railway

If you fancy bumping around the boglands, ride the rails of the Clonmacnoise & West Offaly Line. Operated by Bord na Mona, the Irish Peat Board, the train runs from March through October across the **Blackwater Bog.** Special stops are made so you can watch the turf being cut and "saved." The fare is I£2.50 ($4.80). For more information, contact **Bog Railway**, *Shannonbridge, County Offaly; tel. (353-905)74114.*

The best riverboat cruising

Winding past Clonmacnoise and cutting through the bogs like a broad silver ribbon is the magnificent **River Shannon**. It's the perfect place for fishing, bird-watching, or simply lazing on a summer afternoon. The river is navigable for 120 of its 220 miles to the sea, and cruising is a popular activity. The Emerald Star Line has bases at Portumna and Carrick-on-Shannon, where you can pick up a cruise for a week or longer; prices start at I£300 ($570) per week for a four-berth craft. For reservations, contact **Emerald Star**, *47 Dawson St., Dublin 2; tel. (353-1)679-8166.*

The holiest mountain

Ireland's holiest mountain is **Croagh Patrick** in County Mayo. More than 2,500 feet high, it was from here that St. Patrick reputedly banished all snakes from the island. Each Garland Sunday, the last Sunday in July, 60,000 pilgrims clamber to the summit.

The stoniest wilderness

Stark, strange, and almost brutal to the eye, dotted with megalithic tombs and disappearing loughs, County Clare's **Burren** region seems an unlikely place for a flower show. The landscape is lunar: a vast gray sea of rock stretching for mile upon mile. But look closer—hidden in limestone crevices are orchids, vivid blue gentians, and a profusion of other rare wild flowers. It's a real botanists' paradise.

The strangest festival

If you're looking for romance, head for **Lisdoonvarna** on the southern edge of the Burren, where men are men and women are scarce. Each September, this small spa town hosts a matchmaking festival that boosts the population from 700 to 7,000. And although the matchmaking business isn't as serious as in days gone by, the ballrooms of romance are still filled with dancers until dawn.

Ireland's best accommodation: the castle hotel

The best places to stay in Ireland are the country's castle hotels. Scores of these delightful, historic places dot the countryside.

The finest in all Ireland is **Ashford Castle**, *Cong, County Mayo; tel. (353-92)46003.* President Reagan, among other dignitaries, has stayed here. Situated on the shores of the Lough Corrib, it resembles a huge movie set.

A castle was built on this site as early as 1228. In the 16th century, the troops of Queen Elizabeth battled in the area and stormed through the castle, which later became an English fortress. In the 18th century, a French château was incorporated into the old complex. Nearby are several ancient abbeys, churches, and points of archeological interest. Note the 20-foot fireplace and the fine woodwork.

The castle became a hotel in 1939. A double room is I£52.50 ($89), not including breakfast.

Castle Matrix, *Rathkeale, near Limerick; tel. (353-69)64284,* has seen more than 500 years of history. In 1487, James Fitz-Thomas, the ninth Earl of Desmond, was murdered in the tower. In 1580, Queen Elizabeth sent Sir Walter Raleigh to subdue the outlaw Desmonds. After Raleigh occupied the castle, the English writer Edmund Spenser lived there. In 1641, during the Irish rebellion, the castle was seized by the Irish, but Cromwell's forces soon took it back. In 1709, it was inhabited by German Protestant refugees. In 1756, John Wesley established a Methodist community in it.

The castle fell to ruin over the years but was restored in 1970 by Col. Sean O'Driscoll, an Irish-American architect who converted it into a hotel. Suites have fireplaces and are furnished with Elizabethan and Jacobean antiques. The restaurant serves medieval banquets, and, in the summer, arts and crafts courses are held here. (The cold castle is closed during the winter.) A double room is I£40 ($68), including a "huge fry-up breakfast."

Finally, County Clare's **Gregan's Castle Hotel,** *Ballyvaughan, Clare; tel. (353-65)77005,* is another splendid castle hotel. Each room is beautifully decorated, and the views are unbeatable. A double room starts at I£44 ($74) a night.

The best place to rent a car

You can rent a car at **Shannon Airport** for as little as £20 ($34) per day, including value-added tax (for a two-door Corsa). You receive a discount if you rent for more than 15 days. The fee does not include insurance, which you can waive by making a deposit of approximately I£500 ($860) with the rental company. (A credit card will do.) The deposit is reimbursed after you return the car. The fee does include a radio, a roof rack if you ask for one, and unlimited mileage (but not gas). By renting a car, you automatically become a member of the Irish Automobile Association. You must be over 23 to rent a car in Ireland.

The Best of the Isle of Man

The politically independent **Isle of Man**, located halfway between Ireland and England and only 20 miles south of Scotland, is one of Europe's hidden bests. It is one of the best banking havens in the world. Europe's best ice cream is created here. Manx kippers are world-famous, and Man has been noted by the World Health Organization for its high-quality lamb and beef. The fishing here is terrific. And some of Britain's prettiest walking trails flank the isle's shores.

The Isle of Man, covering a mere 343 square miles, is probably the least-known country in Europe. Still a member of the British Commonwealth, the Isle of Man has been ruled by Ireland, Wales, Norway, Scotland, and England. Though it is part of the British Isles, it is not part of the United Kingdom. The island has its own representative assembly and courts.

The world's oldest legislature

The **Tynwald**, as the Manx legislature is called, is more than a thousand years old and has the longest continuous history of any legislature in the world. *Tynwald* derives from the Norse word *tingvollr*, meaning assembly field.

The **Royal Chapel of St. John the Baptist,** in the town of St. John's, is on the field where the open-air Tynwald Ceremony of the Norsemen began 1,000 years ago. Each year on July 5 (or the Monday after, if the fifth falls on a weekend), the Tynwald assembles at the chapel to sign new laws. Any Manx citizen may present a petition on this occasion.

Man's strangest sight

The Isle of Man's strangest monument in stone is a modern tower in **Corrin's Folly** overlooking Peel Bay. It was built by a man who wanted to be on his feet when Judgment Day arrived. He left instructions to have his glass-lidded coffin stood on its end in front of the tower window. The rest of the family was buried below.

Man's best fishing

Sports fishermen adore the Isle of Man because of its variety of fishing: surf casting, river fishing, and deep-sea fishing.

Sea fishermen can cast their lines for skate, mackerel, and tope from spring through late summer; pollack (the local name is *calig*), conger, dogfish, plaice (a flat fish that is a bottom eater), coalfish, bass, and mullet from June through October; and whiting, brill, monkfish, and flounder in the fall.

The best place for surf casting is the **Point of Ayre**, where you can fish at any tide. The best time, however, is low tide.

Sea-angling boat services are available from Douglas. Freshwater fishing in the Isle of Man is for salmon, sea trout, brown trout, and rainbow trout, primarily in the rivers that flow through the Manx national glens. The main run of salmon and sea trout starts in late summer.

For information on fishing and licenses, contact the offices of the **Isle of Man Board of Agriculture and Fisheries**, *Government Offices, Douglas; tel. (44-624)626262.*

Man's best walking trails

The best walking path is the **Millennium Way**, established in 1979 to commemorate the millennium of the Tynwald. It follows the Regia Via, or Royal Way, one of the earliest recorded highways. In medieval times, it was used by the king and his attendants traveling to the Tynwald from Ramsey. Clearly marked, the Millenium Way is approximately 21 miles long and can be walked by an experienced hiker in a full day.

The Way starts approximately one mile from Ramsey Town Square on the main road to Kirk Michael at the foot of Sky Hill. It ends in Castletown at Castle Rushen, the site of the fortification built by the Norsemen to guard the south of the island.

The world's largest waterwheel

Laxey has the largest waterwheel in the world, with a diameter of 72 feet, 6 inches; a circumference of 217 feet; and a top speed of 2 revolutions per minute. Built in 1854, it was christened the Lady Isabella after the wife of the lieutenant governor. Originally, it was used to pump water out of the lead mines.

Exclusive cats

Man is the only place in the world where you can find the tailless Manx cat. Stop in at the **Manx Cattery**, *Nobles Park, Douglas,* to have your name put on the waiting list for the genuine item. (If you don't actually want a cat, you can just take a look.)

The world's best ice cream

Manx ice cream is the best in the world. This prize-winning concoction is the creamiest and richest we've ever tasted. Visit the **Manx Ice Factory**, *Peel Road, Douglas.*

The isle's best coffee shop and restaurant

The best place for a light meal on the Isle of Man is **Harris's**, *Sefton Hotel; tel. (44-624)626011.* This cocktail bar and coffee shop is both elegant and extremely comfortable. It offers a good menu selection, especially for afternoon tea.

The best restaurant on the Isle of Man is **Boncompte's**, located in the Admiral House Hotel, *tel. (44-624)629551.* The Continental cuisine is excellent, and the atmosphere is sophisticated.

The best ways to get around

The ferry crossing from Heysham, England, to Douglas, the island's port of entry, takes four hours. More expediently, you can take a Manx Airways flight; they depart regularly from London and Dublin. Whether traveling by ferry or plane, do not purchase your tickets in advance. Wait to buy them at a BritRail ticket office; you will save a substantial amount.

Isle of Man Steam Packet Seaways, *tel. (44-524)853802,* runs a ferry from Heysham, England, to Douglas, Isle of Man. The ferry departs daily during the week and infrequently on weekends. It also runs from Liverpool every other day. One-way tickets cost £18 to £27 ($19 to $51) for adults, £45 to £78 ($84 to $146) for cars (depending on the size), and £15 to £25 ($28 to $47) for motorcycles.

Manx Airlines, *tel. (44-71)493-0803* in London, *tel. (353-1)800-626627* in Dublin, or *tel. (44-624)824313* in the Isle of Man, offers flights daily. The cost from London is £130 ($244) round trip. The round-trip cost from Dublin is £105 ($197).

For details on renting a car, contact Cleveland Self-Hire, *1 Albany Road, Douglas; tel. (44-624)628833*. A Nissan Micra is £12 ($23) a day, not including tax and gas.

Hotels with the most charm

Man's most charming hotel is the Admiral House Hotel, *Loch Promenade, Douglas; tel. (44-624)629551*. Not ostentatious, elegant, or expensive, the Admiral House has exceptional furnishings and decor, as well as a warm and inviting library. Request a room facing the promenade and the sea. A double room is £75 ($140) a night.

The Grand Island Hotel is situated along the coast of Ramsey. It offers a health spa and an 18-hole golf course. A double room, including breakfast, costs £90 ($170).

The Palace Hotel, *Central Promenade, Douglas; tel. (44-624)74521*, offers double rooms from £70 to £85 ($131 to $160), not including breakfast.

The Grosvenor Hotel, *The Promenade, Port Erin; tel. (44-624)834124*, offers demi-pension from £19 ($36) per person. This is one of the best hotels in the Isle of Man for the money.

Two other good options are the Ascot, *Empire Terrace, Douglas; tel. (44-624)675081*, and the Mannin, *Broadway, Douglas; tel. (44-624)675335*. Both are economical, offering bed and breakfast for £27 ($50) per person.

For more information on hotels, contact the Isle of Man Tourist Board, *13 Victoria St., Douglas; tel. (44-624)674323*, or the British Tourist Authority, *(212)581-4700* in New York or *(416)925-6326* in Toronto.

The Best of Italy

For all those circumstances that render that classical country illustrious, the seat of great men—the theatre of the most distinguished actions—the exclusive field in which the elegant and agreeable arts have loved to range—what country can be compared to Italy?
—*Arthur Young, 1792*

The Italians live alongside the world's greatest art the way the rest of the world lives next door to tacky neon signs and billboards. Where else but Italy would an insignificant-looking neighborhood church contain paintings by Botticelli? What city but Rome would go about its business amid the ruins of once-great buildings built by ancestors who ruled the then-known world? What people except Italians can be so surrounded by the greatest vestiges of Western civilization—yet so unpretentious?

Rome: the world's most celebrated city

Rome has been the world's most celebrated city for more than two millennia. Before Christ was born, Romans watched gladiators fight lions in the Coliseum. For 1,500 years, Rome has been the center of Christianity. Five centuries ago, Michelangelo painted the Sistine Chapel here. Today, Rome is one of the biggest tourist attractions in the world.

The five most important sights

The **Coliseum** is the greatest architectural remnant of ancient Rome. Shaped like an oval bowl, it was built by Titus and used for monthlong spectacles, including battles between animals and gladiators. Christians were fed to the lions here, according to legend. The structure is well-preserved. Today it is inhabited by hundreds of cats, whose eyes glow from dark archways.

The **Roman Forum** was the chief public square and a center of government in ancient Rome. Only a few ruins remain. With a little imagination, you can look at the columns of the **Temple of the Vestal Virgins** and see a full-fledged Roman temple. Vestal Virgins once lived in this elaborate structure and kept the fire in the center of the temple lit around the clock. If they lost their virginity, these maidens were buried alive.

The Forum also has the remains of the **Curia**, where the Roman senators met, and the **Temple of Julius Caesar.** The **Arch of Titus**, decorated with a seven-branched candelabrum, marks the defeat of the Jews and the destruction of their temple in

Jerusalem. The white stone pillars and arches are surrounded by a green lawn and tall trees with inviting benches beneath them. The main entrance to the forum is on via dei Fori Imperiali.

The **Pantheon**, *Piazza della Rotonda*, a heavy circular structure fronted by a porch with 16 Corinthian columns and topped with a cupola, is the architectural and civic symbol of the city. Marcus Agrippa commissioned it in 27 B.C. as a temple to the gods. The first Christian emperors tried to close the pagan structure, but failed. Later, the popes recognized its popularity and made it into a church in A.D. 606. The Pantheon also has been used as a fish market and a fortress. Raphael and the first two kings of Italy chose to be buried here.

The **Piazza di Spagna** (Spanish Steps) is a square dominated by a pair of curved steps filled with vendors, tourists, artists, street musicians, and Romans on their lunch hours. The ornate, flower-bedecked steps lead from a street filled with high-fashion boutiques to a peaceful residential neighborhood of grand houses. Stendhal, Liszt, Balzac, Wagner, Joyce, Keats, and Shelley all lived on this square. Young people from around the world linger on the steps looking for romance, drugs, and the "real" Rome. Watch out for pickpockets!

To ensure your return to Rome, throw a coin in the 18th-century **Trevi Fountain**, at the base of the steps off the via del Corso on Piazza di Trevi. Money from the Trevi is collected by the city and used to improve tourist attractions. On the average, more than 500,000 lire ($425) is collected from the fountain each week (more in summer months).

The world's second-smallest country

Vatican City, the world's second-smallest country, occupies 1 square mile within the city of Rome. It is the headquarters of the Roman Catholic Church and has its own post office and postage stamps, printing press and newspaper, currency, railway, and radio station. It is governed by the pope and protected by Swiss Guards, whose colorful blue and gold uniforms were designed by Michelangelo.

The Vatican museums have the most impressive art collections in the world. The **Sistine Chapel** is one of the great marvels of the Renaissance. The frescoed ceiling was painted by Michelangelo and has recently been restored. Some art critics view the cleaning as a desecration; others applaud. Judge for yourself. A pedestrian walkway leads through the many museums to the Sistine Chapel, which covers an area of more than 40,000 square yards. En route, keep an eye out for the four rooms painted by Raphael and his assistants in the 16th century, as well as the little Chapel of Nicholas V, with frescoes by Fra Angelico.

St. Peter's Basilica in the Vatican reveals both the grandeur of the Papacy and the impact of Catholicism. When 300,000 people gather to hear the pope's blessing, you understand his power. The basilica was built by Constantine in A.D. 350 on the site where St. Peter was martyred and then buried. Parts of the original building still exist, underground in the crypt. A cupola designed by Michelangelo crowns the church. Be sure to dress modestly when you visit St. Peter's—shorts are forbidden, and women may not wear dresses without sleeves or with hems above the knee. Many travelers are barred from St. Peter's because of improper clothing.

If you would like a papal audience or to attend a special ceremony in St. Peter's, apply in writing to **Prefettura della Casa Pontifica**, *00120 Citta del Vaticano*. When the pope is in Rome, public audiences are held each Wednesday at 11 a.m.

On the edge of the Vatican is an ancient fortress, **Castel Sant' Angelo**, built in A.D. 135 as a mausoleum for the Emperor Hadrian. The sixth-century chapel on top of the mausoleum was built to commemorate an angel who appeared to announce the end of the plague. Corner towers and bastions were added in the 15th and 16th centuries. Pope Clement VII lived in the castle in 1527. The fortress is connected to the Vatican by a long passage.

The best place to dine when visiting St. Peter's

A popular place to dine in the area is **Pierdonati**, *via della Conciliazione 39*. It offers a view of the basilica and has tables set up outdoors when the weather permits. The fettuccine *ai funghi porcini* is excellent.

Rome's most venerated treasure

The **Santo Bambino**, a 2-foot figure carved centuries ago from an olive tree from Gethsemane and then baptized in the Jordan River, is venerated by the Italians for its supposed healing powers. Housed in the chapel of the Santissimo Bambino in the sixth-century **Church of Santa Maria d'Aracoeli**, on the highest point of the Capitoline Hill, the Santo Bambino is brought out four times a year to make sickbed calls. During such excursions, the figure is accompanied by Franciscan monks and an armed escort and sealed behind a bulletproof glass casing. It is said that during a speech given by Mussolini, a Santo Bambino procession passed, and the dictator was left speaking to the backs of a kneeling crowd.

Rome's best markets

Sunday morning, visit the **Porta Portese** flea market. This mile-long sprawl of booths, tables, and ground-cloth displays has everything from glassware and Etruscan relics to Arab carpets. You'll see every manner of Roman here: Gypsy, beggar, well-dressed shopper, street musician, magician, pickpocket. In one section, Arabs sell carpets and blankets. In another, Africans sell wooden sculptures and medicinal cures. Russian Jews have their own section, where they sell linen, caviar, Havana cigars, samovars, and balalaikas.

Campo dei Fiori, a flower market in the middle of the medieval quarter, is a welcome change after days of wandering among ancient monuments and works of art. Every morning, the area is filled with sweet-smelling flower stalls. This is Rome's oldest open market.

Rome's best park

In the northern section of Rome is the city's most remarkable park—**Villa Borghese**. The gardens around the former estate of Cardinal Scipione Borghese were designed in the 17th century. Rome's zoo is here, as well as two museums housed in the cardinal's palace. The main entrance is at Piazzale Flaminio, just outside the Porta del Popolo. You also can get here by walking up the Spanish Steps and following via Trinita dei Monti to the left until you can see all seven hills of Rome.

The most macabre sight

The mass of skulls in the church of **Santa Maria della Concezione dei Capuccini**, *via Veneto 27*, is the most macabre sight in Rome. Monks at this church maintain a crypt that contains more than 4,000 skulls and bones of past Capuchin monks. Two of the five chapels contain floors of earth brought from Palestine. On Nov. 2 (All Soul's Day), the crypt is brightly lit, making it even more gruesome.

Rome's oldest road

The **Appian Way** (via Appia Antica), a 2,300-year-old road paved by the Romans, still exists in places in and around Rome. In 71 B.C., the gladiator Spartacus and the slaves who rebelled against Rome were strung up side by side along this 132-mile route between Rome and Capua. The 6,000 rebels were left to rot.

The **Baths of Caracalla** (Terme di Caracalla) are near the beginning of the Appian Way. Built in the third century, only the walls of the baths remain on this site near the Piazzale Numa Pompilio.

The **Catacombs of St. Calixtus**, *via Appia Antica 110*, are the most famous sight along the route. These burial tunnels were used by the early Christians as hiding places. St. Cecilia, St. Eusebius, and many martyred popes are buried here. Also along the road is the Domine Quo Vadis chapel, about half a mile beyond Porta San Sebastiano. It was built in the ninth century on the site where St. Peter, fleeing Nero, had a vision of Christ telling him not to abandon the Christians. Peter then returned to Rome to face his martyrdom.

Rome's best-kept travel secret: the Aventine

One of Rome's fabled seven hills, the Aventine is rarely traveled by tourists. Mons Aventinus, as it was known in ancient times, was developed by Caesar's contemporaries into a dignified district of majestic temples, fashionable homes, and plush gardens. The rich vegetation and serene setting that attracted the Romans both remain, untouched by the pollution and crowding of the rest of the city. The Aventine's main attraction, however, is its striking churches.

Near the temple to Diana, seven centuries-old churches remain. The most ancient, **Santa Prisca**, was the residence of a Jewish couple, Prisca and Aquila, who allowed Saint Paul and others to worship in their home after their own conversion to Catholicism. The earliest Christians also worshiped at another fourth-century residence near by, now **Santa Sabina**. Along the same street is **Sant'Alessio**, named for the son of a prominent Roman senator who fled the city to avoid an arranged marriage. He returned two decades later, a beggar, to die beneath the front stairwell of his parents' home.

West of Sant' Alessio, past the charming square designed by Piranesi, Piazza de Cavalieri di Malta, is the walled-in, autonomous Knights of Malta, which contains the **Santa Maria del Prioratu**. Special permission is required to visit this church; contact the **Cavalieri di Malta**, *Piazza de CdM, 00153 Rome; tel. (39-6)577-9193 or tel. (39-6)574-3568*. Also worth seeing are the elegant **Sant'Anselmo**, the medieval **San Sabo**, and the sixth-century **Santa Balbina**, which overlooks the Baths of Caracalla.

The best places to stay on the Aventine are three Old World hotels near Santa Sabina: **Hotel Villa San Pio**, *via S. Anselmo 19; tel. (39-6)574-5232*; **Hotel Sant'Anselmo**, *Piazza S. Anselmo 2; tel.(39-6)574-3547*; and **Hotel Aventino**, *via S. Domenico 10; tel. (39-6)578-3214*. Prices range from 134,000 lire ($115) to 175,000 lire ($142), including breakfast.

La Villetta, *Piram viale, Cestia 53, tel. (39-6)574-2004*, is owned and operated by Ada Mercuri Olivetti and her son Aldo. Mamma Olivetti once won first place in a competition among more than 4,000 Roman cooks for her *spaghetti all'Amatriciana*. The prices are moderate.

Rome's six other bests

San Pietro in Vincoli (St. Peter in Chains), *Piazza di San Pietro in Vincoli*, houses Michelangelo's statue of Moses. The church was built in the fifth century to hold the chains that bound St. Peter.

The **Prehistoric and Ethnographic Museum of Rome**, *1 viale Lincoln*, located on the grounds of the Esposizione Universale di Roma (known as the E.U.R.), has some of the finest remains of ancient civilization in existence today. Highlights of the museum include a collection from the Italian school in Crete, statues of priests and warriors from Sardinia, objects found in cemeteries of Etruria, and tombs dating back to 10 B.C. The museum is closed on Mondays.

Carcere Mamertino, *via San Pietro, Cacere, off via dei Fori Imperiali*, today a chapel consecrated to St. Peter, was once a fearsome prison where St. Peter was imprisoned by Nero. The saint baptized his fellow prisoners using water from a spring that appeared miraculously. The dungeons below may be the oldest structures in Rome.

The villa and gardens of Mussolini (the fascist dictator of Italy from 1922 to 1943), called the **Villa Torlonia**, *via Nomentana*, are now a public park, open from dawn to dusk every day. Many of the buildings on the estate date back to the 17th century. The most outstanding are the twin obelisks carved of red granite. The estate includes a 400-seat theater, two simulated ancient Roman temples, a Moorish hothouse, and a Swiss-style châlet.

Also visit the **Casina delle Civette**, once the playhouse of Giovanni Torlonia Jr., a notorious playboy who brought his many girlfriends into the house via secret passages. The house is decorated with owls. The Italian word for owl, *civette*, also means coquette.

The **Keats-Shelley Memorial House**, *Piazza di Spagna 26*, is overlooked by most visitors to the Spanish Steps. It is identified only by a small brass plaque. Keats died here in 1821, when he was 25. Shelley spent much time here visiting his fellow poet. Fragments of Shelley's bones and some of his letters to Keats are on display. Keats' drawing of the Grecian urn that inspired his most famous poem, "Ode on a Grecian Urn," can be seen.

The oldest café in Rome

Antico Caffè Greco, *via Condotti 86*, is one of the oldest cafés in the world. Founded on July 24, 1760, it has been frequented by artists, celebrities, and politicians, including composer Hector Berlioz, Mark Twain (in fact, a statue of Twain decorates the café), Hans Christian Andersen, James Fenimore Cooper, Sir Walter Scott, Henry James, Lord Alfred Tennyson, Richard Wagner, Benjamin Franklin, Henrik Ibsen, Goethe, Schopenhauer, Orson Welles, Federico Fellini, Stalin, and Adolf Hitler. The café was declared a national monument by the Italian government in 1953. Homemade ice cream is served, as well as the best cappuccino in Rome.

Rome's most beautiful bridge

Tiber Island, in the middle of the Tiber River, is connected to the rest of Rome by the **Fabricio Bridge**, known to Romans as the Bridge of Four Heads. A pillar in the middle of the bridge is carved with four faces representing the four builders of the structure, beheaded for not finishing it by the date promised. Tiber Island has been occupied since 292 B.C., when a temple was built in honor of Aesculapius, the Greek god of health.

The most remarkable fountain

The **Fountain of Rivers**, completed in 1651 by Gian Lorenzo Bernini, is the most beautiful fountain in the city. Located in the heart of Rome's picturesque Piazza Navona, it is a mass of rockwork and grottos.

Bernini and Borromini competed for the honor of designing the facade of the Church of Sant' Agnese in Agone on the west side of Piazza Navona. The project was awarded to Borromini. When Bernini was later asked to design the piazza's main fountain, he got even. He designed four colossal figures for the fountain's four corners (representing the Danube, Ganges, Nile, and Plate rivers) and placed them so that none would look upon the facade of Sant' Agnese in Agone. The Nile blocks the view of the church with its hand.

Bests beneath Rome

Santissimi Giovanni e Paolo is a little medieval church built over ancient Roman homes on Celio hill, near the Coliseum. A door in the nave leads to a stairway that descends to the old, brick buildings. Patches of mosaic line the cool walls. Saints John and Paul hid from the Romans here. To get to Santissima Giovanni e Paolo, follow Salita di S. Gregorio from Piazza di Porta Capena until the name of the road changes to Clivo di Sauro.

St. Peter's Basilica is also built above a vault of ancient history—in fact, the basilica stands directly over the tomb of St. Peter himself. You can explore the Roman burial ground here. The Pre-Christian tombs are well-preserved, and on one wall is an elaborate tomb with the inscription "Peter is within." You can visit the necropolis only with special permission, which can be obtained from the **Reverend Fabbrica de San Pietro**, *Ufficio*

Scavi, 00120 Citta del Vaticano. Send him your name and your address and telephone number in Rome.

The best Roman shopping

Luxury shops fill the Piazza di Spagna and line the adjoining streets (via del Babuino, via Vittoria, via della Croce, via Condotti, via Borgognona, via Frattina, and via della Vite). Less expensive shops can be found along via del Corso.

Leather goods, gloves, shoes, purses, wallets, belts, and luggage displayed in windows along via Condotti draw credit cards from the pockets of passers-by like magnets. The jewelry displays at Bulgari are among the most sensational in the world.

Few outsiders know about Rome's department stores. Romans of all social levels shop at the **Coin**, *Piazzale Appio, 7; tel. (39-6)75-73-241,* for high fashion at low prices. The Coin employs its own designers and features stylish collections.

Men should shop at **JCA**, *via Cola di Rienzo 183,* a boutique offering cotton shirts at good prices. **Enzo Ceci**, *via della Vite 52,* specializes in Italian brands of men's clothing and offers classic suits, sport shirts, and sweaters with original designs.

Women can buy hand-painted fabrics made into skirts and blouses at **Convertite 81**, *via delle Convertite 22.* Silk, cotton, and wool sweaters are sold at **Vittoria 3A**, *via Vittoria 3,* where the prices are good.

Leather, especially, is a good buy in Rome. **Boris-Pelletterie**, *Corso Rinascimento 43-45, Piazza Navona,* has purses, wallets, briefcases, and men's bags.

You can have a suitcase or a purse handmade to order in Rome—in three weeks!—at **Di Ceglie**, *via S. Claudio 67.*

The best places to buy red lingerie

Every December, Romans buy new red lingerie to wear when they usher in the New Year. As a result, the city is home to many shops that specialize in red underwear. For the finest lingerie in Rome (red and otherwise), visit the via Frattina area. Try **Vanita**, *via Frattina 70,* which has beautiful lace slips, hand-embroidered silk items, and a good selection of beachwear. More lacy, tantalizing creations can be found at **Tusseda**, *via Frattina 25.* Also visit the elegant shop **Tomassini**, *via Sistina 119,* run by Luisa Romagnoli. Romagnoli's silk slips are works of art. **Gentry**, *via Frattina 100,* sells designers' mens' lines, including Valentino and Cardin.

The world's most beautiful crèches

During the Christmas season, Rome is decorated with crèches rather than lights and Santas. The three most beautiful are on the Spanish Steps, in the Piazza Navona, and in St. Peter's Square.

The oldest Roman crèche, in the **Church of S. Maria Maggiore**, contains figures crafted by Arnolfo di Cambio, the most celebrated architect of the late 13th and early 14th centuries.

However, the crèche most beloved by Romans is at **S. Maria d'Aracoeli**, at the top of 122 stairs on the Capitoline Hill. It features the Santo Bambino. Every afternoon from Christmas Day to Epiphany (Jan. 6), children recite poems in front of the crèche.

Cosma e Damiano, *via dei Fori Imperiali,* houses an 18th-century Neapolitan masterpiece—the only crèche on display year-round.

The best midnight Mass

The most beautiful Christmas midnight Mass in the world is at **St. Peter's Basilica**. The pope celebrates the Mass with the assistance of dozens of cardinals. The Choir of the Sistine Chapel sings, and the Vatican ushers, known as San Pietrini, turn on hundreds of lights. You can write in advance for tickets to Christmas midnight Mass. Contact the **Prefettura della Casa Pontifica**, *Città del Vaticano, 00120.*

Rome's best hotel

The **Hassler**, *Piazza Trinità dei Monti 6, 00187 Rome, Italy; tel. (39-6)679-2651*, which crowns the Spanish Steps, has the best view and the best service. The rooms on the fifth floor have little balconies with tables and chairs and views of the Spanish Steps. If you prefer quiet (the Steps can be noisy), the most peaceful rooms are in the back, overlooking the courtyard.

The Hassler has been in existence since 1855. The hotel feels like a grand old house or a private club. Its lobby is divided into cozy sitting areas. New rooms are painted cheery pastels; old rooms are decorated with mirrors, dark-wood furniture, and leather-covered paneling. Some of the bathrooms are painted with murals of ancient Roman baths. They all have scales, hair dryers, and heated towel racks.

The Hassler's guest book contains the signatures of Liza Minnelli, Charlie Chaplin, Somerset Maugham, and presidents Eisenhower, Truman, and Kennedy. Doubles are 560,000 lire to 750,000 lire ($475 to $635) per night. To make reservations in the United States, contact the **Leading Hotels of the World**, *(800)223-6800* or *(212)838-3110*.

Top contenders for second-best hotel

Le Grand Hotel, *via Vittorio Emanuele Orlando 3, 00185 Rome; tel. (39-6)4709*, truly is a grand hotel. Romans prefer this hotel built above ancient Roman baths. A double room is 450,000 lire ($380).

Hotel Locarno, *via della Penna 22; tel. (39-6)361-0841*, is popular with Italian artists, writers, and actors, but it has not been discovered by tourists. Intimate and inexpensive, it is near the Piazza del Popolo. Built in the 1920s, the Locarno has art nouveau touches. Although it was recently renovated, it doesn't have modern (and intrusive) amenities, such as televisions. A double room is 193,000 lire ($163), including breakfast.

Hotel Lord Byron, *via G. de Notaris 5; tel. (39-6)360-9541*, in the Parioli neighborhood, is one of the most elegant and discreet hotels in Rome. Set in a garden on a hill at the end of a one-way street near the Borghese Gardens, it is luxurious. Rooms have fine linen, refrigerators filled with champagne, and sumptuous marble bathtubs. The hotel restaurant, Le Jardin, is also outstanding. A double room is 380,000 lire ($322) a night, including breakfast.

Hotel Raphael, *Largo Febo 2; tel. (39-6)650-881*, just off the Piazza Navona, hosts Prime Minister Bettino Craxi when he is in Rome. A double room is 385,000 lire ($326), including breakfast.

The best hotel bargains

Scalinata di Spagna, *Piazza Trinita dei Monti 17; tel. (39-6)679-30-06* or *(39-6)679-95-82*, is a cozy place near the Spanish Steps. One of the smallest hotels in Rome, it has 14 rooms on two floors—so make reservations in advance. The hotel has a long terrace with a vista of Rome. Rooms are simply furnished and have good views. A double room is 213,000 lire ($180), including breakfast.

Suisse, *via Gregoriana 54; tel. (39-6)678-3649*, is a comfortable hotel near the Spanish Steps. There is a breakfast room upstairs, and the bedrooms are small but attractive. A double room is 128,000 lire ($108).

Ausonia, *Piazza di Spagna 35; tel. (39-6)679-5745*, is located right on the piazza, and rooms face either the inner courtyard or the square itself. A double room is 110,000 lire ($93).

Portoghesi, *via dei Portoghesi 1; tel. (39-6)686-4231*, is a quiet hotel in Old Rome. The service is good, and the rooms are cozy. A double room starts at 150,000 lire ($127).

Gourmet bests

Alberto Ciarla, *Piazza San Cosimato 40; tel. (39-6)581-8668*, in the heart of the

Trastevere (a colorful working-class neighborhood), is the place for seafood. Try the seafood spaghetti or the seasoned pasta with vegetables. The Tunia wine from Goriza is refreshing. Dinners are about 100,000 lire ($84) per person.

Andrea, *via Sardegna 28; tel. (39-6)48-21-891,* is the best place to go for Italian regional cooking. Instead of ordering from the menu, which is designed for tourists, ask the advice of the owner, Aldo, who will suggest unusual, mouth-watering dishes, such as spaghetti with white truffles. Dinners are 50,000 to 80,000 lire ($42 to $67) per person.

A tiny restaurant called **Cicilardone**, *via Merulana 77; tel. (39-6)73-38-06,* serves enormous dinners for about 50,000 lire ($42). The pasta with broccoli and the vermicelli with cheese and pepper are especially delicious.

Il Drappo, *Vicolo del Malpasso 9; tel. (39-6)68-77-65,* serves creative variations of traditional Sardinian dishes. Near the via Giula, Il Drappo is sophisticated. Try the octopus with wine or the roast breast of veal. For dessert, order the *sedaba*, a cheese fritter topped with honey.

Ristorante da Sabatini, *Piazza S. Maria in Trastevere, 14; tel. (39-6)582-026,* is the homiest restaurant we've come across. This attractive restaurant near the 17th-century Church of San Ignazio has tables in the square. No menu is offered. Instead, a pleasantly round and cheerful *padrona* dishes out a great pot of pasta and oversees the waiters. The shrimp scampi, the specialty of the house, is fresh and delicious accompanied by a large plate of crisp, fresh green salad. The grand finale is a large bottle of Sambuca served with a glass containing coffee beans. You modify the sweetness of the liqueur by crushing a coffee bean between your teeth and sipping the Sambuca through the cracked bean.

Tre Scalini Rossana e Matteo, *via Santi Quattro 30; tel. (39-6)73-26-95,* is an inconspicuous but well-frequented restaurant on a deserted street near the Coliseum. Politicians, bankers, and diplomats are drawn here by the good food and the privacy. Every day a single prix-fixe meal is served for 35,000 lire ($30). Reservations are required.

Night life at its most Roman

In general, Rome's night life is outdoors, centered around three piazzas. **Piazza di Santa Maria** in Trastevere (Rome's Greenwich Village) is filled with street musicians at all hours of the night. **Piazza Navona**, the most beautiful, stretches between three fountains that are surrounded by vendors. The most fashionable crowd, dressed in leather miniskirts and traveling on shiny motorbikes, appears at the cafés in **Piazza del Pantheon**.

The jet set goes to **Cala Regina**, *via L. Luciani, 52; tel. (39-6)322-13-60,* home to a disco and bar, as well as an excellent restaurant.

The most elegant bar in Rome is the outdoor bar of the **Hassler Hotel**, *Piazza Trinità dei Monti 6; tel. (39-6)78-2651.* This enchanted place, pushed against the verdant bluff of the Villa Medici garden, is a perfect place for starting or finishing an evening in Rome. The elegant red marble bar is tended by an amiable and knowledgeable Roman.

Italy's most prestigious wine

Just a short drive from Rome is a 14-century castle overlooking the fertile valleys of Ombrone, Orcia, and Asso. Called **Montalcino**, it is surrounded by a medieval stone wall that boasts the remains of 19 defense towers. But more than medieval artifacts, Montalcino is home to the most prestigious of all Italian wines, the legendary **Brunello di Montalcino.**

Brunello itself is a little more than a century old. But it is rooted in centuries of wine-making tradition. It is made only from Brunello, the local clone of Tuscany's predominant grape, the Sangiovese. It is deep ruby in color and redolent with fruit, a superb accompaniment to roast meats, especially wild game like venison and Canadian goose. It attracts serious wine lovers from around the world.

The best day-trips from Rome

Fifteen miles southeast of Rome are sprawled the ruins of **Hadrian's Villa**. The vast villa covers over 100 acres and dates from A.D. 130. This was Hadrian's retreat from politics. The Praetorian Guard (ancient Rome's version of the Secret Service) insisted that the estate be encircled by a wall. Within these walls, Hadrian recreated the most splendid buildings from his travels. The *piéce de résistance* is a replica of the Egyptian sanctuary of Canopus, a pool that symbolized the canal linking the Temple of Serapis with the Nile. The construction of the theaters, baths, gyms, temples, palaces, and guesthouses, all fashioned after Hadrian's memories, took architects, masons, plumbers, landscapers, and slaves more than 10 years to complete.

A 10-minute car ride from Hadrian's Villa brings you to the rolling hills of Tivoli, or ancient Tibur. Tivoli's claim to fame is the impressive **Villa D'Este**. This sumptuous Renaissance estate of Cardinal Ippolito d'Este, the son of Duke Alfonso and Lucrezia Borgia, contains a three-story palace. The palace, perched on a cliff, overlooks a vast complex of gardens and more than 400 fountains.

A few other sites shouldn't be missed while in Tivoli or nearby. Tivoli's impressive **Romanesque cathedral** survives from the 12th century. (The church went through extensive restoration in the 1600s.) Also, within walking distance, the **Temple of Vesta** remains from the second century B.C., with 10 of its original 18 Corinthian columns still in place. Nearby, the **Villa Gregoriana**, which was built on the original course of the Aniene River, now overlooks the river's waterfalls, which drop 500 feet.

If you're in Tivoli for lunch or dinner, try **La Laterna**, *via Due Giugno 12*. The best *prima piatta* served here is the *cannelloni*; the best *piatta secondo* is the *lombata di vitello*.

Florence—the most beautiful city

Florence is the most beautiful city in this country of lovely places. Ringed by hills, its streets are lined with red-tiled houses. Graceful domes rise from curving, narrow, cobblestoned streets. The ochre-colored walls of the ancient buildings are decorated with weathered gargoyles and faded coats of arms.

Within Florence is some of the greatest artwork in the world. For three centuries, from Giotto to Michelangelo, Florence was the center of the art world. Paintings and frescoes by the great Renaissance masters decorate even the most mundane churches.

The best way to see Florence is on foot. Don't drive through Florence—the convoluted streets are a navigational nightmare. Parking is even worse—spaces are hard to find, and tickets are a way of life. Besides, most everything is within walking distance.

The world's finest Renaissance art

The immense **Uffizi Museum** has the world's greatest collection of Renaissance art, including paintings by Giotto, Raphael, Titian, and Botticelli. The museum also has a room of modern art. Be sure to see the newly restored *Doni Tondo* by Michelangelo and Botticelli's *Birth of Venus*. The room containing Botticelli's *Primavera, Birth of Venus, Madonna della Melagrana,* and *Pallas and the Centaur* is the most impressive.

The best-kept secret in Florence

The **Vasari Corridoio** is a long, covered, secret passage built by Vasari in 1565 for Cosimo I de Medici. It links the Uffizi with the Pitti Palace, now one of Florence's great picture galleries but then Cosimo's residence. It crosses the Arno with the Ponte Vecchio and passes through the Church of Santa Felicità, another Vasari masterpiece, where the Medicis attended chapel.

The largest dome in Christendom

Il Duomo, one of the world's largest cathedrals, is topped with the largest dome in Christendom. Its marble walls are striped with alternating colors. For this reason, it has been called the Cathedral in Pajamas. Built in 1296 by Brunelleschi, its vast walls are decorated with frescoes illustrating Dante's *Divine Comedy* and works by Ucello. Climb up into the dome for a terrific view of Florence. (It is open every day except Sunday between 8:30 a.m. and 12:30 p.m. and between 2:30 and 4:30 p.m.)

Many of the treasures of Il Duomo are stored at **Museo dell'Opera del Duomo,** *Piazza del Duomo 9,* a house behind the church. It contains a pietà by Michelangelo that was never finished and Donatello's *Santa Maria Maddalena,* a nude statue covered only by her hair.

The Gates of Paradise

The **Baptistery,** an octagonal building in Piazza del Duomo dedicated to St. John the Baptist, is famous for its three sets of gilded bronze doors. Michelangelo called the east doors facing the cathedral the "Gates of Paradise." Begun in 1425 by Ghilberti, they weren't completed until 1452, when the artist was 74. They are made up of 10 panels that illustrate the Old Testament. On the Feast of St. John (June 24), the relics of the saint are displayed in the Baptistery, and candles are lit in his honor.

The six most important sights in Florence

Pitti Palace, a huge structure built by Renaissance banker Luca Pitti, is now divided into five museums, including the Palatine Picture Gallery, where works by Titian, Raphael, and Rubens are displayed. The Silver Museum houses Lorenzo de Medici's vases.

Santa Croce, a striped-marble church, has frescoes by Giotto. The most elegant church in Florence, it contains tombs and monuments to Michelangelo, Galileo, Machiavelli, and Dante. Go through the sacristy into the Leather School started by the monks about 30 years ago.

Accademia is where the original of Michelangelo's magnificent *David* stands. You'll want to see this, of course, but be prepared to stand in incredibly long lines. The worst days to visit are Sunday and Tuesday; the best times are 8 a.m. and noon, when the lines are shortest.

Bargello, the national museum, was once a fortress that served as a prison. In centuries past, men were strung out of the tower for their misdeeds. Today, the building contains the best of Florentine sculpture. Several early Michelangelos are housed here, including his first unfinished *David* and his statue of Bacchus. Upstairs are Giambologna's bronze animals created for a Medici garden grotto. This museum doesn't draw the crowds it merits.

The **Basilica of San Lorenzo** and the **Palazzo Medici** were built by the Medici family north of the Duomo. Brunelleschi began work on the church in 1419, incorporating the coat of arms of the Medicis in the design. Donatello's sculpture fills the church, and Filippo Lippi designed the altarpiece. The Medici Chapel, adjacent to the basilica, can be reached only from outside. Actually a mausoleum, the chapel has two sections: the Princes' Chapel, which contains the tombs of six Medici grand dukes, and the New Sacristy (Sagrestia Nuova), built by Michelangelo.

Santa Maria Novella is a grand church with splendid frescoes by Ghirlandaio and Filippino Lippi. They are best seen on a sunny day; the chapels are dark. The wealthy merchants of Florence had special chapels built in their honors in this church. Alberti designed the top half of the facade of the church and one of the chapels. And the choir contains Ghirlandaio's most important frescoes, which his student, Michelangelo, helped to create. The cloister of the church is colored with Uccello's frescoes.

Florence's best bridge

Ponte Vecchio, a bridge dating back to Roman times, is lined with goldsmith shops and street musicians. Butchers and tanners originally plied their trades on this bridge, but they were ousted by the Medici family in favor of the more seemly goldsmiths. During World War II, the commander in charge of the German army's retreat refused to blow up the bridge. Instead, he destroyed the buildings at its base so the rubble would block the span.

The prettiest Florentine church

San Miniato al Monte, one of the oldest churches in Florence, has an inlaid marble facade with 13th-century mosaics. Inside, the pavement is patterned with astrological signs, lions, and doves. The church contains superb Della Robbia terra-cottas. You can hear a Gregorian chant at San Miniato al Monte daily starting at 4:45 p.m.

The most interesting shopping

The **Oltrarno,** or artisan quarter on the left bank of the Arno, is a maze of streets spreading out from the Pitti Palace and around the Church of Santo Spirito. Stop in at the workshops, where picture frames are gilded, furniture is restored, and metals are forged.

Fashionable shopping areas, where the big names in Italian fashion can be visited, are centered around vias Tornabuoni and della Vigua Nuova.

The top art nouveau dealer

Fallani Bet, *Borgognissanti 15,* is the city's top dealer in art nouveau and art deco. The store has a wide variety of art to choose from.

The best hotels in Florence

Villa Medici, *via il Prato 42; tel. (39-55)238-13-31,* is an elegant hotel in the former Sonnino de Renzis Palace. Among other world-famous guests who have stayed at the hotel are the Shah of Iran, Jack Lemmon, and Hubert Humphrey. The rooms are light, airy, and nicely decorated. The fifth-floor apartment has a terrace that looks out over the skyline of Florence.

Elegance greets you as you enter the lobby at the Medici: Oriental carpets warm the marble-tiled floor, the fireplace is copper-hooded, and through an enormous picture window an elaborate garden can be seen. At the center of the garden is an ancient fountain shaped like the Medici family crest. A double room is 280,000 lire ($237) plus 18% tax.

The **Hotel Regency,** *Piazza Massimo d'Azeglio 3, Florence 50125; tel. (39-55)24-52-47,* is certainly the most peaceful hotel in Florence. It is also elegant. Located in a restored old town house on a quiet treelined square, it is only a 10-minute walk from the center of town. The rooms are splendid, and a quiet walled garden is situated behind the hotel. A double room is 280,000 lire to 380,000 lire ($237 to $322).

The most charming small hotel in Florence is the **Tornabuoni Beacci,** *via Tornabuoni 3, 50123 Florence, Italy; tel. (39-55)212-645* or *(800)366-1510,* run by Signora Orlandi-Beacci. This old-fashioned hotel has high ceilings, fine furniture, fresh flowers, and lovely rooms. Located in a 14th-century palace on via Tornabuoni, the Beacci occupies the three top floors of the building. Its windows look out over the mauve and coral rooftops of the city. A double room is 180,000 lire ($150), including breakfast.

Scenes from E.M. Forster's romantic *Room With a View* were filmed at **Pensione Quisisana e Pontevecchio,** *Lungarno Archibulsieri 4; tel. (39-55)216-692* or *(39-55)215-046.* A double room with bath is 150,000 lire ($127), including breakfast.

The best dining

The most surprising Tuscan specialty is steak, which is terrific in Florence. To order it, ask for *bistecca alla Fiorentina.*

Our favorite restaurant in Florence is the **Enoteca Pinchiorri,** *via Ghibellina 87; tel. (39-55)24-27-57.* Located in the 15th-century Ciofi-Iacometti Palace, it has a pleasant courtyard for dining and serves nouvelle cuisine. The sweet-and-sour fish and sweetbread salad are good. The over 60,000-bottle wine cellar is more than comprehensive. Reservations are required. An a la carte dinner is 80,000 lire to 120,000 lire ($67 to $100).

The best Tuscan cuisine is served at an inexpensive restaurant called **Trattoria La Beppa,** *via Erta Canina 6/R.* It's a friendly, family-style place, where everyone sits at long tables. An elaborate antipasto is served, followed by local specialties, such as rabbit, duck, and quail.

Da Noi, *via Fiesolana 46; tel. (39-55)242-917,* is a homey restaurant that requires reservations. Dishes are traditional, yet imaginative. Try the *crespelle* (crepes) stuffed with spinach and ricotta cheese. Save room for one of the marvelous desserts. Credit cards are not accepted.

The best night life

The two best nightclubs in Florence are **Manila,** *Piazza Matteucci, Campi Bisenzio; tel. (39-55)894-121,* and **Tenax,** *via Pratense 46a; tel. (39-55)373-050.* Manila is avant garde and decorated with elaborate graffiti. The crowd is ultrasophisticated. Tenax is in an enormous old warehouse on two floors. The clientele here is also very fashionable.

The best ice cream in Florence

Vivoli's, *via Isola delle Stinche 7,* behind Santa Croce Square, is one of the best places in the world to buy ice cream. The lines are long, but the choice of flavors is great and the ice cream out-of-this-world.

The most magical city: Venice

Venice, a city made up of 118 islets held together by a maze of 150 narrow canals and 400 lacy bridges, has a magical air. The interlocking waterways are plied by graceful wooden gondolas. Domed churches look over the shadowed pedestrian streets, where throngs of people (but no cars) roam.

Venetians took refuge in their watery home after centuries of invasions by the likes of Attila the Hun, the Goths, and the Vandals. In A.D. 687, they elected a president, called a doge. He was the first in a line of 117 doges, each reigning for life, that ended in 1797.

The five most important sights

The heart of Venice is the **Piazza San Marco,** which is dominated by the beautiful basilica on one side and the Doge's Palace on the other. This huge square attracts flocks of pigeons as well as tourists.

Once the doge's private chapel, the **Basilica of San Marco** is now open to the public. Built in the ninth century to house the body of St. Mark, the basilica houses the saint's tomb, paintings by Titian, and the Pala d'Oro, a huge panel behind the altar bedecked with rubies, emeralds, sapphires, pearls, topazes, amethysts, and cloisonné figures, all set in gold. The basilica also has Byzantine treasures. These artifacts and the saint's body were the booty of the fourth Crusade, taken from Constantinople by Doge Enrico Dandolo.

The **Palazzo Ducale** (Doge's Palace) is an ornate structure on the water. Its columns are carved with figures symbolizing the trades. On one side are the Quattro Mori, four Moorish warriors embracing one another. Inside are the doges' apartments, the senate chamber, and the Room of the Council of Ten, which is covered with beautiful paintings. The sinister box outside is intended to receive denunciations of traitors or criminals.

The **Bridge of Sighs** passes between the Doge's Palace and the prison where Casanova was once held. The covered bridge is so named because condemned prisoners sighed as they were led across it to their deaths. They were allowed one last look at Venice from the bridge before their executions.

The **Grand Canal** has been called the finest street in the world. It is lined with 200 marble-covered palaces built between the 12th and 18th centuries. Wagner died in the

Palazzo Vendramin-Calergi, now the Municipal Casino. Lord Byron lived in the Palazzo Mocenigo. Gold leaf was used to coat the balls protruding on the facade of the Ca' D'Oro on the right bank. Its pointed arches were influenced by Islam. A good way to see these palazzi is to take a boat ride along the two-mile length of the canal. Take vaporetto (water-bus) 1 or 4.

The **Galleria dell'Accademia** (Gallery of Fine Arts) houses paintings by Giorgione, Bellini, Tiepolo, Titian, and Canaletto. Admission is free except Sunday.

The Lido—the most fashionable Adriatic resort

Venice is protected from the rage of the Adriatic Sea by a beautiful sand spit called the **Lido.** A fashionable resort, the Lido draws visitors from around the world to its sandy beaches, elegant hotels, and swank casino. To get there, take vaporetto lines 1 and 2 from Venice across the Lagoon.

Before you go to the Lido, read *Death in Venice,* by Thomas Mann. And (if you can afford it) stay at the legendary **Grand Hotel des Bains,** *Lungomare Marconi 17; tel. (39-41)526-5921,* where Mann's character, Hans Aschenbach, spent his last days. Rooms are expensive, from about 400,000 lire ($360) a night for a double.

The romantic islands of the Lagoon

The **Lagoon** is filled with romantic little islands that can be reached by vaporetto. (Boat 12 leaves from the Fondamenta Nuove, near Campo dei Gesuiti, for Murano, Burano, and Torcello.) Burano and Torcello have especially inviting beaches, fishing villages, and small art museums. Murano is famous for its glassmaking.

Burano Island, actually four tiny islets connected by bridges, is a half-hour water-bus ride from the mainland. Everything here is miniature—the canals and bridges are tiny, and the colorfully painted houses look as if they were built for dwarfs. Burano has its own leaning tower, the bell tower of the **Church of San Martino,** *Piazza Baldassare Galuppi.*

However, the island is best-known for its lace making. Wherever you go on Burano, you will see old ladies knitting lace and selling it from outdoor tables. You can buy handmade lace doilies, lace tablecloths, lace mats, hankies, baby bibs, and collars. The **Consorzio Merletti di Burano** (lace museum), *Piazza Galuppi,* is open daily. Admission is 2,000 lire ($1.80).

Murano Island has dozens of workshops where you can watch glass being blown. The **Museo Vetrario,** *Fondamenta Giustinian,* along the main canal, has an immense collection of glass from Roman times to the present. It is closed Wednesdays.

San Francesco del Deserto is a tiny, cypress-covered island inhabited by Franciscan monks. According to legend, St. Francis of Assisi was shipwrecked here in 1220. His wooden staff, which he stuck in the ground, turned into a tree, part of which still can be seen. Gardens and lawns surround the cloister and church. Peacocks and bantams wander the grounds freely.

A surprisingly pleasant island is Venice's cemetery, **San Michele,** which is filled with shade trees, flower gardens, and leaf-covered paths. Ornate tombs and mausoleums are surrounded by gardens and terraces. The ferryboat to San Michele is free on Sundays. The entrance is through the cloister of the island's 15th-century church.

The island of **San Lazzaro** has been the site of an Armenian monastery for 200 years. A priest dressed in a black cassock and sporting a heavy beard will give you a two-hour tour of the cloister, which contains an Egyptian mummy, Armenian paintings, ivories from the Orient, and the room where Lord Byron lived in 1816, when he decided to learn Armenian. One of the rooms contains a collection of rare illuminated manuscripts.

Gondolas—romance supreme

Thomas Mann wrote, "Is there anyone but must repress a secret thrill, on arriving in Venice for the first time—or returning thither after a long absence—and stepping into a

Venetian gondola? That singular conveyance, come down unchanged from ballad times, black as nothing else on earth except a coffin—what pictures it calls up of lawless, silent adventures in the plashing night...And has anyone remarked that the seat in such a bark, the arm-chair...is the softest, most luxurious, most relaxing seat in the world?"

Long gondola rides, unfortunately, must be reserved for the wealthy or the frivolous. The authorized rate starts at 50,000 lire ($42) per 50 minutes—but most gondoliers charge 100,000 lire ($84). They usually charge more after 9 p.m., but you can bargain to get a good price. Gondolas are rented at Piazzale Roma, the San Marco ferry stop, Campo San Moise, and other points along the canals.

At several points along the Grand Canal where you can't cross via a bridge, you can take a short but cheap gondola ride for 500 lire (50 cents). Rides can be taken from south of Campo S. Toma and from Campo del Traghetto to Dorsoduro.

The greatest opera house

Gran Teatro La Fenice, *Campo San Fantin, 30124 Venice, Italy; tel. (39-41)521-0161,* is one of the greatest opera houses in the world. The 18th-century decor is graceful, with chandeliers, plush armchairs, box seats, mirrored corridors, parquet floors, and a grand staircase with marble columns. The acoustics are flawless.

You cannot make reservations for an opera by telephone; you must visit the box office in person between 9:30 a.m. and 12:30 p.m. or one hour before an evening performance.

The most fantastic hotel in Europe

Venice has the most fantastic hotel in Europe, the luxurious **Hotel Cipriani** on Giudecca Island. A polished motorboat fetches guests at the Piazza San Marco. Rooms have private, flower-bedecked terraces that gaze out over the water. Marble bathrooms have sliding, hidden doors that open into the bedroom. Excellent seafood is prepared in the dining room. The Cipriani has Venice's only tennis courts and its largest swimming pool. Mitterand and Kissinger are among the dignitaries who have stayed here. A double room is 740,000 lire to 1.8 million lire ($627 to $1,525) per night. To make reservations in the United States, contact **Leading Hotels of the World**, *747 Third Ave., New York, NY 10017; (800)223-6800.*

Venice's homiest hotels

Pensione Accademia, *Fondamenta Bollani 1058, Venice 30123; tel. (39-41)523-7846,* located in a 17th-century villa, faces a side canal near the Grand Canal at the Accademia bridge. Rooms are elegant, and breakfast and afternoon tea are served at little pink-clothed tables on the patio. Not all rooms have private bathrooms. A double room starts at 190,000 lire ($160).

Hotel Torino, *San Marco 2356, Venice 30124; tel. (39-41)520-5222,* located in a 14th-century palace between San Marco and Santa Maria del Giglio, is noted for its tiny wrought-iron balconies and flowers. A double room starts at 228,000 lire ($193).

La Fenice des Artistes, *Campiello de la Fenice 1936, Venice 30124; tel. (39-41)523-2333,* is a quiet hotel behind the Fenice Opera House. The courtyard, where breakfast and drinks are served, backs up onto a canal. Rooms are comfortable. Try to get one at the back. A double room starts at 210,000 lire ($178).

Hotel Flora, *Calle Bergamaschi 2283/a, Venice 30124; tel. (39-41)520-5844,* attracts English travelers. Although it's centrally located, it is quiet and has a gorgeous garden with ivy-clad walls, fountains, flowers, and tables for breakfast and drinks. Some of the rooms are spacious and decorated with painted furniture; others are plainer. A double room is 200,000 lire ($170).

The best Venetian restaurants

Antica Trattoria Orsetta, *San Polo 3000,* is the best place to go for authentic

Venetian cuisine. The restaurant is hidden in the back streets of Venice and is very difficult to find.

Harry's Bar, *San Marco 1323, 30124 Venice; tel. (39-41)523-6797*, has two Michelin stars and was one of Hemingway's favorites. Only a few minutes from the piazzetta on the Piazza San Marco, it has been owned and run by the Cipriani family for 50 years.

Europe's largest maze

The largest and most complicated maze in Europe is in Stra, 18 miles south of Venice. Here, the odds are a zillion to one that you will get lost. **Il Labirinto**, as it is known in Italy, is part of the stately gardens of the Villa Pisani. This life-size puzzle is one-third the size of a football field and has four miles of paths lined with tall, thick hedges. Napoleon got himself lost in Il Labirinto in 1807 and had to be rescued. If you too get lost, the caretaker, who has been here for 47 years, will rescue you. He can reach the tower at the center of the maze in three minutes. (You may not photograph the maze from any angle.)

Mantua: Venice without the crowds

Mantua has the charm of Venice without the crowds. The River Mincio wraps around the ducal city like a cloak and threads its way through the city via little canals. Graceful bridges cross the winding waterways. Once the seat of one of the most brilliant courts of Europe, today it is one of the best-preserved medieval cities in Italy.

Mantua feels medieval; it has no modern industry and no high-rise buildings. The **Ducal Palace**, built in the Middle Ages, is actually three interconnected buildings. The palace has 500 rooms, seven gardens, and eight courtyards. Frescoes by Pisanello depicting episodes from chivalric tales hang in the Hall of Dukes. Painted in 1440, they were rediscovered in 1969 under two coats of plaster. In the Camera degli Sposi (bridal chamber), built in 1474, hang Andrea Mantegna's frescoes of the Gonzaga family.

A guide is mandatory when you visit the Ducal Palace, but you can explore at your own pace. Take a good guidebook with you. *Mantova Guida Pratica ed Artistica con Pianta della Citta*, by Loretta Santini, is a good one. It is available in English at Mantua bookstores.

After the Ducal Palace, the two most important sights in Mantua are the **Church of Sant' Andrea** and the **Palazzo Te**. The Church of Sant' Andrea has a coffered ceiling and grandiose arches more reminiscent of the Pantheon than a Christian church. This is a good place to get a feeling for the time when the Pagan and Christian worlds met.

The Palazzo Te was a pleasure palace for Federico, the favorite son of Mantua's great lady, Isabella d'Este. Here Federico entertained his mistress for 10 years. The ballroom is decorated with a painting of Federico's favorite horses. Halls are painted with scenes from the Battle of the Titans, the story of David, and the myth of Psyche. Paintings of classical fables cover the scalloped ceiling of Federico's bedroom.

When you tire of sightseeing, enjoy Mantua's delicious egg pasta at **Il Cigno**, *Piazza d'Arco 1; tel. (39-376)327-101*, opposite the Palazzo d'Arco.

Two comfortable hotels in Mantua are the **San Lorenzo**, *Piazza Concordia 14; tel. (39-376) 327-153*, where a double room is 250,000 lire ($212), and the **Hotel Rechigi**, *via Calvi 30; tel. (39-376)320-781*, where a double room is 160,000 lire ($135) a night.

Naples: the most Italian city

Tourists shy away from **Naples**, because of its reputation for crime—although the crime situation here is actually no worse than in New York and other major cities. Because of its rather undeserved bad reputation, Naples is a truly Italian city—free of crowds of gaping foreigners.

A huge, hilly town in the shadows of Mount Vesuvius, Naples is cooled by the breezes of the Gulf of Naples. The city's waterfront is lined with booths where you can stop for a cool drink.

Neapolitans have a lugubrious interest in the macabre. In the **Cappella Sansevero**, for example, is the 16th-century corpse of a family servant mysteriously preserved by the alchemy of the Duke of Sansevero. Thousands of capillaries can be seen through the skin of the body. The chapel, which is hidden on a small side street off Piazza San Domenico Maggiore, also holds an uncanny effigy of the body of Christ covered in diaphanous veils carved by the sculptor Sammartino.

The most important sight

The cathedral in Naples is dedicated to San Gennaro. It was built in the 13th century on the site of a previous basilica dedicated to Santa Stefania. The original basilica was built on the foundations of a Roman temple dedicated to Apollo.

Within the cathedral are an ancient round baptistery, which has a deep baptismal pool and mosaics from the fifth century; the Byzantine basilica of Santa Restituta, attached to the north wall of the duomo; and the 17th-century chapel, which holds San Gennaro's head and blood. The blood has liquefied from its crystalized state the first Sunday in May and Sept. 19 nearly every year since the Middle Ages. Great crowds gather to see this miracle. If the blood does not liquefy, it is believed that a disaster will happen. (Great importance is placed on San Gennaro in Naples. When Mount Vesuvius acts up, for instance, the saint's image is taken to the mountain as a pacifier.)

The world's best antiquities

Il Museo Archeologico Nazionale in Naples houses one of the most important collections of Greek and Roman antiquities in the world, including many of the treasures excavated from Pompeii and Herculaneum. Among these treasures are the *Young Satyr*, a graceful figure carrying a wine casket, and the famous statues of Apollo and Diana, which once stood at Pompeii's Temple of Apollo. You can't miss the *Farnese Bull*, the largest surviving sculpture from antiquity, carved out of a single block of marble.

Naples' best Renaissance museum

Outside Naples is the Capodimonte Museum and Picture Gallery, which houses one of Italy's best collections of paintings from the 14th, 15th, and 16th centuries. Located in an 18th-century palace in the hills northeast of the city and surrounded by a park, it contains works by Bellini, Botticelli, Correggio, and Titian. Capodimonte is also a famous porcelain.

The best people-watching

In the evening, join the Neapolitans in their nightly stroll along the Lungomare, a broad promenade along Santa Lucia Port (subject of the famous folk song *Santa Lucia*).

Also in this area is the Castel dell'Ovo, *via Partenope*, which sticks out like an island in the bay, and the Castel Nuovo, *Piazza Municipio*. Both host evening concerts and exhibitions.

Night life at its hottest

Naples' night life can be found in and around vias Caracciolo and Partenope, commonly referred to as the Margellina Quarter. Within walking distance is the San Carlo Theater, *via San Carlo*, renowned for classical music and dance. Information on the performances here can be obtained at the box office, which is open 10 a.m. until 1 p.m. and 4:30 until 6:30 p.m. every day except Mondays.

Naples' nightclubs and discos usually begin to swing at about 10 p.m., when most people have eaten and are ready for some activity. Il Gabbiano, *via Partenope 26; tel. (39-81)411-666*, attracts beautiful international patrons and usually has live music.

The best ways to thwart thieves

Pickpockets are common in Naples, and they make their livings off tourists. Don't drape your purse over your shoulder. Thieves on motorbikes grab bags as they zoom past, often dragging the person along with the bag. Thieves generally work in pairs. They pull up to people carrying shoulder bags or camera bags. One thug hops off the bike, grabs the loot, and hops back on, and the pair then speeds away.

Avoid carrying a wallet in your back pocket. Leave all jewelry—including watches— in your hotel. It's best to carry limited amounts of cash and your passport and credit cards in the inside pocket of a jacket or a front pocket of your pants.

When driving, never put anything in the back window of the car. Traffic in Naples is dense, and thieves often break rear windows of cars stuck in traffic jams. And don't leave things in parked cars—not even in the trunks. Most rental cars in Italy have Milan tags, and thieves know to look for them around hotels, restaurants, and museums.

The most delicious fare
Avellinese da Peppino, *via Silvio Spaventa 31-35; tel. (39-81)28-38-97,* is a friendly place with cheap but good seafood. Try the *pesce frigole,* a mixture of crayfish, octopus, squid, mussels, and clams. Italian singers serenade you as you dine.

La Cantinella, *via Cuma 42; tel. (39-81)40-48-84* or *(39-81)40-53-75,* is a favorite among Neapolitans. The clams and mussels cooked with garlic, parsley, and tomato and served with linguine are exquisite. Dinner for two is about 89,000 lire ($75). The restaurant is closed Sundays.

La Fazenda, *Calata Marechiaro 58; tel. (39-81)769-7420,* serves the best Neapolitan dishes, including home-raised chickens. This rustic restaurant has spectacular views of the bay and is decorated with a profusion of flowers. It is closed Sundays and for two weeks in August. Dinner for two is about 80,700 lire ($68).

Il Gallo Nero, *via Tasso 466; tel. (39-81)64-30-12,* is in an antique-filled 19th-century villa. Dine on the terrace, where you'll have a splendid view of Mergellina. The fresh fish is terrific. Dinner for two is about 80,000 lire ($67).

Sleeping beautifully
The most luxurious hotels in Naples are the Excelsior and the Vesuvio. The **Excelsior,** *via Partenope 48; tel. (39-81)76-40-111,* has terraced seaside rooms with views of the Castel dell'Ovo and the bay. Its restaurant is good. The rather sparsely furnished and old-fashioned double rooms start at 360,000 lire ($305).

The **Vesuvio,** *via Partenope 45; tel. (39-81)41-70-44,* faces the port of Santa Lucia and has a variety of rooms ranging in style from antique to modern. It has air conditioning and a garage. A double room starts at 330,000 lire ($279).

The strangest sight: the door to the Underworld
Near Naples is one of the strangest sights in Italy—the cave said to have been the door to the Underworld of ancient mythology. Very few people visit the infamous **Grotta della Sibilla,** as it is known.

In the *Aeneid,* the Roman poet Virgil described the cave: "A deep, deep cave there was, its mouth enormously gaping/Shingly, protected by the dark lake and the forest gloom:/Above it, no winged creatures could ever wing their way/With fuming up from its black throat to the vault of heaven:/Wherefore the Greeks called it Avernus, the Birdless Place."

Alessandro, the elderly guide who has given tours and told the tale of the cave for the past 50 years, begins his tour at the entrance of **Lago di Avernus.**

According to the guide, Lago di Avernus was once a volcanic flat with bubbling mud and sulphur fumes that rose into the sky. Because the fumes were poisonous, birds flying over would die and fall into the inferno. (*Avernus* means *no birds* in Latin.) This description matches Virgil's. When Mount Vesuvius erupted, the volcanic action stopped here, and the crater filled with water. The eruption cut off the tunnel leading to the Underworld.

The guided tour takes about an hour. While no set admission is charged, most visitors tip Signor Alessandro at least 1,000 lire (85 cents). Open Friday, Saturday, and Sunday 9 a.m. to 5 p.m. and weekdays 11 a.m. to 3 p.m.

To get to the cave from the via Domitiana in Naples, turn left after the Olivetti factory toward Archo Felice. At the intersection, turn right onto via Miliscola, which goes along the waterfront toward Baia. Go about one mile, past a newsstand, the Lido di Napoli, and the Sibilla Restaurant. A sign points right toward a bumpy road that takes you to a brick wall on your left marked with a white painted sign indicating Grotta della Sibilla.

Volcanic bests

Mount Vesuvius, 15 miles southeast of Naples, can be seen from the city on a clear day. If you'd like to get closer to it, you can actually hike up to the crater. But remember, it was Vesuvius that did away with Pompeii. It last erupted in 1944, and it averages one eruption every 35 years. You can take a chair lift up to the top, or you can drive part way and then walk. Take the Ercolano exit from the Autostrada, then drive 15 kilometers up a zigzagging path across a sort of moonscape. The oval crater, when you finally get there, is 2,000 feet wide and 525 feet deep. Wisps of smoke rise from the top. If you yell your name, Vesuvius will echo it back.

Pompeii and Herculaneum: the world's best ruins

Pompeii and **Herculaneum**, once bedroom suburbs of Roman Naples, were destroyed when Mount Vesuvius erupted in A.D. 79. Today, the ruins are preserved in volcanic ash illustrations of everyday life nearly 2,000 years ago. Explore the shops, baths, and houses of ordinary Roman families.

While Pompeii is packed with tourists, Herculaneum is not. What's more, Herculaneum is closer to Naples and is better preserved than Pompeii. Known as *Ercolano* in Italian, Herculaneum once had 5,000 inhabitants. Much of the town remains unexcavated beneath the modern town of Resina. However, among the ruins that have been excavated you'll see cakes in ovens, eggs in cupboards, chicken bones on kitchen tables, fishnets and hooks on a line, and graffiti on bathroom walls. One of the houses has a small cross, the oldest evidence of Christianity in the Roman Empire. The baths are the most interesting sights. You can see cold, warm, and hot water baths, a gym, and a swimming pool. The skeletons of bath attendants have been preserved intact in the men's cloakroom.

The best-preserved Greek temples

The best-preserved Greek Doric temples stand by the sea in **Paestum**, ancient Poseidonia, not far from Naples. The ancient structures are surrounded by a field of flowers and wild grasses. The three major temples are along the ancient via Sacra. The basilica, which is dedicated to Hera, is the oldest, dating back to the sixth century B.C. Next to the basilica is the Temple of Neptune (450 B.C.), one of the most beautiful Doric temples in the world. It is 6 columns across and 14 columns long. See the frescoes of a diver and a dinner party, the earliest surviving Greek paintings, in the museum across the street from the ruins.

The best of the Amalfi Coast

The **Amalfi Coast**, a mountainous peninsula between the Gulf of Naples and the Gulf of Salerno, is a land of legends. Pirates once used the secluded inlets as hideouts. Spectacular views can be enjoyed from the dizzying summits of the mountains. Serpentine roads wind through cliffside villages. Olive groves and grapevines dot the plains.

In July or August, the Amalfi Coast becomes a madhouse, and it is nearly impossible to drive. The spring and fall are idyllic—warm and uncrowded.

The best coastal views

One of the most breathtaking views on the coast is from the old **Capuchin Monastery** perched on a cliff above Amalfi. An elevator takes you up to the 12th-century building, which today is an inexpensive hotel (rooms are about 100,000 lire, or $85, a night), *via Annunziatella 46; tel. (39-89)87-10-08*. Theodore Roosevelt and Henry Wadsworth Longfellow have stayed here.

You still can visit a chapel and cloisters within the hotel. The foundations of the convent, which is perched on a sheer cliff, date back to A.D. 1000. Bus service connects the hotel with the beach. If you ask, the staff will pack you a picnic lunch.

Another spectacular view is from the little town of **Ravello**, above Amalfi. A bus will take you to this summit via narrow, twisting roads. **Hotel Rufolo**, *via San Francesco 4, 84010 Ravello (Salerno); tel. (39-89)85-71-33*, is a lovely 11th-century building now used as a hotel (with rooms starting at about 200,000 lire, or $170, a night). It has gorgeous gardens filled with hydrangeas and a Moorish cloister overgrown with flowers. During the summer, concerts are staged here. The villa was once the residence of Pope Adrian IV, the only English pope, who reigned from 1154 to 1159. Lord Byron, Greta Garbo, and composer Richard Wagner have stayed in here.

The cathedral in Ravello has sculptures of strange-looking animals and contains a reliquary with the skull of Santa Barbara. The blood of the town's patron saint, San Pantaleone, is preserved in a cracked vessel that never leaks (or so it is said).

The **Hotel Caruso Belvedere**, *via San Giovanni del Torro 52, 84010 Ravello (Salerno); tel. (39-89)857-111*, set 900 feet above the Mediterranean coast, has sweeping views of the sea through its arched terrace. This well-known hotel is in the 11th-century d'Afflito Palace. Wines from surrounding vineyards are served in the restaurant. Most rooms have private bathrooms and private balconies. A double room is about 276,000 lire ($234), including breakfast and dinner.

Hotel Palumbo, *via S. Giovanni del Toro 28, 84010 Ravello (Salerno); tel. (39-89)857-244*, perched 1,200 feet above the coast, also has tremendous views. The 12th-century building was once the Palazzo Confalone. It is a pretty building, with arch and pillar vaulting, stone staircases, tile-inlaid floors, and good paintings. The hotel restaurant serves its own Ravello wines. Three-day stays are requested. A double room is 300,000 lire ($254) a night.

The most romantic hotel in Italy

Hotel San Pietro, *84017 Positano; (39-89)875-454*, is a cantilevered castle built into a cliffside on the Amalfi Coast. It is a veritable wonderland that has become a playground of the rich. Every suite or room faces the sea with a sweeping view. Each room is different, surprising, and eclectic—and every one has a private garden. Balconies, painted tiles, arches, antiques, and bouquets of flowers frame the foaming sea. You can descend through the mountain to swim and sunbathe, watch the fishermen coming and going in their boats, shop for Italian pottery, or just sit back in the evening in awe as the sunset electrifies the bay with scarlet. A double room is 400,000 lire ($340) a night.

Capri: Italy's most beautiful island

Capri is a beautiful but crowded island that can be reached by hydrofoil from Naples, Sorrento, or Pozzuoli. After the boat ride, relax and have a pleasant lunch on the terrace of the Hotel Belvedere Tre Re, on the harbor. Take a funicular from the harbor up to the town of Capri. The best view is from the top of Mount Solaro, where an old monastery stands. To get there, take a bus to Anacapri and then a chair lift to the summit.

The Blue Grotto sea caves are lovely, but touristy. Visit the pagan shrine of the Matromania Cave. Roman Emperor Tiberius built 12 villas on the island to honor the 12 Roman deities. You can best sense his might around Villa Jovis, his headquarters for a decade.

Hotels on the island book up fast, so reservations are a must. One of the most romantic is **Scalanitella,** *via Tragara 8; tel. (39-81)837-0633,* in the town of Capri. A staff member meets visitors upon arrival and leads them along the narrow streets to the little hotel. Cut into a steep and rocky hill, Scalanitella has a Moorish air. Its glistening marble lobby, winding corridors, classical paintings and busts, carved doors, floor-to-ceiling windows, outdoor garden, and little luxuries create a delightful atmosphere. Its pool is one of the best in Capri. The hotel is open Easter through October. A double room is 400,000 lire to 500,000 lire ($339 to $424), including breakfast. Credit cards are not accepted.

The **Quisiana and Grand Hotel,** *via Camerelle 2; tel. (39-81)837-0788,* attracts the jet set with large suites, wide arcades, and an ocean view. Rooms start at 400,000 lire ($360). **Hotel Luna,** *tel. (39-81)837-0433,* combines old-fashioned style with modern conveniences. A double room is from 220,000 to 300,000 lire ($186 to $254).

Good food is served at **La Sceriffa,** *via Acquaviva 29; tel. (39-81)837-7953.* **La Pigna,** *via Lo Palazzo 30; tel. (39-81)837-0280,* is another good bet.

The best of the Italian Riviera

The **Italian Riviera,** which stretches from the French border to Tuscany, is less expensive than the French Riviera and just as pretty. It lies within the prosperous northern region of **Liguria,** which has its own lingo and culture. The heart of Liguria is Genoa, a thriving seaport and a good place to stay if you find coastal resorts too pricey. North of Genoa is the Riviera di Levante (Coast of the Rising Sun). Below and to the east is the Riviera di Ponente (Coast of the Setting Sun).

During July and August, rooms are almost impossible to come by. The best time to visit is spring or fall, when the weather is warm and hotel rooms are vacant.

The oldest resort on the Riviera

San Remo, the oldest resort on the Riviera, is overcrowded and overbuilt. But it has a casino and a yacht basin, and the hotels are affordable despite their Edwardian elegance. (Inexpensive ones are located along the via Matteotti.) The **tourist office,** *Palazzo Riviera,* is helpful if you can't find a room.

Where the crème de la crème rises

Italy's crème de la crème surfaces in **Portofino** during the summer. Very private and romantic, Portofino is one of the most photographed places in the world. Its remarkably deep natural harbor attracts yachtsmen from all over the world. Everyone who is anyone, from Lauren Bacall and Humphrey Bogart to Aristotle Onassis and Ernest Hemingway, has stayed here. Hike out to the lighthouse following the footpath marked *"al faro"* for a spectacular view of the coastline.

Hotel Splendido, *via le Baratta 13; tel. (39-185)269551,* is Portofino's most luxurious hotel. It is perched in a spectacular setting above the yacht harbor, set into a cliff. It has an old-fashioned charm despite its modern swimming pool on the terrace. For reservations in the United States, contact **Relais & Chateaux,** *(800)677-3524* or *(800)743-8033.* A double room costs 533,000 lire ($452).

The Riviera's most charming town

From the docks at the coastal town of Camogli, you can take a boat to **San Fruttoso,** the most charming town on the coast. This tiny fishing village on the Portofino Peninsula is accessible only by sea. It is surrounded by pines, olive trees, and oaks that lead down to the sea. Walk through the cloisters and corridors of the Benedictine Abbey of San Fruttoso di Capo di Monte, which consists of a 13th-century palace, an 11th-century church, and a Romanesque cloister.

Camogli has one of the best hotels along the coast, **Cenobio dei Dogi,** *via Cuneo 34,*

16032 Camogli; tel. (39-185)770-041, set in a manor house on the beach. Once the seat of the bishops of Genoa, this manor has lovely grounds, a beach, a swimming pool, tennis courts, facilities for the handicapped, and central heat. A double room is 240,000 lire to 320,000 lire ($203 to $270) a night.

Cinque Terre: the least crowded

At the southern end of the coast is one of the least crowded, most picturesque areas. The mountains, woods, vineyards, and hilltop villages of the Cinque Terre cover 15 miles of coastline. The area's five villages—Monterosso, Vernazza, Corniglia, Manarola, and Riomaggiore—are perched on the rocky coast north of La Spezia. Taste of the rare local wine, Sciacchetra.

Monterosso is the largest and most crowded town. But it has a beautiful beach at the southern end of the cove. You can rent boats here for about 6,725 lire ($6) an hour. Climb the hill to the Convento dei Cappuccini, which houses Van Dyck's *Crucifixion*. After the strenuous climb, relax at Gigante, Monterosso's best restaurant.

Hiking trails lead from Monterosso to Cinque Terre's quainter towns. A 1 1/2-hour hike along a goat path leads through vineyards and olive groves to **Vernazza**. Another hiking trail leads to **Corniglia**, which has a long, pebbly beach.

If you're up to another hour's walk, follow the trail along the jagged coast to **Manarola**, the most beautiful of the Cinque Terre towns. Here, yellow houses balance on cliffs, and artists and writers seek their muses.

The Alps at their cheapest

The **Dolomites** (Italian Alps) are just as beautiful as their French and Austrian counterparts, but visiting them is far less expensive. The skiing is almost as good as it is to the north, and the hiking can be even better.

Valle d'Aosta is just over the border from France. You can take a cable car to the Italian side from Chamonix, France, for 33,625 lire ($28). The panoramic view from the cable car is beautiful—and a bit scary if you fear heights at all.

Alto Badia, 50 miles south of the Brenner Pass through the Dolomites into Austria, is made up of little Tyrolean villages. This region has the beautiful scenery of Austria, but it also has lower prices, summer skiing, and good Italian restaurants. The best-known and largest among the hamlets is Corvara. Less-crowded are Colfosco, La Villa, Pedraces, and San Cassiano.

The best bargain skiing in the Dolomites

Cortina d'Ampezzo, in the eastern Dolomites, is Italy's most popular ski resort. Although it is very crowded, it has some of the best ski facilities in Italy. The area is huge— you can ski for days without doubling back to redo the same runs. When you tire of skiing, you can ice skate in the remnants of the Olympic Stadium, shop in the town's many boutiques, or dine in one of its many restaurants.

Accommodation here is more expensive than in Mount Livata or Pescasseroli, nearby. The **Cristallo Hotel**, *via R. Menardi 42, Cortina d'Ampezzo 32043; tel. (39-436)4281,* has spacious, well-appointed rooms and a good restaurant. It is open from mid-December through March and during late summer. Rooms are 150,640 lire to 251,515 lire ($127 to $213), including three meals a day.

In **Courmayeur** and **Cervinia**, you can ski in the summer as well as the winter. These towns are well-known—and pricey for Italy. The Val d'Ayas is undiscovered and has lower lift prices (and more challenging runs).

Colfosco, a small, quiet ski village with numerous runs, attracts ardent downhill skiers. The area is best-suited to beginning and intermediate skiers—it offers little cross-country skiing and no deep-powder skiing. Its major advantage over the larger, more crowded ski resorts is that it is part of the **Alta Badia**, a five-village ski association. With a Colfosco lift ticket (which costs about 207,000 lire, or $175, a week), you have access to 75 miles of trails and 53 lifts. You can also buy the Super Dolomite lift pass, which gives you access to 10 major ski areas that include 650 miles of trails and 430 lifts (not all of them easily accessible). For more information, contact **Azienda Autonoma di Soggiono e Tourismo Corvara-Colfosco**, *39003 Corvara, Badia; tel. (39-471)836-176.*

Hotel Colfosco Hof, *39003 Colfosco, Corvara, Badia; tel. (39-471)836-188*, at the first curve of the Grodner Pass, is the most pleasant hotel in the area. It has good hearty food, a pool, a sauna, and a squash court. Rooms are 130,000 lire ($110), double occupancy, including breakfast and dinner.

For more information on skiing in the Dolomites, contact the **Ufficio Informazioni Turistiche**, *Piazza E. Chanoux 8, 11100 Aosta; tel. (39-165)35-655.*

The best hiking

The Dolomites, which are crisscrossed by trails, also boast some of the world's best hiking. Bring hiking boots, a windbreaker, a sweater, socks, and gloves. The best time to hike is August and September, when the snow has melted completely. Don't hike in April and May unless you are an expert. The melting snow causes avalanches.

Pedraces, near the Austrian border, is one of the best places for hiking. For one of the most scenic routes, take a chair lift to the foot of the Croce Mountains and then follow Trail 7.

The **National Park of Abruzzi**, near Pescasseroli, is another beautiful place to hike. The trails, which are named for animals, wander through a forest of pine trees blanketed with snow.

La Pieja, *Opi; tel. (39-863)910-756*, a few miles from Pescasseroli, is one of the best places to stay in the region. A double room is 120,000 lire ($100) in peak season, including breakfast.

The best base for exploring

Aosta is the best base for exploring the Italian peaks. Near mountain trails and several old castles, it has Roman ruins dating from the time of the Emperor Augustus, including a Roman theater, two Roman gates, the Porta Praetoria, and the Arco di Augusto.

The cloister of the medieval **Church of St. Ursus** dates back to A.D. 1000. St. Ursus, responsible for the first conversions to Christianity in the valley, is buried in a crypt below the altar. Modern history can be contemplated at the **Istituto Storico della Resistenza della Valle d'Aosta**, *Xavier de Maistre 22; tel. (39-165)40-846*, which documents the Italian resistance during World War II.

Make hotel reservations early if you plan to be in Aosta in July or August or during the Christmas or Easter season. A good place to stay is **Mancuso**, *via Voison 32; tel. (39-165)34-526.* This family-run hotel is clean and has inviting rooms. The hotel restaurant is good and inexpensive—a double room is only 50,000 lire ($42).

Italy's most beautiful national park

The **Gran Paradiso National Park** in the Valle d'Aosta is 363 square miles of protected area set aside for wildlife. The park has breathtaking scenery, ibex, wild flowers, and hiking trails. **Cogne** is the best base for exploring the park. You can get there from Aosta by bus. From Cogne, walk to Valnontey and then take Trail 2, which climbs to Rifugio V. Sella. The view from the refuge is mind-boggling. Stop to eat or spend the night before setting out on the six-hour trek to Eau Rousse in Valsavaranche. Again, the views are incredible.

Sleeping like royalty in the Italian Alps

A number of old castles have been made into hotels in the mountains of Italy. **Schloss Rundegg**, *via Scena 2, 39012 Merano; tel. (39-473)34-364*, is an old castle nestled in the mountains of southern Tyrol. Parts, including the square towers, date back to the 12th century. The main structure dates to 1580. Public rooms have grand staircases, vaulted ceilings, and arches. Private rooms are furnished with antiques. A pool, sauna, solarium, and massage center are open to guests. Rooms start at 140,000 lire ($118).

The best of the Italian lake district
Italy's Lake Country has steeply rolling hills and a Mediterranean touch. Olive groves and palm trees surround the warm waters.

The largest and clearest lake
Lake Garda is the largest, clearest, and most visited of the Italian lakes. It is surrounded by Mediterranean scenery—rugged, tawny hills dotted with olive and lemon groves and long, shuttered farmhouses. Desenzano, one of the lake's major and most crowded towns, lies on the Venice-Milan train line. From there, it's easy to get to the other lake towns by bus or boat.

Torbole, at the far end of Lake Garda, is the windsurfing capital of Europe because of the steady breezes that blow across the lake.

Europe's deepest lake
Lake Como is Europe's deepest lake. Sadly, it is too polluted for swimming near the main towns of Como and Bellagio. Como is worldly, wealthy, and refined. Its duomo is one of the most famous churches in Italy. Built between 1457 and 1485, it has a lovely rose window and houses Bernardino Luini's (1475-1533) *Adoration of the Magi*.

The artists' favorite
Bellagio, the lake district's art center, invites artists to spend a month or more there developing works in progress. Located at the point where Lake Como intersects with Lake Lecco, it has narrow streets and ancient buildings. The beach is next to the Villa Serbelloni in the center of town.

The most entertaining restaurant
The most entertaining restaurant in the lake district is on an island in the middle of Lake Como. To get there, drive to Menaggio and then to the Isola Comacina. The restaurant is called, imaginatively, **Locanda dell'Isola Comacina**, *tel. (39-344)55-083*. Park your car at the edge of the lake, and a boatman will ferry you out to the island.

When you arrive, introduce yourself to the owner, Benvenuto Puricelli. He will show you to your table and start the food coming your way. You do not choose from a menu. The waiters simply bring you the evening's dishes—including warm bread straight from the oven and a vast selection of fresh vegetables, meat, and fish.

As a finale, Benvenuto turns out the lights and puts a torch to an alcoholic concoction. Then, as the liquor burns, he ladles the brew into the air in fiery garlands while reciting the history of the island. (According to legend, a curse was laid on the island in the 12th century.)

Although the restaurant is still obscure, it is acquiring an international reputation. It is one of Bruce Springsteen's favorites. And the all-inclusive price is only 75,000 lire ($63).

Europe's finest resort hotel
Villa d'Este, *tel. (39-31)511-471*, in Cernobbio on Lake Como, is one of Europe's finest resort hotels. Located in a 15th-century villa begun by Cardinal Gallio, it was later used as a palace by an Empress of Russia, a Princess of Wales, and other members of royalty. In 1873 it became a hotel. It is beautifully furnished and offers concerts, dances, tennis, golf, riding, swimming, water sports, and boating. Open from March to October, the Villa d'Este is very expensive.

The gem of the lakes

Floating in the middle of peaceful **Lago d'Orta** is emerald-green **San Giulio Island**, the little-known gem of the lakes. According to legend, St. Julius (San Giulio) ventured to the forested island in the latter half of the fourth century to rid it of an infestation of snakes and dragons. The island, which is 330 yards long and 175 yards across, hides an age-old settlement and an assembly of Romanesque art treasures. Only one family and the 22 nuns who maintain the island's towering convent live here year-round.

On Wednesday mornings, while mist is still rising off the lake, nuns cross the lake in small fishing boats, as their predecessors did, to attend the weekly open-air market in Orta.

Each year in July, when the population of San Giulio Island reaches 300, townsfolk gather in the main square to sing popular island songs. This ancient tradition is believed to date back to the time of St. Julius, when early Christians gathered in front of the island's basilica to sing hymns.

On Sundays in September, San Giulio sponsors concerts that combine classical and regional folk music. But the island's most colorful festival is Jan. 31, St. Julius Day. From midnight until late into the following evening, there are fireworks, music, and dancing.

On San Giulio, among the elegant villas, terraces, clusters of rich green trees, and fragrant flower gardens of the summer, are some of the finest examples of Romanesque art in all Italy. The Romanesque basilica has undergone several renovations. Its history can be traced to the 11th century, but islanders will tell you that it goes back nearly 700 years earlier, to the time of St. Julius.

Inside the basilica is a remarkable collection of frescoes from the 15th century, most by local painters. The masterpiece of the basilica is the 12th-century Pulpit of the Comacine Masters. Gorgeously ornamented with the symbols of the four Evangelists and splendid animals, the polychrome wooden bas-reliefs are supported by marble columns. The bells of the basilica ring on Sunday mornings and can be heard for miles around.

The island's only restaurant is the **Ristorante San Giulio**, where succulent regional specialties, such as *minestrone alla Milanese* and *costoletta* (a veal dish), are served, along with a fine selection of sparkling white and red wines.

The island has no hotels. Stay at one of the hotels in nearby Orta; contact the tourist office, *(39-322)90-354,* for assistance.

Umbria: the best of the heartland

Undulating **Umbria** is Italy's heartland, stretching between Rome and Florence. This hilly, forested countryside is dotted with Renaissance architectural gems, ancient farmhouses, vineyards, olive groves, and orchards. Umbria's medieval cities perch on hilltops and hang from mountain sides. St. Francis was born in Umbria, and he left his mark throughout the region.

Umbria's strangest sight

The small town of **Bomarzo** is known for the fascinating but creepy garden at the Villa of Orsini. In the late 15th century, Prince Vicino Orsini created these landscaped gardens, which are dotted with bizarre sculptures. Known as Il Sacro Bosco (the Sacred Wood) or the Parco dei Mostri (Park of Monsters), it is filled with statues of half-human, half-animal monsters.

The most beautiful Umbrian town

Orvieto, perched on an enormous rock, is the most beautiful town in the region. It is known for its **duomo**, built in 1229, which has a golden, mosaic-decorated front that glitters when it reflects the sun. Pope Nicholas IV commissioned the duomo to commemorate a miracle. According to Church lore, drops of blood appeared on the Host consecrated by a Bohemian priest who had doubted the Doctrine of Transubstantiation (the belief that during the sacrament of communion the bread actually becomes the body of Christ and the wine His blood). The blood-stained chalice cloth is kept in the cathedral and carried through town during the feast of Corpus Christi and again on Easter Sunday. The duomo has opaque alabaster windows, a rose window designed by Andrea Orcagna, and frescoes begun by Fra Angelico.

The best place to stay in Orvieto is three miles outside town in La Badia. The **Hotel La Badia,** *La Badia, Orvieto Scalo 05019; tel. (39-763)90-359,* a former abbey that dates back to the 1100s, has comfortable rooms with private baths and a first-class restaurant that features produce from the abbey's own farm. This beautiful complex has a swimming pool and tennis courts, as well as a church of Romanesque-Lombard style and a 12-sided tower. The buildings contain frescoes from the 12th, 13th, and 14th centuries. In the 15th century, the abbey was a retreat for cardinals. It has been in the hands of the family of Count Giuseppe Fiumi for the past century. A double room starts at 134,500 lire ($114).

Perugia: a historical treasure house

Perugia is a town of historic treasures. The most fascinating sight is the **via Bagliona Sotteranea,** an underground street filled with the ruins of 15th-century houses. You enter through the Porta Marzia, a second-century Etruscan doorway. Visit the 13th-century **Fontana Maggiore** and stroll along the palace-lined **Corso Vanucci.** The town's **Collegio del Cambio** was frescoed by Perugino and his helpers, one of whom may have been Raphael, in the early 16th century. Upstairs is the **National Gallery.**

Perugia's best hotel is **La Rosetta,** *Piazza d'Italia 19; tel. (39-75)20841.* Located at the top of the Corso Vannucci, near the main sights, it is friendly and efficient, and the food is delicious. Rooms at the back are quieter. A double room is 184,000 lire ($156).

Umbria's most inviting hotel

Torgiano, a walled town complete with towers, boasts the splendid **Baglioni Palace,** which houses a wine museum founded by the local producers of Chardonnay.

The other reason to stop in Torgiano is the **Hotel Le Tre Vaselle,** *via Garibaldi 48, 06089 Perugia; tel. (39-75)988-0447.* Housed in a 300-year-old villa, it has 16th-century wooden doors, thick walls, and hand-hewn ceiling beams and arches. It is a peaceful place on a side street, with spacious bedrooms and views of the countryside. Rooms are decorated with textiles and flowers, and Umbrian specialties are served in the dining room. Try artichoke risotto sage-and-onion bread tarts baked in a wood oven and the traditional Umbrian wafer made in 16th-century molds and flavored with anise. The hotel is often used for conferences of oenologists (wine experts), because it is owned by the Lungarotti Wine Company. A double room starts at 280,000 lire ($237).

In the footsteps of St. Francis

Traces of peace-loving St. Francis are evident throughout **Assisi,** an ethereal mountainside town with medieval houses. Just outside Assisi is the **Basilica Santa Maria,** which includes the fourth-century Chapel of Porziuncola, used by St. Francis and his followers.

St. Francis is buried in the **Basilica of San Francesco**—his remains are kept in the structure's 19th-century crypt. Giotto painted 28 scenes from the life of the saint here. Black-robed pilgrims flock to the basilica from the countryside year-round.

The corpse of St. Clare is exposed and can be viewed in its crystal casket in the crypt of the **Basilica of Santa Chiara,** across town.

Outside Assisi, visit the **Convent of St. Damian,** where St. Francis received his holy orders. See the crucifix that supposedly spoke to St. Francis and the rooms where St. Clare lived, worked, and fought off marauders. Go on to the Eremo delle Carceri, a minute church hollowed out of a rock by St. Francis and his followers in a nearby wood.

Hotel Fontebella, *via Fontebella 25, Assisi 06081; tel. (39-75)812-883,* is located in a 17th-century palazzo in the center of town. Most rooms have a balcony with a view of the city. Guests can play cards and drink cocktails in the comfortable sitting room. The hotel restaurant, Il Frantoio, is expensive. Double rooms are 180,000 lire ($152).

The best of Tuscany

Tuscany has historic towns, fashionable beach resorts, and a leading spa favored by the Italian *bene* (elite). The region that gave us Michelangelo and Leonardo da Vinci continues its artistic traditions, creating marble sculpture and fine gold and leather crafts. Yet it is seldom crowded with tourists.

The oldest Tuscan town

Drive up into the hills above Florence to visit **Fiesole**, one of the 12 great towns of ancient Etruria. Long before there was a Florence, this little town sat above the Arno Valley. In 283 B.C., Etruscan Fiesole was conquered by the Romans, who left behind an amphitheater built in 80 B.C. Classical plays are presented in the restored ruins.

An ochre-colored path leads from the Piazza Mino to the San Francesco Monastery in Fiesole. From the path, you can enjoy one of the best views of Florence. The cloister of the Gothic monastery is filled with Chinese art from the era of Marco Polo.

The town's duomo, built in A.D. 1000, has gray Corinthian columns and Romanesque arches. Paintings by Fra Angelico and Fra Filippo Lippi are displayed at the Museo Bandini.

The best place to dine in Fiesole is the **Hotel Aurora**, *Piazza Mino, 50014 Fiesole; tel. (39-55)59-100.* It has a charming garden and great views, as well as inexpensive Tuscan fare.

Villa San Michele, *via Doccia, 4 Fiesole, 50014 Florence; tel. (39-55)59-451,* is a deluxe hotel in a former Franciscan monastery. Monks' cells have been converted into lavishly decorated bedrooms and suites. Michelangelo is supposed to have designed the building. A double room is 500,000 lire to 650,000 lire ($424 to $550).

The best wine-making estate

Not far from Florence, just off Superstrada 67, is the wine-making **Artimino Estate**, with its 740 acres of vineyards, olive groves, and gardens. In the late 16th century, the villa was commissioned by Grand Duke Ferdinand I to house his court. It became known as La Ferdinanda.

An excellent restaurant, **Biagio Pignatta**, is located on the estate's grounds. It offers Tuscan dishes and the eight wines grown on the estate according to age-old traditions. Wood-burning ovens braise the meats to perfection. The *scaloppina ai carciofi* (veal and artichokes), *bistecca alla Fiorentina* (charcoal-broiled beefsteak), and *faraona alla brace* (broiled guinea hen) are superb. The restaurant is closed on Mondays and Thursdays.

Hotel Paggeria Medicea, *tel. (39-55)87-18-081,* adjacent to the villa, has 37 rooms with wood beams and enormous fireplaces, as well as 20th-century conveniences, such as telephones, televisions, and refrigerated bars. The hotel is in a 17th-century building formerly called Il Corridoio (the Hallway), because it once separated the court residence from the servants' quarters. A double room is 240,000 lire ($203), including breakfast.

The prettiest Tuscan town

Lucca, a small city enclosed within vast ramparts, is the prettiest town in Tuscany. The 12th-century town is beautifully preserved and maintained. Delightfully cool and shaded green walkways follow the massive 16th-century brick and turf walls that surround the town. The curious towers here are typical of Tuscan towns. In the Middle Ages, most patrician houses were dominated by very high and slender towers often crowned with ilex trees (the tower of the Palazzo Guinigi, for example). After exploring Lucca's historic churches, wander through the narrow streets, which are filled with boutiques.

Lucca's grand **Romanesque cathedral** is filled with artistic treasures. Jacopo della Quercia designed the tomb of Ilaria del Carretto, wife of the Lord of Lucca in the early 15th century. A strangely lifelike statue of Ilaria reclines on top of the tomb. Other treasures include Tintoretto's *Last Supper* and Ghirlandaio's *Madonna and Saints*. A life-sized statue of Christ that drifted ashore at the nearby town of Luni is kept in a round chapel in the north nave. Every Sept. 13, the statue is carried through town in memory of the day it miraculously appeared. The facade of the cathedral is carved with religious allegories and fantastic animals. Nicola Pisano's *Deposition* and *Nativity* are above the door on the right.

Inside the **Church of San Michel** is a painting of saints Sebastian, Roch, Jerome, and Helen by Fra Filippo Lippi.

The **Church of San Frediano** houses the mummy of Santa Zita. On April 26, the townspeople place the body in the middle of the church and stroke and kiss its withered limbs.

The best restaurant in town is the **Buca di Sant'Antonio,** *via della Cervia 3, Lucca 55100; tel. (39-583)55881.* Kid roasted on a spit is a specialty. Try the local wine, Rosso delle Colline Lucchesi. Dinner is about 40,000 lire ($34).

Lucca has a shortage of hotels. Of the nine small hotels here, the most comfortable and convenient is the **Albergo Universo,** *Piazza Puccini, Lucca 55100; tel. (39-583)491-543.*

The best-preserved Tuscan town

San Gimignano, with its noble towers, is one of the best-preserved medieval towns in Italy. Unfortunately, tourists flock to this 14th-century gem, crowding the streets. It's difficult to imagine where they all stay—only three hotels are located within the town walls. During the fall, the town is filled with hunters. (Hunting is good in the surrounding hills.)

Fourteen of the 72 towers that once protected this town still stand. At one time, all 72 spires crowded around the main square that surrounds the 13th-century *cisterna* (well). The small square is curiously paved with bricks laid on their narrow sides in a herringbone pattern.

The best (and at one time only) hotel is **La Cisterna,** *Piazza della Cisterna 24, 53037 San Gimignano (Siena); tel. (39-577)940-328,* on the main square. It is an elegant, comfortable, well-run place with an excellent restaurant, La Terrazza. Sit on the terrace to watch the lights blink on in farmhouses and peaceful villages as night falls over the valley.

Tuscany's crown jewel: Siena

The jewel in Tuscany's crown is **Siena,** a beautifully preserved town with wide-open spaces and ancient palaces. It is known for its university, its musical academy, and the annual Palio (a centuries-old horse race). Siena's cathedral, a striped marble structure, reaches high into the sky.

The 14th-century walls that surround Siena were used during World War II to prevent retreating German troops from passing through the city. When the ancient portals were shut, 20th-century tanks couldn't get through!

Siena's most beautiful square is the **Piazza del Campo,** which is bordered by the city's magnificent palaces and the 13th-century Palazzo Pubblico (city hall), which houses the town museum. Built of brick, the city hall is a fine specimen of pointed Gothic architecture. The slim, elegant, 334-foot tower (Torre del Mangia) soars high over the city. Its shadow moves across the brick paving as the day progresses. The Sienese Museum is a good introduction to Siena.

In the evening, join the Sienese in their stroll along the *passeggiata,* or promenade, along the curving Banchi di Sopra. The *passeggiata* leads through the banking district.

Notice the Monte dei Paschiu di Siena, a bank housed in the 14th-century Palazzo Salimbeni. The bank was founded in 1472 and is still in business. Nearby is Palazzo Tolomei, the oldest private palace in Siena, now home to the Cassa di Risparmio di Firenze, another bank.

The most beautiful Sienese artwork is on display at the **Pinacoteca**, which contains Byzantine paintings and works by Simone Martini.

The most exciting time to visit

The most exciting time to visit Siena is during the **Palio**, which is held July 2 and Aug. 16 each year. This bareback three-lap horse race around the shell-shaped Piazza del Campo is one of the most genuine and fascinating of all Italian spectacles. It lasts all of 90 seconds but generates feuds that continue for decades.

The Palio is a competition between 10 of Siena's 17 *contrade,* or districts. During the days preceding the race, the people of Siena revert to the venality of the Middle Ages. Bribery, meddling, and skulduggery are not only permitted but also encouraged. *Contrade* captains are expected to indulge in intrigue as part of their efforts to outdo their rivals. Millions of lire are spent bribing the jockeys.

The Palio has its roots in the Middle Ages, when Siena was an independent republic. At that time, the 17 contrade were separate military societies, each defended by its own military forces. Life in Siena in the Middle Ages was not easy. Homes were small, cold, and badly ventilated and had little light. The streets were narrow and murky and bristled with the threat of ambush. The walls that surrounded the city and those of the high buildings along the streets were blackened by smoke. The danger of epidemic was great, as was the possibility of dying by the sword or dagger. In light of all this, it is no wonder the people looked for escape. The Compagnie Popolari were organized to help provide distraction. These companies, each from a different section of the city, were intended to keep the people happy and free from worries (and thoughts of revolt, no doubt) by initiating games. One of the games the Compagnie Popolari initiated was the Palio.

The best hotels and restaurants

The **Park Hotel,** *via di Marciano 18; tel. (39-577)44-803,* is the best place to stay in Siena. Located in a 15th-century villa, it has modern amenities, such as air conditioning, a heated swimming pool, and central heating. Terraces, gardens, and vineyards surround the villa. Situated on Marciano Hill, it has good views. A double room is 290,000 lire ($245) a night.

Pisa: Tuscany's most famous sight

Pisa, which is famous for its leaning tower, has less-known sights that also are worth seeing: the cathedral, the baptistery, and the Campo Santo. The **duomo** is fronted by white columns that support five tapered arcades. Winged angels peer out from the corners, and mysterious inscriptions can be found on the walls. Inside are Corinthian columns and striped walls. Art in the cathedral includes an ivory Madonna by Giovanni Pisano, Andrea del Sarto's *Sant'Agnese Mourning,* and Giovanni del Biondo's *Flight From Egypt* and *Presentation at the Temple.*

The **baptistery** has gables, arches, and stained-glass windows. A white shaft of light shines through the baptistery dome onto the floor. Sounds echo eerily in the dome.

The **Campo Santo** is a walled cemetery filled with earth brought back from Calvary by the Crusaders. The cemetery walls are covered with terrifying medieval frescoes: *The Triumph of Death, The Last Judgement,* and *Hell.* The last is a picture of snakes, skewered corpses, and demons punishing sinners.

Sicily: Italy at its most exotic

Sicily, an island at the southern tip of Italy, is a land unto itself. The least Italian region of Italy, it has been invaded and settled by Carthaginians, Greeks, Saracens, Normans, and Spaniards over the last 3,000 years. And each group has left its mark on the island's culture. In ancient times, Sicily was part of Greece. Later, it became part of the Roman Empire. After the fall of Rome, it was invaded by northern tribes, Saracens, Byzantines, Normans, French, and Spanish. It didn't become part of Italy until 1860.

Sicily's climate is more like that of northern Africa than that of Europe. So the best time to visit is the spring or fall. (It is blisteringly hot in the summer.)

The best-preserved relics

Some of the best-preserved relics of ancient Greece are scattered across Sicily. Taormina's amphitheater is spectacular, with Mount Etna smoking behind it. The temple in Segesta (a town in western Sicily) is set on a lonely hill facing a huge amphitheater. In Agrigento, the temples to Juno, Concordia, and Hercules are awe-inspiring. Visit Messina, founded by the Greeks in the eighth century, and Siracusa (Syracuse), which has archeological evidence of the ancient Greeks and Romans.

Europe's highest active volcano

Europe's highest active volcano is in Sicily. **Mount Etna** rises 9,840 feet. Don't take the organized tour of Mount Etna—it is a terrible disappointment. The trip takes all day, and you will see nothing but dirt and rocks. The group never goes near the crater.

The least-changed towns

The smaller hill towns in Sicily are some of the least modern in Italy. Donkeys and mules rather than cars and trucks carry loads. Women carry water from wells in jars on their heads. Each morning, a goatherd follows his goats into town. He milks the goats at each door, delivering fresh milk to the residents. Plumbing in some towns in nonexistent, and water is scarce.

Sicily's most charming resort

Taormina is the most charming resort town in Sicily. Set on a ridge with a spectacular view of the bay, its greatest sight is the Greek theater carved out of the hillside, which is still used for productions during summer theater festivals. Palazzo Corvaia, the site of Sicily's parliament in the 14th century, is on the Piazza Vittorio Emanuele. Enjoy a glass of wine and a view of the bay from one of the many cafés along the Piazza 9 Aprile.

The best way to get to Sicily

The most beautiful way to get to Sicily is by ferry or hydrofoil from the southern tip of the mainland at Reggio di Calabria or Villa San Giovanni across the Strait of Messina. The crossing is long and often rough, but always lovely. Boats also connect with Naples, Livorno (Leghorn), Genoa, and Cagliari. You also can fly to Palermo and Catania from major Italian cities.

Sicilian cuisine—Italy's most colorful

Sicily is known for its exotic and colorful dishes, which have a slightly Arabic flavor. One typical dish of the region is *pasta con le sarde*, in which pine nuts and currants lend a Middle Eastern touch to *bucatini* (thick, hollow spaghetti) in a sauce of fresh sardines and wild fennel. The combination of pine nuts and currants is common. Eggplant and sun-ripened fresh tomatoes also are commonly used.

La Scuderia, *viale del Fante 9; tel. (39-91)520-323*, one of the best restaurants in Palermo, serves sophisticated Sicilian cooking. It is expensive by Sicilian standards.

Trattoria Primavera, *Piazza Bologni 2; tel. (39-91)329-408*, also in Palermo, has simple food and low prices. It is closed Fridays. Dinner for one is about 30,000 lire ($25).

The best places to sleep in Sicily

Palermo's luxury hotel is the **Grand Hotel Villa Igiea**, *Palermo 091, Sicily; tel. (39-91)543-744*. Designed to look like a castle, this hotel is right on the sea. It has lovely flower gardens with palm trees and the ruins of an ancient temple. A swimming pool, tennis courts, an elevator, and a bar add to the amenities of the Grand. All rooms have baths. You can have a car sent to pick you up at the train station. A double room starts at 450,000 lire ($380).

Villa San Michele, *tel. (39-942)24-327*, in Taormina is inexpensive. The food is lavish. Ask the staff to pack you a picnic lunch, then walk down the steep hill to spend a day at the beach. A double room at the villa is 140,000 lire ($118).

Unconquered Sardinia, the wildest region

"Unconquered **Sardinia**," as D.H. Lawrence called it, is the least-tamed region in Italy. It is still the land of the *banditti*, family clans, and blood feuds. It has produced such rebels as Antonio Gramsci, theorist and founder of the Italian Communist Party.

Today, Sardinia also attracts movie stars and royalty. Prince Karim bought 35 miles of coastline and established the most luxurious resort in Italy: the **Costa Smeralda**.

Despite an onslaught of foreign tourists and developers, Sardinia is beautiful—hilly and occasionally tropical. The coast has granite cliffs and long, sandy beaches. The water is the cleanest in the Mediterranean. What's more, Sardinia has fascinating Roman ruins at Nora and Tharros, as well as prehistoric stone towers called *nuraghi*.

Cagliari, the best bet

Costa Smeralda has become an expensive luxury resort for the jet set. A better bet is **Cagliari**, on the southern coast, which has inexpensive hotels and a charming medieval district called the Castello. Narrow streets and tall towers cover the hills rising out of the harbor. This friendly town is near the *nuraghi* ruins at Barumini and the sandy beaches of the Costa del Sud. Pink flamingos inhabit the lagoons outside town. The tourist office in Piazza Matteotti can help you find a room.

Cagliari has good seafood restaurants. **Dal Corso**, *viale Regina Margherita 28; tel. (39-70)66-43-18*, serves fresh lobster, eel, shrimp, and fish.

Trattoria Gennargentu, *via Sardegna 60; tel. (39-70)65-82-47*, serves enormous plates of lasagne, shish kebab, and squid for the ridiculously low price of 20,000 lire ($17). The trattoria is comfortable, has plenty of local atmosphere, and serves a good house wine.

A good, cheap place to stay in Cagliari is **Locanda Firenze**, *Corso Vittorio Emanuele 50; tel. (39-70)65-36-78*. It has clean, pleasant rooms, and the management speaks English. The hotel, which is on the third floor, has no elevator. A double room starts at 20,000 lire ($17).

Sardinia's oldest city

Nora, a small city near Cagliari, is the oldest city in Sardinia. Settled by Phoenicians, who left the ruins of their temple behind, it became a bustling Roman town before it died out about A.D. 500. The Roman roads and theater are well-preserved, and the ruins are being excavated. Climb to the Spanish watchtower for tremendous views of the sea, which breaks on either side of the isthmus.

The best beaches

La Costa del Sud, about 31 miles southwest of Cagliari, has unspoiled beaches and hidden coves. The water is turquoise and perfectly clear. Buses run to the coast from Cagliari as far as the beach near the Torre di Chia. But the next beach over, Capo Spartivento, is larger and has two lovely islands that are great for sunbathing.

Sardinia's unique ruins

Don't leave Sardinia without examining its **nuraghi**—ancient stone towers found only in this part of Italy. They were once used as tombs, temples, or forts of refuge. The **Nuraghi of Su Nuraxi** in Barumini, near Cagliari, are the best-preserved in Sardinia. Set on a hill, they are the remains of an ancient village. The huge blocks of stone were designed primarily for defense. The huge central tower dates to about 1300 B.C. The Nuraghi of Su Nuraxi can be visited every day except Mondays.

The town of **Sassari** has the best Sardinian museum, the **Museo Giovanni Antonio Sanna**, *via Roma 64*. See reconstructed *nuraghi*, Sardinian paintings and costumes, Roman statues and mosaics, and an ethnographic section where Sardinian music is played. Open 9 a.m. until 2 p.m. Tuesdays through Saturdays and 9 a.m. until 1 p.m. Sundays.

Two good, inexpensive hotels in Sassari are **Albergo Gallura**, *Vicolo San Leonardo 9; tel. (39-79)238-713*, and **Albergo Giusy**, *Piazza Sant'Antonio 21; tel. (39-79)233-327*. The first is well-run and located in the center of town. The second is very comfortable and located at the far end of Corso Vittorio Emanuele. A double room is 56,000 lire ($47).

The best Roman ruins

Near Sassari, **Porto Torres** occupies the site of the Roman town **Turris Libisonis**. Remains of the Roman settlement, including a circular marble altar and the baths of the Palace of the Barbarian King (Palazzo di Re Barbaro), can be seen next to the train station. Seven arches of an ancient Roman bridge span the River Turritano. The Church of San Gavino is one of Sardinia's most notable monuments. Built in the 11th century, it has 28 columns and a wooden truss ceiling.

Sardinia's most beautiful city

Alghero, the most beautiful and best-preserved city in Sardinia, has a Spanish flavor. Sardinia was united with Aragon in 1325, and the Spaniards left their mark on Alghero, which looks somewhat like Barcelona. Alleys are covered with arches, and some restaurants serve *paella*. Starting at the Bastione della Maddalena in the port, walk around the ramparts and the 16th-century Spanish towers to enjoy the view of the shimmering sea.

Outside Alghero are two beaches with clean, clear water—**Spiaggia di San Giovanni** and **Spiaggia di Maria Pia**. Both are crowded. A short boat trip away is the **Grotto di Nettuno**, which puts Capri's Blue Grotto to shame. The large underwater cavern can be visited by boats that leave from docks in front of Bastione della Maddalena.

One of the best restaurants in Alghero is **Il Pavone**, *Piazza Sulis 3/4; tel. (39-79)97-95-84*. This family-run restaurant serves excellent soups, antipastos, risottos, and seafood. A meal for two is about 44,000 lire ($37). Il Pavone is closed Wednesdays and from Dec. 20 through Jan. 20. Reservations are a good idea.

The Best of Portugal

> I am very happy here, because I loves oranges, and talk bad Latin to the Monks, who understand it as it is like their own. And I goes into society (with my pocket pistols), and I swims in the Taqus all across at once, and I rides on an ass or a mule and swears Portuguese.
> —*Lord Byron, 1809*

Portugal is the best travel bargain in Europe. As beautiful and historic as neighboring Spain, it is far cheaper and less developed. Don't make the mistake of most foreigners and visit only Lisbon. Portugal has much to offer outside this capital city, including quaint old villages surrounded by rolling hills, Moorish cities, long sandy beaches, and mountain vistas.

Portuguese culture has been influenced by the Moors, Catholicism, and a seafaring history. The Portuguese sing the fado, a heart-rending, wailing sort of blues. Their unique cuisine includes *bacalhau*, a dried codfish served a different way every day of the year. Portugal has its own sweet wines, port and Madeira. And the Portuguese have a version of the bullfight gentler than that in Spain. Portuguese matadors wrestle the bull but never kill the animal. At the end of a bullfight, the bull is enticed out of the ring by a cow.

Portugal's cultural center: Lisbon

The capital of Portugal is studded with ancient Moorish quarters and bordered by lovely beaches. Its National Museum of Ancient Art houses one of Europe's best collections. Outside Lisbon are palaces that rival the chateaux of the Loire in France. And at the heart of the city are winding streets that pass medieval churches and inviting cafés.

Built on a series of hills, **Lisbon** has 17 overlooks, called *miradouros*, that offer wide views of the city. The best is at the Castelo de São Jorge, built in the fifth century by the Visigoths and later used as a Moorish stronghold. Another panoramic view is from the top of the statue of Cristo Rei, or Christ the King (a smaller replica of the one in Rio de Janeiro), located on the opposite side of the Tagus River from the city. To get there, cross the Ponte 25 do Abril.

163

Lisbon's seven best sights

Lisbon's most beautiful landmark is the **Basilica da Estrela**, *Largo da Estrela*. Queen Maria I promised God she would build the basilica if he granted her a son. God kept His part of the bargain, and the basilica was built in the late 18th century of luminous pale marble and topped with an enormous stone dome. Maria's tomb is inside. Look for the life-size manger scene carved by Machado de Castro.

The **Se** (cathedral), *Largo de Se*, is downtown's most imposing structure. The 12th-century cathedral was once a fortress and has battlements, two towers, and massive walls. Behind the austere facade are Gothic cloisters and a burial chapel.

Igreja de São Roque is a Jesuit church with an ornate chapel called São Joao Baptista, which is lavishly decorated with amethyst, agate, marble, and entire columns of Chilean lapis lazuli.

The **Gulbenkian Museum**, *ave. de Berna 45*, houses the huge collection of French furniture, Oriental carpets, and great paintings of the eccentric millionaire Calouste Gulbenkian, as well as Beauvais tapestries.

The **Museu de Etnologia**, *avenida Ilha da Madeira*, has one of the finest collections of African art in the world.

Museu National de Arte Antiga, *rua das Janelas Verdes 9*, contains one of Portugal's greatest treasures, the polyptych of the *Adoration of St. Vincent*, painted by Nuno Gonçalves between 1460 and 1470. The six-panel work surrounds a statue of St. Vincent, patron saint of Portugal.

Igreja da Madre de Deus has Europe's best display of antique tiles, called *azulejos*, which line the 16th-century crypt.

Belém: an island of bests

Belém, an island in the middle of the Tagus, west of downtown Lisbon, is surrounded by museums and monuments. The **Torre de Belem**, a five-story tower, is the most outstanding landmark. Built between 1515 and 1521, cannons on this Gothic structure protected the Tagus for centuries. A statue of *Our Lady of Safe Homecoming* on the tower's peak welcomes sailors home from sea.

In 1502, the profits of the spice trade were used to build the magnificent **Mosteiro dos Jeronimos**, a celebration of Vasco da Gama and other Portuguese explorers. This was da Gama's point of return after finding the sea route to India. He is buried in this church, which is backed by a decorative cloister with columns, arches, fountains, and cool stone benches. In front is the *Monument to the Navigators*—erected in 1960 in the shape of a ship's prow.

Belém is also home to the Museum of Folk Art, the National Coach Museum, and the Naval Museum, which houses beautifully restored ships, as well as early airplanes. (The Naval Museum has spurred much controversy because it spoils the view from the Torre de Belém.)

Lisbon's oldest quarter, the Alfama

The only neighborhood in Lisbon not destroyed by the great earthquake on All Saints' Day, 1755, is the **Alfama**, whose tiny medieval streets twist and turn between rows of shops and old houses. The violent earthquake, which struck while most of the city's residents were in church, was followed by 40-foot tidal waves and fires that burned for a week. At least 60,000 people died. Voltaire wrote about it in *Candide*.

The Alfama existed before the Visigoths arrived in the fifth century. It clusters beneath the Castelo São Jorge on one of Lisbon's tallest hills. The cobblestoned streets are so narrow that in some places you must walk single file. Wrought-iron lamps light the streets. Canaries and geraniums brighten the balconies. Laundry waves from lines strung above the streets. Tiles portraying the Virgin Mary, St. Anthony, and St. Martial decorate buildings, some of which date back to the Moors or the Middle Ages.

Walking along **Beco do Mexias**, you pass dozens of tiny shops and come to a doorway that leads to a large fountain where local women do their laundry. Also explore **rua da Regueira**, which is lined with restaurants and shops, and **Patio das Flores**, a little square with houses faced in tile.

Lisbon's most colorful market

Begin your day in Lisbon wandering through the fish market at the foot of the Alfama. Weathered fishermen bring in their catches here, and *varinhas*, or fishwives, march about with baskets of fish on their heads. The *varinhas* wear black skirts with aprons and go barefoot in the summer. Gold hoops dangle from their ears.

Lisbon's best shopping

Veer off the grand avenida da Liberdade onto the rua do Carmo and rua Garrett. This is **Chiado**, Lisbon's shopping district, where you'll find jewelry, Portuguese tiles, leather goods, and wine for reasonable prices.

Lisbon's other main shopping area, **Baixa**, is located between Rossio Square and the river. Here are old bookshops and antique stores. The best place for gold and silver filigree is **Sarmento**, *rua do Ouro 251*. **Por-fi-ri-os Contraste**, *rua da Vitoria 63*, sells the skimpiest bikinis around. **Helio Cinderela**, *rua do Carmo 93*, has good prices on Charles Jourdan shoes and smart leather bags. **Saboia**, *rua Garrett 44*, sells fine men's suits.

Brightly colored *azulejos* are sold at **Fabrica Sant'Anna**, *rua do Alecrin 95*.

Where to find a real steal

A cheap, offbeat place to shop is the **Feira da Ladra** (Market of Female Thieves). This 300-year-old market is similar to huge flea markets in Rome and Paris. Originally, it was literally a market of *sovaqueiras*, or female thieves. The *sovaqueiras* hid illegal wares in their armpits and sold them at stalls then located in Lisbon's central Rossio Square. In 1882, the market was moved to the Campo de Santa Clara, in the shadows of the Pantheon of St. Vincent, where the bodies of the kings of Portugal lie. You can buy just about anything you want at this market. Be on the lookout for bronze, copper, and gold—sometimes you can find great bargains. But be wary, because you also can be ripped off. The market is open Tuesdays and Saturdays.

Portugal's liveliest country market

If you're in Lisbon on the first Sunday of the month, take a detour to the country fair at **Vila Nogueria de Azeitão**, 21 miles south of the city. Portugal's liveliest and largest marketplace, the Azeitão offers everything from livestock and household furnishings to clothing and food. If you miss the fair at Azeitão, the nearby villages of Pinhal, Novo, Coina, and Moita have fairs on succeeding Sundays. Prices at these fairs are lower than those in city stores. Haggling is expected.

The best dishes

Lisbon is famous for its seafood, and the Alfama and the Bairro Alto are the best places to dine on the local *camaróes* (shrimp), *langosta* (lobster), *pesca espada* (swordfish), *salmonete* (red mullet), *linguado* (sole), and *bacalhau*, as well as the ubiquitous *sardinas grilhadas* (fresh grilled sardines), which are delicious. If you see *carne de porco com ameijoas* or *ameijoas na cataplana* on a menu, order it. These are uniquely south Portuguese combinations of pork and sausage with clams.

Drink Sumol (lemon or orange soda), Sagres *cerveja* (beer), or the local wine, Dão or Vinho Verde. Most of the gin and whiskey in Portugal is faked.

The best restaurants

The best restaurant in Lisbon is **Tagide**, *Largo da Academia Nacional de Belas Artes*,

18; tel. (351-1)34-60-570. Michelin gave it a star and especially recommends its salmon paté and the pork. It is closed Saturdays and Sundays. Dinner is 9,000 to 10,000 escudos ($65 to $73).

Tavares, *rua de Misericordia 37; tel. (351-1)34-21-112,* is Portugal's most elegant restaurant. Founded in 1784, it serves traditional Portuguese cuisine. The enormous mirrors and magnificent chandelier are trappings of bygone days. A full-course meal, including Portuguese wine, is 5,000 to 7,000 escudos ($36 to $51).

Casa da Comida, *Travessa das Amoreiras 1; tel. (351-1)68-53-76,* is a Michelin-star winner with a pretty patio. Meals are 8,000 to 10,000 escudos ($58 to $73).

However, the best meal for the best price is at **Conventual,** *Praça das Flores 45; tel. (351-1)60-91-96.* Despite its Michelin star, it charges merely 4,000 escudos to 6,000 escudos ($29 to $43) for dinner.

Fado: Portugal's saddest music

Fado, which means *fate*, is as important to Portugal as flamenco is to Spain—although it is more intense and somber. The best fado is played in the Alfama, the Mouraria (another neighborhood with Moorish traditions), the Bairro Alto (the old section), and the Madragoa (the fishermen's quarter). Fado songs range over many octaves, almost always in a minor key. They are usually sung by women dressed from head to toe in melancholy black and carrying red roses. Male fado singers or guitar accompanists wear black monks' robes.

Some of the songs date back to the 13th century; others are influenced by Portugal's Moorish past (and sound atonal) or by Portugal's seafaring tradition (and are reminiscent of sea chanties). Most are about unrequited love.

Recommended fado restaurants include **Cota d'Armas,** *Beco de São Miguel; tel. (351-1)86-86-82;* **Parreirinha de Alfama,** *Beco do Espirito Santo; tel. (351-1)86-82-09;* **Fado Menor,** *rua das Praças 16;* **Painel do Fado,** *rua S. Pedro de Alcantara 65/69;* **Senhor Vinho,** *Meio-a-Lapa 18; tel. (351-1)39-72-681;* **Lisboa à Noite,** *rua das Gaveas 69; tel. (351-1)34-62-603;* and **A Severa,** *rua das Gaveas 51-61; tel. (351-1)34-64-006.* You must make reservations. Go after a late dinner; shows don't start before 10 p.m.

The hottest night life

One disco that doesn't require a membership is **Whispers,** *Centro Comercial Imaviz (beneath the Sheraton Hotel), avenida Fontes Pereira de Melo; tel. (351-1)57-54-89.* If you don't like rock music, try **Pe Sujo,** *Largo de S. Martinho, 6-7; tel. (351-1)86-56-29,* in the Alfama, where soft Brazilian music is played.

The cheapest fun

If you're trying to save money, you still can spend a pleasant evening in Lisbon—by strolling through the old sections. You'll find plenty of free entertainment. Student choral groups dressed in caps and gowns sing traditional college melodies to the accompaniment of Spanish and Portuguese guitars.

Lisbon's best hotels

The most luxurious hotel in Lisbon is the **Ritz,** *rua Rodrigo da Fonseca 88; tel. (351-1)69-20-20,* set on a hill overlooking Parque Eduardo VII. Rooms at the Ritz are decorated in silks, satins, and suedes. The hotel restaurant, the Grill Room, is one of the city's most popular. A double room is 37,000 to 50,000 escudos ($270 to $365).

The **Principe Real,** *rua de Alegría 53; tel. (351-1)34-60-116,* is a tiny, relatively unknown hotel tucked away in the Barrio Alto. It has great charm and is furnished with lovely antiques and good reproductions. A double room is 13,000 to 21,000 escudos ($95 to $153).

The least expensive places to stay are off of the avenida de Liberdade. **Hotel Jorge V,** *rua Silveira 3; tel. (351-1)35-62-525,* has clean, modern rooms and elevators. Rooms are 8,000 to 12,000 escudos ($58 to $87). A good budget hotel in the old city, near the river, is **Hotel Duas Nações;** *tel. (351-1)34-60-71-01.* A double room is 8,600 escudos ($59).

The best side trips from Lisbon

Queluz, Portugal's version of the Palace of Versailles, is not far from Lisbon. The 18th-century pink rococo palace is filled with Portuguese Empire antiques and surrounded by ornamental gardens. The palace kitchen, Cozinha Velha, is now a famous restaurant.

Cabo Espichel, a windy cape jutting into the Atlantic, is an ancient pilgrimage center. Explore the ruins of the 17th-century baroque church, **Nossa Senhora do Cabo** (Our Lady of the Cape), as well as the arcaded outbuildings that once housed pilgrims. Go around the church to the edge of the cliff, which drops 350 feet into the ocean.

Estoril is a beach resort 13 miles west of the city with a casino that is open from 3 p.m. to 3 a.m. You can take a train to Estoril from Lisbon's Cais do Sodre station. You must show a passport to get into the casino, and men must wear suit coats. The **Hotel Palácio,** *rua do Parque; tel. (351-1)468-0400,* is a gracious old hotel in Estoril near the beach with gardens, a swimming pool, and excellent service. A double room is 31,500 to 39,000 escudos ($230 to $285).

Nearby is a fishing village that has been turned into a sophisticated resort, **Cascais.** A fine sandy beach lines its beautiful bay. Cascais has had an elegant air since 1870, when the court first moved here for the summer. A royal palace was constructed in the former citadel and is still used by the head of state. **Dois Mil e Um** (2001), Cascais' famous disco, offers British and American rock and a good sound system.

Just outside Cascais is one of the strangest sights on the coast—the **Boca do Inferno** (Jaws of Hell). This great hole, formed by the force of the ocean entering under a rock arch, roars when waves crash into it.

Praia do Guincho, five miles west of Cascais, is a long, sandy beach with dunes. Its massive headland is the westernmost point in Europe. It is famous for good fishing and surfing (but beware the undertow).

Setubal is a busy fishing port with 16th- and 17th-century churches and a medieval fortress. Inside the walls of the town's castle, São Filipe, is the attractive **Pousada de São Filipe,** *tel. (351-65)523-844.* Built in 1590, the fortress is 600 feet above the harbor and has many towers and massive battlements. It is entered via a dark, sweeping stone staircase. Underground tunnels and prison cells are now used as wine cellars and storage areas. The chapel is completely tiled. A double room is 22,500 escudos ($165), including breakfast.

Just north of Setubal is **Pousada do Castelo de Palmela,** *Castelo de Palmela, 2950 Palmela; tel. (351-1)23-51-226,* a beautiful castle hotel. A double room is 19,000 escudos ($138) a night.

Sintra—the most romantic town

Sintra is the breathtaking mountain resort made famous by the poet Byron, who wrote, "The village of Sintra is the most beautiful, perhaps, in the world." For centuries, Sintra was favored as a summer refuge by Portuguese royalty. It's a 45-minute train ride from Rossio Station in Lisbon.

Once a mountain stronghold of the Moors, Sintra is dominated by a seventh-century Moorish castle. Situated 1,400 feet above sea level, it has crenelated walls and battlements that extend along rocky cliffs. From the walls, you have a view of the cliffs and the sea.

The most romantic sight in Sintra is the **Pena Palace,** a towering pseudo-medieval palace built in the 19th century. From the windows are views of the coast, the cliffs, and the sea. The palace's 500-acre park, which you enter by crossing a drawbridge, has 400 kinds of trees and plants.

Europe's sunniest spot—the Algarve

Spanning 200 miles of Portugal's southern coast, from Sagres in the west to the Spanish border in the east, the Algarve is Europe's sunniest site, with 300 sunny days per year. During the summer, temperatures range from 68 to 86 degrees Fahrenheit. The hottest days are tempered by refreshing breezes off the Atlantic. Spring and fall have warm weather just right for swimming.

Separated from the rest of Portugal by a spine of mountains, the Algarve was once considered a separate kingdom. The Phoenicians, Greeks, Carthaginians, and Romans all traded here before the Moors took over and ruled for 500 years. The Algarve was the last province taken from the Moors by Portuguese kings, and many towns still more closely resemble the villages of North Africa than those of Europe.

Europe's best golf course

The Algarve has the best golfing in Europe, combining emerald greens and perfect weather year-round. And the best of the Algarve's many courses is **Quinta do Lago**, *Almancil, 8100 Loulé; tel. (351-89)394-271.* Lush fairways of Bermuda grass invite international golfers. The clubhouse and the pool are both welcoming.

Dona Filipa, *Vale do Lobo; tel. (351-89)394-141*, is a grand hotel with views of the greens and the sea. It has a pool and tennis courts for those who tire of golf. A double room is 37,000 to 42,350 escudos ($272 to $311), including breakfast, during peak season.

Hotel Dom Pedro Golf, *8125 Vilamoura, Quarteira; tel. (351-89)389-650*, has a swimming pool and tennis courts. It is popular with golfers. A double room is 13,000 to 20,000 escudos ($95 to $146), including breakfast.

Albufeira—the hottest town

Albufeira, a Moorish town, has the most beautiful bodies and the hottest night life in the region. **Sir Harry's Bar**, an English-style pub on the main square, draws revelers of all ages. But the real action is along rua Candido dos Reis, a cobblestoned pedestrian street that leads from the beach to the plaza. In the evening, the outdoor cafés, the restaurants, and the bars along here are filled. The two most popular bars are **Fastnet**, which is big with the British, and **Twist**, a Scandinavian and German hangout.

The discos in Albufeira get going after midnight. **Sylvia's** is the best, filled with Scandinavians on the prowl and handsome night owls. Across the street is **7 1/2**, which is almost as exciting.

A good, inexpensive place to stay is the **Hotel Rocamar**, *tel. (351-89)58-69-90*, where rooms are 7,000 to 15,000 escudos a night ($59 to $109).

Nature's best show: sea caves and rock formations

Between Albufeira and Portimão, near the cliffside fishing village of Praia do Carvoeiro, nature provides one of its most beautiful spectacles. Drive to the **Nossa Senhora da Encarnaçâo**, a chapel at the summit of a steep hill east of Praia do Carvoeiro. The view of the cliffs and the sea crashing below is breathtaking. Climb down 134 steps through oddly shaped red rocks to see the gaping holes leading into the sea caves, which are engulfed every few minutes by waves. A path leads to a bluff from which you have a clear view of the entrance to an underwater sea cave.

The **Caves of Cape Carvoeiro** are best seen by boat, which you can do during high season. Ask for information at the tourist office in Praia do Carvoeiro or in Portimâo harbor.

The best *cataplana* in Portimão

The largest Algarve city, **Portimão** is a fishing port whose quays are lined with seafood restaurants. Try the dish called *cataplana*. A seafood stew cooked in a thick, hinged container, its exact recipe varies from place to place but always includes clams and usually includes tomatoes, ham, and sausage. The average cost of cataplana is 2,000 to 3,000 escudos ($14 to $22) per person.

The best place for this regional dish is **Avozinha**, *rua Capote 7; tel. (351-82)22922*, a family-run restaurant hidden on a narrow cobblestoned street that climbs uphill from the waterfront. The fish is very fresh, brought from the market at the harbor, just 100 yards away. The *cataplana* here is made of tiny clams, onion, garlic, fresh pork, pimiento, and bacon. The price is 1,300 escudos ($10).

Another good place for *cataplana* is **O Bicho**, *Largo Gil Eanes 12; tel. (351-82)22977*, a working-class establishment with the freshest seafood in town.

Lagos: the saddest past and the sandiest beaches

Ten miles west of Portimão is the town of **Lagos**, once a center of the African slave trade. The **Praça da Republica** is the site of the first slave market established in Europe. Sections of Roman walls remain in the old quarter of Lagos, and you can walk along the walls of the old fortress that guards the harbor. The 18th-century baroque **Chapel of St. Antonio** is known for its ornate gilded wood carvings.

South of town is Ponta da Piedad, a promontory with fine beaches connected by natural rock tunnels. The scenery is striking—the rocks are a reddish color that contrasts with the green of the sea. The boulders have been carved into strange shapes by pounding waves. From the lighthouse is a lovely view of the coast. Hire a boat in town to take you to see offshore grottos.

Sagres: the end of the world

Sagres, the most southwesterly point in Europe, is guarded by the fortress of **Prince Henry the Navigator**. His famous navigational device, the **Compass Rose**, is laid out in the stone.

Prince Henry founded his navigation school here at the beginning of the 15th century. It also was here that he planned his expeditions into Africa and west into the unknown.

Before the great explorations began, sailors believed that **Cabo de São Vicente** (Cape St. Vincent), near Sagres, was the end of the world. The place is marked by a famous lighthouse. Waves crash ferociously on the rocks 250 feet below the lighthouse. If you're going to walk here, bring a windbreaker. Or buy one of the handsome handmade sweaters Sagres women are famous for knitting.

Pousada do Infante, *Sagres; tel. (351-82)64222*, has views of the coast and the lighthouse on the promontory of Cape St. Vincent. Delicious soups are served in the dining room, including *creme de espinafres* (spinach cream soup) and *sopa do mar* (fish soup). The fish is always fresh and well-cooked, and the wine list is extensive. Rooms are 16,000 to 23,380 escudos ($117 to $170).

The best wildlife

Monção is a good base for exploring the **Peneda-Gerês National Park**. The National Forest Department can arrange guided trips through the mountainous 170,000-acre park, where wild horses, stags, and boars roam and where you can spot milestones along the ancient Roman Way. For more information, stop at the tourist office in Monção.

The **Pousada de São Bento**, *Canicada 4850; tel. (351-53)647-190*, is a good place to stay if you want to explore the park. A modern hotel with dizzying views of the Minho Valley, it is cozy in the winter, with the atmosphere of a hunting lodge. It has high ceilings, massive rafters, and large picture windows overlooking the mountains. The swimming pool and tennis courts are inviting in warm weather. A double room is 17,900 escudos ($130), including breakfast, during the summer.

Oporto—the port wine capital

Originally a Roman settlement, **Oporto** has many old palaces, convents, and churches. (The cathedral is famous for its gilded wood altars and grand organ.) But Oporto's true fame comes from port wine. If you wander along the banks of the River Douro, you will see *rabelos*, or barges, bringing the distinctive port wine grapes down from the vineyards.

The area upriver from Oporto is the only place in the world that grows grapes for port, and Oporto is the only place where it is made. You can try port wine and the local Vinho Verde at any restaurant or café in the city. Or you can visit the **Port Wine Institute**, *rua Ferreira Borges; tel. (351-2)200-2522*, or the **Port Wine Solar**, *Quinta da Macierinha-rua-Entre-Quintas; tel. (351-2)697-793*.

Vila Nova de Gaia, on the south bank of the Douro, opposite Oporto, is the center of the port wine trade. You can sample port at the wine bodegas here and learn how it is matured for at least 25 years before being sold.

Portugal's saddest love story

The **Santa Maria Monastery** in the town of Alcobaça is the final resting place of the ill-fated lovers **Dom Pedro** and **Ines de Castro**. When Prince Dom Pedro married his beautiful mistress Ines de Castro, his father, King Alfonso IV of Portugal, was so outraged by the unequal union that he had Ines assassinated in 1355. When he succeeded to the throne, Dom Pedro got his revenge. He dressed the body of Ines in royal attire and forced the noblemen who had killed her to pay homage by kissing her decomposed hand. The lovers are positioned in their ornate tombs so that they will face each other on Judgment Day.

Constructed by Cistercian monks in 1178, the kitchen in the monastery was built above a trout stream so the cooks could have fresh water and fish.

The oldest university town

Coimbra, where Princess Ines was murdered, is one of the oldest medieval university towns in Europe. The city's streets are dotted with students wearing traditional black capes. A steep cobblestoned street leads to the university courtyard, where you can join a tour of the old university buildings, including the Manueline Chapel, with its ornate door and 17th-century *azulejos*, and the library, with its carved and varnished wood embellishments.

The Venice of Portugal

Aveiro, at the northernmost tip of the Costa de Prata, claims to be the Venice of Portugal. It is surrounded by salt flats, beaches, and lagoons and dominated by the Central Canal. Gaily painted *moliceiros* (boats reminiscent of Venice's gondolas) move through the waters gathering algae to be used as fertilizer.

The best place to stay is the **Pousada da Ria**, *Bico do Muranzel; tel. (351-34)48332 or (351-34)48334*. Located by a lagoon, it has bedrooms with views of the water. Eels from the Ria d'Aveiro are the mainstay of the *pousada's* dinner specialties—*caldeirada de enguias* (eel chowder) and *enguias de escabeche* (marinated eels). A double room is 8,700 to 14,300 escudos ($63 to $104).

Buçaco: the most beautiful forest

Buçaco National Park, which has 700 species of trees from around the world, has been considered a holy place for centuries. Benedictine monks built a hermitage here in the sixth century. In 1622, Pope Gregory XV forbade women to enter the oak and pine forest. And the Barefoot Carmelite monks began an arboretum here in 1628.

In 1810, **Buçaco Mountain** was the site of a battle between the combined British and Portuguese forces under Wellington and the French. (Wellington's forces won.) The Portuguese government took over in 1834 and expanded the arboretum. Today, the park covers 250 acres of woodland.

In the center of the park is the royal hunting lodge built by Carlos I (1888-1907). Today it is the **Palace Hotel**, *tel. (351-31)930-101*, an incredibly ornate luxury hotel. A double room is 22,400 to 28,000 escudos ($163 to $205).

Portugal's most spectacular monastery

Portugal's most spectacular monastery is in **Batalha**. King João vowed to the Virgin Mary that he would build a monastery if she helped him defeat the Castillians. The king's army was indeed victorious against the Castillian army in the Battle of Aljubarrota on Aug. 14, 1385, ensuring Portugal's independence for the next 200 years.

The monastery does justice to the momentous victory, with flying buttresses, turrets, a mass of gables, columns, and elaborate tracery. King João and his wife Philippa of Lancaster are buried here along with their children, including Prince Henry the Navigator.

The **Pousada do Mestre A. Domingues**, *tel. (351-44)96260*, next to the monastery and named after the architect of King João, is a comfortable place to stay. The dining room serves excellent seafood, especially the clams and the shrimp. Rooms are 8,700 to 14,300 escudos ($63 to $104), including breakfast.

The prettiest Portuguese town

Obidos, one of the best-preserved medieval fortified towns on the Iberian Peninsula, was traditionally the property of Portuguese queens. It has a feminine look, with tiny whitewashed houses and flower-lined streets. The 12th-century **Obidos Castle** dominates the city. **St. Mary's Church**, where King Alfonso V married his 8-year-old cousin Isabella in 1444, is tiled with blue *azulejos*. The octagonal **Senhor da Pedra Church** has a remarkable second-century stone cross.

The **Pousada do Castelo**, *rua Direita; tel. (351-62)959-105*, housed within the castle walls, is furnished with antiques and has excellent cuisine and extensive wine cellars. Because it has only six rooms, early reservations are recommended. A double room is 13,700 to 22,500 escudos ($100 to $164).

The **Estalagem do Convento**, *rua Dom João de Ornelas, Obidos; tel. (351-62)959-214*, is a medieval hotel in Obidos furnished with tables and chairs from the days of the knights and Crusaders. This is a novel place to stay the night, with little rooms and cobblestoned courtyards. A double room with a shower goes for 6,000 to 10,500 escudos ($43 to $64).

Miraculous Fátima

The village of **Fátima**, where Catholics believe the Virgin Mary appeared to three shepherd children in 1917, is a major shrine and place of pilgrimage. Special ceremonies are held on the 13th day of each month between May and October. Make reservations well in advance if you plan to visit Fatima during that time—throngs descend upon the town.

The two nicest hotels in Fatima are the **de Fatima**, *João Paulo II; tel. (351-49)532-351*, and the **Santa Maria**, *rua de Santo Antonio; tel. (351-49)531-015*. A double room at de Fatima is 7,000 to 10,000 escudos ($51 to $73); a double room at the Santa Maria is 5,000 to 8,000 escudos ($36 to $58).

Portugal's oddest dance

The mountain town of **Miranda do Douro**, perched on a ravine just across the River Douro from Spain, is famous for its *pauliteiros*, who perform a traditional sword dance each year on the Feast of St. Barbara (the third Sunday in August). Dancers carry sticks representing swords and wear kilts, embroidered shirts, and black hats covered with ribbons and flowers. They move in an ancient pattern to the sounds of tambourines and bagpipes. Another regional remnant of bygone eras is Mirandês, a Latin slang that the locals speak among themselves.

The **Pousada de Santa Catarina**, *tel. (351-73)42255*, balanced on the edge of a rocky gorge, has lovely views of the River Douro. Occasionally you'll see a golden eagle. The food, cooked over a wood fire, is good. Try the *guisado de polvo a transmontana,* or octopus ragout. A double room at the pousada is 8,700 to 16,200 escudos ($63 to $119).

Évora—the most Roman

Évora, one of the oldest towns on the Iberian Peninsula, has the best Roman ruins in Portugal. Originally a Roman settlement, the town was later inhabited by the Visigoths. Under the Moors, it became a major trade and agricultural center. And during Portugal's heyday in the 15th and 16th centuries, Evora's university was a magnet for the best scholars and writers of the time. Now a public high school, the old university's great hall is covered with 17th-century tiles.

The Roman **Temple of Diana,** dating from the second century, is well-preserved. Before it was excavated in 1870, it was used as a slaughterhouse! The 1975 bloodless revolution was planned beneath its Corinthian columns.

Notice Evora's quaint street designations—streets bear the names of a countess's tailor, a cardinal's nurse, the lisping man, and the unshaven man. And take a look at the macabre **Igreja de São Francisco,** *Praca 28 de Maio.* It contains a chapel built of 50,000 monks' bones. The Franciscans thought this a good way to encourage meditation upon the transitory nature of life. Above the entrance is a warning, *"Nos ossos que aqui estamos pelos vossos esperamos"*—which means "The bones here are waiting for yours."

Evora's **Pousada dos Loios,** *Largo Conde de Vila Flor; tel. (351-66)24051,* is one of the best in the country. It faces the Temple of Diana and is located in what was the St. Eligius Monastery, consecrated in 1491. The cloisters have been glassed in to form a dining room, which has a vaulted ceiling, horseshoe arches, and a marble font. The bedrooms are converted monastic cells. One of the suites has a baroque antechamber. A double room is 17,000 to 22,500 escudos ($124 to $164).

Portugal's pottery town

Estreméoz has been an artistic center since the 16th century. It is famous for its Alentejo pottery, sold in the main square on Saturdays. Typical wares include narrow-mouthed jars called *barris* and widemouthed jars called *bilhas.* Local artists also create clay figurines of people and animals. Local crafts are displayed at the Rural Museum on the main square.

Madeira: the most fruitful island

About 600 miles off the coast of Morocco lies **Madeira,** a garden paradise that belongs to Portugal. The lush, semitropical volcanic island was discovered by Portuguese explorers in 1419 and soon became a regular port of call for seafarers. Ships coming from the New World and Asia stopped here and left behind specimens of exotic plants, which islanders grew in the rich volcanic soil with great success. The result is an island abounding in tropical fruits (including passion fruit, mangos, papaws, avocados, bananas, and melons), vegetables, and flowers. Madeira's mild temperature ranges from 60 degrees Fahrenheit in winter to 72 degrees Fahrenheit in summer.

The best footin'

The best way to see the interior of the island is to walk along the *levadas,* or footpaths, which follow ancient Madeiran irrigation channels carrying water from high up in the mountains down through the terraced farms to the fields and villages below. The paths are graded 1 to 4, from easiest to most difficult.

For the most difficult walks, you need more than hiking boots—you also need a good head for heights. On one side of the foot-wide paths is the irrigation stream, which may be running 18 gallons per minute, while on the other is a vertical precipice hundreds of feet high. The natives, often carrying high bundles on their heads, scurry fearlessly up the paths.

172

A map of all canal walking paths is available from the **Direcção Regional de Turismo,** *ave. Arriaga 16-18, Funchal.*

Portugal's best thrill

If you're brave enough, make time during your visit to Madeira to take an exhilarating ride in a little wicker fruit cart with steel blades from Monte downhill to Funchal, the island's capital. You use levers to control the wooden carts as they roll like bumper cars down the hill. Once used for practical purposes, such as transporting fruits and vegetables, today the carts are used purely as amusement rides. To arrange a ride, visit the **tourist office,** *ave. Arriga 18; tel. (351-91)29057.*

Bacchus' favorite—Madeira

After such an exploit, you probably will need a drink. Try the island's fortified sweet wine, called **Madeira.** According to the legend, when early settlers reached Madeira (which means *wood*), they burned off the thick forests in a fire that raged for seven years. When vines were planted in the resulting soil, so the story goes, the grapes acquired their characteristic smoky flavor.

During the days of the American Revolution, Madeira could be imported to Colonial America in non-British ships, which made it the drink of independence. It was the favorite tipple of the early American revolutionaries.

Tour the wine bodegas in Funchal to see how Madeira is processed and stored. At the end of the visit, you can sample the stuff.

Funchal's best sights

Funchal's most famous sights, its **botanical gardens,** are brightly colored year-round. Against the natural beauty of these gardens, the works of man fade. The churches in Funchal range from the 15th-century **Capela de Santa Catarina** (in the Manueline style, a Portuguese version of Gothic characterized by nautical-inspired stone carving) to the **Se** (cathedral), with its carved-wood and gilded altars. Church paintings in Funchal and throughout the island show a strong Flemish influence. The **Palace of the Conde de Carvalhal** is now the town hall.

The island's early houses with black stone trim are made of the volcanic rock of Madeira. The customshouse in the harbor (Alfandega) is an often-overlooked site; especially noteworthy are the second-floor carved and painted ceiling and the 17th-century illuminated Bible, on which captains had to swear they had nothing to declare.

The world's second-highest sea cliff

Cabo Girão, on Madeira, is the world's second-highest sea cliff. This promontory has extraordinary views. Go at sunset. (The highest sea cliff in the world is the north coast of East Molokai Island, Hawaii.)

Madeira's best festival

One of the best times to visit Madeira is June, during the **Ribeira Brava Festival of St. Peter.** In celebration of the patron saint of fishermen, residents join in solemn processions, which are followed by dances, including the traditional sword dance.

Madeira's best eats

Good restaurants near Funchal include **A Seta,** which serves barbecued beef and chicken on sword skewers hung from the ceiling, along with mounds of fresh-baked bread and pitchers of red wine.

A Gruta is a particularly inviting outdoor café, where you can sit for hours sipping ice-cold Mateus for about 399 escudos a bottle. The fish is fresh, the bread crusty and warm. Costumed folk dancers sometimes perform. Lunch for two, including wine, salad, fish, coffee, and dessert, is about 1,600 escudos.

In the fishing village of **Camara de Lobos,** perched on a rugged cliff, is the **Restaurant Coral.** From the windows, you can see brightly painted fishing boats bobbing in the water and children mending fishing nets along the jagged coastline. The cost of a meal, including coffee, brandy, and a bottle of good wine is about 2,500 escudos ($18).

The most gracious hotel

Reid's, *Estrada Monumental 139, Funchal; tel. (351-91)23001,* is Madeira's most gracious resort hotel. Set on a cliff overlooking the sea, it has a British colonial flavor. It is surrounded by tropical foliage and flowers and has a private beach, tennis courts, two pools, and boat rentals. A double room is 37,200 to 43,000 escudos ($272 to $314).

The best hotel prices

Madeira is cheap by Caribbean standards. The top-ranked **Casino Park Hotel,** *Aeroporto, Funchal, Madeira; tel. (351-91)33111,* near the Funchal airport, charges 23,000 escudos ($168) for a double room with a mountain view and 26,000 escudos ($190) for a double room with a sea view. (The price is for two people, including breakfast, taxes, service, and use of a pool, a sauna, and tennis courts.)

Apartment hotels, such as the **Estrelicia** and the **Mimosa** (same ownership), *Caminho Velho da Ajuda, Funchal, Madeira; tel. (351-91)30131,* charge about 9,500 escudos ($69) per day, double occupancy, including breakfast. Cheaper are the **Pensão Astoria,** *rua João Gago 10-3, Funchal, Madeira; tel. (351-91)23820* (4,000 escudos, or $29), and the **Pensão Palmeira,** *Porto Santo, Madeira; tel. (351-91)982112* (3,400 escudos, or $25).

Portugal's best accommodation: the *pousada*

The 25 *pousadas* throughout Portugal, many of which have been mentioned in this chapter, offer historic accommodation and fine food. They are housed in converted medieval castles or convents in areas of great natural beauty. For more information or to make reservations, contact **Tinto Basto,** *40 Prince St., New York, NY 10012; (800)345-0739, in the United States,* or **Enatur,** *10 ave. Santa Joanna Princesa, Lisbon 1700; tel. (351-1)848-1221 in Portugal.*

The Best of Scandinavia

Summer, when the sun hardly sets over Scandinavia, is the best time to visit this northern land. After months of darkness, Scandinavians come out of hibernation to celebrate the golden months of June and July with parties that would go on until dawn—except dawn never comes.

Scandinavia—for our purposes Denmark, Norway, Sweden, and Finland—has both cosmopolitan cities and the most enormous wilderness area in Europe. Lapland, which crosses Norway, Sweden, and Finland, is a stunning region with glittering glaciers and bright blue skies. Lapps herd their reindeer across the tundra as they have for centuries. The region's parks offer well-marked trails and huts, where hikers can sleep in comfort.

Denmark: the most accessible country

The southernmost of the Scandinavian countries has a romantic landscape crisscrossed by waterways and dotted with thatched-roof houses. It is easy to imagine the trolls, werewolves, and sorcerers of Danish legend; Hans Christian Andersen was inspired by these legends to write his famous fairy tales.

The most accessible of the Scandinavian countries, **Denmark** is the only one attached to mainland Europe. North of Germany and south of Sweden and Norway, Denmark is made up of the Jutland Peninsula, which shares a border with Germany, and two major islands, Zealand and Funen. Altogether, the Danish islands number 480. Most are uninhabited.

The best way to meet the Danes

Through the **Meet the Danes** program, you can spend an evening in a Danish home in any of eight cities: Århus, Aalborg, Esbjerg, Fredericia, Lønstrup, Odense, Roskilde, or Skive. Local tourist offices can arrange the visit if you give them 24 hours notice. For more information, contact the **Danish Tourist Board**, *655 Third Ave., New York, NY 10017; (212)949-2333.*

Copenhagen: the best fun

Copenhagen (København), on the east coast of the island of Zealand, is a city dedicated to entertainment. What other capital city revolves around an amusement park (**Tivoli Gardens**)? Merrymaking Danes of all ages scream with fear and excitement

175

aboard Tivoli's rides. (The best is Det Flyvende Taeppe, or the Flying Carpet.) The famous Ferris wheel has a far-reaching view.

Built in 1843 on 20 acres in the heart of Copenhagen, Tivoli is more than just an amusement park. It has gardens, lakes, theaters, dance halls, games, bars, and scores of restaurants to suit every budget. At night it is illuminated by 100,000 colored lights, and you can enjoy vaudeville acts, concerts, music, and dancing.

Strøget: the best stroll in Denmark

The longest pedestrian thoroughfare in the world, the **Strøget** (Strolling Place) meanders through the heart of Copenhagen. This mile-long stretch is lined with cafés, banks, department stores, and boutiques selling everything from cheap T-shirts to fine Icelandic sweaters and expensive watches. The most elegant shops are clustered at the eastern end. The **Sweater Market**, *Frederiksberggade 15; tel. (45-3)315-27-73*, sells hand-knit designer sweaters.

The Strøget is actually an area made up of five streets: Frederiksberggade, Nygade, Vimmelskaftet, Amagertorv, and Ostergade. It is between the city's two main squares: Raadhuspladsen and Kongens-Nytorv. All this is made more confusing by the fact that "the Strøget" isn't marked as such on city maps.

The world's largest porcelain factory

The **Royal Copenhagen**, the largest porcelain factory in the world, has a shop on the Strøget at 6 Amagertorv. It is housed in a 16th-century Dutch Renaissance building and offers a fine collection of all four brand names of china. The Royal Copenhagen has been working at its craft for more than two centuries, producing elegant, hand-painted dinnerware and figurines.

The best amber and silver shopping

The best place on the Strøget to shop for amber and silver is the **Danish Silver Shop**, *2 Frederiksberggade*, which offers unique and elegant Scandinavian jewelry. Small amber heart-shaped pendants and solid amber necklaces are half the price charged in other countries.

The two best museums

Copenhagen has 40 public museums and galleries, most within easy walking distance of the Strøget. The largest is the **Nationalmuseet** (National Museum), which has the best display of Viking artifacts in the world. It is behind the Christiansborg Palace, where Parliament meets.

Nearby is **Ny Carlsberg Glyptotek**, which has extensive collections of Roman, Etruscan, and Egyptian art, as well as a respectable number of Impressionist paintings. Its arboretum is a tranquil place where you can sit beneath immense trees and listen to a Gregorian chant.

A beer lover's best

If you love beer and don't mind crowds, visit the **Carlsberg** and **Tuborg** breweries. The tours and beer are free, and it's always a good time—especially after a few tastes.

Copenhagen's two castles

Rosenborg, *Øster Voldgade 4A*, a 17th-century castle, houses the crown jewels and the royal treasures of the Danes. **Amalieborg Castle**, *Amalieborg Square*, is the residence of the royal family. Witness the changing of the guard daily at noon.

Capital night life

Copenhagen's chic set frequents **Annabel's**, *Lille Kongensgade 16; tel. (45-3)311-20-*

20. Fashions straight out of Paris' finest boutiques hang on the bodies here. Officially, Annabel's is a private club, but if you look terribly chic you'll probably get in.

Montmartre, *Nørregade 41; tel. (45-3)311-46-67,* is Copenhagen's largest nightclub, attracting the best jazz bands of Europe. The music is terrific, but it's too crowded to enjoy the dance floor.

Vin & Ølgood, *Skindergade 45; tel. (45-3)313-26-25,* is a rowdy beer-drinking joint with live oompah bands and busty waitresses in leather aprons serving beer in large steins. All age groups can be seen at the trestle tables, arms locked and voices harmonizing (or disharmonizing) in song. No one is left out; this is a good place to go if you're out on your own.

Avoid the bars in the much-touted **Nyhavn,** or sailors' district. They attract rowdy drunks and can be depressing.

The cheapest way to go

The major problem with Copenhagen is that it is expensive. The best way to cut costs is by buying the **Copenhagen Card,** available from the **tourist office,** *22 H.C. Andersen Blvd.,* train stations, Copenhagen's hotels, and travel agents. You can buy cards good for one to three days. They allow entry to 36 museums, unlimited travel on buses and trains within the city, and a 50% discount on the ferry crossing to Sweden. The one-day card is 90 Danish kroner ($15); the two-day card, 145 Danish kroner ($24); and the three-day card, 188 Danish kroner ($31).

The best eating

The most elegant restaurant in town is **Belle Terrasse,** *Tivoli; tel. (45-3)312-11-36,* which has lush gardens and live music. While it is romantic, it is also expensive. Reservations are necessary.

Another good restaurant in Tivoli is **Faergekroen,** *tel. (45-3)312-94-12,* a rustic inn on the lake. Try the Danish specialty called *hvid skieperloen sobs,* a sort of shepherd's pie.

Krog's Fiskerestaurant, *Gammel Strand 38; tel. (45-3)315-89-15,* across the canal from Christiansborg, is the best seafood restaurant.

The best hotels

D'Angleterre, *Kongens Nytorv 34; tel. (45-3)312-00-95,* is the oldest and most fashionable hotel in Copenhagen, located at the far end of the walking street, Strøget. Built in 1795, it has old-fashioned wood-paneled rooms. It also has a good French restaurant and a popular nightclub. A double room is 1,900 to 2,200 Danish kroner ($312 to $361) a night.

Another fine hotel is the **Plaza,** *Bernstorffsgade 4; tel. (45-3)314-92-62,* where rooms are filled with antiques and paneled with mahogany. A double room is 1,525 to 1,925 Danish kroner ($250 to $316) a night. Reserve months in advance.

The **Scandinavia,** *70 Amager Blvd.,* is a large, ultramodern skyscraper hotel run by SAS (the Scandinavian airline). It caters to those prefering Scandinavian modern over Scandinavian provincial. Its restaurants, cafés, and bars are all excellent and popular top-of-the-line stops.

The **Savoy Hotel,** *Vesterbrogade 34, DK-1620; tel. (45-3)131-40-73,* is a very old but modernized hotel that has retained its Old World charm. Here style and service with a smile are still the order of the day. And although it is a quiet place to stay, its proximity to the Strøget puts it in tune with the city as well. The Savoy is also located 10 minutes from the city hall in the center of town. A double room is 870 to 990 Danish kroner ($143 to $162).

Roskilde: the first capital

The ancient city of **Roskilde,** west of Copenhagen, was the capital of Denmark until 1445. It is also the site of the first Danish church, built in A.D. 960. Members of Denmark's royalty are buried in marble and alabaster tombs in the 12th-century cathedral (known as the Westminster Abbey of Denmark), including Harald the Bluetooth, a 10th-century king; Margarethe, once queen of Scandinavia; and Christian X, the Danish king during World War II who wore a yellow star to demonstrate his sympathy for the Jews.

The **Vikingskibshallen** (Viking Ship Museum) at Havnen displays five Viking ships painstakingly pieced together from hundreds of pieces of wreckage. An amazingly well-preserved seagoing cargo ship from A.D. 1000 sits in the main hall.

Lindenborg Kro, *Holbaekvej 90, Gevninge DK; tel. (45-42)40-21-11,* just outside Roskilde, is one of the most pleasant inns in Denmark. The original inn, built 300 years ago, burned in 1967, but a new one was built on the site. A double room is 590 Danish kroner ($97) a night, including breakfast.

Denmark's best castles

If you see only one castle in your lifetime, it should be **Frederiksborg.** This 17th-century treasure trove in Hillerød is surrounded by a moat and has an ornate, gilded chapel with a rare 1610 Compenius organ. Here, Danish kings were crowned. The castle houses the most important national history museum. Every square foot is covered with art and antiques, including four-poster beds, ebony cabinets, coats of arms, and tapestries.

Kronborg Castle at Elsinore is the bleak and imposing castle where Shakespeare set *Hamlet.* It has secret passages and turrets, exactly as you would imagine. Built in 1574 and restored in 1629, it now houses the Danish Maritime Museum.

Nyborg Castle, on the island of Funen, is the oldest royal castle still standing in Scandinavia and is believed to have been built in the 12th century. Until the 15th century, the moated castle guarded one of the most strategic spots in the country. Be sure to see the knight's hall and the old *danehof,* which was used by the medieval parliament, an uneasy alliance between noblemen and clergy. Nyborg can be reached by ferry from Zealand.

Egeskov, near Odense, is the best preserved moated castle in Europe. A Renaissance structure with magnificent gardens, it was built in 1554 on oak pillars in the middle of a small lake. Legend tells of a maiden who bore an illegitimate child to the young nobleman of the castle and was locked in one of the castle towers from 1559 to 1604. The landscaped gardens are open to the public every day. But the castle itself is a private home and can be visited only during chamber music concerts, which are held in the castle's Great Hall during the summer.

Denmark's best bike route

The **Haervejen** (pronounced Hairvine), a marked bike trail, follows an ancient military road along Denmark's spine. It leads through the center of Jutland past menhirs (large monumental stones erected by prehistoric Danes), barrows (mounds of earth or stones over burial sites), rune stones etched with characters from the ancient Scandinavian alphabet, and churches built by the first Danish Christians.

Haervejen runs 170 miles from Viborg in central Jutland south to the Eider River in Germany. For centuries, it was the only road connecting Scandinavia with continental Europe. The official start is at the corner of St. Jørgensvej and Lille St. Mikkelsgade.

Every year, a full-scale, weeklong group trek along the Haervejen is organized for the first weekend in July. For more information on the Haervejen, contact the **Danish Tourist Board,** *655 Third Ave., New York, NY 10017; (212)949-2333,* or the local tourist board in Svendborg, *tel. (45-62)22-25-33.*

A kids' best

Families traveling through Copenhagen should set aside at least one day to visit Denmark's unique theme park, **Legoland.** About 1 million Lego enthusiasts trek to the Danish carpenter Ole Kirk Christiansen's invention, in his hometown of Billund,

Denmark. Specially trained Lego artists used more than 33 million Lego blocks to create 25 acres of colorful fantasy land. Most of the exhibits, displaying historical sights and events from all over the world, are scaled down to one-twentieth of the real-life size. Visitors walk amid a dazzling metropolis of waist-high buildings, dwarf trees, and diminutive shrubs all made of Lego blocks.

Legoland's indoor exhibits are open September through December and April through May. Admission during the indoor season is 12 Danish kroner ($2) for children, 22 kroner ($3.60) for adults. The outdoor exhibits are open from late May through mid-September. Admission during the outdoor season is 25 Danish kroner ($4) for children, 45 Danish kroner ($7.40) for adults. All rides are extra. The park is open 10 a.m. until 8 p.m. For more information, contact **Legoland**, *DK7190 Billund; tel. (45-75)33-13-33.*

The two prettiest Baltic islands

Ærø, a tiny island in the Baltic, is the best place to get a glimpse of the traditional Danish seafaring life. A five-hour trip from Copenhagen by train and then ferry, it is one of many Danish islands in the archipelago north of the German coast.

Brightly painted little fishing villages fringe this 22-mile-long island. Its picturesque beaches are occasionally dotted with nude sunbathers. Inland, thatched-roof farmhouses break the rolling hills. The villages are tiny, but they usually have hotels and bakeries.

Ærøskøbing, on Ærø, is Denmark's most carefully preserved medieval village, dating from the 13th century. Its narrow cobblestoned streets are lined with gingerbread houses roofed with round tiles and painted blue or red. They were once the homes of Ærø's sea captains.

Bornholm, a Danish island between Sweden and Poland, has the world's finest-grained sand and is known for its grandfather clocks and smoked herring. The island's towns balance on sloping rocks. The ruins of a 13th-century castle can be explored at Hammershus Slot. And half-timbered houses and ancient round churches, once used as protection against pirates and enemy armies, still stand here. The greatest round church is in **Ølsker**. Built in 1150, the structure is literally round.

The best natural sight on the island is at **Rø**—a 72-foot rock formation filled with columns, caves, and crevices. Its name means *Sacred Thing*. The most beautiful beach is in **Dueodde** on the south coast, where the sand is incredibly fine, dunes rise 45 feet, and there is a 145-foot lighthouse. If you tire of the sea, explore Bornholm's forest, **Almindingen**, the third-largest in Denmark.

The bluest light in Scandinavia

Skagen, a harbor village at the top of the Jutland Peninsula, was discovered by a group of painters in the middle of the 19th century who were drawn here by the unique play of light in this area of Scandinavia. As one Skagen painter said, "Where two seas meet, the light can't help but be the bluest in creation."

For the cheapest meals in Skagen, go around the red tackle houses to the opposite side. This is where the Danes purchase their seafood, and anything you get here will be good.

Norway: the most rugged

Norway, with the second-lowest population density in Europe, is the most rugged Scandinavian country. It has deep-gouged sharp mountains rising from the jagged coastlines and frigid glaciers glittering beneath the midnight sun. Grass-thatched houses occupy little patches of land on steep hillsides. This is a country that challenges the sportsman, with superb skiing, hiking, sailing, orienteering, hunting, and mountain climbing.

Oslo: the world's most forested capital

Oslo, the capital of Norway, is the most heavily forested capital in the world—

encompassing farms as well as nightclubs. The 175-square-mile city was founded in the 11th century by Viking King Oslo. Because it was completely destroyed by fire in 1824, little medieval architecture remains. The finest residences that survived are along Raadhusgate.

Oslo's most dramatic sight

Akershus Castle, the ancient protector of the city, looms from atop a cliff that juts out into the eastern half of the harbor. The well-preserved medieval structure (built in 1300 by King Haakon V Magnusson) was an impregnable fortress and royal residence for several hundred years. Although it suffered through nine battles, it was never conquered and eventually was transformed into a Renaissance palace by Danish-Norwegian King Christian IV.

Today, the castle is used by the government for state occasions. The bastions offer tremendous views of Oslo. Inside, some of the works of Expressionist painter Edvard Munch are on display.

Scandinavia's oldest church

The oldest church in Scandinavia, **Gamle Aker Kirke**, *Akersbakken 26,* is still in use after 890 years. Daily services are held May 15 through Sept. 10, and Sunday services are held year-round (at 11 a.m.). You can visit the church with an appointment Tuesdays and Thursdays. The tour is free.

Top sights

Next to Akershus Castle is the **Norsk Hjemmefrontmuseum**, Norway's Resistance museum, which documents World War II and Norway's resistance to the Nazis.

Domkirken (Oslo's cathedral), *Stortorvet,* built between 1694 and 1699, has its original altarpiece and pulpit. The stained-glass windows were created by the Norwegian artist Emanuel Vigeland (the younger brother of Norway's most famous sculptor Gustav Vigeland). The bronze doors and ceiling decorations are also impressive, and the cathedral's organ rises five floors. Sunday services are at 11 a.m. and 7:30 p.m.

Raadhuset, Oslo's city hall, completed in 1950, was embellished in a collective effort by Norway's greatest artists and designers. Inside are more than 2,000 square yards of bold, colorful murals, including Munch's *Life*. The walls are a rainbow of colorful stones and woods.

The **Nasjonalgalleriet** (National Gallery), *Universitetsgaten 13,* has paintings by Norwegians, including works by romantic landscape painter John Christian Dahl, statues by Gustav Vigeland, and a wing devoted to Edvard Munch.

The best place to see works by Munch, the Expressionist painter who died in 1944, is the **Munch Museum**, *Tøyengate 53,* filled with 1,000 paintings, 4,500 drawings, 15,000 prints, and notes, letters, and sketches by the artist. His life's works were bequeathed to the museum, so the collection is rotated frequently.

Norway's most memorable sculptures are at **Frognerparken**, a 75-acre park devoted to the works of Gustav Vigeland. In 1921, the city gave the sculptor free rein in the park. The result: a 1,150-piece collection of huge, writhing nude figures illustrating the human struggle. The works were once the subject of much controversy.

The best of the Vikings

Three Viking burial ships excavated on the shores of the Oslo fiord, the clay from which had preserved them since A.D. 800 and A.D. 900, are kept at the **Vikingskiphuset** (Viking Ship House), *Huk Aveny 35; tel. (47-2)43-83-79,* on the Bygdøy Peninsula. The most spectacular is the *Oseberg,* a 64-foot dragon ship with animals carved on its prow. It is believed to have been the burial ship of Harald Fairhair's grandmother and her slave, who were buried in it along with 15 horses, an ox, four dogs, and some artifacts.

The greatest Norwegian adventure

The balsa-log raft *Kon Tiki*, on which Norwegian scientist Thor Heyerdahl sailed 5,000 miles in 1947, is kept at the **Kon Tiki Museum** on the Bygdøy Peninsula. The *Kon Tiki*, designed according to specifications for early Peruvian boats, sailed from Callao, Peru to Raroia, Polynesia to prove that pre-Inca Indians could have crossed from South America to populate Polynesia.

The museum also houses the papyrus *Ra II*, in which Heyerdahl crossed the Atlantic from North Africa to Barbados in 1970, and artifacts from Heyerdahl's voyage to Easter Island.

A close-up view of folk life

Over 100 historic buildings from all over Norway have been transported to the **Norsk Folkemuseum** (Norwegian Folk Museum), a 35-acre area on the Bygdøy Peninsula. Sights there include Raulandstua, one of the oldest wooden dwellings in the country; a hand-built wooden stave church that dates back to 1200; historic log cabins; Lapp artifacts; and a reconstruction of the last apartment of Norwegian playwright Henrik Ibsen.

The highest lookout in Scandinavia

For a dizzying view, climb to the lookout tower at **Tryvannstaarnet**. To get there, take the Holmenkollen subway near the National Theater in Oslo to the end of the line, Voksenkollenn. From there, it's a 15-minute walk uphill to Tryvannstarnet, the highest lookout in Scandinavia.

Another 20-minute walk down the hill leads to the **Holmenkollen ski jump,** one of the most famous in the world and the site of Olympic competitions in 1952. At the base of the jump is the **Ski Museum,** which displays 2,500-year-old ski equipment and equipment used on polar explorations.

Holmenkollen has the widest network of ski trails in the world (more than 1,300 miles of them, many with floodlights to allow nighttime skiing). The best skiers in the world gather for the Holmenkollen Ski Festival each winter to compete in downhill, slalom, cross-country, and ski jumping competitions, drawing thousands of spectators.

The best way to make friends

The **Know the Norwegians** program, sponsored by the **Oslo Travel Association,** *Raadhusgate 19,* and the Lions Club allows you to visit local English-speaking families. Invitations are not arranged during July and August when most Norwegians take a three-week summer holiday.

Eating well

Norwegian cuisine consists primarily of fish. The smoked salmon (*røklaks*) and mackerel (*røkmakrel*) are delicious. However, the meat, especially during fall hunting season, is equally good—try a reindeer or moose steak. The Norwegian *koldtbord* is a buffet that includes everything from herring to roast beef. In Seden, it's known as a *smørgasbrød*.

The best seafood restaurant in Oslo is La Mer, *Pilestredet 31; tel. (47-2)20-34-45.* It is open every day except Sunday after 4 p.m. Meals start at 180 Norwegian kroner ($29).

Mølla, *Sagveien 19; tel. (47-2)37-54-50,* a fish and game restaurant in an old textile mill on the banks of the Akerselva River, was the setting for Oskar Braaten's novels about factory workers at the beginning of the century. It is open daily except Sunday after 3 p.m. Reservations are necessary.

Étoile, *Karl Johans Gate 31; tel. (47-2)42-93-90,* on the top floor of the Grand Hotel, has a beautiful view and serves savory French and Norwegian food. It is open daily from noon until midnight.

Tostrupkjelleren, *Karl Johans Gate 25; tel. (47-2)42-14-70,* is a basement restaurant popular with politicians, journalists, and business people. Meals are 150 to 160 Norwegian kroner ($24 to $26).

Noberto, *Majorstuveien 36; tel. (47-2)46-02-02,* specializes in nouvelle cuisine and is a pleasant respite from traditional Norwegian dishes, although some find its basement locale a distraction.

Oslo nights

Oslo doesn't have enough hotels to house all its visitors, so make reservations well in advance, especially if you are visiting during the summer. **Oslo Promotion,** *Grew Wedels Plaza 4; tel. (47-2)33-43-86,* can make reservations for you if you send an advance deposit with a self-addressed international-reply envelope at least two weeks ahead of your stay. Call for more information.

The **Holmenkollen Park Hotel Rica,** *Kongeveien 26, Holmenkollasen; tel. (47-2)14-60-90,* has cozy albeit tiny rooms with views of the city. The public salon has a huge fireplace, and the exceptionally attractive restaurant serves Norwegian specialties. A double room is 1,395 Norwegian kroner ($226) a night.

The **Scandinavia,** *Holbergs Gate 30; tel. (47-2)11-30-00,* is Norway's largest hotel. Very centrally located near the royal palace, its rooms have views of the city and the fiord. It has a pool, five restaurants, and several bars. A double room is 850 to 1,550 Norwegian kroner ($138 to $252) a night.

Hotel Continental, *Stortingsgaten 24-26, 0161 Oslo 1; tel. (47-2)41-90-60,* has been owned by the same family for generations. It enjoys an excellent reputation as one of the best hotels in Scandinavia. A double room is 890 to 1,750 Norwegian kroner ($144 to $284) a night.

Many consider **The Grand Hotel,** *Karl Johansgate 31,* Oslo's most prestigious hotel. It has spacious rooms, character suites (if you have the money, stay in its Tower Suite, one of the finest anywhere), and charming eateries. Esther Williams stayed here, as did Diana Ross and Miles Davis.

The best sights outside Oslo

Fredrikstad, a fortified town with ramparts, a drawbridge, and a moat, has a flourishing artists' colony. The cobblestoned streets are lined with 18th-century houses and artisans' workshops. You can take an hour-long guided tour of the workshops weekdays between 9 a.m. and 3 p.m. for about 13 Norwegian kroner ($2). Outside town is the 17th-century **Kongsten Fort,** which has secret passages and dungeons.

Tonsberg, Norway's oldest town (founded in A.D. 870), is where Norwegian kings were once crowned. The **Vestfold Folk Museum** at the town's entrance contains relics of the once-mighty whaling industry and of Viking chieftains. A trip to Tonsberg can be combined with a trip to **Sandefjord,** once a great whaling town. This summer resort is just two hours by express train from Oslo. Old whalers work as guides in the **Whaling Museum,** relating stories about the whaling days and explaining the sights.

A 13th-century Norwegian stave church is located in **Heddal,** southwest of Oslo. Only 32 of these tiered timber churches with their pointy shingled roofs are still standing.

The **Brakanes Hotel,** *N-5730,* at Hardanger Fjord in Ulvik, *tel. (47-5)52-61-05,* gives you an incredible view of the fiords; a double room is 800 to 950 Norwegian kroner ($130 to $155).

Bergen: a music lover's best

If you like Grieg's music, you'll love **Bergen.** The city's native son left traces wherever he went. And you can hear his music at the ultramodern **Grieg Hall,** which seats 1,420.

Grieg's music also is played during the international arts festival held in Bergen during the last week in May. (The festival also features opera, ballet, and folklore.) Details are available from the **Festival Office,** *Grieghallen, Lars Hilles Gate 3A; tel. (47-5)230-010.*

Climb up to **Troldhaugen,** the summer villa of the composer in Hop, outside Bergen. The Victorian house contains Grieg's Steinway grand piano (which is used for concerts given at the house during the annual festival). The composer created many of his best works in a cottage on the estate. Grieg and his wife are buried in a cliff grotto here.

Bergen was the seat of the Viking kingdom of Norway until the 14th century and was a member of the Hanseatic League, which linked free towns in northern Germany and adjacent countries for trade and protection. Most of ancient Bergen was destroyed by a fire in 1702. A row of Hanseatic timbered houses, rebuilt along the waterfront after the fire, is all that remains. This area, called **Bryggen,** houses the **Hanseatic Museum,** which illustrates commercial life in Bergen hundreds of years ago.

The oldest building in Bergen, dating back to the 12th century, is a Romanesque church called **St. Mary's.** The baroque pulpit, donated by Hanseatic merchants, is covered with carved figures symbolizing the Virtues. Visit during one of the free organ concerts held at 8 p.m. on Thursday evenings in the summer.

The **Fantoft Stave Church,** built in 1150, is covered with both pagan and Christian designs—serpents, dragons, and crosses. It was built to withstand the winter wind and has overlapping roofs and interlocking gables.

The best of Sweden

Progressive, wealthy **Sweden,** the fourth-largest nation in Europe, is sparsely inhabited. This California-sized country is made up of wheat plains, pine forests, thatched and timbered villages, cosmopolitan cities, historic islands, mountains, waterfalls, 95,000 lakes, and miles of rugged coastline. Best of all, its capital, Stockholm, is the least-traveled (therefore, the least-crowded) of all European capitals.

Stockholm: Mother Nature's favorite

While **Stockholm** has museums and fine old buildings (nearly all the same size and painted mustard yellow), the city's real attractions are natural: the waterways, the beaches, the parks, and the 24,000 little islands of the archipelago that lead to the Baltic Sea (most of them uninhabited). The city is built on 14 islands in Lake Malaren, and, believe it or not, the waterways are clean enough for swimming.

The heart of the city

Founded 700 years ago, Stockholm's roots are visible in the twisting streets of the medieval Old Town, **Gamla Stan.** At the heart of the area is the **Stortorget** (the old marketplace), surrounded by little streets lined with thick-walled, crooked buildings, as well as boutiques, galleries, and inexpensive restaurants.

Gamla Stan is dominated by the 18th-century **royal palace.** (During the summer you can see the changing of the guard here at noon Mondays through Saturdays and at 1 p.m. Sundays.) Parts of the palace can be visited, including the king's throne room, the chapel royal, the royal treasury, and the apartments of state, which have magnificent baroque ceilings and fine tapestries. Look for the crown jewels or the silver throne.

The royal burying ground

On the small island of Riddarholm, next to Gamla Stan, is **Riddarholm Church,** the burial place of Swedish kings and queens. Queen Desideria, the childhood sweetheart of Napoleon Bonaparte, is buried here in a green marble sarcophagus. Born Bernadine Eugénie Désirée Clary (but known simply as Désirée), she married Marshal Jean Baptiste Bernadotte after Napoleon married the sophisticated Josephine. Bernadotte was elected king of Sweden in 1818 (he took the name Carl XIV) and later took part in the battle against Napoleon at Leipzig. Désirée hated the long Scandinavian winters and longed for her native Paris until her death in Sweden in 1860.

Top sights

To the east of Gamla Stan is **Djurgården** (Deer Park), a lake-encircled forested park. Stockholm's great estates and gardens are located here, as well as the Royal Flagship *Wasa,* a man-of-war that sank 20 minutes into its maiden voyage in 1628.

Skansen, an open-air museum on Djurgården, displays more than 150 18th- and 19th-century buildings from all over Scandinavia, including windmills, manor houses, workshops, and a complete town quarter. At the old workshops, you can see how early printing, silversmithing, glassblowing, and leather making were done. During the summer, chamber music concerts are held at the Skogaholm manor house. At night you can dance in the outdoor pavilion.

The **Nordiska Museet** (Nordic Museum), also on Djurgården, is the world's best museum on Scandinavian life, with tools, clothing, and furnishings illustrating life from the 1500s to today.

The **Nationalmuseet** (National Museum of Art), at the tip of a peninsula on Sødra Blasieholmshamnen, has works by Rembrandt and Rubens and a rare collection of Russian icons, most from the 1400s. Room 45 features the works of Rembrandt, including *Portrait of an Old Man* and *Portrait of an Old Woman.*

Stadshuset (the city hall), on the island of Kungsholmen, designed by Ragnar Ostberg, is one of the finest examples of modern architecture in Europe. The poet Yeats said of the building, "No architectural work comparable to it has been accomplished since the Italian cities felt the excitement of the Renaissance." Completed in 1923, the city hall is dominated by a lofty tower topped with three crowns, the symbol of the defunct Scandinavian Union. Its Golden Hall is decorated with 19 million pieces of pure gold mosaic. Banquets following the Nobel Peace Prize ceremony are held here. Climb the tower for a view of Stockholm's islands and waterways.

Drottningholm Palace, on Queen's Island in Lake Mälaren, is the French-style, 17th-century palace of the royal family, surrounded by fountains and parks. The **Drottningholm Court Theater,** the best-preserved 18th-century theater in the world, is located on the palace grounds. Each summer, operas and ballets are staged with full 18th-century regalia. For reservations, contact the theater, *P.O. Box 27050, S-10251, Stockholm.*

The **Moderna Museet** (Museum of Modern Art), on the island of Skeppsholmen, has works by Andy Warhol, Salvador Dali, Picasso, Braque, and Leger.

The best nights out

If you're interested in meeting someone of the opposite sex, the place to go in Stockholm is the **Café Opera,** located in the same building as the national opera across from the Grand Hotel and directly across the bridge from the royal palace. The Café Opera has a dance floor, a bar, and a casino, where men toss away thousands of kronor playing roulette while some of the most beautiful unattached females in the world dance with one another or sit lingering over drinks.

For a different kind of fun, stop by **Grona Lund's Tivoli** (not to be confused with Tivoli in Copenhagen). Enjoy the amusements and go up to the top of the revolving tower for a wide view of Stockholm. Tivoli is open April to September from 2 p.m. to midnight. **Jump In,** a disco in the park, attracts a lively crowd and is open from 8 p.m. to midnight.

Stockholm's best hotels

Nobel Peace Prize winners usually stay at Stockholm's finest, the **Grand Hotel,** *Sødra Blasieholmshamnen 8; tel. (46-8)221020.* It is the best hotel in Sweden and one of the best in the world. The staff is intelligent, thoughtful, and prompt. This luxurious, expensive establishment faces the royal palace and has two restaurants and a bar. Ask for a room facing the water. A double room is 1,030 to 1,364 Swedish kronor ($180 to $239).

Runners-up to the Grand are the **Sergel Plaza,** *Brunkebergstorg 9; tel. (46-8)226600,* where rooms are 1090 Swedish kronor ($190), and the **Royal Viking**, *Vasagatan 1; tel. (46-8)141000*, where a double room starts at 950 Swedish kronor ($166). Another well-regarded hotel is the **Malardrottningen**, *Riddarholmen; tel. (46-8)243600*, across from the Old City. A double room is 500 to 995 Swedish kronor ($87 to $175).

The **Diplomat**, *Strandvagen 7C; tel. (46-8)6635800*, at the edge of the diplomatic quarter, is a small, sophisticated, expensive hotel furnished with antiques. It has a cocktail bar and an elegant teahouse. A double room is 900 Swedish kronor ($157).

Lady Hamilton, *Storkyrkobrinken 5, 2-111 40; tel. (46-8)234680*, in the old town of Stockholm, has rooms furnished with nautical antiques. Nearby church bells mark every quarter hour, but you get used to them after a couple of nights. A double room is 1,800 to 2,080 Swedish kronor ($315 to $364) per night.

If you are looking for a bargain that's full of charm, try **Hotel Anno 1647**, *Mariagrand 3, on the Island of Sodermalm; tel. (46-8)6440480*. The old brick building that dates (surprise!) to 1647 was originally the home of a tailor who achieved a senior position in his guild. It has a fine view of Gamla Stan. A double room is 1,150 Swedish kronor ($200).

How to sleep like a king

If you don't mind staying outside Stockholm, you can sleep like a king in the home of one of Sweden's aristocrats. Sprawling country estates are now open to paying guests on a limited basis. These are not hotels; they are private homes, subject to the whims of owners who may be ambivalent about having guests at their hearth. The following country estates take guests:

Orbyhus, *74060 Orbyhus; tel. (46-295)11061*, north of Uppsala, is the home of the Duchess d'Otrante. Contact Birgitta Tragardh.

Trollenas, *24100 Eslov; tel. (46-413)45100 or (46-413)16010*, at the southern tip of Sweden, is a 400-year-old castle on a sprawling estate. Contact Baron Nils Trolle. A double room is 1,200 Swedish kronor ($210).

Best restaurant, best wine cellar

The Swedes like to eat, which is why Stockholm has so many first-class restaurants. **Ulriksdals Wärdshus**, *Erlichstals Slottspark 1, 17171 Solna; tel. (46-8)850815*, located on the grounds of a royal park a few miles outside Stockholm, has a sweeping view of gardens stretching down to the water. This might have been the setting for the movie *Elvira Madigan*. The current owner, Lauri Nilsson, is the ninth restaurateur to have run an establishment on this spot.

Nilsson has the best—and best engineered—wine cellar in Scandinavia. Press a button, and things happen. A tour takes you from one automated passage to another and finally into the inner sanctum, a kind of bacchanalian boardroom, where Sweden's most posh wine-tasting club gathers to chew bread and spit Mouton Rothschild into crystal bowls. At the center of the room is the pièce de résistance, a high-tech wine spittoon that seems to be a combination of a pagan baptismal and some cruel machine you would find in a dentist's office. The queen of Sweden comes here to taste champagne.

The food at Ulriksdals Wärdshus is superb. Chef Carl-Heinz Krucken specializes in preparing a butterfly of chopped avocado with Swedish caviar and chopped onions. For the main course, try the noisettes of reindeer with raisin and green peppercorn sauce. The cloudberry mousse dessert is delicious.

Close seconds

The **Operakällaren**, *Operahuset; tel. (46-8)24-27-00 or (46-8)11-11-25*, prepares state banquets for the royal palace. Rooms are enormous, with high ceilings, carved oak paneling, and fine paintings. The smorgasbord is excellent. Reservations are necessary.

Another good restaurant in Stockholm is the **Coq Blanc**, *Regeringsgatan 116153*, a spacious and comfortable restaurant decorated with what seem to be thousands of chickens and eggs in various forms of artistic torment. The food is good, especially the morel-stuffed filet of sole and the fried filet of turbot in vermouth sauce.

Wedholms Fisk, *Nybrokajen 17; tel. (46-8)6117874,* has a gray and rather forbidding interior but serves excellent food. Specialties include marmite of fish, shellfish soup, and fricassee of turbot, sole, and salmon with vegetables in champagne sauce.

Fem Små Hus, *Nygrand 10; tel. (46-8)10-04-82,* is a maze of five interconnected buildings and a medieval cellar with vaults, arches, and alcoves. Try the Swedish specialties: reindeer and salmon. Reservations are recommended.

Don't bother looking for a giant smorgasbord. You may find one at Sunday lunch; otherwise, this famous feature of Scandinavian cuisine hardly figures at all in Stockholm's best restaurants. Ditto for Swedish meatballs.

The best side trips from Stockholm
Sigtuna, founded at the beginning of the 11th century on the shores of Lake Mälaren, is Sweden's oldest town, containing remnants of Vikings and early Christians. Low-timbered buildings line Storagatan. Sweden's first cathedral, St. Peter's, is here, along with the 13th-century Monastery of St. Maria.

Uppsala, Sweden's major university town, has a famous 15th-century cathedral and a 16th-century castle. The first Swedish university was founded here in 1477. (The university at Uppsala remains a well-respected institution.)

Walpurgis Eve, April 30, is the best time to visit Uppsala. Alumni and students wearing white caps celebrate the rebirth of spring and the death of winter with a torchlight parade and festivities until dawn. Thousands gather to join in hymns to spring and to hear speeches about the end of winter.

Walpurgis Eve, according to folklore, is when witches ride. It is the night before the birthday of St. Walpurgis, the medieval protectress against magic.

Gamla Uppsala (the old quarter of Uppsala), two miles north of Uppsala, was once a sacred grove, where animals and people were sacrificed to Norse gods. The Viking burial grounds date back to the sixth century. Nearby, on the site of an old pagan temple, is a 12th-century church. An open-air museum illustrating the life of peasants is open June through August.

While you're in the area, visit **Odinsborg,** an old wooden inn where you can drink mead from silver-tipped ornamental oxhorns—as the Vikings did centuries ago. Waitresses wear Viking breastplates over provincial dresses, old murals adorn the walls, the corner fireplace has copper kettles, and the main room is decorated with crude furniture.

Midsummer magic at its best
Dalarna Province in the heart of Sweden has preserved the rites of Midsummer (with a Christian touch, these days) as they were celebrated centuries ago. On **Midsummer Eve,** young people race through forests gathering birch boughs and wild flowers for the maypole. Once the pole is raised, villagers dance around it until dawn, weaving long ribbons that hang from the top.

In the morning, the townspeople go to church in rowboats decorated with greenery. A young girl will dream of her beloved on Midsummer Night if she places a bouquet containing seven wild flowers under her pillow. And if she looks into a reflecting pool on Midsummer Day, the next man she sees will be her loved one. The morning dew supposedly cures all ills.

The most colorful Midsummer celebrations are in the villages around Lake Siljan: Rattvik, Leksand, and Tallberg. In Siljansnas, a church boat race is held on Midsummer Day. In Hjortnas, traditional dancing takes place on the jetty the Saturday night following Midsummer.

Two simple but comfortable hotels in the region are the **Hotel Langbers,** *79303 Tallberg; tel. (46-247)50290* (rooms here are about 300 Swedish kronor, or $52), and the

Romantik Hotel Tallbergsgarden, *79303 Tallberg; tel. (46-247)50850,* where rooms are 390 Swedish kronor ($68). A weekend package at the Romantik Hotel Tallbergsgarden, including meals and two nights' accommodation, costs 815 Swedish kronor ($142).

The world's oldest cross-country ski race

The town of **Mora,** about 4 1/2 hours north of Stockholm by car, is a peaceful place that comes alive suddenly once a year on the first Sunday in March. This is the day of the **Vasalöppet**—the world's biggest and oldest cross-country ski race. As many as 12,000 cross-country skiers race along the course, fueled by the blueberry soup, lime juice, and Swedish meatballs offered by spectators. If you are brave, a good skier, and in good condition, enter the race. For application forms, contact **Vasalöppet,** *Vasagatan 19, S-79200 Mora, Sweden; tel. (46-250)16000.* Arrangements also can be made through major travel agencies.

The rest of the year, you can cross-country ski more peacefully. Rentals are about 171 Swedish kronor ($30) a day, and exquisite trails run along the frozen rivers and fields. Situated on the shores of Lake Siljan, Mora guarantees snow in the winter. It is about as far north as Anchorage.

The **Mora Hotel,** *tel. (46-250)117-50,* is the best place to stay. On weekends, rooms are 600 to 900 Swedish kronor ($105 to $157) per night, including dinner and breakfast. The hotel has a swimming pool, a sauna, a solarium, and a good restaurant called Terrassen.

Visby: the best medieval town

Sweden's best-preserved medieval town, **Visby,** on the country's largest island, Gotland, is protected by a massive, two-mile wall and 44 towers. Punctuating its skyline are 100 churches, 91 of which were built before 1350. Known as the City of Roses, Visby is filled with the sweet-smelling flowers. Nearby are beautiful sandy beaches that are remarkable for their marine stacks, piles of oddly shaped rocks sculpted by wind and water.

The cheapest way to go

The **Sweden Hotel Pass,** a hotel plan offered by several tour groups in the United States, including **Jason Travel,** *(415)957-9102,* and **ScanAm,** *(800)545-2204,* allows you a 50% discount on hotel rooms in Sweden.

Finland: the least spoiled Scandinavian country

Finland is an unspoiled land with the cleanest air in Europe. Its historic towns and cities are simple, elegant, and brightly colored, and its countryside is covered with virgin forests and 62,000 freshwater lakes. Although the population is less than 5 million, this is the fifth-largest nation in Europe. The lengthy coastline is marked by coves and framed by 20,000 small islands. During the summer, Finland is basked in perpetual sunshine.

Finns are known as great sailors and great magicians. Their language is not related to other Nordic tongues, except Lapp. The Finno-Ugric language family is more similar to Hungarian, Turkish, Estonian, and even Eskimo than to Swedish, Norwegian, or Danish. However, Finland has a Swedish-speaking minority, and most Finns have studied English.

Helsinki: where East meets West

The capital of Finland is located halfway between Russia and Sweden and shows signs of both Eastern and Western influences. It has been ruled by both over the centuries. The skyline is marked by the domes of the Lutheran cathedral and a Russian Orthodox church.

A light-colored city built of white granite and surrounded by water on three sides, Helsinki is carefully laid out, with 240 parks and scores of modern buildings, such as the

Temppeliaukion Church, an underground church blasted from solid rock and decorated with purple wood and copper.

The city's most imposing sight

The approach to Helsinki by sea is guarded by the 18th-century **Suomenlinna Fortress**. You can walk the fortress' old ramparts, visit its gardens, and have lunch in its open-air cafés.

A bit of the East

In front of the cathedral is **Senaatintori** (Senate Square), which is so reminiscent of Leningrad that many movies set in that city have been shot here, including *Reds*. The square even holds a statue of Czar Alexander II, a Russian ruler of Finland who is fondly remembered for allowing the Finns some independence. Also on the square is the oldest building in the city: the Sederholm residence, built in 1755.

The best picture of Finnish history

Finnish history is long and involved. A good place to begin absorbing it is the **Suomen Kansallismuseo** (National Museum), which has relics of the seafaring life of Viking times and the migration of the Finnish people northward 1,300 years ago. Located in a 200-year-old wooden building on Mannerheimintie, the city's main artery, the museum was designed by Eeno Saarinen. Opposite the museum is the ultramodern cultural center **Finlandia Hall**.

The world's best fur bargains

Furs are well-made and inexpensive in Finland, the world's biggest seller of farmed furs. Furriers there say you can easily buy a coat and pay for your trip to Finland for what it would cost to buy a similar coat in the United States, for example. Mink coats start at about $5,000; mink jackets at $2,000. In Helsinki, the best places to look are along the Pohjoisesplanadi and Etelaesplanadi, the northern and southern ends of the city's main shopping street, and in the shops at Station Tunnel and Hakaniemi Market Hall.

A sacred tradition: the sauna

Don't miss the chance to enjoy a Finnish sauna, a 2,000-year-old tradition that will make you feel euphoric. You take a sauna in a wood-lined room with layers of benches that climb toward the ceiling (the hottest are at the top). A stove heats the room to about 200 degrees Fahrenheit, and water is thrown on a layer of stones on the stove to produce steam.

Finns consider the oldest saunas the best. Built by early Finno-Ugric tribes, they are log cabins with earth floors, a pile of rocks above a fire, and no chimney.

Most saunas are built by the water—not surprising considering Finland has 188,000 lakes. Country saunas are stoked for hours, until the stones of the hearth are red-hot and the log walls have absorbed the heat and reflect it back.

If you're lucky, you'll be invited to take a sauna at the house of a native, which is a sign of hospitality. Because a sauna involves certain rules of etiquette, you should imitate your host. Allow him to create the first *loyly*, or vapor, by pouring water on the stove. Always ask other bathers if they are ready for a new cloud of steam before taking it upon yourself to create one.

If you're on your own (nearly every hotel has a sauna), take off your clothes and sweat. Then brush yourself lightly with birch branches. When you've had enough, dive into the frigid waters of a lake, roll around in the snow, or take a cold shower. (If you have a heart condition, you should skip that last step.) The ritual can be repeated three or four times. After the last sauna, soap the perspiration off your body.

Don't take a sauna for at least one hour after a meal, and don't drink alcohol before a sauna—it strains the heart. Remove all jewelry, including rings and pierced earrings, because metal gets hot and can burn you.

The best saunas in Helsinki are at the Palace Hotel, the Kalastajatorppa, and the Hesperia. You don't have to be a guest, but you must book in advance.

The best—and most affordable—restaurant

The most delightful restaurant in Helsinki, composed of a wine cellar, a coffeehouse, and several dining rooms, is **Kappeli**, *Etela Esplanadi 1*. Housed in a glassed-in pavilion on the edge of a park, Kappeli is always crowded with local Bohemians chatting over coffee and enjoying the view. Wander around until a table opens up. Dinner with wine is about 127 Finnish markkas ($30).

The best Russian restaurant in Finland

Saslik, *Neitsytpolku 12; tel. (358-0)170-544*, is a little crowded but very cozy. The *zakuski*, assorted appetizers for two, include several smoked, cured, and fresh varieties of fish, caviar with sour cream, meats, cheeses, and vegetables. An order of zakuski can be a meal in itself. The cost is 99 Finnish markkas ($23). For dessert, try the homemade Samarkand ice cream.

The best hotel in Finland

The **Hotel Strand Inter-Continental**, *John Stenbergin ranta 4, 00530 Helsinki*, overlooks the harbor of Helsinki and is ideally located next to the exciting Old City. The Botanical Gardens and the market square are also nearby. But more than a prime location, the Strand offers outstanding service and comfort—and a popular sauna on the top floor. A double room is 970 to 1,020 Finnish markkas ($226 to $238). To make a reservation in the United States, call *(800)332-4246*.

The best side trips

One of Finland's greatest surviving castles is the citadel at **Hämeenlinna**. Built over a long period of time and used for many things, including a prison, it displays a collection of Finnish art. Composer Jan Sibelius was born in this town; his house is a museum displaying his violin, his family's piano, and photos. One of the town's centuries-old wooden buildings houses a historical museum.

Operas are staged in the courtyard of **Olavinlinna Castle** in Savonlinna each July by the Finnish National Opera. Begun in 1475, the castle stands on a small island in a passage connecting two large lakes. Tickets to the operas are 130 Finnish markkas ($30) and should be ordered as early as the preceding October. You can stop by the festival **ticket office**, *Puistokatu 3; tel. (358-57)244-84*, about 4 p.m. the day of the performance to see if tickets are available.

In **Kerimaki**, near Savonlinna, is the largest wooden church in the world. The 150-year-old church seats 3,600 people. Strange, considering the town's population is 2,900. According to legend, the builders were tipsy when they began working on the church. They misread centimeters as inches, making the structure 2 1/2 times the size planned by the architect.

Lapland: Europe's last wilderness

Lapland, where the tundra never completely thaws and the winter darkness is broken only by the glimmering aurora borealis, stretches across the northern halves of Norway, Sweden, and Finland. This is Europe's last true wilderness, suffering long, cold, dark winters. During the summer, however, it is eerily beautiful under the Midnight Sun, reflected by glaciers, waterfalls, rivers, lakes, and mountains. For six weeks in June and July, the sun never sets.

This is the land of the Lapps (or Sami as they call themselves), a nomadic group that herds reindeer for a living and retains old traditions long forgotten elsewhere in

Scandinavia. Some Lapps still wear the traditional costume of blue felt with contrasting bands of red, yellow, and green, often decorated with embroidery. Men wear the "caps of four winds," with four floppy points. Women wear red felt bonnets with flaps over the ears.

Try the Lapp specialties: *poro* (reindeer meat), *lohi* (salmon), and *siika* (whitefish). Also taste the local liqueurs and desserts made from Arctic cloudberries.

The northernmost point in Europe

Nordkapp, Norway's North Cape, is the northernmost point in Europe, the place where the sun doesn't sink below the horizon from May 14 to July 30. This mountain plateau rises 1,000 feet out of the ocean—a bleak but beautiful black cliff. In August, when the sun dips below the horizon for a few minutes, the sky is lit by the Northern Lights, a rainbow of spectacular colors. Even though most people come in July to see the Midnight Sun, August is still the best time to visit. The North Cape is snowbound until early June.

Nordkapp is on Magerøy, an island about 15 miles north of **Honningsvaag,** the northernmost village in the world. During the summer, a Lapp camp with reindeer herds is usually set up at Nordmannset, a little more than a mile outside Honningsvaag.

The northernmost hotel in this northernmost region is the **Sas,** *tel. (47-84)72331,* in Honningsvaag. A modern place, it has great views and rooms for 590 to 990 Norwegian kroner ($95 to $160). Make reservations well in advance.

To fly to the North Cape, take SAS from Oslo to Tromsø or Lakselv and then Wideroe's Airlines to Honningsvaag. Regular bus service runs between Honningsvaag and the North Cape.

The best of Finnmark

Several towns bring civilization of a sort to **Finnmark** (Norwegian Lapland). **Tromsø** is the best base for trappers, whalers, and sealers. (It is also home to Greenpeace, the international volunteer organization that crusades for the environment.) Polar explorers set out from this town, too.

The **Arctic Church,** one of the most impressive pieces of modern architecture in the world, is in Tromsø. Built across the longest suspension bridge in Scandinavia (1,100 yards), it is shaped like an iceberg and made of aluminum that reflects the Midnight Sun.

The best way to visit the Lapps

The town of **Alta** in Finnmark is the best base for excursions into Lapp country. Most Lapps live on the tundra south of here. In Masi, about 44 miles from Alta on the main road to Finland, they wear traditional costumes, although many have taken up a modern way of life.

During the winter, the Lapps live inland. In May and June, they migrate to the coast as they have for centuries, herding thousands of reindeer across rivers and fiords—a spectacular sight. Colorful reindeer roundups usually take place between September and February.

The **Alta Gjestestue,** *tel. (46-864)35-336,* in Alta is an inviting guesthouse where a double room is 430 Norwegian kroner ($70), including breakfast.

The best of Norrland

Norrland, the Swedish word for Swedish Lapland, covers half the area of Sweden. One-quarter of the country is north of the Arctic Circle, and about 10,000 Lapps live here. It is easier to reach than you might imagine. Trains come here from Stockholm. Postal buses continue even farther north and connect with smaller villages and settlements. You can fly to the airports at Umeå, Luleå, and Kiruna. Or you can drive there on Road E4.

Arvidsjaur is modern but has an old Lappish center, with well-preserved, cone-shaped huts. Reindeer are rounded up here in June and July. Pine forests surround the town.

Norrbotten is a Lapp trading and cultural center. A market is held here the first week of February, when traditional Lapp handicrafts (delicately carved wooden utensils, silver jewelry, and colorful and elaborate woven fabrics) are sold.

Kvikkjokk is the gateway to Sarek National Park, the largest wilderness in Europe. There are no roads or trails in the park.

The best hiking trails

Svenska Turistföreningen (the Swedish Touring Club), *STF, Box 25, Vasagaten 48, S-10120, Stockholm; tel. (46-8)22-72-00,* maintains hotels and marked hiking routes for hundreds of miles through Swedish Lapland. About 80 cabins are available with beds and bedding, cooking utensils, and firewood. The cabins can be used for one or two nights only. Cabins are 85 Swedish kronor ($15) for members, 114 Swedish kronor ($20) for non-members (if room is available).

Swedish hikers prefer the **Kungsleden,** or Royal Trail, the longest marked trail in the world, leading from the resort of Abisko to Jakkvik, a total of 210 miles. Cabins are spaced a day apart along the trail, which follows the old nomadic paths of the Lapps.

The National Swedish Environmental Protection Board owns several cabins in **Padjelanta National Park,** where you can stay for 57 Swedish kronor ($10) a night. The mountain's park is known for its unusual flora and many lakes.

The best of Finnish Lapland

Finnish Lapland, the largest and most northerly of Finland's provinces, occupies one-third the area of Finland and lies almost entirely above the Arctic Circle. It adjoins the Lapland districts in neighboring Norway and Sweden, but the landscape contrasts sharply. Some parts are barren, while others are covered by vast forests of pine and spruce and watered by rushing rivers. There are only about four people per square mile.

About 3,500 Sami, or Lapps, live in the northernmost parishes: Utsjoki, Enontekiö, Inari, and Sodankylö. Until the seventh century, Lapps inhabited all of Finland. After the arrival of the Finns from the Volga, they retreated to the north, where they continue their traditional ways.

Finland's best hiking

In the summer, hiking expeditions are led through Lapland by experienced guides. Don't attempt an independent excursion unless you really know what you're doing. And bring the right equipment—boots; protective, warm clothing; and maps, which can be obtained from the **Map Center,** *Karttakeskus, Pasilan Virastokeskus, Opastinsilta 12, 00520 Helsinki.*

A marked 49-mile hiking trail called **Karhunkierros** (the Bear's Ring) runs near Kuusamo, about 124 miles from Oulu, just south of the polar circle. You don't need a guide to follow the clearly marked trail, which passes the most dramatic scenery in the area. You can spend the night free in huts along the trail. However, in July and August, it is a good idea to carry a tent in case the huts are full. Bring food and mosquito repellent as well. Traveling the entire circle takes four to six days. (Shorter trails are also marked.)

The best base for exploring Lapland

Rovaniemi, the capital of Lapland, is a good base for explorations. This modern town five miles south of the Arctic Circle is easy to reach by train or plane from Helsinki. **Lapin Matkailu,** *Maakuntakatu 10, 96100 Rovaniemi; tel. (358-60)346052,* has a reservation service.

The best place to stay in Rovaniemi is **Rantasipi Pohjanhovi,** *Pohjanpuistikko 2; tel. (358-60)33711,* located next to the Kemijoki River. It has two dining rooms, saunas, a swimming pool, and entertainment. Cross-country ski tracks pass right by the hotel. A double room with a bath is 625 to 795 Finnish markkas ($146 to $185), including breakfast.

The **Hotelli Ravintola Oppipoika,** *Korkalonkatu 33; tel. (358-60)20321,* is a modern hotel. A double room with a bath is from 250 to 440 Finnish markkas ($58 to $102).

The best adventure: Lapland in winter

If you like romping in the snow, you'll love Lapland in the winter. Days and nights are spent cross-country skiing, taking reindeer rides, and whizzing across the powder in snowmobiles. Light from the stars and moon reflects off the snow, providing enough visibility for these activities 24 hours a day.

The terrain makes for some of the finest cross-country skiing in the world. Competitive skiers come here from around the world to train. Lapland offers a vast network of maintained ski tracks. Seasoned skiers can book a cabin in one of the fell regions and take on the unmarked countryside. Caution! If you are going out into the wilderness, hire a guide. This is a wild, isolated, and frozen netherworld, and you could easily become lost forever. Arrange guides through the **Finnish Tourist Board,** *655 Third Ave., New York, NY 10017; (212)370-5540.*

A reindeer safari is a great way to discover the land. On a guided trip, you are given a sled (a canoe-shaped contraption of wood planks) and a reindeer. The reindeer wears a harness, which is attached to the sled with a colorful braid. Tucked into blankets, you control the critter with a single rope.

A reindeer safari can last from 20 minutes to an entire week—it's up to you. The longer excursions are definitely for the hardy—you sleep in a tent or cabin and eat reindeer meat (which can be tough) cooked over an open fire.

To explore Lapland at a faster pace, take a snowmobile safari. You wear enormous Arctic overalls, sled shoes, gloves, and a hat. The cold, dry air is exhilarating as you fly through the forests and across the frozen lakes.

The Best of Spain

I would sooner be a foreigner in Spain than in most countries. How easy it is to make friends in Spain!...I defy anyone to be thrown as I was among the Spanish working class and not be struck by their essential decency; above all, their straightforwardness and generosity.
— George Orwell, *Homage to Catalonia*

Spain is the most exotic West European nation. Although it is linked to the European continent at the French border, in many ways it feels more like North Africa. Not until the reign of Ferdinand and Isabella in the 15th century did Spain become part of Europe culturally. But when it did finally join hands with Europe, it became a great power, colonizing much of the world.

No longer mighty, Spain still has Roman ruins, Moorish fortresses, and early Christian cathedrals. The landscape is ruggedly beautiful, the traditions colorful, and the art collections among the greatest in the world. A tour of Spain will lead you from Madrid's gigantic Prado Museum, which rivals the Louvre as the best museum in the world, to the rich and elaborate Alhambra, idyllic sandy beaches, and quaint fishing villages.

Madrid: Spain's most cosmopolitan city

Madrid is a cosmopolitan city with museums, elegant restaurants, and trendy discos. It is worth visiting, despite its pollution problem. Situated more than 10,000 feet above sea level, Madrid is filled with trucks and cars spewing hydrocarbons unhindered by any anti-pollution devices.

The most picturesque quarter

The most picturesque section of Madrid is the labyrinth of narrow streets between **Puerta del Sol** and the **Royal Palace.** Each street has a sign depicting an activity that distinguished it in the past. For instance, Pasadizo del Panecillo has a picture of friars distributing bread to the poor. The best way to explore is on foot. You will find Velazquez's grand statue of Philip IV in the center of the Plaza de Oriente, east of the Royal Palace.

Have a glass of sangria in the vast and uniform old main square of Madrid, the **Plaza Mayor,** near the Royal Palace. You will be surrounded by 17th-century buildings with balconies and arches. Descend the stairway at the southwest corner of the plaza to an area filled with lively bars.

El Prado: the Louvre's greatest rival

El Prado, in the Plaza Canovas del Castillo, is Madrid's number-one attraction. One of the greatest museums in the world, it holds the cream of the collections of Spanish monarchs from the 16th through 19th centuries, including works by Velazquez, Goya, Murillo, El Greco, Breughal, Rubens, and Dürer. The best time to visit the Prado is in the late afternoon, when the sun adds light to the somewhat dim interior.

The most remarkable work at the Prado is *Las Meninas* (*Maids in Waiting*), painted by Velazquez in 1656. This is a painting of the artist painting an unknown subject, probably the royal couple, who are reflected in a mirror behind him. He appears to be painting the viewer, however, because of his direct, straightforward gaze. The artist is surrounded by the royal entourage—the little infanta, *las meninas*, or ladies-in-waiting, dwarfs, and a dog.

The black Goyas, so called because of their dark backgrounds and tragic themes, are housed in a special gallery within the Prado. The Spanish resistance to Napoleon (1808 to 1814) is their theme.

On the ground floor is a special section with tapestries designed by Goya for the Escorial (see below) and his *Disasters of War* etchings, inspired by his experiences during the war against Napoleon.

Opposite the Prado is the new Thyssen-Bornemiszka museum, which houses the collection of the German family formerly housed in Villa Favorita in Lugaro, as well as overflow from the Prado.

Madrid's most impressive palace

El Palacio Real (the Royal Palace) is a baroque structure created under Charles III in 1764. About 50 of the 2,800 rooms are open to the public. They are filled with chandeliers, floral-patterned wallpaper, and colorful rugs. In one room the walls and ceilings are covered with 400 panels of painted porcelain. One of the strangest sights in the palace is what appears to be a doll in a glass case in the private Royal Chapel. Actually, these are the bones of St. Felix, a Christian martyr, wrapped in wax and silk and made to look like a small person. The figure was a gift from the pope to Queen Isabella II. Tours of the palace cost 300 to 400 pesetas ($3 to $4).

El Palacio's **Royal Library** houses more than 300,000 books, including 15th-century books, rare manuscripts, and Queen Isabella's prayer book.

You still can see bullet holes and other signs of the bloody Civil War of 1936-1938 in the tapestries, frescoes, and furniture at the Palacio Real. The victorious Franco regime decided to keep these as reminders of the war (but you won't find this information listed in guidebooks).

Madrid's best market

El Rastro, the flea market that starts at the Plaza Mayor and spills down Madrid's streets on Sundays, is a shopper's mecca. Vendors sell fine cotton shirts from India for 1,320 pesetas ($13), Moroccan belts of brass and leather for 770 pesetas ($8), leather bags for 900 pesetas ($9), and alabaster pots for 165 pesetas ($2), as well as bootleg tapes of U.S. musicians, semiprecious stones, fossils, and antiques.

Throughout the flea market are Gypsies who have a talent for spotting unwary tourists. They will pull you aside and offer you watches, jewelry, and electronic equipment at prices that are too good to be true. Be careful. The watchcases are often empty or filled with cheap materials. The jewelry is fake, and the electronic equipment usually doesn't work. But if they offer you leather goods, you may get a bargain. Look at the items carefully. If they interest you, offer the seller a tenth of the asking price. Haggle!

The best jogging

Parque del Retiro is a great place to take an early-morning jog. Part of the park is designed to look like the pattern on a blue willow plate. Avoid the places designated "*Zona de perros en libertad*" (Zone of dogs in freedom)! You also can rent a rowboat or have a picnic.

The best bull in town

While bullfights may seem barbaric to animal lovers, the Spanish believe the odds between man and bull are even. They see bullfights as a match between man and the untamed elements. The Spanish sense of fair play in a bullfight can be gruesome to the uninitiated. A recent match pitted a matador against the bull who had gouged out his eye. In the rematch, the bull's eye also was removed. An eye for an eye, so they say! The rematch was one of the most heavily attended events in Spanish history. Incidentally, the matador won.

Bullfights can be seen nearly every Sunday and Thursday from Easter through October at **Las Ventas**, *Plaza de Toros Monumental,* or at the smaller ring, **Vista Alegre**. Tickets can be purchased in advance at a counter at Calle Victoria 9, near the Puerta del Sol. But you usually can get a ticket at the door. Shows generally start at 5 p.m. or 7 p.m. (Make sure you buy tickets for the shady side of the ring, even though they are slightly more expensive.)

Tapas—the world's best snacks

Madrileños don't eat dinner until very late—after 10 p.m. It's impossible to order dinner before 8 p.m., which frustrates many foreign visitors. The solution is a little snack called a *tapa*. Madrileños, too, get hungry around 6 p.m., so they nibble on *tapas* (sardines, squid, octopus, olives, fried potatoes, sausage, shrimp, almonds, and any number of other delicious concoctions) with a glass of sherry or sangria in a *tapas* bar.

The most popular *tapas* are those made from chorizo (a Spanish sausage). The best are those that have been aged in a farmer's well and then cooked to kill the bacterial growth. Foreigners, however, should be careful with such local *tapas*. Build up a tolerance slowly for these new foods and their unusual bacterial elements. (Severe disorders have been reported by people who have overindulged in exotic fare on unacclimated stomachs.)

A small version of the *tapa*, a *pincho*, is usually served free with the first drink in any of Madrid's *tapas* bars, known as *mesones* and *tabernas*. The custom is to have only one drink per *taberna* and then move on to the next one. Many of the *tabernas* are located around the Plaza Mayor. Two classics are the Meson de la Tortilla and the Meson del Champiñon, on Cava de San Miguel.

Europe's disco capital

Spain's capital has more discos than anywhere else in Europe. They don't get going until midnight. The music tends to be about five years behind what's playing in London and New York.

The leading disco in Madrid is **Pacha**, *Barcelo 11; tel. (34-1)446-0137,* which attracts a rich young set. Dancers are videotaped and come back the following week to see themselves on tape.

One of the most unusual clubs is **Oh Madrid**, outside town. It has a swimming pool and terraces decorated with beach scenes.

If you tire of rock, New Wave, and the young set, try **Café Berlin**, *Jacometrezo 4; tel. (34-1)231-0810,* which has Madrid's best jazz.

Madrid has Las Vegas-style music halls with top-notch entertainers. **Scala Melia**, *Edificio Melia Castilla, Rosario Pino 7,* is the best.

The finest flamenco

Flamenco dancing has evolved into a unique art form in Madrid. Dinner nightclubs, such as the **Café de Chinitas**, *Torrija 7; tel. (34-1)248-5135,* have superb shows.

Flamenco nightclubs can be expensive, however (about 6,000 pesetas, or $60, with drinks). Often you can watch a show free just by roaming the streets around the Plaza Mayor. Keep your eyes open. You might see an impromptu dance by an Andalusian Gypsy troupe. Often little Gypsy girls will enter into a whirling flamenco with terrific vigor, paced by the insistent clapping of Gypsy boys. Eventually the hat is passed around. A good place to see flamenco dancers is the pedestrian street off Calle Serrano outside the Casa Inglese department store.

The newest thing in Madrid is to do the flamenco, rather than simply sit back and watch it. After 1 a.m., you can join in the heel-tapping, castanet-snapping, hand-clapping whirl of energy at **Al Andalus**, *Capitan Haya 19*, or **El Porton**, *Lopez de Hoyos 25*.

Spain's most luxurious hotel

Hotel Ritz, *Plaza de Lealtad 5; tel. (34-1)521-2857*, is unrivaled for luxury. The late King Alfonso XIII's pet hotel was built in 1910 to regal standards of luxury. Over the years, the hotel became a bit worn around the edges. But in 1984 it was restored when Trusthouse Forte, a British hotel chain, took over. All the old luxuries are still there (Limoges china, handwoven carpets, silverware) and some new ones have been added, such as individual temperature control for each room. The bathrooms at the Ritz are magnificent. Large bouquets of gladioli or exotic birds of paradise give color to the muted greens and grays of the rooms.

When you stay at the Ritz, you are served a breakfast of fresh croissants, Seville marmalade, and hot tea or coffee, served on immaculate white tablecloths with a little vase of pink carnations, shiny starched napkins, and polished silver.

Twice a day, the splendid bowl of fruit on your dressing table is replenished. It is accompanied by a knife, fork, napkin, and finger bowl in which geranium petals float.

The Ritz is in a splendid location, too. The Prado museums and shops are within walking distance.

A night at the Ritz isn't cheap. Double rooms are 40,000 to 755,000 pesetas ($400 to $7,550), but you're paying for exquisite service and handsome surroundings. **Leading Hotels of the World**, *(800)223-6800*, can make arrangements in the United States.

The closest competition

Although topping the Ritz is impossible, Villa Magna and Miguel Angel come closest. Both are expensive luxury hotels with beautiful decor and first-class service.

Villa Magna, *Paseo de la Castellana 22; tel. (34-1)578-20-00*, is quiet, despite its central locale. The hotel's garden is gorgeous, set beneath the balconied, nine-story structure. Rooms are large, with bathrooms, individual thermostats, and huge, comfortable chairs. The hotel is decorated with marble, glass, and stainless steel. The bar is cozy. The hotel also has an elegant lounge, a hairdresser, a sauna, and a shopping area. Rooms start at 52,000 pesetas ($520).

Miguel Angel, *Miguel Angel 31; tel. (34-1)442-00-22*, looks like an ice palace. Enormous chandeliers hang from the ceilings, and the balustrades are crystal. Silk spreads cover the beds, and plush carpet cushions the foot. Perhaps the nicest aspect of the hotel, however, is its marvelous indoor pool surrounded by white furniture. Rooms start at 24,800 pesetas ($248).

The best luxury hotel without the high price

Undoubtedly the best place to stay in Madrid if you want to avoid the exorbitant price at the Ritz is the **Palace Hotel**, *Plaza de las Cortes 7; tel. (34-1)429-75-51*. You will still be pampered, but rooms here cost about 15,825 pesetas ($159).

Sweet nights at sweet prices

Alcalá, *Alcalá 66; tel. (34-1)435-10-60*, is one of our favorites. Near the Retiro Park, it is cozy, with a circular iron hearth. Rooms are air-conditioned, and dual-glaze windows keep out the sounds of traffic. Full-length mirrors and walnut-paneled walls grace the bedrooms. The hotel restaurant is very good also, serving Basque specialties. Double rooms are 10,000 pesetas ($100).

Spain's best restaurant

Zalacaín, *Alvarez de Baena 4; tel. (34-1)561-59-35,* with its 15 cooks, is one of the finest restaurants in Europe. Michelin was so impressed that it gave the elegant restaurant three stars. The food is imaginative and delicious. Dinner is about 15,000 pesetas ($150). Reserve in advance. The restaurant is closed Saturday afternoons, Sundays, Holy Week, and in August.

Spain's restaurant capital

Madrid has become a restaurant capital in recent years. Hundreds of fine restaurants have opened, serving good regional dishes as well as seafood and international cuisine.

The best Castillian cuisine is served at **Casa Botín**, *Cuchilleros 17; tel. (34-1)266-42-17,* and **Posada de la Villa**, *Cava Baja 9; tel. (34-1)266-18-60,* both in Old Madrid. Castillian cuisine is known generally for its use of garlic, onions, and olive oil. Try the roast baby lamb and suckling pig. Both restaurants are more than 200 years old. Dinner in either is 4,000 to 5,000 pesetas ($40 to $50). The restaurants are closed for dinner Sundays.

Casa Lucio, *Cava Baja 35; tel. (34-1)265-32-52,* is one of Madrid's oldest restaurants. Despite its unpretentious service and surroundings, this cozy establishment has attracted the king and the prime minister of Spain. Dinner is about 5,000 pesetas ($50). It is closed Saturday afternoons and in August.

Cabo Mayor, *Juan Hurtado de Mendoza 11; tel. (34-1)250-87-76,* is elegant. One of its best dishes is *ensalada de rape y almejas,* paper-thin slices of raw monkfish and whole clams marinated in lemon, oil, and fennel. The salmon and corn salad is also good. Dinner is around 7,000 pesetas ($70). The restaurant is closed Sundays and from Aug. 15 through Sept. 2.

El Amparo, *Callejon de Puigcerda 18, corner of Jorge Juan; tel. (34-1)431-64-56,* in the exclusive residential neighborhood known as Barrio de Salamanca, serves the unique cuisine of chef Ramon Ramirez, French and Basque. The house wines are exceptional and fairly priced. Dinner is about 10,000 pesetas ($100). The restaurant is closed Saturday afternoons, Sundays, Holy Week, and in August.

Horcher, *6 Alfonso XII; tel. (34-1)522-07-31,* one of the most elegant restaurants in Madrid, serves unusual game dishes. Dinner is around 10,000 pesetas ($100). The restaurant is closed on Sundays.

Jockey, *Amador de los Rios 6; tel. (34-1)319-10-03,* is a fine restaurant that serves Spanish and French dishes. Dinner is 9,000 to 10,000 pesetas ($90 to $100).

The Spanish passion: *paella*

Paella—a delicious concoction of rice with seafood and spices—is a national passion in Spain. It is generally served in huge, heavy black skillets and comes in two varieties: *valenciana* has chicken, sausage, and seafood; *mariscos* has only seafood, no chicken or sausage.

The place for *paella* in Madrid is **El Pescador**, *José Ortega y Gasset 75; tel. (34-1)401-30-26* or *(34-1)402-12-90,* an informal restaurant in Old Madrid near the Puerta del Sol. Long communal tables are shared by diners, who serve themselves *paella* from large pots. If you stop by in midafternoon, you will see fishermen with weathered faces peeling freshly caught seafood for the evening's *paella.* Dinner is about 5,000 pesetas ($50).

The best way to get around

The best way to get around Madrid is the city's fast and efficient subway. Buy your tickets at booths and machines in the stations for only 60 pesetas (60 cents) a ride. (You can buy 10 tickets for 500 pesetas, or $5.) Tickets are inserted into electronic turnstiles that let you enter the system. Don't throw away your ticket—you'll need it to get back out again. The subway is open 6:30 a.m. to 1 a.m.

Spain's most intimidating edifice

El Escorial, on a mountain northwest of Madrid, is a 16th-century monastery-palace. It was the home of Phillip II, who commissioned the Armada to try to conquer England—and failed. A giant, gloomy building with hundreds of rooms and thousands of windows, it is full of history, art, and rare manuscripts. Almost all of Spain's royalty is entombed here, as well as a number of saints, in a cavernous, black-marble room.

Trains to the palace leave 20 times a day from the Atocha station in Madrid. A bus takes visitors from the station to the palace.

Spain's best medieval walled town

Avila, Spain's most beautiful walled town, is just about 90 minutes from Madrid. Perched on a crest and enclosed within massive 38-foot-high walls, Avila is the highest provincial capital in Spain. Six archways lead into this austere and intimidating town, and 90 towers keep watch over the area. It was also the town of St. Teresa, the 16th-century mystic and reformer.

The town has a handful of main tourist sights: the cathedral, the Convent of St. Teresa, and the Basilica of St. Vincent. Visit these first and then explore the streets at random. The best view is from the town walls on the edge of Avila's *parador,* or government-run hotel. Go through the *parador's* garden and climb the flight of stairs to the wall. You will see the River Adaja, the road to Salamanca, and the endless plain. A tourist information office is located opposite the cathedral on the main plaza.

Toledo: the richest history

Toledo, a city rich in history, is an hour's drive from Madrid. In the words of Gerald Brennan in *The Faces of Spain* (1950), "Like Fez, it reeks of the Middle Ages; like Lhasa, of monks."

Lording over the city is a fortress called the **Alcazar.** El Cid, the Lord Champion of the 11th century, whose courageous deeds were described in Spain's epic poem, lived here. Destroyed during the Spanish Civil War, the Alcazar has been reconstructed. It houses a museum of the Spanish Civil War.

Ferdinand and Isabella built a cathedral at the heart of Toledo in the 15th century and filled it with art, sanctuaries, and chapels. For a great view of the city and a small adventure, climb the cathedral's tower and examine its 18th-century bell, which is still in use.

El Greco left his mark on Toledo as well. His famous painting *The Burial of the Conde de Orgaz* is housed in Iglesia Santo Tome (St. Thomas Church) at Angel Santo Tome. The **El Greco House and Museum** (Casa y Museo del Greco), *Paseo del Transito,* contains paintings and memorabilia of the 16th-century artist.

A 14th-century synagogue called El Transito is down the street from El Greco's house. It was once a house of worship for Jews in Toledo. During the Inquisition, it became a church, and its members were forced either to became Christian or flee the country. A museum containing Sephardic religious articles is located in part of the synagogue.

Don't buy any tourist knicknacks in Toledo. Prices here are almost twice as high as elsewhere in Spain. The merchants stalk gullible foreigners.

The best view of this dramatic city is from the **Circunvalación,** a road that runs parallel to the Rio Tajo.

The best sword shopping

Don't leave Toledo without purchasing one of the city's world-famous swords or steel blades. For a good selection, visit **Fabrica Bermejo**, near the Santiago Church beyond the Visagro gates, or **Fabrica Garido**, next to the city's bullring. **Real Fabrica de Armas**, about five kilometers from town on Highway N-401, is another good shop.

The best places to stay

Outside Toledo is a highly recommended *parador*. **El Parador Nacional Conde de Orgaz**, *Cerro del Emperador; tel. (34-25)22-18-50*, is one of the most beautiful in Spain. The two-story hotel has a sweeping view of Toledo. Its restaurant serves Castilian cuisine and international fare. Rooms are air-conditioned, and guests can use the hotel's pool. Rooms are from 13,000 pesetas ($130).

Another good place to stay is the **Hostal del Cardenal**, *Paseo de Recaredo 24; tel. (34-25)22-49-00*. Built in the 18th century as a summer palace for Cardinal Lorenzana, this is a quiet place to stay. A double room is 8,000 pesetas ($80).

The best times to visit

The best times to visit Toledo are during the city's festivals: the **Olive Festival**, held at Mora de Toledo on the last Sunday in April; the pilgrimage to the shrine of **La Virgen del Valle**, held on May 1; the **Feast of San Isidoro** at Talavera de la Reina, May 15-18; the annual fair in August that salutes **La Virgen del Sagrario**; and the fiesta known as the **Rosa del Azafran** (Stigma of Saffron), held on the last Sunday in October at Consuegra.

Barcelona: the most European city

Flower-filled **Barcelona** is sociable, stimulating, and the most European Spanish city. Residents love their town. To them, Barcelona's ancient hegemony over the Mediterranean is only temporarily in eclipse.

The city's Catalan culture, once suppressed by General Franco, is back in full swing—street signs, maps, museum labels, and conversations are again in the distinctive Catalan language.

Adding to Barcelona's charms are low-priced hotels, restaurants, and transportation.

The most interesting quarter

The **Gothic Quarter** (Barrio Gotico), at Barcelona's heart, is filled with shops, bars, nightclubs, and 14th-century buildings. Roman, Gothic, and medieval walls still stand. Wander around—you probably will chance upon crumbling classical arches and statuary.

The barrio's handsome Gothic cathedral is worth a visit, even if you stop in only to see the white geese in the cloister gardens. Interesting contrasts to the medieval buildings are the street lamps, which were designed by Antonio Gaudi, an innovative architect associated with the art nouveau movement. This quarter is a great shopping area, especially if you're looking for trendy clothes and unusual art.

Barcelona's most entertaining avenues

The first thing to do in Barcelona is stroll along **Las Ramblas**. These wide avenues go from the Diagonal (a wide avenue that cuts diagonally across the center of Barcelona) to the Columbus monument at the harbor. (Although the contiguous segments of Las Ramblas have their own names—Rambla Dels Estudis, Rambla de Sant Josep—they are known collectively as Las Ramblas.)

On Las Ramblas near Placa de Catalunya is Orator's Corner, where men gather to discuss the issues of the day. You'll also find the grand opera house, ornate churches, and elegant cafés, as well as Barcelona's intriguing seedy side on Las Ramblas.

This exotic stretch is the place to shop for everything from colorful tropical birds and flowers to postcards showing Barcelona's lewd and kinky night life. A little street called Riera Alta, between Las Ramblas and Calle Ronda San Antonio, hides a wineshop called

Bodega. A little old man runs this dark place lined from floor to ceiling with bottles. If you ask for a sample, he will give you a squirt from a wine skin, or *bota*. He squeezes the *bota*, creating an arc of wine in the air, which you must artfully capture in your wide-open mouth. After dark, a parade of colorfully dressed transvestites joins families and tourists strolling along Las Ramblas near the Diagonal.

One note: Be careful when walking along Las Ramblas—about 30 purse snatchings a day take place here. Don't carry anything valuable with you if you go through the seedy Barrio Chino at the lower end of Las Ramblas.

Spain's most magnificent opera house

About halfway down Las Ramblas on the right is the **Gran Téâtre del Liceu**, *Rambla Catutxins 61; tel. (34-3)318-91-22*, the Barcelona opera. Here Casals first bowed his cello and Caballé hit her first incredible high C. Opened in 1847, it is unassuming on the outside, but inside it is one of the most beautful opera houses in all Europe.

Toulouse-Lautrec's favorite brew

An adventure to try in Barcelona is drinking *absenta*, or absinthe, a potent liquor that is illegal in most countries but perfectly legal in Spain. *Absenta* has given a number of writers and artists their inspiration (and probably rotted their brains), including Toulouse- Lautrec.

This licorice-flavored wood alcohol (not to be confused with Pernod, a much milder drink) is sold at the beautiful Antique Bar on San Pau, near Jeronimo, in the Barrio Chino. The bar is old and ornate and has a sign that reads "Prohibited to Sing."

Limit yourself to two shots of *absenta*, at the most. After three, you won't know where you are or what you're doing there! (And you don't want this to happen when you're in the shady Barrio Chino.)

The best of Picasso

Museo de Picasso, *Calle Montcada near the Barrio Gotico*, has one of the world's most comprehensive collections of Picasso's works, starting from his childhood and continuing through his entire life. Few people take advantage of the free guided tour, available in English, so you rarely have to wait and often can have the guide to yourself.

The most expensive walls in the world

Los 4 Gatos (The 4 Cats) café in Barcelona was frequented by such artists as Picasso and Utrillo. At one time, their paintings hung on the walls there. (They decorated the café when the owner allowed them to use the premises to stage an art show.) This may mean that, at today's prices, these walls were the most expensively covered in the world.

Gaudi's greatest works

Walking around Barcelona, you can't miss the strangely beautiful works of **Antonio Gaudi.** The luxury apartment buildings on and around the Paseo de Gracia were designed by the architect. They are distinguished by their asymmetrical shapes and unusual colors.

Templo de la Sagrada Familia is Gaudi's never-completed but extraordinary church. Its stonework resembling an enormous dribbled-sand castle, the structure towers above the Plaça de la Sagrada Familia. Climb the tiny, twisting and turning, steep stairs in the church towers to enjoy the view from the top.

Work continues to complete the church whenever a bit of money is collected. (Many Gothic cathedrals took centuries to build, too.)

Gaudi died on the street here. He stepped off the curb into the road to look at his work and was hit by a car.

Park Guëll, north of the city, was also created by the imaginative artist and is full of wild, beautiful, and sometimes decaying sculptures and objects. The benches and walls are studded with pieces of pottery and glass, and caves are hollowed out of a hill.

Barcelona's tip-top displays

Barcelona lies in the shadows of an intriguing hill, **Montjuïc**, which is topped with the remains of the 1929 World's Fair. It is a pleasant place to visit—during the day. Don't stroll around by yourself, however, as the park attracts its share of strange characters.

The walk to the top of Montjuïc is long and strenuous (but enjoyable if you are in good shape). If you don't feel up to the hike, take the funicular on weekends and holidays from the Parallel metro station or bus 61, 101, or 201.

The most beautiful of the World's Fair pavilions is a starkly modern structure designed by Mies van der Rohe. Reconstructed last year in celebration of the 100th anniversary of the architect's birth, it was the first of its kind, with chrome, glass, reflecting walls, and an exterior that played an important part in the interior design of the building. Van der Rohe designed the building for the German exhibit, using green marble and golden onyx in the construction. Inside, scarlet velvet curtains sweep across glass walls. White-kid covered chairs once served as thrones. George Kolbe's statue *Morning*, a classical nude, is reflected in the interior pool. The pavilion is open during daylight hours; entry is free.

Pueblo Español, also designed as a pavilion for the 1929 World's Fair, is still in operation. Typical buildings from all over Spain were reproduced in this village, designed as a miniature view of Spain. Houses are of stone, stucco, or intricately laid brick, topped with Spanish tiles and embellished with elaborate balconies. Typical wood carvings, metalwork, pottery, glass, leather, and crafts are sold in the village's 35 shops. A carved wooden salad bowl sells for as little as 681 pesetas(US$7).

Museo d'Art de Catalunya, at the summit of Montjuïc, specializes in Catalan Gothic religious art. The mosaics, frescoes, and artifacts come from isolated churches and hermitages in the Pyrenees. The museum is open Tuesdays through Sundays from 9 a.m. to 2 p.m.

The **Miró Museum** features the work of Joan Miró. Miró, whose paintings were inspired by the art and landscape of Catalonia, is revered by Catalans. His painted-bronze sculptures are displayed on the museum balconies, and his stark, late paintings are in alcoves overlooking the courtyard. Perhaps his best work is *Self Portrait*, begun in 1937 and completed in 1960. He drew himself from a reflection in a convex mirror, creating an enlarged, distorted image. His eyes are starlike. The Miró Museum and Contemporary Art Center is open Tuesdays through Saturdays from 11 a.m. until 8 p.m., Sundays and holidays from 11 a.m. until 2:30 p.m.

Barcelona's best night life

As in Madrid, night life begins well after midnight here. Then it rolls on full-steam until sunrise. Hundreds of bars and nightclubs are located all over the city.

The trendiest nightclub right now is the zany **Otto Zutz**, *Lincoln 15*, where you'll see Barcelona's most beautiful and fashionable. The latest music is played, and the decor is ultramodern: neon, concrete, metal.

Barcelona's jet-setters can be found at a new disco called **Up and Down**, *Numancia and Diagonal*.

Two popular bars are **Network**, *Avenida Diagonal 616*, and **Vaticano**, which was opened by a Catholic priest and plays good music. On the north side of Las Ramblas is the **Born**, named after a huge market surrounded by tiny streets filled with bars, *coctelerias*, and *xampanyerias*, where local wines and champagne are drunk in vast quantities.

Barcelona's best restaurant

The best restaurant in Barcelona is **Neichel**, *Pedralbes 16 bis; tel. (34-3)203-84-08*. Michelin awarded this restaurant two stars. The good news has spread, and reservations are essential. Try the duck paté, the lamb, or the veal with truffle sauce. Closed Sundays, bank holidays, Holy Week, Christmas, and August. Dinner is 7,000 to 8,500 pesetas ($70 to $85).

The finest fish

Barcelona is known for its fish restaurants, where specialties are made with seafood fresh out of the Mediterranean.

The section of Barcelona between the port and the beach, called Barceloneta, has several traditional fish restaurants. One of the best is **Cal Pinxo**, *Final Calle Maestranza,* which also serves a good—and cheap—house wine.

Other favorites

Eldorado Petit, *Dolors Monserdá 51; tel. (34-3)204-51-53,* serves only the freshest produce, fish, and meat, and the wine cellar has a huge selection. Try the crayfish and shrimp or the salmon lasagna with asparagus. Dinner is expensive—8,000 to 9,000 pesetas ($80 to $90)— but worth it.

Azulete, *via Augusta 281; tel. (34-3)203-59-43,* is a favorite among international celebrities. Nouvelle cuisine and very good seafood (especially the salmon) are served. Dinners are 8,000 to 9,000 pesetas ($80 to $90). Closed Sundays.

El Egypto, *Calle Jersulalen 3; tel. (34-3)317-74-80,* behind the Boqueria Market near Las Ramblas, is a favorite. It has delicious and reasonably priced food but slow service.

La Venta, at the top of Tibidabo, has fabulous views of Barcelona and the Mediterranean. Dinner is served outside in the garden, so you can enjoy the panorama.

Jaume de Provença, *Provença 88; tel. (34-3)230-0029,* serves delicious fish. Reservations are necessary. Dinner is 2,250 to 4,450 pesetas ($23 to $45).

Reno, *Tuset 27; tel. (34-3)200-91-29,* serves Catalan haute cuisine in an elegant black dining room. Book well in advance if you want to try this well-known, classic restaurant. Dinner is 8,000 to 10,000 pesetas ($80 to $100) per person.

The best places to sleep

The best hotel in Barcelona is the **Ritz**, *ave. Cortes Catalanas 668; tel. (34-3)318-52-00.* One of the four original Ritz hotels founded by Caesar Ritz, it has been restored to its 19th-century opulence. Rooms are large, all with private bathrooms, and the atmosphere is elegant. But the real drawing card is the efficient, friendly staff. Rooms are 43,000 pesetas ($430) per night.

Another grand hotel is the **Avenida Palace**, *Gran Via 605-607; tel. (34-3)301-96-00.* Less formal than the Ritz, it has comparable service. The lobby is lovely, with gleaming brass, marble, and wood. Rooms have air conditioning, wood furniture, and white chenille bedspreads. However, the dining room is mediocre, and the bar is boring. Doubles are 12,000 to 27,000 pesetas ($120 to $270).

One of our favorite hotels in Barcelona is the relatively inexpensive, but charming, **Hotel Colón**, *ave. Catedral 7; tel. (34-3)301-1404.* You couldn't find a more scenic location—it faces Barcelona's ancient cathedral in the Gothic Quarter. Despite its medieval surroundings, it offers air conditioning and private bathrooms. The best rooms are on the sixth floor. They have terraces with views of the cathedral and the streets below. Prints and gilded mirrors hang on the walls above velvet chairs. The cellar-restaurant, Carabela, is cozy. Rooms are 19,500 pesetas ($195).

Hotel Calderón, *Rambla de Catalunya 27, Barcelona 08007; tel. (34-3)301-0000,* has a rooftop swimming pool with a panoramic view and air-conditioned bedrooms with televisions and private bathrooms. Rooms are 19,000 to 34,000 pesetas ($190 to $340).

Bests outside Barcelona

A **Benedictine monastery** whose Marian shrine has attracted pilgrims for more than 700 years is located in the Montserrat Mountains 38 miles northwest of Barcelona. The Black Madonna (La Morena)—a 12th-century statue of the Virgin Mary—is the focus of the pilgrims' journey.

Seville's greatest pleasures

Seville is a city of simple pleasures: warm sunshine, brightly colored flowers, an expressive river, fragrant orange groves, rustling palm trees, ancient buildings, and shining white houses with patios, flat roofs, and shuttered windows.

In a sense, Seville is the essence of Spain. It has typically ornate and colorful architecture and warm and friendly people. Located on the left bank of the Guadalquivir River, the city is sunny but surrounded by marshland and swamps.

Seville's history is colorful. The Romans conquered the city in 205 B.C. (when it was known as Hispalis), and it became so Romanized that it produced several Roman emperors, including Trajan and Hadrian. Under the Moors, it became splendid, the subject of poetry. During the reconquest of Spain, it was the capital. It became the headquarters of trade with the New World in the 16th century. Cervantes spent his youth here, and his famous *Don Quixote* was born in a Sevillian prison.

The old quarters of the city, with narrow winding streets and tiny squares, were built in medieval times in a way intended to provide the best shelter from the heat of the Andalusian summers. The twists and turns of the narrow streets lead to surprises and unexpected views. The houses in the old part of the city have white limewashed fronts and lots of flowering plants on the balconies.

Spain's most graceful bullfights

Even if you're squeamish, you should see a bullfight in Seville, which is famous for its bullfighters. The Sevillian school of bullfighting teaches a graceful style. Andalusian bulls are bred for the fight and show their stuff in the handsome Maestranza bullring.

Seville's top sight

The most outstanding monument in Seville is the **Giralda.** Built on Roman foundations as a minaret in 1184, it is adorned with four huge gilded-bronze apples. In the 1500s, a belfry with 25 bells was added, as well as the enormous statue representing Faith, which serves as a weather vane.

The world's third-largest church

Seville's cathedral was built on the site of one of Spain's largest mosques, partly destroyed in the 15th century. It is the third-largest Christian church in the world. The Gothic structure has five spacious aisles, and the main chapel is decorated with a magnificent wrought-iron screen. The tombs of King Alfonso X (the Wise) and his mother, Beatrice of Swabia, are here, as well as an urn containing the remains of King Ferdinand.

Many people visit the cathedral without realizing they can also visit the crypt below, which contains the royal coffins of King Pedro the Cruel and Doña Maria de Padilla. The cathedral also contains jewels, vestments, and the sword of King Ferdinand. The Sacristy of the Chalices has paintings by Murillo, Zurbaran, and Goya. Before leaving the cathedral, see the Patio de los Naranjos (Orange Court) and the Christopher Columbus Library. The former was originally the *shan,* or courtyard, of the Mosque. The library contains manuscripts by the discoverer of America.

Best Mudejar architecture

The facade of the old **Alcazar** is one of the finest examples of Mudejar art in Spain. (Mudejars were ex-Moslems who remained after the Reconquest.) It was built on the ruins of King Almotamid's palace. After the conquest of Seville, Ferdinand and Isabella and their successors also lived here. Among the remains is the Patio del Yeso.

The Alcazar as it is today was built by King Pedro the Cruel. Moorish master masons, Sevillian craftsmen, and Toledan decorators took part in creating this building.

The prettiest palace

Casa de Pilatos, or Pilots' House, a typical 15th-century Andalusian mansion, was built as a reproduction of the Praetorium in Jerusalem. The patio, with a graceful fountain and two ornamental statues of Minerva, is one of the most beautiful examples of Spanish Renaissance art in Seville.

Seville's best museum

The **Museum of Fine Arts**, located in a monastery, displays Spanish primitives, a magnificent El Greco, and nearly 50 Murillos.

Granada, the most romantic city

Granada is one of those romantic towns that make you feel like you're living a legend or lost in a movie set. It is most famous for its beautiful Moorish palaces and gardens, collectively called the **Alhambra.**

The palace is delicate, with many-colored ceilings carved with stars. Arched windows look out over the water, and private patios open off bathing rooms. The Patio de la Ria and the upper garden are exquisite. The gardens have intricate waterworks, with channels of water that run alongside the steps. Elaborate fountains dance amid the flowering trees.

Patio de los Leones and the adjoining rooms were the heart of the private apartments of the ruler. Light, filtering through the patio, bathes the rooms and glimmers on the patio's fountains and water channels.

Washington Irving wrote *Tales From the Alhambra* from his apartment on the Lindaraja patio, which looks out on tall cypress trees and a gently gurgling fountain.

The Alcazaba was the guardian of the Alhambra. Its watchtower (Torre de la Vela) is the outstanding feature. In moments of danger, bells rang an alarm. Ferdinand and Isabella flew the banner of Castile from the tower when they took Granada on Jan. 2, 1492. From the tower you can see the entire city and the Alhambra.

The ugliest sight in the Alhambra

Charles V decided to plop a huge marble Renaissance palace into the middle of the Alhambra. His imperial majesty felt the Moors' remains were not majestic enough, so he built his monumental palace (now a museum).

A thousand beautiful nights (the most romantic hotels)

Nightingales sing in the gardens of the **Convent of San Francisco**, *tel. (34-58)22-14-40*, a *parador* inside the walls of the Alhambra. One of the oldest buildings in the Alhambra, it was originally a Moorish palace. Rebuilt in the 14th century by Yusuf I, it became a convent under Ferdinand and Isabella in 1492. The monarchs were buried there for some time. The *parador* has an elegant interior, cloisters, arches, towers, and gardens. Make reservations far in advance. Rooms are 22,000 pesetas ($220) a night.

A good nearby hotel is the **Alhambra Palace**, *Penapartida 1; tel. (34-58)22-14-68*. Rooms are 18,100 pesetas ($181), including breakfast.

North of Granada, at the foothills of the Sierra de Jabalacuz, is the **Parador Castillo de Santa Catalina**, *Apartado 178, Jaen; tel. (34-53)26-44-11*. This castle hotel is known for its atmosphere and fine food. A double room is 11,000 pesetas ($110) a night.

The most passionate dancing

Outside Granada at **Sacromonte**, the summit of Mount Albaicin, are famous Gypsy caves, where, to the beating of hands and the sounds of guitars, Gypsies dance the *zambra*, a colorful and passionate dance. The caves sound primitive, but they are warm in the winter, cool in the summer, and often elaborately decorated.

A word of warning, however. You may be harassed for handouts. And many visitors have been known to leave the caves minus wallets or watches.

Salamanca: Spain's intellectual center

Salamanca is the Oxford or Cambridge of Spain—colored greatly by the country's centralization and religious conformity. The **University of Salamanca**, the oldest in Spain, was founded at the end of the 15th century, almost at the same time as the Spanish Inquisition, by Cardinal Cisneros, adviser to the monarchs who financed Columbus. A plaque on the Patio de las Escuelas, the entrance to the campus, honors Ferdinand and Isabella, those most Catholic monarchs. The campus is now split between the seminary to train priests and the secular university—but many figures on the lay side dress in Roman collars, soutanes, monkish habits, wimples, and coifs.

Perhaps the most telling clue to the way the Renaissance was viewed as both a threat and an opportunity is the large sign at the entrance to the university library, threatening with excommunication those who read books without getting permission from the bishop. All the 16th-century bookshelves lock—and this is not in an effort to stop book thieves!

Near the library is the splendid chapel, which has a painted Renaissance ceiling and is now used for ceremonial occasions. The university buildings are mostly 17th to 19th century, built in tiers around central courtyards. You can visit lecture halls if you enter without disturbing the classes.

Apart from the university, the city also boasts not one but two cathedrals, built partly on top of each other in the local pinkish granite. The older cathedral holds a beautiful retable and the polychrome shrine of Bishop Anaya—both masterpieces.

As is normal in a college town, Salamanca has plenty of cheap eats and cheap digs. If you can't get into the *parador,* do not despair. We have tried the **Alfonso X**, *Tor 64; tel. (34-23)21-44-01,* in Old Town, and it is quite delightful—an international-level hotel built into an old townhouse. Double rooms are 10,000 pesetas ($100).

Good eating includes the Michelin-starred **Chez Victor**, *Espoz y Mina 26; tel. (34-23)21-31-23,* which features cockles in *noilly prat* on homemade noodles and *isla flotante* (floating island). Chez Victor is closed in August (when the university is closed), Sunday nights, and Mondays. A meal here costs about 4,500 to 5,000 pesetas ($45 to $50).

Valladolid, a best for history and architecture buffs

A busy provincial capital in the heart of the Meseta Central, **Valladolid** has medieval churches, university buildings, and traces of Spain's greatest writers and artists. The view of the city as you arrive from the highway is memorable—the cathedral, the university buildings, and church spires.

Valladolid's two literary giants

Valladolid produced two famous Spanish literary figures: Zorrilla and Cervantes. The house where poet **José Zorrilla** was born, on Calle Fray Luis de Granada, is a small whitewashed building that contains his letters, manuscripts, and death mask.

The house of **Miguel de Cervantes** (author of *Don Quixote*), on Calle Miguel Iscar, has been converted into a museum and a public library. The room that Cervantes used as a study is filled with maps and has a painting of the Battle of Lepanto. One of the writer's manuscripts is exhibited, and the furnishings, carpet, and tapestries were his. Two of his works were written here, *El Licenciado Vidriera* and *El Coloquio de los Perros*.

The most important sights

The **College of San Gregorio**, built between 1488 and 1496, is one of the marvels of pre-Renaissance art. It houses the National Sculpture Museum and contains the finest and most valuable carved figures from Castile.

Iglesia de San Pablo, next door, was originally a Dominican monastery built in the 15th century. Inside are two exquisite small doorways and a vaulted ceiling.

La Séo cathedral is quite impressive. Begun by the medieval architect Juan de

Hererra (who also built the Monastery of El Escorial), it was continued in the 18th century but never completed. The interior is sober and grand, with 32 pillars. Next door is a Diocesan Museum, which contains fine images and jewelry.

Spain's castle country

A great number of castles were built outside Valladolid for its defense. **La Mota**, in Medina del Campo, is one of the most beautiful castles in Spain. Built in the 13th century, it was later the home of Ferdinand and Isabella. Over the years it imprisoned Hernando Pizarro, Rodrigo Calderón (the favorite of Philip II), and Cesar Borgia.

Seven miles outside Valladolid stands **Simancas**, originally a bishop's see. It was granted town status in the year A.D. 927. Simancas was a Moorish castle until the 11th century, when it was reconquered by the Christians.

Simancas' cylindrical towers and walls are well-preserved. The inner part of the castle is used as the General Archives of the Kingdom. In its 52 rooms and halls are more than 30 million documents.

Farther down the Douro River is **Penafiel Castle**, a fabulous 14th-century structure that looks down over a historic village. Built in the 10th century, it looks like a huge ship, with 12 buttresses and an interior tower 27 yards high.

Spain's most picturesque city—Cuenca

Cuenca is famous for its ancient hanging houses that jut out over a 600-foot gorge. These *casas colgadas,* as they are called, went unoccupied for 200 years before the government restored them. They date from the 14th century, when they were summer residences of kings and queens. Today, they are national monuments.

One of the houses is now a restaurant that serves delicious trout caught from the Huecar River and crayfish from the Jucar River. From the restaurant's balcony, you can look down into the gorge and watch swallows swooping from cliff to cliff.

Climb the steep, stony streets to the cobblestoned main square with its wrought-iron window grills. Relax in one of the cafés over a glass of *resoli,* the local liqueur made of pure alcohol, coffee, sugar, orange peel, and cinnamon.

A light flickers in the town's lower gate every night in memory of the victory of King Alfonso over the Moors. According to legend, King Alfonso got his troops through the gate by dressing two soldiers in sheepskin and having them slay the gatekeeper. Alfonso's troops then opened the gates and conquered the town without shedding any Spanish blood. A festival is held Sept. 20 to 22 every year in celebration of the victory.

The town is prettiest at night when it is lit by hundreds of lights that cast odd shadows on the crooked buildings and winding streets.

Mérida: the best Roman ruins outside Rome

Mérida, founded in 25 B.C. as a rest home for retired Roman legionnaires (it was then known as Colonis Emerita Augusta), has the most impressive Roman ruins outside Rome itself—and it beats the Provençal ruins (Orange, Arles, Nîmes) hands down. But while it was on the main Roman road in antiquity, Mérida today is a backwater. It is on a road that goes to the Portuguese border, on a river that you can navigate all the way to the sea at Ayamonte—if you have any reason to do so.

Mérida's Roman sights include a multitier bridge over the Guadiana River, which carries both traffic (including modern trucks) and drinking water. The city's monumental aqueduct system, built in granite blocks striped with red clay bricks, is Roman and partially still in use. The city had both a Roman theater (for plays and performances of music for the legionnaires) and a Roman amphitheater (for sports events). The Romans were just like modern soldiers—the sports theater is four times as large as the cultural theater.

The theater was built into a slope of a hill, with seats in a horseshoe facing the stage.

The stage was made of brick and decorated with marble pillars and columns two huge stories high. Statues of the Roman gods are visible between the pillars and the wall. Here and there are little doorways cut into the brick, through which entrances and exits were made. In the middle is a two-story doorway used for spectacular effects (deus ex machina, for example). Behind the facade you can see the actors' dressing rooms, built into the brick structure. You enter the theater (as you do the Coliseum in Rome) through arched stairways.

The huge amphitheater held 40,000 spectators. On the hillside where both structures stand were Roman notables' houses, and the mosaics, paintings, and statuary from these houses can be seen in the Museo Arqueologico. (You pay only one admission price to view the lot.) The bas-reliefs in the museum include depictions of a lute player and of a tavern keeper drawing wine from a barrel.

As if being a major Roman center were not enough, Merida also was a power center under the Moors. The Moorish fortress by the Guadiana is graced by a lovely colonnaded walk, created of ocher and cream stucco with marble pillars. Even more impressive is the *aljibe,* a set of staircases leading to a bath fed water from the river. Despite the Moslem prohibition against alcohol, the frieze on the entrance to the *aljibe* is decorated with bunches of grapes.

The Romans' greatest engineering feat

The Roman **aqueduct** in Segovia is the most powerful example of Roman engineering and architecture in Spain. After centuries of use, it still carries water from the River Frio to the town. Running across the center of Segovia, it has 118 arches and rises 96 feet. It was built in the time of Trajan of uncemented limestone blocks.

Segovia is a beautiful walled town on a rocky ledge above the Eresma River. A 14th-century alcazar (with 19th-century modifications) dominates the town. But the late Gothic cathedral, which dates from the 16th century, vies for attention.

Just south of Segovia is the bridge described by Hemingway in *For Whom the Bell Tolls.*

The Moors' most beautiful city: Córdoba

Córdoba was the capital of Moslem Spain in the eighth century and one of the major cities of the Moslem world. It once had 500,000 inhabitants and 300 mosques; today 255,000 live here, and most of the mosques are gone.

La Mezquita: a Moorish masterpiece

The city's most amazing monument is **La Mezquita,** a masterpiece of Moorish-Spanish architecture topped by a beautiful cupola and boasting an Eastern wall studded with priceless mosaics. Construction of the mosque, which was built on the site of a Visigothic cathedral, was begun in the middle of the eighth century at the orders of Abd-er-Rahman I. Elements of the early cathedral were incorporated into the mosque. Later in the eighth century, Moslems and Christians shared the building, which also was used as a cathedral.

Walk through the Door of Forgiveness into the Orange Tree Patio, an enchanting place with fountains and orange trees. Beyond the patio is a forest of columns—alabaster, jasper, and marble—topped by horseshoe arches. The columns came from North Africa, where they were taken from Roman, Visigothic, and Phoenician ruins.

Christians transformed the mosque into an enormous cathedral after they conquered Córdoba in 1236. But they never really got rid of its Moorish look and feel. The interior is vast, large enough to hold hundreds of Moslems facing east. The ceilings are low, with rounded arches. Striped columns hold up the ceiling. Baroque chapels embellish the edges of the cathedral, trying desperately to make it look Christian. In front of the western wall of La Mezquita is the Episcopal Palace, the residence of the Visigothic governors and later the caliph's alcazar.

The most inviting corners

Outside La Mezquita is **Córdoba's Old Quarter**, which is filled with inviting nooks and crannies. Look for good buys in filigree silver and Córdoba leather in the quarter's little shops.

The **Jewish Quarter** (Juderia), northwest of the Moorish structure, has a 14th-century synagogue, located on Calle Judios. Around the corner, on Calle Averroes and Calle Judios, is a patio where you can watch flamenco dancers.

Glance into Cordoba's patios. You will see white-lime walls draped with trailing plants and embellished with wrought-iron balconies. In the center are wells, marble columns, and fountains surrounded by flowers.

The best hotel in town

The best place to stay in Cordoba is **Residencia Maimonides**, *Torrijos 4; tel. (34-57)47-15-00.* Relatively inexpensive, with rooms from 11,940 to 15,840 pesetas ($120 to $160), it is directly across the street from La Mezquita in the old quarter. It is named after the medieval Jewish philosopher, the most famous son of Córdoba.

Pamplona: the ultimate machismo

Each July in **Pamplona**, the ultimate display of *machismo* takes place. The townsmen pit their lives against hundreds of bulls set loose in the streets and herded toward the bullring. To display their courage, the men run before the bulls, often injuring themselves.

Festivities begin when a rocket is fired from the town hall. Then bands of *txistularis* and bagpipers march through town announcing the running of the bulls. Young people roam the streets singing, dancing, and drinking. The celebration was made famous by Ernest Hemingway in *The Sun Also Rises*.

All this revelry is in the name of the town's patron saint, San Fermin, a bishop and martyr from Pamplona. Buried in Amiens, France, his body mysteriously disappeared. The body was miraculously found six centuries later, and legend says that, although it was midwinter, the trees burst into leaf.

The Costa del Sol: a people-watching paradise

The **Costa del Sol** is the best place in Spain for partygoers, extroverts, and people watchers. However, it's the worst place to go if you are looking for a charming getaway. The Costa del Sol is for you only if you thrive on the excitement of crowds and night life. It's overdeveloped and overcrowded. Its long, sandy beaches are lined with beautiful bodies from all over the world, and its discos are filled with fun-loving dancers ready for a good time.

Young Europeans flock to the coast on their vacations the same way American college students flock to Florida on their Easter breaks. The crowd can be an attraction.

Between Málaga and Algeciras are the most crowded resorts—Torremolinos, Fuengirola, and Marbella. Every imaginable language is spoken.

Marbella: the chicest resort

The chicest town on the coast is **Marbella**—it is also the most expensive. Movie stars and oil sheikhs keep prices high. Puerto Banus has a marina that houses yachts from all over the world. Nueva Andalucia, a community within Marbella, has a fancy casino and chic nightclubs. This is night life at its best

Régine's, *Hotel Puente Romano, Carretera de Cadiz; tel. (34-52)77-01-00*, is the place to find celebrities, including Princess Margaret, Alain Delon, and Gunther Sachs. This basement nightclub is funky and exciting. Rooms here cost 17,000 to 25,000 pesetas ($170 to $250).

Marbella's best hotel

The **Marbella Club Hotel**, *Carretera de Cadiz KM 184; tel. (34-52)77-13-00*, is an expensive but chic jet-set resort. Adnan Khashoggi has an apartment here. The club's Andalusian-style bungalows encircle pools and gardens. Expect to pay 19,000 to 30,000 pesetas per night ($190 to $300).

Torremolinos: the busiest resort

Torremolinos, once a quiet fishing village, is now the busiest resort on the coast. Germans seem to love Torremolinos, flocking there by the hundreds. High-rise hotels and condominiums line the beaches, and restaurants, nightclubs, and boutiques line the streets. The place is packed with tourists all summer long.

The best restaurant is **El Molino de la Torre,** *Cuesta del Tajo 8; tel. (34-52)38-77-56.* Dinners are around 5,000 pesetas ($50).

El Torcal—the strangest landscape

When you tire of the beaches, take a trip inland to **El Torcal,** a plain covered with fantastically shaped boulders. The softest parts of the park's limestone rocks have dissolved over the years, leaving the oddly shaped hard sections of rock. You will think you're on the moon.

The Costa Brava—the most beautiful coast

Spaniards who would rather relax on a secluded beach than gaze at masses of bodies head for the **Costa Brava,** which stretches from Blanes to the French border. The Wild Coast is known for its ferocious, rugged beauty. Pines fringe the rocky cliffs that drop to the fine, sandy beaches. Little towns are sheltered by the coast's protective coves.

Phoenicians, Greeks, Romans, and Arabs all have taken refuge in the Costa Brava's harbors. Ruins left by these early invaders dot the coast, as do fortified villages from the days of pirate invasions. You'll find Phoenician ruins at Rosas, Greek in Ampurias, and a Moorish fortress at Tossa del Mar.

Gerona is the best town for exploring the coast. It is filled with dungeons and ramparts, medieval walls and paintings. The old quarter is dominated by the majestic cathedral, built in the 17th century above Roman ruins. St. Felix Church, next to the cathedral, contains Roman sarcophagi.

The most popular resort

Tossa de Mar, a shiny white town by the sea, is the most popular resort along the Catalan coast. It has an old quarter that predates even Roman civilization and a Moorish alcazar, and it is surrounded by walls that were built in the 12th century.

El Codolar beach, behind Vila Vella, and Playa Llorell beach are the least crowded.

The lap of luxury

If you're looking for luxury, stay in **S'Agaro.** This contemporary residential community attracts the crème de la crème of European society. Paseo de Ronda, which leads to the beach, is lined with gardens, fountains, and statuary.

S'Agaro's **La Gavina,** *Plaza de la Rosaleda; tel. (34-72)32-11-00,* is the most luxurious beach hotel in Spain. The white, Spanish mission-style building is perched on a cliff above a beach. Guests can swim in the pool or play on the tennis courts. Golf is available, and the restaurant is excellent. Rooms are 25,000 to 29,500 pesetas ($250 to $295).

Dalí's favorite town

The Costa Brava attracts artists and writers. **Salvador Dalí,** born nearby, was one of the first major artists to live here—at Port Lligot, Cadaques, near the French border. You can visit his estate, which is marked by gigantic egg-shaped ornaments and has a whimsical garden.

Cadaques is a purely Catalan fishing village where white houses contrast with a dark mountain backdrop. Tourists haven't yet flooded this tranquil town. Mediterranean cooking is served at **Es Baluard**, *Riba Nemesio Llorens 2; tel. (34-72)25-81-83,* a favorite among local artists. The restaurant is closed Oct. 15 to Dec. 15.

Make hotel reservations in Cadaques in advance. The few hotels book up fast. One good place to stay is the **Playa Sol**, *Playa Pianch 5; tel. (34-72)25-81-00.* It has a pool and tennis courts and is reasonably priced—rooms go for 7,000 to 9,000 pesetas ($70 to $90). The hotel is closed in January and February.

The best nude beach

The Costa Brava has a number of lovely secluded beaches perfect for nude sunbathing. **Cabo de Creus** has clean water and little caves hidden among the rocks.

Costa de Almería: the most peaceful beaches

Spain's most peaceful beaches are along the relatively undiscovered **Costa de Almería**. Stretching 120 miles between Almería and Cartagena on the southeastern edge of Spain, the coast retains much of its original charm and still has reasonable prices.

The dry, warm climate and the landscape are somewhat like southern Arizona—with the difference that off the Costa de Almería's precipitous edges the deep blue Mediterranean gleams. Much of the coastline is dotted with little fishing villages, many still lacking modern facilities—which helps keep the tourists away.

Inland, the rusty brown of the Costa de Almeria's dry, terraced mountains is broken by patches of pear cactus, tidy olive groves, and rows of pine trees. Here and there is a crumbling stone farm building (*cortijo*), its faded tile roof askew. Now and then a flock of sheep or goats shuffles across the picture, herded by a craggy shepherd and a floppy sheep dog.

Hollywood Spanish-style

A short drive north of the town of Almería is **Mini-Hollywood**, where replicas of American Wild West streets have been built for spaghetti Westerns such as *The Good, the Bad, and the Ugly.* Such big-budget films as *Lawrence of Arabia* and *Reds* have also been filmed on these dunes. When visiting the region, it is possible to make a little pocket change by acting as an extra in a film being shot. To find out which movies are being filmed, stop in at the offices of **Almantur**, *Carretera de Malága; tel. (34-52)23-48-59,* the tourist promotion board. Staff members there can give you maps showing you film sites.

One of Almeria's best hotels is **El Moresco**, *tel. (34-51)47-80-25,* in a spectacular setting in Mojacar. El Moresco has views in all directions of the mountains, valley, and sea. It also has a rooftop pool. Rooms are about 10,000 pesetas ($100).

The best place to stay in Almeria is the **Gran Hotel Almería**, *ave. Reina Regente 8; tel. (34-51)23-80-11,* a modern place overlooking the harbor. Among other comforts, it has a pool. Rooms are 13,300 to 14,650 pesetas ($133 to $146).

Spain's loveliest cathedral

The largest city in Cantabria is frequently overlooked by travelers, who stick primarily to the coast. **Léon** was the center of the Spanish movement led by El Cid to oust the Moors, as well as one of the great cities along the pilgrim route to Santiago de Campostella.

As you might expect from a city with such important religious traditions, Leon has a splendid cathedral. But you'll be surprised at just how splendid it is. The stained-glass windows here are second only to those of Chartres in France. Because the cathedral was built before the art of using flying buttresses had been mastered, the way the light plays into the Léon cathedral is even more dramatic, being at ground level. The windows are predominantly red and gold (as you might expect in Spain), rather than mostly blue as in Chartres.

In addition to the windows, Léon's cathedral has a beautiful Romanesque cloister with fountains, gardens, and a rood screen by an unknown master, depicting the deposition of the body of Christ.

Léon is the center of the Gallego region, where the people speak a dialect of Spanish closer to Portuguese than Castilian. Léon is not close enough to the sea to provide good fresh fish, and gastronomically it is pretty disappointing.

The best hotel is the **San Marcos**, *Plaza San Marcos; tel. (34-87)23-73-00*, built into the remains of a magnificent 16th-century monastery. This is a rare free-enterprise hotel—most monastery hotels are *paradors*. Prices are high, from 12,000 to 16,000 pesetas ($120 to $160) for a bed-and-breakfast fit for an abbot.

Santiago de Compostela—Spain's pilgrimage center

All roads in northwest Spain (and many roads in France) lead to **Santiago de Campostela**, the greatest pilgrimage center on the Iberian Peninsula. During the Middle Ages, this town was the destination of pilgrims from all over Europe, who came to worship at the tomb of St. James (Santiago), housed in the 11th-century cathedral. Santiago was as important a pilgrimage destination as Rome or Jerusalem.

According to legend, the Apostle James came to this part of Spain to bring Christianity. He landed at Padron on an estuary of the Ulla River. After his death, his remains are said to have been brought back to Spain, where they were lost during invasions by Barbarians and Moors. In the ninth century, a star is said to have appeared marking the point where St. James' remains were buried. They were then taken to Santiago and placed in the cathedral.

Another tale says St. James appeared during a battle against the Moors in A.D. 844, dressed in armor and carrying a white standard with a red cross on it. He fought off the infidels and became known as Matamore, or Slayer of Moors. Later, the saint is said to have fled the Moors by swimming across a river. When he emerged on the other side, he was covered with seashells. For this reason, pilgrims wear cockleshells to show they have been to Santiago de Compostela.

Even if you aren't a pilgrim, Santiago is worth visiting. It is especially beautiful at sunset, when its church spires, hospitals, monasteries, and palaces glint with the sun on their roofs.

The town's Romanesque cathedral and Old Town, where ancient houses and little shops fill the streets, are worth exploring.

The best place to stay in Santiago de Compostela (perhaps the best place to stay in all Spain) is **Los Reyes Catolicos**, *Plaza de España 1; tel. (34-81)58-22-00*. Built in the 16th century by Ferdinand and Isabella as a hospice for pilgrims, the *parador* is in the form of a cross, with an interior square and four patios. Bedrooms have high ceilings and ornate furniture. The nightclub and grill offer dancing. And the cathedral is just across the square. Rooms are 15,000 to 21,000 pesetas ($150 to $210).

San Sebastian: Basque-ing with the best

Beautiful **San Sebastian**, bordered by the Urumea River, Bahia de la Concha, and three hills, is where Europe's wealthiest vacationers play during the summer. Drive to the top of Mount Urgall for a long vista of the bay and the sea. An even better view of the city, the bay, and the sea can be seen three miles west of the city at Mount Igueldo.

San Sebastian is known for its Basque cooking with Spanish and French touches and its original use of seafood.

The best restaurant in San Sebastian is **Arzak**, *Alto de Miracruz 21; tel. (34-43)27-84-65*. Chef Juan Mari Arzak won Spain's National Gastronomy Prize for his river crabs with truffles and lobster sauce, his apple pudding with strawberry cream, and his mousse. Arzak specializes in nouvelle Basque cuisine. The restaurant is closed in June and November and on Sunday nights and Mondays during the winter.

San Sebastian's best hotels

The two most elegant hotels in town are **De Londres y de Inglaterra**, *Zubieta 2; tel. (34-43)426-989*, and **Costa Vasca**, *ave. Pio Baroja 15; tel. (34-43)21-10-11*. Rooms are from 14,000 to 15,500 pesetas ($140 to $155).

Sleeping like a king

Parador Hondarribia, *Plaza de Armas, Fuenterrabia; tel. (34-43)64-21-40*, is an elegant *parador* in a massive Gothic castle between the resort of San Sebastian and the French border, in the little fishing village of Fuenterrabia. It was once the stronghold of Charles V, Holy Roman Emperor and king of Spain (1519-1556).

This dreamy inn has thick stone walls and floors, Gothic arches, exposed beams hung with heraldic banners, and winding staircases that lead to the 16 guest rooms. The kitchen serves tasty local Basque dishes. Rooms are about 10,000 pesetas ($100).

Galicia—the fishermen's favorite

Galicia, the westernmost coast of Spain, is a land of fishermen and damp, green landscapes. It has changed little over the centuries and has yet to draw hordes of tourists, probably because of its damp weather. The coastline is beautiful, a great place for romantic walks.

Vigo, the main fishing port

Vigo is the main fishing port of Galicia. Hemingway described this town as "a pasteboard village, cobbled-streeted, white and orange plastered, set up on one side of a big, almost land-locked harbor."

Vigo lies at the end of a swampy river valley. Sheltered bays and quiet inlets surrounding the town produce the shellfish for which Galicia is famous, as well as sardines, tuna, and hake. During the winter, the port is battered by winter gales.

Snug little bars and restaurants can be found on the steep, winding streets of Vigo. Fishermen drink the local wine, *ribeiro,* and chat among themselves in Gallego, the local Spanish dialect, similar to Portuguese. Early in the morning, Vigo bustles. Fisherwomen wearing clogs push cartloads of fish to market.

White sandy beaches called Samil and America stretch south of Vigo. A road, lined by vines that produce *ribeiro,* hugs the shoreline, dipping into tiny hamlets and climbing the hills. Narrow one-lane bridges cross muddy creeks.

The best place to stay on the coast

Conde de Gondomar, *Bayona; tel. (34-986)35-50-00*, is a *parador* in a dizzying location on the northwest Galician coast. Located in an old fortress surrounded by water, this inn stands between the Vigo and Bayona fiords and has spectacular views of the coast. The guest rooms and lounges are decorated with Renaissance furniture and antique tapestries and clocks. Walk along the top of the fortified walls that ring the property. Or enjoy a seafood dinner in the dining room. The inn's facilities include a swimming pool and tennis courts. Rooms are 10,500 to 13,500 pesetas per night ($105 to $135).

The Canary Islands: Atlantis regained

Scattered off the bulge of West Africa, Spain's 13 **Canary Islands** are blessed with 360 days of sunshine. Only on record-breaking days does the temperature dip below 65 degrees Fahrenheit. As a result of this year-round springlike climate, farmers in the Canaries can harvest four crops a year. The Canaries have markets filled with an incredible variety of fruits and vegetables.

According to legend, the islands are all that remain of the lost city of Atlantis. Roman discoverers named the islands Canaria, from *canus,* after the wild dogs that lived there.

Tenerife, the largest Canary

Tenerife, which covers 1,231 square miles, is the largest Canary. Through the center of the island runs Mount Teide, the highest peak in all Spain, at 12,192 feet.

Throngs of Europeans come here from cold Scandinavia, Germany, and Britain. They romp among the sand dunes and fill the hotels and restaurants all seasons of the year. The burgeoning growth of discos, bars, and multistoried high-rises, along with planeloads of tourists, makes south Tenerife another Costa del Sol. However, the pace of growth is being checked as building requirements become more stringent.

Cosmopolitan Santa Cruz

The most cosmopolitan city in the Canaries is **Santa Cruz**, on Tenerife, the largest port in Spain. The capital city of 200,000 looks for all the world like San Francisco, located at the foot of a gentle slope. It has attractive stores (including designer shops), great restaurants, museums, art galleries, theaters, and even a symphony orchestra.

Shopping in Santa Cruz is a special joy. Because the town is a duty-free port, items can be purchased for prices lower than in their countries of origin. Chinese silks, pearls from Japan, watches, designer clothes, and photographic equipment are some of the best bargains.

Puerto de la Cruz, the prettiest town

On the northwest coast, toward Buena Vista, is the small city of **Puerto de la Cruz.** Built on a rocky coast, it has a 600-acre man-made lake and a chain of natural pools that are terrific for swimming. Yellow and red hibiscus, trailing pink geraniums, 30-foot-tall poinsettias, and other tropical greenery surround the pools, and fountains shoot 20 feet into the air. However, the ocean has no beach.

Perhaps the most entertaining thing about Puerto de la Cruz is its underwater nightclub, where you can sip your drink and look through the water to the stars.

Stroll along the town's pedestrian street to the best ice cream parlor in the Canaries (if not Spain). It has more than 40 flavors and just as many fresh toppings. Imagine cinnamon ice cream smothered in fresh mango and blueberries!

The best times in Tenerife

The two best times to visit Tenerife are July, when a two-week fiesta attracts people from all over Europe, and February, for Carnival.

The island's best hotel

Tenerife's most attractive hotel is **Semiramis**, *Urbanizacion La Paz, Puerto de la Cruz; tel. (34-22)38-55-51,* an imaginatively designed structure overlooking the ocean. Double rooms are 11,000 to 16,400 pesetas ($110 to $164) a night.

The best of Gran Canaria

Gran Canaria is a mountainous island with banana trees, coffee groves, sugarcane, and almond trees. Along the southern coast, from the tourist-ridden Playa San Agustín to the more quiet and chic Puerto Mogan, is an unbroken chain of serious sunbathers, windsurfers, campers, and other winter refugees from all over Europe.

Las Palmas, the capital of this 922-square-mile island, is a duty-free port and a shopper's paradise. Although it's difficult to imagine wearing a fur coat in this warm climate, they are a tremendous bargain in the Canaries, where they are available for 30% to 50% less than in European shops. A good shop is **Voula Mitsakiu**, *Luis Morote 28.*

The most gorgeous resort area in the Canaries is **Maspalomas Oasis**; *tel. (34-28)76-01-70.* It has long, sandy beaches, lagoons, graceful sand dunes, and enormous palm trees swaying in the breeze.

The Oasis Maspalomas shopping center has boutiques, restaurants, bars, banks, car rentals, and book and trinket stalls. Moroccans and other Africans enthusiastically greet you with their wares: camel-skin bags complete with desert aroma, stuffed coiled cobras, and carved ebony elephants. Bikini bottoms are relatively inexpensive, and the selection includes bright colors as well as leopard and zebra prints. But forget about finding matching tops. Topless is the *moda de la playa*.

The most charming village on the island is **Mogan**, a fishing village that rises from the sea on its natural wall of crags and burned earth. Tanned people chat in a half-dozen languages on the streets here. A village artist portrays flamenco dancers on the outside of his house. And the valley is brightened by flowering almond trees and tropical fruits.

Unsurpassable meals
Gran Canaria is a paradise for food lovers. Most restaurants serve delicious meals in gigantic portions for incredibly low prices. This holds true whether you dine in a tiny beach shack or an elegant restaurant. Two generally can feast for a mere $15.

Choose from a variety of fresh meats and fish, including *chulletas de cordero* (thick, juicy grilled pork chops); *solomillo pimentas* (steak smothered with roasted sweet peppers); *tuna casuela* (home-style tuna steaks baked with garlic, onions, and red and green peppers); and local fish, such as *salmonetta* (red mullet) and sole, all prepared with fresh parsley and garlic. Tiny island-grown potatoes called *papas arrugadas* are steamed with sea salt and served with a spicy dipping sauce (*mojo picon*) made of chopped chili peppers, garlic, and oil. A good wine is the velvety Lanzarote.

Our favorite restaurant on the island is the rooftop **Restaurante Rio** in the town of Puerto Rico. Try the *langosta Americana*—grilled rock lobster with mayonnaise. A Latin band plays, and after your meal you can dance until dawn.

Sleeping in the lap of luxury
Maspalomas Oasis, *Playa de Maspalomas; tel. (34-28)76-01-70*, is a huge resort complex with a nightclub, a golf course, horseback riding, tennis, and a health club. It's expensive and popular. Double rooms are 12,000 to 29,000 pesetas ($120 to $290).

Tamarindos, *Playa San Agustín, Las Retamas, 3; tel. (34-28)76-26-00*, is a sophisticated hotel with two swimming pools and a nice beach. A full buffet is set up next to one of the pools. A disco and several bars keep the atmosphere friendly. Double rooms are 28,400 pesetas ($284).

The best of the Balearic Islands
The **Balearic Islands** peek sleepily out of the Mediterranean. Europeans love the islands for their perfect summer weather, easygoing inhabitants, and lovely beaches. Mallorca, Menorca, Ibiza, Formentera, and scores of rocky islets make up the Balearics, which lie 100 miles southeast of Barcelona. The trip from Barcelona can be made in 25 minutes by air or in nine hours by boat.

The islands have changed a great deal since the days when Mallorcans stoned George Sand for wearing pants. You will see artists and jet-setters, punk rockers and tourists, as well as old women in traditional black.

Mallorca—a jet-set getaway
Mallorca offers craggy mountains, Roman temples, and unspoiled beaches.

The biggest Balearic island with the starkest contrasts, Mallorca has office buildings and windmills, highways and ancient villages. Although tourists sunbathe topless, the natives wear traditional costumes. And children inherit thousand-year-old olive trees when the family farms get passed down.

About half the island's residents live in Mallorca's capital, **Palma de Mallorca**. Here, visit the cathedral, Santa Maria, which boasts one of the world's biggest stained-glass windows. Construction of the cathedral began in 1230 and continued for 300 years.

Perfect pearls

If you are a shopping addict, Mallorca should please you. In **Manacor**, *via Roma 52,* you'll find the most beautiful artificial pearls in the world—strings and strings of almost perfect deceptions. You can tour the factory.

Inca, in the heart of the island, produces inexpensive leather goods.

The prettiest town in Mallorca

The most peaceful town in the Balearics is **Deyá**, on the northwest coast. It is a haven for artists and writers who yearn for the romance of the sea yet despair of spending too much time alone with blank paper or canvas. Robert Graves, who wrote *I Claudius,* lived here for years.

A road leads two miles from town through goat fields and over terraces built by the Moors to a beautiful beach. Princess Diana vacations here—but it isn't expensive. The aspiring painter can rent a small cliffside dwelling for very little.

George Sand's bitter refuge

Visit the monastery of **La Cartuja** at Valldemosa, where George Sand and the composer Chopin took refuge for three months during the dreary winter of 1839. Sand's book, *A Winter in Mallorca,* talks bitterly of the island's inhospitality. Set high in the mountains on the west coast, the monastery's beauty belies the misery the two artists felt while living there. They were disliked by locals, who were convinced that Chopin had the plague and were offended by the morals of an unmarried couple who refused to attend Mass. Nonetheless, Chopin composed some of his greatest preludes here.

Built in 1311 as a palace for King Sancho, the place was converted into a monastery after his death. By the time Sand and Chopin lived there, it had become an apartment building. Its pale yellow stone contrasts sharply with the deep green of the surrounding mountains and the blue sky above. Chopin's piano remains in one of the cells.

Also at Valldemosa is an old pharmacy with jars whose contents are labeled with such descriptions as "Nail Pairings of the Great Beast."

Mallorca's best hotels

The island's most beautiful hotel is **La Residencia,** *tel. (34-71)63-90-11.* The place holds less than 100 people. There isn't even a reception desk—just a low table in the lobby. The hotel is composed of two huge stone farmhouses, dating from the 16th and 19th centuries, respectively. A room starts at 19,110 pesetas ($192).

The finest hotel is **Hotel Formentor,** *Playa de Formentor; tel. (34-71)53-13-00,* set in gorgeous hillside gardens. Paths lead down to a private beach. The king of Spain has stayed here, as have other dignitaries. Double rooms are 20,000 to 31,000 pesetas ($200 to $310).

The best of Ibiza

The cobblestoned streets of **Ibiza**, decorated with rainbows of flowers, wind through bright white buildings that lead to the sea. Orange and lemon trees climb terraces to sturdy farmhouses on hilltops. A grove of fig and almond trees curtains sandy beaches. In the evening, lovers stroll to Vedra, the Magic Rock, which reflects the moonlight and is washed gently by the sea.

This island off Spain's east coast has been inhabited by Phoenicians, Greeks, Carthaginians, and Romans. Centuries of invasions by Vandals, Byzantines, and Arabs led to the construction of an enormous fortress here. But the forbidding citadel isn't enough to keep the tourists away.

Now is the time to see Ibiza. Despite efforts to enforce zoning restrictions, houses and apartment buildings are going up at a rate that bodes ill for people who like the island's secluded beaches. Already, hotels line some of the island's most languid beach strips.

Ancient olive groves are being razed for golf courses. And the visitors' appetites for night life have made clubs and bars materialize in out-of-the-way places.

Of course, all this modernizing has its good points (depending on your point of view). Ibiza was the pioneer of nude beaches in Spain, and Agua Blanca beach is an excellent place to get a full-body tan. Cabo Falcon also has a good nude beach called El Cavallet.

Comida San Juan is the best and one of the cheapest restaurants in Ibiza. Local patrons swear by it. Grilled trout is only a few hundred pesos, a fruit plate a few cents. La Marina is almost as good and even cheaper.

El Caliu, a restaurant in a thick-walled farmhouse, has the island's best wine cellar and grilled food. The view of the fields and the sea beyond is lovely. Prices are modest.

The wildest night life in Ibiza is at **Ku**, *San Antonio Road*, a disco that combines swimming, dancing, and eating. It is the source of many a bawdy tale.

The island's most luxurious hotel is the **Hacienda Na Ximena**; *tel. (34-71)33-30-46*, balanced on its own pinnacle at the northern end of the island. It is expensive—from 15,493 to 24,900 pesetas ($155 to $250) for a double room.

Menorca, the most romantic isle

Menorca, the most romantic of the Balearic Islands, is the kind of spot you might want to escape to on your honeymoon, as Princess Grace and Prince Rainier did. Traveling from one end of the island to the other on its narrow, winding roads, you will probably encounter no one, save the unobtrusive sheep on the hillsides. Menorca is lush and hilly, not mountainous.

Menorca is said to have about 120 coves with beaches, mostly unpeopled. The most deserted beach is Sambal, which is four miles long.

Mouth-watering lobster and bouillabaisse are served at Espla, a restaurant famous for its breathtaking location on the waterfront. Another good island restaurant is Buccañeros.

The best hotel on the island is **Port Mahon**, *avenida Fort de l'Eau, Paseo Maritimo*; *tel. (34-71)36-26-00*. It has a pretty view and a swimming pool. Double rooms are 10,000 pesetas to 17,000 pesetas ($100 to $170), including breakfast.

The most Spanish time to visit Spain: Holy Week

The ritual religion of medieval times is resurrected each year in Spain during Holy Week. Candlelight processions mourning the death of Christ file silently through the old quarters of Spain's cities and towns. Statues depicting the life of Christ are carried through the streets. In some areas, residents don the attire of Biblical times and re-enact the life of Jesus.

The biggest Holy Week celebration is in **Seville**. More than 50 orders of priests and laymen march in procession following an ancient route from the Plaza de la Campaña along winding Sierpes Street, past the town hall, and through the Gothic cathedral. They end up in front of the Giralda and the baroque Bishop's Palace. *Pasos* (platforms of wood and silver) carry statues of the Virgin. They are covered with carnations and rock gently on the shoulders of the bearers to the rhythm of *saetas*, short and fervent prayers or hymns.

Not all the ritual is serious. The **Burial of the Sardine** is a nighttime tradition in Murcia that marks the end of Lent. It includes 25 carriages, each with an accompanying group of merrymakers, bands, and *hachoneros*, or men who carry bras. Little toys are thrown to the spectators from the carriages. At the end of the festival, a huge papier-mâché *sardina* is burned at the old bridge in Puento Viejo, and fireworks are set off.

The Burial of the Sardine dates back to the 19th century, when university students, who could afford to eat nothing but sardines, would bury some to celebrate their graduation.

Spain's oldest and strangest ritual

The annual **Pero Palo** festival takes place in Villanueva de la Vera, 20 miles from

Cáceres. On the first night of the festival, the Pero Paleros (young men assigned to the task of creating and then destroying the Pero Palo dummy) take the remains of the previous year's effigy, mend the suit, and fill the figure with straw. Their handiwork is accompanied by a dirge and the playing of drums.

The Pero Palo dummy, which represents the devil, is life-sized, with a wooden head and a pointed black hat. He wears a black suit, white gloves, and a spotted scarf around his shoulders, and he is impaled upon a wooden pitchfork.

On the second day of the festival, Pero Palo is carried around town on the shoulders of the townspeople. He is eventually taken to the plaza, where he is passed through double rows of Pero Paleros and shaken vigorously in a traditional dance.

On the third day, the dummy faces trial. The Pero Paleros select a tribunal and then pin a notice on the dummy's back reading "Condemned to death for high treason by the Popular Tribunal." By the end of the day, the effigy is decapitated. His body is placed in a basket to the sounds of funeral drums.

Finally, the remains of Pero Palo are thrown in the air. He is beaten by townspeople until no straw remains inside him. Then he is carried away in a wheelbarrow and buried to the sound of drum rolls. The wild party that ends the festivities is said to keep the town's birthrate high.

The origins of the Pero Palo trial are unclear. The name *Pero* is a diminuitive of *Pedro*, the name used in many Spanish festivals for the scapegoat effigy.

Spain's best wines

Spanish wines rival French wines and are half the price of their Gallic counterparts. Spain's champagnes are darn good too.

Of the Rioja wines, the two best are Marques de Murrieta and Marques de Riscal. And the rare Castillo Ygay Reserva, made four times a century, is incomparable. The Riscal clarets are delicious; the best of the Riscal reds is the 1922.

Vega Sicilia, which is aged for 10 years, is the best of the Penedes wines (1966 is the best year). Torres is the best brand; the best Torres is the Gran Coronas Black Label.

Spanish sherry is world-famous, yet underpriced. Barbadillo's Sanlucar Manzanilla is the elegant before-dinner drink in Spain. The best-selling dry sherry in the world is Tio Pepe.

The cheapest skiing in Western Europe

Spain is famous for sunshine and bullfights, not snow-covered mountains and ski slopes. However, the skiing in Spain can be quite good, and it's far less expensive and less crowded than in the Alps.

The most popular ski resort is **Baquiera-Beret**, in Lerida province in the Pyrenees. The long ski season here lasts from late November to late April. You can choose from seven slopes of varying difficulty. Facilities include six chair lifts, eight ski lifts, and one baby lift. Ski instruction and equipment rental are available.

Hotels are open from Dec. 1 to May 1. **Hotel Montarto**, *Baquiera-Beret, Salardu, Lerida; tel. (34-73)64-50-75*, is comfortable, has spectacular views of the slopes, and is near the lifts. Rooms are 12,000 to 16,000 pesetas ($120 to $160).

The Best of Switzerland

> Exquisite postal service. No bothersome demonstrations, no spiteful strikes. Alpine butterflies. Fabulous sunsets—just west of my window, spangling the lake, splitting the crimson sun! Also, the pleasant surprise of a metaphorical sunset in charming surroundings.
> —*Vladimir Nabokov*

Mountainous Switzerland is at the peak of Europe. Its mountains are threatening, yet nurturing, encompassing fruitful farms, lakeside resorts, and picturesque old towns. The Rhine, the Rhone, and the Inn rivers originate in Swiss mountain glaciers. The Swiss Alps challenge the world's best mountain climbers, skiers, and hikers. The famous Matterhorn rises above Zermatt, and the Berner Oberland mountain range guards Interlaken. Davos and St. Moritz sit snugly in their Alpine valleys.

Zurich: best financiers, best fun

Zurich, a prosperous banking town, is a two-sided coin. A seat of the Reformation in Switzerland, it later became a center for Dadaism. While it is the home of staid bankers, its German-speaking people also have a jovial, witty side that is evident during the city's festivals. During **Sechselauten** (Zurich's spring festival, held toward the end of April), for example, Zurich's bankers don costumes and celebrate the end of winter by burning a huge straw dummy named the Böögg.

Zurich has hosted writers as well as financiers. Joyce, Mann, Brecht, and Kleist all lived here at various times during their careers.

The cleanest street in the world

The **Bahnhofstrasse**, Zurich's main artery, is the cleanest street in the world. James Joyce once said, "Zurich is so clean that should you spill your soup on the Bahnhofstrasse, you could eat it up with a spoon." The avenue does have its dirty laundry, however. Some of the most powerful bankers in the world, the gnomes of Zurich, work here.

Zurich's best shopping

The Bahnhofstrasse is also known as **Luxury Mile**, because of its expensive, first-class shops. While it's fun to look at 18-carat gold shoehorns and watches, you're better off doing your shopping in Zurich's department stores or along **Marktplatz Oerlikon,** a pedestrian district near Bahnhofstrasse.

Zurich's top sights

On the left bank of the Limmat River is the **Fraumünster,** *Stadthausquaistrasse,* an austere Gothic cathedral enlivened with stained-glass windows by Marc Chagall and Augusto Giacometti.

The *Altstadt* (Old Town), on the right bank of the Limmat River, is a maze of steep cobblestoned streets lined with cafés, sex shops, and nightclubs. A series of 17th- and 18th-century arcaded guildhalls line the Limmatquai and surrounding streets. Inside, the guildhalls are decorated with ornate friezes and ceilings. Most are now restaurants, so you can enjoy lunch as well as the surroundings.

Above it all is Zurich's massive cathedral, the **Grossmünster.** The Romanesque cathedral was a center of the Reformation. Here, Ulrich Zwingli preached against the sale of indulgences, common at that time in the Roman Catholic Church.

Zurich's **Schweizerishches Landesmuseum** (Museum of Swiss History), *Museumstrasse 2,* behind the railroad station, displays prehistoric artifacts, medieval and Renaissance art, and the richly carved furniture of an old peasant civilization.

The **Kunsthaus** (Fine Arts Museum), *Heimplatz 1,* northwest of the opera house, has paintings, sculpture, and graphic art from the Middle Ages to today. The museum has a strong collection of 19th- and 20th-century works by Monet, Munch, Giacometti, Rodin, and Chagall. The Kunsthaus is a large open gallery that is not divided by floors, walls, or stairs.

The **Rietberg Museum,** *Gablerstrasse 15,* in the former Wesendonck Villa on the western shore of Lake Zurich, houses Europe's best collection of non-European art. Most of the collection was donated by Baron von der Heydt. Works are mainly Indian, Southeast Asian, Chinese, Japanese, and African. Richard Wagner was often a guest at this enchanting villa, and his love affair with the hostess inspired him to compose *Tristan and Isolde.* A private park surrounds the museum.

Zurich's coziest café

When you tire of sightseeing, stop at the **Café Schober,** *Napfgasse 4,* which serves a scrumptious chocolate cake. Both students and businessmen enjoy the atmosphere (although the two generations ignore each other here).

The best night life

Most of Zurich's night life centers around the **Niederdorfstrasse** and the **Limmatquai,** where you'll find bars, clubs, and street musicians. The nightclubs in Zurich are expensive—a beer can cost as much as 15 to 20 Swiss francs ($7 to $12). And mineral water is only slightly less expensive. So if you are on a budget, stick to the cafés and bars.

The best restaurants

The best dining in the area is at a restaurant that's just a 20-minute drive from the heart of the city. **Bienengarten,** *Regensbergstrasse 9; tel. (41-1)853-12-17,* is in an old, half-timbered house. Chef and owner Karl Gut spares no effort to make his dishes exceptional. The eight-course meal must be ordered a day in advance.

The restaurant at the Dolder Grand Hotel, **La Rotonde,** *Kurhausstrasse 65; tel. (41-1)251-62-31,* is also superb. Escoffier, one of the first great restaurant critics, praised the cuisine back in 1930. To this day, the restaurant features traditional French cooking of premier quality. The *émincé de filet de veau à la Zurichoise* (finely sliced milk-fed veal in a white wine and parsley sauce) is one of the many delicious dishes here.

Les Vacances-Chez Max, *Seestrasse 53; tel. (41-1)391-88-77,* on Lake Zurich, is famous for its luxurious decor and first-class food and service. The menu includes *soupe* *de homard glacée* and *salade de foie gras aux truffes tièdes.* The restaurant is closed for lunch Sunday and Monday.

Kronenhalle, *Rämistrasse 4; tel. (41-1)251-0256 or (41-1)251-5287,* which was frequented by James Joyce, is more famous for what is on the walls than what is on the tables. Hulda Zumsteg, who ran the restaurant for a half-century, decorated the walls of this brasserie with the works of Braque, Miró, Giacometti, and Leger. You can sit at one of the wide tables designed by Giacometti and enjoy the art while eating a rather overpriced meal. Service is perfect—most of the staff has been here for years.

Kronenhalle has become an institution in Zurich, revered by locals, who favor it as a spot for after-theater and after-work refreshments.

Zeughauskeller, *Bahnhofstrasse 28a and In Gassen 17; tel. (41-1)211-26-90,* a huge restaurant with outdoor dining during the summer, is the best place for traditional Swiss dishes, including potato salad (17 tons of potato salad are sold here every year) and suckling pig. It also has a good selection of local wines. An authentic Zurich guildhouse restaurant, it is cheaper than most Zurich eateries and is popular among business people from neighboring banks.

Au Premier, on the upper floor of the main railroad station, *Bahnhofplatz 15; tel. (41-1)211-15-10,* is an inexpensive restaurant that offers a wide selection of Swiss wines. You can order exactly the amount of wine you want, in carafes of 2, 3, or 5 deciliters (called decis). Local dishes, such as *Kalbsbratwurst,* are offered, as well as fancier fare, such as veal sweetbreads with sherry vinegar or veal steak with morels.

Zurich's best desserts
When you crave something sweet, stop by the **Confiserie Sprüngli,** *Am Paradeplatz, Bahnhofstrasse 21; tel. (41-1)211-0795.* The biggest chocolate maker in Switzerland, it serves delicious fresh white truffles. The chocolate is made with fresh Swiss milk and cream. You can get lunch here, too.

The best hotel in Zurich—and one of the best in the world
The **Baur au Lac,** *Talstrasse 1; tel. (41-1)221-16-50,* was named the best hotel in the world by *Travel & Leisure* magazine and received a Pomme d'Or for its elegance from travel writer William Chamberlayne. Built in 1830, it is not a glitzy palace but a four-story masterpiece of elegance located on the edge of the Zurichsee, not far from the center of town. The Baur au Lac's restaurant, the **Grill Room,** is one of the best in Zurich.

When you stay at the Baur au Lac, you will be in prestigious company. The hotel's guest book has included the King of Sweden, Kaiser Wilhelm II, and Margaret Thatcher. The hotel was built by Johannes Baur, who began life as a baker's apprentice. (Baur's son founded the Hotel School of Lausanne, alumni of which include Charles Ritz and other hotel magnates.) A double room is 520 to 1,700 Swiss francs ($368 to $1,205).

Other top-notch hotels
Whenever he is in town, Henry Kissinger stays in the **Dolder Grand,** *Kurhausstrasse 65; tel. (41-1)251-62-31,* a classic grand hotel. Built in the lavish turn-of-the-century art nouveau style, the hotel looks like a castle. Some of the rooms are modern, others are decorated with antiques. Facilities include a pool, jogging paths through the forest, tennis courts, and a golf course. The rooms at the Grand cost about the same as those at the Baur au Lac, but they tend to be slightly more ostentatious—grander, if you like—and to have better views.

A drawback to the Dolder Grand is that it is not in Zurich itself, but a 10-minute drive from the center of the city. And the decor is dark and heavy. A double room is 440 to 490 Swiss francs ($312 to $347).

Waldhaus Dolder, *Kurhausstrasse 20; tel. (41-1)251-93-60,* the Dolder Grand's less-expensive sister hotel down the hill, has modern but smaller rooms, as well as a good view, a sauna, and an indoor pool. If you stay at the Waldhaus, you can use the sports facilities at the Grand. A double room is 300 to 420 Swiss francs ($212 to $297).

Hotel Florhof, *Florhofgasse 4; tel. (41-1)261-44-70*, is a pleasant, moderately priced hotel in a 16th-century house with a small garden. It is near the Kunsthaus, and the music conservatory is next door. Service is excellent. A double room is 230 Swiss francs ($163).

The **Hôtel du Théâtre**, *Seilergraben 69; tel. (41-1)252-60-62*, is a good place for single travelers to stay in Zurich. The service is especially good, and a double room is only 120 to 135 Swiss francs ($83 to $93).

Bests outside Zurich

Winterthur, a town north of Zurich that dates back to Roman times, is known for its art collections. Oskar Reinhart, an arts patron who died in 1965, left his comprehensive art collection to the town. His collection is divided between the **Oskar Reinhart Foundation,** *Stadthausstrasse 6,* and the **Oskar Reinhart Collection Am Römerholz,** *Haldenstrasse 95.* Works by Swiss, Austrian, and German painters from the 18th through 20th centuries can be seen at the Oskar Reinhart Foundation. The Oskar Reinhart Collection, which is housed in the collector's former house, has paintings covering five centuries, including some of Picasso's paintings from his Blue Period. The collection of 19th-century works by Corot, Delacroix, Courbet, Manet, Renoir, and Cezanne is comprehensive.

Winterthur also has a good **Fine Arts Museum,** which displays works of the 16th century, the local schools of the 17th and 18th centuries, and the Swiss and German painters of the 19th and 20th centuries. It also has paintings of the French schools and sculptures by Rodin, Maillol, Haller, and Marini. A private collection of clocks is displayed in the center of town, at the *Rathaus.*

Four miles outside Winterthur is **Kyburg Castle,** a feudal castle built in the 10th and 11th centuries and passed from the counts of Kyburg to the Hapsburgs. Since 1917, the castle has belonged to the canton of Zurich. It has a collection of furniture and arms and a panoramic view of the surrounding countryside. The castle is open 9 a.m. until noon and 1 until 5 p.m. (4 p.m. in the winter). It is closed Monday.

Geneva: the best place to watch modern history unfold

Geneva, a French-speaking city on shimmering Lac Leman (Lake Geneva), is an international center and the home base of some 200 organizations. This is the best place in Europe to grasp the magnitude of modern history as it unrolls.

The European headquarters of the United Nations is housed in the **Palais des Nations,** *14 ave. de la Paix, Pregny Gateway.* Built in 1936 as the seat of the League of Nations, the Palais des Nations is situated in the Parc de l'Ariana. Marble of various hues was donated by U.N. member countries to create the Salle des Pas Perdus, which leads into the Assembly Room, where U.N. meetings are held. The walls of the Council Chamber, where the most important conferences are held, are decorated with huge frescoes illustrating the achievements of mankind. From the terrace you have a panoramic view of Geneva, the lake, and Mont Blanc. Guided tours of the palace are conducted 9 a.m. until noon and 2 until 4:45 p.m. (5:15 p.m. in the summer) every day except during conferences and the Christmas and New Year holidays.

Not far from the Palais des Nations are the **World Health Organization,** the **International Red Cross,** and the **International Labor Office.** Group visits can be arranged by special request.

The world's tallest fountain

In the center of Lake Geneva is the tallest fountain in the world, the **Jet d'Eau,** which spouts 476 feet. The fountain is striking, backed by the Swiss Alps. For a good view, walk out onto the Quai du Mont Blanc, near the bridge.

The best of *vieille ville*

Most of Geneva's monuments are in Old Town, called here *vieille ville*. The most prominent is **St. Peter's Cathedral.** Built between the 12th and 13th centuries, it was partly rebuilt in the 15th century and has an 18th-century neo-Grecian doorway. The cathedral is huge, but the decor is plain.

St. Peter's has been a Protestant church since 1536, when it became a center of the Reformation. You can see Calvin's seat in the north aisle. And the tomb of the Duc de Rohan, who headed the Reformed Church in France at the time of Louis XIII, is in the first chapel on the south side of the chancel.

The flamboyant Gothic chapel in St. Peter's is more elaborate than the rest of the church. It was built by Cardinal de Brogny in the 15th century and was restored in the 19th century.

Climb the 145 stairs to the north tower of the cathedral. From the top, you have a view of the Jura Mountains, Geneva, the lake, and the Alps.

The **Reformation Monument** was built against a 16th-century rampart of *vieille ville*, in what today is a park. At the center of the 100-yard wall are statues of the four Genevan Reformers: Calvin, Knox, Farel, and de Bèze. The monument was built in 1917 and includes texts that recall the origins of the Reformed Church.

Geneva's **Hôtel de Ville** (town hall), parts of which date back to the 15th century, has an old courtyard with a cobblestoned ramp once used to carry litters to the upper floors. The Geneva Convention (the first convention of the Red Cross) was signed in the Alabama Room on Aug. 22, 1864.

The oldest house in Geneva is the **Maison Tavel,** *6 rue du Puits-St. Pierre,* near the cathedral. The first written record of the house is in 1303, but it was built long before then. The Museum of Old Geneva, which has a display of historic engravings, is located here.

Geneva's best museums

The **Voltaire Museum,** *25 rue des Délices,* is located in Les Délices, where Voltaire lived from 1755 to 1765. It shares the building with the Voltaire Institute, where researchers delve into the life of the famous writer. The drawing room and an adjacent gallery hold Voltaire's furniture, manuscripts, rare editions, and portraits. Look for the terra-cotta model for Houdon's statue of the philosopher and the portrait by Largillière. The museum is open 2 until 5 p.m. during the week. It is closed weekends and Christmas week.

Musée d'Art et d'Histoire, *2 rue Charles-Galland,* contains art from ancient Rome, Greece, and Egypt, as well as European paintings from the 15th through 19th centuries. Especially interesting are the prehistoric objects found in Switzerland and the reconstructed rooms of a castle. The most important artwork in the museum is the 15th-century altarpiece by Konrad Witz depicting the miraculous draught of fishes. It is the first exact representation of landscape in the history of European painting. The museum is open 10 a.m. until noon and 2 until 6 p.m. every day. It is closed Monday morning, Good Friday, Christmas, and New Year's Day.

Le Petit Palais, *2 rue de la Terrasse St.Victor,* features the works of artists from the School of Paris, including Kisling, Van Dongen, Soutine, Chagall, Utrillo, and Valadon. The crypt displays works by 20th-century naif painters, including Henri Rousseau. The Petit Palais is open 10 a.m. until noon and 2 until 6 p.m. It is closed Monday morning, the afternoons of Easter Monday and Christmas, and Jan. 1.

The **Musée de l'Horlogerie** (Watch and Clock Museum), *15 Route de Malagnou,* traces the measurement of time from the Middle Ages to today. On the ground floor are sand timers, sundials, and early watches and clocks. Elaborate, enameled watches from the 19th century, often with musical mechanisms, can be seen on the first floor. Clockmaker Louis Cottier repairs watches in the workshop. The museum is open 10 a.m. until noon and 2 until 6 p.m. It is closed Monday morning.

Lac Leman—the deepest Alpine lake

Lac Leman—the deepest of the Alpine lakes (1,000 feet)—is 45 miles long, is 7.5 miles wide at its widest point, and covers 143,323 acres. The best cruise of Lake Geneva is the "Tour of the Upper Lake," which lasts 12 hours. Official timetables and rates are posted at landing stages throughout Geneva, including Quai du Mont Blanc, Jardin Anglais, and Eaux Vives, opposite the Parc de la Grange.

Chillon, the most poetic castle

Chillon Castle, perched on a rocky island at the opposite end of the lake from Geneva, inspired the poet Byron to write the lyrical poem "The Prisoner of Chillon."

Prior François Bonivard was imprisoned in the castle dungeon for four years for trying to introduce the Reformation to Geneva. The Duke of Savoy, an ardent Catholic, had him chained to one of the pillars. If you visit the dungeon, take a close look at that pillar and the floor around it—you can see the prisoner's footprints traced in the rock. Byron carved his name on the third pillar in Bonivard's cell in 1816.

The fortress was built in the ninth century, but it took on its present-day appearance when it was expanded by the bishops of Sion and embellished by the counts of Savoy from 1150 to the mid-13th century. To get to the castle, you cross a moat on the 18th-century bridge that replaced a drawbridge.

The Great Hall has an imposing 15th-century fireplace, a large collection of pewter, and 13th-century Savoyard furniture. The Banquet Hall's timber ceiling is shaped like an inverted ship's hull. From the keep, you have a view of Montreux, Lake Geneva, and the Alps.

The best local cuisine

The best restaurants in Geneva tend to be French, but Genevan cooking can be delicious as well. Humble fare, it is generally served in informal places. Fish and cheese are the main ingredients.

Raclette—melted cheese that has been scraped off a chunk of grilled Swiss cheese— is a delicious local meal. You can enjoy it in almost any brasserie in Geneva, served with boiled potatoes in their pickets and gherkins.

Fondue is another typically Genevan dish. Also a melted cheese, it is more refined— mixed with garlic, white wine, and sometimes kirsch. The best part of the fondue is the hardened brown cheese at the end, known as *la religieuse* or *la dentelle*.

The best place for fondue is **Café Huissoud**, *51 rue du Stand; tel. (41-22)28-25-83,* which is popular with local business people. The setting is rustic—wooden tables and paper tablecloths—but the selection of Swiss white wines is good. The café is closed Saturday for lunch, Sunday, and evenings April through October. Credit cards are not accepted.

Lake fish is also prepared well in Geneva. (Unfortunately, it no longer comes from Lake Geneva, which is polluted.) The fish is generally deep fried, steamed, or baked. A good place to try it is the **Restaurant du Vieux Port**, *132 Route Suisse; tel. (41-22)755-15-99,* a family-run bistro. The terrine of lake fish is especially good. The restaurant has rustic antique sideboards, beamed ceilings, and a tiny back garden where tables are set in the summer. The restaurant is closed Sunday, Monday, and Dec. 15 through Feb. 28. Credit cards are not accepted.

The best of the French

Parc des Eaux-Vives, *82 Quai Gustave-Ador; tel. (41-22)735-41-40,* is the most famous French restaurant in Geneva. Located in the park of the same name, Eaux-Vives has splendid views and good classic cuisine. The service is always good, and the wine list is the best in Switzerland. The restaurant is closed Monday and Tuesday, April through October.

La Perle du Lac, *128 rue de Lausanne; tel. (41-22)731-79-35,* across the lake, is another superb French restaurant with a view of Mont Blanc. Servings are generous, but the prices are high. The restaurant is closed Monday and Dec. 20 through Feb. 15. (You may want to try the brasserie next door, which serves the same fare from the same kitchen at one-third the price!)

One of the best restaurants in Geneva is the often underestimated Béarn, *4 Quai de la Poste; tel. (41-22)21-00-28.* The *rable de lapereau aux basilic et petites légumes* (rabbit fillets served with liver and kidneys and young vegetables) is superb. Bankers lunch here on the *repas d'affaires,* which changes daily. The market's seasonal fare (fish and game) is presented, uncooked, on a trolley. The restaurant is closed Saturday for lunch, Sunday, and July 15 through Aug. 15.

The best country cooking

In the suburbs of Geneva, you'll find two charming restaurants in former private houses. Le Marignac, *32 ave. Eugene-Lance, 1212 Grand-Lancy; tel. (41-22)794-04-24,* is in a white villa shaded by a weeping willow. Dishes range from country to aristocratic—buckwheat pancakes to caviar. The restaurant is closed Saturday for lunch, Sunday, Feb. 13 through 20, and Sept. 4 through 18.

Le Vieux Moulin, *89 Route d'Annecy, 1256 Troinex; tel. (41-22)42-29-56,* in a former farmhouse, has a cozy dining room with low-beamed ceilings. The menu is diverse. Try the salmon in tomato, basil, and garlic sauce. The restaurant is closed Saturday evening and Tuesday.

Geneva's best hotel

Hotel Le Richemond, *Jardin Brunswick; tel. (41-22)7311-400,* is one of the best hotels in the world. Run by the Armleder family, this imposing, seven-story building has 120 bedrooms that go for 320 to 600 Swiss francs ($226 to $425) a night. The hotel has two fine restaurants, and the wine cellar contains 80,000 bottles.

Adolphe-Rodolphe Armleder founded the Richemond in the 1870s. What makes staying at the hotel so special are the elegant little touches, such as finding your ties hung in order of color and your clothes perfectly folded. Hotel Richemond has served writers Colette and Antoine de St. Exupery, as well as the Russian delegations of the 1930s and the Chinese delegations of the 1950s.

Other good hotels

Another fine hotel in Geneva is the Beau Rivage, *13 Quai du Mont Blanc; tel. (41-22)7310-221,* an immaculate, family-run hotel on the lake. A double room is 420 to 470 Swiss francs ($297 to $333).

Hotel de la Paix, *11 Quai du Mont Blanc; tel. (41-22)732-6150,* is a five-star hotel on the lake with lovely views. A double room is 250 to 500 Swiss francs ($177 to $354).

A less expensive hotel that comes highly recommended is the Hotel Les Armures, *1 rue du Puits-St. Pierre, Vieille Ville; tel. (41-22)28-91-72.* Located on a quiet square near the cathedral, it has one of the oldest restaurants in town. Service is excellent, and the food is good. The building was originally the residence of bishops and counts in the 13th and 14th centuries. The walls are decorated with centuries-old frescoes. But modern amenities have been added. A double room is 275 to 340 Swiss francs ($195 to $241).

The Metropole, *34 Quai General Guisan.; tel. (41-22)21-13-44,* is an attractive hotel with extremely good service. A double room is 310 to 380 Swiss francs ($215 to $263).

Berne—the loveliest city

Switzerland's capital, Berne, is one of the best-preserved medieval cities in Europe. It is filled with turreted buildings and has more fountains per capita than any other city on the Continent. The Alps surround the city, which is divided twice by the Aare River.

Established in 1191 by the duke of Zähringen, Berne was originally a hunting ground. The duke and his cronies decided that the town should be named after the first animal caught on a particular hunt. The unfortunate beast was a bear (*Bär* in German), so the town was called Bärn (Berne is a corruption). A bear appears on the city's coat of arms, and for centuries mascot bears have been kept in the *Bärengraben,* or bear pits.

The best way to explore Berne is to get a map from the tourist office and follow its walking tour along arcaded, cobblestoned roads and through little squares with fountains past all Bern's major sights.

Berne's five top (and topless) sights

St. Vincent Cathedral is an impressive Gothic church with 16th-century statues depicting the Last Judgment. You'll have an incredible view of Berne and the Alps from the top of the 100-meter tower, but you'll have to climb 254 steps to get there.

The **Kunstmuseum** (Art Museum), *Hodlerstrasse 8-12,* has the world's largest Paul Klee collection. (Klee was a native of Berne.) Works by Modigliani and Picasso also are featured.

The **Bernisches Historisches Museum** (Historical Museum), *Helvetiaplatz 5,* displays booty from the Burgundian wars, including the tapestries and embroideries of Charles the Bold, Duke of Burgundy. The museum also has replicas of rural Swiss rooms and objects dating back to the Stone Age.

Zeitglockenturm, the city's medieval clock tower, rings several times a day to the delight of large audiences. Mechanical bears, clowns, and kings perform at four minutes before every hour.

One of the most popular sights in Berne is the city's beach, lined with topless sunbathers. These free-spirited sun worshipers caused a good deal of controversy when they first disrobed (probably because the beach is right beneath Parliament's windows).

Best table, best beds

The best place to eat in Berne is the **Kornhauskeller,** *Kornhausplatz 18; tel. (41-31)22-11-33,* a huge beer cellar with good Swiss food. It specializes in *Berner Platte,* an assortment of boiled meats and sausage served with sauerkraut. At night, a brass band often plays.

Kings and queens stay at the **Bellevue Palace,** *Kochergasse 3-5; tel. (41-31)22-45-81.* This expensive but luxurious place has lovely views and a pleasant terrace where you can have a drink. A double room is 370 to 410 Swiss francs ($262 to $290) a night.

A much less expensive hotel with more traditional Swiss charm is the **Goldener Adler,** *Gerechtigkeitsgasse 7; tel. (41-31)22-17-25,* in the heart of Old Town. A beautiful old inn, it is comfortable and friendly. A double room is only 140 Swiss francs ($99).

Outside Berne are two more good hotels in the region. The **Grand Hotel Regina,** *CH-3818, Grindelwald; tel. (41-36)54-54-55,* offers first-class service in a good location. A double room is 320 to 400 Swiss francs ($222 to $277). And **The Olden Hotel,** *tel. (41-30)43-444,* in Gstaad, has far more charm than many of the luxury hotels in Switzerland. It is favored by the local residents and the international celebrities with homes in the area. A double room is 200 Swiss francs ($138).

Gimmelwald—the most picturesque Swiss town

Gimmelwald (not to be confused with Grindelwald!), a sleepy little town in the mountains near Interlaken, looks like something straight out of *Heidi.* You'll hear cowbells here and see farmers in lederhosen. Cars aren't allowed in Gimmelwald, which explains why it is so peaceful.

To get to Gimmelwald, take the Lauterbrunnen-Grutschalp funicular from Interlaken to Murren, where you'll find several good hotels. You have to hike the rest of the way from Murren.

Once in Gimmelwald, take the cable car to the summit of the Schilthorn, where you can dine in a revolving restaurant with a view across the valley to the German border. This was the setting for a James Bond movie.

Alpine wilderness at its best

The **Swiss National Park** is the best place to enjoy a view of the Alps as God made them, untouched by the hand of man. The Swiss obviously want to keep it this way—fires, camping, pets, and mountain climbing are prohibited, and visitors may not leave designated trails. If you want to sleep in the park, you must stay in one of the designated lodges.

These rules may seem restrictive, but the results are a wonder. The 40,000-acre park is filled with wild valleys of woods and broken by torrential creeks. You'll see deer, ibex, chamois, and marmots—but you won't see any trash dumps or unsightly trailer parks.

Walks through the park are organized at the **Tourist Center,** *Zernez; tel. (41-82)8-13-00.* They are offered from the middle of June through the middle of October and cost 10 Swiss francs ($7) per person. The Sierra Club publishes a little book by William Reifsnyder called *Footloose in the Swiss Alps* that describes the park's trails and accommodations in detail and is updated every few years.

The Valais—Switzerland's best valley

The canton of Valais, situated in the heart of the Alps, is encircled by more than 50 peaks, all more than 4,000 meters high. To the north are the **Bernese Alps**, and to the south rise the **Alpes Valaisannes**. For centuries, the small town of Brig, capital of the Valais, has been a center of trade with Italy, but it is perhaps best known for three other characteristics: its hospitality (a huge and colorful sign decorated with a mountain fräulein welcomes you in German and French as you enter downtown); its Stockalper Castle, Switzerland's largest private residence, built between 1658 and 1678; and its position as the starting point for the beautiful Simplon Pass to the south.

And the Valais does not end in Brig. The **Rhone** continues from here, traveling northeast to a number of tiny towns that give you a true feeling of the area. Make a point of stopping in **Reckingen** to see its 18th-century Baroque church, perhaps the most beautiful building in the Valais. Also travel to **Crans-Montana**, which is actually two towns, **Crans-sur-Sierre** and **Montana**. Although it is perhaps the most touristy place in the entire valley, it is a skier's haven, attracting jet-setters from all over the world.

In the summer, the Valais is green and growing, with acres of terraced vineyards and fruit trees. Wander along the ancient aqueducts and canals, known as *bisses*. For a complete map of all the walking trails in the Valais, contact the **Swiss Hiking Assocation,** *Im Hirsalm 49, 4125 Rienen.*

The most affordable places to stay in the Valais

Unfortunately, the Valais region is as expensive as the rest of Switzerland, but there are ways to cut corners and still enjoy the scenery and sights. One way is to stay in a *zimmer-frei* instead of a hotel. These are similar to bed-and-breakfasts and are very affordable. In the mountains, stay in *cabanes*. These Alpine huts are scattered throughout the Valais. Some are open only to members of climbing clubs, but others are open to everyone.

For specifics on where to stay in the Valais, contact the local tourist offices: **Brig,** *tel. (41-28)23-19-01;* **Montana,** *tel. (41-27)41-30-41;* and **Crans-sur-Sierre,** *tel. (41-27)41-21-32.*

St. Moritz: the world's most famous ski resort

St. Moritz is the most famous, most elegant ski playground in the world. Princess Ira von Fürstenberg and Gunther Sachs are among the celebrities who ski here. And it's easy to understand why—the five mountains at St. Moritz have great slopes. However, as you might expect, skiing here in peak season is expensive.

St. Moritz is the sight of the most treacherous toboggan run in the Alps, the 107-year-old **Cresta Run,** which is for men only. (The British invented it.) St. Moritz is also the only place where polo is played on a lake. Ponies are equipped with spikes.

Most people don't realize that St. Moritz is also a spa. The town is divided into two sections, on two sides of the sky-blue St. Moritz Lake. **St. Moritz-Dorf,** the ski resort, has the world's oldest ski school, dating to 1927. The only vestige of the original village here is the leaning campanile. **St. Moritz-Bad** is the spa quarter. Its curative mineral waters have been sought after since the Bronze Age.

Badrutt's Palace, *tel. (41-82)21101,* is the finest hotel in town. In February, the most elite skiers stay here. It has its own ski school and a private rail link. A double room is 720 to 1,600 Swiss francs ($500 to $1,000).

Less glamorous, less expensive, and more charming is the **Hotel Chesa sur l'En,** *St. Moritz-Bad; tel. (41-82)3-31-44.* A Swiss chalet surrounded by pines, it has a massive front door, a stone-flagged entrance hall, and a richly paneled ornate main hall. You can sleep in the watchtower, if you are a real romantic. King Farouk stayed here during his exile. A double room is 71 to 144 Swiss francs ($49 to $100), and the hotel will be newly renovated after the summer of 1992.

The best place to have lunch is **La Marmite,** at the top of Corviglia. Chef Hartley Mathis prepares haute cuisine for weary skiers. Try the Lady Curzon soup and the truffles. Make reservations. And keep an eye out—you might spot Princess Caroline of Monaco.

The two best night spots are **Kings' Club** at Badrutt's Palace and **Gunther Sachs' Dracula Club.**

The prettiest ski resort: Zermatt

Zermatt may be the most desirable piece of real estate in the world. It is a small, automobile-free village with a picture-postcard tangle of stately hotels. The Matterhorn dominates the town, which has very good skiing. But in season, the queues for the ski lifts are daunting. The hotels and restaurants, too, are crowded.

Zermatt's winter lifts reach as high as 11,500 feet, offering some of Europe's highest slopes and a whopping vertical drop of 6,300 feet. Zermatt's summer skiing is also Europe's best. The most popular run is down to Cervinia on the Italian side, which any strong intermediate skier can do in a morning.

Zermatt is also the best place in Europe for heli-skiing. The best hotels are the **Mont Cervin** (French for *Matterhorn*), which has an indoor pool, a sauna, and day-care facilities, and the **Zermatter Hof,** a modern hotel with a swimming pool, saunas, and a fitness center. Both are expensive.

Hotel Alex, *tel. (41-28)67-17-26,* run by former Matterhorn guide Alex Perren and his wife Gisela, is the center of social life in the winter. Facilities include an indoor swimming pool and indoor squash and tennis courts. A double room is 220 to 400 Swiss francs ($152 to $277).

The **Hotel-Garni Metropol,** *tel. (41-28)67-32-31,* in the center of town on the banks of the Vispa River, has fabulous views. The Taugwalder family, which runs the hotel, recently bought a meadow opposite the hotel so that the views won't be spoiled. Each room has a private bathroom and a balcony facing the Matterhorn. The best are on the south side of the hotel. A double room is 120 to 208 Swiss francs ($83 to $144).

Outside Zermatt, in Villars sur Ollon, is the first-class **Panorama Hotel,** *tel. (41-25)36-21-11.* A double room is 158 to 300 Swiss francs ($109 to $208).

The Matterhorn: the most daunting peak

The Killer Alp, as the **Matterhorn** is known, was scaled for the first time July 14,

1865. Four men were killed in the process. A young British illustrator named Edward Whymper arranged the climb. He, three British friends, a guide from Chamonix, and two guides from Zermatt first reached the peak.

On the return journey, one of the men slipped, dragging three of his fellow climbers with him to their deaths, 4,000 feet below. After the fall, Whymper and his two Swiss guides, theTaugwalders, father and son, reported seeing two crosses shining in a great arc of clouds in the sky.

The Matterhorn (14,688 feet) is intimidating, but you don't have to be an experienced mountain climber to scale its sides. You can climb the daunting mountain with the help of a Zermatt guide. At the Matterhornhütte, the cost of the guide and accommodation is 452 Swiss francs ($313). It takes three to five days to hike the easiest trails. Information on hiking the Matterhorn is available at the **Mountaineering Office,** *tel. (41-28)67-34-56,* near the tourist office.

The best Swiss train rides

A more comfortable and relaxing way to climb the Alps is aboard the **Glacier Express,** which runs from Zermatt to St. Moritz. This train leisurely crosses 291 bridges, passes through 91 tunnels, spans the valleys of the Rhone and Rhine rivers, stops in typical mountain villages, heads into the wild, barren Gotthard region, and then climbs the 6,706-foot Oberalp Pass. The grand finale of the trip is a series of spectacular loops and tunnels that ends at St. Moritz.

The trip takes seven hours and costs $73 one way second-class, $116 one way first-class. For more information, contact **Swiss Travel System,** *608 Fifth Ave., New York, NY 10020; (212)757-5944.*

Cheese lovers' favorite

The **Cheese Express** is the perfect way for cheese lovers to travel through Switzerland. The train goes from Brig to Basel. En route, travelers are treated to a special dinner of fondue, *raclette,* and *walliserteller.* The dining car looks like a huge piece of Swiss cheese on wheels. The train ride costs 94 Swiss francs ($72); the gourmet cheese dinner is 11.80 to 18.50 Swiss francs ($9 to $14). For more information, contact the **Swiss National Tourist Office,** *608 Fifth Ave., New York, NY 10020; (212)757-5944.*

The most spectacular views of the Alps

The most spectacular view of the Alps—indeed one of the most incredible mountain views in the world—is from **Kleine Scheidegg,** a peak near Interlaken. Take a train from Interlaken to Grindelwald and then another train to Kleine Scheidegg—or even higher to Mannlichen.

Kleine Scheidegg has a lodge and an outdoor restaurant, where you can watch mountain climbers dangling in the distance. You can hike back to Interlaken through the Lauterbrunnen Valley if you have the energy. Or you can take a train from Wengen to the valley floor.

The pearl of the Swiss lakes

The pearl of Swiss lakeside resorts is **Montreux,** with its six-mile promenade lined with palm trees and tropical flowers on the shores of Lake Geneva. The climate here is the mildest on the north side of the Alps and produces fig trees, almond trees, cypresses, magnolias, and bay trees.

Montreux is famous for its international music festivals, especially the jazz festival in July, the International Choral Recitals the week after Easter, and the Musical September concerts.

Eden au Lac, *11 rue du Théâtre; tel. (41-21)963-55-51,* a turn-of-the-century hotel on the lake in Montreux, is the best place to stay. Lunch is served in the hotel garden, right on the lake. A double room is 180 to 250 Swiss francs ($125 to $173).

La Rotisserie de Château, *1844 Villeneuve; tel. (41-21)960-20-09,* a towered 17th-century building at the foot of a mountain, was once the residence of the Bouvier family (related to the House of Savoy). Wood-beamed ceilings and other antique touches, as well as the outside terrace, add charm to the rotisserie. The famous Castle of Chillon is nearby. The restaurant is closed Monday and Tuesday.

The best local specialties are served at **La Vieille Ferme**, *tel. (41-21)964-64-65,* a rustic restaurant outside town in Montreux-Chailly. The *raclette* is good, as is the country music. The restaurant is closed Mondays.

The best of Lausanne

Lausanne, another resort on Lake Geneva, is a French-speaking city and a university center. Its universities date back to the 16th century, but its students keep the atmosphere young. Excavations in Lausanne have uncovered Neolithic skeletons and a section of a Roman road where the Geneva-Lausanne highway now comes into town.

The best place to begin exploring Lausanne is **Place de la Palud**, in Old Town. This square is bordered by the Renaissance facade of the town hall and centered around the 16th-century Fountain of Justice.

Behind the fountain is an unusual covered staircase that leads to the town's 12th-century cathedral, one of the finest Gothic buildings in Switzerland. It shelters one of the last night watches in the world, whose duty it is to call out the hour during the night. The south door of the cathedral, known as the Door of the Apostles, is covered with 13th-century sculptures. A 700-year-old rose window illustrates the elements, seasons, months, and signs of the zodiac. Climb the 232 steps to the top of the tower for a view of Lake Geneva and the Alps.

Switzerland's best restaurant

Lausanne boasts the best restaurant in Switzerland (and most of Europe): **Girardet**, *1 Route d'Yverdon; tel. (41-21)634-0505.* Chef Fredy Giradet does amazing things with fish and fresh produce. He is precise, yet inventive. Leave room for the chocolate soufflé. Make reservations far in advance. Dinner is 250 to 300 Swiss francs ($173 to $208).

Lausanne's most romantic hotel

The most romantic place to stay in the region is **Château d'Ouchy**, *2 place du Port; tel. (41-21)26-74-51.* This 12th-century stronghold of the bishops of Lausanne is on Lake Geneva. It was the site of the Louis de Savoie Treaty in 1300 and became a government customhouse in the 1700s. A hotel was built around the castle in 1884, and the Lausanne Peace Treaty was signed here in 1923. The Salle des Chevaliers hasn't changed in 800 years. The hotel offers dancing, tennis, and excursions. A double room starts at 180 Swiss francs ($125).

Switzerland's most beautiful waterfalls

Near Interlaken, in the village of Lauterbrunnen, is the **Staubbach Waterfall**, which plunges 1,000 feet and then dissolves into a fine spray. Lord Byron described the falls as the "tail of the pale horse ridden by Death in the Apocalypse."

Not far away are the **Trummelbach Falls**, which leap and boil, forcing their way through a series of eroded potholes.

The Best of Eastern Europe

Eastern European countries offer as many culture-filled cities, medieval towns, snow-capped peaks, and sandy beaches as their Western neighbors. Yet, in Eastern Europe, hotels and restaurants are cheap, and the people are still curious about foreign visitors. And as Western tourism to the countries of Eastern Europe continues to increase, local governments are working to bolster their fledgling tourist industries; they are building new hotels and opening up new air routes.

The primary attraction for Western travelers to Eastern Europe, however, is the cost. The area remains one of the best travel buys in the world. Still, travel in Eastern Europe is not as inexpensive as it was just a few years ago. Prices are steadily rising and will continue to do so until they eventually become comparable to Western prices. (Please note that all prices in this chapter are quoted in hard currency—the U.S. dollar; the local currencies are in a constant state of flux, and hard currency prices are more dependable.)

Unfortunately, as we go to press the situation in Eastern Europe is extremely unstable and unpredictable. Czechoslovakia is in the process of splitting, Yugoslavia is organizing its new republics, Romania is in the worst economic state in its history, and some of the world's most beautiful and historic cities are being destroyed by civil strife.

The best of Bulgaria

Although Eastern Europe in general is becoming an increasingly popular travel destination, the world has yet to discover Bulgaria. Unlike the traveler to Czechoslovakia or Hungary, the traveler to Bulgaria is still something of a trailblazer, charting virgin territory, as it were. For precisely this reason, Bulgaria is the perfect destination for the intrepid and adventurous explorer, not afraid to endure a bit of discomfort.

The world's best monasteries

Bulgaria is home to some of the world's best monasteries, many of which are located in the mountains. Some are as many as 500 years old. Although the Turks completely

231

subjugated Bulgaria during their occupation from 1393 to 1878, outlawing Christianity and killing off the *boyars,* or aristocracy, they sensibly hestitated to tread deep into the mountains. And it was here that Bulgarian monks built fantastic churches, painted exquisite icons, and printed Bulgarian books.

At the **Rila monastery,** for example, which is situated high in the Rila Mountains, about an hour and a half south of Sofia, the monks printed thousands of Bulgarian books on a printing press brought down the Danube from Vienna. Built in the 10th century and expanded in the early 14th century, the Rila monastery was destroyed in 1833 by fire. To rebuild the monastery, Bulgarians from all over the country contributed jewelry, money, and even belt buckles. The result is a dazzling structure that is part Byzantine fantasy, nestled in a green valley and surrounded on all sides by mountains.

The **Bachkovo monastery,** located near the Assenitsa River, is about 18 miles south of Bulgaria's second-largest city, Plovdiv. Originally governed by 50 Georgian monks, the monastery's holdings stretched as far south as Salonika in modern-day Greece. Destroyed by the Turks in the 16th century, the monstery was rebuilt. It now boasts fine frescoes and a mural depicting the ancient Greeks Aristotle, Sophocles, and Diogenes.

Perhaps the best known of Bulgaria's monasteries is the **Transfiguration,** high above the Yantra River, about four miles from Veliko Turnovo, Bulgaria's second capital. Also destroyed during the Turkish occupation, the monastery was completely rebuilt in 1825 by the self-taught national revival architect Kolyo Ficheto.

Bulgaria's best spas

Bulgaria boasts more than 220 mineral water springs, as well as the fabled mud from the lakes along the Black Sea coast, all believed to hold extensive curative properties. (Keep in mind that there is a tremendous difference between seaside and inland spas. The seaside spas attract thousands of foreigners, looking not only for curative treatment but also for a holiday in the sun. The inland spas, frequented mostly by Bulgarians, offer fewer amenities.)

Bulgaria's warmest and sunniest town, **Sandanski,** lies about 120 miles south of Sofia, at the foot of Pirin Mountain. The climate here is believed to have an incredible recuperative effect. Accommodation at Sandanski is at the four-star Sandanski Hotel, a snow-white, seven-story building set against a background of green hills. A double room is $92 a night.

The spa in **Velingrad** is situated in one of the most beautiful parts of the Rhodope Mountains in southern Bulgaria. The high amounts of negative ions and oxygen released by the rich vegetation and the abundant sunshine account for the curative properties of this spa. The best place to visit nearby is the city of Plovdiv, which has a well-preserved Roman amphitheater and a neighborhood of 19th-century houses that are open as museums, art galleries, or cafés. The best accommodation in Velingrad is at the two-star **Zdravets Hotel.**

The most modern Bulgarian seaside resort, **Albena,** lies about nine miles north of Golden Sands (probably the best-known of Bulgarian seaside resorts), located on the northern part of the Bulgarian Black Sea Coast along a picturesque bay. The best accommodation here is at the four-star Dobroudzha Hotel, where a double is $82 a night.

The best skiing in Bulgaria

The world has yet to realize that Bulgaria offers some of the best skiing in Europe. What's more, Bulgaria's ski resorts are also the most affordable of any on the Continent. Amenities may lag begind those in Switzerland or France, especially when it comes to service, but the low cost of a package deal means you can ski much more for much less money. Add to all of this the sheer novelty of skiing in Bulgaria, which offers a natural rugged beauty you'll find nowhere else.

Bulgaria's best ski resort is **Borovets,** which lies about 43 miles south of Sofia, in the

Rila Mountains. Founded in 1897 by the royal family and named after the surrounding *bor* (or pine), the resort is old and established. Snow covers the forest and slopes for an average of 100 days a year, providing excellent conditions and a long season, which stretches from late November well into May. Accommodation at Borovets ranges from a village of Finnish-built chalets to several large hotels adjacent to the slopes. Rooms are $50 to $70, including breakfast. **The Rila** offers balconies facing the slopes. You can ski directly from the hotel to the chair lift. Another good place to stay is the new four-star hotel, the **Samokov**.

Bulgaria's second-largest resort is **Pamporovo**, which lies about 52 miles south of Plovdiv, in the heart of the Rhodope Mountains. Today, Pamporovo offers seven downhill trails, as well as cross-country runs and six lifts. The season there runs from December through April. Stay at either the **Perelik** or the **Mourgavets**; both offer rooms for $60.

Bulgaria's busiest resort is **Aleko**, on Mount Vitosha. From its slopes, you have tremendous views of the city of Sofia. The resort offers two chair lifts and a gondola, as well as six trails for cross-country skiing. It is in close proximity to Sofia, so that means that you can stay in Sofia and combine sightseeing with skiing. While the skiing is great at Aleko, amenities are not. You're better off staying in Sofia and traveling every day to Aleko for your skiing. The best hotels in Sofia are the **Sheraton** and the **New Otani**.

For more information on any of the resorts mentioned above, contact **Balkanholidays**, *41 E. 42nd. St., New York, NY 10017; (212)573-5530.*

The best of Hungary

Hungary is a world unto itself. While it is at the very heart of the European continent, its language, food, and music are not like those of any other European country. Its people are as unique as its culture. And the country is changing daily—even the official holidays are changing. The nicest change has been in the Hungarian attitude toward foreigners. Travelers are now made to feel completely welcome and at ease.

Hungarians, or Magyars, are descendants of fierce horsemen from the Ural Mountains, who terrorized much of Europe until the ninth century. Hungarians still speak Magyar, which is distantly related to Finnish and Estonian. Their folk music is passionate; strains of the old tunes can be heard in the works of Ferenc Liszt, Bela Bartok, and Zoltan Kodaly.

Budapest: Eastern Europe's loveliest city

The capital of Hungary is one of the most beautiful cities in the world. Its 15th-century streets lead past Renaissance houses that hide pretty interior courtyards. At night, delicate neon signs glow from the old stone facades of the buildings. And Budapest has more museums per citizen than any other city in the world.

Budapest is made up of two sections: **Buda** and **Pest**, which are divided by the Danube River. Once two separate cities, they were united in 1873. Buda, dominated by the spires of the 13th-century Matthias Church, has medieval cobblestoned streets, centuries-old houses, and steep little stairways that climb to the castle. Pest, centered around the neo-Gothic parliament building, is the more modern, business section of the city, with grand 19th-century monuments and memorials.

The best way to get to Budapest is aboard the hydrofoil that glides from Vienna down the Danube and around Czechoslovakia, reaching Budapest at sunset.

The top sights

Buda Castle, *Szent Gyorgy Ter 2,* tops Castle Hill on the Buda side. Generations of Hungarian kings were crowned at this castle, which is embellished with elaborate reliefs. Demolished during bombing raids in World War II, it has been carefully rebuilt. From the courtyard is a splendid view over the Danube. The castle houses the Historical Museum of Budapest, which contains archeological remains of Old Town and exhibits on the history of the palace, and the National Gallery.

However, the most fascinating part of the castle is underground. Labyrinths running below the castle were used to house troops and a hospital during World War I. The tunnels are now a wax museum depicting Hungary's history: the early Roman settlers, the invasion of Attila the Hun and his horsemen from Mongolia in A.D. 430, the Turkish domination of Hungary from 1526 to 1686, the Austrian rulers, and modern history.

Kings Charles and Matthias were crowned at **Matthias Church**, *Szentharomsag ter 2*, as were Empress Maria Theresa and Emperor Franz Josef. High Mass is celebrated every Sunday at 10 a.m., and organ concerts are held in the church on Sunday afternoons.

The **Houses of Parliament**, *Kossuth Ter*, across the Danube in Pest, are a grand imitation of the Houses of Parliament in Westminster. Built 100 years ago, the neo-Gothic buildings are the seat of the Hungarian National Assembly and are used for state receptions.

Also in Pest is the **Hungarian National Museum**, *Muzeum Korut 14-16*, which features a permanent exhibit called "The History of the Hungarian People from the Magyar Conquest to 1849." One room displays a large, lavishly decorated Turkish tent, captured in 1686 when Buda was liberated from the Turkish occupation. Another room shows paintings and sculptures by Hungarian artists from the Middle Ages to the present.

Across from **Heroes Square**, where you'll see a statue commemorating Attila the Hun (a Hungarian hero, believe it or not) and Hungary's 1,000 years as a nation, is the **Museum of Fine Arts**, *Dozsa Gyorgy ut 41*. The museum has more El Grecos than any institution outside Spain, as well as three Rembrandts and major works by Goya, Raphael, Rubens, Franz Hals, Monet, Renoir, and Cézanne. (It also may have a Leonardo sculpture, depending on whether you listen to the Hungarians or the Italians.)

One of the most impressive buildings is the Italian neo-Renaissance **State Opera House.** Statues of Ferenc Liszt, Ferenc Erkel, and other renowned musicians surround the building. Inside, a visual splendor of ceiling frescoes, wall paintings and carved balustrades greets visitors. Recently restored, the State Opera House has presented continuous performances since 1884.

Another favorite area, **Vaci Utca**, attracts visitors and locals alike. In this pedestrian shopping area, large department stores and small specialty shops offer beautiful handcrafted goods. Elsewhere, workers and travelers crowd into busy cafes for *kave-spresso*, traditional *somloi galuska* (sponge cake covered with chocolate sauce and whipped cream), and delicious fruit tortes with fresh cream.

The world's best Gypsy music

Every February in Budapest, the **Gypsy Music Festival** is held. However, you can hear Gypsy music year-round at many restaurants in the city, including Feher Sandor, Lakatos Sandor, Lakatos Gyorgy, Kallai Kis Erno, and Voros Kalman. The best Gypsy music while you dine is at the restaurant called **Matyaspince**, *Marcius 15 ter 7; tel. (36-1)118-169.*

Budapest's best markets

Not far from the Matthias Cathedral, heading toward the river, a lively gypsy market is held on weekends. Gypsies in Hungary deal in secondhand goods and crafts. Among the bargains are leather clothes (jackets, skirts, and tops), embroidery (clothing and tablecloths), and jewelry. Offer to pay half the price they ask in dollars.

The **Vamhaz Indoor Food Market**, *Vamhaz Korut 1-3*, an enormous emporium of glass and iron, sells delicious sausages, salami chunks, and smoked meat, with thick slabs of bread and pickled peppers.

The best restaurants and cafés

The best restaurant in town is **Gundel**, near Heroes Square in Pest, *Allatkerti Utca Ter; tel. (36-1)122-1002*, which sets the standard for fine dining in Hungary.

Our favorite restaurant, however, is **Alabardos**, *Orszaghaz Utca 2; tel. (36-1)156-0851*, which not only offers luxurious dining, but also is cheap. Dinner for two with wine is $50. Guests are seated in a huge Gothic room with a vaulted ceiling; in the summer, you can sit at tables in the cobblestoned courtyard.

Other top-drawer places include **Hungaria** (formerly New York), *Erzebet Blvd. 9-11*, a café-restaurant at Terez Korut, by the train station, and **Feher Galamb** on Castle Hill.

The smartest café in Budapest is **Gerbeaud**, *Vorosmarty ter 7; tel. (36-1)118-1311*, on Vaci Utca. It is also one of the best pastry shops in the city—well worth the usual wait for a table. Built in the mid-19th century, the café boasts crystal chandeliers, heavy drapes, and dark polished wood tables that provide a yesteryear ambiance for enjoying some of the best pastries in Budapest.

The **Hungaria** in Buda and the **Angelika** in Pest also serve mouth-watering pastries.

The best digs

Hungary is one of the few East European nations with a flourishing private sector in bed-and-breakfast accommodation for travelers. Make arrangements for this through **IBUSZ**, *1 Parker Plaza, Fort Lee, NJ 07024; (201)592-8585*. Reservations can be difficult to make, considering the large number of businessmen and Western tourists traveling to this East European nation. Make plans far in advance.

If you want something more elegant than a bed-and-breakfast, Budapest has one of the most stunning hotels of any city in the world: the **Budapest Hilton**, *I Hess Andras ter 1-3; tel. (36-1)175-1000*, built into the ruins of a 13th-century abbey on top of a hill in Buda. It is next to Matthias Church and has views of the city and the river. A double room is $284.

The **Duna-Intercontinental**, *Apaczai cfere janos utca 4; tel. (36-1)117-5122*, the **Atrium-Hyatt**, *Roosevelt ter 2; tel. (36-1)138-3000*, and the **Forum**, *Apaczai cfere janos utca 12-14; tel. (36-1)117-8088*, are beautifully designed palaces all on the Pest side of the Danube. The Duna, within walking distance of the main shopping district, has river views. The Atrium has a glass-covered central court, through which glass-sided elevators soar. The Forum, a four- rather than a five-star hotel, is within easy walking distance of downtown. The price of a double room for all three of these hotels is $225 to $280.

Also on the Pest side, the **Grand Hotel Corvinus Kempinski**, *Erzsbet 7-8; tel. (36-1)2661000*, just opened in the summer of 1992. This five-star hotel is within walking distance of Vaci Utca, an exclusive shopping area. A double room is $220 to $280.

Budapest's incomparable spa hotel, the **Hotel Gellert**, *Szent Gellert Ter 1; tel. (36-1)185-2200*, is famous for its spring-fed baths. Guests are supplied with thick bathrobes and can take an elevator directly to the baths. The radioactive pools are located in mosaic-decorated art deco halls with ornate balconies, massive columns, and skylights. A double room is $170, including breakfast.

Bests beyond Budapest

It is now easier than ever before for the Western traveler to venture beyond Budapest. Hungary is filled with delightful towns and little-known historic sights outside its capital city. **Szentendre**, on the right bank of the Danube, dates from the 1300s. Cobblestoned streets lead to an ancient main square in the inner town, where you'll find shops and market stalls selling embroidered linens, distinctive china and crystal, leather goods, and souvenirs.

Visegrad is another must-see. The Romans occupied Hungary for centuries. In the fourth century, they built a *castrum*, or fortress. A monastery was added in the 11th century. Visegrad, the country's first fortress and watchtower, commands magnificent views of green countryside and the Danube.

To the south is **Pecs**, one of Hungary's oldest cities. A Celtic settlement in the third century, Pecs has become a sophisticated university town. Its main claim to fame is a former Turkish mosque, built in 1580 and since converted to a Catholic church. Pecs also boasts a television tower. You can take an elevator to the top to view the surrounding countryside, a fabulously ornate cathedral, and remarkably well-preserved fourth-century Christian burial chambers, adorned with wall paintings much in the style of the Roman catacombs.

Hungary's best wines

If you don't go anywhere else in Hungary, you must not miss **Eger**, the country's best wine region. It is a delightful city, rich in history, with yet another castle and the most delectable wines on earth. Visit the tiny wine cellars bored into the hillside for a leisurely wine tasting. A nearby *csarda* offers magnificent food at incredible prices. A robust dinner for two with all the wine you can handle costs about $3. Take containers and fill them with good wine for about $1 a liter.

Hungary's Versailles

Not far from Budapest, in Fertod, is **Esterhazy Palace**, the 18th-century home of Prince Nicholaus Esterhazy the Magnificent, who ruled at the height of the Hapsburg monarchy. Joseph Haydn was concertmaster here.

The palace, which was looted by Soviet troops during World War II, has been restored recently and is open to visitors. Nicholas modeled the palace after Versailles, which he had visited on a diplomatic trip.

Hungary's largest cathedral

Esztergom, a town on a narrow side channel of the Danube, contains the largest cathedral in Hungary, built between 1822 and 1856. However, the 19th-century marble cathedral pales in comparison with the Primate's art collection in the attached museum. The Renaissance chapel adjoining the cathedral houses a 13th-century gold cross, upon which Hungarian kings took their oaths. Marcus Aurelius wrote *Reflections* in this town, which was once an important Roman outpost. It was the seat of the Magyar kings in the 12th and 13th centuries and the center of the Hungarian Catholic Church.

Central Europe's largest lake

Hungary's **Lake Balaton**, Central Europe's largest lake, is 48 miles long and 36 feet deep in some places. It is known for its sandy beaches, its warm water (you can swim here from spring through late fall), its resort hotels, and its fine fishing (for 42 kinds of fish). The tastiest of the fish caught here is the giant pike-perch (*fogas*).

Lake Balaton served as a line of defense against the Turks for centuries. The remains of border castles can be seen in Tihany, Nagyvazsony, Szigliget, and Fonyod.

The most popular resorts are on the south shore of the lake, where the water is warmer and the beaches have a softer grade of sand. The north shore is relatively undiscovered and a good place to get away from the crowds; however, the water is colder and the beaches aren't as nice.

(Note that high season for the Lake Balaton region is July 4 through Sept. 5. All hotel prices below are quoted at high-season rates. Off-season, the rates are considerably lower.)

Siofok, the largest town on the southern shore, is also the most crowded. The **Hotel Balaton**, *Petofi setany 9; tel. (36-84)10-655*, is the best place to stay, with reasonable prices. A double room is $77.

Other good places to stay in Siofok are the **Europa**, *Petofi Setany 15; tel. (36-84)13411* (a double room is $77); the **Hotel Lido**, *tel. (34-84)10-633*; and the **Hungaria**, *Petofi Setany 13; tel. (36-84)10-677* (where a double room is $79, including breakfast).

The best restaurant on the lake is just outside Siofolk. **Menes Csarda**, *15 Apaczai Csere J., Szantodpuszta; tel. (36-84)170-803*, serves spicy food cooked according to local custom. The restaurant is housed in a restored stable and is decorated with antique art.

The healthiest place along the lake is the small spa town of **Balatonfured**, on the northern shore. It has 11 medicinal springs that are supposed to be good for the heart and the nerves. This hilly old town is covered with twisting streets. At its center is **Gyogy Ter** (Spa Square), where the waters of volcanic springs bubble under a pavilion.

The most charming hotel in Balatonfured is the old-fashioned **Arany Csillag** (Golden Star), *tel. (36-84)40-323,* a four-story hotel in a small grove of trees. It doesn't have a view of the lake or private baths, but the rooms are airy and clean.

Also in Balatonfured are three one-star hotels: **Annabella**, *Beloiannisz utca 25; tel. (36-86)42-222;* **Margareta**, *Szechenyi utca 29; tel. (36-86)43-824;* and the **Marina**, *Szechnyi utca 26; tel. (36-86)43-644.* All offer double rooms for about $78.

Nearby Zichy Castle hosts the annual **August Horse Show**. This is the best place to observe top riders and horses—Hungary is famous for its equestrian traditions. And riders for this famous horse show dress in medieval costumes. For more information, contact **IBUSZ**, *1 Parker Plaza, Fort Lee, NJ 07024.*

You can bathe in a warm-water lake surrounded by rose-colored Egyptian lotus plants in **Heviz**, a town near Lake Balaton. Fed by a thermal spring, Heviz Lake has a temperature that varies from 82 to 100 degrees Fahrenheit. In cool weather, the warm lake steams, giving it a mysterious air. The mud from the bottom of the lake is also therapeutic; it is dried and exported for mud packs. Cemeteries dating back to Roman times have been found along the lake.

Croatia: the best beaches

Croatia has a spectacular coastline with long sandy beaches, secret coves, and dramatic cliffs. Why battle the crowds and spend a fortune to lie on the beach in Greece, when you can enjoy the same Mediterranean sun and sea for half the price in Croatia? The continuing political strife in this part of the world makes it an unlikely travel destination as we go to press. Nonetheless, the nations that formerly comprised Yugoslavia, particularly Croatia, Slovenia, and Montenegro (still part of the Republic of Yugoslavia), offer stunning landscapes and a rich history. Indeed, this land in turmoil still belongs in our report on the world's best.

Dubrovnik: Croatia's most beautiful city

Dubrovnik, on the Dalmatian Coast, is a medieval walled city that had been so perfectly preserved before recent events that it had been declared a national monument. George Bernard Shaw wrote in 1931, "Those who seek Earthly Paradise should come and see Dubrovnik." Unfortunately, the recent war has destroyed much of the city. Although Dubrovnik was once a city-state to rival Venice, many of its Renaissance palaces and churches have been bombed. Especially breathtaking were the **Doge's Palace**, **Onofri's Fountain**, and the **Church of St. Vlaho**.

Europe's third-oldest synagogue

Zudioska Ulica (Jew Street), near the Ploce Gate on the second floor of a Gothic building, has a 14th-century synagogue, the third-oldest in Europe. In the early 14th century, large groups of Jews found sanctuary in Dubrovnik from persecution in Spain and Italy.

Best sunset, best swimming

The prettiest place to spend the evening in Dubrovnik is the west end of the city, near the **Fortress of St. Ivan**. Young men often gather by the Porporela jetty below the fortress, where three huge iron spikes jut out from the stone wall. To prove their manhood, they swing from one spike to the other and finally drop into the sea. According to a saying in Dubrovnik, a boy has become a man when he has "passed three spikes."

Dubrovnik's two best night spots are **Arsenal**, *Ulica Marshall Tito 7*, in the Old City, and **Lazareti**, *Ulica Franja Supila 6*, outside the Old City. Both have good dance floors.

The best place to swim is at the western end of the city, near **Fort Lovrijena**. Jacques Cousteau has called the water here the purest in the Mediterranean. Offshore is the island of Lokrum, known for its nudist beaches and good swimming.

Dubrovnik's best hotel

The only hotel within the town walls is the **Dubravka**, a former convent. Because it is the most convenient place to stay, it is usually fully booked. Local specialties and fish are served in the hotel dining room. Prices are reasonable.

The best hotel near Dubrovnik is a little place called **Villa Dubrovnik**, *P. Bukovca 8*. Perched on a cliff, this modern hotel has views of the walled town and of the harbor. Pine trees and flowers scent the air. In warm weather, you can dine outdoors on the terrace. It's worth the extra cost to get a room facing the sea. The hotel motorboat can take you into town, which is a 20-minute walk away.

The best of the Dalmatian Coast

Stretching from Zadar to Dubrovnik is the **Dalmatian Coast,** where the people are loud and friendly. The best beaches along this stretch are between Sibenek and Split.

The most beautiful place along the Dalmation Coast is the island of **Hvar** (which means *sun*). Above its harbor, the town spreads across a hill crowned with figs, oleanders, and purple bougainvillea. At the water's edge, a promenade is lined with kiosks selling seafood and hand-woven rugs. Dazzling white stone covers the grounds of the marketplace. You can rent a boat to explore the beaches.

Hvar attracts a good-looking young crowd, which keeps the night life lively. The **Tvrdava Disko,** which is located in the castle, can be seen from a distance—its lights flash from its perch on a hill. From the outdoor dance floor, you have a good view of the town.

The Croatian coastline

Dubrovnik is certainly the best-known city on the Croatian coastline, but it is hardly the only city along this shore.

Porec, farther down the peninsula, is the most pleasant town in the region. Located near spectacular fiords, it has narrow, cobblestoned streets and a maze of red-roofed stone houses. Galleries and studios fill the medieval towers.

The area on the coast known as the Riviera is the place to stay. Spend your Riviera nights at **Club No. 1**, a small, chic club with surrealistic paintings, and your Riviera days sunbathing in the nude at the giant nudist complex south of Porec called **FKK Koversada**, located at the entrance to the Lim Fiord. Day visitors can enjoy the beach for a few dollars (though groups of men might be barred entry).

The most picturesque town along the coast is **Rovinj**, an artists' colony near Porec. This little town, which has a beautiful old church, is built into a hill. Outdoor cafés and restaurants line the harbor. Monte Bar in the Old City serves good Istrian cuisine. The Hotel Eden has an informal casino and several discos.

The best place for peace and privacy is **Rab**, a lush town shaded with evergreens. Located south of the Istrian Peninsula, it has deserted coves where you can swim undisturbed. The residents are friendly. Spend an evening enjoying music by a live band on the terrace of the Hotel Imperial.

The best beach

The nicest beach on the entire coastline is at the south end of the island of **Krk**, a half-hour boat ride from Rijeka. Krk is a strangely beautiful place with a barren valley surrounded by stern, stony hills. The island has a small hotel.

Slovenia—the most glamorous beaches

The **Slovenian Riviera**—the area from the Italian border to the end of the Istrian Peninsula's west coast—is the most glamorous stretch along the coast. It feels like Italy.

Izola and **Piran** are attractive resort towns along the Slovenian Riviera—both resemble old-style Italian resorts. **Portoroz**, a more modern resort, is the most expensive.

Montenegro—the least discovered

Montenegro (Black Mountain) is the least-known and most southerly of the Republic of Yugoslavia's coasts. It follows the Adriatic Sea for 200 miles, from Kotor south to Albania. The scenery is dramatic, varying from high mountains to flat meadows to coastline beaches. The drive down the Old Post Road (now the coastal highway) to Dubrovnik is especially beautiful.

Herceg Novi, in the north, is the oldest town along the coast. It was founded 600 years ago by Tvrtko, the first Bosnian King. The old part of town has ramparts and towers that contrast sharply with the new villas and hotels. Herceg Novi is known as the rainiest spot in Europe. The Topla is a good place to stay.

The area around **Risan** is filled with bays and waterfalls. It is said that Illyrian Queen Teuta, after valiantly trying to fight off the invading Romans in 228 B.C., drowned herself here rather than surrender.

Sveti Stefan: the most exclusive resort

Off the coast of Montenegro is the island of **Sveti Stefan** (St. Stephen), a 15th-century fishing village that became an exclusive resort in 1960. The original fishermen's cottages have been preserved intact, but the interiors have been renovated in luxury. Flower gardens add color to the stone surroundings. The Duke of Bedford came here on his honeymoon; Adlai Stevenson, Kirk Douglas, and Princess Margaret also have been among the resort's guests.

Plitvice Lakes: nature at its best

The **Plitvice Lakes National Park,** halfway between Zagreb and the coast, has been classified by UNESCO as one of the unique natural wonders of the world. Here, 16 magnificent blue-green lakes merge one into the other in a chain of waterfalls that rushes into the Korana River. The highest waterfall is 247 feet. The lakes are surrounded by walking paths, deep forests, beaches, and hotels.

The best hotel in the area is the **Hotel Jezero,** perched in the mountains overlooking the largest of the lakes, Kozjak. The hotel has a large indoor pool, and two ski lifts are located only a mile away.

The best of Czechoslovakia

Czechoslovakia, at the heart of Europe, has suffered the blows of almost every power to hit the Continent. As a result, it is rich in history and culture and filled with 40,000 monuments and 3,000 castles. Its capital, Prague, is one of the most beautiful cities in Eastern Europe, outdone only by Budapest.

Czechoslovakia is an outdoor-lovers' paradise. The Tatra Mountains rise out of the plains to provide excellent skiing and hiking. The 1,000 lakes and ponds that dot Czechoslovakia are chock-full of fish. And the deep, wildlife-filled forests attract campers, backpackers, and hunters.

Czechoslovakia's most beautiful city

Prague, described by Goethe as "The most precious stone in the stone crown of the world," is one of the most beautiful cities in Eastern Europe.

The best way to see Prague is on foot. Start by climbing the 186 steps to the top of the **Prasna brana** (Powder Tower) in Old Town. You'll have a panoramic view of the city from the top. A remnant of the old city fortifications, it was built in 1475 and rebuilt in the 19th century.

Old Town's best treasures
Stare Mesto (Old Town) dates to 1120. Celetna Street leads from the Powder Tower through the heart of Stare Mesto. It passes the **Tyl Theater,** where Mozart's *Don Giovanni* premiered in 1787 and where scenes from the movie *Amadeus* were filmed. Then it skirts the **Church of Our Lady at Tyn,** once a center of early Protestantism. The church's twin spires dominate the skyline.

The street empties into **Staromestske namesti** (the Old Town square). A medieval astronomical clock *(orloj)* has kept time here since 1490. On the hour, figures of Christ and the 12 apostles appear at two little windows above the clock face. Then the skeleton figure of Death, below, tolls the bell. Legend has it that after its completion, the designer was blinded to prevent him from ever creating such a clock again.

The **town hall,** built in 1378, stands above dungeons. Its 15th-century council chamber, decorated with the shields of Prague's medieval guilds, is still used.

Novelist Franz Kafka (1883-1924) was born in the painted house next door to the town hall.

Betlemska kaple (Bethlehem Chapel), *Betlemske namesti 5,* is a reconstruction of the Gothic chapel where the reformer Jan Huss preached his revolutionary ideas from 1402 to 1415. Huss, who was burned at the stake for his views, became a symbol of freedom to the Czech people. There is a monument to Huss in the Old Town square.

The most beautiful bridge
The most beautiful bridge in Eastern Europe connects Prague's Old Town and Mala Strana (Small Town). The **Charles Bridge,** built in 1357 by Charles IV, is lined with baroque statues. The bridge is especially lovely at night, when it is illuminated.

The best of Small Town
Small Town, despite its modest name, contains many of Prague's best sights. Much here is baroque, even though the town was founded in 1257. Arcades and 16th-century houses surround **Malostranske namesti** (Small Town square), which is dominated by **Kostel sv. Nikulase** (St. Nicholas Church), a Jesuit church with a beautiful dome, a belfry, a nave, and ceiling frescoes.

Nerudova ulice (Neruda Street) is the most beautiful street in Small Town. The baroque buildings are identified by signs (a red eagle, for example), as was the custom before numbered streets were introduced.

The magnificent **Valdstejnsky Palac** (Wallenstein Palace), *Valdstejnske namesti,* built in 1624 by Italian architects for the Hapsburg's Gen. Albrecht Wallenstein, now houses the Ministry of Culture. Concerts are held here in the summer.

New Town bests
Prague's **New Town** is not really new by most standards—it was established in 1348. At its heart is **Vaclavske namesti** (King Wenceslas Square), marked by a statue of King Wenceslas and filled with shops, restaurants, and hotels. Prague's best craft shop, **Slovenska Jizba,** located on the square, sells handmade jewelry, glass, porcelain, and folk art.

The **Narodni muzeum** (National Museum), also on King Wenceslas Square, behind the statue of the king, displays neo-Renaissance paintings, artifacts from Czech history, historical and archeological collections, and a famous mineral collection.

Prague's oldest pub, **U Fleku,** *Kremencova 11,* has been in existence at least since 1499. A huge place, it is filled with people singing and drinking its good dark beer.

Karlovo namesti (Charles Square), the biggest square in New Town, is named for

Charles IV, who planned the city. Located in this square is the **Novomestska radnice** (town hall), which was the government center from 1398 to 1784. Antonin Dvorak's mementos are housed in the **Dvorak Museum**, *Ke Karlovu 20,* near Charles Square. During the summer, Dvorak's music is played in the sculpture garden behind the 18th-century house.

The best-preserved ghetto

Jewish merchants settled in the area north of the old town hall as early as the ninth century. As the area grew, it became a center of Jewish culture. The well-preserved Prague Ghetto is now the **State Jewish Museum.**

The **Altneushul** (Old-New Synagogue), built in 13th-century Gothic style, is the oldest surviving synagogue in Europe. Beside it is the **Old Jewish Cemetery,** which holds 12,000 graves piled in layers. Tombs date from 1439 to 1787. If you lay a pebble on a grave here, it is said your dreams will come true.

The most visited tomb is that of the 16th-century scholar **Rabbi Loew,** who created the mythical, magical being called Golem. Today, visitors place scraps of paper with wishes on them in the crack in Loew's tomb. During World War II, Jews hid their valuables in the tomb's cracks before they were transported to concentration camps.

Franz Kafka is also buried in the cemetery. When the Nazis occupied Prague, they sent Kafka's three sisters to a concentration camp, where they were killed. And they destroyed most of Kafka's letters and manuscripts. However, his diaries were overlooked and are now housed among the treasures of the State Jewish Museum.

Klausen Synagogue, *U stareho hrbitova,* has a moving collection of drawings done by Jewish children in concentration camps.

The names of 77,700 Czechoslovak Jews murdered by the Nazis are inscribed on the inside walls of nearby **Pinkas Synagogue.**

Hradcany, the royal quarter

The **Hradcany Quarter** grew up around Hradcany (Prague Castle), the former residence of the kings of Bohemia and today the seat of government. A city within a city, it holds some of Prague's best treasures. The president of Czechoslovakia lives here, in a well-guarded section.

Three walled courtyards open into each other, progressing in architectural design from medieval to 20th century. Off the first courtyard is the former chapel, which houses the treasury. Inside are gold, crystal, and jewels.

The Hradcany also houses the **National Gallery,** which is divided into three chronological sections. The earliest and best, in the former Convent of St. George, houses the state collection of Bohemian Gothic paintings and sculpture.

The third courtyard of the castle contains the imposing **Katedrala sv. Vita** (St. Vitus' Cathedral), the biggest in Prague, and the mausoleum of Czech kings, which holds the crown jewels (including the crown of St. Wenceslas, decorated with a thorn, supposedly from Christ's crown of thorns).

Behind the Hradcany is **Golden Lane,** once the residence of alchemists. The beautiful cobblestoned street, with its small houses, great palaces, and shops, brings the Middle Ages to life.

The bookstore at Number 24 was the residence of Franz Kafka in 1917 (who lived here just after he wrote *The Trial* and before he wrote *The Castle*). Ironically, the bookstore sells no books by Kafka, who has been largely ignored by Czechs.

Nearby is **Strahovsky Klaster** (Strahov Monastery), which houses a museum of Czech literature and beautifully preserved ancient manuscripts and Bibles from all over the world. It is one of the most impressive libraries in Europe. The **Theological Hall,** a vaulted gallery built in 1671, is lined with 17th-century bookshelves. Its white stucco ceilings are embellished with frescoes.

The **Loretta**, another monastery, was founded in 1629 by Princess Lobkowitz. It centers around a replica of the Santa Casa in Loretto, Italy. Paired half-columns and relief panels add to its beauty. Its treasury contains saints' crowns and religious objects made of gold and precious stones.

The oldest fortress
Vysehrad Fortress, believed to have been founded in the ninth century, looms above Prague from sheer cliffs facing Hradcany. The Hussites destroyed much of it—apart from the walls, all that remains are an 11th-century rotunda and the Church of St. Peter and St. Paul. Many of Czechoslovakia's greatest heroes and artists are buried in Vysehrad's cemetery, including Antonin Dvorak, Karel Capek, Jan Neruda, and Bedrich Smetana.

The world's best crystal
Czechoslovakia is known for its lead crystal. **Moser**, *na prikope 12, tel. (42-2)221-851*, is the best place in Prague to shop for crystal. You can order through the store's catalog, which includes patterns preferred by the world's royalty.

The best restaurants
Opera Grill, *Divaeelmin ulice*, is Prague's finest restaurant. An elegant establishment decorated with antique Meissen candelabra, it serves French cuisine. After dinner, brandy is served in giant crystal snifters. The restaurant is closed weekends. Make reservations in advance.

The **Zlata Praha** (Golden Prague), *Curieovych namesti; tel. (42-2)280-0914*, on the eighth floor of the Prague Inter-Continental, has a lovely view of the castle. National specialties—roast duck, sauerkraut, and dumplings—are well-prepared.

Svata Klara (St. Klara), *Prague 7, Ulice Trogskeho Zamku 9; tel. (42-2)84-12-13*, the former wine cellar of Count Vaclav Vojtech, is now a first-class *vinarna* (wine restaurant) that offers a good selection of Moravian wines. You can enjoy dinner in front of a fireplace.

The best hotels
U Tri Pstrosu (Three Ostriches), *Drazickeho namesti 12; tel. (42-2)53-61-51*, is the most charming hotel in town. Located in a 16th-century house at the Small Town end of the Charles Bridge, it has an excellent restaurant. Reservations must be made several months in advance. A double room is $110.

Pariz, *U Obecniho domu 1; tel. (42-2)236-0820*, is a recently reopened art deco hotel with double rooms for $170. The hotel's café and restaurant are decorated with blue mosaic tile.

Hotel Intercontinental, *namesti Curievyeh 43-5, tel. (42-2)231-1812*, is a quick walk from both Wencelas Square and the Charles Bridge on the New town side of the Vltava River. A double room is $250, including bath and breakfast.

The best night life
If you're looking for some insight into how local Czechs spend their evenings out, try **U Fleku** (Fleku's Inn), *Kremencova 9-11*. Or you could stop in for a beer at **U Kalicha** (The Chalice), *Na Bojisti 12; tel. (42-2)29-60-17*. Both these beer halls are lively places to meet people. **Slavia Café**, *Narodni 1*, on the embankment opposite the National Theater, is where local artists and intellectuals hang out.

For Western-style entertainment, try **Night Club**, *tel. (42-2)28-00-912*, on the ninth floor of the Intercontinental Hotel; **Est Bar**, in the Hotel Esplanade, *tel. (42-2)22-25-52*; or **Lucerna**, *Stepanska 61*. All these places offer dancing; some also have cabaret shows.

(Avoid the **Laterna Magika**, *Narodni 40*. The only people you'll meet here are tourists. Its corny extravaganza includes live actors, mimes, films, music, magic, and dance.)

The best castles

Czechoslovakia boasts 3,000 castles, and most are worth seeing. **Hazmburk**, near Ceske Budejovice in the north, is surrounded by a 30-foot-high wall and guarded by two observation towers. (Peregrine falcons have taken up residence in one of the abandoned towers.) The ruins rise out of sheer rock and are surrounded by a valley filled with wheat fields and plum orchards. Be careful—no railings protect you from the 700-foot drop from the ruins to the valley below. You can take a day-trip to this castle from Austria or Southern Germany.

Spilberk Castle in Brno, Moravia, built in 1287 to fend off invaders, was later used by the Hapsburgs to lock up their opponents. During World War II, the Nazis also used the dungeon as a prison. Take a look at the castle's hair-raising instruments of torture. The castle has a good restaurant that serves game dishes along with Moravian wines.

The little town of **Hluboka** has a wedding cake of a château, gleaming white with high, crenelated towers. It is a replica of Windsor Castle in England. Brussels tapestries, fine paintings, glassware, china, antique furniture, and medieval weapons can be seen here.

The best skiing in Eastern Europe

Czechoslovakia has Eastern Europe's best ski area: **Stary Smokovec**, a national park in the High Tatras with jumps, slalom runs, and long cross-country trails. You won't find the crowds and frenzy of St. Moritz here.

In addition to being the best place to ski, Stary Smokovec, which lies in the shadows of the peak called Slavkovsky, is the oldest community in the High Tatras. The first tourist buildings here were built in the late 18th century. The two best hotels in town are the Grand and the Parkhotel.

Romania, the most romantic nation

Romania is a land for romantics. More Gypsies live here than anywhere else in the world. (They call themselves *Romany*.) Romanians claim to be descendants of a lost Roman legion. The Roman poet Ovid was exiled here, on a lagoon north of Constanta. And Vlad the Impaler—the man behind the myth of Dracula—led his bloody life in Transylvania.

Bucharest: the Paris of Eastern Europe

Thousands of years ago, a little Stone Age settlement was established on the trade route that crossed the forest-covered Romanian plains. Today, that settlement is Bucharest, the capital of Romania, and the trade route is the chain of grand boulevards that earned the city the title of the "Paris of Eastern Europe."

The boulevards—N. Balcescu, 1848, Magheru, and Ana Ipatescu—are lined with restaurants and brasseries. Along their southern stretch is the **Princely Palace**, which is surrounded by the trading quarter called **Lipscani**, where narrow medieval streets wind past little shops. The palace, which is now the **National Art Museum**, *Stirbei Voda St NR1*, was inhabited by the notorious Vlad in the 14th century.

The most beautiful hotel in Bucharest is the **Hanul Manuc**. The Russian-Turkish Peace Treaty of 1812 was signed here. **Stavropoleos**, a nearby church built in 1724, has superb wood and stone carvings.

Calea Victoriei, Bucharest's most famous street, passes many of the city's major sights. Starting at the **Operetta Theater**, *Piata Natiunile Unite*, it leads north past Stavropoleos Church to the History Museum of Romania in the former post office. The museum displays the 42-pound golden Hen with Golden Chickens, a fifth-century treasure made of 12 gold pieces.

Like Paris, Bucharest has a triumphal arch. Built in 1922 to celebrate the Allies' victory in World War I, it is located on the wide avenue of Soseaua Kiseleff.

Bucharest's best restaurants

Capsa, *16 Edgar Quintet St.*, is the traditional meeting place for Bucharest's artists. It offers a choice of local or continental cuisine and excellent desserts.

Pescarus, *Aviatorilor Boulevard; tel. (40-0)79-46-40*, located along the Herastrau Park, serves international cuisine on a terrace overlooking a lake in the park.

The **Casa Lido**, *3 Magheru Blvd.; tel. (40-0)155085*, is another restaurant worth visiting; it has a reputation for fine food.

Bucharest's best hotels

The new and deluxe hotel **Bucuresti**, *Caleca Victoriei 63-69; tel. (40-0)14-21-77*, in the center of town, has 800 rooms, two restaurants, two swimming pools, a sauna, and a gym. A double room is $122 to $160.

The **Athenee Palace**, *Strada Episcopiei 1-3; tel. (40-0)14-08-99*, a prewar grand dame, has a slightly faded grandeur. It has two restaurants, a good pastry shop, and very affordable prices. A double room is $44 to $57, including breakfast.

Dracula's castle

While in Brasov, make a day-trip to the town of Poiana Brasov (Sunny Glade) to see **Bran Castle**, the legendary home of Count Dracula. It is actually the home of the Prince of Wallachia, who repelled a Turkish invasion by impaling hundreds of his countrymen on tall stakes and lining the route of the enemy's march. The Turks, frightened by the brutal display, avoided the region. In truth, the Prince stayed at this castle only occasionally.

The best of Poland

Poland doesn't have the tourist amenities of Western Europe—or even the amenities of Hungary or Czechoslovakia—but it does have the Polish people. Self-effacing and fun-loving, they are among the warmest people in all Europe. If you get lost in Poland, a Pole is likely to take you out for dinner and drinks before he points you in the right direction.

Nature, too, welcomes visitors to Poland. The country's 12 natural parks and 500 wildlife preserves contain animals that have disappeared elsewhere in Europe—bison, chamois, bear, moose, and tarpan (small horses). And Poland's 325-mile Baltic seacoast is lined with long, sandy beaches.

Warsaw: worst destruction, best restoration

Warsaw has had the bloodiest history of any Polish city. Hitler ordered that not one stone be left standing in the city following the 63-day Warsaw Uprising against the Nazis. As a result, more than 200,000 people were killed and the city was razed. Between 1940 and 1945, a total of 750,000 of the city's residents died.

The Nazis weren't the first to demolish Warsaw. In the 17th century, the city was razed by the Swedes. It was sacked again in the 18th century. In 1795, Warsaw was given to Prussia. Napoleon took the city in 1806. And the Russians claimed it in 1813.

Although most of Warsaw's old buildings and monuments have been destroyed, many have been beautifully rebuilt. The Old Town section was reconstructed after the war according to prints and old family photographs. It looks much as it did before, with narrow houses, winding streets, and Gothic churches. The district is closed to all traffic except horse-drawn buggies.

At the heart of Old Town is **Market Square**, surrounded by recreated baroque houses, shops, and cafés and filled with flowers. The **Negro House**, Number 36 on the square, was once a center of the slave trade. It is marked by a bust of a black man. It is now the home of the **Warsaw Historical Museum**, where chamber music concerts are held on Tuesdays. The oldest house on the square is the **House of the Mazovian Dukes**, or St. Anne's House, at Number 31. It has the greatest number of Gothic details.

The **Royal Castle**, blown up during the war, is the most beautiful in Poland. Built between the 14th and 18th centuries, it was restored after World War II. It can be seen from Zamkowsky Square along with **King Sigismund's Column**, a symbol of Warsaw. The slender column was the first monument rebuilt after the war. Originally built in 1644, it honors King Sigismund III, who made Warsaw his capital in the late 16th century.

The old walls surrounding the city and a 16th-century tower called the **Barbican** also have been reconstructed. You can see fragments of the old defensive walls along Kamienne Schodki Street. They are defended by the statue of Syrena, a mermaid with a raised sword. According to legend, the mermaid rose out of the Vistula River and told two children playing on the banks to found the city. Their names were Wars and Szawa, hence the Polish name for the city: Warszawa.

The most frightening sights
The horrors of World War II are evident throughout Warsaw. The most frightening reminder is **Pawiak Prison Museum**, *Ulica Dzielna 24/26*, where 35,000 Poles were executed and 65,000 imprisoned.

The walled Jewish ghetto called **Muranow** was flattened by the Nazis. Today, Spartan modern apartments stand in its place. The Monument to the Heroes of the Ghetto stands on a small square at the intersection of Zamenhofa and Anielewicza streets, once the heart of the ghetto. It is a slab of dark granite with a bronze bas-relief.

The **Jewish Historical Institute**, *Swierczewskiego 79*, has exhibits of the ghetto uprising. The **Mausoleum to Struggle and Martyrdom**, *Armii Wojska Polskiego Street*, is located at the former gestapo headquarters and prison.

A less obvious memorial to the war is a manhole cover at the intersection of Dluga and Miodawa streets. Here, 5,300 insurgents left the sewer canal through which they escaped from Old Town during the Warsaw Uprising in September 1944. The horrors of their journey through Warsaw's sewers are graphically depicted in Wajda's film *Canal*.

Poland's prettiest palace
Lazienki Palace and Park is among the most beautiful palaces in the world. In 1766 King Stanislas Poniatowski bought the neoclassical castle, which stood on an island in the middle of a lake, and had it enlarged and remodeled. The grounds also contain the Myslewicki Palace, the White Cottage, an old orangery, a baroque bathhouse, and a theater by the swan-filled lake, complete with artificial ruins.

The Polish Versailles
Wilanow Palace and Park, called Warsaw's Versailles, was built in the late 17th century by King Jan III Sobieski. The building is crowned with parapets, and the facade is carved with deities symbolizing the virtues of the royal family. Inside is the gallery of Polish portraiture and the world's first poster museum.

Warsaw's most famous residents
Stop by the often-overlooked **Maria Sklodowska Curie Museum**, *Ulica Freta 16*. Madame Curie was born here. The scientist was twice awarded the Nobel Prize for her discoveries of the radioactive elements polonium and radium.

Another little-known treasure is the house where **Chopin** was born in 1810. Set in a park in Zelazowa Wola, 33 miles west of Warsaw, the ivy-covered cottage is now a museum. A black Steinway grand piano stands in the corner of the music room. A 19th-century upright grand, which looks something like a harp, stands in another room. Framed musical compositions hang on the walls along with poems Chopin wrote as a boy for his parents. During the summer, Chopin concerts are held here on Sundays.

The best restaurants
The best restaurant in Warsaw is **Bazyliszek**, *Old Town Market Square 5/7*, a wood-

beamed restaurant decorated with Hussar armor. Wild game is served. According to legend, a monster who could kill with a deadly glance once lived in the vaulted cellars. A shoemaker's apprentice did the ogre in by wearing a mirror-covered suit. The monster saw himself and died. Dinner for two is $25 to $35.

Karczma Slupska, *Czerniakowska 127*, features traditional Kashubian (northern Polish) fare in a comfortable setting. Try the nut soup and boar paté. Expect to pay about $15 for two.

The bar at Karczma Slupska is also worth a visit—patrons sit on carousel horses that move up and down and are controlled from behind the bar.

Krokodyl, *Old Town Market Square 19/21*, is a favorite of Fidel Castro, who donated a large stuffed crocodile to the restaurant.

The best hotels
Victoria Inter-Continental, *Ulica Krolewska 11; tel. (48-22)27-80-11*, is Warsaw's top hotel. Its 410 rooms are $172 to $200 per night. The hotel restaurant, Canaletto, specializes in Polish dishes.

Orbis-Europejski, *Ulica Krakowskai Przedmiescie 13; tel. (48-22)265-051*, is a grand four-story building more than 100 years old. It has a delightful café that overlooks the Saxon Gardens and the Monument to the Unknown Soldier. A double room is $65 to $95 per night.

Cracow: the only unscathed Polish city
Cracow is Poland's city of kings and intellectuals. It was the country's capital from 1039 to 1596. Cracow is also the only Polish city that escaped demolition during World War II. Most of its buildings date from the 15th century. The city is dominated by **Wawel Hill**, with its fortified castle and Gothic cathedral. UNESCO described the castle, now a museum, as one of the most beautiful in the world. Poland's kings lived here until 1609, when the royal court moved to Warsaw. Even after the move, Polish kings continued to be crowned here.

Wawel Castle looks like a movie set, with gargoyles hanging from walls, elaborately carved doorways, columns, and brightly painted roof tiles. The castle museum contains the "Szczerbiec," a 13th-century sword used in coronation ceremonies, and the world's largest collection of tapestries—356 in all. The 71 rooms of the castle are richly decorated—one is covered entirely in embossed, hand-painted Spanish leather.

The **Czartaryski Palace** (the National Museum) has collections of tapestries, pottery, weapons, and paintings by old masters, including da Vinci and Rembrandt.

The **cathedral** on Wawel Hill contains the elaborate tomb of St. Stanislaus, Poland's patron. Lovely 15th-century frescoes decorate the cathedral's **Chapel of the Holy Cross**. **Sigismund Chapel**, an 11th-century crypt, contains red marble tombs of royalty, bishops, and national heroes.

Mariacki (the Church of the Virgin Mary) is famous for its bugler. Seven-hundred years ago, a bugler in the church tower was sounding an alarm when he was stopped mid-toot by a Tartar's arrow. Today, a bugle sounds every hour on the hour. The call is cut off suddenly, just as it was centuries ago.

The church also is famous for its 500-year-old altarpiece with life-size figures in gold raiment depicting the assumption of the Virgin Mary.

You enter the Old City via the **Florian Gate**, which is next to a round fort called the Barbican, with walls 10 feet thick and pierced by 130 peepholes. Pedestrians can climb medieval staircases here and view the gargoyles. This area is the site of one of the world's oldest universities, **Jagiellonia University**, which was founded in 1364 and counts Copernicus among its alumni.

All streets in the Old City lead to **Rynek Glowny** (the main marketplace). Once the largest municipal square in Europe, it is the site of political rallies, festivals, and public performances. Hundreds of pigeons share the square with crowds of people.

Oldest new market

Nowy Targ, which means *New Market,* is a town of 10,000 in the foothills of the Carpathian Mountains. The market was new in the 15th century and has operated continuously ever since. Now open every Thursday, the market attracts buyers and sellers from all over Poland. Beginning at the break of day, the market is like a carnival, and fascinates as long as you watch.

Zakopane: Poland's best ski resort

Zakopane, in the Tatra Mountains near the Czech border, a half-hour south of Nowy Targ, is the top ski resort in Poland. At 2,625 feet, it has good ski conditions November through May. A funicular takes you to the top of Gubalowka, a peak above town. And a cable car takes you to the top of Kasprowy Wierch, at nearly 6,514 feet. Zakopane is also a center for sheep-herding mountaineers and has been a mecca for sports and nature enthusiasts since the turn of the century. Summer is for rafting, hiking, fishing, and mountain climbing. And the numerous health spas are popular regardless of the season.

The place to stay in Zakopane is **Orbis Kasprowy**, *tel. (48-1)654-011,* a 300-room hotel with a restaurant, a nightclub, an indoor pool, a sauna, an ice-skating rink, and a mini-golf course. All rooms have private baths and cost $52 to $75.

The **Kawiarnia Mis**, *Bukowina Tatrzanska, Ulica Dluge 154,* is a small country restaurant with six tables for six. It is the creation of Hendryk Kolbusz and his wife and well deserves its high-flown reputation.

Czestochowa, a mecca

Every year on Assumption Day (Aug. 15), hundreds of thousands of pilgrims come to the drab little town of **Czestochowa** on the Warta River to pay homage to a portrait of the Madonna, said to have been painted by St. Luke. The Madonna's cheeks are marred by two slashes that, according to legend, were made by an enraged Tartar who felt the painting getting heavier and heavier as he tried to steal it.

The portrait is kept in a huge monastery called **Jasna Gora** (Hill of Light), founded in 1382 by Paulist monks. Swedish armies were halted here in 1655 and driven out of Poland.

Central Europe's last primeval forest

Bialowieza National Park, the last primeval forest in Central Europe, covers 480 square miles, half in Poland, half in the Soviet Union. A thick wall of 1,000-year-old oaks, pines, and spruce trees, it is home to Europe's only wild bison, as well as moose, lynx, wild tarpans, bears, foxes, deer, and wild boars. You can explore the forest on four-hour excursions in a horse-drawn carriage.

The Best of the CIS

"A riddle wrapped in a mystery inside an enigma." Those are the words that Winston Churchill used to describe the Soviet Union more than 50 years ago. And they are as appropriate today as they were when Churchill first spoke them.

The best adventure travel bargain of our lifetimes

With all its faults and craziness these days, the former Soviet Union is an intensely exciting and interesting place. And if you want an inexpensive travel adventure, it's *the* place to go. Where else could you take an overnight train ride, with sleeper, for 80 cents? Or get lunch for a dime and dinner for a quarter? Where else could you buy a leather coat for $25 and a pair of new leather army boots for $2?

This is the chance of a lifetime. This situation cannot last. Prices must rise to reflect the real economic costs. Or the whole system will sink into such chaos that the trains won't run...and you won't be able to find dinner. Go now for the greatest adventure travel bargain of your lifetime.

The best of Moscow

The most important thing to understand about travel to Moscow, or any other part of the former Soviet Union right now, has nothing to do with travel—it has to do with money. It is possible to travel in the new Commonwealth of Independent States (CIS) spending only a few dollars a day, but you have to learn how to take advantage of the dual monetary system. The commercial, official, and black market rates are all dizzyingly different.

The tourist comes out way ahead by paying with rubles rather than dollars, but, unfortunately, not all shops accept rubles from foreigners. Furthermore, it is illegal to change dollars on the streets. This doesn't mean you shouldn't exchange dollars on the street; it means you should be careful and not get caught.

The best sites

The first thing you must see in Moscow is a ballet at the **Bolshoi Theater.** To find out what's playing, visit Intourist—but don't buy your tickets here. Instead, buy your tickets from scalpers, who gather around the theater 45 minutes before a show and offer tickets for $7 to $8. The second thing you must do in Moscow is attend a traditional Russian banquet at the **Rossiya Hotel.** The banquet, which includes all the caviar and smoked salmon you can eat and all the champagne and vodka you can drink, costs only $6 a person. But you must know the right people—or be willing to offer a bribe to get in.

The **Arbat** has become Moscow's Speaker's Corner. Here you can enjoy the local

249

street artists' scathing political cartoons and listen to the speakers, who rant and rave about anything that happens to be on their minds.

Also visit the country's largest department store, **GUM**, on Red Square. If you overlook the boarded-up shops, empty shelves, and endless queues of unhappy shoppers, GUM is beautiful. TSUM, across the street from the Bolshoi Theater, is just as devoid of merchandise as GUM, and the building is less attractive.

Take a minute to visit the local McDonald's. We don't recommend that you stop in for a meal, but you ought to see the lines—they're incredible.

The cheapest eats

It is possible to get a good meal at a restaurant in Moscow for less than $1. The trick is to know where to find the restaurants, which are hidden away in rundown office buildings and in residential areas where you would not expect to find them. The good restaurants in Moscow do not need to advertise. They know they are in short supply and depend on word-of-mouth recommendations to keep their tables full. As a result, you must ask a local resident to point you in the right direction.

Few restaurants have menus. Your server will tell you what's available—in Russian. You'll need a companion to translate. Also, reservations are a must—but they are not taken over the phone (except by certain hard-currency restaurants, where you pay 15 to 20 times more for the convenience). You must visit the restaurant where you want to eat and leave a deposit.

The best place in the world to buy an original work of art

The best values in Moscow, by far, are in art. Be the first on your block (or in your city) to own an original Russian painting. It will cost you just a few dollars—and there's the chance that it will be worth a small fortune one day. **Arbat Street**, closed to all but pedestrian traffic, is lined with shops and street vendors selling these original pieces of art, as well as souvenirs, clocks, books, linen, and ice cream.

The best of Belorussia

Belarus is home to **Minsk,** a surprisingly attractive town (although it has the reputation of being one of the ugliest cities in the world). The avenues are wide and treelined. And a river flows through town. Many of the public buildings are grand and well-designed. There is a pleasant walkway along the riverbanks (though it is littered by chunks of concrete that have fallen from nearby buildings). There is even a historic section that has been restored and preserved.

The best sites

Walk around Old Town and along the river; you'll pass the city's hotels and art galleries. Also visit the house where Lee Harvey Oswald lived, the site of the first Communist meeting, and the city's monuments, scattered around town.

Visit the city's open markets. It's obvious that the people of Minsk are new at this. They stand all day long trying to sell one dress for the equivalent of 75 cents. This is at the market at the stadium, which charges an admission fee of a few cents and is a good place to trade your dollars for rubles.

A more interesting market is across town at **Storazhovsky Renok.** Here you can find fresh vegetables, fruit, bread, and other food. There's also a lively pet and livestock market here.

The best places to stay

Travelers in Minsk can stay at the **Planeta**, the **Yubeleymaya**, or the **Belarus**. Unfortunately, none is particularly appealing. The rooms are serviceable, but the style is tacky, and the lobbies and public restrooms are dirty and shabby.

The best place to stay in town is in one of the commodious houses in the guarded compound near the park, where guests of the government are put up. The houses are well-built with beautiful wood paneling and parquet floors. And the food is plentiful and good. The challenge is to arrange an invitation.

The most remote regions

Few Westerners have ever seen the remote peaks of the Central Asian Tien Shan and Pamir mountains. Travel here is still highly restricted.

The snow-peaked mountains of the **Tien Shan** (Heavenly) mountain range rise out of the hot and arid Central Asian steppelands to heights of 3,500 and 4,500 meters, extending into China in the east and the Himalayas in the south. Everlasting glaciers, green valleys, emerald lakes, rapid rivers, and ancient towns and cities are hidden in the mountains' valleys.

The Sairam Valley—the best gateway

The mountain valley of **Sairam**, at 1,700 meters, boasts a dry climate, crystal clear water, unusual rock formations, and birch and juniper woods. It acts as a gateway to the mountains in general. The mountains of Sairam are formed of limestone and basalt. The northern and western slopes are precipitous; the southern ones are more gradual and easily accessible.

The best practice climb

Among the most challenging climbs you can make is up **Mount Lenin**. At 7,134 meters, it is one of the highest peaks in this part of the world. It is a good place to practice before tackling the Karakorum or the Himalayas.

The best way to see the mountains

The best way to see the Tien Shan and Pamir mountains is with **ALTEX**, *Alma-Atinsky Prospekt, P.B. 22, 486011, Chimkent, Kazahkstan,* an organization specializing in hiking, rafting, and horseback riding programs in the CIS. Every package includes airfare, ground transportation, accommodation, and meals. The trips emphasize the people of the region, and accommodation is generally in the national Kazakh *yurtas.* The group is based in **Chimkent,** the regional center of southern **Kazahkstan,** one of the crossroads of the ancient silk caravan routes.

The best travel tips

Don't forget to carry a roll of toilet paper with you. It is not yet common in Central Asia. Bathrooms may be quite a shock. Potable water is also a problem in Kazahkstan. Don't drink the tap water. And limit your bottled mineral water intake, because it can be very salty. Bottled soda and juices are your best bet; they're plentiful. Drink boiled water when possible; carry a canteen with you and fill it with boiled water at every opportunity. Carry iodine tablets for when none of the above is available, and Lomotil just in case.

The best accommodation in the CIS

Your best bet is to stay at either one of the country's new bed-and-breakfasts or a facility associated with one of the new homestay programs. Your itinerary remains flexible—you can spend as much or as little time in a city as you want. And the trip can be customized around your specific interests.

The best part is the cost—much less than you'd pay for a typical tour or an Intourist hotel.

Home & Host International, *2445 Park Ave., Minneapolis, MN 55404; (612)871-0596,* offers bed-and-breakfasts for $80 a night, including transfers from the airport and an English-speaking guide. Compare this with the cost of a hotel room booked through

Intourist, which can cost $100 to $400, *not* including the mandatory hotel transfers, billed at $45 each way.

Even cheaper accommodation is available in St. Petersburg. It's now possible to spend the night in this city for as little as $14, including breakfast.

The new hostel-style accommodation is available thanks to Steven R. Caron, a native of California who studied Russian and theater at the University of St. Petersburg. Caron, amazed at the high cost of staying at a typical hotel in the city, learned that St. Petersburg's Financial Trade School had a vacant dormitory just off Nevsky Prospect. He approached the school with his idea of starting a hostel and suggested a joint-venture project, called Russian Youth Hostels and Tourism.

The former dorm has been renovated and now offers 50 beds, three or four in each room. Guests share bathrooms and showers, which are located on each of the four floors. There is constant hot running water except in August (when the government steam plant is shut down). There are also two kitchens and a television room available to guests.

Caron is planning similar budget-style accommodations in Yalta, Moscow, and other major tourist cities throughout the CIS.

Make reservations at the St. Petersburg hostel two to four weeks in advance of your visit. You can fax the hostel at *(7-812)277-5102* or make reservations through the **Finnish Youth Hostel Association,** *tel. (358-0)694-0377; fax (358-0)693-1349.* (The Finnish association is advising the St. Petersburg group.) When making reservations, you must provide the names and passport numbers of all those in your party, the dates of your arrival and departure, and how you will be arriving (by plane, train, or however). Prepayment must accompany all confirmed reservations.

The best way to see the Soviet Far East

The Soviet Far East had been off limits to Western visitors since the 1930s, but no longer. Now you can visit this frontier land as a passenger on the **TransSiberian Express.** You board the train in Khabarovsk. From there, you cross the **Amur River,** travel across the **Olekminsky Range,** follow along the **Shilka River,** and then skirt the edge of the **Gobi Desert.** The next day, after crossing the **Yablonovy Range** at 9,000 feet, the TransSiberian Express enters **Siberia,** circling the southern shore of **Lake Baikal,** the largest freshwater lake in the world. The end of the line is **Irkutsk,** a city founded in 1661 by Cossack pioneers.

For more information, contact **Intourist,** *tel. (70-95)203-6962.*

The Best of China

China? There lies a sleeping giant. Let him sleep!
For when he wakes, he will move the world.
—*Napoleon*

The People's Republic of China (PRC), the largest country in the world, is as big as all the countries in Europe combined. Its civilization flourished when the Occident was struggling its way out of the Dark Ages. Lying on the world's largest continent, China faces the world's largest ocean, the Pacific. It has the world's tallest mountains, the Himalayas, and the world's second-largest metropolitan area, Shanghai; and it controls the world's highest city, Lhasa, in Tibet.

Although 98% of China's population is made up of Han people, the remaining 2% contains nearly 50 million members of minority groups. Tibetans, in their land of monasteries above the clouds, consider the Dalai Lama the head of the Buddhist religion; Mongolian horsemen roam the Gobi Desert; Chinese Muslims (Hui) live in the north; the Miao and Dai people in the south are related to hill tribes of Southeast Asia.

(Note: When reading through this chapter, keep in mind that prices may have changed since the time of publication. Prices in China today are fluctuating wildly.)

The best of Beijing

Beijing (Peking), one of the oldest cities in the world, has been the capital of China for 700 years. People have been living in this area for at least 50,000 years. Peking man, a fossil found in 1918 in a village southwest of Beijing, is one of the oldest relics of early man yet found.

Situated at the end of the route followed by camel caravans for centuries, Beijing is the site of many cities that have come and gone. Kublai Khan built his palace here and called the city Ta-tu (Great Capital). The northern part of the city has remnants of the old Mongol town visited by Marco Polo.

Beijing houses some of the greatest man-made wonders in the world. The Emperor's

253

Forbidden City in the heart of Beijing and the Great Wall on the outskirts of the city are the most notable attractions.

The Forbidden City

The **Forbidden City**, where the emperor of China once lived, is no longer barred to common man. Hundreds pass through the palace museum every day, gaping at the royal opulence. Surrounded by red brick walls and guarded by tile-roofed towers, the palace was built by Ming Emperor Yung Lo in the early 15th century and covers nearly 250 acres. For five centuries, China was ruled from here by the emperor, who was considered the son of heaven. His every wish was granted. His meals were prepared by 5,000 to 6,000 cooks, and concubines, eunuchs, court favorites, and entertainers were kept here.

Surrounded by 35-foot walls and a wide moat, the city contains six palaces, all roofed in yellow tile (yellow was the imperial color), and many gardens and pavilions. See the apartments of the emperor, the empress dowager, and the concubines; the halls of Supreme Harmony, Perfect Harmony, and the Preservation of Harmony; the temples; the libraries; and the art collection. Altogether, the rooms number 9,000.

The best way to prepare yourself for touring the palace is to see Bernardo Bertolucci's film *The Last Emperor*, which tells the sad story of China's last ruler, who was, as a child, virtually a prisoner in the palace.

The world's largest public square

Tiananmen Square (the Square of Heavenly Peace), where Mao Zedong proclaimed the People's Republic of China in 1949, is the largest public square in the world, covering 100 acres and capable of holding 1 million people. As they have for centuries, the Chinese people come to hear government proclamations and to rally and demonstrate.

Ironically, thousands of students demonstrating here, in the Square of Heavenly Peace, were killed in June 1989.

The square is bounded to the west by the Great Hall of the People, which contains a 328-foot-long marble hall and reception rooms where diplomatic meetings are held; to the east by the Museum of Chinese History and the Museum of the Chinese Revolution; to the north by the Tiananmen Gate to the Imperial City, built in 1417 and hung with a portrait of Mao Zedong; and to the south by the Quianmen gate, built in the 15th century. In the center is the 120-foot Monument to the People's Heroes, an obelisk depicting scenes from the revolution and inscribed with quotations by Mao Zedong and Zha En Lai.

Kite flying in the square is a popular pastime and a good way to meet locals. You can buy a colorful Chinese kite in any Friendship Store (government stores for tourists)—an exotic souvenir, unless it gets tangled in the gates to the Imperial Palace.

The most beautiful temple

The blue **Tiantan** (Temple of Heaven), built in the 15th century, is the finest example of Chinese architecture. Actually a complex of buildings, the temple is surrounded by a walled park. The most beautiful building within the complex is the Qi Nian Dian (Hall of Prayer for Good Harvest), set on three marble terraces, each with a 36-foot balustrade, connected to one another by eight flights of stairs. Supported by 28 columns and topped by 50,000 glazed blue tiles, the 123-foot hall was built of wood with no nails. Blue-roofed pavilions flank the temple.

Nearby is the **Huan Qiu Tan** (Round Altar), where each year for centuries on Dec. 20 (the day before the winter solstice), the emperor made a mysterious animal sacrifice that determined the destiny of the nation. The altar is made up of three terraces, each surrounded by a white marble balustrade with 360 pillars.

Beijing's best park

The most famous of Beijing's many parks is **Beihai**, or North Lake, which has pagodas, formal gardens, and three lakes. Created in A.D. 300, the park is the best-preserved ancient garden in China. Young people row on the lakes and whisper sweet nothings on the shores. Closed during the Cultural Revolution, the park reopened 10 years ago.

In the middle of Beihai is an island called **Qionghua**, which is crowned by a Tibetan-style white dagoba (a shrine for sacred relics) built in 1651 to commemorate the visit of a Dalai Lama. The view from the dagoba takes in the park and most of the city. The beautiful **Zhichu Qiao** (Bridge of Perfect Wisdom) leads to the island.

The empress dowager's favorite palace

Yiheyuan (the Summer Palace) on the outskirts of Beijing was the extravagant summer retreat of the infamous Empress Dowager Ci Xi. Located in the Haidian district and surrounded by a walled 692-acre park, the palace was built in 1888 to replace an older and supposedly more beautiful palace that was destroyed by British and French troops in 1860. (All that remains of the original are a marble arch, pillars, and a wall.) The existing palace, too, was burned by Western troops, during the Boxer Rebellion in 1900, but it was restored a few years later.

Stroll along the **Long Corridor**, bordering the lake and exquisitely painted with scenes from Chinese mythology. Visit the royal apartments, which contain jewel-encrusted furniture and beautiful works of art. Climb **Longevity Hill**, at the heart of the palace.

The best undiscovered sights

The **Gulou** (Drum Tower), *Drum Tower Street,* near Shichahai Lake in northern Beijing, is a 15th-century structure in brick and wood, so named because a drum was beaten here to summon officials to audiences with the emperor. For some unknown reason, it is seldom visited by tourists.

Just 100 yards behind is the **Zhonglou** (Bell Tower), similar in design, built about 1745. The night watch announced the hour from here until 1924.

Between the two towers is a charming maze of residential streets that feel like they belong more in a small village than a large city. The stone houses here are tightly packed, topped with tiled roofs, and entered through doors that are thick, old, and decorated with iron. Clay walls surround courtyards that are broken by doors at irregular intervals. The area is safe at any hour, but you may get lost and have trouble finding someone who speaks English and can set you back on the right trail.

Another neighborhood worth exploring is a tangle of streets off **Wangfujing**, one of the main shopping streets, where Manchu nobility once lived. The formidable Empress Dowager Ci Xi was raised in one of the mansions on Xila Hatung. Another landmark in the neighborhood is the **East Church**, built in 1666 by the Jesuits. Pao Fa Hatung is lined with remnants of the **Fa Hua Si Temple** (Temple of Buddha's Glory), built in the 15th century. You can see the original walls, entry gates, and a small antechamber. The rest is gone.

Beijing's best shopping

The easiest place to shop in Beijing is the government-run **Friendship Store**, *Jianguomenwai Avenue,* the largest in China. It has just about anything you could want (jade, ivory, silk hangings, furniture, paintings, cloisonné, carpets, and handicrafts). It is the only place in Beijing that will take care of shipping (which is expensive) and customs.

However, it is more fun to shop at Beijing's **street bazaars**. The most famous is **Donghuamen**, *Wangfujing Street,* behind the Guoji (Beijing) Hotel. Near the Temple of Heaven is the Tan Chiao Bazaar, where fresh fish and vegetables are sold to throngs of people while storytellers, musicians, and street performers entertain.

Wangfujing, around the corner from the Beijing Hotel, is the city's main shopping district. In addition to **Baihuo Dalou**, the main department store, *255 Wangfujing St.,* which is the largest and best-stocked store in Beijing, the neighborhood has scores of little specialty shops.

Zhongguo Pihuo Fuzhuangdian (the China Fur and Leather Clothing Store), *192 Wangfujing St.*, has ready-made fur and leather coats, jackets, hats, and gloves and will make clothing to order as well. **Capital Medicine Shop**, *136 Wangfujing St.*, sells traditional Chinese medicines.

Chinese wind instruments are sold at the **Musical Instruments Store**, *231 Wangfujing St.*, and personalized Chinese stone seals are made at **Wangfujing Kezi Menshibu** (the Wangfujing Seal-Engraving Store), *261 Wangfujing St.* Chinese scrolls and tomb rubbings can be purchased at **The Arts Store**, *265 Wangfujing St.*

Buying antiques in China is a tricky business. Government regulations are strict. Only those items with proper invoice papers and red government seals of approval can be taken out of China.

If you feel up to dealing with the red tape, quite a few shops in China carry fine antiques. In Beijing, the best shops are on **Liulichang**, especially numbers 70 and 80. Here, collectors can find fine porcelain, jade, and wood carvings.

The best silk bazaar

The **Beijing Silk Market** is located in an alley leading from the Friendship Store to the Jianguomenwai Embassy compound. It is a free market run by entrepreneurs who rent space and pay taxes. All goods sold here are made for export to the United States, Germany, and Japan—but if you buy them here, you'll pay a fraction of what you would pay after export. Goods for sale include down ski jackets, silk coats, linens, quilts, lingerie, and name-brand silk clothing. Most stall owners speak at least some English.

The Great Wall

Forty-six miles from Beijing is the **Great Wall**, stretching nearly 4,000 miles through the hills of northern China. It is the only man-made structure that the astronauts have been able to see from the moon. Construction on most of the wall began in 403 B.C. and continued until 206 B.C. Thousands of men, many political prisoners, carried the stones and dirt that make up the gigantic defense. Some of their bodies are buried inside. Once 6,000 miles long, much of the wall has been destroyed.

The section most visited is at **Badaling**, northwest of Beijing, which was constructed during the Ming dynasty (1368-1644). You can walk along the top—it is 18 feet wide and 21 feet tall. Look through the slots in the wall along the top and imagine the terrible battles that once raged against the barbarians from the north. Special trains and buses connect Beijing and the Great Wall.

To avoid all the tourists who gather at Badaling, go a bit farther afield to **Mutianyu**, where a newly restored section of the wall opened in 1986. A great fort with 22 watchtowers was built along this stretch. From the top, you'll have a view of the surrounding mountain slopes, forests, and the town of Mutianyu. To get to Mutianyu, hire a car or take the Dongzhimen Long Distance Bus Line. (Tickets must be purchased one day in advance.)

The Ming tombs

On the way to the Great Wall are the **Ming tombs**, where 13 of the 16 Ming emperors chose to be buried. **Shisanling**, the peaceful valley where the tombs are located, was chosen by the rulers because the winds and the water level ensured that only good spirits wandered the area.

The road to the tombs, known as the **Sacred Way**, is lined with 24 immense statues: 12 animals, real and mythical, and 12 mandarins in ceremonial dress. One of the Qing emperors is said to have wanted to take the statues to line the road to his own tomb. He abandoned the plan after dreaming that the statues are forever loyal to the Ming dynasty and that if he should move them an evil wind would blow across the capital.

Only two of the tombs have been excavated, those of Chang Ling and Ding Ling. The best-preserved and largest tomb is that of Chang Ling (the burial name for Yong Le), who died in 1424. It is entered through a red gate that opens into a courtyard. Another gate leads into a second courtyard, where the marble **Ling En Dian** (Hall of Eminent Favors) is supported by 32 giant tree columns. To get to the sepulcher, you must continue into a third courtyard.

The tomb of Ding Ling (the burial name for Emperor Wan Li) was the first to be excavated. A deep marble vault four stories underground contains the coffins of Ding and two of his wives, who were buried here in 1620. A bronze lion and gigantic marble doors guard the tomb. Inside are the three coffins and 26 chests filled with jewelry.

Beijing's best restaurants

Fang Shan (Imitation Imperial) is *the* restaurant in Beihai Park. The goal of the chefs, who are said to have studied with the last empress's chefs, is to recreate dishes served to the royal families of the past. The restaurant is set on the shores of North Lake. It can be difficult to get reservations.

On the grounds of the Summer Palace, on Longevity Hill overlooking Kunming Lake, is **Ting Li Guan** (Listening to the Orioles Pavilion). This restaurant features dumplings, velvet chicken, and other northern dishes. The **Sick Duck**, *13 Shuaifuyuan* (one block off Wangfujing), takes its name from a nearby hospital, not from the condition of its poultry. It is comfortable and close to the Beijing Hotel.

Beijing's best hotels

The **Beijing Hotel**, *33 East Chang'an Avenue and Wangfujing Street; tel. (86-1)5137766*, takes the honorable first position. Not too long ago, it was the only good place in Beijing, and it's still the most exclusive. Foreigners cannot book rooms directly—you must go through an influential Chinese contact. Rooms are modern and spacious, many with color televisions, radios, and refrigerators. Some have balconies with views of the Forbidden City. A double room is $40 to $65.

Xiang Shan (the Fragrant Hills), *Xiangshan Park, Haidian District; tel. (86-1)2565544*, a 40-minute drive outside town and halfway to the Great Wall, was designed by the famous Chinese-American architect I.M. Pei. Jackie Kennedy was one of the hotel's first guests.

A grand, white fortress of a place, Xiang Shan has beautifully landscaped gardens and skillfully lit rooms. Double beds (an unusual feature in Chinese hotels), an outdoor swimming pool, and a health club are special features. While the Fragrant Hills is not conveniently located if you want to visit Beijing every day, it is surrounded by lovely countryside and situated near little-known shrines and monuments. For this reason, it may be the best place to stay on your *second* trip to Beijing. A double room is $60.

Zhu Yuan (Bamboo Garden Hotel), *24 Xiaoshiqiao, Jiugulou Street; tel. (86-1)444661*, in an attractive residential neighborhood in the northern section of the city, has bamboo gardens, rookeries, air conditioning, and color televisions. It is near the Drum Tower and was once home to Kang Sheng, one of the Gang of Four. A double room is $40.

The **Holiday Inn Lido Beijing**, *Jichang and Jiang Tai roads; tel. (86-1)5006688*, is Beijing's version of an American resort hotel. It has a bowling alley, restaurants and lounges, a health club, a swimming pool, and rooms with air conditioning, private bathrooms, color televisions, and direct-dial telephones. While it is comfortable, the Lido is outside town on the road to the airport. Whoever chose the color combinations must have been colorblind (mustard yellow and pea green). A double room is $45 to $115.

The **Shangri-La Hotel**, *29 Zizhuyuan Road; tel. (1)8412211*, is another Western-style luxury hotel. It has an extensive health center with a pool, a sauna, a solarium, a squash court, and tennis courts. The business center is also well-developed, with meeting facilities of up to 1,000. A double room is $100 to $180; suites start at $300.

The best of Guangzhou

Still known to most English-speaking people as Canton, **Guangzhou** is a popular point of entry for foreign tourists visiting China—it is only three hours from Hong Kong by train. (By the way, you can buy lovely pure silk Chinese scarves on the Guangzhou train from Hong Kong for a mere $2.)

Unlike the rest of China, which stayed free of outside influence until well into the 19th century, Guangzhou began dealing with foreign traders in A.D. 714. Thus, a foreigner has never been much of a rarity here. Besides Shenzhen, China's Special Economic Zone, Guangzhou is the most capitalist (and Western-influenced) city in China.

Early on, the Chinese government thought it best to canton the barbarians, as foreign traders were known, so they wouldn't corrupt the rest of the kingdom—hence, the name Canton. Arab, Portuguese, English, French, and American traders who sailed up the Pearl River were isolated and cantoned in their own areas. After their victory in the First Opium War, the Europeans were given an island in the Pearl River off Canton's waterfront, called **Shamian.** French and Victorian buildings still can be seen here.

Another result of foreign influence: Guangzhou has one of China's largest Muslim communities and the nation's oldest mosque, dating from A.D. 627.

This old city remains a trading capital, and the mixture of local and foreign influences is as exotic today as it must have been to residents and traders of the Middle Ages.

Top sights

Zhenhailou (Tower Overlooking the Sea), a five-story red pagoda built in 1380 on the highest hill in Yuexiu Park, was originally a temple. Today it is the Guangdong Historical Museum—fitting, considering the pagoda's involvement in Guangzhou's history. It served as a watchtower during the Opium War, when it was seized by French and British troops, and again during the 1911 revolution.

If you climb all the way to the top of the tower, you will be rewarded with a cup of green tea and a view of the park and the city. The museum's exhibits are displayed in chronological order from prehistoric times to the modern day.

The graceful **Five Goats Statue,** a reminder of Guangzhou's mythical beginnings, is also in Yuexiu Park. According to legend, the city was founded by five gods bearing stalks of rice who rode to earth on five goats, the rice symbolizing a promise that the city would never go hungry. (That promise wasn't kept.) Guangzhou is still known as Yangcheng, or Goat City.

Cultural Park, near the Pearl River, covers 20 acres and includes an aquarium, an opera house, a concert hall, seven exhibition halls, three television screens for the public, two open-air theaters, a roller-skating rink, a teahouse, a pingpong area, and flower gardens.

Chen Clan Academy, a 19th-century compound, is one of the world's best examples of late imperial southern Chinese architecture. The roof and walls are decorated with terra-cotta sculptures, and the windows, doors, columns, and roof beams are carved. This family-run school of Confucian studies was built around an ancestral temple, where you still can see an altar and a shrine.

At the Chen Clan Academy, you can buy bottles, decorated inside with Shantou paintings, a characteristic art form of southern China. These tiny glass bottles, about 3 inches high, are elegant and antique in style. Pictures are drawn within the bottles, which have pea-sized mouths. Fine scenery, all sorts of characters, flowers, birds, insects, and fish are painted on the inside surface. Golden patterns on the outside surfaces of the bottles enhance their beauty. Each sells for a mere $20. These bottles are appreciable art treasures, seldom seen except in museums.

China's largest garden

The largest garden in China, the **South China Botanical Gardens,** is found just northeast of Guangzhou. Covering 750 lush acres, it boasts one of the best botanical collections anywhere in the world.

The oldest mosque and the best cathedral

Foreign visitors brought foreign religions to Guangzhou, and, as a result, the city has two buildings that may seem out of place in a country with a Buddhist past and a Communist present. On Zhongshan Road, near the intersection with Haizhu Road, is the **Huaisheng Mosque**, the oldest in China. It was built in A.D. 627 by an uncle of the prophet Muhammed, who is said to have brought the first Koran to China. It is now the mosque of China's largest Muslim community, which is estimated at 4,000. On the Yide Road, near the popular Renmin Daxia Hotel, is a Gothic-style cathedral that was designed by the French architect Guillemin and built in 1860. During the Cultural Revolution, this building was used as a warehouse; however, it was renovated and reconsecrated in 1979 and now holds regular Sunday services.

The best shopping

International traders still flock to Guangzhou for the **Chinese Export Commodities Fair**, held Oct. 15-30 and April 15-30 in the big exhibition hall near the Dong Fang Hotel.

If you are interested in more modest retail purchases, wander along **Renmin Road**, home of the Nanfang department store complex, the biggest in the city. Number 8 is a well-stocked poster store, number 14 is a tea shop, number 20 is a housewares store, and number 60 is a barbershop that brings a bit of the American West to Southeast Asia. You can unearth fine antiques on **Hongshu Road**, in an antiques warehouse that has just about anything you could want.

While shopping, stop for a snack at the most popular dumpling shop in town, the **Nanfang**, *number 35*.

The world's most exotic market

The **Quingping Market**, just over the bridge from Shamian Island, has an incredible assortment of animals intended for the table. It is divided into two sections: one for vendors of traditional Chinese medicines and one for vendors of produce, meats, and live animals to be butchered. Dogs hang from hooks. Kittens are sold by the pound. Dead rats are sold as food. Wild boars are caged. Owls, mice, and snakes await slaughter.

Some of the beasts at this market are seen in the West only in zoos. The pangolin, for example, is on the endangered species list. Small, Bambi-like deer are slaughtered before your eyes. And internal organs you have never heard of are for sale.

China's best food

Guangzhou's cuisine is the best in China and the best-known in the West, where Cantonese restaurants are common. However, exported Cantonese cuisine is not the real thing. In Canton, the ingredients are exotic, including snake, dog, frogs, and rats. The people of Guangzhou have an expression that explains, "The things flying in the sky, except the planes, can be eaten. The things on the ground with four legs, except the tables, can be eaten."

If you are feeling adventurous enough to try monkey brain (more power to you!), try **She Canguan**, *41 Jianglan Lu*. Guangzhou's most palatable contribution to the world is *dim sum*, or *dyan syin*, a Chinese brunch that consists of a long series of small courses (sometimes 10 or more), served in the course of one or two hours. Most of the dishes are different varieties of dumplings filled with pork, seafood, or vegetables.

Banxi, *East Xiangyang Road*, is Guangzhou's biggest and best *dim sum* restaurant. **Yuyuan**, *90 S. Liwan Road*, is also good. Try the chicken steamed in Maotai and the crab-paste dumplings. Or, if you prefer atmosphere, eat at **Nanyuan**, *120 Qianjin Road;* it offers dining in a splendid garden.

The best hotels
The **White Swan Hotel**, *1 South St., Nol Shaman Island; tel. (86-20)886968*, was China's first five-star hotel. Rooms are decorated in jade-colored silk and filled with walnut furniture. The hotel opened in early 1983 and quickly distinguished itself with its many guest services (including a 24-hour laundry), its 30 dining rooms, its trilingual staff, and its astounding variety of fitness activities. The hotel also offers its guests the services of a tiny but strong Chinese masseusse, who will give you a great acupressure massage, including walking on your back, for $20 an hour.

The lobby is one of the most beautiful anywhere. And the hotel has reasonably priced shops selling Chinese silk rugs, hand-painted screens, gigantic carved jade boats, and silk paintings. The building is situated on Shamian Island in the Pearl River, where a legendary hero is said to have been spirited away by a white swan. Free shuttle service is available to the hotel from the train station. A double room is $60 to $150.

The most romantic temporary address in Guangzhou is the **Dong Fang Hotel**, *120 Liuhua Road; tel. (86-20)669900*—not so much for its appearance, which is strictly Soviet revival, but for its inhabitants. Journalists, consular personnel, and powerful international businessmen have stayed in the rooms here. The dining room serves everything from Wiener schnitzel to Indian curries, from Japanese tempura to American apple pie. A double room starts at $50.

Two of China's most luxurious hotels are outside Guangzhou, on the slopes of Baiyun (White Cloud Mountain): the **Shanzhuang** and the **Shuangxi**. Guests stay in large villas with sunken baths, private gardens, and lovely sitting rooms. Chinese government officials and high-ranking foreigners are among the guests.

The best side trips from Guangzhou
Nine miles from Guangzhou is **Bai Yun Shan**, which rises 1,400 feet and has a panoramic view of the city, the countryside, and the river. At the top are teahouses and pavilions, where you can recover from the six-hour climb. Don't stray from marked paths—the government doesn't want Americans getting too close to the nearby defense installations.

China's best mineral springs are in **Conghua**, 50 miles north of Guangzhou. The eight springs are about 104 degrees Fahrenheit and are said to cure chronic ailments. They are worth visiting even if you feel fine just for the views—they are surrounded by mountains, lichee orchards, plum trees, and bamboo groves.

Zixingyan (Seven Star Crags) is a series of natural rock towers connected by arched bridges and little pathways. Five small lakes and several caves lie in the shadow of traditional pavilions, which provide shelter. You can get to Zixingyan by bus or taxi in three hours.

Shanghai: China's largest city
Shanghai was the most powerful city in China before the Communists took over in 1949. Merely a fishing village in the 17th century, it gained its wealth from trade as a treaty port opened by the Europeans during the Opium Wars. Controlled by the British from 1842 until 1949, Shanghai still has a Western air and has been compared to New York and Rome. Before the Chinese Revolution, it had a lively stock market and great wealth.

Today, Shanghai is one of the largest cities in the world—and, with more than 15,000 coal-burning factories, the most polluted. Until a few years ago, it was considered China's most important city economically. (Now Shenzhen has China's—and the world's—fastest-growing economy.) Covering 2,344 square miles, metropolitan Shanghai is striving to catch up with high growth rates in the south. Still, Shanghai remains China's most cosmopolitan city.

The prettiest neighborhood
Shanghai's most charming corner is **Old Town**, the Chinese ghetto during the British

occupation. Between Jinling, Renmin, and Zhonghua roads are narrow streets, thatched huts, tiny shops, and outdoor markets with piles of fresh produce. In the northeast section of Old Town is a bazaar where you can buy beautifully carved walking sticks and traditional Chinese handicrafts. A little farther north are the Temple of the Town Gods and the Garden of the Purple Clouds of Autumn. Be careful; it's easy to get lost in this maze.

Forget the fancy restaurants and eat in the area's little food shops. (But don't drink the water.) Chinese lunchtime fare is cheap and fun to eat.

The best opium dens and brothels

Until 1949, the area west of People's Park, off Fuzhou Road, was the heart of Shanghai's world-famous red-light district known as **Blood Alley**. Before it was cleared out, it was inhabited by thousands of opium addicts and prostitutes. Liberation Lane alone, then known as Meet-With-Happiness Lane, had 34 brothels worked by more than 1,000 women. From 1949 until 1954, the brothels and opium dens were closed, the prostitutes given new work and new identities, and the addicts detoxified.

Yu Yuan: the happiest garden

At the heart of Old Town is **Yu Yuan Garden** (Garden of Happiness), built in 1577 by a city official as a peaceful retreat for his aging father. It includes more than 30 halls and pavilions, all with charming names: Pavilion for Paying Reverence to Weaving, Fairyland of Happiness, Tower for Observing Waves, and Tower for Appreciating the Moon. A tall, white brick wall topped with stone dragons divides the garden into three separate areas. Each section is designed to create the illusion of space and depth via artificial hills, ponds, bridges, and miniature gardens. A small lake at the center of the garden is crossed by zigzag bridges and bordered by teahouses and pavilions. The scene inspired the famous Blue Willow china pattern.

When you tire of the crowds in Yu Yuan Garden, take a break at **Wuxing Ting** (Five-Star Pavilion), a teahouse just opposite the garden.

The Temple of the Town Gods

Not far from Yu Yuan is **Cheng Huang Miao** (Temple of the Town Gods), devoted, as its name implies, to the ancient town gods. Once, every Chinese town had such a temple. This is one of the few that remain. Behind the temple is a garden with a lake, pavilions, and artificial hills. **Qiu Xia Pu** (the Garden of the Purple Clouds of Autumn) was laid out during the Ming dynasty.

The liveliest promenade

The most delightful place to stroll in Shanghai is **Wai Tan** (the Bund), the area around Zhongshan Park, Zhongshan Road, and the Wusong River, near Old Town. The park is green with shade trees and decorated with rock and flower gardens. During the British occupation, the Chinese were forbidden to be in this area. The tall buildings that line the Bund once housed international banks and corporations; now they house the Bank of China and government offices.

Evening is the best time to stroll along the Bund, when city lights reflect in the water. If you are energetic, come here in the morning and join the locals in their daily Tai Chi Quan exercises.

China's best art collection

The three stories of the **Shanghai Museum of Art and History**, *Henan Road*, house the finest art collection in China. The first floor has bronzes from the Shang and Western Zhou dynasties (1523 B.C.until 771 B.C.). The most interesting objects are the instruments of torture. The second floor has ceramics from the Neolithic era to the present, including life-size terra-cotta statues of warriors and a horse from Emperor Qin Shi Huangdi's tomb in Xi'an. Scrolls from the Tang, Song, Yuan, Ming, and Quing dynasties are kept on the third floor, where good reproductions are sold.

The best Buddhas
The **Jade Buddha Temple**, in northwest Shanghai, has two statues of Buddha, each carved out of a single piece of white jade. They were brought by a monk to China from Burma in 1890. Several other statues fill the halls of the temple. Twenty-four monks still live here.

The oldest and biggest temple
Shanghai's oldest and largest temple is **Longhua**, in the southern suburbs. Built before A.D. 687, it has four main halls, drum and bell towers, and a seven-story pagoda next door. The best time to see the temple and pagoda is early spring, when the peach trees blossom.

The best way to meet the people
If you wander the back streets of Shanghai and take public transportation rather than taxis, you will get a glimpse of the lives of the locals. The masses of Shanghai live in tiny, unheated one-story apartments. It's common for a middle-class family to live in two rooms and share cooking and washing facilities with six other families. Because their homes are so small, most people's daily lives take place outdoors, regardless of temperature: morning ablutions in icy water, Tai Chi Quan exercises, cooking, haircuts, pingpong, and card games.

The best entertainment
The **Shanghai Acrobatic Theater**, *400 Nanjing Xi Lu; tel. (86-21)564051,* presents highly skilled and exciting shows every day except Tuesday. You should see this impressive show, but realize that it is a production intended entirely for tourists and part of every package tour in the city.

The best undiscovered entertainment
The best place to people-watch and to listen to great jazz is the nightclub in the Peace Hotel. The band members play as if they've been playing together forever. The music is good and the atmosphere unbeatable. You can get the band to play your favorite tunes all night—just buy them a carton of Marlboro cigarettes.

The most exotic foods
Food is sold helter-skelter on the streets of Shanghai. Shortly before New Year's, the sidewalks are piled with carcasses of pigs ready for the butcher. The below-freezing temperatures keep the meat from spoiling. At New Year's, men sell pancakes cooked over barrel stoves in the streets and set out chickens in cages or baskets of eggs.

Snake is a specialty. Customers choose their favorite snakes from squirming masses on the snakemongers' tabletops. Restaurants devoted exclusively to this delicacy are located throughout Shanghai.

The best Shanghai cuisine
Shanghai has more than 600 restaurants serving 14 kinds of regional foods. The best place to look for restaurants serving regional specialties is along **Nanjing Dong Road.**

The best place for authentic Shanghai cuisine is **Lao Fandian Restaurant,** *242 Fuyou Road.* In the heart of the Old City, this is a good place to stop after a day's sightseeing. Another good place for local fare is **Laozhengxing** (Old Prosperity) **Restaurant,** *566 Jinjiang Road,* a small, well-respected place famous for its turtle, crab, and fish.

If you tire of the exotic fare, take refuge at the Peace Hotel's dining room, which has the best cream puffs in China.

The best hotels

The **Heping** (Peace) **Hotel** (formerly the Cathay), *20 Nanjing Road East near the Bund; tel. (86-21)3211244,* is the aging bastion of the cosmopolitan life Shanghai once enjoyed. Its high ceilings, spacious 1930s-style suites with attached servants' rooms, and gilded dining room once hosted Chinese and European guests. A double room is $45 to $56.

Another old hotel, the **Jinjiang**, *59 Maoming Road; tel. (86-21)2582582,* is in a group of mansions surrounded by a wall in the French Quarter. The grounds are beautifully landscaped. This is where Richard Nixon and Zha En Lai signed the Shanghai Communiqué in 1972, opening the door between the West and China. A double room is $37 to $53.

While the rooms at the **Shanghai Mansions Hotel**, *20 Suzou North Road; tel. (86-21)246260,* are nothing special, the suites are spectacular, some with grand pianos and private balconies. The view from the rooftop terrace is panoramic. The one drawback is that at night the horns of river barges can be startling.

One of the two best *new* hotels in Shanghai is the **Hua Ting Sheraton**, *1200 Cao Xi Bei Lu; tel. (86-21)38-6000,* which offers modern luxury and superior service. Facilities include a tennis court, swimming pool, and health club, as well as an excellent business center. The other good new hotel is the **Shanghai Hilton International**, *250 Huashan Road; tel. (86-21)56-3343,* which also offers deluxe modern facilities, including eight restaurants.

Shenzhen—the most open door in China

Shenzhen, the coastal region just across the border from Hong Kong, is China's most successful economic experiment. This Special Economic Zone, as it is known, is rapidly becoming a thriving metropolis.

The best miniature recreation of a place

Shenzhen is home to one of the best sites in China: **Splendid Miniature China**, a huge park where all of China is laid out in miniature. It displays models of the best of China, including the Imperial Palace in Beijing (China's largest), Zhaozhou Bridge in Hebei (the most ancient stone arch bridge), the Ancient Star Observatory in Beijing (the oldest astronomical observatory), the Great Wall, and the terra-cotta soldiers and horses near Xi'an.

In most any other country in the world, we would tell you to shy away from a splendid miniature recreation of the place. Tourist trap, we'd warn. But China is a special case. Travel here is so difficult and slowgoing that most travelers would never be able to see everything this ancient country has to offer.

Admission is $11. For more information, contact **China Travel Service Ltd.**, *21st Floor, CTS House, 78-83 Connaught Road, Central, Hong Kong; tel. (852)853-3888; fax (852)8541383,* or the **Shenzhen Splendid China Development Company Ltd.**, *Overseas Chinese Town, Shenzhen Special Economic Zone, People's Republic of China.*

Shenzhen's best hotel

As Shenzhen struggles to transform itself into a modern metropolis, beautiful hotels are springing up where chicken coops and rice paddies stood only a few years ago. One of the newest and finest is the **Forum**, *67 Heping Road, Shenzhen, Guangdong Province, People's Republic of China; tel. (86-755)586-333; fax (86-755)561-700.* It has seven restaurants, comfortable rooms, and 24-hour room service.

Hangzhou: the best silks and embroideries

Hangzhou, which lies on the startlingly beautiful Xi Hu (West Lake), is known for its silks, embroideries, tea, and gourmet restaurants. You can watch silk being made at the

Hangzhou Silk Dyeing and Printing Mill, where nearly 5,000 workers produce silk by reeling fibers off silkworm cocoons and then print designs on the finished fabric. Mulberry trees, where silkworm cocoons are found, grow in profusion in the surrounding countryside.

Longjing (Dragon Well) tea is picked and dried at the **West Lake People's Commune,** where you can watch the work or try your hand at tea-leaf picking.

Four islands with pavilions and temples float in West Lake. The largest and most beautiful is **Gu Shan** (Solitary Hill) in the northwest. The second largest, **Three Pools Mirroring the Moon,** is beautiful on moonlit nights, when the pagodas along the water, lit with candles and sealed with thin paper, look like moons on the water.

Suzhou, the Venice of China

With its maze of canals bordered by small whitewashed houses and weeping willows, **Suzhou** is the most romantic town in China. Venetian Marco Polo felt at home here. And China's most famous romantic novel, *The Dream of the Red Chamber,* is set in a Suzhou mansion. Gnarled sycamore branches bend low over the town's narrow cobblestoned streets, where high walls shield private gardens.

Suzhou's other claims to fame are its gardens—150 in all. The two loveliest are **Zhuozhengyuan** (the Humble Administrator's Garden) and **Liuyuan** (the Tarrying Garden), both of which have all the elements of traditional Chinese gardens: pavilions, ponds, bridges, rock sculptures, and temples. They are two of China's four nationally protected gardens (the other two being the Summer Palace in Beijing and the Imperial Mountain Resort in Changde).

Most of Suzhou's shops are grouped close together in the downtown area. One of the best places to shop is the Friendship Store, which caters exclusively to foreigners. Here you find a large and varied selection of silk (Suzhou is known for the quality of its silk), dry goods, and clothing. Collectors will drool over the extensive selection of unusual Chinese antiques. Local handicrafts also are featured, including fragrant sandalwood fans and double-faced embroidery.

Guilin and the Li River: beauty defined

The sharp peaks so often depicted on Chinese scrolls exist in **Guilin,** known for its magnificent natural beauty. Set in the Karst Hills of southern China, Guilin has shrouded limestone peaks and subterranean caverns.

You can visit some of the spectacular caves in the hills around Guilin. Reed Flute Cave in the northwest suburbs was once a refuge for villagers escaping enemy armies and bandits. Inside is a grotto, **Shuijinggong** (Crystal Palace), that holds 1,000 people. A trail leads through the cave past stalactites and stalagmites, ending at a terrace with a view of the mountains, farms, and Li River.

A Stone Age matriarchal people lived in **Zengpiyan Cave,** where 14 human skeletons have been found, as well as skeletons of elephants, boar, and deer. The cave is open to visitors.

Seven Star Park contains six caves. The most famous is **Long Lin** (the Dragon Refuge Cave), which has walls carved with ancient inscriptions.

The best river cruise

The best way to see this region is to take a cruise on the **Li River.** As you float downriver, look for Elephant Trunk Hill, Old Man Mountain, Folded Brocade Hill, and Crescent Moon Hill. You'll be able to recognize each by its name.

You will pass lush tropical scenery—fruit trees, bamboo groves, sugarcane, and rice paddies—as well as a 1,300-year-old banyan tree.

Boats leave at 7:30 or 8:30 a.m., depending on the season, and sail for five hours, docking for a time at a small village called Yangdi, at the base of two mountains. This is a good place to shop. Local peasants meet the boat, anxious to sell their produce and handicrafts, at bargain prices.

For more information on Li River boat cruises, stop by the **Tourist Office**, *14 Ronghu Bei Road, Guilin.*

The best of the black market

Because of the increasing number of tourists, Guilin is the heart of a flourishing black market in currency, one that is rapidly spreading to every corner of the PRC. This black market is a boon to travelers, who, in many cases, are required to pay a higher rate than the locals for the same services.

Zhongshan Lu, Guilin's main commercial thoroughfare, provides a substantial sidewalk trade in foreign exchange certificates (FECs), which are bank notes given to foreigners when they convert their home currencies. The whole dual-currency phenomenon is the result of the government's Friendship Stores, which accept only FECs. The Chinese currency, the renminbi (RMB), is literally "people's money," the official coin of the realm. RMBs are negotiable everywhere except Friendship Stores.

To purchase rationed items, the Chinese are eager to sell their RMBs for FECs at a premium. The usual premium is 20%, but foreign students from the Beijing Language Institute report 50% premiums offered around the institution's gates, practically around the clock. On the streets the operation is fronted by "change-money" women, who approach anyone who looks like a Westerner, a Japanese, or an overseas Chinese with offers of *"fifaty-siksaty"* for FECs.

A word of caution: While selling FECs is a great way to stretch the budget, it's illegal. A little discretion will prevent hassles later. Everyone entering China is required to complete a customs declaration form stating the amount of hard currency brought into the country. On leaving China, you can convert any unused FECs to foreign currency. But don't exchange more FECs than you could have purchased legally with dollars. In other words, you don't show a profit.

Xi'an: once the world's largest city

Once the largest city in the world, **Xi'an,** in north central China, is filled with archeological wonders. The most famous is the recently discovered tomb of China's first emperor, Qin Shi Huangdi, which is guarded by 8,000 life-size terra-cotta soldiers.

Chang An, as the city was known in ancient times, was the capital of 11 dynasties, and the hills to the north of the city are filled with ancient tombs. Qin Shi Huang Di, who completed the Great Wall in the third century B.C., chose Xi'an as his capital. Under the Tang dynasty, from the seventh through the 10th centuries, it became the largest city in the world, with a population of about 1 million.

Today, the masses are returning to Xi'an, this time as tourists. In fact, more foreign visitors are appearing in the city than at any time since the eighth century.

While Xi'an is an industrial city congested with throngs of bicyclists, remnants of the city's loftier past remain. A medieval city wall can be seen in places. Two pagodas, Big Wild Goose and Small Wild Goose, watch over the city from a distance. (The view from the top of Big Wild Goose takes in the city and the green fields beyond.) And the city museum has the Forest of Steles, 1,000 standing stone tablets inscribed with ancient poems, essays, and images.

Xi'an has a large Muslim population and a functioning **Great Mosque,** *Huajue Xiang Road,* founded in A.D. 742. This, too, is a remnant of the city's past, when trade routes from all over the world led here. The best day to see the mosque is Friday, when about 2,000 Chinese Muslims arrive to pray in the splendid Ming dynasty prayer hall.

The best collection of ancient artifacts

The **Shaanxi Provincial Museum,** in a former Confucian temple in the south of the city, has the best collection of ancient artifacts in China. It is made up of three main buildings and three annexes and can hold 4,000 separate exhibitions. The Forest of Steles mentioned above is the museum's most important display. Also important is the stone menagerie, a collection of gigantic statues of real and imaginary animals that once guarded royal tombs.

Xi'an's top sights

At the center of Xi'an is a Ming dynasty bell tower that provides a convenient vantage point when scouting out street routes. Within sight is Xi'an's drum tower (inside is the city's best antique shop), marking the city's Hui, or Chinese Muslim, neighborhood. The aquiline features and bearded faces of the men here bear witness to their Arab ancestry. Arab and Persian merchants and mercenaries came to Chang An during the Tang dynasty (A.D. 618 to A.D. 907). The men of this neighborhood often congregate on the tranquil grounds of the Chinese-style mosque.

Throughout old Xi'an are many small shops offering handmade products. Follow the hammer taps to the tinsmith. Simple enamelware, army canteens, straw hats, oilcloth umbrellas, and chopsticks are some of the souvenirs you can buy here. Roast chicken is sold by Hui street peddlers, whose lamplit stands dot the street corners in the evenings.

Stop at the **Hua Xing Hot Springs**, outside town, where, according to a local joke, Chiang Kai-Shek left his dentures when running from the Chinese Red army. (He was arrested here in 1936.) The lush oasis was popular with the Chinese emperors, who bathed in the hot springs with their concubines and built a number of palaces in the area. After the court moved from Xi'an, the palaces were turned into a Taoist monastery.

Today, some of the buildings are used as a spa. The springs, discovered 2,800 years ago, have a temperature of 110 degrees Fahrenheit and are said to be curative.

The **Xing Jiao Temple**, located southeast of Xian, is the burial site of a Tang dynasty monk, the patron saint of the Silk Route. Xuan Zhuang traveled to India and back in A.D. 627 on a quest for Buddhist scriptures.

China's greatest archeological find

The 8,000 life-sized terra-cotta warriors found in Lingtong County, 20 miles east of Xi'an, are the 20th century's most exciting archeological find. In 1974, a group of well-diggers accidentally unearthed the ancient figures, which had stood guard at the tomb of Emperor Qin Shi Huangdi for 2,000 years.

The first emperor of China, Qin Shi Huangdi united warring states and completed the Great Wall, as protection against northern barbarians. His tomb is divided into three vaults. The first contains the infantry, each statue with an individualized face. The second and third contain an additional 2,000 figures of men, horses, and chariots. The emperor himself is buried a distance away, hidden in a maze of corridors and gates.

The emperor began to build the army of life-sized soldiers when he came to power at age 13. Over a period of 36 years, Qin conscripted three-quarters of a million countrymen to build 6,000 figures and ordered the statues to guard his tomb. (The model soldiers acted as substitutes for real soldiers, who in earlier times would have been buried with their emperor.)

The figures have stood for centuries 20 feet underground in an area the size of a football field. Most are lined up in marching positions as they would have been on a military campaign, while others are being pulled in chariots by teams of horses. The painted soldiers are modeled after Qin's live honor guard and carry real swords, spears, and crossbows, set to be triggered by invaders. Despite the decoys and booby traps, however, looters raided Qin's tomb four years after he died.

The best food and spirits

Sichuan Restaurant, *Jiefang Lu, near the train station; tel. (86-29)714863,* is Xi'an's most inviting restaurant. No less than 125 varieties of *jiaozi* (Chinese ravioli) are served here, with such names as Buddha's Claw and Make Money. Try the local liquor with your dinner, a pale spirit with the unappetizing name *Kueihua Chen Chew* (yellow osmanthus thick wine). This sweet but potent brew has a way of obliterating your memory.

China's best hotel

The 2-year-old **Golden Flower Hotel**, *8 Chang'le Road W., Xi'an, Shaanxi; tel. (86-29)332981*, offers rooms that are vast by present-day standards in China, well-lit, tastefully decorated, and equipped with two queen-sized beds, televisions, and video machines. The staff is well-trained and speaks English.

Facilities at the Golden Flower include secretarial and translation services, money changing, and a gift shop. The hotel runs tours and a fleet of taxis, and the concierge can negotiate restaurant reservations, prices, and menus. The hotel restaurant offers Sichuan and Shaanxi food. Double rooms are $135 a night. (Lower rates are available in the off-season.)

The most exotic destination: the Silk Route

The legendary **Silk Route** is far from silken. Ancient caravans following the route braved trackless deserts, towering mountains, and staggering distances to barter with foreign merchants or to spread new religions. Although some of this terrain is paved today, it remains a difficult passage. However, the payoff for undertaking the trip is great: the stark beauty of the landscape; the friendly, freedom-loving Uygurs; the colorful bazaars; and the incomparable religious art.

This 3,720-mile network of routes has spanned Eurasia since the second century B.C. Beginning at China's ancient capital Chang An (modern Xi'an), it snakes to Kashgar in western China and then splits. The main route climbs the Himalayas and continues west to Samarkand (the southern part of what used to be the Soviet Union), Persia (now Iran), and Rome. One alternate route dips down to Pakistan.

The Chinese leg of the route is probably all you'll have the time and fortitude to travel. Guided tours are practical for those with limited tolerance or language skills.

Making the best of it

The first leg of the Silk Route is a 13-hour train journey from Xi'an to Lanzhou. This ordeal is more palatable if you make a reservation for "hard-sleeper," the class between "hard-seat" and "soft-sleeper." You will have your own berth, but you won't be secluded from the other passengers. Bring food, tea, and a lidded teacup; attendants will provide hot water.

The best place to stay in Lanzhou is the megalithic Chinese-built **Friendship Hotel**, *14 Xijin Xi Lu*. Rooms, which are comfortable, if cavernous, with well-worn, deep-seated armchairs with lace arm covers, fragile pink lampshades, and heavy velvet curtains, cost a mere $25 and have private bathrooms.

Just across the road from the hotel is the Provincial Museum, which has magnificent pieces of decorated pottery dating back 6,000 years. The most important is the 1,800-year-old "Flying Horse of Gansu," which really looks as if it is flying.

Buddhist bests

Twenty miles from Lanzhou are the **Bilingsi Buddhist Caves**, which are definitely worth visiting. China International Travel Service (CITS) arranges inexpensive tours to the caves, which were dug into the face of a 180-foot cliff about 1,500 years ago by Buddhist monks. They are full of Buddhist statues, sculptures, and murals. From here, the Silk Route crosses the Wei River Valley into the arid province of Gansu, where it flanks the Great Wall for 700 miles. Eventually, it comes to **Jiayuguan**, a fortress built by Ming dynasty rulers in 1372 as their western outpost.

Northwest of Jiayuguan are the **Thousand Buddha Grottoes** at Dunhuang, an oasis stuck in the middle of the Gansu Desert. In the old days, this dusty little place was a vital staging post for camel caravans going east and west—here the northern and southern branches of the Silk Route met. Only 40 of the 500 cave temples are open to the public. Each enshrines superb paintings and sculptures that were commissioned over a period of 1,500 years by rich and pious pilgrims and merchants as gestures of thanks for a safe journey on the Silk Route. Bring a flashlight to see the details of the works.

The best of the desert

The **Taklamakan Desert**, which the route follows on the southern border, translates from Uygur to mean "Once you go in, you never get out." The desert is haunted not by the specters that the ancients feared but by the sounds of underground nuclear testing. A long, parched trip via bus and train will lead you out of the desert and into Turpan, a cultural oasis where grape arbors shade courtyards.

The friendliest folks

Descendants of the Uygurs make up the region's largest—and friendliest—ethnic group (besides the Han Chinese). Their language is Turkish, their religion Islam. Cool evenings, when the people are outdoors, are the best times to meet the Uygurs. Invitations to their adobe huts are not unusual.

The best of the past

Nearby ruins of two ancient Silk Route cities still have recognizable streets, town walls, and buildings. **Gaochang**, the larger of the two cities, was the capital of the Uygur kingdom in the ninth century. It once hosted Marco Polo and is a vast and slightly terrifying place.

Jiaohe, perched above a riverbed, was a Chinese garrison until it came under local control. Its main road is still clearly visible.

Join with other travelers and hire a minibus to take you to the ruined cities. In groups of 12, it costs about $4 per person.

The Silk Route's best guesthouse

The best place to stay in Turpan is the **Turpan Guesthouse**, *Qingnian Road, not* the garish new Tourgroup Hotel up the road. The guesthouse is one of the great joys of the Silk Route. Plan to stay several days. Relax on the vine-covered verandas, sipping cool beer, snacking on grapes, and contemplating the past splendors of the Silk Route.

China's least-desirable digs

The **Turpan Depression**, which surrounds the town of Turpan, has been called one of the strangest places on earth. It lies nearly 500 feet below sea level and can get so hot in the summer that people live in the underground cellars of their houses. An underground irrigation channel was built 2,000 years ago to bring melted snow from the Tian Shan Mountains in the north (hence, the profusion of well-watered melon and grape crops in the middle of the desert).

Ugliest city, loveliest carpets

A few hours beyond Turpan is **Ürümqi**, one of the ugliest, most polluted cities in China. One thing saves this industrial city—it has the country's best carpet market. To find it, go to the **Hua Qiao Hotel** (popular with overseas Chinese), *51 S. Xinhua Road; tel. (86-991)70530,* head toward the city center, and turn into the fourth lane on the right. At the end is a bustling little market with noodle restaurants, kebab stalls, teahouses, clothes shops, and a magnificent array of carpets.

The best of Switzerland in the desert

Once you have visited the market, head out of town toward **Heaven Lake**, a bit of Switzerland halfway up Bogda Shan (the Mountain of God). The trip takes four hours.

Deep blue Heaven Lake is surrounded by pine forests and snow-capped peaks. The Kazakhs, herders, and horsemen (not to be confused with the Russian Cossacks) set up their yurts (dome tents) in the cool meadows here during the summer.

If you can't face returning to Ürümqi, you can rent a yurt from a Kazakh nomad for less than $1 a night per person. Or you can stay at the Heavenly Lake Hotel, on the shore of the lake, for $12.

The best horsing around

While in Ürümqi, you may be invited to see the *boz kashi*, a contest of horsemanship. Riders must carry a headless goat or lamb from one end of a field to another. Because this spectacle appears to lack either a referee or rules, it's best to view it from a safe perch.

China's westernmost city

From Ürümqi, you can fly to **Kashgar**, China's westernmost city and the end of the Chinese portion of the Silk Route. (If you continue on from here, you will end up in Pakistan.) But taking the three- or four-day bus trip in the company of Uygurs, Mongols, Tibetans, and Han Chinese better duplicates Silk Route sojourns of long ago. The buses make frequent stops that give you a chance to sample the area's plentiful melons.

They say Kashgar is farther from the sea than any other town on earth. When you get there, you'll believe it. The streets are narrow and dusty, lined with adobe houses. You will hear muezzin cries and smell the smoke-filled kebab markets. Kashgar has been around for 2,000 years and is one of the most important cities on the Silk Route, at the borders of Russia, Afghanistan, India, and Pakistan. When Marco Polo passed through Kashgar, he called it "the starting point from which many merchants set out to market their wares all over the world."

One thing above all must be seen in Kashgar: the **Sunday Market**. When you plan your trip, make sure you will be in town on a Sunday. Hundreds of thousands of people (mostly Uygurs) swarm to an area on the outskirts of town, where they buy and sell everything you can imagine—and much you can't. The most exciting part of the market is where Kazakh horsemen test-ride horses in an enclosure full of donkeys, sheep, goats, cows, and camels.

Near the market is **Id Kah Mosque**, one of the largest in China. Built in 1442, it dominates the old town and draws thousands of worshipers every Friday. If you aren't in town on a Sunday, many of the goods available at the market can also be purchased at the bazaar near the Id Kah Square.

When you tire, relax over a meal at the **Tian Nan Restaurant**, tucked behind the hotel of the same name, 300 yards east of the imposing Mao statue. The food is excellent (which is evidenced by the number of Han Chinese who crowd the restaurant).

The best hotel in Kashgar is the **Kashgar Guesthouse**, on the eastern side of town. It is comfortable, but a bit too far from the center of things. Double rooms are $20.

The **Seman Hotel**, *Seman Lu,* is more central. Its old wing was once Kashgar's Russian Consulate. Little seems to have been repaired since the Russians left in 1949, but the dilapidated rooms are rather charming. They have the biggest and best bathtubs you'll find within 1,000 miles! What's more, you'll be provided with plenty of hot water. Rooms in the older wing are $10; rooms in the newer wing are $20.

Hong Kong is the best place to arrange a trip along the Silk Route. Typically, such tours cost $2,200 and last two weeks.

Dali—China's newest vacation spot

One of the most popular new destinations in Yunnan province, which only recently opened to tourists, is the town of **Dali**, a handsome historical city in a spectacular setting. Look one way and you see the snow-capped Cangshan (White-Haired Mountain); look the other way and you see the blue Erhai (Ear Lake). Between the mountain and the water are well-irrigated green fields dotted with villages.

The majority of Dali's natives—about 80%—are of Bai nationality. For hundreds of years, they formed a kingdom independent of China that flourished until conquered by Kublai Khan in 1253. A stone tablet commemorates the event.

The Bai people are extremely friendly and will greet you constantly with "Hi." Women wear traditional colorful clothing, including ornately decorated backpacks for carrying small children.

When Chinese emperors moved the provincial capital to Kunming, Dali sank into oblivion. Because of this, the town is well-preserved, with narrow cobblestoned streets and old buildings of wood, plaster, and stone. A short walk takes you down the main street from one Ming dynasty gate to the other. The gates have been impressively rebuilt, but most of the wall that surrounds Dali is now little more than earthworks with rice planted on the top.

You can buy colorful clothing at the marketplaces in and around Dali. The largest is held every Monday at **Shapin**, on the north side of the lake, about 18 miles from Dali. In addition to pigs, seed, and farming tools, you can buy coins, handkerchiefs, and fabrics. Tailors in Dali can stitch up clothing to order.

Beyond the wall, two competing entrepreneurs rent out bikes for less than $1 a day. The bikes are crude one-speeds, and the roads are very bumpy.

Finagle a boat ride across the lake and watch the fishermen with their nets. Hike up the mountains, where many old temples are still in use. To relax your tired muscles, get a vigorous massage at Dali's public bathhouse.

Food in Dali is cheap and good. The **Peace Café**, next to Number 2 Hotel, caters to travelers. The **Garden Café**, a family restaurant, serves locals as well as visitors. Late at night, three generations of the owner's family gather in the back room to eat, squabble, watch television, and make a lot of noise.

April is the best time to visit Dali, when the town holds its **Third Month Fair**, an annual festival that dates back 1,000 years. People come from miles around for their once-a-year trip to town.

Getting to Dali involves a nine-hour bus ride from Kunming, the capital of Yunnan province. Flights to Kunming depart from Hong Kong, Beijing, Guangzhou, Shanghai, and Rangoon.

Xishuangbanna: tropical China

The southernmost region of China's Yunnan province, **Xishuangbanna**, is more like Thailand than China. Bordering Burma and Laos, this is a lush, tropical land with hillside tea and rubber plantations, markets full of exotic fruit, and coconut-palm-shaded villages where women dress in brilliantly colored sarongs.

The liveliest time to visit is during the **New Year Water Splashing Festival** (celebrated according to the Buddhist calendar in mid-April). Festivities in Jinghong, the capital, include dragon-boat races on the Mekong River, Dai music and dancing, bamboo rockets, and a riot of water splashing. If you plan to visit during the festival, make reservations far in advance. Both flights from Kunming to Jinghong and accommodations become scarce.

A better time to visit is off-season, when you can enjoy the tranquil countryside and the gentle ways of the attractive Dai people (one of Yunnan's largest and most prosperous minority groups).

Jinghong is a small, sleepy town of broad streets bordered by palm trees. Buddhist monks in saffron robes bicycle slowly along the streets, while Dai women carrying pretty parasols congregate in the open markets. If you are lucky, one of the Dai will present you with a sticky cake of glutinous rice wrapped in palm leaves, a common sweet snack in Xishuangbanna.

About 35 miles west of Jinghong lies **Menghai,** one of the great tea regions of China and home of the most famous temple site in the province: the **Octagonal Pagoda.** This tiny gem of intricate architecture was built in the 17th century.

Far to the south, five miles from the Burmese border, lies **Damenglong,** a village with a 13th-century white pagoda and a lively Sunday market. Here you can see a panoply of other minority people, who come to trade with the local Dai: Lahu women in brightly colored bodices; Bulang with colored tufts of wool for earrings; and women of the Hani and Aini tribes (who are similar to Thailand's Akha people) bedecked in breastplates and headdresses of silver and metal coins, embroidered black leggings, belts of cowrie shells, and short black miniskirts that have an alarming tendency to fall off.

Another market is held at **Menghan,** southwest of Jinghong, which you can get to by slow boat on the brown Mekong River. It's a one-hour trip downstream, with stops to pick up villagers. Women can be seen on the river's edge panning for grains of gold.

The life of the Dai in these villages is slow and traditional. They live along the northern shore of Menghan's Virtuous Dragon Lake in large wooden houses built on stilts. You can see men making bamboo baskets and girls weaving cloth. In the Buddhist temple, boy monks learn their sacred texts. Chickens and pigs roam the dusty village paths, and buffalo plow the fields. Inside the thatched-roof wood and bamboo houses, gold-toothed Dai women prepare banquets: purple rice, spiced zucchini, sesame beef, and fried bumblebees.

The easiest way to reach Xishuangbanna is to fly from Kunming to Simao (75 minutes) and then take a bus or taxi the 100 miles to Jinghong. You'll pass spectacular scenery, including rice plains, hillsides of tea and rubber, and dense jungles.

Hainan, the Red Hawaii

Hainan Island off the coast of China is slated to become the Hawaii of the Far East. The island is off the southernmost part of China, not far from Vietnam, and is nearly as big as Taiwan. Recently, it was made a separate province. (It had been part of Guangdong.)

Despite its coconut groves and pristine golden beaches, the island has a few problems. Telephones are unpredictable. Until recently the only airstrip on its south coast was a military field, although a new airstrip has been opened. Passengers are ferried in venerable Russian planes. Sanya, slated to be the tourist center, has only 500 hotel rooms, none with a private bath.

Lhasa: the world's highest capital

Lhasa, Tibet, at 12,087 feet above sea level, is the world's highest capital. Set in royal blue skies above the clouds, it is so high that tourists are given oxygen bags when they arrive. Unfortunately, the monks here and the Chinese police have been coming into confrontation. The city is closed to individual travelers and can be visited only by groups.

When the political problems subside, make your way to this autonomous region of China. The City of the Sun, as it is known, is high in the Gyi Qu Valley, just 100 miles north of India. Summers here are hot and humid, winters bitingly cold. The best times to visit are spring and fall.

The former seat of the Dalai Lama, the head of Tibetan Buddhism, Lhasa is filled with palaces and temples. Behind these grandiose man-made monuments are towering snow-covered mountains that make the Rockies seem mundane.

The **Potala,** where the Dalai Lama lived until he was ousted by the Communists in 1959, is an enormous 17th-century edifice that dominates the entire valley. The 13-story, 1,000-room palace is a museum today. Inside are gigantic, bejewelled Buddhas, murals illustrating Buddhist legends, and solid gold crypts containing the remains of former Dalai Lamas. The 10,000 chapels are decorated with human skulls and thighbones. Beneath the

271

palace are torture chambers, where criminals and dissidents were kept in dungeons or stung to death by scorpions.

The **Deprung Monastery**, which is about three miles outside Lhasa, is where lesser religious leaders lived. The stone building, constructed in 1416 and set precariously against a mountainside, was once the largest cloister in the world. Although thousands of monks once lived here, the monastery is now inhabited by 300.

The **Jokhang Temple** houses two enormous gold and bejewelled Buddhas. Built 1,300 years ago, it is still visited by pilgrims who can be seen prostrate in front of the temple at dawn and dusk. Beautiful from the outside, the temple is smelly inside, because of the fermented butter burned by monks as part of their religious ceremonies.

One of the best bazaars in all China takes place around the outside. Pilgrims from across Tibet congregate in the Barkhor and walk around it clockwise, praying, shopping, and socializing as they move along. A fantastic variety of goods is sold in the Barkhor, including prayer wheels, silver inlay boxes, and Tibetan musical instruments. Be prepared to bargain fiercely.

The best hotel in Lhasa is the **Holiday Inn**, *93 W. Bejing Road; tel. (86-3)22221.* Rooms are air-conditioned and equipped with televisions, telephones, and oxygen tanks. Prices are relatively high, as all supplies must be transported by truck for miles up the mountain. Double rooms are $46 to $74.

The best way to travel

If you have the time, the most pleasant way to travel through China is by boat. Several boat routes allow you to make the circiut of the major Chinese cities. One goes from Guangzhou to Wuzhou, a small town en route to Guilin, in 20 hours. The price, including a seven-hour bus trip to Yangshuo, is less than $10.

Everyone on these boat trips gets his own berth, either an upper with a window view of the Pearl River or a lower-level berth with easier access. No one sits in the aisles. Thick mats and quilts are provided in the dormitorylike setting. You'll enjoy lovely views and great people-watching opportunities.

The cheapest way to get to China

Hong Kong is the cheapest place to buy a package tour to China. You can save a few thousand dollars by flying to Hong Kong on your own and joining a tour group heading for China from there.

CITS, *Room 108, Swire Road, Central, Hong Kong; tel. (852)810-4282,* and *23-33 Nathan Road, Kowloon; tel. (852)366-7201,* is among the most reliable agencies sponsoring tours from Hong Kong to China. Also try the **Hong Kong Student Travel Bureau,** *120/2 Des Voeux Road, Tai Sang Bank Building; tel. (852)725-3898,* and **China Youth Travel,** *151 Des Voeux Road; tel. (852)541-0975.* Make sure the Hong Kong agent you deal with is officially authorized to issue you a visa.

The Best of Hong Kong and Macau

Hong Kong, the pearl of the Orient, is the most dynamic city in the world. The bustling colony is as hectic as New York—without the crime and unemployment. It is a thriving financial center, a shopper's paradise, and a gourmet's delight. Everyone works in this city, where fortunes are still made and lost overnight and almost anything can be bought—at a bargain price.

Hong Kong is a unique mixture of British and Chinese cultures. A British Crown Colony and a free market port, it is a gateway between worlds: Eastern and Western, ancient and modern, communist and capitalist, poor and wealthy.

In 1997, Hong Kong will revert to Chinese sovereignty. However, in an agreement signed in 1984, the Chinese government has pledged to allow Hong Kong to continue its economic system and way of life until 2047.

Hong Kong has more people per square mile than any other spot on earth (and more Mercedes, too). And most of its 6 million people are crammed into tall buildings in an area just a few miles wide and long. However, despite its claustrophobic urban crowds, Hong Kong has more open space than cities half its size. And you can travel easily from the city to the rural countryside, where the dramatic terrain is inspiring.

The best view of Hong Kong

One of the world's greatest views is that of **Hong Kong Harbor** from **Victoria Peak**. Guarded by a tall fortress of mountains, behind which looms the awakening giant China, Hong Kong Harbor is alive with ships and boats from every corner of the earth. Rimmed by skyscrapers, the harbor is dotted with picturesque Chinese junks, hydrofoils, Russian cargo ships, big navy vessels, and the tiny sampans of those who make their livings from the sea. Some of these boats carry people who have never stepped foot on land.

Out in the water beyond the traffic jams of the central harbor rises a large emerald mountain called **Lantau Island**. And if you look hard or climb very high, you'll see 236 other such islands floating in the South China Sea.

You can either take a trolley up to Victoria Peak or, if your legs are up to it, make the trek on foot. The mile-long Governor's Walk takes you through junglelike growth around the top of the mountain.

273

The biggest bazaar in the world

Hong Kong is the biggest bazaar in the world. With no import duties on anything except cigarettes, liquor, automobiles, and cosmetics, the city also has some of the best prices in the world. Clothes, watches, jewelry, and Chinese goods should be at the top of your shopping list. Hong Kong is no longer the best place in the world to shop for electronic equipment or cameras; you often can get better prices in Singapore or New York. (Avoid the hotel shops, which are the most expensive).

Have a suit made—in a day

Hong Kong's major industry is textiles, so clothing is a good buy. Once *the* best place in the world to have a suit made, Hong Kong now has great competition from Singapore. Nonetheless, tailors here are world-famous for their inexpensive, quality work—overnight, if you like. However, it is better to allow time for at least two fittings. If you have no particular tailor in mind, begin by approaching tailors who display the HKTA logo (a red junk in a circle). The **Poon Keung Workshop,** *Room 11, Haiphong Mansion, 3/F Haiphong Road, 101 Nathan Road, Kowloon; tel. (852)368-8461,* is one of the best places to get a custom-made suit in Hong Kong. The proprietor not only tailors fine suits for a dozen shops but also operates a worldwide catalog service.

Name brands at bargain prices

Silks, cottons, linens, furs, and jeans are also great buys. You can buy jeans on the street for one-third the price you'd pay in the United States. One of Hong Kong's best-kept secrets is its factory outlets, which carry overruns or rejects of items with well-known labels manufactured originally for export to the United States or Europe. The merchandise is available for a fraction of what you'd pay in the United States.

Two well-known outlets are **Oriental Pacific,** *Room 601-6 6/f, Sands Building, 17 Hankow Road, Tsimshatsui; tel. (852)724-2633,* and **Shoppers' World Ltd.,** *Room 708, Sands Building, 17 Hankow Road, Tsimshatsui; tel. (852)769-8075.*

The outlet offering the greatest selection is **Four Seasons Garments,** *Kaiser Estate, Phase II, 1/f, G1, 51 Man Yue St., Hunghom, Kowloon; tel. (852)363-2218.* Also known as the Silk Factory, this place sells every kind of glamorous silk item imaginable.

Linen, imported from China and exquisitely embroidered, is a bargain at Stanley Market and China Arts & Crafts stores.

The most affordable furs

If you want to buy a fur coat, do it in Hong Kong, where prices are competitive. **Jindo Ltd.,** *World Financial Center, Harbour City, Tsimshatsui; tel. (852)369-8698,* claims, "We make the world's finest furs rather more affordable."

The best of everything Chinese

For anything Chinese, shop at one of the Chinese Arts & Crafts stores, which you'll find throughout Kowloon and Central. (One is located at the Star House by the ferry terminal in Tsimshatsui.) Don't be put off by the department store atmosphere. You can't bargain here, but you'll find many high-quality Chinese goods, including art, crafts, jewelry, clothing, carpets, furniture, porcelain, silk, furs, leather, watches, cosmetics, shoes, cameras, electric appliances, and Chinese medicines. Chinese-style dresses, made in Western proportions, are a particularly good deal.

The best-known street market

The most famous of Hong Kong's many street markets is the **Stanley Market,** on the south side of the island. Stanley is an old fishing village with a large expatriate community. Silk dresses, sunglasses, fresh fruits, rattan furniture, porcelain ware, shoes, and luggage are all available for incredible bargain prices.

The best place in the world to lose your glasses

Hong Kong is the best place to lose your eyeglasses. Friendly, efficient opticians have offices throughout the city that display the HKTA logo. Competition makes for bargain prices on lenses and frames.

Antique bests

Shop for antiques on **Hollywood Road**, about two streets up from Queen's Road Central. This picturesque area has the atmosphere of a Chinese city from the 1930s. Follow the road around the hill to the old Cat Street quarter, where you can browse through the **Cat Street Galleries**, *Lok Ku Road*. Antique porcelain, traditional Chinese furniture, wall scrolls, old Chinese photographs, jade, ivory, carved wood, vases, and other curiosities fill the crowded stalls. Remember to get a red wax seal if you plan to export any antiques you buy.

Ivory buys

Ivory has been carved in China for 3,000 years, and in Hong Kong you will find ivory in both modern and traditional designs. Each province has its own style of carving.

Rickety stairs lead to the ivory factories lining Hollywood Road and Tsimshatsui. At the tops of the stairs are rooms where Chinese sit carving ivory. In the showrooms are shelves upon shelves of ivory statues, jewelry, chopsticks, and ornaments. Intricately carved balls are the most popular items. Remember, though, that it is illegal to bring even small amounts of ivory into the United States.

Shopping for gems

Hong Kong boasts more jewelry shops per square mile than any other city in the world, and it is the world's third-largest diamond-trading center. Because you pay neither sales tax nor import duty on gems or jewelry, you'll find good buys not only on diamonds but also on gold, pearls, emeralds, sapphires, coral, jade, and lapis lazuli. You can bargain, too. Stick to shops displaying the HKTA logo in their windows.

The world's most famous jade market

The **Jade Market**, located under Kansu Street in the Yau Ma Tei section of Kowloon, is the heart of the world's jade trade. You'll recognize the big-time dealers—they're the Chinese with newspapers covering their hands. They bargain by tapping each other's hands beneath the papers, which keeps competitors from seeing what the bids are. You're not likely to get a bargain here unless you know a lot about jade.

The best Buddhas

The **Temple of Ten Thousand Buddhas** actually contains about 12,800 of the statues. **Yuet Kai**, the gold-plated monk on exhibit, is actually a mummy, sealed in gold leaf and serenely dressed in his saffron robe. Also look for the scarlet Buddha, a bright red statue of the philosopher. The temple is near the train station at Shatin.

The busiest Buddhist temple

Wong Tai Sin Temple, Hong Kong's busiest Buddhist temple, is perhaps the best choice for foreigners interested in having their fortunes told. You have a choice of 150 fortunetellers, whose booths are lined up in a winding concrete alley like dominos. Some of these fortunetellers speak English; otherwise, you'll have to depend on a translator.

The best place for bird lovers

Birds are an important part of Chinese life. And **Bird Street**, a small alley in Kowloon, is where the Chinese buy their feathered friends. Hundreds of them—whistling, singing, talking, screaming—are for sale, along with elaborate bamboo cages and live insects (bird food). The street's real name is Hong Lok Street. It is a few blocks west of the intersection of Argyle Street and Nathan Road.

The best place for a workout

Bowen Road is a quiet, tree-shaded path about 400 feet above sea level on Hong Kong Island. Along it you'll see people jogging, playing badminton, and performing Tai Chi. Following the path as it winds around the island, you'll hear (and maybe encounter) bands of monkeys playing in the subtropical forest.

The world's most noteworthy new building

If you are interested in architecture or money, visit the **Hongkong & Shanghai Bank,** *1 Queen's Road Central.* This high-tech edifice, built of steel, glass, and aluminum, and designed by British architect Norman Foster, cost $641 million. Rather than resting upon the framework, each section is suspended from it. Only the supports and service shafts touch the ground. What normally would be the ground floor is open space, connected to the bank by twin escalators—the longest freely supported escalators in the world. They look like ramps reaching down from a spaceship and are sealed off when the bank closes by means of a sliding glass underbelly.

Hong Kong's most popular spectator sport

Horseracing is Hong Kong's most popular spectator sport and, with the exception of the local lottery, the territory's only legal form of gambling. Races regularly attract crowds of more than 45,000. And the betting is great. The record stands at $14 million in one day.

Visitors to the territory are invited to get in on the action. The Hong Kong Tourist Association offers a Come Horseracing tour September through June that allows anyone older than 18 who has not been in Hong Kong for more than three weeks to experience a day at the races. The tour includes transportation to and from the racetrack, entry to the visitors' box, the services of a guide, and lunch or dinner. The cost is HK$350 ($45).

To make reservations to join a Come Horseracing tour, take your passport to the tourist association's **Information and Guest Center,** *Shop 8, Basement, Jardine House, Connaught Place, Central,* or the *Star Ferry concourse, Tsimshatsui, Kowloon.* Reservations can also be made through a travel agent and many hotels.

The perfect Hong Kong night

The perfect place to begin a night in Hong Kong is at the **Mandarin Oriental**, with a glass of champagne at the circular bar. This is a great place to meet people. Next walk over to the Star Ferry and take the short ride across the harbor to the Peninsula Hotel. Walk around the beautiful old lobby, and if you're hungry, enjoy a delicious Chinese dinner at Spring Moon on the second floor. Next, walk over to the Regent, where you can have dessert while looking at the most beautiful night view of Hong Kong Harbor. Your last stop should be the nightclubs of Lan Dwei Fong, where people of all ages and nationalities mix and mingle. Be sure to try "1997," a lively place named for the year when Hong Kong will return to China.

Hong Kong's hottest spots

Hong Kong's night life is varied. Posh hotel nightclubs offer sophisticated music and dancing. For the best Western-style entertainment, visit **Lan Kwai Fong Street,** in the heart of Central, where *gweilos* (Westerners) abound. One of the hottest discos is **1997,** *9 Lan Kwai Fong; tel. (852)810-9333.* A restaurant that serves Middle Eastern and Meditteranean fare, **Mecca 97,** and a nightclub, **Post 97,** are located in the same building.

The best time to visit

Although the **Chinese New Year,** at the end of February, is a good time to visit, most stores and cultural offices are closed at this time. The next-best times to visit are during the colorful **Dragon Boat Festival** in June and the **Cheung Chau Island Bun Festival**, when special buns are distributed to ensure good luck and prosperity. The Bun Festival usually takes place in late May, but the date depends on the Chinese calendar.

The most tranquil escapes

If you're looking for relief from the frantic pace of the city, retreat to Hong Kong's quiet coves, beaches, and small villages. You can reach them by ferry from the city center. Lantau, Lamma, and Cheung Chau islands have beautiful beaches and seafood restaurants. **Lamma** is the best getaway spot—it has no cars or motorcycles, and its villages have no more than a few hundred inhabitants. It is known as Hong Kong's Stone Age Island.

The world's best Chinese food

Hong Kong, not China, has the world's best Chinese food. The best Chinese cooks fled here in 1949.

The finest Cantonese restaurant is the **Man Wah,** *Mandarin Hotel; tel. (852)522-0111.* Another excellent restaurant is **Tan Wong Kok,** *Carpo Commercial Building, 18-20 Lyndhurst Terrace, Central; tel. (852)541-30713.*

Among the most delicate Chinese foods are the bite-size *dim sum,* served for breakfast or lunch in steaming bamboo baskets. The **Luk Yu Tea House and Restaurant,** *26 Stanley St., Central,* an old restaurant decorated Chinese-style, is one of the best places to eat *dim sum.* Elderly Chinese men dressed in long gray robes sit for hours over tea, reading Chinese newspapers and choosing from the delicacies brought around on *dim sum* carts.

The world's oldest eggs

The oldest eggs in the world are served in Hong Kong. *Pay daan,* known as 1,000- or 100-year-old eggs, are actually only about three months old. *Pay daan* are buried in dung, and their whites turn to a clear, gellike substance. Despite their odd name and dirty appearance, many find them quite good.

Hong Kong's best seafood

The freshest seafood dinner in Hong Kong can be had at **Lei Yue Mun**, a fishing village on a tiny peninsula in east Kowloon. You take a ferry over to an enclave of fish stalls, where you can wander among hundreds of tanks and tile pools filled with fish, crabs, multicolored lobsters, prawns, eels, scallops, and myriad other live sea animals. Watch your dinner flop on the floor as you bargain with vendors; then make your way to one of the 20 restaurants around the market, where you can have your seafood cooked to order for a reasonable charge.

The most romantic dining

Dining afloat is one of Hong Kong's most novel gastronomic experiences. You can have a meal on one of the big floating restaurants in Aberdeen or on board a tiny sampan in a makeshift restaurant with room for six to eight people. Sampans are for rent at the Causeway Bay Typhoon Shelter. They will pull alongside the dock to cook your meal, serve your drinks, and even serenade you. All this is not cheap, of course.

The best of the West

The two best places to go in Hong Kong for Western-style food are **Gaddi's,** *Salisbury Road, Tsimshatsui; tel. (852)366-6251,* in the Peninsula Hotel, and the **Plume,** *Salisbury Road, Tsimshatsui; tel. (852)721-2111,* in the Regent Hotel. The Plume has an extraordinary view of the harbor and about 10,000 bottles of wine in its cellar—which probably qualifies it as the best wine cellar in Asia.

The best hotels in the world
Service is what sets hotels in the Orient apart from those in the rest of the world—
and the service in Hong Kong is unsurpassed anywhere. The Crown Colony, we would
argue, is home to the best hotels in the world. The **Peninsula**, *Salisbury Road, Tsimshatsui;
tel. (852)366-6251,* is a unique establishment, reminiscent of the best days of the British
Empire. Rooms are HK$2,250 to HK$22,000 ($290 to $2,850). The **Regent**, *Salisbury
Road, Tsimshatsui; tel. (852)721-2111,* is an expensive and luxurious hotel with a commanding view of the harbor. Rooms are HK$1,520 to HK$16,000 ($196 to $2,072).

The **Mandarin**, *5 Connaught Road, Central; tel. (852)522-0111,* is cited by businessmen as the best hotel in the world, with a reputation for personal, discreet service.
Rooms are HK$1,650 to HK$20,000 ($213 to $2,850).

The **Hong Kong Hilton**, *2 Queen's Road, Central; tel. (852-5)233-111,* is an elegant,
well-run hotel in a superb location right in the heart of the business district between the
Hong Kong & Shanghai Bank and the new headquarters of the Bank of China. Rooms are
HK$1,510 to HK$6,000 ($195 to $777).

The **Island Shangri-La**, *Pacific Place, Supreme Court Road; tel. (852) 877-3838,* is
Hong Kong's newest, tallest, and most luxurious hotel. The guest rooms are the island's
most spacious. You feel that you are far from the frenetic pace of the city—yet you are right
in the central business district. The decor is beautiful, featuring a 14-story-high Chinese
landscape, created by 40 painters of the Beijing Arts and Crafts Research Institute, which
decorates the Atrium.

If you are looking for reasonable rates in the best location, stay at the **Salisbury YMCA**,
41 Salisbury Road, Kowloon; tel. (852) 369-2211. This is no ordinary YMCA. Located right
around the corner from the Peninsula Hotel, near the Star Ferry and the Nathan Road
shopping district, the YMCA offers attractive, air-conditioned rooms with color televisions, minibars, room safes, and more. Rooms are HK $450 to HK$980 ($63 to $125).

A quiet retreat
If you're looking for a reasonably priced place to stay, away from the tourists and
crowds of Central Hong Kong, make reservations at the **Trappist Monastery Retreat
House**, *P.O. Box 5, Peng Chao; tel. (852) 987-6292.* For only HK$100 ($15), including
three meals a day, you will get a simple but comfortable room looking out onto a beautiful
garden. No radios or typewriters are permitted in the retreat house, though, which is
operated by Trappist monks, and lights are turned out at 10 p.m.

The easiest place to get to in Asia
You won't have any trouble getting to Hong Kong. All the world's major international
airlines fly into the city or have offices there, and about 1,000 flights go in and out of Kai
Tak International Airport each week. The airport has a great location, right in the middle
of Kowloon, which makes for dramatic landings, particularly at night.

The world's best cheap transportation
The **Star Ferry** is the best way to cross Hong Kong's harbor. At HK$1.20 for a first-
class fare (about 15 cents), it's one of the cheapest and most scenic journeys in the world.
In the eight minutes it takes to go from Central to Tsimshatsui, you'll experience the
essence of Hong Kong. Twilight is the best time to take the ride.

The best way to see Hong Kong
The best way to see Hong Kong is on foot. Driving is too hectic. Besides, Hong Kong
is so compact and so efficiently laid out that you'll have no trouble traveling around the
city. Public transportation is the best way to explore the surrounding countryside.

After you go through customs at Kai Tak Airport, pick up a free Hong Kong Tourist
Association (HKTA) map at one of the stands outside the customs area. The street names

are in English and Chinese, and the map indicates hotels, office buildings, markets, and important sights.

The **Mass Transit Railway** (MTR) is fast, efficient, clean, and cheap. Most trips cost HK$3 to HK$7 (40 cents to 90 cents). If you are planning on using the railway frequently, buy a Common Stored Value ticket for HK$50 or HK$100 ($6 to $13). Tourist tickets are also available for HK$25 ($3.25), but you only get a HK$20 ($2.50) value.

Macau—Asia's oldest European colony

Macau is one of the last remnants of the 16th-century Portuguese empire, renowned for its gourmet food, exotic setting, and outrageous gambling. Officially a Chinese territory under Portuguese administration (until it reverts to China in 1999—two years after Hong Kong), Macau has a tangible sense of history that is preserved in its beautiful colonial buildings.

For centuries, it was a place where smugglers, pirates, prostitutes, drug lords, sailors, and flesh merchants made their home. Today, Macau is a refuge from the hustle and bustle of Hong Kong. However, Macau, too, has an exciting night life, with a flavor all its own.

The best gambling tables in Asia— and the ugliest hotel in the world

Macau is famous for its casinos. The biggest is the **Casino de Lisboa**, *avenida da Amizade*, in the Lisboa Hotel. The Lisboa is probably the ugliest hotel in the world, designed to look like a roulette wheel, which it wears like a crown upon its head. The **Macau Palace**, known as the Floating Casino, is a more exotic place to gamble. This red and gilded Chinese boat is moored on the inner harbor off avenida de Almeida Riveiro.

Games include both those familiar to Westerners, such as blackjack, and Chinese games, such as *dai-siu* and keno. Slot machines are known locally as "hungry tigers."

The best place to honeymoon

Macau's **Pousada de São Tiago**, *avenida da Republica; tel. (853)378111*, became a hotel in 1980—it was built 350 years ago as a fortress (the Fortaleza da Barra). Every historical feature was preserved during the transformation, including the Portuguese marble, hand-painted tiles, ancient stone walls, gentle cascades, hand-carved mahogany, and even the trees that shade the multilevel terraces.

Overlooking the South China Sea, enveloped in warm, salty breezes, the *pousada* is an ideal romantic hideaway, perfect for a honeymoon. You could have your wedding here, too—small weddings can be arranged in the chapel (which holds only 15 people). The *pousada* is complete with restaurants, gardens, a pool, and reading rooms—you never need to venture beyond its grounds. The *pousada* has 20 rooms and three suites, starting at $125 per night.

Macau's most memorable monument

The ruins of the **Church of St. Paul** are Macau's most memorable monument. Built by the Jesuits in 1602, the beautiful church was mostly destroyed by a typhoon-fanned fire in 1835. All that remains is its baroque facade, covered with Catholic saints, Chinese dragons, and a Portuguese caravan. It is an imposing sight, with a broad granite stairway.

The oldest shrine

The **A Ma Temple** is the territory's oldest temple, built before the Portuguese came to Macau. According to legend, A Ma, the goddess of fishermen, was the sole survivor of a fishing boat caught in a severe storm.

The temple is a series of shrines built at various levels on the Barra hillside and linked by winding paths and steps. The shrine has a mysterious religious atmosphere, with its painted rocks, prayer sticks, tiny shrines, and statue-filled pavilions. Keep a close eye on your purse or wallet. Beggars congregate here, and signs warn against pickpockets.

The best place to get away from it all

Take a day to visit Macau's two outlying islands, **Taipa** and **Colonne**. These quiet retreats offer tree-shaded lanes, wide sandy beaches, small Chinese villages, and lush forests. Both islands are easily accessible, connected by a causeway to Macau City.

Macau's best hike

The **Rua da Praia Grande** is a lovely promenade alongside the South China Sea— a great place to stroll at night. Along the elegant walk you'll see the pink Government House, a typical example of colonial Portuguese architecture. There are also benches where you can rest beneath huge banyan trees.

If you are feeling adventurous and fit, follow one of the steep paths leading up to the lighthouse. Birds, frogs, and dogs will greet you as you climb the hill. At the top, you'll have a bird's-eye view of the city, with its bright lights and neon far below.

Macau's best restaurant

The best restaurant in Macau, if not all of Asia, is **Pinocchio's**, *4 Rua do Sol, Taipa Island; tel. (853)327128*. This garden restaurant off the village of Taipa's main street draws crowds from Hong Kong on weekends. Try the superb roast quail, chili crab, prawns, roast suckling pig, and baby lamb.

Macau's oldest restaurant

Fat Siu Lau, *64 Rua da Felicidade; tel. (853)373580*, which opened in 1903, is the oldest restaurant in Macau. It serves excellent Macanese cuisine, an exotic mixture of Chinese and Portuguese food and wines. The fresh seafood dishes are exceptionally good.

The best way to get to Macau

Because Macau doesn't have an airport, you can get to it only from Hong Kong or the People's Republic of China. The **Far East Jetfoil** from Hong Kong is the best option. Tickets cost from HK$72 to HK$108 ($9 to $14), depending on the day and hour you go, and the trip takes about an hour. Hovercraft, hydrofoil helicopters, and ferry services also run frequently between Hong Kong and Macau. Make reservations in advance, especially on weekends and holidays.

The best times to go

The best times to visit Macau are spring and fall. Unless you want to visit this island when it is jam-packed with people, avoid the Chinese New Year and the November Grand Prix. For more information, contact the **Macau Tourist Information Bureau**, *3133 Lake Hollywood Drive, Los Angeles, CA 90068; (213)851-3402 or (800)331-7150 in the United States*. In Macau, contact the **Department of Tourism**, *11 Largo do Senado; tel. (853)315566*.

The Best of Japan

A case might be made for Japan as Pandora's box.
—*John Gunther,* Inside Asia, *1939*

Japan is at once one of the best-known yet least-understood countries in Asia, a unique combination of Eastern and Western cultures. The Japanese go to great lengths to provide Western travelers with American-style hotels and modern amenities; yet, the Westerner may be excluded from a geisha club or a traditional Japanese inn. In the space of a few miles, you can race with the dizzying traffic of Tokyo's Ginza district and then revel in the silence of a remote Buddhist temple.

An ancient country, Japan is also the most modern nation in Asia. It is at once tranquil and chaotic, trend-setting and traditional. Young people wearing the latest fashions share sidewalks with elderly people in ancient costumes. Japanese businessmen taking the international market by storm also take time to meditate in centuries-old temples.

The best of Tokyo

Japan's capital and largest city is the most expensive city in the world. Tokyo is not known for its beauty. Indeed, the central districts are an architectural study in neon and chrome. But the city has hidden temples and flower gardens that preserve the serene, traditional side of Japanese culture.

The metropolis of Tokyo sprawls to the horizon, covering 800 square miles and comprising 26 cities, six towns, nine villages, and several islands. Curiously, this industrial city also has 20,679 farmers.

The best ways to travel

The subway system in Tokyo is excellent. Its routes are color-coded, and most stations are marked in Roman letters. The bus network is efficient as well, but information is printed only in Japanese. Taxis are luxurious, many with television sets and doors that open and close by remote control.

Despite all this, walking is the best way to see Tokyo. Even at night, the streets in this virtually crime-free city are safe. However, many of the streets are not named, and buildings aren't always numbered, so it is easy to get lost. If you do get lost, you're in luck as long as it's on a weekday between 9 a.m. and 5 p.m. or Saturday between 9 a.m. and

281

noon. During those times, you can stop by a police box and call the **Tokyo Information Center,** *tel. (81-33)503-2911.* A member of the English-speaking staff will be able to help you.

The number-one sight

At the heart of Tokyo is the **Imperial Palace,** a 28-acre retreat surrounded by a moat filled with swans. The palace stands on the site of Edo Castle, built in the 15th century by Lord Dokan Ota. From the 1500s to 1868, when it was the residence of the Tokugawa shoguns, it covered 608 acres and was defended by a 10-mile wall with 111 gates, 20 turrets, and 30 bridges. The city of Tokyo grew around the edifice, which has been destroyed and rebuilt several times.

Behind the palace walls are a silkworm farm, rice paddies, and a mulberry field. Visitors can enter the palace only twice a year: on Jan. 1 and on the emperor's birthday.

You can visit the **Imperial Palace East Garden** every day except Monday and Friday from 9 a.m. to 3 p.m. You'll think you are in the shoguns' Japan, not a modern city. Still standing are four of the gates that once led into ancient Edo Castle. The Kitakibashimon, the entrance to the castle tower, is the most imposing, its stone bulwarks reflected in the deepest part of the moat.

The **Kitanomaru Koen** and **Chidorigafuchi Suijo Koen** parks are open to the public year-round. The Kitanomaru Koen Park contains the National Museum of Modern Art; the Crafts Gallery, located in the former headquarters of the Old Imperial Palace Guard; the Science and Technology Museum; and the Nippon Budokan (built for the 1964 Olympics), a concert hall that looks like a Buddhist temple but hosts performances by such rock stars as Rod Stewart.

The Imperial Palace is encircled by a 4.6-mile bike trail. Five hundred free bikes are available at the police station in the Imperial Palace Plaza if you'd like to make the *tour du palais.* Or you can join the locals in a jog around the palace's perimeter. The Imperial Hotel provides its guests with complimentary running gear and shoes for this purpose.

For the best view of the palace and its gardens, have lunch or dinner in the 10th-floor restaurant at the nearby Palace Hotel. Another good view is from the 36th floor of the Kasumigaseki Building, southwest of the palace. On a clear day, you can see all the way to Mount Fuji.

The loveliest shrines and temples

Beyond the palace grounds and up a hill is the **Yasukuni shrine,** *3-1-1 Kudan Kita, Dhiyoda-ku,* dedicated to the souls of those who have fought and died for Japan. Surrounded by parklike grounds, its entrance is marked by a huge, yoked wooden gateway called a *torii.* Walk through the mazelike shrine, with its many pillars. Toss some coins in the box by the door, clap your hands to awaken the spirits within, and say a prayer. Flocks of doves seem somehow symbolic. Inside the shrine is a museum containing war memorabilia.

The **Asakusa Kannon temple,** at the heart of the Asakusa neighborhood, is dedicated to Kannon, the Buddhist goddess of compassion. According to legend, the temple was built in A.D. 628 by three fishermen who had discovered a statue of the goddess in their fishing net. It is marked by a 10-foot red paper lantern that weighs 220 pounds. An enormous incense vat sends sweet-smelling smoke into the air from the courtyard in front of the temple. When cupped in one palm and patted on the body, the smoke is said to cure ailments. The flocks of doves that fly around the temple are considered sacred messengers of Kannon. Many of Tokyo's temples hold annual festivals, but the one held here May 16 to 18 is the largest in the city.

The **Hie shrine,** *2-10-5 Nagata-cho,* is dedicated to Oyamakuni, the monkey god, who grants fertility and good relationships and wards off evil. The best time to visit the shrine is every other June (odd years), during the Sanno-sai Festival, when miniature shrines are carried through the neighborhood.

The **Meji shrine**, *Shibuya-ku*, is one of the most popular Shinto shrines in Tokyo. Founded in 1920, it is dedicated to the Emperor Meiji (1868-1912), who ended the 600-year rule of the shoguns and opened Japan to the West. The shrine is surrounded by a 180-acre garden, and before it stands Japan's largest *torii*. The shrine's best feature is its iris garden, which bursts into color in June and July. Horsemen wearing samurai costumes compete in the yearly archery contest held here.

The **Sengakuji temple**, *Takanawa*, is the burial site of the 47 samurai of Asano Naganoni, Lord of Ako. They died for their master after avenging his death. Naganoni had made the mistake of drawing his sword when the court chamberlain insulted him. As punishment, he was forced to commit suicide. His faithful samurai then cut off the head of the chamberlain, for which they too had to commit suicide. Their story is re-enacted in the Kabuki play *Chushingura*. The faithful still come to lament the death of the samurai by lighting joss sticks on stone memorials in the temple gardens.

Tokyo's best park

On weekends, Tokyo residents flock to busy **Ueno Park**. Weekdays are less crowded. Try to visit the park during the Cherry Blossom Festival, from late March through mid-April, when the trees are breathtaking.

The **Ueno zoo** is worth visiting, if only for its pandas. Also visit the **Shitamachi History Museum**, at the far end of the park, featuring everyday objects donated by Tokyo residents.

The Ginza: Tokyo's best shopping

The **Ginza district**, southeast of the center of the city, is world-famous for its enormous department stores and exclusive little shops. Cars and trucks are barred from this district on weekends, when shoppers take over the streets and merchandise is moved onto sidewalks. Ginza (which translates as *Silver Mint*) is named for the Japanese mint, which was once located south of Kyobashi Bridge.

In addition to the usual fare, Takashimaya, a department store in the Ginza, has restaurants, tearooms, boutiques, a kimono department, and an art gallery that exhibits shows from top international museums. The best time to experience the formal hospitality of this store is at 10 a.m., when it opens and the salespeople line up and bow to you.

For an experience in high-tech shopping, visit **Seibu**. In addition to designer clothes and imported ice cream, Seibu has 177 closed-circuit televisions that entertain shoppers with rock music videos, breaking waves, and cherry blossoms.

The most colorful place to shop in the Ginza is the **Tsukiji fish market**, a 50-acre stretch of wholesale fish stalls. This is a great place to take photos. You will see all the fish that make their way into Tokyo's sushi bars, some familiar, some not. Wear waterproof shoes.

The most memorable neighborhoods

Shinjuku, especially around busy Shinjuku Station, is a maze of small alleys crammed with bars, restaurants, and coffee shops. It is popular with the student crowd. An interesting contrast to these energetic, off-beat establishments is Shinjuku Central Park, a peaceful wooded area with gardens, the largest man-made waterfall in Japan, and a clear view of Shinjuku.

On the west side of the city is the **Harajuku district**, a prime spot for people watching, especially if you want to watch Tokyo's youth wearing the latest fashions. At the heart of Harajuku is Omotesando Street, lined with fashionable boutiques, restaurants, and cafés.

You can buy anything, from a tape recorder to a stuffed peacock, at **Asakusa**, a bustling shopping and entertainment area made up of dozens of crosshatched alleys and covered passages, for less than elsewhere in Tokyo. The western end of Asakusa has theaters, burlesque shows, bathhouses, and restaurants. A large boulevard on the edge of the area is home to the Kokusai Theater. Tickets to plays here are inexpensive, despite the extraordinary sets. Surprisingly, behind the glitz, Asakusa is also one of Tokyo's most traditional areas.

Japan's best baseball (*besuboru*)

One of the most popular destinations in Tokyo is in the Korakuen district, southwest of Ueno Park: the **Korakuen baseball stadium**. With two baseball leagues and 12 teams, the Japanese are passionate *besuboru* (baseball) fans, and the stadium is often sold out through the entire season. (The Japanese baseball season is roughly equal to ours.)

The best theater in Japan

The three traditional forms of theater in Japan are Kabuki, Noh, and Bunraku, all of which can be seen at their finest in Tokyo. The **National Theater of Japan**, *4-1 Hayabusa-cho, Chiyoda-ku; tel. (81-33)265-7411*, is the best for Kabuki and Bunraku. It was designed by Hiroyuki Iwamoto, based on a centuries-old design for Kabuki theaters.

Kabuki plays have fantastic plots, elaborate costumes, a lot of action, and singing. All parts are played by men, and performances go on for hours. (You don't have to sit through an entire performance. It is acceptable to leave or arrive in the middle.) Musicians are seated on stage, and stagehands wearing black hoods bring actors their props during performances.

The largest Kabuki theater in Tokyo is **Kabukiza**, in the Ginza. (However, as mentioned above, the best place to see Kabuki is at the National Theater, because performances are translated and explained via earphones.)

Bunraku—puppet versions of Kabuki—are heroic tales of samurai enacted by life-size puppets. A small theater in the National Theater is designed especially for Bunraku.

Noh plays, which date back to the 12th century, are highly stylized and symbolic dramas. The stage is bare except for a backdrop showing a huge pine tree. Actors wear masks and speak in falsetto voices. The best place to see Noh plays are small Noh theaters, including **Ginza Nohgakudo**, *6-5-15 Ginza, Chuo-ku; tel. (81-33)571-0197* (for performances every even-numbered month); the **National Noh Theatre**, *4-18-1 Sendagaya, Shibuya-ku* (for performances every first Wednesday at 1 p.m. and every third Friday at 6 p.m.); **Kanze Nohgakudo**, *1-16-4 Shoto, Shibuya-ku; tel. (81-33)469-5241* (for performances on the first Sunday every month at 11 a.m. and the second Thursday on even-numbered months at 5 p.m.); and **Hosho Nohgakudo**, *1-5-9 Hongo, Bunkyo-ku; tel. (81-33)811-4843* (for performances every second Sunday and every third Saturday at 1 p.m., except in July and August, and on Wednesday in odd-numbered months at 6 p.m.).

The world's best flower arranging

Ikebana, the Japanese art of flower arrangement, follows strict aesthetic and philosophical principles. Flowers are placed to symbolize heaven above, earth below, and man in the middle. Ikebana was developed in the eighth century, when it was practiced at the Imperial Court. Today, the art can be seen in every temple and many households throughout Japan. The **Ohara School of Ikebana**, *7-17 Minami-Aoyama, 4-chome, Minato-ku; tel. (81-33)499-1200*, offers a two-hour course in traditional Japanese flower arranging, Monday through Friday mornings.

Tea ceremony secrets

The Japanese make even the English look careless when it comes to making tea. O-cha (green tea) is served ceremoniously on important occasions, at the beginning of conversations, at temples, and at the end of meals. The many details of the ceremony have been carefully preserved throughout the centuries. Tea is served without sugar in small cups without handles as participants sit silently in a circle. The tea is ground into a fine powder and then, after steeping, whisked until it foams. The cups are held and contemplated before the tea is sipped. Every movement has a symbolic significance.

You can see tea ceremonies at a number of hotels in the city, including the **Imperial Hotel**, *1-1-1, Uchisaiwaicho, Chiyoda-ku; tel. (81-33)504-1111*, for 1,100 yen ($9); **Hotel Okura**, *2-10-4, Toranomon, Minato-ku; tel. (81-33)582-0111*, for 1,030 yen ($8); and **Hotel New Otani**, *4-1, Kioicho, Chiyoda-ku; tel. (81-33)265-1111, ext. 2443*, for 1,030 yen ($8). Tea ceremony classes are offered at **Kenkyusha Eigo Centre**, *1-2, Kagurazaka, Shinjuku-ku; tel. (81-33)261-8840*, where 10 courses cost 34,000 yen ($264), not including an enrollment fee of 10,000 yen ($77); **Chado Bunka Shinko-kai**, *Sado-kaikan, 3-39-17, Takadanobaba, Shinjuku-ku; tel. (81-33)361-2446*, where a month of classes costs 7,500 yen ($58), not including an enrollment fee of 10,000 yen ($77); and **Etsu**, *3-12-3, Koenji Minami, Suginami-ku*, where a month of classes costs 4,000 yen ($31) and a one-day class costs 2,000 yen ($15), not including an enrollment fee of 4,000 yen ($31).

Super sumo

The best place to witness sumo is the Ryogoko district in northeast Tokyo, home to more than 30 stables for the immense wrestlers who wander the streets dressed in kimonos and topknots. You can watch them competing (wearing slightly less) at the new sumo stadium called New Kokugikan.

Sumo tournaments take place in mid-January, mid-May, and mid-September. If you can't make it to the tournaments, have your hotel call a stable to ask permission for you to watch a morning practice session. Two stables to try are **Kasugano-beya**, *1-7-11 Ryogoku, Sumida-ku; tel. (81-33)631-1871*, and **Takasago-beya**, *1-16-5 Hashiba, Taito-ku; tel. (81-33)876-8866.*

Bathing at its best

In Japan, a bath is not just a bath. It is a ceremony. Tokyo has 1,865 public *sento* (bathhouses)—which indicates the importance of the bath to the Japanese. Sixteen of the baths are fed by natural hot springs. You can enjoy one for 320 yen ($2.50)—but you must follow the rules.

Shoes are left in lockers by the front door, and clothes are exchanged for small towels, with which you attempt to cover yourself as you walk to the communal bath. (Men and women bathe separately.) Before climbing into the steaming water, wash yourself with soap and water using your little towel. Little stools are lined up in front of a row of faucets near the pool. This is where you soap up. Remember to rinse yourself thoroughly—it is a terrible faux pas to get soap in the clear water of the bath. Once you are clean, climb into the *furo* (tub) and soak. Be prepared for some scrutiny. After all, not many Westerners are seen here. One good bathhouse is Azabu Onsen, in the Juban district near Roppongi.

The best restaurants

Chinzanso, *10-8 Sekiguichi 2-Chrome, Bunkyo-ku; tel. (81-33)943-1111*, is an enormous restaurant set in a magnificent garden. Dinner is about 10,000 yen ($77).

Kushi Hachi-ten, *10-9 Roppingi, 3-Chrome, Minato-ku; tel. (81-33)403-3060*, was Jimmy Carter's favorite restaurant when he passed through Tokyo. Dinner is about 10,000 yen ($77), including drinks.

Iseju, *14-9 Kodenmacho, Nihonbashi; tel. (81-33)663-7841*, the oldest restaurant in Tokyo, established in 1869 by the Takamiyama family, serves the world's best sukiyaki.

Hundreds of restaurants in Tokyo are named **Yabu-Soba**, but the one at *2-10 Kanda Awaji-cho, Chiyoda-ku; tel. (81-33)251-0287*, is the best. *Soba* is the traditional noodle soup eaten by everyone in Japan with astonishing speed and slurping noises. Try the *mori-soba* with wild vegetables. Dinner is about 2,000 yen ($15).

Sushi is also found everywhere and is eaten as often for breakfast as for dinner.

Tokyo's best sushi is served at **Kybei**, *8-5-23 Ginza; tel. (81-33)571-6523.* Warning: The prices match the quality. Dinner is about 7,500 yen ($60).

The best place for eel is **Chikuyo Tei**, *8-14-7 Ginza; tel. (81-33)542-0787.* The eel, grilled (*kaba-yaki*) or cooked with a sweet sauce (*shiro-yaki*), is served in a teahouse atmosphere—you sit on the floor on tatami mats. Well-prepared eel is one of the most expensive meals in Tokyo. Expect to pay about 12,000 yen ($85) for a meal for two.

For a good Western meal, try **Maxim's**, *Sony Building, 5-3-1 Ginza, Chuo-ku; tel. (81-33)572-3621.* This replica of the Paris restaurant is staffed by Paris-trained cooks and waiters. This is the best French restaurant in Japan; it's also one of the most expensive. Meals are up to 25,000 yen ($200).

Asia's most dangerous food

If your culinary curiosity is stronger than your common sense, try fugu (poisonous blowfish), considered the greatest Japanese delicacy. The meat is fine, but the innards are deadly. (About 30 Japanese per year die eating fugu.) The fish is served as *fugusashi* (raw flakes eaten with a soy, orange, and chive sauce), *birezake* (sun-dried fins dipped in hot sake), and *fuguchiri* (*fugu* soup). You should eat fugu only during a month with an R in it (as with oysters) and only when prepared by a licensed fugu cook.

Sake at its best

Tokyo has a number of *nomiya* (sake houses), where you can sample this peculiarly Japanese brew. **Sasashu**, *2-2-2 Ikebukuro, Toshima-ku; tel. (81-33)971-9363,* is the best, serving little goodies along with the warm white wine. **Chichibu Nishiki**, *2-13-14 Ginza, Chuo-ku; tel. (81-33)541-4777,* is the most attractive sake house, a historic building filled with antiques.

Tokyo's best (and most traditional) hotels

The best accommodation in Japan is at a *ryokan*, a traditional Japanese inn. They are virtually unchanged since the times of the samurai, with translucent paper windows, sliding doors, mat floors, alcoves, polished wood, and intricate gardens. (They do, however, have electricity, running water, and modern toilets.)

When you arrive at a *ryokan*, you are greeted at the entrance (where you leave your shoes), then escorted to your room, served tea, and given a freshly laundered cotton kimono. The rooms are furnished with tatami mats, cushions, and scrolls. Sliding-glass walls usually overlook Japanese gardens. After the ritual bath in a sunken wooden tub, dinner is served in your room by a maid in a kimono, who later prepares your futon bed.

Ryokans in Tokyo vary widely in price. **Fukudaya**, *6 Kioicho, Chiyoda-ku; tel. (81-33)261-8577,* is expensive, starting at 50,000 yen ($400) per person, including two meals. **Atamiso**, *4-14-3 Ginza, Chuo-ku; tel. (81-33)541-3621,* is 10,000 yen ($77) per person. **Tokiwa Ryokan Shinkan**, *7-27-9 Shinjuku, Shinjuku-ku; tel. (81-33)202-4321,* is 7,000 yen ($50).

A slightly cheaper but less intimate version of the *ryokan* is the *minshuku*. These inns are frequented primarily by vacationing Japanese. You are not always given a kimono or served your meals in your room, but a night in one of Japan's 27,000 *minshuku* costs only about 5,000 yen ($40) per person, including two meals. For reservations, contact the **Japan Minshuku Center**, *B1 Kotsu Kaikan Building, 2-10-1 Yurakucho, Tokyo 100; tel. (81-33)216-6556,* or the **Japan Minshuku Association**, *Eighth Floor, Kokusai kanko kaikan, 1-8-3 Marunouchi, Chiyoda-ku; tel. (81-33)232-5310.*

Tokyo's top Western-style hotels

Hotel Okura, *2-10-4 Toranomom, Minato-ku; tel. (81-33)582-0111,* next to the American Embassy, offers both Western- and Japanese-style suites, the latter with tatami mats, futons, and shoji screens. The hall is brightened with enormous, elaborate flower arrangements. Shops, restaurants, and a swimming pool are available to guests. Service is impeccable. A double room starts at 26,000 yen ($200).

The **Imperial Hotel**, *1-1-1, Uchisaiwaicho, Chiyoda-ku, Tokyo 100; tel. (81-33)504-1111*, is next door to the Imperial Palace, overlooking its grounds and Hibiya Park. Dating back to the Meiji era, it is now a thoroughly modern building that comprises some of Tokyo's best shops and restaurants. A double room starts at 38,000 yen ($285); suites are 62,500 yen ($560).

The **Keio Plaza**, *2-2-1 Nishi Shinjuku, Shinjuku-ku, Tokyo 160; tel. (81-33)344-0111*, was the first high-rise in Tokyo and has magnificent views. The hotel restaurant, Ambrosia, features performances by a pianist. A double room is usually 27,000 yen ($200), but special deals are available.

Gajoen Kanko, *1-8-1 Shimo-Meguro, Meguro-ku; tel. (81-33)491-0111*, is an old-fashioned hotel with ornate doors and 1940s decor. A double room is 20,400 yen ($150).

The **Hyatt**, *2-7-2 Nishi Shinjuku, Shinjuku-ku; tel. (81-33)349-0111*, overlooks Shinjuku Central Park and has views of Mount Fuji. Live music is played in the lobby every night. A double room is 34,000 yen ($254).

The best places for romance—with a twist

Just outside Tokyo are **rabu hoteru** (love hotels), where you can choose from rooms with exotic themes: water beds that look like space shuttles, revolving roulette-wheel beds, or beds built into copies of the Sphinx. Most rooms have mirrored ceilings and large television screens. Rooms are 2,500 yen to 3,750 yen ($20 to $30) an hour (cheaper after 10 p.m.).

Although the tourist boards are not likely to give you the names of specific love hotels, they are not hard to find—they are everywhere. They resemble American motels. And their garages are designed with curtains, in order to hide visitors' cars and protect their privacy.

The best of Tokyo at night

Tokyo's liveliest night life is in the **Roppongi district**, where clubs stay open until 6 a.m. Wandering the maze of streets, you'll find everything from intimate jazz cafés to huge hostess clubs. The nightclub hostess, although often clad in a kimono, is not to be confused with the geisha, who presides only at private parties, usually to entertain businessmen.

Geishas undergo intensive training in the arts of dance, music, and song. They serve at parties as entertainers, waitresses, and witty conversationalists. Hostesses, on the other hand, are employed by nightclubs to pour sake, provide conversation, and sometimes serve as dance partners. Neither the geisha nor the hostess is a prostitute.

Tokyo's hottest disco is the **Lexington Queen**, *B1, Third Goto Building, 3-13-14 Roppongi, Minato-ku; tel. (81-33)401-1661*, which attracts such celebrities as Sylvester Stallone, Stevie Wonder, and Rod Stewart. It is big with the fashion and film crowds. The cover charge is 3,000 yen ($24) for women and 4,000 yen ($31) for men.

Two other good discos are **Le Rat Mort**, *Ginza; tel. (81-33)571-9296*, and **May Flower**, *Ginza; tel. (81-33)563-2426*.

At **Club Fontana**, *31524 Roppongi; tel. (81-33)401-1419*, you can listen to a pianist and a vocalist. The entrance fee is 7,000 yen ($56).

For chic dancing and drinking, visit the **Potato Club**, *Akasaka; tel. (81-33)588-0950*, which has live music. An evening here is 10,000 yen ($77).

Akasaka is another good district for nightclubs. One is **Club Charon**, *tel. (81-33)586-4480*, which is inexpensive. Although it's crowded, it's a good place to enjoy live jazz and mingle in Tokyo's artistic circles.

The seediest side

The seedy side of Tokyo's night life is in the **Shinjuku district**. The streets here are crammed with neon signs for X-rated movie theaters, brothels, often called Turkish baths, and little local bars, where *mama-san* will serve you cheap *mizuwari* (watered-down whiskey).

These local bars are also the places to experience *karaoke*. Well-whiskied customers with microphones and accompanying tape recordings entertain the bar with their favorite love songs. Talent is of little consideration in these late-night shows. What counts is volume. (*Karaoke* has been forbidden in many residential areas.)

Yoshiwara, known as the Turkish massage district, is Tokyo's lust-ridden den of iniquity.

Mount Fuji: the world's best sunrise

Those who have seen the sun rise from the top of **Fuji-san** (Mount Fuji) claim it is a mind-altering experience. Mount Fuji, which the Japanese consider a goddess, hides its dazzling beauty in a cloak of clouds most days. When the cloak is lifted, the 12,390-foot peak glitters white. You can climb the mountain only from the end of June through the beginning of September. Six trails lead to the top.

A short train or bus ride from Tokyo brings you to **Fuji-Hakone-Izu National Park**. Although the climb takes four to six hours, most of the trails are easy to hike, and the view is spectacular. Fellow trekkers, who sport everything from the latest fashions to the long white robes of religious pilgrims, are interesting additions to the view.

You can spend the night in communal stone huts along the way and wake up in time to see the sunrise. Or you can begin hiking at night and reach the peak above the clouds just as the rising sun illuminates the sky. Wear sturdy shoes or boots and bring along warm, waterproof clothing and a flashlight. It is windy at the summit.

Kyoto: Japan's most beautiful city

For more than 1,000 years, **Kyoto** was the political, cultural, and religious capital of Japan, and the city's heritage is still evident in its 1,600 temples, 200 shrines, and well-preserved traditions of architecture and craftsmanship. After trying to make your way through Tokyo, you'll find Kyoto's gridlike street plan a pleasure. Kyoto, about three hours from Tokyo, merits a visit of several days. The city's treasures are many.

Kyoto's most important sights

The **Imperial Palace** and its 220-acre park are the city's central attractions. Built by Emperor Kammu in A.D. 794, it has been destroyed several times by fire, but the existing building follows the original design. To visit the palace, you must get a pass at least 20 minutes and sometimes up to two weeks in advance. Register for a pass at the **Imperial Household Agency**, *Kyoto Gyoen, Nai Kamigyo-ku; tel. (81-75)211-1215*. Bring your passport.

The **Heian shrine**, with its impressive torii gate, was built in 1895 to commemorate the 1,100th anniversary of Kyoto's founding. The shrine itself is a replica, 12 times reduced, of the original Chinese-style Imperial Palace, set in Kyoto's most beautiful gardens. In the spring, you can walk among weeping cherry trees and azaleas; in the fall, chrysanthemum displays decorate the stepping stone pond. The shrine is a favorite spot for weddings, and often you will catch a glimpse of a bride and her party, all dressed in kimonos.

Kinkaku-ji (Temple of the Golden Pavilion), in the northwest corner of the city, is Kyoto's prettiest temple. Surrounded by a lake, its exterior walls are gilded. The existing temple is a reconstruction of the original one, built in 1397. Trees shade the structure, and you can see mountains in the distance.

Southwest of Kinkaku-ji is **Ryoanji** (Temple of the Peaceful Dragon), founded in 1473. Its famous stone garden is simple yet thought-provoking. Stones are raked in Zen patterns (the sea, the desert, or the mountains), which are said to aid meditation.

The **Kyoto National Museum**, *527 Chayamachi, Higashiyama-ku; tel. (81-75)51-*

1151, houses an impressive collection of Chinese paintings from the Ming and Ch'ing dynasties, as well as treasures from Buddhist temples and Shinto shrines. Admission is 300 yen ($2).

The **Toji temple**, which is five stories and 183 feet high, has the tallest pagoda in Japan. The temple's stone house (*azekura*), built of wood without using nails, houses an unrivaled collection of art treasures. On the 21st of each month, the Toji flea market, where you'll find everything from household items to miniature bamboo cages with singing crickets, is held here.

Nijo Castle, situated on 70 acres and surrounded by stone walls and a moat, was built in 1603 as the Kyoto residence of Leyasu, the first shogun of the Tokugawa family. Of the palace's five buildings, don't miss the Ohiramai and its Great Hall, decorated with paintings by Tanyu Kano. Corridors in the Imperial Messenger's chamber are constructed so that anyone stepping on the floor will trigger a sound resembling the song of the Japanese bush warbler, warning guards of approaching intruders. The shogun's apartments, in the fifth building, contain hidden chambers, where samurai guarded their master out of sight of palace guests.

Sanjusangendo (Temple of 33 Niches), a few blocks east of Kyoto Station, was founded in 1132 and is a national treasure. It is so-named because the facade is divided into 33 niches, one for each of the goddess Kannon's 33 personifications. The goddess is embodied here in a 10-foot statue, the *Thousand-Armed Kannon*.

Saiho-ji (Moss Temple), founded in 1339, is an incredible green. Its pond is shaped like the Chinese character for *heart and mind*.

The **Katsura Villa** is widely admired as the crowning achievement of Japanese architecture. Begun in 1590 by Kobori Enshu for the military dictator Hideyoshi, it is silent, austere, and perfectly balanced.

The **Shugakuin**, a villa in the foothills of Mount Hiei, has three large stepped gardens. Built in 1629 as a retirement home for Emperor Gomizuno-o, the buildings are fragile, simple, and airy. Both the Katsura Villa and the Shugakuin can be visited by permission of the **Imperial Household Agency**, *address above*.

The craft quarter

Kyoto's old **Nishijin district** is the place to buy famous Nishijin silk brocade, which is still handwoven. You can hear the sounds of silk looms along the narrow back streets. Displays of the district's handwork can be seen at the **Nishijin Textile Museum**, *Omiya Imadegawa, Kamigyo-ku*.

Another Kyoto specialty is Kiyomizuware pottery, produced by a 16th-century technique. Kiyomizuware is sold everywhere in Kyoto, but a concentration of particularly good shops is located along Teapot Lane near the Kiyomizu temple.

A good place to watch a variety of craftsmen at work on damascene metalware, woodblock prints, dolls, and porcelain is the **Kyoto Handicraft Center**, *Kumano Jinja Higashi, Sakyo-ku*. You'll also see painters, weavers, and goldsmiths here. The restaurant on the top floor has a good view of the city.

Yuzen cloth, decorated by using a special 300-year-old dying process, is another Kyoto specialty. To achieve its perfect color, the cloth must be washed in the cold running waters of the Kamo River. Walk along the river between the Nijo-dori and Shijo-dori bridges for a good view of this activity.

The world's best knives

Aritsugu, *Gokomachi Nishi-iru, Nishikikoji-dori, Nakagyo-ku; tel. (81-75)221-1091*, in the heart of the market district in central Kyoto, has been supplying Japan with swords and knives since 1560. Fujiwara Aritsugu, who began the family business, was the sword maker to the imperial household and supplied feudal warriors with their weapons.

Today, cooking knives, which are direct descendants of the original Aritsugu swords, form the core of the business. The assortment is bewildering: the *deba-bocho,* for slicing through fish, meat, and bones; the *usuba* and the *nakiri,* for chopping and slicing vegetables; knives with rosewood or black synthetic composition handles; and knives banded with buffalo horn to help prevent cracking.

Aritsugu's knives range from 4,375 yen ($35) for a *deba-bocho* with a 5-inch blade to more than 12,500 yen ($100). Terakubo Wasaburo, the director of the shop, can instruct you on the proper care and storage of your knives.

Kyoto's best restaurants

Kyoto's restaurants tend to be smaller, more old-fashioned, and more intimate than those in Tokyo.

Sagano, *45 Susuki-no-banba-cho, Nanzen-ji, Sakyo-ku; tel. (81-75)771-8709,* which offers 10 kinds of tofu dishes, is unknown to non-Kyoto residents. Dinner is served overlooking the garden and costs about 2,500 yen ($20). This restaurant is particularly cozy in the rain. It is open from 11 a.m. until 7 p.m.

Another excellent tofu restaurant is **Okutan,** *86-30 Fuku chi-cho, Nanzen-ji, Sakyo-ku; tel. (81-75)771-8709,* where you are served by kimono-clad waitresses. Order the *yudofu* or the *shojin-age* for deliciously prepared Zen-style vegetables. Dinner costs about 2,500 yen ($20), and the restaurant is open 10:30 a.m. until 7 p.m. except Thursdays.

Junidanya, *Shijo Hanami Koji; tel. (81-75)561-0213,* is also small and intimate. If you can't read the Japanese menu, you can order in English.

Good places to look for a restaurant are the English-language *Kyoto Restaurant Guide,* published by the Kyoto Restaurant Association, and the *Kyoto Gourmet Guide.*

Japan's best hotel

The **Tawaraya,** on a quiet back street in Kyoto, *tel. (81-75)211-5566,* is a Japanese paradise. Dim and cozy, it has 19 rooms that are booked year-round. You must remove your shoes at the door, where you are welcomed with a warm washcloth, tea, and a *yukata,* a light, cotton version of the kimono. (Your street clothes are neatly packed away.)

Bedrooms at the Tawaraya open onto a wooden platform overlooking the garden. Guests sit on *zabuton,* square cushions placed on the tatami mats that cover the floor. The bathroom looks out onto its own garden. All utilitarian items, such as televisions, telephones, and tea-making sets, are hidden. There are no room keys, and futons are kept in the closets. You're served eight-course dinners on a lacquered table. A staff of 38 keeps things running smoothly.

You must make reservations at least two months in advance. (You can make reservations from the United States through the **Ryokan Reservation Center of Pacific Select Agency,** *(800)722-4349* or *(212)972-8748,* or a travel agent.)

The best Western-style hotels

The most luxurious hotel in Kyoto is the new **Takaragaike Prince Hotel,** *Takaragaike, Sakyo-ku; tel. (81-75)712-1111,* in the northern suburbs.

Two other good Western-style hotels are the **Miyako,** *Sanjo Keage, Higashiyama-ku; tel. (81-75)771-7111,* and the **International Kyoto,** *284 Nijo, Abura-koji, Nakagyo-ku; tel. (81-75)222-1111.* Both are opposite the Nijo Castle.

Three hotels with both Western- and Japanese-style rooms are the **Kyoto Royal,** *tel. (81-75)223-1234;* the **Fujita,** *tel. (81-75)222-1511;* and the **Kyoto,** *tel. (81-75)211-5111,* where rooms are 15,000 yen ($117).

The hottest night life

Gion is Kyoto's answer to Tokyo's Asakusa district. The city's best theaters are located here. Gion is also the best place to attend a geisha party. Make arrangements through your hotel or travel agent. Settle on the price beforehand—these are usually costly evenings.

Gion Corner, *First Floor, Yasaka Kaikan Hall; tel. (81-75)561-1115*, was established by the Kyoto Visitors Club. Classes here teach various aspects of Japanese traditional arts. In two evening shows, demonstrations are given of the tea ceremony, flower arrangement, Bunraku puppet plays, *kyomai* (Kyoto-style dance), court music, and *koto* music, which is played on a 13-string instrument.

Nihon Seibukan, *60 Shimogawa izumikawa-cho, Sakyo-ku; tel. (81-75)701-3121*, is an exercise hall for karate, kendo, and judo. Geisha dances are performed during April and May at the **Pontocho Kaburenjo** (Kamogawa Dance), *Pontocho-dori 3 jo, lower level, Nakagyo-ku; tel. (81-75)221-2025*; the **Kitano Kaikan** (Kitano Dance), *Shinsei-cho; tel. (81-75)461-0148*; and the **Gionkobu Kaburenjo** (Cherry Blossom Dance), *Hanamikoji Gion; tel. (81-75)541-3391*, theaters. You can watch Kabuki performances at **Minami-za**, *Higashizame, Shijo-ohashi, Higashiyama-ku; tel. (81-75)551-1522*; Noh performances are staged at **Kanze Kaikan**, *Okazaki, Sakyo-ku; tel. (81-75)771-6114*. Call the **Kyoto Information Center**, *Kyoto Tower Building, Higashi-Shiokojicho, Shimogyo-ku; tel. (81-75)371-5649*, for exact dates and times.

Osaka: bests beneath the grime

Osaka, the industrial center of Japan, seems an ugly city at first glance. But if you look behind the city's utilitarian facade and grime, you will discover its traditional temples and shrines, secluded in their gardens; a mighty castle; and two good museums.

Visit the 10th-century **Temmangu shrine** on July 24 and 25, when the annual Tenjin Festival is held. On these nights, the normally solemn shrine to Tenjin, the god of learning, is transformed, as lantern-lit boats sail down Osaka's canals accompanied by a fireworks display.

The 16th-century **Osaka Castle**, located southeast of the Temmangu shrine, was built by the warlord Hideyoshi, who ordered huge stones for its construction, some of which are still in place. One of the stones, called Higo-ishi, is 47 1/2 feet long and more than 19 feet high.

Tennoji Park, in the southern part of the city, contains a zoo, botanical gardens, the Shitennoji temple, and Keitakuen, one of the best examples of a Japanese strolling garden.

Two excellent museums of Chinese and Japanese art are the **Fujita Art Museum**, *10-32 Amishima, Miyakojima-ku, Osaka-city; tel. (81-6)351-0582*, and the **Masaki Museum of Art**, *2-9-26 Tadaokanaka, Tadaoka-cho, Senboku-gun; tel. (81-725)21-6000*.

Treelined **Mido-suji** is Osaka's best street for strolling and window shopping, but for serious shopping you're better off in one of the city's shopping districts or arcades. An underground labyrinth of stores is located in Kita, near Umeda Station. Shinsai-Bashi-Suji is another well-known shopping street. Also visit the shopping arcade between Shinsai-Bashi-Suji and Ebisu-Bashi-Suji.

Osaka's best restaurants

For luxury dining with some unusual surprises, visit **Wakatake**, *1-18-31 Shinsaibashi Chuo-ku; tel. (81-6)271-0005*. The service is irreproachable and the food excellent, but the main attraction is the garden, which has a large sculptured *lingam* (holy penis), as well as more traditional pavilions and a bathhouse. Dinner costs about 25,400 yen ($198).

For Osaka's best eel, try **Hishitomi**, *7-8 Sousemon-cho, Minami- ku; tel. (81-6)211-1159*. Order the *unagi-teishoku*. Dinner is from 11,000 to 14,000 yen ($85 to $109) per person.

For local atmosphere and good grilled specialties, try **Goenya**, a chain of 12 inexpensive restaurants. The best in Osaka is at *30 Sennen-cho, Minami-ku; tel. (81-6)5731*. The place stays open until 3 a.m., and a meal costs less than 1,250 yen ($10).

The best accommodation
Two deluxe hotels in Osaka are the **Royal Hotel**, *Nakanoshima; tel. (81-6)448-1122*, where a double room is 26,000 yen ($195), and the **Miyako Hotel Osaka, Minami; tel. (81-6)773-1111**, where a double room is 26,000 yen ($195).

The liveliest entertainment
Kokuritsu Bunraku Gekujo (National Puppet Theater), *1-12 Nihonbashi, Minami-Ku, Osaka-city; tel. (81-6)212-1081*, is considered the original home of the 300-year-old art of puppeteering. The best Bunraku shows in Japan are presented here. Bunraku is not just for children. The stories are colorful and exotic, designed for adults.

Kabuki performances are given in the five-story **Shin-Kabukiza**, *4-3-25 Nanba, 20 Chuo-ku, Osaka; tel. (81-6)631-2121*, in the southern part of the city. The Takarazuka all-girl revue, Japan's most famous all-girl opera, performs at the Grand Theater in Takarazuka City, 40 minutes by train from Osaka.

The best bars and nightclubs can be found in Sonezaki Shinchi in Kita, near the Umeda arcade.

Hiroshima: the world's most sobering city
Hiroshima, the place where the first atomic bomb was dropped in 1945, is a sobering site. Heiwa O-dori (Peace Boulevard) leads to the **Hiroshima Peace Memorial Museum**, *1-2 Nakajima-cho, Naga-ku; tel. (81-82)241-4004*, south of Peace Park. The center features the Peace Tower and a museum of objects left after the explosion, as well as photographs of the bombed city and its victims.

The Industrial Promotion Hall, the building believed to have been directly below the center of the blast, also is located here. It has been left standing, gutted from the explosion, as a reminder of the bomb. On Aug. 6, the day of the bombing, Hiroshima holds its annual Peace Festival in the Peace Memorial Park.

You can reach the city of Hiroshima, set on a bay of the Inland Sea, by a two-hour bullet train ride. The stretch between Okayama and Hiroshima (when traveling from Osaka or Kyoto) is considered the most beautiful train ride in Japan.

The best place for singles
A worthwhile excursion from Hiroshima is to the island of Miyajima to see the Shinto shrine **Itsukushima**, known among the Japanese as one of Japan's three great sights. (The other two are Amanohashidate and Matsushima.) The island is dedicated to a Shinto goddess who, according to legend, is extremely jealous. For this reason, married couples might want to think twice about visiting the shrine. Singles can take the train or bus from Hiroshima to Miyajimaguchi, where a ferry will take them to the island. Offshore stands the red painted torii, the gate of the Shinto shrine.

The shrine itself and its smaller galleries are on stilts above the water—when the tide is high, both the shrine and the torii appear to be floating on the water. The sight is most spectacular in April, when the cherry blossoms are out, and in the fall, when the maples turn glowing red. These are also the most crowded times.

For an incredible view of Hiroshima surrounded by mountains and the Inland Sea, take the ropeway from Momiji-dani Park behind the Itsukushima shrine to the highest peak on the island, Mount Misen. From this height, you also can see the ninth-century Gumonjido temple.

Hiroshima's best hotels
The three best Western-style hotels in Hiroshima are the **Hiroshima Grand**, *4-4 Hatchobori, Naka-Ku; tel. (81-82)227-1313*, which has double rooms for 18,000 yen ($144); the **Hiroshima Kokusai**, *3-13 Tate-Machi, Naku-Ku; tel. (81-82)248-2323*, where a double room is 12,000 yen ($96); and the **Hiroshima River Side**, *7-14*

Kaminoboicho, Naka-Ku; tel. (81-82)227-1111, where a double room is 14,000 yen ($112). The best *ryokan* is **Minakiso,** *1-7 Mitaki-ocho, Nisuhi-ku; tel. (81-82)237-1402,* which charges 18,750 yen to 40,000 yen ($150 to $320) per person, including two meals.

Nagoya: Japan's best pearls

Japan's best pearl farms are in **Nagoya,** between Tokyo and Kyoto. You can get from Tokyo to Nagoya Station in just two hours on the super-express trains on the Shinkansen line. The station is the commercial center of the city, with stores and restaurants located in the network of underground passageways that connect to neighboring buildings.

The heart of the pearl industry is just south of Nagoya in Ago Bay and five other bays off Ise-shima National Park. To learn about the process of pearl cultivation, visit Toba, where pearls are developed, harvested, and prepared for sale. *Ama* (women divers), ranging in age from adolescence to their early 40s and dressed in white cotton bodysuits, face masks, and caps, collect the oysters, making six or seven dives an hour to depths of up to 100 feet. The oysters are then seeded and suspended in cages from bamboo rafts. More than 200 million pearls each year are harvested after about six months, sorted, and polished.

Ama demonstrate their diving methods at the Toba Aquarium and on Irukajima, also in Toba Bay. Nearby Pearl Island has a model pearl farm that you also can visit.

Nagoya's two most important sights are its castle and the Atsuta shrine. **Nagoya Castle** is topped by a famous pair of golden dolphins and crowned with a five-story inner tower.

The **Atsuta shrine** is considered one of the most important Shinto shrines in Japan, housing the **Kusanagi-no-Tsurugi** (Grass-mowing Sword), one of the nation's Three Sacred Treasures. (The other two are the Sacred Jewels at the Imperial Palace in Tokyo and the Sacred Mirror of Ise Grand Shrines.) Nagoya also claims one of the largest zoos in the Orient, in Higashiyama Park.

Nagoya's best Western-style hotels are the **Meitetsu Grand,** *1-2-4 Meieki, Nakamura-Ku, Nagoya; tel. (81-52)582-2211,* where a double room is 17,000 yen ($136); **Nagoya Castle,** *3-19 Hinokuchicho, Nischi-Ku; tel. (81-52)521-2121,* where a double room is 22,000 yen ($176); **Nagoya Kanko,** *1-9-30 Nishiki, Naka-Ku; tel. (81-52)231-7711,* where a double room is 22,000 yen ($176); and **Nagoya Miyako,** *4-9-10 Meieki, Nakamura-Ku; tel. (81-52)571-3211,* where a double room is 20,000 yen ($160).

Japan's strangest festival

Japan's strangest festival is the **Konomiya Naked Festival,** held every Jan. 13 in Inazawa City, near Nagoya. This festival, first held in A.D. 780 to ward off the plague, is still thought to drive out devils. Each year, one man is chosen to act as a divinity who takes on the sins of others and purges them. The divine man appears naked before a crowd of also naked men at the Owari Okunitama shrine and exorcises spectators' demons. The male worshipers surge forward to touch the holy man and transfer their sins to him.

The best fishing and parasols

The most colorful fishing spectacle in Japan takes place in **Gifu,** 30 minutes by train north of Nagoya. From mid-May to mid-October, cormorant are fished at night along the Nagara River. Boats are hung with fire baskets to attract ayu, a kind of river smelt. The fishermen then command large tame birds, tied to long leashes, to dive in and retrieve the fish from the illuminated river.

Gifu is also famous because it contains one of the few remaining *bangasa,* or Japanese parasol factories, where you can watch paper and silk dancing parasols being made and individually painted. If you buy one, the factory will take care of shipping it home for you.

Kyushu: Japan's best seaside resort

Kyushu, the southernmost of Japan's islands, is a popular summer resort for Japanese vacationers. Because few Western visitors make their way here, it is a good place to sample

Japanese culture as well as sandy beaches. Stay in a *ryokan* in one of the remote towns in the area and explore the secluded coves at your leisure.

Kitakyushu, the largest city on the island, is a good place to find a hotel and make travel arrangements. The island's nicest drive is from Kitakyushu to Fukuoka, which takes you along the coast and through Genkai-Quasi National Park. En route are oddly shaped rock formations and pine groves that dot the white sand beaches.

At the southernmost tip of the island is **Ibusuki,** a popular seaside resort. The **Ibusuki Kanko Hotel,** *3755 Junicho, Ibusuki, Kagoshima Prefecture; tel. (81-9932)22131,* a Western-style hotel facing north to Mount Sakurajima, is a good place to stay. You can lie by the pool in the shade of banana trees and dine in hotel robes and slippers in the Jungle Theater restaurant. A double room is 10,625 yen ($85).

Another good restaurant is in the **Ibusuki Royal Hotel,** *42-32-1 Junicho, Ibusuki; tel. (81-9932)32211,* where a double room is 12,500 yen ($100).

Ibusuki's seawall is lined with small *ryokan.* The beaches cover underwater hot springs, and in certain spots attendants will dig holes so you can immerse yourself from toe to chin in warm sand.

The best of **Fukuoka's** many parks is **Ohori,** a large open parkland surrounding a tidewater lake formed from the moat of an old castle. Bridges link the surrounding park with smaller island parks in the lake. In the background is a forest with remnants of the stone walls of Fukuoka Castle.

Nagasaki: Japan's first open door

Curving around the mouth of the Urakami River, **Nagasaki** is considered Japan's first open door. This was the first major port to trade with the Portuguese and Dutch in the 16th century. European influences are still visible in the city's old forts, brick buildings, and cobblestoned streets.

Nagasaki was also the first place in Japan to accept Christianity. However, in the 16th and 17th centuries, the Christian communities here were forced underground. Monuments to martyred Christians can be found throughout the city. The most impressive is the **Oura Catholic Church,** built in 1865 to commemorate 26 Christians who were crucified here in the 16th century. The church is the oldest example of ecclesiastical Gothic architecture in Japan.

Glover Mansion is the house where Madame Butterfly (from the opera of the same name) waited for her lover's return. Set on a hilltop, the house has a panoramic view over the harbor.

Nagasaki is also known as the second city on which the Americans dropped the atomic bomb. Peace Park and the Atom Bomb Museum are monuments to the horror.

Good Western hotels in Nagasaki are the **Nagasaki Grand,** *5-3 Manzai-Machi, Nagasaki; tel. (81-958)231-234,* where a double room is 13,000 yen ($104); **New Nagasaki,** *tel. (81-958)266-161;* **Nagasaki Tokyu,** *1-18 Minamiyamate-Machi; tel. (81-958)251-501,* where a double room is 19,000 yen ($152); and the **New Tanda Hotel,** *2-24 Tikiwa-Machi; tel. (81-958)276-121,* where a double room is 17,000 yen ($136).

Suwa-so, on a hillside overlooking the city, is a *ryokan* visited by Japan's royal family.

Nagasaki's most threatening volcano

A short ride by bus or ferry from Nagasaki brings you to the active volcano **Mount Aso** in Aso National Park. A toll road leads most of the way up the side of the volcano. You can reach the rim by foot or ropeway, unless the area has been closed by volcanologists. Standing at the rim, you will see white smoke and gases spurting from the bottom of the crater and feel the ground rumbling.

Hokkaido: Japan's best skiing

The 1972 Winter Olympics were held in **Hokkaido,** Japan's northernmost district.

It was then that the world discovered the region's ideal skiing conditions.

Skiing in Japan is luxurious. Everything is civilized and efficient. For your après-ski enjoyment, try a relaxing *o-furo* (hot bath) with a massage and hot sake.

The two best places to ski are **Teine**, good for slalom skiing, and **Eniwa**, good for downhill skiing. **Mount Moiwa**, 30 minutes southwest of the city by bus, is also popular, overlooking the capital and the Sea of Japan.

The region's biggest city is **Sapporo**, which has a wide choice of hotels, as well as taxis and buses to take you to the slopes.

The **Akakura Kanko Hotel**, *Myoko-Kogen, Naki-Kubiki-gun; tel. (81-255)87-2501,* in Niigata prefecture, is one of the best in Sapporo, with an excellent restaurant. Tables are set with crisp white linen and sparkling crystal and silverware. You can ski right from the back door, and a connecting system of lifts and slopes extends for miles through the mountains. A double room is 22,500 yen ($180).

Three other good ski hotels are the **Yamagata Grand**, *1-7-42 Honcho, Yamagata 990; tel. (81-236)41-2611*, with double rooms for 14,500 yen ($116); **Sapporo Park**, *3-11 Nishi Minami-10, Chuo-ku, Hokkaido 64; tel. (81-11)511-3131*, with double rooms for 23,500 yen ($188); and the **Sapporo Grand Hotel**, *4 Nishi Kita-1, Chuo-ku, Hokkaido 060; tel. (81-11)261-3311*, where a double room is 24,000 yen ($192).

Numerous lodges and *minshuku* (guesthouses) are located throughout Japan's ski country. They cost about 3,750 yen to 6,250 yen ($30 to $50) a night per person, including breakfast and dinner. Accommodation is Japanese-style—which means you sleep on a futon and share a room with three or four other people. Rooms are heated and often have televisions. Baths are communal, and toilets are down the hall. The food, Japanese country cooking served boarding-house style, is plentiful and good.

You can rent ski equipment at most Japanese resorts. The selection is good at larger establishments. Boots are the main worry for Americans; few Japanese wear size 10, for example. A set of equipment (boots, skis, and poles) rents for about 3,750 yen to 4,375 yen ($30 to $35) a day. Lift passes cost 3,125 yen to 3,750 yen ($25 to $30).

It's easy to book a ski trip once you're in Japan. Trains depart for snow country from Tokyo's Ueno Station every half-hour during ski season (but reservations are necessary). The closest slopes are three to four hours north.

Hokkaido's minority

Hokkaido is also known as the home of the **Ainu**, a fast-disappearing people originally from Honshu who have been forced north into the mountains. The Ainu are Caucasians, who, unlike other Japanese, have light skin and hairy bodies. The men often have thick beards, and the women have blue tattoos around their mouths. The best place to see their huts and their rituals of worship—the Ainu practice a form of nature worship influenced by Shintoism—is the small colony in **Asahikawa**, Hokkaido's second-largest city. You also can visit a display village in **Shiraoi**, near Noboribetsu Spa on the south coast.

Karuizawa: the best mountain resort

Karuizawa, two hours north of Tokyo, is the mountain escape of Japan's powerful elite who come here to play tennis or golf, to horseback ride, and to sail on the lakes. Since future emperor Akihito met and married the untitled Michiko Shoda at the Karuizawa Kai tennis club in the late 1950s, Karuizawa has been seen by many as a fairy-tale town where anything is possible—even falling in love with a prince.

The countryside is embellished with waterfalls and streams and dotted with elegant villas. In the summer, classical music concerts are staged outdoors.

Generally, the hotels in Karuizawa have great restaurants. The Kuruizawa Prince complex holds about 13 restaurants, including an informal Japanese grill and an excellent French restaurant where diners eat overlooking a pond while being entertained by a harpist. The Suehiro (a steak house) is a favorite, as is the Akasaka Hanten, a Chinese restaurant with a pleasant garden.

The elegant **Karuizawa Prince**, *Karuizawa, Karuizawa-machi, Kitasaku-gun, Nagano Prefecture 389-01; tel. (81-267)46-1111*, offers three types of accommodation: the original hotel, log cabins, and a fancy new annex overlooking a pond and a golf course.

Hoshimo Onsen Hotel, *2148 Oaza Nagakura, Karuizawa-Machi, Kitasaku-gun; tel. (81-267)45-5121*, has hot springs as well as comfortable rooms for 10,000 yen ($77).

Tsuruya Ryokan, *678 Kyu-Karuizawa, Karuizawa-machi, Kitasaku-gun, Nagano Prefecture 389-01; tel. (81-263)93-2331*, is a cozy little Japanese inn.

Asia's most alluring women

Geishas are highly talented entertainers, well versed in all the traditional arts of Japan. They are not prostitutes. They are good conversationalists who serve food and drinks and provide high-caliber singing and dancing. Geisha parties, often organized by Japanese businessmen, feature pretty entertainers dressed in kimonos, elevated clogs, whiteface makeup, and elaborate hairdos. Generally these parties are for men, but women can be included.

The Akasaka district in Tokyo has a concentration of exclusive houses where geishas perform. Company presidents and others who can afford the high cost frequent these places.

You can see young apprentice geisha, called *maiko*, near Gion Corner and Ponto-cho in Kyoto. The young women appear at 6 p.m., dressed in their colorful costumes, and shuffle in tiny steps from their residences to their places of work.

Your travel agent can arrange for you to attend a geisha party in Kyoto or Tokyo. But you could pay up to 100,000 yen ($800) per person.

The
Best
of India

> This is indeed India! The land of dreams and romance, of fabulous wealth and fabulous poverty, of splendour and rags, of palaces and hovels, of famine and pestilence, of genii and giants and Aladdin lamps, of tigers and elephants, the cobra and the jungle, the country of a hundred nations and a hundred tongues, of a thousand religions and two million gods, cradle of the human race, birthplace of human speech, mother of history, grandmother of legend, great-grand-mother of Tradition.
>
> —*Mark Twain, 1897*

India is an exotic, ancient, multicolored land covering an area of 1,261,597 square miles. The size, variety, and grandeur of this country make it a feast for visitors. Every region is different. The bordering Himalayas contain the highest peaks in the world, including Mount Everest. The Ganges Plain is one of the world's greatest stretches of flat land—as well as one of the world's most densely populated regions. There are towns dating back to 3000 B.C. and mosques that draw pilgrims by the thousands. The country's diverse population of 683 million shares the land with elephants, tigers, camels, and millions of sacred cows.

The religions of India are as varied as its climate. You'll find Hindus, Muslims, Sikhs, Buddhists, Jainists, Jews, Christians, Zoroastrians, and former headhunters. The different groups are lively and colorful, each with its own festivals, dances, cultures, and cuisines. Each has left its artistic mark on India—ancient, elaborately carved temples are located throughout the country.

We will explore India counter-clockwise, beginning with Delhi and moving southwest toward Bombay, southeast to Madras, northeast to Calcutta, and finally to the farthest corners of India for a look at the continent's least-known regions.

Delhi, the oldest Indian city

When Bombay and Madras were mere trading posts, Delhi was the capital of a 500-year-old empire. India was ruled from Delhi by various Hindu dynasties, then the Moguls, and finally the British. And it was here that India was granted its independence.

Eight cities have flourished where Delhi is today. And each of the city's former rulers has made significant architechural contributions.

Today, Delhi is divided into two cities: Old Delhi, once the Mogul capital, which is filled with ancient forts, temples, and monuments; and New Delhi, the present capital, which has wide boulevards, modern office buildings, parks, and hotels.

Tour Delhi from south to north, because growth has moved steadily northward. Bring a sweater if you plan to travel during the winter, when temperatures drop to 40 degrees Fahrenheit.

The Seventh Wonder of Hindustan

Ten miles south of Delhi is **Qutb Minar,** a 234-foot victory tower known as the Seventh Wonder of Hindustan. One of the earliest monuments of the Afghan period in India, and built in pre-Muslim Delhi, it has stood for 800 years. You can climb the 11th-century tower via a spiral staircase.

At the foot of the tower lies the **Quwwat-ul-Islam Mosque.** The first mosque built in India, it was erected in the 12th century on the foundations of a Hindu temple. The mosque contains the **Iron Pillar,** which has remained rust-free for more than 1,500 years.

Delhi's top sights

East of the Qutb Minar is the fortress and tomb of the first Tughlaq king (1230 to 1400), Tughlaqabad. A seven-mile, inwardly sloping wall guards the tombs of the founder and his son, mosques, palaces, and hundreds of residences. The fortress has a panoramic view of the surrounding countryside.

Two miles south is the Suraj Kund, the largest Hindu monument near Delhi. It is believed that a sun temple once stood here.

Following the road back toward Delhi you'll come to the **mausoleum of Emperor Humayun,** erected in the 16th century. This was the precursor of the Taj Mahal, and it features rose-colored sandstone walls inlaid with white marble and surrounded by gardens. Opposite the tomb is a place of pilgrimage, the **shrine of Nizam-ud-din,** which encloses a mosque covered with a fine Byzantine dome.

A few minutes away is the **Purana Qila,** a fort standing on the site of Indraprastha, a mythological Delhi of prehistoric times. The present fort, built in the 16th century, frames one end of the two-mile vista leading to the Presidential Palace.

Pass through the **War Memorial Arch** honoring Indian soldiers who died in World War I. This leads to the fabulous **Rajpath,** the broadest avenue of Delhi, lined with government buildings. **Parliament House** is a huge circular structure with an open colonnade. The **Presidential Palace,** built in this century, has 340 rooms and covers 330 acres.

The strange **Jantar Mantar Observatory,** *Parliament Street, Tolstoy Marg,* was built in 1725 by Maharaja Singh II of Jaipur to view the sun, moon, and stars. Every year on the March 21 and Sept. 21 equinoxes, the sun shines through a slit in the wall.

Jama Masjid, India's largest mosque, has three white marble domes and two 134-foot minarets. Typical of Mogul architecture (it was built in the 17th century), its 450-square-foot courtyard is paved with marble.

Facing the mosque is the **Red Fort,** the finest example of Mogul architecture, built in 1648 behind red sandstone walls. Once the imperial palace of Emperor Shah Jahan (1627-1657), today it houses the Museum of Archeology. It is open to the public during daylight hours.

Rajghat (Shrine of Mahatma Gandhi), southeast of the Red Fort, is where Gandhi was cremated in 1948 following his assassination. A black marble slab in the garden is inscribed with the leader's last words, "Oh, God."

Delhi's best shopping

Chandni Chowk, the city's marketplace, is a web of narrow streets that surround the Red Fort. Here you can shop for shoes, cows, pungent Oriental spices, jewelry, ivory carvings, and rich brocades, and then you can have your stars read or your hair cut.

The best zoo in India

Delhi Zoological Park, next to Purana Qila on Mathura Road, is home to rare white tigers. Magnificent gardens brighten the park, which has an especially extensive collection of birds. The zoo is open until 6 p.m.

India's most colorful festival

Try to time your visit to Delhi to coincide with **Ram Lila**, when gigantic effigies of Ravana and his minions are burned on the last day of the 10-day **Dussehra Festival** to symbolize the destruction of evil. According to Hindu mythology, the evil Ravana kidnapped the wife of the good Lord Rama. Commemorating the story of Lord Rama, Ram Lila is one of the biggest events in Delhi.

Dussehra usually falls in October and includes colorful dramas and dances reenacting the stories of gods and demons.

The best dancing

The **Bhangra Dance** of the Punjab, a community dance marked by its energy and hilarity, can be seen in Delhi. Men dance in a line on one side, wearing brightly colored turbans, vests, and pants, while women dance on the other. For specific information on when and where performances are held, contact the **Government of India Tourist Office**, *30 Rockefeller Plaza, Room 15, North Mezzanine, New York, NY 10020; (212)586-4901.*

The best hotels in Delhi

The **Ashok**, *50-B Chanakyapuri; tel. (91-11)600121*, is a modern hotel with a pool, miniature golf, gardens, tennis courts, an art gallery, and an open-air theater that features performances by a highly rated Indian contemporary dance company. Theater seats are RP60 ($2.25). A double room is RP2,160 ($80).

The **Imperial**, *Janpath; tel. (91-11)3325332*, at the edge of town, is surrounded by a palm garden. Rooms are large, with private bathrooms and air conditioning. A double room is RP2,025 ($75), suites are RP5,400 ($200). A pool and tennis courts are open to guests. The restaurants are good.

Oberoi Maidens, *7 Sham Nath Marg; tel. (91-11)2525464*, is a gracious old hotel with colonial-style bedrooms and private baths, a swimming pool, tennis courts, and gardens. A double room is RP2,025 ($75). The hotel disco, Sensation, is a good place to go at night.

The Taj Mahal—one of the world's greatest wonders

South of Delhi, in the town of Agra, is the **Taj Mahal**, one of the world's greatest wonders. Built in white marble by Emperor Shah Jehan as a mausoleum for his queen, Mumtaz Mahal, it is most beautiful at sunset and under moonlight.

Twenty-two years went into the construction of this palace, which was completed in 1652. Beautiful formal gardens and a reflecting pool lead to the arched entrance. An enormous dome, accompanied by two smaller domes, tops the structure, and four minarets mark the corners. It is said that the architect's right hand was cut off upon the completion of the Taj Mahal so that he could not duplicate his creation.

Rajasthan: India at its most traditional

Southwest of Delhi is a desert land broken up occasionally by jungle. Here are some of the most ornate temples in India. **Rajasthan**, which translates as *Abode of Kings*, is the home of the Rajputs, an ancient people whose mythology includes tales of chivalry and romance. You can recognize Rajputs by their colorful clothing: the men wear pink and yellow turbans, and the women wear full skirts and half-bodices and wrap themselves in long mantles.

Jaipur: the rosiest spot in India

The buildings of **Jaipur**, the capital of Rajasthan, are made of rose-colored stone. Founded in 1727 by the brilliant Maharaja Jai Singh II, who built an observatory with a remarkably accurate 90-foot gnomon (an object whose shadow serves to indicate time), Jaipur is protected by a crenellated wall with seven gates. The city's spacious streets are filled with exotic animals, including peacocks, elephants, buffalo, and camels.

The most beautiful building in Jaipur is the **City Palace**, which is now a museum housing rare manuscripts, arms, and paintings. The loveliest structure within the palace walls is the lofty **Chandra Mahal**, a seven-story building with a view of the city. While there, wander through the **Man Singh II Museum**. Also visit the **Jantra Observatory**, constructed in 1718.

Next to the palace are the **Jai Niwas Gardens**, filled with fountains, statues, and artificial lakes where well-fed crocodiles swim.

Hawa Mahal, or Palace of the Winds, *Siredori Bazaar*, with its delicate overhanging balconies and perforated windows placed one above the other in a symmetrical pattern, is another important landmark in Jaipur. Although it looks like a palace, it is actually a facade behind which women of the court could watch processions without being seen themselves.

Guarding the city from the hills above is **Nahargarh**, or Tiger Fort. You can get there from the Amber palace by jeep or by rickshaw.

Amber: a little-known treasure

The 17th-century palace at **Amber** stands high above a lake, its towers and domes reaching to the sky. An arched gateway leads into the courtyard, where a broad flight of stairs climbs to the royal apartments. Inside are Persian mosaic walls, filigreed doors, fountains, aqueducts, and high ceilings covered with mirrors. Beneath the palace are vaults said to hide the treasures of Jaipur.

You can visit the palace astride an elephant. Musicians play as you make the slow climb to the palace apartments.

Mount Abu—India's most beautiful sunset

While **Mount Abu** is most famous as an archeological and religious landmark, you should come here for another reason as well: to see the sunset. From **Sunset Point** you can see much of Rajasthan illuminated by the pink glow of the setting sun.

Mount Abu, which is due south from Jodhpur, was originally a center of the cult of Siva. The Jains (a Hindu sect that abhors the killing of animals) still make pilgrimages to this mountain, which is known in Hindu legend as the son of the Himalayas. Between Abu's peaks are five Jain shrines, the most beautiful of which was built of pure white marble by Vimal Shah in the 11th century. Inside, marble elephants carrying statues of Vimal Shah and his family climb from the pavilion to the domed porch, which is intricately carved and supported by eight sculptured columns.

Udaipur: India's most romantic city

Udaipur, known as the City of Dreams, is the most romantic city in India. Founded in the 16th century by Maharana Udai Singh, supposedly a descendant of Sri Ram (the hero of the Ramayana epic), Udaipur is bastioned by a wall and five spiked gates. Inside the walls are whitewashed houses painted with murals.

The ruler of the city, known as the Maharana, or Sun of the Hindus, lives in a sparkling palace surrounded by a lake. Amber, jade, and colored glass sparkle on the palace pinnacles. Inside are ivory doors, marble balconies, stained-glass windows, and mirrored walls. You can visit every day, 9:30 a.m. until 4:30 p.m.

Udaipur's second most beautiful sight, after the palace, is **Sahelion-ki-Bari Park**, one of the best examples of Hindu landscaping. The park is filled with ornamental pools, fountains with water spouting from elephant trunks and bird beaks, and black stone monuments.

How to travel like a maharaja

Maharaja's Palace on Wheels, a reincarnation of the elegant train that once carried maharajas and viceroys, is the most pleasant way to travel through Rajasthan. The plush cars have been restored, and each coach is equipped with individual sleeping cabins, bathrooms, showers, a kitchen, and an attendant dressed in traditional Rajasthani clothing. The train has two dining cars and a library/bar.

The trip takes eight days and seven nights and includes stops at Jaipur, Udaipur, Jaisalmer, Jodhpur, the Taj Mahal, and the bird sanctuary at Bharatpur. The train leaves from Delhi Cantt Station every Wednesday at 10:45 p.m.

For more information, contact the **tourist office**, *30 Rockefeller Plaza, Room 15, North Mezzanine, New York, NY 10020*, or **Tours of Distinction**, *Central Reservations, Rajasthan Tourism, Chandralok Building, 36 Janpath, New Delhi; tel. (91-11)321820.*

The best of Ahmedabad

Founded in 1411, **Ahmedabad** was once considered the finest city in India. Of the many Muslim monuments there, the finest is **Ahmed Shah's Masjid Mosque**, which contains his colored marble tomb, 250 massive pillars, carvings, and inscriptions. The shah's queens lie in ornate tombs across the street.

Another Muslim architectural feat is the Haibat Khan Mosque, built in the 16th century by the Rani, one of the two wives of Mahmud Begara, after her son was executed for "misbehavior."

Also see the stone carving of a slave of Ahmed Shah in the **Mosque of Sidi Sayvid** and the **Mausoleum of Shah Alam** at Batwa.

The **Sun Temple of Modhera**, 60 miles northwest of Ahmedabad, is the best of the many temples built by the Solanki kings of Anhilwad Patan. The grandeur of this temple is enhanced by its wide steps and pillared porch. The shrine was designed so that the image of Surya (the sun god) is illuminated by the rising sun and the equinoxes.

Kashmir: India's most beautiful region

North of Delhi, wedged between China and Pakistan, is the most beautiful region in India, the **Vale of Kashmir**. At 5,200 feet, it is circled by mountains (the Himalayas to the southwest, the Karakorams to the north). It feels as if it is cut off from the rest of the world. Snow-capped peaks appear to float above the clouds. Houseboats and lotus leaves bob in spring-fed lakes. Flowers fill the meadows. The fair-skinned residents look surprisingly European, despite their veils and nose rings.

Mogul emperors (descendants of Genghis Khan) were partial to Kashmir and built lavish palaces and gardens in the valley. In the colonial days, this was one of the few places in India where Europeans were not allowed to build. (They resorted to living in houseboats instead of houses.) For centuries, caravans from China and elsewhere passed through Kashmir on their way to the southern reaches of India, giving it an international flavor.

The best time to visit Kashmir is April or May, when the spring flowers are in bloom. But every time of year has its charms. The leaves turn scarlet in the fall, and the fields are lush during the summer. Winter brings deep snows and good skiing conditions.

Srinagar, the capital of Kashmir

Srinagar, the capital of Kashmir, has flowering rooftops (the roofs are made of earth, which bursts into bloom in the spring). Painted shutters and dyed-wool doors brighten the brown houses that line the river. Houseboats with canopied roofs sail the river toward the Dal and Nagin lakes, where they anchor. The men wear fur caps, the women veils to cover their hair. Turbanned old men smoke hookahs on the sidewalks.

Srinagar's most important landmark is a small **temple to Siva** at the peak of a 1,000-foot hill, which can be climbed by steep stone steps. The view from the top encompasses the town, the river Jhelum, and Dal Lake.

The **Palace Hotel,** *tel. (91-194)71241,* overlooks the lake. A 100-acre terraced garden surrounds the hotel. There is a golf course on the property, and the hotel restaurant and bar are recommended. A double room is RP1,620 ($60).

Broadway, *Maulana Azad Road; tel. (91-194)75621,* another recommended hotel in Srinagar, has a swimming pool and a good restaurant. A double room is RP810 to RP1,080 ($30 to $40).

Shahenshah, *Boulevard Road; tel. (91-194)71345,* is a reasonably priced hotel in Srinagar with a pool, a garden, and a good restaurant. A double room is RP1,080 ($40).

Garden paradises, beautiful lakes

The Dal and Nagin lakes are bordered by two beautiful gardens: the **Shalimar Bagh** (Garden of Love), which was designed 400 years ago by one of the Great Moguls for his queen; and the **Nishat Bagh** (Garden of Pleasure), which has terraces of flowers and avenues of cascades.

Lake Manasbal, also in this area, is covered with lotus blossoms. **Lake Wular** is the largest lake in the region.

The holiest spot

In the mountains above the Liddar Valley is the sacred cave of **Amarnath,** reached by steps cut into the rock by pilgrims. Situated at 13,000 feet, the cave is surrounded by snow and ice most of the year. The night of the full moon in the month of Sravan (July or August) is considered the luckiest time to visit.

The world's highest golf course

The highest golf course in the world is at **Gulmarg** (8,700 feet), once a summer hill station popular with British colonialists. (A hill station was a mountain village where Europeans took refuge during the hot season.) Gulmarg's seven-mile Circular Path offers a dizzying view of the Vale of Kashmir and Srinagar.

India's best skiing

Kashmir has beautiful, pristine ski slopes, but its facilities, including the number of lifts and T-bars and the selection of rental equipment, are limited, which can be frustrating to good skiers. The conditions are improving, however, and for the more adventurous skier Kashmir offers heli-skiing.

Contact the Institute of Skiing and Mountaineering in Gulmarg or ask at your hotel for more information. The **Hotel Highland Parks** offers ski packages during the winter months. A double room is RP2,025 ($70).

The best of Bombay

Bombay is India's most modern, prosperous, and cosmopolitan city, an industrial metropolis and one of Asia's busiest seaports. Despite its industry, Bombay is also a beautiful city, backed by mountains and hugging the Arabian Sea. Hilly islands dot the harbor.

The best introduction to Bombay is a cruise along **Marine Drive,** also known as the Queen's Necklace. Tracing the coastline, it is the city's main boulevard and offers views of the sea and the Bombay skyline.

Wander Bombay's intriguing neighborhoods on foot. Venture beyond the Colaba market—a village of the Kolis, one of the original fishing tribes of the region. Old traditions are maintained here, and the women dress in colorful saris and flowers.

Chowpatty Beach, with its statue of Tilak, a great political leader of this century, is the political center of Bombay. This meeting place by the sea is always crowded with people fishing, playing, and eating at food stalls. The entertainment here is free: yogis buried in the sand, soapbox orators, fishermen hauling in their nets. The fortunetellers here are said to be disconcertingly good.

Not far from the beach is **Mani Bhavan** (the Mahatma Gandhi Memorial), which has photographs of the master of passive resistance, along with books he wrote.

The **Prince of Wales** in Fort Bombay has a good collection of Nepalese and Tibetan art, as well as 18th-century miniatures, jade, crystal, and china. It is open every day except Monday, 10 a.m. until 6:30 p.m. March through June, and 10 a.m. until 5:30 p.m. July through February.

The **Hanging Gardens**, where you can find respite from the noise of the city, have a beautiful view of the city. Here you can walk among bushes cut to resemble elephants, monkeys, cows, oxen, or giraffes.

The greenery on the left as you go beyond the gardens is part of the **Parsee Towers of Silence**, where locals dispose of their dead. The area is concealed by a park surrounded by a high wall. Bodies are carried to the top of towers, where they are left to be devoured by vultures. The Parsees originally came from the city of Pars in Persia, 1,300 years ago. Today their descendants are a key part of the fabric of life in Bombay.

In Byculla, an old residential area, is **Veermata Jijabai Bhonsle Udyan** (the Victoria Gardens), a park full of trees and plants. The park also includes the city zoo, the Victoria and Albert Museum, and a gigantic statue of an elephant that once guarded the Elephanta Caves outside Bombay. Visit the park between dawn and dusk, but if you want to see the zoo or the museum, make sure you arrive before 6 p.m. Tuesday through Saturday you can rent a boat or ride an elephant or camel from 8 until 9:30 a.m. and 4 until 5:30 p.m. Compared with the noise and crowds of most of Bombay, this is a peaceful place to escape to for a while.

Juhu Beach, 12 miles northwest of Bombay, is the best place to cool off after wandering through the city. To get to the lake, you cross **Mahim Creek**, a fishing village with ancient boats. After your swim, you can watch the performing monkeys.

Bombay's best buys

Bombay's shops display beautiful pure silk saris for $10 to $100 and silver earrings for $15. Bargain for the best prices.

The city's two most colorful markets are **Mahatma Jyotiba Phule Market** (Crawford Market), *Dadabhai Naoroji and L. Tilak roads*, and **Thieves Market**, near Mohammed Ali Road. The first is a good place to buy fruits and vegetables, cotton, animals, and flowers. It is also a great place to take photos. Thieves Market is a junk-lovers delight, offering everything from old car parts to fine antiques. Both markets are open from early morning until late evening.

The best time to visit

The best time to visit Bombay is during **Ganesh Chaturthi**, a festival that glorifies Ganesh, the god of good omens. Hindus worship images of the deity, which are later sunk in a lake. A spectacular procession follows. The festival is usually held in September.

Eating well

The best restaurant in Bombay is the Indian restaurant in the Taj Mahal Hotel, a five-star establishment with good curry.

Delhi Darbar, *Holland House, Colaba; tel. (91-22)2020235*, near the Regal Cinema, has Bombay's best Mughlai (Muslim/Indian) foods. The mutton is excellent.

Khyber Restaurant, *145 Mahatma Gandhi Road; tel. (91-22)273227*, offers Continental dishes as well as Indian, vegetarian, and Mughlai fare. It is open for lunch until 4 p.m. and for dinner until midnight.

Sri Ratan Tata Institute, *30 S. Patkar Marg; tel. (91-22)274537*, features Parsee foods and tempting pastries.

Satkar Caterers, *Indian Express Building; tel. (91-22)2043259* and *Landmark, 35*

N.S. Patkar Marg; tel. (91-22)8226077, is a favorite with locals, serving vegetarian dishes, South Indian specialties, and Punjabi dishes. The patio at the Indian Express Building is pleasant.

Berry's Restaurant and Bar, *Veer Nariman Road; tel. (91-22)2048954,* opposite the Stadium House, near Churchgate Station, is well-regarded for its food. The Indian specialties are good. The restaurant is open until midnight.

Bombay's best hotels

The finest hotel in Bombay is the **Taj Mahal Intercontinental,** *Apollo Bunder, Colaba; tel. (91-22)2023366,* where Old World charm is combined with modern amenities. Rooms at this waterfront hotel, which are decorated with antiques and artwork, have views of the city and the harbor, air conditioning, and private baths. French, Chinese, and Indian dishes are served in the hotel's four restaurants. A double room is RP4,590 ($170).

Oberoi Towers, *Nariman Point; tel. (91-22)2024343,* is a luxurious hotel with fountains, marble walls, a health club, a swimming pool, six restaurants, and a shopping arcade. A double room is RP4,590 ($170).

Less ostentatious is the **Grand,** *17 Sprott Road, Ballard Estate; tel. (91-22)2618211,* where the rooms are still spacious, with private baths and air conditioning. The Grand has a cozy, old-fashioned air about it, and it is popular with European travelers. A double room is $35.

Hotel Nataraj, *135 Netaji Subhash Road; tel. (91-22)2044161,* was once a private club. Today, it is a homey hotel near the sea. All the rooms have attached bathrooms and air conditioning. A double room is RP1,100 to RP1,500 ($40 to $55).

The Elephanta Caves—the most important site outside Bombay

The most important side trip from Bombay is to the island of **Elephanta,** six miles across the harbor, where five cave temples a visit have been excavated. No one knows who carved the temples, which were created between the fifth and sixth centuries.

The caves contain beautiful, life-size sculptures of Hindu gods. The most impressive is a 15-foot sculpture of three-headed Mahesamurti, a trinity made up of the gods Brahma, Siva, and Vishnu. Outside the main cave is an enormous columned veranda, approached by steps and sculptured elephants. To best appreciate the subtleties of the religious statues and carvings here, read up on Hindu mythology before your trip. Bring a flashlight if you want to see anything.

The holiest village

Mahabaleshwar, a tiny village on a hill nine hours south of Bombay by bus or train, was once considered so holy that Englishmen were not allowed on any part of the hill. (In 1824, General Lodwick broached it anyway.) Five streams of water representing the sources of five holy rivers flow through the Krishnabai Temple. They combine and travel through a sculpture of a cow's mouth into two cisterns where Hindus take holy baths. Mahashivaratri, a festival of Siva held in February or March, brings throngs of pilgrims.

Climb to nearby **Pratapgarh Fort,** built in 1656, for a view that extends all the way to the coast. On the western side of the fort a precipice drops 2,000 feet to the Konkan plain below. Prisoners once met their deaths here.

The **Frederick Hotel,** *Bombay-Goa Road,* is the nicest in town, with private bathrooms, tennis courts, and a golf course.

Little Portugal: Goa

South of Bombay is **Goa,** a Portuguese colony from 1510 to 1961. It has a mixture of local and Portuguese charms and some of the most beautiful ocean and river beaches in India. In addition to all this, Goa has perfect weather (except during monsoon season, June through September). Whitewashed houses and Catholic churches give Goa a

European look. Traders first traveled to Goa seeking spices.

St. Francis Xavier came here in 1540 and converted many of the people to Catholicism. Although he died in China, his body was returned to Goa. His embalmed remains lie in a silver, gem-encrusted casket in the **Basilica of Bom Jesus** in Panaji. Once every 10 years the saint's body is displayed. If you look closely, you will notice that his big toes are missing—they were bitten off by religious fanatics. His arm, too, is gone—it was sent to the pope. Built in 1593, the basilica is Goa's primary example of Portuguese architecture.

Nearby is the magnificent, all-white *sé* (cathedral), noted for its five bells. Its Golden Bell is the largest of its kind in the world. A small chapel in the back of the cathedral contains a crucifix on which a vision of Christ is said to have appeared in 1919.

Goa's delights are physical as well as spiritual. The silvery beaches along the Malabar Coast are incomparable. The best are near Panaji, the capital. **Dona Paula** is the most chic. Across the Mandovi River from Panaji is the spectacular **Calangute Beach. Colva Beach,** on the south coast near Margao, is also beautiful. At some of Goa's beaches, the swimming is spoiled by fierce undertows. Ask around before you test your strength against the sea.

The best place to stay if you are a beach lover is the **Dodge Holiday Village,** *Candolim Bardez, tel. (91-832)7515* run by the Taj Group, on Calangute Beach. You can sleep in a cottage near the sea, use the sports facilities, and lounge in hammocks on the beach, as well as restaurants and bars. A double room is RP1,485 ($55).

If you would rather stay in Panaji, try the **Fidalgo,** *18 June Road; tel. 6291,* or the **Mandovi,** *D.B. Bandodkar Marg; tel. 6270,* both reputable hotels with double rooms costing RP875 ($35).

The world's oldest Buddhist sculptures

The Buddhist caves of **Ajanta** were carved into the face of a 259-foot rock cliff 2,000 years ago and contain the oldest Buddhist art in the world. Frescoes cover the walls, ceilings, and pillars of the 25 monasteries and five temples here.

The **Ellora Caves** form another fantastic complex of Buddhist, Jain, and Hindu temples carved side by side from rock. The 34 elaborately carved and frescoed caves were constructed between A.D. 600 and A.D. 1200. The Hindu temple Kailasa is the most beautiful, with enormous pillars, painted ceilings, and grand statues. It took 100 years to quarry the 3 million cubic feet of rock here.

Aurangabad is the best base for visiting the caves. Stay at the **Rama International Hotel,** *R-3 Chikalthana; 82455,* where a double room is RP1,500 to RP1,775 ($55 to $65) and the staff is efficient. The manager personally meets guests at the airport.

Daily flights run between Bombay and Delhi via Aurangabad. By train, you can get to Aurangabad aboard the Punjab Mail and the Panchavati Express from Bombay to Manmad. Daily bus service connects Aurangabad with Ellora, Ajanta, and Jalgaon.

Bus tours to the Ellora Caves from Aurangabad are conducted by the Maharashtra Tourism Development Corporation. Tour guides will pick you up at Aurangabad Railway Station at 9 a.m. and return you there at 6:30 p.m.

The Maharashtra Tourism Development Corporation also provides four-day excursions to Ajanta-Ellora-Aurangabad from Bombay. The cost is less than RP810 ($30), including transportation, guides, and accommodation. Buses leave daily.

The most sacred Jain hill

Shatrunjaya (the Place of Victory), a hill by the river of the same name, is the most sacred of five hills considered holy by the Jains. It is covered by 863 Jain temples. You must remove all leather before you will be permitted to climb the hill. To see the temple jewels or to take photos, you must ask permission from the Munimji, Anandji Kalyanji Trust, in Palitana. Your hotel can give you the daily viewing times for the jewels and help you get permission to take pictures. The temples are closed in the monsoon season (the summer months) and after dark.

The best place to stay while visiting the hill is the nearby town of **Palitana**, due south of Ahmedabad in the province of Gujarat. **Hotel Sumeru**, *Station Road*, is pleasant, with a pretty garden and good vegetarian food.

The best lion viewing

The **Gir Forest**, on the coast of the Arabian Sea in Gujarat, is the last stronghold of the Asiatic lion (only about 200 remain in the world). The best time to see the king of beasts is during the hot months, from March through May, when they frequently congregate at watering holes, but the forest is open to the public from December until June.

To make arrangements to visit the forest, contact the **Regional Manager**, *Gir Tourism Development Corporation, Rang Mahal, Diwan Chowk, Junegadh*. Gir Tourism Development Corporation offers two-day trips for RP950 ($35), including transportation (by jeep), binoculars, guides, and accommodation. You cannot shoot the lions, but you can hunt the other game in the area (blue bull, spotted deer, gazelle, and antelope).

The most splendid ancient ruins

The empty shell of the once-courtly kingdom of **Malwa** sits atop a plateau in Mandu, northeast of Bombay. Known centuries ago among Muslims as the City of Joy, today it is a ghost town. Raj Bhoja first noticed the charms of the location, which is cut off from the world below, and built a retreat here in the 10th century. The Muslims took over in the 13th century and expanded the city until it covered eight square miles, the whole surrounded by massive walls.

The oldest monument is the mosque, which is to the right as you enter the grand Delhi Gate. The most beautiful is the tomb of Hoshang Shah (1405-1432), a white marble structure with a great dome and four turrets. The buildings are divided into three main groups: the Royal Enclave, the Village Group, and the Reva Kund Group.

You can stay overnight at the modern **Travellers' Lodge**, which has eight rooms with attached bathrooms. It is located on the main road on the way to the Village Group. The **Taveli Mahal**, once the royal stables, is located closer to the fort.

The least-known Buddhist caves

A drive through the jungle from Mandu brings you to **Bagh**, where sixth-century Buddhist caves rival those at Ajanta (but they're not as crowded). Sadly, the beautiful wall paintings have been somewhat damaged over time.

The river Bagmati flows in front of the humid sandstone caves. The foliage has been cut back to prevent sneak attacks by pythons and tigers.

Only four of the nine caves have survived. Hewn from solid rock, each has a veranda, a large central hall, gloomy monks' cells, and a prayer hall. The second cave has a maze of passageways and hidden chambers. It contains larger-than-life sculptures of the Buddha and his disciples and paintings of animals and flowers. The most beautiful paintings are in the fourth cave, Rang Mahal, which on its veranda has a mural of life-size figures.

Sanchi—the best Buddhist art

Northeast of the Bagh Caves, near the Bhopal, is **Sanchi**, one of the world's most important centers of Buddhist art. Emperor Asoka built his most beautiful monuments here on a hilltop overlooking the forest. (The emperor's son, Mahendra, left Sanchi for Sri Lanka, where he worked to spread the influence of Buddhism.) After the decline of Buddhism in India, the town lay forgotten until 1818, when it was rediscovered. Restoration was begun in 1912 by Sir John Marshall. Of the eight stupas (sacred mounds) originally built on the hill, only three remain.

What catches the eye first in Sanchi is the **Great Stupa,** a 106-foot second-century round burial mound with elaborately decorated gateways. Balustrades encircle its roof and base, and it is surrounded by a fence with four ornate gates. The bas-reliefs on the yellow stone gates are the most beautiful early Buddhist works of art that exist today. Don't expect to understand the elaborate religious illustrations—one archeologist published three enormous volumes on Sanchi.

The **Travellers' Lodge** is a pleasant little inn near the caves with eight air-conditioned rooms and a restaurant. A double room is RP270 ($10).

India's greatest man

If you head south from Sanchi through the jungles, you will come to the tiny town of **Sevagram**, where Mahatma Gandhi established his ashram (retreat) in 1933 and began putting his doctrines into practice. The Hindu leader established a self-sufficient community, with a dairy, a tannery, and a cloth-weaving. He refused to acknowledge the caste system, with its untouchables and "unclean" occupations. His simple hut is preserved exactly as he left it. At the Nai Talimi Sangh School in Sevagram, students continue to follow Gandhi's way of life, growing their own food and weaving their own cloth.

The best place to stay (if you share Gandhi's values of simplicity and modesty) is the guesthouse at the ashram, where food is served communally. For reservations write to **Sarve Seva Sangh**, *Sevagram, Wordha, Maharashtra.*

If you prefer creature comforts, stay at **Mt. Hotel**, *Commercial Road, Nagpur,* 50 miles away. (Nagpur is known for its fragrant orange groves.)

Madras—the most traditional city

The state of **Tamil Nadu**, at India's southern tip, is more traditional than the rest of the country. Because it is so far south, this region was untouched by the many invaders who once assailed the north. Founded by the Dravidians more than 5,000 years ago, Tamil is the home of India's oldest sculptures.

The capital of the region, **Madras**, is as colorful as the cotton cloth it is famous for producing. The fourth-largest city in India, it sprawls across 68 square miles.

India's best beach

Hugging the coast of the Bay of Bengal, Madras has one of the most beautiful beaches in India, if not the world: **Marina Beach**. It has fine sand and is lined with walkways and gardens.

The best sights

Fort St. George, built in 1640 by the British, is the best place to begin a tour of Madras. Twenty-foot walls loom over the city, which acts as the government center of Tamil Nadu. Inside is **St. Mary's Church**, the oldest Anglican church in Asia, built in 1680. The **Fort Museum** contains memorabilia of the East India Company, as well as costumes, coins, and china.

Madras National Art Gallery houses the famous 10th-century bronze statue of a dancing Nataraja-Siva and rare Mogul, Rajput, and South Indian paintings.

Next door is the **Government Museum**, which has the best bronze collection in India, as well as rare second-century Buddhist sculptures.

Madras Snake Park and Conservation Center in the beautiful **Guindy Deer Park** is home to cobras, pythons, and other exotic reptiles. The surrounding Deer Park shelters black buck and spotted deer.

Tradition says that the apostle Thomas (Doubting Thomas) came to Madras as a missionary and was martyred on St. Thomas Mount in A.D. 78. The **Cathedral of St. Thome**—the first Christian church in India—is a Gothic structure built on the site of a chapel said to have held the remains of St. Thomas.

Kapaliswarar Temple, dedicated to Lord Kapaliswarar (Siva), was built by the Dravidians. It was destroyed in 1566 during a war but rebuilt 300 years ago. Its gopura (pyramid-shaped entrance) marks the city's horizon.

Madras is home to the world headquarters of the **Theosophical Society,** an international organization promoting the interplay of religion, science, and philosophy. The banyan tree in the garden of the society's building is the oldest in India, shading 40,000 square feet.

The best dancing

Madras is the best place to see the classic **Bharata Natya** dance, in which dancers exhibit perfect control over every muscle in their bodies. (They can actually move their necks while keeping their heads motionless.) Originally a temple dance, this is the most ancient dance form in India. And it is performed to the accompaniment of musical instruments and singing.

The beauty of the Bharata Natya lies in the grace of its symmetrical patterns and in the emotions portrayed by the elaborate gestures and facial expressions of the dancers. Check the local newspapers—*The Hindi* and *Indian Express*—for show listings. You can watch Indian dancing every night during tourist season in the Mysore Room of the Taj Coramandel. (During the summer, performances often are canceled.)

Madras' most important side trips

The ancient city of **Mahabalipuram** has the world's largest bas-relief, *Penance of Bhaghirata,* an 80- by 20-foot work in stone. The city's other claim to fame is its group of seven pagodas, which look like flat-topped pyramids and are guarded by statues of an elephant, a lion, and a bull. The walls of the pagodas are illustrated with images from Hindu mythology.

Mahabalipuram was once the main harbor of the Pallava empire, which died out about 1,200 years ago. Hindu sculpture can be found in the cave temples carved from the rock here. When you tire of the ancient works of art, relax on Mahabalipuram's gorgeous beach.

Kanchipuram, the capital of the ancient Pallava empire, has 1,000 temples and 124 shrines. It is an important place of pilgrimage for Hindus. The **Kailasanatha Temple,** believed to be 1,200 years old, contains excellent seventh- and eighth-century paintings. Smaller but prettier is the **Varadarajaswamy Temple.** The best Hindu murals, which illustrate various wars, are in the **Vaikunthanatha Perumal Temple.**

One of the oldest cities in the south, **Kumbakonam,** on the banks of the Cauvery River, has 18 temples decorated with lively Hindu sculptures. Once every 12 years pilgrims invade the city for the bathing festival.

A half-hour away is **Thanjavur,** lying at the foot of India's greatest temple, **Brihadiswara,** whose tower rises more than 200 feet. The tower's dome rests on an 80-ton block of granite brought in from a village four miles away.

Forty miles south of Madras is the breathtaking ninth-century **Temple of Nataraja** at Chidambaram. Two of the temple's four granite gopuras are covered with sculptures illustrating the 108 positions of Natya Sastra, the Indian science of dancing. No one knows how the granite was brought to the temple, for there is no granite for 50 miles around.

India's most elegant hill station

Ootacamund, recently renamed Udhagamandalam (but still affectionately known as Ooty), is a small, elegant hill station in the Nilgiris, the famed Blue Mountains of southern India. Situated nearly 8,000 feet above sea level, Ooty appealed to the royalty and the wealthy of many cultures, each of which left its imprint, but none more indelibly than the British. English is the major tongue here, and Ooty feels for all the world like a Victorian town in the heart of England.

The best way to reach Ooty is to rent a car and driver and travel through the

Mudamalai jungle along the intricate hairpin turns that wind through parrot-and monkey-crowded bamboo jungles. It is a dramatic surprise to make the last turn and find yourself in a bit of England. Ooty's flowers are celebrated throughout India. Garden clubs present a floral spectacle each May, mingling familiar English varieties with exotic blooms.

Less than 50 miles away is a large wild-animal sanctuary. Not far from the hill station, entire families of monkeys scamper about, panhandling from passers-by, running off with fruit from trees or market stalls, and gazing at humans as intently as the humans stare at them. Now and then you'll catch a glimpse of an elephant, and you'll see birds everywhere. An excellent and inexpensive place to stay is the **Savoy Hotel**, *tel. 4234142*. Faded but still elegant in its full Victorian regalia, the Savoy is a treasure. Its gardens are famous throughout India. A double room is RP1,620 ($60).

Orissa: India in a nutshell

For a capsule view of India, visit the state of **Orissa**, on the Bay of Bengal. You can explore mountains, jungles, valleys, plains, tribal villages, coconut groves, and 250 miles of beach in this area of 60,000 square miles.

The recorded history of Orissa begins in 260 B.C., when the edicts of the Emperor Asoka were carved in rock in Dhauli, five miles from Bhubaneswar, the capital. The peak of Orissan civilization was reached between the 4th and 13th centuries, when thousands of temples and monuments were built. The British took over in 1803.

The **Adivasi**, a tribal group in Orissa, are descendants of the inhabitants of Orissa before the Aryan invasion 3,000 years ago. Over the centuries they have been pushed into the heart of Orissa, the least fertile section of the state. Now they are protected by the government.

Orissa's main sights

Bhubaneswar is a picturesque town with a myriad of temples, some dating back to 300 B.C. They are covered with spirals, turrets, decorations, and sculptures depicting good and evil, morality and immorality. The **Great Lingaraj Temple**, built in A.D. 1000, is the finest Hindu temple in India, with a tower that can be seen for miles. Outside town are Udayagiri and Khandagari hills, where caves were carved by Jain monks as far back as the first century B.C.

Konarak (the Black Pagoda), outside Bhubaneswar, is one of the most beautiful sights in India. More than 1,000 workers took 12 years to build the 100-foot-high temple. Dedicated to the sun, the 13th-century Konarak rests on a base of 24 wheels pulled by seven horses. The roof is topped by a three-tiered spire. The entire temple is covered with carvings and sculptures.

Puri, a site of Hindu pilgrimages, is one of the four holiest places in India. Hindus believe that if you stay here for three days and three nights, you will attain eternal life. The enormous **Jagannath Temple**, dedicated to the Lord of the Universe, was built in the 12th century. While non-Hindus are not allowed to enter the structure, you can get a good view inside the 20-foot temple walls from atop the neighboring Raghunandan Library.

The most colorful (and most crowded) time to visit Puri is June, during the **Rath Yatra Festival**, when the image of Lord Jagannath is taken from its temple and carried in a canopied car by thousands of pilgrims to Gundicha Mandir, the god's Garden House.

Puri is also a great place to shop. If you know how to bargain, you can get good buys on statues, toys, and shoes.

The place to stay in Puri is the **South Eastern Railway Hotel**, *Chakratirtha Road; tel. 2063*, which is near the beautiful but polluted beach.

Incredible Calcutta

Calcutta is incredible—a huge and growing industrial metropolis inhabited by the Bengalis, an emotional and artistic people who produce many of the best books, dramas, and films in India. The city is a convenient base for exploring the Himalayas, Sikh temples, and the temples of Orissa and Bhutan. No one can claim to really know India without visiting Calcutta.

If you arrive in Calcutta by train, you will see families camping on the platforms of Howrah Station, water vendors, newsboys, rice peddlers, tea-serving waiters, running children, and shouting porters.

When you leave the station and cross the **Howrah Bridge,** you will encounter cars, bicycles, cows, rickshaws, oxcarts, trucks, and crowds of people. Below the bridge, on the banks of the Hooghly River, live Calcutta's masseurs and barbers.

Calcutta's best sights

On the other side of the Howrah Bridge (the third-largest single-span bridge in the world) is **Old Calcutta,** the core of the city, which grew out of three tiny villages: Sutanati, Govindpur, and Kalikata (Anglicized as Calcutta). Kalikata was once a sacred spot with two temples. Aside from the temples, however, the area is unsavory.

Victorian Calcutta sprang up around **Fort William,** built in 1780. At the south end of Maidan Park, in front of the fort, is **Victoria Memorial,** completed in 1921 and filled with relics of British rule.

North of **Dalhousie Square** (now called B.B.D. Bagh) and surrounded by busy bazaar streets is the **Nakhoda Mosque,** which holds up to 10,000 people.

The **Indian Museum,** *Chowringhee Road,* is the oldest in India and one of the most comprehensive in the Orient. Its archeology section is the largest in Asia and one of the most important in the world, with a large and representative collection of antiquities illustrating the cultural history of India from prehistoric times to the Muslim period. The museum also has a fine collection of Indian coins, gems, and jewelry. It is open 10 a.m. until 4 p.m.

Parasnath Jain Temple, *Badris Temple Street,* built by the court jeweler in 1867, glitters with crystals and precious stones. A French crystal chandelier hangs above the gleaming mosaic-tile floor. The temple lamp has burned continuously for 112 years. A landscaped garden surrounds the structure. You can visit the temple 6 a.m. until noon and 3 until 7 p.m.

Calcutta has a fabulous **zoo** with white Bengal tigers, monkeys, reptiles, and white peacocks, among other exotic beasts and birds.

The **Botanical Gardens** cover 273 acres with mahogany trees, Royal Cuban palms, an orchid house, and other exotic flora. Its crown jewel is its banyan tree, the largest in the world, with a circumference of 1,000 feet. The garden was established in 1786 by the East India Company.

In the evening, stroll along **The Maidan,** a two-mile stretch of green lawn bedecked with statues of Indian heroes. When the sun sets, the locals use this as a rendezvous point. If you feel lucky, try out the Maidan Racetrack.

Calcutta's best shopping

New Market, *Lindsay Street,* is one of the largest markets in India, with 2,500 stalls selling everything from cheap tin pots to fine silks. The market's real name, the Sir Stuart Hogg Market, is, not surprisingly, seldom used. The market was built in 1874. It is open from the early morning until about 8 p.m. every day except Saturday afternoon and Sunday.

Best restaurants

Vineet Restaurant, *1 Shakespeare Sarani; tel. (91-33)440-788* has live Indian music between 6:30 and 11 p.m. Indian-vegetarian South Indian, and continental foods are served.

Peter Cat Restaurant, *18 Park St; tel. (91-33)298-841,* is a peaceful, pleasantly decorated place that serves Indian and continental food 10 a.m. until midnight.

Shenaz Restaurant and Bar, *2A Middleton Row; tel. (91-33)270-494,* is a romantic little place with good *tandoori* and Indian specialties. The restaurant is open 10 a.m. until 11:30 p.m. Make reservations.

Abhinandan, *24 Park St., Second Floor;* is a vegetarian restaurant with live music. It is open noon until 11 p.m. weekdays and 9 a.m. until 11 p.m. Sundays and holidays.

Gay Rendez-Vous, *71 Strand Road,; tel. (91-33)285-680,*has a lovely view of the Hooghly River and serves both Indian and Western cuisine. It is open 10:30 a.m. until 9 p.m.

Mocambo Restaurant, *25B Park St.; tel. (91-33)294-152,* has good *tandoori* dishes and dancing. It is open 10 a.m. until midnight.

Remember that you cannot eat meat or drink alcohol on Thursdays in Calcutta.

Calcutta's finest nights

Calcutta's best hotel is the **Oberoi Grand,** *15 Jawahar Lal Nehru Road; tel. (91-33)292-323,* which is centrally located and has rooms with beautiful private baths and refrigerators. Guests may use the swimming pool, health club, in-house astrologer, and disco. The hotel has four restaurants and a shopping arcade. A double room is RP3,375 ($125).

New Kenilworth Hotel, *1 Little Russel St.; tel. (91-33)448-394,* is more affordable. A double room is RP2,970 ($110). A fine old hotel, it has marble floors, a well-kept lawn, and rooms with private baths and air conditioning. The garden bar is pleasant, and the two restaurants are good.

The most sacred river

The **Ganges River,** considered sacred by Hindus, is believed to originate in the hair of the god Siva. Regardless of its origins, the water is indeed pure, running downhill from the Himalayas.

Hindus believe that bathing in the Ganges washes away sin. The holiest place to bathe is **Allahabad,** where the Ganges and the Yamuna (or Jumna) rivers meet. This is also considered the holiest place to scatter the ashes of cremated loved ones.

The **Magh Mela,** India's biggest religious bathing festival, is held at Allahabad in the spring. During the festival, pilgrims stay in tents along the river, holy men lie on thorns and give sermons, barbers shave the heads of those who intend to bathe in the river, and women throw rose petals and marigolds into the water. The fair has a commercial aspect as well. On the banks of the river, vendors set up food stalls and little booths featuring souvenirs and religious pictures.

If you decide to join the pilgrims in their holy bath, you can't just walk into the water—the river has no beaches. You must take a boat to the middle of the river and dive in from there.

The bathing festival is largest every 12th year, when millions convene to celebrate the **Kumbh Mela,** the most important religious ceremony.

The area's best hotels are the **Yatrik,** *33 Sadar Patel Marg,* and **Barnetts,** *14 Mahatma Gandhi Marg.*

Darjeeling: for the most daring

The train ride to **Darjeeling** is spectacular and dizzying. The 52-mile trip begins at New Jalpaiguri, near Bagdogra, which is a 55-minute flight from Calcutta, and takes about six hours. For the first few miles, the train rushes through dense jungle. Then the steep climb begins. The train chugs through lush tea plantations, clinging to the mountainsides. When it passes through the center of Kurseong, children jump the running boards and make faces at passengers.

From there the train climbs to Ghoom, 8,000 feet the site of a Tibetan monastery.

Monks here worship a 15-foot image of the Coming Buddha and fly prayer flags.

Darjeeling, which lies four miles farther north and about 1,000 feet lower, has an absolutely amazing view of the Himalayas. **Kanchenjunga Mountain** is especially awe-inspiring; the Hindus believe it is the god Siva lying down.

Darjeeling is built in a series of steps. At the top are hotels, cafés, and shops. Halfway up are smaller hotels, Indian restaurants, and more shops. The people of Darjeeling live at the bottom. Nepalese, Tibetans, and Lepchas, in their colorful tribal costumes, crowd the bazaars and markets. Women wear nose ornaments and huge necklaces.

At the center of the town is **Observatory Hill**, where the Mahakala Cave is located. The view is beautiful. Also visit the **Lloyd Botanical Gardens**, which are devoted to the flowers of the Himalayas, and the **Bhutia Busty Tibetan** and the **Aloobari**, two Buddhist monasteries.

Darjeeling also boasts the smallest and highest **racetrack** in the world, where ponies run the course three times before finishing a race. Seven miles from Darjeeling is **Tiger Hill** (8,482 feet), from which you can see Mount Everest on clear days. The best time to see the mountain is sunrise, when the white mountain peaks turn rose.

You can learn to mountain climb in 40 days at the **Himalayan Mountaineering Institute,** *Jawahar Road West,* in Darjeeling. The instructor climbed Mount Everest with Sir Edmund Hillary in 1953. The institute has a museum that displays climbing equipment. It is open 8:30 a.m. until 1 p.m. and 2 until 4:30 p.m.

India's most exotic areas

India's most exotic and remote areas, **Assam** and **Nagaland,** in the extreme north-east corner of the country, are off-limits to foreigners. But if the Indian government lifts the travel restrictions, take the opportunity to visit. These are the most fascinating places in India, inhabited by little-known tribes, some of whom were headhunters a generation ago. This is a paradise for wildlife enthusiasts, hunters, and fishermen. The region has incredible waterfalls, high peaks, and wild rivers.

The **Kaziranga Wild Life Sanctuary** is the best place for big-game hunting in India, if not the world. Because the grass here is 16 feet high, the only way to see the sanctuary is astride an elephant. The sanctuary protects several species of deer, birds, wild boars, jackals, buffaloes, elephants, and tigers.

If the travel restrictions are lifted, you will be able to make arrangements to visit the sanctuary by applying to the **Divisional Forest Officer,** *Sibsagar Division, Jorbat,* three weeks in advance of the date you want to travel there. (Call the Indian Consulate to find out the most recent restrictions and where to contact the Forest Officer.) This allows enough time for reservations to be made for rooms and elephants. It's a two-hour flight from Calcutta to Jorhat, where the Forest Department car meets visitors to take them to Kaziranga, 40 miles away. It's a tough 135-mile ride from Gauhati. Don't wear white or bright colors, which frighten the animals.

The best travel planning

India is immense, so it is important to plan your trip carefully. Bombay, Delhi, Calcutta, and Madras are the best places to begin your travels.

Most travelers to India *must* have a visa. Applications for visas should be made on prescribed visa application forms before you leave and should be accompanied by a valid passport. Visas are valid for three months.

Foreign visitors receive special assistance and concessions in India. Booking and information sections for foreigners, which are located in railway stations and the major offices of Indian Airlines, enable you to avoid the usual long waiting lines and can greatly reduce the costs of transportation throughout India. In states where alcohol is banned, foreigners can apply for a liquor permit. The Indian government is anxious to promote tourism.

Keep in mind that certain parts of India, which are politically sensitive or strategic, are designated by the government as "restricted" or "protected" areas. Foreign tourists can enter them only with special permits from the Foreigners' Regional Registration Offices (in Bombay, Calcutta, Delhi, and Madras).

You also need a permit if you plan to stay more than 15 days in the Andaman Islands. This can be obtained through local travel agents in Calcutta or directly from the **Home Ministry**, *North Block, New Delhi*. Western Kahmir is not a recommended destination for travelers, and some areas of the Andanans are restricted. Check at your local consulate or in New Delhi for current restrictions. To visit Bhutan, you need a permit from the Bhutan Government.

You can visit Sikkim for four days with a permit issued by the **Deputy Secretary Ministry of Home Affairs**, *North Block, New Delhi*. It takes about six to eight weeks to process the permit, so make your plans well in advance.

Permits also are required to photograph railway stations or trains.

The best way to travel

Traveling by air can save a lot of time and irritation in India, which is, after all, a subcontinent. **Air India** has been building up its services and is now one of the largest domestic carriers in the world. More than 240 flights daily from 73 cities are offered from the four major bases of Delhi, Bombay, Calcutta, and Madras. Air travel is relatively inexpensive.

The best deal for foreigners is Indian Airlines' $400 **Discover India ticket**, which allows unlimited travel for 21 days. The ticket can be purchased when you book your trip to India. If you buy it on arrival, you must pay for it with foreign currency. Call *(91-11)4620566* for details.

The best time to go

The best time to go to India is between November and the end of March. This avoids the rainy season and the severe heat of October and April in northern India and the hill stations of southern India. It's wise to plan your travels around the weather. Making your way through India demands tremendous energy; trying to make your way through India during the rainy season or in severe heat can be miserable.

The Best of Southeast Asia

Thailand—the most exotic Oriental country

Thailand can rightly claim to be the most exotic Oriental country. Unlike many of its neighbors, it has never been colonized. Nevertheless, Thailand has always been open to foreign influences. Its king plays the jazz clarinet, many of its royals were educated in England and Switzerland, and wealthier Thais speak English.

This openness and friendliness toward foreigners makes Thailand an ideal vacation spot. The Thai people are so friendly and polite that they make you feel right at home. Moreover, Thailand is cheap; it's possible to find accommodation here for as little as $10 a night. (When reading through this section, be aware that many hotels in this part of the world add a service charge and taxes to the prices quoted. Be sure to inquire about these additional charges when making reservations to avoid an unpleasant surprise when the bill comes.)

Bangkok—the most sophisticated city

Bangkok, Thailand's largest city, is a mix of beauty, crowds, sophistication, and sin. It is, at once, polluted and congested downtown—and quiet and serene in its outlying corners.

Bangkok's best attractions

Bangkok has more than 400 temples; you can't help but run into them wherever you go. And they are all worth seeing. The most famous include **Wat Pho**, the oldest and largest in Bangkok; **Wat Phra Kaeo**, the Temple of the Emerald Buddha in the Grand Palace; and **Wat Arun**, situated by the Chao Phraya River. Wat Arun is open daily, 8 a.m. until 4:30 p.m.; admission is 10 baht to14 baht (40 to 50 cents).

Bangkok's **Floating Market** is also a must—even though it has become tourist-trodden in the last several years. You can arrange a tour from the Oriental Hotel's pier, departing about 7 a.m., for 300 baht ($12.50). Another good—and lesser-known—floating market is at **Khlong Damnoen Saduak**, about 65 miles west of Bangkok. Tours can be arranged from all major hotels. In addition to a floating-market tour, arrange a *klong* (canal tour); for details, ask at any pier in the vicinity of the Oriental Hotel.

Thailand's royal barges

For centuries, visitors have marveled at the sight of Bangkok's royal river barges. Unfortunately, Royal Barge Processions, a breathtaking tradition for many years, are rare today. The last major procession honored the bicentennial of Bangkok in 1982, and it will likely be years before the royal barges ply the waters of the Chao Phraya River again.

But you can still see them on display at the **Royal Barge Museum**, on Klong Bangkok

315

Noi near the Phra Pinkloa Bridge and Arun Amarin Road. The museum and its barges, all restored and reconstructed, are housed in a cavernous shed. The best way to get there is by river taxi or as part of a general canal trip. Admission to the museum is 10 baht (80 cents). The shed is open daily, 8:30 a.m. until 4:30 p.m.

The most slithery farm

The **Bangkok Snake Farm**, *Rama IV and Henri Dunant roads; tel. (66-2)252-0161-4*, at the Thai Red Cross Society, is by far Thailand's most interesting farm. This is where cobras, kraits, spotted vipers, and other poisonous snakes are fed and milked for their venom. Milking snakes is not an exciting process. The snake's mouth is simply forced open, and the venom squirts out into a small petri dish. However, it is not meant to be a form of entertainment. It is part of a life-saving process. The Queen Saovabh Memorial Institute, the scientific division of the Thai Red Cross Society, provides snake-bite serum for much of the world.

What follows the milking process *is* very exciting. When it's showtime, the handlers use long poles to remove the snakes from the pits and place them on the ground. The audience sits only a few feet away, but several feet off the ground, and watches as the handlers encourage the snakes to hiss and slither, display their hoods, and strike and spit venom. Although it's all done very casually, rest assured that the handlers don't take their jobs lightly—one recently lost his life.

There are two shows daily; admission is 40 baht ($1.75).

Thailand's best golf course

Thailand is fast emerging as a favorite year-round venue for the world's golfers. The country already boasts some 50 courses, and additional courses are in the works.

The best golf course in Thailand is the **Rose Garden Golf Course**, 45 minutes from Bangkok. It has been awarded a Silver Medal by *Golf Magazine USA* for being one of the best golf courses in the world. It is renowned as Thailand's best-managed and most attractive, and the caddies are exceptionally well-trained and savvy. The cost for a day on the course varies from 280 baht to 480 baht ($12 to $20), depending on when you play. Clubs can be rented for an additional 200 baht ($8).

The best market in Southeast Asia

Be sure to visit the **Chatuchak** weekend market. Take a hotel car to the market and ask the driver to wait, as taxis can be difficult to find.

Haggle ferociously over the prices and realize that not all of the antiques are real. Don't buy the pirated videotapes; they will not play on Western-format televisions.

The most luxurious places to stay

The **Oriental**, *48 Oriental Ave.; tel. (66-2)236-0400*, has been called the best hotel in the world, a haunt of millionaires and beautiful women. Although lately showing signs of decay, it remains a traditional and beautiful place to stay. A double room is 5,600 baht ($220).

The Oriental is also known for its **Thai Cooking School**, which conducts classes year-round, Monday through Friday, 9 a.m. until noon. The five-day course costs 49,375 baht ($1,975), including accommodation at the hotel, all classes, materials, and two meals daily.

Close runners-up are the **Regent**, *155 Rajdamri Road; tel. (66-2)251-6127*, which has rooms from 4,500 baht ($180), and the brand-new **Sukhothai**, *13/3 S. Sathorn Road,; tel. (66-2)287-0222*, which has rooms starting at 4,300 baht ($168).

The **Dusit Thani**, *946 Rama IV Road; tel. (66-2)236-0450*, located only minutes from Bangkok's famous Patpong (bar) district, is also a good place to stay. It is less expensive than other luxury-class hotels in the city. A double room is 3,600 to 6,300 baht ($140 to $247).

The best bargain hotel
The **Nana Hotel,** *4 Soi Nana Tai, Sukhumvit Road; tel. (66-2)252-0121,* is a good—and attractive—budget hotel. A double room is only 963 baht ($39) a night.

The oldest settlement
Chiang Mai is the hill capital of northern Thailand, home to a million people. Founded in 1296, it is one of the oldest continually inhabited settlements in Thailand. It was at one time an independent kingdom, surrounded by a moat and fortified gates. The best way to get to Chiang Mai from Bangkok is by air; a round-trip flight is $100.

Chiang Mai's greatest attractions
Wat Phra That Doi Suthep, a temple high on a mountain peak, and **Phuping Palace,** the summer residence of the royal family, are two beautiful and ancient monuments that alone make the visit to Chiang Mai worthwhile.

The best place to shop
The best place to shop in the city is the **Night Market,** just off Thaphae Road. It's also the cheapest: Cassette tapes, for example, go for 25 baht ($1). Also available at bargain prices are rugs, clothes, and leather goods. This is also the place to buy a pair of boots made out of chicken skin, should your tastes run in that direction, as well as silver and Burmese lacquer and handcrafts.

The best pastime
From Chiang Mai, you can arrange to go elephant trekking. Avoid the big, touristy elephant camp; instead, ask a tuk-tuk or taxi driver to take you to one of the smaller camps, farther up in the hills (about 45 minutes outside the city). It will be the adventure of your life.

The driver sits on the elephant's head, and usually two people share the seat strapped across the animal's back. The elephants can go anywhere; they can cross streams on tiny stepping stones with the grace and balance of gymnasts. As they step down, you are tilted at a 90 degree angle to the ground. The motion may make you sick at first, but soon your body will become accustomed to it.

The second-best pastime
In a spectacular setting at the foot of the famous Doi Suthep mountain, just 10 minutes from the center of the city, sits the **Lanna Golf Club.** The course is moderately difficult, with more than 20 lakes and water hazards and with elevated greens planted with Bermuda grass. The cost for a day of golfing is 250 baht ($10); a set of clubs rents for 200 baht ($8).

The best place to stay
Stay at the **Chiang Mai Orchid,** *100-102 Huay Kaew Road; tel. (66-53)222-099,* a lovely, first-class establishment, where a double room is 3,296 baht to 3,531 baht ($132 to $142) a night.

The best place to buy silk in Thailand
Although Jim Thompson's silk shops are the best-known in Thailand—with good reason—they are also the most expensive. (They are easily located all over the major Thai cities.) If you're looking for a bargain, try one of the city's smaller shops. Although the quality is not as good, the prices are much cheaper.

We recommend **Shinawatra Parnich,** *72 Chiangmai-Sankumpaeng Road; tel. (66-53)331-187,* and **Shinawatra Thaisilk,** *145/1-2 Chiangmai-Sankumpaeng Road; tel. (66-53)331-712.*

Asia's hottest resort

If you're male, single, and tired of Bangkok's Patpong, there's no better place to vacation than Thailand's Pattaya Beach. The prices are absolutely bargain-basement (you can get a first-rate meal for 225 baht, or $9), and the nightlife is wilder than the wildest London, New York, or Hong Kong has to offer.

For centuries Pattaya was a sleepy fishing village astride the invasion routes across the Gulf of Siam. According to local lore, the legendary Thai King Taskin's soldiers once put ashore here on their way to conquer what is now southern Thailand. Two hundred years later, Pattaya was a favorite destination for American GIs on leave from Vietnam. Today, it is a mecca for sun worshipers and sybarites from all across Asia and Europe.

The most undiscovered—and cheapest—place to stay in Thailand

The island of Koh Phi Phi, off mainland Thailand, is an island paradise that offers not only long, secluded beaches and gorgeous scenery but also the cheapest accommodation in Thailand. Beach bungalows cost $5 to $20 a night. Meals are as little as $3. And best of all, you don't need reservations. The place is such a well-kept secret that you can just show up and request a room.

The Philippines—the friendliest nation

The Philippines has always been known for the friendliness of its people, who speak 67 different dialects. This has not changed in recent years, despite the turmoil the country has suffered.

And the country is certainly as beautiful as ever. Made up of about 7,100 island paradises stretching toward China and Japan in the north and Malaysia and Singapore in the south, the Philippines offers a combination of exciting cosmopolitan cities, white-sand beaches, and achingly blue waters.

Manila's best sites

Manila, the capital of the Philippines, is a hustling, bustling international city on the island of Luzon and a good base for excursions to the surrounding countryside. The city is within two hours of beautiful resorts and beaches. See the **Pagsanjan Falls**, about an hour outside Manila, where you can take a scenic boat tour of the rapids along 100-meter-high falls. Also visit the **Hidden Valley Springs**, a series of mineral springs in Alaminos, Laguna, that are buried in a 90-meter crater and surrounded by lush vegetation.

Other attractions near Manila include the **Malacañang Palace,** by the Pasig River; **Coconut Palace**, which was built, in part, using coconut trees and is the national symbol of life and abundance; **Makati**, the financial center of the country; and the **San Agustin Church** in Intramuros, the oldest church in Manila.

The best place to stay in Manila

The **Manila Hotel**, *Rizal Park, P.O. Box 307; tel. (63-2)470-011 or (800)44-UTELL in the United States,* is a, luxury hotel in a good location. The staff is attentive. A double room is 6,295 pesos ($250) a night.

The best hotel outside Manila

The best place to stay in Laguna, just outside Manila, is the **Villa Escudero**, *P.O. Box 4, San Pablo,* which offers exceptional service, atmosphere, and comfort. This coconut plantation, less than two hours by road from the capital city, gives you a glimpse of typical village life. Even if you can't stay the night, take time to visit the grounds.

The summer capital of the Philippines

The cool, mountainous region of **Baguio City**, located in the province of Benguet, offers a break from the city crowds. Only three or four hours from Manila by car, or 50 minutes by jet, Baguio City is becoming increasingly popular among travelers, who appreciate the region's incredible views and cool climate.

The best place to stay in the city is the **Bagula Park Hotel**, *Harrison Road, Baguio City*. Also recommended are the **Vacation Hotel**, *tel. (63-74)442-4545*, and the **Safari Lodge**, *tel. (63-74)442-2419*, both of which face the Baguio Botanical Gardens on Leonard Wood Road. A double room at the Vacation Hotel is 690 pesos ($28); a double room at the Safari Lodge is 300 pesos ($14).

The most attractive city in the South

Cebu City, the "Queen city of the South," is a beautiful and graceful city, located on the island of Cebu in the Visayas, south of Manila. It is the oldest city in the Philippines founded by the Spaniards. Ferdinand Magellan, who landed on its shores in 1521, fell in love with the place and eventually died there. He planted Magellan's Cross, which is now more than 460 years old and still standing. It is the symbol of the Rajah Humabon and his queen's acceptance of Christianity.

The most festive time to visit Cebu City is during its festival of Sinulog, a weeklong religious celebration held every January.

The best of the oldest in Cebu

The image of **Santo Niño de Cebu** is the oldest religious relic in the country; it was given to Queen Juana by Magellan in 1521. The **Basilica Minore del Santo Niño**, built in 1565, is the oldest church in the Philippines and was built on the site where the image was found.

The oldest street in the country, **Colon Street**, is also in Cebu. Located in Cebu's Chinatown, in the center of the city, it was built by Spanish soldiers.

The Philippines' last frontier

The best place in the Philippines to enjoy water sports is on the island of **Palawan**, 70 minutes by plane southwest of Manila. This island is known as the Philippines' last frontier, a paradise for sailors, sunbathers, deep-sea divers, and fishermen.

The island is surrounded by coral reefs, and the waters are filled with fish. Manta rays are common. New marine species have been discovered in the waters off the exclusive El Nido Resort on the island's northern shore.

The best place to stay on Palawan

The best place to stay in Puerto Princesa, the capital of Palawan, is the **Badjao Inn**, *Rizal Avenue Extension, tel. (63-4821)2761*. The hotel has a beautiful garden, and you can't beat the price. A room with a fan is 135 pesos ($6); a room with air conditioning is 210 pesos ($9).

The best seafood

The best seafood on the island is served at the **French Café Puarto**, *277 Rizal Ave.*

The best places for water sports

The upscale **El Nido Resort**, *Miniloc Island, El Nido,* is *the* place on Palawan for deep-sea diving. Designed to resemble a native village, this resort was named for the birds' nests *(nido)* found on the surrounding cliffs.

El Nido is several hours by car from the airport at Puerto Princesa. For $70, you can hire a jeepney at the airport to take you out to the resort. The best way to get there, however, is to charter a plane from Manila. Charter flights are offered by **Ten Knots Philippines Inc.**, *Ground Floor, Makati Stock Exchange Building, Ayala Avenue, Makati, Metro Manila; tel. (63-2)818-2623; fax (63-2)817-2848*. A double room at El Nido is $88, including meals and the use of deep-sea diving equipment.

Another good spot for water sports is the area around Port Barton, which is peppered with beach resorts. We recommend **Mantaray Resort**, *Capsalay Island, Port Barton*, which has three rooms that cost only $39 a night, including meals.

The best time to visit
The best time to visit the Philippines is between December and May, especially April or May. The rest of the year is typhoon season.

Laos–the most serene
It's hard to get to Laos, and once you're there, it's hard to get around. Only recently have Americans been able to travel here at all. But it is worth the effort. What you'll remember most about Laos is its serenity: There are no hawkers on the streets; in fact, there are no vehicles on the streets—at least no four-wheeled vehicles. Instead, the streets of Laos are given over to bicycles and tuk-tuks.

Laos' largest town–the best set for a spaghetti Western
In 1963, UPI war photographer Tim Page described **Vientiane**, Laos' ancient capital, as resembling "a set for a spaghetti Western or a Graham Greene thriller." Thirty years later, nothing has changed.

The best restaurant in Vientiane
The best place to eat in Vientiane is the **Nam Phu Restaurant**, behind the Lan-Xang Hotel. This French-style Laotian restaurant is famous for its venison steak and Bulgarian red wine. Reservations are recommended, as this reasonably priced restaurant is always crowded with visiting diplomats, who have few other options.

Asia's most beautiful temples
Laos is notable for possessing the most beautiful Buddhist temples in Southeast Asia—temples that have not fallen to explosives, tourism, or redevelopment, as have most of those in Burma, Vietnam, Cambodia, China, and Hong Kong.

Twice daily, weather and inclination permitting, Laos Aviation flies from Vientiane to Luang Prabang, Laos' most beautiful town and the site of **Wat Xiengthong**, one of the most impressive temples in all of Southeast Asia, with its courtyard filled with bougainvillea and its location on the Mekong River.

The best place to arrange your trip
The best place to arrange a trip to Laos is Bangkok, where several tour operators specialize in tours to this remote country. **Diethelm Travel**, *Kian Gwan Building II, 140/1 Wireless Road; tel. (662)255-9150; fax (662)256-0248*, one of the city's largest and best-known, has a reputation for getting you there—usually on schedule—with the least amount of inconvenience. It is possible to book directly with Diethelm Travel or through **Siam Exclusive Tours**, *Building One, Seventh Floor, 99 Wireless Road; tel. (66-2)256-6153-5*.

The most economical ride
Although daily flights are scheduled in and out of Laos, it's far less expensive and far more adventurous to take the overnight train from Bangkok to Nong Khai in northern Thailand on the Thai/Laotian border. An express train departs Bangkok Railway Station at 8:30 p.m. and arrives in Nong Khai at 7:30 the next morning. Save the picturesque daytime train ride for the trip home, as the border closes at 5 p.m., and you can't take a day train to Nong Khai from Bangkok and return in the same day.

Palau, the most undiscovered in the Pacific
In the far western Pacific, about 800 miles southwest of Guam and 500 miles east of

the Philippines, the 36-mile-long, 15-mile wide, reef-encircled tropical archipelago known as Palau remains largely the secret of world-class scuba divers and marine experts, who count it among the wonders of the world.

About 9,000 Palauans live on Koror, capital of the not-quite-independent Republic of Palau. It boasts 18 miles of paved road, nearly 200 taxis, a speed limit of 25 miles per hour, and no passing. The longest stretch of road wanders 8 1/2 miles from Palau International Airport to the Palau Pacific Resort. Life on the islands of Kayangel and Angaur, which mark the northern- and southernmost tips of the archipelago respectively, revolves around fishing along the reef or in the lagoon and the cultivation of taro, tapioca, coconuts, and bananas.

The jewels of Palau

The pièce de résistance of Palau is the group of 200 Rock Islands, scattered in strings between Koror and Peleliu. Found nowhere else in the world, these jungle-covered knobs of solid coral and limestone, undercut at tide level because of the water-soluble limestone, look from a distance like so many green mushrooms floating on a turquoise sea. The islands fringed by white sand are ideal for picnicking or snorkeling.

The best dive sites

Scuba divers in Palau should head straight for the outer reefs, including the Big Drop-off, Blue Corners, Blue Hole, and Turtle Cover, where you can descend to incredible depths in search of dazzling coral formations and exotic sea life.

The best dive shop

Koror has no shortage of dive shops and tour operators, but you can't go wrong with **Sam's Tour Service,** *tel. (680)488-1720; fax (680)488-1471.* Sam Scott is the American stepson of Ibedul, high chief of Koror. He can help you arrange it all—diving in the coral reefs of the Rock Islands, exploring shipwrecks from World War II, sightseeing, fishing, boat charters, or even a night search for alligators in the mangrove swamps of Babeldaop. A full day of scuba diving costs $80, a half day is $50.

The best places to stay

Stay at the deluxe **Palau Pacific Resort,** *tel. (680)488-2600,* or the somewhat worn **Nikko Hotel,** *tel. (680)488-2486* ,which commands breathtaking views of the Rock Islands. The restaurant at the Nikko Hotel offers international foods and seafood specialties daily, 6:30 a.m. until 10 p.m.

The best bargain accommodation

The best buy in town is the **DW Motel,** run by a friendly Palauan named Dave Williams and his family. Close to downtown Koror and within walking distance of the central business district, the DW offers large and airy rooms with air conditioning and refrigerators for $28 to $33 a night.

The best restaurants

Take at least one meal at the **Fuji Restaurant,** located downtown next to the West Plaza Hotel. The Fuji serves seafood, local specialties, and international dishes Monday through Saturday, 6 p.m. to 10 p.m. Most meals in Palau range from $5 to $15.

The **Carp Restaurant** near the government fish dock serves Japanese-style dishes, in addition to crab and lobster varieties, Monday through Saturday 11 a.m. until 9 p.m. and Sunday 9 a.m. until noon.

The **Pirate's Cove,** otherwise known as the **Royal Belau Yacht Club,** at the fish dock, welcomes all. It serves an international selection of foods, seafood, and pizza specialties and is open daily 9 a.m. until 2 p.m. and 4 to 11 p.m.

Myanmar—a destination for the most adventurous

Myanmar is becoming a more accessible destination for the adventurous traveler. It is not a journey to be taken lightly, but an adventure suitable only for the strong of body and spirit. Nonetheless, it is worth the effort it takes to get there. Those who see it invariably describe it as one of the few places left in the world where you can get a feel for what Asia "used to be like."

The busiest city

Yangon (formerly Rangoon), Myanmar's capital, is a gray city of prewar buildings, faded grandeur, and wide streets cluttered with lampposts, loiterers, and round-fendered cars. Street vendors sell cold drinks made of sugarcane and water, dipping the gray-green liquid from big glass tanks. (Don't be tempted.)

The best attractions

The glowing **Sule Pagoda** in the center of town is an impressive spectacle at night. But it pales in comparison with the 2,500-year-old **Shwedagon Pagoda**. High on a hill, the Shwedagon is reached either by elevator or by a breathless climb up an enormous stairway lined with hawkers and souvenir vendors. At the top is a Disneyland-like arena of jeweled spires, gold-plated domes, and gilded statues. People mill about in their bare feet trying to sell flowers, fortunes, and medical advice.

The Strand—Myanmar's oasis

Yangon's **Strand Hotel**, *92 Strand Road; tel. 81530,* has been recently renovated and is considered the best hotel in all Myanmar. It is a white-pillared relic from the days of British rule. The ceilings are high, the stairways wide and polished, and the elevator an ornate, wrought-iron cage. In the dining room, waiters in white jackets serve mutton and potatoes from dented silver platters. In the hotel bar, a pianist plays Henry Mancini while sparrows nest in the light fixtures. It is an oasis.

The most historic city

Mandalay is a sprawling, walled city of historic monasteries, bridges, moats, and, of course, more pagodas. Men in sarongs pedal trishaws through the dusty streets. It isn't a beautiful city, but it is a good jumping-off point for excursions along the Irrawaddy River.

The best ruins

Pagan is one of the wonders of Asia, a sprawling landscape littered with thousands of ancient ruins. During the Golden Age of Pagan, in the 11th century, riches were spent on pagodas, shrines, and temples. It is believed that these buildings numbered 13,000 when Kublai Khan sacked the place in 1287. A major earthquake in 1975 caused more damage, but most of the important structures have since been restored.

The ancient city of Pagan is now deserted except for a tiny village. Surrounding the village are the remains of the ancient temples. If you join the other travelers here, moving from one temple to another on foot or rented bicycle, you'll have the opportunity to glimpse dark, cold rooms filled with marble Buddhas and terra-cotta tiles.

The best resort hotel in Myanmar

The **Candacraig Hotel**, *East Ridge Road*, in Maymyo, is a 19th-century hill station that used to serve as the officers' residence of the Bombay-Burma Trading Company. Its restaurant serves English food.

The best ways to travel to and through Myanmar

The best route to Myanmar is, as always, through Bangkok, where a number of small agents, most with family contacts in Myanmar, specialize in arranging travel to this hard-to-reach country.

While independent travel is possible in Myanmar, the amount of time you will be allowed to travel alone varies according to the whims of the government. Nonetheless, it is well worth the trouble to, if possible, avoid the travel agencies and go it alone.

Make your airfare arrangements with **Thai International**, which flies from Bangkok to Myanmar three times a week. A round-trip, tourist-class ticket costs 5,955 baht (US$230). Pay the additional 445 baht (US$17) for an upgrade to business class on the return flight; the unlimited champagne on this one-hour trip will seem like heaven after roughing it in Myanmar.

All internal flights are with **Myanmar Airways**, known for the poor condition of its planes and its frequent fatal crashes. But you don't have any choice if you want to cover long distances.

Myanmar Airways offers daily flights between Yangon and all other cities open to travelers (which, right now, include Bago, Bagan, Mandalay, Taunggyi, Mawlamyine, Sittwe, Pathein, Pyi, and Pyin Oo Lwin). The alternative is to travel by train, but train travel in Myanmar is time-consuming and sometimes unreliable. It is not possible to rent a car on your own, but day-trips can be arranged with a car and driver. In some areas, you can travel by bus, boat, or horse and buggy (not a tourist treat, but the primary means of local transportation).

Singapore—the clockwork city

Singapore is an exciting, pulsating place, very cosmopolitan, very well-run, and incredibly clean. In fact, you can be fined $2 for spitting on the sidewalk. But gone are the days of sprawling British colonial homes. Today, the 225-square-mile island is sparsely dotted with these vestiges of a more relaxed, distinctive past, and the 2.6 million people living here are discovering that space is precious. Modern Singapore is a city of high-rise structures.

Colonial Singapore is north of the Singapore River. **Empress Place** is decorated with the statue of Sir Stamford Raffles (the Brit who founded Singapore and made it the trading port that it is today), overlooking the river where the explorer first stepped onto the island. The newly restored **Raffles Hotel**, *1 Beach Road; tel. (65)337-1886,* is a must, a symbol of colonial Singapore. A double room is S$700 ($390). Have a Singapore Sling on the terrace (touristy, but fun). **Chinatown** is an interesting area to explore, full of mosques and temples.

The best places to stay

The 90-year-old **Goodwood Tark**, *22 Scotts Road; tel. (65)737-7411,* is known for its true Singaporean service and its elegant rooms. Its 5-hectare site near the Orchard Road shopping district is convenient. A double room is S$400 to S$495 ($223 to $276).

Another good place to stay is the more reasonably priced **Carlton Hotel**, *76 Bras Basah Road at the corner of Victoria Street; tel. (65)338-8333.* The decor is beautiful, the service good. A double room is S$280 to S$330 ($156 to $184).

The world's greatest shopping

There are two reasons Singapore offers the best shopping in the world. First, a better selection cannot be found anywhere. Second, the government's harsh policy toward unscrupulous merchants makes this a safe place to spend your money.

Tanglin, Orchard, and **Scotts** roads are the obvious places to begin a shopping spree. Prices are fixed charge cards are welcome, and shopkeepers are friendly and speak English. Bring your walking shoes—or better yet, buy a pair at one of the shops in the area.

The best place to buy a carpet

The best place to buy a carpet in Singapore is at an auction. Open to the public, auctions are announced in the local paper. They are usually held in hotel ballrooms. Attend several auctions before purchasing anything; it pays to listen and learn. The carpets sold are from Afghanistan, Turkey, and Pakistan. Weavers tend to reproduce their everyday experiences in their works.

The best custom-made clothing

Singapore is also the best place for custom-made clothing. Here, prices are cheaper, the selection of fabrics is greater (you'll find an especially wide selection of cottons, silks, and polyester fabrics), and the workmanship is at least as good as that of anyplace else in the world. And there is certainly no shortage of tailors. (Allow four to five days for a custom-made suit.)

A man's cotton/polyester summer suit, including stitching and cloth, costs about $195 in other major cities, including Hong Kong. The same suit in Singapore is only $155. **Justmen** in the *Tanglin Shopping Center, 01-36/39 Tanglin Shopping Center,* is a good place for men's tailoring.

A women's wool suit is about $170 at the **Bagatelle Shoppe** in the *Specialist Center, 277 Orchard Road.*

The world's tallest hotel

An absolute must is afternoon tea at the **Compass Rose** on the top of the Stamford Westin, which, at 73 stories, is the world's tallest hotel. It boasts fantastic city and harbor views.

New Guinea—the second-largest island in the world

New Guinea, the second-largest island in the world (Greenland is the largest), looks in profile like a bird taking flight. The head of the bird, a place the Dutch named Vogelkop (*bird's head*), is now called Irian Jaye and is part of Indonesia. The other end of the island is Papua New Guinea. Either end of the island makes a perfect destination. But overall, the eastern half, the "bird's tail," has the most to offer. Myriad islands litter the Bismarck Sea off the north coast. And there are mountains, some snow-covered, some with valleys so remote that the life they contain has not changed noticeably since the Stone-Age. Mighty rivers, such as the Fly and the Sepik, coil their way through lowland jungles to the sea in this land that is home to 700 languages and many cultures.

One of the world's greatest adventures

If you're looking for an adventure, you couldn't do better than to set off from Port Moresby, the capital of Papua New Guinea, and fly to Milne Bay, the bird's tail, 250 miles to the east. From there, you can negotiate the coastline all the way from the fabled Trobriands to the upper reaches of the Sepik River.

You can make the journey in two ways. You can either hunt down locally run trading vessels, take a flight with Air Niugini, and ride a bus from Lae to Madang. Or, if sailing on tiny, Spartan vessels and being jolted around on dusty buses doesn't appeal to you, consider the *Melanesian Explorer,* an expeditionary ship that begins its voyages off the northeast coast and heads south after a few days through the D'Entrecasteaux Islands— tiny green places with talcum-white beaches. The journey eventually ends 200 miles upriver, where you can take a plane to the highlands town of Mount Hagan, from which it is another hour by plane back to Port Moresby.

For information on the *Melanesian Explorer* and the newer *Melanesian Discoverer,* contact the **Melanesian Tourist Services Pty. Ltd.,** *P.O. Box 707, Madang; tel. (685)82-27-66; fax (685)82-35-43, or 302 W. Grand Ave., Suite 10B, El Segundo, CA 90245; (310)785-0370; fax (310)785-0314.*

Malaysia—the most bountiful country

Malaysia is known for its extreme beauty, including gorgeous beaches and spectacular mountains. Athough it does not have the history of other countries in Southeast Asia, it is one of the most developed and prosperous nations in this part of the world. Kuala Lumpur, the capital (complete with luxury hotels and skyscrapers), is a pleasant stopover from your explorations in other parts of the country. It is a modern city, but colonial-era buildings are evident everywhere.

The best three excursions from Kuala Lumpur

While in Kuala Lumpur, you should take three day-trips. First, visit **Malacca** (Melaka), 149 kilometers south of the capital city. This splendid old port city on the infamous, formerly pirate-infested Straits of Malacca, boasting a rich Portuguese, Dutch, English, Chinese, and Malaysian heritage, is a fertile shopping ground for antique enthusiasts. To visit, rent a car and driver in Kuala Lumpur or join one of the day tours that depart from all the major hotels. The journey itself, through plantation after plantation of rubber trees and oil palms, is worth the trip.

A shorter (13 kilometers out of Kuala Lumpur) but equally rewarding journey takes you to the limestone **Batu Caves**, a Hindu pilgrimage center notable for its swarms of bats, whose guano adds to the eerie mystical atmosphere inside the caves. Frequent and inexpensive minibuses from Kuala Lumpur take travelers to the Batu Caves. Or you can hire a car and driver.

Another must is the island of **Penang**, which lies off the east coast of the Malasian peninsula. It is the oldest British settlement in Malaysia. Georgetown, its major town, is a compact, attractive city, known for its good food. From here, you have easy access to the rest of the island and its beautiful beaches, rubber-tree plantations, and forests (filled with monkeys and bananas).

The most romantic colonial-style hotel

Penang's **Eastern & Oriental Hotel**, *10 Farquhar St., Penang; tel. (60-4)63543*, at the waterfront end of Jalan Penang, is unreservedly Malaysia's most romantic colonial-style hotel, a vestige of the former British rule. Even if you're staying in more modest accommodation, stop by the Eastern and Oriental for a gin and tonic on the terrace. A double room starts at $100.

The best of Indonesia

Indonesia is a nation teeming with 160 million people and more than 9,000 islands. Although now mainly Muslim, these islands have a rich history of Buddhism and Hinduism, which can be seen in the ruins of ancient temples and cities scattered among the lush tropical landscape. Its capital, **Jakarta**, located on the main island of Java, is the least attractive of all the cities in Indonesia; its only real claim to fame is that it has more monuments in the city proper than any other city in the world. Once you've escaped Jakarta, you'll discover that Indonesia offers some of the most beautiful scenery in the world.

The best island to visit—Bali

No other island in the archipelago can compare with **Bali**. Bali has everything: stunning beaches, ancient temples, and an active volcano. The best beach is **Nusa Dua**. See it, but don't stop there. Explore the island's lush interior and its temples. The best base for this is the village of **Ubud**. Ubud, discovered by Dutch artists in the 1920s, is still home to a thriving colony of Indonesian artists and wood sculptors, each with an individual style.

If your pocketbook can handle it, stay at the ultraexclusive **Amandari Resort**, where a double room is $300 to $800 a night. If it can't, stay at one of the area's many good guesthouses, where a room is only $15 to $25 a night. You can hire a cab to drive you around the surrounding countryside. It's cheaper to negotiate a rate with the driver for an entire afternoon or day (expect to pay $20 for four hours) than to pay for individual trips. Just tell the driver to show you the temple and the volcano; it will be money well-spent.

The world's biggest Buddhist monument

Java's ancient city of **Jogyakarta** is home to the world's largest Buddhist monument, the circular ruin of **Borobodur**. The stone friezes that circle the monument tell the life story of the Buddha and his search for enlightenment. Legend has it that originally only the initiated were permitted to view the higher levels, as they are said to contain the key to a happy life.

The best place to stay is the **Hotel Ambarukmo Palace**, *Jalan Laksda Adisucipto; tel. (62-274)88488.* A double room is $80.

The Best of Africa

The best travel tips

Before you begin your travels through Africa, prepare yourself for an astonishing level of corruption. (The local term for bribes is *dash*.)

A word about currencies... Many West African countries use the CFA franc (connected to the French franc); Nigeria uses the naira (N); and South Africa uses the rand (calculated at both a commercial and a financial rate). Airports are usually good places to exchange your money.

The world's best safaris

East Africa, one of the last strongholds of the lion, the elephant, the gorilla, and other exotic beasts, is the best place in the world to go on safari. Enormous national parks where the great beasts roam freely, uninhibited by the progress of mankind, have been established throughout the region.

Kenya and **Tanzania** are the best countries for viewing wildlife; they offer comfortable accommodation and have mild climates with warm, sunny days and cool nights. Hunting is now banned in Kenya and many other African countries, where the typical safari has been replaced with the viewing safari. Plan your adventure for July through March to avoid the rainy season.

Zambia and **Zimbabwe** are also good safari destinations; they are less known by Westerners and therefore less spoiled. Zambia is the only country where walking safaris are still common. And Zimbabwe is one of the few African countries where hunting safaris are still permitted.

Your first step in planning a safari should be to read up on the subject. Michael Tomkinson has written an excellent guide called *Kenya, A Holiday Guide*, available from Ernest Benn Ltd. in London.

The most accessible game park is **Masai Mara**, on the border between Kenya and Tanzania, in the **Rift Valley**. It has the largest diversity of game—rolling hills dotted with herds of elephants, antelopes, baboons, and lions. Masai tribespeople, who wear beautifully colored cloth garments, also inhabit the area.

The **Ngorongoro Crater** and **Serengeti Plain** are part of the **Ngorongoro Conservation Area**, a 3,200-square-mile tract of Masai land. Together, these two areas have the largest concentration of game in the world.

The least expensive prearranged safaris leave from London. **Sunrise Travel and Tours**, *10 Maddox St., London; tel. (44-71)495-3673*, offers a 14-day trip, including a seven-day safari, for £825 to £1,600 ($1,500 to $3,000), including airfare from London to Nairobi.

Also try **United Touring International**, *400 Market St., Suite 260, Philadelphia, PA;*

(215)923-8700; fax (215)985-1008. It offers a 13-day safari of Kenya, including a trip to the former home of Karen von Blixen (author of *Out of Africa*), starting at $1,999.

Another U.S. firm, **Saga Holidays,** *(617)262-2262* in Boston, Massachusetts, offers a 22-day safari for $2,500, including airfare.

However, the cheapest safaris of all are arranged in Kenya. For less than $275 you can join a five-day camping safari that includes travel by land rover, tent accommodation, and good food. Tour agents are located along the main streets of Nairobi. Camping safaris are not always advertised; you might have to ask for information. Try **Atkin Tours & Travel Ltd.**, *IPS Building, Kimathi Street, P.O. Box 43987; tel. (254-2)333669* or *(254-2)331667,* or **Inside Africa Safaris Ltd.**, *P.O. Box 59767; tel. (254-2)337154.*

Worldwide Journeys and Expeditions, *146 Gloucester Road, London, England; tel. (44-71)370-5032,* arranges safaris designed to avoid the typical tourist destinations. The 17-day Zambia Safari includes walking tours of Luangwa Valley, which has the best unspoiled parks in Africa, as well as a visit to Victoria Falls. The price is £2,000 ($3,800), including airfare from London.

Kenya: the most inviting country

Kenya's 225,000 square miles of mountains, plains, and coastline provide an extraordinary variety of terrain. This country is beautiful and—once you have arrived—inexpensive. Kenya is perhaps the most inviting country in Africa—it is English-speaking, politically stable, and easily accessible.

Not only valued for its beauty, the land includes some of the most fertile tropical soil in the world. Although famous for its large exportation of coffee and tea, Kenya is also one of the world's leading horticultural countries. Germany and the Netherlands are among the biggest customers for its carnations and many varieties of roses. Fruits and vegetables flourish as well.

In Kenya, you can experience both the sophistication of the big city and the savage excitement of the bush country. The population of this nation defies generalization, composed of British colonial descendants, black Muslims with a Middle Eastern culture, Luo and Kikuyu farmers, Somali nomads, and tall, inscrutable Masai warriors. The majority of the population is now Christian—but this general category comprises extreme Pentacostalism and melanges of Christianity with indigenous religions as well as traditional Roman Catholicism and Episcopalianism.

Before a Kenyan football team will play a game, a witch doctor must be hired to set up nail fetishes around the goalposts to stop the opposing team from scoring any goals. In 1987, Kenyan courts were hearing a case involving a widow's suit against her brothers-in-law, who wanted to bury her late husband according to tribal ritual. Had his brothers-in-law buried him under the Luo ritual, the dead man's property would have gone to the tribe—and not his family. Even among modern city families, the Kikuyu custom of female circumcision (excision of the woman's clitoris) is tolerated, although not supported, by the government.

Swahili, the official language of Kenya, combines African grammar with Arabic words. Because it is the language of trade, you will hear it in the markets and on the streets of Kenya. However, English is spoken by government officials, bankers, and international businessmen.

The best place to view the heavens

Because of its location across the equator, Kenya is one of the best places in the world to stargaze. The cloudless deserts and high, isolated Mount Kenya also contribute. Being on the equator means that every constellation in the sky is visible every night of the year. They simply change positions. What was on the western horizon at sunrise is on the eastern horizon 12 hours later, along with the sun. Mount Kenya and Lake Turkana in northern Kenya are the best viewing sites.

Africa's metropolis: Nairobi

"Nairobi is the Paris of the East African coast," said Negley Farson in *Behind God's Back* (1940). The towers of the city shine in the hot noon sun and stand guard in the cool, fresh night air. The harsh contours of modern office buildings are camouflaged by cascades of bougainvillea (a genus of South American climbing shrub), clumps of carnations, and banks of orchids. Residents harmonize with this tropical gaiety in brightly printed and tie-dyed garments.

Kenya's best museum

The **National Museum of Nairobi**, *on Museum Hill off Uhuru Highway*, has the world's foremost collection of fossils of human evolution. The museum houses many archeological discoveries of the late Dr. Richard Leakey, as well as 184 watercolor paintings by Joy Adamson, author of *Born Free*. Children can enjoy a special "please touch" exhibit. The admission charge is 57.6 Kenyan shillings ($1.80) for adults, 19.2 Kenyan shillings (60 cents) for children. The museum is open daily 9:30 a.m. until 6 p.m.

Snake Park, across the street from the National Museum, is also of interest to nature enthusiasts, containing more than 200 species of snakes.

Kenya's best art gallery

Paintings, sculptures, batiks, and photos by the best artists in Kenya and other African countries can be seen at **Gallery Watatu**, *Lonrho House, Standard Street; tel. (254-2)228737*. The gallery displays and sells works Monday through Friday, 9 a.m. until 5 p.m., and Saturday, 9 a.m. until 12:30 p.m.

The best animal viewing

A visit to the Animal Orphanage in **Nairobi National Park** five miles outside town is a good way to prepare for a wilderness safari. The orphanage is most famous for its lion and leopard cubs, which are as endearing as kittens—as long as they are tiny.

Nairobi's best shopping

In the center of Nairobi is the **Nairobi City Market**, where you can barter for animal carvings and usually come out ahead. The **African Heritage Shop**, *Kenyatta Avenue*, sells animal carvings, textiles and jewelry. **Colpro Outfitters**, *Kenyatta Avenue*, is the place to go for safari gear.

Here are some Swahili words that may prove useful: *Bei gani* (How much?); *Ni ghali* (It is expensive); *Taf adhali nipunguzie bei* (Please give me a discount).

The best way to send a message

At the **Thorn Tree Message Center** in Nairobi, you can leave a free message for anyone anywhere in the world. By the sidewalk café at the **New Stanley Hotel**, *Kimathi Street and Kenyatta Avenue; tel. (254-2)33233*, is a thorn tree with bulletin boards affixed on four sides. You can fill out blank message forms with personal messages, advertisements, or announcements.

The most exotic meals

Food is a bargain in Nairobi. Foods of all nationalities are served, as well as local specialties, such as *ugali*, a corn and bean dish, and *ino*, a mixture of seeds. The best place to try traditional Kenyan foods is **African Heritage Ltd.**, *Kenyatta Avenue and Muindi Mbingu Street*. Among specialties served in the rear garden are grilled whole tilapia fish and roast lamb for 80 Kenyan shillings ($2.50) each; beef kabobs with salad are 88 Kenyan shillings ($2.75).

The best restaurant in town is the **Carnivore**, *Langata Road; tel. (254-2)501775*, where the specialty is—you guessed it—meat. You can try an unlimited amount of exotic skewered meats (anything from antelope to zebra) for 272 Kenyan shillings ($8.50).

The **Mount Kenya Safari Club**, *P.O. Box 35, Nairobi,* where a meal of pan-fried Nile perch, potatoes, and salad costs 176 Kenyan shillings ($5.50), is the most elegant place to dine.

Good Indian curry, made with African ingredients, can be found in restaurants throughout Kenya. Many of the Indians, imported by British colonialists as administrators, were Muslims, which is why the curries are made with beef (which Hindus are not allowed to eat). Try Kenya colonial curry (which will probably be cooked by an African rather than an Indian, because many Indians emigrated to England after Kenya gained its independence). Curry is usually served with a proliferation of accompaniments: chutneys and fried and roasted breads as in India; bananas, coconuts, mangoes, and other fruits; very hot red pepper sauce; peanuts; and even soy sauce.

Nairobi's best beds
Nairobi's best hotel is a remnant of the colonial days called the **Norfolk**, *Harry Thuku Road, P.O. Box 40064; tel. (254-2)335422.* It is Kenya's answer to the famous Singapore Raffles Hotel, with individual bungalows in a tropical formal garden.

Another good place to stay—if you can arrange an invitation—is the private **Muthaiga Club**, where members can arrange accommodation for their friends.

The **Hotel InterContinental**, *Uhuru Highway, P.O. Box 30353, City Hall Way; tel. (254-2)33-55-50*, charges 2,080 Kenyan shillings ($65) for a double room, as does the **Mount Kenya Safari Club**. If you can stand the name, the **Hotel Comfy** can put you up in a double room for only 736 Kenyan shillings ($23).

The least expensive place to stay is the **Hotel Ambassadeur**, *Moi Avenue, P.O. Box 30399; tel. (254-2)336803*, providing bed and breakfast for two for 1,152 Kenyan shillings ($36). The hotel boasts a fine Indian restaurant called **Safeer**.

The best revolution
The revolving restaurant at the top of the **Kenyatta Conference Center** (the highest building in Nairobi) has a spectacular view of the city, particularly at sunset.

The best java
Kenya produces the best coffee in the world and is one of the world's leading exporters of Arabica coffee. The **Coffee Board of Kenya**, *Mama Ngina Street*, serves the most tempting coffee in town, as well as light snacks. A snack of coffee, *mandazi* (fried dough), and *samosa* (meat pie in the Indian fashion as interpreted by Kenyan cooks) is only 6.4 Kenyan shillings (20 cents).

Coffee was introduced to Kenya by the French Holy Ghost Fathers (who liked a good cup of coffee) in the 1890s. It was developed in the region north of Nairobi. African farmers were forbidden to grow coffee until 1954. It is now Kenya's main export crop (which causes problems when the coffee crop fails). The berries are handpicked twice a year.

The second leading export crop is tea—another crop Africans were forbidden to grow. Today the region around Limuru supports more than 100,000 African smallholders, who grow enough tea to make Kenya the third-largest producer in the world, after India and Sri Lanka.

The country's best dancers
The best places to watch tribal dancing in Kenya are the country's **bomas**, miniature replicas of Kenya's 40 tribal villages, located seven miles outside Nairobi, on Langata Road. They are also good places to shop for wood carvings. Admission is 115 Kenyan shillings ($3.60) for adults, 58 Kenyan shillings ($1.80) for children.

The loveliest drive from Nairobi

The best way to see the countryside around Nairobi is by car, at your own pace. Following is the best itinerary, recommended by an old Kenya hand.

Drive three hours north of Nairobi to **Nanyuki**, stopping along the way to see the grave of Lord Baden Powell, founder of the Boy Scouts, in Nyerere. On his tomb is a circle with a dot in the middle, the scout symbol for "gone home."

Nanyuki is situated 8,000 feet high on the slope of snow-topped Mount Kenya, which sits smack on the equator. Once you have become acclimated to the altitude, you will find this an ideal base for observing Kenya's wildlife.

Take time to stay at either the **Sportman Arm's Club** or the **Mwingo Gate Hotel** (formerly the Safari Club). Visit Africa's most exciting racetrack.

From Nanyuki, head north to **Archer's Post**, a spring in the middle of the desert. If you are traveling independently, this is the end of the line. Solo travelers are not permitted to venture farther out into the Northern Frontier district. (This is for your own protection.)

To venture deeper into the desert, join an organized tour and continue north to **Marsabit**, a tree-covered mountain in the middle of the Kaisul desert; this is where game animals come to drink during the dry season.

Backtrack to Nanyuki and then take the road to **Nakuru**, which runs along the edge of the Rift Valley. You will see flamingos and views of mountains and the plain. This is where early traces of man were discovered.

En route, stop at the **Nyahururu waterfall** (formerly called Thomson's Fall). Stay at the **Thomson's Fall Lodge**, a bit of old England, where you can take tea on the lawn while watching the water fall. A few miles away is the courthouse where Jomo Kenyatta, leader of the independence movement, was tried.

A bird watcher's best

Lake Nakuru Park, 100 miles northwest of Nairobi, is the habitat of more species of birds than all the British Isles; it is also home to millions of pink flamingos. The best accommodation here is at the **Lake Nakuru Lodge**, *P.O. Box 561; tel. (254-2)85446.*

Lake Naivasha is also an excellent place for bird watching. More than 340 species can be spotted near this beautifully situated lake. Dominated be the shadow of Mount Longonot, an extinct volcano, Lake Naivasha also provides water sports and hiking opportunities. Joy Adamson wrote her best-selling novel *Born Free* here.

Accommodation is available at the **Lake Naivasha Hotel**, *South Lake Road, P.O. Box 15; tel. (254-2)20013,* which is a collection of cottages on the lakeshore, each with a private veranda overlooking the water.

The best of Kenya's beaches

Kenya has 300 miles of glorious beaches along the Indian Ocean. The Swahili, a people of Arab and African ancestry and culture, live along the coast and for centuries have been astute traders.

The white-sand beaches, edged with palms, are protected from pollution and sharks by reefs. Beyond the palm trees is the forest, inhabited by leopards, Colobus monkeys, and brightly colored birds.

World-class craftsmanship

Kenya has become one of the leading exporters of handicrafts, including soapstone, stone, and wood carvings and sisal baskets (popularly known as *kiondos*). Wood carvings, however, top the list. Wamunyu, a small township about 60 miles east of Nairobi, is the birthplace of this growing industry. It began with Mutisya Munge in the early 1840s, and today over half of Wamunyu's population of 20,000 are wood-carvers.

You can visit wood carving studios in Wamunyu, Mombasa, and Nairobi, where you can watch rows of men effortlessly creating exquisite statues. Visitors can buy items at wholesale prices.

Mombasa: gateway to the coast

Mombasa, gateway to the coast, is Kenya's second-largest city, combining African, Indian, and Arab cultures. Its narrow side streets, impassable by car, are lined with Indian temples, bazaars, and houses decorated with intricately carved wood doors. Curry scents the air, and the Muslim women are veiled in black *buibuis*.

While in Mombasa, stay at the **Castle** in Old Town or the **Outrigger** by the yacht club. To make reservations, contact **Alliance Hotels**, *College House, University Way, P.O. Box 49839, Nairobi; tel. (254-2)337501.*

The best way to get to the beach

Although it is possible to fly to Mombasa via Kenya Airways, old-timers prefer to take the overnight train from Nairobi. This train offers a good meal, a private sleeper, and a porter who wakes you up at 6:30 a.m. with a delicious cup of locally grown tea or coffee.

Malindi: the best modern beach resort

Malindi, an island 74 miles north of Mombasa, is known for its modern hotels, lively nightclubs, and ocean sports, including big-game fishing, sailing, water-skiing, skin and scuba diving, and underwater photography. It also has a half-dozen nature preserves; the Malindi Marine National Park, where you can see technicolor fish, the moray eel, and octopi; and Gedi, the ruin of an abandoned Islamic settlement in a thick tropical forest inland.

The best hotel on Malindi is **Lawford's**, *P.O. Box 20, Malindi; tel. (254-12)32113*, which offers two restaurants and two swimming pools.

The best way to get to Malindi is by plane—taxis are expensive, and buses are slow.

The least-developed islands

From Malindi, you can take a boat to the barely developed and sparsely inhabited out islands of **Manda, Kiwayuu**, and **Pate**. Pate Town can be reached only if the tide is right. Faza and Siyu, also on Pate Island, are more accessible.

The best-preserved Swahili town

The island of **Lamu** is a perfectly preserved 18th-century Swahili town, where men and women still wear the traditional dress—women are veiled and men wear *kofia* (white embroidered caps).

Don't expect to tour Lamu by car. The only car in town is reserved for use by the island's government representative. The best way to travel is by dhow. (*Dhows* are handmade sailboats.)

The islanders are obviously Islamic. There are outdoor Koran schools and 29 mosques. Don't try to photograph the island residents; it is a violation of the Orthodox Muslim religious injunction against graven images.

Africa's deepest valley

The **Rift Valley**, a geological fault that originates in Syria and runs to South Africa, is best seen in Kenya. Sheer cliffs several thousand feet high rise above the valley floor, which is 50 miles wide in places. Changes in climate and topography when one descends the valley slopes are abrupt. Coffee plantations are everywhere. Large herds of relatively tame animals graze along the valley edges.

Kenya's best watering holes

Comfortable (even luxurious) lodges have been built near many of the country's watering holes. If you don't think you're up to a safari, opt for a holiday at one of these lodges. Instead of roughing it in the wilds, you'll be relaxing, while elephants, lions, hippos, and monkeys come up to you. All you need is a pair of binoculars.

The best watering hole is **Kilaguni**, 200 miles south of Nairobi in the giant Tsavo National Park. Animals can be viewed day and night, game drives and walks around Mzima Springs are available, and camping facilities are available for true adventurers. **Kilaguni Lodge**, *P.O. Box 30471; tel. (254-2)336858*, has a swimming pool, safari vehicles, and a restaurant and bar overlooking the watering hole. A double room is 2,976 Kenyan shillings ($93), including meals.

The most famous of the watering holes is Kenya's original, **Treetops**, *c/o Block Hotels, P.O. Box 47557; tel. (254-2)33580*, 80 miles north of Nairobi in the Aberdares Mountains. You climb (slowly) to cedar huts where you are welcomed by servants, who spoil you, and by baboons, which pester you if you don't keep the windows shut. As night falls, wild animals visit the water hole below the lodge; the scene is periodically floodlit. Treetops is the most expensive watering hole lodge in Kenya, at 4,768 Kenyan shillings ($149) a night, including all meals.

The Ark, *P.O. Box 449, Nyeri; tel. (254)55620*, near Treetops, is comparable in amenities to its more famous counterpart—but it's slightly less expensive, at 3,616 Kenyan shillings ($113) a night, including full board. In addition, many argue that the game viewing is better at The Ark than at Treetops; a tunnel leads you to a hide right next to the watering hole.

Africa's most spectacular peaks

Kenya is home to the two most spectacular mountain peaks in Africa: **Mount Kilimanjaro** and **Mount Kenya** (known as Nyandarua among the Kikuyu). The eternal snows of these equatorial peaks seem like the stuff of legend even after you climb them. Mount Kilimanjaro can be climbed from the Tanzanian side of the border or the Kenyan.

A five-day trip from base to peak, Mount Kilimanjaro is the most challenging. The **Uhuru Peak** (20,000 feet) can give climbers quite a rush of success. Tourist agencies in Tanzania will organize a climb of the mountain. No climbing is allowed during the rainy season in April and May.

In the language of the Masai, who live in its shadow, Kilimanjaro means *White Mountain*. The Masai climb only to an altitude of 10,000 feet, where the air gets thin. It's another 9,340 feet from there to the top. It can be done, thanks to an easy trail, encouraging Tanzanian guides, and comfortable Norwegian huts.

The standard hike to the top takes five days. From the park entrance at 6,000 feet, the first day's hike is along a gently rising trail for three to four hours until you reach Mandara Hut. Tropical forest animals inhabit this lower altitude.

After five to seven hours of walking, you come to Horombo Hut at 12,000 feet. It has one notable difference from the first hut: the view of the snow-capped Kibo Peak above and the ocean of clouds washing the base of the mountains below.

The third day demands a climb to 14,000 feet over a stream marked "Last Water" and across wind-blown dusty terrain. It takes another three hours to climb to 15,600 feet, where the cold, dark, and uncomfortable Kibo Hut awaits you.

By tradition, you must reach the mountaintop in time to see the sunrise. So at 1 a.m. you will be awakened to trudge to Uhuru Peak. You will feel nauseous, lethargic, and sore. But when you see the sunrise from the mountain's peak, it will all seem worthwhile.

Mount Kenya, a snow-covered peak on the equator, is more scenic and easier to climb than Mount Kilimanjaro, due to the lower altitude. (It's 17,000 feet high.) Both are volcanos, but unlike the case with its southern neighbor, Mount Kenya's fires have long been extinct. The two highest peaks—Batian at 17,058 and Nelion at 17,022 feet—are named after 19th-century Kenyan medicine men. They stand like huge black tombstones and are the domain of technical climbers of rock and ice. The average climber takes an easier route to Mount Lenana at 16,355 feet.

From the entrance gate at 9,500 feet, another 500-foot ascent brings you to the hut at Met Station Lodge, where a troop of Sykes monkeys entertains.

Before passing the tree line the next morning, you might see black and white Colobus monkeys flinging themselves madly through the trees overhead. At an area called the Vertical Bog, from 11,000 to 13,000 feet, the serpentine trail is covered with soggy peat and leads eventually to the foot of the glacier.

You sleep in the Kami Hut, made of corrugated iron, until 4 a.m., when you begin the trek across ice-coated boulders, using flashlights to light the way. A guide is essential to chop steps with an ice ax. By dawn, you will reach the top.

Hikes of Mount Kenya must be arranged through **Naro Moru River Lodge**, *P.O. Box 18, Naro Moru; tel. (254-176)62023.* Three- to seven-day trips can be arranged for 1,600 Kenyan shillings ($50) per person per day. You can rent any equipment you will need at the lodge.

Tanzania: the best of the wild

Tanzania is Kenya's southern neighbor. This country is the result of the fusion of the offshore island of Zanzibar, once an Arab stronghold, and the mainland (called Tanganyika in colonial days), inhabited by the Bantu and other African ethnic groups. The political unrest this fusion created was complicated by the country's adoption of Ujamaa, a form of socialism promoted by President Julius Nyerere. Tanzania is still suffering economic woes from its turbulent past; the country is desperately poor, hungry for tourism, and cheap.

Because it is so inexpensive (guides can be hired for 375 Tanzanian shillings, or $1.25, a day), Tanzania is beginning to draw tourists to its enormous game parks. Tanzania is really where the wild things are. The famous **Serengeti Plain**, where you can witness the spring wildlife migration every year, has the largest concentration of game in the world.

Seronera Wildlife Lodge, *P.O. Box 3100, Arusha,* in the center of the park, has an airstrip and a swimming pool carved from natural rock. **Lobo Wildlife Lodge**, *P.O. Box 3100, Arusha,* is an entire building carved from natural rock.

One of the undiscovered wonders of Tanzania is **Selous**, the largest game reserve in the world. This unspoiled, undeveloped wilderness is populated by more than 1 million animals, including Africa's greatest elephant and lion populations. Animals are less visible to visitors at this park, though, due to the immense area of the reserve.

Luxury accommodation is offered in Selous at **Mbuyu Safari Camp**, *Bushtrekker Safaris, P.O. Box 5380, Dar es Salaam,* a hotel constructed around a baobab tree.

Be cautious when visiting **Dar es Salaam**, Tanzania's capital. It is a city rife with criminals who prey on tourists. And before you enter Tanzania, ask government officials for exact information on how much currency you must exchange. The rules are complicated and strict. The black market exchange rate in Tanzania is much higher than the official rate.

Zimbabwe: best hunting, best waterfall

Zimbabwe, formerly Rhodesia, is the best place to go on a hunting safari (for which a hunting license is required). However, peaceable safaris are also offered.

Victoria Falls, located on the border with Zambia, is over a mile wide. The **Zambezi River** falls 300 feet here, creating a spray visible for miles. Spectacular rainbows arc over the cliffs.

American passport holders theoretically do not require visas to enter Zimbabwe, but there have been instances when travelers on their own have been stopped and imprisoned in Harare, the capital, for not having a visa. Traveling with a group tour is advisable.

Rwanda: the best place to observe gorillas

Perched high in the Rift Valley Mountains west of Tanzania, tiny landlocked **Rwanda** is the best place in the world to see mountain gorillas.

To visit the heart of gorilla country, you must hike through dense bamboo forests to an altitude of 10,000 feet. Professional guides lead small groups and carry rifles in case you meet wild buffalo, elephants, stray leopards, or poachers.

The hour-long trek begins easily, ascending through fields of flowers and potatoes before you enter the forest, where the trail becomes steep, narrow, and slippery. Just when you're out of breath, the path ambles across flat mountain meadows—but not for long before making another jungle climb.

It takes a while to find the gorillas. They roam over a wide area and move more easily than humans through the dense vegetation—their physiques are better suited to bending and swinging than ours.

When the guide sights a troop of gorillas, he motions to hurry forward quietly. You can hear the gorillas snorting and cracking the vegetation beneath them. The guide makes low vocalizations to assure the gorillas' leader of friendliness before deciding if the great apes seem willing to allow visitors. If they are, you can crouch silently within feet of the primates for about 60 minutes. You are warned not to stare at the 500-pound creatures; they interpret this as a sign of aggression. In the unlikely event of an attack, the best defense is no defense—just lie flat.

The best ways to get there

Direct flights from Belgium, France, and Kenya are available to **Kigali**, the capital of Rwanda. There, you can rent a car or take an inexpensive but crowded bus to the gorillas' habitat, **Virunga Volcanoes National Park**. The most picturesque town to stay in is **Gisenyi**, which is on Lake Kivu, an hour's drive from the park.

To minimize disturbance to the gorillas' habitat, tour groups are restricted to six people. Tours must be booked in advance through the Rwandan Office of Tourism and National Parks in Kigali, and there is a 10- to 20-day waiting list.

The cost is approximately 11,451 Rwandan francs ($80) per person, excluding the customary 10% tip to porters. Bring your own food, water, and camping equipment from Kigali.

With fewer than 250 of these gorillas in the wild, they are listed as an endangered species. Because gorillas are susceptible to human diseases, a visitor with even a bad cold may not be allowed to visit the troop. Children under 15 may not participate.

Uganda: birthplace of the Nile

Still recovering from the political terror of the Idi Amin regime from 1971 to 1986, Uganda's tourism industry is still in its infancy. Nonetheless, Uganda is worth visiting for two reasons. First, it is cheap. Second, its people are hospitable.

Eighty kilometers from **Kampala**, Uganda's capital, lies Lake Victoria, the largest lake in Africa and the second-largest lake in the world. Here you can witness the beginning of the Nile's long journey to the Mediterranean Sea.

About 150 miles downriver, **Kabalega National Park** is home to not only hippos, crocodiles, and other aquatic life but also the famed **Murchison Falls**. Here, the great river is crammed through a 20-foot fissure in the rocks and led down a 1,000-foot drop.

While in Kampala, visit Kabaka's Palace and Kasubi's Tomb. These are where the royal chiefs of the Buganda tribes were interred. There is also a traditional marketplace where you can purchase traditional Ugandan goods.

The **Nile Hotel Complex** in Kampala is the best place to stay in Uganda. It has parklike grounds with tennis courts, swimming pools, and restaurants.

The Seychelles: paradise found

Some say the **Seychelles**—an island country 1,000 miles east of Kenya in the Indian Ocean—was once the Garden of Eden. Because of its government's strict environmental guidelines, some of its islands are among the least spoiled on earth. Tall palms line these sandy beaches that stretch along the pale-blue Indian Ocean. The people are an exotic mixture of African, Arab, French, British, Indian, and Chinese.

Ninety percent of all Seychellese live on the island of **Mahé**. The high mountain peaks at **Morne Seychellois National Park**, in the center of the island, offer views of the other islands.

Authors Somerset Maugham, Ian Fleming, Alec Waugh, and Noel Coward have been lured by the beauty of the islands. Most of them stayed at the **Northolme Hotel**, *Mahé, Glacis, P.O. Box 333; tel. (248)47-222.* The original hotel building is no longer in use, but guests can visit it and see the rooms labeled with names of former guests. Today's visitors are housed in a new building patterned in the old style and equipped with modern conveniences. The Northolme also has a French and Creole restaurant. A double room is 995 rupees ($190).

Another hotel on Mahé is the **Coral Beach**, *Beau Vallon Beach; tel. (248)47036.* This bed-and-breakfast has double rooms for 770 rupees ($146) a night.

The second-largest island of the Seychelles, **Praslin**, is home to the rare black bulbul parrot and the Coco-de-mer palm, which produces a large double coconut shaped somewhat like a woman's derrière and is said to have special fertility powers. **Vallée de Mai** on Praslin is the best place to glimpse rare birds and see the Coco-de-mer, and **Anse Lazio** is the Seychelles' most spectacular beach. **Baie des Chevaliers** is more secluded and can be reached by boat or airplane. (Air Seychelles charges 270 rupees, about $51, round trip.)

The best place to stay on Praslin is **Maison des Palmes**; *tel. (248)33411,* a guesthouse on Grande Anse Beach with individual cottages that have private baths and terraces. A twin room is 410 rupees ($78) a night, including breakfast.

The forests of **Silhouette Island** contain plants and animals found nowhere else in the world. And the island's beaches are ideal for swimming and snorkeling. The 250 islanders raise cattle, goats, coconuts, sugarcane, cinnamon, vanilla, and fruit. There are no roads, only paths. The island has a superb hotel, the **Silhouette Island Lodge**, *P.O. Box 608, Victoria; tel. (248)24003,* which has thatched bungalows for 860 rupees to 1,180 rupees ($163 to $224).

The most picturesque and expensive of the Seychelles is the coral **Denis Island**, only 30 minutes by plane from Mahé. (Air Seychelles charges 990 rupees, or $171.) You can stay in thatched cottages by the sea at **Denis Island Lodge**, *P.O. Box 404, Denis Island; tel. (248)23813,* for 1,355 rupees to 1,500 rupees ($246 to $275). Creole food is served at the buffet.

Banyan trees surround the **Plantation House** on **Fregate Island**, *P.O. Box 330, Fregate; tel. (248)22717.* A double room at this colonial inn near an orchard and a beach is 500 rupees ($95) a night, including meals. Air Seychelles charges 270 rupees ($49) for the round-trip flight.

The least developed of the inhabited Seychelles is **La Digue**, with no cars but plenty of bicycles. Enormous boulders and tall palms line the surf. And 30 pairs of rare paradise flycatchers live in the Indian almond trees. If you like to snorkel or scuba dive, contact **Gregoire's Watersports**, *Gregoire's Island Lodge, La Digue; tel. (248)34233.* You can stay at **Gregoire's Island Lodge**, *Anse Reunion, La Digue; tel. (248)34233,* on the beach, for 864 rupees to 945 rupees ($164 to $180) a night, including meals.

Cousin, Bird, and Aride islands draw flocks of rare birds. More than a million sooty terns nest on Bird Island from May to November every year. The endangered bush warbler lives on Cousin. Aride is home to the world's largest colonies of lesser noddy and roseate terns.

Bird Island Lodge, *P.O. Box 404; tel. (248)44449,* has cottages with private baths and terraces for $150 a night, including English breakfast, Creole lunch, and European dinner.

South Africa: a world of contrasts

With sanctions recently lifted, South Africa is opening up as a whole new paradise for international travelers. The country is a land of contrasts. **Johannesburg**, it's capital, is its industrial, financial, and cultural center. The nouveau riche (and many foreigners) are settling here in droves, originating the city's nickname as the "City of Gold." But this is hardly the essence of South Africa. Each direction you travel will reveal a different and beautiful landscape, and another culture. From the rocky expanses and beautiful beaches of the west coast to the subtropical forests of the east coast, South Africa is teeming with energy and beauty. And once you get there, you'll find that travel in general is very affordable; you can stay in five-star hotels for as little as $60 a night.

The best beds

The best accommodation in the country is organized through **Bed 'N Breakfast**, *Eighth Avenue, Melville 2092, P.O. Box 91309; tel. (482)22067.* It operates a network of bed-and-breakfasts, through which South Africans offer their own homes to travelers.

Cape Town: South Africa's oldest city

With Table Mountain as its backdrop, Cape Town is not only South Africa's oldest city but also its most beautiful. In fact, it is boasted as one of the most beautiful cities in the world. Its diverse architecture reflects the city's Victorian background, as well as its 20th-century influences.

South Africa's oldest—and best—museum

The **South African Museum**, *Government Laan Road*, is South Africa's oldest museum. It features an extensive natural history collection of mammals, reptiles, birds, fish, and insects. The whale gallery, life-size Bushman models, and planetarium are also worth a look.

World-renowned wineries

The wineries east of Cape Town are world-renowned. If you're a connoisseur of the fruit of the vine, you'll want to make time to visit this region while in South Africa. Stay the night at the **Lanzerac Estate**, *P.O. Box 4, Stellenbosch 7600; tel. (27-2231)71132,* an original Dutch homestead. The cost is 23.27 rand to 36.37 rand ($64 to $100) a night for a room furnished with original Cape antiques.

The most challenging maze

Larger than the legendary maze at Britain's Hampton Court, the new garden maze in Cape Town at **Three Anchors Bay** offers some of the world's most challenging hedges. Admission to the **Serendipity** is 8 rand ($22) for the entire family.

South Africa's smallest province

Although **Natal** is South Africa's smallest province, it offers beautiful countryside, as well as bustling city life. **Durban**, Natal's capital, is known for its Golden Mile, where five-star hotels and diverse restaurants abound. You'll also find an abundance of nightclubs, discos, or concert halls, theaters, and galleries—something for everyone.

The best way to experience Zulu life

Just north of Durban is **Eshowe**, where three Zulu *kraals* accommodate visitors in authentic beehive huts, giving you the chance to experience firsthand the lifestyle, rites, and rituals of tribal life. Also visit the **Zululand Historical Museum** (at Fort Nonquai).

The best beaches

With more than 100 gorgeous white-sand beaches to choose from, the Cape Peninsula has some of the best coastline in Africa. Discerning sun worshipers prefer **Clifton** beach, with its mountainous backdrop. Another favorite is **Muizenberg**, a seaside resort town within 35 kilometers of beach.

The most plants
If plants are your fancy, the Cape Peninsula is the place for you. It has more indigenous plant species per square meter than anyplace else on earth. The **National Botanic Gardens of Kirstenbosch**, on the eastern slopes of **Table Mountain**, is a prime viewing location.

Africa's largest game preserve
Along the northeastern border (adjacent to Moçambique) lies **Kruger National Park**, Africa's largest game preserve. The 12,000 square miles of land is home to more species of wildlife, birds, and plants than any other park in Africa. The park is less than four hours by car from Johannesburg; local flights are also available, to get you there more quickly.

The best adventure
The newest nature thrill available in South Africa is underwater shark watching. Four shark spotters at one time can spend three hours in sturdy cages, watching the great whites circling in search of prey. Seven days of shark watching cost 1,636 rand ($4,500). Contact **Exotic Drive Tours**, *45 Rosmead Ave., Kenilworth, Cape Town 7700.*

The best ways to see South Africa
If you're looking for flexibility and independence, the best way to see South Africa is from the driver's seat of a rented motor home. This makes a lot of sense, especially because camping space is often easier to book than cottages at national parks throughout the country. One of the best companies is **CI Leisure Rentals**, *P.O. Box 137, Pinetown 3600,* with offices in Johannesburg, Cape Town, and Durban; rates are 400 rand to 436 rand ($1,100 to $1,200) per week.

Another adventurous way to see South Africa is on board the world's most luxurious steam train, *Rovos.* You can spend four days and three nights exploring the former gold-rush country of the eastern Transvaal for 727 rand ($2,000), all-inclusive.

Madagascar: home of the ring-tailed lemur
Madagascar, off the southeastern coast of Africa in the Indian Ocean, is the fourth-largest island in the world. It is also one of the least visited, famous primarily for its large lemur population.

The capital of Madagascar, **Antananarivo** (known locally as Tana), is a good place to start your exploration. This charming little city offers hundreds of tiny shops and the Zuma marketplace. Every Friday, this giant market overflows with people looking for bargains in leather, jewelry, and other local goods. Pickpockets and muggers roam the streets, so keep your belongings close.

Also venture over to **Nosy Be Island**, off the northwest coast of Madagascar. Coffee, vanilla, and ilang-ilang trees (their oil is used to make perfumes and soaps) are grown here. Stay at the **Andilana Beach Hotel**.

The best lemur watching
If you came to Madagascar looking for the infamous ring-tailed lemurs, visit the **Berenty Lemur Reserve** in Fort Dauphin. Large, clean guesthouses are available on the grounds, and lemurs run rampant. The furry little creatures here are so tame they take food right from your hand.

The best beds
You can find clean, convenient accommodation on Madagascar for less than 19,000

francs ($10) a night: the **Hotel Select**, *avenue 18 de juin*; **Hotel Terminus**, *ave. de la Libération 2; tel. (261)25440;* and the **Bridge Hotel**, *avenue Marguerite Barbier*, are all good places to stay.

Even the luxury hotels on the island are less than 152,000 francs ($80) a night. The **Acropole**, *71 ave. Lenine; tel. (261)23380*, has quality rooms and a restaurant that serves good Malagasy and French food. The **Hotel Colbert**, *rue Prince Ratsimamanga; tel. (261)20202*, has air-conditioned rooms and a restaurant and casino.

The best travel tips

Because of its tropical setting, Madagascar does experience a lengthy rainy season (November through March). Avoid visiting during this period, when inland travel becomes difficult. The local buses and taxis are suitable methods of getting around the island, but avoid the *proper* buses (which hold about 30 people, not very comfortably). They tend to be slow and do not handle the unsurfaced roads well.

The island trains are inexpensive and faster than buses, but you must make reservations in advance. They run daily except Sunday.

Senegal: a French holiday favorite

Senegal is a paradise of European sunseekers, who make up the majority of visitors to this West African country. Americans have yet to discover Senegal, although it is the African country geographically closest to the United States, a mere 6 1/2-hour flight from New York. The Senegalese government is working to attract more American visitors by expanding the denationalized tourist industry.

Senegal offers 350 miles of beach, two national game parks (open seasonally), a bird reserve, sailing, and fishing—as well as history and a pleasant climate (relatively speaking—remember, this is West Africa). Because it juts out into the Atlantic, pleasant breezes waft through the country, and the heat is less unpleasant than in neighboring countries.

The Senegalese Dance Troupe is world-acclaimed, and the local handicrafts are beautiful: precious jewelry crafted by hand, printed and woven fabrics, and snakeskin and crocodile leather goods.

The three negative aspects of this African country are the panhandlers, the dangerous ocean currents, and the unpleasant creatures of the surf, including sharks and jellyfish.

Dakar: the best Paris of Africa

Several cities claim to be the "Paris of Africa," but **Dakar** best fits the description. Good restaurants and outdoor cafés can be found throughout the French-speaking capital. The architecture shows signs of French influences, including wrought-iron balconies and little courtyards. But mosques also punctuate the cityscape, and little dirt streets weave between the grand boulevards.

The best of Senegalese art

The best place to see the art of Senegal is the **Musée d'Art Nègre-Africain** (African Art Museum), *Place Tascher*. The entire first floor of this museum is devoted to Senegalese culture, displaying clothing, furniture, jewels, costumes, and instruments. The museum is open Tuesday through Sunday 8 a.m. until noon and 2 until 6 p.m.

Local galleries also exhibit the works of contemporary Senegalese artists. The best is **Galerie 39**, *avenue Pompidou*, which displays paintings, drawings, and textile work.

The most important monuments

Dakar's two great architectural monuments are its cathedral and the Grand Mosque. The **cathedral**, *Boulevard de la République and avenue du Président Lamine Gueye*, is one of the finest examples of Senegalese architecture. The **Grand Mosque**, *Allée Coursin*, built in 1964, is one of the largest mosques in Africa. (You must be content to view it from outside, because visitors are not permitted to enter.)

The most international shopping

Dakar is filled with fascinating markets that combine African, Arabian, and European traditions. The one drawback is that all the city's markets are expensive.

The most colorful is **Sandaga**, an enormous place covering several city blocks with little stalls selling everything from fruit and meat to cloth and sandals. This is where the locals shop—it is about as authentic as you'll get. Another typical market is **Marché Tilène**, *avenue Blaise Diagne*.

Local designers create garments decorated with batik and embroidery and then sell their clothing in boutiques throughout the city. Recommended boutiques include **Fara**, *rues Assane N'Doye and Wagane Diouf*, and the **Deco Shop**, *rues Carnot and Blanchot*.

Marché Kermel, *near place de l'Indépendance*, is Dakar's European-style market, where you can buy high-quality imported goods, as well as clothing and souvenirs. Haggling is not recommended. The market is open daily.

Caritas Tissage Traditionnel, *Route de Ouakam*, is a weavers' workshop that sells belts, bedspreads, purses, and clothing. Prices are reasonable. Again, haggling is not recommended.

The best digs in Dakar

Novotel Dakar, *avenue Sarraut, B.P. 2973; tel. (221)23-10-90*, which belongs to the French Novotel chain, boasts two restaurants, two bars, a swimming pool, and tennis courts. A double room is CFA14,850 ($56).

La Croix du Sud, *20 ave. Albert Sarraut; tel. (221)23-29-47*, has a view of the flower market. A double room is CFA24,000 ($90).

Dakar's best cuisine

Senegalese food tends to be spicy, often garnished with *sauce piment* (hot pepper sauce). Most entrées consist of rice combined with meats and sauces. French cuisine is also available in Dakar. Because alcohol is forbidden to Muslims, only non-alcoholic beverages—mostly teas—are served in restaurants.

La Région du Fleuve, located near the Foreign Ministry and operated by a Frenchwoman and her African husband, is decorated with African masks and textiles and serves African fare. Meals are inexpensive. The restaurant is closed Wednesdays.

La Croix du Sud, *20 ave. Albert Sarraut; tel. (221)23-29-47*, is an elegant but expensive French restaurant. All produce for the meals is imported from France. The restaurant is closed Sundays.

The best entertainment in Dakar

The Senegalese National Theater Company and the Mudra Dance Group, in addition to many other groups, appear at the **Sorano** (the National Theater), *Daniel Sorano Building, boulevard de la République*.

The darkest history

Just 20 minutes from Dakar is the **Island of Gorée**, once the most important transit center for slave traders, who bought Africans for shipment to America. It was from this appalling place that hundreds of thousands of shackled prisoners were loaded onto ships for the so-called Middle Crossing. The first crossing carried rum from the American colonies to Africa to pay for black gold; the final crossing was of sugar to New England to make the rum. A small museum on the island has chilling displays of shackles, chains, and other unpleasant instruments of the trade.

Senegal's best beach

Cap Skirring in Joal is an unspoiled, dazzling white beach fringed by coconut trees. **Club Med,** *tel. (221)93-51-35* or *(212)750-1687 in the United States,* has a highly recommended outpost here. Watch out for sharks (not just the human kind). The resort is closed during the summer (monsoon season).

The least expensive place to stay is **Le Campement**, a government-run accommodation made up of little concrete huts on the water. For a few dollars, you can spend the night on foam pads under clean sheets and enjoy good local food.

The best seashells

The **Island of Fadiouth**, 60 miles from Dakar, is so covered with seashells that the populace uses them as building material. Everything here is made of shells: a cemetery, a church, granaries built on stilts. Natives follow a traditional, self-sufficient, African lifestyle, making their own cloth and growing their food. You can reach the island from the mainland region of Joal via the wooden bridge or in a pirogue (a wooden canoe).

The best place to view game

Basse Casamance, a 12,350-acre game park near Ziguinchor in southeast Senegal, has thick forests inhabited by 52 species of mammals and 172 species of birds. You can visit on guided boat or car tours. A limited number of guests can spend the night in the park at Impluvium Lodge, where light meals and drinks are served.

The best bird sanctuary

One of the most important bird sanctuaries in the world is the 25,000-acre **Djoudj Park**, in the Saloum Delta, where you can see 180 species, including pelicans, herons, flamingos, and egrets. You can observe from a mirador without scaring the birds away.

Mauritanian Blue People camp on the edge of the park from time to time, providing a rare opportunity to see these Berbers.

You, too, can camp here, in a hut in the Campement de Djoudj.

The best duck hunting

Less benevolent bird watchers prefer **Maka Diama** (150 miles north of Dakar), a paradise for duck hunters, who from Dec. 15 to April 15 are licensed to shoot here. In addition to ducks, bags include fancolin, guinea fowl, hare, and quail.

Togo: a microcosm of Africa

Togo, a small west coast country, is sub-Saharan Africa in miniature, with plains alive with game, plantations fertile with crops of cocoa and coffee, and mud-brick villages where the old traditions remain unchanged.

Originally a German protectorate, and then a French colony, Togo is now an independent country. **Lomé**, the capital, offers a wide choice of restaurants, while the coast boasts idyllic beaches.

In Lomé, women hold powerful economic and political positions, and every village has a women's union. The powerful Nana Benz—made up of matronly merchants—wields considerable force in the politics of this country (and has overthrown at least one government). The women sell everything imaginable in the marketplace—from a fully equipped Mercedes Benz to a pair of plastic slippers. Many of the older Nana Benz members are illiterate—but they can calculate their margins and execute foreign-exchange transactions in their heads. Although the language of Togo is officially French, the people also can converse in Pidgin English.

Where to go in Togo

The best way to get a taste of the native life in Togo is to visit **Le Grand Marché** in the center of Lomé, where the smell of roasting meats and tangy spices permeates the air and tie-dyed caftans and printed pagnes are sold. These colorful swaths of cloth are used to make the dresses, shirts, and headdresses worn by West Africans, but they also can be used as unique tablecloths, draperies, or sheets back home. (The textiles are on the second floor of the market.)

For an in-depth look at Togo's culture, visit the **National Museum**, housed in the headquarters of Togo's only political party, the Rassemblement du Peuple Togolais (R.P.T.), a building decorated with reliefs sculpted by a leading Togolese artist. Museum exhibits include shells (which were formerly used as currency), pottery, musical instruments, and ceremonial relics. The museum is open Monday through Friday 8 a.m. until noon and 3 until 5 p.m. Admission is free.

The Odef Craft Center, *tel. (228)21-51-59*, attracts the best of the area's traditional wood carvers. The center also has a selection of macramé, batik, fiber, and clay works.

The best place to settle a score

Voodoo is practiced in **Bé**, a residential area on the east side of Lomé. At **Bé Market**, near the Hotel de la Paix, you can buy unusual charms—bones, little figurines, skulls—from both pagans and Muslims. The charms are said to bring success or money, to defeat a rival in love, or to attract a lover.

Togo's most interesting village

Deep in the **Tamberma Valley** live the Tamberma people, who continue a lifestyle unchanged by the passage of time. Famous for their masonry, they live in cool *tata* dwellings constructed by hand from clay and wood. The houses are situated in a compound that is surrounded by a circle of conical towers connected by a wall. The towers are used primarily to store grain.

The Tamberma spend most of their time outdoors on patios—they even do their cooking outdoors. They wear little clothing and smoke long pipes. The women are marked by scars in intricate patterns; they are tattooed when they are 8 days old to protect against miscarriages and stillbirths.

The best hotels in Togo

The best hotel in Togo is the **Hotel de 2 Fevrier Sofitel**, *B.P. 131, Lomé; tel. (228)21-00-03*, which rivals any posh American hotel. The 36 stories of this glass building include two restaurants, two bars, a nightclub, and a casino. A double room is CFA81,000 ($305).

Hotel Sarakawa, *B.P. 2232; tel. (228)21-65-90*, is a favorite of the French, a five-star hotel with restaurants, a disco, and recreational facilities. A double room is CFA30,000 to CFA35,000 ($113 to $132).

Less expensive is the **Hotel Le Benin**, *tel. (228)21-24-85 or (228)21-24-87*, where the price for a double room is CFA14,000 to CFA20,000 ($53 to $75). This hotel is Togo's training ground for restaurant personnel—the dining room serves fine cuisine for low prices.

Nigeria: the most populated African country

Don't spend much time in Nigeria's capital, **Lagos**. It is an appalling place. Built on a lagoon, the city has a mushrooming population, but it lacks the infrastructure to deal with it. Roads, sewage, garbage collection, and water are all becoming problems. The results are a perpetual traffic jam and generally unpleasant conditions. Telephones seldom work, and electricity is erratic. Most of the Westerners in Lagos are diplomats and businessmen, who leave for the country as quickly and as often as they can.

In the days of high oil prices, Lagos was the most expensive city in Africa; now it is cheap—the one point in its favor. Cars and airplane tickets, however, have become more expensive. (This is helping to lessen the congestion on the highways and at the airport.)

Another thing in Lagos' favor is its restaurants, which are good—and cheap. Dinner at one of the best restaurants is about N120 ($7) per person. Recommended are **Chez Antoine**, *61 Broad St., Tabriz; tel. (234-1)66-48-81*, which serves French and Lebanese cuisine but is closed Sunday, and **Club Bagatelle**, *208/212 Broad St.; tel. (234-1)66-24-10*, which serves Indian and Middle Eastern cuisine.

The Federal Palace Hotel, *Victoria Island; tel. (234-1)610030,* is the best place to stay in town. It has a good restaurant/nightclub, the Atlantic, which serves Italian food. A double room is N700 ($32).

But you shouldn't let Lagos spoil your opinion of all Nigeria. The country has much more attractive cities, notably Ife, Ibadan, Jos, Onitsha, and Kano. And a new capital is being built in Abuja, which is roughly the geographic center of the country.

Kano: the best place to explore Islamic history

In the Old City of **Kano**, an oasis on the edge of the Sahara Desert, you can step back into the Islamic past. A mud wall inscribed with Islamic scriptures and Hausa engravings here is believed to protect the faithful from intrusion from the outside world. Livestock wander freely through the streets, along with men and women in flowing, Islamic robes and headdresses. Camel caravans of the nomadic Tuareg, dressed in immaculate sheaths and tall turbans, roam the streets.

Men in pastel *baba riga* robes and women in drab wrapper dresses trot freely with goats and lambs along winding footpaths in a maze of mud huts. The only modern addition to the Old City is the heavily guarded electric gate built into the mud wall surrounding the centuries-old Emir's Palace.

The towering 40-foot Nassarawa Kofar mud gate connects the Old City with Kano's hastily constructed replica of a Western commercial center, where business is transacted but aesthetics are forgotten.

Climb to the top of the Dalan or Goren Dutse hills for a view of the city skyline against the Sahara desert.

The drawbacks

Kano has been the center of much of the political turmoil that has wracked Nigeria since it became an independent country. From this city, Muslims waged holy wars against rival groups for control of the country, which has the largest population in Black Africa.

Perhaps this history explains the terrible delays and red tape at Kano's international airport. Soldiers toting submachine guns guard the hangarlike terminal, where a sea of scuffling, sweating bodies crashes against two tiny immigration desks. One correspondent reported waiting six hours to get out of the airport after landing. She finally had to pay a bribe to get through.

Water is scarce and must be boiled, strained, and purified. Sometimes, running water is not available.

The best Hausa food

If you enjoy sampling unfamiliar foods, try the local *sire* or *souya*, sold every evening at dozens of food stands all over town. Watch at dusk for small flaming fires where chunks of meat, tomato, onion, and pepper roast on skewers.

You can enjoy authentic tribal food at restaurants throughout Kano. Try the **Akesan Restaurant** and restaurants in the Ikeja, at the Usman Memorial, and in the international hotels. Prices are generally expensive, but the meals are worth it.

Hotels: smaller is better

The cost of a hotel room in Kano is usually not worth the price. The major hotels are no better than any of the smaller hotels in town (except that they usually have recreational facilities), and they are twice the price. All hotels are subject to water, electricity, and food shortages, but the smaller hotels are cleaner and offer more courteous service.

The two best hotels in Kano are the **Daula**, *150 Murtala Muhammed Way, PM Bay*, and the **Central**, *State Road*. The key to getting a room at a hotel is often a small bribe, not a confirmed reservation.

The best side trips

If you want to shake the dust of Kano off your shoes for a few days, visit one of the three ultramodern spa resorts an hour south of the city. The **Baguada** and **Tiga Lake** resorts and the **Rock Castle Hotel** offer iced drinks under the palms.

Or take a trip to **Daura**, a town two hours north of Kano, where the nomadic desert culture that once dominated the Sahara continues unchanged.

Kano is an excellent base for safaris. The **Yankari Game Reserve** is a four-hour drive due south in the state of Bauchi. East of Yankari is the **Jos zoo**. Both nature reserves offer safaris that take you to see thousands of native species.

Yoruba: best markets, best art

Yoruba cities, such as **Ibadan**, which is as large as Lagos but much nicer, are the African cities most welcoming to tourists. Ibadan boasts the best market in Nigeria, called Dugbe, and has a large Lebanese population made up of Middle Easterners who came to Africa to trade and stayed to open restaurants.

Benin City, the Yoruba capital, boasts the the best market for souvenirs in Nigeria. Its other claim to fame is **Oba's Palace**, which is difficult to get into—you must apply for permission in advance. (An *oba* is a Yoruba ruler.)

Far more accessible is the public **Ife Palace complex**, another former home of a Yoruba ruler. Ife is the center of a flourishing art colony, where printmakers have adapted skills once used on cloth to produce gorgeous woodcuts.

Top travel tips

Nigeria doesn't have to be the bureaucratic nightmare it is often reported to be. You just have to be prepared. Before arriving at the international airport in Lagos, make sure you have a visa, a passport, a yellow fever vaccination certificate, and a return ticket. You will have to pay a minimal airport tax when you leave.

The Côte d'Ivoire: the richest African country

The **Côte d'Ivoire** has the highest standard of living in sub-Saharan Africa and is one of the continent's most politically stable nations. Originally a French colony, the Côte d'Ivoire (the government refuses to answer to the English name, Ivory Coast) is now an independent democratic republic (although it retains a strong French influence).

In the Côte d'Ivoire, you can examine Ashanti and Senoufu art at the National Museum, observe wild animals at West Africa's largest game reserve, and bathe in the sun and water of the African Riviera. The country also boasts Africa's only ice-skating rink.

Africa's most European city

In **Abidjan**, capital of the Côte d'Ivoire, splendid African ladies dress in brightly colored long dresses and head wraps and carry baguettes fresh from the bakery—on their heads. This metropolis is reminiscent of European cities. Unfortunately, the beauty of the city has been diminished by recent downtown development. But beautiful sites remain along the lagoon, by the seashore, and in the suburbs.

Musée National, *boulevard Nangui-Abrogoua*, houses more than 20,000 works of art, including jewelry, statues, ritual costumes, and furniture. It is open Tuesday through Sunday 9 a.m. until noon and 3 until 6 p.m.

Marché Sénégalais, *boulevard de la République*, and **Marché de Cocody** sell art and handicrafts imported from all areas of Africa. Both are open every day. The **Treichville Market** is a treat for veteran shoppers who know how to bargain. The second floor of the market, which is open daily 7 a.m. until 2 p.m., features special regional textiles.

A forest reserve called **Banc National Park** is just within the city limits. Its 7,500 acres are scored with trails that lead past exotic—and labeled—flora.

The best local dishes

Most Ivorian cuisine is based on the plantain, which looks like a banana but isn't, and the yam, which looks like a sweet potato but isn't. From both, the Ivorians make a stew called *foutou*, a mush covered in a nut or palm-seed sauce. *Aloco*, fried plantains, is another specialty. Drink specialties are *bandji*, made with palm extract, and *lemonroudji*, a concoction of lemon and ginger. Meat and fish are usually fresh and grilled on outdoor barbecues. Try fresh fruit for dessert.

The best African restaurants are in the Treichville section of Abidjan. For good meat and fish, try **Kedjenou**. For Ivorian-style cuisine, try the Marquis restaurants: **Le Senat** and **La Bache Bleue**, both in Marcory in Abidjan.

The best native dances

A troupe of 35 dancers performs the ritual dances of the Côte d'Ivoire at **Le Wafou**, *Boulevard de Marseille 7km; tel. (225)36-96-22*, an expensive cabaret on the lagoon. Dinner is served here also.

The best night life

Treichville has the best discos in Abidjan. Try **l'Acetylène**, *tel. (225)32-50-24*; **Treich Can-Can**, *37 blvd. Delafosse; tel. (225)32-17-91*; and **Zorba le Grec**, *tel. (225)22-66-29*. (These places have a fast turnover, so they may be gone by the time you read this.)

The best places to stay in Abidjan

Hôtel Ivoire, *08 B.P. 001, Abidjan 01, boulevard de la Corniche, Cocody; tel. (225)44-10-45 or (800)327-0200 in the United States,* is an immense luxury hotel that houses 14 boutiques, five restaurants, five bars, a supermarket, a cinema, a concert hall, sports facilities, a casino, a man-made lake, and the only ice-skating rink in Black Africa. A double room is CFA45,000 ($170).

Le Forum Golf Intercontinental, *boulevard Lagunaire, La Riviera, Cocody, 08 B.P. 18; tel. (225)43-10-44, (225)43-10-51 or (800)327-0200 in the United States,* on the banks of the lagoon, has a nightclub, a pool, a restaurant, and, of course, golf facilities. A double room is CFA29,000 ($109).

The best place to view wildlife

Comoe National Park, 440 miles north of Abidjan—a comfortable distance only by air—is a government wildlife reserve where you can see buffalo, antelope, wild boar, baboons, and a very few lions. The reserve is open December through May. Food and drink are available here, but they are expensive.

The best place to stay is the **Comoe Safari Lodge Hotel**, which has a restaurant, a bar, a pool, and organized excursions. Traditional dances are performed on the premises.

The best place to buy textiles

A modern textile center is located in the provincial town of **Bouaké**, 235 miles from Abidjan. Here, the area's oldest textile factory, **Ets. Gonfreville**, manufactures cotton goods. **Solinci**, a lingerie factory, is also located in town. Both are open to the public on Thursday. But you can buy seconds any day of the week from the factories at the **Bouaké Market**. Look the goods over carefully, but usually they have been rejected only for minor flaws. Among the goodies are household linens.

In Bouaké, stay at the **Hôtel du Centre**, *B.P. 54; tel. (225)63-32-78,* where a double room is CFA7,000 ($36). Although the hotel's rooms are simple and plain, its location is excellent; next to the hotel is the **Artisan's Center,** where you can buy leather crafts, cane furniture, ivory sculpture, jewelry, and Baoulé masks. (The Baoulé are a traditional carving tribe whose work is less known than that of peoples elsewhere in Africa.) Traditional masks are used in initiation ceremonies and to ward off misfortune.

Sierra Leone—the best of the British in West Africa

If sightseeing isn't really your cup of tea, visit West Africa's former British colony, Sierra Leone. This country has no outstanding attractions, but it does offer beautiful tropical scenery, a dry climate, and a friendly population, made up of 18 different ethnic groups. Perhaps the best part (at least if you're a foreign visitor) is that Sierra Leone has one of the unhealthiest economies in West Africa, so your foreign currency will go a long way.

Although English is the official language of Sierra Leone, a form of English called Krio, enriched by several West African languages, is more widely spoken.

Freetown: the heart of Sierra Leone

Freetown, the capital of Sierra Leone, offers the best opportunities for accommodation and dining in this quiet country. And its peninsula is the only place along the West African coast where mountains rise near the sea, providing beautiful views. It's also one of the few areas where the water is safe for swimming.

The best beds in Freetown

The **City Hotel**, *Lightfoot Boston Street*, is a run-down, chaotic hotel built in the 1920s. Once an architectural gem, the City Hotel remains intriguing for fans of author Graham Greene. Greene wrote *The Heart of the Matter* in a room at this hotel during World War II. The other attractive thing about the City is the price—a double room is $1 a night.

The newly renovated **YMCA**, *32 Fort St.*, is the best of all the YMCAs in West Africa. For $5 a night, including breakfast, you have use of a library, a TV room, and a fully equipped kitchen. There are only six rooms, so be sure to make reservations.

If your priority is the beach, stay at the **Cape Sierra**, *P.O. Box 54; tel. (232)37269,* just off the water. A double room is $5 a night; during low season, you can rent a private bungalow for even less.

The best place to try African cuisine

If you're in the mood for ethnic food, and a lot of it, try **Provilac**, *Congo Cross Road.* Every Wednesday at lunch, Provilac serves an all-Sierra Leone buffet for $2. The best dishes include potato-leaves sauce, okra sauce, palm oil stew, groundnut stew, and pepper soup.

Freetown bests

Across the street from the City Hotel is the city's major landmark, the **Cotton Tree**, more than 500 years old. Next to the Cotton Tree is the **Sierra Leone National Museum**.

A must for hikers is the half-hour climb to **Leicester Peak**. The highest point in Freetown (595 meters), this mountain offers a spectacular view of the bay area and the peninsula.

The most popular beach in Sierra Leone is the **River No. 2 Beach**, 45 minutes south of Freetown. Many consider it one of the most beautiful beaches on the entire West African coast.

The Best of North Africa

North Africa is a mixture of civilizations: the pharoahs of Egypt, whose history dates back to the beginning of time; the exotic Moroccans, whose intriguing culture mystifies Westerners to this day; and the elusive Algerians, who live in a land yet to be discovered—trapped in time.

The best of Egypt

For 4,000 years, the pharoahs of Egypt reigned over a civilization with a stability and technology that have yet to be duplicated. Recently, a team of Japanese engineers tried to build a pyramid just 35 feet high using the ancient Egyptian methods. They couldn't finish it. Thus, the pyramids of Egypt are eternal reminders of the lost wisdom of a great civilization.

A few days among the tombs and temples of Egypt will convince you that the pharoahs had something we have now lost. But a few days among the guides and the multitudes of poor asking for baksheesh (tips) may also convince you that what the pharoahs succeeded in building was merely a nation of the greatest tourist attractions known to man.

While Egypt is largely a desert nation, most of its people live on the water—along the banks of the Nile, by the Red Sea, or on the Mediterranean. So one of the best ways to see this country is by boat. One of the geographic peculiarities of this land is that the southern half of it is known as Upper Egypt; the northern half is Lower Egypt.

Cairo: the greatest paradox

Founded in the 10th century by invading Muslims, this noisy, crowded city thriving in the shadow of the pyramids is one of the most intriguing capitals in the world. **Cairo's** mixture of poverty and riches exemplifies the paradox of the Middle East, which is made up of nations straddling the Third World and the Western world. Minarets rise imperiously from 10th-century mosques, cars hurtle recklessly down narrow streets, poor families live in the graveyards of wealthy relatives, and merchants crowd the bazaars selling Arabian Night perfume and "genuine" Pharaonic scarabs.

Metropolitan Cairo, jam-packed with one-quarter of Egypt's population, is split by the Nile into two districts: Cairo on the east bank and Giza (a suburb on the edge of the Giza Plateau) on the west. In between are two small islands: Zamalek and Roda. Zamalek (also called Gezira) lies across from the northern, more upscale New City, with its Tahrir Square—Cairo's downtown—and its Islamic section and tourist bazaar of Khan el-Khalili. Roda is parallel to the southern, squalid Old Cairo, which includes the Coptic neighborhood bordered by the Fatimid Wall built in 1087.

The best view of Cairo
Most people come to Cairo to see the pyramids; in the process, they often miss the city itself. The best place to get your bearings is atop the 600-foot **Cairo Tower** in Zohria Garden on Zamalek. The view from the observation deck stretches to the pyramids. (Skip the mediocre restaurant.)

Cairo's two best museums
Two museums on the island provide insight into modern Egypt: the **Mukhtar Museum** shows the works of Mahmud Mukhtar, the father of modern Egyptian sculpture, and the **Gezira Museum** displays rare paintings, sculptures, and Islamic and Coptic artifacts.

The most fashionable neighborhood
Walk around the fashionable neighborhood of **Heliopolis** in the New City, where Egyptian President Mubarak lives. Buildings mix Western and Islamic architecture. Notice the Palace of Prince Husayn, the arcades on Abbas Boulevard, and the Palace of Empain, a copy of a Hindu temple with an electronically controlled tower that rotates to follow the path of the sun.

In search of the *Arabian Nights*
Islamic Cairo, with its magic lanterns and flying carpets even better than those of Baghdad, has preserved the atmosphere of the *Arabian Nights.* It takes several mornings of walking to really see the area. Visit some of the 500 mosques here—remember that not all of them are open to non-Moslems and that you won't be allowed to enter any mosque until after prayer.

When visiting a mosque, dress conservatively and don't draw attention to yourself; women should cover their heads. You must remove your shoes at the door. (Give the man who watches them 25 piastres, or 8 cents.) Anyone who opens special doors or explains things in detail also should be tipped. Some mosques charge an admission in Egyptian pounds.

The world's oldest university
Cairo's most famous mosque is certainly the **Al-Azhar Mosque**, on the corner of Al-Azhar and Al-Muizz streets. Built in A.D. 972, it was the world's first university, and today it serves more than 90,000 Moslem students. Restored in bits and pieces, the mihrab in the center aisle is from the 10th century. You can take photographs here, as in any mosque, as long as you don't focus on any one person.

The holiest mosque
Across the street from Al-Azhar Mosque is **Sayiddna al-Husayn,** Cairo's most venerated Moslem shrine. It is closed to non-Moslems, but you can examine the finely decorated exterior walls. Inside rests the head of al-Husayn, grandson of the prophet Muhammad (transported to Cairo in a green silk bag from Iraq).

Westernization has hit even Sayiddna al-Husayn. Just inside the door is a green neon light reading "Allah."

The Citadel
South of the Al-Azhar is the **Citadel,** a monolithic complex that dominates Cairo's skyline. Built in the late 12th century by Salah al-Din on the Mokattam hill range, it has a strategic view of the capital.

The 19th-century ruler Muhammad Ali added a mosque to the Citadel, one of the great features of Cairo. The silver domes and marble and alabaster decorations are rivaled only by the building's vast interior.

The Citadel houses the Mostafa Kamel Museum and the Military Museum.

Cairo's oldest mosque

Southwest of Salah al-Din Square is the city's oldest mosque: **Ibn Tulun,** *Calen el-Salikban Street.* It was built in A.D. 879 by Ibn Tulun, who seceded from the Islamic Empire and built himself the largest mosque in Egypt, decorating it with sweeping contours and intricate inscriptions. The mosque's courtyard covers almost seven acres, and the building's lacy stuccowork surrounds inscriptions from the Koran. Climb the external staircase to the top of the tower, from which you have a view of the city and the pyramids to the west. You can visit Ibn Tulun from 8 a.m. until 6 p.m.

The most beautiful windows

The mausoleum complex of **Qalaun,** *Gonar al-Qaid Street,* in northern Sharia al-Muizz, is famous for the colors in its stained-glass windows. During the times of the Crusades, Egypt was the world's center of glasswork, and the incredible craftsmanship of these windows set a standard for all Islamic tombs and Gothic churches in Europe.

The best Islamic art

The **Museum of Islamic Art**, off Ahmad Maher Square at the corner of Port Said and Muhammed Ali streets, is an overlooked treasure. This museum houses a little of everything, from Persian carpets to Islamic glassware to Kufic script wood carvings. Because most visitors to Egypt dwell on Pharaonic art, the Museum of Islamic Art is rarely crowded. The exhibits are arranged by craft, so it's easy to trace stylistic developments over time, giving yourself a mini-art history course. Don't miss the Koran engravings. The museum is open Saturdays through Thursdays, 9 a.m. until 4 p.m.

Giza: the most tranquil district

Giza Square, in the heart of Cairo's Giza district on the west bank, marks the beginning of Pyramids Road. Cross Al-Gamaa Bridge to get to the Al-Urman Botanical Garden and the Cairo zoo. To the north is Dokki, Giza's fashionable residential neighborhood, which contains several embassies and two good museums.

The **Museum of Modern Art**, *18 Ismail Abu'l-Futuh St.,* exhibits postwar Egyptian art and has an excellent sculpture garden. The **Agricultural Museum,** at the western end of the 6th of October Bridge, contains the only remaining mummified bull.

The best of Old Cairo

South of Tahrir Square is **Old Cairo**, which surrounds the old Roman fort Babylon outside Fatimid Wall. You'll find evidence of Greco-Roman culture and early Christianity throughout the quarter. From the time of the last pharaoh to the first mosque, Egypt was part of the Greco-Roman world and Christianity, which in Egypt emerged as the Coptic Church.

The world's finest Coptic art

The **Coptic Museum**, built on the site of the Roman fort in Qasr al-Shama, has the finest Coptic art collection in the world. The buildings, courtyards, and gardens of the museum tell the story of early Christianity from the third through the seventh centuries. See the intricately woven robes and curtains for which the Copts were renowned. The museum is open Saturdays through Thursdays, 9 a.m until 4 p.m.

The most beautiful Coptic church

In front of the Coptic Museum are the remains of the fort that took invading Muslims seven months to overpower. The **Church of al-Muallaqa** was built atop the gate of the fort, giving it the name the Hanging Church. Also known as the Church of St. Mary, this is the most beautiful of Cairo's Coptic churches. The pointed arches and carved relief are interesting changes from the Gothic style commonly associated with Christian churches.

Climb the 24 stairs to see the interior. The famous pulpit stands on 13 slender columns (symbolic of the 12 apostles and Jesus, with the black column representing Judas). Unlike in mosques, baksheesh is not paid in churches. Photographs are prohibited.

The three most charming churches
North of al-Muallaqa, on Mari Girgis Street, is the **Church of Mari Girgis** (St. George), noted for its fine stained-glass windows. To the left of the church is a staircase descending into an old alley, at the end of which is the elegant Church of Abu Serga. The crypt below is supposed to be where Joseph, Mary, and baby Jesus stayed during their flight to Egypt. (The crypt is now flooded and closed to the public.)

To the right of Abu Serga is the **Church of St. Barbara**, an ornate structure with striped-marble steps. According to legend, the order was given to destroy one church and restore the other, but the caliph's architect couldn't decide which to destroy. He paced back and forth between the two buildings until he died of exhaustion—so the caliph restored both churches.

Egypt's oldest synagogue
Near the Church of St. Barbara is the **Ben Ezra Synagogue**, the oldest in Egypt. The interior is beautifully decorated, and the custodian is a humorous, talkative fellow. You can follow the steps to the spot where the pharaoh's daughter is said to have found the infant Moses.

The Cities of the Dead
The vast and forbidding **Cities of the Dead,** where thousands live in and around graveyards, are to the northeast and south of the Citadel. The poor use parts of mausoleums as their homes and parts of tombs as clotheslines or soccer goals.

Wealthy citizens are buried in the northern cemetery, and their graves are marked with elaborate tombs. Especially fine is the tomb of Umm Ahuk. The many-ribbed dome caps an ancient pointed archway.

The most impressive monument in the southern cemetery is the **mausoleum of Imam Al-Shafi'i,** *Imam Al-Shafi'i Street.* Built in 1211, the mausoleum contains an 800-year-old carved cenotaph. The nearby tomb of Shagarat al-Durr was built for Shagarat, the Moslem queen who poisoned two husbands and her son to remain in power. The mausoleum is decorated with Kufic carvings and a mihrab with Byzantine glass mosaics.

Egypt's most important museum
The **Egyptian Museum,** like the British National Museum and the Smithsonian, exhibits an entire culture on several carpeted floors. Located in Tahrir Square just down the road from the enormous Ramses Hilton, the Egyptian Museum (commonly called the Cairo Museum) is the world's unrivaled warehouse of Pharaonic art. More than 100,000 pieces are crammed together with little order; the most exquisite are not always highlighted. The famous mummy room has been closed for religious reasons; however, the museum has enough ankhs, scarabs, and statues to fill several days of exploring.

The second floor houses the treasures found in Tutankhamon's tomb, the only one that escaped plundering, because of its hidden location. When viewing the incredible gold statues, alabaster lamps, and general ostentation, remember that Tutankhamon died young and his treasure was comparatively small.

The Cairo Museum is always crowded but less so when the tour groups break for lunch. It is open daily 9 a.m. until 4 p.m. Cameras are prohibited.

The most colorful markets
In Cairo, you can buy not only an aphrodisiac but also an anti-aphrodisiac, made from baby crocodiles. The two Arabic phrases you'll want to know when shopping are *Bikam*

hadha? (How much does this cost?) and *Hatha Kathir* (That's too expensive). The main shopping areas are **Zamalek**, **Dokki** (in Giza), and **Heliopolis** (northeast of the New City).

Khan el-Khalili is the largest bazaar in Egypt, with hundreds of shops grouped by trade: gold merchants, silversmiths, and spice sellers. The 14th-century courtyards buzz with the sounds of haggling. You will find the best buys on *galabiyyas*, full-length cotton robes worn by Egyptian men, and local crafts. **Nassar Brothers**, *Khan Al Khalily Street; tel. (20-2)907-210*, is the best place for precious and semiprecious stones.

Every Friday morning, a camel market is held in **Imbaba** (on Zamalek Island). Traders sell and swap hundreds of Sudanese camels, horses, sheep, and goats, as well as food, wagons, jeans, and baskets. (You can buy a camel for about 1500 Egyptian pounds, or $450.) The sights and smells are strong: you may witness a camel giving birth or a goat being butchered and skinned for immediate barbecue. Remember to bargain. And don't pet the camels—they spit and bite.

The **Bab Zuwayla district** of Old Cairo teems with people and livestock. Peddlers transport their goods by bicycle and truck and on foot. Saffron, cumin, coriander, and hibiscus perfume the air. Along the Street of the Tentmaker, men sit crosslegged, plying their needles in the traditional art of appliqué stitchery. Also to be found are food, silk carpets, gold jewelry, clothing, ceramics, baskets, and two fez factories. Bab Zuwayla is more commercialized than **Khan el Khalili**, which is across the street, but just as colorful.

Finally, you can't leave Cairo without purchasing a cartouche, the quintessential Egyptian souvenir. These Pharaonic 18-karat gold pendants are personalized with your name or initials translated phonetically into hieroglyphics. Prices are $70 to $180. The best place to shop for a cartouche is **Ohnig of Cairo** in the **Egyptian Museum**.

Cairo's best cuisine

In a city where butchers slap flies off pieces of meat to show them to customers, only certain restaurants can be trusted. However, if you're willing to venture beyond the hotel restaurants, you will find that the food in Cairo is exotic and inexpensive. Typical Egyptian dishes include *mulokhiya*, a gelatinous soup made with a spinachlike herb; *fool*, a big brown bean; *feteer*, which resembles pizza; *taboula*, ground wheat and parsley salad; and *kofta*, tiny grilled meatballs.

Andrea, *59 Mariouthia St.; tel. (20-2)385-4441*, an outdoor farm restaurant near the pyramids, serves delicious grilled chicken and some of the best *mazza* (a collection of appetizers) in Cairo.

Nearby **Felfela Village**, *off Pyramids Avenue; tel. (20-2)383-7950*, offers fine Egyptian cuisine and occasional folklore shows. Dinner here and at Andrea costs 17 Egyptian pounds ($5).

Abu Shakra, *69 Kasr el-Nil St.; tel. (20-2)848-860*, specializes in shish kebab and *kofta*. Two can dine for less than 17 to 20 Egyptian pounds ($5 to $7).

A full-course Egyptian meal is best at **Aladin**, *26 Sherif St.; tel. (20-2)755-694*, in the **Cairo Sheraton**, a watering hole popular among foreign journalists. Kebabs, barbecues, and *om ali*—a spicy bread pudding—are tasty and filling.

The best seafood restaurant in Cairo is **Hag Mohammed el-Samak**, *Abdel-Aziz Street; tel. (20-2)901-337*, across from the Omar Effendi department store. The grilled fish is good at this restaurant, which is decorated with art deco furnishings.

The most romantic meals in Cairo are served on Nile boats. The food is a little more expensive (about 66 Egyptian pounds, or $20, a meal), but the atmosphere is worth it. The two best floating restaurants are **Scarabee**, *16 July 26th St., Azakabia*, opposite the **Shepheards Hotel**; *tel. (20-2)393-9675*, and the **PharaohHotel**, *12 Lotfi Hassouna St., Dukki; tel. (20-2)347-619*. Both have floor shows and large crowds, so make reservations.

The most recommended hotels

Maintaining its 20-year reputation as the best hotel in Cairo is the **Nile Hilton**, *Tahrir*

Square. Across the street from the Egyptian Museum, it is well-run and elegant. It has luxurious rooms and the best pool in the city. Rooms start at 500 Egyptian pounds ($151).

Located at the northern tip of Roda Island, the **Meridien Hotel**, *Corniche El-Nil; tel. (20-2)845-444*, is quieter but also first-class. All rooms have Nile views.

Nearby is the world-famous **Shepheard's Hotel**, *Corniche El Nil; tel. (20-2)355-3800*, which has developed a reputation as a hideaway for international spies. A double room with a view of the Nile is 416 Egyptian pounds ($126) a night.

The Club Med, *Em Manial Palace, Kasr Mohommed Aly; tel. (20-2)844-083 or (20-2)846-014*, in nearby Mena, is outstanding.

Good hotels need not all be five-star. **The President Hotel**, *22 Taha Hussein Street; tel. (20-2)3416-751, (20-2)3413-195*, or *(20-2)3400-718*, in the residential section of Zamalek, is spacious and clean. The rooftop restaurant has an extensive wine cellar. A double room is 158 Egyptian pounds ($48) a night including breakfast.

The best night life

At night, when the temperature drops, Cairo's night life gets hot. Discos are crowded, especially on Thursday nights. The popular ones include **After Eight**, *6 Kasr El Nil St.; tel. (20-2)983-000*, and **Rasputin**, *Green Pyramids Hotel, Helmiat Alahram Street; tel. (20-2)856-775*. The **Atlas Hotel**, *2 Mohamed Roushdi St.; tel. (20-2) 918311*, has good rock'n'roll music. **Al-Capo**, *22 Taha Husayn St.*, is a great place for live music. **Al-Sokkareya**, *Abd'l-Hamid Badawy Street, Heliopolis*, has singers and musicians, a penny arcade and fortune-tellers, good drinks, and the popular *sheesha* (water pipe), all in an Egyptian garden.

Surprisingly, night life in Cairo can be liveliest during Ramadan, a month-long holiday during which devout Moslems fast from sunrise to sunset. After dark, however, they indulge in large meals and take to the streets around al-Azhar and the Nile, where you'll find street theater performances, magic shows, and noisy crowds.

The Nile Hilton, Marriott, and Sheraton hotels have casinos, where gambling takes place in American currency.

If you want glitzy belly dancing, try the **Belvedere** in the Nile Hilton, *tel. (20-2)740-777*, or the **Two Seasons Supper Club** in the **Ramses Hilton**, *1115 Corniche El-Nil; tel. (20-2)744-400*.

More authentic floor shows can be seen at the clubs along Pyramids Road, which cater to Egyptians.

The popular folk-dancing Rida Troupe performs at the **Balloon Theater**, *El-Nil Street, Agouza; tel. (20-2)711-718*.

If you'd rather spend a peaceful, romantic evening, take a felucca (small sailboat) on the Nile. Feluccas can be rented just south of the Kasr El-Nil Bridge on the east bank for about 20 Egyptian pounds ($6) an hour. Across the corniche from the Shepheards Hotel, boats are available from midnight to dawn for 26 to 33 Egyptian pounds ($8 to $10). It's felucca etiquette to bring food for a picnic to share with your navigator.

The best ways to get around Cairo

Getting around Cairo is simultaneously easy and bothersome. Overcrowded buses (commonly called VOAs, for Voice of America—they were bought with American aid) are cheap and run everywhere, but they can be recommended only to the most adventurous. They don't stop—they only slow down for you to jump on or off.

The newly built metro offers fast, inexpensive service, but only in the southern area of the city. The happiest traveler is the one who has mastered the art of Cairo taxis, which come either metered or unmetered. Either bargain the cost before you get into a cab or at the end of the ride pay the driver a fair amount—usually 13 to 17 Egyptian pounds ($3-$7) for a ride within the city and 17 to 21 Egyptian pounds ($4-$7) to travel from downtown to the pyramids.

Chaffeured cars can be hired for the day outside either Hilton. You also can rent a car to drive yourself around. This may be practical in the rest of Egypt, but in Cairo it's dangerous. The famous race-car driver Mario Andretti said that the one place he'd never drive is Cairo. Traffic lights here were built to be ignored. Cars speed through intersections, slowing only momentarily to warn pedestrians by honking their horns or flashing their headlights.

Giza: the best and the tackiest of Egypt

Not five miles west of Cairo, the pyramids of Giza are easily reached via Pyramids Road by taxi or buses 8 and 900. The best route is through Mena village. Toward the southern edge of this town is a broad plaza where tourist buses park. Here, clear of buildings, you have an uninterrupted view of the Sphinx with the pyramids behind and overhead.

The best time to visit Giza is at dawn, when sunlight makes the area glow and you feel the power that overwhelmed even Napoleon. If you show up before the tourists arrive, you can try to climb the outside of the Great Pyramid. It's necessary to hire a guide to take you up; you must pay him again to take you back down. Although technically illegal, this is common practice.

The greatest pyramid

The tallest pyramid in Egypt, the **Pyramid of Cheops** (or the Great Pyramid), was finished in 2690 B.C. and stands 448 feet tall. It contains 2.3 million separate blocks of stone, each weighing 2.5 tons. Millions have visited and climbed Cheops, from French novelist Gustave Flaubert to a Parisian wallpaper manufacturer, who left an advertisement on the top.

Scientists believe that Cheops (or Khufu) built the pyramid for some reason besides pure ostentation. Theories that the ancient Egyptians knew the earth was round and calculated the circumference are supported by the pyramid. Measurements taken in the 1930s revealed that the proportions of the Great Pyramid are the same as the proportions of the earth's Northern Hemisphere. Scientists don't know whether this information was used in ancient navigation and astronomy, but it suggests an advanced culture.

The Grand Gallery of Cheops, with its 28-foot ceiling, is unusually devoid of decoration. It is one of the main reasons for the Great Pyramid controversy—it is the largest chamber in Cheops but contains absolutely nothing to suggest worship or religion.

The gallery leads to the King's Chamber, which contains the bottom half of the sarcophagus. (A lid was never found.) The king was never buried here, because the passages in the pyramid were too narrow for the sarcophagus to be brought in after the pyramid was completed.

The most beautiful pyramid

Next to Cheops is the **Pyramid of Chepren** (Khafre), Cheops' son. This pyramid is actually about 10 feet shorter than the Pyramid of Cheops, even though it seems taller because it's on higher ground. Its construction is not symbolic—only the Great Pyramid is thought to have any astronomical significance.

Chepren, however, is the most beautiful of the pyramids, because part of its limestone casing remains. The interior is spacious, and the ornate sarcophagus sinks into the floor up to its lid.

The least-crowded pyramid

The **Pyramid of Mycerinus** (Menkaure) is a 15-minute walk south of Cheops and Chepren. Because it is "only" 210 feet tall, it attracts relatively few tourists. Mycerinus, Chepren's son, began the pyramid about 2472 B.C. but died before the outermost stones were placed.

The world's oldest boat
Next to the northern face of Cheops is the museum housing the *Solar Barque*, the oldest boat in the world. Discovered in 1954, the 128-foot-long boat is presumed to have been built to carry Cheops to the Underworld.

The boat's construction is ingenious. Its hull is made from hundreds of jigsawlike pieces of wood that were fitted and then sewn together with rope. When the hull was put into water, the wet wood swelled while the rope shrunk, creating a watertight fit.

The world's greatest riddle
Northeast of the Great Pyramid crouches the most famous statue on earth: the giant **Sphinx.** Carved out of a single ridge of rock, it has the head of a man and the body of a lion and measures 240 feet long and 66 feet high. The face is missing its nose and beard, because the statue was used for target practice during the Turkish Occupation in the 1700s.

Because it is commonly believed that the face of the Sphinx represents Chepren, some conclude that the statue is 4,500 years old. Other scientists, however, believe it is much older. Geologists have concluded that the severe erosion of the body could not have been caused by wind and sand. Water, they say, must have been the cause. Egypt was flooded at the end of the last Ice Age, about 10,000 B.C.; therefore, the Sphinx must have been built prior to that time, which is thousands of years before mankind is thought to have had tools.

The Sphinx continues to crumble—it recently lost a chunk of its shoulder. Scientists are debating how to save it. See it while you can.

Also explore the **Valley Temple of Chepren** at the foot of the Sphinx. The core contains limestone blocks, each weighing more than 100 tons; the method used to lift these huge blocks into place is unknown. The floors of the temple are made of slabs of alabaster. Though small, the temple is well-preserved, and its construction is unique in all Egypt.

The most romantic views
Perhaps the most romantic thing to do in Egypt is to ride Arabian horses around the pyramids at dusk. Two stables near the Sphinx rent and lease horses. Rates are 4.5 to 9 Egyptian pounds ($10 to $20) an hour, depending on how well you bargain.

The hokiest show
At night you can attend a sound-and-light show on the Giza Plateau. The pyramids and Sphinx are illuminated as the narrator tells the story of Egypt. It's as hokey as you'd expect, but few people regret attending. Admission is 4 to 6 Egyptian pounds ($9 to $13). The English shows are held at 6:30 p.m. Mondays, Wednesdays, and Fridays.

The best hotels in Giza
Most people stay in Cairo and visit the pyramids from there; however, waking up to see the Great Pyramid catch the first rays of dawn outside your window is a special pleasure.

The best hotel in Giza is the **Mena House Oberoi,** *Pyramids Road; tel. (20-2)387-4999,* which is within walking distance of the pyramids. It was once a weekend palace for the Khedives, the Turkish viceroys who governed the area from 1867 to 1914, then a meeting place for Churchill and Roosevelt. Since 1973, it has been a luxury hotel. The management has kept the old wooden balconies and added air conditioning, restaurants, bars, and a swimming pool. A double room is 743 to 990 Egyptian pounds ($225 to $300) a night.

A less expensive hotel is the **Holiday Inn Sphinx,** *P.O. Box 45; tel. (20-2)854-700.* It sounds like a motel that has fake pyramids in every room, but it's actually the most reasonably priced place to stay in Giza. The rooms are new and pleasant, and almost every one has a view of the pyramids. A double room starts at 297 Egyptian pounds ($90).

Saqqara: the world's oldest stone complex

Saqqara, a necropolis 24 miles south of Cairo, is the oldest stone complex in the world, dating back to 2611 B.C. Although they'd never before worked with stone on such a grand scale, the Egyptians created a masterpiece here. As Egyptologist John West put it, "Starting architecture off with Saqqara is like starting automobiles off with the 1984 Porsche." The complex was designed by the legendary Imhotep, an Egyptian Leonardo.

The most important sight at Saqqara is the **pyramid complex of King Zoser**, which contains the world's oldest pyramid. Predating the Great Pyramid by a century, the 200-foot **Step Pyramid** was built of six mastabas (traditional rectangular tombs) of diminishing size. Inside are religious inscriptions.

The complex often uses stonework to imitate organic material; the ceiling of the entranceway to Zoser, for example, simulates a roof of split logs. And the colonnade contains columns that look like they're made of papyrus stalks. (These may be the first stone columns built.) The colonnade leads into the Great Court, where Zoser and his successors ran races as part of a ritual physical fitness test called *heb-sed*.

To the south of the complex are the ruins of the **Pyramid of Unas**. The dilapidated outer stones make you wonder at the people waiting in line to get in. However, once you're inside, you'll understand—the interior is decorated with the finest hieroglyphic reliefs in Egypt. The **Pyramid Texts**, as they're known, tell the story of—and give advice concerning—the trip to the afterlife. Carved delicately out of slabs of white alabaster, the outstanding hieroglyphs in the tomb chamber are highlighted in blue paint dating back to 2330 B.C.

Surrounding the Pyramid of Unas are shacks covering stairways to the Persian tombs. (During Persian rule, mummies were buried in shaft tombs to prevent robbery.) See the Tomb of Ti, with its unusual wall decorations, and the Serapium, an ornate monument where the Persians buried sacred cows.

You can catch a minibus in Cairo to take you to Abu Sir in Giza Square at 6 a.m.; it drops you off about a mile from Saqqara. Or you can take a taxi directly to the site for about 16.5 Egyptian pounds ($5).

Luxor: ancient Thebes and modern city

Built on the site of ancient Thebes, **Luxor** remains one of Egypt's most popular cities. As in most Egyptian cities, the grand sights here are crowded with natives looking to hustle naive tourists.

Ancient Thebes was the capital of Egypt during the Middle Kingdom, when Amon was the most popular of the Egyptian gods. Today the metropolitan area comprises the east bank (Luxor) and the west bank (Thebes). Luxor is small enough that you can see it on foot. The three main thoroughfares are Sharia Al-Mahatta, Sharia El-Nil, and Sharia Al-Karnak.

The most noble temple

The principal sight in Luxor is the **Temple of Karnak**. *Noble* is the only word that aptly describes this gigantic building. Its unusual design stems from its history: From the beginning of the Middle Kingdom until the time of Alexander the Great, each pharaoh added something new to the temple's architecture. A double row of ram-headed sphinxes guards the entrance to the Great Court, the temple's largest room, built about 1000 B.C.

Pass through the mighty outer pylon (an entranceway between two flattened pyramids) into the corner of the Great Court, which is surrounded by huge columns and flanked by the Triple Shrine of Amon on one side and the Temple of Ramses III on the other.

355

Continue on through Hypostle Hall, which features the Obelisk of Queen Hathsheput, carved from exquisite pink granite, and enormous columns that have been imitated in several Egyptian temples. Next is Transverse Hall, with 134 monolithic columns.

Pass the southern buildings and pylons to the sanctuary. Filled with carved reliefs covering the mammoth stone blocks, this is the heart of the Karnak Temple. Past this are rooms, sarcophagi, and a sacred lake that is overshadowed by an enormous stone scarab. Take an entire afternoon to appreciate this.

The most unusual temple
The Avenue of the Sphinxes (which, as its name suggests, is lined with sphinxes) leads from Karnak to the most unusual temple in Egypt: the **Temple of Luxor**. Built with virtually no right angles, Luxor's rooms are set crookedly against one another. Six giant statues of Ramses II mark the main doorway, which is cut into the 80-foot Pylon of Ramses. Carved reliefs on the pylon illustrate Ramses' battle with the Hittites (tribes from Asia Minor who battled Egypt for control of Syria). Beside the pylon is a huge granite obelisk, the twin of one that stands in the Place de la Concorde in Paris.

Inside the temple court is the **Mosque of Abu el-Haggag**, a small building contrasting oddly with the general splendor of the temple. You'll pass the Colonnade of Amenhotep III, with its 14 pillars, on your way to the Sanctuary of Alexander the Great, which contains bas-reliefs of Alexander worshiping Amon.

A banana best
In the late afternoon, take a felucca to **Banana Island**, a palm-studded islet three miles upriver from Luxor. Here you can indulge in all the oranges, lemons, and, of course, bananas you can eat for 1 Egyptian pound.

Luxor's best hotels
One of the two best hotels in Luxor is **Hotel Etap Luxor**, *Corniche El-Nil Street; tel. (20-95)382-160,* where every room has a Nile view. A double room is $65 a night. The other best hotel is the **New Winter Palace**, *Corniche El-Nil Street; tel. (20-95)755-216,* where a double room is 231 to 297 Egyptian pounds ($70 to $90).

The **Luxor Hotel**, *Maabed El Karnak Street; tel. (20-95)382-400,* is cheaper. It's decorated with bizarre Egyptian art-deco prints. A double room is 172 Egyptian pounds ($52).

Luxor's best restaurant
The best restaurant in town is **Mont Azza**, overlooking Luxor near the Winter Palace.

The greatest collection of tombs
Across the Nile, in **Thebes**, is the greatest collection of tombs on earth. You can reach the hills of the west bank from Luxor via two tourist ferries. Once in Thebes, your best bet is to hire a taxi for about $11 (plus baksheesh). Or consider a donkey. Thebes is too big and too hot to visit on foot. A donkey is certainly slower than a taxi, but it is also less than half the cost and can take you through areas too narrow for cars. (Also, it's much more fun.) The trail from the Valley of the Queens over the ridges to the Valley of the Kings makes an especially memorable donkey trip.

The best way to see the Valley of the Kings
Some 64 rulers are buried in the **Valley of the Kings**. Because the locations of the graves were selected haphazardly, a little effort is needed to see the seven most impressive tombs in chronological order.

Begin with the **tomb of Tuthmosis III**, the walls of which are covered with the complete text of the *Book of the Duat*, the most important guide to the afterlife. Next is the **tomb of Amenhotep II**. The walls here are covered with glare-producing glass.

You can skip the famous **tomb of Tutankhamon**. Although its discovery in 1922 was front-page news (and the mysterious deaths of the exploration team started the Curse of the Mummy lore), it is the smallest and plainest of all the tombs—all the treasure was moved to the Cairo Museum. In addition, this tomb is always ridiculously overcrowded.

Next are the Ramses tombs. The **tomb of Ramses I** is followed by the **tomb of Seti I**, which is possibly the best-preserved on the west bank. The lower section of the burial chamber displays an incredible vaulted ceiling decorated with the 12 signs of the zodiac.

The **tomb of Ramses III** contains 10 unusual side chambers that show scenes from daily life (which are not found in other tombs). The artwork in the tomb of **Ramses VI** is more garish and fantastic than that in earlier tombs—Ramses VI ruled during the decadent 20th dynasty. This tomb also is noted for its ancient Greek and Coptic graffiti. One marking translates roughly as "Hermogines of Amasa was here."

The best of the Valley of the Nobles

The **Valley of the Nobles** is divided into five ticket regions. To see the best tombs, buy tickets 6, 7, and 8. The **tomb of Khaemet** has some of the best detail. The **tomb of Ramose** shows the radical departure Egyptian art took under Akhnaten. Reliefs show the pharaoh in scenes from family life, displaying affection, and showing his physical deformity.

The **tomb of Nakht** contains well-preserved paintings, some biographical, some inexplicable. The **tomb of Usheret** is notable for female figures, defaced by a Christian monk who lived in the burial chamber in the seventh century. The **tomb of Intefoger** has strangely insulting portraits. One shows an adult yelling at a child, "Your mother was a female hippopotamus!"

The Ramasseum

The **Colossi of Memnon**, two 70-foot statues, guard the **Temple of Ramses II**, also known as the Ramasseum. The temple contains the fallen Colossus of Ramses, which the poet Shelley described as "two vast and trunkless legs of stone, half sunk, a shattered visage." However, even the ruins are impressive—one ear measures 3.5 feet. The rest of the Ramasseum is in better condition, with relics depicting the Battle of Kadesh, astronomical charts, and rituals.

The tomb of the eight primordials

According to legend, beneath the **Temple of Medinet Habu**, which contains temples of Ramses III and Thutmose III, are buried the **eight primordials**—the Egyptian gods that existed before creation (as did the Greek gods Rhea and Kronos). Ramses' temple has pictures chiseled eight inches into the stone.

"The Most Splendid of All"

North of the Ramasseum is the cliffside Temple of Hatsheput, known in Arabic as **Deir El-Bahari**, which translates as "The Most Splendid of All." Considered one of the most important architectural wonders of the world, Deir El-Bahari is the only monument to have been built partly against the cliff and partly into it. This is also the only temple in Egypt, and the first building in history, made to blend with and complement the landscape.

Hatsheput (circa 1473 B.C.) was the only queen to dare crown herself pharaoh. The temple's broad walkway, the chapels to Anubis and Hathor, and the inscriptions here depict her descent from the god Amon.

Hathor: the magnificent temple

About 35 miles north of Luxor lies Dendera and the magnificent **Temple of Hathor** (the cow goddess and deity of healing), built about 200 B.C. A massive gate leads into the great courtyard of the temple, where the ceilings are decorated with the signs of the zodiac. Pass into the column-filled Hypostle Hall, the walls of which are covered with reliefs carved by priests seeking to preserve secret texts when Egyptian culture fell to the Roman Empire. The results are hieroglyphics so complex that archeologists cannot decipher them. A staircase leads to two rooftop chapels. One contains the famous circular zodiac.

The Mysterious Corridor surrounds the sanctuary, opening off into 11 chapels, one of which has a small opening in the floor that leads to the crypts. The purpose of this subterranean hallway is unknown, but its highly stylized reliefs are fascinating. If the crypts are closed, a guard will open them for you if you offer baksheesh.

Abu-Simbel: the most remote temple

At the far end of the Nile, 150 miles south of Aswan in the Nubian desert, is an awe-inspiring temple that seems to rise out of nowhere. Four 65-foot colossi of Ramses II guard the entrance to the structure, which was originally cut out of a cliff. Between and beside his legs are smaller statues of his queens and daughters.

As remarkable as the temple itself is the fact that it was taken apart and moved. In the 1960s, it was dissected stone by stone and moved by archeologists after they learned it would be flooded by the new High Dam at Aswan. The still beautiful temple lost some of its magnitude with the move. Formerly, it was part of a cliff overlooking the roaring Nile. Today, it is set beside calm Lake Nasser.

Scientists took great pains to place the temple exactly as its original builders did so that during equinoxes the rising sun shines directly through the entrance, lighting statues 180 feet back in the sanctuary. Unfortunately, the statues have been badly mutilated. (No one knows by whom.)

Travel like Cleopatra

The best way to explore Egypt is aboard a **felucca**, the traditional sailboat that glides along the Nile. Because the river cuts through most of Egypt's towns and villages, following it gives you a complete view of the country. As you bob along, you'll pass women doing wash in the river, fishermen pulling in their nets, and children playing along the river's bank.

Between Aswan, where most felucca journeys begin, and Luxor, where most of them end, the Nile passes many of Egypt's most important ancient monuments and temples. During this 140-mile sail, a felucca stops at one monument a day.

Of course, on a felucca journey, you must be prepared to rough it. Usually, you have no bathroom facilities—other than the Nile. And meals, while hearty and usually tasty, are prepared over a campfire. Your bed is on board, beneath the stars.

Spring and fall are the best times to sail. Be sure to bring sunscreen, a hat, toilet paper, and a flashlight. Women should not wear bikinis or skimpy bathing suits—they cause problems in an Islamic country. It takes about three weeks to cruise the entire length of the Nile. However, the Aswan-Luxor stint takes only about five days.

Feluccas can be cheap or expensive. Shop around, and don't be afraid to bargain. If you arrange the trip yourself in Egypt, plan to spend about 23 Egyptian pounds ($7) per person per day plus 7 Egyptian pounds ($2) per day for food, permits, and tips.

Feluccas line the riverfront in Aswan and Luxor. Ask around on the waterfront at the Cataract Hotel in Aswan. Hotel clerks often can recommend a place to rent a boat. It is a good idea to get references.

Alexandria: the least Egyptian city

Alexandria was a very un-Egyptian city when it was founded by Alexander the Great in 330 B.C. It flourished as the cultural center of the world for 300 years, until the great library accidentally burned down during the reign of Julius Caesar, destroying more than a half-million irreplaceable manuscripts. Modern Alexandria is an international city, small and clean and known for its Greco-Roman relics and its sandy beaches.

The **Greco-Roman Museum,** *Sharia el-Mathaf,* houses a collection of artifacts from the days of Greek and Roman rule, including bas-reliefs, pottery, statues, jewelry, and marble pieces. Don't miss Room 9, which displays relics of the cult of the crocodile god Pnepheros, including a mummified crocodile. The museum is open daily except Fridays from 9 a.m. to 4 p.m.

At the western end of town are the **catacombs of Kom el-Shoqafa,** burial chambers carved into rock 100 feet belowground. Built in the second century for a wealthy family that still practiced the ancient religion, the catacombs represent the last burst of native Egyptian sacred art. However, because the artisans were trained in Italy, the Egyptian gods have unmistakably Roman bodies. Reliefs depict a Roman-style Osiris making an offering to the deceased. Lesser gods hold bunches of grapes and Medusa heads. One statue of Anubis is even dressed in Roman armor. The museum is open daily from 9 a.m. to 4 p.m.

Near Nasr Station is a beautifully preserved white marble **Roman amphitheater,** the only known Roman era amphitheater remaining in Egypt. Behind it lie a cistern and Roman bath. In 1963, when construction workers were building the foundation of an office building, the ruins were unearthed; archeologists continue to uncover artifacts here.

A relatively modern attraction in this ancient city of Alexandria is the 19th-century summer residence of the Egyptian royal family, the **Ras el-Tin Palace.** King Farouk forfeited its Throne Room, Gothic Hall, and Marble Hall when he abdicated in 1953 for a life of exile in Italy.

The **Fine Arts Museum,** *18 Menasha St.,* contains both a collection of modern Egyptian art and Alexandria's public library. Not far from the Mosque of Abul Abaas, along the corniche, it is the largest Islamic building in the city and has a beautiful courtyard. According to legend, the priest Abul Abaas rose from his tomb here to catch bombs falling on Alexandria during World War II.

At the western end of the corniche, where the Lighthouse of Pharos (one of the original Seven Wonders of the World) once stood, is the **Fort of Qait Bay.** Built by Sultan Bay in the 15th century from the remains of the lighthouse, the fort commands a sweeping view of Alexandria. Inside are a scale model of the 400-foot lighthouse and a naval museum.

The best case of mistaken identity

A 98-foot granite column erected in Alexandria in 297 A.D. was named **Pompey's Pillar** by Crusaders during the 13th century. Actually, the rose-colored column is a monument to the emperor Diocletian that was built by his troops. The most famous monument of ancient Alexandria, the pillar sits in a small public park on a hill where Diocletian once had a temple dedicated to the bull god Serapis.

The best way to get to Alexandria

Located 110 miles north of Cairo, bordering the Nile Delta, Alexandria can be reached easily by bus, plane, train, or car. For about 23 Egyptian pounds ($7), Golden Rocket buses carry you between Cairo's Giza Square and Alexandria's Zaghloul Square. Make reservations if you plan to use the daily air-conditioned trains that travel between Cairo's Ramses Station and Alexandria's Masr Station. (The cost is 20 to 25 Egyptian pounds, or $6 to $8.) Shared taxis take the same route, but they cost about $1 less. EgyptAir's flight from Cairo departs daily at a cost of 115 Egyptian pounds, or $35.

The Egyptian Riviera

In the summer, Moslem Egyptians crowd Alexandria's beaches, where the temperature is an average 15 degrees cooler than in Cairo. The beaches are beautiful and the water clear, but Egypt's **Riviera** is crowded and cluttered. And remember, this is a Moslem beach, so don't wear bikinis or daring swimsuits.

Corniche, the 15-mile road along the coast, is lined with houses, hotels, shops, and palm trees. At the eastern tip of Alexandria's stretch of beaches is the **Montaza Palace and Gardens**, a huge complex that includes gardens, beaches, and hotels. Just east of Montaza is **Ma'amura**, a cleaner, relatively isolated beach where the people have more Western tastes in swimwear. However, true beach lovers will best enjoy Egypt's beach resorts along the Sinai and Red Sea.

The best dining in Alexandria

Alexandria has several excellent restaurants. **Morgan**, *El-Gueish Boulevard; tel. (20-3)61-184,* is an elegant seafood restaurant on the shore.

Lord's Inn, around the corner from the San Stefano Hotel, offers continental cuisine in a gourmet setting.

For the best Pakistani food outside Pakistan, try **Tikka Grill**, located on the waterfront near the Abul Abaas Mosque.

Expensive by Egyptian standards, meals at both the Lord's Inn and the Tikka Grill run 66 to 99 Egyptian pounds ($20 to $30) for two.

Santa Lucia, *40 Safia Zaghoul St.,* is a good French restaurant. **Restaurant Elite**, *43 Safia Zaghoul St.,* has inexpensive pizza and strong espresso. Ignore the menu and opt for the daily specials, which are written on the wall.

Egypt's best seafood restaurant

For the best seafood in Egypt, drive to the small town of Abu Kir, about 10 miles east of Alexandria. Here, four blocks from the central mosque, on the waterfront, is a famous restaurant called **Zephyrion**, *tel. (20-3)860-758.* In business since 1929, Zephyrion has fresh fish, large salads, imported beer, and succulent shrimp.

Alexandria's best hotels

The best hotels in Alexandria cost only 182 to 281 Egyptian pounds ($55 to $85) a night. You won't have as great a choice as in Cairo, but you won't have to fight the crowds either.

The **Ramada Renaissance**, *544 El Gueish St., Sidi Bishr; tel. (20-3)866-111,* has a pool, great views, and air conditioning. A double room is 112 to 221 Egyptian pounds ($67 to $75).

Two rival beachfront hotels are the **Sheraton Montazah**, *Corniche Road, El Montazah; tel. (20-3)969-220,* where a double room is 224 to 277 Egyptian pounds ($68 to $84), and the **Palestine**, *Kasr El Montazah; tel. (20-3)547-4033,* where a double room is 254 to 314 Egyptian pounds ($70 to $95) a night.

More modest accommodation can be had at **El Alamein**, *PLM Azur; tel. (20-03)492-1228.* It's not on the beach, but a double room costs only 115 Egyptian pounds ($44). **Al Haram**, *162 El Gueish St., Cleopatra; tel. (20-3)964-574,* is in a nice old stone building. A double room is 83 Egyptian pounds to 116 Egyptian pounds ($25 to $35) a night.

It isn't wise to stay too cheaply in Egypt; budget hotels must be chosen carefully. However, we do recommend the **Hotel Marhaba**, *10 Orabi Square.* It's quiet and immaculate and charges only 27 Egyptian pounds ($8). Another cheap but acceptable place is **Hotel Leroy**, *25 Talaat Harb St.; tel. (20-3)4833-439,* located on the top floors of an office building. Rooms are clean; some have breezy balconies. A double room is 30 Egyptian pounds ($9).

Sinai: the most unusual landscape

Four wars have been fought between Israel and Egypt on the **Sinai Peninsula**. As of

1967 it was Israeli territory, but the Sadat-Begin Treaty returned it to Egypt in 1982. You now can enter the southern Sinai Peninsula, which, with its high granite mountains and deep chasms, has some of the most unusual landscapes in the world. It's also the site of two popular beaches and one of the most famous mountains in history.

The Sinai is heavily militarized. Police want you to keep to the main roads, but you can obtain permission to visit parts of the desert interior with a Bedouin guide. (You might even catch a glimpse of military exercises.) The Sinai heat can be unbearable, sometimes reaching 110 degrees Fahrenheit.

You can't make direct telephone calls in Sinai—you must go through the operator at **Al-Arish**, *tel. (20-68)0100.*

Buses are the most affordable way to get to the Sinai. They cost 33 to 66 Egyptian pounds ($10 to $20) and depart Abassiya Station in Cairo for St. Catherine, Nuweiba, and Dahab. Most stop at Sharm El Sheikh, the southernmost town on the peninsula, where you won't find anything much to do or see.

A car allows you more flexibility when exploring the Sinai. The main roads are well-maintained, but the drive from Cairo to Nuweiba is a good seven hours—and you won't find anywhere to stop along the way for gas or water.

Flying is fastest and easiest. **Air Sinai**, *15 Kasr El Nil St.; tel. (20-2)750-663 or (20-2)760-948*, flies from Cairo to St. Catherine for 165 Egyptian pounds ($50) or to Sharm El Sheikh for 205 Egyptian pounds ($62).

Dahab: a golden town

When the Israelis occupied this town, they named it **Zahav** (Gold). It is split into two parts: a terrific beach and a Bedouin village of thatched huts and palm trees. The beach is never crowded and almost always sunny. In town, you can rent scuba gear for exploring the coral reefs.

Villagers allow travelers to stay with them in their huts for as little as 23 Egyptian pounds ($7). This is a great way to get to know the people and to experience firsthand their lifestyle. But remember, the huts have neither toilets nor running water, and Bedouins are superstitious about having their pictures taken.

More luxurious accommodation is available at the **Dahab Holiday Village**, where air-conditioned beachfront rooms cost 76 Egyptian pounds ($23) a night. The hotel restaurant serves dinner for about 17 Egyptian pounds ($5).

Nuweiba: the best beach

Nuweiba, a tourist village about 10 miles north of Dahab, has an even better beach. That's good, because this town doesn't have much else to offer, and the nearby Bedouin villages don't invite visitors. The bus to Nuweiba lets you off at the **tourist office**, *tel. (20-66)768-832.*

You can rent scuba gear or sailing equipment at the Sailing Club. The best reefs are along the southern part of Nuweiba's beach. For more secluded diving, walk a quarter-mile south to what the locals call the Stone House. Rental prices are good—gear, a boat dive, and a guide cost only 132 Egyptian pounds ($40).

The best camel treks

Bedouins from Dahab run camel treks into the desert. If you bargain hard, 12 Egyptian pounds will get you a one-day journey to the oasis Wadi Gnay.

Mount Sinai: the most commanding mountain

God gave Moses the Ten Commandments atop **Mount Sinai**, a remote mountain in the Sinai desert. A religious landmark, the mountain is dotted with tents and small chapels.

The most interesting and difficult route to the 7,000-foot peak that the Arabs call

Gebal Musa is up the 3,500 **Steps of Repentance,** supposedly carved out by just one monk to fulfill his pledge of penitence. An easier way to reach the peak is to take the camel path that begins directly behind the monastery. When the path and steps meet, look down at the 500-year-old cypress tree that marks Elijah's Hollow, where the prophet Elijah heard the voice of God. (There are now two chapels in the hollow.) At the mountain's summit is a small church, usually surrounded by dozens of tourists and pilgrims in sleeping bags.

You, too, can bring a sleeping bag and sleep on the mountain (but remember—it gets chilly). When you awaken, you'll see both Africa and Asia from the peak.

More comfortable places to stay include the monastery's hostel (17 Egyptian pounds, or $5, a cot) and **St. Catherine Salam,** *tel. (20-10)240-28-32,* a hotel in town with rooms for 56 Egyptian pounds ($20) and up. A national tourist office is located in this hotel.

A Byzantine best
At the base of Mount Sinai is **St. Catherine's Monastery,** the oldest unrestored Byzantine complex in the world. Emperor Justinian had it built in 342 A.D. on the site of the Burning Bush, where God first recruited Moses to lead the Hebrews out of Egypt.

Fortresslike walls protect St. Catherine's Monastery (named after the saint martyred in Alexandria). Inside are jewel-studded crosses, hand-carved furniture, and the Chapel of the Burning Bush. The monastery's library contains enough early Christian manuscripts to rival the Vatican, and the marvelous mosaic of the *Transfiguration of Christ* is one of the great treasures of early sacred painting. Don't miss the Ossary, a separate building containing the bones of all the monks who have died at St. Catherine's over the centuries.

The best snorkeling in the Middle East
The best snorkeling in the Middle East is at **Yemenieh Reef,** off Aqaba, a Jordanian town just across the gulf from Nuweiba. Here, you can see 40 kinds of coral not found anywhere else in the world. Scuba and skin divers commonly cross the gulf to Aqaba (captured from the Turks in 1917 by the legendary Lawrence of Arabia), which has beautiful beaches and an excellent aquarium in its Marine Research Center. Ferries depart daily from Nuweiba for Aqaba at 11 a.m. and 3 p.m. for 248 Egyptian pounds ($75) round trip. You'll need a passport, of course, to make the crossing.

The **Nuweiba Holiday Village,** near the ferry terminal, has comfortable lodgings for 182 Egyptian pounds ($55). Farther south is a cheaper, nameless hotel that charges 106 Egyptian pounds ($32) for a double room. Next door is a set of bungalows, where you can stay for 23 Egyptian pounds ($7) per person (up to three people to a bungalow).

Hurghada: Egypt's best coral reefs
The sleepy little town of **Hurghada,** which lies 240 miles south of Suez and about 350 miles from Cairo, is one of the best places in the world for unspoiled scuba and snorkeling expeditions. The coral reefs here are the most beautiful in Egypt, and dozens of boats are available to take you to any one of the tiny reef islands. At Giftun El **Saghir,** a small island off Hurghada, the water is so clear that you can see 100 feet down to the rocky bottom. At the offshore island of **Shaab Um Qamar,** divers sometimes catch lobsters at night with their bare hands.

Everything in Hughada centers around two landmarks: **Al-Dhar Mosque** and **Ugly Mountain,** which is, indeed, ugly. Hurghada is a good place to fish; it is teeming with barracuda, swordfish, sailfish, and tuna. You can rent bikes for a few dollars a day from a shop just north of the Al-Dhar Mosque. And about two miles north of that is the Red Sea Museum, which has a large collection of sea life, including sharks and sea lions.

The most comfortable place to stay in Hurghada is the **Hurghada Sheraton,** *48 B*

Giza St., Orman Tower Building; (800)325-3535, which has air-conditioned double rooms for 231 to 300 Egyptian pounds ($70 to $100) a night.

What the cheaper places lack in air conditioning they make up for in personality. At **Hurghada Happy House,** between the Al-Dhar Mosque and the main avenue, *tel. (20-62)405-40,* Captain Muhammed Awad rents beds for 16.5 Egyptian pounds ($5) a night and tells the best fishing stories in town. For 10 Egyptian pounds ($4) more, the captain will take you on his boat to the House of Sharks, a reef pulsating with lionfish, sharks, eels, and other sea creatures.

Tips on baksheesh

Baksheesh is a way of life in Egypt. Although only a minority of Egyptians pester foreigners, those who do expect baksheesh for the slightest things—opening a door, for example—and even more baksheesh for doing nothing. In a bazaar, you will be followed by a half-dozen children with outstretched palms.

You should always travel with a pocketful of loose change and 1-pound notes. However, give baksheesh only for services rendered. In most cases, 25 piastres (8 cents) will do, but in rare instances, such as being shown a sight after hours, 1 Egyptian pound (30 cents) is proper.

Two useful terms concerning baksheesh are *Shukran* (Thanks) and *Emshee!* (Get lost!).

The best of Morocco

Morocco is a land of casbahs, veiled women with painted toenails, belly dancers, minarets, and ancient *souks.* Its ancient cities have modern European sections, with tree-lined avenues, Parisian boutiques, sidewalk cafés, and luxury hotels. But each also has a *medina,* or old quarter, where you must navigate your way through a maze of narrow, twisting, cobblestoned steets, arabesque archways, and cluttered bazaars.

Tangier—Morocco's port city

The port of **Tangier** on the country's northwestern tip, attracts French, German, British, American, and especially Spanish travelers, who come via the hovercrafts that make daily trips between Tangier and Gibraltar and southern Spain. Its commanding position on the Straits of Gibraltar has made it a strategic military state, coveted by everyone from the Phoenicians to modern-day Spanish, British, French, and Germans. In 1923, Tangier was declared an international zone. In 1957, it became part of Morocco. Ask anyone who knows Morocco well, however, and he will tell you that Tangier is not Morocco. Its customs and culture, which retain vestiges of all those who have invaded it over the centuries, are too diverse to be truly Moroccan.

In addition to cafés, where Arabs and tourists alike sit for hours over cups of strong black coffee or sweet mint tea, Tangier has miles of uncrowded, golden beaches fringed by the Mediterranean to the north and the Atlantic to the west.

The legendary Garden of Hesperides, Tangier was once a haven for black marketeers and smugglers. Today, because of its low income tax and favorable climate, it has become a refuge for the world's wealthiest citizens.

The best marketplace

Tangier's casbah, or walled fortress, is very much the center of life here. It is built on the highest point of the city and juts up against the *medina.* You can reach it from the **Bab el Assa,** at the end of Rue Ben Raisouli in the *medina.* The white arched gateway into the casbah leads to an open courtyard called **Tabor Square,** which leads to Dar al Makhzen, the former sultan's palace (now a museum).

The casbah is really a huge marketplace. It is packed with people—vendors, shoppers, tourists. It is noisy. And it is filled with the smells of mint, spices, fresh camel meat, and fruits and vegetables.

The best place to stay

A relaxing and intimate place to stay in Tangier is **El Minzah Tangier**, *85 Rue de la Liberte; tel. (212-9)937844* or *(800)448-8355 in the United States.* A double room is 1,007 dirhams ($126) a night.

The best castles

On the outskirts of the city are the splendid villas of Gianni Agnelli (Italy's Fiat magnate) and the late Malcom Forbes. The king of Saudi Arabia owns two palaces, one in Tangier and the other across the Mediterranean in Marbella, Spain.

The late dime-store heiress Barbara Hutton lived for years in a storybook palace tucked away in a corner of the mysterious casbah. The palace has been made a museum and is one of the city's major attractions.

The most magnificent city

Rabat, the present-day capital of Morocco, is home to one of the magnificent palaces of King Hassan II. Its entrances are protected by the personal guard of the royal family. You can see the full splendor of the guard on Friday morning, the Moslem holy day. It escorts the king, who rides in a gilded coach drawn by four white horses, across the palace grounds to the mosque. The weekly ritual is a dramatic reminder that King Hassan is not only the head of state but also the religious leader of the country.

Ancient Fez

The old walled city of **Fez**, wrapped in a pink fog, is four hours by car from Rabat. Founded in A.D. 800, Fez is a renowned religious center. For 11 centuries, it was the epitome of cultural, artistic, and religious life in Morocco.

The *souk* of the woodcarvers in Fez is filled with the pleasant scent of cedar. Not so the *souk* of the tanners. Here, young men in short pants, standing thigh-high in steaming cauldrons of red, yellow, and purple dye, leap from vat to vat, dipping, pulling, and kneading the sodden camel, goat, and sheepskin pelts in the noxious liquids

The world's oldest university

Karaouine University, which dates to A.D. 859, is the oldest university in the world. Today it is a mosque that attracts Moslems in droves. They believe that seven pilgrimages to Karaouine are the spiritual equivalent of one trip to Mecca.

The best place to stay

The best place to stay in Fez is the **Palais Jamai**, *Bab El Guissa; tel. (212-5)634331* or *(800)888-4747 in the United States,* a former sultan's palace located at the entrance to the bustling *medina.* It is one of Morocco's most luxurious hotels. Lavish tile murals, fine cuisine, and an unbeatable situation above the city combine to produce an extraordinary hotel in a fomer 19th-century palace. A double room is 680 dirhams to 840 dirhams ($83 to $103) a night.

The biggest palace

Mekès, less than 40 miles from Fez, is home to the sultan's gigantic palace, complete with storerooms, gardens, military barracks, and stables. At the beginning of the 18th century, this unbelievable complex housed the court and the imperial family of 600 wives and 1,500 children, as well as at least 50,000 slaves, servants, and eunuchs. The stables accommodated 12,000 horses, each with its own stall and valet. All this splendor is now mostly in ruins, destroyed by an earthquake in 1755.

The most imperial city

The imperial ciy of **Marrakech** was chosen by the sultans as capital of the 1,200-year-old Sheriffien Empire, which stretched from Spain to Timbuktu. Founded on the arid Haoux plain in the 11th century, Marrakech was a caravansary, a major port of call on the Sahara desert for camel caravans that linked Ghana with Fez and Algiers.

Today Marrakech is a city of brownish-pink houses, towering ramparts, and graceful minarets. This capital city boasts a dry, warm climate, luxurious hotels, colorful marketplaces, and an old walled quarter.

The liveliest spot in town

The heart of Marrakech is a vast public square adjacent to the *medina* known as **Djemma El Fna**, or Place of the Dead, which is in fact the liveliest spot in town. Long ago, the sultans displayed the heads of criminals and enemies defeated in battle around this huge square. Today it is filled with bazaars where you can shop for almost anything.

But more than a market, Djemma is the largest outdoor show in all North Africa. Storytellers, mimes, medicine men, sword swallowers, male belly dancers, and snake charmers perform for the crowds, each competing for the small coins that spectators toss in appreciation.

The most colorful festival

One of the most striking spectacles in the Arab world takes place in Marrakech in June. The **National Folklore Festival**, which draws visitors from all over the world, is held amid the red-ochre ruins of the El Badii Palace.

The performers in the National Folklore Festival are not professionals. They are villagers, country people from the Sahara desert and the Atlas Mountains who have been selected by the festival directors to take part in the two-week extravaganza.

For the performances, the stage is covered with layers of intricately woven Moroccan carpets spread to create an *Arabian Nights* setting. On either side of the stage, huge striped tents are set up to house the performers waiting their turn. In the foreground, separating the stage from the audience, is the outer edge of a rectangular pool, where, centuries ago, sultans frolicked with their harem favorites.

The performances begin suddenly, with lines of colorfully garbed dancers surging forward from both sides of the stage, their shoulders twitching to the beat of the drums. Soon, the desert air is filled with their songs and hypnotic chants. Spotlights accentuate the splendid costumes and coined headpieces and necklaces. All the images are reflected in the pool.

Black dancers from the Sahara dressed in white pantaloons and red vests leap and whirl frantically to the rhythm of the shrill reed flutes. They are followed by barefooted acrobats in green trousers, who somersault high in the air as cymbals crash. The stage seems to explode with motion and song.

The best mint teas

Mint, in Moroccan, means *hospitality.* No guest gets away from a Moroccan household without several glasses of hot mint tea. Actually a mixture of green tea, anisette, vervain, marjoram, and mint, the tea is made according to strict rules. First, 2 to 3 teaspoons of green tea are placed in a pot. The pot is held high to aerate the tea, which is then served in tiny glasses. Guests must, according to custom, have three glasses.

One of the best places for tea in Marrakech is the **Dar Marjana**, *15 Derb Ettir, Ang Bab Doukkada; tel. (212-4)448688.* And tea is served with formality in the ornate courtyard of the elegant **Arab Palace.**

The best beaches in Morocco

Agadir, in southwest Morocco, is the country's playground. It has a white-sand beach and all the sun and water sports anyone could want. And unlike most of the world's beach towns, Agadir doesn't scream commercialism and tourism.

Destroyed by an earthquake in 1960, Agadir has been completely rebuilt. But its main attration is still its beach, which is a pleasant 10-minute walk from the center of town. To get there, you meander down a terraced hillside covered with greenery and flowering plants. Along the beach runs a wide walk of marble, which is lined with open-air cafés facing the water. In the background are the **Anti-Atlas Mountains.**

Agadir enjoys more than 300 days of sun a year. And the temperature is always between 66 and 82 degrees Fahrenheit. Its white-sand beaches are as beautiful as you'll find anywhere, and its water as blue. It is easy to see why European sunseekers flock here year-round.

Agadir can be expensive and crowded because of its thriving tourist industry, however. If you're looking for space and a bit of private beach, head north from Agadir, where you'll find sandy coves every few miles.

The best silver factory in Morocco

Situated south of Agadir, along a caravan crossroads in south Morocco, is **Tiznit**. This tiny town is best known for its silver jewelry, which is made by local Berbers from the silver mined nearby.

The rooms in what the townspeople refer to as their "silver factory" are filled with handmade silver jewelry, serving trays, pots, and trinkets. In the front of the rooms sit small boys, apprentices who work in the factory in the morning and go to school in the afternoon. Expect to haggle, but you'll end up with good silver at cheap prices.

The tiny, muddy passageways that make up Old Town are crowded with street vendors offering rugs, pottery, jewelry, and spices. Everything is for sale. (Nothing is refrigerated.)

The best of Algeria

Algeria, Africa's second-largest country, is a sea of sand drifts. It is also a place where anything Western is in high demand; Algerians are willing to pay handsomely for Western goods of all kinds. The chief black market commodity is whiskey; you can resell a bottle of whiskey for six times your purchase price.

There is still a definite discrimination against women in Algeria; men eat at the table, while women cook and remain in the kitchen, for example. Change is coming slowly here, giving travelers a rare opportunity to experience a centuries-old culture.

The most fundamentalist town

In the very fundamentalist town of **Ghardaïa**, the few women on the streets are clothed and veiled from head to foot. They have one eyehole, through which they peer cautiously. Ghardaïa is the most prosperous town in the country and is inhabited, as it has been for more than 900 years, by the Mozabites, a strict Moslem sect that broke from the mainstream of Islam in the seventh century. The people use the same underground irrigation canals, live in the same cubelike houses, and worship in the same mysterious mosques as did their ancestors.

The world's biggest sandpile

The golden sand in the west is called the **Grand Erg Occidental**. Its white counterpart in the east is called the **Grand Erg Oriental**. Erg can be translated as "sand sea" or "desert of sand dunes." Either way, you get the idea. The vastness of it all will overwhelm you at times.

The best way to see Algeria

The **Trans-Algerian Highway** is the only road that crosses Algeria from border to border. It passes through the Sahara desert and covers the 1,100 miles from Morocco to Tunisia. The Highway is well-maintained. Gas stations are adequately spaced along the road. (But don't ever pass one without filling up.) Spare auto parts are a rare commodity, however, so carry with you anything you think you might need.

The greatet attraction of traveling the highway is the chance it gives you to see the Sahara desert. Great sand dunes, with ridges perfectly carved by the wind, seem to go on forever, dwarfing the occasional camel train or group of palm trees.

A best for horse lovers

Horse lovers can spend two weeks in the saddle in Algeria. Riding is English-style, luggage is carried by a support car, and nights are spent at hotels, inns, private homes, or camps. Most tours involve four to six hours of riding a day. The best tours are arranged by an American company, **FITS Equestrian,** *685 Latten Road, Solvang, CA 93463; (800)666-FITS* or *(805)688-9494*, which charges $1,975 for a two-day trip.

The Best of Israel

> The world of Palestine always brought to my mind a vague suggestion of a country as large as the United States. I do not know why, but such was the case. I suppose it was because I could not conceive of a small country having so large a history.
> —*Mark Twain, 1869*

The Land of Milk and Honey holds a special place in history. A professor at the Hebrew University once wrote a study comparing Israel to a newborn child that has emerged from a centuries-old womb. Israel is a 20th-century country built on a 4,000-year-old prophecy; even the modern high-rise buildings carry a history of conflict.

A war-torn desert nation, Israel is thriving today. Bordered by four seas, the promised land has dozens of uncrowded beaches and a fertile Mediterranean coast that rivals the French Riviera. The country's three largest cities offer night life and historical landmarks.

The national *aliyya* (settlement) programs attest to Israeli concern for growth and building; however, this dedication has not come without problems. Israel is bordered to the north by Lebanon and to the east by Jordan, its enemies since the country was established in 1948. The Golan Heights and Jericho, for example, are Israeli-occupied territories.

Israel is small—about the size of Rhode Island—but it offers a diversity of terrain, weather, and people. You can ski the slopes of Mount Hermon, swim in the Mediterranean, and hike in the desert all in the course of one day. Yemenite, American, South African, Ethiopian, and Moroccan Israelis mingle with one another and with 1 million Arab Israeli citizens.

Jerusalem, the eternal capital

Israel is best visited in two trips: one to see **Jerusalem** and one to see the rest of the country.

The capital city has been the center of both conflict and faith for 3,000 years. Divided by Israel and neighboring Jordan for 20 years, the city was reunited after the 1967 war.

369

It is the largest city in Israel. Expansion and construction mark the New City; inside Old Jerusalem, heavy industry is banned and archeological research continues.

Jerusalem's heart: the Old City

The 40-foot-high crenelated wall encircling the Old City is surrounded by a belt of grass and bushes. Most of Jerusalem's sights are inside this wall, which has eight gates. **Golden Gate** is thought to lie over the Closed Gate of the First Temple, the entrance through which the Jewish Messiah is expected to pass. **Jaffa Gate** is the most convenient entrance to the New City and houses a helpful tourist center. At **Damascus Gate** you can buy a ticket (about $1) to ascend the rampart onto the top of the wall, where you'll have a view of the entire Old City.

Among the Old City's attractions are the Dome of the Rock (Mosque of Omar), the Church of the Holy Sepulcher, and the Via Dolorosa (Way of the Cross). The **Dome of the Rock,** an ornate shrine standing on Temple Mount, is usually filled with Moslems facing Mecca and praying. Inside is the rock from which Mohammed is said to have ascended to heaven. The **Church of the Holy Sepulcher** contains the tomb where Christ was laid to rest after the crucifixion, as well as the tomb of Joseph of Arimathea.

The **Via Dolorosa** is the path along which Jesus walked from the court of Pilate to the hill of Golgotha. You can retrace His steps; the 14 stations, or places of devotion, where Jesus rested along the way, are marked. Not far away is the **Coenaculum,** the room of the Last Supper, and to the east stands the Garden of Gethsemane, where Christ prayed the night before his crucifixion.

The **Wailing Wall,** the western wall (and sole remains) of the Second Temple, is the holiest structure in Judaism. Jews have gathered here for centuries to pray and bemoan the temple's destruction. If you write a prayer on a scrap of paper and slip it between the stones of the wall, it is said God will hear you more quickly. Jewish boys' bar mitzvahs are held here nearly every day. And at night, floodlights cast shadows on the ancient stones, and you can hear old men murmuring in prayer.

The nearby **Mount of Olives** has a famous Jewish cemetery, and the Greek Orthodox Church there houses the **Tomb of the Virgin Mary.** According to Christian tradition, the mount was the site of Jesus' Ascension; according to Jewish tradition, the Mount of Olives is where the Messiah will resurrect the dead. At dawn, **Temple Mount** has a golden glow.

Near the Old City walls is **Mount Zion,** the site of King David's tomb. (It's a bare room.)

More interesting is **Hezekiah's Tunnel,** built about 1000 B.C. so water could be brought in when the city was under siege. Begin at the **Gihon Spring** and slosh through the tunnel all the way to the **Pool of Shiloah.**

The **Museum of the Potential Holocaust,** *31 Usishkin St., on the Mount of Remembrance,* displays contemporary anti-Semitic works from such groups as the American Nazi Party and the Klu Klux Klan. The museum is open Sunday through Thursday 9 a.m. until 5 p.m. and Friday 9 a.m. until 2 p.m. For more information, call *(972-2)752-611.*

The Hadassah Hebrew University Medical Center and its synagogue are decorated with stained-glass windows designed and painted by Marc Chagall.

The best of the New City

The first thing to see in the New City is the **Knesset,** Israel's parliament, which is decorated with mosaics by Chagall. You can catch a lively debate (in Hebrew) when the Knesset is in session Sunday and Thursday, 8:30 a.m. until 2:30 p.m. Be sure to bring your passport, and expect to be searched thoroughly when you enter.

Two blocks away is the **Yad Vashem,** a monument honoring the 6 million Jews killed in World War II. The photos and documents trace Hitler's rise and focus on those who fought back, particularly the Warsaw Ghetto.

Walk through the picturesque **Yemenite Moshe Quarter,** which has been renovated into residential and artists' neighborhoods. The nearby village of En Karem is the birthplace of John the Baptist. Take note of the beautiful Church of St. John, with its soaring tower.

The **Rockefeller Museum**, *Suleiman and Jericho roads, tel. (972-2)282-251*, displays Middle Eastern artwork from the last two millenia. The Billy Rose Sculpture Garden contains works by Picasso and Degas, as well as Israeli artists. It is open 10 a.m. until 5 p.m. Sunday through Thursday and 9 a.m. until 2 p.m. Friday. The **Israel Museum**, *Rehov Ruppin; tel. (972-2)698-211*, which incorporates the Bezalel Museum, has a large collection of Jewish folk and ceremonial art. Main areas devoted to archeology, Judaica, and Israeli painting mix with major exhibits from abroad. The Dead Sea scrolls are displayed here, at the Shrine of the Book. The museum is open Sunday, Monday, Wednesday, and Thursday, 10 a.m. until 5 p.m., Tuesday, 4 until 10 p.m., and Friday and Saturday, 10 a.m. until 2 p.m. Take bus 9, 17, or 24.

The best entertainment

While in Jerusalem, try to attend a performance of the Israeli Philharmonic, which stages winter concerts at **Binyanei Haoma**, *Yafo Street*, or the popular Jerusalem Dance Company. A less-known dance troupe is Kol U'Demama (Sound and Silence), an art-dance ensemble with both hearing and deaf dancers. It is the only group of its kind in the world. The **Cahanna Ticket Agency**, *tel. (972-2)222-831,* can provide tickets to most cultural events.

The most festive times to visit

In the summer, musicians, dancers, and actors from around the globe converge on Jerusalem for the **Israel Festival of Music and Drama**. The holiday of Simchat Torah, which usually falls in early October, is marked by **Hakafot** ceremonies—which consist of singing, dancing, and parading the Torah through the streets. In Jerusalem, Hakafot festivities take place in the Liberty Bell Garden area, located on Recham HaMelekh (King David) Street. (The Liberty Bell was set up to fête the U.S. Bicentennial.)

Christmas and Hanukkah are special times in Jerusalem. Christmas is marked by a weeklong festival of choral music called the **Liturgica**, and Hanukkah begins with a public candle-lighting ceremony at the Western Wall. The largest Christmas tree in the city is set up and lit at the West Jerusalem Y.M.C.A. Eastern Orthodox Christmas celebrations include a parade with bagpipers. On Dec. 24 at 12:30 p.m., people gather at Jaffa Gate for the Procession of the Latin Patriarch, commemorating the journey of the Three Wise Men. Anyone can join the procession, which winds its way from the Old City to Bethlehem, about seven miles south. Once in Bethlehem, choirs accompany the priest into St. Catherine's Church for High Mass. If you're thinking of spending Christmas in the holiest of cities, make reservations months in advance, and don't even think of staying in the King David Hotel.

Jerusalem's best bargains

The **Arab bazaar** in the Old City offers Jerusalem's best bargains. (Haggling is the rule.) Throw rugs and Bedouin-style dresses are among the most popular items. A good buy for a dress is $25. You can get a *keffiyah* (Arab head scarf) for about $4.

The best jewelry shop in Jerusalem is **Tarshish**, *18 King David St.*, where you can buy intricate Yemenite jewelry. Tarshish is open until 5 p.m. every day except Friday and is located right across from the King David Hotel. For handcrafted jewelry made with malachite and Israeli glass, go to the jeweler/artisan Uri Ramot; he, along with other jewelers and weavers, displays his goods along the **Khutsot Hayotser** (Arts and Crafts Lane) just outside the Jaffa Gate.

The best dining

For Mideastern cuisine, go to the **Caravan**, located about a half-mile before the entrance to Bethlehem along the road from Jerusalem. Chef Abu-Isaac's succulent *mezze* (appetizers), cubed shashlik, and lamb kabobs stuffed with onions are delicious and inexpensive. Don't try making reservations; the restaurant has no telephone.

The **National Palace Restaurant**, in the National Palace Hotel, *tel. (972-2)282-139,* is another good place to get an Arabian meal. Ask your waiter what he recommends—this is considered proper. Order a selection of *mezze*—you'll be served a plate of appetizers ranging from olives to brain salad (it's good). The shish kebab and the grilled mutton marinated in yogurt are delicious. Before your meal, try a glass of arrack, an anise-flavored brandy mixed with water and ice. Dinner for two is about $25, including drinks and tip.

Caty's Restaurant, *16 Rivlin St.; tel. (972-2)234-621,* popular with the smart set, has first-class French food plus some North African specialties. Brooke Shields has eaten here.

Ticho House, *9 Haravkook St.; tel. (972-2)245-068,* part of the Israel Museum, is a pleasant café in the former home of artist Anna Ticho, whose works are on display. The villa has a Persian garden and a collection of Hanukkah lamps. The kitchen is kosher and serves good crêpes, soups, and salads.

Shemesh on Ben Yahudah Street, is an elegant eatery decorated with figurines of the sun (which is the literal translation of *shemesh*). The stuffed veggies and various kabobs, as well as the mezzes (the best is the hummus with tahini) are excellent. And the prices are moderate; dinner is $15.

In Jerusalem, a restaurant doesn't have to be expensive to be good. The **Shulchan Restaurant**, *2 Kikar Remaz,* across from the train station at the Khan Theater; *tel. (972-2)719-602,* serves quiches, salads, and hearty soups by the fireplace for less than $15.

Middle Eastern food sold by street vendors is even cheaper. For less than $2, you can fill up on *felafel, mezze,* and *fuul* (beans).

Premier hotels

The city's premier hotel is the **King David**, *23 King David St.; tel. (972-2)221-111* or *(212)752-6120 in the United States,* famous for its celebrity guests. Considered one of the classic hotels of the Middle East, the King David has more than 250 rooms, air conditioning, tennis courts, a pool, and a sauna. A double room is $285 to $315. Make reservations far in advance.

The **American Colony Hotel**, *Naplus Road, P.O. Box 19215; tel. (972-2)282-421,* once the home of a Turkish Pasha, is a luxurious hotel walled off from the hectic streets of Jerusalem. Rooms have gold and blue ceilings, antique Arab and Turkish furnishings, and modern bathrooms. Archeological finds are displayed in the lobby. The garden and the swimming pool are inviting. Ask for a room in the old building; the new building is not as interesting. A double room is $70 to $280 a night, including breakfast.

Overlooking the Old City is the **King Solomon Sheraton**, *32 King David St., near the YMCA; tel. (972-2)241-433,* with more than 100 rooms and great service. A double room is $100 to $150.

Less expensive is the **Windmill**, *3 Mendele St.; tel. (972-2)663-111,* a peaceful hotel with air-conditioned rooms. A double room starts at $90. You can get a discount if you book before 3 p.m.

Babylonian night life

For a good time in Jerusalem, go to **Herod's Bar**, *28 King David St.,* near the YMCA, which has a young crowd and, occasionally, belly dancing. The **Jerusalem Khan**, *David Remez Square,* is an entertaining nightclub. It's open 9:30 p.m. until midnight every night. The **Taverna** is another good club with a floor show, and the cellar bar at the **American Colony Hotel** has good jazz bands.

Most of the city closes down on Friday afternoons (Friday is the Moslem Sabbath, and Jewish shopkeepers must begin to prepare for their Sabbath), but you can catch an earful of jazz on Fridays at 1:30 p.m. at the **Pergod Theater**, *94 Bezalel St.; tel. (972-*

2)231-765. And the **Tourist Bureau**, *tel. (972-2)282-295*, conducts synagogue tours on Friday afternoon.

For more information, contact the **Jerusalem Tourist Information Center**, *24 King George St.; tel. (972-2)241-281* or *(972-2)241-282*.

The best side trips

Outside Jerusalem is the intercultural village **Neve Shalom** (Oasis for Peace), an experiment in peaceful coexistence among Arabs, Christians, and Jews, which has received several Ford Foundation grants. Visit Neve Shalom's School for Peace and the educational center for intergroup relations. Few tourists know about the village.

A visit to **Hebron** is a good day-trip (if the West Bank is quiet). Egged (a cooperative bus company) buses 34, 440, and 443 (which you can catch at the Jerusalem Central Bus Station) will take you to Hebron's main square, outside the Cave of Machpelah, where the three patriarchs—Abraham, Isaac, and Jacob—are buried with their wives (except Rachel). This is a major shrine for Jews and Moslems. The large, fortresslike synagogue above the cave opens to a long hallway. On the right is the tomb of Jacob and Leah. Across the courtyard is a tomb covered with calligraphy commemorating Abraham and Sarah. The Machpelah is closed to non-Moslems on Friday.

Bethlehem: Christianity's birthplace

Bethlehem, the birthplace of Jesus and King David, is only seven miles south of Jerusalem. This town of 25,000 is so touristy that post offices stay open on Christmas Day so tourists can mail postcards. On the road from Jerusalem is the **Garden Tomb**, where, according to the Gospels, Christ was buried.

The frenetic heart of Bethlehem is crowded **Manger Square**. On the east side of the square is the imposing **Church of the Nativity** (the oldest church in Israel, built by Constantine in A.D. 326), which you enter through a low doorway designed to stop visitors on horseback. Twelve pillars decorated with images of the apostles hold up the oak ceiling. Armenian, Greek, and Franciscan priests take care of the church. Descend into the cave beneath, where Jesus was born. The manger is holy to both Christians and Moslems.

Other important sights are the **Milk Grotto**, where the Virgin Mary is said to have dropped milk when nursing the baby Jesus, miraculously turning the cavern rocks white; **Rachel's tomb**, a small domed shrine built in 1860 and visited by Moslems, Jews, and Christians; and **Shepherds' Field**, just outside town off Shepherds' Street, believed to be the place where shepherds were told by angels that Christ had been born.

The colorful souk (market) is crowded, but worth a trip just to visit **Barakat Antiques**, *4648 King David St.*; this is the finest antique shop in Israel.

The **Casa Nova Inn**, *10 Casa Nova St.; tel. (972-2)282-791*, just east of Manger Square, is a newly renovated pilgrims' inn. Rates begin at only $25 for a comfortable room with a private bath. This includes not only a Continental breakfast but also a five-course afternoon dinner and a late supper. This is by far the best place to stay in Bethlehem; not only is it cheap, but it is also undiscovered and free of tourists.

Tel Aviv: Israel's busiest city

Tel Aviv is Israel's bustling metropolis, the fastest growing city on the Mediterranean coast. Most countries have their embassies here. Established in 1909 as a suburb of ancient Jaffa, Tel Aviv has become a second capital. It is situated conveniently, only an hour's drive from both Haifa and Jerusalem.

Tel Aviv's top museums

Tel Aviv Museum, *next to the Municipal Central Library at 27 King Saul St.; tel. (972-3)257-361*, houses a comprehensive collection of art, a sculpture garden, and a children's wing. The museum is open Sunday, Monday, Wednesday, and Thursday, 10 a.m. until 5 p.m.; Tuesday, 9 a.m. until 1 p.m. and 4 until 10 p.m.; Friday, 10 a.m. until 2 p.m.; and Saturday, 7 p.m. until 11 p.m.

Diaspora Museum, *Beit Hatefutzot, on the campus of Tel Aviv University; tel. (972-3)425-161*, uses films, computers, and audiovisual displays to trace the history of the Jewish people and the birth of Israel. It's open Sunday, Monday, Tuesday, and Thursday, 10 a.m. until 5 p.m., and Wednesday, 10 a.m. until 7 p.m.

The **Eretz Museum** (Museum of the Land), *Ramat Aviv; tel. (972-3)415-244*, displays glass, coins, ceramics, and other archeological finds. It is open Sunday through Thursday, 9 a.m. until 2 p.m., Tuesday, 4 a.m. until 7 p.m., and Saturday, 10 a.m. until 2 p.m.

The tallest tower in the Middle East
The **Migdal Shalom** (Shalom Tower), *Allenby Road*, is the tallest structure in the Middle East. Its 34th-floor observation terrace provides a bird's-eye view of the city. It also houses the Israel Wax Museum.

Israel's Miami Beach
Tel Aviv's seafront smacks of Miami Beach. It is lined with tourist hotels, outdoor cafés, shops, and restaurants, especially in **Kikar Namir** (Namir Square).

Tel Aviv's best park
Yarkon Park, an urban oasis in the northern part of the city, can be reached by Egged buses 1, 4, and 5. During the daylight hours, you can rent a rowboat on the HaYarkon River; contact **Irgun HaYarkon**, *tel. (972-3)448-422.*

The best shopping
Tel Aviv's main streets, Allenby, Ben Yehuda, and Dizengoff, are lined with cafés and boutiques. A connoisseur's choice of Israeli handicrafts, including chunky silver jewelry, pottery, and embroidered caftans, is available at **Maskit**, *Ben Yehuda Street off Frishman Street.* Dizengoff Street, lined with trees and cafés and bistros that rival those of Paris, is the place to shop for high fashion and diamonds (cut and polished in Netanya, 19 miles to the north).

Israel's best night life
Tel Aviv's discos are the best in the country. Try **Colosseum**, *Kikar Atarim*, where you can dance until 4 a.m.

Music and theater flourish in Tel Aviv. The 3,000-seat **Mann Auditorium** is the home of the world-famous Israeli Philharmonic, which gives 180 concerts a year, often with such acclaimed Israeli-born musicians as Itzhak Perlman and Pinchas Zuckerman. Habimah, the famous repertory group, and the Cameri Theater offer first-class productions of classical and contemporary drama. The ticket office is on *Ibngzirol Street.; tel. (972-2)527-9797;* purchase tickets as far in advance as possible.

The most delicious dining
The best restaurants in Tel Aviv can be found along the old port. **Restaurant Yamit**, *18 Kikar Kedumim; tel. (972-3)825-353*, has an outdoor terrace with a view of the sea and serves good drinks. It is open from 10 a.m. until midnight A good place for Yemenite food is the **Zion Restaurant**, *28 Peduyim St.; tel. (972-3)658-714*, which is open 11:30 a.m. until midnight. Dizengoff Street cafés remain open on the Sabbath. Especially recommended is **Cherry's**, *145 Ben Yehuda St.; (972-3)524-0134*, which is open from 7 a.m. until 2 a.m. and serves breakfast, lunch, and dinner. For a great meal on Saturday, visit the **Taj Mahal**, *12 Kikar Kedumim; tel. (972-3)821-002;* it is open for lunch from noon until 3 p.m. and for dinner from 7 p.m. until midnight.

374

The best hotels

Considered by many to be the best hotel in Israel, the **Tel Aviv Sheraton**, *115 Hayarkon St.; tel. (972-3)286-6222*, has spacious, air-conditioned rooms, restaurants, discos, and shops. It is within walking distance of the beach and Dizengoff Street shops. A double room is $185 to $200.

Others argue that the **Dan Hotel**, *99 Hayarkon St.; tel. (972-3)5241-111*, is the best in Israel. On the beach close to the city, it is one of the oldest hotels in Tel Aviv. A double room is $195 to $264.

More modestly priced accommodation is available at the **Hotel Tamar**, *8 Gnessin St.; tel. (972-3)5286-997*, where a clean, Spartan room is $30. Slightly better and cheaper still is **Hotel HaGalil**, *23 Bayit Josef; tel. (972-3)5655-036*, where a double room is $17 to $26. This hotel, near Souk HaCarmel, offers rooms with private balconies.

The **Greenhouse**, *201 Dizengoff St.; tel. (972-3)5235-994*, is the best hostel in Tel Aviv; it offers dorms, double rooms, and private apartments with showers for $10 to $40. Call in advance; availability is limited. **Immanuel House Christian Hospice**, *Jaffa; tel. (973-2)821-459*, is a quiet, friendly place built by Peter Ustinov's father. It also has a dorm room, singles, and doubles for $10 to $50. Plan ahead in the busy season.

Jaffa: an offbeat best

Jaffa, the Biblical port town, is now part of Tel Aviv. Its winding lanes are filled with shops, restaurants, and nightclubs. The reconstructed Old City houses an artists' colony, private and public art galleries, and studios. Shops and boutiques here remain open until midnight. The flea market off Aleystion Street is where everyone ends up; it is as colorful as it is inexpensive.

Old Jaffa, with its intimate restaurants and romantic cafés, is a splendid counterpoint to the dangerous and rocky coastline on its border. **Toutoune**, *1 Simpat Mazel Bagim; tel. (972-3)820-693*, is an outstanding restaurant that serves excellent French cuisine on the roof of an old Turkish house. It is rivaled only by **Via Maris**, *6 Kikar Kdumim; tel. (972-3)828-451*, where you can sit on a vine-covered terrace and enjoy delicious seafood and a view of the floodlit town. Both restaurants open for dinner around 6 p.m. and serve until midnight.

Jaffa comes alive at night, especially on Hayarkon Street near the old port and in the new cafés and restaurants around city hall.

Ashkelon: defying fate

Located on the Mediterranean coast 30 miles south of Tel Aviv, **Ashkelon** is a flourishing port city—despite the Biblical prophecy that "Gaza shall be deserted, and Ashkelon shall become desolation" (Zephaniah 2:4). In response to the prophecy, the center of town is named Zephaniah Square.

Ashkelon, associated with Samson and his battles with the Philistines, is one of the three famous Philistine city-states. The seaside National Antiquities Park here has ancient ruins, including pillars and walls dating back to Canaanite times. The most extensive ruins are Roman, and the haphazard collection of columns, statues, and capitals is highlighted by the Boulouterion, the third-century square filled with marble statues of Atlas, Nike, and Isis.

You can rent a bungalow for $20 or a caravan for $28, including use of a public shower. Contact the campground, *P.O. Box 5052; tel. (972-51)736-777*.

Ashkelon is big on tennis. Its tennis center has 17 courts, and the Ashkelon Tennis Tournament plays to a crowd of 2,000. For more information, contact the **Ashkelon Tourist Center**, *tel. (972-51)732-412*.

The world's best spa: the Dead Sea

The greatest natural wonder of Israel is one of the healthiest as well. At 400 meters below sea level, the **Dead Sea** region is the lowest point on earth. As a result, it has one of the driest climates in the world, and its pure and pollen-free air is especially good for those with allergies or respiratory problems. (People with skin disorders also come here for the therapeutic ultraviolet rays.) Because this region has the highest atmospheric pressure on earth (which reduces the danger of sunburn), it is one of the most relaxing places to sunbathe—and it has more than 300 cloudless days a year.

The main wonder is the sea itself, with 10 times as much salt as any ocean in the world. The surface of the calm brown water is periodically broken by the green-white salt mounds. It is considered the only sea in which you cannot drown, because the salt-laden water makes you float like a cork. Don't try to swim if you have cuts—the salt will irritate them.

The shores of the sea are lined with resorts and historic sites—few tourists realize just how lively the Dead Sea is.

Mezad Zohar, near Jericho on the Dead Sea coast, is an ancient stronghold surrounded by fantastic rock formations. Natural freshwater bathing pools mark green oases.

Ein Gedi, *tel. (972-57)84757*, about 11 miles north of Masada, is the oasis where David hid from King Saul. Now a kibbutz facing the Dead Sea, it contains waterfalls, a nature reserve, hot springs, and an archeological site. A double room at the guesthouse is $80.

A revitalizing visit to the Dead Sea spa is a must. Spend a week at the five-star **Moriah Dead Sea Spa Hotel**, *tel. (972-57)584-221*, enjoying Dead Sea hydrotherapy and treatment in pools and mud. When you are fed up with the brackish water, you can swim in fresh water (indoors or out) or use the hotel's various sports facilities. Rates will vary depending on the package and the season, but a two-week package (that includes a treatment for arthritis) is $1,500.

If you're going to the Dead Sea, also visit **Arad**. Located a half-hour from the Dead Sea, but 3,500 feet higher, Arad sits on a plateau overlooking an ancient Roman fort. This Biblical city, renovated in the 1960s, is a mixture of old and new. The nearby Tel Arad excavations include a temple dating back to King Solomon and a fortress that was rebuilt six times before Julius Caesar was born.

The best Dead Sea digs

The best areas to stay in while visiting the Dead Sea are En Boqeq and Arad. The **Margoa Arad**, *Moav Street, P.O. Box 20; tel. (972-57)957-014*, has a nightclub, a cinema hall, and a private pool. A double room is $80 in high season.

The two outstanding hotels in En Boqeq are **Ein Bokek**, *tel. (972-57)584-331*, which has a pool, a nightclub, and tennis courts, and the **Moriah Gardens Hotel**, *tel. (972-57)584-351*, a four-star hotel with an outdoor pool, an indoor seawater pool, a private beach, and a famous spa fed by waters of the Zohar Hot Springs. A double room at either is $130 to $145.

The **Ein Gedi kibbutz**, *tel. (972-57)84-757*, has a reasonably priced guesthouse. The 92 rooms have televisions and radios and cost only $80, including two meals.

For more information on hotels in the area of the Dead Sea, contact the **Arad Tourist Information Office**, *tel. (972-57)958-144*; it is open 9 a.m. until 5 p.m.

Masada—the most dramatic

Masada, the famous hilltop fortress built by King Herod, is one of Israel's most important sights. Commanding a view of the pink mountains of Moab, Masada was the last stronghold of the Jews when Rome invaded the country. In 73 B.C., after three years of fighting, the Romans finally broke through Masada's defenses only to find that the 960 rebels had committed mass suicide rather than surrender to slavery. Built on a cliff that drops 1,300 feet, Masada is dramatic in both history and appearance.

The peak can be reached either by foot (follow the Snake Path) or by cable cars, which run every 15 minutes from the eastern side of the mountain. The bathhouses, storehouses, water cisterns, and Herod's three-tiered palace have been restored. See the mosaics in the lavish palace halls; the world's largest collection of first-century Roman and Jewish coins; the world's oldest synagogue; and the Mikvot, the world's oldest extant ritual immersion baths, predating baptism by 100 years.

Jericho—the world's oldest city

Jericho, the world's oldest city, was a walled community as early as 7000 B.C. According to the Old Testament, Joshua toppled Jericho's walls with trumpet blasts. Since then, the city has been rebuilt and destroyed several times. Lush scenery surrounds this oasis. Explore the many levels of the ruins and the remains of the magnificent palaces.

Haifa—the prettiest city

Although **Haifa** is heavily industrialized, it is one of the most beautiful cities in Israel. The nation's third-largest city and main port, it has been compared to San Francisco. Hugging a beautiful bay on the Mediterranean, it encompasses the hilly suburb of Mount Carmel.

Israel's biggest museum

The **Haifa Museum Complex**, *26 Shabatai Levi St.; tel. (972-4)523-255*, is one of the largest in Israel, with three separate exhibits: Israeli modern art, ancient art, and Jewish folklore and ethnology. Visit 10 a.m. until 5 p.m. Tuesday through Thursday. Also visit the **Haifa Illegal Immigration and Naval Museum**, *204 Derech Allenby; tel. (972-4)536-249*. It illustrates the history of Jewish migration to Palestine when it was under British mandate. (Although the British outlawed further migration, Israelis managed to smuggle their relatives in for another 20 years.) The museum is open 9 a.m. until 4 p.m. Sunday through Thursday, 9 a.m. until noon Friday and Saturday.

Highest tech in the Middle East

The **Technion** (Israel Institute of Technology), *Neve Sha'anan; tel. (972-4)230-111*, is the university that makes Israel the most technologically advanced nation in the Middle East. Covering 300 acres and including 50 buildings, it has a panoramic view of the city, the bay, and, on clear days, Lebanon. Students from all over the world can be seen strolling the campus lawns. Stop by the Coler-California Visitor Center on campus, where a robot welcomes you and a free film is shown about the technological discoveries made here.

The world's most internationally minded religion

Haifa is the world center of **Baha'i**, a religion that broke away from Islamic mysticism in the 19th century. The Baha'i believe in the unity of all religions and advocate an international language and government.

Few travelers visit the beautiful gold-domed **Baha'i Shrine and Gardens**, halfway up Mount Carmel. (You can get there via Bus 23 from Hanevi'im Street.) The Bab, the herald of the primary Baha'i prophet, Bahaullah, is buried in the shrine. (Bahaullah is buried a few miles north of Haifa in Akko.) You must remove your shoes to enter the shrine. The gardens are filled with statues of animals and graceful cypress trees. You can visit 9 a.m. until noon.

The **Baha'i International Archives** and the **Baha'i Universal House of Justice** are also located in Haifa. The archives were modeled after the Parthenon, and the House of Justice is noted for its 58 marble columns and its hanging gardens. Unfortunately, neither attraction is open to tourists.

Israel's largest national park

Mount Carmel, the site of Elijah's confrontation with the priests of Ba'al, is the site

377

of Israel's largest national park, with 25,000 acres of eucalyptus and cypress forests, picnic areas, and a restaurant. At the peak of the mountain are hanging gardens. Beautiful homes cling to the slopes. Mount Carmel also has some of Haifa's best hotels. Climb the mountain just before sunset, when the sun is a flaming red ball, dipping below the horizon.

The best restaurants

Haifa's speciality is seafood. The two best places to enjoy it are downtown: **Neptune,** *19 Pinhas Margolin St.; tel. (972-4)535-205,* and **Misabag,** *29 Pinhas Margolin St.; tel. (972-4)524-441.*

The best place for a traditional home-style Jewish meal is **Shmulik & Dany,** *7 Habankim St.; tel. (972-4) 514-411.* This popular establishment papers its walls with rave reviews and fine paintings. Try the roast duck, the house specialty.

Peer, *1 Atlit St.; tel. (972-4)665-707,* is a good Arabic restaurant open for breakfast, lunch, and dinner.

The best place for European food is **Bankers Tavern,** *2 Habankim St; tel. (972-4)528-439.*

Haifa's best hotels

Haifa's best hotel is the five-star **Dan Carmel,** *85-87 Sderot Hanassai; tel. (972-4)386-211,* with the most luxurious rooms and the best view of Haifa Bay in the city. A double room is $150 to $180.

Almost as good and less expensive is **Yaarot Hacarmel Rest House,** *Mount Carmel; tel. (972-4)229-144,* where a double room is $50 to $60.

Nof, *101 Sederot Han Nasi, Carmel; tel. (972-4)354-311,* has a panoramic view and luxurious rooms. The restaurant serves excellent kosher food. A double room is $95.

Another good hotel in Carmel is the **Shulamit,** *15 Kiryat Sefer St.; tel. (972-4)342-811.* A double room is $80 to $95.

Highlights near Haifa

Ten miles south of Haifa is **En Hod,** a famous artists' colony that is open to the public. It is situated on Atlit Beach, where a castle juts up from the water. This was the site of the Crusaders' last stand before they were expelled from the Holy Land.

Nahariyya, a half-hour north of Akko (Acre), is an old-fashioned village where horse-drawn carriages are still the mode of transportation. This friendly town is a popular Israeli honeymoon resort. A small stream flows through the center of town into a wide beach, where legend has it that man first learned to make glass. Sailors made a huge bonfire on the sand, so powerful and hot that it turned part of the beach into glass.

Israel's best beach

Akko is one of the oldest (it existed more than 3,500 years ago) and most picturesque cities in the world. Surrounded by thick seawalls on the tip of a point of land, the city is fringed with palm trees and punctuated with minarets. Only 14 miles north of Haifa, it was an important Phoenician port and later served as a capital for the Crusaders.

On the southern edge of Akko is the **Argaman,** or purple beach, the most beautiful beach on the coast, with crystal-clear water.

Akko was the site of the largest prison break in history. On May 4, 1947, 251 prisoners were freed from the prison known as the Fortress by Jewish underground fighters. The movie *Exodus,* which is about the escape, was filmed here. Part of the prison, known as the Museum of Heroes, contains Jewish memorabilia and the cell where Bahaullah was imprisoned in the 1860s. The other part of the prison is a mental hospital.

Most of Akko's sights are in the Old City, including the remains of an underground Crusader town, the Al-Jazzar mosque (the third largest in Israel), caravansarais, and Oriental markets. If you admire architecture, you will be dazzled by the ramparts, minarets, spires, and domes. The city's high walls, alleys, and stairways are thick with fragrances from the Arab market.

Akko is considered the holiest place on earth by people of the Baha'i faith. Their prophet, Bahaullah, is buried here, at the shrine at Bahji. He was brought to the Ottoman-Victorian house here to die after spending two years in the Fortress. His ornate tomb is covered with flowers and gold designs. The house (now his shrine) contains memorabilia of the leader. The surrounding gardens are lush and peaceful.

Concerts are held from time to time at Knights' Hall in **Crusader Castle.** The Haifa Symphony Orchestra performs here, 10 feet below ground because of the good acoustics. During mid-October, the Knights' Hall hosts the **Akko Theater Festival.**

The **Argaman Motel,** *P.O. Box 153, Akko Beach; tel. (972-4)916-691,* has one of the most beautiful views of the sea in Israel, with the walls of the Old City in the foreground. Rooms are spacious, with air conditioning, balconies, telephones, and modern bathrooms. The hotel is located next to the gas station on the Road of the Sea, near Argaman Beach. A double room is $65, including breakfast.

Caesarea—built to rival Baghdad

South of Haifa is **Caesarea,** built by King Herod in the first century B.C. to rival Baghdad. Once the port could hold an entire Roman fleet. Today, it is an impressive recreation center, with horseback riding, swimming, and one of the few 18-hole golf courses in Israel. Concerts, both classical and rock, are held in the Roman amphitheater.

The extensive historical remains in Caesarea include a Roman hippodrome, part of the Roman harbor and aqueducts, and the remains of a Crusader town, walls, and moat. Archeological digs continue constantly in Caesarea.

The beach in Caesarea is pleasant. The famous Sharon Coast runs from Caesarea down to Tel Aviv—this is where the lilies of Sharon bloom in the sand during the fall.

If you stay in Caesarea, your best bet is the **Dan Caesarea Golf Hotel,** *tel. (972-63)62-266,* which has three restaurants, a pool, tennis courts, a sauna, and a Turkish bath. The beach and shops are nearby. A double room is $150 before July and up to $200 after July, including breakfast.

Galilee—pastoral perfection

Galilee, in northeast Israel, is a green region dotted with small cities and world-famous historical sites. It borders the **Sea of Galilee,** which is also called Lake Kinneret (which translates as violin-shaped harp), because of its shape.

Greatest knowledge, best baths

Tiberias is the largest city on the shore and a good base from which to tour the area. This holy city, full of synagogues and churches, was founded 2,000 years ago in honor of the purity of Caesar Tiberias (who turned out to be an extremely decadent ruler). For 200 years after the fall of Jerusalem, it acted as the center of Jewish learning, and it was here that the books of Jewish law, the Mishnah and the Gamorah, were written.

Tiberias is also a winter resort, where foreigners and natives have traveled for hundreds of years to enjoy the therapeutic hot springs. After you've wandered through the city's bazaars, shops, and monuments, a visit to the health resort Hamme Teverya will limber up your aching muscles.

The best restaurant in Tiberias is the little-known Lido. Located right on the water, it serves delicious Near Eastern food. Try the grilled St. Peter fish.

You won't find much in the way of night life in Tiberias. Across the Dead Sea, however, the En Gev Music Festival is held every year during Passover.

In the footsteps of Jesus

Outside the city are numerous landmarks easily reached by bicycle, taxi, bus, or boat.

Capernaum (Kefar Nahum) was the site of Jesus' first miraculous cures, as well as where He found His first disciples. Nearby is the **Mount of Beatitudes**, where Jesus delivered the Sermon on the Mount. **Qursi**, on the opposite side of the lake, has the remains of a beautiful church and monastery built on the site where Jesus drove the devils out of a possessed man and into a herd of swine.

Tabgha, traditional site of the miracle of loaves and fishes, has an ornate church with a Byzantine mosaic floor. And in nearby **Hittim** is the Nebi Shueib, the Druze holy place. **Jethro**, the father-in-law of Moses, is buried here.

Near the sea is **Kafr Kanna**, with its impressive Fransiscan and Greek churches. Have a glass of wine here; this is where Jesus performed His first miracle, changing water into wine.

To complete your religious/historical tour of Galilee, visit **Nazareth**, just to the south. The childhood home of Jesus is filled with shrines, including Mary's Well, the Church of St. Joseph, and the Basilica of the Annunciation. Completed in 1966, the basilica is an ornate shrine to which almost every church in the world contributed. And just southeast of Nazareth is an archaeological site that shouldn't be missed. **Bet Shean** is the oldest of the old. Towering above the excavation site is a tell, a mound composed of the remains of successive settlements. The one at Bet Shean consists of 18 cities superimposed one atop the other, attesting to more than 5,000 years of continuous occupation from roughly the fourth millennium B.C. to the early Arab period (in the seventh century).

Safed—mysticism and magic

Take a short trip north to the intriguing hillside town of **Safed** (Zefat), one of the Four Holy Cities of Israel. Jewish refugees expelled from Spain took refuge in this town, which clings to the steep slope of Mount Canaan, in 1492, and Safed became a center for the study of Cabala—Jewish mysticism and magic. (Cabala is so arcane that men may not study it until they are 35 years old and married.)

Six of Safed's old synagogues are named after the city's most learned rabbis of Cabala. The most famous of these is the **Ha'Ari Synagogue**, traditionally guarded by the ghost of Rabbi Luria. (Luria developed a branch of mysticism in the 16th century now known as Lurianic Cabala. The people of Safed named him Ha'Ari, or the Lion.)

Explore the Synagogue Quarter on foot—the streets are too narrow for automobiles. Safed was the site of the first printing press in Israel in 1563. The former Arab Quarter houses a thriving artist's colony, where, among the winding lanes, dozens of painters and artisans work in the sunshine as it glares off the white stone. Most artists open their studios daily to visitors.

Safed's **Rimon Inn**, *tel. (972-69)30-665,* off the standard tourist route in the Artists' Quarter, has secluded rooms with spectacular views. A double room is $100 to 130, including breakfast.

For information about walking tours, contact the **Safed Tourist Information Center**, *50 Jerusalem St.; tel. (972-6)930-633.*

The best horsing-around in Galilee

Kfar Hittin Ranch, *Ms. Shadmot Dvora, Galil Hatchton 15240; tel. (972-67)795-921,* a member of the Israel Camping Union, offers a horseback-riding tour of Galilee. You follow a trail that leads to a lookout on Ginossar Hill, an ancient synagogue near Zukei Arbel, the Ginossar Valley, and through a riverbed to the Sea of Galilee. You'll have a breathtaking view of the Jordan River.

Eilat—the world's best scuba diving

During the winter, fashionable Israelis flock to this port town at the southernmost tip of Israel, on the coast of the Red Sea. The beaches are filled with tanned bodies; the water just offshore is filled with marine life that exists nowhere else—tropical fish the origin of which is lost in time. The Red Sea is part of the African Rift, which runs through East Africa to the gold mines of the Rand in South Africa. **Eilat** has marvelous facilities for skin and scuba diving. One of the best places to rent gear is the **Lucky Divers' Eilat Scuba Center**.

Eilat has one of the best underwater observatories in the world for viewing exotic aquatic life. In spring, the city becomes a bird watchers' paradise, as dozens of migrating species make a stopover here. The colorful annual festival at Eilat (usually held in March) is marked by water sports and moonlight pageants.

If you're a nature lover, explore the Eilat zoo and **Hai-Bar**, an 8,000-acre wildlife preserve where animals from Biblical times are being returned to their natural habitats. Hai-Bar also contains the ruins of Nabataean cities (Nabataea was a small kingdom from 200 B.C. to 300 B.C.) and remnants of the oldest Christian churches in the world. Your hotel should be able to arrrange tours or give you directions.

Neviot, Israel's only nude beach, about 30 miles south, is less crowded than Eilat's beaches.

The best food and lodging

The most elegant restaurant in the city is **La Coquille**, *tel. (972-07)73-461*. It is expensive but luxurious. Located on the North Beach near the Gala Eilat, it offers the finest French food on the Red Sea. It is open 7 p.m. until 1 a.m.

Two good seafood restaurants are **La Bohème**, *Coral Beach; tel. (972-07)37-422*, which is open for lunch and dinner, and the **Last Refuge**, *Hof Aimog Jetty on Coral Beach; tel. (972-59)724-37*, which is only open for dinner.

The best hotel is the **Sonesta Suites Hotel**, *Haraba Road; tel. (972-59)376-222*, with a tennis court, a pool, and a private beach. A double room is $111, including breakfast..

The **Red Sea Sport Hotel**, *Coral Beach; tel. (972-07)7373-145*, is an excellent little hotel with a pool. A double room is $110.

The Golan Heights—the most tension-ridden area

The Israeli-occupied **Golan Heights** is a tension-ridden area, where Palestinians and Israeli soldiers eye each other nervously. Nevertheless, this northwestern region has some of the most interesting archeological treasures in the Middle East. And it is possible to visit the area with a private guide.

Although rusty tanks and occasional passing soldiers color the sandy landscape, **Qazrin**, the municipal center of Golan, is an attractive town. The helpful **Golan Field School**, *tel. (972-06)961-352*, can answer your questions and, when space provides, will give you a lift in one of its buses. Located at the north end of town, the **Golan Archeological Museum**, *tel. (972-6)961-350*, is well laid-out and has informative displays. It is open 9 a.m. until 4 p.m. Sunday through Thursday and 9 a.m. until 1 p.m. Friday and Saturday.

If you can't get a ride with the Golan Field School, Egged runs a $24 tour of the Golan area. It departs Tiberias on Tuesdays, Thursdays, and Saturdays at 8:30 a.m. The tour includes visits to ancient and Christian sites, as well as a stop at Qatzrin, the newest Israeli city. This area is one of the few places where a rented car will come in handy.

Hazor—Israel's biggest archeological site

Hazor, about 10 miles north of the Sea of Galilee, is the biggest excavated archeological site in Israel. The original city, which served as the capital of Biblical Canaan, dates back to 2500 B.C. Centuries after Joshua and the Israelites leveled the city, Solomon rebuilt it. The excavations at Hazor span 4,000 years of history and 22 cities layered one atop the other.

The Hykssos (Hittite) fortress, palaces, tablets, and chariot remains on display show the cruelty of the Hittites, who led the way in using chariots and became the world's first conquerors.

The Best of Australia

> Earth is here so kind that just tickle her with a hoe and she laughs with a harvest.
>
> —*Douglas William Jerrold, 1849*

The world's oldest and smallest continent, Australia offers something for everyone. Nature lovers are fascinated by the Outback, with its rugged terrain and unusual animals. Divers explore the Great Barrier Reef, the largest coral reef in the world, stretching 1,260 miles along Australia's northeast coast. This coast is also the place to enjoy the world's best surfing. Sydney and Melbourne have big-city restaurants, night life, and shopping. And enormous cattle stations cover the interior of the country.

Australia is the world's most isolated country. Because of this, animals, birds, insects, and plants unknown to the rest of the world have evolved here. Nowhere else will you see kangaroos and koala bears, for example. Also because of the country's isolation, the aborigines, who have one of the most intriguing and ancient cultures in the world, were able to continue their way of life—living in harmony with nature—for thousands of years before Europeans arrived. Still largely uninhabitable and unexplored, this continent's vast desert heartland, known as the **Red Centre**, is made up of four great deserts that together occupy 1.2-million square miles.

Australia was formed when Europe and North America were still evolving. The last great geological shifts here took place 230 million years ago. However, some places in Australia date back 1 billion years. Ancient artifacts are stored in the **Great Western Plateau**, in the heart of Australia. A rock found near Marble Bar contained the remains of 3.5 billion-year-old organisms, the oldest forms of life yet discovered. And a dinosaur left his footprint in the rock near Broome.

Only slightly more than 15 million people live in this area roughly the size of the continental United States. Yet this is one of the most highly urbanized nations in the world—almost 85% of all Australians live in or around the cities. Furthermore, Australia boasts one of the world's highest standards of living.

Sydney: the number-one sight

Sydney—a huge city sprawling across 670 square miles and housing 3.5 million people—is the largest, oldest, and most cosmopolitan city in Australia. It is also naturally beautiful, built around a harbor and cradled by the fabulous "Blue Mountains."

Light-colored buildings and red-tile roofs stand out against the blue water and sky. Flowers bloom year-round. And the ocean laps at 150 miles of shoreline.

Life revolves around the harbor and the sea, where thousands of boats vie for space. Scantily clad sun worshipers flock to the city's 30-odd beaches, where topless bathing is the norm. (Three beaches also allow nude bathing.) But Sydney's beaches are never as packed as those at U.S. resorts.

During the Australian summer (from November through February), the city is hot and the humidity is suffocating—which is fine if you intend to spend all your time on the beach but uncomfortable if you are want to explore the city. Sydney's many hills, combined with the heat, are hard on visitors who aren't familiar with the transport system. However, during the winter, Sydney is mild and pleasant.

The summer heat brings Sydneyites outdoors and forces them to shed their clothes. At night, the inner streets of Sydney are overflowing with people, who eat outdoors and often party on until dawn.

The best view of Sydney

The best view of Sydney is from the 48th-floor, glassed-in skywalk at the **Australia Square Tower,** which is the tallest building in the Southern Hemisphere. You'll be able to see the entire city, the Blue Mountains, and Botany Bay. What's more, the tower (which isn't square but round, constructed of steel, cement, and glass) has the fastest elevators in the Southern Hemisphere.

While you are in the building, stop off at the sixth-floor **Opal Skymine,** where you can see films about life in the Australian opal mines and supposedly buy gems at field prices.

If you can afford it, lunch at the **Summit Restaurant,** on the 47th floor, the largest revolving restaurant in the world. Needless to say, the view is superb—even if the fare isn't.

The best way to see Sydney

The **Sydney Pass** is the best bargain for sightseeing in Sydney. The pass allows you three days of unlimited use of the Sydney Explorer bus, the harbour shuttle, three different harbour cruises, all other Sydney ferry services, all Sydney buses, and the airport express bus. The pass is A$39 ($30) for adults, A$29 ($23) for children, and A$95 ($74) for families.

The world's most unusual opera house

When work began on Sydney's ultramodern winged **opera house** in 1957, local residents, who called it the New South Whale and the Operasaurus, said it wouldn't fly. Much to its critics' chagrin, the opera house turned out to be the most beautiful in the world, praised from London to Hong Kong.

Designed by Danish architect Joern Utzon, the A$102 million ($140 million) structure on Bennelong Point, surrounded by Sydney's harbor, is topped by interlocking wing-shaped roofs that glitter with more than 1 million Swedish ceramic tiles. The acoustics are the best in the world.

Take a tour of the building to see the treated timber panels, the tinted glass through which you have a view of the harbor, and the bright blue curtains. The opera house has a total of 980 rooms, four of which are performance halls, where concerts, operas, ballets, plays, and recitals are held. Rock'n'roll groups perform as well as symphony orchestras. Tours are available from 9 a.m. until 4 p.m. and cost A$8.50 ($6.50) for adults, A$5 ($4) for children and students. Backstage tours are A$12 ($9.50). Book through **Visitor's Services,** *tel. (61-2)250-7250.*

Sydney's oldest quarter

The **Rocks,** a renovated area on the west side of Circular Quay, was notorious for its rough residents in the mid-1800s. Convicts, sailors, prostitutes, soldiers, whalers, and gangsters gathered on this rocky ridge, known as the Cradle of Sydney. For a map of the no-longer-seedy area, visit the **Information Center,** *104 George St.,* near the Overseas Passenger Terminal.

At the heart of The Rocks is **Argyle Place,** a peaceful park surrounded by pastel houses dressed with wrought-iron grills and balconies. The **Church of the Holy Trinity,** better known as the Garrison Church, was built in 1840. The second-oldest church in Sydney, it is the earliest example of Gothic architecture in Australia, with Gothic arches, mullioned windows, and a red cedar pulpit.

Sydney's oldest house, **Cadman's Cottage,** built in 1816, is just off Argyle Street. Circular Cove once came nearly to the door of this little homestead, built by John Cadman, superintendent of government boats.

The **Argyle Arts Centre,** *18 Argyle St.,* was built in 1820 by convicts as a three-story warehouse. Today the sandstone building houses craft shops and antique stores. Notice the hand-hewn timber. (Convict labor came cheap.) You can buy hand-blown glass, beeswax candles, and pottery here. The center is open from 10 a.m. until 5:30 p.m.

From Argyle Street, take the **Argyle Cut,** a dank 300-foot tunnel hollowed out of solid stone by prisoners 140 years ago. It leads to Miller's Point.

The best picnicking

The best places to get away from the cement and steel that make up Sydney are the Domain and the Botanic Gardens, separated from each other by a highway. The **Domain** is a park with an emerald lawn perfect for picnics and naps on Sunday afternoons. Soapbox orators harangue crowds here with their personal views of the world. The **Botanic Gardens** are known for their exotic flora, including giant Moreton Bay fig trees and hothouses filled with orchids and ferns.

Australia's best art gallery

Near the Botanic Gardens is the **Art Gallery of New South Wales,** *Art Gallery Road; tel. (61-2)225-1700,* divided into two sections, one housing Renaissance to 20th-century art, the second housing Impressionist and modern works. The new wing, with its angled white walls and views of the harbor, is more attractive. Look for works by Australian artists William Dobell, Sidney Nolan, and Russell Drysdale. The gallery is open Mondays through Saturdays 10 a.m. until 5 p.m. and Sundays noon until 5 p.m.

The Southern Hemisphere's best private gallery

Holdsworth Galleries, *86 Holdsworth St.,* is the biggest art gallery south of the equator, with a great collection of contemporary Australian artists that changes every three weeks. Among the displays are paintings and sculptures by Sidney Nolan, Sali Herman, Margaret Olley, and Arthur Boyd. The gallery is as lovely as the works it contains. Admission is free. It is open daily until 5 p.m.

The world's most beautifully situated zoo

Taronga Zoo and Aquarium, on a peninsula jutting into Mosman Bay, has the most beautiful setting of any zoo in the world. It offers a view of the harbor (**Taronga** means *water view* to the aborigines) and 75 acres of bushland. Among other strange creatures, you can see koala bears, emus, platypuses, dingoes, kookaburras, and wombats. A special underground part of the zoo houses nocturnal animals, which you can see under red light. The rain forest aviary is also worth seeing. The zoo is open 9 a.m. until 5 p.m.

The worst prison

Fort Denison, on a little island in the harbor, was known as Pinchgut among Australia's early convicts, because of the starvation rations meted out here. The fort was never actually used to protect Sydney, although that was its original purpose when it was built in 1857. You can still see cannons and cannonballs in the round Martello Tower, which is used as a tidal observation station. Tours of the fort depart Wharf Two on Circular Quay three times a day Tuesdays through Sundays. Call the **Maritime Services Board,** *tel. (61-2)247-2733,* a half-day in advance to make reservations. Admission is A$8 ($6.20) for adults, A$5.50 ($4.30) for children.

Sydney's best beach

Sydney has 34 ocean beaches, each with its own style. If you are looking for peace and quiet, try Whale, Avalon, or Bilgola. But if you want to see a Sydney beach at its best—filled with perfect bodies, sun-streaked blonds, surf bums, and joggers, all in a sunny mood—go to Bondi.

Bondi (pronounced Bond-Eye) has produced many world-champion surfers. The half-mile crescent of sand and surf is filled from dawn to dusk with surfers, sunbathers, and swimmers. Snacks and drinks are available at Bondi Junction, near the beach.

Bondi's neighbor, **Tamarama Beach,** is smaller, prettier, and more peaceful.

Sydney's best shopping

Paddington, or Paddo as it is called, is the best place to shop in Sydney. The area is much like Washington, D.C.'s Georgetown, with restored town houses and colorful little shops.

The major draw is the **Village Bazaar,** held each Saturday from 9 a.m. to 4 p.m. on the grounds of the Uniting Church in Australia. The bazaar feels for all the world like California in the 1960s, filled with lots of long-haired youths. But look closer and you also will see busy matrons searching for dinner. More than 120 stalls sell handicrafts, antiques, clothing, imported goods, and art. This is one of the best places in Australia to find authentic Australian-made goods at bargain prices.

Although the bazaar can be a shopping spree in itself, it should be considered only the starting point of a shopping journey through Paddington. Along Oxford Street, the main thoroughfare, and its side streets, you will discover antique shops, boutiques, art galleries, bookstores, craft shops, jewelers, and record shops.

Paddo's best shops include **Jack O'Beans,** *264 Oxford St.,* an elegant antique store; the **Australian Centre for Photography,** *257 Oxford St.,* for Australian and international photo art; **Game Birds,** *108 Oxford St.,* for made-to-order leather and lace fashions; **Cooee Australian Emporium,** *98 Oxford St.,* for custom-designed jewelry; and **Angelo's,** *112 Oxford St.,* for handmade boots and shoes.

Sample homemade Russian chocolates at **W. Pulknownik's,** *Oxford and Elizabeth streets.*

To get to Paddington from downtown Sydney, take the 380 bus from Circular Quay to Oxford Street or bus 378 from Railway Square.

The best times to visit

Each year, Sydney hosts a number of different festivals. The entire month of January is one big festival, with plays, exhibitions, operas in the parks, sailboat races, and food and wine fairs. Then come the Royal Sydney Easter Show, which is a huge country fair with animal exhibitions; Royal Gardens Week; Carnivale; and the Blessing of the Fishing Fleet. And don't miss the Gay Mardi Gras, one of the biggest gay festivals held anywhere in the world.

Sydney's favorite pastimes

Surfing (which many schools teach as a physical-education course) and windsurfing are the two passions of Sydneyites. A sign on trains admonishes, "Surfers, be considerate. Don't block aisles with your boards."

Australia's best restaurant

Outside Sydney is the **Berowra Waters Inn,** *Berowra Waters; tel. (61-2)456-1027,* the finest restaurant in Australia. Chef Gay Bilson produces innovative Australian dishes. Unfortunately, you can't get here by road; you must fly or take a boat. The restaurant is open for lunch Friday through Sunday and for dinner Friday and Saturday.

Sydney's best dining bets

Sydney's best restaurant is **Oasis Seros,** *495 Oxford St., Paddington; tel. (61-2)361-3377,* a simple but stylish place that serves light food made from fresh ingredients. The china, crystal, and cutlery are elegant, and an enormous bouquet of flowers adorns the mantelpiece.

A small Italian restaurant known as **No Name,** *81 Stanley St.; tel. (61-2)357-4711,* has delicious food, an unpretentious atmosphere, and low prices. It's located in a little house on Chapel Street, a short street in East Sydney near the intersection of Crown and Stanley streets.

The best place for seafood is **Doyle's on the Beach,** *11 Marine Parade, Watson's Bay; tel. (61-2)337-2007.* Enormous platesful of battered fish are served. And the setting is lovely—a sandy beach lined with little boats. The only drawback is that the restaurant's charms are known, and it's crowded.

Also at Watson's Bay is the **Fisherman's Lodge,** a pleasant restaurant housed in a 19th-century mansion. The **Endeavor at Mosman,** across the Harbor Bridge, is in an old ship.

Bellevue Hotel, *159 Hargrave,* in Paddo, has a back-garden barbecue and live entertainment.

Sydney's top hotels

Sydney's finest hotel is the **Regent,** *199 George St.; tel. (61-2)238-0000.* Overlooking the opera house and the harbor, it has luxurious rooms and an attentive staff. A double room is A$205 to A$280 ($160 to $218). In the United States, make reservations through **Leading Hotels of the World,** *(800)223-6800.*

Three close seconds are the **Sheraton-Wentworth,** *tel. (61-2)230-0700,* where a double room is A$240 to A$270 ($187 to $210); the **Inter-Continental,** *117 Macquarie St.; tel. (61-2)230-0200;* and the **Parkroyal Hotel,** *tel. (61-2)977-7666,* where a double room is A$220 to A$260 ($170 to $203).

Outside the business district, near King's Cross, is the discreet and elegant **Sebel Town House,** *23 Elizabeth Bay Road, Elizabeth Bay; tel. (61-2)358-3244* (also represented by Leading Hotels of the World). This place is popular among celebrities, whose signed photographs paper the walls at the bar. A double room is A$190 ($148).

Another attractive small hotel is the **Russell,** *143a George St.; tel. (61-2)241-3543,* where Rachel Ward stays when she's in town.

The hottest night life

Although Sydney's drinking laws are strict, the local residents manage to have a rowdy good time anyway. Bars close at 11 p.m. during the week, after midnight on weekends and holidays (depending on the area). But many Sydneyites belong to private clubs, where you can get beer into the wee hours of the morning. The clubs often have live shows, slot machines, and food.

Sydney's chic set—good-looking models, visiting rock stars, and well-dressed socialites—makes a point of being seen at **Arthur's Bar and Restaurant,** *155 Victoria St., Potts Point; tel. (61-2)358-5097;* **The Cauldron,** *207 Darlinghurst Road, Darlinghurst; tel. (61-2)331-1523;* and the **Freezer,** *11 Oxford St., Paddington; tel. (61-2)332-2568.*

If you'd like to barhop but don't want to drive or risk getting lost, go to the **Holiday Inn Menzies,** *14 Carrington St.,* where 20 pubs share one roof. Each has its own character and clientele, from snooty and expensive to cheap and blue-collar.

The liveliest neighborhood at night is **King's Cross,** a combination Greenwich Village and red-light district, where Darlinghurst, Potts Point, and Elizabeth Bay meet. Darlinghurst Road and Macleay Street are the main thoroughfares. Sydney's best bar is here, the **Bourbon and Beefsteak,** *Darlinghurst Road; tel. (61-2)357-1215.* The piano bar provides entertainment in the early evening, and jazz combos jam later on.

Sydney's oldest pub is in the **Hero of Waterloo Hotel,** *81 Lower Fort St.,* in The Rocks. Built in 1804 as a jail, it became a rousing pub in the rip-roaring 1800s. Today it is a peaceful place to have a drink while sitting beside a fireplace.

The **Manzil Room,** *15 Springfield Ave., King's Cross,* has live music until dawn all week.

The bluest mountains

The **Blue Mountains** really are a vivid blue. Oil released by the mountains' eucalyptus trees reflects the blue light rays of the sun on these saw-toothed peaks, just 50 miles from Sydney. Head for **Katoomba,** where you can take the Scenic Railway, the steepest in the world, up the mountains. Or you can ride the Scenic Skyway, a cable car dangling above a deep chasm. Nearby are the enormous Jenolan Caves and the giant waterfall at Govett's Leap, near Blackheath.

Australia's best skiing

The **Snowy Mountains,** 300 miles southwest of Sydney, are much higher than the Blue Mountains. Covered with snow from June to late August, they are a great place to ski. Australia's highest peak is here, **Mount Kosciusko** (known as Mount Kozzie locally), which rises 7,314 feet.

Although skiing in Australia is as spectacular as skiing in the Alps (Australia has more snow than Switzerland), it is much less expensive. An all-inclusive six-day ski package can cost as little as A$500 ($390). And it's one big party. Aussies drink until dawn, then manage to ski the 25 miles of trails flawlessly.

The Snowy Mountains are worth a visit off-season as well, when prices are even lower and you can take a 1 1/2-mile chair lift to the top of Mount Crackenback. The fishing, swimming, and hiking can't be beat.

The world's most imaginative water festival

Surf Carnivals are hosted by the Surf Lifesaver's Association; they are perhaps the world's most imaginative water festivals. Not only do the macho members of the Surf Club compete in paddling wooden boats against a crashing surf, diving for plastic batons, and squatting on surfboards while hand paddling their way across the finish line, but the senior members of the Lifesavers Association, in units of 12, are judged for posture, pace, and unity. For more information, contact the **Surf Lifesavers Association of Australia,** *128 The Grand Parade, Brighton-le-Sands, New South Wales 2216; tel. (61-2)597-5588.*

Capital Canberra

Canberra, the national capital, is a city planner's dream. Designed to function expressly as Australia's capital, it is free of traffic and unsightly shopping malls. At its heart is a large man-made lake. Throughout the city are parks, and the broad avenues are lined with trees. An American named Walter Burley Griffin designed the city in 1913, after winning an international competition for the job. However, Australia's parliament didn't actually meet here until 1927.

While it is not on the coast and doesn't have sunny beaches, Canberra is fast becoming an artistic and intellectual enclave. It boasts the new National Gallery, one of the finest art museums in Australia, and great restaurants and bars.

Canberra's top sights

The city's best-known landmark is the **Captain Cook Memorial Water Jet,** which shoots 6 tons of water 450 feet into the air from 10 a.m. to noon and 2 p.m. to 4 p.m. every day. Part of the fountain is a 9-foot globe illustrating the routes followed by Captain Cook.

More important, however, is the **Australian War Memorial**, on Anzac Parade, a beautiful structure honoring the 100,000 Australians who died fighting in the world wars. Bronze panels inscribed with their names cover two enormous walls. The memorial contains excruciatingly realistic paintings of the wars, as well as old biplanes, tanks, and bombs. The **Australian National Gallery**, on the shores of the lake, has an outstanding collection of works by both Australians and foreigners. It also has a good restaurant with a lovely view of the lake. The memorial is open daily.

Canberra's **carillon** is one of the largest in the world, with 53 bells, the largest weighing more than 6 tons. A gift from Britain, the tall white pillar stands at the northern end of the Kings Avenue Bridge. Recitals are given on Sundays and Wednesdays.

The **Institute of Anatomy** on the campus of the Australian National University has a good museum illustrating the culture of the aborigines and the natives of New Guinea.

The **Botanic Gardens**, *Clunies Ross Street,* is a maze of footpaths and bridges that guide you over little ponds and through gardens with carefully labeled Australian plants and flowers.

For a glimpse of Australia's early pioneer life, visit **Blundell's Farmhouse**, *Wendouree Drive,* off Constitution Avenue. Built in 1858, the cottage's three rooms are filled with pioneer furnishings. It is open from 2 p.m. until 4 p.m. daily and 10 a.m. until noon on Wednesdays.

Twenty-five miles southwest of Canberra is the 12,000-acre **Tidbinbilla Nature Reserve**, where you can see local flora and fauna and feed the kangaroos. This unspoiled bushland is open daily from 9 a.m. to 6 p.m.

The best eating and sleeping

Charlie's, *Bunder Street,* is an elegant restaurant with French cuisine and especially good soups. Politicians eat here when Parliament is meeting.

Rascals, *33 Petrie Plaza,* is a restaurant with the atmosphere of a disco. A good place for after-theater supper, it stays open until 2 a.m. The decor is pleasant, with low ceilings and stained-glass windows. Prices are moderate.

Gus's Café, *Bunda Street,* is a tiny place with a pleasant outdoor terrace surrounded by flower boxes. You can linger over a meal here, reading Gus' selection of magazines and newspapers. Save room for the cheesecake, which is out of this world.

Tall Trees, *21 Stephen St., Ainslie; tel. (61-62)479200,* two miles from Canberra, is an inviting lodge named for the tall trees that surround it. All rooms have views of the gorgeous gardens and are supplied with electric blankets. (It gets cold here during the winter.) The lodge has a laundry room and a lounge with a television and tea-making equipment. A double room is A\$32 to A\$78 (\$25 to \$61).

Chelsea Lodge, *526 Northbourne Ave.,* is a bed-and-breakfast in a villa with a pleasant veranda. Breakfast is good. All rooms have televisions; two have private bathrooms. A double room is A\$22 (\$17), including breakfast.

The best of Melbourne

Melbourne rivals Sydney as Australia's most attractive city. Both coastal cities have 3 million residents. However, Melbourne is more of a European city and offers more cultural opportunities than Sydney; it also has fewer tourists and lower prices.

Melbourne's weather is less pleasant than Sydney's. It rains more frequently, and winters can be grim, drizzly, and gray, without the excitement of snow.

While Sydney's beauty is natural, Melbourne's is man-made. Because it is a planned city, Melbourne's road network forms a grid pattern, making travel within the city easy. The city's architecture is sophisticated, especially along wide and gracious **Collins Street**, the banking capital of Australia. Lush parks and the Yarra River add greenery to the cityscape.

Although Melbourne was founded in 1835 by a group of Tasmanian entrepreneurs, it didn't actually take off until 1851, when it became the center of Australia's biggest and longest gold rush. A product of the time, Melbourne is mostly Victorian in appearance.

Melbourne's must-sees

The National Museum, the Museum of Science, the state library, and LaTrobe Library are combined in one huge, interconnected complex between Swanston and Russell streets. The strangest sight in the entire complex is the stuffed body of a well-loved Australian racehorse, Phar Lap, who died a mysterious and shady death in the United States. Also look for Australia's first car and first airplane.

Melbourne's creepiest sight is the **Old Melbourne Gaol**, *Russell Street.* Built in 1841, it was used as a prison until 1929. More than 100 prisoners were hanged here. The somber building is now a museum, with death masks of notorious criminals and records of the early convicts transported to Australia from Britain. (Some were exiled for incredibly minor crimes.)

The **National Gallery**, housed in the Cultural Centre Complex on St. Kilda Road, has a good art collection and exhibits from overseas. The Great Hall has a beautiful stained-glass ceiling, and fountains fill the central courtyard. The gallery is closed Mondays.

King's Domain is an enormous park that houses the Shrine of Remembrance, a World War I memorial; Governor LaTrobe's cottage, the original Victorian government house prefabricated and sent from England; and the Sidney Myer Music Bowl, an outdoor concert hall.

The **Royal Botanic Gardens**, also within King's Domain, are the most beautiful in Australia. Laid out beside the Yarra River, they include lakes, a rainbow of flowers, and a surprising number of wild animals, including water fowl, cockatoos, and possums. You can have tea and scones by the lake.

The best shopping

Melbourne's center for shopping buffs is located between Swanston and Elizabeth streets, on Collins and Bourke. This is where you'll find Myers, Australia's biggest department store. Bourke Street is a pedestrian mall, but be careful; trams pass through here at alarming speeds.

Aboriginal Handicrafts, *Ninth Floor, 125 Swanston St.; tel. (61-3)650-4717,* is the best place for honest-to-goodness handicrafts made by Australia's oldest residents. It is open daily from 10 a.m. until 4:30 p.m.

The best bets for fitness freaks

On weekends, you can rent a bicycle at the Botanical Gardens or Como Park and then bike the trail along the Yarra River.

If canoeing is more your style, you can rent a canoe or a rowboat at Studley Park in Kew for A$16 ($12.50) an hour for two people. The **Studley Park Boathouse**, *tel. (61-3)853-8707,* is open from 9:30 a.m. until 5:30 p.m.

The best place to jog is the 2 1/2-mile running track around King's Domain Park. The Tan Track, as it is known, is where Melbourne's fitness freaks race at dawn and dusk.

The world's strangest football game

Australian football—a game all its own that is based on Gaelic football—is a strange combination of soccer and rugby. You can see this one-of-a-kind game at the Melbourne

Cricket Ground in Yarra Park, one of Australia's biggest sports stadiums. The best football game, if you can get tickets, is the Grand Final in September, Australia's biggest sporting event.

Melbourne's best restaurants

Without question, Melbourne beats Sydney when it comes to restaurants. **Fanny's**, *243 Lonsdale Street; tel. (61-3)663-3017*, is one of the best restaurants in Australia, a cozy little place with international fare. If you want an elegant night out, eat upstairs. If you'd rather save your Australian dollars, eat in the little bistro downstairs. It is less chic but serves the same food at much lower prices.

The city's best seafood restaurant is **Jean Jacques by the Sea**, *40 Jacka Blvd., St. Kilda; tel. (61-3)534-8221.*

Mietta's Melbourne, *7 Alfred Place; tel. (61-3)654-2366*, is a lovely restaurant in an old Victorian building. A piano bar is located downstairs. **Stephanie's**, *405 Tooronga Road; tel. (61-3)822-8944*, is another romantic place, in an elegant historic mansion.

Melbourne is famous for its ethnic cuisine. Chinatown (Little Bourke Street), for example, is a thriving neighborhood with pagoda-style buildings. The aroma of hanging ducks and ginseng fills the air. The best restaurant here is **Flower Drum**, *17 Market Lane; tel. (61-3)662-3655.*

Turkish and Mideastern restaurants are sprinkled along Sydney Road. The Richmond district, just east of downtown Melbourne, off Swan Street, is also heavily ethnic, with Greek, Turkish, Argentine, Indian, Vietnamese, and Mexican restaurants. Lygon Street, near the university, is a busy row of Lebanese and Italian restaurants.

The best hotels

One of the great landmarks of Melbourne is the **Windsor Hotel**, *Spring Street; tel. (61-3)630261.* Recently restored, the Victorian hotel has a domed Grand Dining Room, decorated with silk wallpaper and crystal chandeliers. Visiting statesmen stay here. A double room is A$103 to A$115 ($80 to $90).

The **Regent**, *Collins Place, 25 Collins St.; tel. (61-3)653-0000*, is a work of modern art, with a sky-lit atrium filled with little white bulbs. Occupying the top 15 floors of a 50-story building, the hotel has panoramic views of the city. Jackie Collins stayed in the Kensington Suite on the top floor, which has windows from floor to ceiling. A double room is A$280 to A$1,800 ($218 to $1,400).

Rockman's Regency, *Lonsdale and Exhibition streets; tel. (61-3)662-3900*, has suites with private jacuzzis that hold five people at a time. The bar is nice, but it's open only to guests. John McEnroe stays here. A double room starts at A$195 ($152).

The dullest night life

In Melbourne, lights generally go out well before midnight. However, you can enjoy the arts at the city's new theater complex and concert hall. Luciano Pavarotti praised the Melbourne concert hall as the finest in the world.

Melbourne does have one New York-style dance spot. **Inflation**, *60 King St.; tel. (61-3)614-6122*, has a gigantic video screen and a huge dance floor. The crowd is lively.

Palace, *Lower Esplanade, St. Kilda; tel. (61-3)534-0655*, is also a fun place.

The best of Perth

Perth, the largest city on Australia's west coast, is the most isolated city in the world. Adelaide, the closest town, is more than 1,000 miles away. It takes three days to get to Perth by train from Sydney. Because of their isolation, the 1 million residents of Perth are close-knit and friendly.

Perth has many parks and wide-open spaces, miles of great beaches, good hotels, and a wide variety of ethnic restaurants. But best of all, it has the most ideal weather in

Australia, more like the Mediterranean than Down Under. Although it's not as hot as Sydney, it offers more continuous hours of sunshine.

Perth's pride

King's Park, a 1,000-acre wilderness area, tops Mount Eliza and offers panoramic views of Perth. At its heart is a fountain dedicated to pioneer women. If you lose track of the time, check the floral clock.

King's Park is a place to stroll at your leisure, enjoying some of Australia's exotic flora and fauna. When you tire, stop for a snack at the park's restaurant.

Other top sights

The **Art Gallery,** *47 James St.,* is one of the best art museums in Australia. It is a dramatic modern building that cost $10 million to build. Masterpieces by Van Gogh, Cézanne, Picasso, and Monet are displayed, as well as works by contemporary Australian artists. Look for the "Art of the Western Desert," created by the Panunya, a tribe of aborigines.

The **Old Mill,** at the end of Narrows Bridge in South Perth, ground flour during the gold rush in the 1800s. Today it houses colonial tools and artifacts.

Perth's best restaurants

The best Chinese food in Perth is **Choi's Inn,** *68 Roe St., tel. (61-9)328-6350.* The restaurant serves Mandarin fare and is located in Perth's Chinatown.

Perth's best seafood restaurant is **Jessica's Fine Seafood,** *Shop 1, Merlin Centre, 99 Adelaide Terrace; tel. (61-9)325-2511,* which has a view of the Swan River. Try the grilled dhufish, a firm, sweet fish found only in Western Australia.

Other good bets are the **River Room** at the Sheraton Perth; the **Oyster Bar,** *20 Roe St., Northbridge;* **Lombardo's,** *Fishing Boat Harbor, Fremantle;* and **Oyster Beds,** on the Swan River at Fremantle. Oyster Beds is especially nice because the Swan River flows directly under the restaurant.

Perth's most pleasant hotels

Celebrities stay at the **Parmelia Hilton,** *Mill Street; tel. (61-9)322-3622.* Excellent service is the main attraction. A double room at the Hilton starts at A$190 ($148).

The **Observation City Resort,** *Esplanade, Scarborough; tel. (61-9)245-1000,* was built on the beach and has spectacular views. A double room starts at A$155 ($121).

Other good hotels are the Orchard, the Parkroyal, the Langley, and the Sheraton Perth.

Perth's best bets

Burswood Restaurant and Casino, *Great Eastern Highway; tel. (61-9)362-7777,* is the largest resort complex in the Southern Hemisphere and the second-largest gaming floor anywhere in the world.

The best of Queensland

Queensland, Australia's northeastern province, is a diverse land made up of many different worlds: the fluorescent Great Barrier Reef in the Coral Sea, the aboriginal reservations; the Daintree Rain Forest, the gold and opal mines in the desert fringe, and the sacred natural art galleries in the pitiless Outback.

The best of Brisbane

Complete with a surfing subculture (at nearby Surfer's Paradise on the Gold Coast), **Brisbane** is often compared to Los Angeles. Homes in Queensland's sprawling capital city sport red-tile roofs and blue swimming pools. The hot sun fosters a casual dress code—men often wear shorts, knee socks, and ties to work. In the fields they wear kepis, military hats with wide brims that snap to the crowns on one side.

Founded as a penal colony for convicts supposedly too tough to be sent to Sydney, Brisbane originally was home to Australia's mining and agricultural industries. Today, tourism is making a bid for first place in the local economy.

While in Brisbane, stop by **Queensland Aboriginal Creations**, *135 George St.*, run by the Department of Aboriginal and Islanders Advancement. You can buy tribal masks, musical instruments, weapons, and bark paintings.

For a boost to your patriotic ego, stop by the memorial called **They Passed This Way**, *Lyndon B. Johnson Place, Newstead Park*, erected as a tribute to the United States after General MacArthur made his headquarters here during World War II.

Forest Park is an oasis of eucalyptus trees and tropical birds just outside Brisbane. Carefully designed walking paths lead through the park and its Botanical Gardens. Stop by the **Sir Thomas Brisbane Planetarium**, the largest in Australia.

The best place to see cuddly koalas is the **Lone Pine Sanctuary**, *Fig Tree Pocket*, west of Brisbane. About 100 of the little bears live here, along with kangaroos, emus, and other Australian animals. You can hold the koalas and feed the kangaroos by hand.

The place to stay in Brisbane is the **Sheraton Brisbane Hotel**, *249 Turbot St.; tel. (61-7)835-3535*. Rooms are beautifully furnished and offer views of the Brisbane River.

Another good bet is the **Hilton International Brisbane**, *190 Elizabeth St.; tel. (61-7)231-3131*.

Surfer's Paradise: the best of the Gold Coast

Just south of Brisbane is **Surfer's Paradise**, the largest and liveliest resort on Australia's 20-mile Gold Coast. The sandy beaches are perfect, the water warm, the surf, as you would expect, terrific—and behind it all are the MacPherson Mountains. Believe it or not, the beach here is even better than in Hawaii. However, the crowds can be unbearable, especially around Christmas and Easter.

A good place to stay is the **Hub Hotel**, *21 Cavill Ave.; tel. (61-75)31-5559*, actually a motel near the beach. Each unit has its own balcony, bathroom, refrigerator, and television. A double room is A$50 ($39) per person.

Cairns: a tropical best

Cairns (pronounced "Cans") is a beautiful fully restored tropical town filled with the aromas of coffee, sugarcane, and orchids. You can walk from one end of Cairns to the other. The jungle encroaches wherever someone hasn't mowed his lawn or raked pesky mangoes from his yard.

A languid town, Cairns sprawls along the northern fringes of the Great Barrier Reef, overlooking blue Trinity Bay. The ramshackle houses, surrounding jungle, and fields of sugarcane lend the town its colonial mystique. Palm trees sway in the wind, and tropical fruits are mainstays of the local diet. Trading ships line the oceanfront.

Cairns can be a best or a worst for women, because it is home to many more men than women. Pubs are often partitioned into separate rooms for men and women, and signals can get crossed if the boundaries are violated.

For decades, Cairns has been a fishing capital of the world, abounding in barramundi, shark, and marlin. It's also the stepping-off point for the world's best black marlin fishing grounds. Although they aren't particularly good eating, black marlin put up one heck of a fight, making for a good battle.

Cairns' real attraction is the nearby **Great Barrier Reef**, which is described below.

Cairns' best hotels

Cairns does have a celebrated hotel or two, including **Harbourside Village**, *209 The Esplanade; tel. (61-70)51-8999*, where a double room is A$125 ($62); the **Pacific In-**

ternational, *43 The Esplanade; tel. (61-70)51-7888*, where a double room is A$90 ($70); and the good old **Hilton International,** *Wharf Street; tel. (61-70)52-1599,* where a double room is A$220 ($109).

Palm Cove, not far from Cairns, has a jet-set resort called the **Reef House**, where bougainvillea scents the air and palm trees rustle in the wind. The resort's restaurant is good.

Australia's best caravan park

Australia's best—and most exotic—caravan park is **Ellis Beach**, 25 km north of Cairns. It is situated among coconut palms, with views of Double Island and right next to the rain forest.

The Great Barrier Reef

Extending 1,260 miles, from New Guinea to the Tropic of Capricorn, the **Great Barrier Reef** passes along the coast of Queensland. Containing more than 2,000 coral reefs, coral islands, and cays, the reef is home to the world's greatest variety of marine life, nearly 1,400 kinds of sea creatures. It is a must-see if you are in Australia. The coral forms stunning natural patterns, and clear and brightly colored fish swim in unison.

Scuba divers from around the world come here to swim among the exotic fish. If you'd rather, you can walk across much of the reef at low tide, when the water recedes. (Wear tennis shoes, the coral is sharp.) Or you can go beyond the danger zones around this coral paradise and swim to your lungs' content.

Australia's best island

Green Island, *tel. (61-70)51-4644,* is the best place to stay while exploring the reef. You can see the submarine world through windows at the island's **Underwater Coral Observatory** or from one of the glass-bottom boats that depart the island regularly.

The beaches that edge the mile-square island are empty except for driftwood trees. Cool coconut palm groves offer refuge from the hot sun. Blue and white herons prance along the sand paths. Even the pigeons here are beautiful—they're green and yellow, not the soot color of North American pigeons. Between the chirping crickets and slapping palms, Green Island is a lively spot.

The cheapest way to get to the island is to book a trip with Great Adventure Tours in Cairns. For about A$25 ($20), you get a boat ride to and from the reef. If the six-hour stay is too short, you can rent a bungalow from **Hayles Resort** for A$60 ($47) per night. Other reef resorts cost triple that.

Another beautiful reef resort is **Dunk Island**, where you can sleep in a beach-front cottage for A$130 ($100). You can spend your days snorkeling, swimming, walking in the rain forest, and playing golf and tennis.

Queensland's best market

Take the train from Cairns to **Kuranda**, which has an outdoor market selling Indonesian batiks, native opals, and sapphires. The town is a short walk from the market, past the reconstruction of a settlers' village and an aboriginal art gallery that sells bark paintings. (These barks cost less and look better than those in Sydney or Melbourne.)

Tarzan's favorite: Queensland's rain forests

Not far from Brisbane are misty rain forests where orchids scent the air and parrots sing from thick canopies of leaves hundreds of feet in the air. More than 800 kinds of trees grow in these forests, many with buttressed trunks that form church-size caves. Giant ferns, orchids, ginger plants, and organ-pipe fungi grow together in a thick web that blocks out the sun. You can swing like Tarzan from thick vines. Butterflies, tree frogs, snakes, and bugs make their homes here. (The best time to visit is during the less-buggy dry season, from May to November.)

The rain forest closest to Brisbane is at **Mount Glorious,** a 45-minute drive away. Slightly farther on, at **Mount Tamborine,** are six rain forest parks. While hiking here, stop at the Maiala Rain Forest Café to enjoy English tea served with fresh scones, jam, and thick cream, while savoring the fragrance of jasmine and watching colorful parrots. Just 2 1/2 hours south of Brisbane is the **Lamington Plateau,** where you can stay at Binna Burra or O'Reilly's Lodge.

The densest and least-spoiled rain forests are 1,000 miles north of Brisbane (closer to Cairns): Kurando, Lake Eachem, Lake Barrine, Daintree River, and Cape Tribulation.

Hayles Tours runs a private bus service from Cairns to Cape Tribulation. The one-store town is near a good youth hostel with compound huts that surround a free-form swimming pool and a patio of logs sliced in cross sections. The restaurant serves fresh fish on ginger rice topped with coconut milk and flanked by mango strips—all for A$5 ($4).

Peacocks and parrots roam Cape Tribulation, which begins the **Daintree Rain Forest,** said to be the oldest on earth. The controversial new road that cuts through the forest is threatened by roots reaching down from branches to reclaim the red mud.

Wear long pants, long sleeves, and a hat to protect yourself from bugs and thorny plants. (Look out for ticks, which are unusually tenacious here; the wait-a-while plant, which has savage thorns; snakes; and leeches.)

Two tour agencies to try for guided trips in the area are **Traffic Wings,** *tel. (61-70)353-555,* and **AAT Kings,** *tel. (61-70)311-155.* They are both in Cairns.

For information on transportation to the rain forests, contact the **Queensland Government Travel Centre,** *196 Adelaide St., Brisbane, Queensland 4000.*

Australia's oldest residents

The aborigines lived in Australia for at least 39,000 years before Britain sent its prisoners to colonize the country. On the shores of Lake Mungo in western New South Wales, evidence remains of a cremation that took place 30,000 years ago. And caves on the Nullabor Plain and a Bass Strait island were occupied 20,000 years ago. Anthropologists estimate that 300,000 aborigines lived in Australia before 1770. They spoke 500 different languages.

The aborigines believe in Dreamtime, an age that existed at the dawn of creation and is still present, a timeless otherworld linking the past, present, and future. Mythological characters from Dreamtime, painted by the aborigines on rocks, can be seen in the **Nourlangie Rock Northern Territory** and at other places throughout the country.

North of Cairns, in Laura, is the **Quinkon Reserve,** which boasts three rock galleries. Some of the paintings date from 13,200 B.C. The cracked and overhanging rocks were chosen because they face east and the rising sun.

The best of the three galleries is the **Split Rock Gallery,** a natural gallery displaying ancient aboriginal cave paintings. Two routes lead from Cairns to the gallery. The easier of the two is through the Outback; the more interesting but riskier route is via the well-named Cape Tribulation through the jungle. You will need an odometer to find the rock walls that are decorated with the murals, because all traces are invisible from the road.

Aborigines continue the artistic ways of their forefathers, decorating weapons, tools, and totems with colorful religious patterns and figures. Tribal dancers hold on to the steps and music symbolizing events in Dreamtime. The best-known dance is the Corroboree, performed by dancers covered with white paint and wearing leafy pompoms around their knees. Australia's 160,000 aborigines maintain their tribal traditions mainly in northern and central Australia. (Queensland is populated with more aborigines than any other state.) About two-thirds of the aborigines are living a relatively modern lifestyle in the big cities. They are the poorest group in Australia, plagued by health problems, alcoholism, and culture shock.

Wujal Wujal, an aboriginal reserve, is in the Daintree Rain Forest, 30 miles from the nearest town of Helensvale. This village of impoverished shacks is littered with crashed cars, mysteriously parked on end, nose down, against trees. This position represents the ritual return to Dreamtime in aboriginal paintings.

The world's most mysterious rock

An island-size red monolith called **Ayer's Rock** lies in the heart of Australia. The largest rock on earth, it draws thousands of curious visitors and is part of a national park run by tribal elders and white officials. Situated in the Northern Territory, 200 miles southwest of Alice Springs, it could be considered the navel of the Australian Outback.

The Pitjantjatjara tribespeople call the rock *Uluru* and attach religious significance to it. On the north surface of the rock is a series of caves and grooves known as the Skull. Tribespeople believe this area of the rock served as the camp of their ancestors in Dreamtime before the world began. They perform initiation ceremonies here.

Resorts have been built near the rock. The best is the **Sheraton Ayers Rock**, *Yulara Drive; tel. (61-89)562200.* Painted in the red hues of Ayer's Rock, it is kept cool by a huge white awning that stretches over the entire complex.

Yulara, 15 miles from the rock, has the **Four Seasons Hotel**, *tel. (61-89)56-2100*, and campgrounds.

Between Alice Springs and Ayer's Rock are the **Desert Oaks Resort Centre**, *tel. (61-89)560984;* the **King's Canyon Frontier Lodge**, *tel. (61-89)567442;* and the **Curtin Springs Roadside Inn**, *tel. (61-89)562906.*

The best time to visit Ayer's Rock is during the Australian winter, from May through September, when rain makes the desert flower. Temperatures are in the 70s, rather than 140 degrees Fahrenheit as they can be in the summer.

A taste of the Outback

Australia's great **Outback**, a vast, hot, wilderness land in the heart of the continent, is inhabited by leathery stockmen and ancient aborigines. A little-known land, it stretches from the heart of Australia to the northwest. It was once known as the Back of Beyond. Cattle graze on million-acre ranches, or *stations* as they are known, on dusty turf that conceals diamonds, iron, aluminum, and uranium.

To really get to know the Outback, arrange a farm or ranch stay. For more information, contact **Bed and Breakfast Australia**, *15 Yarabah Ave., Gordon, Sydney, New South Wales 2072; tel. (61-2)498-5344.*

Or live like a ranch hand at **Escott Lodge Resort**, *Escott Station, Burketown; tel. (61-77)455-108*, a rambling cattle ranch in the wilds of northern Queensland. You'll stay in a rustic guest cottage on the homestead, eat with the ranch hands, and get acquainted with the cattle.

Don't expect a luxurious, California-style dude ranch. The place has a bar, a swimming pool, and electricity, but you are not pampered with resort-type service. You won't spend your days enjoying planned recreational activities—life on a ranch involves hard work. If you're up to it, tag along with the stockmen and watch the bulls being castrated. Or you can help out with more palatable jobs, such as breaking horses, catching crocodiles, and fishing. You also can canoe on the Nicholson River and go on a wild-pig shoot. Bed and board is A$30 ($23) a day.

The most gem-studded land

The Outback, in places, is paved with gems. Towns in the region have such names as Sapphire, Rubyvale, and Emerald and are connected by dirt roads made from piles of earth heaped up by old-time miners. From time to time, valuable gems overlooked by miners are found in the dirt.

Finding a sapphire, emerald, or ruby could turn a vacation into a jackpot. A book on Australian gems advises that "although it's not recommended that gem hunters should begin to dig up roads in search of stones, many fine gemstones have been found on the sides of roads." The odds against finding a gem on the road are like those against winning big in Las Vegas. But in the road, you don't have to pay to play.

It's not as easy as stepping from your vehicle and picking up a rock or two along the road; however, you could get lucky. Roy Spencer, a 12-year-old boy, did. He picked up the Black Star of Queensland, a 1,156-carat sapphire, in a field. It was cut to a 733-carat star sapphire valued at $450,000.

It's hard to see stones in the road. That sparkle you spy is most likely quartz or shards of glass from countless windshields that have been shattered along the way. Giant road trains—tractor trailers that tow huge dollies packed with freight or cattle—roar along the dirt tracks, shooting up rocks that demolish windshields. Because of this, most Australian vehicles that travel through the bush are outfitted with wire windshield guards or curved plastic shields.

The best way to set off on an Outback mining journey is to rent a camper in Sydney and then head north for the gem fields. Vans rent for about A$32 ($25) a day plus 9 cents a mile. They are well-equipped, but you will need a few extra items, such as a shovel, a block and tackle, a spare gas can, a thermos, and some plastic bowls. Small refrigerators that run on 220 volts, generators, or porta gas are provided. Finding water can be a problem. The bore water brought up by windmills is drinkable, but it acts as a laxative. Carry your own supply.

Mining licenses cost $15, but you don't need one for just a few days. Just don't try your luck on any claims you see pegged out.

Emerald is the first of the gem-field townships. Beyond this town are the fields near the mining village of **Sapphire**, a dingy huddle of slapped-together shacks and tents. The main post office is a tiny one-room shanty. The Rough and Ready Pub is just down the dirt road.

If you don't manage to find a gem on your own, you can buy some in this region and sell them in the United States for a fine profit. One Yankee miner recently gave up on the quest for gems and bought one instead—a star sapphire (in Sapphire, of course) for A$30 ($23). Back in the United States, the stone was appraised at twice that.

If you'd rather search for the world-famous Australian opal, head for Coober Pedy or Lightning Ridge, in the center of the country, where 90% of the world's opals are mined. Coober Pedy is an underground town on the edge of the formidable Simpson's Desert. Miners in this 120-degree desert live in underground caves, where the temperature is an even 65 degrees Fahrenheit. Water is trucked in and sold at 15 cents a gallon.

Opal buyers throng to this settlement to buy wholesale opal rock clusters or polished opals. Dutch buyers predominate.

Western Australia—the most faraway land

Western Australia, the westernmost province, is about as far from Sydney and the east coast as you can get. This gigantic region's beauty is natural. Only 300,000 people live outside Perth, in an area four times the size of Texas.

The hottest town in Australia is in this province. **Marble Bar** has an average annual temperature of 96 degrees Fahrenheit.

The most beautiful sights in Westralia, as this region is known, are the fields of wild flowers. No ordinary fields these. They roll to the horizon, a patchwork quilt of blue, purple, red, and orange. Between August and October, more than 7,000 native species (some not found anywhere else on earth) blossom here. The most famous fields are near Albany on the southern coast and Geraldton, north of Perth.

Westralia also houses Australia's best ghost town. **Coolgardie**, once home to 15,000 rowdy, brawling gold miners, is now deserted except for tourists. Old covered wagons remain on the main street, where 29 hotels and bars once thrived. **Goldfields Exhibition,** *Bayley Street,* displays memorabilia from the gold rush of the 1890s, which brought nearly 200,000 miners to Westralia.

Kalgoorlie was the area's largest mining town, with two stock exchanges, seven newspapers, and some of the most expensive real estate in the country. Kalgoorlie still mines gold, but the pace has slowed.

The **Kimberley Plateau** raises its flat head in the northern corner of Westralia, covering a region larger than California but home to only 6,000 brave souls. The green Fitzroy River carves a gorge through the limestone plateau, its water filled with sharks, crocodiles, and stingrays. Caves once used by the aborigines as burial grounds can be seen at Windjana.

Australia's best foods

Australia's culinary delights often have strange names—but don't let that stop you from trying them. Look for Moreton Bay bugs and Victorian yabbies (both are crustaceans, not insects); Queensland snapper, coral trout and Red emperor; Sydney rock oysters; barramundi; John Dory fish; Tasmanian scallops; and shrimp from anywhere along Australia's 35,000-mile-long coastline. If you can find it, try some kangaroo-tail soup. For dessert, order pavlova, a delicious fruit, whipped cream, and meringue concoction.

Australian wines can be good. They have been compared favorably to those produced in France. The Baroosa Valley near Adelaide and Hunter Valley near Sydney are the prime wine-producing regions. The whites are superior to the reds.

Top travel tips

The best way to save on the cost of rail travel within Australia is to purchase an Austrailpass, similar to the Eurailpass, before you leave home. First-class and economy versions are available, and the cost depends on class and the length of your stay rather than distance traveled. For more information, contact the **Australian Travel Service,** *100 N. First St., Suite 301, Burbank, CA 91502; (800)423-2880.*

The best way to see the Outback is by train. Two routes are especially scenic.

The transcontinental **Indian-Pacific** runs from Sydney on the Pacific Ocean to Perth on the Indian Ocean. This route cuts through the Great Dividing Range and the pasture country to the west, the mining country around Broken Hill, along the shores of the Great Australian Bight, and across the vast expanse of the dry Nullabor Plains. The trip takes three days and costs A$693 ($540) first class. (It's worth the extra money—economy class tends to be uncomfortable, noisy, and unpleasant.) Book a few months in advance— berths are in demand, particularly in September and October, when the wild flowers are blooming.

The **Ghan** runs from Adelaide on the south coast to Alice Springs in the center of Australia, skirting the beautiful Simpson Desert and its dry salt lakes. This overnight journey is about A$353 ($275) first class, one way, including meals. The train has an entertainment car with slot machines, a hairdresser, a gift shop, VCR rentals, and video games for children.

The Best of New Zealand

The great drawback to New Zealand comes from the feeling that after crossing the world and journeying over so many miles, you have not at all succeeded in getting away from England.

—*Anthony Trollope, 1873*

New Zealand is a land of spectacular scenery: shooting geysers, cloud-shrouded mountain peaks, bubbling hot springs, deep blue fiords, and secluded coves. It is also a land of extremes, with both tropical beaches and icebergs.

The Kiwis, as the people of New Zealand are affectionately known, love their land and are among the most ardent conservationists in the world. They are as varied and interesting as the landscape they seek to preserve. The Maoris, a Polynesian people who lived here long before the Europeans arrived, maintain their ancient traditions. The Europeans, too, preserve their old ways. Scottish dances seldom seen even in Scotland are danced by kilted sheep farmers.

This is the best place in the world for nature lovers, thrill seekers, and sports buffs. You can raft down a wild mountain river, battle a fighting rainbow trout, explore magnificent fiords, climb or ski the Southern Alps, or hike the awe-inspiring Milford Track.

New Zealand, which is made up of three main islands (North, South, and Stewart) and a number of smaller ones, stretches 1,000 miles along the southern tip of Polynesia. Its nearest neighbor is Australia, 1,300 miles to the northwest.

New Zealand's largest city

Auckland, huddled on an isthmus separating Waitemata and Manukau harbors, has 14 volcanos, each with tremendous views. The best panorama is from **Mount Eden**, the highest point in the city. Hike up the cow path or road and picnic in the volcano's grassy bowl while enjoying the view.

Known as the Queen City among its inhabitants, Auckland has restaurants, cinemas,

399

shops, theaters, concerts, and art galleries. It also has 102 mainland beaches and 23 secluded islands. The Hauraki Gulf is a favorite among boaters (and Auckland has a lot of boaters—one in every four homeowners also owns a boat).

The world's best Polynesian museum

The **War Memorial Museum,** built in memory of the New Zealanders who died fighting in World War I, houses the world's best collection of Maori and Polynesian artifacts, some dating back to A.D. 1200. The pièce de résistance is a 98-foot war canoe carved from a giant totara tree. It carried 80 Maori warriors at a time.

The best Kiwi art

The world's biggest collection of paintings by New Zealand artists is at the **Auckland City Art Gallery,** *Kitchener and Wellesley streets; tel. (64-9)379-2020.* Especially worth seeing are works by John Webber and William Hodges, both of whom accompanied Captain Cook on his voyages in the South Pacific in the 18th century. The gallery is open 10 a.m. until 4:30 p.m.

Animal bests

Animal lovers should make time to visit the **Auckland Zoo,** where the nocturnal, flightless kiwi bird can be seen, as well as **Lion Safari Park** in Massey.

Auckland's best picnicking

The best places to picnic are the **Domain,** a large shaded park, and **Albert Park,** which adjoins the University of Auckland. Pack your picnic basket with mango juice, which is as common here as orange juice is in the United States, and good local cheeses.

The best bargains in town

Lamb is as cheap in Auckland as Kentucky Fried Chicken is in the United States. It can be found on cafeteria lunch menus, on the dinner table several nights a week, and at restaurants.

Good, inexpensive shops are located downtown, near Quay and Queen streets. Just east of the intersection is the **Old Customhouse,** which has been converted into a mall with a movie theater, arts and crafts shops, a tavern, and a bookstore. Built in 1889, the Customhouse is one of the few examples of Victorian architecture in Auckland.

A 10-minute walk west from the corner of Queen and Quay is the **Victoria Park Market,** located in the city's former trash dump. (It's quite picturesque, believe it or not!) You can buy kiwifruit for a few cents apiece, fresh fish, and inexpensive clothing. The market is open every day.

Polynesian bests

Karangahape Road (known as K Road) is where Auckland's Polynesian population shops. You can buy brilliantly colored cloth and tropical foods here alongside matrons from Samoa, Fiji, Tonga, and the Cook Islands.

(Auckland has the largest Polynesian population of any city in the world. More than 70,000 residents have Maori ancestry, and 58,000 Pacific islanders have immigrated here.)

Auckland's best dining

Most of the better restaurants in Auckland don't have liquor licenses. But you usually can bring your own wine (which brings down the price of dinner considerably).

Auckland's best restaurant is **Antoine's,** *333 Parnell Road; tel. (64-9)798-756,* a French restaurant in a sun-drenched colonial house with linen-covered tables. Wine is served here. Ring the doorbell to enter.

Other bests include **Harbourside Seafood Bar and Grill,** *First Floor, Ferry Building,*

99 Quay St.; tel. (64-9)307-0556, **Cin Cin On Quay**, *Ferry Building, 99 Quay St.; tel. (64-9)307-6966*, and **Sails**, *The Anchorage, Westhaven; tel. (64-9)789-890.*

Other good New Zealand and Polynesian restaurants are located on Ponsonby Road, near K Road.

The best hotels

Auckland's only five-star hotel is the newly built **Regent of Auckland**, *P.O. Box 3938; tel. (64-9)309-8888.* A queen-sized room is NZ$265 ($150) per night.

Other good hotels are the impersonal but efficient **Hyatt Auckland**, *Waterloo Quadrant and Princes Street; tel. (64-9)797-22*, and the **Sheraton Auckland**, *83 Symonds St.; tel. (64-9)795-132.* Both are centrally located and have double rooms for NZ$270 ($153). If you need to stay close to the Akl airport, book a room at the **Hotel du Vin**, *Lyons Road, Mangatawhiri Valley; tel. (64-9)233-6314.* It's only 35 minutes away, and a double room is NZ$276 ($156).

The best place to argue politics

The bar at the **Abbey Hotel**, *Wellesley and Albert streets*, is known as the watering hole for Auckland's literati. A British-style lounge, it is frequented by sociable intellectuals, always looking for a lively battle over ideology. If you plan to get involved in the nightly squabble (it's all in good fun), be sure to read up first. The Kiwis have a good grasp of current events.

The Quay, a key travel hub

The **Quay**, in addition to offering a view of Harbor Bridge, is a transportation center. You can get a "Bus-About" pass here that allows you to ride public buses at reduced fares. You also can catch a ferry here to take you to the islands and beaches in Hauraki Gulf.

New Zealand's best train trip

If you want to see the beautiful countryside of New Zealand in first-class comfort and style, buy a ticket on the *Silver Fern*, one of the best trains in the world. The *Silver Fern* runs daily from Auckland to Wellington and back. The cost is NZ$61 ($34) one way. For more information, contact **Frangipani Tours**, *(800)458-1130* in the United States.

Capital Wellington

The growing city of **Wellington**, the capital of New Zealand, sprawls along the southern tip of North Island. For a view of Wellington's harbor and skyline, ascend **Mount Victoria**. (A Maori burial ground was bulldozed to make room for the viewing platform.) White wooden houses cover the green hills surrounding the city. The beaches of the Inner Harbor are popular, and on summer weekends the harbor is filled with yachts.

Wellington is a cultural center, with two professional theater companies, numerous amateur dramatic and musical societies, the New Zealand Symphony Orchestra, and the Royal New Zealand Ballet Company. The recently completed Michael Fowler Center and St. Paul's Cathedral (built in 1866) both sponsor plays and concerts.

From **Lambton Quay**, bright red cable cars carry pedestrians 397 feet over the suburbs to the beautiful **Botanical Gardens**.

The **National Museum and Art Gallery** in the suburb of Newtown has superb Maori artifacts, items used by Captain Cook, geological collections, colonial history displays, and works of art by national and international masters.

Wellington's best restaurants include **At the Bay**, *Marine Parade, Days Bay; tel. (64-4)562-8882*, which offers a variety of New Zealand specialties; **Grain of Salt**, *232 Oriental Parade, Oriental Parade; tel. (64-4)384-8642*, which is one of the top—and most expensive—restaurants in the city; and **Il Casino Restorante**, *108 Tory St., TeAro; tel. (64-4)385-3947*, which has good Italian food.

The city's best French restaurant is the **Petit Lyon Restaurant,** *8 Courtney Place; tel. (64-4)384-9402.*

The best place to stay in Wellington is the **Parkroyal,** *corner of Grey and Featherstone streets; tel. (64-4)472-2722.* A double room is NZ$315 ($178).

The highlights of North Island

North Island is the cradle of New Zealand. It was here that the Europeans first landed and faced off with the native Maori. The island's beauty belies its violent past— it is fringed with beautiful, palm-shaded beaches and blessed with hospitable weather year-round. Explore it from north to south.

New Zealand's northernmost point

Cape Reinga, the country's northernmost point, affords a magnificent view of the Pacific Ocean and the Tasman Sea. Its graceful white lighthouse seems frail and vulnerable, facing the rage of two great bodies of water from the ridge of a narrow point of land.

The Maoris believe this is where spirits of the dead depart for their journey back to the ancestral land, which they call Hawaiki.

The cape is a pleasant 3 1/2-hour drive on Highway 1 or a one-hour flight from Auckland. It is a great place to spend the night if you enjoy camping—the area lacks hotels. Try the campgrounds at Houhora and Taputupoto bays.

The best beaches

Doubtless Bay is a crescent of perfect sandy beaches that draws throngs on holidays. **Houhora** is a beach favored by fishermen, picnickers, campers, and smugglers.

Ninety Mile Beach (which is only 57 miles long) is a seemingly endless stretch of golden sandy beaches lined with dunes and embroidered with seashells. This is the scene of a popular fishing contest each summer and the prime spot to find toheroa, a much sought-after shellfish.

The best boating

Whangaroa Harbor, with its rocky pinnacles with biblical names, is the place to go for boating and deep-sea fishing. This is where the Boyd Massacre occurred in 1809. A local tribe did away with the passengers and crew of the *Boyd,* the shell of which still can be seen here.

The largest private museum

The **Wagener Museum,** *tel. (64-9)409-8850,* at Houhora Heads, is the country's largest private museum, containing rare pre-European Maori artifacts, an excellent natural history display, and extensive exhibits from the Victorian era.

The hottest beach

The **Coromandel Peninsula,** on the east coast of North Island, has New Zealand's hottest (and strangest) swimming spot: **Hot Water Beach.** Named for the hot springs that seep through its sand, the beach literally steams. You can create your own thermal pool by digging into the sand.

The peninsula is also a mecca of alternative lifestyles and naturalists. The back-to-nature movement remains as healthy here in the 1990s as it was in the United States in the 1960s. You can see how hippies have evolved over the past 30-odd years— bringing communal life into the electromagnetic age by constructing recording studios on their farms, for example. The marijuana smoked in New Zealand allegedly originates on this peninsula.

Best view, best springs

Kaikohe has spectacular views of both the Tasman and Pacific coasts, as well as a museum called Pioneer Village. Nearby is **Ngawha Springs**, with waters that have the highest mineral content in the world and are known for their curative qualities.

The most magnificent trees

Magnificent native kauri trees stand along the road that runs through the 6,100-acre **Waipoua Kauri Sanctuary.** The largest is the mighty Tane Mahuta (Lord of the Forest), which is estimated to be 1,200 years old. The oldest is the 2,000-year-old Te Matua Ngahere (Father of the Forest).

Waikato: the best of the Maoris

North of **Hamilton**, which is the capital of New Zealand's rural Waikato region and the largest inland city, is the center of Maori culture. **Turangawaewae Marae** is the focal point of a Maori revival movement organized in the 1920s by Princess Te Puea Herangi, who established a complex of buildings on the river. The complex includes traditionally carved meetinghouses and a concert hall. It is not generally open to the public, but you can see it from across the river at the bridge downstream.

The sacred burial ground of the Waikato Maoris is 2 1/2 miles downstream at **Mount Taupiri.**

The scene of the last battle of the Wakato Land Wars in 1864 is southwest in **Orakau.** Maori leader Rewi Maniapoto and 300 men, women, and children fought off 1,400 colonial soldiers for three days before they lost their fortified village.

The finest Maori carved meetinghouse is in Te Kuiti in southern **Waitomo.** Maori leader Te Kooti Rikirangi built the wooden structure to thank the local Maniapoto people, who gave him refuge when he was in danger.

King Country, as the region is known, is largely a resort for outdoor enthusiasts. Tour companies based in Te Kuiti and Taumarunui offer canoeing, horseback riding, hunting, jet boating, and fishing expeditions. Safari expeditions operate from Te Kuiti.

The rose of New Zealand

The magnificent rose gardens of **Te Awamutu**, southwest of Hamilton, have earned this town the title Rose Town of New Zealand. The roses are best seen in November during the annual Rose Festival. New Zealand's oldest and loveliest church is here; **St. John's Anglican Church** was built in 1854.

New Zealand's largest lake

Lake Taupo, at the heart of North Island, is the largest New Zealand lake, extending over 232 square miles and filling an old volcanic crater. The trout fishing is terrific in the lake and the rivers and streams that feed it. You can fish here year-round.

One of New Zealand's most attractive lodges is on the banks of Lake Taupo. **Huka Lodge**, *Huka Falls Road, Taupo; tel. (64-7)378-5791*, is a five-star hotel with a rustic atmosphere. A double room is NZ$385 ($218).

The best adventures

At the southern end of Lake Taupo are the renowned trout-fishing and river-rafting waters of the Tongariro and Wanganui rivers, Kaimanawa State Forest Park, and Tongariro National Park, all accessible from Turangi.

Tongariro National Park, with its snow-capped mountain peaks, is a superb ski resort in winter and a scenic place to hike in summer. An extensive network of paths and huts makes it easy to explore the park and its historic Maori sights. The volcanic peaks of Tongariro, Ruapehu, and Ngauruhoe are the focal points.

The **THC Château,** *Mount Ruapehu; tel. (64-7)892-3809*, is a luxurious hotel at the heart of the park's spectacular mountains. A double room is NZ$157 ($89); villas are NZ$225 ($127).

On the Wanganui River, you can embark on boat trips, guided canoe treks, and white-water rafting expeditions. This is also the site of an annual motorboat race. A luxury paddle boat travels along the river to the Holly Lodge Estate Winery, where wine tastings are held.

Rotorua: a heavenly Hades

"I was pleased to get so close to Hades and be able to return," said playwright George Bernard Shaw after visiting the area around **Rotorua City**—the boiling, bubbling, steaming center of North Island.

Located on this volcanic rift that once inspired great fear, Rotorua is New Zealand's number-one tourist spot, surrounded by thermal springs, Maori villages, and 10 trout-filled lakes. Boiling mud, erupting geysers, steaming terraces of sulphur, and colorful silica deposits combine to create an otherworldly landscape.

Rotorua has the greatest concentration of Maori residents of any New Zealand city. The historic Maori village of **Ohinemutu**, on the lake, has a 19th-century traditional meetinghouse that took 12 years to carve. The Christian church, **St. Faith's**, built in 1910, has a window with a Maori Christ, elaborate carvings, and a bust of Queen Victoria presented to the Maoris by Britain for their loyalty to the crown.

On Geyser Flat in Whakarewarewa is New Zealand's greatest geyser, **Pohutu** (Splashing), which shoots 100 feet into the air several times a day. The smaller geyser next to it usually erupts just before Pohutu does.

Rotorua is popular among trout fishermen. Professional fishing guides are available. If fishing isn't your thing, you can visit wildlife sanctuaries, government gardens, the Buried Village, and the Agrodome, where sheep- and dog-handling demonstrations are given.

Rotorua City was established as a sanatorium in 1880, when the New Zealand government leased the land from the Maoris. **Tudor Towers**, which houses a museum and an art gallery, was the original bathhouse. To its right are the **Polynesian Pools**, whose sulphurous waters are still used at the Queen Elizabeth Hospital to treat rheumatism and arthritis. Another good hot pool is **Hinemoa**, on Mokoia Island, in the middle of Lake Rotorua.

New Zealand's most beautiful drive— and the best place to greet the morning sun

The road around the **East Cape** is one of the most rugged yet beautiful coastal drives in New Zealand, passing small historic settlements, pleasant coves and beaches, and wild countryside that remains rich in Maori tradition and culture. Some of the finest Maori carvings can be seen in the traditional meetinghouses of this district, which is the first in the world to greet the morning sun.

The world's only mainland gannet reserve

The world's only mainland gannet (a large yellow-headed seabird) sanctuary is to the south of Cape Kidnappers, where large flocks can be seen between April and October. The reserve can be reached by four-wheel-drive vehicles or on foot.

The world's best sheep-shearing contest

Masterton, on the southern tip of North Island, hosts the annual Golden Shears competition—a sheep-shearing contest that attracts shearers from all over the world. For details, contact **Mr. N. Grieve,** *P.O. Box 40, Masterton.*

South Island: the most beautiful

New Zealand's most spectacular scenery is on **South Island**. At **Punakaiki,** for example, nature has carved limestone rocks into what look like giant stacks of pancakes. The Tasman Sea rushes into bore holes in these oddly shaped rocks, making great shuddering booms. The island's most memorable sights are described below, starting at the north end, following along the Pacific coast, crossing the Southern Alps, and then following the Tasman coast.

The best boat charters

Ferries from North Island land in **Picton**, a busy little port in South Island's incredibly beautiful Marlborough Sounds, 597 miles of waterways sheltered by bays and coves. Picton is the base for charter boat companies that take you cruising, fishing, and diving.

The best places to stay on South Island

The **Timara Lodge**, *Road #2; tel. (64-3)572-8276,* is the best place to stay in Blenheim, but it's not cheap. A double room is NZ$265 to NZ$450 ($150 to $255). The **California Guesthouse,** *29 Collingwood St., Nelson; tel. (64-3)548-4173,* about 50 miles from Blenheim, in Nelson, is another good place to stay on South Island. It's also less expensive—NZ$95 to NZ$135 ($53 to $76) a night, including breakfast.

The least-traveled trail

New Zealand is crisscrossed by well-marked trails leading through spectacular scenery. One of the least known, and therefore least crowded, is the **Nydia Trail,** along the Marlborough Sounds. Passing through genuine wilderness, the trail has no access road. A mail boat that serves farms and vacation homes also delivers hikers to any starting point along the 80-mile trail. If prearranged, the mail boat will pick you up again farther north. Check with the ranger station or public information office in the harbor town of Havelock for maps and to arrange transportation.

One of the best routes along the trail begins at Shag Poing in Kauma Bay. Heading north, you cross two fast-running jade-green rivers near a deer farm. (The Japanese buy the velvet of the deer antlers and use it as an aphrodisiac.) The trail then climbs the first of several 1,000-foot saddles with a view of the valley below. You can quench your thirst at a waterfall before continuing across a stretch of private property. Keep an eye out for wild goats and boars—and take cover if you spot any.

At intervals of about five hours, the trail passes a series of bays: Stanley, Duncan, Penzance, and Elaine. The last is a good place to meet the mail boat and return to Havelock.

Don't attempt to travel the Nydia without an accurate map and a compass. The trail is barely marked and rarely tramped.

The wildest coastline

South of Picton, at **Kaikoura**, the Pacific coast is at its wildest. The town is on a narrow peninsula buffeted by the ocean and protected by rocky cliffs and a narrow beach. Nearby are limestone caves and seal colonies. The Kaikoura Mountains are a dramatic backdrop. The peninsula is popular among fishermen and known for its large crayfish.

The most English town

Nestled at the base of Banks Peninsula on the edge of the Canterbury Plains is the garden city of **Christchurch**, a very English town. The river that meanders through its center, past old stone buildings and terraced houses, is called the Avon.

The best hotel in Christchurch is the **Parkroyal Christchurch,** *corner of Durham and Kilmore streets, 1544 Christchurch; tel. (64-3)657-799.* The food is exceptional and served with a smile. A double room is NZ$240 to NZ$290 ($136 to $164).

The **Cotswold Inn,** *88-90 Papanui Road; tel. (64-3)355-3535,* is pleasant, with authentic period furnishings. A double room is NZ$90 to NZ$108 ($51 to $61).

Two other good places to stay are the **Elizas Manor House**, *82 Bealey Ave., tel. (64-3)668-584*, where a double room is NZ$73 ($41), and the **Riverview Lodge**, *361 Cambridge Toe; tel. (64-3)652-860*. A double room at the Lodge is NZ$70 to NZ$90 ($40 to $51).

The best fishing

The **Canterbury** region, especially the town of Methven, is a mecca for salmon and trout fishermen. During the summer, quinnat salmon run in the Rangitata and Ashburton rivers near Geraldine. Three major salmon-fishing contests are held each year on the Rangitata, Rakaia, and Waitaki rivers.

New Zealand's only castle

The Edwardian and Victorian houses of **Dunedin,** on the southernmost Pacific coast, embrace Otago Harbor, a 12-mile fiord. On one of the hills overlooking the city is New Zealand's only castle, **Larnach,** built in 1871 by J.M. Larnach, minister of the crown. The castle took 14 years to build, its ceilings 12 years to carve. The strangely European edifice was built to impress Larnach's French wife. Perhaps it didn't work; she committed suicide in Wellington's Parliament building years later. The castle has been restored, and its 43 rooms are open to the public.

Dunedin has several good restaurants, including the elegant **La Scala,** *tel. (64-3)455-4555,* and **Blade's,** *tel. (64-3)477-6548,* an inexpensive place where you bring your own wine.

The world's largest flying bird

The world's largest bird of flight, the rare royal albatross, can be seen in all its glory at **Taiaroa Head,** at the tip of Otago Peninsula near Dunedin. The graceful bird has a 10-foot wingspan and hovers above the sea like a kite. The oldest-known wild bird in the world is an albatross. Since 1937, when she was banded, this albatross has returned here each year.

About 20 pairs of royal albatrosses circle the globe each year, at speeds of up to 66 miles per hour, to roost at Taiaroa. They mate for life and produce one chick every two years. You can observe the birds up close from a newly opened lookout. For more information, call the **Dunedin Visitor Center,** *tel. (64-3)474-3300.*

The world's largest marbles

North of Dunedin, on a beach near the fishing village of **Moeraki,** are the intriguing Moeraki boulders known as **The Devil's Marbles,** strange spherical rocks weighing several tons. The huge round stones were formed 60 million years ago by the accumulation of lime salts.

The shortest route across the Alps

The shortest route across the Southern Alps passes through the Alpine playground that is **Arthur's Pass National Park.** The picturesque mountain village of Arthur's Pass is a great base for mountain climbing, hiking, hunting, skiing, and breathing fresh mountain air.

If you'd like to savor the area, stay a few nights at the **Chalet,** *P.O. Box 5, Main Road; tel. and fax (64-516)89-236,* a Swiss Alpine-style chalet with five rooms.

The Tasman Coast—a nature lover's best

The **Tasman Coast,** on the other side of the island, is a good place to go if you like hiking, mountain climbing, rafting, or watching animals. It has three major national parks and is flanked by rugged mountains and washed by turbulent rivers.

New Zealand's best glaciers

The 217,000-acre **Westland National Park** has New Zealand's two most beautiful glaciers: Fox and Franz Josef. Arrange a (strenuous) guided hike across the icy masses at the park headquarters in the town of Franz Josef. (The native forest is crisscrossed with 68 miles of trails.) Or take a helicopter or ski plane over the shining glaciers.

New Zealand's highest peak: Mount Cook

Mount Cook, at 12,349 feet, is New Zealand's highest mountain. Sir Edmund Hillary, the first man to climb Mount Everest, trained here. The mountain is at the heart of **Mount Cook National Park**, which also features the beautiful 18-mile Tasman Glacier (and four other very high, very large glaciers). Ski planes operate regular flights to the head of Tasman—an exhilarating experience.

One of the best hotels in the area, the **Hermitage**, *Glentanner; tel. (64-3)435-1809 or (800)835-7742 in the United States*, is a chalet at the foot of Mount Cook. Nearby are bases for heli-skiing, glacier skiing, cross-country skiing, and mountaineering. A double room is NZ$190 to NZ$240 ($107 to $136).

The most spectacular park

Fiordland National Park, at the southern tip of South Island, is one of the largest national parks in the world. Much of it remains unexplored. Lonely fiords lap at the mountains, while waterfalls tumble thousands of feet into the densely forested valleys. The fourth-largest waterfall in the world, **Sutherland Falls**, drops 1,873 feet through the forest. The gateway to the park is the town of **Te Anau**, which is the place to go for hotels and restaurants.

Fiordland Travel Limited, *P.O. Box 1, Te Anau, New Zealand; tel. (64-3)249-7416*, offers boat and bus tours of Doubtful Sound that take you to see Lake Manapouri, the Wilmot Pass, and many beaches in Fiordland Park.

The eighth wonder of the world

According to Rudyard Kipling, the **Milford Sound**, which leads from Fiordland National Park to the sea, is the eighth wonder of the world. And who are we to argue with Kipling? The scenery is indeed spectacular: misty peaks, white waterfalls tumbling down green cliffs, and cottony clouds reflected in the mirrorlike water. The sound is dominated by 6,247-foot **Mitre Peak**, a pyramidlike mountaintop. And it is fed by the spectacular **Bowen Falls**, which drop 531 feet.

The most beautiful walk in the world

The 33-mile **Milford Track**, which makes its way through Fiordland National Park to the Milford Sound, is the most beautiful walk in the world. To get here, take a boat across Te Anau Lake to Glade House. Leading through rain forests, meadows, and mountain passes, the trail passes wild rivers, deep fiords, and crashing waterfalls. The clearly marked track takes five days to hike; it is suitable even for the novice.

You can hike independently or join a group (which costs NZ$726, or $412). Accommodation is in shelters along the way. Only a limited number of hikers (82) are permitted on the trail each day, so write to the **Independent Hikers**, *Department of Conservation, P.O. Box 29, Te Anau*, as far in advance as possible (up to one year) to make arrangements. Reservations also can be made by travel agents in the United States through the New Zealand Central Reservations Office in California or through the **Southern Pacific Hotel Corporation**, *(213)557-2292*. The hiking season is late October through mid-April.

The most southerly Alpine pass

Haast Pass is the most southerly, and the most historic, of the trans-Alpine passages, following an ancient Maori route through a rugged, breathtaking landscape. The contrast between the east and west sides of the pass is dramatic—**Westland** is lush; **Otago,** on the other side of the pass, is a dry region, relieved by lakes.

The pass runs through **Mount Aspiring National Park,** a 100-mile reserve that covers most of the southern Alps. Looming above the park is 9,961-foot Mount Aspiring. Many of the park's activities (hiking and fishing, for example) are centered in its headquarters at Lake Wanaka.

The most beautiful lakes

Mackenzie Country (named for a Scottish shepherd who tried to hide stolen sheep in this isolated area at the heart of South Island) is a rural area known for its six glacial lakes, the largest of which are Tekapo, Pukaki, and Ohau. Lake Tekapo is an unbelievable turquoise color (the result of powdered rock ground by the glaciers feeding the lake). All the lakes offer great fishing.

Queenstown: the most sophisticated resort

Nestled on the shores of clear blue Lake Wakatipu is Tyrolean-style **Queenstown.** Once a sleepy lakeside town, Queenstown has become the country's most sophisticated resort, with restaurants, hotels, an airport, and ski slopes. Any adventure is possible here: jet boating, white-water rafting, canoeing, sailing, jet skiing, water skiing, horseback riding, snow skiing, back-country safaris, and helicopter flights. You can cruise Lake Wakatipu on the *TSS Earnshlaw* steamer or follow its southern border aboard the Kingston Flyer steam train.

The **Quality Inn A Line,** *27 Stanley St.; tel. (64-3)442-7700,* is a nice hotel with a restaurant overlooking Queenstown Bay. A double room is NZ$140 ($79).

The **Lakeland Regency,** *Lake Esplanade; tel. (64-3)442-7600,* has scenic views, its own restaurant, a pool, and private bathrooms. A double room is NZ$118 ($66).

The **Nugget Point Club,** *Arthurs Point Road; tel. (64-3)442-7273,* is a luxury sporting resort. A double room is NZ$225 ($127).

Stewart Island, the most unspoiled

Across Foveaux Strait from South Island is **Stewart Island,** an untouched haven of dense forest with birds, animals, and flowers. (Its Maori name is Rakiura, which translates as *Heavenly Glow.*) The tiny fishing village of **Oban** is the main town on the island. Bush walks and paths spread out from it to strategically placed huts throughout the northern part of the island.

Stewart Island is a bird watcher's paradise. You can see tuis, bellbirds, wekas, tomtits, and wood pigeons. And you can hear their songs year-round from the woods and meadows. **Codfish Island,** off the west coast of Stewart Island, is also a great place to view birds.

Buffeted by both the Arctic and the Pacific oceans, Stewart Island's early settlers had a hard life. Many abandoned the island, fed up with the harsh storms and the cold winters, and left behind their homes, sawmills, tin mines, and whaling stations.

The place to stay is the **South Seas Hotel,** in the middle of Oban, where the island's inhabitants meet for a beer. If you're not interested in a beer, just enjoy the view of the harbor.

The world's best summer skiing

Summer skiing in New Zealand is much cheaper than winter skiing in the United States or Europe. Lift tickets are NZ$42 ($23), about half the price of those at U.S. or European ski resorts. And hotels and restaurants are much less expensive.

The largest ski area

The largest and most popular ski area in New Zealand is the **Whakapapa Skifield** in

Tongariro National Park on North Island. The slopes descend from Mount Ruapehu, a dormant volcano. Skiers are warned that part of the ski area is in a mudflow danger zone.

The park is a comfortable one-day drive from Auckland. Head south on State Highway 4 and then turn onto Provincial Highway 48, which takes you into the park and eventually up to the slopes. If you arrive early in the morning, the road to the top of Ruapehu is usually clear of snow and ice, allowing you to drive all the way to the parking area. Midday, however, usually brings fresh snow, and you may be forced to leave your car below and ride up the hill on a goat (a comfortable, four-wheel-drive bus).

An adult full-day lift ticket is from NZ$36 to NZ$42 ($20 to $23); a half-day ticket is about half that, and a season pass is NZ$495 ($280). These fees allow you to use the platter lift, four chair lifts, four T-bars, two pomas, and seven rope tows. With a capacity of 10,000 skiers per hour, these lifts provide access up to 7,200 feet. Whakapapa has slopes for every level of skier, including a superb national downhill course for experts.

Skiing across the top of the last face of the High Traverse, you can look up into the chimney at the end of the run. The chimney isn't very long, but when you drop in from the top you can't see the slope below—and you have no retreat. It's a bit like stepping into an empty elevator shaft. A thrill for even the most jaded skiers.

On the flanks of **Mount Ruapehu**, accommodation ranges from the luxurious Château Tongariro to the rustic cabins at Skotel, from high-class hotels and club chalets to a trailer park. If you want to stay at the Château Tongariro, make reservations well in advance. An elegant restaurant in the basement serves delicious steak and seafood specialties.

The longest ski season

Mount Hutt, *tel. (64-3)302-8811,* on South Island, has New Zealand's longest ski season, extending from May through November. It boasts the earliest operating date of any ski field in the Southern Hemisphere. The field itself is set in a huge bowl that collects snow. Early in the season is the best time to ski powder snow; little patches of powder hide in the shadows of ridges.

Mount Hutt has several great routes that offer 700 vertical meters of skiing and a range of slopes and snow types. Facilities include one chair lift and four T-bars. You can heli-ski here, too, with the help of Methven Heliski, which flies to the upper Rakai Ranges. Ski lessons at Mount Hutt are NZ$80 ($45), including the lift ticket; half-day ski lift passes are NZ$30 ($17).

New Zealand's wooliest bargains

New Zealand supports a flock of 70 million sheep. So it shouldn't be a surprise that fleece is a way of life for many and the backbone of the New Zealand economy. An army of home knitters stands by to turn the raw material into sweaters, gloves, hats, and scarves. The handiwork of New Zealanders pays off in apparel that is sturdy and well-designed.

The wool varies from breed to breed, but most is incredibly dense and full of lanolin, which makes it water-resistant (and gives knitters baby-soft hands). Undyed yarn, enough to make three to four sweaters, can be bought for NZ$100 ($56).

For those who like their wool still on the hide, New Zealand is also one of the world's greatest marketplaces for sheepskin. A sheepskin throw rug is less than NZ$75 ($42).

The best travel bargain

A New Zealand **Railways Travelpass** makes traveling through New Zealand easy and affordable. Unlimited travel, including the boat between North and South islands, is NZ$469 ($266) for 15 days or NZ$629 ($356) for 22 days. For information, write **Travelpass,** *c/o Passenger Business Group, New Zealand Railways Corporation, Private Bag, Wellington, New Zealand.*

The Best of the United States

America is more wild and absurd than ever.
—*Edmund Burke*

Nothing that you say about the whole country is going to be true.
—*Alistair Cooke*

Americans go to great lengths and expense to travel to the far corners of the earth in search of the world's bests. The irony is that they can find many of them right in their own back yards. People from around the world flock to the United States to see New York, Washington, D.C., San Francisco, New Orleans, the Rocky Mountains, the Grand Canyon, and Niagara Falls.

New York is one of the most exciting cities in the world. California is where the world's trends are set. The Grand Canyon is one of the world's major wonders. Texas is a world unto itself. Hawaii has the world's best surfing. Alaska is one of the world's last frontiers. And decisions affecting the entire globe are made in Washington, D.C.

Where to begin? If you like big cities, go to New York or Chicago. If you prefer nature, go to Yellowstone and Yosemite national parks. Beach lovers should head for Southern California.

We will begin our look at the United States on the East Coast with New York City, continue on to New England, and then head south along the East Coast. Next we will head west through Texas and the Southwest. Then we will explore the Rockies and California, before heading north on the Pacific Coast. We won't overlook the Midwest, including Chicago. And last, but not least, we will describe the bests of Alaska and Hawaii. (This order is not meant as a rating.)

New York City: America's number-one sight

Ask any foreign visitor where he would most like to go in the United States and his reply most likely will be New York City. People around the globe dream of visiting New York, America's great melting pot, a stew of colorful traditions and peoples. New York

411

is also the creative center of the United States. Ambitious young Americans hoping to make it big make their way to the Big Apple—the country's best dancers, artists, writers, musicians, and fashion designers. This mixture of exotic, ambitious, and energetic people makes New York electric.

Manhattan: the heart of the City

Manhattan Island, the liveliest of New York's five boroughs, is the heart of the City, as New Yorkers call their town. The famous **Midtown** area, stretching from 34th to 59th streets, contains the most important sights, including the Museum of Modern Art, Rockefeller Center, St. Patrick's and St. Bartholomew's cathedrals, Times Square, Grand Central Station, the United Nations, Macy's and Bloomingdales (two of the most important department stores in the world—although recently Macy's declared bankruptcy), and the Empire State Building.

The southern tip of the island houses most of the city's historic sights, as well as the financial district. Farther north are ethnic neighborhoods: Little Italy, Chinatown, and the Lower East Side. SoHo, an artists' haven, is west of Little Italy. North of SoHo is Greenwich Village, the famous student and artist district, which has become more polished and expensive in recent years. Andy Warhol and Arthur Miller frequented Chelsea, just north of the Village. East of Chelsea is Gramercy Park, with its 19th-century mansions and brownstones.

The **Lower East Side**, between Houston and Canal streets and Allen and Essex streets, is a Jewish and Latino community with great bargain clothing stores. The best are on **Orchard Street**. For Jewish treats, visit **Yonah Schimmel's Knishery**, *137 E. Houston St.; (212)477-2858*, or **Moishe's Bakery**, *181 E. Houston St.; (212)475-9624*, open every day.

Chinatown, surrounding Mott Street, is the largest Chinese community east of San Francisco, with hundreds of Chinese restaurants and stores. The **Chinese Museum**, *8 Mott St.*, explains the history and culture of New York's Chinese community and leads tours through the neighborhood.

SoHo's best galleries are the **Museum of Holography**, *11 Mercer St.*, and **O.K. Harris**, *383 W. Broadway*. The shops along Canal Street, especially **Canal Jean**, have the best and most interesting buys.

Greenwich Village is filled with homes and haunts of American writers and artists. Louisa May Alcott once lived at 132 MacDougal St. Anarchists from the 1920s met at 137 MacDougal St. in the Liberal Club. Eugene O'Neill saw his first plays produced at the Provincetown Playhouse. Edgar Allen Poe lived at 85 W. Third St. Look for Picasso's colossal sculpture *Sylvette* on Bleecker Street.

Washington Square Park is the place to go to see first-class street performances. For a bit of spare change, you can watch comedians, musicians, and other performers do their stuff here. (You'll also see sunbathers, drug pushers, office workers, and lovers.)

If money interests you, visit the **Financial District**. Tour the **Federal Reserve Bank** (The Fed), located between Nassau and William streets, and the **New York Stock Exchange** (free), where you can see the trading floor from the visitors' gallery. **Federal Hall**, facing the Stock Exchange, is where George Washington took his oath of office.

The symbol of freedom

The recently restored **Statue of Liberty**, on an island off the tip of Manhattan Island, has become a symbol of America at its best—welcoming with open arms immigrants from poor and oppressive nations. The best view of the statue, a gift from France, is from the **Staten Island Ferry**, which leaves from the ferry dock on South Street. For a trip to the statue itself, take a ferry from **Battery Park**.

The best city park: Central Park

New York's **Central Park** is the best city park in the world—and one of the biggest.

412

Here, New Yorkers escape the pace of their frenetic city. This playground for all ages has a zoo, a carousel, an ice-skating rink, a boating lake, gardens, soccer fields, horseshoe courts, baseball diamonds, tennis courts, jogging paths, basketball courts, wading pools, bird-watching, bike rentals, marionette shows, concerts, lawn bowling, horse-and-buggy rides, and refreshment stands. Free Shakespearean plays are performed during the summer. Be careful in the park at night, when it is frequented by prostitutes, drug dealers, and muggers.

The top sights

The **Empire State Building**, *Fifth Avenue,* between 33rd and 34th streets, was for years the tallest building in the world. Designed by Shreve, Lamb, and Harmon, it was built in 1930-1931. From the top of this 102-story building, you have a breathtaking view of New York. The building is open from 9:30 a.m. to midnight daily.

Radio City Music Hall, *50th Street and Sixth Avenue,* next to Rockefeller Center, is New York's most extravagant theater. The long-legged, feathered Rockettes and their cancan are the main attractions. The interior is art deco.

St. Patrick's Cathedral, *51st Street and Fifth Avenue,* is the largest Roman Catholic cathedral in the United States. Built between 1858 and 1879, it was designed by James Renwick. This Gothic Revival church has 12 side chapels and contains the shrine of St. John Neumann (1811-1860), the first American male to be canonized.

The **United Nations**, *between 42nd and 48th streets,* on the East River, is a large complex with a garden and an esplanade. Free tickets to General Assembly meetings are available in the lobby 30 minutes before each 10:30 a.m. and 3 p.m. meeting (weekdays). Tours are held daily.

Former Beatle John Lennon lived in the **Dakota Apartments**, *Central Park West,* between 72nd and 73rd streets, until his murder there Dec. 8, 1980. This elegant apartment building, home to many celebrities, was built in 1884.

New York's best museums

The **Metropolitan Museum of Art**, *Fifth Avenue and 82nd Street; (212)535-7710 or (212)879-5500,* houses more than 3 million works of art, including the Rockefeller Collection of Primitive Art, European paintings, and Egyptian art. The Met, as it is known, is New York's number-one museum and a must-see. The museum is closed Monday.

The **Museum of Modern Art**, *11 W. 53rd St.; (212)708-9480,* has the best collections of modern art in the world. Permanent shows range from Impressionist to contemporary. It is closed Wednesday.

The **Cloisters**, *Washington Avenue and West 193rd Street; (212)923-3700,* in a rebuilt medieval monastery in Fort Tryon Park in upper west Manhattan, displays Romanesque and Gothic art. Highlights are the Unicorn Tapestries, the Cuxa Cloister, and the Treasury. It is closed Monday.

The **Guggenheim Museum**, *Fifth Avenue and 89th Street; (212)360-3500,* a modern spiral building designed by Frank Lloyd Wright, displays the best of contemporary art, including works by Kandinsky, Miró, Calder, and Klee. The Guggenheim has just reopened after extensive restoration and boasts the addition of a new wing.

The **American Museum of Natural History**, *Central Park West at 79th Street; (212)769-5000,* houses the fossilized remains of prehistoric animals, as well as reconstructed homes of present and past civilizations. See the show of stars at the planetarium.

The **International Center of Photography**, *1130 Fifth Ave. at 94th Street,* is America's only major museum of photography. The **Jewish Museum**, *Fifth Avenue at 92nd Street,* has a comprehensive collection of Jewish ceremonial art. The Jewish museum is closed Friday and Saturday.

The **Museum of the American Indian**, *3753 Broadway and 155th Street; (212)283-2420,* is the largest Indian museum in the world.

El Museo del Barrio, *1230 Fifth Ave. at 104th Street; (212)831-7272,* is devoted to Latin American art and culture.

The **Museum of the City of New York,** *103rd Street and Fifth Avenue; (212)534-1672,* illustrates the city's past.

The **Museum of Broadcasting,** *1 E. 53rd St.; (212)752-7684,* is one of the least known and most interesting museums in the city, showing old television shows and playing old radio recordings.

The **Whitney Museum,** *945 Madison Ave. at 75th Street; (212)570-3676,* is a futuristic structure housing modern American art by Hopper, Soyer, de Kooning, Motherwell, and Warhol. The Whitney is known for its innovative special exhibits.

The City's best shopping

Fifth Avenue is lined with some of the world's chicest and most expensive stores. Look at the gigantic gems in Tiffany's windows. Take stock of the latest fashions on display at Bergdorf Goodman and Saks. Or stop in at F.A.O. Schwartz, where you can spend from $20 to $20,000 for a toy. Also look for Cartier, Gucci, Steuben Glass, Godiva Chocolates, and the famous Trump Tower.

Other elegant shopping streets include Madison, Park, and Seventh avenues and 39th, 56th, and 57th streets.

If you prefer bargains over elegance, go to Orchard and Delaney streets. **Annemarie Gardin Inc.,** *498 Seventh Ave.,* where prices are very low, is open Monday through Friday only from 9 a.m. to 5 p.m. The **Better Made Coat and Suit Company,** *270 W. 38th St.,* has designer labels for less than designer prices.

The world's best diamond market

The **Diamond Exchange,** *47th Street and Sixth Avenue,* is responsible for more than 80% of the world's wholesale diamond trade. The exchange is dominated by the Orthodox Jewish community.

New York's best food markets

Zabar's, *2245 Broadway; (212)787-2000,* has the greatest variety of delicacies and the biggest crowds, attracting 30,000 customers per week. The coffee is roasted by Saul Zabar himself. Twenty-six kinds of salami, 42 kinds of mustard, and 30 varieties of honey are sold. Zabar's is open every day.

Balducci's, *424 Avenue of the Americas; (212)673-2600,* has fresh produce and herbs, pasta, homemade dishes, and candy. Prices are high.

Dean & Deluca, *560 Broadway; (212)431-1691,* is another deli with an incredible variety, including edible ferns in season. The Italian foods are good. The Dean & Deluca café is located at 121 Prince St.

New York's best beaches

While New York isn't known as a beach town, it does have 20 miles of beaches. The best are **Rockaway Beach** (not Far Rockaway, which is seedy) and **Jones Beach;** the worst is **Coney Island,** which has become a slum. Take the A or CC subway train to Rockaway, the Long Island Railroad to Jones. **Brighton Beach** is a Russian enclave called Odessa by the Sea.

The best way to see a live television show

Free tickets to live television shows are offered occasionally at the **New York City Visitors Bureau,** *2 Columbus Circle; (212)397-8200.*

The best entertainment

Midtown, on the west side, is New York at its most entertaining. You'll see everything from Broadway shows to X-rated movies. The **Theater District** stretches from 44th to 54th streets on Broadway. The most beautiful theaters are the **St. James**, *246 W. 44th St.*, the **Shubert**, *44th Street*, the **Booth**, *45th Street*, and the **Majestic**, *44th Street*.

Lincoln Center is the hub of New York's haute couture. More than 13,000 spectators can be accommodated in the center's six buildings: Avery Fisher Hall, the New York State Theater, the Metropolitan Opera House, the Library and Museum of Performing Arts, the Vivian Beaumont Theater, and the Julliard School of Music. Daily tours of the center cost $6.50 for adults, $5.50 for senior citizens, and $3.50 for children. The **Metropolitan Opera House** is spectacular, with gigantic Chagall murals, a beautiful central fountain, and glittering chandeliers.

The best on and off Broadway

If you're looking for lights, luster, and glitter, see a show on Broadway. For a more intimate or avant-garde evening, see an off-Broadway show. In either case, you'll be seeing some of the world's best theater.

At **TKTS**, *Duffy Square, 47th Street and Broadway; (212)354-5800*, you can get tickets to on- and off-Broadway shows for half-price—but you have to buy tickets for shows that same day. **Hit Shows**, *630 Ninth Ave.; (212)581-4211*, sells "two-fers" for a discount. **QUIKTIX** at **Joseph Papp's Public Theater**, *425 Lafayette St.; (212)598-7100*, sells tickets at half-price at 6 p.m. on the night of a performance (as do many other theaters, on and off Broadway).

Joseph Papp's New York **Shakespeare Festival** performs at the Delacorte Theater in Central Park from June through September. Tickets are given out free at 6:15 p.m. for the 8 p.m. performance. Arrive at 5 p.m. and bring a picnic to ensure a good place in line.

The world's best opera company

The **Metropolitan Opera Company**, *(212)362-6000*, is the largest in the world, with a cast that sometimes includes Joan Sutherland and Luciano Pavarotti. The sets are incomparable. From September through April, the company performs at the Metropolitan Opera House in Lincoln Center. During the summer, free performances are given in city parks.

The best dance and music

The **New York City Ballet**, *(212)870-5570*, is the oldest ballet company in the United States. It presents classics, including the *Nutcracker Suite* at Christmas, at Lincoln Center.

The **American Ballet Theater**, *890 Broadway; (212)477-3030*, directed by Mikhail Baryshnikov, engages such stars as Baryshnikov himself.

The **Joffrey Ballet**, *(212)265-7300*, and the **Alvin Ailey Dance Company**, *(212)767-0590*, are innovative troupes that perform in the City Center, *130 W. 56th St.*. Joffrey does classic revivals. Ailey concentrates on modern dance.

The **New York City Opera**, *(212)870-5570*, managed by Beverly Sills, presents bold productions, often in English. Foreign-language operas have supertitles.

The **New York Philharmonic**, *(212)875-5000*, is well-respected, performing works from Bach to Bernstein from September through May at Lincoln Center.

The best jazz joints

New York's best places to hear jazz include the **Blue Note**, *131 W. Third St.; (212)475-8592*; **Sweet Basil**, *88 Seventh Ave. S.; (212)242-1785*; the **Village Vanguard**, *178 Seventh Ave. S.; (212)255-4037*; the **Bottom Line**, *15 W. Fourth St. at Mercer Street; (212)228-6300* (all in Greenwich Village); and the **West End Café**, *2909-011 Broadway; (212)662-8830*, near Columbia University.

The best contemporary music

The **Ritz**, *119 E. 11th St.; (212)956-3731*, rocks with the tunes of such musicians as Chuck Berry.

The **Lone Star Café**, *240 W. 52nd St.; (212)245-2950*, has good country-western and blues music, a surprise in the middle of such a cosmopolitan city.

The **Back Porch**, *488 Third Ave.; (212)685-3828*, has a terrific pianist.

Brazilian music is played at **Sounds of Brazil**, *204 Varick St.; (212)924-5221*.

New York's best restaurant

The **21 Club**, *21 W. 52nd St.; (212)582-7200*, in the heart of midtown Manhattan, has an elegant dining room for those who wish to keep a low profile. Dr. Armand Hammer and Aristotle Onassis have been patrons.

This establishment began as a speakeasy during Prohibition; Jack Kriendler and Charlie Berns opened the club on New Year's Day in 1930. Away from the scrutiny of federal agents, it became a haven for politicos, actors, and journalists. Tallulah Bankhead once said there wasn't much point in getting up on Sunday, because 21 is closed. Dinner for two at 21 is about $100, not including drinks.

Other superb restaurants

The **Quilted Giraffe**, *550 Madison Ave.; (212)593-1221*, serves the innovative creations of Barry and Susan Wine. The beggar's purses are especially good, little crepes filled with *crème fraîche* and caviar. The prix-fixe menu is $75, not including drinks. The restaurant is closed Sunday and Monday.

The **Four Seasons**, *99 E. 52nd St.; (212)754-9494*, is a popular place for lunch. The menu varies with the season, a combination of classic and contemporary cuisines. Dinner for two is about $130, not including wine from the restaurant's extensive wine list. Save room for the chocolate-chocolate mahogany cake.

Lutèce, *249 E. 50th St.; (212)752-2225*, is the best French restaurant in New York. Only the finest ingredients are used, and the preparation is imaginative. The prix-fixe menu is $60.

Café des Artistes, *1 W. 67th St.; (212)877-3500*, has been a New York institution since the 1930s. Try the potted and roasted duck *confit*. The restaurant is open daily for dinner and Sundays for brunch.

Le Cirque, *58 E. 65th St.; (212)794-9292*, is one of the best French restaurants in Manhattan, an elegant, spacious place with impeccable cuisine. Its *crème brulée* is the best in the United States. Reservations are required. Le Cirque is closed Sundays.

Enoteca Iperbole, *137 E. 55th St.; (212)759-9720*, has the largest wine cellar in the United States. Try the pheasant with your wine. The restaurant is closed Sundays.

The best ethnic restaurants

The best Mexican restaurant in New York (and one of the best in the United States) is **Rosa Mexicana**, *1063 First Ave.; (212)753-7407*. Try the red snapper in cilantro sauce. The restaurant is open every night.

Benito's II, *163 Mulberry St.; (212)226-9012*, in Little Italy, is one of the city's best Italian (Sicilian) restaurants. **Elaine's**, *1703 Second Ave.; (212)534-8103*, is also good, especially popular among publishers and writers. Nancy Reagan and friends lunch at **Primavera**, *1578 First Ave.; (212)861-8608*. And **Sandro's**, *420 E. 59th St.; (212)355-5150*, should not be overlooked. Chef Sandro Fioriti goes all out with spices and imagination when preparing his pasta. The fried ricotta with tomato sauce is tasty. Sandro's is open daily after 3 p.m.

The **Russian Tea Room**, *150 W. 57th St.; (212)265-0947*, near Carnegie Hall, has Russian specialties and a glamorous clientele. Try the blini with caviar, the borscht, and the icy vodka drinks. The restaurant is open daily.

416

The **Ukrainian Restaurant**, *140 Second Ave.; (212)529-5024*, is humble and cheap—but the food is excellent.

Darbar, *44 W. 56th St.; (212)432-7227*, is the best Indian restaurant in town, an elegant place with white-linen tablecloths and correct service.

New York's best hotels

The best place to stay is the **Carlyle**, *35 E. 76th St.; (212)744-1600*, an old-fashioned, Old World hotel with perfect service. The attention to detail is remarkable. A double room is $275 to $350.

Morgans, *237 Madison Ave.; (212)686-0300*, is an exclusive hideaway for celebrities, including Margaux Hemingway and Rod Stewart. An enthusiastic young staff (owner Steve Rubell says he hired no New Yorkers) takes care of guests' needs. Andy Warhol paintings adorn some of the rooms. Guests are guaranteed admission to the Palladium. A double room is $235.

The **Algonquin**, *59 W. 44th St.; (212)840-6800*, is a first-class, old-fashioned hotel. A double room is $160 to $170.

The **Helmsley Palace**, *455 Madison Ave.; (212)888-7000*, is a modern skyscraper rising out of a 19th-century mansion. The lobby and dining rooms are elegant old rooms with antiques. Bedrooms are spacious and modern, with fantastic views of New York. A double room is $190 to $320.

The **Ritz Carlton**, *112 Central Park S.; (212)757-1900*, is a very English, very luxurious modern establishment with views of Central Park and a central location near the main shopping areas. The popular Jockey Club dining room is here. A double room is $170 to $380.

The **Pierre**, *Fifth Avenue at 61st Street; (212)838-8000*, is a peaceful place, where celebrities stay when they want privacy. The view is of Central Park. A double room is $310 to $430.

The new **Park 51 Hotel**, *152 W. 51st St.; (212)765-1900 or (800)237-0990*, is a bit of old Europe in the middle of Manhattan. Each of the 180 rooms is decorated differently, but all have bathrooms of Italian marble. Hotel services include courtesy limousine service to Wall Street and use of nearby health-club facilities. The concierge is especially helpful. A night at the Park 51 costs from $175 to $240.

The best budget hotel

The best hotel for your money in New York is the **Paramount**, *235 W. 46th St.; (212)764-5500*, with a progressive European atmosphere and decor and first-class service. All this for only $125 a night. The Paramount is becoming *the* place to stay in the City.

The best of New York state

Don't spend all your time in the City; **New York state** also is worth seeing. Unspoiled forest and rolling farmland still exist in this fertile state, which is watered by lakes Champlain, George, Erie, and Ontario, as well as the Hudson River. The Adirondack and Catskill mountains offer retreat from the noise and pollution of New York City.

Niagara Falls: the best honeymoon spot

You'll hear **Niagara Falls** long before you see it. This 180-foot waterfall, which pours 40 million gallons of water a minute, is actually made up of three great torrents: Canada's **Horseshoe Falls**, the **American Falls**, and **Bridal Veil Falls**. Horseshoe is the most spectacular, so you should definitely see this natural wonder from both the U.S. and Canadian sides.

The best way to see Niagara is aboard the *Maid of the Mist*, which departs Prospect Park and the landing on the American side. The half-hour cruise costs about $4. Another good way to see the falls is from the Observation Tower in Prospect Park.

You also can view the cascade from below. Take an elevator 125 feet down to the **Scenic Tunnels**, which lead to a two-level observation deck near Horseshoe Falls. Wear a slicker; it's wet.

Bridges and wooden walkways lead across the base of Bridal Veil Falls, within 25 feet of the river, to the **Cave of the Winds** below Goat Island. The roar of the water and the heavy spray are overwhelming.

Look for accommodation on the Canadian side, 20 minutes north on Niagara Parkway, in the 164-year-old town **Niagara-on-the-Lake**. This lovely retreat is the home of the Shaw Festival. The **Oban**, *160 Front St.; tel. (416)468-7811*, is one of the oldest inns—rooms start at $95. The **Moffat Inn**, *60 Picton St.; tel. (416)468-4116*, where a double room is $159 to $199, and the **Prince of Wales**, *6 Picton St.; tel. (416)468-3246*, where a double room is $106 to $220, are also pleasant places to stay.

The best of the Adirondacks

You can hike in the **Adirondacks** for days without leaving the wilderness. The most beautiful area is between lakes Placid and Saranac, where the forest is untouched and the streams are pure.

Adirondack National Park is the largest wilderness area east of the Mississippi, bordered by lakes George and Champlain. One of the most beautiful sights in the park is the **Ausable Chasm**, on Route 9 near Interstate 87, a mile-long gorge near Lake Champlain.

Fort Ticonderoga, used during the French and Indian War and the Revolutionary War, guards the junction of lakes Champlain and George. A museum today, it is open May through October.

Lakes Placid and Saranac, at the heart of the Adirondacks, offer canoeing, boating, and fishing. Lake Placid has tremendous skiing—good enough for Olympic athletes, in fact, who competed here in 1980.

The best place to stay on Saranac Lake is **The Point**, *Star Route, Saranak Lake, Box 65; (518)891-5674*, an 11-room inn with a private beach. Originally a camp, The Point is elegant now, decorated with fine paintings. The bedrooms are enormous. You can sail or canoe on the lake, hike or cross-country ski through the woods, or play tennis, golf, badminton, billiards, pingpong, or croquet. A double room is $625 to $775, including use of all facilities.

High Peaks Base Camp, 13 miles from Lake Placid, *Springfield Road; tel. (518)946-2133*, is situated on 200 acres ringed by the Sentinel Wilderness Range and the Hurricane Mountain Primitive area. It has miles of cross-country ski trails and is just five miles from the downhill ski slopes at Whiteface Mountain. Enjoy a home-cooked meal in the Wood Parlor. The price is unbelievable—$18 for a bunk, $45 for a double room. Weekly rates are $65 to $90.

The **Rose Inn**, *Route 34N, P.O. Box 6576, Ithaca; (607)533-7905*, is also a charming place to stay, 10 minutes outside of Ithaca. The light-rose, Italianate mansion is set on 20 acres of gardens, a pond, and an apple orchard. All the rooms are decorated differently, with a variety of antiques and Victorian furniture. The cuisine here is fabulous. Each guest chooses his appetizer and entrée at the time of booking. A double room is $90 to $220.

The Baseball Hall of Fame

Cooperstown, in central New York state, is a small town with a big drawing card—the **Baseball Hall of Fame**. Three floors of baseball memorabilia fill this museum, a mecca for baseball fans. You can see enlarged photographs of the world's best baseball players, sculptures of Babe Ruth and Ted Williams carved from single pieces of laminated basswood, and roughly 1,000 artifacts and photos from the early Negro baseball leagues. Also on display are baseball cards from 1900, Lou Gehrig's uniform, and Joe DiMaggio's locker.

Cooperstown has several good restaurants. The best is the **Dining Room**, *171 Main*

St.; (607)547-2211, where you can indulge in homemade fare and rich desserts.

Our favorite place to stay is **Angelholm,** *14 Elm St.; (607)547-2483,* a restored home built nearly 175 years ago. This bed-and-breakfast has only four bedrooms, and baths are shared. But a complete breakfast is included in the price of a room ($70 to $80).

Lake Champlain's bests (and beasts)

Between New York, Vermont, and Quebec lies **Lake Champlain,** where more than 200 sightings of a controversial monster called Champ have been reported. Champ's existence is debatable, but the beauty of the lake and its islands is not.

Lake Champlain's major islands—North Hero, South Hero, and Isle La Motte—are dotted with sugar maple and oak trees, red barns, and silos. Although they look serene, they have had a tumultuous history. The French, British, and Americans warred over the lake, because of its importance as a natural highway from New York to Canada.

Samuel de Champlain discovered the islands in 1609, claiming them for the French. Later, the British claimed them, and finally the Americans. The turning-point battle of the War of 1812 was fought at Plattsburgh, where nearly 30,000 British troops were defeated by 2,000 Americans.

Isle La Motte is the site of the first settlement in Vermont, **Fort St. Anne,** which was built by the French in 1666 for defense against the Indians. Today open-air Masses are held here. **Fort Blunder,** built by the Americans in 1777, was so named because its builders didn't realize it was on Canadian soil.

The best of New England

One of the oldest and most historic areas of the United States is **New England,** where quaint, shingled homes and simple churches have a unique charm. Boston harbors intellect, art, ethnic variety, and beauty. Cape Cod has the most beautiful coastline on the Atlantic. And the mountains of northern New England are green and rolling.

The best of Boston

Boston, one of the most livable cities in America, is a collection of interconnected small towns. Despite its folksy atmosphere, it is sophisticated, with a large intellectual community and many universities and colleges. It is also the best place to trace American colonial history. Historic figures, such as Samuel Adams, Paul Revere, and Ben Franklin, lived here. Walk by the **Old North Church,** where lanterns were hung to signal an attack by the British during the Revolutionary War. Or climb **Bunker Hill,** the site of one of the war's major battles. And visit the place where Boston Tea Party participants dumped British tea into the harbor.

American writers Ralph Waldo Emerson, Henry David Thoreau, Louisa May Alcott, and Daniel Webster found inspiration in Boston. In more recent years, Boston has spawned the Kennedys. And many of America's best minds have graduated from nearby Harvard University.

The easiest way to see the best of Boston

The easiest way to see Boston is to follow the **Freedom Trail**—a red brick or painted line that leads past the city's greatest landmarks. The trail takes you past the **Old State House,** where the Boston Massacre occurred; the **Old North Church,** where the light was hung to signal Paul Revere; the **Old South Meeting House,** where the Boston Tea Party was planned; the **Boston Tea Party Ship and Museum;** and the **Granary Burial Ground,** where the victims of the Boston Massacre are buried.

Boston's must-sees

The best view of the city is from **Bunker Hill,** but you'll have to climb 294 steps to enjoy it.

Beacon Hill is an elegant neighborhood with trees, cobblestoned streets, and beautiful old brownstones. Louisa May Alcott once lived at 10 Louisburg Square. Blue bloods now live where Puritans originally settled.

The **Black Heritage Trail** passes 16 important landmarks of black history over the past 300 years.

The **State House**, a gold-domed building in Beacon Hill, is open to visitors.

The world's oldest public library
Boston's **Public Library** is the oldest in the world, founded by Benjamin Franklin and decorated with paintings by Sargent.

Boston's best museums
The **Museum of Fine Arts**, *(617)267-9377*, near Northeastern University, has Egyptian, Impressionist, and Americana collections.

The **Isabella Stuart Gardner Museum**, *280 Fenway; (617)734-1359*, is a small Venetian-style palace filled with great works of art, including Titian's *The Rape of Europa*, Raphael's *Pieta*, and paintings by Rembrandt, Sargent, Whistler, and Matisse. The museum is closed Monday.

Boston's **Institute of Contemporary Art**, *955 Boylston St.; (617)266-5151*, in a former fire station, displays works by contemporary artists.

The museum at the **John F. Kennedy Library**, *Morrisey Boulevard; (617)929-4567*, contains photos and documents about John and Robert Kennedy.

The world's largest fish tank
The **New England Aquarium** on Central Wharf is the world's largest fish tank, containing the world's greatest collection of sharks.

Boston's best parks
Boston is a city of parks. The best is the **Boston Common**, with its inviting green lawns, sunbathers, frisbee players, musicians, picnicking families, and swan-filled ponds.

Boston's **Public Gardens**, between Arlington, Boylston, Beacon, and Charles streets, are just across from the Boston Common.

The **Arnold Arboretum**, a 265-acre park on the Arborway in Jamaica Plain, is one of America's oldest parks, containing 6,000 varieties of trees.

Boston's best laughs
The **Comedy Connection**, *76 Warrenton St.; (617)426-6339*, backstage at the Charles Playhouse, has uproarious comedians every night. **Catch a Rising Star**, *Harvard Square, Cambridge; (617)661-9887* or *(617)661-0167*, and **Stitches**, *835 Beacon St.; (617)424-6995*, are also good. The cover charge for the city's comedy clubs is $5 to $12.

The most festive times to visit
Patriot's Day (April 19) is celebrated with the re-enactment of Paul Revere's ride. The hero sets out from the North End and gallops past the Old North Church yelling, "The British are coming, The British are coming." In Concord, Minutemen re-enact the battle of the Old North Bridge. This is also the day of the Boston Marathon.

Boston's best ice cream
Every Boston-area neighborhood has its favorite ice-cream parlor. The best is **Toscanini's**, *899 Main St.; (617)491-5877*, in Cambridge, a small shop serving 16 homemade flavors, including ginger, grape-nut raisin, Vienna finger cookie, and Belgian chocolate.

420

A roster of great restaurants

The best seafood restaurant in Boston is **Anthony's Pier 4**, *140 Northern Ave.; (617)423-6363*, which is decorated with pieces of scrimshaw and old navigational equipment. Order the lobster.

The most elegant restaurant in town is **Aujourd'hui**, in the Four Seasons Hotel, *200 Boylston St.; (617)338-4400*, where New England fare is spiced up with European and Asian accents. White linen and Royal Doulton china dress the tables.

The most romantic restaurant is **Café Budapest**, *90 Exeter St.; (617)266-1979*, where exotic flowers decorate the Old World dining rooms, and spicy Central European dishes scent the air.

One of the oldest restaurants in Boston is the **Locke-Ober Café**, *3 Winter Place; (617)542-1340*, which opened in 1875. Try the filet of lemon sole *bonne femme*.

Boston's finest hotels

The oldest hotel in America and Boston's best is the **Omni Parker House Hotel**, *60 School St; (617)227-8600*. Dickens, Emerson, and Longfellow all stayed here. The famous Parker House roll was first baked here more than a century ago. Ho Chi Minh once worked at the Parker house as a busboy. A double room starts at $195.

The **Ritz Carlton**, *15 Arlington St.; (617)536-5700*, is an elegant place with a dignified staff and luxurious rooms. The hotel restaurant offers exquisite meals and lovely views of Boston's Public Gardens. A double room is $199 to $380.

The **Copley Plaza**, *138 St. James Ave.; (617)267-5300*, is an elegant 460-room hotel opened in 1912. While it is grand, it has an intimate air, with a library where you can take tea. The bedrooms are spacious and richly furnished. The Copley has three restaurants, three bars, and shops. A double room is $190.

The best of Cambridge

Across the Charles River from Boston is **Cambridge**, a charming area encompassing Harvard University (the oldest in the nation), the Massachusetts Institute of Technology (MIT), and lots of bookstores and movie houses.

The trendiest shops and restaurants are on **Harvard Square**, where you'll also find street performers, five ice-cream parlors, and seven bars. **Harvard Yard**, part of the campus, is quieter and more dignified.

The **Harvard University Museum**, *24 Oxford St.*, is actually four museums: the Peabody Museum of Archeology and Ethnology, the Museum of Comparative Zoology, the Mineralogical and Geological Museum, and the Botanical Museum. The museum's Ware Collection of glass flowers is the finest array of decorative glasswork in the world.

The **Fogg Art Museum**, *32 Quincy St.*, is the best university art collection, a formidable assortment of Oriental and late 18th-century European art.

One of the largest comic book stores in the United States is the **Million Year Picnic**, *99 Mount Auburn St.*

The **Grolier Bookstore**, *6 Plympton St.*, is the oldest poetry bookstore in the country.

Two historic towns

Just outside Boston are two towns that played essential roles in American history: Lexington and Concord.

Paul Revere rode through **Lexington** the night of April 18, 1775, warning that British troops were approaching. On Lexington Green, the first shots of the Revolutionary War were fired and the first blood was drawn.

Founding fathers Samuel Adams and John Hancock slept at the **Hancock-Clarke House**, *36 Hancock St.*, today a museum.

Concord is the town next door, where Minutemen gathered to head off the British.

The Old North Bridge over the Concord River is the site of the Revolutionary War's first battle. It was made famous by these words: "Here once the embattled farmers stood and fired the shot heard round the world."

Concord produced some of America's most famous writers. Louisa May Alcott lived with her family at the Wayside and wrote *Little Women* at the Orchard House. You can visit the **Ralph Waldo Emerson House**, *28 Cambridge Turnpike*. Nathaniel Hawthorne rented the **Old Manse**, *Monument Street*, but bought **Wayside**, *Lexington Road*.

The **Concord Museum**, *Lexington Road and Cambridge Turnpike*, displays possessions of Emerson and Thoreau.

Cape Cod: the most beautiful coastline

Cape Cod, a hook-shaped sandy peninsula in southeast Massachusetts, has the most beautiful coastline on the Atlantic: sand dunes covered with sea oats, silvery driftwood, seagulls basking in the sun, huge rocks, and the crashing ocean. The Cape Cod National Seashore protects 44,600 acres of the cape from development.

The liveliest town

Provincetown, at the northern tip, is the cape's hot spot, a maze of clapboard houses, some dating back to the 18th century, galleries, guesthouses, and shops. Popular and busy, it draws artists, gays, and families. The town lies within the Cape Cod National Seashore and is surrounded by dunes, ocean beaches, marshes, and woods.

Commercial Street, the main thoroughfare, is lined with art galleries, shops, and crowds of pedestrians, bikers, cars, horse-drawn buggies, hawkers, and skateboarders. Here, also, is the **Provincetown Playhouse**, where Eugene O'Neill spent a lot of time.

Provincetown has a long history. Although Plymouth claims to be the oldest colony, the pilgrims actually landed at Provincetown first, before heading on to Plymouth, where they settled. A monument to these hardy souls sits atop a 100-foot hill at the heart of town. The 252-foot granite column can be climbed via 116 steps. From the top, you can see for 50 miles on a clear day.

Provincetown boasts one of the few links-style golf courses in the United States, the **Highland Golf Club**, *Highland Road, Truro; (508)487-9201*. You can play for $10.

For dancing, go to **Captain John's**, *Shankpainter Road; (508)487-3899*. More novel entertainment can be found at the **Surf Club**, *MacMillan Wharf; (508)487-1367*, where you can marvel at the Provincetown Jug and Marching Band—four musicians who play 20 instruments, including washboards, jugs, and kazoos.

The **Moors**, *Bradford Street; (508)487-0840*, has good Portuguese dishes and fresh seafood, but it is a seasonal restaurant.

Our favorite inn is **Bradford Gardens**, *178 Bradford St.; (508)487-1616*, built in 1820, one block from the beach. The two-story main house and the four additional cottages are decorated with fireplaces and old-fashioned furnishings. Double rooms are $89 to $150 during peak season, including a gourmet breakfast. The hotel is seasonal, so call before arriving.

New England's oldest settlement

Plymouth, where the *Mayflower* landed in December 1620, is the oldest European settlement in New England. Half the colony died the first terrible winter here. **Plymouth Rock**, the landmark boulder marking the spot where the pilgrims disembarked, is kept behind bars at **Pilgrim Hall**, *Water Street*. The Plymouth of 1627 and the Wampanoag Indian summer campsite have been recreated here in a Williamsburg-style complex called **Plimouth Plantation**, where actors play the parts of the pilgrims and Indians. Explore the *Mayflower II*, a reproduction of the original.

The **Sleepy Pilgrim**, *182 Court St.; (508)746-1962*, is a pleasant 12-unit motel with double rooms for $57. It is open April through December.

The best whale watching

Whale-watching cruises depart Plymouth and Provincetown for the Stellwagen Bank north of Cape Cod, one of the few areas in the United States where great whales can be seen on a regular basis. Each year, thousands of these beautiful giants take up residence on the 20-mile-long shoal. Fifteen kinds of whales have been seen in these waters, as well as dolphins, porpoises, and rare birds. Marine biologists accompany the cruises to identify and describe the fish and birds and explain their behavior. The price is about $20 for adults, $14 for children, and $16 for senior citizens and students.

Groups offering cruises from Plymouth include **Captain Tim Brady & Sons**, *(508)746-4809*. Whale-watching cruises from Provincetown include **Portuguese Princess**, *(508)487-2651*, and **Provincetown Whale Watch**, *(508)487-3322*.

Provincetown Inn, at the tip of Provincetown, *(508)487-9500*, offers a whale-watching package that includes a cruise, two dinners, two breakfasts, and two nights lodging for $120 per person, double occupancy in high season, $69 in low season.

Also visit the **Whale Discovery Museum**, *(508)747-0015*, in Plymouth. Admission is $5 for adults, $3.75 for children.

The most beautiful island

Martha's Vineyard Island, off the coast of Cape Cod, is the most beautiful on the Atlantic Coast, protected by bluffs and dunes. Rocky and sandy beaches edge the island. Inland are pine forests and peaceful lakes and ponds, where you can canoe among rare seabirds. At the far end of the island are the brightly colored cliffs of Gay Head and a small Indian reservation. Shingled Cape Cod houses nestle among the island's rolling hills, and bayberry scents the air.

You can catch a ferry to Martha's Vineyard from the Cape Cod town of **Woods Hole**. If you plan to bring a car, make reservations well in advance; you'll have to wait in line for hours if you don't.

Edgartown is the most elegant town on the island, its narrow streets lined with expensive shops and guesthouses.

Oak Bluffs is a honky-tonk town, less stuffy than most of the towns on the island. Gingerbread houses make this slightly seedy town look quaint. The largest carousel in the world, the Flying Horses, is here.

Gay Head is the most beautiful spot on Martha's Vineyard. It is also home to the remaining Indians on the island, who live on a reservation nearby. An Indian-operated lunch counter at the top of the cliffs serves the best milk shakes anywhere. The view from the patio is the best on the island.

Seafood is fresh and plentiful on Martha's Vineyard. For lobster, go to the **Homeport** restaurant, *Menemsha; (508)645-2679*, where dinner is about $23, including appetizer and dessert. Bring your own wine. Reservations are advised.

If you're feeling more adventurous, buy your own fresh lobster and a steamer in Menemsha, a small fishing village, and prepare your own feast. Freshly caught lobsters sell for just $5 a pound. Or stop in at any of the restaurants in these towns frequented by the local fishermen; most all of them offer lunch specials including one or two small lobsters, french fries, and salad for less than $10.

Edgartown is home to the island's two most elegant restaurants: L'Etoile and Warriners. The seafood at **Warriners**, *Post Office Square; (508) 627-4488*, is good, and the wine list is extensive. But it's a bit stuffy, and it's closed Wednesday nights. **L'Etoile**, *Charlotte Inn, 27 S. Summer St.; (508)627-5187*, is pretty, and the service is superb.

Our favorite inn is the **Kelly House**, *121 N. Water St.; (508)627-4394*, in Edgartown. A cozy place decorated in the style of the 1890s, it is open year-round. Double rooms are $205 to $510. The dining room is good and inexpensive.

The **Captain Dexter House**, *100 Main St., Vineyard Haven; (508)693-6564*, is a good inn with reasonable prices. (Double rooms are $95 to $140 during the summer, including Continental breakfast.) This old sea captain's home was built in 1843 and is filled with antiques. But it is seasonal, so call ahead.

Nantucket—the most exclusive

Nantucket is a lovely island east of Martha's Vineyard. This wealthy resort has long, sandy beaches and quaint, cobblestoned streets. If you love to shop, you'll love Nantucket. Look for Nantucket woven baskets and scrimshaw jewelry (carved from whale teeth). **Seven Seas Gifts** is a good gift shop with an enormous variety.

The best way to see Nantucket is by bike. Pedal out to **Seaskonset Beach** (pronounced Skonset) and check out the island's many old lighthouses.

Nantucket was the greatest whaling town in the United States during the 18th and 19th centuries. Visit the **Nantucket Whaling Museum** and **Hadwen House** and **Peter Foulger House**, old whaling homes that are open to the public.

The island's best restaurant is the **Jared Coffin House**, *29 Broad St., (508)228-2400*, which is internationally acclaimed. It is open April through December.

Two pleasant old inns are the **Carriage House**, *5 Ray's Court; (508)228-0326*, in a converted 1865 carriage house, and the **Ships Inn**, *13 Fair St.; (508)228-0040*, in a sea captain's house built in 1812. Both have antique furnishings. A double room at the Ships Inn is $95 to $100 in high season, including Continental breakfast; a double room at the Carriage House is slightly more expensive. Both are seasonal.

New Hampshire's bests

The highest peak on the East Coast is **Mount Washington** in the White Mountains of New Hampshire. Located in the **White Mountain National Forest**, this 6,288-foot mountain is a popular ski resort. Take the train to the top. **Crawford Notch State Park**, nearby, has sparkling waterfalls. Take Route 3 to the flume at the southern end of Franconia Notch. This glacier-covered chasm has 70-foot walls. A rock formation called The Old Man of the Mountains looks over Profile Lake.

Mount Washington Hotel and Resort, *Bretton Woods; (603)278-1000*, is the most peaceful of the Shite Mountain resorts. Excellent stables, a championship golf course, fishing, skiing, and tennis are offered. A double room is $95.

Maine's main sights

The best thing about **Portland, Maine**, is the area surrounding it. Casco Bay, the Casco Bay Islands, and Sebago Lake are typical New England areas, with quaint houses and good boating and swimming. Portland also has great lobster, good night life, and the poet Longfellow's house. **Cap'n Newick's Lobster**, *740 Broadway St., South Portland; (207)799-3090*, is the best place in town for lobster (although the decor isn't much).

Bar Harbor

Bar Harbor, Maine, once a mecca for the wealthy, welcomes a broader spectrum of visitors today. The quaint harbor town shares **Mount Desert Island** (so named by Champlain in 1604 because of its rocky summit) with **Acadia National Park**, an expanse of mountains, spruce forests, rugged coastline, and deep lakes. Along the shore is Somes Sound, the deepest fiord on the East Coast. The air is pure, and the drinking water is the best we have ever tasted. The local restaurants serve fresh lobster for next to nothing.

Acadia National Park is surrounded by a 10-mile park road loop. Along the road are **Thunder Hole**, where waves rush into a rocky canyon producing a thundering boom and sending up towers of foam; **Jordan Pond**, an idyllic, mirrorlike pond reflecting the Bubbles, two rounded mountains; **Jackson Memorial Library**, the world's largest center for mammalian genetic research; and **Sand Beach**, the island's only sandy swimming area.

It's worth rolling out of bed early to see the sun rise from the summit of **Cadillac**

Mountain, a windswept bald spot, the highest on the island, with views of forests, ocean, and neighboring islands. If you do get here at dawn, you are the first person in the United States to see the sun rise.

The best place to dine on the island is the **Jordan Pond House,** *Park Loop Road, Acadia National Park; (207)288-9561,* a rambling old house. You can dine on the lawn when it's warm or by the fireplace when it's not.

A good place to stay is the **Bluenose,** *90 Eden St., Bar Harbor; (800)445-4077,* set on a cliff just outside town. Rooms have French doors that open onto private balconies overlooking Frenchman's Bay. The pool is heated, a real asset in chilly Maine. And there is also an indoor pool. A double room is $145 to $175.

Newport: best jazz, best sailing

Newport, Rhode Island has New England's finest mansions (which belong to such families as the Astors and the Vanderbilts), as well as the region's top music festival and sailing events. (Before the America's Cup was won by Australia, the regatta began here, at the mouth of the Narragansett Bay.)

For two weeks every July, Newport hosts a music festival with concerts featuring premier and recently discovered works and thematic programs, such as "Emperor's Court," works composed in Austria-Hungary during the reign of Franz Josef. The spectacular mansions of Newport are converted to concert halls for this 21-year-old event. The long list of debuts by major talents at this festival is indicative of its quality. You can get tickets through the **Music Box,** *(401)849-6666.*

The best restaurant in town is the **White Horse Tavern,** *Marlborough and Farewell streets; (401)849-3600,* America's oldest tavern. Built in 1673, it later became a tavern run by a notorious Red Sea pirate. It doesn't open for lunch on Tuesdays.

A good place to stay the night is **Mill Street Inn,** *75 Mill St.; (401)849-9500,* where double rooms are $195 to $300 during the summer, including Continental breakfast.

The most interesting inn in the area is the **Jail House Inn,** *13 Marlborough St.; (401)847-4638.* Built in 1772, it served as the Newport jail for over 200 years. The 22 "cells" have been converted into modern, sunny suites with views of downtown Newport. A double room is $55 to $125, depending on the season. Continental breakfast is included.

Classic New England in Vermont

Rural **Vermont** offers the rolling Green Mountains, lovely Lake Champlain, covered bridges, bridle trails, farmland, and little villages.

Stowe, in northern Vermont, is the state's biggest vacation center. It is best visited during its Winter Carnival in mid-January, which includes ice sculpture and winter sport competitions. **Mount Mansfield** provides downhill and cross-country skiing and hiking on its Long Trail.

Arlington, in southwestern Vermont, is home to the Norman Rockwell exhibition and to our favorite inn in the area, the **Arlington Inn,** *Historic Route 7A, P.O. Box 369; (802)375-6532.* The feel and decor of the Arlington is pure Victorian; the exterior architecture is Greek Revival. Each of the 13 rooms has a fireplace, as well as a reading chair or sitting area. Bed and breakfast is $50 to $125.

The quintessential New England town is **Newfane,** Vermont. North of Brattleboro, this town is gorgeous in the fall, when autumn leaves splatter it with color and the air smells of apples. In winter, neighbors gather around the potbelly in Union Hall.

The **Old Newfane Inn** (1787) dates back to when Vermont was a republic. **Union Hall,** built in 1832, was once a house of worship. The **Newfane Store** sells homemade cider and fudge. The famous **Marlboro Music Festival** is held nearby each summer, on the campus of Marlboro College. A double room at the **Old Newfane Inn,** *Court Street; (802)365-4427,* on the green, costs $105.

One of Vermont's best resorts is **Stratton Mountain Resort,** *(802)297-2200,* in the

425

Green Mountains. Lessons are given in downhill and cross-country skiing, golf, tennis, and fishing.

Said to be the most photographed village in Vermont, **Lower Waterford** is home to one of the best places to stay in the entire state. The **Rabbit Hill Inn,** *Route 18; (802)748-5168* or *(800)76-BUNNY,* makes you feel right at home. When you arrive, tea or cider is served in the formal dining room, and dinner is served by candlelight. Many of the rooms include four-poster beds, sitting areas, and fireplaces. A double room is $159.

New Jersey: the most maligned state

New Jersey is the most maligned state in the Union, probably because most people know only the long and ugly turnpike. Despite odorous industrial cities, such as Newark and Elizabeth, New Jersey does deserve its description as The Garden State. A patchwork quilt of farm communities and historical parks, New Jersey offers the top per-acre value for agricultural production.

The state's beaches are natural and white and extend the entire length of the coast. At the heart of New Jersey are the **Pine Barrens,** an unspoiled wooded area. Northern New Jersey has pretty lakes, and in the northwest are mountains leading into the Poconos. Along the Delaware border are historic towns dating back to the Revolutionary War.

More than 100 clashes occurred on New Jersey soil during the Revolutionary War, including pivotal battles in Trenton, Princeton, and Monmouth.

Princeton: New Jersey's prettiest town

Princeton, a beautiful, historic town founded in the 17th century, is the site of an Ivy League university, stately private mansions, and an intimate downtown area. In addition to housing **Princeton University,** the town is the home of the Institute of Advanced Study founded by Einstein, the Princeton Theological Seminary, and Westminster Choir College, famous for its choir.

Built around Princeton University, a center of thought since 1756, the town has been embellished by such wealthy benefactors as Andrew Carnegie (who funded the building of a lake used as a training area for the Princeton rowing crew and as an ice-skating rink in winter). Another benefactor refurbished the central downtown square (called **Palmer Square**) in a Tudor motif, complete with an old-fashioned inn. Palmer Square is especially lovely at Christmas, when the giant pine at its center is decorated. Princetonians gather around the tree to sing carols.

Nassau Hall at the university was the seat of the Continental Congress from June to November 1783.

Buy a gourmet picnic lunch from the **Squire's Choice,** *Palmer Square,* and enjoy it on **Princeton Battlefield,** where George Washington's army won a victory on Jan. 3, 1777, against the British, or in **Marquand Park,** which has more variety than most botanical gardens. Late in the summer, community theater groups stage plays on the battlefield beside the four marble columns left standing from a home burned down during the Revolutionary War. The cool pines protect the audience from the summer sun.

The **Annex Restaurant,** *Nassau Street; (609)921-7555,* is an Italian restaurant where you can get a relatively inexpensive but delicious meal. After 10 p.m., you can mingle with professors and students at the bar.

The **Nassau Inn,** *10 Palmer Square; (609)921-7500,* at the center of town, has several dining rooms, including the **Yankee Doodle Tap Room,** which offers live music. Initials carved in the inn's tabletops date back to 1919.

The best of the Jersey shore

One hundred miles of boardwalk and beaches trim the New Jersey coast, offering both honky-tonk towns and quiet enclaves.

Atlantic City: a gambler's best

Almost every American knows the streets of **Atlantic City**, a honky-tonk town famous for its gambling, by heart—they are on the *Monopoly* game board. Before the Civil War, Atlantic City was the seaside getaway for the high society of New York and Philadelphia. The town fell on hard times during the mid-20th century. However, in 1978, Resorts International opened the first casino here, and since then the town has been revived. A dozen casinos have opened along the boardwalk and on the bay.

The former Million Dollar Pier has been reborn as **Ocean One**, a shopping and dining arcade. Like visitors of 100 years ago, you can ride a canopied wicker chair on wheels from one end of the boardwalk to the other, stopping to see saltwater taffy being pulled.

The best restaurant in town is the **Knife and Fork**, *Pacific and Albany avenues; (609)344-1133*, near Bally's Grand. Service is fabulous; customers are treated like royalty. The seafood dishes are excellent, especially the bouillabaisse, which is chock-full of fish, including large pieces of lobster.

Cape May: a Victorian surprise

At the southern tip of the Jersey shore is a Victorian surprise: **Cape May**. Victorian mansions with wide porches, gables, and elaborate woodwork line the streets. Many are guesthouses. The wide sandy beach is inviting.

The **Barnard-Good House**, *238 Perry St.; (609)884-5381*, is a Victorian house with a wraparound porch decorated with lacy wood trim. The parlor has an antique pump organ and a hand-carved and tiled false fireplace. An iron, pewter, and brass gasolier hangs above the dining room table. The breakfast served here is delicious—fresh juice, omelets, croissants, homemade breads, and crepes. Each of the six bedrooms is decorated differently; some have four-poster beds, others have bathrooms with antique tubs. It is seasonal.

The **Summer Cottage Inn**, *613 Columbia Ave.; (609)884-4948*, was built in 1867 as a summer home. Verandas and tall ceilings keep the house cool. This Victorian bed-and-breakfast is decorated with walnut- and oak-inlaid floors and period wallpaper. Afternoon tea is served in the sitting room, where wicker furnishings are placed around the fireplace. Three of the bedrooms have private baths. A double room is $105 to $115.

A best for Bruce fans

Bruce Springsteen fans should visit the **Stone Pony**, in Asbury Park, where he and Southside Johnny got their starts. Rock'n'roll stars still come through here now and then. Otherwise, the Stone Pony's marquee lists up-and-coming regional bands that you might see on the charts some day.

New Jersey's best inn

The **Woolverton Inn**, *Woolverton Road, Stockton; (609)397-0802*, is on the New Jersey/Pennsylvania line at the Delaware River. Shaded by two spacious front porches and big old trees, this stone manor house was built in 1793 by John Prall, who ran a quarry in what is now the garden. In 1957, Sir John Terrell, the owner of the popular Music Circus, bought the property, and many of the celebrities performing in the Music Circus have stayed here. Every room is filled with antiques. Some bedrooms have canopied beds, others have four-poster beds. A double room is $66 to $135.

Philadelphia: a historian's best

Philadelphia is the most historically important city in the United States. Founded in 1681 by William Penn as a Quaker colony, Philadelphia is where Thomas Jefferson wrote the Declaration of Independence, signed at Independence Hall, and where the Bill of Rights was adopted at Congress Hall. The Continental Congress met in Philadelphia, which was the national capital from 1777 to 1800.

All the city's major historic sights are in **Independence National Historic Park:** Independence Hall; the Liberty Bell; Carpenter's Hall, where the First Continental Congress met in 1774; City Tavern, a reconstruction of the tavern where delegates of the Continental Congress gathered; Congress Hall; Graff House, where Thomas Jefferson lived; Old City Hall; and the Betsy Ross House.

Bordering the one-mile-square park is **Society Hill,** Philadelphia's oldest neighborhood, which has been completely restored. Society Hill was named for the Free Society of Stock Traders, a company created by William Penn. However, most people presume it was named for the somewhat snooty residents.

The most important sights

The Declaration of Independence and the Constitution were signed at **Independence Hall,** *Chestnut Street.* Half-hour tours are offered. Across the street is the **Liberty Bell Pavilion,** where you can touch the cracked bell that rang out in July 1776 to proclaim the Declaration of Independence. (The bell cracked in 1835 and again in 1846.)

The **Betsy Ross House,** *Arch Street between Second and Third streets; (215)627-5343,* is where musket balls were made for the Continental Army and flags were made for the Pennsylvania Navy. In the house are Betsy Ross' spectacles, snuffbox, and Bible.

The **National Portrait Gallery,** *420 Chestnut St.,* houses paintings of great American figures, many painted by artist Charles William Peale. It is open 9 a.m. until 5 p.m. daily; admission is free.

Penn's Landing is the largest freshwater port in the world. You can visit several ships here, including the *Gazela Primeiro,* a Portuguese square-rigger built in 1883; the *Moshulu,* the largest all-steel sailing ship afloat; and the *SS Olympia,* Admiral Dewey's flagship for the battle of Manila Bay during the Spanish American War.

The **Edgar Allan Poe House,** *532 N. Seventh St.; (215)597-8780,* is where Poe wrote *The Raven, The Tell-Tale Heart,* and *The Murders in the Rue Morgue.*

Germantown: the most historic neighborhood

Philadelphia's most historic neighborhood is **Germantown.** In 1688, its residents made the first formal protest against slavery in this country. The British quartered their troops here during the Revolutionary War. In the 18th century, Philadelphian society built mansions in the area. The most elegant is **Cliveden,** *6401 Germantown Ave.; (215)848-1777,* built in 1763 for Benjamin Chew, a friend of the Penns. The mansion is open to visitors Tuesday through Saturday 10 a.m. until 4 p.m. and Sunday 1 p.m. until 4 p.m.; admission is $4.

The **Wyck Mansion,** *6026 Germantown Ave.; (215)848-1690,* and the **Stenton Mansion,** *Windrim Avenue and 18th Street; (215)329-7312* (which served as Washington's headquarters for a time), are also beautiful. The Wyck Mansion is open 1 p.m. until 4 p.m. Tuesday, Thursday, and Saturday, April through December. The Stenton Mansion is open Tuesday through Saturday 1 p.m. until 4 p.m. April through Christmas. Both charge $3 for admission.

The city's best museums

The **Philadelphia Museum of Art,** *26th Street and Benjamin Franklin Parkway; (215)763-8100,* houses one of the best art collections in the United States. Especially good are the John G. Johnson Collection of European old masters and the paintings by Eakins. The building is a 1928 reproduction of the Parthenon. See Ruben's *Prometheus Bound,* Van Eyck's *St. Francis Receiving the Stigmata,* and Brueghel's *Village Wedding.* Admission is $6, and the museum is open Tuesday through Sunday 10 a.m. until 5 p.m. and until 8:45 p.m. Wednesday.

The **Barnes Foundation Museum,** *300 N. Latches Lane, Merion Station; (215)667-0290,* displays a superb collection of Impressionist paintings, including works by Renoir,

Cézanne, and Matisse. The museum is open Friday and Saturday 9:30 a.m. until 4:30 p.m. and Sunday 1 until 4:30 p.m. It is closed in July and August. Children under 12 are not admitted. Admission is $1.

The rare book department of the **Philadelphia Library**, *Logan Square; (215)686-5322*, is a treasure trove of letters, manuscripts, and original prints, including letters by Dickens, folios by Shakespeare, and Edgar Allen Poe manuscripts.

The **Franklin Institute**, *20th Street and Benjamin Franklin Parkway; (215)448-1200*, is a hands-on science museum founded in 1824, where you can walk through a giant human heart, check out a steam engine, or watch a giant clock that works by gravity. This is the best museum for children in the entire country. Admission is $8.50 to $13.50 for adults, $7.50 to $11.50 for children.

The **Norman Rockwell Museum**, *601 Walnut St.; (215)922-4345*, in the Curtis Building, houses more than 600 reproductions of the painter's works and 324 of his *Saturday Evening Post* covers. The museum is open daily 10 a.m. until 4 p.m. and Sunday 11 a.m. until 4 p.m. Admission is $2.

The **Pennsylvania Academy of Fine Arts**, *Broad and Cherry streets; (215)972-7600*, contains famous American paintings, including Benjamin West's *Penn's Treaty With the Indians* and Winslow Homer's *Fox Hunt*. The Academy is closed Monday; admission is $3.

The **Rodin Museum**, *22nd Street and Benjamin Franklin Parkway; (215)763-8100*, has the most complete Rodin collection outside Paris. It is closed Monday; admission is $6 for adults, $3 for children and students.

The **Rosenbach Museum**, *2010 Delancey Place; (215)732-1600*, has the Rosenbach family collection of rare books, antiques, paintings, and drawings. The original manuscript of James Joyce's *Ulysses*, first editions of *Don Quixote*, a rough draft of *Lord Jim*, and Keats' famous love letters to Fanny Brawne are kept here. The museum is closed Monday; the last tours of the day begin at 2:30 p.m. Admission is $3.50 for adults and $2.50 for children and students.

Three tip-top restaurants

Le Bec-Fin, *1523 Walnut St.; (215)567-1000*, is an elegant restaurant with only 14 tables. The prix-fixe menu includes six courses and changes with the season. Seatings are at 6 and 9 p.m. The restaurant is closed Sunday.

The **Garden**, *1617 Spruce St.; (215)546-4455*, as its name implies, has a lovely garden for dining outdoors. It also has five inviting dining rooms. Try the roast chicken flambé. The restaurant is closed Sunday.

Old Original Bookbinders, *125 Walnut St.; (215)925-7027*, is the place for seafood. This Philadelphia fixture was founded at the end of the Civil War by Samuel Bookbinder and has always been popular. Nearly every president since Lincoln has eaten here.

Philadelphia's best hotels

The crème de la crème of Philadelphia hotels is the **Four Seasons**, *18th and Benjamin Franklin Parkway; (215)963-1500*, an elegant institution with 24-hour room service, a health spa, an indoor pool, complimentary shoeshines, valet parking, a restaurant, and a lounge. A double room is $235 to $285.

The **Sheraton Society Hill**, *One Dock St.; (215)238-6000*, is centrally located in Society Hill, near the historic sights. Facilities include an indoor pool, a health spa, a restaurant, an entertainment lounge, and 24-hour room service. A double room is $175 to $195.

The best of Washington, D.C.

Washington, D.C. has more open space than any capital city in the world. At its heart is the **Mall**, a two-mile expanse of lawn stretching from the Capitol to the Lincoln Memorial and from the George Washington Monument to the Jefferson Memorial. The city's main roads are wide as well, giving a sense of that valued American commodity—elbow room.

Capital sights

The **Capitol,** a domed white building topped by a statue of an Indian symbolizing freedom, is Washington's bull's eye. The main avenues begin here and head out toward the suburbs like spokes on a bicycle wheel. The building is open to the public; you can sit in on congressional hearings. Free tours are offered every 10 minutes to the congressional visitors' galleries of the Senate and the House of Representatives.

From the visitors' gallery of the **Supreme Court Building,** behind the Capitol, you can watch as the laws of the United States are shaped. Sixteen marble columns line the front of this classic Greek-style structure. Six-ton bronze doors guard the main entrance, which is flanked by two huge statues: *The Contemplation of Justice* and *The Guardian, or Authority, of Law.* The court is in session from October through April.

The **White House** is the nation's number-one residence. The best way to see the president's house is to have your congressman arrange a tour. If that's not possible, take one of the regular (and free!) tours conducted in the morning. Be prepared for a long wait. You'll see the public rooms, not the rooms where the first family actually lives. For more information, call *(202)456-2200.*

The **Library of Congress,** *First and Independent streets S.E.,* is one of the world's most comprehensive libraries, with 83 million books, magazines, maps, photos, and films. It is made up of one main building and two annexes and grows at a rate of 7,000 items per day. The original Library of Congress building opened in 1897, a grand Italian Renaissance structure with a dome, columns, murals, and carved balustrades. Three Gutenberg Bibles, a collection of Stradivarius violins, and rare books and prints are kept here. All adults can use the facilities for research, but you cannot take books out. A librarian can explain how to find materials.

Ford's Theater, *511 10th St. N.W.; (202)347-4833,* where Lincoln was assassinated, is still in use. Plays are presented October through May.

The Smithsonian: America's treasure-house

The stated purpose of the **Smithsonian Institute,** founded by Congress in 1846, is "the increase and diffusion of knowledge among men." In its quest to fulfill this goal, the institution has expanded many times and now comprises 15 museums, galleries, a theater, and a zoo. All the Smithsonian museums are open daily 10 a.m. until 5:30 p.m.; admission is free.

The most fascinating of the Smithsonian museums is the **National Air and Space Museum,** *606 Independence Ave. between Sixth and Seventh streets.* It houses the Wright brothers' *Kitty Hawk,* Lindbergh's *Spirit of St. Louis,* and spacecraft. Don't miss the three-dimensional movies on flight.

The **Hirshorn Museum,** *Eighth Street and Independence Avenue N.W.,* contains the most comprehensive collection of modern sculptures in the world. The circular building has ramps that lead upward in a spiral past works of art. Outside the Hirschorn, on the Mall, is the museum's sculpture garden, which contains works by Rodin.

The **Freer Gallery of Art,** *12th Street at Jefferson Drive S.W.,* displays Far Eastern art and artifacts and a splendid collection of works by James Whistler. The president's inaugural reception is held in the garden.

The **National Gallery of Art,** *Sixth and Constitution avenues N.W.,* hosts first-rate art shows. The East Wing, opened in 1978, is an architectural feat, a triangular shape that comes to a perfect point. The West Wing houses one of the world's greatest collections of 19th-century European paintings. It is open Monday through Saturday from 10 a.m. until 5 p.m. and on Sundays from 11 a.m. to 6 p.m.

The **National Museum of Natural History,** *10th and Constitution avenues,* has dinosaur skeletons and the Hope Diamond.

The **National Museum of African Art**, *950 Independence Ave.,* has one of the best collections of African art in the world, as well as an extensive collection of photos and films about Africa.

The **National Museum of American History**, *12th Street and Constitution Avenue N.W.,* displays the earliest American bicycles, the ruby slippers worn by Judy Garland in *The Wizard of Oz*, a 240-pound brass pendulum, tapes of the Watergate hearings, tapes of old *Superman* television shows, recordings of radio shows from the 1940s, and reproductions of log cabins.

The nation's greatest monuments

The **Washington Monument** is the tallest and can be seen from most places in the capital. To enjoy the view from the top, you'll have to wait in a seemingly endless line.

The **Lincoln Memorial** is the most impressive of the monuments. This imposing statue of Honest Abe looks over the reflecting pool. The words of the Gettysburg Address are engraved in the marble walls around him. It is most beautiful at night, when spotlights bring out Lincoln's craggy features.

The **Jefferson Memorial** is the most beautiful, a white marble structure softened by a dome and reflected in the Tidal Basin. It is loveliest in the spring when the cherry trees surrounding it are in bloom.

The **Kennedy Center for the Performing Arts** commemorates President Kennedy. Tour the building and its many theaters even if you don't see a show.

The most moving monument is the **Vietnam War Memorial**, a long black marble wall sunk into the earth, on which the name of every American soldier killed in Vietnam is inscribed. War veterans from around the country make pilgrimages to the site.

The grandest cemetery

Arlington National Cemetery is the final resting place of thousands of soldiers and famous Americans. The tomb of the Unknown Soldier and the graves of John and Robert Kennedy, Pierre L'Enfant (the architect who designed the city), and Chief Justice Oliver Wendell Holmes are also here. The cemetery is located across Memorial Bridge.

Mount Vernon: the most beautiful home

George Washington's home, **Mount Vernon**, is located in a beautiful spot along the Potomac, in Virginia. The pillared colonial mansion house of the tobacco plantation has a gorgeous view of the river. See the slave cemetery, a sad reminder of the days when some Americans were not free. To get to the house, drive south from Alexandria. The house is open daily from 9 a.m. to 4 p.m.; admission is $7 for adults, $6 for senior citizens, and $3 for children.

The most beautiful parks and gardens

Dumbarton Oaks Museum and Garden, *1703 32nd St. N.W.,* has the city's most beautiful gardens. The museum has a choice collection of Roman and Byzantine art and a display of Columbian jewelry. The French and Italian gardens become more informal as they descend the hill toward woods. The museum is closed Mondays.

The **National Zoological Park**, *the 3000 block of Connecticut Avenue N.W.,* is one of the largest zoos in the country. And it's free. The giant pandas were a gift from China. In warm weather, the monkeys play outside on jungle gyms.

Joggers, bikers, hikers, and horseback riders get away from the city in **Rock Creek Park**. If you follow the wooded trails, you will find yourself alone in the forest. It's hard to believe you're in the middle of the city.

The **Chesapeake and Ohio Canal National Historic Park** provides 185 miles of biking and hiking trails along the Potomac River.

The capital's finest fare

Jean-Louis, at the Watergate Hotel, *2650 Virginia Ave.; (202)298-4488*, is the most elegant restaurant in Washington, a favorite of former President Reagan. Chef Jean-Louis Palladin prepares prix-fixe meals with an endless array of courses. As you might expect, it's expensive.

The **Palm**, *1225 19th St. N.W.; tel. (202)293-9091*, is an elegant restaurant, the best in town for steak.

Dominique's, *1900 Pennsylvania Ave. N.W.; tel. (202)452-1126*, serves exotic and tasty game dishes. It offers a prix-fixe menu for $16.95, as well as an a la carte menu.

Washington's best ethnic food

Au Pied du Cochon, *1335 Wisconsin Ave. N.W.*, is a good, inexpensive French bistro.

Le Gaulois, *Pennsylvania Avenue*, near George Washington University, is a popular French restaurant. Make reservations, or you'll wait in line forever.

Thai Taste, *Connecticut Avenue at Calvert Street*, is a good Thai restaurant with reasonable prices. Expect to wait in line if you come here on a weekend.

The **Iron Gate Inn**, *1734 N St. N.W.*, has terrific Mideastern food. The outdoor courtyard is charming.

Washington's most elegant hotels

The **Sheraton Carlton**, *525 New Jersey Ave. N.W.; (800)325-3535 or (202)638-2626*, on 16th and K streets, is only two blocks from the White House. A double room is $170 to $285.

The **Four Seasons**, *2800 Pennsylvania Ave. N.W.; (202)342-0444*, in Georgetown, is the oldest and, until recently, the most elegant hotel in Washington. A double room is $305.

The **Vista International Hotel**, *1400 M St. N.W.; (202)429-1700*, is built around a 14-story atrium. This hotel's facade is a 130-foot-high window. The six floors of suites were personally decorated by Givenchy. A double room is $198.

The **Washington Plaza Hotel**, *Massachusetts and Vermont avenues; (800)424-1140*, is five blocks from the White House and five blocks from the Convention Center. Oriental art decorates the lobby of this nine-story building, which has one of the nicest swimming pools in Washington. A double room is $96 to $170.

The **Stouffer Mayflower Hotel**, *1127 Connecticut Ave. N.W.; (800)468-3571*, was one of the greatest hotels in the world when it opened in 1925. John F. Kennedy, Lyndon B. Johnson, and Harry S. Truman stayed here. A double room is $250.

The **Capitol Hilton**, *16th and K streets N.W.; (202)393-1000*, was renovated recently but still has its has old marble walls. A double room is $224 to $275, including Continental breakfast. **Trader Vic's**, a well-known restaurant in the same building, serves seafood and fancy alcoholic drinks.

The **Hay-Adams**, *H and 16th streets; (800)424-5054*, facing the White House, is the best-situated hotel in Washington. The lobby has rich walnut paneling and two 17th-century tapestries. A double room is $225 to $390.

The **Omni Shoreham**, *Calvert Street and Connecticut Avenue N.W.; tel. (800)843-6664 or (202)234-0700*, is surrounded by 11 acres of parks and woods. Built in 1930, the hotel's 770 rooms have been renovated. Double rooms are $215.

The **Watergate Hotel**, *2650 Virginia Ave. N.W.; tel. (800)424-2736 or (202)393-0930*, was the scene of the famous Watergate burglaries during the Nixon years. Museum-quality Oriental art and top-class restaurants draw visitors. Double rooms are $240.

The best night life

Blues Alley, *1073 Wisconsin Ave. N.W.; (202)337-4141*, in Georgetown, is a great place to see big-name acts. Because the room is so small, you are sure to have a good view of the stage.

432

One Step Down, *2517 Pennsylvania Ave. N.W.; (202)331-8863,* has good jazz musicians on weekends. The cover charge is $12 on the weekends and $5 during the week.

The Bayou, *K Street; (202)333-2897,* in Georgetown, has live local and national bands. The cover charge is $5 to $15.

You can hear live jazz at Lautrec's, *2431 18th St.; (202)265-6436.* On the weekends, there is tap dancing atop the bar.

Kilimanjaro, *1724 California Ave. N.W.; (202)328-3838,* in Adams Morgan, offers live bands, reggae, and steel drums.

Cities, *18th Street,* in Adams Morgan, is a restaurant with a really hot disco upstairs, where everyone is dressed to the hilt. The restaurant is fun. The decor, which revolves around a city theme, changes monthly; one month the place looks like Nairobi, the next month like Paris.

If you prefer a quieter evening, see a Shakespearean play at the Lansburgh Theater, *450 Seventh St. N.W.; (202)393-2700.* Or take in a show at the Kennedy Center, *North Hampshire Avenue and F Street; (202)467-4600;* the National Theater, *1321 Pennsylvania Ave. N.W.; (202)628-6161;* or Arena Stage, *Sixth Street and Maine Avenue S.W.; (202)488-3300.*

The best of Dixie
The U.S. South offers a traditional yet laid-back lifestyle all its own. Southern hospitality is alive and well below the Mason-Dixon Line.

Williamsburg: America's best colonial town
Williamsburg, Virginia, is a completely reconstructed colonial town. Originally, Williamsburg was an outpost of Jamestown, the first permanent English settlement. By the late 1600s, it was the capital of Virginia. However, when the capital was moved to Richmond during the Revolutionary War, Williamsburg was forgotten. In 1926, John D. Rockefeller had the town restored. Today, costumed actors act out the roles of Williamsburg's early settlers.

William and Mary, the second oldest college in the country, is located in Williamsburg. The Sir Christopher Wren Building is the oldest classroom building in the United States.

Old plantations line the banks of the James River near Williamsburg, remnants of colonial days. Carter's Grove is the most beautiful. A dirt road leads from Williamsburg through plantation fields to this Georgian mansion, located on U.S. Route 60.

Berkeley Plantation—not Plymouth—between Williamsburg and Richmond on Route 5 was the site of the first Thanksgiving in 1619. Both Benjamin Harrison and William Henry Harrison were born here.

Charlottesville
Charlottesville, Virginia, sits in the foothills of the Blue Ridge Mountains. Its softly rolling countryside is peppered with acres of mature forests. It is less than 20 minutes from the Shenandoah National Park and Skyline Drive and just around the corner from the University of Virginia, founded by the area's most famous resident, Thomas Jefferson. Although the Charlottesville of today has been "discovered" by the world's rich and famous, the city remains at heart a small, Southern town—a place where Southern hospitality, gentility, and even chivalry are alive and well.

The South's best inn
Just 10 minutes from downtown Charlottesville is the Clifton Inn, *Route 13, Box 26; (804)971-1800.* The 40-acre estate was once part of the Shadwell Plantation, birthplace of Thomas Jefferson. The Clifton possesses not only beauty and history but also a certain charm that truly sets it apart from other inns and hotels. At the Clifton, you are greeted as an old friend and invited to make yourself at home. The main floor of the house is

433

entirely open to guests, who can help themselves to a snack from the kitchen's always-full cookie jar and guest refrigerator.

A double room at the Clifton is $138 to $188, with full breakfast and afternoon tea.

Atlanta: the South's most important city

Atlanta, the city that suffered the most during the Civil War, has become the South's most prominent city. The federal headquarters of Reconstruction following the war is modern and bustling.

Reverend Martin Luther King Jr. began his crusade against racism in Atlanta, which became one of the first southern cities to erase the vestiges of the old slave system. King and his father were pastors at **Ebeneezer Baptist Church**, *407 Auburn Ave. N.E.* King's tomb is in the churchyard there.

Paces Ferry Road is one of the prettiest residential sections in the area. Magnificent estates line the road. The finest is the **governor's mansion**, *391 W. Paces Ferry Road*, with its antiques, gardens, and fountains. The **Atlanta Historical Society** property, *3101 Andrews Drive*, includes the Swan House, an elegant mansion; the Tullie Smith House, a restored antebellum farmhouse and McElreath Hall, which has historic exhibits.

The Margaret Mitchell Room in the **Fulton Public Library**, *Carnegie Way and Forsythe Street; (404)730-1700*, houses autographed copies of *Gone With the Wind*.

Uncle Remus fans should see the **Wren's Nest**, *1050 Abernathy St.; (404)753-7735*, where Joel Chandler Harris lived.

Atlanta's best restaurants and hotels

The **Abbey**, *163 Ponce de Leon Ave.; (404)876-8831*, is meant to look like an abbey, with stained-glass windows and waiters wearing monks' robes. The food is sinfully good and rich. Try the *feuilleté d'agneau* (lamb in a pastry crust).

The **Dining Room**, *3434 Peachtree Road N.E.; (404)237-2700*, just outside Atlanta in Buckhead, has uncompromising service and scrumptious food and wine. Afternoon tea is served. A two-course dinner is $44, a three-course dinner $56; a three-course dinner with wine is $78. All meals are served with dessert.

Two of the finest hotels in the South are the **Westin Peachtree Plaza**, *Peachtree Street and International Boulevard; (404)659-1400*, and the **Hyatt Regency**, *265 Peachtree St.; (404)577-1234*. The Plaza has a lake, birds, and floating cocktail lounges. The Hyatt has a 27-story atrium and revolving bars. A double room in either begins at $195.

Savannah and Charleston: the best of the Old South

Savannah and Charleston retain the charm of the Old South, with pastel houses and near-tropical greenery. **Charleston** is a museum, with old homes, historic monuments, and gardens. Mansions line Church, Meeting, and Battery streets. The two most splendid are the **Nathaniel Russell House**, *51 Meeting St.; (803)724-8481*, and the **Edmonston-Allston House**, *21 E. Battery St.; (803)722-7171*.

The **Charleston Museum**, *360 Meeting St.; (803)722-2996*, is the oldest in America. The **Gibbes Gallery**, *135 Meeting St.; (803)722-2706*, has a collection of works by American artists. Also visit **Fort Sumter**, where the Civil War began when South Carolina attacked the Union stronghold.

Stay at the **Maison Du Pre**, *317 E. Bay St.; (803)723-8691*, in the historic district of Charleston. A double room is $95 to $200, including Continental breakfast, afternoon tea, and newspapers.

Savannah, Charleston's sister city, has a pirate past but an aristocratic Southern ambiance. For two centuries, piracy and shipping flourished here. Today, mansions and gardens dot the town, and the renovated waterfront is filled with shops and restaurants.

Visit the **Ships of the Sea Museum**, *503 E. River St.; (912)232-1511*, which displays ship models and figureheads. Also see the **Owens-Thomas House**, *124 Abercorn St.;*

(912)233-9743, and the **Davenport House**, *Columbia Square; (912)236-8097*. The Owens-Thomas House was built in 1816 and has formal gardens and a restored kitchen. The Davenport House is older and has a beautiful china collection. The grave of Tomochichi, the Indian who allowed settlement in the area, is at Wright Square.

The **First African Baptist Church**, *Franklin Square*, built in 1788, is one of the oldest black churches in the country.

Savannah's best restaurant is **Wilkes Dining Room**, *107 W. Jones St.* Mrs. Wilkes says grace at each table. Long lines wait to enjoy the food at this inexpensive place.

The **Johnny Harris Restaurant**, *1651 E. Victory Drive*, serves the best barbecue in the South. Stay at the **Gastonian**, *220 E. Gaston St.; (912)232-2869*. With two adjoining mansions built in 1868, the Gastonian is the epitome of Southern innkeeping. A double room is $98 to $225, including breakfast.

The best swamp: Okefenokee

This huge wildlife sanctuary is home to rare birds and alligators. Immense cypress trees spread their roots in the black water. Known as the Land of the Trembling Earth by Indians, Okefenokee is surrounded with legend. The northern entrance is south of Waycross, Georgia. For information on swamp excursions, call *(912)283-0583*.

The country-western capital: Nashville

Nashville, the town from which most of America's greatest country musicians hail, is a mecca for country music fans.

The **Grand Ole Opry** is where country music achieved its fame. The Opry opened in 1943 at the Ryman Auditorium, drawing country music fans from far and wide. In 1974, it moved to the newer, bigger **Grand Ole Opry House**, *2802 Opry Lane Drive, just off I-40; (615)889-6700*. The best seats in the house cost $15.62—and they are in high demand, so call early for reservations.

Nashville's top sights

Centennial Park is the place to laze as you listen to local jazz musicians do their thing. The 140-acre park, located on the fringe of downtown Nashville, has a lake and a rose garden and is always filled with people throwing frisbees and playing soccer.

Centennial Park's reproduction of the Greek Parthenon gave Nashville its nickname, the Athens of the South. This impressive structure was built in 1897 to celebrate Nashville's centennial. Housed inside the Parthenon are a collection of oil paintings by American artists from the late 1800s and a statue of Athena—a Nashville sculptor's rendering of a demolished statue described in a fifth-century B.C. critique. For more information on the park, call *(615)862-8431*.

The **Hermitage**, *4580 Rachel's Lane, off Old Hickory Boulevard near I-40; (615)889-2941*, was the home of Andrew Jackson, the seventh president of the United States, built in 1819. Here, Jackson made the decision to move the Cherokee from their homeland to Oklahoma. Some 18,000 Indians passed not far from his house as they marched the Trail of Tears in 1838. The house escaped harm during the Civil War; it was guarded by Federal troops. The house is open daily; admission is $7 for adults, $3.50 for children.

The **Country Music Hall of Fame**, *4 Music Square E.; (615)256-1639*, houses Elvis' solid gold Cadillac and other memorabilia. Across the street is a pool shaped like a guitar. Admission is $6.50.

Fort Nashborough, *First Avenue below Church Street*, is a recreation of the original settlement of Nashville. It's open from 9 a.m. to 4 p.m. daily.

Top entertainment

Although Nashville is home to country music, that's not the only kind of entertainment you'll find here.

The **Tennessee Performing Arts Center (TPAC)**, *505 Deaderick St.,* offers Broadway road shows and performances by the Nashville Ballet and the Tennessee Repertory Theater. For ticket and scheduling information for the Tennessee Repertory Theater, and other TPAC events, call **TicketMaster,** *(615)714-2787.*

For live music (including blues, jazz, rock, and country), go to the **Bluebird Café,** *4104 Hillsboro Road; (615)383-1461.* Get here early or reserve a table. There is a cover charge of $5 to $10 after 9 p.m.

The best restaurants

Julian's, *2412 W. End Ave.; (615)327-2412,* offers the best a la carte classic French cuisine in Nashville. Because the rooms are small, with only one table per room, privacy is ensured. Dinner for two is $70 to $80, not including wine.

Arthur's, *1001 Broadway in the Union Station Hotel; (615)255-1494,* in the mall at Green Hills, is an elegant four-star restaurant with a prix-fixe seven-course meal for $39.50 per person, not including wine. Princess Anne, President Ford, and country music stars have dined here. Arthur's won the 1988 *Travel-Holiday* magazine award for the best restaurant.

The best hotel

The most luxurious accommodation in town is at the **Hermitage,** *231 Sixth Ave. N.; (800)251-1908* or *(615)244-3121,* built in 1910. This hotel, voted the most romantic in Nashville, offers only suites: Choose from contemporary, traditional, and Oriental. Hotel limousines will meet you at the airport. A double room is $59 to $67.

Memphis—home of the king of rock'n'roll

Memphis, located on the banks of the mighty Mississippi, was home to Elvis Presley (known affectionately as The King) and is the cradle of blues music. The music lives on on Beale Street and at Graceland, Elvis' home.

Take a guided tour of **Graceland.** You'll see the King's vast car collection, his trophy room, and the Meditation Gardens, where he and his family are buried. Elvis paid $100,000 for the house in 1957, when he was 22 years old. Die-hard Elvis fans come here to mourn at the singer's grave, often wearing Elvis costumes (white pantsuits, dark glasses, and slicked-back hair). The cost of the tour is $7.95 for adults, $4.75 for children under 12. For more information, call *(901)332-3322* or *(800)238-2000.*

New Orleans: the best party town

New Orleans is famous for its outrageous Mardi Gras, when residents don splendid costumes and hold all-night parties and balls. But it also has some of the nation's best food. And it is one of the prettiest cities in the country.

The **French Quarter** is the oldest, loveliest, and zaniest section of town. Wrought-iron balconies and railings decorate French- and Spanish-style buildings. Female impersonators dance in the bars. Artists, musicians, and partiers roam the streets. **Jackson Square,** the heart of the French Quarter, is marked by St. Louis Cathedral and a statue of Andrew Jackson. The **Moonwalk** provides a view of the river. Streetcar tours along the Mississippi are available at *(504)569-2899* for $1.25, and excellent river tours are available on the Cajun Queen and the Creole Queen, *(504)524-0814.* You can choose either a day cruise or a dinner and jazz cruise. The **French Market** has colorful shops with local crafts and fruits for sale.

The **Garden District,** above Canal Street, is also a good place to visit. This was the center of 19th century American aristocracy, and the homes in the area are of Victorian and Greek Revival design.

Most of the city's bars, which stay open 24 hours a day, are located along **Bourbon Street.** College students, transvestites, bums, tourists, and locals stroll up and down the

436

street in a never-ending, colorful parade. **Royal Street** has good art galleries and shops.

Lafitte's Blacksmith Shop, on Bourbon Street, is New Orlean's most historic saloon. It originally belonged to the pirate John Lafitte, who sold his booty here and plotted to rescue the exiled Napoleon.

Also visit **Café du Monde**, *800 Decatur St.; (504)581-2914*, and treat yourself to its famous beignets and café au lait.

The best museums in New Orleans

The **Cabildo**, *(504)568-6968*, near Jackson Square, houses a death mask of Napoleon. This building was at various times the seat of French, Spanish, and American rule of the Louisiana Territory. It is closed at this time but will reopen Labor Day weekend 1993.

The **Chalmette National Historic Museum**, *St. Bernard Highway; (504)589-4428*, is the site of the Battle of New Orleans (1815), where Andrew Jackson defeated the British.

The **Musee Conti**, *917 Conti St.; (504)525-2605*, is one of the world's finest. The voodoo display and the haunted dungeon are the best.

The **Voodoo Museum**, *724 Dumaine; (504)523-7685*, has a voodoo altar and educational displays.

Mardi Gras: the biggest party

Mardi Gras—a famous celebration that includes balls, parades, and a costume contest—begins shortly after Christmas and lasts until Lent. Most of the activity is in the French Quarter and along Canal Street. The most popular event is a transvestite **He Sheba Contest**. Make reservations well in advance.

The best jazz festival

The New Orleans **Jazz and Heritage Festival** lasts for 10 days in late April and early May, featuring jazz, blues, gospel, and Cajun music. Big-name performerss, such as Fats Domino, the Fabulous Thunderbirds, and Wynton Marsalis, have played. Tickets are $7 per day in advance, $10 per day at the gate. For information, contact the **New Orleans Jazz and Heritage Foundation Inc.**, *P.O. Box 53407, New Orleans, LA 70153; (504)522-4786*.

Booklovers' favorite festival

The **Tennessee Williams/New Orleans Literary Festival** is a must for all booklovers. It takes place in the middle of March.

The best way to dine

The **Grill Room**, at the Windsor Court Hotel, *300 Gravier St.; (504)523-6000*, is the most elegant place in town. It has hosted Nancy Reagan and Princess Anne. The menu and wines are superb. The restaurant is open daily for lunch and dinner.

Arnaud's, *813 Bienville St.; (504)523-5433*, in the French Quarter, is the best Creole restaurant. The decor glitters: crystal chandeliers, antique ceiling fans, beveled windows, and delicate china. Try the oysters Bienville, and save room for the crepes suzette.

The best bars

In the **Napoleon House**, *500 Chartres St.; (504)524-9752*, pictures of the emperor hang on the wall beneath ceiling fans.

The **Old Absinthe House**, *240 Bourbon St.; (504)523-3181*, once served absinthe, an extract of wormwood that is now outlawed because it causes insanity. Here pirates, artists, and gentlemen drank absinthe from a fountain. Today, the bar offers a tasty Absinthe Frappe made with anisette or Pernod.

Pat O'Brien's, *718 St. Peter St.; (504)525-4823,* has a pianist, lots of singles, and an unusual fountain.

Antoine's, *713 St. Louis St.; (504)581-4422,* has New Orleans' best wine cellar. **K-Paul's Louisiana Kitchen,** *416 Chartres St.; (504)524-7394,* serves gin marinated with jalapeno peppers. At the **Maple Leaf,** *8316 Oak St.; (504)866-9359,* you can hear zydeco, Tex-Mex, blues, and ragtime. And the **Preservation Hall,** *726 St. Peter St.; (504)523-8939,* is famous for its Dixieland Jazz. (The Hall doesn't serve drinks; although you can bring your own with you.)

The best hotels

Pontchartrain, *2031 St. Charles Ave.; (504)524-0581,* is the most romantic hotel in town. Double rooms are $150 to $180.

A pleasant, more affordable place to stay, is the **Frenchmen Inn,** *417 Frenchmen St.; (504)948-2166,* in two townhouses built in 1860. Rooms are decorated with antiques and have balconies overlooking the courtyard, the pool, and the patio. Double rooms are $84 to $124, including breakfast.

Soniat House, *1133 Chartres St.; (504)522-0570,* is one of the most elegant and delightful of New Orleans' little hotels. The rooms have all the amenities of luxury hotels, with such added touches as antiques, Oriental rugs, fireplaces, and polished hardwood floors. Rooms are expensive, though—$415 to $425, including breakfast.

Florida: the most tropical state

Florida is the closest most North Americans get to the tropics. Thousands of Yankees and Canadians descend on the Sunshine State during the winter and spring to escape the snow and cold of their home states. It's the easiest winter escape, complete with sandy beaches, palm trees, tropical drinks, resort hotels, seafood restaurants, and lively crowds.

The most peaceful beaches

Most people think of the Atlantic Coast when they think of Florida. But some of the prettiest and least crowded beaches are along the Gulf of Mexico. **Pensacola Beach,** on the panhandle, has fine, white sand and temperate, clear water. **Fort Walton Beach** is attractive and has a 1,200-foot observation pier. Farther south are the white sand beaches of **Belleair** and **Clearwater.** The finest sand is at **Madeira** and **Redington** beaches. **Long Boat Key** is posh and not too crowded. **Point O'Rocks,** an isolated beach near Siesta Key, is famous for its colorful rocks. **Venice Beach** is known for the sharks' teeth that wash up on shore. **Fort Myers Beach** has the most beautiful sunsets. And **Sanibel** and **Captiva** islands are the best places in the state to look for seashells.

Our favorite hotel on the Gulf of Mexico is the **Don CeSar** on St. Petersburg Beach, *(813)360-1881,* an amazing pink Spanish-style castle surrounded by palm trees overlooking the ocean. Once the hideaway of F. Scott Fitzgerald, it is the playground of celebrities. Rooms are $190 to $245 during the winter.

The **Belleview Biltmore,** *25 Belleview Blvd., Belleair-Clearwater; (800)237-8947* or *(800)282-8072,* is a spa. Here you can soak in whirlpools and Swedish showers and work up a sweat in the exercise room. A double room is $130 to $160.

The **Buccaneer Inn,** *595 Dream Island Road; (813)383-1101,* is the best restaurant on Longboat Key, situated on a marina. The house specialty is prime rib cooked very rare and then roasted over live charcoal.

Where the action is: the Atlantic Coast

The Gulf of Mexico is nice, but the surf and the crowds are more exciting on the Atlantic. **Daytona Beach** has 23 miles of sandy beach and a boardwalk. High-rise hotels and condominiums line the ocean. Alas, cars can drive on the beach (a real nuisance).

The most beautiful dunes and beaches along the Atlantic Coast are at **Ponte Vedra** and **South Ponte Vedra** beaches, where two exclusive resorts are located: the Sawgrass and the Ponte Vedra Inn.

The quietest East Coast beach is **New Smyrna**, between Daytona Beach and Titusville. One of the state's last unspoiled beaches is **Playalinda**, part of the Canaveral National Seashore.

Southern Florida's Atlantic Coast has some of the world's most famous resort towns: **Palm Beach**, **Fort Lauderdale**, and **Miami Beach**. College students flock here for spring vacation, and Americans in general migrate here during the winter.

Our favorite place to stay on Florida's Atlantic Coast is the **Breakers**, *South County Road, Palm Beach; (407)655-6611.* The lobby of this grand Italianate resort has frescoed vaulted ceilings and 15th-century Flemish tapestries. The original Breakers, built in 1903, burned, as did the second. The present building was built in 1926. The National Register of Historic Places lists the Breakers as "culturally significant in its reflection of 20th-century grandeur." It has two 18-hole golf courses, a private beach with cabanas, 14 tennis courts, an outdoor saltwater pool, a sauna, lawn bowling, croquet, and programs for children. The hotel dining room is large, and its 100,000-bottle wine cellar is one of the world's biggest.

Fort Lauderdale has some of the finest beaches south of Daytona—and the best night life. The **Candy Store Disco**, *1 N. Atlantic Blvd.; (305)523-7005,* is a lively spot.

The **Bonaventure Resort Spa**, *250 Racquet Club Road; (305)389-3300,* is surrounded by palm trees and waters. You can put your body through a Swiss needle shower, a Shiatsu massage, or an herbal wrap. A double room is $85 to $300, depending on the season.

Miami Beach is the most famous resort, drawing 13 million visitors each year to its luxurious beachfront hotels. South Beach's **Lummus Park** is the best beach area. Eighth Street in **Little Havana** is lined with great Cuban restaurants. The affluent **Coral Gables** neighborhood has more elegant restaurants. And in the middle of Coral Gables sits a gem of a hotel, the **Hotel Place St. Michel**; *162 Alcazar Ave.; (305)444-1666.* A double room is $75 to $125, depending on the season.

The Keys: Florida at its best

The 100-mile chain of gorgeous islands known as the Florida Keys stretches into the Gulf of Mexico from Florida's southern coast. Beaches in the Keys are less commercial, less spoiled, and more relaxed than most of Florida's other beaches.

Four towns dot the islands: Key Largo, Islamorada, Marathon, and Key West. **Key West**, at the tip of the Keys, is known as a place for all-out parties; **Key Largo** is peppered with beaches in small coves; **Smathers** is the longest; **Memorial** has a 100-yard pier over the water; and **South** is the most peaceful. Tavernier and Plantation islands have pretty Atlantic beaches. Big Pine Key has white sand coves on the Gulf side.

The best place to stay in the Keys is the **Marriott Casa Marina**, *1500 Reynolds Ave., Key West; (305)296-3535 or (800)228-9290,* literally the last resort in the United States, situated at the south end of the southernmost city in Florida. Originally, it was a stopover for travelers heading to Havana, Cuba. This posh four-story resort hotel has vaulted ceilings, polished mahogany, arched windows, sea views, and landscaped gardens. Hemingway liked this hotel, as did Harry Truman. During the Cuban Missile Crisis in 1962, the hotel housed American troops. In 1978, it was renovated and returned to its original splendor. A double room is $230 to $335 during peak season.

St. Augustine: America's oldest settlement

Decades before Plymouth or Jamestown, the Spanish established **St. Augustine**, America's oldest permanent settlement, in 1565. In 1740, the fortified town fought off the English. Its fortress, **Castillo de San Marcos**, built in 1672 of coquina rock, has been preserved and can be visited. The courtyard is surrounded by guardrooms, storerooms, a jail, and a chapel.

The **Oldest Store Museum**, *4 Artillery Lane; (904)829-9729,* has tools and machines from the 1800s, including high-wheeled bicycles, a steam-powered tractor, a Gibson Girl corset, and animal-powered treadmills. Admission is $3 for adults, $1.50 for children, and $2.50 for senior citizens.

The **Kenwood Inn**, *38 Marine St.; (904)824-2116,* is a charming old inn in the historic section of St. Augustine. Built in 1865, it has been restored and is furnished with antiques and reproductions. Guests can use the inn's pool. Double rooms are $55 to $85, including Continental breakfast.

Wakulla Springs—America's deepest
Johnny Weissmuller grappled with alligators at **Wakulla Springs** in his famous Tarzan role. Located 10 miles south of Tallahassee, this deep spring has no bottom, or so divers claim, which is why the water is so incredibly cold. If you want to get away from the Florida heat, this is the place. Mastadon bones have been found in this spring.

A beautiful old resort hotel, the **Wakulla Springs Lodge**, *(904)224-5950,* overlooks the spring, surrounded by giant oaks draped with Spanish moss. The lodge is decorated with wood-beamed ceilings, marble floors, massive doors, and antiques. and the food in the dining room is good. A double room is $52 to $78 year-round.

Texas: the Lone Star State
Texas, the second-biggest state (after Alaska), is a land of extremes. Here, the J.R. Ewings of the world gamble great fortunes, while the women dress in furs, despite the scorching heat, and keep the makeup manufacturers of the world in business. At the same time, cowboys roam the stark, wide-open ranges. And Mexicans risk their lives to cross the border illegally. Going to Texas can be as much a cultural experience as visiting a foreign country.

Houston: the fastest-growing city
Houston has grown faster than any other American city, sprawling across 532 miles. Twenty-five oil companies have their headquarters in the city's skyscrapers.

The coolest way to tour hot, humid Houston is through the **Houston Tunnel System**, a series of air-conditioned passageways that connect all the major buildings downtown. For a map of the tunnels, which are lined with shops and restaurants, stop by the Houston Library, Penzoil Place, or the Texas Commerce Bank.

Penzoil Place is Houston's cultural showpiece. Designed by the prominent architect Philip Johnson, this glass complex includes the Jesse H. Jones Hall for the Performing Arts and the Alley Theater. The Jesse H. Jones Hall is home of the Houston Symphony Orchestra, the Grand Opera, and the Houston Ballet Company. Its lobby features Richard Lippold's *Gemini II* sculpture.

Hermann Park contains the Museum of Natural Science and Burke Baker Planetarium, the Houston Zoological Gardens (where you can see a colony of vampire bats), and the Miller Outdoor Theater. Nearby are the **Museum of Contemporary Arts**, *5216 Montrose Blvd.; (713)526-3129,* which is free, and the **Museum of Fine Arts**, *1001 Bissonet; (713)639-7300.* Admission to the latter is $3 for adults, $1.50 for students.

Also worth seeing are the **Bayou Bend**, *1 Wescott St.; (713)529-8773,* off Memorial Drive, the former home of Ima Hogg, daughter of the first native-born Texas governor, and the **San Jacinto Museum of History**, *3800 Park Road; (713)479-2421,* located at the base of the San Jacinto Monument (which is taller than the Washington Monument) on the San Jacinto Battlegrounds. Admission to the Bayou Bend is $2.

One of the world's greatest sports complexes is Houston's immense **Astrodomain**, *(713)799-9555,* which includes the Astrodome.

The **Menil Collection**, *1515 Sul Ross St.; (713)525-9400,* is a wide-ranging gallery with prehistoric to modern art and special exhibits on tribal cultures. The gallery is closed Monday and Tuesday.

Houston's best rodeo
Every February, the **Houston Livestock Show and Rodeo** is held in the Astrodome. The largest show of its kind in the world, it draws cowboys from all over North America.

Houston's best restaurants
Brennan's, *3300 Smith; (713)522-9711*, is a well-loved Houston institution with fine food and bargain prices. Try the eggs Creole or the catfish with roasted pecans; save room for praline parfait.

Charley's 517, *517 Louisiana; (713)224-4438*, has imaginative fare, including fresh venison and buffalo. The wine list is extensive.

La Reserve, *Inn on the Park, Four Riverway; (713)871-8181*, is an elegant restaurant surrounded by reflecting pools where black swans glide. Inside are beveled ceiling mirrors, antiques, and crystal chandeliers. The menu changes daily but always includes fresh fish, beef, game, and produce.

Houston's best hotel
The best hotel in town is the **Ritz Carlton**, *Post Oak Park, 1919 Briar Oaks Lane; (713)840-7600* or *(800)231-9802*, a beautifully decorated place with a homey feel. Little extras make it special: handmade soaps, fresh fruit and chocolates in the bedrooms, and brass razors. Double rooms start at $190.

Dallas: fact is better than fiction
Dallas is famous for J.R. Ewing of the television series *Dallas*, the Dallas Cowboys and their cheerleaders, and the assassination of John F. Kennedy. What many people don't know is that it is the most sophisticated city in the South.

Be prepared for the **Dallas-Fort Worth Airport**, the world's largest—larger than Manhattan Island.

The saddest sight
The most sobering sight in Dallas is the spot where John F. Kennedy was shot, a grassy knoll at Market and Main streets marked by a large black granite marker. The **John F. Kennedy Museum** opened in November 1988 to mark the 25th anniversary of his assassination. It is located on the sixth floor of the School Book Depository, where Lee Harvey Oswald hid and took aim at the president.

Dallas' best sights
Dallas City Hall, *1500 Marilla; (214)670-3957*, rises 560 feet and surrounds a pleasant plaza.

The **Dallas Zoo**, *621 E. Clarendon Drive; (214)946-5154*, has the finest collection of rare birds in the nation. It is open daily; admission is $5, $1 for senior citizens and children.

Thanksgiving Square has a bell tower, the Chapel of Thanksgiving, and the Hall of Thanksgiving, which exhibits costumes and artifacts from seven continents.

The **Museum of Fine Arts**, *1717 N. Harwood St.; (214)922-1200*, displays classic, pre-Columbian, European, and American paintings and sculpture. The museum is closed Mondays; admission is free.

The best collection of museums
State Fair Park, *off I-30 East*, has five museums within walking distance of one another. **Science Place** is one of the best science museums in the United States, housing exhibits on astronomical phenomena, human anatomy, shells, and the workings of radios. The **Dallas Hall of State** covers 400 years of state history. The **Age of Steam Railroad Museum** exhibits an old Dallas depot, a streetcar, an old passenger train, and the world's

largest steam locomotive. The **Museum of Natural History** features the wildlife of the Southwest. The **Dallas Aquarium** and the **Dallas Planetarium** are favorites with children.

Dining bests in Dallas

Lawry's The Prime Rib, *3008 Maple Ave.; (214)521-7777*, serves the best roast beef in Texas, carefully dry aged 14 to 21 days and then roasted on a bed of rock salt. It is carved and served warm at your table. When it was founded 50 years ago, Lawrence Frank and Walter Van de Kamp agreed that their restaurant should be elegant but friendly—no snooty waiters and no foreign languages on the menu.

The **Routh Street Café**, *3005 Routh St.; (214)871-7161*, has a five-course prix-fixe menu for $49 that includes American, Mexican, and Continental cuisines. This renovated prairie-style house has an art deco decor. Reservations are required.

Dallas' best digs

Mansion on Turtle Creek, *2821 Turtle Creek Blvd.; (214)559-2100 or (800)527-5432*, a 1920s mansion-turned-hotel, is cozy, with wood fires, leaded windows, and a good dining room. The lobby has polished floorboards, a domed ceiling, and tall arched windows. A double room is $290 to $350.

Austin: the most laid-back city in Texas

A large student population and a rebellious history make Austin the most laid-back and freethinking city in Texas. It is also one of the prettiest.

Austin's top sights

The **Texas State Capitol**, *Congress Avenue*, built in 1888, is colossal. It is open 24 hours a day when the legislature is in session, and free tours are conducted from 8:30 a.m. to 4:30 p.m. The **Texas Archives and Library Building** is located on the capitol grounds.

The **Laguna Gloria Art Museum**, *3809 W. 35th St.; (512)458-8191*, has the city's best art collection. Concerts, plays, and festivals are held on the grounds, which are lovely. The museum is closed Mondays; admission is $2, $1 for students and senior citizens.

The **Lyndon Baines Johnson Library**, *2313 Red River St.; (512)482-5136*, contains the former president's speeches.

Austin's Area Garden Center, *2220 Barton Springs Road*, in Zilker Park, has gardens, a 19th-century pioneer cabin, a log-cabin school, and an old blacksmith shop.

A country-western Hollywood

Young country-western musicians flock to Austin to try to make it big. Willie Nelson and Jerry Jeff Walker are among those who have succeeded. **The Terrace**, *200 Academy Drive*, was formerly owned by Willie Nelson and now is rented out for occasional events. The **Broken Spoke**, *3201 S. Lamar*, is the best place for foot stompin'.

A bed for the night

The best place to stay in Austin is the **Driskill Hotel**, *604 Brazos St.; (512)474-5911*, a renovated 19th-century building. Double rooms are $119.

San Antonio: the best of Tex-Mex

San Antonio is the site of the battle of the **Alamo** between 200 Texans (including Davy Crockett) and 4,000 Mexicans led by Commander Santa Anna. The Texans turned a mission building into a fort and fought to free Texas from Mexico. When the siege ended, all but six Texans were dead. Crockett survived, but he was later killed on the orders of Santa Anna. "Remember the Alamo" became a battle cry. The people of San Antonio still commemorate March 6, the day the siege ended.

Founded in 1718 as a Spanish military mission, the city is now more than half Mexican-American. The Tex-Mex atmosphere is thick and spicy.

The best Mexican food north of the border is prepared in San Antonio. Try **The Hacienda** at Los Patios, *2015 N.E. Loop 410; (512)655-6171*, which has the best location, or **Casa Rio**, *430 E. Commerce St.; (512)225-6718*, which is the oldest and most popular.

The best of the missions

Spanish Franciscan missionaries built five missions in San Antonio to convert local Indians to Christianity. Two of them, the Alamo and Mission San Jose, are downtown.

The **Alamo**, *Alamo Plaza*, is actually the Mission San Antonio de Valero, with a chapel and barracks. The **Mission San Jose**, *6539 San Jose Blvd.*, is the largest. It has its own irrigation system, built by the Spaniards, and a beautiful rose window. Mass is still held here, and a mariachi band plays on Sundays.

The **Mission San Francisco de la Espada**, *10040 Espada Road*, has a beautiful chapel. A mile-long aqueduct, built between 1731 and 1745, supplies it with water. The **Mission San Juan Capistrano**, *9102 Grof Road*, built in 1731, differs from other, more architecturally elaborate missions in its simplicity.

The best museums

The **San Antonio Museum of Art**, *200 W. Jones Ave.; (512)978-8100*, is housed in the restored Lone Star Brewery building, which has towers, turrets, ornate columns, and huge rooms. The collection includes pre-Columbian, American Indian, Spanish Colonial, Mexican, and European art and Texas furniture. Admission is $4, $1.75 for children, and $2 for senior citizens.

The new **Lone Star Brewing Company**, *600 Lone Star Blvd.*, displays animal heads, horns, and antlers, as well as birds and fish. You can sample free beer at the Buckhorn Bar.

The best restaurant and hotel

San Antonio's best restaurant is **La Louisiane**, *2632 Broadway; (512)225-7984*, which is beautifully decorated and has good French cuisine.

Amerisuites, *11221 San Pedro Ave.; (512)342-4800*, is a good, inexpensive hotel with double rooms for $60 to $82, including Continental breakfast. The hotel has a heated pool and a whirlpool.

The Southwest: nature at its most powerful

The **Southwest** region of the United States is an area of awe-inspiring natural beauty, much of which is preserved in the region's national parks. The most famous is the **Grand Canyon** in Arizona. If you think the reality can't possibly match the Grand Canyon's reputation, you're wrong. This is a sublime place, carved over the course of eons by the Colorado River. The descent to the bottom is rugged. From the base, the canyon looks like some otherworldly Shangri-La, a rainbow of colors and powerful bastions.

The best place to stay while you explore is **El Tovar Hotel**, *(602)638-2401*, on the South Rim, an elegant but rustic lodge perched on the edge. Rooms are $111 to $251. All other hotels are outside the park limits and do not have views of the canyon. For more information, contact the **Grand Canyon South Rim Visitors Center**, *(602)638-7888*.

Zion National Park, in Springdale, Utah, is less famous. It is so named because its beauty reminded Mormon pioneers of paradise. The best view in all the Southwest is from **Angel's Landing**, a 2 1/2-mile trail from the Grotto picnic area in the park. For information, contact the park's **Visitors Information Center**, *(801)772-3256*.

Bryce Canyon National Park, five hours south of Salt Lake City, has a delicacy that differentiates it from other canyons. Some consider it the most beautiful, with its lacy rock formations. For information, contact the **Visitors Center**, *(801)834-5322*.

Phoenix—the best oasis

The power of nature in the Southwest—the giant rocks and the lack of water—is unrelenting. **Phoenix** is a welcome oasis in the middle of this desert. The capital of Arizona is actually a chain of resort towns. The Valley of the Sun, ringed by mountains, is inhabited by 1 1/2 million people, many of them wealthy retirees. Outside Phoenix are 23 reservations, home to 50,000 Indians.

Both the best view and the best meal can be found at **Etienne's Different Point of View**, *Pointe Tapatio Resort, 11111 N. Seventh St.; (602)863-0912.* This restaurant at the top of a mountain has a 360-degree view of the city and the surrounding desert. Try to dine at sunset.

Frank Lloyd Wright designed the valley's greatest hotel, the **Arizona Biltmore**, *24th Street and Missouri; (800)228-3000 or (602)955-6600.* Gold leaf lines the ceilings. The color scheme and decor are Southwestern, with stained glass, murals, paintings, and Indian tapestries. The Biltmore has two 18-hole golf courses, 18 tennis courts, three swimming pools, a health club, and a sauna. A double room is $220 to $650.

The best of Tucson

Tucson, surrounded by the Sonora Desert, has both the easygoing atmosphere of a small town and the cultural offerings of a big city, including opera, a symphony, theater, and art. With an influx of newcomers from the East Coast, Tucson is losing some of its Hispanic and Southwestern flavor. But old Spanish festivals are still held, and good Mexican restaurants can be found throughout the town.

Most of Tucson's sights are within walking distance of the University of Arizona campus. The **Arizona State Museum**, *(602)628-5774,* for example, has a collection of Southwest Indian artifacts and exhibits on area plants and animals. It is open daily and is free. The **Arizona Historical Society**, *949 E. Second St.,* illustrates the state's history, with colorful exhibits about early settlers and outlaws.

El Presidio is a walled fortress built by Spanish settlers. Nearby are the **Spanish Colonial Pima County Courthouse**, built in 1928, and the **Tucson Museum of Art**, *140 N. Main Ave.; (602)624-2333.* The museum is closed Monday; admission is $2 every day except Tuesday, when it is free.

Old Town Artisans, *186 N. Meyer St.,* next to El Presidio, displays Western handicrafts, including Navajo rugs, in a 19th-century adobe building. It is open daily.

Fourteen miles west of Tucson is the **Arizona-Sonora Desert Museum**, *(602)883-2702,* where you can see jaguars, mountain lions, beavers, and bighorn sheep, as well as a cave and a garden with 300 kinds of plants. Admission is $7.95 for adults, $3.50 for children.

The **Mission of San Xavier del Bac**, nine miles south of Tucson on Mission Road on the Tohano O'Adham Indian Reservation, was founded in 1692 by the Jesuits. It is one of the most beautiful churches in the Southwest, a white Mexican Renaissance structure surrounded by brown desert. Visit during the Mariachi Mass, held at 12:30 on Sundays during the winter. This adobe structure has frescoes, carved figurines of saints, and two lions that wear satin bow ties.

Tuscon's best restaurant is the **Tack Room**, *Rancho Del Rio Resort, 2800 N. Sabino Canyon Road; (602)722-2800,* in an old adobe hacienda in the desert. Try the veal or the rack of lamb Sonora. Breads and desserts are homemade.

The best place for closet cowboys

If you've always dreamt of riding horses across the desert, visit the **Tanque Verde Guest Ranch**, *14301 E. Speedway Blvd.; (602)296-6275.* Located 12 miles from Tucson, this hostelry, a working ranch until the 1920s, welcomes you into ranch life. You can eat well, swim in the indoor pool, and ride horses. A double room is $240 to $300.

444

The best cliff dwellings

Most travelers travel to Machu Picchu and Chichen Itza to see ancient Indian ruins. However, the most extraordinary pre-Columbian ruins are to be found in the United States. The mysterious Anasazi Indians built beautiful, complex cliff dwellings in the **Four Corners** region of the American Southwest long before Europeans arrived. Great cities were carved out of reddish-gold sandstone cliffs by these unknown people, whom the Navajo named the Anasazi, or Ancient Ones. Their civilization flourished from the time of Christ until 1300, then disappeared without a trace.

No one knows exactly what became of the Anasazi, but you can explore their ancient dwellings, perched in gigantic cliffside caves on plateaus in the open plain, at times five stories high with as many as 800 rooms. (The caves are tiny as compared with the sheer cliffs that loom above them.) The caves went unseen by the white man until December 1888, when they were discovered by two cowboys searching for stray cows.

The most extensive cliff dwellings (4,000 in all) are in the 52,000-acre **Mesa Verde National Park** in Colorado. The largest and most famous cliff dwelling is **Cliff Palace**, where about 250 people lived in the 13th century. Its towered ruins look like a fantasy castle protected by a gigantic cave 100 yards wide and 30 yards deep, almost perfectly preserved because it is shielded from the elements by the cliff overhang. It is one of the five dwellings in the park that you can visit.

Hiking is limited in the park, but you are permitted to walk along five marked trails. The best is the loop called **Petroglyph Trail.**

During the winter season, ranger-guided tours of **Spruce Tree House**, one of the cliff dwellings, are conducted daily. And the **Archeological Museum** is open from 8 a.m. to 5 p.m. For more information, contact the **Park Superintendent**, *Box 8, Mesa Verde National Park, CO 81330; (303)529-4461.*

Mesa Verde National Park is a two-hour drive from the airport at Durango, Colorado, where rental cars are available.

The best place to stay is the **Far View Lodge**, *Box 277, Mancos, CO; (303)529-4421*, near the cliff dwellings. Each room has a private balcony with a view. Double rooms are $84 during the summer; in May and October, you can get a double room for two nights for $69.

You also can see Anasazi dwellings at the Navaho National Monument in **Monument Valley Tribal Park**, near Kayenta, Arizona. Unfortunately, overuse is wearing down the three dwellings there—Inscription House, Betatakin, and Keet Steel. Inscription House has been closed, and entrance to Betatakin and Keet Steel houses is limited.

The best of modern-day Indian country

Modern-day Indians maintain their traditions throughout the Southwest. Their pueblos are living communities, not museums.

The **Navajo reservation** in Monument Valley covers 16 million acres, mostly in northeastern Arizona. Over 260,000 people make up the Navajo nation. They are shepherds, silversmiths, weavers, and tour guides. One of the oldest (active) Navajo trading posts in the area is **Hubbell's**, a national historic site. For more information on the Navajos, contact **Recreational Resources Department**, *Navajo Tribe, Box 308, Window Rock, AZ 86515; (602)871-4941.*

The **Hopi reservation** is enclosed by Navajo country. The 10,000 Hopis (whose name means *Peaceful Ones*) occupy 1.4-million acres of land. Believed to be the descendants of the Anasazi, the Hopis are farmers and craftspeople. They believe spirits live in the nearby San Francisco Peaks.

The Hopis live on three main mesas. The Indians on **First Mesa** produce the best pottery. Those on **Second Mesa** create beautiful baskets, kachina doll carvings, and silver jewelry. The Hopis on **Third Mesa** are known for decorative wicker plaques.

Old Orabi on Third Mesa vies with Acoma Pueblo as the oldest inhabited town in the United States. The centuries-old village of **Walpi**, high on the edge of First Mesa, has tiny winding streets and houses crowded into the cliffs. For more information, contact the **Hopi Cultural Center**, *Box 67, Second Mesa, AZ 86043; (602)734-2401.*

Santa Fe: the nation's oldest capital

Set atop a 7,000-foot plateau at the base of the Sangre de Cristo Mountains in northern New Mexico is **Santa Fe.** The air is pure, the adobe homes are ancient, and the people are a mixture of Spanish, Indian, and Anglo.

The oldest capital in the nation is inhabited by families who have been here for 14 generations. Outside the city are weathered mountains and old Indian pueblos. The desert is dotted with cacti and piñon pines.

Spanish conquistadors arrived here 400 years ago and named the town La Villa Real de la Santa Fe de San Francisco. The Spanish town was built on the site of abandoned Pueblo Indian villages that had been built 300 years before the arrival of the conquistadors.

The central plaza of Santa Fe was laid out by the Spanish in 1610. The **Palace of the Governors,** built of adobe in 1610, is the oldest public building in North America. It houses the **Museum of New Mexico** and occupies the entire north side of the plaza. Along its porch, Indians spread blankets and sell handmade jewelry and pottery.

An inn has existed at the site of the **Hotel La Fonda,** off the plaza, since before the opening of the Santa Fe Trail. A faded sign on the hotel wall marks the end of the trail.

Around the corner is **St. Francis Cathedral,** completed in 1886. The two gold towers of this stone structure glow in the sun. Inside is a 16th-century wooden statue called *La Conquistadora,* said to be the oldest madonna in North America. A block away is the Loretto Chapel, which houses the circular miraculous staircase built without nails or other visible means of support by an unknown carpenter. Legend says the carpenter was St. Joseph. The chapel itself was modeled after the Ste. Chapelle in Paris.

The best fiesta

The **Fiesta de Santa Fe,** held in September, has music, dancing, and candlelight processions that begin at the cathedral. Zozobra, a 40-foot puppet representing Old Man Gloom, is burned to the delight of the crowds.

The biggest bomb

The scientists responsible for the atomic bomb met at 109 E. Palace St. beginning in 1943. Members of the **Manhattan Project** entered here and then went out a back way to Los Alamos. A plaque on the wall says, "All the men and women who made the first atomic bomb passed through this portal to their secret mission at Los Alamos. Their creation in 27 months of the weapons that ended World War II was one of the greatest achievements of all time."

The best restaurants

The **Pink Adobe,** *406 Old Santa Fe Trail; (505)983-7712,* in a 300-year-old adobe building, serves native specialties with creative variations. It is closed on major holidays.

Arturo Jaramillo and his family serve some of the region's best traditional food at **Rancho de Chimayo,** *(505)351-4444 or (505)351-4375,* in the village of Chimayo. Reservations are advised.

The best accommodation

The **Bishop's Lodge,** *Bishop's Lodge Road; (505)983-6377,* is set on 1,000 acres in the foothills of the Sangre de Cristo Mountains and offers horseback riding, tennis, swimming, and a fine dining room. Archbishop Latour in Willa Cather's *Death Comes for the Archbishop* retreated here. In reality, the archbishop's name was Lamy, and he left his little chapel with painted glass windows. At the turn of the century, the archbishop's retreat was purchased by newspaper tycoon Joseph Pulitzer, who added two houses to the estate before selling it to James R. Thorpe. Thorpe turned it into a dude ranch. A double room is $130 to $260.

Taos: an artists' best

Artists and writers flock to **Taos**, the most picturesque town in the Southwest. About 3,000 people live here at the foot of Mount Wheeler, the highest peak in the state. **Taos Plaza**, built in 1617, became an artists' colony in the 1890s and is still inhabited by artists today. Museums around the plaza include the 200-year-old **Blumenschein House**, *LeDoux Street*, where pioneer artist Ernest Blumenschein lived from 1919 to 1962. The **Harwood Foundation Museum and Library** contains the paintings of the first Taos artists. The **Kit Carson Museum** was bought by the scout in 1843. Also on the plaza are the **Millicent Rogers Museum of Southwestern Arts and Crafts** and the **D.H. Lawrence Shrine and Ranch**, where the writer lived in the 1920s.

Just north of Taos on Route 68 is the most striking and best-preserved adobe pueblo in New Mexico. This town, which dates from 1100, is home to about 2,000 Taos Indians. Wooden ladders lead to the five-story tiered homes. For more information, contact **Taos Pueblo Tourism Director**, *P.O. Box 1846, Taos, NM 87571; (505)758-8626.* For a chuckwagon tour of the reservation, organized by the **Taos Indian Horse Ranch**, call *(505)758-3212.* You must make reservations two weeks in advance.

The best place to stay in the area is the **Sagebrush Inn**, *(505)758-2254*, where Georgia O'Keeffe painted some of her best canvases. The adobe walls are 24 inches thick, and the interior ceilings are supported by log beams. Spanish-tile floors and fireplaces give the inn a rustic look. Navajo Indian rugs and works by Taos artists decorate the lounge. The inn has a swimming pool and tennis courts.

The best of the Rockies

Glacier National Park, *(406)888-5441*, in northwest Montana contains some of the most spectacular and least-touched scenery in the **Rocky Mountains**, including glaciers, high peaks, lakes and streams, and a great variety of wildlife (including grizzly bears, so be careful). The park straddles the Continental Divide. **Going to the Sun Road** is a 50-mile stretch leading to hiking trails.

Glacier Park Lodge, *(406)226-5551*, in the park, draws nature lovers, fishermen, hikers, and backpackers. This scenic resort also offers naturalist programs, golf, horseback riding, swimming, cruises, and nightly entertainment. Rooms are $82 to $150 per night.

Rocky Mountain National Park, *(303)586-2371*, is the best place in Colorado for hiking and horseback riding. Two hours from Denver, the park has 20 peaks rising more than 12,000 feet. You'll see bighorn sheep, deer, and elk on the park grounds. Admission to the park is $5.

Yellowstone National Park, *(307)344-7381*, is the world's greatest geyser area, with more than 200 geysers and 10,000 hot springs. The most famous geyser is **Old Faithful**, which erupts at regular intervals. **Steamboat** is the largest geyser in the world, lasting 20 minutes and shooting higher than 300 feet. Admission for vehicles is $10, for people on foot $4. Both passes are good for 10 days.

The **Yellowstone River** has carved a canyon through the rock at Yellowstone National Park. Waterfalls and lakes reflect the blue sky. More than 1,000 miles of trails crisscross the park. Be careful if you hike the backcountry; grizzly bears have become a problem. You'll also see moose and bison. Park employees say swimming in the warm waters of Firehole River can be exhilarating; however, this isn't encouraged, because you can be scalded. Yellowstone is the oldest national park in the United States, established in 1872.

The best skiing in the United States

Taos, New Mexico, and Jackson Hole, Wyoming, are challenging ski areas that are remote enough not to attract big crowds. Both have serious ski schools, but neither has much après-ski activity. Taos does have French-run inns and an Indian culture. Jackson Hole has views of the magnificent Tetons, and from time to time you'll see a graceful elk leaping through the snowfields. Grand Targhee, the backside of the Tetons, offers world-class powder and empty slopes. The resort at Sun Valley, Idaho, has all the amenities but little charm. Snowbird, Utah, has the best powder skiing in the country.

The best of California

During the past century, Americans have flocked to California with visions of fame, fortune, and freedom. They have been drawn by dreams of striking it rich or of making it big in Hollywood. The energy created by these imaginative and ambitious people has made this state one of the most productive in the Union—and one of the most unusual.

The best of San Francisco

San Francisco is the most inviting city in the United States—even if it also is one of the most expensive. It's beautiful, surrounded on two sides by water—the Pacific Ocean and San Francisco Bay. When the fog rolls in, the city becomes mysterious and soft. When the sun shines, the city glitters. Situated atop steep hills, San Francisco has been the setting for many a chase scene in the movies. Nearly every neighborhood has a hill with a spectacular view. This city is remarkably clean—and very cosmopolitan.

The Golden Gate Bridge, which crosses the Golden Gate Strait between the Pacific Ocean and San Francisco Bay, is the city's most famous landmark. Actually a reddish color, the bridge is especially beautiful when partially shrouded in fog. The bridge connects the city to exclusive Marin County, home of Sausolito's artists' colony. It is also one route to the Napa Valley wineries.

The Golden Gate Promenade in Aquatic Park is a 3 1/2-mile hike to the bridge that passes beaches, a yacht harbor, the Palace of Fine Arts, the Presidio Army Museum, and Fort Point.

Golden Gate Park offers 1,017 acres of hiking trails and bridle paths. Free concerts are held in the Music Concourse on Sundays at 2 p.m. One of the city's major art museums, the MH de Young Memorial Museum, which has a splendid Rodin collection, is in the park. Next door is the Asian Art Museum. The California Academy of Sciences, which features the Wattis Hall of Man, the Steinhart Aquarium, and the Morrison Planetarium, is also located here.

The most interesting neighborhoods

San Francisco's Chinatown is the largest Chinese community in the United States. Walking these streets, you can actually imagine you are in China. Most of your fellow pedestrians are Oriental. The signs are in Chinese. Little shops sell silk Chinese jackets and little black slippers. Food stores have unidentifiable items in their windows. And the architecture of the buildings is Chinese; many were built long ago by the first Chinese immigrants, brought to America to help build the railroad. The best time to visit is during the Chinese New Year celebration in January or February. The highlight is the Dragon Parade, but there also are marching bands, fireworks, and a beauty pageant. For more information on the festival, call (415)982-3071.

Nob Hill, an area with plush hotels and a lovely park, is San Francisco's most elegant neighborhood. The Stanford Court Hotel, 905 California St.; (415)989-3500, serves high tea and delicious dinners. Leland Stanford, a railroad mogul, once owned this mansion. Huntington Park, between Taylor and Mason streets, with a lovely view of Grace Cathedral, is the most romantic place for a picnic.

North Beach, between Chinatown and Fisherman's Wharf, is home to hippies, the

Italian community, and many of the city's best restaurants and bars. The Cathedral of Saints Peter and Paul looms above the neighborhood, making sure its residents keep their faith. You are likely to see elderly men playing boccie in the parks. The most colorful time to visit is during the Blessing of the Fishing Boats the first weekend in October, when the community parades from the cathedral to Fisherman's Wharf.

San Francisco's best time
Holy City Zoo Comedy Club, *408 Clement St.; (415)386-4242,* features good country, rock'n'roll, and folk musicians, as well as uproarious comedians. All the fun takes place in an 80-year-old high-ceilinged farmhouse.

Superb restaurants
Nob Hill Restaurant, *The Mark Hopkins, Number One Nob Hill, 999 California St.; (415)391-9362,* is the best in San Francisco. It has a gentlemen's club atmosphere, with wood paneling and a quiet dining room.

Le Castel, *3235 Sacramento St.; (415)921-7115,* in an old San Francisco home, has delicious poached salmon. Make reservations at this popular restaurant, which is closed Mondays.

The **Mandarin,** *900 N. Point St.; (415)673-8812,* is the city's best Chinese restaurant. And it has a spectacular view of San Francisco Bay. This is the place to get Peking duck. Save room for the mandarin glazed bananas for dessert.

McCormick & Kuleto's; *(415)929-1730,* is decorated like a steamship, with a wood and brass decor. Tables have excellent views of the bay.

Favorite inns
Our favorite inn in San Francisco, home to some of the best inns in the United States, is the **White Swan,** *845 Bush St.; (415)775-1755,* in the heart of town. Each room is individually decorated, with four-poster beds, fireplaces, antique chairs and desks, and shelves and shelves of books. Guests are provided with thick terry bathrobes, and at night the sheets are turned down and chocolates are left on the pillows. Soft teddy bears lounge on the beds, and the air smells of the homemade cookies being baked in the kitchen. Breakfasts are enough to keep you going until dinner. Afternoon cocktails and hors d'oeuvres are served in the cozy sitting room. The young staff is extremely helpful and friendly. A double room is $145 to $160, including breakfast, tea, and cocktails.

La Petite Auberge, *863 Bush St.; (415)928-6000,* has a French motif. Fresh flowers scent the rooms, and floral wallpaper, French country antiques, quilts, handmade pillows, and working fireplaces make them cozy. Continental breakfast and afternoon tea are served in the dining room. A double room is $105 to $155.

The **Archbishop's Mansion Inn,** *1000 Fulton St.; (415)563-7872,* is the lavishly restored home of the archbishop of San Francisco. In 1934, the pope spent the night here. Rooms, which are named after operas, are decorated with carved beds, fireplaces, and antiques. Breakfast and a complimentary cocktail are included in the cost of the room. Smoking is permitted only in the drawing room. A double room is $100 to $285.

The **Mansion Hotel,** *2220 Sacramento St.; (415)929-9444,* is the most amusing place to stay, owned and operated by zany Bob Pritikin, who entertains visitors with his musical saw on weekend evenings. The hotel is decorated with oddball antiques and is set in a grand old home that was built in 1877 by Senator Chambers. His daughter Claudia haunts the house, or so they say. The art collection is museum-worthy, the furniture Victorian, and the service first-class. A double room is $129 to $159.

The **Sherman House,** *2160 Green St.; (415)563-3600,* was originally the home of 19th-century music publisher Leander Sherman. The hotel is complete with marble fireplaces and butlers to light them, canopy drapes on the feather beds, and thick terry bathrobes next to whirlpool baths. A double room is $210 to $700.

The best side trip
Sausalito, across Golden Gate Strait by bridge or ferry, is a pretty port and beach resort. The population of this former Bohemian haven doubles on summer weekends. Situated between San Francisco and Mount Tamalpais, Sausalito has lovely views, unusual crowds, great bars and restaurants, and a profusion of shops.

Sausalito's two best hotels are the **Alta Mira,** *(415)332-1350,* where doubles are $100 to $170, and the **Casa Madrona,** *(415)332-0502,* where doubles are $90 to $200.

Los Angeles: the most eclectic city
Although **Los Angeles** is often obscured by smog and deafened by the din of traffic, it has the stuff of which dreams are made: Hollywood, Beverly Hills, Malibu, and Marina del Rey. This is the stage for the jet-set world of the Beautiful People.

Hollywood: the best of the limelight
Northwest of downtown Los Angeles is the center of the entertainment world: **Hollywood.** Major film and television studios are here, as well as great cinemas and theaters. **Hollywood Boulevard** is a fascinating mishmash of shops and people. **Grauman's Chinese Theater** is a garish building. Outside the theater, in the cement, are the foot- and handprints of famous Hollywood movie stars. **Sunset Boulevard,** or The Strip, is lined with nightclubs, bars, and performance halls, and **Melrose Avenue** is lined with pleasant restaurants, where you can stargaze. Hollywood is seedy at night, frequented mainly by prostitutes.

The best studios
Universal Studios, *Universal City; (818)508-9600,* the birthplace of box-office hits and prime-time television shows, offers the most elaborate tour, lasting seven hours. It costs $24.50 for adults, $19 for children under 12, and it's free for children under 3.

NBC Television Studios, *3000 W. Alameda Ave., Burbank; (818)840-3537,* is smaller, but you can sit in on TV tapings free.

Free tickets to some show tapings are offered by all the television studios on a first-come, first-served basis. You can get them at the Visitors Information Center in the Greater Los Angeles Visitor and Convention Bureau. Or send a self-addressed, stamped envelope to **ABC-TV,** *4151 Prospect, Hollywood CA 90027; (213)557-7777;* **CBS-TV,** *7800 Beverly Blvd., Hollywood CA 90036; (213)460-3000;* or **NBC-TV,** *3000 W. Alameda Ave., Burbank CA 91523; (818)840-3537.*

L.A. sights
The oldest buildings in the city are in the **Pueblo de Los Angeles State Historical Park,** a 19th-century area in the northwest section of downtown. The **Old Plaza,** with 100-year-old trees, stands at the center. You can tour the Avila Adobe, the Pico and Sepulveda houses, and ancient Chinese gambling and opium dens.

Visit the **Huntington Library, Art Gallery, and Botanical Gardens,** *1151 Oxford Road, San Marino, CA; (818)405-2100.* The library houses one of the world's most important collections of rare books, including a Gutenberg Bible and original editions of *The Canterbury Tales,* Thoreau's *Walden,* and Benjamin Franklin's autobiography. The art gallery contains 18th- and 19th-century British paintings, including Thomas Gainsborough's *Blue Boy* and Sir Thomas Lawrence's *Pinkie.* The botanical gardens are immense, with desert, Japanese, and Elizabethan sections. The library and gallery are closed Monday.

The **J. Paul Getty Museum,** *17985 Pacific Coast Highway; (310)458-2003,* in Malibu, is located in the mansion of the late billionaire, a replica of a first-century Roman villa situated on a cliff overlooking the coast. Inside are pieces of Greek and Roman sculpture, 18th-century French decorative art, and European paintings. The museum is open

Tuesdays through Sundays, 10 a.m. until 5 p.m.

The **Watts Towers,** *1765 E. 107th St.,* are eight spirals of varying heights, taking on the shape of a boat, built single-handedly by Simon Rodia out of pieces of trash. The old man took 33 years to build these works.

Venice: the craziest beach

Venice, a crowded, crazy, somewhat seedy beach area on the edge of Los Angeles, is the best place in the city to people watch. **Ocean Front Boulevard,** a coastal walkway, is lined with vendors, street musicians, roller skaters, drug addicts, lovers, beachboys, gays, senior citizens, artists, and tourists from all over the world. Venice was so named because of its many canals and Italian-style buildings. Abbot Kinney attempted to build an American Riviera here at the turn of the century, with canals and gondoliers.

Disneyland: the world's best theme park

Disneyland, outside Los Angeles, is the world's original theme park. (Walt Disney World outside Orlando, Florida, was built later.) The oldest and still the best, it brings Mickey Mouse to life, offers trips through the stars, and creates a disconcertingly convincing haunted house. By 1992, Disneyland had had an estimated 320 million visitors.

The best song and dance

The **Los Angeles Philharmonic** plays at the **Hollywood Bowl,** *2301 N. Highland Ave., Hollywood; (213)850-2000,* during the summer. The rest of the year, it plays at the Dorothy Chandler Pavilion in the **Music Center,** *First Street and Grand Avenue.*

Troubadour, *9081 Santa Monica Blvd., West Hollywood; (213)276-6168* or *(213)276-1158,* hosted Linda Ronstadt, Miles Davis, Joni Mitchell, and Blood, Sweat, and Tears before they hit the big time.

The **Roxy,** *9009 Sunset Blvd., West Hollywood; (213)276-2222,* is a fashionable night spot and a testing and recruiting ground for the music industry. The cover charge is $10 to $12.

The **Comedy Store,** *8433 Sunset Blvd., Hollywood; (213)656-6225,* hosts well-known comedians, including Richard Pryor, Steve Martin, and Robin Williams. There is usually a cover charge of $6 to $14.

The best restaurants

The **Polo Lounge,** in the Beverly Hills Hotel, *9641 Sunset Blvd.; (213)276-2251,* is where celebrities are made—and then fade. The many windows of this fishbowl offer views of a swimming pool and tropical plants. The Polo Lounge attracts the likes of Barbra Streisand, Gore Vidal, and Joan Collins. If the celebrities don't interest you, concentrate on the food, which is scrumptious.

Le Dome, *8720 Sunset Blvd; (213)659-6919,* serves better down-home French country cooking than you'll find in France. The *choucroute garnie* is delicious, and the wine list is good. The restaurant is closed Sundays and Saturdays at lunchtime.

The **Dynasty Room,** *Westwood Marquis, 930 Hilgard Ave.; (213)208-8765,* is a gourmet restaurant, with classic Continental cuisine. The decor is lovely, with crystal chandeliers and T'ang Dynasty pottery.

Scandia, *9040 Sunset Blvd., West Hollywood; (213)278-3555,* is the best Scandinavian restaurant in the United States. Have brunch or a late supper after the theater at this popular place.

L.A.'s heavenly hotels

Celebrities who don't live in Beverly Hills stay at the Beverly Wilshire or the Beverly Hills hotels. The **Beverly Wilshire Hotel,** *9500 Wilshire Blvd; (213)275-4282,* has cobblestoned pavements and Louis XIV gates. The older wing, called the Wilshire, is a lavish neo-Renaissance building. The newer Beverly Wing is decorated with French tapestries, Spanish furniture, and Italian marble. Prince Charles stayed in the most opulent suite, the Christian Dior. A double room is $255 to $550.

The **Beverly Hills Hotel**, *9641 W. Sunset Blvd.; (213)276-2251*, a pink-stucco Spanish villa, is surrounded by palm-shaded lawns where movie stars lounge. Less-famous folks have a hard time getting a room here. A double room is $250 to $320.

The **Bel Air**, *701 Stone Canyon Road, Bel Air; (213)472-1211*, is a pink mission building with red-tiled roofs and a courtyard fountain. Despite its old-fashioned appearance, it has many modern luxuries. Dolly Parton likes the Bel Air. A double room is $265 to $435.

The **Terrace Manor**, *1353 Alvarado Terrace; (213)381-1478*, is a Tudor-style house built in 1903 by the owner of a glass factory, who fitted the windows with art nouveau leaded stained glass. Victorian antiques look stately against the mahogany and oak wall panels. Caruso recordings are played while cocktails are served in the parlor in the late afternoon. The price of a room at the Terrace ($70 to $100) includes dinner and the entrance fee to the Magic Castle.

Bacchus' favorite: Napa Valley

The beautiful **Napa Valley**, 40 miles north of San Francisco on Highway 101, produces America's best wines. September through November, the area's wineries are busy harvesting grapes. More than 60 wineries in Napa and Sonoma counties invite visitors to tour their facilities and sample their wines. The best tour is the three-hour exploration of the **Robert Mondavi Winery**, designed for people who already know something about wine.

A lovely place to stay in the valley is **Beazley House**, *1910 First St., Napa; (707)257-1649*, a two-story shingled residence built in 1902. The Beazley House is noted for its woodwork and stained-glass windows. Sherry, coffee, and tea are served to guests in the living room, next to a large fireplace. A double room is $125 to $180.

America's most beautiful drive

The drive along the Pacific Coast from San Francisco south to Big Sur is the most spectacular in the United States. **Highway 1** is a dizzying twisting ribbon edging high cliffs above the pounding surf. Many movie chase scenes have been filmed on these precipitous roads. Stop from time to time to look over the edge at the deep blue water and empty beaches below. Because the undertow along the coast is so fierce, swimming is usually forbidden. In places, you'll hear colonies of sea lions barking on the rocks. The most spectacular scenery is at **Big Sur**. Waves crash through holes worn in giant rocks, and fierce winds whip along the sand. When you get here, ask how to get down to the beach. The roads often aren't marked.

The **Ventana Inn**, *Highway 1, Big Sur; (408)667-2331* or *(408)624-4812*, is a modern cedar structure. Rooms have carved arched headboards and handmade Nova Scotian quilts. Some have fireplaces, saunas, and Japanese hot tubs. The hotel has a heated swimming pool. Continental breakfast is served in the lobby, and a complimentary cheese and wine buffet is offered in the afternoon. The inn's restaurant has good food and a view of the ocean and mountains. A double room is $165 to $350.

America's best golf resort

Pebble Beach, 120 miles south of San Francisco and 337 miles north of Los Angeles, has America's best golf course. **Pebble Beach Golf Links** has hosted three U.S. Open golf tournaments (1972, 1982, and 1992), two U.S. Amateur Golf Championships, and the annual AT&T Pebble Beach National Pro-Am. It is 6,357 yards long, very narrow, and draped across a magnificent landscape.

The **Cypress Point Club**, also in Pebble Beach, is the most exclusive golf course in the world and one of the prettiest. You must be invited to play here.

This area is worth a visit even if you aren't a golfer. **Carmel,** a quaint beach town with chic shops and inviting inns, is nearby. The best view of the sun setting over the Pacific Ocean is from the beach in Carmel. Residents flock here each evening to watch the red orb sink behind the sea. And the **Del Monte Forest,** stretching along the coast, offers some of the most scenic—and expensive—real estate in the world. The forest is surrounded by **17-Mile Drive,** a loop that passes beaches, sea lions, blowholes, grand estates, and scenic overlooks.

The **Lodge at Pebble Beach,** *17 Mile Drive, Pebble Beach; (408)624-3811,* is a gorgeous resort with tennis, swimming, horseback riding, saunas, hiking, fishing, and hunting. A double room starts at $280 a night in the summer.

The premier auto show in the world is the **Pebble Beach Concours d'Elegance,** held on the lawn of the Lodge at Pebble Beach.

The tallest tree in the world

Redwood National Park in northwest California contains the world's tallest tree, 367 feet high. Magnificent stretches of virgin redwood forest, many of the trees 2,000 years old, are the main attraction. The park borders the Pacific coastline, where sea lions, seals, and birds live unthreatened.

The highest falls in North America

The falls located in **Yosemite National Park,** in east central California, are the highest in North America (dropping 2,425 feet). They are among many natural spectacles in the **Sierra Nevada,** the cliffs and pinnacles of which were formed by glaciers. The famous photographer Ansel Adams took many of his best-known photographs in this park.

The **Ahwahnee Resort** in Yosemite, *(209)252-4848,* built in 1927, has views of the falls and Glacier Point. The six-story pseudo castle is decorated with Western and Indian motifs. Movie stars and heads of state have stayed here. The 77-foot Great Lounge has two fireplaces. Facilities include a pool, tennis courts, horseback riding, hiking trails, and winter sports. A double room is $200.

The Northwest: nature at its best

The **Pacific Northwest** has managed to keep its natural beauty from being commercialized and overdeveloped. The rugged, untouched coasts of Washington and Oregon are breathtaking. The mountains are protected by national parks. The cities are lively without polluting the countryside.

The Northwest gets a lot of rain. If you can put up with the drizzle, you'll love its result. This is the greenest place in North America. Grass is an emerald color. Pine trees grow straight and tall, to heights unheard of on the East Coast.

Seattle: where the grass is greenest

Seattle is one of the nation's most gorgeous cities. Surrounded by mountains on nearly all sides, it sits on Puget Sound and Lake Washington. The Cascade and Olympic mountains are only two hours away, and the lone white peak of Mount Rainier can be seen from anywhere in the city. In addition to all its natural wonders, the city also offer restaurants, bars, and cultural activities.

The best view of the city is from the **Space Needle** in Seattle Center, a remnant of the 1962 World's Fair.

The most bizarre place in Seattle is **Ye Olde Curiosity Shop,** *Pier 54; (206)682-5844,* where shrunken heads and mummified humans are displayed

The best place for restaurants and night life is **Pioneer Square,** the renovated section of Old Seattle. **Grand Central Arcade,** *First Avenue and Occidental Street,* has the best shops.

The best tour of the city is the **Underground Seattle Tour,** which leaves from 610 First Ave. and shows you the remains of the original city, which burned in 1889.

Seattle's finest food

Pike Place Farmer's Market, *First Avenue and Pike Street,* has stalls filled with colorful fresh vegetables and fruits. It also has good restaurants. One of Seattle's best is **Chez Shea,** *(206)467-9990,* a cozy room on the top floor of the Corner Market Building. You can enjoy gourmet food while looking out over Puget Sound and the Olympic Mountains. **Café Sport,** *(206)443-6000,* at the north end of the Pike Place Market, is a casual restaurant with good seafood.

Le Gourmand, *425 N.W. Market St.; (206)784-3463,* is an intimate restaurant with three-course prix-fixe meals. It is open Wednesday through Saturday.

The **Georgian Room,** *Four Seasons Olympic Hotel, 411 University; (206)621-7889,* is a stately dining room serving nature's best.

Seattle's best inn

Chambered Nautilus Bed and Breakfast Inn, *5005 22nd Ave. N.E.; (206)522-2536,* is a rambling old house on a steep hill with views of the Cascade Mountains. Country antiques are sprinkled throughout the house, and most rooms have their own porches. Wine and tea are served by the fireplace in the parlor. Breakfast is served in the dining room and usually includes fresh-baked bread or muffins. A double room is $72 to $95.

The best of the wilderness

Mount Rainier, a 14,410-foot mountain in **Mount Rainier National Park,** has more glaciers than any other mountain on the U.S. mainland. The 4 1/2-mile **Skyline Trail** is the longest loop trail on the mountain. From Panorama Point, you can see glaciers and the summit. Mount Rainier was sacred to the Yakima and Klickatt Indians, who believed evil spirits inhabited a crater lake at the summit and caused storms and avalanches.

You can stay in Mount Rainier National Park at the **Paradise Inn,** *Highway 706; (206)569-2275,* which looks out over Mount Rainier and the valley below. This rustic inn was built in 1916 of notched cedar logs, with no nails. The open-beamed lobby has 50-foot cathedral ceilings and two stone fireplaces. The inn is open May through October.

The **Olympic National Forest** has wildly beautiful beaches along the Pacific Ocean. Inland, the Hoh, Queets, and Quinault river valleys have nontropical rain forests. Up to 140 inches of rain fall here each year, and moss covers everything. **Mount Olympus** rises 7,915 feet, challenging mountain climbers.

Stay at **Quinault Lodge,** *(206)288-2571,* a big lodge on Lake Quinault in Olympic National Park. Facilities include a pool, sauna, boats, hiking trails, and fishing areas. A double room is $75 to $99.

To truly understand the power of nature, visit **Mount St. Helens,** a volcano that erupted in 1980 causing mass destruction. You can tour the barren, burned-out area around the mountain. This peak is 50 miles northwest of Portland, Oregon.

America's deepest lake

Crater Lake in Oregon, which fills a 1,932-foot crater, never freezes, because of its depth. Located 6,000 feet above sea level, it is surrounded by snow-capped mountains. This beautiful, deep blue lake is five hours south of Portland. While the park is open year-round, only the south and west entrance roads are open during the winter. And Rim Drive is open only from July 1 through late September or October, depending on the snowfall. For more information, call *(503)594-2211.*

You can spend the night by the lake in cottages operated by **Crater Lake Lodge,**

(503)594-2511. The cottages are equipped with cold running water, blankets, and electricity, and prices range from $69 to $80 per person.

The best of the Great Lakes

In the middle of America's northern prairies are the **Great Lakes.** Surrounding these five mammoth, freshwater lakes are some of the nation's best farmland and most prosperous cities. **Lake Superior** is the deepest, the most treacherous, and the most beautiful. **Lake Michigan** is the best for fishing, swimming, and sailing. And its high western dunes are excellent for hang gliding.

Chicago: the biggest city

The greatest thing about this rough-and-tumble town is its beautiful, clean beaches. Its architecture is memorable also, showing off the genius of Frank Lloyd Wright and his ilk. The second-largest city in the United States, **Chicago** has three of the world's tallest buildings. And its neighborhoods are varied, filled with ethnic groups.

The best architecture

Chicago was the birthplace of modern architecture as developed by Louis Sullivan, his disciple Frank Lloyd Wright, and other members of the unofficial Chicago School of Architecture. Many of this group's first skyscrapers are still standing, next to taller, more modern buildings designed by the likes of Mies van der Rohe and Helmut Jahn. The **Archicenter**, *224 S. Michigan Ave.; (312)922-3432*, is the place to learn about Chicago's diverse architecture. For tour information, call *(312)922-TOUR.*

The tallest building

Standing proudly over Chicago is the **Sears Tower**, *233 S. Wacker*, the world's tallest building. Its 110 stories are reached by 103 elevators and lit by 16,000 windows. It covers an entire block. You can visit the sky deck on the top floor, from which, on a clear day, you can see as far as Wisconsin to the north, Indiana to the south, and Michigan to the east.

The most magnificent mile

The 16-block stretch of Michigan Avenue between the Chicago River and Oak Street is called the **Magnificent Mile**—with good reason. Here are Chicago's best and most exclusive department stores, as well as hundreds of small specialty shops and many of the best restaurants in Chicago.

Along the Magnificent Mile is **Water Tower Place**, *835 N. Michigan Ave.; (312)440-3165*, by far Chicago's best—and most beautiful—indoor shopping mall, eight stories of shops and restaurants.

The **Chicago Water Tower** and the **Pumping Station**, *Michigan and Chicago avenues*, were the only buildings that survived the Great Chicago Fire of 1871.

The best museums

The **Art Institute of Chicago**, *Michigan Avenue at Adams; (312)443-3600*, is a world-class art museum with the finest collection of Impressioinist paintings in this country and an outstanding collection of Renaissance, Oriental, and post-Impressionist art. Admission is $6 (free on Tuesday).

The **Field Museum of Natural History**, *Roosevelt Road and South Lake Shore Drive; (312)922-9410*, is a huge museum with a collection of jewels, Egyptian mummies, and freestanding dinosaur skeletons. Admission is $4 (free on Thursdays).

The **Museum of Broadcast Communications**, *800 S. Wells; (312)987-1500*, pays tribute to Chicago's glory days, when many national radio and television broadcasts originated here. You can watch or listen to more than 400 classic radio shows and over 900 television shows.

The **Museum of Contemporary Art**, *237 E. Ontario; (312)280-2660*, features art being created today. Admission is $4 (free on Tuesdays). The museum is closed on Mondays.

With more than 2,000 displays—including a coal mine, a World War II German submarine, and the Apollo 8 command module—the **Museum of Science and Industry**, *57th Street and South Lake Shore Drive; (312)684-1414*, is the most popular in the city. The **Omnimax Theater** features a five-story domed screen that puts the viewer in the middle of the action. Admission to the museum is free; admission to the Omnimax Theater is $4.50 for adults, $3 for children.

The **Oriental Institute**, at the University of Chicago, *ll55 E. 58th St.; (312)702-9520*, is a first-rate museum of artifacts from the ancient Near East (Egypt, Mesopotamia, Iran, and the Holy Land). Highlights are Egyptian mummies, fragments of the Dead Sea scrolls, and a huge winged bull from the throne room of King Sargon II of Assyia. Admission is free. The institute is closed Monday.

One of Chicago's newest museums, the **Terra Museum of American Art**, *666 N. Michigan Ave.; (312)664-3939*, which opened in 1987, has a strong collection of works by American Impressionists.

The most colorful neighborhoods

Hyde Park, the home of the University of Chicago, is an intellectual's dream, with six bookstores (four new, two used) and hundreds of people itching for a good conversation. Hyde Park is also home to the Museum of Science and Industry, the Oriental Institute, and Frank Lloyd Wright's famous Robie House. Every June, Hyde Park hosts its annual **57th Street Art Fair**.

The wealthiest part of town, known as the **Gold Coast**, is an area of old mansions and luxury apartment buildings, conveniently close to Lake Michigan, Oak Street Beach, and the Magnificent Mile.

Chicago's old Bohemia was Old Town, where many of the city's artists and hippies lived. But as Old Town gentrified, rising rents drove the artists, actors, and writers out. The new Bohemia is **Lake View**, the neighborhood around Belmont and Clark, which is filled with restaurants, bookstores, small theaters, coffee shops, and used-clothing stores.

Chicago's newest neighborhood is **River North**, an old warehouse district that in the past 10 years has become a chic loft area. Bounded by the Chicago River on the south and Chicago Avenue on the north, River North is an area of fashionable shops, trendy nightclubs, and popular new restaurants.

An art gallery district—not unlike SoHo in New York City—thrives along West Erie, Huron, and Superior streets, between Wells and Sedgwick.

The best parks and zoos

Chicago has 29 miles of lakefront parks. Lake Michigan offers clean water and pleasant swimming. The most popular beaches are **Lincoln Park** and **Oak Street**. Smaller, rockier, and less crowded are the beaches in **Hyde Park**, between 49th and 57th streets.

Grant Park, on the waterfront between Roosevelt Road and Randolph Street, east of Michigan Avenue, is attractive. The Grant Park Orchestra gives free outdoor concerts here on Wednesday, Friday, and Saturday evenings. At night, a light display dances across the **Buckingham Fountain**, which sprays 90 feet into the air.

On the grounds of the **Lincoln Park Zoo**, *2200 N. Cannon Park; (312)294-4662*, are beaches, yacht harbors, and the Lincoln Park Conservatory, which is the city's music capital. Good music can also be heard in the bars and theaters along Clark Street and Lincoln Avenue. Look out for muggers.

The **Brookfield Zoo**, *First Avenue and 31st Street; (708)485-2200*, in Brookfield, recreates the Sahara Desert and the Australian Outback, as well as the habitat of the Siberian tiger. Admission is free on Tuesdays and Thursdays.

The best town for theater

Twenty years ago, Chicago had no live theater to speak of. However, today more than 100 groups perform in the city. In fact, Chicago's theater scene rivals even those of New York and London. Although many are shoestring operations performing in storefronts and church basements, Chicago also has a respectable number of strong, well-established theaters.

No other Chicago theater group comes close to the **Steppenwolf Theater,** *1650 N. Halsted; (3l2)335-1650.* Many of its best shows have gone on to perform off-Broadway in New York City.

Chicago's best laughs

For about 30 years, **Second City,** *1616 N. Wells; (312)337-3992,* the best comedy theater in the city, has provided Chicago with consistently popular comedy revues. John Belushi, Shelley Long, Gilda Radner, and Alan Arkin all began their careers here. If you want to go, make reservations at least a week in advance.

Second City recently opened a second stage, **Second City ETC,** *1608 N. Wells,* and a third stage, *1701 W. Golf Road.* Both are just as funny.

The most outrageous entertainment

Believe it or not, one of Chicago's most popular night spots is the **Baton Lounge,** *436 N. Clark; (312)644-5269,* an outrageous club, where funny, ravishing female impersonators attract an eclectic crowd. Straight and gay, young and old all come to see such local legends as Chili Pepper and Leslie. Reservations are essential. The Lounge is closed Monday and Tuesday.

The best jazz and blues

For music lovers, Chicago is synonymous with jazz and blues. And **Joe Segal's Jazz Showcase,** in the Blackstone Hotel, *636 S. Michigan Ave.; (312)427-4300,* has been the place to hear great jazz in Chicago for decades.

No blues bar comes close to the **New Checkerboard Lounge,** *423 E. 43rd St.; (312)624-3240,* where such blues greats as Buddy Guy and Junior Wells perform regularly and rock stars such as Mick Jagger and Keith Richard drop by. (Sometimes they even jam with the old bluesmen.) The club itself is friendly and safe, but it is located in a dangerous neighborhood—so park near the club or take a cab. Don't take a bus or the subway—Chicago's South Side is rough.

If you love the blues but prefer to stay in a safer neighborhood, visit the **Kingston Mines,** *2548 N. Halsted; (312)477-4646,* in the heart of Lincoln Park. The Kingston Mines attracts many of the acts that play at the New Checkerboard Lounge as well as newer bands during the week.

The best classical music and opera

Under the leadership of its conductor, Daniel Barenboim, the **Chicago Symphony Orchestra** (CSO) has become a world-class orchestra, popular not only in its home city but also in Europe and the Orient. The CSO performs in **Orchestra Hall,** *220 S. Michigan Ave.,* across the street from the Art Institute of Chicago. For a schedule, call *(312)435-8122;* for ticket information, call *(312)435-6666.*

The **Lyric Opera,** *20 N. Wacker Drive; (312)332-2244,* is world-famous for its grandly staged operas.

The best deep-dish pizza

A quick way to start an argument in Chicago is to ask who has the best pizza in town. Everyone has his favorite place for pizza. The world-famous Chicago-style pizza was first served in the late 1940s at **Pizzeria Uno,** *29 E. Ohio Ave.; (312)321-1000.* And everyone agrees (even in Chicago) that Pizzeria Uno and sister restaurant **Due,** *619 N. Wabash Ave.; (312)943-2400,* still serve great pizza.

The best barbecued ribs
Chicago, not the South, has the best barbecued ribs in the world. At **Ribs 'n Bibs,** *East 53rd Street; (312)493-0400,* you can get a bucket of mouth-watering ribs for $23.76.

The best ethnic restaurants
A city of ethnic groups—Poles, Irish, Lithuanians, Serbs, Croatians, Italians, and Hispanics—Chicago has hundreds of great ethnic restaurants. The best is a Serbo-Croatian restaurant called the **Golden Shell,** *10063 South Ave. N.; (312)221-9876,* on Chicago's far southeast side. The food is great, and on weekends authentic folk bands and belly dancers perform.

The best gourmet restaurant
In a city of excellent restaurants, **Le Français,** *269 S. Milwaukee Ave.; (708)541-7470,* in the nearby suburb of Wheeling, is la crème de la crème. Close to O'Hare International Airport and a 45-minute drive from the Chicago Loop, Le Français serves a classically French menu that will please the most finicky gourmet palate. The restaurant is closed Sunday.

The best grand hotel
The **Mayfair Regent,** *181 E. Lake Shore Drive; (312)787-8500,* is Chicago's first-class hotel, the place where important businessmen want to be seen. The penthouse restaurant has a wide view of the lake, as do most of the rooms. A double room is $200 to $425.

The best little hotel
The **Tremont Hotel,** *100 E. Chestnut St.; (312)751-1900,* just off the Magnificent Mile, is one of Chicago's most elegant little hotels. A short walk from Michigan Avenue and the Oak Street Beach, the Tremont couldn't be more conveniently located. Double rooms are $170 to $240.

The Great Lakes' best resort
Mackinac Island, Michigan, where Lake Huron meets Lake Michigan, is a beautiful, peaceful place with no automobiles, just horse-drawn carriages and bicycles. Indians once lived here in lodges that are preserved in an open-air museum. During the Revolution, British forces built a fort here, now restored and open to the public. The island became a fashionable resort in the late 19th century, and it was the second area (after Yellowstone) to become a national park.

Today, the island is a refuge for city dwellers, a place for sailing, golfing, horseback riding, and tennis. Victorian homes and white church steeples dot the town. Sailboats bob in the lakes, and the waterfront is filled with shops and restaurants.

The **Grand Hotel,** *(906)847-3331* (call collect for reservations), on Mackinac Island, was built in 1887 by railroad and steamship companies. Constructed in Greek Revival style, with a long veranda supported by columns, it has a lovely pool (where Esther Williams swam in *This Time for Keeps*), as well as a golf course and tennis courts. The food is good, but the main dining room is stuffy. Tea is served in the parlor. Double rooms are $135 to $235.

The **Island House,** *(906)847-3347,* is an old Victorian resort on Mackinac Island. The enormous white building is fringed with shaded porches and topped with corner turrets and dormer windows. Built in 1852, it is the island's oldest hotel. Breakfast and dinner are served in the hotel dining room. You can sleep late and then have cocktails on the front porch while savoring the view of the straits. Double rooms start at $115.

The newest hotel on the island is **Mission Point Resort**, *(800)833-7711*, set on 18 acres of Lake Huron shoreline. It has a heated outdoor swimming pool, two hot tubs, three tennis courts, a fully equipped health and fitness center, a pool hall, and an arcade. The main lobby is a spacious circular room with five huge stone fireplaces and a soaring, vaulted ceiling of 40-foot hand-hewn timbers. Rooms overlook Lake Huron. Double rooms begin at $160 during peak season.

Alaska: the wildest (and coldest) state

Alaska is the last frontier in the United States. Having more unexplored territory than the rest of the 49 states combined, Alaska's virtues lie not in its few major cities but in the beauty of its frozen landscape, home to only 300,000 fishermen, prospectors, and Eskimos. Our largest state has excellent fishing, unlimited trails, and an endless reserve of wildlife.

Alaska is a land of superlatives. **Mount McKinley**, at 20,320 feet, is the tallest mountain in North America. Astounding amounts of gold and oil have been discovered in this state. And Alaska is the last area in the country where native populations keep their traditional ways, undisturbed by the white man. Alaska has the longest winter in the United States, lasting from October to April. June and July have days of continuous light. This is the best time to visit—unless you really like the snow.

Alaska's most spectacular sight

The most spectacular sight in Alaska is **Glacier Bay National Monument**, where myriads of ice boulders float in fiords bordered by thick forests. The park was covered by ice thousands of feet deep until just 200 years ago. Nowhere else can you get so close to glaciers. In this ever-changing area, humpback and killer whales spout, porpoises and seals play, and bears, mountain goats, and more than 200 species of birds, including the bald eagle, live. The waters are filled with trout, salmon, and halibut. During the summer, Glacier Bay is a rainbow of flowers.

The top of the world

Across the **Arctic Circle** is the land of the Eskimo, where the sun never sets during summer. All you can see for miles is vast, gently rolling tundra.

Barrow is the northernmost point of the continent, located 330 miles north of the Arctic Circle. North America's largest Eskimo settlement is here—Barrow covers 88,000 square miles. This is also the whaling capital of the Arctic.

Kotzebue is the trading center of the Arctic. Part of the ancient land bridge that once joined Siberia and North America, it has been a major settlement and trade center for 6,000 years. **Front Street**, the city's main street, is also the beach, where fishing boats pull up and fish and meat are hung on racks to dry. You can shop here for jade, ivory carvings, furs, native handicrafts, and artifacts.

The Pribilof Islands

The **Pribilof Islands**, in the Bering Sea, are home to North America's largest seal herd and the biggest seabird colony in the world. (More than 190 bird species have been sighted.) Each summer, 1.7 million northern fur seals migrate here to bear their young.

The best of the Alaskan panhandle

The history of Alaska began in its panhandle, a scenic fishing, timber, and mining area filled with thousands of wooded islands, mountains covered by glaciers, and waterfalls. The entire southeast of the state is the huge, wild **Tongass National Forest**. One of its glaciers, the Malaspina, is as big as Rhode Island. Lonely, isolated towns are blocked from the mainland by the Coastal Mountains.

459

Juneau, the capital

Juneau, the capital of Alaska, was founded 100 years ago as a fishing and gold-mining town. It has 18,000 residents, who are watched over by Mount Roberts and Mount Juneau. Behind the state capitol is **Gold Creek**, where a mining museum shows what it was like to tunnel through the mountains. North of town is the splendid **Mendenhall Glacier.**

Juneau's best hotel is the **Westmark Juneau**, *51 W. Egan Drive; (907)586-6900* or *(800)544-0970*, across from the waterfront. Beautifully carved wood decorates this hotel, which has modern furnishings, cable television, and a good restaurant and lounge. Double rooms are $144 during the summer and $114 during the winter.

The best drive

The most spectacular drive from Juneau is north to **Haines.** Forty miles of road wind through the mountains to the border. **Klukwan**, near Haines, has the largest concentration of bald eagles in North America. The **Chilkoot Trail**, which begins in the gold-rush town of Skagway, is littered with wagon wheels, horse skeletons, and commemorative plaques that trace the steps of gold-crazed miners.

Luxury in Alaska

The most luxurious place on the panhandle is a hot-springs resort on Chichagof Island called **Tenakee Springs.** The springs (about 107 degrees Fahrenheit) are therapeutic. The town is made up of wooden houses on stilts connected by plank walkways. Stay at the Victorian **Tenakee Inn and Tavern**, *(907)736-9238*; call ahead, it's seasonal.

Sitka: where Russia meets America

Alaska's tourist center is **Sitka**, at the base of Mount Edgecumbe. When Alaska was part of Russia, this was its capital. You can still see the Slavic influence, especially in the Russian Orthodox cathedral. Visit the **Sitka National Historical Park**, at Lincoln Street and the Indian River. Here, Russians captured a Tlingit Indian stronghold in 1804. You can see totem poles, the battlefield, and a museum with displays of Tlingit and Russian culture.

The **Westmark Shee Atika**, *330 Seward St., Sitka; (907)747-6241*, is decorated with native art, including a wall mural illustrating Tlingit history. A sunken living room surrounds the fireplace. The best views are from the rooms on the fifth floor. Double rooms start at $98.

Where the people are: Anchorage

Half of Alaska's population (about 180,000 people) lives in **Anchorage**. This big city boasts two daily newspapers, performances by celebrities and internationally recognized orchestras, theater, fast-food joints, glass and steel buildings, supermarkets, and department stores.

The best thing about Anchorage is its night life. This is where those with cabin fever go to let off steam. Bars, massage parlors, restaurants, nightclubs, and strip joints keep the money changing along Fourth Avenue and Spenard Road.

Visit the **Anchorage Museum of History and Art**, *121 W. Seventh Ave.; (907)343-4326.*

Shop for native crafts at the **Alaska Native Arts and Crafts**, *333 W. Fourth Ave.; (907)274-2932.* Look for the soft, warm clothing of Alaska at the **Oomingmak Musk Ox Cooperative**, *604 H St.; (907)272-9225.*

The best time to visit Anchorage is during the **Winter Carnival**, held each year in mid-February.

Alaska's best restaurants and hotel

Even hotel restaurants in Alaska, which is known for its seafood, are surprisingly good. The best restaurant is the **Crow's Nest**, at the Captain Cook Hotel in Anchorage. Other good restaurants include **Elevation 92,** *Third Avenue and K Street,* and **Simon and Seaforths,** *410 L St.*

The state's best hotel is the **Anchorage Westward Hilton,** *(907)272-7411,* which will seem like paradise after the rough cold of the Alaska wilderness. A double room is $110 to $240.

The largest island: Kodiak (with the biggest bears)

Kodiak, the largest island in the United States, is also the largest fishing port and the home of the king crab. This island, where you will see Russian architecture, has the oldest European settlement in Alaska. The Kodiak bear is the world's largest species of bear.

A heavenly sight

One of the most beautiful sights in Alaska can be seen from anywhere in the state. Electromagnetic fluctuations in the atmosphere and the magnetic pull of the North Pole create the magnificent spectacle of the **Aurora Borealis,** a rainbow of colors that glimmers on the horizon.

Hawaii: America's paradise

The most beautiful place in the United States is halfway around the world—**Hawaii.** Long, sandy beaches, palm trees, jungles, exotic people, luxurious resorts, and the some of the world's best surfing combine to make this state a true paradise.

Maui, the second-largest of the Hawaiian Islands, has both luxury resorts and large undeveloped areas. The **Kaanapali Beach Resort** has restaurants, shops, and hotels. The **Hyatt Regency Maui** is splendid. Its open-air lobby is decorated with antique Asian vases. The Kapalua Bay Hotel is more subtle.

On the east coast of Maui is **Hana,** a ranch town (the drive here is breathtaking). Maui's best adventure is a helicopter ride over the **Haleakala volcano.** You will see waterfalls and sacred pools, as well as the grave of Charles Lindbergh. You also can join a bicycle tour down Mount Haleakala. A van carries you to the rim of the volcano, where you enjoy breakfast and the sunrise. Then you coast downhill for 38 miles.

The most civilized island is **Oahu,** where Honolulu is located. The **Kahala Hilton** is superb, as is the **Halekulani.** Visit the Iolani Palace, the Bishop Museum, and Pearl Harbor.

Hawaii, the biggest island

Waterfalls, black-sand beaches, cliffs, surf, soft trade winds, and beautiful views make **Hawaii** gorgeous. The Big Island, as it is known, is also the most historic, settled by Polynesians more than 1,000 years ago. The island has plantation towns, royal homes, missionary churches, and burial grounds. Its extraordinary resort hotels, which draw people from around the world, lie on the **Kohala Coast.**

Hawaii is a 93-mile-long diamond-shaped island with four active volcanoes. A trip around the island leads past fields of sugarcane, rain forests with wild orchids, steam vents, volcanoes, black-sand beaches, petroglyphs, ancient temples, coffee trees, shacks, grasslands, and cacti.

While exploring Hawaii, you may also see the Night Marchers, ghost warriors who chant along the ancient **King's Trail,** which winds through several resorts. The **Puuhonua O Honaunau National Historical Park** was a place of refuge, where Hawaiians could escape the king's wrath in ancient times. Near the town of **Hawi** is the birthplace of Kamehameha, the first king to rule all the islands. Nearby is the **Mo'okini Heiau,** a temple dating back to A.D. 480, still cared for by the Mo'okini family, which has watched over it since it was built.

The beach town of **Kailua** has reasonably priced hotels, fishing charters, shops, and stone churches built in the 1800s. **Hulihee Palace,** now a museum, provides a view of the harbor. Built as a summer palace for Hawaiian royalty, its architecture is a curious blend of elements from New England, France, England, and Hawaii.

Hawaii Volcanos National Park encompasses the island's two active volcanos: **Kilauea** and **Mauna Loa**. An 11-mile drive circles Kilauea's huge collapsed summit, or caldera, which passes near man-size lava tubes and the **Halemaumau**, a fire pit where the goddess Pele is said to live. The most beautiful drive is along the **Chain of Craters Road**, which winds 25 miles down Kilauea and takes you as close as you are permitted (and as close as you would want to get) to **Puu Oo Vent**, which erupts regularly.

Mauna Kea is the best place on earth to conduct infrared studies. This peak is 13,796 feet above a huge, dark ocean, protected from the lights of civilization; it is also above 40% of the earth's atmosphere. The **Manua Kea Observatory** has six astronomical telescopes.

If you can afford it, stay at the **Kona Village Resort**, *P.O. Box 1299, Kailua-Kona; (808)325-5555 or (800)421-0000.* A double room is $360 to $640, including all meals.

Kauai: the lushest isle

Kauai, the fourth-largest Hawaiian island, is the most beautiful. *The Thorn Birds, Raiders of the Lost Ark,* and *South Pacific* were filmed here. The **Na Pali Coast**, which can be reached by helicopter, is the island's most spectacular area.

The air seems green on this lush island. Waterfalls cascade down sharp peaks into the **Hanalai River**. Orchids and ginger line the river, which meanders through taro fields toward the sea. Three beautiful parks line Hanalei Bay: Hanalei Beach Park, Hanalei Pavilion, and Waioli Beach Park. Two large peaks, Hihimanu and Namolokama, watch over the valley.

Waimea Canyon is often called the Grand Canyon of the Pacific. It is 3,600 feet deep and 10 miles long. Its valleys are green, and its ridges are blanketed with flowers. The **Kukui Trail** leads down 2,000 feet to the fertile canyon floor, where you can explore ancient Hawaiian ruins.

The wettest place on earth is **Mount Waialeale**, where 450 inches of rain fall each year. On the western slope of this 5,080-foot peak lies the **Alakai Swamp**, a 10-mile area where birds and plants (but no mosquitoes) flourish. The **Pihea Trail** (which translates as *Din of Voices*) leads to the swamp, where giant ferns and tree-size violets grow.

Hawaii's most luxurious resorts

Honolulu has two grand hotels: the **Moana**, *2365 Kalakaua Ave.; (808)922-3111,* where a double room is $195 to $300, and the **Royal Hawaiian**, *2259 Kalakaua Ave.; (808)923-7311 or (800)325-3535,* where a double room starts at $235.

The Moana, one of Hawaii's first hotels, opened in 1901. Robert Louis Stevenson came here to write. The 75-room white clapboard hotel is of classic South Seas design, with some verandas furnished with wicker furniture. It is on the beach.

The Royal Hawaiian is a pink Moorish-style palace built in the 1920s. The hotel's first guest was Princess Kawanakoa, who would have been queen of Hawaii if the islands had been left alone. The hotel is on the beach and has a pool.

The **Kahala Hilton**, *5000 Kahala Ave., Honolulu; (808)734-2211,* is a first-class hotel with a beach and a swimming pool. It also has a pool filled with dolphins. The hotel's beachfront restaurant is good. A double room starts at $220.

The **Mauna Kea Beach Hotel**, *1 Mauna Kea Beach Drive, Kohala Coast; (800)882-6060,* was built in July 1965 by Laurance Rockefeller on the white sands at Kaunaoa Bay. A double room is $260 to $390.

Kona Village, *P.O. Box 1299, Queen Ka'ahumanu Highway, Kailua-Kona; (800)367-5290,* is on a kipuka, an area of land left untouched by surrounding lava flows. This recreation of a South Seas island community was built by Johnno Jackson. Jackson sailed to this protected cove for years before opening the resort, where coats and ties are banned. You stay in individual thatched huts in a tropical setting. A double room is $360 to $640.

462

The Best of Canada

The aloofness of Canada, not less inhabited perhaps, but so far less humanized than Asia, struck me with awe, and an immense admiration for the courage that had tackled it.
—*Freya Stark, 1951*

Canada, which covers 3.8 million square miles, is the second-largest country on earth. Within its wide boundaries are a rainbow of cultures and a kaleidoscope of natural sights. To the west are cloud-piercing mountain peaks, the rugged Pacific coastline, and cities with large Chinese communities. In the east are quaint British towns, French-speaking Quebec, and secluded islands. The interior is home to cowboys, rodeos, and ranches.

Canada is a nature lover's dream, offering some of the world's best skiing, fishing, boating, hiking, bird-watching, and hunting. But it offers the best of big-city life as well. Montreal, Toronto, Edmonton, and Vancouver are metropolises with fine restaurants, high-fashion boutiques, cosmopolitan populations, artistic communities, and good theater and dance companies.

The best of Montreal

Montreal, is the world's second-largest French-speaking city (after Paris). Parisian sophistication and Canadian friendliness blend here. The air smells of good coffee and French cooking.

Located on Montreal Island in the St. Lawrence River, the city faces the entrance to the St. Lawrence Seaway. Dominating the city is Mont Réal (Mount Royal), for which the city is named.

The city is informally split in two: the English section in the west and the French section in the east. Street names reinforce this division.

The oldest section

The oldest section, which hugs the waterfront, is called, appropriately, **Vieux Montreal** (Old Montreal). The seed of the city was an Indian village called Hochelaga. French

463

settlers took it over in 1642 and called their town Ville Marie de Montreal. The French town was surrendered to the British 118 years later, in 1760. For one year (1775 to 1776), the British ceded the town to the Americans. The quarter has been patiently restored and is filled with antique shops, cafés, and boutiques. The cobblestoned alleyways are lined with artists and their easels on summer evenings. It's a pleasant place to wander or stop for a snack.

A futuristic contrast

At the other end of the time scale is **Man and His World,** a permanent miniversion of the international exposition EXPO '67. Situated on an island in the St. Lawrence River, it is a fascinating, ultramodern collection of spheres and towers, some of which are slowly rusting and falling apart.

Montreal's prettiest churches

The **Basilica of Notre Dame,** *Place d'Armes,* is an elaborate neo-Gothic affair with two tall spires. Built in 1829, the church houses an immense organ with 5,772 pipes. The altar, too, is monumental. And the wood carvings are carefully detailed. The basilica was designed by New York architect James O'Donnell, whose grave is in the church. The **Sacred Heart Chapel,** adjacent to the basilica, has stained-glass windows illustrating the history of Montreal. The church is open daily.

Notre-Dame-de-Bonsecours, *400 St. Paul St. E.,* in Vieux Montreal, is the city's oldest church, built in 1657, destroyed by fire, then rebuilt in 1771. The facade is from 1895. Located near the water, it is also known as the Sailor's Chapel. It is closed Monday.

Underground Montreal: the warmest shopping

Because Montreal can be buried in as much as 100 inches of snow during the winter, many of the city's shops have taken refuge in a seven-mile mall beneath the city. Designed by architect I.M. Pei and developer William Zeckendorf in the 1950s, the underground complex has shops, sports facilities, theaters, exhibits, restaurants, apartments, hotels, and banks. Best of all, it's all heated.

The nucleus of the complex is **Place Ville Marie,** where shops surround a sculptured fountain. Corridors link Ville Marie with similar complexes at Place Bonaventure and Place du Canada. The three areas together contain 280 shops, 20 restaurants and bars, and entrances to three hotels.

Place des Arts is a lavish performing-arts center, home of the Montreal Symphony Orchestra and the Montreal Opera. To get there, take the metro to the Place des Arts stop.

The best of Montreal at night

Montreal doesn't close until 3:30 a.m., a liberty that spoils other cities for many Montrealers. The center of the city's nighttime activity is charming and sophisticated **Crescent Street,** Montreal's version of the Latin Quarter in Paris. Prince Arthur, Duluth, and St. Denis streets are also lined with bars, cafés, and restaurants.

On summer nights in early July, you can take in the jazz festival at the Théâtre St. Denis, and in late August you can enjoy the film festival at cinemas throughout the city.

For something unique, go to a *boîte à chanson,* a Quebec-style café with French folk music.

The finest French cooking

The best restaurant in Montreal is **Les Mignardises,** *2037 rue St. Denis; tel. (514)842-1151.* Chef Jean Pierre Monnet creates masterpieces, and the service is superb. Dinner is C$60 to C$100 ($52 to $87) per person, with wine. The restaurant is closed Sundays.

Chez la Mère Michel, *1209 Guy St.; tel. (514)934-0473,* is cozy, with an outstanding French provincial menu and a pretty garden patio. Try the *homard soufflé Nantua* (fresh lobster added to mousseline potatoes and served on a bed of spinach). The restaurant is closed Sundays and Monday mornings.

Les Chênets, *2075 Bishop St.; tel. (514)844-1842,* is decorated with original works of art. The dishes, too, are masterpieces, smothered in delicious sauces. The selection of Cognac and Armagnac brandies is the best in the Americas.

The best hotels

Montreal's best hotel is the **Ritz Carlton,** *Sherbrooke West; tel. (514)842-4212.* A luxurious, Continental-style hotel, it is near fashionable boutiques, restaurants, and galleries. A double room is C$135 to C$250 ($96 to $219).

Less expensive hotels include **L'Hôtel de la Montagne,** *tel. (514)288-5656,* where a double room is C$99 to C$129 ($86 to $113), and the **Hotel Château Versailles,** *tel. (514)933-3611,* where a double room is C$109 to C$149 ($95 to $130).

But we think the best (and certainly the most affordable) accommodation in Montreal is at the city's bed-and-breakfasts. For a list, contact **Downtown Bed and Breakfast,** *3458 Laval Ave., Montreal H2X 3C8; tel. (514)932-9690 or (514)289-9749.*

Quebec: the French heart—and the only walled city

Quebec City, the capital of the French-speaking province of Quebec, is the focal point of French Canadian nationalism. It is also the first French settlement in North America (95% of the population is French) and the oldest city in the New World (the walled fortress was founded by Champlain in 1608). Quebec is the only walled city in North America. It is set high on Cape Diamond, 350 feet above the St. Lawrence River.

The best of Vieux Quebec

In **Vieux Quebec** (Old Quebec), you'll see 17th- and 18th-century stone houses similar to those in the villages of Normandy and Brittany in France.

The heart of Vieux Quebec is the beautiful **Place d'Armes.** A good introduction to the history of Quebec is the sound-and-light show at the **Musée du Fort.** The **Seminary,** dating from 1663, houses a museum containing a rare collection of Canadian money, including Indian wampum and playing cards used as legal tender in colonial times. In the museum at the **Hotel Dieu,** you can see the stone vaults where Augustinian nuns took refuge during the 1759 siege. The skull of French general Montcalm is on view at the **Ursulin Convent Museum.**

Looming over the Place d'Armes is the **Château Frontenac,** *tel. (418)692-3861,* a magnificent Victorian hotel with turrets and towers. Built in 1892, it perches at the top of Cape Diamond, a 300-foot bluff. A double room is C$119 to C$240 ($104 to $210).

Next door is the **Jardin des Gouverneurs,** originally the private garden of the Château St. Louis. It is best known for its statue of General James Wolfe and Marquis de Montcalm, erected in 1828. On it is written, "Their courage gave them the same lot; history, the same fame; posterity, the same monument."

Canada's most important battlefield

The **Plains of Abraham** in Quebec were the site of a battle that determined the fate of Canada. On Sept. 13, 1759, the British army under Wolfe defeated the French under Montcalm, and Canada was turned over the British. (However, the French inhabitants held on to their language and culture.) Both Wolfe and Montcalm were killed during the battle. According to legend, at the end of the battle, a voice was heard across the plains crying, *"Je me souviens"* (I remember), which became the motto of the province of Quebec.

Today the battlefield is part of the 230-acre **Parc des Champs de Bataille.** From the observation post, you'll have a wide view of the field and the river.

The **Quebec Museum,** *tel. (418)643-2150,* is also on the park grounds. It contains displays illustrating Quebec's history, paintings by Quebecois artists, and a section devoted to 17th-century decorative arts. The museum is open 10 a.m. until 5:45 p.m. daily except Monday, when it is closed.

The oldest section

The oldest section of the city is around Place Royale in a district known as **Lower Town**. When Champlain started his colony here, it was a trading post, with a store, a few houses, and fortifications. In later years, Place Royale became the center of the fur-trading industry. As colonists and missionaries arrived, the settlement gradually moved uphill, to Vieux Quebec.

Today, Lower Town is a busy port. Designated a historic area by the Canadian government, the section surrounding Place Royale is being restored. It has the greatest concentration of 17th- and 18th-century buildings in North America.

The oldest church in Quebec, **Notre Dame des Victoires**, is located on Place Royale. This small stone church built in 1688 is decorated inside with elaborate woodwork. The altar is carved in the shape of an old fort. The church is open daily.

A funicular will take you from Place d'Armes down to Place Royale, where you can walk along cobblestoned streets past 17th-century buildings and sunny squares. **Rue de Trésor** is the best place to stroll; painters sell their masterpieces along here.

The best French architecture

Quebec's **Assemblée Nationale** (parliament buildings)—bounded by rue Dufferin, boulevards St. Cyrille and St. Augustin, and Le Grande Allée—are imposing French structures built in 1877 and 1886. Twelve bronze statues commemorating famous Canadians rest in niches in the facade. They are the works of the Quebec sculptor Hébert. Guided tours are conducted daily during the summer and on weekdays during the winter.

The best time to visit

The **Carnival de Quebec**, a 10-day celebration beginning on the first Thursday in February, is the most festive time to visit the city. A huge party to commemorate the end of winter, it includes two parades, fireworks, and winter sports. The official mascot is a 7-foot snowman called Le Bonhomme Carnival.

If you plan to visit during Carnival, you will be competing for hotel rooms with more than a half-million people from all over North America. Make reservations. If you can't find a room, contact the **Carnival Lodging Committee**, *tel. (418)524-8441.*

Quebec's best restaurants

The best restaurant in town is **À le Table de Serge Bruyère**, *Livernois Comples (upstairs), 1200 rue St. Jean; tel. (418)694-0618,* where a special prix-fixe menu of seven courses is served (C$40.25, or $35). Try the filet of Quebec lamb with green shallots and fresh tomatoes. Reservations are required. The restaurant is open daily.

Restaurant Louis Hebert, *668 Grande Allée Est; tel. (418)525-7812,* is also good, serving light French fare. Set in a 17th-century fieldstone building, it has a French provincial atmosphere, with calico lampshades and an outdoor terrace. It is open daily.

The best place for local French-Canadian fare is **Aux Anciens Canadiens**, *34 rue St. Louis; tel. (418)692-1627.* Located in the former home of the 19th-century historical novelist Philippe Aubert de Gaspé (which was built in 1675), the restaurant serves Canadian yellow pea soup, *tourtière* (meat pie), and maple syrup pie with heavy cream. Reservations are suggested. The restaurant is open daily.

The best hotels

The most elegant place to stay is **Le Château Frontenac**, *1 ave. des Carrières; tel. (418)692-3861.* It is grand, historic, and expensive (rooms are C$119 to C$240, or $104 to $210). The cocktail lounge and many of the rooms have views of the St. Lawrence. However, because this is a tourist hotel, expect to be one of many Americans.

Auberge du Trésor, *20 rue Ste. Anne; tel. (418)694-1876*, is a 300-year-old inn on the Place d'Armes. Its 20 guest rooms have private bathrooms, televisions, and air conditioning. Prices are moderate, from C$55 to C$95 ($48 to $83).

Le Château de Pierre, *17 ave. Ste. Geneviève; tel. (418)694-0429*, is a 15-room mansion built in 1853. Its large rooms all have color televisions and air conditioning. A double room is C$55 to C$100 (US$48 to US$87).

The best of provincial French Canada

Most American visitors, smitten by Quebec City's charms, overlook the nearby countryside (unless they snow ski in the Laurentides, Quebec's Little Switzerland). This is a big oversight. Farmstays are available in fascinating villages, where people wake up with the roosters.

An island lost in time

Nearby **Ile d'Orléans** is a lovely island with historic Quebecois homes, old farming villages, and French restaurants. Until 1935, the island could be reached only by boat. Because of this, it retained its old French ways longer than its neighbors. Many of the houses here are from the 17th and 18th centuries. Most residents are farmers and descendants of French immigrants from Normandy and Brittany.

Miraculous cures

Farther on is the village of **Ste. Anne de Beaupré**, whose massive cathedral is a famous Catholic shrine. Invalids from all over the world come here to be cured—the fountain in front of the church is said to cure many diseases. There must be something to this claim, to judge from the plethora of crutches, canes, and walkers left behind by cured believers—some of the paraphernalia is hung from the church's ceiling. Built in 1922, the cathedral holds 10,000 people.

A best for *les artistes*

Just an hour north of Quebec City, on the north shore of the St. Lawrence River, is a bustling resort for artists and patrons called **Baie St. Paul**. Dozens of galleries display works of the Group of Seven—painters who portray the Charlevoix region.

The Gaspe Peninsula

An hour northeast of Baie St. Paul, the port of Rivière du Loup marks the beginning of the **Gaspe Peninsula**, a French fishing and farming region. The Gaspe begins dramatically. Mountains plunge into the sea. Little fishing towns brave the pounding surf. Although rugged, the peninsula is accommodating—many manor houses have been converted to inns.

Gaspe is an old French fishing village, three hours north of Rivière du Loup on the northern tip of the peninsula. The French spoken here, *joual*, sounds to the French of France as Middle English would sound to us. Gaspe is where Cartier first stepped ashore in North America in 1534. A large granite cross marks the spot. The **Gaspe Museum** has exhibits on the history and folklore of the area.

Around the point from Gaspe is **Bonaventure**, founded by French-speaking Acadians fleeing British troops in 1755. Nearby are limestone rock formations that reach out of the sea—popular among small-boat sailors and seabirds. You can walk to **Percé Rock** at low tide. **Ile Bonaventure** is a boat ride away. This bird sanctuary was once a pirate hideout.

One of Quebec province's best restaurants perches 1,000 feet above Percé Rock. **L'Auberge du Gargantua**, *tel. (418)782-2852*, serves excellent French provincial cooking. Specialties include periwinkles in court bouillon, fresh fish, and giant crab. But the best dish is the bouillabaisse Gargantua. Reservations are required. The restaurant is open daily.

Ottawa, a capital city

Canada's capital, **Ottawa**, is a small beautiful city with only 303,747 inhabitants. Set high on a bluff overlooking the confluence of the Ottawa, Gatineau, and Rideau rivers, it has lovely views in all directions. Man has added to the scenery: the Gothic parliament buildings create a romantic skyline. The Rideau Canal is pretty, cutting through the city.

Ottawa has a British flavor. The language is predominantly English, and you're more likely to be served scones than croissants. Established by Queen Victoria in 1858 as the capital of the United Provinces of Canada, the city is filled with elaborate Victorian architecture. It became the capital of modern Canada in 1867.

Ottawa's top sights

Parliament Hill, on a bluff over the Ottawa River, is the pedestal for the spectacular parliament buildings, with their tall copper roofs. The 302-foot **Peace Tower** dedicated to Canadians who lost their lives in World War I forms part of the main entrance to the buildings. Its walls and floors are made of stones from the battlefields. Its tower contains a 53-bell carillon. You can go to the Visitor's Galleries in the House of Commons and the Senate. Or take a tour of the Center Block, which passes through the Memorial Chamber, the library, and the Peace Tower lookout. During the summer, you can watch the changing of the guard on the lawns of Parliament Hill daily at 10 a.m.

The **National Gallery of Canada** is located in the **Lorne Building,** *Elgin Street,* between Albert and Slater streets. It contains six floors of galleries devoted to European and Canadian art, displaying works by Canada's Group of Seven, including Paul Kane's paintings of Indians and Cornelius Kreigoff's paintings of pioneers. European masters Rembrandt, Chardin, El Greco, Cézanne, Van Gogh, Monet, and Picasso are also represented.

Bytown Museum, near the junction of the Rideau Canal and the Ottawa River, is filled with artifacts of the Ottawa Indians: furniture, clothes, guns, tools, and toys.

Ottawa's best hotels

The best hotel in town is **Château Laurier,** *Confederation Square; tel. (613)232-6411.* An institution in Canada since 1912, it is a favorite among politicians and big-time businessmen. The hotel's restaurant, the Canadian Grill, is dignified. A double room is C$119 to C$249 ($104 to $218).

The **Ottawa Hilton,** *150 Albert St.; tel. (613)238-1500,* has all the modern luxuries: whirlpool baths, tanning rooms, and saunas. The rooms have been renovated recently, and the dining room and wine bar are popular. This is one of Ottawa's most expensive hotels—a double room is C$129 to C$195 ($113 to $171).

The **Park Lane,** *111 Cooper St.; tel. (613)238-1331,* is a moderately priced hotel. A double room is C$70 to C$109 ($61 to $95).

The best of Shakespeare

Try to make it to Stratford's annual summer **Shakespearean Festival.** The town, which is modeled on Stratford, England, has swans, green lawns that sweep down to the river, and pretty cottages. You can picnic in **Queen's Park** beneath tall shade trees. Past the Orr Dam and the 90-year-old stone bridge is the **Shakespearean Garden,** a formal English garden with a sundial that was presented to the town by a former mayor of England's Stratford-upon-Avon. For more information, contact the **Stratford Festival Office,** *P.O. Box 520, Stratford, Ontario N5A 6V2; tel. (519)273-1600.*

The most curious place to dine in Stratford is **The Church,** *Brunswick and Waterloo streets; tel. (519)273-3424,* which has delicious food and churchlike decor—organ pipes, an altar, a vaulted roof, and stained-glass windows. Reservations are required.

Shrewsbury Manor, *30 Shrewsbury St.; tel. (519)271-8520*, a charming old Victorian house, has been turned into a bed-and-breakfast. A double room is only C$50 ($43) per couple.

Niagara from the other side

Just 20 minutes from Niagara-on-the-Lake, down Niagara Parkway, is the Canadian side of **Niagara Falls**, which is both prettier than the U.S. side and less crowded. You can take an elevator below the falls at Table Rock House. And the ship *Maid of the Mist* takes you practically under the falls. Boats leave from the dock on the parkway just down from the Rainbow Bridge. The cost is C$5 ($4.30) for adults, C$3 ($2.60) for children.

The best place to stay is the **Foxhead Hotel**, *5685 Falls Ave.; tel. (416)374-4444*, which has a perfect view of the falls. A double room is C$69 to C$190 ($60 to $166), depending on the season.

The best of Toronto

Toronto, situated on the Great Lakes, is the largest city in Canada. Towering buildings, such as the CN (Canadian National) Tower, the world's tallest freestanding structure, punctuate the city's dramatic skyline. Canada's most modern city, Toronto boasts avant-garde architecture, especially on Eaton Square and at the O'Keefe Center.

Despite its modern appearance, Toronto is old, occupying the site of a French fort (1749-1759) in an area purchased by the British from the Indians in 1787. It was settled largely by Loyalists who left the Thirteen Colonies during and just after the Revolutionary War. Americans raided the city twice, destroying parts of it during the War of 1812. Then known as York, it was renamed Toronto in 1834.

Toronto is an Indian word meaning *place of meeting*, which is appropriate considering the huge and varied ethnic groups that populate the city. Because of the diversified population, the choice of restaurants is astounding.

Toronto is second only to New York in number and variety of stage productions. It has a progressive urban spirit and a sophisticated cosmopolitan outlook, without the big-city problems of Chicago and New York.

The world's tallest building

Toronto's most visible landmark, the **CN Tower**, has an observation deck at 1,136 feet that affords a panoramic view of the city. At the top is the revolving Top of the Tower restaurant (the highest and largest revolving dining room in the world) and a communications tower. On a clear day, you can see for about 75 miles.

Toronto's top sights

The best place to begin exploring the city is at its heart: **City Hall**, a modern superstructure that looks something like the landing pad for a spaceship. Topped with a white dome and flanked by 20- and 27-story curved towers, the building's twin clamshell design won an international competition for Finnish architect Viljo Revell, one of 530 contestants.

The 9-acre plaza in front of City Hall, called **Nathan Phillips Square**, was named after the Toronto mayor responsible for the project. It provides a community meeting place for concerts and self-appointed orators. In the winter, the reflecting pool doubles as a skating rink. The focal point of the square is a Henry Moore sculpture called *The Archer*. When city fathers balked at buying it, the people of Toronto raised the money to buy it themselves. Moore was so touched by their enthusiasm that he donated many of his works to the Art Gallery of Toronto.

Across the street is **Old City Hall**, an imposing Romanesque fortress that houses the Provincial Courts. Built in 1899, it has marble columns, stained glass, and grained flooring from Georgia. The building is embellished with carved gargoyles, said to be furtive caricatures of city councillors with whom the architect battled in the 1890s.

In Queen's Park, the **Provincial Parliament Building** stands on the site of a former lunatic asylum. Wander through the pink sandstone complex and listen to the lawmakers debating in the legislative chambers.

Casa Loma is a 98-room medieval-looking castle created by financier Sir Henry Pellant. Built between 1911 and 1914, this extravagance boasts gold-plated bath fixtures, a gigantic pipe organ, and one of the largest wine cellars in North America. An 800-foot underground tunnel leads to stables furnished in marble, mahogany, and Spanish tile.

Old Fort York, *Garrison Road,* was built in 1793, destroyed during the War of 1812, and then rebuilt. The officers' quarters, center blockhouse, and battlements have been refurbished. Members of the Fort York Guard are dressed in uniforms of British troops of the era.

Also visit the city's new baseball stadium, the **Skydome**. It has a retractable roof, several restaurants—including a Hard Rock Café, and a hotel. You can even get McDonald's food from the vendors in the bleachers.

The finest art
The **Art Gallery of Ontario** is renowned for its collection of works by Canadian artists and for its important collection of Henry Moore sculptures.

The **Royal Ontario Museum**, *Avenue Road and Bloor Street West,* displays Chinese art and artifacts, extensive ethnological collections, dinosaurs, fossils, and minerals.

The **McMichael Canadian Collection of Art**, in Kleinburg, about 25 miles north of Toronto, has 30 gallery rooms constructed from timbers that once enclosed pioneer homes and barns. More than 1,000 paintings by the Group of Seven and their contemporaries are on display, along with West Coast and Woodland Indian and Inuit works.

The most inviting parks
Toronto has 15,000 acres of parkland displaying signs that say "Please walk on the grass." **Toronto Islands Park** can be reached by ferry from across the harbor. **Exhibition Place**, *Lakeshore Boulevard West,* is the site of the Canadian National Exhibition, held from the third week in August to the first Monday in September. **High Park**, near the west end of the Queen streetcar route, is a lovely place for sailing, picnicking, and strolling.

The best shopping
The hub of downtown shopping is **Eaton Center**, an 860-foot-long shopping center docked on Yonge Street. The mall is shaped like a large ocean freighter, with a series of railings, big exposed ducts, greenhouse glazing, and three-dozen sculptured geese swooping from the glass-domed ceiling. The Eaton Center does more gross sales than any other shopping mall in North America.

The retail giants Simpsons and Eaton's are anchored at each end of the mall, with 300 shops, banks, boutiques, and fast-food outlets on three levels in between.

The best entertainment
Ontario Place, along the lakefront, is an overwhelming futuristic entertainment complex built over the water on three man-made islands. It includes a disco, a roller rink, a marina, numerous restaurants, and snack bars. The main attraction is the **Cinesphere**, a ball-shaped theater where films are projected on a six-story curved screen, the world's tallest.

Harborfront, another recreational development, stretches 1 1/2 miles from York Street to just past Bathurst. Divided into four sections, the attractions include antique shops, art galleries, cafés, studios, theaters, picnic facilities, and a multicultural media center.

Toronto has its own symphony and is home to both the Canadian Opera Company and the National Ballet. The **O'Keefe Center**, *Front and Yonge streets*, is a modern hall with seating for 3,200. The **St. Lawrence Center**, *Front and Scott streets*, contains an 830-seat theater that accommodates a resident repertory company, visiting theater groups, and opera and dance companies.

Incomparable cooking

Toronto's best restaurant, and the granddaddy of haute cuisine in Canada, is **Winston's**, *104 Adelaide St. W.; tel. (416)363-1627*. You'll feel like royalty here, surrounded by magnificent decor. Try the lamb or the *escalope de veau*, and save room for crepes suzette. The wine list is extensive. Dinner is about C$70 ($61), with wine. Reservations are required. Winston's is closed Sundays and holidays.

Canada's best Thai restaurant is **Bangkok Garden**, *18 Elm St.; tel. (416)977-6748*, a beautifully decorated place. Try the steamed gingerfish or the mussels in spicy coconut sauce. The restaurant is closed Sundays.

The most charming restaurant in town is **Le Bistingo**, *349 Queen St. W.; tel. (416)598-3490*, a fashionable French restaurant with scrumptious desserts. It is closed Sundays and major holidays.

The best place for French Continental cuisine (with a touch of California) is **Chiaro's**, *37 King St. E.; tel. (416)863-9700*, in the newly renovated King Edward Hotel. Dishes are not only light and delicious but also beautifully presented. Try the tea-smoked Atlantic salmon and fruit ices. Chiaro's is closed Sundays and holidays.

Il Posto, *York Square, 148 Yorkville Ave.; tel. (416)968-0469*, is Toronto's best Italian restaurant, with imaginatively prepared pasta dishes. The restaurant is closed Sundays.

The best hotels

The **Royal York Hotel**, *100 Front St. W.; tel. (416)368-2511*, is the biggest hotel in the British Commonwealth. A landmark since 1929, it is a favorite among royalty, movie stars, and visiting prime ministers. Service is superb. A double room is C$149 to C$219 ($130 to $192).

Toronto's most charming hotel is the **King Edward**, *37 King St. E.; tel. (416)863-9700*. This Edwardian-style classic was recently renovated. A double room is C$219 to C$289 ($192 to $253).

The **Sheraton Center**, *123 Queen St. W.; tel. (416)361-1000*, outdoes itself with imaginative decor. A three-story waterfall cascades in the lobby, and the hotel complex houses 40 stores, two theaters, 10 restaurants, and six bars. Outside are lovely gardens. And, of course, modern luxuries, such as saunas and indoor and outdoor pools, have not been forgotten. A double room is C$79 to C$235 ($69 to $206).

A pleasant moderately priced hotel is the **Delta Chelsea Inn**, *33 Gerrard St. W.; tel. (416)595-1975*, between Yonge and Bay streets. A double room is C$92 to C$180 ($80 to $157).

The best of New Brunswick

Along New Brunswick's 1,400-mile shoreline are some of the oldest cities and towns in Canada, founded by Loyalist refugees from the American Revolution. The coast is also home to small Acadian French towns. Forests cover 84% of the province. Life is serene. Along the **Fundy Coast**, residents pass the time predicting the weather and discussing the price of seafood.

Campobello Island, a president's favorite

Campobello Island is where President Franklin Roosevelt retreated from the tensions of his job. His house is open to the public. The **Roosevelt Campobello International Park**, a joint Canadian-American preservation effort, is open May to October from 9 a.m. to 6 p.m. Benedict Arnold also lived on Campobello Island for a time, at Snug Cove.

St. Andrews, a moving town

St. Andrews is a Loyalist settlement with a unique history. The first settlers built their town at Fort George (later Castine, Maine). When that area became part of the United States, the townspeople actually lifted their homes and moved them to the Canadian side of the border. Today St. Andrews is a peaceful summer haven with swimming, golfing, and tours of Passamoquoddy Bay.

St. Andrews Blockhouse National Historic Site, at the northwest end of Water Street, is the only surviving wood fortress of several built for the town's defense during the War of 1812. Also see **Greenock Church**, a pretty church built in 1824.

Visit the aquarium at Huntsman Marine Laboratories, northwest of town on Brandy Cover Road, and the **Ross Memorial Museum**, *188 Montague St.,* in an old house filled with antiques, paintings, and curios.

The best place to stay in town is the quirky **Rossmount Inn**, *tel. (506)529-3351.* The Victorian house is decorated with a mishmash of Persian rugs, English wallpaper, and French art. Smoking is not permitted on the grounds. Credit cards are accepted, but it is seasonal, so call before you go.

The best bird-watching

New Brunswick is an excellent place for bird-watching. More than 350 species of birds can be seen; you need only a pair of binoculars and a North American field guide. During the winter, New Brunswick attracts such rare birds as the Bohemian waxwing, pine grosbeak, common redpoll, and purple finch.

For bird watchers, the event of the year is the **Christmas Bird Count**, sponsored by the National Audubon Society. As many observers as possible are needed on the count day, which usually falls during the last two weeks of December. Write to the **New Brunswick Museum**, *Natural Science Department, 277 Douglas Ave., St. John, New Brunswick E2K 1E5,* for the names and addresses of count compilers.

The New Brunswick Federation of Naturalists sponsors field trips several times a year. For more information, write to the **New Brunswick Museum**, *address above.*

St. John: the oldest town

St. John is the oldest incorporated town in Canada, inaugurated in 1785. Actually, it was founded by Samuel de Champlain on St. John the Baptist Day (June 24) in 1604. The Loyalists turned this city into one of the world's greatest shipbuilding ports. Vessels from every country call here.

The St. John River's **Reversing Falls** will leave you wondering. The falls, which appear to flow backward, are actually rapids beneath the bridge on Highway 100. A Tourist Information Center here shows a film explaining the phenomenon. Usually the river empties into the Bay of Fundy. But as the tide rises, the estuary water reverses the river current, creating climbing rapids.

New Brunswick's best seafood

Shediac, which holds a six-day Lobster Festival every July, is known for its incredibly fresh and inexpensive lobster. The city is also known for having New Brunswick's warmest water, thanks to sand bars and shallow depths.

Paturel Shore House, *tel. (506)532-4431,* on the ocean next to a seafood-packing plant, is the best place in the area to get seafood. Take Highway 15 east from Shediac and watch for signs to Cape Bimet and Paturel. Lobster is caught locally and prepared to your specifications. The lobster stew (C$7, or $6.15) can be a meal in itself.

The best place to stay is **Chez Françoise**, *93 Main St.; tel. (506)532-4233*, where rooms are C$60 ($53).

Nova Scotia: more Gaelic than Scotland

Nova Scotia, a 375-mile peninsula separated from New Brunswick by the Bay of Fundy, is more Gaelic than its grandfather, Scotland. The province, which is made up of two main sections, Nova Scotia proper and **Cape Breton Island**, drew boatloads of Scotsmen during the wave of immigration from the Highlands in the 18th century. The Cape Breton immigrants left before they felt the full impact of King James VI's law of 1616, which prohibited the use of Gaelic and the wearing of kilts. Today, even in such remote regions of Scotland as the Isle of Skye, the use of Gaelic is rare. However, on western Cape Breton Island, most adult residents have Gaelic-speaking parents. (Nova Scotia is actually a better place to learn Scottish Gaelic than Scotland. You can take summer classes at St. Anne's in Cape Breton. For more information, contact the **Scottish Studies Department** in Ontario, *tel. (519)824-4120.*)

Fiddlers in this province retain a Scottish style abandoned by most Scottish musicians long ago. "This, not Scotland, is the real McCoy," says Celtic record distributor Dan Collins of Shanachie Records. The stretch along the coast of Cape Breton from the causeway at Port Hastings to Margaree Forks, known as the **Ceilidh Trail**, is the place to go to enjoy traditional music and dance. Check with the proprietors of pubs in the area for details.

Every July, Antigonish hosts the annual **Highland Games**, during which contestants compete in the cabor (log) toss, among other things. For more information, contact the **Nova Scotia Department of Tourism**, *(800)341-6096.*

The Micmac Indians also sponsor annual summer games, which have evolved from a reunion, lasting three months, held since the 18th century. Originally, a continental Indian congress met and planned survival tactics against the encroaching Europeans. It succeeded at least to a degree—to this day, the Micmacs on rural reservations retain their native language.

The Micmac summer games include tributes to St. Ann, such as dances to the beat of the sacred drum, and field games, including archery, canoeing, and *waltes*, a dice game.

To arrange a visit to the Micmac summer games, call the **Micmac Association of Cultural Studies**, *tel. (902)539-8037.*

The best treasure hunting

Oak Island, Nova Scotia, has frustrated treasure hunters for nearly 200 years. Convinced that Captain Kidd and his fellow pirates hid their loot here, many fortune seekers have tried the hunt and failed. Millions of dollars have been spent and six lives lost trying to find the treasure. So far, nothing has been found.

The oldest colony: Newfoundland

Newfoundland is at once the newest of the Canadian provinces and the oldest of the British colonies. Sir Humphrey Gilbert landed on this North Atlantic island in 1583 and claimed it for Queen Elizabeth. But it didn't become part of Canada until 1949.

Legions of hunters, hikers, fishermen, campers, boaters, and photographers take advantage of the natural bounties of this northern province's 47 provincial park wilderness areas and two national parks: Terra Nova in the east and Gros Morne in the west.

The **Marine Atlantic Reservations Bureau**, *121 Eden St., Bar Harbor, ME 04609; (800)341-7981*, operates a year-round vehicle and passenger ferry service between North Sydney, Nova Scotia, and Port-aux-Basques, Newfoundland. During the summer, an additional service operates between North Sydney and Argentia, 78 miles from St. John's.

Gros Morne: the most beautiful scenery

Gros Morne National Park is a jaw-dropping wilderness area on the west coast of Newfoundland. The 750-square-mile park has the most spectacular fiords in North America. Gros Morne (which translates as *Big Knoll* in French) is a flat-topped extinct volcano rising 2,000 feet from the Gulf of St. Lawrence. Climb the 2 1/2-mile **Names Callaghan Trail** to the top of Gros Morne for the best view of the tundra and the roaring sea below. Look for moose, caribou, bald eagles, black bears, and beaver.

Hike along the elevated boardwalk through the marshes to **Western Brook Pond**. At the end of the path is a dock, where you can catch a tour boat and cruise the pond. (You can register for a boat tour at the park's visitor center.) Boats sail beneath towering rocky cliffs to a misty 2,000-foot waterfall. Three boat trips depart daily, weather permitting, from mid-June to mid-September. Boat capacity is 25 to 30 people. The fare is C$23 ($20) for adults, C$6 ($5) for children. To get to the pond, drive north of the visitor center on Highway 430 for about 18 miles, past Sally's Cove.

Canada's loveliest drive

Canada's most beautiful drive is **Highway 430**, north of Gros Morne, on the coast of the **Great Northern Peninsula**. The waters of jagged fiords lap at the steep Long Range Mountains. At the northern tip of the peninsula, hundreds of icebergs rise as much as 300 feet out of the water. You can get more information from the Information Center in Wiltondale, which is open 9 a.m. until 9 p.m. in the summer.

Canada's best archeological sites

The Great Northern Peninsula is the site of some of Canada's most interesting archeological sites. **Porte-aux-Choix** has a 5,000-year-old Red Paint Indian burial mound and the remains of later Inuit cultures. Three Red Paint burial mounds have been excavated here, uncovering the remains of 100 people, weapons, and artifacts. The relics can be seen in the visitor center, which is open from June through Labor Day. (The Red Paint lived here about 2340 B.C. Later, Dorset Eskimos, known for their fine stone tools, lived here for 2,000 years. About A.D. 1100, the Beothuck Indians took over the region.)

At the tip of the Great Northern Peninsula is **L'Anse aux Meadows National Historic Park**, the site of a Viking settlement dating from A.D. 1000 (492 years before Columbus). These early Norse settlers built six thatched houses, three of which have been reconstructed. Historians believe the first European child born in America was Snorri Thorfinnson, born here to Icelandic trader Thorfinn Karlsefni in A.D. 1005. The child is mentioned in Viking sagas.

While visiting the park, stay at the **St. Anthony Motel**, *P.O. Box 465, St. Anthony, NF, A0K 4S0; tel. (709)454-3200.* A double room is C$60 ($53).

The best of the Beothucks

For a glimpse of the life of the Beothuck Indians, head east on the **Trans-Canada Highway** (Highway 1) to Grand Falls. The **Mary March Museum**, *Cromer Avenue*, is dedicated to the study of these people, who inhabited the region when the first European settlers of the 1600s came ashore. Mary March was the last of the unassimilated Beothucks, and her knowledge was the foundation of the museum.

While in Grand Falls, stay at the **Mt. Peyton Hotel-Motel**, *214 Lincoln Road, Grand Falls, NF A2A 1P8; (800)563-4894* (for reservations only) or *(709)489-2251.* A double room is C$78 ($68).

Terra Nova: the best wildlife

Terra Nova National Park, *tel. (709)533-2801,* southeast of Gander, is famous for its Atlantic beaches and its wildlife (including moose, black bear, red fox, Canada geese, beaver, and lynx). Keep an eye out for the park's unusual pitcher plant, which is carnivorous. You can rent cabins, canoes, and bikes at the park headquarters.

The best of France in the New World

Off the southern coast of Newfoundland are two French islands: **St. Pierre** and **Miquelon.** You must clear customs to travel to these islands, but a passport is unnecessary if you have identification.

Both islands truly feel like forgotten French towns, with French architecture, fashion, and culture. French wines are a good buy here, even though the islands lost their tax-free status recently.

The best place to stay on St. Pierre is **Hôtel Robert**, a small old-fashioned hotel; it has a local phone number, *(41)2419*, but it is impossible to call from the United States. A double room costs C$86 ($75). For reservations at any of the hotels in St. Pierre, contact **SPM Tours**, *tel. (709)722-3892.*

The most romantic town

St. John's, a natural rockbound harbor on the Avalon Peninsula, is Newfoundland's most romantic town. Quaint houses with brightly colored facades recall the town's wild past, when pirates raided and great feasts were held. While St. John's is one of the oldest towns in North America, inhabited by fishermen since the 15th century, its buildings are Victorian. Earlier dwellings all were destroyed by fire.

Signal Hill, which looms above the harbor, was the site of the first trans-Atlantic reception of a radio signal, sent by Guglielmo Marconi on Dec. 12, 1901. About two-thirds of the way up Signal Hill is **Queen's Battery**, built in the late 18th century. Across the narrows from Queen's Battery is **Fort Amherst**. The battery and the fort, together with a chain that stretched across the narrows, were effective in closing the port to enemies.

St. John's has two beautiful churches: the twin-spired **Roman Catholic Basilica** and the **Anglican Cathedral**, one of the best examples of Gothic architecture in North America.

If you're looking for restaurants, shops, and people, stroll downtown along Duckworth and Water streets. (**Water Street** is known as the "oldest main street on the continent," because it served as a pathway for the early explorers.)

To dine in an old-time colonial atmosphere, visit the **Woodstock Colonial Inn**, *tel. (709)722-6933.*

Most hotels in St. John's are expensive. The best are the **Hotel Newfoundland**, *tel. (709)726-4980* or *(800)268-8136 in Canada,* located on Cavendish Square (rooms are C$144 to C$173, or $126 to $151), and the **Stel Battery Hotel**, *tel. (709)576-0040* or *(800)267-STEL,* which has panoramic views. A double room at the Stel Battery is C$59 to C$99 ($51 to $86).

The best of Alberta

The peaceful and vast prairies of **Alberta** retain much of the open space and freedom that drew settlers into the Canadian wilderness a century ago. Alberta's prairies stretch for miles, a flat quilt at the foot of the Canadian Rockies.

While Alberta does have thriving, colorful cities, most of this vast 255,285-square-mile province is unpopulated—it has fewer inhabitants than the city of Philadelphia. And most of the population (more than half) lives in Edmonton and Calgary.

Calgary: the best cow town

Calgary is both a colorful remnant of the Wild West and a huge, modern city. Known as Cowtown, because of its cattle industry, Calgary is a thriving business center located less than an hour from the Rockies. This lively, crazy town is best known as the home of the **Calgary Stampede**, a wild rodeo of horse racing and high jinks.

Calgary got its start as a Royal Canadian Mounted Police post in 1875, back in the days when buffalo hunters, whiskey traders, pioneers, and Indians required the likes of Sergeant Preston of the Yukon to keep them in line. The post was founded at the junction of two rivers, the Bow and the Elbow. Colonel J.F. Macloud, the commander of the Mounties who founded the post, named it Calgary after his favorite fishing spot on the Bay of Mull in Scotland. The log fort attracted 600 settlers.

Four years later, the Canadian Pacific Railway reached Calgary in its rush to "save the West from the Yankees." The population of the post promptly doubled, as Chinese were brought in from the Pacific to lay railway tracks and European settlers—mostly English—poured in from the Atlantic Coast.

Tremendous beef herds were built up around Calgary, and it soon became a cattle metropolis. With the discovery of oil at nearby Turner Valley in 1914, Calgary boomed. The province of Alberta (the nation's richest) provides 85% of Canada's oil. (The province is so rich, in fact, that residents don't have to pay any provincial taxes.)

Outside the downtown area, Calgary is beautiful. The Rocky Mountain foothills begin to the west. The prairie stretches forever to the east. Northeast of Calgary are the **Drumheller Badlands**, where dinosaur skeletons have been found. Southwest is the **Glenmore Reservoir**, surrounded by parks and trails. Farm towns and huge cattle ranches begin south of the city.

The best rodeo

If you want to brave the **Calgary Stampede**, make sure you have reservations—the city swells with participants and spectators. (To make reservations, contact **Calgary Exhibition & Stampede**, *P.O. Box 1860, Calgary, AB T2P 2M7; tel. (403)261-0101.*)

The stampede is big and rough, drawing an immense and enthusiastic crowd. Cowboys from all over the continent ride bucking broncos and bulls, rope calves, and wrestle steers for prizes. The **Stampede Stage Show** features chorus girls, clowns, bands, and glamour. The funniest event is the **Chuckwagon Race**, in which old-time cowboy chuck wagons race around the track. The total prize money for the 10-day meet is C$337,000. Sudden Death, the last heat, takes place the final night and is worth C$50,000.

The best view of the city

The revolving restaurant at the top of the 626-foot **Calgary Tower**, *Ninth Avenue and Center Street; tel. (403)266-7171,* has the best view in town. You can see the Rockies when it's clear. If you don't want to pay for dinner, enjoy the view from the observation deck.

Calgary's top sights

Fort Calgary, *750 Ninth Ave. S.E.; tel. (403)290-1875,* is a 40-acre natural history park on the site of the original Mounted Police fort. Exhibits explain the history of Calgary. The fort is open daily year-round. Tours can be arranged for a nominal fee.

The **Glenbow Museum**, *130 Ninth Ave. S.E.; tel. (403)264-8300,* has extensive displays of Indian and Inuit art and artifacts. The art gallery has carvings and ceramics from all over the world. The museum is closed Mondays.

Explore **Heritage Park**, west of *14th Street and Heritage Drive S.W.; tel. (403)255-1182,* an authentic pre-1915 Alberta town. Original pioneer buildings from all over Alberta have been transported here, including a log church, a blacksmith's shop, a newspaper office, and a bakery. The park is open May through mid-October.

The best shopping

If you have a secret urge to look like Roy Rogers, head to **Western Outfitters,** *128 Eighth Ave. S.E.; tel. (403)266-3656.* (If you're planning to attend the Calgary Stampede, this is the place to pick up your spurs!)

The best food

The most elegant restaurant in Calgary is the **Owl's Nest**, *320 Fourth Ave. S.W.; tel. (403)266-1611.* Before dinner, women are given roses. Have the British Columbia salmon, Beluga caviar, lobster, or quail. Reservations are suggested. Major credit cards are accepted.

The finest of Alberta's beef is served at the **Rimrock Room**, *Palliser Hotel, Ninth Avenue and First Street S.W.; tel. (403)262-1234.*

Calgary's best hotel

The **Palliser**, *133 Ninth Ave. S.W.; tel. (403)262-1234,* is an institution in Calgary, built in 1914 by the Canadian Pacific Railroad. The gracious old hotel has brass doors, marble pillars, and chandeliers. A double room is C$180 ($157).

Canada's most beautiful national parks

Banff and Jasper national parks, on the border between British Columbia and Alberta, are among the most beautiful nature reserves in the world. Together, they comprise 6,764 square miles in the Rocky Mountains. Imagine snow-topped peaks, deep-green forests, cascading rivers, mountain sheep, bears, and silent blue lakes.

Banff is the older of the parks, Jasper the larger. They run together and stretch from Mount Sir Douglas in the south to the Resthaven Mountains in the far north. Many nature trails climb into their remote valleys and peaks. Banff lies 81 miles from Calgary via Highway 1; Japser is 225 miles from Edmonton on Route 16.

Highway 93, from Banff to Jasper, which passes the Athabasca glacier, is spectacular. You'll see bighorn sheep, mountain goats, and bears from the road.

The 160-square-mile **Columbia ice fields** spread across Jasper. Rent a snowmobile in the park and take off to explore them. Jasper also boasts Alberta's highest peak, **Mount Columbia** (12,294 feet), and the spectacular **Athabasca Falls**, which rush through a narrow gap.

The **Banff Springs Hotel**, *Spray Avenue; tel. (403)762-2211,* which has views of the mountains and two rivers, is the best place to stay while exploring the parks. Established in 1928 to bring visitors to the nearby hot springs, the castlelike hotel has four dining rooms, an espresso bar, cocktail lounges, and a post office. Its golf course is considered one of the most scenic in the world. A double room is C$160 to C$250 ($140 to $219).

Edmonton: the best boomtown

Edmonton has been a boomtown three times in its life: The fur trade brought hundreds of trappers and trackers in the 18th century, the gold rush attracted thousands in the 1890s, and the discovery of oil and natural gas brought industrial development in the 1960s. Despite its spurts of sudden growth, Edmonton is well-designed, with 11,000 acres of parks. And city leaders have made a tremendous effort to preserve historic buildings.

Edmonton's best festival

Klondike Days, which celebrate the days of gold prospecting, take place in late July. Everyone must dress in period costumes (those who don't may find themselves temporarily incarcerated in the Klondike clink!), the streets are filled with performers, and parades make their way through the streets. The new coliseum hosts rock'n'roll and Western entertainment.

Edmonton's best sights

Fort Edmonton, a replica of the fur-trading post established in 1795, stands in a 158-acre park off Whitemud Freeway in the suburbs. It is complete with a stockade, a fur-processing plant, a clay oven, McDougall's General Store, the Northwest Mounted Police

Jail, and a Masonic temple. The original trading post has been replaced with **Alberta's Legislative Building**, *109th Street and 97th Avenue*, which was built in 1912.

The **Muttart Conservatory and Horticulture Center**, *98th Avenue and 96th Street*, is a complex of four ultramodern pyramid-shaped greenhouses that act as a botanical incubator. Each pyramid has a specific climate and is filled with flora of appropriate regions. The complex is open daily.

The **Edmonton Civic Center**, *100th Street and 102nd Avenue*, is a gigantic structure containing the Edmonton Art Gallery, City Hall, a convention center, the law courts building, and the Centennial Library.

Edmonton's best restaurants

Hy's Steak Loft, *10013 101st Ave.; tel. (403)424-4444*, serves superb steaks. (Alberta is famous for its beef.) The restaurant is closed Sundays. Reservations are required.

Vi's, *9712 111th St.; tel. (403)482-6402*, has good, hearty food for a reasonable price. Try the thick homemade soup; finish your meal with the chocolate-glazed pecan pie. The restaurant is open daily.

The best hotel

The **Westin Hotel**, *100th Street at 101st Avenue; tel. (403)426-3636*, is where Princess Di and Prince Charles stayed when they visited in 1983. The swimming pool and sauna are inviting, and the restaurant is one of the best in the city. A double room is C$90 to C$170 ($78 to $149).

Play cowboy for a while

Rafter Six, *Seebe; tel. (403)673-3622*, is a typical guest ranch 50 miles west of Calgary. The package cost is C$69 to C$99 ($60 to $86) per person per day.

The best of British Columbia

British Columbia, Canada's westernmost province, has snow-capped mountains that rise out of the Pacific, providing backdrops for Vancouver and Victoria. In the north of this region are tiny settlements lost in a stark wilderness; in the center are wide-open ranchlands that cowboys call home. Throughout the area, glacier ice fields jut into birch and maple forests.

More than 1 million acres of British Columbia have been set aside for five national parks. The area also contains 11 million acres of provincial parks.

Throughout this coastal province are **petroglyphs**, rock drawings made by unknown tribes long ago, which are carefully preserved by the government. Mementos of the early fur traders, explorers, and pioneers can be seen at **Fort Langley**, a restored fur trading post in Fort Defiance on Vancouver Island, and at **Fort James**, near Prince George. Artifacts of the Cariboo gold rush of the 1860s are preserved at **Barkerville**. And the Royal Mounted Police left its mark at **Fort Steel**.

Vancouver: a best city

Vancouver is surrounded on all sides by snow-capped mountains, and glass-sided skyscrapers are reflected in the glittering blue harbor. The air is pure, and the climate is mild. At the western edge of the city, cliffs drop to the sea. Totem poles stand near the Strait of Georgia, a reminder of the Northwest Indians, who were the first inhabitants of this region. Canada's third-largest city, Vancouver has 1.3 million residents.

The city's main thoroughfare is **Georgia Street**, where you'll find the old Hotel Vancouver, the Vancouver Art Gallery inside an old granite courthouse, and entrances to underground shopping malls.

Near Georgia Street, between Howe and Hornby, is **Robson Square**, a three-block complex designed by Arthur Erickson. Inside the square are international kiosks, a skating rink, and terraced gardens with pools and waterfalls. At the edge of the square is a seven-story glass pyramid—the **Law Courts Building**. During the week, you can wander into an open courtroom, sink into an upholstered chair, and watch a hearing.

Stanley Park, just north of downtown, is a wilderness playground with performing whales and a zoo. The best way to see this immense, 1,000-acre preserve is by bike. (A 6-mile scenic drive circles the park.) **Stanley Park Rentals**, *676 Chilco St.*, just outside the park, rents 10-speed and tandem bicycles.

Gastown, east of the Sea Bus terminal, is the birthplace of Vancouver. This renovated 19th-century area is filled with pubs, restaurants, galleries, and boutiques. Stop by **Hill's Indian Crafts**, *Water Street*, for baskets, moccasins, carvings, jewelry, prints, and sweaters.

South of Gastown, along Pender Street, is **Chinatown**. Sidewalk stalls sell Chinese food and knicknacks, and herbalists offer deer horns, dried sea horses, and exotic teas. The **Chinese Cultural Center**, *Pender Street*, has maps of the area. Stroll through the **Dr. Sun Yat-Sen Classical Garden**, 2 1/2 acres of miniature fountains, pavilions, ponds, and bridges.

Granville Island has galleries, theaters, cafés, and an open market. Have dinner at **Bridges**. Afterward, stop by Granville Island Hotel's **Pelican Bay Lounge** to enjoy some jazz. Return downtown from Granville aboard the False Creek Ferry, which departs from a dock near Bridges.

The stern-faced totem poles in the **Museum of Anthropology** at the University of British Columbia are a sharp contrast to the modern lines of the museum itself, which was designed by Erickson.

The best restaurants

Chartwell, *Georgia and Howe streets; tel. (604)689-9333*, in the Four Seasons Hotel has a superb menu that features game and seafood. The wine list is extensive. The restaurant is closed Sundays. Reservations are highly recommended.

Umberto's is an institution in Vancouver, with three restaurants serving three different cuisines. The original, *1380 Hornby St.; tel. (604)687-6316*, specializes in northern Italian cuisine. **Al Porto Umberto**, *321 Water St.; tel. (604)683-8376*, has fresh local seafood. And **Il Giardino**, *1382 Hornby; tel. (604)669-2422*, serves fowl and wild game. All three are excellent.

The **Only**, *20 E. Hastings St.; tel. (604)681-6546*, serves the freshest seafood in town. A cheap, informal place in a down-at-the-heels neighborhood, it has booths and counter seats, all with views of the gas burners and frying pans where the fish is cooked. No liquor is served, and credit cards are not accepted. The restaurant is closed Sundays.

Vancouver's best beds

Vancouver's best hotel is **Delta Place**, *645 Howe St.; tel. (604)687-1122*, which offers every luxury and convenience imaginable, from a gourmet restaurant to a health club. A double room is C$205 to C$225 ($179 to $197).

The **Bayshore Inn**, *1601 W. Georgia St.; tel. (604)682-3377*, once hosted Howard Hughes, who took over the top two floors. Yachtsmen stay here, mooring their boats at the hotel dock. Doormen in red jackets and tall fur hats guard the doors. Rooms have floor-to-ceiling windows with lovely views of the water and the city. Shops, lounges, restaurants, and a pool are available to guests. A double room is C$115 ($100).

If you're watching your budget, stay at the **Sylvia Hotel**, *1154 Gilford St.; tel. (604)681-9321*. This nine-story hotel, which has a good dining room, is popular, so make reservations in advance. A double room is C$53 to C$77 ($46 to $67).

Vancouver Island: the most beautiful

Vancouver Island, which stretches 170 miles along the western coastline of British Columbia, is sheltered along its southern border by the state of Washington's Olympic

Peninsula. You can take a ferry from Vancouver City to Nanaimo.

Most of the half-million people on Vancouver Island live along its east coast, which is rich in timber, farmland, and fishing streams, or at the southern tip in the city of Victoria. The wild and rugged west coast is sparsely inhabited, with few villages. It is deeply cut by fiords and piled high with mountains. The south end of the island is mountainous, reaching a height of 7,200 feet; the north end is flat.

Victoria, the provincial capital, was first settled by Europeans in 1843. It has been the site of coal mining, logging, fur trading, and fishing.

One of the most beautiful sights on the island is **Butchart Gardens,** near Victoria, across the Saanich Peninsula from Sydney. Originally (in 1905), this area was a limestone quarry; today it offers entertainment on summer evenings.

Victoria, the most British city

"A tweedy, daffodilish, green-fingered sort of place, a golfish, fly-fishing, 5 o'clock teapot place." That's how Canadian author Bruce Hutchinson described **Victoria,** which feels more British than any other city in the Americas. While it is the largest city on Vancouver Island, the atmosphere is relaxed. The air smells of flowers and the sea. The climate is mild, less rainy than on the island's west coast.

Go behind the **Tweed Curtain,** as it is known, along Oak Bay. Enjoy the thick British accents and stop for tea at the Oak Bay Beach Hotel, the Blethering Place Tearoom in Oak Bay Village, or the dining room in the Butchart Gardens Mansion.

Activity in Victoria centers around the harbor, which is surrounded by Victorian buildings, including the Empress Hotel, the Provincial legislative buildings, the old steamship terminal (now a wax museum), and the Belmont Building. The Visitors and Convention Bureau, an art deco building, offers maps and information.

Victoria's **Provincial Museum** traces life before and after glaciers covered Vancouver Island with a sheet of ice 3 1/2 miles thick. Walk through the rain forest, which includes a reconstructed 19th-century town and an Indian longhouse.

Outside the Provincial Museum complex is **Thunderbird Park,** which has a collection of coastal Indian totem poles. You can watch Indian craftsmen carving reproductions of traditional designs. Just beyond the park is the **Helmcken House,** the oldest house still standing in British Columbia.

The **Tong-Ji Men** (Gate of Harmonious Interest), at the corner of Fisgard and Government in Chinatown, is a 30-foot arch with 4,500 ceramic tiles and 1,008 decorative panels that was made in Taiwan.

Craigdarroch Castle, *Joan Crescent,* was built in 1885 by the multimillionaire coal baron Robert Dunsmuir for his wife Joan. A nonprofit society is refurbishing the castle, which was auctioned off for a dollar after Joan's death.

Along Rockland Avenue is the **Government House,** where the lieutenant governor of British Columbia resides. Its gardens are more than 100 years old.

Most restaurants in Victoria serve mostly bland English fare—fish and chips and the lot. Two exceptions are **Periklis,** *531 Yates St.,* where you can enjoy Greek food, and **Foo Hong,** in Chinatown, a popular and inexpensive lunch spot.

Stay at the Gothic **Empress Hotel,** *721 Government St.; tel. (604)384-8111,* which is great fun but rather touristy and expensive. Built in 1906 on the harbor, it has lovely views as well as a bar, a restaurant, and a disco. Have high tea in the afternoon. A double room is C$230 ($201).

A good, moderately priced hotel is **Helm's Inn,** off Government Street, near the Provincial Museum, *tel. (604)385-5767.* A comfortable, nicely decorated double room is only C$48 ($42).

The most shopping space

Nanaimo, the second-largest city on Vancouver Island, has the largest amount of retail shopping space per capita of any city in Canada. The city is also filled with preserved pioneer buildings and sites, which you can see on the historic walking tour.

Stroll around Nanaimo's waterfront, where you'll see the **Bastion**, the former Hudson's Bay Company Fort, erected in 1852 by settlers as protection against raiding Indians. **Fishermen's Wharf** has an abundance of fresh seafood. The **Georgia Park Promenade** leads to the modern seaplane base and on to Swy-A-Lana Lagoon and Maffeo Sutton Park.

Georgia Park is dedicated to the Indian tribes who first inhabited this area and features a display of authentic Indian canoes and totem poles. **Swy-A-Lana Lagoon** features a man-made tidal pool. Next to the lagoon, native Indians operate a traditional carving shed, where you can watch craftsmen carving masks and other artifacts.

The world's best bathtub race
Nanaimo's annual **Bathtub Race** in mid-July is a zany spectacle. Hundreds of daring tubbers challenge the wild waters of the Georgia Strait in a 30-mile race to the beaches of Vancouver. It's hilarious.

The most romantic town
One of the loveliest places on the island is **Parksville**, a little town off Route 19 on the east coast. From the highway, the town doesn't look like much—a few trailers and gift shops. But behind the ever-present towering pines are wide beaches with calm, clear waters. On the horizon are purple, snow-topped mountain ranges. The beach extends out for nearly a mile at low tide, and sea lions cavort not far from land. The water is surprisingly warm as early as May.

Tigh Na Mara, *1095 E. Island Highway, V9P 2E5; tel. (604)248-2072*, has the most romantic accommodation on Vancouver Island. You stay in log cabins (with fireplaces) next to the beach and have use of a jacuzzi, canoes, paddle boats, and rowboats. Rooms are C$59 to C$129 ($51 to $113).

The best whale watching
You can track the great gray whale each spring as it migrates northward along the west coast of Vancouver Island. The first migrants appear in late February; by mid-April, the waters are filled with hundreds of them. As many as 40 or 50 gray whales like the area so much that they spend the summer here.

The best time for whale watching is from late February through June. The whales can be spotted from the headlands of Pacific Rim National Park, from the restaurant at Wickaninnish Bay, or from the rocky shores of Little Beach, Big Beach, or Amphitrite Point in Ucluelet. However, the best way to watch is from the deck of a charter boat that specializes in whale-watching trips.

You'll usually see only a small portion of the whale. When spouting, whales roll forward and seem to lift partly out of the water, revealing their scarred gray backs and the bumps of their vertebrae, which are known as knuckles. While diving in deep water, they occasionally show their graceful, barnacle-encrusted tails, displays called fluking. When they poke their heads out of the water for a look around, they are spy-hopping. The most breathtaking sight is when whales breach, jumping almost completely out of the water to land on their backs with a huge splash.

Canadian Princess Resort offers whale-watching cruises that depart from Vancouver and Victoria. A two-day, one-night cruise costs C$89 ($78) per person; a three-day, two-night cruise is C$154 ($135). For more information, contact the resort at **Oak Bay Marina Ltd.**, *1327 Beach Drive, Victoria, BC V8S 2N4; tel. (604)598-3366*, or *Ucluelet, BC; tel. (604)726-7771.*

Subtidal Adventures, *P.O. Box 253, Ucluelet, BC V0R 3A0; tel. (604)726-7061 or (604)726-7336*, also offers a whale-watching cruise. The three-hour trip runs from 9 a.m. to 1 p.m. in March and April. The cost is C$24 ($21) for adults, C$19 ($16) for children.

The highest city

British Columbia boasts the highest city in Canada: **Kimberley**, in the Rocky Mountains just north of the U.S. border. This mining town-turned-ski resort resembles a Bavarian Alpine village. The townspeople sponsor a **Julyfest** modeled after the German Oktoberfest (but held earlier in the year) that includes parades, folk dances, beer tents, and international entertainment.

Kimberley's real claim to fame is its excellent downhill skiing. The city's mountain rises 2,300 feet and has 32 runs served by chair lifts and T-bars. The mountain also has one of North America's longest lighted ski runs (1,600 feet). For information on ski packages, contact **Kimberley Ski Resort**, *P.O. Box 40, Kimberley, BC V1A 2Y5; tel. (604)427-4881.*

Canada's only desert town

Osoyoos is a Spanish-influenced desert town in a 252-mile desert pocket east of Vancouver. It is watered by deep Lake Osoyoos, where you can fish for trout and bass. You can swim here, too, if you don't mind sharing the water with painted turtles. Try your luck panning for gold in the Okanagan Valley above Osoyoos.

The most authentic Indian village

Hazelton (known as Kiran-maksh among the Indians), in the heart of British Columbia, is a modern Indian town next to a reconstructed Gitskan Indian village built to look as it did before the arrival of the white man. The village, called **Ksan**, has six longhouses, totem poles, and birchbark canoes. The House of Treasures contains the tribal regalia of Gitksan chiefs. A campground and trailer park adjoin the village.

Canada's best skiing

Skiing in Canada is as exhilarating as skiing in the Alps. British Columbia and Alberta have some of the most spectacular peaks in the world, beginning on the Pacific coastline. The Canadian Rockies are rugged, wild, and challenging. And Quebec's Laurentians offer aprés-ski activities with a French flavor.

The best heli-skiing

Heli-skiing, a relatively new sport, uses helicopters instead of chair lifts to allow you to avoid lift lines and to reach empty slopes in remote places. Canada boasts some of the best heli-skiing opportunities in the world.

Kootenay Heli-skiing, *P.O. Box 717, Nakusp, BC V0G 1R0; tel. (604)265-3121 or (800)663-0100*, offers trips into the open bowls and steep treelined runs of the unspoiled Selkirk and Monashee mountains. (Because the terrain is difficult, you must be an accomplished skier to participate.) Seven-day packages, available from Jan. 3 to April 17, cost from C$3,295 ($2,890), depending on the season and accommodation.

Whistler Heli-skiing, *P.O. Box 368, Whistler, BC V0N 1B0; tel. (604)932-4105*, offers packages out of Whistler and Bralorne that take you into the four surrounding mountain ranges.

Mike Wiegele Helicopter Skiing, *P.O. Box 249, Banff, Alberta, Canada T0L 0C0; tel. (403)762-5548 or (800)661-9170*, takes you to the Cariboos and Monashees in the Canadian Rockies.

The best powder skiing: British Columbia

British Columbia's ski slopes are a sparkling, powder-covered paradise. And they are varied, including the Rockies, Bugaboos, Purcells, Selkirks, Chilcotin, Cariboo, and Monashees. The longest fall-line runs in North America are here, as is the highest serviced vertical drop.

Whistler, a trendy, fast-growing resort with gorgeous powder-bowl skiing above the tree line, has the longest vertical drop in the Americas (4,278 feet). Nearby **Blackcomb Mountain**, *(604)932-3141*, opened recently. For more information, contact **Whistler Resort Association**, *4010 Whistler Way, Whistler, BC V0N 1B4; tel. (604)932-4222.*

Alberta's best slopes

Calgary, Alberta, the jumping-off point for some of the world's finest downhill and cross-country skiing, hosted the 1988 Winter Olympic Games. About an hour from Calgary are the magnificent Rocky Mountains and **Mount Allan**, the site of many Olympic events. Thirty minutes farther into the mountains is **Banff National Park**, with beautiful terrain reminiscent of Lake Tahoe and Yosemite National Park.

Banff, the best resort

Banff is the area's best ski resort, with both the easiest and most difficult trails and superb facilities. **Mount Norquay** has some of the best beginner trails in the park, as well as three of the most difficult runs in North America: the North American, the Bowl, and the Lone Pine. The **Lone Pine** is a favorite among residents of Calgary, but it often intimidates tourists. The **North American** and the **Bowl** have acted as training grounds for many of Canada's world-class downhill racers. The mountain rises from 2,680 feet to 7,005 feet; the longest run measures 1.6 miles.

The best time to visit Banff (unless you dislike crowds) is during the **winter festival**, which has been held every January since 1917. Teams from around the country meet for the Mountain Madness Relay Race—a pentathlon of downhill skiing, running, skating, snowshoeing, and cross-country skiing.

The **Banff Springs Hotel** is the best ski lodge in Canada. Built in 1888, it was once the world's largest hotel. Not only does it look like a castle, but it operates like one, too. A medieval banquet—complete with period costumes and mead—is staged once a week in the imposing two-story Mount Stephen Dining Hall.

The longest season

Another ski area popular among Calgarians is **Sunshine Village**, about 20 minutes from Mount Norquay. Located at the tree line in an Alpine bowl, it is known for its powder snow. It has the longest ski season in the region, lasting through mid-June—an average snowfall of 30 feet enables the resort to stay open so long. Trails range from tight tree-lined runs to open bowls at the top. Sunshine's runs cover 1,200 acres, with a vertical drop of 3,420 feet to an on-the-mountain village. Stay at the **Sunshine Inn**.

Sunshine Village's **Nordic Center**, which opened in 1982, offers excellent high-country touring and programs for the novice and the telemark cross-country skier. Tracks to look for include the Spray River Loop, the Cascade Fire Road, the Red Earth Creek, the Pipestone Loop, and a telemark trail on Moraine Lake Road.

The world's biggest ski jump

The world's biggest ski jump is in **Thunder Bay, Ontario**, the newest hot spot for ski-jump fans. Four major Alpine areas have scores of slopes, including dozens of cross-country trails, for both beginners and experts. Canada's famous ski-jump champions practice here. Daily air service is available from Toronto, Winnipeg, Sault Ste. Marie, and Minneapolis.

North America's oldest ski slopes

The **Laurentians** (*Laurentides* in French), 40 minutes north of Montreal, boast the oldest ski areas in North America. The world's first rope tow was installed here in 1932 in the Quebec village of Shawbridge. Since then, these mountains have catered to skiers from around the world.

Mount Tremblant, the highest peak in the Laurentians, has a spectacular view of lakes, valleys, and forests. Its 3,000-foot vertical drop makes all kinds of skiing possible. **Gray Rocks** also offers tremendous skiing. **St. Sauveur** is the place to ski and be seen.

If you're looking for accommodation in the Laurentians, try **Station Mount Tremblant**, which can handle up to 800 guests. **Manoir Pinoteau** has the best view of Tremblant and serves excellent food.

The world's best fishing

Some say Canada, which is bordered by three oceans and the Hudson Bay and dotted with thousands of lakes, rivers, and streams, has the best fishing in the world. Inland waters are filled with major freshwater fish, while the Atlantic and Pacific coasts run with striped bass, bluefin tuna, shark, and other deep-sea fish. Generally, the farther north you go, the better the fishing. In the Yukon and Northwest Territories, the open-water fishing season runs from June to late September. Water in these Arctic regions is ice-cold, and the fish fight harder, making the sport more challenging and exciting.

British Columbia: the best fishing year-round

In British Columbia, which many claim has the best fishing in Canada, you can fish year-round. With so many miles of streams and rivers and thousands of lakes spread across a sparsely populated land, it is a fisherman's paradise. Despite all this, the region isn't crowded.

Five species of salmon can be caught in the coastal waters off British Columbia. Pacific-Gulf Charters offers three-day packages in British Columbia for about C$449 ($393), including accommodation, fishing equipment, and meals. Contact **Oak Bay Marine Group**, *1327 Beach Drive, Victoria, BC V8S 2N4; tel. (604)598-3366 or (800)663-7090.*

Fred Kuzyk is one of the best fishing guides in the business. His company, **Coho Fishing and Guiding Services**, *104 E. 49th Ave., Vancouver, BC Canada V5W 2G2; tel. (604)324-8214*, can organize every detail of your trip, including all the necessary fishing licenses. All packages include transportation, accommodation, meals, equipment, tackle, and guide.

The wildest fishing

The Atlantic coast of **Labrador** is a wild and woolly place to pit yourself against trout and salmon. **Powell's Outfitters Limited**, *Charlottetown, Labrador, Canada A0K 5Y0; tel. (709)949-0214*, can arrange a wilderness trip for you, providing accommodation in a lodge.

The northwestern woods of Ontario provide another remote and beautiful place to fish. **Reserve-A-Resort**, *P.O. Box 647 (T), Kenora, Ontario, Canada P9N 3X6; tel. (807)468-6064* (call collect), can arrange fishing trips here.

The happiest hunting grounds

Canada has a profusion of wildlife: brown bears and grizzly bears in British Columbia and the Laurentian Mountains of Quebec, buffalo in Alberta, and elk and moose in Saskatchewan. The Northwest Territories and the Yukon have polar bears, musk oxen, caribou, seals, walruses, and penguins. Most of the animals are protected. Hunting laws are detailed and involve specific seasons and registrations. For more information, contact the Ministry of Natural Resources of the area where you want to hunt.

The most adventurous hunt

Adventurous and experienced hunters can track polar bears in the Northwest Territories with the help of Eskimo guides. However, the total quota of polar bears that can be hunted is 400 a year, and the local Eskimos decide how many of these are to be shot by tourists. You must use an Eskimo guide, and you can't use mechanical vehicles in your hunt. Plan on two weeks of travel over huge ice ridges via dogsled.

If the polar bear quota is filled, plenty of other game can be hunted in the Northwest Territories: musk ox, caribou, reindeer, wolf, wolverine, mink, lynx, otter, beaver, seal, walrus, and whale.

The best hunting camps and lodges

For a real wilderness adventure, stay at an Indian camp in Ontario, where a sure-footed Indian guide can show you the trails. **Big Trout Lake Indian Band** operates a lodge, where you can hunt moose, bear, and grouse. Access is by aircraft. For more information, contact **Tom Morris**, *Bugg River Camp, Big Trout Lake, Ontario P0V 1G0.*

Sylvester Jack, *P.O. Box 210, Atlin, BC V0W 1A0*, operates a big-game hunting camp in northwestern British Columbia. He can guide you on sheep, bear, and moose hunts.

Canada's best sailing

Nova Scotia is a Shangri-La for boaters. Its calm harbors and rolling hills are a perfect refuge for Atlantic sailors. Boaters can dock at **Armdale Yacht Club**, *Halifax, North West Arm*; **Bedford Basin Yacht Club**, *Halifax*; **Bras d'Or Yacht Club**, *Baddeck*; **Canadian Forces Sailing Association**, *P.O. Box 280, Shearwater*; **Chester Yacht Club**; **Dartmouth Yacht Club**, *Bedford Basin*; **Lennox Passage Yacht Club**, *D'Escousse*; **Lunenburg Yacht Club**, *Herman's Island*; and **Royal Western Nova Scotia Yacht Club**, *Montague Row, Digby.*

The rugged island is filled with boat charter and rental companies. **Whale Cruisers Cheticamp Ltd.** (Capt. Bill Crawford), *P.O. Box 10, Grand Etang, Nova Scotia B0E 1L0; tel. (902)224-3376*, offers whale-watching cruises and scenic boat tours and charters that depart Government Wharf at Cheticamp Harbor at 9 a.m., 1 p.m., and 6 p.m. during July and August. Special group rates and charters can be arranged.

The most exciting rafting

Aventures en Eau Vive, *RR 2, Calumet J0V 1B0; tel. (819)242-6084*, arranges rafting groups on the Rouge River from April through October for C$73 to C$77 ($64 to $67) per day on weekends, C$69 to C$74 ($60 to $64) per day during the week, and C$140 ($122) for a two-day camping and rafting trip.

The best on horseback

What better way to see the wilds of Canada than on horseback? The best way to go is with **Trail Riders of the Canadian Rockies**, *P.O. Box 6742, Station D, Calgary, Alberta, Canada T2P 2E6; tel. (403)263-6963*, a nonprofit group that leads riders through the uninhabited valleys of Banff National Park. A six-day trip is C$680 ($596), including accommodation in Indian tepees, horses, saddles, meals, and guides.

The best ways to get around

VIA Rail Canada, *tel. (800)561-3949*, is an efficient, comfortable, and scenic way to travel across Canada. Tickets are relatively inexpensive: Vancouver to Halifax is C$514 ($451); Montreal to Edmonton is C$330 ($290); Ottawa to Montreal is C$28 ($25); and Edmonton to Toronto is C$291 ($256).

The **Canrailpass** offers unlimited transportation on VIA trains in a designated region at a fixed cost. A 30-day pass costs C$428 ($376) during the summer.

The Best of Mexico

After Mexico, I shall always associate balconies and politicians—plump men with blue chins wearing soft hats and guns on their hips. They look down from the official balcony in every city all day long with nothing to do but stare with the expression of men keeping an eye on a good thing.

—Graham Greene, 1939

Mexico is a North American's best choice for an inexpensive vacation in a warm and exotic foreign country. It is also perfect for sun worshipers, hardy adventurers, high rollers, and those on a tight budget. Mexico offers beautiful beaches, unexplored wilderness, cosmopolitan cities, historic monuments, and good food—all for next to nothing.

In general, Mexico's telephone system functions poorly. It is not uncommon, for example, to get a busy signal time after time, even though the number you are calling is not in use. Keep this in mind when trying to make travel plans here; it can be a frustrating proposition.

Most Mexican hotels and some of the larger restaurants accept dollars as well as pesos. However, we recommend exchanging dollars for pesos at a bank and paying in pesos; banks give a much better exchange rate than hotels and restaurants.

Keep in mind that prices in this chapter may have changed by the time you read it, because the inflation rate in Mexico is high.

Mexico City: the world's largest landlocked city

Mexico City is the largest city in Mexico, with the largest population of any city in the world. It is the cultural, political, and commercial hub of the country. Located on a plateau, it is surrounded by mountains. Colonial architecture gives it a Spanish air.

The best place to put the city in perspective is the rooftop bar of the 44-floor **Latin American Tower**, *Eje Central Lázaro Cárdenas*.

487

The best museums

The best place to begin your tour of the city is the **Museo de la Ciudad** (City Museum), *Pino Suarez 30*. Formerly the Palace of the Counts of Santiago (early Spanish conquistadors who came to the New World seeking their fortunes), it documents Mexico City's history in chronological order from the Aztecs through the 20th century. The museum is open Tuesdays through Sundays from 9 a.m. until 5 p.m., and a small admission fee is charged. Tours in English are conducted every day.

The **National Museum of Anthropology**, *Paseo de la Reforma*, in Chapultepec Park, houses most of Mexico's excavated pre-Columbian treasures, including artifacts from the Palenque tombs, Mexico's most spectacular Mayan site. The architecture and figurines at Palenque strangely resemble those at ancient Oriental sites in Cambodia, which is possible evidence of a direct ancestral link.

The museum also houses an Aztec calendar stone that divides the year accurately into a 52-week cycle, providing evidence of early Indian civilizations' ability to use astronomy to divide time. On the second floor, a display depicts present-day Indian lifestyles in Mexico. Bilingual guides are available for tours. The museum is open Tuesday through Friday 9 a.m. until 5 p.m. and Saturday and Sunday 10 a.m. until 6 p.m. Tours in English are conducted daily.

The **Bellas Artes Museum**, *Lázaro Cárdenas*, has a permanent collection of Mexico's world-famous murals, including a duplicate of the Diego Rivera mural commissioned for the Rockefeller Center in New York City. (Because Rivera depicted John D. Rockefeller as a greedy capitalist, the copy in New York is now covered by another less provocative mural.)

If you visit the Bellas Artes Museum on a Sunday or a Wednesday, you can see a performance by **Ballet Folklórico**, a lively folk ballet company. The glass curtain hung across the stage was commissioned from Tiffany's. The museum is open 10 a.m. until 6 p.m. daily except Monday.

The best of the Hapsburgs in Mexico

In Chapultepec Park, once the royal hunting grounds of the Aztecs, is **Chapultepec Castle**, once the imperial residence of the Hapsburgs, whose quarters are now on display. This unlikely bit of Austria-Hungary in the heart of Mexico was engineered by Napoleon III of France, who in 1864 installed the Hapsburg prince Maximillian as the governor of Mexico. Needless to say, this ill-thought-out bit of colonialism didn't work. In 1867, this outpost of Napoleon's empire collapsed, Maximillian was killed, and his widow went mad.

The castle, which is a museum today, also displays a collection of 19th-century art and costumes. It is open to the public 9 a.m. until 6 p.m. daily except Monday. A small admission fee is charged.

The best handicrafts

Mexico is known for its regional crafts, including leatherwork, furniture, blown glass, ceramics, pottery, textiles, tinwork, and woodcarving. At the **National Museum of Art and Popular Industry**, *avenida Juarez 44*, you can inspect the country's handicrafts and then purchase your favorites at the museum shop. Prices are relatively cheap, and the quality is usually good. The museum is open daily.

The zocalo: the heart of the city

Many of Mexico City's attractions are on the zocalo, the main city square. The grandest is the **National Palace**, which houses most of Mexico's government offices. It is a beautiful example of colonial architecture, especially dramatic when illuminated during Mexico's many holidays. Inside are Diego Rivera murals depicting this country's history through the Revolution of 1910. The National Palace is open 9 a.m. until 6 p.m. daily except Monday.

Mexico's grandest cathedral

The **Cathedral of Mexico**, the largest in the country, is also on the zocalo. Built over a 200-year period beginning in the 16th century, the cathedral incorporates many architectural styles. Its massive sanctuary houses 16 chapels, 27 altars, and a valuable collection of religious artwork from the Spanish colonial period.

The **Altar of the Kings** is a highly ornamental creation built in the wild baroque style known as churrigueresque, which was introduced by Spanish architect and artisan José Churriguera. Popular in the late 17th century, this style ignored the restraint employed by Renaissance artists and used elaborate designs and rich materials, such as gold and silver.

The greatest archeological find

Located just off the zocalo is the greatest accidental archeological find of the century: the **Great Temple of Tenochitlán**. Unearthed in 1978 by the Mexican Power and Light Company, it was once the holiest temple of the Aztecs. It depicts the legend of the god Huitzilopochtli, who avenged the murder of his mother Coatlicue by his sister Coyolzauhqui on the Hill of the Serpents. Although many of the artifacts found here are displayed in museums around the country, the site is still impressive, with intricate, artistic wall sculptures. Admission is free. The site is closed Mondays.

The city's best house

The 17th-century **Casa de los Azulejos** (House of Tiles), *Calle Madero 4*, which is completely covered in tiles, was built by the son of one of the counts of Orizaba. The young man became wealthy despite his father's prediction that he would never have a house of tiles (a Spanish saying that meant he would never be successful). To spite his father, he bought a house and had it completely covered in tiles.

The House of Tiles is now a department store called Sanborns.

Mexico City's best shopping

The best shopping in Mexico City is at the huge open-air markets. **Lagunilla**, *avenida Allende*, is a massive, sprawling market that sells everything from false teeth to expensive jewelry. The best day to shop is Sunday, when Lagunilla combines with the **Thieves' Market** to become the largest market in Mexico City.

The **San Juan Crafts Market**, *Ayuntamiento*, a modern three-story complex of artisans' shops, sells kitschy artwork. A better place to shop is the **Bazaar Sabbado**, *San Jacinto 11*, a more fashionable Saturday bazaar in the suburb of San Angel. This is where some of the best craftsmen sell their wares, everything from jewelry to paintings. The bazaar is set up in the refurbished remains of a 17th-century convent.

Look for fine leatherwork at **Aries**, *Florencia 14*, which sells everything from boots to knife holders.

Good (but expensive) silver products are available at **Tane**, *Amberes 70*, and **Flato**, *Amberes 21*. Wherever you buy silver, always check the back for the Mexican double eagle mark or the number 0.925, which guarantees that the product contains the proper amount of silver.

Although it is better to buy textiles in the regions where they are made (the quality and prices are better), Mexico City has shops selling excellent government-approved items. At **Girasol**, *Calle Genova 39*, for example, you can buy sarapes, wool blankets, wall hangings, and shawls. The best are made of lightweight white wool. You also can buy *huipils*, white cotton dresses embroidered with tiny flowers; *rebozos*, long multicolored scarves made of silk or wool; and *guayabera* shirts, light, gaily decorated shirts popular among Latin American men.

Mexico City's best restaurants

Hosteria Santo Domingo, *Belisario Dominguez 72; tel. (52-5)510-1434*, is the best restaurant in town. Located in a perfectly preserved 19th-century building, it serves traditional Mexican dishes. The *chillis in nogada* (a Poblano pepper stuffed with walnuts, cream, pomegranate seeds, and mince) is especially good.

The **San Angel Inn**, *Palmas 50; tel. (52-5)548-6840*, is the most beautiful restaurant in Mexico, situated in a 250-year-old building that has been completely restored. It has hosted Pancho Villa, Pavlova, Caruso, and Gershwin. Chef Manual Lozano cooks up a good *pompano en papillote*. Men are required to wear jackets.

The **Hacienda de los Morales**, *Vasquez de Polanco Mella 525; tel. (52-5)540-3225*, is an elegant, reasonably priced restaurant specializing in both Continental and Mexican cuisine. Reservations are a must at this beautifully restored 16th-century hacienda.

La Fonda el Refugio, *Liverpool 166; tel. (52-5)525-8128*, is decorated with primitive art and locally blown glass. The Tuesday special is delicious: *mole poblano* (thin tortillas fried and stuffed with shredded chicken and covered with *mole*, a rich sauce made with 25 ingredients, including hot peppers, tomatoes, raisins, and chocolate). Finish your meal with *café de olla* (black coffee served with brown sugar, cinnamon, and cloves). Dinner for two is 150,000 pesos ($50). Reservations are recommended.

Meson del Cid, *Humboldt 61; tel. (52-5)521-1940*, is a three-level dining room that serves open-hearth cooking. Baby suckling pig *à la segovia* is the house specialty. The pheasant *à la meson del cio* is good, too.

The **Del Lago Restaurant**, *Nuevo Bosque de Chapultepec; tel. (52-5)515-9585*, has a clear view of Chapultepec Lagoon through its grand windows. Trees and hanging plants give the interior an outdoor look. The seafood is good. Save room for dessert, and order the *mango flambé au tequilla*.

The capital's best hotels

Camino Real, *Mariano Escobedo 700; tel. (52-5)203-2121 or (800)228-3000*, is the only deluxe hotel in Mexico City. Located at the edge of Chapultepec Park, its seven-acre spread includes pools, tennis courts, three entertainment bars, a disco, a coffee shop, and two restaurants. A double room is 490,000 pesos to 765,000 pesos ($160 to $250) a night.

Gran Hotel Howard Johnson, *ave. 16 de Septiembre #82, Colonia Centro, 07000 Mexico City; tel. (52-5)510-4040 or (800)654-2000 in the United States*, is centrally located, is comfortable, and has excellent service. It has cage elevators and a Tiffany glass ceiling in the lobby. A double room is 220,000 pesos to 245,000 pesos ($71 to $85) a night.

The **Hotel Majestic**, *Francisco Madero 73; tel. (52-5)521-8600*, is another good hotel. From its rooftop terrace, the view of the city is panoramic. The Mexican color guard marches by the hotel every day at 6:30 p.m. A double room is 170,000 pesos to 185,000 pesos ($54 to $60).

Hotel de Cortes, *ave. Hidalgo 85; tel. (52-5)585-0322 or (800)528-1234*, a restored 18th-century hacienda, is a moderately priced hotel—a double room is 230,000 pesos ($75) a night. The hotel is clean, comfortable, and efficient. It is also popular, so make reservations well in advance.

The **Maria Cristina**, *Lerma 31; tel. (52-5)546-9880*, is a small hotel with a pretty garden and a piano bar. A double room is less than 140,000 pesos ($45) a night.

The hottest night life

The **Bellas Artes**, *Plaza Central Alameda*, presents the Ballet Folklorico on Wednesdays and Sundays at 9 p.m. You also can attend a concert, symphony, ballet, or opera. Check the *Mexico City News* for the schedule.

Popular nightclubs include **Can Can**, which has a lively floor show; **Magic Circus**, *Rodolfo Gaona 3*; the **Disco Club** at El Presidente, *Campos Eliseos 218*; and **Hotel Aristos**, *Paseo de la Reforma 276* (the place to go to hear rock bands). The leading gay bar in the city is **9**, *Londres 156*.

Single women aren't usually allowed in clubs or bars in Mexico City by themselves. The only bars lone women may frequent are hotel lounges.

The best day-trips

Midway between Mexico City and Tula, the capital of the ancient Toltec Indians, is the **Tepotzotlán Monastery**, a beautiful example of Spanish architecture, encrusted with intricate gold carvings made by local Indians. You can visit Wednesday through Sunday 11 a.m. until 6 p.m.

Cholula was the site of thousands of human sacrifices. In fact, although it was built long before the Aztec civilization flourished, this gory monument was still in use when the Spanish came. Hearing that they were to be killed here, Hernan Cortes and his entourage killed thousands of Aztecs. The site is open daily.

The pyramids of **Teotihuacan**, built sometime between A.D. 400 and A.D. 800, make up the largest, most complete archeological site in this hemisphere, covering more than 35 square miles. The Indians who built the pyramids, probably Mayans or their predecessors, marked time in 52-year cycles, building a new pyramid on top of the old one every cycle. The site includes hundreds of small temples, two large ones (the Pyramid of the Sun and the Pyramid of the Moon), and a large enclosed arena that was probably used for religious spectacles or ceremonial ball games. From mid-October to mid-May, a narrated sound-and-light show begins at 7 p.m. in English and at 8:15 p.m in Spanish. The site is open daily. A small admission fee is charged.

San Miguel de Allende: the best artisans' town

Situated in a small valley surrounded by hills, **San Miguel de Allende** has retained its colonial charm while blossoming into a center for the arts. Burros line the streets, and flowers fill every corner. Homes are hidden behind tall, bougainvillea-draped stucco walls. And art galleries, cafés, and restaurants serve the thriving expatriate community.

Located on the high central plateau about 250 miles northwest of Mexico City, San Miguel is in the agriculturally rich Bajio region on the colonial route. The entire town is a historic national monument; all architecture conforms to the colonial style.

La Parroquia, the imposing pink cathedral on the main zocalo, is a 19th-century Indian mason's interpretation of a French Gothic cathedral. The bells chime every 15 minutes.

San Miguel earned its reputation as an international arts center in 1938, with the opening of the first English-speaking school, the **Instituto Allende**, *Bellas Artes, Centro Cultural El Nigromante*. The institute is now the largest Latin American fine arts school for English-speaking students.

The city is also the home of the **San Miguel Writing Center**, *Ancha de San Antonio 20, GTO 37700 San Miguel de Allende; tel. (52-465)201-90*. The teachers here are all published writers.

A favorite among expatriates, San Miguel is home to an eccentric blend of Yankee artists, writers, gays, and retired folks.

Buying handicrafts and antiques

This is one of the best places in Mexico to buy handicrafts. Most shops are within three blocks of the main square. Its a good idea to visit several before buying—quality varies. Although you can do some bargaining, most of the prices are set.

Casa Maxwell, *Canal 14*, and **Llamas Brothers**, *Zacateros 11*, are two of the best handicraft shops in San Miguel. They're also both quite expensive. Two cheaper shops are **La Ventana**, *Canal Street*, and **La Balaiza Mercantil**, *Mesones 42*.

San Miguel is also a good place to buy antiques. Although no pre-Columbian antiques may be sold legally in Mexico, you can buy Spanish antiques from the colonial period. Try the antique shops that line the main square. Be careful—many items offered for sale are merely convincing reproductions.

The best restaurants

The best restaurant in San Miguel de Allende is the **Villa Jacaranda**, *Aldama 53; tel. (52-465)21015* or *(52-465)20811*. The food is superb, but the atmosphere alone makes the place worth a visit. Set in a vast stone hacienda, the quiet and relaxing restaurant is surrounded by gardens filled with flowers and trailing vines. Try the house specialty, drunken chicken, which is breast of chicken sautéed in onions and peppers. At brunch, try the *chilis nogadas,* a tangy blend of peppers covered in a sweet cream sauce. Order the crisp, dry local white wine called Calafia. Dinner for two costs 110,000 pesos ($55).

The restaurant at the **Casa de Sierra Nevada**, *Hospicio 35; tel. (52-465)20415,* is the most elegant in town. Dinner for one person costs 65,000 pesos to 70,000 pesos ($28 to $30).

La Posada Carmina, *Cuña de Allende 7; tel. (52-465)20548,* set in a cool, inviting courtyard filled with flowers, is also good. On Thursdays, try the specialty, a cheese and vegetable salad, or the *paella Valenciana.* You don't need to make reservations. A meal for two costs 35,000 pesos ($15).

El Patio, *Correo 10,* is a good place for a quick lunch. Although the food is ordinary, the setting is pleasant. You can enjoy live music at the bar. Dinner for two is 75,000 pesos ($37).

The sweetest dreams

La Posada San Francisco, *Plaza Principal 2,* right on the main square, *tel. (52-465)566-9688,* is within walking distance of just about everything in San Miguel. A spacious suite, suitable for a family of four, costs 220,000 pesos ($110) per night. The hotel serves delicious breakfasts for 15,000 pesos ($8) for two.

Casa de Sierra Nevada, *Hospicio 35; tel. (52-465)21895,* is an old Spanish villa. A double room, which is luxurious, costs 280,000 pesos to 550,000 pesos ($140 to $275) a night. The hotel has an excellent restaurant.

The spiciest nights

Cantinas, nightclubs, and cocktail lounges in San Miguel stay open until 1 a.m., and many will stay open later at the request of guests. The **Ring**, *Calle de Hidalgo 25,* is a disco popular with the over-35 crowd. **Laberintos Discoteque**, *Calle Ancha de San Antonio 7,* is popular with a younger set and has loud music. You must pay a cover charge.

Mama Mia, *Umaron 8,* has live music, from Andean folk to jazz, Wednesday through Monday on its patio. **La Princesa**, *Recreo 5,* is a quiet place, where you can listen to music while enjoying an early evening drink.

The steamiest side trips

Just a few miles from San Miguel, in **Taboada**, you can soak in steaming hot springs while a waiter serves you drinks. And at **La Gruta** (in El Cortijo) you can swim in an Olympic-sized heated pool or take a steam bath in a cave of hot mineral water.

The best place to hear the flutter of butterfly wings

A three-hour drive from San Miguel de Allende is the colorful old mining town of **Angangueo**. And only an hour from Angangueo, up a steep, unpaved road, is the **Monarch Butterfly Sanctuary**, now open to the public. The park's 12,000 acres became a protected area in 1986 in response to warnings from conservation groups that logging operations threatened to destroy the area's unique butterfly habitat and migration site. The butterflies seclude themselves in the *abies religiosas* (a type of fir tree) at the summit of the 10,000-foot climb. When you climb to the top, you are overwhelmed by the noise created by the fluttering wings of 10 million butterflies.

For information about organized tours to the sanctuary, contact **Columbus Travel**, *(800)225-2829.*

Taxco: the silver capital

Taxco is a mining town in the mountains. About a day's ride outside of Mexico City and off the main tourist route, it is less crowded than Guanajuanto or Cuernavaca. It is also *the* place to buy silver jewelry.

William Spratling introduced silversmithing to Taxco in 1929. Now the town has more than 300 fine jewelry shops. And the mines show no signs of cutting off the supply of metal.

Original Spratling pieces are difficult to come by, but most of the jewelry sold throughout Taxco is styled upon his original models. All silver products, from jewelry to candelabra, cost about 25% less than American counterparts and about 50% less than European pieces.

The best jewelry shops are **Los Castillos**, *Plazuela Bernal 10*, and **La Mina**, *Avendia J.F. Kennedy*, on the site of an old silver mine.

The most colorful times to visit Taxco are during Holy Week and the National Silver Fair, at the beginning of December. Make reservations far in advance.

Taxco's best tables

La Ventana de Taxco, *Hotel Hacienda del Solar; tel. (52-762)20587*, in a pink stone house on a hill just south of town, serves delicious Italian food for reasonable prices. Tables look out at the red-roofed houses of Taxco and the mountains beyond. The view is loveliest at sunset. Hollywood publicist Ted Wick, who lives in town, once owned this building—he still plays the grand piano in the lounge.

La Pagaduriá del Rey, *Calle H. Colegio Militar; tel. (52-762)2-3467*, serves steaks, seafood, and Mexican food. The menu is limited, and the restaurant opens whenever the staff feels like it, but the food is good. A meal for two is 100,000 pesos ($35), not including tip or wine.

The best hotels

The most beautiful hotel in Taxco is **Rancho Taxco-Victoria**, *Carlos J. Nibbi 5-7; tel. (52-762)2-0010*, with large rooms, a pleasant restaurant, a bar, a swimming pool, and beautiful gardens. A double room is 13,000 pesos ($50) a night.

Hotel de la Borda, *Cerro del Pedregal 2; tel. (52-762)2-0025*, is cozy, with a pool, restaurant overlooking the city, and large bathrooms. A double room is 160,000 pesos ($50) per night.

Fiesta Montetaxco, *off Route 95; tel. (52-762)2-1300*, a mountainside hotel on the north side of town, has 160 rooms and 50 villas and suites. It offers color televisions, air conditioning, a pool, spa facilities, a golf course, a tennis court, horseback riding, and a restaurant with nightly entertainment. A double room is 285,000 pesos to 310,000 pesos ($142 to $205) a night.

Cuernavaca, where spring springs eternal

Cuernavaca is the city of eternal spring, with temperatures that hover around 75 degrees Fahrenheit year-round and lush vegetation. The Mexicans were not the first to recognize this city as an ideal resort. The Aztecs also used Cuernavaca (or Cuauhnáhuac, as the city was originally called) as a retreat.

Cortes recognized its appeal as well. He built **El Palacio de Cortés**, his personal residence, here. This massive fortress is now home to the **Cuauhnáhuac Historical Museum**, which houses murals by Rivera, Siquieros, and Orozco.

Cuernavaca has become expensive by Mexican standards, in part because of the year-round expatriate community. Prices are substantially higher than in Taxco or San Miguel de Allende, and the area is more touristy than other cities.

See the cathedral that Cortes founded in 1529, the summer palace of the Hapsburgs, and the beautiful Borda Gardens, where a botanical festival is held each year in April.

Cuernavaca's best restaurants

Las Manañitas, *Ricardo Linares 107; tel. (52-73)14-14-66*, is set in an exotic tropical garden where peacocks, cranes, macaws, and myna birds roam among diners. Try the shrimp Patricia or the Patzcuaro whitefish with Lorenzo sauce.

The **Château René**, *Atzingo 11; tel. (52-73)17-23-00*, serves excellent French and Italian food. Dinner for two is 90,000 pesos ($45).

Harry's Bar, *Gutenberg 3; tel. (52-73)127679*, attracts a lively crowd. House specialties are barbecued ribs and chicken. A meal for two is 60,000 pesos ($30).

Yucateco, *Francisco Villa 112; tel. (52-73)13-3758*, serves Mayan food. House specialties include *panuchos* and chicken *pibil*. Dinner for two is less than 50,000 pesos ($25).

The best hotels

The most luxurious place to stay in Cuernavaca—and the most expensive—is the **Hotel Hacienda Cortes**, *Plaza Kennedy 90, Atlacomulco; tel. (52-73)15-1844*. This resort hotel has tennis courts, spa facilities, pools, lounges, two restaurants, lovely gardens, and weekend concerts. A double room is 275,000 pesos ($88) a night.

Las Mañanitas, *Ricardo Linares 107; tel. (52-73)12-4646*, a longtime favorite of the rich and famous, is another luxurious hotel with an excellent restaurant. Peacocks strut proudly through the gardens surrounding the hotel. A double room is 230,000 to 700,000 pesos ($75 to $225) a night. Credit cards are not accepted.

Posada Jacarandas, *Cuauhtemoc 805; tel. (52-73)15-7777*, is a large estate with a lovely outdoor restaurant, two sunken grotto pools, tennis courts, a small golf course, beautiful gardens, and spacious suites with fireplaces, terraces, and televisions. A double room is only 220,000 pesos ($71) a night.

Oaxaca: the best Indian ruins

Oaxaca, the most Indian region, is the best place to explore present-day Indian culture as well as ancient Indian ruins. The colonial city of Oaxaca is a good base. Plan to stay at least a few days—there is a lot to see.

The age-old tradition of weaving lives on in the village of **Teotitlán del Valle.** You can watch weavers at work and then buy decorated carpets and serapes for 60,000 pesos to 600,000 pesos ($30 to $300).

About eight miles outside Teotitlán del Valle is the **Yagul** site, dating from about A.D. 700. Earlier this century, precious Zapotec artifacts were taken from this series of multiple tombs. The site includes a hill fortress, a group of palaces and temples, and a ball court.

Mitla, the City of the Dead, is 26 miles outside Oaxaca. Built by the Zapotecs, Mitla was later enlarged by the Mixtecs. Although this is a touristy spot (Indian women mill around trying to sell souvenirs), it is also impressive, with intricate mosaics and strange stone carvings on the walls.

In the opposite direction from Oaxaca is another impressive archeological site: **Monte Albán.** This massive group of Zapotec ruins covers 15 square miles. The Temple of Dancers and the ceremonial ball court are the two most impressive sites. However, you can spend hours wandering among literally hundreds of ceremonial altars, winding staircases, and stone carvings. The site is open daily 8 a.m. until 6 p.m.

To see what was found in the tombs of Mitla and the ruins of Monte Albán, visit the **Regional Museum** in Oaxaca, *Calle M. Alcalá*, where most of the treasures are kept.

Keep in mind that when exploring the region of Oaxaca, you should use your camera guardedly; the natives don't like to have their pictures taken.

Oaxaca's best buys

The region of Oaxaca is a good place to shop. Prices for textiles, jewelry, and handicrafts are much lower than those in Cuernavaca and Mexico City. Visit the village of **Tlacolula** on a Sunday, when a huge market is set up by Indian vendors and artisans selling clothing, pottery, rugs, wall hangings, and gold jewelry styled upon the original Zapotec and Mixtec patterns. Visit the village of **Atzompa** on a Tuesday for superb green-glazed ceramics. The village of **Ejutla** is famous for its intricately carved knives, **San Bartolo Coyotepec** for its black pottery, and **Octolan** for its straw baskets.

If you prefer to shop in stores rather than open markets, visit **Casa Brena**, *Pino Suarez 58*, or **Aripo**, *Garcia Vigil 809*.

Oaxaca's best food and lodging

El Asador Vasco, *Portal de Flores 10; tel. (52-951)6-2092*, overlooking the zocalo, is the best restaurant in town. Chef Juan Hernandez takes cuisine seriously, and his restaurant is worth a special trip. Both Spanish and Mexican dishes are served. Try the house specialty, *cazuelas*, small casseroles of baked cheese, mushrooms, and garlic. Entrees are 30,000 pesos ($15). The restaurant is closed Sundays.

El Sol y La Luna, *Murguia 105; tel. (52-951)6-2933*, is a combination coffeehouse, restaurant, and gallery. Although the restaurant is small and you may have to wait for a table, it's worth the wait. Entrees are 25,000 pesos to 35,000 pesos ($12 to $17). The restaurant is closed Sunday.

No matter where you eat, your meal probably will include chocolate. Oaxaca is known for it. Try the famous *mole* sauce (a mixture of chocolate, cinnamon, chili peppers, and bananas), which is served on meat and poultry.

Although hotels here don't have the amenities of those in the resort cities, they are clean, comfortable, and cheap. The **Victoria**, *Km 545, Carreterra Pan Americana, Apt. Postal 248; tel. (52-951)52633*, atop a hill overlooking town, is one of the best, with a heated pool, tennis courts, a disco, and large breakfasts. A double room starts at 243,000 pesos ($83).

El Presidente, housed in the former Santa Catalina Convent, *Cinco de Mayo 300; tel. (6)0611 or (800)HOTELS-1*, is comfortable and serves an excellent luncheon buffet that is open to both guests and visitors. A double room is 124,000 pesos ($55) per night.

Oaxaca travel tips

The best way to get from Mexico City to Oaxaca is on one of Mexicana's daily flights. Round-trip airfare is $105. Once in Oaxaca, rent a car to get to the archeological sites.

Guadalajara: Mexico at its best

Guadalajara is the home of the Mexican hat dance, mariachi bands, tequilla, Mexican horsemen, and rodeos. It is also a bustling, sophisticated city with a large American community, attracted by the easy lifestyle and the pleasant climate.

This is a good place to admire Spanish colonial architecture. Many of the buildings in the **Plaza Tapatía** have been restored to their former glory. Hospicio Cabañas, built in 1801 as an orphanage, has been renovated and converted into the Cabanas Institute, a center for the arts. Its chapel contains Orozco's famous mural, *Four Horsemen of the Apocalypse*. Other colonial buildings of interest include the cathedral at the center of the city, the Jalisco Supreme Court, the Government Palace, and the Legislative Hall.

Gaudalajara is a city of parks. The largest, **Parque Agua Azul**, *Gonzales Gallo and avenida Independencia*, has an open-air theater, a bird sanctuary, and special sections designed for children and the blind. The park also houses the House of Handicrafts, which contains superb examples of colonial furniture, ceramics, blown glass, tinwork, and textiles produced in the state of Jalisco. Most of the products are for sale at reasonable, fixed prices.

Mexico's largest open-air market

The huge **Libertad Market**, *Calzada Independencia*, is the largest open-air market in Mexico. After shopping, retire to the **Plaza de los Mariachis**, across the street, and listen to the strolling musicians while sipping a cool drink.

The best places to dine to music

For a late lunch, try the **Guadalajara Grill**, *López Mateos Sur 3771; tel. (52-36)31-56-22*, where the band strikes up at 3 p.m. or 4 p.m. and then again about 10 p.m. The Guadalajara serves Mexican food. Another favorite is the **Cazuelas Grill**, *ave. López Mateos Sur 3755; tel. (52-36)31-57-80*, a family-run, traditional restaurant. There are two shows daily, at 1:30 and 6:30 p.m.

Luxurious hotels

Most hotels in Guadalajara are more like resorts, with extensive recreational facilities and restaurants and bars on the premises.

El Camino Real, *ave. Vallarta 5005; tel. (52-36)478400*, is a luxurious hotel with lovely gardens, a putting green, a tennis court, a bar, and a restaurant. A double room is 342,000 pesos ($110) a night.

The new **Hyatt Regency**, *avenida Lopez Mateos; tel. 36-22-7778*, boasts the only indoor skating rink in Mexico. A double room is 390,000 pesos ($125) a night.

The best day-trips

Tlaquepaque, a suburb of Guadalajara, has a wide selection of artisans' shops selling textiles, blown glass, and brass. Lunch at the **Restaurant Sin Nombre**, *Francisco Madero 80; tel. (52-36)354520*, which serves a creative mixture of Provençal and Mexican food. Dress is casual, and entrees are about 30,000 pesos ($15). Daily entertainment includes a vocal trio, singing waiters, and mariachis.

Jalapa: the flower garden of Mexico

Jalapa, the capital of Veracruz, is known as the flower garden of Mexico, because of its many parks. This small and friendly colonial city is seldom visited by tourists, even Mexican.

The city is 4,700 feet above sea level, and all the streets run at steep angles. Walking is thoroughly exhausting, so hire a taxi to take you sightseeing. Taxis are plentiful, and the rates are regulated—you can go anywhere in the city for less than $1.

Begin your tour in the main square. Visit the **Palacio de Gobierno** (Government House), which houses the famous *Liberation* mural by Diego Rivera, depicting man's struggle through life, and the massive colonial cathedral, built in 1773.

El Mercado Jauregui, one of the four local markets, has booths selling food, furniture, clothes, and flowers.

After the crush of the market, visit the small **Barrio Xalitic**, said to predate Christopher Columbus. Women scrub their clothes in the public water trough, and children play in a small park among tapped springs and small Christian shrines.

At centrally located **Parque Juarez**, vendors sell balloons, flowers, and food, and boys offer to shine your shoes. Steer clear of the food sold by vendors; it looks good but is known to cause Montezuma's revenge.

Try some of Jalapa's famous coffee at the café in the park, shaded by red-and-white striped umbrellas. The café serves an excellent *lechero*—hot milk poured into rich coffee extract and sweetened.

Mexico's best symphony

Jalapa boasts the best symphony orchestra in Mexico. For 10,000 pesos ($5), you can listen to two hours of both classical music and contemporary creations in the modern **State Theater**, *tel. (52-281)74177*. During intermission, members of the audience are allowed backstage to meet the orchestra.

The best hotels

The **Maria Victoria**, *Zaragosa 6; tel. (52-281)86011*, is the best hotel in Jalapa. It has a good restaurant and a bar. A double room is 105,000 pesos ($52) a night.

The **Hotel Villa del Mar**, *Boulevard Avila Camacho, Veracruz; tel. (52-29)313366*, is an attractive and inexpensive place to stay. A double room is only 121,000 pesos ($60).

The **Hotel Jalapa**, *tel. (52-281)82222*, is also a good place to stay in the center of town. A double room is 220,000 pesos ($110).

Chihuahua: home of the best bandito

Chihuahua was home to Pancho Villa (Doroteo Arranga), the Mexican Robin Hood. The house where the beloved bandito lived is a museum of the revolutionary era as well as Villa's life. (In 1910, Villa joined rebels and fought for President Madero and against General Huerta and President Carranza. He and his men killed American citizens in Columbus, New Mexico in 1916 and were pursued unsuccessfully by the U.S. Army for 11 months.) Villa's house was inhabited until just four years ago by his aging widow. The featured artifact on display is the bullet-riddled Dodge in which Villa was assassinated in 1923.

Chihuahua's best sites

Also in Chihuahua is the **Museo de Arte Popular**, which has an exhibit on the Tarahuamara culture, with woven blankets, full-sleeved blouses, whirling skirts, carved wooden masks decorated with goat hair, and palm baskets. Attached to the museum is a gift shop, where you can buy copies of these items as well as books on the indigenous cultures of Mexico and Mexican history.

El Palacio del Gobierno (Government Palace) is noteworthy for its gorgeous murals by Pina Mora, depicting the history of Mexico, including the arrival of the first priests, the Spanish Conquest, and the Mexican Civil War and its heroes.

The **Museo Regional** is housed in a beautiful art deco mansion with well-preserved stained-glass windows and elaborately carved mantels. Parts of the mansion have exhibits of Mormon and Mennonite settlements in Chihuahua. The toy display includes Tarahuamara miniatures, Mennonite playthings, and antique dolls.

You can see a replica of an adobe house from the ancient Paquime Indian culture in the northern part of Chihuahua, at **Casa Grandes**.

The world's grandest canyon—and most exciting train ride

Chihuahua's **Barranca del Cobre** (Copper Canyon) is four times larger and 300 feet deeper than the U.S. Grand Canyon. Its mountain peaks rise 10,000 feet, and its valleys drop 1,500 feet.

Until 1961, when the Chihuahua al Pacifico train line opened, the canyon was inaccessible and known only to isolated Tarahumara Indians living in caves. The train line climbs from sea level at Los Mochis on the Pacific to 8,000 feet before decending to Chihuahua. It passes the most spectacular scenery in Mexico—sheer cliffs that change color as the sun sets, giant rock formations, deep gorges, and mountain peaks. You can catch the train every day in Chihuahua at 7 a.m. or in Los Mochis at 6 a.m. The cost of a one-way trip from start to finish is 18,000 pesos ($80).

The best place to stay in the canyon is **Hotel Cabañas Divisadero-Barrancas**, *Calle 7, No. 1216*, in Divisadero, midway along the route. This rustic log-cabin hotel is perched on the rim of the canyon and affords dizzying views. Several Indian families live in caves nearby. These timid people sell handwoven baskets for less than 11,000 pesos ($5), wood carvings, and necklaces. Surrounding the hotel are trails that the Indians follow to the bottom of the canyon, 5,000 feet below.

Acapulco: Mexico's most sophisticated resort

Since the 1920s, the rich and famous have retreated to **Acapulco** every winter. The tropical Pacific Coast resort is famous for its fine beaches, luxury hotels, and deep-sea fishing facilities. Slim, tanned bodies line the beach, and colorful parasails float above it.

Acapulco isn't quite as nice as it used to be. It has become a smoggy, crowded city with bumper-to-bumper traffic. And on the hills above the city, crowded, dirty barrios have developed that house the cheap labor serving the many hotels and restaurants.

But you can forget all that, if you choose, by not driving and by frequenting such places as the **Crazy Lobster**, a seafood restaurant on La Condesa Beach, where the langostas and margaritas are as perfect as the view.

Blackbeard's, *Costera Miguel Alemán; tel. (52-74)84-25-49*, also on La Condesa Beach, is another popular restaurant. Have the fish kabobs and the house rum with pineapple juice. **Villa Demos**, *ave. Del Prado 6*, serves good Italian food in a tropical garden.

The place to stay, if you can afford it, is **Las Brisas**, *Carretera Escénica Clemente Mejia 5255; tel. (52-748)41650, or (800)228-3000 in the United States*. Guests stay in individual casitas on a hill overlooking Acapulco Bay, surrounded by bougainvillea and hibiscus. Each little cottage has its own pool. A double room is 619,600 to 1,765,860 pesos ($300 to $970).

Another good—and slightly more affordable—hotel in Acapulco is the **Villa Vera**, *Lomas del Mar 35, P.O. Box 560; (800)44-UTELL in the United States*. Originally a private home, this hotel stresses service and intimacy. It is private; it is discreet; it is charming. Its decor is white stucco, old stonework, fountains, and grottos, with touches of deep blue. The rooms are furnished with touches of old Mexico and the Orient. A double room is 498,300 pesos ($249) a night.

Puerto Vallarta: the most charming resort

Puerto Vallarta, that sleepy little fishing village discovered by Hollywood in 1964, has developed into one of Mexico's foremost resort towns. And unlike Acapulco, Puerto Vallarta hasn't yet lost its traditional charm. Native vendors push their wares in barrows up cobblestoned streets. Local fishermen roast pompano and red snapper on the beach. And Indian women pound their laundry on rocks by the stream.

The town doesn't have fine examples of Spanish architecture or a preponderance of pre-Columbian ruins, but it does have 25 miles of beaches, superb restaurants, and luxurious hotels.

The fishing is good here, too. Marlin season is November through January. And every November an international fishing competition is held off the coast of Manzanillo. You can charter a deep-sea fishing boat in town at the bay.

Puerto Vallarta was carved out of the jungle, which still encroaches on the town. You can join a jungle tour for about $6. Most involve a three-hour van ride through back country. Douse yourself with insect repellent—these mosquitoes eat gringos.

Eating well

La Perla, *Camino Real Hotel; tel. (52-322)30123*, is the best restaurant in town, with an international cuisine and a fine wine list. You can try gourmet treats, such as poached quail eggs with red caviar or crayfish salad with broccoli and morels. La Perla is open 7 p.m. until 11 p.m.

Carlos O'Brian's, *Paseo Diaz Ordaz 786; tel. (52-322)21444*, is a popular restaurant—long lines form hours before the 7 p.m. opening. The food is delicious, and the margaritas are strong. Dinner for two is 45,000 pesos ($20).

Las Palomas, *Paseo Diaz Ordaz 594; tel. (52-322)23675*, along the Malecon, is open for breakfast, lunch, and dinner. Steak and lobster are served, and 1950s dance music is played late into the evening. A meal for two, including wine, is 68,000 pesos ($30).

Chico's Paradise, 30 minutes south of Puerto Vallarta off Mismaloya Road, is perched high above a waterfall in the midst of the jungle. House specialties include drunken shrimp, which is baby shrimp marinated in beer, wine, orange juice, and herbs; barbecued ribs; a steak and lobster combination; and Chico's black-bean soup.

The best hotels

The best hotel in Puerto Vallarta is **Garza Blanca**, *Playa Palo Maria; tel. (52-322)21023*. You can stay in suites right on the beach or in a villa with its own garden and pool for 35,000 pesos ($150) a night.

El Camino Real, *Playa de las Escatacas; tel. (52-322)30123 or (800)228-3000 in the United States*, two miles south of Puerto Vallarta, is also an area best. A double room is 493,680 pesos to 1.2 million pesos ($240 to $600) a night, but rooms are spacious, with two double beds, a large bathroom, a fully stocked refrigerator, and a small lounging area. Buffet lunches are served.

Hotel Plaza Careyes, north of town, is quiet and elegant, with eight miles of beach, a disco overlooking the ocean, and facilities for water sports. A double room is 338,000 pesos ($160) a night.

Plaza las Glorias, *avenida de las Garzas; tel. (52-322)2-2224*, is another five-star hotel in Puerto Vallarta. Each room has a full-service bar and cable television. Guests can use the John Newcombe Tennis Center next door. A double room is 160,000 pesos ($80) a night.

Molino de Agua, *Ignacio Vallarta 13; tel. (52-322)2-1907*, has comfortable bungalows around a jungle garden. A double room is 198,000 pesos ($99) a night.

The Pacific at its best

Acapulco and Puerto Vallarta are busy resort towns, much changed from the sleepy little fishing villages they once were. However, you still can experience the peaceful ways of the Pacific in **San Blas**, 40 minutes south of Mazatlan, off Highway 15.

This is a land of endless summer, with rain forests, orchids, and warm waves. Life is lazy, and no one worries about the time. The cafés serve giant shrimp and fresh fish roasted over coals. For a few cents, you can take a bus from San Blas to **Matanchin Bay**, the most beautiful beach on the Pacific, where the waves are giant and clear and carry surfers miles before breaking.

When you tire of the beach, take a jungle boat for a few dollars into the marshy forest. You will see iguanas, blue herons, and parrots. The boat stops at a little cantina overlooking a deep pool. Have a beer and a swim.

The best whale watching

In October, hundreds of gray whales migrate from the Bering Straits to the warm lagoons of the **Baja Peninsula** to mate and have babies. The best place to see them is **San Ignacio Lagoon**, halfway down the peninsula on the Pacific Coast. The whales are so friendly that they'll probably come right up to you.

The bright green lagoon is mirrorlike, ringed with sandy hills and rocks. The hazy Santa Clara Mountains stand in the background. Because whale watching has become so popular here, it is carefully regulated by the Mexican government. San Ignacio, Ojo de Liebre, and Guerrero Negro are official sanctuaries. Boats must have permits to enter, and only two are permitted in at a time.

Baja Discovery, *P.O. Box 152527, San Diego, CA 92195; (619)232-1600*, arranges camping and whale-watching expeditions in San Ignacio. Five-day trips are $1,135, including airfare, camping equipment, transportation, one night in the La Pinta Hotel in San Ignacio, and meals. All-inclusive eight-day trips are $1,650.

The best of the Mexican Caribbean

Until the early 1970s, Mexico's idyllic Caribbean coast was undeveloped, inhabited only by Mayan Indians. Then the Mexican government realized the area's potential as a resort and began developing the Yucatan Peninsula. The empty island of Kankune became **Cancun**—the trendiest resort town in Mexico. Its neighbors, Cozumel and Isla Mujérès, also have benefited from the exposure, sprouting luxury hotels and restaurants and attracting tourists in larger numbers each year.

Considering their temperate climate, white-sand beaches, and clear waters, it's amazing that these spots took so long to attract notice. The weather is mostly sunny from October through April, and even during the rainy season (July through September), showers are often only brief afternoon events. If you tire of the sand and surf, you can visit the nearby Mayan ruins at Tulum, Coba, and Chichén Itzá.

While Cancun and Cozumel are developed resort towns, with superb restaurants, luxurious hotels, excellent beaches, and facilities for water sports, Isla Mujérès is less sophisticated, still a place for Mexican families on holiday. One recent visitor reported that some of the islanders were less than friendly. However, Isla Mujérès does have a Mayan temple and excellent scuba diving.

The most seductive beaches

The Caribbean side of Cancun has the best beaches, with sand as soft as talcum powder, aquamarine water, and exhilarating waves. The beach in front of the **Hyatt Caribe** is especially pretty, shaded by coconut palms and studded with lounge chairs that can be used by anyone, not just guests at the hotel. If you tire of the beach, splash in the Hyatt's series of pools connected by a canal that is crossed by a little bridge.

Cancun's best beach playground is at the **Camino Real**, *tel. (52-988)30100,* a hotel on a point of land. On one side, the Caribbean crashes against an inviting beach; on the other is the calm Bahia de Mujérès, where you can snorkel among fluorescent fish. The hotel has a saltwater pool fed by the bay and inhabited by giant tortoises and tropical fish. You can snorkel here or sun on the raft in the middle. Then wash the salt off your body in the ice-cold futuristic freshwater pool. (You don't have to be a guest to use the pools here either.)

On Cozumel, the beaches north and south of San Miguel are superb. Most of the island's hotels hug these beach coves, so guests walk directly from their rooms onto the beach each morning. Because the currents off Cozumel are tricky, you should never swim alone.

Isla Mujérès' most beautiful beach is **El Garrafón**. The beaches at Tortugas and Marias are less crowded, though.

Super snorkeling, super diving

Outside Cancun, on the road to Tulum, is an idyllic lagoon called **Xel-Há**, where you can enjoy the best snorkeling in the Mexican Caribbean. Netting keeps the sharks out, while letting all the colorful fish in. You can glide among the rocks, circle around the edge, or explore coves on the far side. You will see electric-blue fish, yellow fish with black stripes, and schools of tiny darters moving in unison. Although the lagoon is deep, the water is so crystal clear that you can see to the bottom. You can rent equipment here, but the flipper sizes are limited.

The best scuba diving is off the coast of Isla Mujérès, which is surrounded by reefs. You can rent equipment at **Mexico Divers**, *avenida Rueda Medina,* on the waterfront for 68,000 pesos ($30) a day.

About 500 yards off Cozumel, along **El Cantil**, is a series of reefs where you can dive to see tropical fish and underwater wrecks. Water visibility averages 100 feet, perfect for photographs. You can rent diving equipment in San Miguel from **Aqua Safaris**, *ave. Melgar 39A; tel. (52-987)2-0101,* or **Dive Cozumel**, *tel. (52-988)2-0002.* Tanks and weights rent for 22,500 pesos ($10) an hour, regulators for 22,500 pesos ($10), and fins, masks, and snorkels for 11,250 pesos ($5).

Most hotels charge higher prices for their diving facilities, but the on-site convenience is sometimes worth it. And some hotels offer scuba lessons. At the Stouffer Prezidente in

Cozumel, for example, a two-hour lesson is 110,000 pesos ($55) and a four-day progressive scuba seminar with a certified instructor is 700,000 pesos ($350). A one-day guided diving tour from Cozumel to Palancar Reef costs 100,000 pesos to 128,000 pesos ($50 to $64), including equipment.

Cancun's best scuba diving is in the waters off its southern point. You can arrange guided diving expeditions and equipment rental through your hotel for 68,000 pesos ($30).

The best of the mysterious Mayans

Remnants of the great civilization of the Mayans, who mysteriously disappeared long before Europeans appeared in Mexico, can be explored near Cancun. Descendants of the Mayan workers can be seen on the streets of the city and in surrounding villages—friendly, small, dark-eyed people with round faces. Many live as they have for centuries in one-room, palm-thatched huts furnished with hammocks and a table.

However, no traces remain of the ancient Mayan priests and mathematicians, who designed and built the great monuments and developed a calendar more accurate than the Gregorian.

Chichén Itzá is worth the three-hour drive from Cancun. The most famous and complete of the ancient ceremonial sites, it was built by the Toltecs (an invading Indian group) on top of a smaller Mayan site. The 1,000-year-old temple complex includes burial grounds, sacrificial altars, and royal ball courts. Plan to get here early in the day, and wear low-heeled shoes and sunscreen.

The most impressive monument at Chichen Itza is the **Temple of Kukulcan**, which is a perfect calendar as well as an engineering feat. The 91 steps to the top of each of the pyramid's four faces plus the one step to the temple at the top add up to 365, the number of days in a year. Fifty-two panels decorate the sides of the pyramid, one for each year of the Mayan century. The 18 terraces equal the 18 months of a Mayan year. During the spring and fall equinoxes, the sun creates a shadow on one face of the wall that resembles a serpent, the sign of the god Kukulcán.

Although the climb is steep, the view from the top of the pyramid makes it worthwhile. Ascending is actually easier than descending the tall, narrow steps. The easiest way to get back down to the ground is to walk sideways, holding onto the chain provided for that purpose. Experts say this is the correct way to descend anyway, as it is considered impolite to turn your back on the gods.

Another impressive sight at Chichén Itzá is the ceremonial **ball court**, used by the Mayans to play a game that was a cross between soccer and basketball. The goal was to get the ball through one of two hoops placed 25 feet high on opposing walls. The winning captain was beheaded as a sacrifice to the gods. However, before he was dropped down the 390-foot sacrificial well (which you still can see), the sacrificee was given hallucinogenic drugs and wine. And he was consoled with the fact that he was guaranteed a place in heaven.

To get to Chichén Itzá from Cancun, you can rent a car and drive yourself (but be careful of villagers and their animals, who cross the country roads with abandon). Or you can hire a taxi and a guide to take you there for about $120 a day. Another alternative is to join a bus tour at your hotel. These cost about $89 a person, including a guide and lunch. Beer and Coke (only) are sold on the buses for a pittance.

The walled city of **Tulum** is on a cliff overlooking the sea. The piles of ancient rock are brightened by flowering trees. Parts date back to A.D. 500. Climb the steep, narrow steps to the top of the main pyramid, the **Temple of the Descending God**. Below, white-sand beaches stretch in either direction. Human sacrifices were once pushed over this cliff. Note the carving of the upside-down god. Some say it is the god of rain; others claim that it is a being from outer space descending to earth.

You can arrange a bus tour from Cancun to Tulum and Xel-Ha for 125,000 pesos

($62). Tours to Tulum and Chichén Itzá can be arranged from Cozumel for 225,000 pesos ($112).

The largely uncharted city of **Cobá**, about 30 miles west of Tulum, boasts the tallest pyramid in the Yucatan—at 1,150 feet, it is twice the height of El Castillo at Chichén Itzá. Once it has been completely studied, Coba may prove the most important Mayan city of all. It once had as many as 40,000 inhabitants, and more than 7,000 stone structures have survived. Carvings of the Descending God can be seen on the temple that tops the pyramid. From the summit you can see Coba's five lakes, surrounded by jungle.

Uxmal is the best-preserved of the Mayan cities on the Yucatan Peninsula. It's also one of the prettiest, with reservoirs rather than wells. Built and abandoned three times between A.D. 325 and A.D. 900, it boasts richly carved temples. One of the most intriguing buildings here was named the **Nunnery** by conquistadors, who knew little about the Mayans. Some scholars believe the name is almost correct, because the building housed priestesses, who would be sacrificed to the god Chac. Others say it was just an administrative center.

The ancient Mayan ways also linger in **San Cristobal de las Casas.** The former colonial capital is located 6,500 feet high in the mountains of the southern state of Chiapas. Besides market days, the best times to visit San Cristobal and its mountain villages are during religious festivals. Masked dancers perform to traditional music played on harps, flutes, and drums; farces are acted out mocking the forces of evil; and horse races and fireworks are staged. (Keep in mind that hotel prices are increased during these festival times. And you must make reservations at least a couple of weeks in advance.)

Major festivals are staged during Carnival and Holy Week. In addition, the following holidays are observed: **Martes (Tuesday) of Carnival,** when Chamula (a neighboring village to San Cristobal de las Casas) enacts a purification ritual, with dancers leaping over open fires; **July 22-24,** when Chamula celebrates the festival of its patron saint, San Juan, in ceremonies that are both Catholic and Mayan; **July 24-25,** when San Cristobal honors its patron saint with a torchlight parade; and **Dec. 30-Jan. 1,** when ceremonies are held to mark the changing of village officials.

The best place to stay in San Cristobal de las Casas is the **Posada Diego de Mazaiegos,** *Calle Ma. Adelina Flores 2; tel. (52-967)81825.* All the rooms have fireplaces, and the hotel is located just off the main plaza. A double room is 60,000 pesos ($30).

A fisherman's paradise

Fishing is fabulous in the Mexican Caribbean. From March through mid-July, the sailfish run. From May through early June, the bonito and dolphin run. From May through September, it's the wahoo and kingfish. And barracuda, bluefin, mackerel, white marlin, and grouper can be fished year-round.

The best place to arrange a charter is in **Puerto Juarez,** where rates are $125 to $250 a day for two. Isla Mujérès also has good rates—you can arrange an all-inclusive deep-sea fishing expedition for four people for $200 a day through **Mexico Divers.** Rates are much higher in Cancun and Cozumel—from $250 to $350 a day.

The best shopping in the Mexican Caribbean

Shopping in the Caribbean takes patience, persistence, and a poker face. The basic rules of haggling apply. First ask the price of something and then offer half as much. The shopkeeper inevitably will reply that what you're offering won't even cover the costs of the materials. Your best response is to shrug your shoulders and walk away. The shopkeeper probably will follow after you.

In Cancun

Cancun's major market area is downtown along **avenida Tulum.** As you walk by this open-stall market, which stretches for about two blocks, the shopkeepers call to you—some even reach out to grab you by the arm as you pass. Blankets, sweaters, silver bracelets, and straw hats are thrown across boxes and tables in these stalls, and nothing is marked with a price. Feel free to rummage, but wait to ask for help until you're sure of what you want to buy. Once you have the attention of a salesperson, you won't get rid of him easily.

One of our editors found a handmade cardigan sweater in this market. The salesperson (a 16-year-old boy) asked for 225,000 pesos ($100). She offered 90,000 pesos ($40). The boy laughed. But when she walked away, he grabbed her arm. She eventually bought the sweater for $40.

The sweaters and blankets at this market are good quality, but the gold and silver may be less so. Buy a piece of jewelry (if you can get a good price) because you like it, not because you think you're investing in gold. Real silver is marked with a government symbol that shows an eagle with a snake in its mouth leaning against a cactus.

If you'd rather avoid the market, good shops are located along avenida Tulum. **La Casita,** for example, stocks traditional Mexican clothes and silver and coral jewelry.

El Parian, Cancun's main square, also is a good place to shop. One store there, **Anakena,** sells Mayan art.

Little boys on the streets sell marionettes dressed in Mexican costume that make good gifts for children and cost next to nothing.

In Isla Mujérès

The place to go for handmade, brightly embroidered cotton dresses is **Isla Mujérès.** As you step from the boat onto the dock, you'll be bombarded by people selling blankets, lace tablecloths, necklaces, and conch shells. However, the better merchandise is in the shops in town. These shops keep their doors open to the sun, and the maracas and hats seem to pour from the shops onto the streets and sidewalks. The pastel blue and green dresses, which hang in the doorways and wave in the wind, go for 68,000 pesos ($30). One of our editors found a pair of silver earrings shaped like roses, with fine individual petals, for 11,250 pesos ($5). You can bargain in some of these shops, but not all.

In Cozumel

In Cozumel, **Bazaar Cozumel,** *Boulevard Rafael E. Melgar,* sells high-quality Mexican art, including silverwork, tapestries, and pottery, at good prices. And **Plaza del Sol** has about a dozen craft and jewelry shops.

Cancun's best restaurants

El Pescador, *Tulipanes,* off avenida Tulum, is immensely popular, with long lines for dinner. The food is good and the ambiance colorful. Vendors selling everything from roses to Mexican hats stop by the tables. It's all in good fun. And the prices are great.

Hacienda el Mortero, *tel. (52-988)3-1133,* set in a quiet, elegant hacienda, serves excellent Mexican cuisine. You can't go wrong, no matter what you order. Dinner for two, not including drinks, tip, or tax, is 100,000 pesos ($50).

Although you may have to wait a half-hour to be seated, **Maxime,** *tel. (52-988)3-0438,* is worth it, especially if you tire of Mexican food. The fare is French, and house specialties include *terrine de canard au poivre vert, feuilleté d'escargot,* and *soufflé orange.* Dinner for two is 79,000 pesos ($69).

Papagayo, *Claveles 31,* is a charming and inexpensive restaurant made up of little Tiki huts. Try the Papagayo omelet, seafood tacos, lime soup, and margaritas. A meal is only 34,000 pesos ($17).

Los Alemandros, *avenidas Bonampak and Sayil; tel. (52-988)40807,* serves good local Yucatec food.

Cancun's best hotels

The **Camino Real,** *tel. (52-988)3-0100 or (800)228-3000 in the United States,* is the best hotel in town. It has more than 300 rooms, two good restaurants, a saltwater swimming pool, water sports, tennis courts, and one of the hottest discos on the island. Double rooms are 420,000 pesos to 540,000 pesos ($210 to $270) a night during high season (December through May).

The **Exelaris Hyatt Regency**, *tel. (52-988)3-0966*, offers villas as well as hotel rooms, four restaurants, tennis courts, facilities for water sports, and a pool with a waterfall. A double room costs 400,000 pesos ($200) a night.

The **Casa Maya**, *tel. (52-988)3-0555* or *(800)221-6509* in the United States, is a huge hotel that is well-suited for families. Its rooms are spacious, with walk-in closets and large bathrooms. The hotel offers moped rentals, pools, restaurants, and tennis courts. A double room is 260,000 pesos ($130) a night.

The **Club Lagoon**, *tel. (52-988)3-1111*, is a quiet group of adobe dwellings on Laguna Nichupte. The hotel has two good restaurants and two bars. A double room is 154,000 pesos ($77) a night.

Cozumel's best fare

Santeago's Grill, *Adolfo Rofado Sala 15; tel. (52-987)221-37*, has good Mexican food, including seafood and meats. Entrees are 35,000 pesos ($27).

Pepe's Grill, *avenida Rafael Melgar*, serves superb seafood in a romantic setting. A buffet-style dinner for two is 56,000 pesos ($25).

El Portal, *Malecon; tel. (52-987)203-16*, is an inexpensive place for a good breakfast.

Cozumel's best hotels

Although other luxury hotels have arrived in the last few years, **El Presidente**, *tel. (52-987)203-22*, remains the best, with large rooms, a pretty beach, a pool, tennis courts, and an excellent dining room. A double room is 360,000 pesos to 460,000 pesos ($180 to $230) a night.

The **Sheraton Sol-Caribe**, *North Zone; tel. (52-987)207-00*, has good diving facilities, an excellent dining room, and three tennis courts. A double room is 320,000 pesos to 360,000 pesos ($160 to $180).

The **Galapago Inn**, *South Zone; tel. (52-987)206-63*, is a small, quiet hotel with access to good diving areas. A double room is 142,000 pesos ($66) a night, including three meals a day.

The **Cabanas del Caribe**, *P.O. Box 9; tel. (52-987)200-17*, boasts fabulous beaches and a tropical garden. A double room is 198,000 pesos ($99).

Isla Mujérès' best restaurants

Maria's Kankin, *El Garrafon Park; tel. (52-988)314-20*, five miles outside town, serves excellent French cuisine in elegant, peaceful surroundings. Dinner for two is 68,000 pesos ($30).

Restaurant Gomar, *Hidalgo 5; tel. (52-988)201-42*, is romantic, with both indoor and terrace dining. The lobster and fresh fish are your best bets. Dinner for two is 56,000 pesos ($25).

Isla Mujérès' best hotels

Crystalmar Beach Club, *Paradiso Laguna Mar Lote 16; tel. (52-988)200-07 or (800)622-3838 in the United States*, is one of the best places to stay in Isla Mujérès. There is a secluded tropical beach nearby, rooms are equipped with complete kitchenettes, and diving and snorkeling are available. Double rooms are 160,000 pesos to 200,000 pesos ($80 to $100) during peak season.

Posada del Mar, *avenida Rueda Medina; tel. (52-988)20300*, is a comfortable, small hotel across from the beach. It has tennis courts, a pool, a restaurant, a bar, a laundromat, and air conditioning. A double room is 124,000 pesos ($55) a night.

The best travel tips

Although both Cancun and Cozumel have efficient, inexpensive bus service, you might as well travel by taxi—fares seldom exceed 7,800 pesos ($3.50), and Cancun's green and white taxis are equipped with meters. The cabs in Cozumel do not have meters, so make arrangements with the driver before you get in. The fare here should be less than 2,250 pesos ($1).

Minibuses transport tourists and their luggage from the airport to hotels for less than 6,800 pesos ($3) per person.

Cancun, Cozumel, and Isla Mujérès all offer moped and auto rentals. The Casa Maya and Krystal hotels on Cancun charge about 100,000 pesos ($50) for a day's rental. On Cozumel, you can rent a moped from Reuben's for about 34,000 pesos ($15) a day. On Isla Mujérès, you can rent a motorbike at **Motorent Cárdenes**, *avenida Guerrero; tel. (52-988)200-79*, for 40,000 pesos ($20) a day.

In Cancun, you can rent a car from **Avis**, *tel. (52-988)423-28;* **Budget**, *tel. (52-988)407-30;* **Econorent**, *tel. (52-988)414-35;* or **Holiday**, *tel. (52-988)410-61*. Each starts at about 79,000 pesos ($69) a day with a 125-mile limit. Hertz and Avis are represented on Cozumel, where they charge about 110,000 pesos ($55) a day.

The best—and cheapest—getaway

Americans looking for a short getaway filled with sun and fun should look south to Cancun. Inexpensive package trips to this Mexican resort area are available from the Baltimore/Washington area. **American Express**, *(800)241-1700*, can arrange a seven-day trip, including round-trip airfare and hotel accommodation, for $667. Apple Vacations offers even less expensive packages; prices range from $489 to $629 for three- to seven-night deals.

The Best of Brazil

> Delight is a weak term to express the feelings of a naturalist who, for the first time, has wandered by himself in a Brazilian forest. The elegance of the grasses, the novelty of the parasitical plants, the beauty of the flowers, the glossy green of the foliage, but above all the general luxuriance of the vegetation, filled me with admiration. A most paradoxical mixture of sound and silence pervades the shady parts of the wood. The noise from the insects is so loud that it may be heard even in a vessel anchored several hundred yards from the shore; yet within the recesses of the forest a universal silence appears to reign.
> —*Charles Darwin, 1832-1836*

Brazil—the largest South American country—is watered by the Amazon rain forest, the largest in the world, and drained by the Amazon River, which carries more water than any other river in the world. The country's spectacular shoreline—which is lined with broad beaches and high mountains that circle the harbors—rivals any shoreline in the world. But Brazil has more to offer than spectacular scenery. It boasts the continent's most exciting city, Rio de Janeiro, and South America's largest industrial city, São Paulo.

Brazilians are beautiful, an exotic blend of Indian, African, and European ancestry. Half the population is under 25, adding to the beauty quotient but creating social and economic problems.

A fun-loving nation, Brazil has the world's best Carnival, with glittering costumes, immense processions, mesmerizing music, and gala balls. And year-round, its beaches boast the world's most scantily clad sun worshipers.

Restaurants in Brazil are excellent and cheap. Food supplies are abundant and varied, and the chefs are talented. Once you have tried the national dish, *feijoada* (a spicy black-bean stew), take advantage of the international cuisine. You can enjoy gourmet meals for next to nothing.

Brazil has the highest inflation rate in the world—20% a month in 1992. So prices rise rapidly. As of press time (spring 1992), five-star hotels charged about $250. However, you should take prices quoted herein as rough guides only, considering the incredible inflation rate and the constantly changing value of the cruzeiro to the dollar.

Rio: Brazil's cultural center

Rio de Janeiro is Brazil's most cosmopolitan city. It is most famous for its pre-Lenten

507

Carnival, but it has much more to offer than simply a festival. A beautiful city surrounded by low mountains, Rio hugs Guanabara Bay, which is rimmed with palm-lined beaches and dotted with 84 islands. Jet-setters from around the world soak in the sun all day and dance in the nightclubs all night.

The world's best Carnival

People from around the world flock to Rio for its **Carnival**, a four-day extravaganza that concludes Ash Wednesday. Poor Cariocas (residents of Rio) often put a year's savings into their costumes for the round of wild parties and balls.

Carnival officially begins when the mayor hands the key to the city to King Momo, the mock king of the festivities, who appears at all major Carnival events (parades, balls, costume contests) and orders everyone to have fun. King Momo is elected every year by the residents of Rio; the primary requirement is that he be very fat.

Samba schools are the focus of glittering processions beginning at 6 p.m. Sunday and Monday and continuing until noon on Shrove Tuesday. These enormous groups compete for prizes and go to great lengths to come up with the most fantastic and outrageous costumes and themes. The competition is always passionate, and at times it gets violent.

Traditionally, each of the city's samba schools (which number up to 5,000 members each) paraded through the streets of downtown Rio displaying their floats and gaudy costumes. A few years ago, the rowdy parades were taken off the streets and put into the **Sambo'dromo**, a stadium about a half-mile long and about as wide as a street. Brazilians and visitors of all backgrounds pay up to $1,000 to crowd into this structure and watch the samba schools perform. It is the equivalent in spectacle of a half-time show at the Super Bowl, but the majorettes are topless. And the show lasts 17 hours.

If you can't get tickets to the Sambo'dromo, just walk through the streets. Bandstands are erected on street corners, where samba bands give impromptu concerts and people in skimpy costumes shake their stuff.

Rio's elite, disguised in fantastic costumes, attend elaborate balls. The best are at the Canecão nightclub, the Yacht Club, the Flamenco Football Club, La Scala, and Sugarloaf Mountain. Local nightclubs also arrange elaborate parties, with samba bands and costumes.

Tickets for Carnival balls and parades go on sale in November and sell out early.

The most exotic New Year's celebration

As colorful as Carnival—but less known—is Rio's New Year's celebration. Just before midnight, thousands of white-robed worshipers carrying candles gather on the city's beaches to make offerings to the goddess of the sea, Lemanja. At midnight, fireworks go off, and crying, singing worshipers rush into the ocean carrying flowers and gifts for their deity.

The best view from Christ's feet

Rio's best-known landmark is the huge statue of **Christ the Redeemer**, overlooking the harbor from the top of Corcovado Mountain, 2,250 feet above sea level. A little train takes you to the statue.

From this vantage point on the top of the mountain, the view of the harbor is spectacular, particularly as the day turns to dusk, then dark, and the city below begins to glitter against the aquamarine blue of the sea. Have a drink in the café at the top of the mountain.

Another beautiful view of Rio is from the top of **Pao de Açucar** (Sugarloaf Mountain), a rock rising 390 feet above the bay. A cable car makes the trip from 8 a.m. until 10 p.m. for about $5.

Rio's best garden

Rio's **Jardim Botânico** (Botanical Garden) has 7,000 varieties of tropical plants. Palm-lined paths wind their way past ponds covered with lily pads.

Rio's best museum

The **Quinta da Boa Vista** (National Museum), *São Cristóvão*, in the former Imperial Palace, displays objects that once belonged to the royal family, along with the Bendego meteorite, one of the largest ever found on earth, and an impressive Amazon Indian display.

Surrounding Quinta da Boa Vista is a quilt of lawns, flower beds, and hothouses that can be explored by horse-drawn carriage.

Brazil's best books

The **National Library**, founded in 1810, has a collection of 1 million volumes in various languages, including a parchment copy of the Guttenberg Bible (one of four existing) and an astonishing collection of Hebraica.

The most authentic neighborhoods

Lapa, an old, slightly crumbling neighborhood, has narrow streets with wrought-iron balconies. The old townhouses have been converted into shops and pensions.

Santa Teresa, near Corcovado Mountain, gives a glimpse of Rio as it was at the turn of the century. Beautiful old houses, completely neglected, flank cobblestoned avenues shaded by broad, ancient trees. The neighborhood has no restaurants or nightclubs. Nor has any visible effort been made to restore or preserve this lovely part of the city.

South America's best beaches

Rio has spectacularly beautiful beaches—Botafogo, Copacabana, Ipanema, Leblon, São Conrado—where women wearing the world's skimpiest bikinis bask in the sun. Called *tangos,* the bikinis here consist of three tiny triangles of fabric held in place by lengths of string.

The prettiest beach is the one most distant from the center of the city, **São Conrado**, where the Hotel Intercontinental has taken root. This beach is not as crowded as Copacabana and Ipanema, and the water is cleaner.

São Conrado is also the best place to go hang gliding—or just to watch the colorful gliders hover in the air for hours, held aloft by updrafts coming off the ocean and up the mountainside. They look like huge butterflies leisurely enjoying the afternoon sun.

Copacabana, lined with luxury hotels, restaurants, and nightclubs, is the chicest beach in South America. It is the longest and widest in Rio. Stroll along **avenida Atlântica**, which is tiled with mosaics and lined with first-class hotels and expensive shops.

Close rivals of Copacabana are Ipanema (which is less congested and draws a younger crowd), Leblon, and Barra da Tijuca. The southern part of Ipanema is a fashionable residential area.

About 90 miles north of Rio is Cabo Frio, where forts and a 17th-century convent provide a dramatic backdrop to a wide, almost deserted beach.

A word of caution: Never take valuables to the beach—leave them in your hotel safe. Thieves from the nearby *favelas* (slums) roam the beaches looking for easy pickings. They move fast.

Brazil's best cuisine, two hours north of Rio

Two hours north of Rio are the beaches of **Buzios**, the playgrounds of the elite. Called the jewel of the Brazilian Riviera, Buzios is filled with expensive boutiques. The pace is languid. People sleep until noon and dine in the wee hours of the morning. You can walk to the beach from anywhere in this little fishing village. Houses have no doors, and drums can be heard everywhere.

Buzios' cuisine is considered the finest in Brazil. An elaborate dinner for two at one of the town's best restaurants can cost more than a night at a local hotel. But it's worth it. Restaurants to try in Buzios include **Au Cherval Blanc**, *ave. Jose Bento Ribeiro Dantas*

181, and **French Satyricon,** *ave. Jose Bento Ribeiro Dantas 412*, both of which serve local fish specialties and Italian food.

At Satyricon, you can enjoy a complimentary appetizer of eggplant roasted in garlic, quail eggs (hard-boiled), baked red and yellow peppers, and warm bread. Follow all of this with fresh marimba seasoned with hot red peppers you pluck from a plant on the table.

The best place to stay in Buzios is the **Nas Rocas Club Hotel,** *Ilha Rasa Marina Porto; tel. (55-246)231303*, which is worth the few extra dollars you'll pay over the cost of standard lodging. A double room is 317,552 cruzeiros to 353,232 cruzeiros ($178 to $198).

Other recommended places to stay in Buzios include **Pousada La Mandragora,** *tel. (55-246)23-1454*; **Pousada Dos Buzios,** *ave. Jose Bento Ribeiro Dantas 21; tel. (55-246)23-1155*, near Armacao Beach; **Pousada Barracuda,** *Ponta da Sapata; tel. (55-246)23-1214*, near Manguinhos Beach; and **Pousada La Chimere,** *pca Eugenio Honold 36; tel. (55-246)23-1460*, near Ossos Beach. Rates are available upon request.

The world's largest stadium

Maracana Stadium, the world's largest sports arena, which holds more than 200,000 people, is the locale of Rio's wild soccer matches. The games are second in importance only to Carnival here. Buy a Cadiera Especial ticket for 5,000 cruzeiros ($2)—this allows you to enjoy the matches in an area fenced off from the mobs of raucous fans. Most hotels offer packages that provide transportation to and from the stadium as well as seats for the games.

Your best bet

The **Jockey Club** holds horse races Thursday nights and weekends. The most important is the Grande Premio Brasil, held the first Sunday in August. Everyone who is anyone shows up in fancy dress to watch South America's best horses run.

The best way to see the bay

The best way to see **Guanabara Bay** is to take a day or half-day cruise among its islands. Boats dock along avenida Nestor Moreira, next to the Sol e Mar restaurant. Paqueta, where Rio's lovers meet, is the loveliest island. Cars aren't allowed here, only bikes and carriages. A ferry to Paqueta takes about an hour and a half; the hydrofoil takes 30 minutes.

Rio's best drive

The road that winds through Rio's mountain backdrop, passing through Itatiaia National Park toward Visconde de Maua, is breathtaking. En route is **Petropolis,** once the emperor's summer palace, which has been preserved complete with royal belongings, including the Brazilian imperial crown. You must remove your shoes to visit the interior of the palace, which is open to the public from noon until 5:30 p.m. daily except Monday. About an hour farther along is **Teresopolis,** a national park that attracts mountain climbers.

The best shopping

The best shopping in Rio is for leather goods. You'll find good deals at all the city's department stores, including **Rio Sul,** on the west side of the tunnel leading from avenida Princesa Isabel. Or stroll along avenida Atlantica in the evening, where you'll find a wide assortment of leather products.

Feirarte (formerly known as the Hippie Market) is a good place to buy arts and crafts. It is held Sundays at Praça General Osorio in Ipanema.

Rio's best restaurants

Rio has an endless list of outstanding eateries. The city's best gourmet restaurants include **Le St. Honoré**, *Meridien Hotel; tel. (55-21)275-9922*, inspired by Paul Bocuse; **Le Pré Catalán**, *Rio Palace Hotel; tel. (55-21)521-3232*, created by Gaston Lenôtre; and **Le Bec Fin**, *ave. Copacabana 178A; tel. (55-21)542-4097.*

For authentic Brazilian food, the best restaurant in town is **Moenda**, *Trocadero Hotel, Second Floor, ave. Atlantica 2064, Copacabana; tel. (55-21)257-1834.* The decor is not deluxe, but the food is scrumptious. Try the *feijoada completa.* Prices are moderate.

Ouro Verde, *tel. (55-21)542-1887*, attached to the hotel of the same name, is one of the best restaurants in Copacabana. The most romantic is **Copacabana**, *tel. (55-21)255-7070*, in the Copacabana Hotel. **Enotria**, *rua Constante Ramos; tel. (55-21)237-6705*, serves delicious northern Italian food.

In old Rio, try **Chale**, *rua da Matriz 54; tel. (55-21)286-9548*, or **Maria Thereza Weiss**, *rua Visconde Silva 152; tel. (55-21)286-3866.* Both are in old colonial houses full of Brazilian antiques.

In new Rio, try **La Tour**, *rua Santa Luzia*, a revolving restaurant at the top of the Aeronautical Club building near the U.S. Consulate.

Rio also has good barbecue restaurants, called *churrascarias*. These all-you-can-eat places serve grilled meats—pork, beef, marinated chicken livers—with salad and rice. The food is inexpensive and usually superb.

The best *churrascaria* is **Gaucha**, *rua Laranjeiras 114; tel. (55-21)285-5767.* **Porcao**, *Barra; tel. (55-21)521-0999*, past São Conrado, is also good.

Rio's best seafood is served at the **Sol e Mar**, *ave. Nestor Moreira 11; tel. (55-21)295-1896*, in Botafogo, which has a view of the bay. A string quartet entertains as you enjoy your South Atlantic fish.

The city's best Portuguese restaurant is the elegant **Antiquarius**, *rua Aristides Espindola 19; tel. (55-21)294-1496*, in Leblon. Inexpensive Portuguese food is served at a no-frills eatery called **Adegao**, *Campo de São Cristovão; tel. (55-21)580-7288.* A lunchtime favorite is **Penafiel**, *rua Senhor dos Passes; tel. (55-21)224-6870.*

Rio's best hotels

Rio's most inviting hotel, in a glitzy modern way, is the **Meridien**, *Copacabana; tel. (55-21)275-9922.* A double room is 338,960 cruzeiros ($190), including breakfast.

Other first-class hotels include the **Rio Palace**, *Copacabana Beach, tel. (55-21)521-3232* ($220 for a double room); **Caesar Park**, *Ipanema, tel. (55-21)287-3122* ($255 for a double room); and **Marina Palace**, *Leblon, tel. (55-21)259-5212* ($155 for a double room).

The **Copacabana Palace**, *ave. Atlantica 1702; tel. (55-21)255-7070*, is the grand old lady of Rio's hotels, the first major hotel built on Copacabana Beach. Until recent years, jet-setters from around the world returned here year after year. However, despite cosmetic surgery, the old girl can't match the attractions of newer hotels on Copacabana and Ipanema beaches, and the Copacabana Palace is not as popular as it once was. A double room is 258,680 cruzeiros to 338,960 cruzeiros ($145 to $190).

The **Ouro Verde Hotel**, *ave. Atlântica 1456; tel. (55-21)542-1887*, is on the beach in Copacabana and has a good French restaurant. It used to be the best hotel in Rio, with the atmosphere of a genteel British men's club. But it too has become a bit shabby. A double room is 144,000 cruzeiros to 155,208 cruzeiros ($80 to $87).

The best budget hotel

The centrally located **Carlton**, *rua Joao Lira 68, 22430 Leblon; tel. (55-21)259-1932*, is recommended as a budget hotel, but it doesn't scrimp on service. A double room is 14,000 cruzeiros ($7).

The hottest night life

Rio's residents don't sit down to dinner until 9 p.m. or so. By the time dinner is finished, it's nearly 11 p.m. This is when the city's night spots wake up.

The most popular *discotecas* (discos) are Hippopotamus, Caligula, and Help. They are like discos everywhere, with loud music, light shows, and lively crowds. Many are organized as private clubs; you need a reservation, and in some cases a reference, to get in. Ask the concierge at your hotel to make a reservation for you.

Rio's *gafieiras* are a better bet if you want to see authentic Brazilian night life. These large dance halls draw people of all ages. The places have little or no decor, the bands vary, and the crowds are noisy. But the noise is distinctly Brazilian, and the crowds are charmingly unsophisticated. One of the more sophisticated *gafieiras* is **Asa Branca**, *ave. Meme de Sa 17; tel. (55-21)252-0966*, a fairly new dance hall owned by one of Rio's most energetic entertainment moguls, Chico Recarey.

One of the best clubs for live entertainment is **Karoake de Canja**, *ave. Ataulfo de Paiza 375; tel. (55-21)511-0484*.

You'll find a more sophisticated piano bar and a live band at **Café Un, Deux, Trois**, *rua Bartolomeu Mitre 123; tel. (55-21)239-0198*. **Biblos**, *ave. Epitacio Pessoa 1484; tel. (55-21)521-2645*, is a good place to dance. There's a $5 cover charge.

If you're in the mood for a quiet evening, try the **Bâteau Mouche Bar**, next to the Sol e Mar. The tunes date back to the 1940s, and there's dancing, of course.

For a Las Vegas-type show, take in the spectacles at **Plataforma**, *rua Adalberto Ferreira 32; tel. (55-21)274-4022*, or **Scala Rio**, *ave. Afranio de Melos Franco 296; tel. (55-21)239-4448*.

South America's most modern city: Brasilia

Brasilia is a futuristic fantasy situated in the middle of the great central plain of Brazil. The white structures of this capital city are striking, set against the rich red soil. The capital is laid out in the shape of an airplane, with government buildings down the middle and residential and commercial areas along the two wings.

Brasilia came into existence in 1960. President Juscelino Kubitschek decided the nation's capital should be in the center of the country, rather than on the coast, and began construction of the city, which took three years to complete. He drew on the talents of urban planner Lucio Costa, who designed the city, and architect Oscar Niemeyer, who designed the city's major buildings.

However, the seeds of Brasilia were sown in the 1800s by St. João Bosco, who wrote in his memoirs, "Repeatedly a voice spoke out, saying: When they come to excavate the mines hidden in the breasts of these mountains (between the 15th and 20th parallels), here the promised land will arise, giving forth milk and honey. It will be of unimaginable riches, and this will happen before the second generation passes...before 120 years go by."

Bosco's vision inspired Brazilian leaders to stipulate in the constitution of 1891 that the new capital should be established in the area between the 15th and 20th parallels, the location of modern-day Brasilia. The saint is commemorated at **Dom Bosco Church**, which has tall and brilliant blue stained-glass windows.

Brazil's tallest tower

Brasilia has one of the tallest telecommunications towers in the world, the 600-foot **Torre de Televisão**. Take an elevator to a platform at 225 feet or another elevator to a restaurant and bar, both of which offer an extensive view of the city.

The best place to begin

Catetinho, the temporary residence of President Juscelino Kubitschek in 1956 and Brasilia's first building, is the best place to begin a tour of the city. The white-clapboard house on stilts was built in 10 days for the former president, when he and city planners were plotting the city's future. It is modestly furnished, with a bed and a plain wooden table, around which city planners gathered.

Brazil's ultramodern cathedral

The architecturally noteworthy **National Cathedral** is an ultramodern structure designed in the shape of the crown of thorns. A statue of St. Peter is suspended from the roof in the Passage of Reflection, which leads to the underground nave. A pool, which surrounds the concrete building, is reflected in the nave's glass roof panels, giving the interior an airy brightness.

The prettiest palace

One of Brasilia's most famous buildings is the **Itamarati Palace,** which rises out of the beautiful water gardens that hold the city's well-known sculpture, the **Meteor.** The reflecting pool is filled with yard-wide lily pads called Victoria Regia, native to the Amazon. Inside the palace is a splendid collection of Brazilian art, including works by Portinari, the country's premier painter.

Brazil's boldest architecture

The **National Congress Complex** looks more like an outer-space colony than a political center. The long, narrow building is reached by ramplike staircases and topped by two eggshell domes (one inverted) known as the cup and saucer. The building glows at sunset.

The **Planalto Palacio** is the city's most graceful building, its roof supported by marble arches, its facade mirrored in a reflecting pool. Next door, a man-made waterfall washes the face of the Justice Ministry.

The **Palacio dos Arcos** (the Ministry of Foreign Relations) is considered the city's most beautiful building.

The president's house

The **Palacio da Alvorada,** the home of the president of Brazil, is outside town on Lake Paranoá. The sumptuous building has glass walls, rosewood floors, and panels of gilded tile. To visit the palace, which is open to the public most weekends, obtain a pass from the **Palacio do Planalto,** *Praça Dos Tres Podres, Brasilia DS, 70150; tel. (55-61)211-1200.*

Modern masterpieces

Brasilia is known for its modern sculptures, displayed outdoors in public places. The most famous is the **Meteor,** at the Itamarati Palace, which was mentioned above. Also important are the **Warriors,** in front of the Planalto; the **Water Nymphs,** at the Alvorada; and the **Mermaid,** in front of the Navy Ministry on the Esplanada dos Ministérios.

Brasilia's best dining

The *churrascarias* along the lake are good places to eat. The best is **Churrascaria do Lago,** *tel. (55-61)223-9266.*

Good international cuisine is served at the **Piantella,** *tel. (55-61)224-9408,* which has live music.

First-class hotels

Brasilia's best hotel is the first-class **Nacional,** *Setor Hoteleiro, Sul Lote 1; tel. (55-61)321-7575,* which has a lovely central view of the government buildings. A double room is 170,000 cruzeiros to 220,000 cruzeiros ($95 to $123).

Hotel Das Americas, *Setor Hoteleiro, Sol 4, Building D.; tel. (55-61)321-3355,* in the southern hotel area, is air-conditioned. Rooms are supplied with refrigerators. A double room is 164,128 cruzeiros to 167,696 cruzeiros ($92 to $94).

Brazil's best theater

The **Teatro Nacional** (National Theater) in Brasilia has one of the most flexible modern stages in South America, as well as two auditoriums. The building was designed to look like an elongated Aztec pyramid.

São Paulo: South America's richest city

São Paulo, a city of nearly 13 million, is the industrial center of Brazil and the largest city in South America. It employs the largest labor force in Latin America, with more than 400,000 workers, and it has the highest standard of living in Brazil. It is also home to the largest number of Japanese in the world outside Japan.

South America's biggest cathedral

The **Catedralo Metropolitano of São Paulo** is the largest cathedral—and one of the most beautiful—in South America. The vaulted neo-Gothic structure holds 8,000 worshipers and dominates the **Praça da Sé** (Cathedral Plaza), where fountains gurgle and Paulistas gather. The cathedral's extensive underground crypt contains the remains of past ecclesiastical figures.

South America's biggest zoo

São Paulo's **zoo**, *ave. Miguel Estefano 4241, Auga Funda; tel. (55-11)276-0811,* is the largest in South America, with more than 400 animals and 600 birds. It is open daily 9 a.m. until 6 p.m.

After visiting the zoo, stop by the **Jardim Botanico**, *ave. Miguel Estefano 3031,* an orchid farm that displays more than 35,000 species. It is open Tuesday through Sunday 9 a.m. until 5 p.m.

South America's best art gallery

The **Museu de Arte de São Paulo**, *ave. Paulista 1578; tel. (55-11)251-5644,* has a collection of Western art from the Gothic Age to the present, the only such collection in South America. The museum has Raphael's *Resurrection,* painted when the 16th-century artist was just 17, a Rembrandt self-portrait, and 13 works by Renoir.

The closest thing to Japan in the Americas

São Paulo's **Liberdade**—south of Praça da Sé along Praça da Liberdade and rua Galvão Bueno—is the closest thing to Japan in the Americas. Entered through red lacquer gates, it has tranquil rock gardens, Japanese grocers, and herbal-remedy stores. To realize the importance of São Paulo's Japanese population (nearly 800,000 strong), visit the **Museu da Imigração Japonesa** (Japanese Immigration in Brazil Museum), where exhibits explain the 75-year history of Japanese immigration.

The world's second-best religious art museum

São Paulo's **Museu de Arte Sacra** (Sacred Art Museum), *ave. Tiradentes 676,* is second only to the Vatican when it comes to collections of Western religious art. Room after room of the museum is filled with carved altars, gold altarpieces, statues, and paintings.

The top sights

Ibirapuera Park was built for São Paulo's fourth centennial celebration. Inside the grounds is an exact reproduction of Japan's Katura Palace. Willows border the lakes, and eucalyptus groves scent the air.

Casa do Bandeirante, *Praça Monteiro Lobato,* is an 18th-century pioneer house preserved for tourists. You can see firsthand the Spartan lifestyles of early settlers, who slept in hammocks and used trunks as tables. On the grounds are oxcarts and three mills for sugarcane and corn. The house is open Tuesday through Sunday 9 a.m. until 5 p.m.

You can see how Brazil's wealthier colonists lived at the **Museu da Casa Brasileira**

(Brazilian Home Museum), *ave. Brigada Faria Lima 774.* Built in 1945, the mansion contains photos and sketches of early homes, as well as antique furniture and religious pieces.

In the old center of town, near the financial district, several churches and a Byzantine Franciscan convent still stand, as well as São Paulo's oldest building, a Jesuit chapel built in 1554.

Another attraction (so to speak) is the largest snake farm on the continent, the **Instituto Butantã**, *ave. Vital Brasil 1500,* where venom is collected for medicinal uses. It is open 9 a.m. until 5 p.m Tuesday through Sunday.

Shopping bests

São Paulo is known for its shopping. The best buys include clothing, antiques, and Brazilian jewels. The steep rua Augusta, lined with little boutiques selling native art and unusual clothing, is a good place to begin your shopping spree. In addition, the city has many large shopping malls, which offer a glittering array of high-quality merchandise. The two biggest are **Iguatemi**, *Faria Lima,* and **Ibirapueraon**, *avenida Ibirapueraon.* The jeweler Henry Stern has an office in São Paulo as well as in Rio.

A huge Sunday fair is held along the **Praça da Republica.** A colorful street fair is held Tuesday and Thursday through Saturday in **Pacaembú Stadium**, *Praça Charles Miller.* Unrecognizable tropical fruits and vegetables are sold, as well as such exotic items as octopus and orchids.

The best restaurants

O Profeta, *Alameda Dos Aicas 40; tel. (55-11)549-5311,* serves food from all over Brazil. The specialties are fish and *feijoadas.*

The best place in São Paulo for *feijoadas* is **Bolinha**, *ave. Cidade Jardim 53; tel. (55-11)852-9526,* a popular place that usually has long lines (reservations not accepted). Have a drink at the bar and watch the people while you wait.

If you tire of Brazilian food, you can have a good French meal at **Marcel's**, *rua Epitácio Pessôa 98; tel. (55-11)257-6968.* Chef Jean Durand is good friends with Paul Bocuse, with whom he shares a love of delicate dishes. The restaurant is closed Sunday. Credit cards are not accepted.

Terraço Italia, *ave. Ipiranga 344; tel. (55-11)257-6566,* has a spectacular view of the city as well as good food.

São Paulo also has good *churrascarias* (**Rodeio**, *rua Haddock Lobo 1498; tel. (55-11)883-2322,* which has a great cowboy atmosphere, is the best) and a great many ethnic restaurants. The city's Oriental section is 5 miles square and loaded with Asian restaurants. To the east is an area of typical Italian restaurants run by descendants of immigrants who came to Brazil to grow coffee and wine.

The best beds

Maksoud Palace, *Alameda Campinas 150; tel. (55-11)251-2233,* is the most luxurious hotel in São Paulo, with a swimming pool, a sauna, squash courts, eight restaurants, and a Scandinavian smorgasbord. Top-floor rooms have maid, butler, and valet service. Built in 1979, it is a modern 22-story structure surrounding an atrium, where a 1-ton sculpture by the Brazilian artist Toyota hangs. A double room is 291,926 cruzeiros to 335,269 cruzeiros ($163 to $187).

The chicest hotel in São Paulo is **Caesar Park**, *rua Augusta 1508; tel. (55-11)285-6622,* surrounded by lush vegetation. The lobby is an elegant place for a rendezvous. Breakfast is served in the garden, and at night a band plays in the rooftop bar. A double room is 265,156 cruzeiros to 325,071 cruzeiros ($148 to $182).

The **Mofarrej Sheraton**, *Alameda Santos 1437; tel. (55-11)284-5544,* is a five-star European-style luxury hotel. A double room is 293,201 cruzeiros ($164).

The **São Paulo Hilton**, *ave. Ipiranga 165; tel. (55-11)256-0033*, has a pool, a sauna, four restaurants, five bars, and jewelry and gift stores. But it is touristy and near the red-light district. A double room is 216,714 cruzeiros ($121).

The **Othon Palace Hotel**, *rua Libero Badaro 190; tel. (55-11)239-3277*, is reasonably priced and conveniently located in the center of the financial district. A double room is 187,600 cruzeiros ($105).

The best places for music and dance
São Paulo's most popular nightclub, **Club 150**, *Alameda Campinas 150, Maksoud Hotel; tel. (55-11)251-2233*, is a good place to listen to jazz.

St. Paul, *Alameda Lorena 1717; tel. (55-11)282-7697*, is the best place to go if you're traveling single. Couples are admitted only on weekends.

Plataforme 1, *ave. Polista 424; tel. (55-11)287-1234*, has a samba show with beautiful dancers. Patrons also can dance. Dinner is served. Because it's located on the 42nd floor (the penthouse), it offers a spectacular view. The club is open Monday through Saturday beginning at 8:30 p.m.

Barracao de Zinco, *ave. Ibirapuera 2441; tel. (55-11)531-6740*, is a samba house where you can dance with native Brazilians. Drinks and appetizers are served.

Salvador—center of voodooism
Salvador de Bahía is the center of the **candomblé** cult, created by African slaves who were forced to practice Catholicism but wanted to preserve their own religion. The slaves merged their gods with Christian saints and biblical characters and worshiped both. The deity of lightning, Chongo, for example, was combined with St. Barbara, also associated with lightning. And Iemanjá is another name for the Virgin Mary. Candomblé has become an accepted part of Roman Catholicism. Salvador has 166 churches and 4,000 candomblé *terreiros* (temples).

You can attend a candomblé ceremony (as long as you don't bring a camera or cross your hands or feet, which is considered unlucky). The god to be honored at the ceremony has a special costume, the colors of which are donned by candomblé followers. Men and women are seated opposite each other. As the ritual progresses, worshipers fall to the ground in convulsions, their bodies apparently possessed by the spirits being conjured up. They speak in voices completely unlike their own.

Most ceremonies begin at 8:30 p.m. and continue until 11 p.m. or midnight.

Another ritual dating back to the days of slavery is the *capoeira,* a dance-fight. This strange and beautiful performance was begun by slaves, who, forbidden to fight, learned to disguise their aggressions in the graceful form of a dance.

Traditional Christianity is also colorful in Salvador. Celebrations of regional Catholic holidays, including the Procession of Our Lady of the Seamen, the Procession of Bonfim, and the Feast of the Second of July, are elaborate.

The best place to enjoy Carnival
Carnival is even more colorful in Salvador than in Rio, although it is less-known. And it is longer, beginning one month before Lent. Participants pay homage to Iemanjá, the goddess of the sea, and don the *mortalha,* a costume made of bed sheets. Groups, called *afoxes,* dance to drums and throw a powder called *efu,* which is made from the horns of sheep and supposedly possesses mystical powers.

The most beautiful churches
Igreja da São Francisco, *Praça Pae. Anchieta 1; tel. (55-71)243-2367*, is one of the most beautiful baroque churches in the world. Built in the 18th century by Franciscans, the interior walls are covered with gold leaf and hand-carved rosewood. Portuguese stone was imported to construct the church and Portuguese tiles to illustrate the life of St.

Francis. Men can visit the monastery next door, but women can only peer through the door.

Salvador's cathedral, **Terreiro de Jesus**, is massive and also covered in gold leaf. The Jesuits built the cathedral from 1657 to 1672, before they were ousted from Brazil. It is closed to the public during Carnival.

The most popular church in the city is the **Igreja de Nosso Senhor do Bonfim** (Church of Our Lord of the Good Ending), *Adro do Bonfim*. It is dedicated to Oxalá, the father of candomblé gods and goddesses, who is also known as Jesus. Worshipers often wear silver and white, the colors of Oxalá. A tiny room in the back of the church contains creepy testimonials to the power of faith—wax castings of injured or sick human body parts that have been miraculously cured.

A beautiful little **Carmelite church**, *Largo do Carmo; tel. (55-71)243-1935*, founded in 1585, has been made into a museum that displays religious objects in precious metals and stones and an exhibit explaining candomblé.

Igreja da Boa Viagen (Church of the Good Voyage), *Boa Viagen Beach; tel. (55-71)226-1800*, is known for its 18th-century Portuguese mosaics.

The oldest church in Salvador is **Igreja e Mosteiro de Nossa Senhora da Graça**, *Largo da Graça; tel. (55-71)247-4670*. The 18th-century church includes part of a monastery built in 1557.

Igreja e Convento de Santa Tereza, *rua do Sodré 25; tel. (55-71)243-6310*, was built in the 17th century for the Shoeless Carmelites' Order of St. Teresa. It has been restored and made into the Museu de Arte Sacre. The museum is open Tuesday through Saturday 10 a.m. until 11:30 a.m. and 2 p.m. until 5:30 p.m.

The best shopping

Mercado São Joaquim, *avenida Jequitaia*, is the largest market in Salvador, selling everything from vegetables to magic herbs. You can find great bargains. The market is open from 6 a.m. to 6 p.m. daily except Sundays, when it closes at 1 p.m.

Mercado Modelo, *Praça Cairu*, is a great place to shop for gifts. Choose from silver and rosewood charms to ward off the evil eye (some for as little as $1). Or you can buy *balagandãs*, little silver fruits once given to slave women who shared their masters' beds.

Salvadore's best food

In addition to religion, African culture also has influenced local cuisine, most of which you'll find fantastic, some of which you'll find strange. It is characterized by creoles and jambalayas, spicy and served with rice. The primary ingredients are pork, seafood, and coconut.

Solar do Unhão, *avenida do Contorno; tel. (55-71)321-5588*, is in an old stone sugarcane factory washed by the Bahía de Todo los Santos (Bay of All Saints), which gives Bahía its name. Brazilian politicos and jet-setters come here.

Casa da Gamboa, *rua Gamboa de Cima 51; tel. (55-71)321-9776*, is located in a colonial house with antique furniture and lace curtains. Bahían specialties are served. The restaurant is closed Sundays.

The best hotels

Luxor Convento do Carmo, *Largo de Carmo 1; tel. (55-71)242-3111*, is the most charming hotel in town, occupying the former convent of a 16th-century Carmelite church. Guests sleep in nuns' cells, which have been outfitted with decadent modern additions, such as air conditioning, color televisions, and refrigerator-bars. The central courtyard has a large pool. Although the hotel is not near the beaches, it is a convenient base for exploring town. The hotel restaurant, **Forno o Fogão**, serves good local fare.

Quatro Rodas Salvador, *Farol de Itapuã; tel. (55-71)249-9611*, is located on the beach 40 minutes from town. It has an ocean-view rooftop nightclub, two excellent restaurants, a bar, tennis courts, a concert hall, and satellite television. A double room is 187,000 cruzeiros ($104).

The best moderately priced hotels in Salvador are the **Praia Mar**, *ave. 7 de Setembro 3577; tel. (55-71)247-7011*, which has rooms for 121,312 cruzeiros to 174,832 cruzeiros ($68 to $98), and the **Grande Hotel da Barra**, *rua Forte de Sao Diago 2; tel. (55-71)247-6011*, where a double room is 71,360 cruzeiros to 80,280 cruzeiros ($40 to $45). Both have pools and restaurants.

Niagara's superior

Iguaçu Falls, at the border with Argentina and even bigger than Niagara Falls, is a spectacular sight. One of the world's greatest waterfalls, it is on the Iguaçu River, near its confluence with the Paraná River. Iguaçu Falls is actually made up of 200 separate falls, some very tiny. The biggest is Devil's Throat, 330 feet high. (*Iguaçu* means *great waters* in the language of the local Guaraní tribes, who were once cannibalistic and the subject of the movie *Missionary*.)

To best see the falls, take the elevator down to the river's edge and walk out onto the platform that reaches into the middle. From this angle, you will see rainbows glimmering through the water.

Nearby is the great **Itaipú Dam** and the world's largest hydroelectric power complex.

The best place to stay is the **Hotel das Cataratas**, *Rodovia das Cataratas, Km. 28; tel. (55-455)74-2666*, which overlooks the falls. It has a pool, a restaurant, and a bar. A double room is 156,992 cruzeiros to 176,616 cruzeiros ($88 to $99). The **Hotel Bourbon**, *Rodovia das Cataratas, Km. 2.5; tel. (55-455)23-1333*, is also good, although it is slightly more expensive. A double room is 203,376 cruzeiros to 235,488 cruzeiros ($114 to $132).

The world's largest rain forest: the Amazon

The world's largest rain forest and the world's wildest river share the same name: the **Amazon**. The river flows 3,550 miles, is fed by 1,000 smaller rivers and tributaries, and is home to 2,000 species of fish (including the life-threatening piranha, with its razor-sharp teeth, and the candiru, which swims up human orifices and lodges itself in the body).

The forest is home to exotic animals, such as the tapir and anaconda. You'll see colorful parrots deep in the jungle. About 158 Indian tribes live in the Amazon. When they first visited the New World, Christopher Columbus and Sir Walter Raleigh both reported hearing of Amazon warrior women, who, like the characters in Greek legend, lived independently of men.

Encompassing an area of 2.3-million square miles, the Amazon is overwhelming. The only practical way to see it is by boat—few roads make their way through the dense jungle. Don't expect to see all the Amazon's mysteries when traveling down the river—at points the river is so wide that the shore cannot be seen on both sides.

The best ways to see the Amazon

The Brazilian government hosts one-way Amazon cruises twice a month on the **ENASA Line**, *ave. Presidente Vargas 41, Belém; tel. (55-91)223-3011*. These ships, modern catamarans, have state-rooms, dining areas, and air conditioning. The trip takes six days from Belém to Manaus, five days from Manaus to Belém.

If you're interested in a jungle excursion, take a trip on a smaller boat. Riverboats (with room for four to 20 passengers) depart weekly from Manaus for three-day adventures that return to Manaus. Some riverboats are equipped with what is called jungle air conditioning (cooling provided by old generators) and individual cabins. Others simply supply hammocks, and you sleep on deck in the open air. (The hammocks are not as uncomfortable as you might expect, because mosquitoes and other bugs do not, in fact, ravage the river.) The boats stop at various jungle sites, where English-speaking guides lead the way across the terrain.

Another way to explore the jungle is to stay at a jungle lodge, which can be either Spartan or deluxe. You can arrange for a van to pick you up at Manaus and drop you off for two or three days at a lodge.

Another alternative is a private boat, which can be found by asking around the docks of Belem near the Ver-O-Peso Market. When traveling on these private boats, you must bring your own hammock.

It is best to plan these adventures from the United States. For more information, contact one of the following tour operators: **LADATCO**, *2220 Coral Way, Miami, FL 33145; (800)327-6162 or (305)854-8422 in Florida;* **LATOUR**, *15-22 215th St., Bayside, NY 11360; (800)327-6162 or (718)229-6500;* or **Brazil Nuts**, *1150 Post Road, Fairfield, CT 06430; (800)553-9959 or (203)259-7900.*

The best medical advice

Take proper medical precautions against malaria before and during a trip to the Amazon. Anti-malaria pills, such as Aralen (chloroquinephosphate, 500 milligrams), are available with a prescription. Yellow fever shots are also required for travel in the Amazon.

The best of Belém, gateway to the Amazon

Belém—the gateway to the Amazon—is a modern city with vestiges of its colonial past. Nearby, at the mouth of the Amazon, is **Marajo Island**, which is bigger than all of Denmark. Archeologists are studying burial grounds on Marajo, where remnants of a long-lost people can be seen. The island also has huge buffalo farms and herds of wild buffalo, whose ancestors escaped the captivity of earlier farms. Buffalo hunts are organized out of Belem.

The newest and most expensive hotel in town is the **Hilton**, *ave. Presidente Vargas 862; tel. (55-91)223-6500,* across from the Praça da Republica. A double room is 258,680 cruzeiros ($145). It is possible to make reservations from the United States; call *(800)445-8667.*

A block away, on avenida Presidente Vargas, is the **Excelsior Grão Para**, *tel. (55-91)222-3255,* with small, rather drab, but inexpensive rooms (107,040 cruzeiros, or $60). The recently renovated **Hotel Regente**, *ave. Governador José Malcher 485; tel. (55-91)224-0755,* is an inexpensive three-star place. A double room is 119,528 cruzeiros ($67).

Manaus: at the heart of the rain forest

If you want to really experience the Amazon, go to **Manaus**. The architecture in this town is a mix of European styles and modern wooden structures that is blended into the jungle surroundings. The waterfront market sells live animals and birds and voodoo and Indian artifacts. Because Manaus is a free port, you can buy imported merchandise for at least two-thirds less than elsewhere in Brazil.

Manaus is the best base for taking day excursions upriver into narrow tributary channels. **Capitania do Porto** (Office of the Port Captain), *rua Marques de Santa Cruz,* has information on boat trips, including several one- and two-day trips up the River Negro. A one-day trip costs 4,550 cruzeiros ($1.85), including guides, lunch, and drinks. Four or more people can hire a smaller boat for 1,300 cruzeiros (50 cents) a head for trips on the river or into the small, jungle-roofed canals. Hunting and fishing safaris also can be arranged. (Because less rain falls during July to December, this is the best time to hunt.)

The best hotel in Manaus is the five-star **Tropical**, *tel. (55-92)238-5757,* on the beach of Ponta Negra outside town. It is well worth its price. Owned by Varig Airlines, the Tropical is situated on a 10-acre site, cleared from virgin jungle, running along the River Negro from Manaus. It has a private zoo. Architect Adolpho Linden designed the hotel to look like a Portuguese colonial country house. A double room is 240,840 cruzeiros ($135).

You can arrange expeditions to explore the Amazon River and the jungle from the hotel. The hotel's restaurant is first-class, known for its superb regional fish dishes. For reservations, contact **Varig Airlines,** *tel. (55-92)234-0251,* or the hotel.

Rooms at the older **Hotel Amazonas,** *Praça Adalberto Vale 4,* in downtown Manaus, are comfortable. A double room is 237,272 cruzeiros ($133). The least expensive place to stay is the **Hotel Monaco,** *rua Silva Ramos 20; tel. (55-92)622-3446,* where a double room is 89,200 cruzeiros to 107,040 cruzeiros ($50 to $60).

South America's most spectacular wildlife

Travelers are just beginning to discover **Pantanal**, a region similar to the Florida Everglades, located south of the Amazon in western Brazil. Pantanal has the most spectacular concentrations of wildlife in South America, if not the world. A tremendous place for birding and fishing, Pantanal can be reached from either Campo Grande or Cuiaba via a jeep safari or a riverboat trip. The same groups that arrange trips to the Amazon (listed above) organize trips to Pantanal.

The world's best colored gems

Brazil is the world's major purveyor of colored gems. Aquamarine, topaz, amethyst, and turmaline stones are abundant, and they cost 20% to 25% less in Brazil than in New York, for example. Emeralds are also in great supply—large deposits have been discovered recently. Settings and mountings are also tremendous bargains because of the low cost of labor.

Two good places to shop for colored gems are **H. Stern,** *tel. (55-21)259-7442,* and **Amsterdam Sauer,** *tel. (55-21)210-3123*—the largest dealers in Brazil. H. Stern offers free round-trip transportation from all major hotels in Rio to its headquarters in Ipanema. It also conducts tours of its lapidary, goldsmith workshops, and gem museum, which features a 42-pound aquamarine.

The Best of Latin America

The best of Uruguay

We believe Uruguay is one of the most attractive countries in South America—and it's certainly one of the most undiscovered. This tiny country, especially its capital city of Montevideo, is reminiscent of European countries. With one important difference—the cost of living, which is considerably lower than that in any country on the Continent. To give you an idea: a liter of milk is 1,274 new pesos (40 cents), a kilo of bread is 6,370 new pesos ($2), a dozen eggs are 3,185 new pesos ($1), and a liter of Coke is 3,185 new pesos ($1). A first-run movie in Montevideo, the capital, is 9,555 new pesos ($3). A bus ride is about 1,115 new pesos (35 cents). You can hire a part-time maid for 6,370 new pesos ($2) to 15,925 new pesos ($5) an hour. Gardeners, laborers, and washerwomen can be employed for about the same salary.

Furthermore, health care is very affordable. At the medical clinic in Atlantida, for example, you pay only 40,000 new pesos ($12.50) a month to enjoy complete benefits, everything from major surgery to house calls.

The Uruguayan countryside is lovely—long stretches of open fields planted with corn and wheat and peppered with cattle and sheep. And because of the tropical climate, palm trees, cacti, rubber pants, and ferns grow wild along the roadsides—along with the famous pampas grasses.

The beaches along the **Costa de Oro** (Gold Coast), which extends from Montevideo to **Punta del Este**, the country's major seaside resort, are beautiful—sandy and clean. The water of the **Río de la Plata** (which is so broad you'll think it's an ocean) is a shimmering silver (hence the name). The people are friendly and welcoming. Even strangers are greeted with an embrace and a kiss on the cheek.

Montevideo, the best port

Montevideo is a port city; in fact, it is considered the best port in Latin America. Large freighters from around the world dock here, then transport their cargo to smaller ships that can make it into other, smaller Latin America harbors. The large sprawling city has a single hill, from which it takes its name. (Montevideo means literally *I see a hill*. This was the phrase uttered by the first Spanish explorers to see these shores.)

The best sites

In the center of downtown Montevideo, in the middle of **Plaza Independencia**, is the tomb of the country's national hero, General Josef Artigas, who led the fight more than 100 years ago for Uruguay's independence from Spain. The tomb is guarded 24 hours a day by soldiers in red, white, and black uniforms. Try to visit in the morning for the changing of the guards.

521

The streets of the city are lined with vendors selling all manner of junk, much of it worthless. The one thing you should shop for on the streets is a *mate*. This is a gourd made into a cup. You use it, along with a silver straw, to drink *yerba*, a kind of herbal tea that originated among the *gauchos* on Uruguay's frontier. (They had no tea, so they invented one from the grasses growing wild in the fields.) Everywhere you go, you'll see Uruguayan men and women sipping from their *mates*. You can buy a gourd for about 6,370 to 9,555 new pesos ($2 to $3); the straw costs a bit more, depending on the quality of the silver plating. You can buy the *yerba* at any grocery store for about 7,963 new pesos ($2.50) a kilogram.

The best places to stay in Montevideo

For years, the **Victoria Plaza**, well-situated on the Plaza Independencia, *tel. (598-2)92-02-37, fax (598-2)92-16-28,* had been *the* place to stay in Montevideo. At one time, it was probably wonderful. But it's old and a little rough around the edges these days. The staff and service are excellent, but the rooms are only adequate. (Perhaps the most notable thing about the Victoria Plaza is that it is where 16-year-old Uruguayan debutantes hold their coming-out parties.) A double room is 318,500 to 382,200 new pesos ($100 to $120).

The Victoria Plaza has some stiff competition from a new hotel that has just opened down the street, however. The **Balmoral**, *Plaza Libertad; tel. (598-2)92-23-89,* is a first-class establishment; we recommend it as the best place to stay in the entire country. The bathrooms are large and modern, the beds have mattresses and box springs (a rarity here), room service is standard (another rarity), and modern computers and printers whir in the lobby. The manager is an endearing young man who studied hotel management in Europe and the United States (and used to work for the Victoria Plaza). Furthermore, the Balmoral is less expensive than the Victoria Plaza—a double room is 254,800 new pesos ($80).

The world's best beef

Uruguay is known for its beef. The country's cattle produce some of the world's best beef—and the country's people consume this meat in tremendous quantities. Don't visit Uruguay if you're a devout vegetarian—you'll starve.

One of the most typical Uruguayan specialties is the *asado,* a barbecue that includes steak, ribs, sausages, intestines, and brains. The best place to sample the *asado* is at Montevideo's port market area. This is a lively, entertaining place to eat lunch, especially on the weekends. The little streets and alleyways are filled with artisans selling their work and musicians singing to the accompaniment of homemade instruments. You'll also see human billboards; these men don large posters advertising a local restaurant or business and then walk the market's streets, rhythmically beating sticks or pieces of metal together to call attention to themselves.

The best hotel outside Montevideo

Outside Montevideo, along the road to Colonia, is a treasure of a hotel called **Nirvana**, located in an area known as the **Colonia Suiza** (Swiss Colony), a region populated by descendants of the Swiss and German soldiers who settled here following World War II.

The **Hotel Nirvana**, *tel. (598-552)4052; fax (598-552)4175,* newly renovated, is a large white structure amid fields of grass and flowering shrubs and trees. The view is quite picturesque as you make your way up the drive. The furnishings are simple but elegant. The dining room is superb. There's a swimming pool on the grounds, as well a cottage where cheese is made and sold in summer. A double room is 286,650 new pesos ($90), including tax and breakfast.

The country's best spa

In **Piriápolis**, east along the coast from Montevideo, the place to stay is the **Argentino Hotel Casino**, right on the water at Playa de Piriápolis, *Ramblas de los Argentios; tel. (598-*

432)2796. One of the hotel's wings is given over to the Centro PiriaVital, a Romanian health spa founded by a Romanian doctor who has trained local Uruguayans in ancient East European health and fitness techniques. Visitors to the spa are put on an eight- to 24-day program of exercise, hydrotherapy, mud baths, and massage. The cost is from 3.8 million to 8.9 million new pesos ($1,195 to $2,795), including accommodation at the hotel and all meals.

Uruguay's best restaurant

La Posta del Cangrejo, *tel. (598-42)70021,* the country's most internationally renowned hotel, is located in **Punta del Este,** northeast of Piriápolis. The hotel's restaurant, situated right on the water, is considered the finest in the country. (President Bush has dined here). It is expensive, but the food is worth the price.

Each room at the hotel is decorated differently. A double room with a sea view is 286,650 new pesos ($90) a night, including breakfast.

The best fort

The **Fortin de Santa Rosa,** *Rua Interbalnearia; tel. (598-372)7376,* is situated along the Costa de Oro just west of Atlantida. The small white fort is just off the highway, but you'll feel like you're miles from everything. Relax in the courtyard while enjoying traditional afternoon tea with scones and jam.

The best part about the fort is that you can stay there. The rooms are tastefully decorated, and the beds are draped with mosquito netting (a necessity). A double room is 191,100 new pesos ($60), including breakfast and tax.

The best of Costa Rica

What you'll find most surprising when visiting Costa Rica is that, despite all its natural beauty, despite all the favorable press it has received for years now, despite its low cost of living, despite its Edenic climate, and despite its friendly populace, this tropical paradise has not yet been overrun with tourists. Yes, there have been many more visitors to Costa Rica in recent years than a decade ago, for example. But compared with the world's other tropical paradises, Costa Rica remains largely undiscovered.

The country boasts some of the best-preserved countryside in Latin America. There are acres upon acres of pristine forest and jungle. And there are long stretches of totally deserted and undeveloped beaches, on both the Caribbean and the Pacific coasts.

Two other characteristics set Costa Rica well apart from its Central American neighbors: a high literacy rate (one of the highest in the world) and the absence of an army.

San José: the best modern city in Costa Rica

We're not going to sugarcoat the issue. The primary drawback to Costa Rica is its capital city, San José, which is crowded, noisy, run-down, polluted, and crawling with pickpockets. At one time, though, San Jose must have been beautiful. The old sections of the city are filled with large, ornate buildings that were originally residences but have been converted into office space.

The one thing you should take time to see in San José is the **Téatro Nationale,** a beautiful building inside and out. When you walk into the lobby, be sure to look up, to see one of the most beautifully painted ceilings outside Rome.

The best way to get around San José

The best way to see San José is by foot. The city is arranged in a grid, with *calles* running from north to south and *avenidas* running from east to west. However, if you do decide to walk your way around San Jose, we offer one caveat: Don't assume that pedestrians have the right of way. Costa Rica has the highest number of traffic fatalities per year of any country in the world. And when you step off a curb in San José, you'll understand why.

The best way to exchange money

San José is the best place in the country to exchange your money. And if you deal in San José's black market, you'll get 5% to 7% more for all currency you exchange.

Actually, there are two black markets in the city. The first is operated by money changers on the streets who approach anyone who looks like a tourist. Avoid these shysters; they will cheat you.

The other black market operates out of downtown office buildings. Many travel agents and tour operators, for example, run money-changing operations on the side. The only way to find out about these people is by word-of-mouth. Inquire discreetly of your host or guide or of someone at your hotel.

The best place to eat in San José

Bar Centrale, *Calle Centrale and avenida 6; tel. (506)22-52-52,* is small and simple. The food and service are good. Lunch for two is 966 colons ($7), and a beer is 69 colons (50 cents). Beer at the Bar Centrale, as at most places throughout the country, is served with a *boca,* a piece of barbecued meat and a little salad.

The best beds in San José

The best place to stay in the city is the **Amstel,** *Calle 7, P.O. Box 4192; tel. (506)22-46-92,* where a double room is 6,210 colónes ($45). The service is first-rate, and the food at the hotel restaurant is good.

Another good place to stay is the **Costa Rican Inn,** *Calle 9 between avenidas 1 and 3; tel. (506)21-27-62.* A double room here is also cheap—only 3,000 colónes ($22), and the decor is nicer than at most Costa Rican hotels.

San José's best English bookstore

Casey's Book Exchange, *Calle Central between avenidas 7 and 9; tel. (506)21-79-95,* stocks hundreds of used paperbacks and attracts dozens of expats who come in to browse and chat. Casey himself may offer you a cup of coffee and exchange gossip with you about literary and local matters.

Costa Rica's most beautiful drive

Bone-rattling though it is, a ride across the **Inter-American Highway** from San José to Limon takes you through some of the most startlingly beautiful scenery in the world, including the state-protected Braulio Carrillo National Park, dense with wet tropical forests and acres of banana and coffee plantations. Winding up and down these mountainsides, snaking through these lush valleys, you'll begin to wonder how this Edenic, tropical paradise managed to escape a huge influx of tourists.

Costa Rica's best beach—Cahuita

Cahuita beach is notable for its split personality: it has one beach of white sand and one beach of black sand. A wrecked Spanish galleon lies on a nearby coral reef; you can swim out to explore it.

The best place to eat in Cahuita

The **Cahuita National Park Restaurant,** *tel. (506)58-15-15, ext. 201,* situated right on the beach, is nothing more than a platform with a straw roof and wooden tables and chairs, but the view is spectacular, the service is friendly, and the food is good. Island music plays in the background for the student-age clientele. A meal is 828 colons ($6), and a beer is 138 colons ($1).

The best place to stay in Cahuita

Down the road from the Cahuita National Park Restaurant is a place called **Cabinas Atlantida**, *tel. (506)58-15-15, ext. 213.* It's hidden back off the road but worth going out of your way to find. Each of the 30 cabins comes with a private bathroom, breakfast, and the use of a bicycle (necessary for beach hopping). Picnic tables and hammocks are set up on the grounds. There's even a mascot—a spider monkey who roams freely. A double room is only 4,830 colons ($35).

Sarchi: the best wooden crafts

Sarchi, a small artisans town, filled with the shops of local craftsmen, exists solely as a tourist attraction. However, the wooden furniture here is so well-made and so affordable that touristy Sarchi is worth the visit. You can buy a handmade, high-backed wooden rocking chair for 6,900 colons ($50). Oxcarts, the most popular—and most expensive—souvenir, brightly painted symbols of Costa Rica's history, go for 27,600 to 41,400 colons ($200 to $300) apiece. Prices are often higher for *gringos* than for *Ticos*, so, if possible, have your guide or host do your buying for you. Haggling is discouraged.

The most developed beach

Jaco, south of San José, is the most developed beach in the country. Hotels and *cabanas* here are 6,900 to 13,800 colons ($50 to $100) a night. Jaco is especially popular with Canadians, who have invested heavily in development here. Construction is evident everywhere; new hotels, restaurants, souvenir shops, and surf shops are springing up every month.

The country's only jacuzzis

Guanacaste, on the northwest Pacific coast, recently opened its **Flamingo Marina Resort Hotel and Club**, *tel. (506)31-62-62; fax (506)20-14-83,* built by a Canadian who bought the property about 25 years ago. He sat on his investment until he thought the time was just right for the kind of first-class (and expensive) resort he wanted to build. The Flamingo is the only hotel in the country that boasts jacuzzis in some of the suites. Other facilities include tennis courts, a swimming pool, and a poolside bar. A double room is 13,110 colons ($95) a night.

The best—and most affordable—Tico hospitality

The best way to see Costa Rica is as the guest of a Tico. And this is easier to arrange than you might imagine. Simply contact **Costa Rica Home & Host**, *P.O. Box 185, 1000 San José; tel. (506)25-47-52; fax (506)24-58-84.* This organization will match you with a local family, with whom you can spend a few days or a few months. The cost of the program is 15,870 colons ($115) a day for one person, 29,670 colons ($215) a day for two people. (Special rates can be arranged for long-term stays.) Included in the cost of a homestay are meals with the family, all transportation, and entrance fees to parks and museums.

The best travel tips

Costa Rica is a tiny country; you can travel from one coast to the other in a single day. To do so, rent a car or a jeep. We recommend **Elegante Rent A Car** (also known as Tico Rent a Car), *Calle 10, San José; tel. (506)21-00-66; fax (506)21-57-61,* which also has offices in Puntarenas, Jaco, Quepos and Guanacaste and at the airport. The cost of a rental is 2,898 colons ($21) a day and 28 colons (20 cents) a kilo, not including insurance.

You can also travel around Costa Rica by bus. Buses are available to most regions throughout the country, but they are slow, crowded, and uncomfortable.

The country's only train trip

At one time, trains traveled from one coast to the other, with connections in all the major towns. Today, a single train runs from San José to Puntarenas. It departs the **Pacific Coast Train Station,** *avenida 20 and Calle 2,* every day at 7 a.m. and 3 p.m. It is slow-going, but it is also a chance to see some of the country's most picturesque landscapes.

The best of Ecuador

Ecuador is the most affordable country in the world. Dinner for two at a good restaurant is 14,330 sucres ($10). Gas is 688 sucres (48 cents) a gallon. A taxi ride from the airport to downtown Quito is 4,299 sucres ($3). And a bus ride almost anywhere in the city is 115 sucres (8 cents). Live-in maids are available for only 42,990 sucres ($30) a month, and life's other little luxuries are just as affordable. In Guayaquil, for example, a masseuse will make a house call for 14,330 sucres ($10) an hour. A home manicure and pedicure is 1,433 sucres ($1). And you can go to the theater for 717 sucres (50 cents).

Ecuador is located between Colombia and Peru on the Pacific coast of South America, directly on the equator. (*Ecuador* is Spanish for *equator.*) It offers an endless summer, with year-round temperatures between 65 and 89 degrees Fahrenheit.

It also offers good and inexpensive health care; many of the doctors in Quito have been trained in the United States or West Germany, but they bill at Ecuadorian prices.

Guayaquil—Ecuador's largest city

Guayaquil, Ecuador's largest city, bustling with activity year-round, is also one of the country's major exporting ports. Ecuador is the largest exporter of bananas and the second-largest exporter of shrimp in the world.

Guayaquil's best digs

The best hotel in Guayaquil is the **Hotel Oro Verde,** *9 de Octubre y Garcia Moreno; tel. (593-4)327-999.* Your only complaint will be the temperature; the Swiss management seems to use air conditioning to recreate an Alpine environment. Otherwise, the deluxe hotel is a pleasure. A double room is 214,950 sucres ($150).

Another good place to stay is the **Uni Hotel,** on the corner of Clemente Vallen and Chimborazo, *tel. (593-4)327-100,* especially if you're traveling with your family and want the independence of your own kitchen. These comfortable apartments are available for short- and long-term rental.

The best markets

The city's major supermarkets, **Supermaxi** and **Mi Comisariato,** carry abundant fresh fruits, vegetables, fish, and seafood. Excellent fresh milk and European-style yogurt are available from a farmers' co-op called **Chiveria.** And **Top Cream** makes a gourmet ice cream.

To shop at either of the two supermarket chains, you must become a member. Simply purchase a *cupo* card, which also entitles you to a 10% discount on your groceries.

The best day-trips

Within a couple of hours of Guayaquil are **Salinas** and **Playas,** two good weekend getaways. Playas was once a fishing village; today it is a popular beach resort. Salinas is more modern; it, too, is highly regarded by locals for its beaches. It also offers some of the best fishing in the country, for tuna, black marlin, and billfish.

Buses run from Guayaquil to both Playas and Salinas several times a day.

Cuenca, the country's third-largest city, is four hours away by car. The narrow, winding streets here are filled with *artesinia* shops. And the Old Town area has churches that date from the 16th and 17th centuries.

The best of capital Quito

Quito, today the capital of Ecuador, has the feel of an 18th-century colonial town;

much of its colonial architecture remains. It has been called the "Florence of the Americas."

The best rentals in Quito

In Quito, you can rent a new, beautifully furnished two-bedroom, two-bathroom apartment in the posh avenida Gonzalo Suarez area, near the Intercontinental Quito Hotel, for 573,200 to 1.1 million sucres ($400 to $800) a month.

The country's best crafts

About two hours north of central Quito is the town of **Otavalo**, situated among several Indian villages. The handiwork of these Indian craftsmen is respected around the world. A market is held every Saturday morning, where you can purchase the Indians' handiwork, including woven goods and gold jewelry.

Ecuador's highest mountain—and greatest adventure

The best adventure in Ecuador is a climb up the country's highest mountain, the 6,300-meter **Chimborazo volcano**. Start your journey on horseback in **Pogyos**. As you make your way up the mountain, you can make camp at Quebrada Colorado (Red Gorge); Abraspungo; Chuquipogyo, on the volcano's eastern slopes; Riobamba; the Valley of Totoras, on the mountain's southern slopes; and by the Edward Whymper Refuge, at the foot of the Thielman Glacier on the western slopes, where the British mountaineer began the first successful ascent of the Chimborazo volcano in 1880.

En route, your trek will take you across the Valley of Rubbish, where local Indians gather ice from the glacier, wrap it in hay, and then sell it in the mountain villages. Between the Whymper Refuge and the trek's end back at Pogyos, you follow part of the ancient Inca road through El Arenal (the Great Sand Pit), a vast, high desert.

Riobamba, one of the towns along your trek, is the center of an extensive Indian region. The Spanish established their first capital nearby, and Riobamba became the repository of an extraordinary collection of religious paintings, sculpture, and goldwork. (All of it was saved from the 1797 earthquake that destroyed most of the original city.) Riobamba is also famous for its Saturday market, where you can shop for ponchos, shawls, leather goods, and baskets.

The best of Venezuela

Venezuela is a land of contrast that has remained unchanged for thousands of years. The country boasts the world's largest falls, Angel Falls (979 meters), impenetrable rain forests, and an abundance of wildlife and lush vegetation. Then there's Caracas, Maracaibo, and other coastal towns, where the concrete and skyscrapers remind you that you are still in the 20th century.

The other notable thing about Venezuela is its economy, which is growing at the fastest rate of any in the Americas (9.2% in 1991).

The fastest-growing city—Caracas

Caracas, Venezuela's capital, is modern, boasting an efficient and inexpensive metro system, as well as theaters, concert halls, and sports arenas. See the **Casa Natal del Libertador**, *Calle Traposos*, the birthplace of Simon Bolívar and a museum; the **Museo de Bellas Artes**, *Plaza Morelos, Parque Los Caobos*, which has an excellent collection of contemporary art; and the **Museo de Arte Contemporáneo**, *Edificio Anauco, in Parque Central*, which has an exceptional display of cyber-kinetic art.

Also see the **Parque Los Chorros**, a lush park with freshwater cascades, streams, and tropical vegetation, and **La Casona**, between La Carlota and Santa Cecelia districts, *tel. (58-2)284-6322*, formerly a colonial cacao plantation. Today, La Casona is a restored mansion.

The best hotels in Caracas
The best hotels in Caracas are the **Caracas Hilton**, *Plaza Morelos Sur 25 El Conde; tel. (58-2)574-1122*, and the **Tamanico Inter-Continental**, *avenida Principal, Las Mercedes; tel. (58-2)91-45-55.* A double room at either is 9,921 to 12,236 bolivars ($150 to $185).

The best cuisine in Caracas
For typical Venezuelan cuisine, try **El Portón**, *avenida Pichincha*, a restaurant decorated with Venezuelan handicrafts and featuring entertainment on the weekends. The goat and rabbit specialties are gourmet delights. Dress is casual, and the clientele is mainly Venezuelan.

Another favorite is **Barba Roja**, *avenida Tamanaco*, in the Rosal section. The food is Spanish with an emphasis on fish. The decor is rustic. Try the *hayaca navideña*, a pastry made of light corn flour. Portions at Barba Roja are enough for two.

The dustiest village
Fernando de Apure, the capital and main town in the Venezuelan llanos, the vast interior plains of the country, is a 40-minute plane ride from Caracas. It is a dusty, tropical frontier village.

The best place to stay when visiting this area is the Doña Barbara ranch, a 95,000-acre ranch with some of the most abundant wildlife in the Americas, including flocks of scarlet ibis, storks, egrets, herons, kingfishers, hummingbirds, and vermilion flycatchers, as well as deer, caimans, iguanas, piranhas, turtles, anteaters, capybaras, and howler monkeys. The best way to see the grounds of the ranch is on horseback. For reservations, contact **Francisco J. Estrada**, *Paseo Libertador, Edificio La Torraca, P.B. y Mezzanina Aptdo. 55, San Fernando de Apure; tel. (58-47)25-003; fax (58-47)27-902.* Doubles are 6,879 bolivars ($104) per person, including meals, beverages, horseback riding, and insurance.

Merida: Venezuelans' favorite city
If you ask a Venezuelan what his favorite city is, nine times out of 10, he'll name **Merida**. The climate in this city, which is located about an hour west of Caracas at the foot of the Andes, is close to ideal. Merida lies in the Chama River valley, where small farms bordered with ancient stone walls are still cultivated by oxen. The roads are lined by local craftsmen who sell alpaca blankets, sweaters, and other handicrafts. Merida is also home to an impressive, though austere, cathedral and the University of the Andes.

Venezuela's best beaches
Tucacas, on the Caribbean coast, was a sleepy fishing village only a few years ago. Today there are a half-dozen high-rise condominiums and a five-star resort under construction. But the town has managed to retain its village atmosphere and its pristine beaches. You can bask on nearly deserted stretches of sand and snorkel over reefs crowded with coral, sponges, and tropical fish. The beaches here are part of Morrocoy National Park, which also maintains a bird sanctuary.

Another good option is **Cumaná**, southeast of Margarita Island, with an isolated coastline protected by Mochimo National Park. Cumaná was the first settlement founded by the Spanish on the mainland of South America, in 1520. Now it's an important fishing center. While visiting the many undiscovered beaches in Cumaná, stay at the **Cumanagota Hotel**, *avenida San Luis at Universidad; tel. (58-93)24-591*, where a double room is 2,315 bolivars ($35) a night. The hotel boasts a large pool, an outdoor terrace, a tropical garden, a sea view, and a broad beach.

Other best beaches in this area include Cautaro, Cautarito, Los Matos, Puerto la Cruz, and Margarita Island. Rocky cliffs make them accessible only by sea.

The best bone-jarring trails—the Gran Sabana

The journey through **Canaima National Park** in Venezuela's Gran Sabana is a succession of surprises. There are not tour buses, no airplanes, no schedules. There are few tourists. The only thing you can count on here is the scenery—which is world-class.

The most famous landmark in Canaima is **Angel Falls**, which plunges 1,000 meters from Auyan-Tepui (Devil's Mountain). Thousands of tourists fly by Angel Falls every year—or fly in to stay at the comfortable Canaima camp a few miles from the falls.

The Gran Sabana (or Grand Savanna) is the remains of an ancient plateau in southeastern Venezuela. Almost uninhabited, the heart of the savanna is protected by Canaima National Park, the third-largest national park in the world. Don't attempt to journey through the Gran Sabana without a guide who knows his way across this unmarked and unmapped terrain.

The Gran Sabana is most glorious at dawn. Endless treeless plains stretch for miles in every direction, and breathtaking valleys, *tepúis*, and mountains form a panoramic background. In the sterile soil, only fragile tufts of grass and stunted shrubs grow—much like the vegetation in the Arctic. But along rivers and ravines, rhododendrons, azaleas, and trees filled with orchids and noisy parrots form a sharp contrast to the otherwise drab landscape.

It is not easygoing, making your way through the Gran Sabana. By car, it can take two hours to cover 10 miles. You'll be bounced over the most rutted, cratered, narrow, and boulder-strewn road you'll ever travel. You have to be prepared to rough it. Swim when a pool appears, eat when food is available, and sleep when you can find a bed. You will be rewarded with one of the grandest adventures of your lifetime.

To arrange a trip through the Gran Sabana, contact *Teresa Xiques*, **Turismo Ye'Kuana**, *avenida Casanova, Edificio Cediaz, Torre Oeste, Piso 11, Oficinia 113, Caracas; tel. (58-2)762-37-90; fax (58-2)762-66-81.* A six-day, five-night trip, including airfare from Caracas, ground transportation, meals, and accommodation, is 36,377 bolivars ($550) per person. Trips depart weekly, and little advance registration is required. Another adventure outfitter specializing in trips to the Gran Sabana is **Turven Tropical Travel Service**, *Calle Real de Sab. Grande, Edificio Union, Piso 1, Oficinia 13, P.O. Box 60627, Caracas; tel. (58-2)95-11-032; fax (58-2)95-11-176.* This group offers four-day camping trips for 19,842 bolivars ($300) per person.

The best of Chile

Chile offers a mild climate, friendly people, excellent wines, and some of the best skiing and white-water rafting in the world. In addition, the political situation is stable and the prices are low.

The best place to eat in the capital

In Santiago, eat at **Aquí Está Coco**, *La Concepcion 236; tel. (56-2)465-985.* The seafood is especially good. The adventurous should try the national dish, called *erizos*, a mixture of sea urchins that can be quite tasty when prepared in the right sauce.

The most arid place on earth

North of Antofagasta is the small port town of **Taltal**. It lies at the edge of the **Atacama desert**, which covers the northernmost end of Chile. Reputedly the most arid place on earth, there are whole stretches of this desert where rain does not fall for years at a time. In the interior of the desert, nothing lives—no grass, no cactus, no lizards, no birds. It is fascinating landscape.

The best surfing

Surfers should head to **Pichilemu**, site of the 1990 international surfing and body board championships. Watching from a cliff overlooking the beach, you'll see row after row of breaking waves, as many as 12 to 15 at a time.

This is a primitive beach town, so don't expect much. The best hotel is the **Motel Las Cabanas,** *San Antonio 48, Casilla 50; tel. (56-74)68-10-68,* run by Eliana Guzman Lyon. A room is only 10,491 pesos ($30) a night, including breakfast.

The best of the Lake District

Chile's Lake District is north of Puerto Montt and far south of Santiago. Although Spanish is the official language in the region, many here speak Germany.

The most ambitious trip through the Lake District is to pick up a car in Santiago and drive all the way south to Puerto Montt. However, many car rental companies tack on one-way drop-off charges in the hundreds of dollars.

The better option is to fly into Puerto Montt, pick up a car there, and drive a circuit around the region. The main highways are paved and in good condition. The secondary roads vary greatly in condition, from smooth and paved to dirt and gravel. All of the roads are well-marked.

In addition to lakes, the Patagonia region is filled with volcanos and rivers. Given all the waterways and all the rain, the region is incredibly green, reminiscent of New Zealand.

The Lake District's best bed and board

An idyllic bed-and-breakfast in Puerto Montt, *Leuterio Ramirez 415, Puerto Chico, Casilla 301, Puerto Varas,* opened by two German sisters now in their late 50s, offers the best accommodation in the country for less than 6,994 pesos ($20) a night. Breakfast is served in a large country kitchen; before the meal, the sisters hold hands and give thanks with a German song.

Chile's best luxury hotel

The luxury hotels in the south of Chile cater to Chilean and Argentinian vacationers. The **Hotel Termas,** *Puyehue, Osorno,* situated on Lake Rupanco, has elegant rooms, piped-in Beethoven music, an Olympic-size swimming pool, hot baths, and mud massages. A double room is 20,982 to 30,774 pesos ($60 to $88), including three meals.

South America's best summer skiing

In Chile, the snow begins to fall in June and July, and from mid-August through September, the weather and snow conditions are dependable, the slopes are not crowded, and all the ski resorts offer their lowest prices of the year. Furthermore, the scenery of the Andes is as spectacular as any in the Alps.

The safest slopes

At **La Parva,** only 35 miles from Santiago, you can ski right from your door to the base of the lift. From there you can choose from nine poma lifts and two chair lifts. Wide-open and friendly, this is a safe place to be adventurous. Snowboarders can twist and turn over the edges of wind-curled cornices, and the miles of treeless mountains are perfect for heli-skiing.

A week at La Parva, *tel. (56-2)233-2476,* costs 146,874 to 190,587 pesos ($420 to $545), depending on the season, including lift tickets and all meals.

The biggest slopes

Valle Nevado is the biggest, newest, and most talked about ski resort in South America, with 33 square miles of skiable terrain. These slopes offer the solitude of cross-country skiing *and* the conveniences of a downhill resort. Weekly rates at Valle Nevado, *tel. (56-2)698-0103,* start at 279,760 pesos ($800).

The granddaddy of ski resorts

The first skiers at **Portillo**, the granddaddy of South American ski resorts, were Norwegian mountaineers who arrived in 1890 to study the construction of a railroad between Chile and Argentina. The first lift was built in 1937 and had wooden towers. In 1947, this was replaced by a chair lift, and in 1949 the first hotel was built.

Portillo offers some of the most challenging terrain and ski lifts in South America. Because avalanches periodically wiped out lift towers on the steep upper slopes (where the best skiing is), the French invented the *Va et Vient* lift. Also known as the Sling Shot, this contraption shoots four people standing abreast on a poma lift straight up 2,442 feet.

Two people can spend a week at Portillo, *tel. (56-2)231-3411*, for 375,928 pesos ($1,075), including accommodation, all meals, and lift tickets.

South America's longest ski lift

The longest ski lift in the country is 8,200 feet; it takes 25 minutes to complete the trip. And **Termas de Chillan**, *tel. (56-2)251-2685*, the slope on which the ski lift operates, offers 15,000 acres of challenging runs, with the most varied terrain and snow conditions in Chile. There are volcanos above, while below are thermal springs belching steam from the mountainsides.

The best white-water rafting

The rapids on Chile's **Rio Bio-Bio** include some of the most challenging stretches of navigable cataracts anywhere in the world.

The Bio-Bio is 400 miles south of Santiago; getting to the river is an adventure in itself. You travel on a 50-year-old train, decorated with mahogany and brass, that rattles slowly south and inland, toward Patagonia and the river.

The river begins high in the Andes. Rafters and kayakers meet up with it a few miles from the source, in a little cowboy town called **Lonquimay**. At first the Bio-Bio is little more than a stream, an emerald-green trickle flowing through a valley of flowered meadows and pine-scented forests.

The most difficult rapids

When the river approaches **Nireco Canyon**, the narrow path becomes cluttered with boulders. And a few miles downstream from the entrance to the canyon, rising straight up from eye level, is a curving wall of solid basalt. Here are the rapids for which the Bio-Bio is famous: the Milky Way, Lost Yak, Lava South, and Cyclops. The rapids are big and rocky, and to make navigation even more difficult, the force of the river pushes you constantly toward house-sized slabs of volcanic stone. This section of the Bio-Bio has taken its toll, and rafting here is not for the inexperienced. Two Bio-Bio rafters have drowned, and another was impaled on a 10-foot oar.

Flush Canyon, with its five rapids (named after the poker hand, because rafting here is a real gamble), also offers challenging runs. After the **Valley of the Thousand Waterfalls**, the river's pace slows.

The oldest living things on earth

Chile's magnificent evergreen giants, called *alerce*, are the largest trees in the Southern Hemisphere. These trees grow only in South America in a temperate rain forest far from the equator, where the ecosystem is different from what you'd find in a tropical rain forest, such as the Amazon basin. Temperatures are much cooler, the growing season is shorter, and plants and animals must be well-adapted to harsh living conditions—or perish.

All of these factors have combined to produce an ancient (old growth) forest, with groves of giant old trees, some of which exceed four meters in diameter. This is especially amazing when you realize that each tree grows only one millimeter in diameter each year. These trees were here long before Columbus discovered the Americas.

The best of Argentina

Argentina has historically suffered the curse of politics; its most recent coup attempt was Dec. 3, 1990. Argentine politics have been characterized by cruel military dictators, pointless border disputes with Chile, civil strife, high inflation, corruption, and general instability. But the country still has its charms.

No country in the world is as naturally suited for farming as Argentina, the second-largest country in Latin America. It has more than a million square miles of territory. An extraordinary three -quarters of this is suitable for cultivation, and the topsoil is as much as a yard deep. Argentina is also an exporter of oil and gas (to Chile), and its mines offer an abundance of minerals.

The richest region

The richest 10% of Argentine terrain is in La Pampa, the only part of the country that is cultivated. (The Argentines are careful about protecting their lands and are stingy about the areas they farm). La Pampa is a treeless plain of the central, temperate-climate zone, with richness other countries can only dream about.

Buenos Aires—the Paris of the poor

Nobody lives in poverty with the style and flair of the Argentines; even in its impoverished state, Buenos Aires is as full of pizzazz as Paris itself. And Buenos Aires is a city of neighborhoods—that is what makes it so hospitable.

The **Plaza Dorrego**, in the heart of San Telmo, is Buenos Aires' answer to the Latin Quarter. Weekdays it is quiet, but on the weekends it is transformed into a bustling antiques market. Walk down avenida de Mayo to see the **Casa Rosada**, the pink presidential palace. It is here that thousands of workpeople cheered political leaders Juan and Evita Péron. The square is surrounded by monuments. Also visit **La Recoleta**, Evita's final resting place. Across from the cemetery's entrance is the place to see and be seen for the *porteño* ultrarich. Dressed in the latest Paris fashions, glamorous people wile away their days at the outdoor cafés here.

La Boca is the city's oldest Italian section. It is also the poorest neighborhood in the city, distinguished by its colorfully painted wooden houses. The heart of the neighborhood is a touristy walkway, **El Caminito**, where painters hang out. La Boca's side streets are jammed with bakeries and butcher shops.

The best antiques

Calle Defensa is packed in with antique dealers; the heirlooms of once-wealthy merchant families—their fine china, their brocade upholstered chairs, and their fanciful English hunting prints—are for sale here. And the prices are so low that they would embarrass most antique dealers.

The best café

The city's oldest café is also its best. The **Café Tortoni**, founded in 1858, situated on the avenida de Mayo, epitomizes all the melancholy and faded glory of Buenos Aries. Its walls are covered with paintings and photographs from the city's artistic past. In the back is a poetry corner and a gaming room.

The best tango

The **San Martín Municipal Theater** is the best place in Buenos Aires to see a traditional tango.

The best hotels

The **Claridge Hotel**, *Tucumán 535; tel. (54-1)322-7700*, within walking distance of all the downtown sights, maintains vestiges of the city's old charms. (Choose the Claridge over the Plaza; the Plaza is better known but does not have the character of the Claridge.) A double room at the Claridge is 113 to 163 pesos ($115 to $165).

The best skiing in Argentina
The internationally famous resort called **Valle de Las Leñas** offers outstanding hotels, fine cuisine, and the best ski-lift service in the world. South of here is **Parque Caviahue**, on the east side of the Caviahue volcano, and even farther south is **Primeros Piños**, a tiny ski area off the beaten path. It is still relatively undiscovered, so don't expect extensive facilities.

In the lakeside village of San Martín de los Andes is **Chapelco**, which offers nine lifts, including South America's only ski gondola, and the best bowls and chutes of the region.

The world's southernmost skiing
The southernmost skiing in the world is in **Ushuaia**, where you can choose from five small ski centers. It is a beautiful and safe place to ski. And its residents are gracious. But the best thing about skiing here is the cost. Lodging and dining are inexpensive. And a lift ticket is only 4.95 to 19.80 pesos ($5 to $20) a day.

The best of Peru
Peru is physically spectacular, caught between the Pacific and the stupendous Andes Mountains. Covering 60% of the country is the Amazon basin, located to the east of the Andes; the gateway to this region is the former missionary town of **Iquitos**.

In the southern half of the country is **Cuzco**, a Peruvian region high up in the Andes. From there, the Incas ruled much of South America. Using this as a base, the archeologically inclined can head for the mountains and Machu Picchu.

The most hidden city
Several hours from Cuzco lies **Machu Picchu**. Surrounded by thick jungle, this is the only Inca city that the Spanish invaders never found (although they knew of its existence). This is hardly surprising. Even today, the road to Machu Picchu is not easy. You can make the trip either by foot or by train, for the most breathtaking scenery in all Peru. On foot, the trip is rugged, taking you along the Inca Trail through the Andean hills—but the view is worth it.

Also walk up a neighboring peak, **Huayna Picchu**, for a bird's-eye view of the lost city. Machu Picchu is set amid mountains, rivers, and lush green vegetation. It's a sight you won't forget.

The best accommodation
You have two choices for accommodation in Machu Picchu. You can stay at the **Turistas Hotel**, which costs about 65 new sols ($55) per night. Or you can venture to **Gringo Bill's**, where the "honeymoon suite" is only 8 new sols ($10) a night. Staying here is like camping out with electricity and running water. But it gives you a much better glimpse into what life in this town is like.

The best of Cuzco
Cuzco is a small city nestled in a valley against the rugged backdrop of the Andes Mountains. It was once the capital of the Inca Empire, and many Inca vestiges remain. The Spanish retained the superb stonework after conquering the country—they built their homes on top of the original Inca foundations.

Cuzco's primary site is its Renaissance cathedral, which many believe is the finest church in the Americas. It was built on the site of an Inca temple to the god of creation, Viracocha. Situated in the main square, it is a hub of activity. Here, the people of Cuzco sell everything from handmade turquoise jewelry to hand-woven woolen belts. Also see

Cuzco's 328 shrines, marvels of masonry built by Indian craftsmen. The shrines correspond to former Inca religious sites. (The Inca calendar had 328 days.)

Peru's most famous jungle city

Iquitos retains vestiges of the rubber-boom days, when latex barons lit their cigars with dollar bills and sent their laundry to England for washing. The city's main plaza is bordered by a metal house designed by Gustave Eiffel (of the tower in Paris). The house is now rusted and abandoned.

Iquitos sprang up overnight in this rain forest nearly 100 years ago, and it garnered such fame that European opera stars risked shipwreck and dysentery to perform in this Amazon city. Today, it is again Peru's largest jungle city, with modern shops, restaurants, and hotels. And it is becoming increasingly popular as a tourist destination.

The best beds

The luxury **Amazonas Plaza Hotel,** *tel. (51-14)41-01-36,* formerly a Holiday Inn, has central air conditioning, a swimming pool, a bar, a restaurant, and efficient service. A double room is 48 new sols ($40).

The government-run **Hotel Turistas** is worn but charming; it still houses the country's movers and shakers when they come to town. It is inexpensive, and its restaurant serves fine fare. A double room is 36 new sols ($30).

The world's best jungle

The **Manú national park** is surrounded by the finest pristine jungle anywhere in South America—if not the world. Comprised of more than 5 million square acres, the park is located in the Mother of God (Madre de Dios) department in southeastern Peru, at the end of one of the Amazon's tributaries. This park is so remote that within it dwell two of the tribes of Peruvian Indians yet to be contacted by the outside world. Their villages have only been seen by plane.

The Best of the Caribbean

The Caribbean Sea is speckled with dozens of beautiful little worlds—islands rimmed with white sand, coral reefs, and palm trees. Each is unique. Some have volcanos, others are as flat as pancakes. On some, the residents speak French; on others, the people speak Spanish, Dutch, or English. A few of the islands have luxurious resorts with gambling casinos and fine restaurants that draw the jet set. Others are remote, with thick jungles and few inhabitants. Although technically not in the Caribbean, the Bahamas and Bermuda have been included because of their tropical lifestyle and beaches.

(Because most Caribbean islands accept U.S. dollars as well as their own local currencies, prices for hotels, restaurants, and travel are quoted in dollars only throughout this chapter.)

St. Barthélemy—the beaches of the rich and famous

St. Barthélemy has the most gorgeous beaches in the Caribbean. This millionaire's island is dotted with the vacation homes of such illustrious families as the Rockefellers and the Rothschilds. Mick Jagger, Peter Jennings, Beverly Sills, Mikhail Baryshnikov, and Billy Joel frequent the island. They are drawn to St. Barts (as the island is affectionately known) by the seductive langor of its lifestyle and its sophisticated French atmosphere.

The island's most beautiful beach is **Anse du Gouverneur**, on the south coast. The sand is as soft as talcum powder, and jagged cliffs protect the beach on two sides, giving it a secluded air. It is never crowded.

Despite the jet-setters who frequent the island, life on St. Barts is homey and small-scale. However, it has become pricey. One of the island's most exclusive resorts is **Sapore di Mare**, *Lurin, 97133 St. Barthélemy, French West Indies; tel. (590)276173*, founded by a financier on the board of the American Ballet.

St. Barthélemy is one of only two completely free trading ports in the Caribbean (the other is St. Martin), and it sells French perfume and champagne at prices lower than in Paris.

The Cayman Islands—a mecca for scuba divers

The most varied scuba diving in the Caribbean is off the **Caymans**, three islands (Grand Cayman, Cayman Brac, and Little Cayman) surrounded by almost continuous rings of reefs. This spectacular underwater frontier contains 325 coral-encrusted shipwrecks, some rumored to contain pirates' treasure. The water is crystal clear, with a visibility of 200 feet. Craggy coral formations extend to the North Canyon Wall, where the ocean floor drops off a mile deep.

More than 20 diving companies offer scuba-diving lessons and gear rental in the Caymans. The oldest and largest on Grand Cayman is **Bob Soto's Diving,** *tel. (809)949-2022,* run by owner Ron Kipp out of four locations, including the Holiday Inn on Seven Mile Beach.

The inhabitants of the Caymans are among the best seamen in the world and are heavily recruited by international freighting companies. Until tourism became their bread and butter (beginning in the 1960s), every able-bodied man went to sea at age 18.

Aside from scuba diving, the national pastimes are barhopping and churchgoing. Barefoot Man (a local legend—reminiscent of Jimmy Buffet) and other island bands play nightly except Sunday at the **Grand Cayman Holiday Inn.** Another popular night spot is **Silver's Nightclub** at the Treasure Island Hotel.

Blue laws close bars at midnight on Saturday. Bars can open again at noon on Sunday; however, on Sunday, live music can't be performed.

The **Tortuga Club,** *P.O. Box 496; tel. (809)947-7449,* on the east end of Grand Cayman, is the most romantic place to stay. It offers reasonably priced package tours, and units cost $200 a night.

Our other choice for the best place to stay on Grand Cayman is the **Hyatt,** an incredible property that includes three restaurants, gift and specialty shops, a charter boat company (Red Sail Sports), a golf course, tennis courts, a pool, and villas that can be rented on a long-term basis. A double room is $165 to $450; a villa rents for $275 to $690, depending on the season. For reservations, call (809)949-1234.

The best duty-free shopping

The Cayman Islands have recently expanded into a bargain center for high-quality goods. Shopping centers have arisen to accommodate the needs of the Caymans' relatively affluent population—and to cater to tourists. You'll find fashion boutiques, scuba equipment shops, beauty salons, and gift stores. Better yet, prices of goods in duty-free shops are often as much as 40% cheaper than those in U.S. shops. You can buy a $7,000 Rolex watch for $5,000, a Wedgewood five-piece setting for $73, and a Waterford crystal goblet for $32.

Jamaica: the sensuous island

Jamaica is a sensuous place, a land of sunshine, ganja, reggae, colonial houses with verandas, and thick tropical jungle. The pace is slow and languid. The sexiest place on the island is the **Blue Lagoon,** where Brooke Shields starred in a romantic movie by the same name.

Jamaica's longest, most beautiful white-sand beach is **Negril,** discovered by hippies almost two decades ago. The hippies have gone, but Negril is still a place for the younger set. The beach is lined with hotels, including the Hedonism II (a name that reflects its philosophy of life). Nude sunbathing is allowed on a section of the beach.

At the westernmost point on the island is **Rick's Café,** propped 10 feet from the edge of a cliff. The water below is deep and clear, prompting thrill seekers to dive from the top of the cliff into the water 30 or 40 feet below. Try to get here in time for the sunset, the most fantastic in the Western Hemisphere. Other popular tourist areas are **Montego Bay, Ocho Rios, Port Antonio,** and **Runaway Bay.**

The most beautiful of Jamaica's great houses (mansions left from the colonial days) is **Rose Hall,** in Montego Bay, once inhabited by the infamous white witch Anne Palmer. It was bought by John Rollins, the former lieutenant governor of Delaware, in the 1960s and restored with meticulous attention to the original detail.

Avoid **Kingston,** unless you go with a friend who knows the city well. Some sections of the city can be downright dangerous. If you decide to spend time in Kingston, the best place to make contacts is the **Pegasus Hotel,** the meeting place for Kingston's expats.

Many Jamaican resorts are all-inclusive: room, meals, liquor—even cigarettes— are covered by one prepaid price. These resorts fall into family and couples-only categories.

The best places to hear reggae

Jamaica's reggae is an urban outgrowth of the Rastafarian religion, which grew up on this island among a group of escaped African slaves called Maroons. To hear reggae, visit **Montego Bay** and **Negril.** Appearances by top reggae artists, including Third World, The Mighty Diamonds, and Dennis Brown, are advertised in local newspapers. Outdoor concerts are held every Friday at Cornwall Beach in Montego Bay.

If you have Jamaican friends, ask them to take you to clubs outside the tourist areas. These are cheaper and feature smaller reggae bands. But you shouldn't frequent these clubs unless you are accompanied by a Jamaican. And don't object to the ever-present ganja.

The best beds in Jamaica

The best place to stay in Jamaica is the **Sans Souci,** *Ocho Rios; tel. (809)974-2353,* about two hours down the coast from the Montego Bay airport. It has multilevel pools and terraces connected by leafy walks. The entrance is imposing, with a guardhouse. The outer walls are beige and pink. Inside, the decor is casual—white rattan and wicker furniture on a tile floor in the foyer, overhead fans, and a mahogany bar fancifully done up as the Ballroom Bar. Rooms are $185 to $330 a night.

The Sans Souci features a local band that performs Bob Marley tunes with the same ease and grace it handles Elvis hits. When the band takes a break, the pianist in the bar, who is a dead ringer for Sam in the movie *Casablanca,* takes over. You'll hear *As Time Goes By* at least once during the course of the evening.

The **Half Moon Club,** *tel. (809)953-2211,* is near the airport at Montego Bay. Dining rooms, hallways, and verandas are done in the open plantation style. The service and food are good. Guests can use a Robert Trent Jones-designed golf course, pools, tennis and squash courts, and water-sports equipment. The private beach is one mile long. A double room is $162 to $252, depending on the season.

For convenience and moderate prices, try the **Holiday Inn,** *tel. (809)953-2485,* at Montego Bay. It also has three restaurants to choose from.

The world's most expensive coffee

Blue Mountain Coffee, the world's most expensive, is grown in Jamaica on the Blue Mountain range. It's also sold there, for far less than you'd pay anywhere else in the world (but still pricey—a half-pound bag sells for $10). Be sure to enjoy at least one cup.

The best of the Bahamas

Just a few hours from New York or Miami are the 700 islands of the **Bahamas,** an idyllic chain of islands stretching from Bimini, just 50 miles off the coast of Florida, toward Haiti. The islands are mostly flat and bordered by white-sand beaches. Only 20 of them are inhabited. **Nassau,** the biggest tourist center, acts as the seat of government. It is not particularly attractive, plagued by crime, unemployment, and resentment.

However, Nassau does have a splendid health club, the **Royal Bahamian Hotel,** *West Bay Street, Cable Beach; tel. (809)327-6400.* A first-class hideaway, this $7 million complex offers guests use of a gym, a whirlpool, a sauna, steam baths, a massage room, tennis courts, swimming pools, and a private white-sand beach. What's $135 to $280 per night when good health is at stake?

The best hotel in Nassau

If you must stay in Nassau, make reservations at the **Carnivals Crystal Palace Resort and Casino,** *tel. (800)222-7466,* an oceanfront hotel 10 minutes from the airport downtown. It is on 3/4 mile of property, with 13 restaurants, four of them gourmet; discos; spas; and sports facilities. A double room is $110 to $130 a night.

The world's best planned paradise

The best thing to do when you get to Nassau is leave. Cross the bridge from Nassau to **Paradise Island**, leaving the shabby, graffiti-stained city behind. You will be engulfed in growth as green and thick and dark as a jungle.

This is a planned playland for vacationers. All the trappings are here: quick and easy access from the United States; a benevolent Junelike climate year-round; accommodation of every degree of luxury; sandy beaches and calm, clear water; a championship golf course; tennis courts; restaurants and nightclubs; and a large casino.

One of the most beautiful places on the island is **Versailles Gardens**, located behind the Ocean Club Hotel. This landscaped series of terraced gardens stretches across the island from the hotel grounds to the water's edge. The gardens were begun years ago by Dr. Axel Wenner-Gren, who owned the island (then named Hog Island) and wanted to recreate the gardens at the Château de Versailles in France. When Wenner-Gren sold the island in 1960, the new owner, Huntington Hartford, continued to develop the gardens, adding statues, fountains, and—the crowning touch—a 14th-century Augustinian cloister brought all the way from France.

Night life on Paradise Island is Las Vegas revisited. Most of the action is at the **Paradise Island Resort and Casino,** a loud and gaudy place with a casino and nightclubs. Your best bet is the variety show at the **Tradewinds Lounge,** located within the Paradise Island Resort and Casino. The show is corny but worth seeing for Bill Bonaparte, a steel drummer.

The finest (and oldest) hotel on Paradise Island is the **Ocean Club,** *P.O. Box N4777; tel. (809)363-2501.* It's a small, tasteful 71-room place. A doorman, in top hat and tails, stands by to greet you. The hotel's restaurant, the Courtyard Terrace, is beautiful and romantic. A double room is $155 to $355.

The **Paradise Paradise Resort,** *tel. (809)363-2542,* attracts a young, lively crowd with free water sports. A double room is $155 per night.

To make reservations at the above hotels from the United States, call *(800)321-3000* or *(305)895-2922.*

The most comfortable hotel on the Exumas

You'll be treated like family at the **Peace and Plenty Hotel,** *P.O. Box 55, Georgetown; tel. (809)336-2551* or *(809)336-2552.* The rooms are comfortable, and each one looks over the Elizabeth Harbor. A double room is $78 a night.

The purest of the U.S. Virgins

St. John, the smallest of the U.S. Virgin Islands, seems to be escaping the fate of its overdeveloped sisters. Two-thirds of its mere 20 square miles are set aside as national parkland. Campsites dot the park, just a few yards from the surf.

The favorite pastime on St. John is snorkeling. One of the best places to watch the fish is **Watermelon Bay**, past the ruins of the Annaberg sugarcane factory near Leinster Bay.

At the tip of Frances Bay is **Mary's Point**, a haunted promontory. Legend has it that during the revolt against the Danes in 1733, slaves leapt to their deaths from the cliff above to avoid being captured. They believed their souls would return to Africa.

Maho Bay—a 14-acre private campground—is our favorite place to stay on the island. When Maho Bay was first built, materials were carried to the site by hand to keep the natural beauty intact. Innovative water and sewage systems help to conserve precious supplies (though St. John still must import 1 million gallons of water a day). Hot water is not available.

The 102 cottages at Maho Bay are actually canvas tents on 16-foot platforms connected by a labyrinth of walkways. Each includes a sleeping area with two beds, a living room with one bed, a cooking area, and a porch with a table and chairs. Electric lamps, bed linens, blankets, and towels are provided.

If you aren't up to camping, try **Caneel Bay Plantation,** *St. John, U.S. Virgin Islands 00830; tel. (809)776-6111,* the most luxurious place to stay on St. John. The 170-acre 18th-century sugar plantation is dotted with tennis courts and exotic plants. Cottages are clustered around seven beaches. The posh cottages don't have air conditioning or telephones. A double room is $200 to $325. To make reservations in the United States, contact **Rockresorts Reservations,** *501 E. Camino Real, Boca Raton, FL 33432; (800)223-7637.*

Anguilla—the most peaceable island

On **Anguilla,** one of the Caribbean's least-discovered islands, you apologize shyly if you pass someone on the beach. Anguilla has no discos, no casinos, no high-rises—just lots of beach and solitude.

The Anguillans are a peaceful people with a peaceful history. Slavery didn't pay here. Cotton and bananas wouldn't grow, and the workers were a strain on water supplies. So plantation owners left the islanders to lead their own lives.

In 1969, when the English Parachute Regiment landed in Anguilla to put down what was thought to be a revolt, the parachutists were met by Anguillans waving Union Jacks. The islanders wanted to remain a Crown Colony.

Serene beaches border the island. The best is at **Shoal Bay Villes,** a two-mile stretch that is popular but still uncrowded. The ocean bottom is evenly sloped to a distant string of rocks that attracts sea creatures and snorkelers. Underwater, you can look around for coral gardens, reefs of elkhorn, and star and flower coral, as well as squirrelfish, sergeant fish, and damselfish. Snorkeling and rafting equipment can be rented at **Happy Jack's,** *tel. (809)497-2051,* a restaurant in the Shoal Bay Villes complex.

The **Malliouhana Hotel,** *Meads Bay; tel. (809)497-6111 or (800)372-1323 in the United States,* is the most exclusive and expensive hotel in the Caribbean. (Guests have included Kissinger and Onassis.) The hotel has Mediterranean and Far Eastern furnishings, hardwood and tile floors, brass fixtures, and balconies off every room. The 30 acres surrounding the hotel are dotted with swimming pools perched high on the cliffs. A double room is $320.

A more rustic, less expensive place to stay is the **Mariners,** *Sandy Ground; tel. (809)497-2671.* The hotel complex is made up of nine gingerbread cottages on the beach, each with trellised doorways and tiled floors. A double room is $125.

The most romantic hotel in the Caribbean

Tucked into Maunday Bay on Anguilla is the ultimate Caribbean hideaway. With its villas of soft white arches, tiled roofs, and covered terraces that face long, creamy beaches, **Cap Juluca,** *P.O. Box 240; tel. (809)497-6666,* offers secluded island beauty. Your neighbors are likely to be crowned princes and heads of state. Cap Juluca is so desirable that the waiting list runs a year in advance—unless you're a repeat guest. The sunset sail on Cap Juluca's yacht to offshore cays with a silver service picnic prepared by the crew is particularly recommended. Other noble pursuits include Sunfish sailing, Hobie cat voyages, windsurfing, deep-sea fishing, and water skiing. A double room is $240 to $475.

St. Kitts and Nevis: the first British colonies

St. Kitts and **Nevis,** an independent two-island nation since 1983, were the first British colonies in the Caribbean. They retain a British-colonial flavor, with English inns, sugar plantation houses, and a lovely 19th-century port. St. Kitts has forested volcanic hills and sheltered beaches. Nevis is quiet and civilized.

St. Kitts' best hotel is the **Golden Lemon**, *Dieppe Bay; tel. (809)465-7260,* an elegant place with ceiling fans, canopied beds, and a walled garden. The Kennedys have stayed here. A double room is $350, including meals.

The best place to stay on Nevis is the **Montpelier Plantation Inn**, *tel. (809)469-5462,* which is popular among writers and artists. Fruits and vegetables grown on the grounds are served at mealtimes. Rooms are $175 to $350, including meals.

St. Martin/Sint Maarten: the most divided island

The French and Dutch **St. Martin/Sint Maarten** is the most varied of the Caribbean islands. It has tropical scenery and a European culture. In fact, it has two European cultures.

Sint Maarten, the Dutch half of the island, has luxurious Dutch inns frequented by the royal family of the Netherlands. Cruise ships dock in the Philipsburg Harbor to allow passengers to take advantage of duty-free prices on jewelry, linens, crystal, and cameras.

The French half of the island is more affordable (although several of the large new hotels tend to be expensive) and has better restaurants. Artists come to **Marigot**, St. Martin's waterfront square, to set up their easels. Small fishing boats pull into port with the day's catches; vendors sell their wares under brightly colored umbrellas; and travelers meet at La Vie en Rose to chat over fresh, exquisitely prepared seafood. Accommodation ranges from luxury resorts in the French-Mediterranean style to downright cheap guesthouses.

Away from the main towns, you'll find secluded bays and long sandy beaches protected by coral reefs. In the center of the island, mountain peaks rise sharply. Palm trees grow alongside orange bougainvillea and magenta hibiscus. The sun shines year-round, and temperatures hover around 80 degrees Fahrenheit. The only international golf course is under construction at Port de Plaisance on the Dutch side. The course will run across the island to the French side.

Thanks to the island's French legacy, dining is a pleasure worth taking time to enjoy. More than 150 restaurants are spread over both sides of the island. Our favorite is **La Caravelle** in Philipsburg. The entrance is on Front Street opposite the Caribbean Hotel. The romantic covered terrace is candlelit and looks out over the ocean.

The best hotels in St. Martin/Sint Maarten are La Samanna, Mullet Bay, Caravanserai, Oyster Pond, and L'Habitation. La Belle Creole is one of the island's most charming hotels, built in the form of an old Mediterranean village.

Martinique: the most sophisticated

Martinique is the most sophisticated and developed island in the Caribbean, with gourmet restaurants and nude beaches. It is lush, covered with flowers. Fort-de-France is known as the Paris of the western Atlantic, with the same wrought-iron grillwork and narrow-street charm as the European city. And Martinique (along with Guadeloupe) has the best Creole food in the region. French luxury goods are sold at bargain prices, and luxury to rock-bottom accommodations are available.

One of the Caribbean's liveliest Carnivals (after Trinidad's and St. Vincent's) is held in Martinique. The week before Lent bubbles with color, music, and parties. Each day has a special significance. On Devil Day, for example, children dress in red to ward off the devil. Near the end of the week, a Carnival queen is crowned, people line the streets to watch the grand parade, and parties continue through the night.

Fort-de-France—the Paris of the western Atlantic

Fort-de-France, Martinique's capital, is a cosmopolitan city, where the people speak French. However, only a short drive outside the city are places where you'll have to wait for cows to cross the streets and you'll have to compete with the jungle for the land. Creole, not French, is the language of choice.

In Fort-de-France, seek out the tiny bakeries, where French pastries and breads are sold at reasonable prices. Don't miss the **Pre-Columbian Art Museum**, *rue de la Liberté*, and the nearby **Schoelcher Library**, with a statue of the local abolitionist (who was from Alsace). Along **rue Victor Hugo** are shops selling island crafts and paintings and French imports.

The island's best beaches

Martinique has both silvery beaches and rocky cliffs. Inland are rain forests and a volcano. The island's most appealing beaches, as well as several petrified wood savanna forests, are in **Ste. Anne**. The church in the center of town is planted with beautiful tamarind trees. Ste. Anne has two good restaurants: Chez Jack and l'Etoile de Mer.

Off Martinique's coasts are the wrecks of 13 ships, which can be explored by scuba divers. For equipment, visit the Carib Scuba Club in Carbet.

Martinique's most powerful mountain

Climb Martinique's extinct volcano, **Mount Pelée**. Ask for a guide at the town hall. Needless to say, the view from the mountain is spectacular. For a glimpse of the fierce power of Mount Pelée, visit the ruins of the town of St. Pierre, destroyed by the volcano in 1902.

The island's most famous resident

La Pagerie, on the Southwest Peninsula, is the birthplace of Empress Josephine. A museum here contains mementos and love letters to her from Napoleon. It is open Tuesdays to Sundays from 9 a.m. to 5:30 p.m. The entrance fee is FFr15 ($2.80).

Martinique's best digs

The best place to stay in Martinique is **Hôtel Plantation de Leyritz**, *Basse-Pointe; tel. (596)785-392,* an isolated 18th-century French-colonial plantation that has been made into a hotel with a first-class health spa that offers beauty and health therapy, horseback riding, and French food. A double room is $130.

Trinidad—the Caribbean's best Carnival

Trinidad—a cosmopolitan island, oil-rich and industrialized—rivals Rio as host of the world's best Carnival. Its Carnival parades have developed into an art form as carefully choreographed and costumed as any Broadway musical. They have casts of thousands.

Participants in Trinidad's spectacular parades are grouped into theme bands. As many as 3,000 people can be part of one costume band, while steel bands have 80 to 100 musicians, playing up to 500 steel pans.

The steel band competition begins about three weeks before Carnival and culminates on the Saturday before, when the champions are chosen from the island's 100-odd bands. The musicians are so talented (and their drums so well-tuned) that they have been known to play classical symphonies with expertise.

The Carnival activities climax in the big parade on Shrove Tuesday. Revelers work themselves into a frenzy and join the bands in their dances.

For information on Carnival, contact the **Trinidad and Tobago Tourist Board**, *25 W. 43rd St., Suite 1508, New York, NY 10036; (212)719-0540.*

The best place to stay in Trinidad and Tobago is at the **Man of War Cottages**, *Charlotteville; tel. (809)660-4327.* This facility offers truly exceptional accommodation right in the rain forest. Bird-watching and hiking are at your fingertips. A double room starts at $45 a night.

St. Vincent—Trinidad's biggest rival

The island of St. Vincent in the British Isles is the place to go for the last Carnival of the year, known as *Vincy Mas*. It's a 10-day kaleidoscope of color, music, costumes, and street dancing, held every June, when visitors from all over the world descend on this tiny nation to indulge in all the glitter and pageantry.

Originally a Christian celebration, Vincy Mas used to be held just prior to Lent. Like other Carnivals, it was the last hurrah before the 40-day period of fasting and penitence in February and March. By the 1960s, St. Vincent's Carnival had grown into a more elaborate fête featuring costumed bands meant to depict various cultures. By 1977, when the celebration's date was switched to the week preceding the first Monday in July, all religious ties had dissolved.

For information on how to plan your Carnival visit, contact the **St. Vincent & The Grenadines Department of Tourism**, *P.O. Box 834, Kingstown, St. Vincent, B.W.I.; tel. (809)457-1502.*

The Grenadines—the Tahiti of the Caribbean

St. Vincent and the **Grenadine Islands** are billed as the Tahiti of the Caribbean, because of their tropical beauty. Here, Captain Bligh brought the breadfruit that survived the mutiny on the *Bounty*. The 100 islands making up the Grenadines are connected by local mail boats, and all offer inexpensive accommodation.

Mustique is the Grenadine hideout of celebrities, including Princess Margaret. Try the **Cotton House**, *tel. (809)456-4777,* a hotel in an 18th-century cotton warehouse built of stone and coral. Rooms are expensive, though—about $475 a night in winter. The hotel restaurant, Roft, and Basil's Bar are good.

The easiest—and cheapest—Caribbean destination

Puerto Rico boasts the most extensive air service in the Caribbean, with daily flights from all major North American cities. And because it is a U.S. territory, American visitors don't have to worry about passports or changing money.

The island's beaches are lined with modern, self-contained resorts, as well as budget hotels and charming guesthouses. But the island also has a huge modern city with a historic core—**San Juan**. Old San Juan, a cluster of cobblestoned Spanish streets with old houses and churches, is built in and around a fort. The city offers posh boutiques, horse races, cockfights (if your tastes run in this direction), casinos, flamenco dancing, Las Vegas-style shows, discos, and brothels.

The most historic hotel in San Juan

El Convento, *100 Cristo St., P.O. Box 1048, San Juan; tel. (809)723-9020,* is in a beautiful Spanish-style building with many antiques but modern facilities. A convent dating from 1600, it is a historic landmark in Old San Juan, now restored with most of the original architecture, tiles, and beams left intact. A double room is $95 a night.

Puerto Rico's best town

One of Puerto Rico's most charming towns is **Rincon**, on the unspoiled southwest coast. A friendly fishing town, it draws American retirees, with its easygoing pace and low prices. Panoramic roads curve down from the green hilltop farms to the Caribbean beaches. Trade winds from the east dump moisture on the 4,500-foot-high rain forest. In the morning, you can help fishermen pull their nets onto the beach. While the main plaza has a supermarket, a bakery, a tropical bar, and restaurants, the town does not have high-rise hotels, casinos, gourmet food, fancy boutiques, or tourists.

Rincon's beach is shaded by palm trees and backed by squatters' shacks surrounded by mango, banana, citrus, papaya, and breadfruit trees.

In 1987, Rincon was blessed with a *parador*—a government-owned country inn. For information, call *(800)443-0266.*

The best hotel in town is the **Villa Antonio**, *P.O. Box 68, Route 115, Rincon, PR 00743; tel. (809)823-2645,* which has rooms starting at $53 a night.

Puerto Rico's best-kept secret

Puerto Rico's best-kept secret is **Vieques**, a little-known 21-mile-long island due east of the big island. A U.S. naval base is located here, and from time to time bomb tests are held.

Despite this, Vieques is a nice vacation cove. Wild horses and cattle roam the roads, hills, and empty beaches. Small boats cruise **Phosphorescent Bay** on moonless nights, allowing you to see the brilliant streaks emitted by phosphorescent organisms. Mahogany and rubber trees reach through the ceiling of the small rain forest. And white-sand beaches, some near colorful coral reefs, slip into clear calm waters.

Home to 8,000 Spanish-speaking natives and 100 U.S. sailors and Marines, Vieques is an informal, low-key, and low-cost hideaway. You can hire a ketch for scuba diving through **Vieques Divers** in Esperanza for $40 per person, including food and drinks.

To get to Vieques, either take a plane from San Juan or drive from San Juan to Fajardo and then take the ferry to Vieques. For information, call *(809)741-8198.* For information about a camping site on the island, call *(809)722-1551.*

The most central place to stay is **Parador Villa Esperanza**, *tel. (809)741-8675,* in the little fishing village of Esperanza. Double rooms are $65 a night. The marina has mooring facilities and tennis courts. To the right of the front door is restaurant row.

Landlubbers might prefer **Casa del Frances**, *P.O. Box 458, Vieques, PR 00765; tel. (809)741-3751,* a guesthouse that features horseback riding. This former plantation has French doors, pillars, balconies, an atrium, a large pool, and an outdoor bar with tropical plantings. It is a mile or so from the beach and Esperanza. Winter rates are $143 a night for a double room, including breakfast.

Haiti: the most exotic island

It's unfortunate **Haiti** is politically unstable and dreadfully poor, because it is the most unique island in the Caribbean. The Haitians' exotic culture is a blend of French, African, and voodoo traditions. You can see African dances, attend one of the most colorful Mardi Gras celebrations, and indulge in Creole feasts. Accommodation ranges from luxury villas and antique mansions to quaint hostelries, including **Habitation Leclerc**, the West Indian palace of Napoleon's sister Pauline. Jackie Onassis and Catherine Deneuve have stayed here. **Cap Haitien** is one of the most beautiful cities in the West Indies, with artists' studios and a port.

The voodoo capital

Haiti's dramatic mountains and flawless black and white beaches set the stage for the true drama of the island: voodoo. Superstition and ritual abound, even among the most educated inhabitants. Haitians believe the island gods are all around you, moving through the air and living in the mountains, rivers, seas, rocks, caves, and sacred trees.

Spirit-worship rituals are performed by priests or priestesses, known by their followers as *hungans*. Accompanied by the hypnotizing rhythm of sacred drums, bells, and rattles, the *hungans* dance and chant, beckoning the spirits to possess them and their followers.

The climax of these ceremonies is always the blood sacrifice, when an animal's sacred powers are believed to be released. The adorned and painted animal, typically a chicken, is mutilated, dismembered, and placed on the altar as an offering to the gods. Sometimes the blood is collected and drunk by the worshipers to sate the thirst of the spirit.

As the frenzy of the drumbeats and the singing increases, the believers become possessed, and their bodies begin to convulse and contort. Once the believers are in the trance state, the spirits speak through them, giving advice and threatening evildoers in the assembly.

To display the miraculous powers of the spirits, called *loas,* the possessed may repeatedly stab themselves, handle red-hot coals or bars of iron, or eat broken glass, apparently causing themselves no harm.

If you would like to see a voodoo ceremony, ask for information at your hotel or from your travel agent.

Magical nights

Haiti's best hotel is the **Grand Hotel Oloffson,** *Port-au-Prince; tel. (509)234000,* where rooms are named after celebrities who have stayed in them—Mick Jagger, Marlon Brando, Graham Greene, and Anne Bancroft. A double room is $59 to $99 a night.

If you want a good, and extremely inexpensive, hotel with attentive service and a comfortable atmosphere, stay at the **Pension Craft,** *Place de l'Eglise, Jacmel; tel. (509)882641.* A double room is $35 to $52 a night.

The Dominican Republic—the first settlement

Columbus called the **Dominican Republic** the most beautiful island in the world when he landed here in 1492. One year later, his brother Bartholomeo established here the first permanent European settlement in the Americas, New Isabella (known today as Santo Domingo). Historic monuments, monasteries, and fortresses remain from the colonial days, giving the island a Spanish air.

The Dominican Republic covers 1,900 square miles, approximately two-thirds of the island of **Hispaniola,** which it shares with Haiti. It has lovely beaches, lively night life, excellent restaurants, and many hotels. The tallest mountains in the Caribbean (more than 10,000 feet) are here.

Santo Domingo, the oldest city

Santo Domingo, the capital of the Dominican Republic, is the New World's oldest European-style city. It has one of the largest botanical parks in the world and an enormous zoo. Visit the **Casas Reales Museum,** downtown, to see treasures recovered from the *Concepcion,* a 16th-century Spanish galleon. The cathedral, **Santa Maria la Menor,** is also worth seeing. The **National Pantheon,** *Calle Las Damas,* houses the bodies of the country's heroes and martyrs.

The **Alcazar,** often called the Columbus Fortress Palace, was home to Don Diego Columbus (Christopher's son) from 1509 to 1516. It was restored in 1957.

The city's most unusual restaurant is the **Meson de la Cava,** *Paseo de los Indios; tel. (809)533-2818,* located in a cave with stalactites and stalagmites.

Another unusual restaurant is **La Roca,** *tel. (809)586-2898,* in the town of Sosua, originally settled by Marranos (hidden Jews who pretended to be Catholics). The cuisine is similar to the dishes of Ladino Jews (who speak a form of Spanish) in Greece and Turkey.

One of the best and least expensive places to stay in Santo Domingo is the 16th-century **Hostal Nicolas de Ovando,** *53 Calle las Damas, Santo Domingo; tel. (809)687-3101.* A double room is $55 a night.

The Caribbean at its most posh

The poshest resort in all the Caribbean is the **Casa de Campo,** *tel. (809)523-3333,* at La Romana in the Dominican Republic. Frank Lloyd Wright designed the main building, and the interior was designed by Oscar de la Renta. Celebrities, including de la Renta, have private mansions on the grounds.

Accommodations at the resort include private villas along the golf course and sea. Waitresses wear long white gowns with pink bows, and you can hire a horse and buggy to take you dining. The nephew of the maharaja of Jodhpur introduced polo to the Dominican Republic, and you'll find the best riding horses in the Caribbean at the Casa de Campo resort. A double room is $255 a night.

Curaçao—the best of Holland in the Caribbean

Curaçao, the largest island in the Netherlands Antilles, is a bit of old Holland in the New World. **Willemstad**, the capital, resembles Amsterdam, complete with canals and 17th-century canal houses; the tallest pontoon bridge in the Caribbean (named after Queen Juliana); Indonesian restaurants; and a museum featuring wooden shoes and Delft tiles.

History buffs should visit the Willemstad forts. **Fort Nassau** is situated in the ramparts above town. **Fort Amsterdam**, on the sea, is the site of the Governor's Palace and the 18th-century Dutch Reformed Church, which still has an English cannonball embedded in its walls.

See **Ronde Klip** in northeast Curaçao, a privately owned *landuis*, or plantation, and **Jan Kok Landhuis**, built in 1650 and used as a restaurant.

The prettiest natural sight in Curaçao is in **St. Christoffelberg**, where wild orchids grow. (You have to climb 1,213 feet to the highest spot on the island to see the flowers.)

The oldest Jewish settlement in the New World

The Dutch tradition of religious tolerance spread early to the New World, and in 1651 a group of Jews established the oldest Jewish settlement in the Americas on this island. Services are held Friday nights and Saturday mornings at the synagogue, **Congregation Mikve Israel-Emanuel**, near Schottegat Harbor. Also visit the Jewish graveyard, **Beth Haim**, also the oldest in the Americas.

The most exotic cuisine

Curaçao features a mélange of Dutch, Latin American, and Indonesian cuisines.

Outside Willemstad, on the western tip of the island, is **Westpunt**, a fishing port, the place to go for excellent seafood restaurants, including **Jaanchie's** and **Playa Forti**. Dutch-French food is served at **De Taveerne**, not far from Willemstad, in an 18th-century manor house complete with antiques of the period.

Saba: the most scenic

Although **Saba**, a five-square-mile volcanic island, has no beaches, it is incredibly scenic. Twenty-eight miles from St. Martin in the Netherlands Antilles, this rugged, mountainous island is a wall of jagged black and gray rock that shoots up 3,000 feet from the white caps of the surf. Its summit is lost in the clouds. Roads snake through picturesque villages with such names as Hell's Gate, Windwardside, and The Bottom. Small white houses with red-tile roofs peek through the thick tropical vegetation produced by the rich volcanic soil. Because most of the houses are built on slopes, each one has a magnificent view. Cultivated crops cut into the sides of steep hills like steps.

Saba has no casinos and no high-rises, and you won't find air conditioning. But lush rain forests hug the mountainsides, mist shrouds the summits, and gabled Dutch architecture distinguishes the small towns. If you stay overnight, the local radio station probably will announce your visit.

Saba is world-famous for its scuba diving, with more than 25 different diving areas. Diving instruction and certification are offered at **Saba Deep**, a diving shop at the LAI Chance Harbor, which is owned and operated by two Americans.

After all that exercise, you'll want a good meal. Try **Scout's Place** or **Lime Time**. Local specialties are curried barbecued goat and lobster.

Saba's most popular hotel is **The Captain's Quarters**, *tel. (599-4)2201,* formerly the residence of a famous Saban sea captain. This comfortable hotel has one of the few swimming pools on the island. The food at the restaurant is delicious and moderately priced.

Aruba—the world's most beautiful beaches

The southwest coast of the island of Aruba is fringed by seven miles of white-sand beaches, considered the most beautiful in the world. In fact, *Sports Illustrated* was so impressed with the beaches of Aruba that it featured them in past Swimsuit Issues. For information on the island, contact the **Aruba Tourism Authority,** *P.O. Box 1019, L.G. Smith Blvd. 172, Eagle Beach, Aruba; tel. (297-8)23777.*

Aruba's best beds

The **Hyatt Regency Hotel,** *Palm Beach; (800)233-1234, fax (297-8)21682,* is an elegant and dramatic-looking hotel. A double room starts at $120. Also outstanding are the **Sonesta Hotel Beach Club and Casino,** *Oranjestad; tel. (297-8)36000,* and the **La Cabana All-Suite Hotel,** *Eagle Beach; tel. (297-8)39000.*

The best place to eat

The **Waterfront,** *Swain Wharf; tel. (297-8)35858,* is an upscale seafood restaurant. It's a good idea to make reservations.

Montserrat—the best refuge

Montserrat is a lush green island that was colonized primarily by Irish Catholics from nearby St. Kitts in the early 17th century. (Because of its Irish heritage, Montserrat is known as the Emerald Isle. It is now a British colony, but Irish influences remain.)

In the 17th century, Montserrat became known as a safe place to avoid Protestant persecution, and it drew Catholic refugees from neighboring islands and Virginia. The most important heritage left by religious dissent on Montserrat is a sense of privacy and freedom.

Plymouth, the island's largest town, is remarkably quiet. Chickens cross the road here as often as do people. Shops along **Parliament Street** sell handmade cotton goods and local fruits. Stop by **Anthony's Church** to see its exquisite interior, as well as the 200-year-old tamarind tree outside. Try Montserrat's rum liqueur punch at **Perk's Factory.**

Montserrat's black-sand beaches (which set it apart from other Caribbean islands) were formed from volcanic ash. The only white-sand beach is also one of the best (and least accessible): **Rendezvous Beach.** (The other beaches are gray.) To get to the beach, board a local charter from the **Vue Point Hotel,** *tel. (809)491-5210.* The Vue Point is also a lovely place to stay; a double room is $166 to $236.

Montserrat has miles of hiking trails across its mountains. The most spectacular is the one to the **Great Alps Waterfall,** a 70-foot cascade. A slightly more difficult walk takes you along **Galway's Soufrère,** where water bubbles out of the ground.

The world's best recording studio

Rock stars Elton John, Phil Collins, Sting, Stevie Wonder, Duran Duran, Paul McCartney, and James Taylor have been drawn to Montserrat by George Martin's recording studio, **Air Studios,** recognized as one of the best in the world.

Bermuda—a perfect family getaway

Although most people visit the Caribbean to lie in the sun, this may not be your primary objective if you are traveling with children. If you want to travel in the Caribbean—and you plan to have your family in tow—head for Bermuda, the best place in the Caribbean to entertain kids. Following is a guide to the best things on Bermuda to do with your family.

➤ Ride the ferry. Ferries run from Hamilton Harbor to Somerset and the Royal Naval

Dockyard, at the southern tip of the island. They depart Hamilton from 6:15 a.m. until 6 p.m. Monday through Friday, 8:50 a.m. until 11 p.m. Saturday. The ride to the Dockyard takes an hour and costs $1. This is one of the best ways to see the harbor and the southern section of the island. And children are welcome.

➤ Take the bus to St. George's, at the other end of the island. This is the most historical spot in Bermuda. Settled in 1609, St. George's was the capital of the island until 1815. You may want to forgo a photograph at the stocks and pillory (unless you don't mind waiting in line behind every tourist on the island), but don't miss the ducking stool, a fiendish contraption used to punish nagging wives. Any wife found guilty of spreading rumors or engaging in the crime of gossiping was sentenced to the appropriate number of ducks in the harbor. For the poor disgraced woman, it was a punishment worse than death.

➤ Take a ride in a glass-bottom boat. Many are offered; all depart Hamilton Harbor. **Bermuda Water Tours**, *P.O. Box HM 1572, Hamilton HMGX, Bermuda; tel. (809)295-3727,* for example, offers a "Glass-Bottom Boat Daniel's Head Reef and Wreck Adventure" ($20 per person; children under 2 free).

➤ Ride in a horse-drawn carriage through Hamilton and the surrounding suburbs. Carriages pull up in front of Hamilton Harbor beginning at noon each day and wait for passengers. The cost is $15 per half-hour.

➤ Visit the aquarium, the zoo, and the National History Museum, all in Hamilton Parish. The complex is open daily, 9 a.m. until 4:30 p.m. Admission is $4 for adults; $1 for children ages 5 to 11; free for children under 5.

The best place to stay in Bermuda—without the children

The **Elbow Beach Hotel**, *P.O. Box 455, Paget, Hamilton; tel. (800)223-7434,* is a jet-set—and romantic—place to stay on the island. You can choose either a spacious room in the main hotel or an ocean-view suite tucked away in the hotel's botanical gardens. A private ocean beach is at your doorstep, as well as a beautiful pool, a health club, and six distinctive bars. Rooms at the hotel cost $196 to $256 a night.

Cuba: waiting to be discovered—again

Until Fidel Castro came to power, Cuba was traditionally the Caribbean's most popular vacation destination. Less than 100 miles from Florida, Cuba is also the largest island in the region and has a population of more than 10 million.

Today this island awaits a new influx of tourists. Canadians and Europeans are already enjoying some of the most beautiful beaches in the hemisphere. New five-star hotels have been built on Varadero Beach by Spanish and Jamaican investors. Two of the best are the **Varadero Super Club**, recently opened by a Jamaican company, and the **Punta Arena-Paradiso** complex, *tel. 63917,* which includes two luxury hotels in two separate buildings, sharing many of the same facilities.

The most historical hotel

The **Internacional** (today the Oasis Internacional), *Havana; tel. 63011,* was *the* place to stay before Castro. Built in the 1950s, it was a world-famous hotel for the jet set, and it is now being reopened in renovated splendor.

The best way to explore the islands

What better way to explore the Caribbean islands than by sailboat? And you don't have to sell the family jewels to afford a trip like this. Prices for bareboats (you bring your own provisions and sail the boat yourself) range from $175 to $360 per day during the summer and from $340 to $575 during the winter, depending on the size and type of boat.

Unlike Greece and its islands, the Caribbean knows no winter. And unlike their counterparts in the South Pacific, the Caribbean islands are close enough to each other to make knowledge of a sextant unnecessary.

A charter company will check your sailing skills to make sure you can operate its expensive vessel safely before agreeing to rent to you. The company may decide to appoint a professional skipper to accompany you (at extra cost) or refuse to rent you a vessel altogether if you don't have enough experience handling sailboats.

If you want relatively calm waters and a few hours of sailing each day, consider the British Virgin Islands. The entire chain is only 50 miles long, and large charter fleets are based on St. Thomas, in the U.S. Virgin Islands, and Tortola, in the British Virgin Islands. The islands are small, with scores of quiet bays off sandy beaches. One of the nicest places to anchor is **Cane Garden Bay** on Tortola's north shore, a narrow fiord cut into tall, steep hills. You can row a dinghy ashore for a dinner of fresh lobster and a steel drum concert at **Stanley's Welcome Bar**, right on the beach.

If you are in for more adventurous sailing and more diversion, consider the Leeward or Windward islands. Beginning with St. Martin, about 80 miles east of the Virgin Islands, the Lesser Antilles island chain turns south. Distances between the islands are greater here than in the Virgins, and the ocean swells that roll in from Africa can make the interisland passes wet and rough.

The months from July through November are hurricane season. High season is from mid-December to mid-April, when the weather tends to be settled, the trade winds reliable, and the prices high.

The Moorings, *P.O. Box 139, Road Town, Tortola, British Virgin Islands* or *19345 U.S. 19 North, Suite 402, Clearwater, FL 34624; (800)535-7289,* is the oldest and most reliable bareboat outfit operating in the Caribbean. Marinas are located in the British Virgin Islands and Hurricane Hole, St. Lucia.

Discovery Yacht Charters, *(809)494-6026,* operates from the full-service marina at a new 26-acre resort complex on Nanny Cay, *tel. (809)494-2512* in Tortola.

North South Charters, *(800)387-4964,* is a good company also located in the British Virgin Islands. It rents bareboats and bareboats with skippers.

The World's Top Retirement Havens

The idea of retiring to another country is becoming increasingly popular among people all over the world, who are realizing that by looking far afield when choosing a retirement destination, they can enjoy a substantially improved standard of living—for less than it would have cost them to retire to their own home-towns.

International Living, a monthly publication that regularly reports on international retirement, has created an index of the world's top retirement havens called the *Global Retirement Index.* It examines the 20 countries in the world that make the most sense as retirement destinations. Each is ranked in seven categories of interest to anyone planning for his retirement, and then each category is weighted to reflect how important it is to the foreign retiree. Finally, an overall average, or final ranking, is calculated.

Following is an explanation of the seven categories considered in the 1992 index:

1. Cost of living

This score is based on statistics from the *Indexes of Living Costs Abroad, Quarter Allowances,* and *Hardship Differentials,* published by the State Department, and on material published by *Business International.*

Cost of living, which takes into account the cost of property, utilities, groceries, gasoline, household goods, and other expenses, is one of the most important factors to consider when choosing an overseas retirement destination.

In *IL's Global Retirement Index,* countries with low costs of living, including Ecuador and Venezuela, receive high scores in this category; countries with high costs of living, including Switzerland and Ireland, receive low scores.

2. Culture

This is the most subjective of the seven categories. It considers the number of museums and cinemas per capita, the number of newspapers per 1,000 citizens, the number of third-level students per 10,000 citizens, and the national literacy rate. It also takes into account the variety of cultural offerings, the freedom of artistic expression, and the international reputation and recognition enjoyed by the country for its cultural achievements during the past year.

3. Infrastructure

This category considers the number of automobiles per capita, the number of telephones per capita, the length of railroad track in usable condition, the number of airports, the availability of telecommunications, and the quality of a country's roads and highways. While a country's infrastructure should be taken into account by anyone considering retiring there, it is not as important as other factors; this category is weighted lightly when the final rankings are computed.

4. Stability

This measure of unrest in each country is based primarily on Interpol data, including statistics on each country's rate of reported violent crime. Also considered is each country's status in State Department travel advisories, as well as Amnesty International's annual report on human rights violations. This category also takes into account the civil liberties and political rights granted by each government.

While the United States, Thailand, and the Philippines, for example, have suffered from unrest recently, this did not dramatically affect their scores in this category. The unrest in these countries has not been widespread, and, although you should be aware of it, it should not keep you from considering these places as attractive retirement destinations.

5. Health

Considered in this category are infant mortality rates, the number of physicians per capita, the number of hospital beds per capita, available daily calories per capita, and life expectancy. Also taken into account (and weighted heavily) is the cost of a typical office visit to a family-practice doctor.

In some countries in our index, including Costa Rica, France, and Ireland, residents enjoy low-cost or even free medical care at government-run hospitals or through national health insurance programs. In some cases, foreign residents can participate in the programs by paying monthly fees.

6. Climate

Countries with warm weather year-round, little rainfall, and low risks of natural disasters come out on top in this category, compiled using data from *The Weather Almanac*.

7. Special benefits

This category is as important as cost of living to anyone planning for his international retirement. It considers governmental provisions that make living in each country easier, more affordable, and more enjoyable for foreign retirees. It takes into account property rights for foreign residents, property and income tax rates as they relate to foreigners, provisions (especially reduced rates of import duty) for bringing personal belongings into the country, restrictions on the exchange and transfer of currency, restrictions on employment for foreign residents, voting rights for foreigners, and transportation discounts for senior citizens. Countries where English is commonly spoken received extra points in this category.

Greece has recently liberalized its banking and property regulations as they relate to foreign residents, and both Spain and France are re-examining their income tax laws for foreigners. Mexican officials report that they hope to sign a double-taxation agreement with the United States by the end of 1992. Meanwhile, Costa Rica has done away with many of its *pensionado* provisions for retirees. All of these developments, which have a direct effect on the quality of life enjoyed by foreign residents in these countries, should be researched carefully when comparing one foreign retirement haven against another.

1992 Global Retirement Index

Following are highlights of *International Living*'s 1992 Global Retirement Index:

The five best

The five best retirement destinations in the world according to our index are as follows:

Uruguay	81	United States	79
Venezuela	80	Greece	79
New Zealand	80		

The world's most affordable countries

Ecuador	100
Venezuela	100
Guatemala	91
Mexico	91
Philippines	90

1992 Global Retirement Index

	Cost of Living	Culture	Infrastructure	Stability	Health	Climate	Special Benefits	Final Score
Belize	81	64	22	86	95	41	32	65
Chile	84	75	51	67	89	75	69	78
Costa Rica	65	69	52	100	99	65	57	71
Ecuador	100	62	24	94	79	91	52	77
France	57	91	73	98	95	70	58	70
Greece	81	69	50	71	92	59	82	79
Guatemala	91	46	15	49	66	80	74	72
Hungary	86	75	63	94	87	41	53	74
Ireland	53	80	68	99	93	93	92	78
Israel	70	76	63	50	92	73	61	71
Mexico	91	73	40	91	72	75	55	74
New Zealand	76	65	84	96	80	84	85	80
Philippines	90	65	28	45	67	18	59	66
Portugal	70	78	44	98	81	86	66	73
Spain	60	88	63	91	92	59	83	75
Switzerland	25	93	100	98	58	59	68	56
Thailand	78	69	21	93	78	52	61	70
United States	78	90	89	98	83	55	74	79
Uruguay	80	77	38	97	100	86	74	81
Venezuela	100	67	30	70	83	100	61	80

What it costs to visit the doctor

Belize	Government insurance*	Mexico	$20 to $40
Chile	Less than $20	New Zealand	$20 to $40
Costa Rica	Government insurance*	Philippines	Less than $20
Ecuador	Less than $20	Portugal	$20 to $40
France	Less than $20	Spain	Less than $20
Greece	Less than $20	Switzerland	More than $60
Guatemala	Less than $20	Thailand	Less than $20
Hungary	Less than $20	United States	$20 to $40
Ireland	Less than $20	Uruguay	Government insurance*
Israel	Less than $20	Venezuela	Less than $20

*These countries offer programs to foreign residents whereby in exchange for paying a monthly fee, they can be treated at government-run clinics and hospitals free of charge.

The world's safest countries

Following are the numbers of reported incidents of crime per 100 citizens for each country in our index:

Belize	10	Greece	3.12	Mexico	6.01	Switzerland	5.13
Chile	1.37	Guatemala	20	New Zealand	12.51	Thailand	0.35
Costa Rica	0.84	Hungary	12	Philippines	0.33	United States	5.03
Ecuador	0.29	Ireland	2.9	Portugal	0.47	Uruguay	1.03
France	6.71	Israel	6.01	Spain	2.67	Venezuela	0.84

	Property Rights for Foreign Residents?	Property Tax Rates	Import Belongings Without Import Duties?	No Currency Controls?	Can Foreigners Be Employed?	Voting Rights for Foreigners?	Transportation Discounts?
Belize	Y	Higher than 3%	N	N	N	N	N
Chile	Y	Lower than 1%	N	Y	Y	Y	N
Costa Rica	Y	1% to 2%	Y**	Y	Y+	N	N
Ecuador	Y*	Higher than 3%	Y	Y	Y	N	N
France	Y	Higher than 3%	Y	Y	Y	N	Y
Greece	Y	Lower than 1%	Y	Y	Y	N	Y
Guatemala	Y	Lower than 1%	Y**	Y	Y	N	Y
Hungary	Y*	1% to 2%	N	Y	Y	Local Elections	Y
Ireland	Y	Lower than 1%	Y	Y	Y	Local Elections (EC Members Only)	Y
Israel	Y	Lower than 1%	Y**	N	Y	Local Elections	Y
Mexico	Y*	1% to 2%	Y	Y	Y	N	Y
New Zealand	Y*	Lower than 1%	Y	Y	Y	N	N
Philippines	N	Lower than 1%	Y	Y	Y	N	Y
Portugal	Y	1% to 2%	Y	Y	Y	N	Y
Spain	Y	Lower than 1%	Y	Y	Y	Local Elections (EC Members only)	Y
Switzerland	N	Lower than 1%	Y	Y	Y	Local Elections	Y
Thailand	Y	Higher than 3%	Y	Y	Y	N	Y
United States	Y	2% to 3%	Y	Y	Y	N	Y
Uruguay	Y	1% to 2%	Y	Y	Y	N	N
Venezuela	Y	Higher than 3%	Y	Y	Y	N	N

*Only in some areas, or with other restrictions   **Up to a fixed value   +Can own or manage a business but cannot receive income

The World's Best Employment Opportunities

In most countries, laws protect jobs for nationals, making it difficult for foreign residents to find employment. Still, attractive job opportunities are available to anyone who wants to work in a foreign country—you just need to know where to look. Following are details on the world's best employment opportunities as we go to press.

1. Be an English teacher in Czechoslovakia

"It all started just after the revolution (in 1989). All of a sudden, there was a tremendous interest in learning to speak English."

So explains Tom Holan, who works for Education for Democracy, a non-profit group that has placed about 1,200 English-language teachers in Czechoslovakia.

While interest in learning English is growing by leaps and bounds, there is a great shortage of English-language teachers. And therein lies an opportunity for any native speaker of this now valuable language. If you're interested in spending a few months—or a few years—exploring Czechoslovakia, you should have no trouble finding a job to support your travels.

To find a job as an English-language teacher in Czechoslovakia, you can either contact a placement agency or go directly to one of the many private language schools that are sprouting up in all the major cities. It's difficult to arrange a position before arriving in the country. Most are advertised only locally, on bulletin boards for example. A good place to look is the bulletin board at the American Hospitality Center, near Prague's Old Town Square. Openings are also advertised in the new English-language newspaper, Prognosis.

However, it's safer to go through a placement agency, especially if you're looking for a long-term assignment. But, by going this route, you give up some flexibility—you won't be able to choose the school where you'll be placed. One good placement agency is **Education for Democracy**, *P.O. Box 40514, Mobile, AL 36640; (205)434-3889* in the United States, or *Dom Zahranicnych Stykov, Acedemic Info Agency, Hviezdoslavovo Namesti*

14, 81329 Bratislava; tel. (42-7)332192 in Czechoslovakia, which specializes in teaching English to adult businessmen. Another is a state organization, *Dum zahrancicnich styku, MSMT CR, Senovazne Namesti 26, 11121 Prague 1* in the Czech Republic, or *Sworovava 12, 811 09 Bratislava* in the Slovak Republic, which currently has about 200 teachers placed in public schools throughout the country. Another placement agency, **The Society of Friends,** *Staromestske Namesti 22, 11121 Prague 1,* has about 70 teachers placed in Prague.

For help in arranging your trip to Prague (and the necessary visas), contact the **Embassy of the Czech and Slovak Federative Republic,** *3900 Linnean Ave. N.W., Washington, DC 20008; (202)363-6315.*

2. Temp your way through London

Temporary secretaries, or temps, are a significant, growing labor force in London, where most firms hire temps to fill in for secretaries on short-term sick leave or vacation. So if you're planning an extended stay in London and need a job, temping may be the answer. It allows you a steady income, and it also gives you flexibility. Perhaps most important, it gives you a firsthand view of business life in Britain.

Temping can be tough. It's not for you if you need security. You're always jumping from company to company. You must be resilient and confident, able to march into a firm and make yourself at home among strangers.

The average temporary assignment runs from two days to two weeks. All you really need to find work as a temp is minimal word processing experience. If you can take shorthand and type about 60 words per minute, you can count on senior level placement and top pay rates.

The following agencies place temporary secretaries throughout London:

➤ **Alfred Marks,** *151 Regent St., London W1R 7LA, England; tel. (44-71)491-4645*
➤ **MacBlain Nash and Associates,** *Carrington House, 130 Regent St., London W1R 5FE, England; tel. (44-71)872-8885*
➤ **Covent Garden Bureau,** *8 Maddox St., London EE1, England; tel. (44-71)495-8822*

3. Be a French au pair

If you are between the ages of 18 and 30 and unmarried, you can live and study in France as an au pair. Au pairs do baby-sitting and light housework for French families in exchange for room, board, and pocket money. During their free time, au pairs study French at area schools—at the expense of their employers.

Most au pairs are expected to work about five hours a day. You need a long-stay visa to work as an au pair—which you can arrange only after you have arranged a position with a French family.

To arrange for an au pair position, contact **L'Accueil Familial des Jeunes Etrangers,** *23 rue du Cherche-Midi, 75006 Paris; tel. (33-1)42-22-50-34,* or **Au Paris-Homestay International,** *Suite 750, 1015 15th St., Washington, DC 20005; (202)408-5380.*

4. Teach at an international school

During the past few years, the number of positions available at the world's 504 international schools has increased dramatically. Qualified people are in great demand. In addition, positions are also available with church-affiliated schools, company schools, internships, and private English-language instruction programs.

Superintendents for international schools are looking for candidates who are certified to teach and who have two or more years of successful teaching experience. Some schools waive these requirements if they find an English-speaker with knowledge of a specific subject; upper-level mathematics and science teachers are particularly difficult to find, for example.

Language ability and travel experience are not absolutely essential. Superintendents do, however, like candidates who have experience in extracurricular activities, which are an important part of the curriculum in overseas schools.

Most international schools hire their teachers at recruiting fairs, which are held every year in the United States, Europe, Africa, and Asia. The major ones, held in February and early March, are sponsored by the **International Schools Services**, *Rofzel Road, P.O. Box 5910, Princeton, NJ 08543; (609)452-0990*, and by the **University of Northern Iowa**, *Overseas Teacher Placement, SFC 19, Cedar Falls, IA 50614; (319)273-2083*. For more information, contact the **European Council of International Schools (ECII)**, *Hampshire, England; tel. (44-730)68244.*

The World's Best Educational Opportunities

The best way to learn a foreign language

The best place to study a foreign language is in a country where it is spoken. You learn more from the day-to-day experiences of living in that country than you can from any amount of time spent in a classroom. Much more valuable than a class in French grammar, for example, is the act of going into a French marketplace and discussing brands of cheese with a cheese merchant or how to cook squid with a fish seller.

What's more, many language schools around the world offer packages that, in addition to tuition, include bed and board with a local family. This can be one of the most affordable ways to enjoy an extended stay in a foreign country. It is possible to study Spanish in Guatemala, for example, for $125 a week, including language study, room, and board. That's about $18 a day, less than it would cost to pay for a hotel room and three meals a day at a restaurant.

➤ **French in Paris.** The most reasonably priced programs are offered by the **Alliance Française de Paris**, *101 Blvd. Raspail, 75270 Paris Cedex 06; tel. (33-1)4544-3828.* You spend 3 1/2 hours a day in the classroom, studying vocabulary, grammar, literature, and business French. You can arrange accommodation at inexpensive hotels on the Left Bank.

➤ **Italian in Florence.** The **Centro Fiorenza**, *Università degli Studi, Santo Spirrito 14, 50125 Florence; tel. (39-55)239-8274, fax (39-55)287-148,* offers 10-week sessions that include 2 1/2 hours a day in the classroom and additional hours each day in a language lab.

➤ **Japanese in Tokyo.** The **International Education Center**, *Japanese Language Institute, 21 Yotsuya 1-chome, Shinjuku-ku, Tokyo 160; tel. (81-3)3359-9621,* offers a three-month intensive summer session, as well as classes throughout the year. Word-study scholarships are available, and the organization can help you find housing nearby.

➤ **Spanish in Spain.** The **Colegio de España**, *Calle Compañia 65, 37008 Salamanca; tel. (34-23)214-788,* offers a four-week intensive course, four hours a day. Room and board can be arranged for as little as 1,350 pesetas ($13.60) a day for a shared room in the home of a local family. The **University of Malaga**, *Calle Can Angustin No. 6, 29080 Malaga; tel. (34-52)21-40-07,* offers four-week courses at beginner, intermediate, advanced, and superior levels.

➤ **Spanish in Guatemala.** The **Proyecto Linguistico Francisco Morroquin**, *Apartado 237, Antigua 03901, Guatemala, Central America; tel. (50-29)320-406,* offers four-week courses for 2,500 quetzals ($500), including room and board with a Guatemalan family.

557

Classes are held in parks, museums, ruins, and nearby Mayan villages. Make reservations three or four months in advance.

➤ **German in Stuttgart.** The **University of Stuttgart,** *7000 Stuttgart-1, Keplerstrasse-7, Stuttgart; tel. (49-711)1210,* offers intermediate and advanced German language classes, as well as courses in German literature. The cost is DM760 ($490), including tuition, housing, some meals, excursions, and fees.

➤ **Hebrew in Israel.** You can spend three to six months living on a kibbutz in Israel, enjoying a firsthand look at life in Israel and receiving an education in Hebrew, for only $645. Participants in this program are assigned to one of Israel's collective farms, where they are expected to pitch in and earn their keep. In between classroom study, students must do their part to help keep the farm running. This kibbutz study program is open to men and women age 18 through 35 and in good health. You do not have to be Jewish to participate. For more information, contact the **Kibbutz Aliyah Desk,** *27 W. 20th St., New York, NY 10011; (212)255-1338.*

The best self-instruction language tapes

An alternative to arranging for language lessons in a foreign country is to study the language at home with the help of a self-instruction language tape program. The best we've discovered are available from **Audio Forum,** *96 Broad St., Guilford, CT 06437.* You can purchase tapes offering quick introductory courses, in-depth courses, courses tailored to the needs of business travelers, courses designed for children, and cassette-only programs that don't include workbooks or texts.

The world's best cooking schools

➤ **In Britain. Miller Howe,** *Royrigg Road, Windermere LA23 1EY; tel. (44-053)944-2536,* a popular resort in the Lake District, offers informal four-day classes that teach the art of making cheese, pâte, tarts, Christmas cakes, and a variety of pork dishes.

➤ **In France. La Varennes,** *Chateau du Fey, Ville Cien, 89300 Joigny, France; tel. (86-63)18-34,* offers a variety of one-week classes at the Château du Fey in Burgundy. Each week of study focuses on a different cuisine, such as bistro cooking; the regional specialties of Burgundy and Alsace, Provence and Gascony, or Brittany and Perigord; contemporary French cuisine; or entertainment menus. La Varenne also offers a five-week Professional Diploma course from May through October.

➤ **In Hong Kong. Chopsticks Cooking Center,** *Cecilia Au-Yang, director, 108 Boundary St., Ground Floor, Kowloon; tel. (852)3368433*

➤ **In Ireland. Ballymaloe Cookery School,** *Shanagarry, County Cork; tel. (353-21)646785; fax (353-21)646909*

➤ **In Italy. Giuliano Bugialli's Cooking School in Florence,** *tel. (39-55)581-292,* is one of the finest cooking schools in the world, offering courses in regional Italian cooking. Each weekly program includes five four-hour classes; each class covers about 35 recipes.

➤ **In Thailand.** The **Oriental Hotel** in Bangkok, *48 Oriental Ave.; tel. (66-2)236-0420,* conducts classes in Thai cooking year-round. The five-day courses demonstrate the preparation of Thai *khong waang* (hors d'oeuvres), main and side dishes, desserts, and condiments.

The World's Best Real Estate Buys

As we go to press, the world's real estate markets continue to struggle. Still, there are good buys to be had—in choice properties. Following are our picks for the six best places in the world to purchase property.

1. Charlottesville, Virginia, the United States

Property in this tiny corner of Virginia has appreciated steadily in value for as long as anyone can remember, and there's no reason to think that this trend will change. In fact, there's every reason to be sure it will continue. All indicators point toward prosperity and growth.

Few regions of the world offer such a combination of natural beauty, fertile farmland, mature forest, rich history, and a lively, cosmopolitan atmosphere. Charlottesville is unique—unique enough, it seems, to be recession-proof.

The area is best-known for its sprawling country estates, each sporting miles of spanking-white board fence and huge, breezy manor houses. Many also boast million-dollar price tags.

Today's rich and famous have discovered Charlottesville (Thomas Jefferson's hometown). But you'd never know it unless you were told. At its heart, Charlottesville is a small Southern town—and strictly enforced building restrictions and construction codes almost guarantee that it will remain this way.

A home in Charlottesville is a sound investment—and a chance to substantially improve your standard of living. Taxes are low. Health care is first-rate. The climate is pleasant. The transportation system is efficient and dependable. And the people are friendly.

And not all of the homes cost a million dollars or more. We recently investigated the opportunities and discovered many homes on the market for less than $100,000. For more information, contact **Roy Wheeler Realty Co.**, *One Board's Head Lane, Charlottesville, VA 22903; (804)979-9200;* ask for James Bonner.

2. The Valais, Switzerland

Switzerland has the healthiest economy of any country in the world (according to International Living's 1992 Quality of Life Index). It offers an excellent standard of health and health care. And it is a very civilized country, offering recreational and cultural diversity and an excellent educational system. But more than all of that, Switzerland is beautiful. The Valais region, in particular, boasts some of the world's most spectacular and varied scenery. The air is clean, and the streets are litter-free.

Given all of this, we heartily recommend this region of Switzerland as a perfect place to buy a home—with two caveats.

First, it's expensive. While Switzerland boasts one of the highest standards of living of any country in the world, it also suffers from one of the highest costs of living.

Second, and more important, it is not easy for foreigners to take up residence in Switzerland. Under the terms of the Lex Friedrich (Federal Resolution on the Purchase of Real Estate by Persons Abroad), foreigners must obtain a permit to purchase real estate in Switzerland. And it is becoming increasingly difficult to obtain one of these permits.

However, we have discovered some particularly appealing properties in the Valais that are available for sale to foreigners. These aparthotels (or condominiums) are expensive (as is most property in Switzerland), but they are impressive, with every possible amenity and ski lifts that come nearly to their front doors. Each complex is situated literally at the foot of the Alps. The views from the balconies are impossible to describe. For more information, including details on how many aparthotels remain available for sale, contact **Lee Euler**, *(410)234-0515, ext. 35.*

3. Vanuatu

Vanuatu, a string of 80 islands in the Pacific, is one of the world's premier tax havens. It also boasts some of the most exotically beautiful scenery in the world. It's like Hawaii 60 years ago, before the tourists came.

In addition, Vanuatu offers prime real estate—at good (although no longer cheap) prices—and the potential for substantial profits. Prices have risen steadily for the past five years, as the world has begun to see the potential in this tiny corner of the globe. The French have purchased businesses and restaurants on the island. And the Japanese recently undertook a major upgrading of the international airport in Port Vila, Vanuatu's capital city. They also bought and renovated the nation's top resort, Le Lagon.

But it's not too late to take advantage of the opportunities here. Real estate prices are expected to rise; anyone investing now could still expect substantial returns. And what makes the prospect even more appealing is Vanuatu's status as a tax haven. By taking advantage of the country's secrecy laws, you can arrange to have your rental income sent anywhere in the world and in any currency—completely tax free. Furthermore, you can protect yourself and your privacy by purchasing property through a company name rather than your own.

For more information, contact **Moore Stephens**, *P.O. Box 95, Moore Stephens House, Kumul Highway, Vila; tel. (678)22159; fax (678)22776.* Note that it is not possible to telephone directly to Vanuatu from many parts of the world. You must place your call through an international operator.

4. Bulgaria

Bulgaria probably would not be first on your list when considering where in the world to purchase real estate; nonetheless, this little country, situated on the Black Sea, deserves consideration. Bulgaria is well-positioned to benefit from the dramatic changes taking place throughout Eastern Europe as a whole. And there are attractive properties to be had—luxury downtown apartments, seaside villas, chalets in the mountains. You could be the first on your block to own a holiday home on the shores of the Black Sea.

Furthermore, prices are cheap—at least in dollar terms. While properties today are selling for 10 to 30 times what they sold for only a year or two ago, there are still tremendous bargains to be had. And prices are sure to continue to appreciate at this alarming rate for some time to come.

The primary obstacle to purchasing real estate in Bulgaria is overcoming all of the red tape. Foreigners can own real estate in Bulgaria only with the special permission of the country's finance minister. It's best to work with a partner in Bulgaria, who can go to auctions for you, keep you informed of the market, and help you wade through the bureaucracy. Transactions are usually made in cash. Financing is not unheard of, but if you are paying in dollars, you will have more trouble arranging a mortgage than if you are paying in levs.

One word of caution. Bulgaria is suffering fi om an economic crisis, which has bred a grab-the-money-and-run attitude among both Bulgarians selling their homes and attorneys/real estate agents handling the transactions. Proceed with caution. For more information, contact **Max-M**, *22 J. Gagarin St., Bl. 154, vh. A, Sofia, Bulgaria; tel. (359-2)70-44-71; fax (359-2)72-01-83,* or **Agencia Za Nedvizhimi Imoti**, *42 Osmi Primorski Polk St., Varna, Bulgaria; tel. (359-52)22-70-75.*

5. Punta del Este, Uruguay

An apartment in downtown Punta del Estate, Uruguay's premier beach resort, with a view from the balcony of the resort, the beach, the Silver River on one side, the Atlantic Ocean on the other, and Uruguay's Costa de Oro stretching off in the distance.

Once you've seen it (or even imagined it), you'll understand why these apartments are being snatched up in great numbers by Argentines living just across the river in Buenos Aires. This is prime real estate, among the most attractive in the world.

Not long ago, this prime real estate was also dirt cheap. But no longer. Prices have risen substantially—but it will be some time before they reach their peak. If you bought a house now, you would surely double your money within a few years.

And if you've no desire to live in Uruguay, you could easily rent your place to Argentines and Brazilians, who are willing to pay $2,000, $4,000, even $7,000 a month for the privilege of vacationing at South America's finest summer playground. Uruguay, particularly Punta del Este, is one of the few places in the world where you can actually make money on a rental property. For details, contact **Elizabeth W. Smith**, *N. 36720 Highway 101, Lilliwaup, WA 98555; (206)877-5009,* or *Casilla de Correo 56047, Punta del Este 20100; tel. (598-42)88914.*

6. The French Pyrenees

Real estate prices in the French Pyrenees represent some of the few bargains left in all France. You'll spend two-thirds as much for a home in the Pyrenees as you would for one in Provence—and about half as much as you would for a home in Paris.

These majestic mountains, which make up a huge natural barrier that separates France from the Iberian Peninsula, jut nearly as high as the Alps. But, unlike their taller counterparts, the Pyrenees remain uncrowded, pristine, and relatively inexpensive. Furthermore, the Pyrenees offer spectacular beauty, skiing, fishing, kayaking, and sailing, and a peaceful, relaxed atmosphere that is hard to come by in the rest of Europe.

The architectural style common in the Pyrenees is unlike that found anywhere else in Europe, as well. And it varies from valley to valley (of which there are about 42). In general, the quality and character of the houses available in this part of France are outstanding. For details on properties currently on the market in the Pyrenees, contact **Propriétés Rouissillon**, *Benjamin House, 10 Portland St., Birmingham B6 5RX, England; tel. (44-21)327-3654; fax (44-21)327-0438.*

The 1992 Quality of Life Index

Every January, **International Living**, *824 E. Baltimore St., Baltimore, MD 21202; (410)234-0515; $29 a year,* the monthly publication on traveling, living, retiring, and investing abroad, compiles its Quality of Life Index, which ranks nearly every country in the world in the following categories: Cost of Living; Prosperity; Health and Health Care; Culture, Recreation, and Entertainment; Freedom; and Infrastructure. Follwing are highlights of the 1992 Index.

Best places in the world to live
United States
Switzerland
United Kingdom
Germany
Japan
Luxembourg
Netherlands
Denmark
France
Austria
Belgium
Australia
Canada

Worst places in the world to live
Chad
Central African Republic
Burkina Faso
Ethiopia
Niger
Guinea
Afghanistan
Equatorial Guinea
Mali
Iraq
Mauritania
Dijbouti

World's most expensive countries
Syria
Switzerland
Central African Republic
Gabon
Finland
Iraq
Sweden
Iran
Congo
Japan
Liechtenstein

World's most affordable countries
Ecuador
Venezuela
Guyana
Colombia
Egypt
Guatemala
Mexico
Philippines
Kenya
Czechoslovakia
South Africa
Paraguay
Zimbabwe
Swaziland

World's most prosperous countries
Switzerland
Japan
Sweden
Finland
United States
Germany
Denmark
Norway
France
Canada

World's least prosperous countries
Burma (Myanmar)
Ethiopia
Cuba
Chad
Burundi
Benin
Swaziland
Central African Republic
Congo
Haiti
Guinea
Cambodia

World's best infrastructures
Switzerland
Liechtenstein
Monaco
Japan
United States
Australia
Luxembourg
New Zealand
United Kingdom
Sweden

World's worst infrastructures
Rwanda
Central African Republic
Papua New Guinea
Burkina Faso
Bhutan
Uganda
Guinea
Burundi
Laos
Somalia
Niger
Lesotho
Liberia

World's healthiest nations
Iceland
Luxembourg
Belgium
Denmark
Finland
Switzerland
United States
France
Netherlands
Norway
Canada
Sweden
Germany
Japan
Australia

World's least healthy nations
Ethiopia
Afghanistan
Nepal
Guinea
Burkina Faso
Mozambique
Bangladesh
Chad
Sierra Leone
Niger

World's most cultured nations
United States
Italy
France
United Kingdom
Germany
Japan
Switzerland
Spain
Denmark
Netherlands

World's least cultured nations
Ethiopia
Chad
Burkina Faso
Afghanistan
Mali
Djibouti
Mozambique
Somalia
Malawi
Laos

1992 Quality of Life Index

Country	INFRA SCORE	FREEDOM SCORE	COL SCORE	CULTURE SCORE	PROSPERITY SCORE	HEALTH SCORE	FINAL SCORE
Afghanistan	5	9	84	9	16	20	24
Albania	33	5	69	35	12	56	35
Algeria	38	49	67	44	20	73	49
Andorra	82	100	79	65	51	93	78
Angola	7	17	81	26	18	42	32
Antigua & Barbuda	29	76	73	58	25	86	58
Argentina	51	88	74	75	51	87	71
Australia	86	100	67	78	64	96	82
Austria	78	100	65	85	68	95	82
Bahamas	43	88	60	67	43	84	64
Bahrain	30	29	65	36	47	82	48
Bangladesh	6	53	87	40	18	30	39
Barbados	45	100	71	68	33	88	67
Belgium	76	100	62	85	69	99	82
Belize	21	92	81	64	22	77	59
Benin	4	19	54	32	6	48	27
Bermuda	71	100	71	68	58	88	76
Bhutan	2	29	64	17	12	43	28
Bolivia	28	76	84	58	30	56	55
Botswana	7	92	82	37	46	63	55
Brazil	31	85	67	71	35	75	61
Brunei	15	21	67	33	40	84	43
Bulgaria	29	65	78	69	22	82	57
Burkina Faso	2	29	57	8	11	24	22
Burma (Myanmar)	5	15	75	43	5	43	30
Burundi	2	17	71	22	6	47	28
Cambodia	7	17	85	34	8	40	32
Cameroun	23	21	42	40	10	53	31
Canada	70	100	69	80	75	96	82
Cape Verde	20	29	84	32	12	70	41
Caymans	45	92	70	65	45	83	67
Central African Republic	1	21	26	23	7	44	20
Chad	8	14	37	8	4	30	17
Channels	66	100	71	72	67	93	78
Chile	50	78	84	75	55	87	71
China	29	17	85	73	21	79	51
China (Taiwan)	61	65	62	73	44	87	65
CIS	41	75	57	73	27	62	56
Colombia	28	53	94	59	25	74	55
Comoros	5	17	55	18	12	53	27
Congo	17	19	32	39	7	62	29
Costa Rica	51	100	58	69	43	85	68
Cuba	31	17	64	72	4	83	45
Cyprus	45	86	85	70	48	90	71
Czechoslovakia	60	95	89	74	45	84	75
Denmark	69	100	61	88	78	98	82
Djibouti	4	29	48	10	13	47	25
Dominica	19	87	86	54	42	81	62
Dominican Republic	26	84	86	57	29	71	59

Country	INFRA SCORE	FREEDOM SCORE	COL SCORE	CULTURE SCORE	PROSPERITY SCORE	HEALTH SCORE	FINAL SCORE
Ecuador	23	83	100	62	29	71	61
Egypt	24	50	92	62	22	76	54
El Salvador	26	56	77	52	24	71	51
Equatorial Guinea	6	4	70	17	15	35	24
Estonia	41	71	71	69	30	89	62
Ethiopia	4	29	77	7	3	13	22
Fiji	53	83	82	57	18	80	62
Finland	83	100	30	79	81	97	78
France	72	100	57	91	76	97	82
French Guiana	12	65	79	47	30	82	53
Gabon	19	29	28	36	17	46	29
Gambia	28	84	79	21	24	47	47
Germany	70	100	65	89	80	96	83
Ghana	22	29	75	37	10	54	38
Greece	49	92	81	69	41	93	71
Grenada	38	86	77	45	44	86	63
Guatemala	14	68	91	46	30	49	50
Guinea	2	14	69	22	8	24	23
Guinea-Bissau	5	31	83	18	11	39	31
Guyana	12	41	94	49	19	75	48
Haiti	8	15	76	38	8	49	32
Honduras	42	76	78	46	19	64	54
Hong Kong	81	65	69	68	60	91	72
Hungary	62	95	86	75	43	85	74
Iceland	72	100	65	65	70	99	79
India	31	82	86	59	30	58	58
Indonesia	19	45	87	62	21	56	48
Iran	38	29	32	43	45	82	45
Iraq	26	4	30	37	12	38	25
Ireland	67	99	53	80	65	95	76
Isle of Man	58	100	70	62	64	94	74
Israel	62	83	70	76	55	92	73
Italy	62	100	61	92	71	95	80
Ivory Coast	41	29	58	34	29	62	42
Jamaica	21	84	83	59	24	71	57
Japan	90	100	34	89	90	96	83
Jordan	10	61	82	46	19	76	49
Kenya	9	25	89	43	22	53	40
Korea (North)	17	9	82	43	13	81	41
Korea (South)	64	68	78	56	60	89	69
Kuwait	51	50	64	37	34	89	54
Laos	2	13	84	16	13	56	31
Latvia	43	77	71	69	31	87	63
Lebanon	40	29	71	49	19	81	48
Lesotho	3	29	87	19	20	54	35
Liberia	3	27	71	18	14	50	30
Libya	20	17	83	25	28	78	42
Liechtenstein	97	100	34	84	74	95	81
Lithuania	39	77	71	69	29	87	62

Country	INFRA SCORE	FREEDOM SCORE	COL SCORE	CULTURE SCORE	PROSPERITY SCORE	HEALTH SCORE	FINAL SCORE
Luxembourg	83	100	65	79	72	99	83
Macao	42	78	79	71	32	89	65
Madagascar	8	54	81	35	14	52	41
Malawi	8	14	83	15	18	40	30
Malaysia	27	72	79	53	34	80	57
Maldives	19	29	79	50	18	50	41
Mali	7	21	58	9	18	34	25
Malta	50	100	72	52	41	89	67
Mauritania	7	10	64	18	16	35	25
Mauritius	20	50	84	46	24	78	50
Mexico	39	73	91	73	34	80	65
Monaco	90	100	60	71	73	93	81
Mongolia	18	45	87	50	22	73	49
Morocco	26	39	80	50	38	64	49
Mozambique	5	23	72	12	18	29	26
Namibia	23	79	71	30	20	64	48
Nauru	14	90	57	32	73	83	58
Nepal	6	45	82	36	12	21	34
Netherlands	74	100	70	86	69	97	83
New Zealand	83	100	76	65	49	93	78
Nicaragua	32	45	74	56	19	66	49
Niger	3	14	53	17	13	33	22
Nigeria	5	29	71	18	29	46	33
Norway	82	100	48	79	77	96	80
Oman	41	30	62	25	37	70	44
Pakistan	16	68	88	31	19	47	45
Panama	45	87	87	60	23	80	64
Papua New Guinea	2	83	67	20	19	59	42
Paraguay	34	80	89	64	49	78	66
Peru	18	62	76	59	17	63	49
Philippines	27	76	90	65	20	51	55
Poland	43	95	76	74	25	93	68
Portugal	43	95	70	78	46	94	71
Qatar	49	32	67	40	67	87	57
Romania	23	19	67	45	14	43	35
Rwanda	1	21	72	29	19	36	30
San Marino	79	100	69	65	54	92	76
Saudi Arabia	36	25	70	42	38	81	49
Senegal	19	61	50	35	15	48	38
Seychelles	31	42	60	49	33	79	49
Sierra Leone	7	29	77	24	11	32	30
Singapore	56	53	67	68	61	87	65
Somalia	3	9	82	14	15	41	27
South Africa	57	62	89	81	29	71	65
Spain	62	100	60	88	62	92	77
Sri Lanka	18	38	85	58	21	71	48
St. Kitts and Nevis	32	100	77	60	23	80	62
St. Lucia	17	92	72	56	22	83	57
Sudan	7	12	76	25	14	44	30

Country	INFRA SCORE	FREEDOM SCORE	COL SCORE	CULTURE SCORE	PROSPERITY SCORE	HEALTH SCORE	FINAL SCORE
Surinam	25	68	69	54	24	84	54
Swaziland	5	29	89	28	7	52	35
Sweden	83	100	31	81	89	96	80
Switzerland	99	100	25	89	99	97	85
Syria	17	17	20	35	23	77	28
Tanzania	7	33	84	47	15	51	39
Thailand	20	80	78	69	31	70	58
Togo	12	29	70	19	17	51	33
Tonga	35	61	75	43	14	81	52
Trinidad and Tobago	28	100	81	58	24	85	63
Tunisia	26	61	88	56	23	76	55
Turkey	43	70	77	72	23	78	61
Uganda	2	37	80	29	11	46	34
United Arab Emirates	45	45	67	37	65	92	59
United Kingdom	83	100	62	90	71	95	83
United States	88	100	78	93	80	97	89
Uruguay	37	92	78	77	25	86	66
Venezuela	29	85	100	67	46	78	68
Vietnam	8	30	79	35	13	65	38
Western Samoa	11	92	82	36	18	70	51
Yemen	10	45	71	17	20	51	36
Yugoslavia	29	20	73	62	23	89	49
Zaire	7	14	56	25	13	45	27
Zambia	8	50	79	32	13	55	39
Zimbabwe	32	70	89	50	20	63	54

Currency Exchange Table

Following are current exchange rates for all currencies mentioned in the book (as of July 15, 1992).

Country	Currency	Currency per US$
Algeria	Dinar	22.42
Argentina	Peso	.99
Australia	Dollar	1.3365
Austria	Schilling	10.44
Brazil	Cruzeiro	3613
Britain	Pound	.5206
Bulgaria	Leva	23
Canada	Dollar	1.1927
Chile	Peso	349.71
China	Renminbi	5.47
Costa Rica	Colon	138
Cote d'Ivoire	CFA Franc	327.76
Croatia	Dinar	200
Czechoslovakia	Koruna	26.84
Denmark	Kroner	5.7135
Ecuador	Sucre	1433.01
Egypt	Pound	331.92
Finland	Markka	4.0640
France	Franc	5.0085
Germany	Mark	1.4835
Greece	Drachma	182.30
Guatemala	Quetzal	4.26
Hong Kong	Dollar	7.7310
Hungary	Forint	75.85
India	Rupee	28.21
Indonesia	Rupiah	2025.11
Ireland	Punt	.5569
Isle of Man	Pound	.5051
Israel	Shekel	2.3799
Italy	Lira	1124.57
Japan	Yen	125.20
Kenya	Shilling	33.50
Laos	Tip	700
Malaysia	Ringgit	2.4975
Mexico	Peso	3115

Country	Currency	Currency per US$
Morocco	Dirham	8.10
Myanmar	Kyat	6.0326
New Zealand	Dollar	1.8248
Nigeria	Naira	18.25
Norway	Krone	5.8285
Papua New Guinea	Kina	.9269
Peru	New Sol	1.19
Philippines	Peso	24.5
Poland	Zloty	12867.03
Portugal	Escudo	126.31
Romania	Lei	314
Rwanda	Franc	120
Senegal	CFA Franc	327.76
Seychelles	Rupee	4.82
Singapore	Dollar	1.6125
Slovenia	Tolar	85
South Africa	Rand	2.7473
Spain	Peseta	94.45
Sweden	Krona	5.3840
Switzerland	Franc	1.3410
Tanzania	Shillings	294.5
Thailand	Baht	25.29
Togo	CFA Franc	327.76
Uruguay	New Peso	3185.01
Venezuela	Bolivar	66.14
Yugoslavia	Dinar	316.86
Zimbabwe	Dollar	4.958

Index

Africa

Aberdares Mountains (Kenya) 333
 The Ark 333
 Treetops 333
Abidjan, Côte d'Ivoire 344
 Banc National Park 345
 Clubs
  l'Acetylène 345
  Treich Can-Can 345
  Zorba le Grec 345
 Hotels
  Forum Golf Intercontinental 345
  Hôtel Ivoire 345
 Museums
  Musée National 344
 Native dances
  Le Wafou 345
 Restaurants
  La Bache Bleue 345
  Kedjenou 345
  Le Senat 345
 Shopping
  Marché de Cocody 344
  Marché Sénégalais 344
  Treichville Market 345
Abidjan, Côte d'Ivoire 344
Antananarivo, Madagascar 338
Archer's Post (Kenya) 331
Banc National Park (Côte d'Ivoire) 345
Basse Casamance (Senegal) 341
Bé, Togo 342
 Bé Market 342
Benin City, Nigeria 344
 Ife Palace complex 344
 Oba's Palace 344
Berenty Lemur Reserve (Madagascar) 338
Bouaké, Côte d'Ivoire 345
 Hotels
  Hôtel du Centre 346
 Shopping
  Artisan's Center 346
  Bouaké Market 345
  Ets. Gonfreville 345
  Solinci 345
Cap Skirring (Senegal) 341
 Le Campement 341
 Club Med 341
Cape Peninsula (South Africa) 337
 Clifton beach 337
 Muizenberg beach 338
Cape Town, South Africa 337
 Hotels
  Lanzerac Estate 337
 Museums
  South African Museum 337
 Three Anchors Bay 337
  Serendipity maze 337
Club Med (Senegal) 341
Comoe National Park (Côte d'Ivoire) 345
 Comoe Safari Lodge Hotel 345
Côte d'Ivoire 344
Dakar, Senegal 339
 Art galleries

Galerie 39 339
 Cathedral 339
 Grand Mosque 340
 Hotels
  La Croix du Sud 340
  Novotel Dakar 340
 Museums
  Musée d'Art Nègre-Africain 339
 Restaurant
  La Région du Fleuve 340
 Shopping
  Caritas Tissage Traditionnel 340
  Deco Shop 340
  Fara 340
  Marché Kermel 340
  Marché Tilène 340
  Sandaga 340
 Theaters
  Sorano 340
Dar es Salaam, Tanzania 334
Daura, Nigeria 344
Denis Island (Seychelles) 336
 Denis Island Lodge 336
Djoudj Park (Senegal) 341
Durban, South Africa 337
Eshowe, South Africa 337
 Zululand Historical Museum 337
Freetown, Sierra Leone 346
 Cotton Tree 346
 Hotels
  Cape Sierra 346
  City Hotel 346
  YMCA 346
 Leicester Peak 346
 Museums
  Sierra Leone National Museum 346
 Restaurants
  Provilac 346
Fregate Island (Seychelles) 336
 Plantation House 336
Gisenyi, Rwanda 335
Ibadan, Nigeria 344
Island of Fadiouth (Senegal) 341
Island of Gorée (Senegal) 340
Johannesburg, South Africa 337
Jos zoo (Nigeria) 344
Kabalega National Park (Uganda) 335
Kampala, Uganda 335
 Nile Hotel Complex 335
Kano, Nigeria 343
 Akesan Restaurant 343
 Hotels
  Central 344
  Daula 344
  Rock Castle Hotel 344
Kenya 328
Kigali, Rwanda 335
Kiwayuu (Kenya) 332
Kruger National Park (South Africa) 338
La Digue (Seychelles) 336
 Bird Island Lodge 336
 Gregoire's Island Lodge 336
 Gregoire's Watersports 336

Lagos, Nigeria 342
  Hotels
    The Federal Palace Hotel 343
  Restaurants
    Chez Antoine 343
    Club Bagatelle 343
Lake Naivasha (Kenya) 331
Lake Naivasha Hotel (Kenya) 331
Lake Nakuru Park (Kenya) 331
    Lake Nakuru Lodge 331
Lamu (Kenya) 332
Leicester Peak (Sierra Leone) 346
Lomé, Togo 341
  Hotels
    Hotel de 2 Fevrier Sofitel 342
    Hotel Le Benin 342
    Hotel Sarakawa 342
  Museums
    National Museum 342
  Shopping
    Le Grand Marché 341
    Odef Craft Center 342
Madagascar 338
  Hotels
    Acropole 339
    Bridge Hotel 339
    Hotel Colbert 339
    Hotel Select 339
    Hotel Terminus 339
Mahé (Seychelles) 336
  Hotels
    Coral Beach 336
    Northolme Hotel 336
  Morne Seychellois National Park 336
Maka Diama, Senegal 341
Malindi, Kenya 332
Manda (Kenya) 332
Marsabit (Kenya) 331
Masai Mara game park 327
Mombasa, Kenya 332
  Hotels
    Alliance Hotels 332
    Castle 332
    Outrigger 332
Morne Seychellois National Park (Seychelles) 336
Mount Kenya (Kenya) 333
    Naro Moru River Lodge 334
Mount Kilimanjaro (Kenya) 333
Murchison Falls (Uganda) 335
Nairobi, Kenya
  Bomas 330
  Hotels
    Hotel Ambassadeur 330
    Hotel Comfy 330
    Hotel InterContinental 330
    Mount Kenya Safari Club 330
    Muthaiga Club 330
    New Stanley Hotel 329
    Norfolk 330
  Museums
    Gallery Watatu 329
    National Museum of Nairobi 329
  Nairobi National Park 329
  Restaurants
    African Heritage Ltd. 329
    Carnivore 329
    Coffee Board of Kenya 330
    Kenyatta Conference Center 330
    Mount Kenya Safari Club 330
    Safeer 330
  Shopping
    African Heritage Shop 329

    Colpro Outfitters 329
    Nairobi City Market 329
  Snake Park 329
  Thorn Tree Message Center 329
Nakuru, Kenya 331
Nanyuki, Kenya 331
    Mwingo Gate Hotel 331
    Sportman Arm's Club 331
Natal (South Africa) 337
Ngorongoro Conservation Area 327
    Ngorongoro Crater 327
    Serengeti Plain 327
Nigeria 342
Nosy Be Island (Madagascar) 338
    Andilana Beach Hotel 338
Nyahururu waterfall (Kenya) 331
    Thomson's Fall Lodge 331
Pate (Kenya) 332
Praslin (Seychelles) 336
    Anse Lazio 336
    Baie des Chevaliers 336
    Hotels
      Maison des Palmes 336
    Vallée de Mai 336
Resorts (Nigeria)
    Baguada 344
    Tiga Lake 344
Rift Valley 327, 332
River No. 2 Beach (Sierra Leone) 346
Rwanda 334
Safaris 327
    Companies
      Atkin Tours & Travel Ltd 328
      Inside Africa Safaris Ltd. 328
      Saga Holidays 328
      Sunrise Travel and Tours 327
      United Touring International 327
      Worldwide Journeys and Expeditions 328
Selous game reserve (Tanzania) 334
    Mbuyu Safari Camp 334
Senegal 339
Serengeti Plain (Tanzania) 334
    Lobo Wildlife Lodge 334
    Seronera Wildlife Lodge 334
Seychelles 335
Shark watching 338
Sierra Leone 346
Silhouette Island (Seychelles) 336
    Silhouette Island Lodge 336
South Africa 337
    Travel information and contacts
      Bed 'N Breakfast 337
      CI Leisure Rentals 338
      Exotic Drive Tours 338
Table Mountain (South Africa) 338
    National Botanic Gardens of Kirstenbosch 338
Tamberma Valley (Togo) 342
Tanzania 334
Togo 341
Tsavo National Park (Kenya) 333
    Kilaguni 333
      Kilaguni Lodge 333
Uganda 335
Uhuru Peak (Kenya) 333
Victoria Falls (Zimbabwe) 334
Virunga Volcanoes National Park (Rwanda) 335
Voodoo 342
Watering holes 332
    Kilaguni (Kenya) 333
    The Ark (Kenya) 333
    Treetops (Kenya) 333
Yankari Game Reserve (Nigeria) 344

Yoruba (Nigeria)   344
Zambezi River (Zimbabwe)   334
Zimbabwe   334

Australia

Ayer's Rock   396
  Hotels
    Curtin Springs Roadside Inn   396
    Desert Oaks Resort Centre   396
    King's Canyon Frontier Lodge   396
    Sheraton Ayers Rock   396
Canberra   388
  Australian War Memorial   389
  Blundell's Farmhouse   389
  Botanic Gardens   389
  Captain Cook Memorial Water Jet   388
  Carillon   389
  Galleries
    Australian National Gallery   389
  Hotels
    Chelsea Lodge   389
    Tall Trees   389
  Museums
    Institute of Anatomy   389
  Restaurants
    Charlie's   389
    Gus's Café   389
    Rascals   389
  Tidbinbilla Nature Reserve   389
Laura   395
  Quinkon Reserve   395
Melbourne   389
  Boating
    Studley Park Boathouse   390
  Clubs
    Inflation   391
    Palace   391
  Collins Street   389
  Hotels
    The Regent   391
    Rockman's Regency   391
    Windsor Hotel   391
  King's Domain   390
  LaTrobe Library   390
  Museums
    Museum of Science   390
    National Gallery   390
    The National Museum   390
  Old Melbourne Gaol   390
  Restaurants
    Fanny's   391
    Flower Drum   391
    Jean Jacques by the Sea   391
    Mietta's Melbourne   391
    Stephanie's   391
  Royal Botanic Gardens   390
  Shopping
    Aboriginal Handicrafts   390
Nourlangie Rock Northern Territory   395
Outback   396
  Emerald   397
  Hotels
    Bed and Breakfast Australia   396
    Escott Lodge Resort   396
  Sapphire   397
Perth   391
  Hotels
    Observation City Resort   392
    Parmelia Hilton   392
  King's Park   392
  Museums
    Art Gallery   392

Old Mill   392
  Restaurants
    Choi's Inn   392
    Jessica's Fine Seafood   392
    Lombardo's   392
    Oyster Bar   392
    Oyster Beds   392
    River Room   392
Queensland   392
  Brisbane   392
    Forest Park   393
    Kuranda   394
    Lone Pine Sanctuary   393
    Reef House   394
    Sir Thomas Brisbane Planetarium   393
    They Passed This Way   393
  Cairns   393
  Daintree Rain Forest   395
  Ellis Beach   394
  Hotels
    Harbourside Village   393
    Hilton International   394
    Hilton International Brisbane   393
    Hub Hotel   393
    Pacific International   393
    Sheraton Brisbane Hotel   393
  Lamington Plateau   395
  Mount Glorious   395
  Mount Tamborine   395
  Shopping
    Queensland Aboriginal Creations   393
  Surfer's Paradise   393
  The Great Barrier Reef   394
Resorts
  Burswood Restaurant and Casino   392
Snowy Mountains   388
  Mount Kosciusko   388
Split Rock Gallery   395
Surfing
  Surf Lifesavers Association of Australia   388
Sydney   383
  Argyle Arts Centre   385
  Argyle Cut   385
  Argyle Place   385
  Australia Square Tower   384
  Beaches
    Bondi   386
    Tamarama Beach   386
  Blue Mountains   388
    Katoomba   388
  Botanic Gardens   385
  Cadman's Cottage   385
  Chocolates
    W. Pulknownik's   386
  Church of the Holy Trinity   385
  Clubs
    Arthur's Bar and Restaurant   387
    Bourbon and Beefsteak   388
    The Cauldron   387
    Freezer   387
    Hero of Waterloo Hotel   388
    Holiday Inn Menzies   387
    The Manzil Room   388
  Domain   385
  Festivals
    Blessing of the Fishing Fleet   386
    Carnivale   386
    Gay Mardi Gras   386
    Royal Gardens Week   386
    Royal Sydney Easter Show   386
    Surf Carnivals   388
  Fort Denison   385

Galleries
   Art Gallery of New South Wales 385
   Holdsworth Galleries 385
Hotels
   Inter-Continental 387
   Parkroyal Hotel 387
   Regent 387
   Russell 387
   Sebel Town House 387
   Sheraton-Wentworth 387
King's Cross 388
Opal Skymine 384
Opera house 384
Restaurants
   Bellevue Hotel 387
   Berowra Waters Inn 387
   Doyle's on the Beach 387
   Endeavor at Mosman 387
   Fisherman's Lodge 387
   No Name 387
   Oasis Seros 387
   Summit Restaurant 384
Shopping
   Angelo's 386
   Australian Centre for Photography 386
   Cooee Australian Emporium 386
   Game Birds 386
   Jack O'Beans 386
   Paddington 386
   Village Bazaar 386
Taronga Zoo and Aquarium 385
The Rocks 384
Travel
   Information Center 385
   Maritime Services Board 386
   Sydney Pass 384
   Visitor's Services 384
The Great Barrier Reef 394
   Green Island 394
   Resorts
      Dunk Island 394
      Hayles Resort 394
   Underwater Coral Observatory 394
Travel
   Australian Travel Service 398
   Ghan 398
   Indian-Pacific 398
Western Australia 397
   Coolgardie 397
      Goldfields Exhibition 397
   Kalgoorlie 398
   Kimberley Plateau 398
   Marble Bar 397
Wujal Wujal 395
Yulara 396

Austria

Arlberg 11
Festivals
   Austrian National Music Festivals 8
   Haydn Festival 1
   International Chamber Music Festival 1
   Salzburg Festival 1
Hallein 10
Innsbruck 7
   Alpine Zoo 7
   Goldener Adler 7
   Goldenes Dachl 7
   Hiking
      Club Innsbruck 8
   Hofkirche 7
   Hotels

Goldener Adler 8
Hungerburgbahn 7
Maria-Theresien-Strasse 7
Nordkette 7
Kitzbühel 11
   Hotels
      Schloss Lebenberg 11
Krimml Waterfall 11
Lake District 10
   St. Gilgen 11
   Wolfgangsee 10
Landeck 11
Obergurgl 11
Salzburg 8
   Alter Markt 8
   Dom 9
   Glockenspiel 9
   Hellbrunn Palace 9
   Hohensalzburg 9
   Hotels
      Gastschloss Mönchstein 10
      Hotel Elefant 10
      Hotel Kaserbräu 9
      Hotel Schöne Aussicht 9
      Schloss Haunsperg 10
      Simony Hotel 10
   Judengasse 8
   Mirabell Palace 9
   Old quarter 8
   Residenz 9
   Restaurants
      Eschlböck-Plomberg 9
      Stiftskeller Sankt Peter 9
      Weisses Kreuz 9
Skiing
   St. Anton 12
   Zürs 12
Tourist Information
   Austrian National Tourist Office 1
Vienna 1
   Clubs
      Griechenbeisl 6
      Jazzland 5
      Queen Anne 5
      Reiss Bar 5
      U4 5
   Hofburg Palace 1
      Chapel of St. George 2
      Hofburgkapelle 2
      Imperial Treasury 2
      Michaelertor 2
      Schweizerhof 2
   Horsemanship
      Spanish Riding School 2
   Hotels
      Amadeus 6
      Bristol 6
      Hotel im Palais Schwarzenberg 6
      Imperial 6
      Kaiserin Elisabeth 6
      Römischer Kaiser 7
      Sacher 6
      Schloss Dürnstein 6
      Mayerling 7
   Museums
      Akademie der Bildenen Kunste 3
      Graphische Sammlung Albertina 3
      Kunsthistorisches Museum 3
      Naturhistorisches Museum 3
      Neue Hofburg 4
      Österreichische Galerie 3
   Pastry shops

Demel's 5
Gerstner 5
Heiner's 5
Prater Park 3
Restaurants and cafés
Café Central 4
Café Hawelka 4
Café Schwarzenberg 4
Gottfried 5
Hauswirth 5
Korso 6
Sacherstube 5
Zu den Drei Husaren 5
Ringstrasse 1
Schönbrunn Palace 2
Skiing
Stubai Glacier 8
St. Stephen's Cathedral 2
Staatsoper 4
Ticket information (Boys' choir)
Verwaltung der Hofmusikkapelle 4
Ticket information (opera)
Bundestheaterverband 4
Vienna Boys' Choir 4
Zurs
Hotels
Zorserhof 12

Brazil

Amazon 518
Belém 519
Hotels
Excelsior Grão Para 519
Hilton 519
Brasilia 512
Catetinho 512
Dom Bosco Church 512
Hotels
Hotel Das Americas 513
Nacional 513
Itamarati Palace 513
Meteor 513
National Cathedral 513
National Congress Complex 513
Palacio da Alvorada 513
Palacio do Planalto 513
Palacio dos Arcos (Ministry of Foreign Relations) 513
Planalto Palacio 513
Restaurants
Churrascaria do Lago 513
Piantella 513
Sculpture
Mermaid 513
Meteor 513
Warriors 513
Water Nymphs 513
Theaters
Teatro Nacional 513
Torre de Televisão 512
Buzios 509
Hotels
Nas Rocas Club Hotel 510
Pousada Barracuda 510
Pousada Dos Buzios 510
Pousada La Chimere 510
Pousada La Mandragora 510
Restaurants
Au Cheval Blanc 509
French Satyricon 510
Candomblé cult 516
Carnival 508

Guanabara Bay 510
Iguaçu Falls 518
Hotel Bourbon 518
Hotel das Cataratas 518
Itaipú Dam 518
Manaus 519
Hotels
Hotel Amazonas 520
Hotel Monaco 520
Tropical 519
Marajo Island 519
Pantanal 520
Shopping
Amsterdam Sauer 520
H. Stern 520
Rio de Janeiro 507
Avenida Atlântica 509
Beaches
Copacabana 509
São Conrado 509
Christ the Redeemer 508
Clubs
Asa Branca 512
Bâteau Mouche Bar 512
Biblos 512
Café Un, Deux, Trois 512
Karoake de Canja 512
Plataforma 512
Scala Rio 512
Hotels
Caesar Park 511
Carlton 511
Copacabana Palace 511
Marina Palace 511
Meridien 511
Ouro Verde Hotel 511
Rio Palace 511
Jardim Botânico (Botanical Garden) 508
Jockey Club 510
Lapa 509
Maracana Stadium 510
Museums
Quinta da Boa Vista (National Museum) 509
National Library 509
Pao de Açucar 508
Petropolis 510
Restaurants
Adegao 511
Antiquarius 511
Le Bec Fin 511
Chale 511
Copacabana 511
Enotria 511
Gaucha 511
Maria Thereza Weiss 511
Moenda 511
Ouro Verde 511
Penafiel 511
Porcao 511
Le Pré Catalán 511
Sol e Mar 511
Le St. Honoré 511
La Tour 511
Sambo'dromo 508
Santa Teresa 509
Shopping
Feirarte 510
Rio Sul 510
Salvador de Bahía 516
Churches
Carmelite church 517
Igreja de Nosso Senhor do Bonfim 517

Igreja de São Francisco   516
Igreja e Convento de Santa Tereza   517
Igreja e Mosteiro de Nossa Senhora da
  Graça   517
Terreiro de Jesus   517
Hotels
  Forno o Fogão   517
  Grande Hotel da Barra   518
  Luxor Convento do Carmo   517
  Praia Mar   518
  Quatro Rodas Salvador   517
Restaurants
  Casa da Gamboa   517
  Solar do Unhão   517
Shopping
  Mercado Modelo   517
  Mercado São Joaquim   517
Salvador de Bajía
Igreja da Boa Viagen   517
São Paulo   514
  Casa do Bandeirante   514
  Catedralo Metropolitano of São Paulo   514
  Clubs
    Barracao de Zinco   516
    Club 150   516
    Plataforme 1   516
    St. Paul   516
  Hotels
    Caesar Park   515
    Maksoud Palace   515
    Mofarrej Sheraton   515
    Othon Palace Hotel   516
    São Paulo Hilton   516
  Ibirapuera Park   514
  Instituto Butantã   515
  Jardin Botanica   514
  Liberdade   514
  Museums
    Museu da Casa Brasileira   514
    Museu da Imigração Japonesa   514
    Museu de Arte de São Paulo   514
    Museu de Arte Sacra   514
  Pacaembú Stadium   515
  Praça da Sé (Cathedral Plaza)   514
  Restaurants
    Bolinha   515
    Marcel's   515
    O Profeta   515
    Rodeio   515
    Terraço Italia   515
  Shopping
    Ibirapueraon   515
    Iguatemi   515
    Praça da Republica   515
  Zoo   514
Teresopolis National Park   510
Travel information and contacts
  ENASA Line   518
  LADATCO   519
  Varig Airlines   520

Britain

Aberystwyth, Wales   37
  Cooper's Arms   37
  Holyhead   37
Arisaig, Scotland   40
  Arisaig House   40
Arran, Scotland   41
  Brodick Castle   41
  Holy Island   41
Bannockburn, Scotland   42
Bath, England   30

Ben Nevis (Scotland)   40
Birmingham, England   27
  New Hall   27
Bracora, Scotland   40
Brighton, England   33
  Royal Pavilion   34
Buckinghamshire, England   34
  Stowe   34
Caernarfon (Wales)   35
Cambridge, England   24
  King's College Chapel   24
Camelford, England   28
Camelot   28
Canterbury, England   27
Chagford, England   29
  Barton's   29
Cheltenham, England   30
  Hotel de la Bere   30
  Promenade   30
Chester, England   30
  Chester at Home   31
Cornwall, England   28
  Hotels
    Allhays Country House   28
    Falmouth Hotel   28
    Truro Farm   28
Cotswolds   29
  Sudeley Castle   30
Dartmoor National Park   29
  Inns
    Burrator House   29
    Gidleigh Park   29
Derbyshire, England   32
Devon, England
  Barton's   29
  Dartmoor National Park   29
Dover, England   27
Edinburgh, Scotland   37
  Chapel of St. Margaret   37
  Edinburgh International Festival   38
  Gladstone's Land   38
  Holyrood   38
  Hotels
    Caledonian   38
  Royal Mile   37
Fife, Scotland
  Golden Lion Hotel   39
  Stirling Castle   39
Glasgow, Scotland   38
  Art collections   38
    Burrell Collection   38
    Hunterian Museum   39
    Kelvingrove   38
  Hotels
    Central   39
  Restaurants
    Ubiquitous Chip   39
    Willow Tea Room   39
Glencoe, Scotland   40
  Inverlochy Castle   41
Glenfinnan, Scotland   40
Gloucestershire, England
  Beckford Silk   25
  Cheeses   25
Grasmere, England   33
Grimspound, England   29
Harlech (Wales)   36
Harris (Scotland)   42
Haworth, England   31
  Black Bull House   31
Hay-on-Wye, Wales   36
Hebrides (Scotland)   41

Arran 41
Harris 42
Iona 42
Isle of Islay 41
Lewis 42
Mull 42
Skye 41
Staffa 42
Travel information and contacts
    Highlands and Islands Travelpass 42
    Scottish Rail Pass 42
    Hi-Line 42
Highlands (Scotland) 39
Ben Nevis 40
Glencoe, Scotland 40
Inverlochy Castle 41
Scenic drives
    Arisaig, Scotland 40
    Bracora, Scotland 40
    Glenfinnan, Scotland 40
Horse racing
National Horse Racing Museum 26
Newmarket, England 26
Hungerford, England 26
Below Stairs 26
Bow House Antiques 26
Hungerford Arcade 26
Pandora's Box 26
Styles 26
The Collector's Shop 26
Inverary, Scotland 40
Episcopal Church of All Saints 40
Inverary Castle 40
Inverness, Scotland 40
Ben Nevis 40
Culloden House Hotel 40
Iona (Scotland) 42
Isle of Wight (England) 27
Kemerton, England 25
Tilly M 25
Keswick, England 33
Castlerigg Stone Circle 33
Killin, Scotland 39
Lake District (England) 33
Hotels
    Castlerigg Stone Circle 33
    Sharrow Bay Hotel 33
    Wasdale Head Inn 33
Ledbury, England
Hope End 27
Lewis (Scotland) 42
Standing Stones of Callanish 42
Loch Morar, Scotland 40
Loch Tay, Scotland 39
Lochranza (Scotland) 41
Brodick Castle 41
London, England 13
Banqueting House 14
Berwick Street 16
Big Ben 13
Bloomsbury 16
Buses
    Eccleston Bridge 24
    National Express 24
    Victoria Coach Station 24
Chapel of St. John 14
Chelsea 16
Cleopatra's Needle 15
Clubs
    The Comedy Store 22
Coram's Fields 16
Covent Garden 15

Crown Jewels 14
Cutty Sark 14
Freud's home 16
Hampstead 16
Hampton Court Palace 18
Hotels
11 Cadogan Gardens 23
Bailey's Hotel 21
Beaufort 23
Brown's 20, 23
Claridge's 23
Connaught Hotel 21, 23
Cranley Place Hotel 23
Dorchester Hotel 20, 21
Ebury Court 23
Hyde Park 23
Inverness Court 24
St. James's Court 24
Wilbraham 23
House of Commons 15
House of Lords 15
Jermyn Street 19
Keats' home 16
Leicester Square 16
Little Venice 17
Museums
Lace Hall 20
London Transport Museum 16
Madame Tussaud's 16
Severn's Building 20
Theatre Museum 16
National Gallery 14
Nelson Column 14
Number 10 Downing Street 14
Parliament 13
Piccadilly Circus 15
Poets' Corner 14
Pubs
Anchor Tavern 22
Brahms and Liszt 22
George and Vulture 22
Prospect of Whitby 22
The Flask 22
The Trafalgar 22
Ye Olde Cheshire Cheese 22
Restaurants
Bailey's Hotel 21
Bloom's 21
Bombay Brasserie 21
Grill Room 21
Liberty's 21
Nam Long 21
Reuben's 21
Simpson's in the Strand 21
Terrace Restaurant 21
Ritz 15
Royal Academy of Fine Arts 15
St. Paul's Cathedral 15
St.-Martin-in-the-Fields 14
Shopping
Antiquarius 18
Camden Lock 17
Camden Passage 18
Crafts market 16
Hamley's 19
Hildich & Key 19
Irish Linen Company 19
Jermyn Street 19
Kite Store 19
Lobbs 19
London Brass Rubbing Centre 18
Maggs Brothers 18

New Caledonian Market 18
Nottingham 20
Paxton & Whitfield 19
Petticoat Lane Flea Market 18
Stovel & Mason 19
Swaine & Adney 19
The Bayswater Road Art Exhibition 17
Tricker's 19
Turnbull & Asser 19
Wildsmith 19
Soho 16
Speakers Corner 16
St. James' Church 15
Tate Gallery 14
10 Downing Street 14
Theater
 Albany Empire 17
 Leicester Square Ticket Booth 17
 Royal Opera House 16
Tours
 British Tours 20
 Citisights of London 20
 Double-decker bus tours 20
 Jason's Trip 17
 London Travelcard 20
 London Visitor and Convention Bureau 20
 London Walks 20
 Take-A-Guide 20
 The Driver Guides Association 20
 Waterbus Company 17
Tower of London 14
Trafalgar Square Post Office 15
Westminster Hall 14
Whispering Gallery 15
Whitehall 14, 15
Wine bars
 Ebury Wine Bar 21
Travel information and contacts
 Travelcard 20
 Visitor and Convention Bureau 20
 Walks 20
Lowlands (Scotland) 42
 Bannockburn 42
 Stirling Bridge 42
Manaton, England 29
Mazes
 Grey's Court 26
 Hampton Court Palace 18
Mount Snowdon (Wales) 36
Newmarket, England 26
 National Horse Racing Museum 26
North York Moors National Park (England) 31
Offa's Dyke (Wales) 36
Orkney Islands (Scotland) 42
Oxford, England 25
 Ashmolean 25
 Bear Inn 25
Oxford University 25
 New College 25
Oxfordshire, England 35
 Blenheim Palace 35
Pembrokeshire Coast National Park 36
Penzance, England 28
Port Charlotte, Scotland 42
Portcurno, England 28
 Minack Theater 28
St. Andrews, Scotland 39
 Links Management Committee of St. Andrews 39
 Old Course 39
Scotland 37
Segontium (Wales) 35
Shakespeare, William 30

Shanklin, England 27
Skiing
 Cairngorm mountains (Scotland) 39
Skye 41
 Cullins 41
Snowdonia National Park (Wales) 36
Staffa (Scotland) 42
 Fingal's Cave 42
Stirling, Scotland 39
 Golden Lion 39
Stone rows 29
Stratford-upon-Avon, England 30
 Royal Shakespeare Company 30
 Dirty Duck Pub 30
Tenby, Wales 37
 Imperial Hotel 37
Tetbury, England 29
 Close 30
 St. Mary the Virgin 30
Thirsk, England 31
 Yorkshire Gliding Club 31
Tintagel, England 28
Ullswater, England 33
 Sharrow Bay Hotel 33
Wales 35
 Castles
  Caernarfon 35
  Cardiff Castle 35
  Harlech 36
  Segontium 35
Welshpool, Wales 37
Wem, England 26
Westminster Hall 14
Whisky, Scotch 42
Whispering Gallery 15
Whitehall 14, 15
Wilbraham 23
Wildsmith 19
Willow Tea Room 39
Winchcombe, England 30
Windsor, England 27
 Eton College 27
 St. George's Chapel 27
 Windsor Castle 27
York, England 31
 Thorntons 32
 York Minster 31
Yorkshire (England) 31
 Black Swan Hotel 31
 Yorkshire Gliding Club 31

Canada

Alberta 475
 Banff 477
  Banff Springs Hotel 483
  Bowl 483
  Lone Pine 483
  Mount Norquay 483
  North American winter festival 483
 Calgary 475
  Calgary Stampede 476
  Calgary Tower 476
  Chuckwagon Race 476
  Fort Calgary 476
  Glenbow Museum 476
  Heritage Park 476
  Owl's Nest 477
  Palliser 477
  Rimrock Room 477
  Stampede Stage Show 476
  Western Outfitters 476
 Drumheller Badlands 476

Edmonton 477
  Alberta's Legislative Building 478
  Edmonton Civic Center 478
  Fort Edmonton 477
  Hy's Steak Loft 478
  Klondike Days 477
  Muttart Conservatory and Horticulture Center 478
  Vi's 478
  Westin Hotel 478
Glenmore Reservoir 476
Mount Allan 483
Rafter Six 478
Sunshine Village 483
  Nordic Center 483
  Sunshine Inn 483
Aventures en Eau Vive 485
Baie St. Paul 467
Banff 477
  Banff Springs Hotel 477
Big Trout Lake Indian Band, Ontario 485
British Columbia 478
  Barkerville 478
  Blackcomb Mountain 483
  Coho Fishing and Guiding Services 484
  Fort James 478
  Fort Langley 478
  Fort Steel 478
  Granville Island 479
    Bridges 479
    Pelican Bay Lounge 479
  Hazelton 482
  Kimberley 482
    Julyfest 482
    Kimberley Ski Resort 482
  Kootenay Heli-skiing 482
  Ksan 482
  Mike Wiegele Helicopter Skiing 482
  Oak Bay Marine Group 484
  Osoyoos 482
  Petroglyphs 478
  Sylvester Jack 485
  Vancouver 478
    Bayshore Inn 479
    Chartwell 479
    Chinatown 479
    Chinese Cultural Center 479
    Delta Place 479
    Dr. Sun Yat-Sen Classical Garden 479
    Gastown 479
    Georgia Street 478
    Hill's Indian Crafts 479
    Law Courts Building 479
    Museum of Anthropology 479
    Only 479
    Robson Square 478
    Stanley Park 479
    Sylvia Hotel 479
    Umberto's 479
  Vancouver Island 479
    Bastion 481
    Bathtub Race 481
    Butchart Gardens 480
    Craigdarroch Castle 480
    Empress Hotel 480
    Fishermen's Wharf 481
    Foo Hong 480
    Georgia Park 481
    Georgia Park Promenade 481
    Government House 480
    Helmcken House 480
    Helm's Inn 480

Nanaimo 480
Oak Bay Marina Ltd. 481
Parksville 481
Periklis 480
Provincial Museum 480
Subtidal Adventures 481
Swy-A-Lana Lagoon 481
Thunderbird Park 480
Tigh Na Mara 481
Tong-Ji Men 480
Victoria 480
Whistler 482
  Whistler Heli-skiing 482
  Whistler Resort Association 483
Cape Breton Island 473
  Ceilidh Trail 473
Gaspe 467
  Bonaventure 467
  Gaspe Museum 467
  Percé Rock 467
Grand Falls 474
  Mary March Museum 474
  Mt. Peyton Hotel-Motel 474
Great Northern Peninsula 474
  L'Anse aux Meadows National Historic Park 474
  Highway 430 474
  Porte-aux-Choix 474
  St. Anthony Motel 474
Ile Bonaventure 467
Ile d'Orléans 467
Jasper 477
  Athabasca Falls 477
  Columbia ice fields 477
  Mount Columbia 477
Labrador 484
  Powell's Outfitters Limited 484
Laurentians 483
  Gray Rocks 484
  Manoir Pinoteau 484
  Mount Tremblant 483
  St. Sauveur 484
  Station Mount Tremblant 484
Miquelon 475
Montreal 463
  Crescent Street 464
  Hotels
    Downtown Bed and Breakfast 465
    Hotel Château Versailles 465
    L'Hôtel de la Montagne 465
    Ritz Carlton 465
  Man and His World 464
  Place Ville Marie 464
  Religious sites
    Basilica of Notre Dame 464
    Notre-Dame-de-Bonsecours 464
    Sacred Heart Chapel 464
  Restaurants
    Les Chênets 465
    Chez la Mère Michel 464
    Les Mignardises 464
  Vieux Montreal 463
New Brunswick 471
  Campobello Island 471
  Christmas Bird Count 472
  Fundy Coast 471
  New Brunswick Museum 472
  Reversing Falls 472
  Roosevelt Campobello International Park 472
  St. Andrews 472
    Greenock Church 472
    Ross Memorial Museum 472
    Rossmount Inn 472

579

St. John   472
Shediac   472
    Chez Françoise   473
    Paturel Shore House   472
Newfoundland   473
    Gros Morne National Park   474
    Marine Atlantic Reservations Bureau   473
    Names Callaghan Trail   474
    St. John's
        Fort Amherst   475
        Hotel Newfoundland   475
        Queen's Battery   475
        Roman Catholic Basilica   475
        Signal Hill   475
        Stel Battery Hotel   475
        Water Street   475
        Woodstock Colonial Inn   475
    St. John's Anglican Cathedral   475
    Western Brook Pond   474
Niagara Falls   469
    Foxhead Hotel   469
Nova Scotia   473
    Highland Games   473
    Micmac Association of Cultural Studies   473
    Oak Island   473
    Yacht clubs
        Armdale Yacht Club   485
        Bedford Basin Yacht Club   485
        Bras d'Or Yacht Club   485
        Canadian Forces Sailing Association   485
        Chester Yacht Club   485
        Dartmouth Yacht Club   485
        Lennox Passage Yacht Club   485
        Lunenburg Yacht Club   485
        Royal Western Nova Scotia Yacht Club   485
Osoyoos   482
Ottawa   468
    Bytown Museum   468
    Hotels
        Château Laurier   468
        Ottawa Hilton   468
        Park Lane   468
    Lorne Building   468
    National Gallery of Canada   468
    Parliament Hill   468
    Peace Tower   468
Parc des Champs de Bataille   465
    Plains of Abraham, Quebec   465
    Quebec Museum   465
Parc des Champs de Bataille, Quebec   465
Percé Rock   467
    L'Auberge du Gargantua   467
Quebec City   465
    Assemblée Nationale   466
    Carnival de Quebec   466
    Carnival Lodging Committee   466
    Hotels
        Auberge du Trésor   467
        Le Château de Pierre   467
        Château Frontenac   465
        Hotel Dieu   465
    Jardin des Gouverneurs   465
    Lower Town   466
    Musée du Fort   465
    Notre Dame des Victoires   466
    Place d'Armes   465
    Restaurants
        Au Table de Serge Bruyère   466
        Aux Anciens Canadiens   466
        Restaurant Louis Hebert   466
    Rue de Trésor   466
    Seminary   465

Ursulin Convent Museum   465
Vieux Quebec   465
Reserve-A-Resort   484
St. Pierre   475
    Hôtel Robert   475
    SPM Tours   475
Ste. Anne de Beaupré   467
Scottish Studies Department, Ontario   473
Stratford   468
    Queen's Park   468
    Shakespearean Festival   468
    Shakespearean Garden   468
    Shrewsbury Manor   469
    Stratford Festival Office   468
    The Church   468
Terra Nova   474
    Terra Nova National Park   474
Thunder Bay, Ontario   483
Toronto   469
    Casa Loma   470
    City Hall   469
    CN Tower   469
    Exhibition Place   470
    High Park   470
    Hotels
        Delta Chelsea Inn   471
        King Edward   471
        Royal York Hotel   471
        Sheraton Center   471
    Museums
        Art Gallery of Ontario   470
        McMichael Canadian Collection   470
        Royal Ontario Museum   470
    Nathan Phillips Square   469
    O'Keefe Center   471
    Old City Hall   469
    Old Fort York   470
    Ontario Place   470
        Cinesphere   470
    Provincial Parliament Building   470
    Restaurants
        Bangkok Garden   471
        Chiaro's   471
        Il Posto   471
        Le Bistingo   471
        Winston's   471
    Shopping
        Eaton Center   470
        Harborfront   470
    Skydome   470
    St. Lawrence Center   471
    Toronto Islands Park   470
Trail Riders of the Canadian Rockies   485
Trans-Canada Highway   474
VIA Rail Canada   485

The Caribbean
Anguilla   539
    Cap Juluca   539
    Happy Jack's   539
    Malliouhana Hotel   539
    Mariners   539
    Shoal Bay Villes   539
Aruba   546
    Aruba Tourism Authority   546
    Hyatt Regency Hotel   546
    La Cabana All-Suite Hotel   546
    Sonesta Hotel Beach Club and Casino   546
    Waterfront   546
Bahamas   537
    Nassau   537
        Carnivals Crystal Palace Resort and Casino   538

Royal Bahamian Hotel   537
Paradise Island   538
Bermuda   546
    Bermuda Water Tours   547
    Elbow Beach Hotel   547
Caymans   535
    Grand Cayman
        Bob Soto's Diving   536
        Grand Cayman Holiday Inn   536
        Hyatt   536
        Silver's Nightclub   536
        Tortuga Club   536
Cuba   547
    Internacional   547
    Punta Arena-Paradiso   547
    Varadero Super Club   547
Dominican Republic   544
    Hispaniola   544
    Santo Domingo   544
        Alcazar   544
        Casa de Campo   544
        Casas Reales Museum   544
        Hostal Nicolas de Ovando   544
        La Roca   544
        Meson de la Cava   544
        National Pantheon   544
        Santa Maria la Menor   544
Exumas   538
    Peace and Plenty Hotel   538
Haiti   543
    Cap Haitien   543
    Grand Hotel Oloffson   544
    Habitation Leclerc   543
    Pension Craft   544
Jamaica   536
    Blue Lagoon   536
    Blue Mountain Coffee   537
    Hotels
        Half Moon Club   537
        Holiday Inn   537
        Pegasus Hotel   537
        Sans Souci   537
    Kingston   537
    Montego Bay   536, 537
    Negril   536, 537
    Ocho Rios   536
    Port Antonio   536
    Rick's Café   536
    Rose Hall   536
    Runaway Bay   536
Marinas and Charters
    Discovery Yacht Charters   548
    North South Charters   548
    The Moorings   548
Martinique   540
    Fort-de-France   540
        Pre-Columbian Art Museum   541
        Rue Victor Hugo   541
        Schoelcher Library   541
    Hôtel Plantation de Leyritz   541
    La Pagerie   541
    Mount Pelée   541
    Ste. Anne   541
Montserrat   546
    Air Studios   546
    Galway's Soufrère   546
    Great Alps Waterfall   546
    Plymouth   546
        Anthony's Church   546
        Parliament Street   546
        Perk's Factory   546
    Rendezvous Beach   546

Vue Point Hotel   546
Netherlands Antilles   545
    Curaçao   545
        Beth Haim   545
        Congregation Mikve Israel-Emanuel   545
        De Taveerne   545
        Fort Amsterdam   545
        Fort Nassau   545
        Jaanchie's   545
        Jan Kok Landhuis   545
        Playa Forti   545
        Ronde Klip   545
        St. Christoffelberg   545
        Westpunt   545
        Willemstad   545
    Saba   545
        Lime Time   545
        Saba Deep   545
        Scout's Place   545
        The Captain's Quarters   545
Puerto Rico   542
    Esperanza   543
        Parador Villa Esperanza   543
        Phosphorescent Bay   543
    Rincon   542
        Villa Antonio   543
    San Juan   542
        El Convento   542
    Vieques   543
        Casa del Frances   543
        Vieques Divers   543
Nevis   539
    Montpelier Plantation Inn   540
St. Barthélemy   535
    Anse du Gouverneur   535
    Sapore di Mare   535
St. Kitts   539
    Golden Lemon   540
St. Martin   540
    La Caravelle   540
    Marigot   540
St. Vincent & The Grenadines   542
    Mustique   542
        Cotton House   542
Trinidad and Tobago   541
    Man of War Cottages   541
    Tourist Board   541
U.S. Virgin Islands   538
    St. John   538
        Caneel Bay Plantation   539
        Maho Bay   538
        Mary's Point   538
        Rockresorts Reservations   539
        Watermelon Bay   538

China

Bai Yun Shan   260
Beijing   253
    Beihai   255
        Qionghua   255
        Zhichu Qiao   255
    Forbidden City   254
    Gulou   255
    Hotels
        Beijing Hotel   257
        Holiday Inn Lido Beijing   257
        Shangri-La Hotel   257
        Xiang Shan   257
        Zhu Yuan   257
    Religious sites
        East Church   255
        Fa Hua Si Temple   255

Huan Qiu Tan   254
Tiantan   254
Restaurants
Fang Shan   257
Sick Duck   257
Ting Li Guan   257
Shopping
Arts Store   256
Baihuo Dalou   255
Beijing Silk Market   256
Capital Medicine Shop   256
Donghuamen   255
Friendship Store   255
Liulichang   256
Musical Instruments Store   256
Wangfujing   255
Wangfujing Kezi Menshibu   256
Zhongguo Pihuo Fuzhuangdian   256
Tiananmen Square   254
Wangfujing   255
Yiheyuan   255
Long Corridor   255
Longevity Hill   255
Zhonglou   255
Bilingsi Buddhist Caves   267
China Youth Travel   272
Conghua   260
Dali   270
Garden Café   270
Peace Café   270
Third Month Fair   270
Gaochang   268
Great Wall   256
Badaling   256
Mutianyu   256
Guangzhou   258
Hotels
Dong Fang Hotel   260
Shanzhuang   260
Shuangxi   260
White Swan Hotel   260
Restaurants
Banxi   259
Nanyuan   259
She Canguan   259
Yuyuan   259
Shamian   258
Shopping
Chinese Export Commodities Fair   259
Hongshu Road   259
Nanfang   259
Quingping Market   259
Renmin Road   259
Sites
Chen Clan Academy   258
Cultural Park   258
Five Goats Statue   258
Huaisheng Mosque   259
South China Botanical Gardens   258
Zhenhailou   258
Guilin   264
Long Lin   264
Shuijinggong   264
Zengpiyan Cave   264
Zhongshan Lu   265
Hainan Island   271
Hangzhou   263
Gu Shan   264
Three Pools Mirroring the Moon   264
West Lake People's Commune   264
Heaven Lake   269
Hong Kong Student Travel Bureau   272

Jiaohe   268
Jiayuguan   267
Kashgar   269
Id Kah Mosque   269
Kashgar Guesthouse   269
Seman Hotel   269
Sunday Market   269
Tian Nan Restaurant   269
Li River   264
Ming tombs   256
Ling En Dian   257
Sacred Way   256
Shanghai   260
Hotels
Heping (Peace) Hotel   263
Hua Ting Sheraton   263
Jinjiang   263
Shanghai Hilton International   263
Shanghai Mansions Hotel   263
Nanjing Dong Road   262
Restaurants
Lao Fandian Restaurant   262
Laozhengxing (Old Prosperity) Restaurant   262
Wuxing Ting   261
Shanghai Acrobatic Theater   262
Shanghai Museum of Art and History   261
Sites
Blood Alley   261
Cheng Huang Miao   261
Jade Buddha Temple   262
Longhua   262
Old Town   260
Qiu Xia Pu   261
Wai Tan   261
Yu Yuan Garden   261
Shapin   270
Shenzhen   263
Forum   263
Shenzhen Splendid China Development Company Ltd.   263
Splendid Miniature China   263
Shisanling   256
Silk Route   267
Suzhou   264
Liuyuan   264
Zhuozhengyuan   264
Taklamakan Desert   268
Thousand Buddha Grottoes   268
Tibet   271
Lhasa   271
Deprung Monastery   272
Holiday Inn   272
Jokhang Temple   272
Potala   272
Turpan   268
Ürümqi   268
Hua Qiao Hotel   268
Xi'an   265
Golden Flower Hotel   267
Great Mosque   265
Hua Xing Hot Springs   266
Shaanxi Provincial Museum   265
Sichuan Restaurant   266
Xing Jiao Temple   266
Xishuangbanna   270
Damenglong   271
Jinghong   270
Menghai   271
Octagonal Pagoda   271
Menghan   271
New Year Water Splashing Festival   270
Zixingyan   260

CIS

Amur River 252
Belarus 250
Gobi Desert 252
Homestays
    Home & Host International 251
Hostels
    Finnish Youth Hostel Association 252
Irkutsk 252
Lake Baikal 252
Minsk, Belarus 250
    Hotels
        Belarus 250
        Planeta 250
        Yubeleymaya 250
    Markets
        Storazhovsky Renok 250
Moscow 249
    Arbat 249
    Bolshoi Theater 249
    Restaurants
        Rossiya Hotel 249
    Shopping
        Arbat Street 250
        GUM 250
Olekminsky Range 252
Shilka River 252
Siberia 252
Tien Shan Mountains 251
    Chimkent 251
    Kazahkstan 251
    Mount Lenin 251
    Sairam 251
Travel
    Intourist 252
    TransSiberian Express 252
Yablonovy Range 252

Eastern Europe

Albena, Bulgaria 232
Aleko, Bulgaria 233
Balatonfured, Hungary 237
    August Horse Show 237
    Gyogy Ter 237
    Hotels
        Annabella 237
        Arany Csillag 237
        Margareta 237
        Marina 237
Bialowieza National Park, Poland 247
Borovets, Bulgaria 232
    Hotels
        Samokov 233
        The Rila 233
Bucharest, Romania 243
    Calea Victoriei 243
    Churches
        Stavropoleos 243
    Hotels
        Athenee Palace 244
        Bucuresti 244
        Hanul Manuc 243
    Museums
        History Museum of Romania 243
        National Art Museum 243
    Princely Palace 243
    Restaurants
        Capsa 244
        Casa Lido 244
        Pescarus 244
    Shopping

Lipscani 243
    Theaters
        Operetta Theater 243
Budapest, Hungary 233
    Buda 233
    Buda Castle 233
    Gypsy Music Festival 234
    Heroes Square 234
    Hotels
        Atrium-Hyatt 235
        Budapest Hilton 235
        Duna-Intercontinental 235
        Forum 235
        Grand Hotel Corvinus Kempinski 235
        Hotel Gellert 235
    Houses of Parliament 234
    Matthias Church 234
    Museums
        Hungarian National Museum 234
        Museum of Fine Arts 234
    Pest 233
    Restaurants
        Alabardos 235
        Angelika 235
        Feher Galamb 235
        Gerbeaud 235
        Gundel 234
        Hungaria 235
        Matyaspince 234
    Shopping
        Vaci Utca 234
        Vamhaz Indoor Food Market 234
    Theaters
        State Opera House 234
Bulgaria 231
Cracow, Poland 246
    Churches
        Chapel of the Holy Cross 246
        Mariacki 246
        Sigismund Chapel 246
    Czartaryski Palace 246
    Florian Gate 246
    Jagiellonia University 246
    Museums
        Czartaryski Palace 246
    Shopping
        Rynek Glowny 246
    Wawel Castle 246
    Wawel Hill 246
Croatia 237
Czechoslovakia 239
Czestochowa, Poland 247
    Jasna Gora (Hill of Light) 247
Dalmatian Coast, Croatia 238
    Hvar, Croatia 238
Dracula's castle 244
Dubrovnik, Croatia 237
    Church of St. Vlaho 237
    Clubs
        Arsenal 238
        Lazareti 238
    Doge's Palace 237
    Fort Lovrijena 238
    Fortress of St. Ivan 237
    Hotels
        Dubravka 238
        Villa Dubrovnik 238
    Onofri's Fountain 237
    Zudioska Ulica 237
Eger, Hungary 236
Esztergom, Hungary 236
Fertod, Hungary 236

Esterhazy Palace   236
Hazmburk Castle, Czechoslovakia   243
Herceg Novi, Yugoslavia   239
Heviz, Hungary   237
Hluboka, Czechoslovakia   243
Hungary   233
Hvar, Croatia   238
   Tvrdava Disko   238
Krk, Croatia   238
Lake Balaton (Hungary)   236
Monasteries
   Bachkovo   232
   Rila monastery   232
   Transfiguration   232
Montenegro, Yugoslavia   239
Mount Vitosha, Bulgaria   233
Pamporovo, Bulgaria   233
   Hotels
      Mourgavets   233
      Perelik   233
Pecs, Hungary   235
Plitvice Lakes National Park, Yugoslavia   239
   Hotel Jezero   239
Poiana Brasov, Romania   244
   Bran Castle   244
Poland   244
Porec, Croatia   238
   Clubs
      Club No. 1   238
      FKK Koversada   238
Prague, Czechoslovakia   239
   Charles Bridge   240
   Churches and synagogues
      Altneushul (Old-New Synagogue)   241
      Betlemska kaple (Bethlehem Chapel)   240
      Church of Our Lady at Tyn   240
      Katedrala sv. Vita   241
      Klausen Synagogue   241
      Kostel sv. Nikulase   240
      Loretta   242
      Pinkas Synagogue   241
      Strahovsky Klaster   241
   Clubs
      Est Bar   242
      Lucerna   242
      Night Club   242
      U Fleku   240, 242
      U Kalicha   242
   Golden Lane   241
   Hotels
      Hotel Intercontinental   242
      Pariz   242
      U Tri Pstrosu   242
   Hradcany Quarter   241
   Karlovo namesti   240
   Laterna Magika   242
   Museums
      Dvorak Museum   241
      Narodni muzeum   240
      National Gallery   241
      State Jewish Museum   241
      Strahovsky Klaster   241
   Nerudova ulice   240
   New Town   240
   Novomestska radnice   241
   Old Jewish Cemetery   241
   Prasna brana   239
   Restaurants
      Opera Grill   242
      Slavia Café   242
      Svata Klara (St. Klara)   242
      Zlata Praha (Golden Prague)   242

Shopping
   Moser   242
   Slovenska Jizba   240
Small Town   240
   Malostranske namesti   240
   Stare Mesto (Old Town)   240
   Staromestske namesti   240
   Theological Hall   241
   Tomb of Franz Kafka   241
   Tomb of Rabbi Loew   241
   town hall   240
   Tyl Theater   240
   Vaclavske namesti   240
   Valdstejnsky Palac   240
   Vysehrad Fortress   242
Rab, Croatia   238
Risan, Yugoslavia   239
Romania   243
Rovinj, Croatia   238
St. Stephen, Yugoslavia   239
Sandanski, Bulgaria   232
Siofok, Hungary   236
   Hotels
      Europa   236
      Hotel Balaton   236
      Hotel Lido   236
      Hungaria   236
   Restaurants
      Menes Csarda   236
Ski resorts
   Bulgaria
      Aleko   233
      Borovets   232
      Pamporovo   233
   Czechoslovakia
      Stary Smokovec   243
   Poland
      Zakopane   247
Slovenia   239
Slovenian Riviera   239
   Towns
      Izola   239
      Piran   239
      Portoroz   239
Sofia, Bulgaria   233
   Hotels
      New Otani   233
      Sheraton   233
Spilberk Castle, Czechoslovakia   243
Sveti Stefan, Yugoslavia   239
Szentendre, Hungary   235
Velingrad, Bulgaria   232
   Zdravets Hotel   232
Visegrad, Hungary   235
Warsaw, Poland   244
   Barbican   245
   Chopin's birthplace   245
   Hotels
      Orbis-Europejski   246
      Victoria Inter-Continental   246
   House of the Mazovian Dukes   244
   King Sigismund's Column   245
   Lazienki Palace and Park   245
   Market Square   244
   Mausoleum to Struggle and Martyrdom   245
   Muranow   245
   Museums
      Jewish Historical Institute   245
      Maria Sklodowska Curie Museum   245
      Pawiak Prison Museum   245
      Warsaw Historical Museum   244
   Negro House   244

Restaurants
    Bazyliszek 245
    Karczma Slupska 246
    Krokodyl 246
  Royal Castle 244
  Wilanow Palace and Park 245
Zakopane, Poland 247
  Hotels
    Orbis Kasprowy 247
  Restaurants
    Kawiarnia Mis 247

France

The Alps, France 59
  Chamonix 59
  Compagnie des Guides 59
  Mont Blanc 59
  Route des Grandes Alpes 60
Alsace 65
  Colmar 66
  Eguisheim 66
  Restaurants
    Maison Kammerzell 65
  Riquewihr 66
  Rocher de Dabo 66
  Route du Vin 66
  Strasbourg 65
  Vosges Mountains 66
Basque Country, France 71
  Biarritz 71
  Hotels
    Hôtel du Palais 71
  St. Jean-Pied-de-Port 71
Bordeaux 63
  St. Emilion 63
  Syndicat d'Initiative 63
  Wine cellars
    Château Prieuré-Lechine 64
  Wine stores
    Badie 63
    Vignes et Vins de France 63
    La Vinothèque 63
Brittany 60
  Carnac 61
  Gulf of Morbihan 61
  Locmariaquer 61
  Restaurants
    Lorand-Barre 61
  St. Malo 60
    Hotel, the Central 60
Burgundy 64
  Beaune 64
  Chevaliers du Tastevin 65
  Grand' Salle 64
  Hospice 64
  Hospice de la Charité 64
  Hotel-Dieu 64
  Hotels
    Château d'Igé 65
    Hostellerie de la Poste 65
    Hôtel de la Poste 65
  Restaurants
    L'Espérance 64
Cathedrals
  Amiens 57
    Comité Régionale de Tourisme de Picardie 57
  Chartres 57
  Rheims 57
Centre Commercial de la Part-Dieu 59
Champagne
  Epernay 57
  Montagne de Rheims 57

Châteaux
  Blois 63
  Chambord 62
  Château Beychevelle 64
  Château Beynac-et-Cazenac 67
  Château Cos d'Estournal 64
  Château d'Amboise 62
  Château de Chissay 63
  Château de Pray 63
  Château Margaux 64
  Chenonceaux 62
  Domaine de Beauvois 63
  Vaux-le-Vicomte 57
Côte d'Azur 67
  Antibes 68
  Cannes 68
    Palm Beach Casino 68
  Grande Corniche 68
  Hotels
    Hôtel du Cap-Eden Roc 68
    Hôtel Negresco 68
    St. Yves 68
  Nice 67
  Restaurants
    Le Chantecler 68
    L'Oasis 68
  St. Tropez 67
Dordogne 66
  Brantôme 67
  Hotels
    Château de Roumegouse 67
  Limoges 66
  Oradour-sur-Glane 66
  Perigord 66
  Rocamadour 67
EuroDisney 58
Grande Corniche 68
Honfleur 61
  Hotels
    Lechat 61
Lake Annecy 60
  Hotels
    Hotel de l'Abbaye 60
Loire Valley, France 62
Lyons
  Hotels
    La Cour des Loges 59
    Maurice Bernachon 58
  Restaurants
    Henry 58
    Léon de Lyons 58
    L'Industrie 58
    Paul Bocuse's 58
    Vettard 58
  Shopping
    Centre Commercial de la Part-Dieu 59
    La Maison des Canuts 59
    Minouche Picot 59
Maurice Bernachon 58
Medicis Fountain 51
Mercure Galant 54
Mère Poulard 61
Michelin 46
Minouche Picot 59
Monaco 68
Mont St. Michel 61
Monte Carlo, Monaco 68
  Hotels
    Hôtel de Paris 68
  Night clubs
    No Rock 68
  Restaurants

Louis XV   68
Nice   67
Normandy   61
   D-Day beaches   62
   Deauville   61
   Etretat   61
   Honfleur
      Hotel, Lechat   61
   Hotels
      Lechat   61
      Mère Poulard   61
   Mont St. Michel   61
   Restaurants
      Mére Poulard   61
Paris   43
   American Library in Paris   49
   Berthillon   51
   Bois de Boulogne   51
   Carnets   57
   Les Catacombes   51
   Conciergerie   45
   Dalloyau   51
   Eiffel Tower   43
   Gastron Lenôtre   51
   Gibet de Montfaucon   48
   Hotels
      Esmeralda   56
      Hôtel d'Angleterre   56
      Hôtel de Crillon   56
      Hôtel des Deux Iles   56
      Hôtel George V   56
      L'Hôtel   56
      Plaza-Athénée   56
      Royal Alma   56
      The Ritz   55
   Jardin du Luxembourg   51
   Latin Quarter   47
   Les catacombes   51
   Marais   46
   Markets
      Beauvau St. Antoine   50
      Boulevard de Charonne   50
      Carmes   50
      Enfants Rouge   50
      La Chapelle   50
      Le Jules Vallès   49
      Le Marché aux Puces   49
      Le Marché Cambo   50
      Le Marché Malik   50
      Le Marché Serpette   50
      Père Lachaise   50
      Port-Royal   50
      Raspail   50
      Rue de Seine   50
      St. Didier   50
      St. Quentin   50
      Ternes   50
      Woodrow Wilson   50
   Medicis Fountain   51
   Michelin   46
   Montmarte   46
   Museums
      Centre Beaubourg   44
      Historical Museum of France   46
      Hotel de Cluny   46
      Hôtel de Rohan   46
      Louvre   44
      Musée Carnavalet   45
      Musée de Thermes   46
      Musée des Arts de la Mode   45
      Musée d'Orsay   45
      Musée Marmottan   45

      Musée Rodin   45
      Palais Soubise   46
      Picasso Museum   45
      Victor Hugo House   46
   Night clubs
      Les Bains-Douches   53
      Castel's   53
      Caveau de la Huchette   53
      Crazy Horse   53
      French Lovers   54
      La Nouvelle Eve   54
      Le Petit Journal   53
      Le Slow Club   53
      New Morning   53
   Notre Dame Cathedral   44
   Opéra de la Bastille   53
   Paris by Cycle   46
   Paris Opéra   53
   Paris Vélo   46
   Père Lachaise Cemetery   44
   Pigalle   53
   Place des Vosges   46
   Pont Alexandre III   48
   Restaurants and cafés
      Ambassade d'Auvergne   55
      Le Babylone   55
      Bofinger   52
      Brassérie Lipp   52
      Café de Flore   52
      Café de la Rotonde   52
      Le Café Costes   52
      Le Carré des Feuillants   54
      Charlot Ier   54
      Chez Francis   52
      Chez Georges   55
      Chez l'Ami Louis   55
      Chez Pauline   54
      Chez Pierrot   55
      La Coupole   52
      Les Deux Magots   52
      Le Dôme   52
      Dominique   55
      Le Drouot   55
      L'Epi d'Or   54
      Le Foux   55
      Mercure Galant   54
      L'Oulette   54
      Pasta et Vino   54
      Ramponneau   54
      Restaurant Chartier   55
      Robouchon   54
      La Tour d'Argent   54
      Le Train Bleu   55
   Sacrè-Coeur   45
   Le Sainte Chapelle   45
   Shopping
      Chanel   48
      Christian Dior   48
      Givenchy   48
      Irlande   48
      Jean Patou   48
      Passage Molière   49
      Philippe Venet   48
      Shakespeare & Co.   49
      Yves St. Laurent   48
   St. Germain-des-Près   45
   Tuileries Gardens   51
   University of Paris   47
   Versailles   57
Provence   69
  Aigues-Mortes   70
  Arles   69

Avignon 69
  Palais des Papes 69
  Pont d'Avignon 69
Camargue 70
Grasse 70
  La Parfumérie Gallimard 70
  La Parfumérie Fragonard 70
Hotels
  Hôtel d'Arlatan 69
  Hôtel d'Europe 69
  Jules César 69
  Mas de la Fouque 70
  Mas du Clarousset 70
Nîmes 70
Restaurants
  Auberge de France 69
  Le Vaccarès 69
St. Trophîme 69
Village des Bories 69
Rouen 62
Roussillon 70
  Carcassonne 71
  Collioure 70
Hotels
  Hôtel de la Cité 71
Perpignan 70
Sète 70
Rue de la Grange-aux-Belles 48
Stes. Maries de la Mer 70
Skiing
  Chamonix 59
  Les Contamines-Monjoies 60
    Hotel, Le Gai Soleil 60
St. Tropez 67
Trains
  Le Train Bleu 55
  Trains à Grande Vitesse, TGV 59

Germany

Aachen 84
  Schloss Friesenrath 84
  Spielcasino Aachen 84
  Steigenberger Hotel Quellenhof 84
Ahr region
  Lochmühle 87
  Weinstube Sankt Peter 87
Ahr Valley 87
Alps 94
  Garmisch-Partenkirchen 94
    Schneefernerhaus 94
  Zugspitze 94
Augsburg 97
  Fuggerei 97
Baden region 87
  Perkeo 87
  Weinstube im Schloss Heidelberg 87
Baden-Baden 85
Bavaria 89
Bergstrasse-Odenwald Nature Park 97
Berlin 73
  Akademie der Künste 76
  Alte Bibliothek 75
  Clubs
    Café Keese 76
    Metropol 76
    Riverboat 76
    Wirthaus zum Löwen 76
  Fernsehturm 73
  Hotels
    Bristol-Hotel Kempinski 77
    Hotel Ambassador 77
    Hotel Belvedere 77

    Metropol 77
    Palast 77
    Schloss Hotel Gerhus 77
  Humboldt University 75
  Ishtar Gate 74
  Kreuzberg 76
    Mehringhof complex 76
  Museums
    Altes Museum 74
    Bode Museum 74
    Egyptian Museum 75
    Gemäldegalerie 75
    House at Checkpoint Charlie 74
    Museumsinsel 74
    National Gallery 74
    Pergamon 74
    Zeughaus 75
  Pergamon Altar 74
  Philharmonie 76
  Restaurants
    Blockhaus Nikolskoe 77
    Bristol Kempinski Hotel Grill 77
    Conti Fischstuben 77
    Ermeler Haus 77
    Hecker's Deele 77
    I-Punkt 77
    Rockendorf's 76
  Shopping
    Die Nolle 76
    Kaufhaus des Westens 76
  Sites
    Charlottenburg Mausoleum 75
    Deutsche Staatsoper 74
    Europa Center 74
    French (Huguenot) Cathedral 74
    Kaiser-Wilhelm-Gedächtniskirche 74
    Lutheran Cathedral 74
    Marienkirche 75
    Saint Nicholas Church 75
    Schloss Charlottenburg 75
  Tiergarten 75
Black Forest 84
  Black Forest Crest Road 84
  Bühler-Höhe Hotel 85
  Route 500 84
Bodensee 84
Bremen 82
  Cathedral 82
  Der Ratskeller 82
  Grashoff's Bistro 82
  Grosse Halle 82
  Hotels
    Marriot 83
    Park Hotel 83
  Schiffahrtsmuseum 83
  Schnoor Viertel 82
  Statue of Roland 82
Buchenwald
  Buchenwald Concentration Camp 99
Cologne 83
  Cologne cathedral 83
  Hlg. Aposteln 83
  Hlg. Maria im Kapitol 83
  Hlg. Pantaleon 83
  Hotel Bristol 84
  Rhine Park 83
  St. Gereon 83
  Weinhaus im Walfisch 83
Deutsche Alpenstrasse 97
Dresden 98
  Albertinum 98
    Grünes Gewölbe 98

Frauenkirche 98
Hotels
   Astoria 98
   Königstein 98
Prager Strasse 98
Restaurants
   Meissener Weinkeller 98
   Oberlausitzer Topp'l 98
Semper Opera 98
Zwinger Palace 98
East Frisian Islands 88
   Amrum 89
   Borkum 89
   Fremdenverkehrsverband Nordsee Niedersachsen-
   Breme 89
   Juist 89
   Memmert 89
   Sylt 89
   Westerland 89
Fairy-Tale Trail 97
Feldberg 85
Frankfurt 77
Clubs
   Der Jazzkeller 79
   Operncafé 79
   Peter Dunker 79
   Volkswirt 79
Hotels
   Hessischer Hof 79
   Hübler 79
   National 79
   Schlosshotel Kronberg 79
   Steigenberger-Hotel Frankfurter Hof 79
Museums
   Historisches Museum 79
   Städel 78
Restaurants
   Dippegucker 78
   Gutsschänke Neuhof 78
   Restaurant Français 78
   Weinhaus Brückenkeller 78
Sachsenhausen Quarter 78
Sites
   Dom (Cathedral) of St. Bartholomäus 78
   Frankfurt's zoo 78
   Palmengarten 78
   Römer 78
German Wine Academy 87
Hamburg 80
Clubs
   Colibri 81
   Erotica 81
   Moonlight 81
   Salambo 81
Deichstrasse 80
Historic Emigration Office 81
Hotels
   Hotel Abtei 82
   Hotel Atlantic Kempinski 82
   Hotel Prem 82
   Vier Jahreszeiten 81
Museum of Hamburg History 80, 81
Reeperbahn 81
Restaurants
   Fischerhaus 81
   Haerlin 82
   Landhaus Scherrer 81
   Schümanns Austernkeller 81
Warehouse City 80
Harz 89
Heidelberg 79
   Electoral Palatinate Museum 80

Haupstrasse 79
Heidelberg Castle 80
   Grosses Fass 80
   Pharmaceutical Museum 80
   Weinstube Schloss Heidelberg 80
Hotels
   Der Europäische Hof 80
   Zum Ritter Sankt Georg 80
Philosopher's Walk 80
Kehlsteinhaus 95
Lorelei 88
Mad King Ludwig 95
   Linderhof Castle 95
   Neuschwanstein 95
Meersburg 85
   Hotel Bad Schachen 85
Meissen 98
Mittenwald 96
Moselle Valley 86
Munich 89
   Alte Peterskirche 91
Beer halls
   Augustiner 93
   Augustinerkeller 93
   Aumeister 93
   Chinesischer Turm 93
   Donisl 93
   Hofbräuhaus 93
   Mathäser Bierstadt 93
   Platzl 93
Clubs
   Musicland 93
   Park Café 93
   Schwabing 93
   Unterfahrt 93
Dachau Concentration Camp 92
Englischer Garten 91
Frauenkirche 90
Glockenspiel 90
Hotels
   Hotel Vier Jahreszeiten Kempinski 93
Marienplatz 90
Museums
   Alte Pinakothek 90
   Deutsches Museum 90
   Domicile 93
   J.A.M. 93
   Leopoldstrasse 92
   Marstallmuseum 92
   Munich Municipal Museum 91
   Neue Pinakothek 90
   P-Eins 93
   Residenzmuseum 90
   Schatzkammer 90
   Städtische Galerie im Lenbachhaus (Municipal
   Gallery) 91
Oktoberfest 89
Olympic tower 90
Restaurants
   Altes Hackerhaus 93
   Die Aubergine 92
   Franziskaner und Fuchsenstuben 93
   Nürnberger Bratwurstglöckl 93
   Weichandhof 93
Schloss Nymphenburg 92
Shopping
   Loden-Frey 91
   Marssstrasse 92
Nibelungenstrasse 97
Nuremberg 94
Oberammergau 95
   Alois Lang 95

Passionsspielhaus 95
Partenkirchen 97
Potsdam 99
    Interhotel Potsdam 99
    Sanssouci 99
Rheingau region 86
    Rüdesheim 86
Rheinpfalz region 86
Rhineland
    Hotel Burg Reichenstein 87
    Klostergut Jakobsberg 87
    Rheinfels 87
    Schlosshotel auf Burg Rheinfels 87
Romantic Road 96
Rothenburg ob-der-Tauber 96
    Baumeisterhaus 96
    Eisenhut 96
    Ratsstube 96
    Ratstrinkstube 96
Sababurg
    Hotel Sababurg 98
Speyer 86
    Café Hindenburg 86
Stuttgart 86
    Wirtshaus zum Götzenturm 86
Triberg 84
    Heimat Museum 85
    Park-Hotel Wehrle 85
    Uhrenmuseum 85
Trier 88
    Petrisberg Hotel 88
Worms 88

Greece

Athens 101
    Acropolis 101
    Acropolis Museum 102
    Agora 102
    Arch of Hadrian 103
    Benaki Museum 103
    Byzantine Museum 103
    Dafni Monastery 105
    Ergastirion Aporon Gynekon 104
    Ethniki Pronia Institute 104
    Hadrian's Library 102
    Hotels
        Diomia 105
        Grande Bretagne 103, 105
        Hotel Phaedra 105
        Meridien 105
        St. George Lycabettus 105
    Ikotechnia 104
    Kaesariani Monastery 105
    Kerameikos 102
    Kolonaki 104
    Kolonaki Square 103
    Lykabettos 103
    Monastiraki 104
    National Archeological Museum 102, 104
    National Organization of Handicrafts 104
    National Parliament Building 103
    Odeon of Herodes Atticus 102
    Omonia Square 104
    Pandrossou 104
    Parthenon 102
    Plaka 102
    Restaurants
        Apotsos 104
        Balthazar 104
        Dyonissos 104
        Erotokritos 104
        Five Brothers 104

    G.B. Corner 104
    Orfanides 104
    Psaropoulos 104
    Salamandra 104
    Savories 104
    Vasilena 104
    Xynos Taverna 104
    Roman Forum 102
    Stoa of Attalus 102
    Syntagma Square 103
    Temple of Athena Nike 102
    Temple of Olympian Zeus 103
    Theater of Dionysos 102
    YMCA 104
Atlantis 110
Automobile and Touring Club of Greece 114
Cape Sounion 105
    Aegean Hotel 105
    Temple of Poseidon 105
Corfu 112
    Achilleion Palace 112
    Cavalieri Corfu 112
    Hora 112
    Kassiopi 112
    Paleokastritsa 112
    Paliokastritza 112
    Pink Palace 112
Corinth 107
Crete 112
    Elounda 113
    Hania 113
        Elounda Beach Hotel 113
        Hotel Doma 113
    Knossos 113
    Samarian Gorge 113
Cyclades Islands 107
    Delos 109
    Mykonos 108
        Hotel Aphrodite 109
        Hotel Paralos Beach 109
        Kouneni 109
        Leto 109
        Little Venice 108
        Mykonos Disco Bar 109
        Niko's 108
    Santorini 109
        Hotel Villa Renos 110
    Xenia 108
Delphi 107
    Taverna Vakhos 107
    Vouzous Hotel 107
Dodecanese Islands 110
    Patmos 110
    Rhodes 110
        Fortress of the Knights of St. John 110
        Grand 110
        Kontiki 110
        Rhodes Casino 110
        Rodos Palace Hotel 110
Halkidi Peninsula 106
    Petralona Cave 106
Kastoria 106
Lesbos 111
    Xenia 111
Markessa 106
Meteora 107
Mount Athos 105
Mount Olympus 106
    Olympios-Zeus 106
    Xenias 106
Mount Parnassus 106
    Hotel Anemolia 106

Mycenae   107
Nafplion   107
Olympic Airways   114
Peloponnese   107
    Epidaurus   107
    Nafplion   107
    Olympia   107
    Sparta   107
    Summer Festival of Music and Drama   107
    Xenia Palace   107
Piraeus Port Authority   114
Samos   112
Santorini   109
Sporades Islands   111
    Skiathos   111
        Skiathos Palace   111
        Xenia   111
    Skopelos   111
Trikala   106
Tzitzines   104
Volos Port Authority   114
Yacht Brokers and Experts Association   115

Hong Kong and Macau

1997   276
Hong Kong
    Bird Street   275
    Bowen Road   276
    Cat Street Galleries   275
    Far East Jetfoil   280
    Festivals
        Cheung Chau Island Bun Festival   277
        Chinese New Year   276
        Dragon Boat Festival   277
    Hollywood Road   275
    Hong Kong Harbor   273
    Hongkong & Shanghai Bank   276
    Hotels
        Hong Kong Hilton   278
        Island Shangri-La   278
        Mandarin   278
        Peninsula   278
        Regent   278
        Salisbury YMCA   278
        Trappist Monastery Retreat House   278
    Information and Guest Center   276
    Jade Market   275
    Jindo Ltd.   274
    Lamma   277
    Lan Kwai Fong Street   276
    Lantau Island   273
    Mass Transit Railway   279
    Nightclubs
        1997   276
        Lan Kwai Fong Street   276
        Mandarin Oriental   276
        Mecca 97   276
        Post 97   276
    Outlets
        Four Seasons Garments   274
        Oriental Pacific   274
        Shoppers' World Ltd.   274
    Poon Keung Workshop   274
    Restaurants
        Gaddi's   277
        Lei Yue Mun   277
        Luk Yu Tea House and Restaurant   277
        Man Wah   277
        Plume   277
        Tan Wong Kok   277
    Stanley Market   274
    Star Ferry   278

Temple of Ten Thousand Buddhas   275
Victoria Peak   273
Wong Tai Sin Temple   275
Yuet Kai   275
Macau   279
    A Ma Temple   279
    Casino de Lisboa   279
    Church of St. Paul   279
    Colonne   280
    Department of Tourism   280
    Far East Jetfoil   280
    Macau Palace   279
    Macau Tourist Information Bureau   280
    Pousada de São Tiago   279
    Restaurants
        Fat Siu Lau   280
        Pinocchio's   280
    Rua da Praia Grande   280
    Taipa   280

India

Ahmedabad   301
    Ahmed Shah's Masjid Mosque   301
    Mausoleum of Shah Alam   301
    Mosque of Sidi Sayvid   301
    Sun Temple of Modhera   301
Assam   312
Aurangabad   305
    Ajanta Caves   305
    Ellora Caves   305
    Rama International Hotel   305
Bagh   306
Bombay   302
    Chowpatty Beach   302
    Festivals
        Ganesh Chaturthi   303
    Hanging Gardens   303
        Parsee Towers of Silence   303
    Hotels
        Grand   304
        Hotel Nataraj   304
        Oberoi Towers   304
        Taj Mahal Intercontinental   304
    Juhu Beach   303
    Mahim Creek   303
    Mani Bhavan   303
    Marine Drive   302
    Markets
        Mahatma Jyotiba Phule Market   303
        Thieves Market   303
    Restaurants
        Berry's Restaurant and Bar   304
        Delhi Darbar   303
        Khyber Restaurant   303
        Satkar Caterers   303
        Sri Ratan Tata Institute   303
    Shopping
        Prince of Wales   303
    Veermata Jijabai Bhonsle Udyan   303
Calcutta   309
    Botanical Gardens   310
    Dalhousie Square   310
    Fort William   310
    Hotels
        New Kenilworth Hotel   311
        Oberoi Grand   311
    Howrah Bridge   310
    Markets
        New Market   310
    Museums
        Indian Museum   310
    Nakhoda Mosque   310

Old Calcutta 310
Parasnath Jain Temple 310
Restaurants
  Abhinandan 311
  Gay Rendez-Vous 311
  Mocambo Restaurant 311
  Peter Cat Restaurant 310
  Shenaz Restaurant and Bar 311
  Vineet Restaurant 310
The Maidan 310
Victoria Memorial 310
Zoo 310
Chidambaram 308
Temple of Nataraja 308
Darjeeling 311
Aloobari 312
Bhutia Busty Tibetan 312
Kanchenjunga Mountain 312
Lloyd Botanical Gardens 312
Mountain climbing
  Himalayan Mountaineering Institute 312
Observatory Hill 312
Racetrack 312
Tiger Hill 312
Delhi 297
Bhangra Dance 299
Delhi Zoological Park 299
Hotels
  Ashok 299
  Imperial 299
  Oberoi Maidens 299
Iron Pillar 298
Jama Masjid 298
Jantar Mantar Observatory 298
Mausoleum of Emperor Humayun 298
Parliament House 298
Presidential Palace 298
Purana Qila 298
Qutb Minar 298
Quwwat-ul-Islam Mosque 298
Rajghat 298
Rajpath 298
Ram Lila 299
  Dussehra Festival 299
Red Fort 298
Shopping
  Chandni Chowk 298
Shrine of Nizam-ud-din 298
War Memorial Arch 298
Elephanta 304
Ganges River 311
Allahabad 311
  Magh Mela 311
Hotels
  Barnetts 311
  Yatrik 311
Kumbh Mela 311
Gir Forest 306
Travel
  Regional Manager 306
Goa 304
Basilica of Bom Jesus 305
Beaches
  Calangute Beach 305
  Colva Beach 305
  Dona Paula 305
Hotels
  Dodge Holiday Village 305
Kanchipuram 308
Kailasanatha Temple 308
Vaikunthanatha Perumal Temple 308
Varadarajaswamy Temple 308

Kashmir 301
Amarnath 302
Gardens and Lakes
  Lake Manasbal 302
  Lake Wular 302
  Nishat Bagh 302
  Shalimar Bagh 302
Golfing
  Gulmarg 302
Hotels
  Broadway 302
  Palace Hotel 302
  Shahenshah 302
Skiing
  Hotel Highland Parks 302
Srinagar 301
  Temple to Siva 301
Kumbakonam 308
Mahabaleshwar 304
Hotels
  Frederick Hotel 304
Pratapgarh Fort 304
Mahabalipuram 308
Malwa 306
Hotels
  Travellers' Lodge 306
Taveli Mahal 306
Nagaland 312
Ootacamund 308
Hotels
  Savoy Hotel 309
Orissa 309
Bhubaneswar 309
  The Great Lingaraj Temple 309
Hotels
  South Eastern Railway Hotel 309
Konarak 309
Puri 309
  Jagannath Temple 309
  Rath Yatra Festival 309
The Adivasi 309
Palitana 306
Hotels
  Hotel Sumeru 306
Shatrunjaya 305
Panaji 305
Hotels
  Fidalgo 305
  Mandovi 305
Rajasthan 299
Amber 300
Jaipur 300
  Chandra Mahal 300
  City Palace 300
  Hawa Mahal 300
  Jai Niwas Gardens 300
  Jantra Observatory 300
  Nahargarh 300
Mount Abu 300
Museums
  Man Singh II Museum 300
Sunset Point 300
Udaipur 300
  Sahelion-ki-Bari Park 300
Sanchi 306
Great Stupa 306
Hotels
  Travellers' Lodge 307
Sevagram 307
Hotels
  Mt. Hotel 307
  Sarve Seva Sangh 307

Taj Mahal   299
Tamil Nadu   307
  Madras   307
    Bharata Natya   308
    Cathedral of St. Thome   307
    Fort Museum   307
    Fort St. George   307
    Government Museum   307
    Guindy Deer Park   307
    Kapaliswarar Temple   308
    Madras National Art Gallery   307
    Madras Snake Park and Conservation Center   307
    Marina Beach   307
    St. Mary's Church   307
    Theosophical Society   308
Thanjavur   308
  Brihadiswara   308
Travel
  Air India   313
  Discover India ticket   313
  Divisional Forest Officer   312
  Tours of Distinction   301

Ireland

Aran Islands   123
  Dun Aengus   123
  Inisheer   123
  Inishmaan   123
  Inishmore   123
Ballaghisheen Pass   122
Blackwater Bog   124
Bray   119
Burren   125
Castle Hotels
  Ashford Castle   125
  Castle Matrix   125
  Gregan's Castle Hotel   126
Clarinbridge
  Paddy Burke's Oyster Tavern   123
Cliffs of Moher   122
Clonmacnoise   124
Conair Pass   122
Cork   121
  Ballymaloe House   121
  Blarney Castle   121
  English Market   121
  President's Restaurant   121
  Shandon Church   121
County Donegal
  Magee's Tweed Shop   124
County Galway
  Aille Cross Equitation Centre   123
  Connemara Trail   123
  Great Fair of Ballinasloe   123
County Wicklow   120
Croagh Patrick   125
Dingle Peninsula   122
Donegal   124
Dublin   117
  Dublin Trail   117
  Guinness Brewery   118
  Hotels
    Jurys Dublin Hotel   120
    Shelbourne Hotel   120
  James Joyce   117
  Martello Tower and Museum   117
  Moore Street Market   119
  Museums
    Kilmainham Jail Historical Museum   118
    National Gallery   118

National Museum   118
Paul Cooke's Shop   118
Pubs
  Abbey Tavern   119
  Baggot Inn   119
  Brazen Head   118, 119
  Culturalann na hEireann   119
  Davy Byrne's   119
  Long Hall   118
  Mulligan's   117
  Palace Bar   118
  Slattery's Pub   119
  The Bailey   119
Restaurants
  Bewley's   117
  King Sitric   120
Sites
  St. Michan's Church   119
  Bedford Tower   118
  Dublin Castle   118
  General Post Office   118
  Phoenix Park   119
  Records Tower   118
The Book of Kells   117
Trinity College   118
Ennis   121
  Bunratty House   122
  Old Ground   122
Enniskerry   120
Gallerus Oratory   122
Glencar   122
Glendalough   120
Kerry
  Ballyseede Castle Hotel   122
  Parknasilla-Great Southern   122
Killarney   122
Kinsale   121
Limerick   123
  Bunratty Castle   123
Lisdoonvarna   125
Mount Charles   124
Ring of Kerry   122
River Shannon   125
  Emerald Star   125
Rossbeigh Beach   122
Shannon Castle Tours   123
Skellig Rocks   122
Slea Head   122
Sligo   123
  Hargadons   124
Sybil Head   122
Ventry   122
Waterford   120
  Joseph Know   121
  Kelly's Ltd.   121
  Shaw's   121
Wexford   120
  Crown Bar   120
  Killiane Castle   120

Isle of Man

Corrin's Folly   127
Hotels
  Admiral House Hotel   129
  Ascot   129
  Grand Island Hotel   129
  Grosvenor Hotel   129
  Mannin   129
  Palace Hotel   129
Laxey   128
Manx Cattery   128
Manx Ice Factory   128

Millennium Way   128
Point of Ayre   128
Restaurants
    Boncompte's   128
    Harris's   128
Royal Chapel of St. John the Baptist   127
Travel
    Cleveland Self-Hire   129
    Isle of Man Steam Packet Seaways   128
    Manx Airlines   129
Tynwald   127

Israel

Akko   378
    Akko Theater Festival   379
    Beaches
        Argaman   378
    Crusader Castle   379
    Hotels
        Argaman Motel   379
Ashkelon   375
    National Antiquities Park   375
Bethlehem   373
    Barakat Antiques   373
    Casa Nova Inn   373
    Church of the Nativity   373
    Garden Tomb   373
    Manger Square   373
    Milk Grotto   373
    Rachel's tomb   373
    Shepherds' Field   373
Caesarea   379
    Dan Caesarea Golf Hotel   379
Dead Sea   376
    Arad   376
    Ein Gedi   376
    Hotels
        Ein Bokek   376
        Ein Gedi kibbutz   376
        Margoa Arad   376
        Moriah Gardens Hotel   376
    Mezad Zohar   376
    Spas
        Moriah Dead Sea Spa Hotel   376
Eilat   381
    Diving
        Lucky Divers' Eilat Scuba Center   381
    Hai-Bar   381
    Hotels
        Red Sea Sport Hotel   381
        Sonesta Suites Hotel   381
    Restaurants
        La Bohème   381
        La Coquille   381
        Last Refuge   381
En Hod   378
Galilee   379
    Bet Shean   380
    Capernaum   380
    Hittim   380
    Jethro   380
    Kafr Kanna   380
    Kafar Hittin Ranch   380
    Mount of Beatitudes   380
    Nazareth   380
    Qursi   380
    Restaurants
        Lido   379
    Sea of Galilee   379
    Tabgha   380
    Tiberias   379
Golan Heights   381

Golan Field School   381
Hazor   381
Museums
    Golan Archeological Museum   381
    Qazrin   381
Haifa   377
    Baha'i International Archives   377
    Baha'i Shrine and Gardens   377
    Baha'i Universal House of Justice   377
    Hotels
        Dan Carmel   378
        Nof   378
        Shulamit   378
        Yaarot Hacarmel Rest House   378
    Museums
        Haifa Illegal Immigration and Naval Museum   377
        Haifa Museum Complex   377
    Restaurants
        Bankers Tavern   378
        Neptune   378
        Peer   378
        Shmulik & Dany   378
    Technion   377
Hebron   373
Jaffa   375
    Restaurants
        Toutoune   375
        Via Maris   375
Jericho   377
Jerusalem   369
    Binyanei Haoma   371
    Clubs
        American Colony Hotel   372
        Herod's Bar   372
        Jerusalem Khan   372
        Pergod Theater   372
        Taverna   372
    Cultural Events
        Cahanna Ticket Agency   371
    Festivals
        Hakafot   371
        Israel Festival of Music and Drama   371
        Liturgica   371
    Hotels
        King David   372
        King Solomon Sheraton   372
        The American Colony Hotel   372
        Windmill   372
    Museums
        Museum of the Potential Holocaust   370
        The Israel Museum   371
        The Rockefeller Museum   371
    New City
        Knesset   370
        Yad Vashem   370
        Yemenite Moshe Quarter   370
    Old City
        Church of the Holy Sepulcher   370
        Coenaculum   370
        Damascus Gate   370
        Dome of the Rock   370
        Gihon Spring   370
        Golden Gate   370
        Hezekiah's Tunnel   370
        Jaffa Gate   370
        Mount of Olives   370
        Mount Zion   370
        Pool of Shiloah   370
        Temple Mount   370
        Tomb of the Virgin Mary   370
        Via Dolorosa   370

Wailing Wall   370
Restaurants
  Caravan   371
  Caty's Restaurant   372
  National Palace Restaurant   372
  Shemesh   372
  Shulchan Restaurant   372
  Ticho House   372
Shopping
  Arab bazaar   371
  Khutsot Hayotser   371
  Tarshish   371
Masada   376
Mount Carmel   377
Nahariyya   378
Neve Shalom   373
Safed   380
  Ha'Ari Synagogue   380
  Hotels
    Rimon Inn   380
Sea of Galilee   379
Tel Aviv   373
  Clubs
    Colosseum   374
  Hotels
    Dan Hotel   375
    Greenhouse   375
    Hotel HaGalil   375
    Hotel Tamar   375
    Immanuel House Christian Hospice   375
    Tel Aviv Sheraton   375
  Mann Auditorium   374
  Migdal Shalom   374
  Museums
    Diaspora Museum   374
    Tel Aviv Museum   373
    The Eretz Museum   374
  Restaurants
    Cherry's   374
    Restaurant Yamit   374
    Taj Mahal   374
    Zion Restaurant   374
  Shopping
    Maskit   374

Italy

Alghero   161
  Beaches
    Spiaggia di Maria Pia   161
    Spiaggia di San Giovanni   161
  Grotto di Nettuno   161
  Restaurants
    Il Pavone   161
Alta Badia   151, 152
Amalfi Coast   148
  Capuchin Monastery   149
  Positano   149
  Ravello   149
Aosta   152
  Churches
    Church of St. Ursus   152
  Gran Paradiso National Park   152
  Mancuso Hotel   152
  Museums
    Istituto Storico della Resistenza della Valle
      d'Ao   152
Artimino Estate   156
  Hotel Paggeria Medicea   156
Artimo Estate
  Biagio Pignatta   156
Assisi   155
  Churches

Basilica of San Francesco   155
Basilica of Santa Chiara   155
Basilica Santa Maria   155
Convent of San Damian   155
Hotels
  Hotel Fontebella   155
Bellagio   153
Bomarzo   154
Burano Island   143
  Church of San Martino   143
  Consorzio Merletti di Burano   143
Cagliari   160
  Hotels
    Locanda Firenze   160
  Restaurants
    Dal Corso   160
    Trattoria Gennargentu   160
Camogli   150
  Hotels
    Cenobio dei Dogi   151
Capri   149
  Hotels
    Hotel Luna   150
    Quisiana and Grand Hotel   150
    Scalanitella   150
  Restaurants
    La Pigna   150
    La Sceriffa   150
Capuchin Monastery   149
Cervinia   151
Cinque Terre   151
Cogne   152
  Gran Paradiso National Park   152
Colfosco   151, 152
Corniglia   151
Cortina d'Ampezzo   151
  Cristallo Hotel   151
Cortina d'Ampezzo   151
La Costa del Sud   160
Costa Smeralda   160
Courmayeur   151
Dolomites   151
  Cogne   152
  Hotel Colfosco Hof   152
  National Park of Abruzzi   152
  Towns
    Alta Badia   151
    Aosta   152
    Cervinia   151
    Colfosco   151
    Cortina d'Ampezzo   151
    Courmayeur   151
    Merano   152
    Pedraces   152
    La Pieja   152
    Valle d'Aosta   151
Fiesole   156
  Hotels
    Hotel Aurora   156
    Villa San Michele   156
  Restaurants
    Hotel Aurora   156
Florence   139
  Accademia   140
  Baptistery   140
  Churches
    Baptistery   140
    Basilica of San Lorenzo   140
    Il Duomo   139
    San Miniato al Monte   141
    Santa Croce   140
    Santa Maria Novella   140

Clubs
  Manila 142
  Tenax 142
Hotels
  Hotel Regency 141
  Pensione Quisisana e Pontevecchio 141
  Tornabuoni Beacci 141
  Villa Medici 141
Museums
  Accademia 140
  Bargello 140
  Museo dell'Opera del Duomo 140
  Pitti Palace 140
  Uffizi Museum 139
Oltrarno 141
Palazzo Medici 140
Ponte Vecchio 140
Restaurants
  Da Noi 142
  Enoteca Pinchiorri 141
  Trattoria La Beppa 142
  Vivoli 142
Shopping
  Fallani Bet 141
Vasari Corridoio 139
Gran Paradiso National Park 152
Hadrian's Villa 139
Herculaneum 148. *See also* Mount Vesuvius
Hiking 152
Isola Comacina
  Locanda dell'Isola Comacina 153
Italian Riviera 150
  Camogli 150
  Corniglia 151
  Manarola 151
  Monterosso 151
  Portofino 150
  San Fruttoso 150
  San Remo 150
  Vernazza 151
Lago d'Orta 154
Lake Como 153
  Hotels
    Villa d'Este 153
  Restaurants
    Locanda dell'Isola Comacina 153
Lake District
  Islands
    Isola Comacina 153
    San Giulio Island 154
  Lakes
    Lago d'Orta 154
    Lake Como 153
    Lake Garda 153
  Towns
    Bellagio 153
    Torbole 153
Liguria 150
  Italian Riviera 150
Lucca 156
  Churches
    Church of San Frediano 157
    Church of San Michel 157
    Romanesque cathedral 157
  Hotels
    Albergo Universo 157
  Restaurants
    Buca di Sant'Antonio 157
Manarola 151
Mantua 145
  Churches
    Church of Sant' Andrea 145

Ducal Palace 145
  Hotels
    Hotel Rechigi 145
    San Lorenzo 145
  Palazzo Te 145
  Restaurants
    Il Cigno 145
Merano 152
  Hotels
    Schloss Rundegg 152
Montalcino castle 138
  Brunello di Montalcino 138
Monterosso 151
Mount Etna 159
Mount Vesuvius 148
Murano Island 143
  Museo Vetrario 143
Naples 145
  Castel dell'Ovo 146
  Castel Nuovo 146
  Churches
    Cappella Sansevero 145
  Clubs
    Il Gabbiano 146
    Margellina Quarter 146
  Grotta della Sibilla 147
  Herculaneum 148
  Hotels
    Excelsior 147
    Vesuvio 147
  Lago di Avernus 147
  Lungomare 146
  Margellina Quarter 146
  Mount Vesuvius 148
  Museums
    Capodimonte Museum and Picture Gallery 146
    Il Museo Archeologico Nazionale 146
  Pompeii 148
  Restaurants
    Avellinese da Peppino 147
    La Cantinella 147
    La Fazenda 147
    Il Gallo Nero 147
  Theater
    San Carlo Theater 146
Nora 160
Orvieto 154
  Duomo 154
  Hotels
    Hotel La Badia 155
Paestum 148
Palermo 160
  Hotels
    Grand Hotel Villa Igiea 160
  Restaurants
    La Scuderia 159
    Trattoria Primavera 159
Pedraces 152
Perugia 155
  Collegio del Cambio 155
  Corso Vanucci 155
  Fontana Maggiore 155
  Hotels
    La Rosetta 155
  Museums
    National Gallery 155
  Via Bagliona Sotteranea 155
Pisa 158
  Baptistery 158
  Campo Santo 158
  Duomo 158
Pompeii 148. *See also* Mount Vesuvius

Porto Torres   161
Portofino   150
  Hotels
    Hotel Splendido   150
Positano   149
  Hotels
    Hotel San Pietro   149
Ravello   149
  Hotels
    Hotel Caruso Belvedere   149
    Hotel Palumbo   149
    Hotel Rufolo   149
Rome   131
  Appian Way   133
  Arch of Titus   131
  Baths of Caracalla   133
  Cala Regina   138
  Casina delle Civette   135
  Catacombs of St. Calixtus   133
  Churches
    Carcere Mamertino   134
    Church of S. Maria Maggiore   136
    Church of Santa Maria d'Aracoeli   133
    Cosma e Damiano   136
    S. Maria d'Aracoeli   136
    St. Peter's Basilica   135, 136
    San Pietro in Vincoli   134
    San Sabo   134
    Santa Balbina   134
    Santa Maria del Prioratu   134
    Santa Maria della Concezione dei Capuccini   133
    Santa Prisca   134
    Santa Sabina   134
    Sant'Alessio   134
    Sant'Anselmo   134
    Santissimi Giovanni e Paolo   135
    Sistine Chapel   132
    St. Peter's Basilica   132
  Coliseum   131
  Curia   131
  Fabricio Bridge   135
  Fountain of Rivers   135
  Hotels
    Ausonia   137
    Hassler   137
    Hotel Aventino   134
    Hotel Locarno   137
    Hotel Lord Byron   137
    Hotel Raphael   137
    Hotel Sant'Anselmo   134
    Hotel Villa San Pio   134
    La Villetta   134
    Le Grand Hotel   137
    Portoghesi   137
    Scalinata di Spagna   137
    Suisse   137
  Keats-Shelley Memorial House   135
  Museums
    Prehistoric and Ethnographic Museum of
      Rome   134
  Pantheon   132
  Parks
    Villa Torlonia   134
  Piazza del Pantheon   138
  Piazza di Santa Maria   138
  Piazza di Spagna   132
  Piazza Navona   138
  Restaurants
    Alberto Ciarla   137
    Andrea   138
    Antico Caffè Greco   135
    Cicilardone   138

    Hassler Hotel   138
    Il Drappo   138
    Ristorante da Sabatini   138
    Tre Scalini Rossana e Matteo   138
  Roman Forum   131
  Santo Bambino   133
  Shopping
    Boris-Pelletterie   136
    Campo dei Fiori   133
    Coin   136
    Convertite 81   136
    Di Ceglie   136
    Gentry   136
    JCA   136
    Porta Portese   133
    Tomassini   136
    Tusseda   136
    Vanita   136
    Vittoria 3A   136
  Temple of Julius Caesar   131
  Temple of the Vestal Virgins   131
  Trevi Fountain   132
  Vatican City   132
    Castel Sant' Angelo   132
    Pierdonati   133
    Prefettura della Casa Pontifica   132
    St. Peter's Basilica   132
    Sistine Chapel   132
  Villa Borghese   133
San Francesco del Deserto Island   143
San Fruttoso   150
San Gimigano
  Hotels
    La Cisterna   157
San Gimignano   157
San Giulio Island   154
San Guilio   154
San Lazzaro   143
San Remo   150
  Tourist office   150
Sardinia   160
  Alghero   161
  Cagliari   160
  Costa Smeralda   160
  Hotels
    Albergo Giusy   161
    La Costa del Sud   160
  Nora   160
  Nuraghi   160
    Nuraghi of Su Nuraxi   161
  Towns
    Porto Torres   161
    Sassari   161
    Turris Libisonis   161
Sassari   161
  Hotels
    Albergo Gallura   161
  Museums
    Museo Giovanni Antonio Sanna   161
Sicily   158
  Catania   159
  Mount Etna   159
  Palermo   159
  Taormina   159
Siena   157
  Hotels
    Park Hotel   158
  Palio   158
  Passeggiata   157
  Piazza del Campo   157
  Pinacoteca   158
Skiing   151

Stra
  Il Labirinto 145
Taormina 159
  Hotels
    Villa San Michele 160
Tivoli
  Restaurants
    La Laterna 139
  Romanesque cathedral 139
  Temple of Vesta 139
  Villa D'Este 139
  Villa Gregoriana 139
Torbole 153
Torgiano 155
  Baglioni Palace 155
  Hotels
    Hotel Le Tre Vaselle 155
Turris Libisonis 161
Tuscany 156
  Artimino Estate 156
  Towns
    Fiesole 156
    Lucca 156
    Pisa 158
    San Gimignano 157
    Siena 157
Umbria 154
  Towns
    Assisi 155
    Bomarzo 154
    Orvieto 154
    Perugia 155
    Torgiano 155
Valle d'Aosta 151
Venice 142
  Bridge of Sighs 142
  Burano Island 143
  Churches
    Basilica of San Marco 142
  Grand Canal 142
  Harry's Bar 145
  Hotels
    Grand Hotel des Bains 143
    Hotel Cipriani 144
    Hotel Flora 144
    Hotel Torino 144
    La Fenice des Artistes 144
    Pensione Accademia 144
  Lagoon 143
  Lido 143
  Museums
    Galleria dell'Accademia 143
  Palazzo Ducale 142
  Piazza San Marco 142
  Restaurants
    Antica Trattoria Orsetta 144
  San Francesco del Deserto 143
  San Lazzaro 143
  San Michele 143
  Theaters
    Gran Teatro La Fenice 144
Vernazza 151

Japan

Ainu 295
Asahikawa 295
Aso National Park 294
Eniwa 295
Fuji-Hakone-Izu National Park 288
Fuji-san (Mount Fuji) 288
Fukuoka 294
  Ohori Park 294

Geishas 296
Gifu 293
Hiroshima 292
  Hotels (Western-style)
    Hiroshima Grand 292
    Hiroshima Kokusai 292
    Hiroshima River Side 292
  Museums
    Peace Memorial Museum 292
Hokkaido 294
Ibusuki 294
  Hotels (Western-style)
    Ibusuki Kanko Hotel 294
    Ibusuki Royal Hotel 294
Ikebana 284
Itsukushima Shrine 292
Karuizawa 295
  Hotels (Japanese-style)
    Tsuruya Ryokan 296
  Hotels (Western-style)
    Hoshimo Onsen Hotel 296
    Karuizawa Prince 296
  Restaurants
    Akasaka Hanten 296
    Suehiro 296
Kitakyushu 294
Konomiya Naked Festival 293
Kusanagi-no-Tsurugi 293
Kyoto 288
  Gion Corner 291
  Gion district 290
  Hotels (both Japanese- and Western-style rooms)
    Fujita 290
    Kyoto 290
    Kyoto Royal 290
  Hotels (Japanese-style)
    Ryokan Reservation Center 290
    Tawaraya 290
  Hotels (Western-style)
    Miyako 290
    Takaragaike Prince Hotel 290
  Imperial Palace 288
  Japanese dance performances
    Gionkobu Kaburenjo 291
    Kanze Kaikan 291
    Kitano Kaikan 291
    Minami-za 291
    Pontocho Kaburenjo 291
  Katsura Villa 289
  Museums
    Kyoto National Museum 288
    Nishijin Textile Museum 289
  Nihon Seibukan 291
  Nijo Castle 289
  Nishijin district 289
  Restaurants
    Junidanya 290
    Okutan 290
    Sagano 290
  Shopping
    Kyoto Handicraft Center 289
    Nishijin district 289
  Shrines
    Heian shrine 288
  Shugakuin 289
  Temples
    Kinkaku-ji 288
    Ryoanji 288
    Saiho-ji (Moss Temple) 289
    Sanjusangendo (Temple of 33 Niches) 289
    Toji temple 289
Kyushu 293

Mount Aso 294
Mount Fuji 288
Nagasaki 294
    Atom Bomb Museum 294
    Glover Mansion 294
    Hotels (Japanese-style)
        Suwa-so 294
    Hotels (Western-style)
        Nagasaki Grand 294
        Nagasaki Tokyu 294
        New Nagasaki 294
        New Tanda Hotel 294
    Oura Catholic Church 294
    Peace Park 294
Nagoya 293
    Hotels (Western-style)
        Meitetsu Grand 293
        Nagoya Castle 293
        Nagoya Kanko 293
        Nagoya Miyako 293
    Nagoya Castle 293
    Shrines
        Atsuta shrine 293
    Zoo 293
Osaka 291
    Hotels (Western-style)
        Miyako Hotel Osaka 292
        Royal Hotel 292
    Museums
        Fujita Art Museum 291
        Masaki Museum of Art 291
    Osaka Castle 291
    Restaurants
        Goenya 291
        Hishitomi 291
        Wakatake 291
    Shopping
        Ebisu-Bashi-Suji 291
        Kita district 291
        Mido-suji 291
        Shinsai-Bashi-Suji 291
    Shrines
        Temmangu shrine 291
    Tennoji Park 291
    Theater
        Kokuritsu Bunraku Gekujo (National Puppet
            Theater) 292
        Shin-Kabukiza 292
Sapporo 295
    Hotels (Western-style)
        Akakura Kanko Hotel 295
        Sapporo Grand Hotel 295
        Yamagata Grand 295
Shiraoi 295
Shopping
    Aritsugu 289
Ski resorts
    Eniwa 295
    Mount Moiwa 295
    Teine 295
Teine 295
Tokyo 281
    Clubs
        Club Fontana 287
        Le Rat Mort 287
        Lexington Queen 287
        May Flower 287
        Potato Club 287
    Ginza district 283
    Harajuku district 283
    Hotels
        Rabu hoteru (love hotels) 287

Hotels (Japanese-style)
    Atamiso 286
    Fukudaya 286
    Japan Minshuku Center 286
    Tokiwa Ryokan Shinkan 286
Hotels (Western-style)
    Gajoen Kanko 287
    Hotel Okura 286
    Hyatt 287
    Imperial Hotel 287
    Keio Plaza 287
Imperial Palace 282
Korakuen baseball stadium 284
Museums
    Shitamachi History Museum 283
New Kokugikan sumo stadium 285
Nomiya (sake houses)
    Chichibu Nishiki 286
    Sasashu 286
Ohara School of Ikebana 284
Parks
    Chidorigafuchi Suijo Koen 282
    Kitanomaru Koen 282
    Ueno Park 283
Restaurants
    Chikuyo Tei 286
    Chinzanso 285
    Iseju 285
    Kushi Hachi-ten 285
    Kybei 286
    Maxim's 286
    Yabu-Soba 285
Roppongi district 287
Shinjuku district 283, 287
Shopping
    Asakusa district 283
    Seibu 283
    Tsukiji fish market 283
Shrines
    Hie shrine 282
    Meji shrine 283
    Yasukuni shrine 282
Sumo stables
    Kasugano-beya 285
    Takasago-beya 285
Sumo stadiums
    New Kokugikan 285
Tea ceremonies
    Chado Bunka Shinko-kai 285
    Etsu 285
    Hotel New Otani 285
    Hotel Okura 285
    Imperial Hotel 285
    Kenkyusha Eigo Centre 285
Temples
    Asakusa Kannon temple 282
    Sengakuji temple 283
Theater
    Ginza Nohgakudo 284
    Hosho Nohgakudo 284
    Kabukiza 284
    Kanze Nohgakudo 284
    National Noh Theatre 284
    National Theater of Japan 284
Ueno zoo 283
Yoshiwara district 288

Latin America

Argentina 532
    Buenos Aires 532
        La Boca 532
        Café Tortoni 532

Calle Defensa   532
El Caminito   532
Casa Rosada   532
Claridge Hotel   532
Plaza Dorrego   532
La Recoleta   532
San Martín Municipal Theater   532
Chapelco   533
La Pampa   532
Parque Caviahue   533
Primeros Piños   533
Ushuaia   533
Valle de Las Leñas   533
Cahuita Beach   524
Cabinas Atlantida   525
Cahuita National Park Restaurant   524
Chile   529
Atacama desert   529
Flush Canyon   531
Lake District   530
Lake Rupanco   530
Hotel Termas   530
Lonquimay   531
Nireco Canyon   531
La Parva   530
Pichilemu   529
Motel Las Cabanas   530
Portillo   531
Rio Bio-Bio   531
Santiago   529
Aquí Está Coco   529
Taltal   529
Termas de Chillan   531
Valle Nevado   530
Valley of the Thousand Waterfalls   531
Costa Rica   523
Cahuita Beach   524
Costa Rica Home & Host   525
Elegante Rent A Car   525
Guanacaste   525
Flamingo Marina Resort Hotel and Club   525
Inter-American Highway   524
Jaco   525
San José   523
Amstel   524
Bar Centrale   524
Casey's Book Exchange   524
Costa Rican Inn   524
Pacific Coast Train Station   526
Téatro Nationale   523
Sarchi   525
Ecuador   526
Chimborazo volcano   527
Cuenca   526
Guayaquil   526
Chiveria   526
Hotel Oro Verde   526
Mi Comisariato   526
Supermaxi   526
Top Cream   526
Uni Hotel   526
Otavalo   527
Playas   526
Pogyos   527
Quito   526
Riobamba   527
Salinas   526
Peru   533
Cuzco   533
Huayna Picchu   533
Iquitos   533, 534
Amazonas Plaza Hotel   534

Hotel Turistas   534
Machu Picchu   533
Gringo Bill's   533
Turistas Hotel   533
Manú National Park   534
Uruguay   521
Costa de Oro   521
Fortin de Santa Rosa   523
Montevideo   521
Balmoral   522
Colonia Suiza   522
Nirvana   522
Plaza Independencia   521
Victoria Plaza   522
Piriápolis   522
Argentino Hotel Casino   522
Punta del Este   521, 523
La Posta del Cangrejo   523
Río de la Plata   521
Venezuela   527
Caracas   527
Barba Roja   528
Caracas Hilton   528
Casa Natal del Libertador   527
La Casona   527
Museo de Arte Contemporáneo   527
Museo de Bellas Artes   527
Parque Los Chorros   527
El Portón   528
Tamanico Inter-Continental   528
Cumaná   528
Cumanagota Hotel   528
Fernando de Apure   528
Francisco J. Estrada   528
Gran Sabana   529
Angel Falls   529
Canaima National Park   529
Turismo Ye'Kuana   529
Turven Tropical Travel Service   529
Merida   528
Tucacas   528

Mexico

Acapulco   497
Blackbeard's   498
Las Brisas   498
Crazy Lobster   498
Villa Demos   498
Villa Vera   498
Angangueo   492
Baja Peninsula   499
Cancun   500
Hotels
Camino Real   500, 503
Casa Maya   504
Club Lagoon   504
Exelaris Hyatt Regency   504
Hyatt Caribe   500
Restaurants
El Pescador   503
Hacienda el Mortero   503
Los Alemandros   503
Maxime   503
Papagayo   503
Shopping
Anakena   503
avenida Tulum   502
La Casita   503
El Parian   503
Chichén Itzá   501
Ball court   501
Temple of Kukulcan   501

Chihuahua 497
  Barranca del Cobre (Copper Canyon) 497
    Hotel Cabañas Divisadero-Barrancas 497
  Casa Grandes 497
  Museo de Arte Popular 497
  Museo Regional 497
  El Palacio del Gobierno 497
Cholula 491
Cobá 502
Cozumel 500
  El Cantil 500
  Dive Cozumel 500
  Hotels
    Cabanas del Caribe 504
    Galapago Inn 504
    El Presidente 504
    Sheraton Sol-Caribe 504
  Restaurants
    Pepe's Grill 504
    El Portal 504
    Santeago's Grill 504
  Shopping
    Bazaar Cozumel 503
    Plaza del Sol 503
Cuernavaca 493
  Cuauhnáhuac Historical Museum 493
  Hotels
    Hotel Hacienda Cortes 494
    Las Mañanitas 494
    Posada Jacarandas 494
  El Palacio de Cortés 493
  Restaurants
    Château René 494
    Harry's Bar 494
    Las Manañitas 494
    Yucateco 494
    La Gruta 492
Guadalajara 495
  Hotels
    El Camino Real 496
    Hyatt Regency 496
  Libertad Market 495
  Parque Agua Azul 495
  Plaza de los Mariachis 496
  Plaza Tapatía 495
  Restaurants
    Cazuelas Grill 496
    Guadalajara Grill 496
Isla Mujéres 500
  El Garrafón 500
  Hotels
    Crystalmar Beach Club 504
    Posada del Mar 504
  Mexico Divers 500
  Restaurants
    Maria's Kankin 504
    Restaurant Gomar 504
Jalapa 496
  Barrio Xalitic 496
  Hotels
    Hotel Jalapa 497
    Hotel Villa del Mar 497
    Maria Victoria 497
  El Mercado Jauregui 496
  Palacio de Gobierno 496
  Parque Juarez 496
  State Theater 496
Matanchin Bay 499
Mexico City 487
  Ballet Folklórico 488
  Bellas Artes 490
  Clubs

  9 490
  Can Can 490
  Disco Club 490
  Hotel Aristos 490
  Magic Circus 490
Hotels
  Camino Real 490
  Gran Hotel Howard Johnson 490
  Hotel de Cortes 490
  Hotel Majestic 490
  Maria Cristina 490
Latin American Tower 487
Museums
  Chapultepec Castle 488
  Museo de la Ciudad (City Museum) 488
  Museo des Bella Artes 488
  National Museum of Anthropology 488
  National Museum of Art and Popular Indus-
    try 488
Restaurants
  Del Lago Restaurant 490
  La Fonda el Refugio 490
  Hacienda de los Morales 490
  Hosteria Santo Domingo 489
  Meson del Cid 490
  San Angel Inn 490
Shopping
  Aries 489
  Bazaar Sabbado 489
  Flato 489
  Girasol 489
  Lagunilla 489
  San Juan Crafts Market 489
  Tane 489
  Thieves' Market 489
Sites
  Altar of the Kings 489
  Casa de los Azulejos 489
  Cathedral of Mexico 489
  Great Temple of Tenochitlán 489
  National Palace 488
Monarch Butterfly Sanctuary 492
Oaxaca 494
  Hotels
    El Presidente 495
    Victoria 495
  Mitla 494
  Monte Albán 494
  Restaurants
    El Asador Vasco 495
    El Sol y La Luna 495
  Shopping
    Aripo 495
    Atzompa 495
    Casa Brena 495
    Ejutla 495
    San Bartolo Coyotepec 495
    Tlacolula 494
  Teotitlán del Valle 494
  Yagul 494
Puerto Juarez 502
Puerto Vallarta 498
  Hotels
    El Camino Real 499
    Garza Blanca 499
    Hotel Plaza Careyes 499
    Molino de Agua 499
    Plaza las Glorias 499
  Restaurants
    Carlos O'Brian's 498
    Chico's Paradise 498
    Las Palomas 498

La Perla 498
San Blas 499
San Cristobal de las Casas 502
　Martes (Tuesday) of Carnival 502
　Posada Diego de Mazaiegos 502
San Ignacio Lagoon 499
San Miguel de Allende 491
　Clubs
　　Laberintos Discoteque 492
　　Mama Mia 492
　　La Princesa 492
　　Ring 492
　Hotels
　　Casa de Sierra Nevada 492
　　La Posada San Francisco 492
　Instituto Allende 491
　La Parroquia 491
　Restaurants
　　Casa de Sierra Nevada 492
　　El Patio 492
　　La Posada Carmina 492
　　Villa Jacaranda 492
　San Miguel Writing Center 491
　Shopping
　　La Balaiza Mercantil 491
　　Casa Maxwell 491
　　Llamas Brothers 491
　　La Ventana 491
Taboada 492
Taxco 493
　Hotels
　　Fiesta Montetaxco 493
　　Hotel de la Borda 493
　　Rancho Taxco-Victoria 493
　Restaurants
　　La Pagaduriá del Rey 493
　　La Ventana de Taxco 493
　Shopping
　　Los Castillos 493
　　La Mina 493
Teotihuacan 491
Tepotzotlán Monastery 491
Tlaquepaque 496
　Restaurant Sin Nombre 496
Tulum 501
　Temple of the Descending God 501
Uxmal 502
　Nunnery 502
Xel-Há 500

New Zealand

Auckland 399
　Albert Park 400
　Auckland Zoo 400
　Bars
　　Abbey Hotel 401
　The Domain 400
　Gallery
　　Auckland City Art Gallery 400
　Hotels
　　Hotel du Vin 401
　　Hyatt Auckland 401
　　Regent of Auckland 401
　　Sheraton Auckland 401
　Lion Safari Park 400
　Mount Eden 399
　Museums
　　War Memorial Museum 400
　Old Customhouse 400
　Quay 401
　Restaurants
　　Antoine's 400
　　Cin Cin On Quay 401
　　Harbourside Seafood Bar and Grill 400
　　Sails 401
　Shopping
　　Karangahape Road 400
　Travel
　　"Bus-About" pass 401
　Victoria Park Market 400
Codfish Island 408
North Island 402
　Beaches
　　Coromandel Peninsula 402
　　Doubtless Bay 402
　　Hot Water Beach 402
　　Houhora 402
　　Ninety Mile Beach 402
　Cape Reinga 402
　East Cape 404
　Hotels
　　Huka Lodge 403
　　THC Château 403
　Kaikohe 403
　Lake Taupo 403
　Masterton 404
　Museums
　　Wagener Museum 402
　Ngawha Springs 403
　Ohinemutu 404
　　St. Faith's 404
　Pohutu 404
　Rotorua City 404
　　Hinemoa 404
　　Polynesian Pools 404
　　Tudor Towers 404
　Te Awamutu 403
　　St. John's Anglican Church 403
　Tongariro National Park 403
　Waikato 403
　　Hamilton 403
　　Mount Taupiri 403
　　Orakau 403
　　Turangawaewae Marae 403
　　Waitomo 403
　Waipoua Kauri Sanctuary 403
　Whangaroa Harbor 402
Resorts
　Queenstown 408
Skiing
　Mount Hutt 409
　Whakapapa Skifield 408
　　Mount Ruapehu 409
South Island 404
　Arthur's Pass National Park 406
　Canterbury 406
　Christchurch 405
　Dunedin 406
　　Larnach 406
　Fiordland National Park 407
　　Sutherland Falls 407
　Haast Pass 407
　　Otago 408
　　Westland 408
　Hiking
　　Independent Hikers 407
　Hotels
　　California Guesthouse 405
　　Chalet 406
　　Cotswold Inn 405
　　Elizas Manor House 406
　　Hermitage 407
　　Lakeland Regency 408
　　Parkroyal Christchurch 405

Quality Inn A Line 408
Riverview Lodge 406
Timara Lodge 405
Kaikoura 405
Mackenzie Country 408
Milford Sound 407
Bowen Falls 407
Mitre Peak 407
Milford Track 407
Moeraki 406
The Devil's Marbles 406
Mount Aspiring National Park, 408
Mount Cook 407
Mount Cook National Park 407
Nydia Trail 405
Picton 405
Punakaiki 404
Restaurants
Blade's 406
La Scala 406
Taiaroa Head 406
Tasman Coast 406
Te Anau 407
Westland National Park 407
South Islands
Hotels
Nugget Point Club 408
Stewart Island 408
Hotels
South Seas Hotel 408
Oban 408
Travel
Frangipani Tours 401
Railways Travelpass 409
Travelpass 409
Wellington 401
Botanical Gardens 401
Hotels
Parkroyal 402
Lambton Quay 401
Mount Victoria 401
Museums
National Museum and Art Gallery 401
Restaurants
At the Bay 401
Il Casino Restorante 401
Grain of Salt 401
Petit Lyon Restaurant 402

North Africa
Abu Kir, Egypt 360
Restaurants
Zephyrion 360
Abu-Simbel (Egypt) 358
Agadir, Morocco 365
Al-Arish, Egypt 361
Alexandria, Egypt 358
Catacombs of Kom el-Shoqafa 359
Fort of Qait Bay 359
Hotels
Al Haram 360
El Alamein 360
Hotel Leroy 360
Hotel Marhaba 360
Palestine 360
Ramada Renaissance 360
Sheraton Montazah 360
Museums
Fine Arts Museum 359
Greco-Roman Museum 359
Pompey's Pillar 359
Ras el-Tin Palace 359

Restaurants
Lord's Inn 360
Morgan 360
Restaurant Elite 360
Santa Lucia 360
Tikka Grill 360
Roman amphitheater 359
Algeria 366
Ghardaïa 366
Grand Erg Occidental 366
Grand Erg Oriental 367
Trans-Algerian Highway 367
Anti-Atlas Mountains (Morocco) 366
Aswan, Egypt 358
Baksheesh 363
Banana Island (Egypt) 356
Cairo, Egypt 347
Agricultural Museum 349
Al-Sokkareya 352
Bab Zuwayla district 351
Cairo Tower 348
Camel market
Imbaba 351
Churches
Church of al-Muallaqa 349
Church of Mari Girgis (St. George) 350
Church of St. Barbara 350
Citadel 348
Cities of the Dead 350
Clubs
After Eight 352
Al-Capo 352
Atlas Hotel 352
Belvedere 352
Rasputin 352
Two Seasons Supper Club 352
Folk dancing
Balloon Theater 352
Giza Square 349
Heliopolis 348
Hotels
Meridien Hotel 352
Nile Hilton 351
Ramses Hilton 352
Shepheard's Hotel 352
The Club Med 352
The President Hotel 352
Islamic Cairo 348
Khan el Khalili district 351
Mausoleum of Imam Al-Shafi'i 350
Mosques and shrines
Al-Azhar Mosque 348
Ibn Tulun 349
Sayiddna al-Husayn 348
Museums
Coptic Museum 349
Egyptian Museum 350, 351
Gezira Museum 348
Mukhtar Museum 348
Museum of Islamic Art 349
The Museum of Modern Art 349
Old Cairo 349
Qalaun mausoleum complex 349
Restaurants
Abu Shakra 351
Aladin 351
Andrea 351
Cairo Sheraton 351
Felfela Village 351
Hag Mohammed el-Samak 351
Pharaoh Hotel 351
Scarabee 351

Shepheards Hotel   351
Shopping
   Bab Zuwayla district   351
   Cartouche   351
   Dokki   351
   Heliopolis   351
   Imbaba   351
   Khan el Khalili   351
   Nassar Brothers   351
   Ohnig of Cairo   351
   Zamalek   351
Synagogues
   Ben Ezra Synagogue   350
Camel market
   Imbaba   351
Cartouche (souvenir pendant)   351
Dahab, Egypt   361
   Hotels
      Dahab Holiday Village   361
Dendera, Egypt
   Temples
      Temple of Hathor   357
Egypt   347
Egyptian Riviera   360
   Corniche   360
   Ma'amura   360
   Montaza Palace and Gardens   360
Felucca   358
Fez, Morocco   364
   Hotels
      Palais Jamai   364
   Karaouine University   364
Ghardaïa, Algeria   366
Giza, Egypt   353
   Hotels
      Holiday Inn Sphinx   354
      Mena House Oberoi   354
   Pyramid of Cheops (the Great Pyramid)   353
   Pyramid of Chepren   353
   Pyramid of Mycerinus   353
   Solar Barque   354
   Sphinx   354
   Valley Temple of Chepren   354
Grand Erg Occidental (Algeria)   366
Grand Erg Oriental (Algeria)   366
Hurghada, Egypt   362
   Al-Dhar Mosque   362
   Giftun El Saghir   362
   Hotels
      Hurghada Sheraton   362
      Hurghada Happy House   363
   Shaab Um Qamar   362
   Ugly Mountain   362
Luxor, Egypt   355
   Colossi of Memnon   357
   Eight primordials   357
   Hotels
      Hotel Etap Luxor   356
      Luxor Hotel   356
      New Winter Palace   356
   Mosque of Abu el-Haggag   356
   Restaurants
      Banana Island   356
      Mont Azza   356
   Temple of Luxor   356
   Temples
      Deir El-Bahari   357
      Ramasseum   357
      Temple of Hatsheput   357
      Temple of Karnak   355
      Temple of Medinet Habu   357
      Temple of Ramses II   357

Thebes   356
Valley of the Kings   356
   Tomb of Amenhotep II   356
   Tomb of Ramses I   357
   Tomb of Ramses III   357
   Tomb of Ramses VI   357
   Tomb of Seti I   357
   Tomb of Tutankhamon   357
   Tomb of Tuthmosis III   356
Valley of the Nobles   357
   Tomb of Intefoger   357
   Tomb of Khaemet   357
   Tomb of Nakht   357
   Tomb of Ramose   357
   Tomb of Usheret   357
Marrakech, Morocco   364
   Djemma El Fna   365
   National Folklore Festival   365
   Tea houses
      Arab Palace   365
      Dar Marjana   365
Mekès, Morocco   364
Morocco   363
   Agadir   366
   Anti-Atlas Mountains   366
   Marrakech   364
   Tangier   363
   Tiznit   366
Mount Sinai (Egypt)   361
   Hotels
      St. Catherine Salam   362
   St. Catherine's Monastery   362
   Steps of Repentance   361
Nuweiba, Egypt   361
   Hotels
      Nuweiba Holiday Village   362
Rabat, Morocco   364
Saqqara, Egypt   355
   Pyramid complex of King Zoser   355
   Pyramid of Unas   355
   Pyramid Texts   355
   Step Pyramid   355
Sinai Peninsula (Egypt)   360
   Travel information and contacts
      Air Sinai   361
Tangier, Morocco   363
   Bab el Assa   363
   El Minzah Tangier   364
   Tabor Square   363
Tiznit, Morocco   366
Trans-Algerian Highway (Algeria)   366
Yemenieh Reef (Egypt)   362
Zahav, Egypt   361
Zamalek Island (Egypt)   351

Portugal
Albufeira (Algarve)   168
   Bars
      Fastnet   168
      Sir Harry's Bar   168
      Twist   168
   Discos
      7 1/2   168
      Sylvia's   168
   Hotels
      Hotel Rocamar   168
Alfama (Lisbon)   164
   Beco do Mexias   165
   Patio das Flores   165
   Rua da Regueira   165
Algarve   168
   Caves of Cape Carvoeiro   169

Golfing
    Dona Filipa   168
    Hotel Dom Pedro Golf   168
    Quinta do Lago   168
    Nossa Senhora da Encarnaçâo   168
Aveiro   170
    Pousada da Ria   171
Batalha   171
    Pousada do Mestre A. Domingues   171
Belém   164
    Mosteiro dos Jeronimos   164
    Torre de Belem   164
Buçaco Mountain   171
Buçaco National Park   171
    Hotels
        Palace Hotel   171
Cabo Espichel   167
    Nossa Senhora do Cabo   167
Cascais   167
    Boca do Inferno   167
    Clubs
        Dois Mil e Um   167
    Praia do Guincho   167
Coimbra   170
Estreméoz   172
Évora   172
    Hotels
        Pousada dos Loios   172
    Igreja de São Francisco   172
    Temple of Diana   172
Fátima   172
    Hotels
        de Fatima   172
        Santa Maria   172
Funchal   173
Lagos (Algarve)   169
    Chapel of St. Antonio   169
    Ponta da Piedad   169
    Praça da Republica   169
Lisbon   163
    Basilica da Estrela   164
    Clubs
        Pe Sujo   166
        Whispers   166
    Hotels
        Hotel Duas Nações   167
        Principe Real   167
        Ritz   166
    Igreja da Madre de Deus   164
    Igreja de São Roque   164
    Museums
        Gulbenkian Museum   164
        Museu de Etnologia   164
        Museu National de Arte Antiga   164
        National Museum of Ancient Art   163
    Restaurants
        A Severa   166
        Casa da Comida   166
        Conventual   166
        Cota d'Armas   166
        Fado Menor   166
        Hotel Jorge V   167
        Lisboa à Noite   166
        Painel do Fado   166
        Parreirinha de Alfama   166
        Senhor Vinho   166
        Tagide   166
        Tavares   166
    Se   164
    Shopping
        Baixa   165
        Chiado   165

        Fabrica Sant'Anna   165
        Feira da Ladra   165
        Helio Cinderela   165
        Por-fi-ri-os Contraste   165
        Saboia   165
        Sarmento   165
Madeira   173
    Cabo Girão   174
    Camara de Lobos   174
    Direcção Regional de Turismo   173
    Funchal   173
        Botanical gardens   173
        Capela de Santa Catarina   173
        Palace of the Conde de Carvalhal   174
        Se   173
    Hotels
        Casino Park Hotel   174
        Estrelicia   174
        Pensão Astoria   174
        Pensão Palmeira   174
        Reid's   174
    Restaurants
        A Gruta   174
        A Seta   174
        Restaurant Coral   174
    Ribeira Brava Festival of St. Peter   174
    Wine   173
Miranda do Douro   172
    Pousada de Santa Catarina   172
Monção   170
    Peneda-Gerês National Park   170
    Pousada de São Bento   170
Obidos   171
    Hotels
        Estalagem do Convento   171
        Pousada do Castelo   171
    Obidos Castle   171
    Senhor da Pedra Church   171
    St. Mary's Church   171
Oporto   170
    Port Wine Institute   170
    Port Wine Solar   170
    Vila Nova de Gaia   170
Portimão (Algarve)   169
    Restaurants
        Avozinha   169
        O Bicho   169
Pousadas   175
Queluz   167
Resorts
    Estoril   167
    Hotels
        Hotel Palácio   167
Sagres   169
    Cabo de São Vicente   169
    Compass Rose   169
    Hotels
        Pousada do Infante   169
        Prince Henry the Navigator   169
Santa Maria Monastery   170
Setubal   167
    Hotels
        Pousada de São Filipe   167
        Pousada do Castelo de Palmela   167
Sintra   167
    Pena Palace   168
Vila Nogueria de Azeitão   165

Scandinavia

Ærø, Denmark   179
    Ærøskøbing   179
Alta

Hotels
  Alta Gjestestue 190
Alta, Finland 190
Arvidsjaur, Sweden 191
Bergen, Norway 182
  Fantoft Stave Church 183
  Festival Office 182
  Grieg Hall 182
  St. Mary's 183
  Troldhaugen 183
Biking (Denmark)
  Haervejen 178
Billund, Denmark 178
  Legoland 178
Bornholm, Denmark 179
  Almindingen 179
  Dueodde 179
  Rø 179
Bryggen, Norway 183
  Museums
    Hanseatic Museum 183
Castles, Denmark
  Egeskov 178
  Frederiksborg 178
  Kronborg Castle 178
  Nyborg Castle 178
Copenhagen 175
Copenhagen, Denmark 175
  Amalieborg Castle 176
  Breweries
    Carlsberg 176
    Tuborg 176
  Clubs
    Annabel's 176
    Montmartre 177
    Vin & Ølgood, 177
  Hotels
    D'Angleterre 177
    Plaza 177
    Savoy Hotel 177
    Scandinavia 177
  Museums
    Nationalmuseet 176
    Ny Carlsberg Glyptotek 176
  Nyhavn 177
  Restaurants
    Belle Terrasse 177
    Faergekroen 177
    Krog's Fiskerestaurant 177
  Rosenborg 176
  Royal Copenhagen 176
  Shopping
    Danish Silver Shop 176
    Sweater Market 176
  Strøget 176
  Tivoli Gardens 175
  Tourist office 177
  Travel
    Copenhagen Card 177
Dalarna Province 186
  Hotels
    Hotel Langbers 186
    Romantik Hotel Tallbergsgarden 187
  Midsummer Eve 186
Dalarna Province, Sweden 186
Denmark 175
Enontekiö, Finland 191
Finland 187
Finnish Lapland 191
Finnmark, Finland 190
Fredrikstad, Norway 182
  Kongsten Fort 182

Hämeenlinna, Finland 189
Heddal, Norway 182
Helsinki, Finland 187
  Finlandia Hall 188
  Hotels
    Hotel Strand Inter-Continental 189
  Museums
    Suomen Kansallismuseo 188
  Restaurants
    Kappeli 189
    Saslik 189
  Saunas
    Hesperia 189
    Kalastajatorppa 189
    Palace Hotel 189
  Senaatintori 188
  Suomenlinna Fortress 188
Hiking (Finland) 191
  Karhunkierros 191
Hiking (Sweden)
  Kungsleden 191
  Svenska Turistföreningen 191
Homestays
  Meet the Danes 175
Honningsvaag, Finland 190
  Hotels
    Sas 190
Inari, Finland 191
Kerimaki, Finland 189
Kvikkjokk, Sweden 191
Lapland, Finland 189
Mora, Sweden 187
  Hotels
    Mora Hotel 187
  Skiing
    Vasalöppet 187
Nordkapp, Finland 190
Norrbotten, Sweden 191
Norrland, Sweden 190
Norway 179
Oslo, Norway 179
  Akershus Castle 180
  Domkirken 180
  Frognerparken 180
  Gamle Aker Kirke 180
  Holmenkollen ski jump 181
  Hotels
    Holmenkollen Park Hotel Rica, 182
    Hotel Continental 182
    Scandinavia 182
    The Grand Hotel 182
  Museums
    Munch Museum 180
    Nasjonalgalleriet 180
    Norsk Folkemuseum 181
    Norsk Hjemmefrontmuseum 180
    Ski Museum 181
  Raadhuset 180
  Restaurants
    Étoile 181
    La Mer 181
    Mølla 181
    Noberto 182
    Tostrupkjelleren 181
    Tryvannstaarnet 181
  Viking ships
    Kon Tiki Museum 181
    Vikingskiphuset 180
Padjelanta National Park, Sweden 191
Roskilde, Denmark 177
  Hotels
    Lindenborg Kro 178

Museums
Vikingskibshallen 178
Rovaniemi, Finland 191
Hotels
Hotelli Ravintola Oppipoika 192
Rantasipi Pohjanhovi 192
Sandefjord, Norway 182
Museums
Whaling Museum 182
Savonlinna, Finland 189
Olavinlinna Castle 189
Sigtuna, Sweden 186
Skagen, Denmark 179
Sodankylö, Finland 191
Stockholm, Sweden 183
Clubs
Café Opera 184
Jump In 184
Djurgården 184
Drottningholm Palace 184
Drottningholm Court Theater 184
Gamla Stan 183
Grona Lund's Tivoli 184
Homestays
Orbyhus 185
Trollenas 185
Hotels
Diplomat 185
Grand Hotel 184
Hotel Anno 1647 185
Lady Hamilton 185
Malardrottningen 185
Royal Viking 185
Sergel Plaza 185
Museums
Moderna Museet 184
Nationalmuseet 184
Nordiska Museet 184
Skansen 184
Restaurants
Coq Blanc 185
Fem Små Hus 186
Operakällaren 185
Ulriksdals Wärdshus 185
Wedholms Fisk 186
Riddarholm Church 183
Royal palace 183
Stadshuset 184
Stortorget 183
Sweden 183
Tonsberg, Norway 182
Vestfold Folk Museum 182
Tromsø, Finland 190
Arctic Church 190
Ulvik, Norway 182
Hotels
Brakanes Hotel 182
Uppsala, Sweden 186
Gamla Uppsala 186
Inns
Odinsborg 186
Walpurgis Eve 186
Utsjoki, Finland 191
Visby, Sweden 187

Southeast Asia
Amadari Resort 325
Baguio City, Philippines 318
Hotels
Bagula Park Hotel 319
Safari Lodge 319
Vacation Hotel 319

Bali (Indonesia) 325
Amandari Resort 325
Nusa Dua 325
Ubud 325
Bangkok, Thailand 315
Bangkok Snake Farm 316
Golf courses
Rose Garden Golf Course 316
Hotels
Dusit Thani 316
Nana Hotel 317
Oriental 316
Regent 316
Sukhothai 316
Museums
Royal Barge Museum 315
Shopping
Chatuchak 316
Floating Market 315
Khlong Damnoen Saduak 315
Temples
Wat Arun 315
Wat Pho 315
Wat Phra Kaeo 315
Thai Cooking School 316
Cebu City, Philippines 319
Basilica Minore del Santo Niño 319
Chiang Mai Orchid 317
Colon Street 319
Santo Niño de Cebu 319
Chiang Mai, Thailand 317
Elephant trekking 317
Hotels
Lanna Golf Club 317
Phuping Palace 317
Shopping
Night Market 317
Shinawatra Parnich 317
Shinawatra Thaisilk 317
Temples
Wat Phra That Doi Suthep 317
Indonesia 325
Jakarta, Indonesia 325
Jogyakarta, Indonesia 326
Borobodur ruins 326
Hotel Ambarukmo Palace 326
Koror, Palau
Hotels
DW Motel 321
Nikko Hotel 321
Palau Pacific Resort 321
Restaurants
Carp Restaurant 321
Fuji Restaurant 321
Pirate's Cove 321
Royal Belau Yacht Club 321
Travel information and contacts
Sam's Tour Service 321
Kuala Lumpur, Malaysia 325
Batu Caves 325
Laguna, Philippines 318
Villa Escudero 318
Laos 320
Travel information and contacts
Diethelm Travel 320
Siam Exclusive Tours 320
Vientiane 320
Luang Prabang 320
Temples
Wat Xiengthong 320
Makati, Philippines 318
Malacca, Malaysia 325

Malaysia 324
Mandalay, Myanmar 322
Manila, Philippines 318
  Coconut Palace 318
  Hidden Valley Springs 318
  Hotels
    Manila Hotel 318
    Villa Escudero 318
  Malacañang Palace 318
  Pagsanjan Falls 318
  San Agustin Church 318
Maymyo, Myanmar 322
  Candacraig Hotel 322
Myanmar 322
New Guinea 324
Pagan, Myanmar 322
Palau 320
Palawan, Philippines 319
  Badjao Inn 319
  El Nido Resort 319
  French Café Puarto 319
  Mantaray Resort 320
  Ten Knots Philippines Inc. 319
Penang, Malaysia 325
  Hotels
    Eastern & Oriental Hotel 325
Philippines 318
Puerto Princesa, Philippines 319
Silk dealers
  Shinawatra Parnich 317
  Shinawatra Thaisilk 317
Singapore 323
  Chinatown 323
  Empress Place 323
  Hotels
    Carlton Hotel 323
    Goodwood Tark 323
    Raffles Hotel 323
    Stamford Westin 324
  Restaurants
    Compass Rose 324
  Shopping 323
    Bagatelle Shoppe 324
    Justmen 324
    Orchard 323
    Scotts 323
    Tanglin 323
Vientiane, Laos 320
  Restaurants
    Nam Phu Restaurant 320
Yangon (formerly Rangoon), Myanmar 322
  Hotels
    Strand Hotel 322
  Schwedagon Pagoda 322
  Sule Pagoda 322

Spain

Alhambra 204
  Hotels
    Alhambra Palace 204
    Convent of San Francisco 204
    Parador Castillo de Santa Catalina 204
Avila 198
Balearic Islands 214
  Clubs (Ibiza)
    Ku 216
  Hotels (Ibiza)
    Hacienda Na Ximena 216
  Hotels (Menorca)
    Port Mahon 216
  Hotels (in Mallorca)
    Hotel Formentor 215

La Residencia 215
Ibiza 215
Mallorca 214
  La Cartuja 215
  Deyá 215
  Palma de Mallorca 214
Menorca 216
Restaurants (Ibiza)
  El Caliu 216
  Comida San Juan 216
Shopping (Mallorca)
  Manacor 215
Baquiera-Beret 217
  Hotels
    Hotel Montarto 217
Barcelona 199
  Antonio Gaudi 200
  Clubs
    Born 201
    Network 201
    Otto Zutz 201
    Up and Down 201
    Vaticano 201
  Gothic Quarter 199
  Gran Téâtre del Liceu 200
  Hotels
    Avenida Palace 202
    Hotel Colón 202
    Ritz 202
  Las Ramblas 199
  Montjuïc 201
  Museums
    Miró 201
    Museo d'Art de Catalunya 201
    Museo de Picasso 200
  Park Guëll 200
  Restaurants
    Los 4 Gatos 200
    Azulete 202
    Cal Pinxo 202
    El Egypto 202
    Eldorado Petit 202
    Hotel Calderón 202
    Jaume de Provença 202
    Neichel 201
    Reno 202
    La Venta 202
  Templo de la Sagrada Familia 200
Cáceres 217
  Pero Palo festival 217
Canary Islands 212
  Gran Canaria 213
    Mogan 214
    Las Palmas 213
  Maspalomas Oasis 213, 214
  Restaurante Rio 214
  Tamarindos 214
  Tenerife 213
    Puerto de la Cruz 213
    Santa Cruz 213
  Semiramis 213
Córdoba 207
  Hotels
    Residencia Maimonides 208
  Jewish Quarter 208
  La Mezquita 207
  Old Quarter 208
Costa Brava 209
  Beaches
    Cabo de Creus 210
    Cadaques 210
      Salvador Dalí's home 209

Gerona 209
Hotels
  La Gavina 209
  Playa Sol 210
Restaurants
  Es Baluard 210
S'Agaro 209
Tossa de Mar 209
Costa de Almería 210
Hotels
  Gran Hotel Almería 210
  El Moresco 210
Mini-Hollywood 210
Costa del Sol 208
Cuenca 206
Galicia 212
Hotels
  Conde de Gondomar 212
Vigo 212
Gerona 209
Gran Canaria
Shopping (Las Palmas)
  Voula Mitsakiu 213
Granada 204
Alhambra 204
Léon 210
Cathedral 210
Hotels
  San Marcos 211
Madrid 193
Bullfighting
  Las Ventas 195
  Vista Alegre 195
Clubs
  Al Andalus 196
  Café Berlin 195
  Café de Chinitas 196
  Oh Madrid 195
  Pacha 195
  El Porton 196
  Scala Melia 195
El Escorial 198
Hotels
  Alcalá 197
  Hotel Ritz 196
  Miguel Angel 196
  Palace Hotel 196
  Villa Magna 196
Markets
  El Rastro 194
Museums
  El Prado 194
Parque del Retiro 195
Plaza Mayor 193
Puerta del Sol 193
Restaurants
  El Amparo 197
  Cabo Mayor 197
  Casa Botín 197
  Casa Lucio 197
  Horcher 197
  Jockey 197
  El Pescador 197
  Posada de la Villa 197
  Zalacaín 197
Royal Palace 193
Marbella 208
Hotels
  Marbella Club Hotel 209
  Régine's 208
Mérida 206
Montserrat Mountains 202

Benedictine monastery 202
Murcia 216
Festivals
  Burial of the Sardine 216
Pamplona 208
El Palacio
  Royal Library 194
El Palacio Real 19
Resorts, Spain
  Torremolinos 209
  Tossa de Mar 209
Salamanca 205
Hotels
  Alfonso X 205
Restaurants
  Chez Victor 205
University of Salamanca 205
San Sebastian 211
Hotels
  Costa Vasca 212
  De Londres y de Inglaterra 212
  Parador Hondarribia 212
Restaurants
  Arzak 211
Santiago de Campostela 211
Santiago de Compostela
Hotels
  Los Reyes Catolicos 211
Segovia 207
Roman aqueducts 207
Seville 203
Alcazar 203
Casa de Pilatos 204
Cathedral 203
Giralda 203
Holy Week Celebration 216
Giralda 203
Museum of Fine Arts 204
Skiing
  Baquiera-Beret 217
Toledo 198
Alcazar 198
Circunvalación 198
El Greco House and Museum 198
Festivals
  Feast of San Isidoro 199
  Olive Festival 199
  Rosa del Azafran 199
  La Virgen del Sagrario 199
  La Virgen del Valle 199
Hotels
  Hostal del Cardenal 199
Shopping
  Fabrica Bermejo 199
  Fabrica Garido 199
  Real Fabrica de Armas 199
  El Torcal 209
Torremolinos 209
  El Molino de la Torre 209
Valladolid 205
Castles
  La Mota 206
  Penafiel Castle 206
  Simancas 206
College of San Gregorio 205
Iglesia de San Pablo 205
José Zorrilla 205
La Séo 206
Miguel de Cervantes 205

Switzerland

Berne 225

Hotels
    Bellevue Palace 226
    Goldener Adler 226
    Grand Hotel Regina 226
    The Olden Hotel 226
Museums
    Bernisches Historisches Museum 226
    Kunstmuseum 226
Restaurants
    Kornhauskeller 226
St. Vincent Cathedral 226
Zeitglockenturm 226
Geneva 222
    Chillon Castle 224
    Hôtel de Ville 223
    Hotels
        Beau Rivage 225
        Hôtel de la Paix 225
        Hôtel du Richemond 225
        Hôtel des Armures 225
        Metropole 225
    International Labor Office 222
    International Red Cross 222
    Jet d'Eau 222
    Lac Leman 224
    Maison Tavel 223
    Museums
        Musée d'Art et d'Histoire 223
        Musée de l'Horlogerie 223
        Le Petit Palais 223
        Voltaire Museum 223
    Palais des Nations 222
    Reformation Monument 223
    Restaurants
        Béarn 225
        Café Huissoud 224
        Le Marignac 225
        Parc des Eaux-Vives 224
        La Perle du Lac 225
        Restaurant du Vieux Port 224
        Le Vieux Moulin 225
    St. Peter's Cathedral 223
    World Health Organization 222
Gimmelwald 226
Hiking
    Swiss Hiking Assocation 227
Lac Leman 224
Lausanne 230
    Hotels
        Château d'Ouchy 230
    Place de la Palud 230
    Restaurants
        Girardet 230
Matterhorn 228
Montreux 229
    Hotels
        Eden au Lac 229
    Restaurants
        La Rotisserie de Château 230
        La Vieille Ferme 230
St. Moritz 227
    Clubs
        Gunther Sachs' Dracula Club 228
        Kings' Club 228
    Cresta Run 228
    Hotels
        Badrutt's Palace 228
        Hotel Chesa sur l'En 228
    Restaurants
        La Marmite 228
    Skiing
        St. Moritz-Dorf 228

Spas
    St. Moritz-Bad 228
Staubbach Waterfall 230
The Alps, Switzerland 227
    Glacier Express 229
    Kleine Scheidegg 229
    Swiss National Park 227
    Mountaineering Office 229
Travel
    Cheese Express 229
    Swiss National Tourist Office 229
    Swiss Travel System 229
Trummelbach Falls 230
Valais 227
    Alpes Valaisannes 227
    Bernese Alps 227
    Crans-Montana 227
    Crans-sur-Sierre 227
    Montana 227
    Reckingen 227
    Rhone 227
Winterthur 222
    Kyburg Castle 222
    Museums
        Fine Arts Museum 222
        Oskar Reinhart Collection Am Römerholz 222
        Oskar Reinhart Foundation 222
Zermatt 228
    Hotels
        Hotel Alex 228
        Hotel-Garni Metropol 228
        Mont Cervin 228
        Panorama Hotel 228
        Zermatter Hof 228
Zurich 219
    Altstadt (Old Town) 220
    Bahnhofstrasse 219
    Clubs
        Limmatquai 220
        Niederdorfstrasse 220
    Fraumünster 220
    Grossmünster 220
    Hotels
        Baur au Lac 221
        Dolder Grand 221
        Hôtel du Theatre 222
        Hôtel Florhof 222
    Museums
        Kunsthaus 220
        Rietberg Museum 220
        Schweizerishches Landesmuseum 220
    Restaurants
        Au Premier 221
        Bienengarten 220
        Café Schober 220
        Confiserie Sprüngli 221
        Grill Room 221
        Kronenhalle 221
        La Rotonde 220
        Les Vacances-Chez Max 220
        Zeughauskeller 221
    Sechselauten 219
    Shopping
        Luxury Mile 219
        Marktplatz Oerlikon 220

The United States

Adirondacks (New York) 418
    Adirondack National Park 418
        Ausable Chasm 418
    Fort Ticonderoga 418
    Hotels

High Peaks Base Camp   418
Rose Inn   418
The Point   418
Alaska   459
Anchorage, Alaska   460
  Festivals
    Winter Carnival   460
  Hotels
    Anchorage Westward Hilton   461
  Museums
    Anchorage Museum of History and Art   460
  Restaurants
    Crow's Nest   460
    Elevation 92   461
    Simon and Seaforths   461
  Shopping
    Alaska Native Arts and Crafts   460
    Oomingmak Musk Ox Cooperative   460
Arctic Circle (Alaska)   459
  Barrow   459
  Kotzebue   459
  Front Street   459
Arlington, Vermont   425
  Arlington Inn   425
Atlanta, Georgia   434
  Atlanta Historical Society   434
  Ebeneezer Baptist Church   434
  Governor's mansion   434
  Hotels
    Hyatt Regency   434
    Westin Peachtree Plaza   434
  Margaret Mitchell Room   434
  Fulton County Public Library   434
  Paces Ferry Road   434
  Restaurants
    The Abbey   434
    The Dining Room   434
  Wren's Nest   434
Atlantic City, New Jersey   427
  Knife and Fork   427
  Ocean One   427
Aurora Borealis (Alaska)   461
Austin, Texas   442
  Austin's Area Garden Center   442
  Clubs
    The Broken Spoke   442
    The Terrace   442
  Hotels
    Driskill Hotel   442
  Lyndon Baines Johnson Library   442
  Museums
    Laguna Gloria Art Museum   442
    Texas Archives and Library Building   442
  Texas State Capitol   442
Bar Harbor, Maine   424
  Acadia National Park   424
    Cadillac Mountain   424
    Jackson Memorial Library   424
    Jordan Pond   424
    Jordan Pond House   425
    Sand Beach   424
    Thunder Hole   424
  Bluenose   425
  Mount Desert Island   424
Big Sur, California   452
  Hotels
    Ventana Inn   452
Boston, Massachusetts   419
  Beacon Hill   420
  Black Heritage Trail   420
  Bunker Hill   419
  Comedy clubs

Catch a Rising Star   420
Comedy Connection   420
Stitches   420
Freedom Trail   419
Granary Burial Ground   419
Hotels
  Copley Plaza   421
  Omni Parker House Hotel   421
  Ritz Carlton   421
Museums
  Boston Tea Party Ship and Museum   419
  Institute of Contemporary Art   420
  Isabella Stuart Gardner Museum   420
  John F. Kennedy Library   420
  Museum of Fine Arts   420
New England Aquarium   420
Old North Church   419
Old South Meeting House   419
Old State House   419
Parks
  Arnold Arboretum   420
  Boston Common   420
  Public Gardens   420
Patriot's Day   420
Public Library   420
Restaurants
  Anthony's Pier 4   421
  Aujourd'hui   421
  Café Budapest   421
  Locke-Ober Café   421
State House   420
Toscanini's   420
Bryce Canyon National Park
  Visitors Center   443
Bryce Canyon National Park (Utah)   443
Cambridge, Massachusetts   421
  Fogg Art Museum   421
  Grolier Bookstore   421
  Harvard Square   421
  Harvard University Museum   421
  Harvard Yard   421
  Million Year Picnic   421
Cape Cod, Massachusetts   422
  Provincetown   422
    Bradford Gardens   422
    Captain John's   422
    Commercial Street   422
    Highland Golf Club   422
    Moors   422
    Portuguese Princess   423
    Provincetown Inn   423
    Provincetown Playhouse   422
    Provincetown Whale Watch   423
    Surf Club   422
Cape May, New Jersey   427
  Barnard-Good House   427
  Summer Cottage Inn   427
Carmel, California   453
  Del Monte Forest   453
  17-Mile Drive   453
Charleston, South Carolina   434
  Edmonston-Allston House   434
  Fort Sumter   434
  Hotels
    Maison Du Pre   434
  Museums
    Charleston Museum   434
    The Gibbes Gallery   434
  Nathaniel Russell House   434
Charlottesville, Virginia   433
  Hotels
    Clifton Inn   433

Chicago, Illinois   455
  Architecture
    The Archicenter   455
  Buckingham Fountain   456
  Chicago Symphony Orchestra   457
  Clubs
    Baton Lounge   457
    Joe Segal's Jazz Showcase   457
    Kingston Mines   457
    New Checkerboard Lounge   457
    Second City   457
  Festivals
    57th Street Art Fair   456
  Gold Coast   456
  Hotels
    The Mayfair Regent   458
    Tremont Hotel   458
  Hyde Park   456
  Lake View   456
  Lyric Opera   457
  Magnificent Mile   455
  Museums
    Field Museum of Natural History   455
    Museum of Broadcast Communications   455
    Museum of Contemporary Art   456
    Museum of Science and Industry   456
    Oriental Institute   456
    Terra Museum of American Art   456
    The Art Institute of Chicago   455
  Omnimax Theatre   456
  Orchestra Hall   457
  Parks and zoos
    Brookfield Zoo   456
    Grant Park   456
    Hyde Park   456
    Lincoln Park   456
    Lincoln Park Zoo   456
    Oak Street   456
  Restaurants
    Due   458
    Golden Shell   458
    Le Français   458
    Pizzeria Uno   457
    Ribs 'n Bibs   458
  River North   456
  Sears Tower   455
  Steppenwolf Theater   457
  Water Tower Place   455
Chilkoot Trail (Alaska)   460
Clearwater, Florida   438
  Hotels
    Belleview Biltmore   438
Concord, Massachusetts   421
  Concord Museum   422
  Old Manse   422
  Ralph Waldo Emerson House   422
  Wayside   422
Cooperstown, New York   418
  Angelholm   419
  Baseball Hall of Fame   418
  Dining Room   418
Coral Gables, Florida   439
  Hotels
    Hotel Place St. Michel   439
Crater Lake (Oregon)   454
  Hotel
    Crater Lake Lodge   454
Dallas, Texas   441
  Dallas City Hall   441
  Dallas Zoo   441
  Dallas-Fort Worth Airport   441
  Hotels

    Mansion on Turtle Creek   442
  Museums
    Age of Steam Railroad Museum   441
    Dallas Aquarium   442
    Dallas Hall of State   441
    Dallas Planetarium   442
    John F. Kennedy Museum   441
    Museum of Fine Arts   441
    Museum of Natural History   442
    Science Place   441
    State Fair Park   441
  Restaurants
    Lawry's The Prime Ri   442
    Routh Street Café   442
  Thanksgiving Square   441
Florida   438
  Beaches
    Belleair   438
    Captiva   438
    Clearwater   438
    Daytona Beach   438
    Fort Myers Beach   438
    Fort Walton Beach   438
    Long Boat Key   438
    Madeira   438
    New Smyrna   439
    Pensacola Beach   438
    Playalinda   439
    Point O'Rocks   438
    Ponte Vedra   438
    Redington   438
    Sanibel   438
    South Ponte   439
    Venice Beach   438
Fort Lauderdale, Florida   439
  Bonaventure Resort Spa   439
  Candy Store Disco   439
Four Corners (Southwest)   445
Glacier Bay National Monument (Alaska)   459
Glacier National Park
  Hiking
    Going to the Sun Road   447
  Hotel
    Glacier Park Lodge   447
Glacier National Park (Montana)   447
Grand Canyon (Arizona)   443
  El Tovar Hotel   443
Great Lakes   455
Haines, Alaska   460
Hawaii   461
Hawaii, Hawaii
  Chain of Craters Road   462
    Puu Oo Vent   462
  Hawaii Volcanos National Park   462
  Hawi   461
  Kailauea   462
    Halemaumau   462
  Kailua   461
    Hulihee Palace   461
  King's Trail   461
  Kohala Coast   461
  Mauna Kea   462
    Kona Village Resort   462
  Mo'okini Heiau   461
  Puuhonua O Honaunau National Historical
    Park   461
Hawaii Volcano National Park   462
  Kialauea   462
  Mauna Loa   462
Highway 1 (California)   452
Honolulu, Hawaii   461
  Hotels

Kona Village   462
Moana   462
Royal Hawaiian   462
The Kahala Hilton   462
The Mauna Kea Beach Hotel   462
Hopi Reservation (Arizona)   445
First Mesa   445
Walpi   446
Hopi Cultural Center   446
Second Mesa   445
Third Mesa   445
Old Orabi   445
Houston, Texas   440
Astrodome   440
Bayou Bend   440
Hermann Park   440
Hotels
Ritz Carlton   441
Houston Tunnel System   440
Museums
Menil Collection   440
Museum of Contemporary Arts   440
Museum of Fine Arts   440
San Jacinto Museum of History   440
Penzoil Place   440
Restaurants
Brennan's   441
Charley's 517   441
La Reserve   441
Rodeos
Houston Livestock Show and Rodeo   441
Juneau, Alaska   460
Gold Creek   460
Hotel
Westmark Juneau   460
Mendenhall Glacier   460
Kauai, Hawaii   462
Alakai Swamp   462
Hanalai River   462
Kukui Trail   462
Mount Waialeale   462
Na Pali Coast   462
Pihea Trail   462
Waimea Canyon   462
Key Largo, Florida   439
Key West, Florida   439
Hotels
Marriott Casa Marina   439
Klukwan, Alaska   460
Kodiak, Alaska   461
Lake Champlain (New York)   419
Fort Blunder   419
Fort St. Anne   419
Isle La Motte   419
Lake Michigan   455
Lake Superior   455
Lexington, Massachusetts   421
Hancock-Clarke House   421
Long Boat Key, Florida   438
Restaurants
Buccaneer Inn   438
Longboat Key, Florida   438
Los Angeles, California   450
Clubs
The Comedy Store   451
Disneyland   451
Hollywood   450
Grauman's Chinese Theater   450
Hollywood Boulevard   450
Melrose Avenue   450
Sunset Boulevard   450
Hotels

Bel Air   452
Beverly Hills Hotel   451, 452
Beverly Wilshire Hotel   451
The Terrace Manor   452
Museums
Huntington Library, Art Gallery, and Botanical
Garden   450
J. Paul Getty Museum   450
Music and Entertainment
Los Angeles Philharmonic   451
Music Center   451
The Roxy   451
Troubadour   451
Old Plaza   450
Pueblo de Los Angeles State Historical Park   450
Restaurants
Le Dome   451
Polo Lounge   451
Scandia   451
The Dynasty Room   451
Television studios   450
Watts Towers   451
Lower Waterford, Vermont   426
Rabbit Hill Inn   426
Mackinac Island, Michigan   458
Mission Point Resort   459
The Grand Hotel   458
The Island House   458
Martha's Vineyard Island, Massachusetts
Captain Dexter House   423
Edgartown   423
Gay Head   423
Kelly House   423
Oak Bluffs   423
Restaurants
Homeport   423
L'Etoile   423
Warriners   423
Woods Hole   423
Maui, Hawaii   461
Haleakala volcano   461
Hana   461
Hotels
Halekulani   461
Hyatt Regency Maui   461
Kaanapali Beach Resort   461
Memorial, Florida   439
Memphis, Tennessee   436
Graceland   436
Mesa Verde National Park (Colorado)   445
Cliff Palace   445
Hotels
Far View Lodge   445
Museums
Archeological Museum   445
Park Superintendent   445
Petroglyph Trail   445
Spruce Tree House   445
Miami Beach, Florida   439
Little Havana   439
Lummus Park   439
Monument Valley Tribal Park (Arizona)   445
Mount Mansfield, Vermont   425
Mount McKinley (Alaska)   459
Mount Olympus (Washington)   454
Mount Rainier (Washington)   454
Hotels
Paradise Inn   454
Mount Ranier National Park   454
Skyline Trail   454
Mount St. Helens (Washington)   454
Mount Vernon, Virginia   431

Mount Vernon   431
Nantucket, Massachusetts   424
  Carriage House   424
  Hadwen House   424
  Jared Coffin House   424
  Nantucket Whaling Museum   424
  Peter Foulger House   424
  Seaskonset Beach   424
  Seven Seas Gifts   424
  Ships Inn   424
Napa Valley, California   452
  Hotels
    Beazley House   452
  Robert Mondavi Winery   452
Nashville, Tennessee   435
  Centennial Park   435
  Country Music Hall of Fame   435
  Fort Nashborough   435
  Hotels
    Hermitage   436
  Music
    Bluebird Café   436
    Grand Ole Opry   435
  Restaurants
    Arthur's   436
    Julian's   436
  Tennessee Performing Arts Center   436
  The Hermitage   435
Navajo Reservation (Arizona)   445
  Hubbell's   445
New England   419
New Hampshire   424
  Crawford Notch State Park   424
  Mount Washington   424
  Mount Washington Hotel and Resort   424
  White Mountain National Forest   424
New Jersey   426
  Pine Barrens   426
  Stone Pony   427
  Woolverton Inn   427
New Orleans, Louisiana   436
  Bars
    Antoine's   438
    K-Paul's Louisiana Kitchen   438
    Lafitte's Blacksmith Shop   437
    Maple Leaf   438
    Napoleon House   437
    Old Absinthe House   437
    Pat O'Brien's   438
    Preservation Hall   438
  Bourbon Street   436
  Festivals
    Jazz and Heritage Festival   437
    New Orleans Literary Festival   437
  French Quarter   436
  Garden District   436
  Hotels
    Frenchmen Inn   438
    Pontchartrain   438
    Soniat House   438
  Jackson Square   436
  Mardi Gras   437
    He Sheba Contest   437
  Moonwalk   436
  Museums
    Chalmette National Historic Museum   437
    Musee Conti   437
    The Cabildo   437
    Voodoo Museum   437
  Restaurants
    Arnaud's   437
    Café du Monde   437

    The Grill Room   437
  Royal Street   437
New York, New York   411
  Beaches
    Brighton Beach   414
    Coney Island   414
    Jones Beach   414
    Rockaway Beach   414
  Chinatown   412
  Clubs
    Back Porch   416
    Lone Star Café   416
    Ritz   416
    Sounds of Brazil   416
  Dakota Apartments   413
  Diamond Exchange   414
  Empire State Building   413
  Federal Hall   412
  Federal Reserve Bank   412
  Financial District   412
  Greenwich Village   412
  Hotels
    Algonquin   417
    Carlyle   417
    Helmsley Palace   417
    Morgans   417
    Paramount   417
    Park 51 Hotel   417
    Pierre   417
    Ritz Carlton   417
  Jazz clubs
    Blue Note   415
    Bottom Line   415
    Sweet Basil   415
    Village Vanguard   415
    West End Café   415
  Lower East Side   412
  Manhattan Island   412
  Markets
    Balducci's   414
    Dean & Deluca   414
    Zabar's   414
  Midtown   412
  Moishe's Bakery   412
  Museums
    American Museum of Natural History   413
    Chinese Museum   412
    Cloisters   413
    El Museo del Barrio   414
    Guggenheim Museum   413
    International Center of Photography   413
    Jewish Museum   413
    Metropolitan Museum of Art   413
    Museum of Broadcasting   414
    Museum of Holography   412
    Museum of Modern Art   413
    Museum of the American Indian   413
    Museum of the City of New York   414
    Whitney Museum   414
  Music and theater
    Alvin Ailey Dance Company   415
    American Ballet Theater   415
    Booth   415
    Joffrey Ballet   415
    Lincoln Center   415
    Majestic   415
    Metropolitan Opera Company   415
    Metropolitan Opera House   415
    Midtown   414
    New York City Ballet   415
    New York City Opera   415
    New York Philharmonic   415

St. James   415
   Shakespeare Festival   415
   Shubert   415
   Theater District   415
New York City Visitors Bureau   414
New York Stock Exchange   412
O.K. Harris   412
Orchard Street   412
Parks
   Battery Park   412
   Central Park   412
   Washington Square Park   412
Radio City Music Hall   413
Restaurants
   21 Club   416
   Benito's II   416
   Café des Artistes   416
   Darbar   417
   Elaine's   416
   Enoteca Iperbole   416
   Four Seasons   416
   Le Cirque   416
   Lutèce   416
   Primavera   416
   Quilted Giraffe   416
   Rosa Mexicana   416
   Russian Tea Room   416
   Sandro's   416
   Ukrainian Restaurant   417
St. Patrick's Cathedral   413
Shopping
   Annemarie Gardin Inc.   414
   Better Made Coat and Suit Company   414
   Canal Jean   412
   Fifth Avenue   414
SoHo   412
Staten Island Ferry   412
Statue of Liberty   412
Ticket offices
   Hit Shows   415
   Joseph Papp's Public Theater   415
   QUIKTIX   415
   TKTS   415
United Nations   413
Yonah Schimmel's Knishery   412
Newfane, Vermont   425
   Hotels
      Old Newfane Inn   425
   Marlboro Music Festival   425
   Newfane Store   425
   Old Newfane Inn   425
   Union Hall   425
Newport, Rhode Island   425
   Jail House Inn   425
   Mill Street Inn   425
   Music Box   425
   White Horse Tavern   425
Niagara Falls   417
   American Falls   417
   Bridal Veil Falls   417
   Cave of the Winds   418
   Horseshoe Falls   417
   Scenic Tunnels   418
Niagara-on-the-Lake, Canada   418
   Hotels
      Moffat Inn   418
      Oban   418
      Prince of Wales   418
Oahu, Hawaii   461
   Hotels
      Kahala Hilton   461
Okefenokee, Georgia   435

Olympic National Forest (Washington)   454
   Quinault Lodge   454
Palm Beach, Florida   439
Pebble Beach, California   452
   Auto Show
      Pebble Beach Concours d'Elegance   453
   Cypress Point Club   453
   Pebble Beach Golf Links   452
   Resorts
      The Lodge at Pebble Beach   453
Philadelphia, Pennsylvania   427
   Betsy Ross House   428
   Edgar Allan Poe House   428
   Germantown   428
      Cliveden   428
      Stenton Mansion   428
      Wyck Mansion   428
   Hotels
      Four Seasons   429
      Sheraton Society Hill   429
   Independence Hall   428
   Liberty Bell Pavilion   428
   Museums
      Barnes Foundation Museum   428
      Franklin Institute   429
      Norman Rockwell Museum   429
      Pennsylvania Academy of Fine Arts   429
      Philadelphia Library   429
      Philadelphia Museum of Art   428
      Rodin Museum   429
      Rosenbach Museum   429
   National Portrait Gallery   428
   Penn's Landing   428
   Restaurants
      Garden   429
      Le Bec-Fin   429
      Old Original Bookbinders   429
   Society Hill   428
Phoenix, Arizona   444
   Arizona Biltmore   444
   Etienne's Different Point of View   444
Plymouth, Massachusetts   422
   Captain Tim Brady & Sons   423
   Pilgrim Hall   422
   Plimouth Plantation   422
   Plymouth Rock   422
   Sleepy Pilgrim   422
   Whale Discovery Museum   423
Portland, Maine   424
   Cap'n Newick's Lobster   424
Pribilof Island (Alaska)   459
Princeton, New Jersey   426
   Marquand Park   426
   Nassau Hall   426
   Palmer Square   426
   Princeton Battlefield   426
   Princeton University   426
   Restaurants
      Annex Restaurant   426
      Nassau Inn   426
      Squire's Choice   426
      Yankee Doodle Tap Room   426
Redwood National Park (California)   453
Rocky Mountains   447
San Antonio, Texas   442
   Alamo   442
   Hotels
      Amerisuites   443
   Missions
      The Alamo   443
      Mission San Francisco de la Espada   443
      Mission San Jose   443

Mission San Juan Capistrano   443
Museums
   Lone Star Brewing Company   443
   San Antonio Museum of Art   443
Restaurants
   Casa Rio   443
   The Hacienda   443
   La Louisiane   443
San Francisco, California   448
   Chinatown   448
   Golden Gate Bridge   448
   Golden Gate Park   448
   Golden Gate Promenade   448
   Holy City Zoo Comedy Club   449
   Hotels
      Archbishop's Mansion Inn   449
      La Petite Auberge   449
      Mansion Hotel   449
      Sherman House   449
      Stanford Court Hotel   448
      White Swan   449
   Huntington Park   448
   Museums
      Asian Art Museum   448
      California Academy of Sciences   448
      MH de Young Memorial Museum   448
   Music Concourse   448
   Nob Hill   448
   North Beach   448
   Restaurants
      Le Castel   449
      McCormick & Kuleto's   449
      Nob Hill Restaurant   449
      The Mandarin   449
Santa Fe, New Mexico   446
   Festivals
      Fiesta de Santa Fe   446
   Hotel
      Bishop's Lodge   446
   Hotel La Fonda   446
   Manhattan Project   446
   Museums
      D.H. Lawrence Shrine and Ranch   447
      Millicent Rogers Museum of Southwestern Arts
      and Crafts   447
      Museum of New Mexico   446
   Palace of the Governors   446
   Restaurants
      Pink Adobe   446
      Rancho de Chimayo   446
   St. Francis Cathedral   446
Sausalito, California   450
   Alta Mira   450
   Casa Madrona   450
Savannah, Georgia   434
   Davenport House   435
   Gastonian Hotel   435
   Museums
      Ships of the Sea Museum   434
      Owens-Thomas House   434
   Restaurants
      Johnny Harris Restaurant   435
      Wilkes Dining Room   435
Seattle, Washington   453
   Chambered Nautilus Bed and Breakfast   454
   Museums
      Ye Olde Curiosity Shop   453
   Pioneer Square   453
   Restaurants
      Café Sport   454
      Chez Shea   454
      Le Gourmand   454

Pike Place Farmer's Market   454
   The Georgian Room   454
Shopping
   Grand Central Arcade   454
Space Needle   453
Underground Seattle Tour   454
Sierra Nevada (California)   453
Sitka, Alaska   460
   Hotels
      Westmark Shee Atika   460
   Sitka National Historical Park   460
Skiing
   Jackson Hole, Wyoming   448
      Grand Targhee   448
   Snowbird, Utah   448
   Sun Valley, Idaho   448
   Taos, New Mexico   448
Smathers, Florida   439
South, Florida   439
St. Augustine, Florida   439
   Castillo de San Marcos   439
   Kenwood Inn   440
   Oldest Store Museum   439
St. Petersburg, Florida   438
   Don CeSar   438
Stowe, Vermont   425
Taos, New Mexico   447
   Museums
      Blumenschein House   447
      Harwood Foundation Museum and Library   447
      Kit Carson Museum   447
   Sagebrush Inn   447
   Taos Plaza   447
   Taos Pueblo Tourism Director   447
   Tours
      Taos Indian Horse Ranch   447
Tenakee Springs (Alaska)   460
   Tenakee Inn and Tavern   460
Texas   440
Tongass National Forest (Alaska)   459
Tucson, Arizona   444
   Arizona Historical Society   444
   Arizona State Museum   444
   El Presidio   444
   Hotels
      Tanque Verde Guest Ranch   444
   Mission of San Xavier del Bac   444
   Museums
      Arizona-Sonora Desert Museum   444
      Old Town Artisans   444
      Tucson Museum of Art   444
   Restaurants
      Tack Room   444
   Spanish Colonial Pima County Courthouse   444
Venice, California   451
   Ocean Front Boulevard   451
Vermont   425
   Stratton Mountain Resort   425
Wakulla Springs, Florida   440
   Hotels
      Wakulla Springs Lodge   440
Washington, D.C.   429
   Arlington National Cemetery   431
   Capitol   430
   Ford's Theater   430
   Hotels
      Capitol Hilton   432
      Four Seasons   432
      Hay-Adams   432
      Omni Shoreham   432
      Sheraton Carlton   432
      Stouffer Mayflower Hotel   432

615

Vista International Hotel   432
Washington Plaza Hotel   432
Watergate Hotel   432
Jefferson Memorial   431
Kennedy Center for the Performing Arts   431
Library of Congress   430
Lincoln Memorial   431
Mall   429
Monuments
  Jefferson Memorial   431
  Lincoln Memorial   431
  Vietnam War Memorial   431
  Washington Monument   431
Mount Vernon   431
Nightclubs
  Bayou   433
  Blues Alley   432
  Cities   433
  Kilimanjaro   433
  Lautrec's   433
  One Step Down   433
Parks and gardens
  Chesapeake and Ohio Canal National Historic
    Park   432
  Dumbarton Oaks Museum and Garden   431
  National Zoological Park   431
  Rock Creek Park   431
Restaurants
  Au Pied du Cochon   432
  Dominique's   432
  Iron Gate Inn   432
  Jean-Louis   432
  Le Gaulois   432
  Palm   432
  Thai Taste   432
  The Palm   432
  Trader Vic's   432
Smithsonian Institute   430
  Freer Gallery of Art   430
  Hirshorn Museum   430
  National Air and Space Museum   430
  National Gallery of Art   430
  National Museum of African Art   431
  National Museum of American History   431
  National Museum of Natural History   431
Supreme Court Building   430
The Capitol   430
Theaters
  Arena Stage   433
  Kennedy Center   433
  Lansburgh Theater   433
  National Theater   433
White House   430
Williamsburg, Virginia   433
  Berkeley Plantation   433
  Carter's Grove   433
  William and Mary   433
Yellowstone National Park (Wyoming)   447
  Old Faithful   447
  Steamboat   447
  Yellowstone River   447
Yosemite National Park (California)   453
  Ahwahnee Resort   453
Zion National Park (Utah)   443
  Angel's Landing   443

Credit Repair Kit

5th Edition

by Melyssa Barrett, Steve Bucci, and Rod Griffin

for dummies®

A Wiley Brand

Credit Repair Kit For Dummies®, 5th Edition

Published by: **John Wiley & Sons, Inc.,** 111 River Street, Hoboken, NJ 07030-5774, www.wiley.com

Copyright © 2021 by John Wiley & Sons, Inc., Hoboken, New Jersey

Published simultaneously in Canada

For general information on our other products and services, please contact our Customer Care Department within the U.S. at 877-762-2974, outside the U.S. at 317-572-3993, or fax 317-572-4002. For technical support, please visit https://hub.wiley.com/community/support/dummies.

Wiley publishes in a variety of print and electronic formats and by print-on-demand. Some material included with standard print versions of this book may not be included in e-books or in print-on-demand. If this book refers to media such as a CD or DVD that is not included in the version you purchased, you may download this material at http://booksupport.wiley.com. For more information about Wiley products, visit www.wiley.com.

Library of Congress Control Number: 2020949887

ISBN 978-1-119-77106-7 (pbk); ISBN 978-1-119-77107-4 (ebk); ISBN 978-1-119-77108-1 (ebk)

Manufactured in the United States of America

SKY10023060_120720

Contents at a Glance

Foreword xvii

Introduction 1

Part 1: Getting Started with Credit Repair 7
CHAPTER 1: Introducing Credit Repair, Credit Scores, and Your Life on Credit 9
CHAPTER 2: Turning Your Credit Around 27
CHAPTER 3: Cleaning Up Your Credit Reports 43
CHAPTER 4: Getting the Best Help for Bad Credit for Free 63
CHAPTER 5: Coping with Debt Collection 77
CHAPTER 6: Working with Collectors, Lawyers, and the Courts to
Manage Debt Obligations 101

Part 2: Reducing Credit Damage from Major Setbacks 119
CHAPTER 7: Reducing Credit Damage in a Crisis 121
CHAPTER 8: Filing for and Recovering from Bankruptcy 145
CHAPTER 9: Repairing Credit Damage in the Wake of Identity Theft 165

**Part 3: Rebuilding Credit, No Matter Where
or When You Begin** 175
CHAPTER 10: Starting or Restarting Your Credit in Real Life 177
CHAPTER 11: Ending Life's Negative Credit Surprises 199
CHAPTER 12: Protecting Your Credit During Major Life Challenges 213

Part 4: Making Sense of Credit Reporting and Scoring 243
CHAPTER 13: Discovering How Credit Reporting Works 245
CHAPTER 14: Understanding Credit Reports and Scores 261
CHAPTER 15: Monitoring Your Credit Reports and Scores 295

Part 5: Successfully Managing Your Credit for Life 307
CHAPTER 16: Putting Yourself in Control of Your Credit 309
CHAPTER 17: Taking a Sustainable Approach to Your Credit 317
CHAPTER 18: Safeguarding Your Credit with a Spending Plan 329
CHAPTER 19: Understanding Equity and Diversity in Credit 355
CHAPTER 20: Knowing Your Rights to Protect Your Credit 367
CHAPTER 21: Protecting Your Identity 387

Part 6: The Part of Tens 403

CHAPTER 22: Ten Consumer Protections Everyone Needs to Know 405

CHAPTER 23: Ten Strategies for Dealing with Student Loans 415

CHAPTER 24: Ten Ways to Deal with a Mortgage Meltdown 425

Index 435

Table of Contents

FOREWORD xvii

INTRODUCTION 1

    About This Book. 2

    Foolish Assumptions. 3

    Icons Used in This Book 4

    Beyond the Book. 4

    Where to Go from Here 5

PART 1: GETTING STARTED WITH CREDIT REPAIR. 7

CHAPTER 1: **Introducing Credit Repair, Credit Scores,**
and Your Life on Credit 9

    Repairing Bad Credit. 10

        Settling debts 10

        Resetting your goals 11

        Rebuilding your credit by using it 11

        Using a cosigner or becoming an authorized user. 12

        Finding sources of free help 12

        Dealing with collectors 13

    Weathering a Major Crisis 13

        Mortgage meltdowns 13

        Medical debt. 15

        Student loans 16

        Car loans 16

    Understanding Diversity in Credit. 16

    Filing Bankruptcy. 16

    Protecting Your Credit and Your Identity. 17

        Getting familiar with credit laws 17

        Receiving free reports and filing disputes 18

        Signing up for credit monitoring. 18

        Setting alarms, alerts, and freezes 19

        Identifying identity theft. 19

    Maintaining Good Credit Throughout Life. 20

        Establishing credit for the first time 20

        Making credit changes at life's stages 21

        Avoiding pitfalls 21

    Managing Credit in Today's Unforgiving Economy. 22

        Planning for success 22

        Reviewing your credit report. 23

        Knowing your credit score 23

        Considering credit a renewable resource 24

CHAPTER 2: **Turning Your Credit Around** 27

Understanding How Your Actions Impact Your Credit Score 28
Using a Cosigner to Raise Your Score. 29
Turning Small Purchases into Big Credit 30
Maximizing Your Credit Score with Major Expenditures. 33
Leveraging your mortgage. 34
Financing your car. 36
Paying back student loans 37
Understanding How Good Debt Builds Good Credit 38
Achieving goals with the help of credit. 38
Sending a message to potential lenders 39
Giving nonlenders a sense of how you handle responsibility 39
Selecting the Best Tools for Building Your Credit. 40
Spending your way to better credit with a spending plan. 40
Tracking your progress: Paying attention to your
credit report and score. 41

CHAPTER 3: **Cleaning Up Your Credit Reports** 43

Understanding the True Value of Good Credit 44
Reviewing Your Reports for Problems 47
Using the Law to Get Your Credit Record Clean and
Keep It That Way 50
Identifying and Disputing Inaccurate Information 53
Understanding the dispute process 53
Correcting all your credit reports 54
Contacting the creditor. 59
Adding Positive Information to Your Credit Report 60
Asking your landlord to report your rent payments 60
Adding your utility and cellphone payments to your report. 60
Opening new credit accounts 61
Adding a 100-word statement. 61

CHAPTER 4: **Getting the Best Help for Bad Credit for Free** 63

Knowing Whether You Need Help 64
Gauging your need for outside assistance 64
Handling situations on your own 65
Identifying Help You Can Get for Free 67
Getting help with your mortgage 68
Considering credit counseling. 69
Working with an attorney. 74

CHAPTER 5: **Coping with Debt Collection** 77

Handling Those Collection Phone Calls 78
Knowing what collectors can do 78
Knowing what collectors can't do 80

Deciding whether to answer the phone. 81

Preparing to answer collection calls. 81

Knowing what not to say 82

Taking Charge of the Collection Process 83

Asking for proof that the debt is yours .84

Knowing when debts fade away: Statutes of limitations. 84

Negotiating a payback arrangement 86

Keeping your promise. 87

Identifying Escalation Options That Help. 89

Asking to speak to a manager 89

Approaching the creditor 90

Fighting harassment 91

Communicating with Customer Service Before Being Placed for
Collection 92

Contacting your creditor promptly. 93

Explaining your situation 94

Offering a solution. 95

Covering all the bases. 96

Keeping Collectors in Check. 96

Calling in a credit counselor. 96

Referring the matter to your lawyer. 97

Freeing Up Money to Pay a Collector 97

Utilizing a spending plan 97

Cutting the fat from your monthly spending. 98

Avoiding Collectors Altogether 98

Getting organized 99

Stopping the paycheck-to-paycheck cycle 100

CHAPTER 6: **Working with Collectors, Lawyers, and
the Courts to Manage Debt Obligations**. 101

Getting a Handle on Charge-Offs 102

So what is a charge-off? 102

Making sense of unpaid charge-offs. .103

Making charge-off payments. 104

Coming to a Debt Settlement Agreement .105

Considering a debt settlement offer. .105

Hiring a debt settlement firm 106

Reaching expiration dates on debts. .106

Finding Out about Judgments and What They Mean to You. 107

Understanding Wage Garnishments 110

Dodging wage garnishments. 110

Figuring out how much can be garnished 112

Stating Your Case in Court 112
Managing IRS Debts, Student Loans, and Unpaid Child Support 114
 Handling IRS debts 114
 Educating yourself about student loans 115
 Putting your kids first: Child support 117

PART 2: REDUCING CREDIT DAMAGE FROM MAJOR SETBACKS 119

CHAPTER 7: Reducing Credit Damage in a Crisis 121
Assessing the Damage from a Mortgage Meltdown 122
Understanding How Mortgages Differ from Other Loans. 124
 Spotting a foreclosure on the horizon .124
 Counting to 90 125
Knowing Where to Turn for Help 126
 Finding good help for free 126
 Working with your mortgage servicer 126
 Avoiding help that hurts. 127
Alternatives to Going Down with the Ship. 128
 What to do first 129
 What to do for more serious problems .129
 What to do to end matters. 130
 Managing a foreclosure 131
 Strategic default: Stopping payments 132
Dealing with Deficiencies 134
Preparing for "Credit Winter". 136
Curing Medical Debt 136
 Understanding new reporting and scoring rules 137
 Reviewing your options for paying medical bills. 137
 Discovering how insurers get your medical information 138
 Monitoring insurance claims for errors .138
 Dealing with denied medical claims 139
Managing Student Loans 139
 Default timelines 140
 Loan forgiveness programs 140
 Where to get help 141
 The impact of the CARES Act on student loans. 141
Avoiding Car Repossession 141
 Repossession: What you can do 143
 Dealing with auto loan default deficiencies. 143
Coping with So-Called Acts of God and Other Things
That Are Not Your Fault 144

CHAPTER 8: **Filing for and Recovering from Bankruptcy** 145

Deciding Whether Bankruptcy Makes Sense for You 146
  Deliberating the bankruptcy decision 146
  Adding up the pluses and minuses 150
  Considering a debt management plan first 152
Understanding Bankruptcy, Chapter and Verse 154
Qualifying for and Filing for Bankruptcy 155
  Qualifying for Chapter 7 155
  Qualifying for Chapter 13 157
Managing Your Credit After a Bankruptcy 159
  Telling your side of the story 159
  Reaffirming some debt 161
  Repairing your credit score 161
  Establishing new credit 163
  Moving forward with a game plan 163

CHAPTER 9: **Repairing Credit Damage in the Wake
of Identity Theft** 165

Taking Fast Action When Identity Theft Occurs 165
  Communicating with the right people 166
  Protecting your identity through the FACT Act 169
  Sending out a fraud alert 171
  Blocking fraudulent credit lines 171
Getting and Using Credit After Identity Theft 172
  Closing and reopening your accounts 172
  Altering your PINs, passwords, and radio transmissions 173
  Changing your Social Security number and driver's license
  number 174

PART 3: REBUILDING CREDIT, NO MATTER
WHERE OR WHEN YOU BEGIN 175

CHAPTER 10: **Starting or Restarting Your Credit in Real Life** 177

Debunking Misinformation about Banking and Credit 178
  Why you need credit 179
  Why credit is safe 180
Obtaining Credit: Starting Out on the Right Foot 181
  Establishing a credit file without a Social Security number 182
  Setting goals before you set out 183
  Establishing a relationship with a financial institution 185
  Using prepaid and reloadable cards 186
  Fattening up your credit file 187
  Avoiding high interest, fees, and scams 189

Overcoming Credit Fears and Mistakes 190
Qualifying for First-Time Cards and Lending. 192
    Getting a credit card 192
    Using savings for credit 194
Considering Credit for Students and Military Members 195
    Giving credit to students 195
    Following military credit rules 197

CHAPTER 11: **Ending Life's Negative Credit Surprises**. 199
Keeping Your Credit from Hurting Your Job Prospects 200
Dealing with Rental Application Checks. 201
    Knowing what's on your reports 202
    Taking action 203
Qualifying for a Mortgage 203
    Ordering your credit report and score. .204
    Looking at your credit file like a lender .205
Preparing to Purchase a Car 205
    Arming yourself with information. 206
    Reviewing what to consider when you're at the dealership 207
Unveiling the Relationship between Your Credit and
Your Insurance Premiums 208
    Understanding insurance scores 209
    Getting a copy of your insurance score and
    insurance claim report 209
    Figuring out what to do with your newfound knowledge 210
    Taking other factors into account. 211

CHAPTER 12: **Protecting Your Credit During Major**
Life Challenges 213
Tying the Knot in Life and in Credit: A Couples' Guide
to Building Good Credit 214
    Engaging in prenuptial financial discussions. 214
    Considering joint accounts. 216
    Managing joint debt 218
    Avoiding money conflicts 219
Protecting Your Finances in a Divorce 220
    Taking precautions when a split-up looms 220
    Preparing your credit before heading to court. 221
    Protecting your credit in a divorce decree and beyond. 222
Keeping Credit Strong While Unemployed 226
    Preparing your credit for the worst-case scenario. 226
    Using credit when you don't have a job. 226
    Protecting your credit lines 228

Curing Medical Debt 229
    Reviewing your options for paying medical bills. 230
    Discovering how insurers get your medical information 234
    Monitoring insurance claims for errors 235
    Dealing with denied medical claims 236
Resolving Credit Issues After the Death of a Spouse or Partner 238
    Understanding what happens to joint credit when
    you're single again. 238
    Knowing exactly what your liability is. 239
    Building your credit record on your own. .240
Fitting Credit into Retirement 240
    Budgeting on a fixed income. 241
    Using credit for convenience 241

**PART 4: MAKING SENSE OF CREDIT REPORTING
AND SCORING**. 243

CHAPTER 13: **Discovering How Credit Reporting Works**. 245
Grasping the Importance of Your Credit Report. 246
What Is a Credit Report, Exactly?. 247
    Revealing the facts about your financial transactions 248
    Providing insight into your character 252
The Negatives and Positives of Credit Reporting 253
    The negatives. 253
    The positives 255
Your Credit Report's Numerical Offspring: The Credit Score 255
    Cracking credit score components 256
    The reasoning behind risk factors 259

CHAPTER 14: **Understanding Credit Reports and Scores**. 261
Getting Copies of Your Credit Reports. 262
    Where to get your reports 263
    What you need to provide 264
    When to get copies of your credit reports. 265
Tracking Down Specialty Reports: From Apartments
to Casinos to Prescriptions 268
Perusing Your Credit Reports 271
    Identifying information: It's all about who you are. 272
    Accounts summary: An overview of your financial history 272
    Bankruptcy public records: The most serious element
    in a credit report 273
    Credit inquiries: Tracking who has been accessing your file. 273
    Account history: Think of it as a payment CSI. 274
    Your optional 100-word statements: Making sure
    your voice is heard 281

Correcting Any Errors You Find 283
    Contacting the credit bureau 283
    Contacting the creditor 283
Getting and Understanding Your Credit Scores 284
    Ordering your score 285
    Telling a good score from a bad one 287
    Connecting pricing to your credit score .290
    Knowing the reason for reason statements 292

CHAPTER 15: **Monitoring Your Credit Reports and Scores** 295
How Credit Monitoring Really Works 296
Understanding the Types of Monitoring Services Available 297
Making a Case for and against Third-Party Credit Monitoring 299
    Monitoring on your own 300
    When paid monitoring may be worth the time and money 301
    Recognizing the protection you have already 302
Getting Your Money's Worth from Monitoring Services 303
Setting Alarms, Alerts, and Freezes 304
    Alarms 305
    Fraud alerts 305
    Credit freezes 305

**PART 5: SUCCESSFULLY MANAGING YOUR
CREDIT FOR LIFE** 307

CHAPTER 16: **Putting Yourself in Control of Your Credit** 309
Determining Your Credit Style 310
Balancing Spending, Savings, and Credit Use 312
    Spending on your terms 312
    Saving for financial emergencies 312
    Using credit to enhance your life 313
Remembering the Importance of Planning When
It Comes to Your Credit 313
    Zeroing in on the plans others have for your money 314
    Developing your own plans for your future 314

CHAPTER 17: **Taking a Sustainable Approach to Your Credit** 317
Going Green: Treating Credit as a Renewable Resource 318
    Recognizing your credit environment 318
    Taking a closer look at the parts that make up your
    credit ecosystem 319
Sustaining Your Credit Ecosystem for Life 321
    Funding college 321
    Home sweet home 322
    Credit on wheels 322

Steering Clear of Credit Pollution 322
    Endangering your payment history 323
    Clear-cutting your credit in bankruptcy 323
    Outlasting a long, cold credit winter. 325
Surviving and Reviving After a Credit Catastrophe. 325
    Understanding what happened 325
    Rebuilding your credit ecosystem. 327

CHAPTER 18: **Safeguarding Your Credit with a Spending Plan** 329
Appreciating the Benefits of a Solid Spending Plan 330
Deciding on Goals: Imagining Your Future as You Want It to Be 332
    Setting the stage for planning 332
    Categorizing your goals 333
    Putting your goals in order 334
Building Your Vision of Your Future 334
    Step 1: Counting up your income 335
    Step 2: Tallying what you spend 336
    Step 3: Making savings part of your spending plan 341
    Step 4: Managing your credit to improve your spending plan . . .345
    Step 5: Looking at your insurance options 346
    Step 6: Planning for the IRS 348
    Step 7: Planning for retirement. 349
Using Cool Tools to Help You Build and Stick to a Spending Plan . . .351
    Web-based financial calculators 352
    Budgeting websites. 352
    Smartphone apps 353
    Spending plan assistance 353
Adjusting Your Priorities and Your Plan 354

CHAPTER 19: **Understanding Equity and Diversity in Credit** 355
Benefitting from Financial Inclusion. 357
Participating in the Financial System 358
Taking or Retaking Control of Your Credit. 358
Educating Yourself on How the System Works. 359
Tackling Debt 362
    Student loans. 363
    Payday loans 363
    Collections 364
    Bankruptcy 364
Working Toward the Goal of Homeownership 364

CHAPTER 20: **Knowing Your Rights to Protect Your Credit** 367

    Why You Have the Right to Credit Protections 368

    The CARD Act: Shielding You from Credit Card Abuse............369

    The Consumer Financial Protection Bureau:
    The New Cop on the Financial Beat 372

    Safeguarding Your Credit Data through the FACT Act............372

    The FDCPA: Providing Protection Against Debt Collectors 375

        Controlling the contacts 375

        Finding out about the debt 375

        Stopping a collector from contacting you 376

        Spotting prohibited behavior.............................376

        Suing a collector......................................377

    The CROA: Getting What You Pay For.........................378

        Knowing what credit repair organizations must do...........378

        Understanding what credit repair companies can't do 379

    Exploring Other Protections 379

        The ins and outs of payday loans 380

        The details of debt settlement............................382

        The scoop on the statute of limitations 384

CHAPTER 21: **Protecting Your Identity** 387

    Keeping Thieves at Bay....................................388

        Getting on the technology train 388

        Looking out for phishing scams 389

        Safeguarding your computer data 391

        Keeping passwords secret 392

        Protecting your mail 393

        Storing financial data in your home 393

        Putting your credit information on ice.....................394

        Shielding your credit card number 395

    Catching Identity Thieves in the Act 397

        Watching for early-warning notices 397

        Early warnings from the IRS..............................399

        Handling a collections call 400

        Detecting unauthorized charges..........................400

        Being denied credit or account access.....................401

        Noticing missing account statements......................401

PART 6: THE PART OF TENS 403

CHAPTER 22: **Ten Consumer Protections Everyone
Needs to Know** 405

    The Fair Debt Collection Practices Act 406

    The Bankruptcy Abuse Prevention and Consumer
    Protection Act...406

Your Lawyer 407
Coronavirus Aid, Relief, and Economic Security (CARES) Act 408
Statute of Limitations Laws 409
Your State Attorney General 409
The Consumer Financial Protection Bureau 410
The Credit Card Accountability, Responsibility,
and Disclosure Act. 411
The Fair and Accurate Credit Transactions Act. 412
The Federal Trade Commission. 413

CHAPTER 23: **Ten Strategies for Dealing with Student Loans** . . . 415
Knowing How Student Loans Are Reported Differently
Than Other Loans 416
Dealing with the Collection Process 416
Identifying the Best Repayment Option for Your Situation. 417
Taking Your Loans to Bankruptcy. 418
Dealing with the Prospect of Default 418
Gaining Student Loan Forgiveness 419
Lowering Your Bill While You're in School 421
Keeping Up with Your Loans After You're Out 422
Setting Limits During the Planning and Application Process 423
Getting Help if You're in the Military. 423

CHAPTER 24: **Ten Ways to Deal with a Mortgage Meltdown**. 425
Knowing When You're in Trouble 426
Knowing How Your State's Laws Treat Foreclosures 427
Nonrecourse or recourse. 427
Judicial or nonjudicial 427
Deciding Whether to Stay or Go 428
Walking away 428
Working with the lender to exit. 429
Staying the course. 429
Tightening Your Spending to Stay in Your Home 430
Prioritizing Your Spending to Build Cash. 431
Lessening the Damage to Your Credit 431
Knowing Who to Call. 432
Beware of Scams. 432
Beefing Up Your Credit. 432
Consulting an Attorney. 433

INDEX. 435

Foreword

Chances are, at this very moment, you're within arm's reach of a small, yet powerful device: your smartphone. This relatively tiny, yet complex machine was once considered an optional luxury. Now, in 21st-century America, it's a necessary utility for everyday life. Our cellphones give us access to nearly everything imaginable — food, information, transportation, vacation options. You name it, and it's available at your fingertips! Though it has profound potential to make our lives easier, we leave so much of its capability on the table without ever fully realizing its benefits. Worse, we have a tendency to abuse it, all because we didn't approach it with respect and understanding.

Credit is the same way.

Credit is the fuel that helps drive most of the major milestones in life — purchasing your first home, leasing a new car, launching your own business, even getting a job offer. Credit impacts so much of our lives, yet many of us are unaware of its potential and the vast possibilities it offers *if* we learn to leverage it properly and use it for our betterment.

Today, more than 191 million Americans have access to credit through a credit card or have unknowingly begun building their credit profile through other means. Yet most people are unaware of what this means for their lives today, and more important, their futures. They understand its basic functions, but they don't access its best features simply because they don't know how.

As an entrepreneur, philanthropist, and nonprofit leader, I understand just how important this subject is to so many Americans and the future of the American Dream, especially the underbanked and underserved. For far too long, many people on the margins never received the memo on financial literacy and credit management. Unknowingly, they began to borrow against their future and locked themselves out of much-needed opportunities. But the beauty of our country is that we all have a chance to make our hopes and aspirations become a reality, even after we've messed up, if given the right tools and opportunity.

Melyssa Barrett, Steve Bucci, and Rod Griffin offer both of those through *Credit Repair Kit For Dummies.* This book empowers you with the knowledge and mindset needed to make the most of your credit and live your best life. But you must apply the lessons learned and dedicate yourself to living them out daily.

This edition of this book is special because it takes into account the ongoing challenges that our nation continues to face regarding financial equity, diversity, and inclusion. With an exciting new chapter, three experts address these issues head on and invite every reader, from every background, to learn the rules of the credit game, participate, and win. Regardless of race, creed, culture, or class, you have the power to make your dreams come true.

We're all rooting for you!

John Hope Bryant
Founder, Chairman, and CEO
Operation HOPE

Introduction

The credit crisis has been replaced by the credit "chronic." Now more than ever, your ability to weather and recover from the next crisis depends on your credit. You've already lived through a series of financial explosions that caused a "credit winter" and that gave way to a fragile and uneven credit spring thaw. You've heard of the meteor that killed off the dinosaurs by causing a prolonged winter environment around the globe, and of the consequences of an atomic war called a nuclear winter? Well, the same thing can happen to your credit regardless of what causes it. For many people, credit loosens and tightens cyclically. For others, it has been a challenge through good times and bad. Equal access to credit and the benefits it brings have never been fully assured for those new to credit, including immigrants, minorities, and the working poor.

Credit access may have thawed over the last few years, but only for those people who have a solid credit report and credit score. Loan interest rates may be low, but criteria for obtaining the best credit terms are not. Jobs may be readily available or scarce depending on the economy, but regardless, failing a credit review can keep you unemployed in the best of times. Your need for great credit never ends. This book is meant to help you successfully rebuild and manage your credit. Rather than taking an academic approach to the subject of credit, it helps you succeed at integrating credit into your *real* life. It enables you to make great credit an outcome of the decisions you make every day as you pursue life and happiness. I call it your *credit-life connection.*

Given today's increasing reliance on credit reporting and credit scores for lending and non-lending decisions making, you need better credit and a higher credit score to access today's credit products, which are an essential part of leading a rewarding life in today's society. Not only are the criteria for the best access to credit very selective, but the penalties for ignorance and failure have multiplied.

And if all this isn't enough, the non-lending use of credit reports is growing seemingly by the day. Updates to this book tell you about new consumer databases that collect information about your medical history, prescription drug use, rental history, banking data, and more. Employers, insurance companies, landlords, and lenders use this information to decide whether to hire or promote you, what insurance rates to give you, whether to rent you an apartment, and whether to offer you new banking products. You need to know what's in these files, and that's one of many things we tell you how to do in this book.

Credit Repair Kit For Dummies comes at a critical time. Credit plays an ever-changing and increasingly important role in your life, regardless of whether you use a credit card. Insurance, employment, home buying or renting, and getting an education with student loans are more dependent than ever on you having good credit. Plus, although the rewards for good credit have never been higher, the penalties for failure — foreclosure, eviction, job problems, mounting debts, collections — have never been greater. For these reasons and more, millions of people are looking for up-to-date, useful, and proven answers from a trusted and knowledgeable resource. If you know the rules of the credit game, you'll get a winning score. That's why we wanted to bring you the best, non-biased information in the industry based on our decades of experience and research.

About This Book

The approach we outline in this book is different because it's low-cost and simple and drives right to the heart of the matter. With this book, you can manage your credit by applying just a few key concepts. Unlike the talk-show approach of making one philosophy fit all after a 15-second question-and-answer period, this book takes the time to give you the concepts and tools you need so that you can apply them to your specific situation and come up with an answer that's custom-tailored to you.

So why this book?

>> **Because although credit problems can seem incredibly complex and unfair, you can have good credit with a few simple actions that anyone can master.** We give you all the tools and insight you need to rebuild your credit (or build it up for the first time).

>> **Because you may need the advice of an experienced advisor to guide you through a mortgage problem.** This book tells you how to find a good resource for credit or bankruptcy counseling.

>> **Because your credit may be in detention due to crushing student loans.** This book can help you find the right solution and then rebuild your credit score as quickly as possible.

>> **Because you want to get a job or promotion; buy a reliable car to get to your job; start a business; insure your home, apartment, or car; or further your education.** If any of these situations applies, you need a good credit record.

>> **Because you may be one of the millions of people who become victims of personal data theft each year.** This book provides valuable information to salvage and protect your identity.

>> **Because you may be on the brink or even over the cliff of credit trouble.** This book gives you budgeting and spending advice that can pull you back from the edge.

>> **Because the time is right for you to regain control of your credit and your financial peace of mind.** This book helps you do just that.

Foolish Assumptions

We assume that you're reading this book because you know that repairing your credit is important, but you may not know all the ins and outs of making credit work for you. Whether your credit is not so great and you want to know how to improve it or your credit is just plain nonexistent and you want to establish it on your own terms, you'll benefit from this book. An understanding of your credit and how the credit system works may be especially important during life's transitions. We assume that this book can be of value to you if you're

>> Concerned about your credit report and who may be looking at it

>> Concerned about the credit status of a loved one

>> Considering what to do about overwhelming debt

>> Wondering how to deal with medical bills

>> Unsure about the credit impact of remaining in your home or walking away

>> Starting over again after filing for bankruptcy

>> Taking on or paying back a student loan

>> Concerned that your personal information may have been compromised or stolen

>> Already in or soon to be in a marriage or partnership

>> Recently divorced or in the process of divorcing

>> Reestablishing credit after the loss of a spouse or partner

>> Hunting for a job or hoping for a promotion

» Establishing credit for the first time

» Wanting to know how to maintain good credit after you get back on track

We assume that you don't have a formal education in credit or personal finance. Even if you do, however, we believe that you can still find practical insights in this book based on our experience and that of others we've helped.

Icons Used in This Book

Icons are those little pictures you see sprinkled in the margins throughout this book. Here's what they mean:

REMEMBER

This icon denotes critical information. Considering the state of our own over-crowded memories, we wouldn't ask you to remember anything unless it was really important.

TECHNICAL STUFF

This image of a credit professional — okay, fine, of the Dummies Man — shows up whenever we go into more detail on a concept or rule. If you don't care about the details of how something works or where it came from, feel free to skip these gems.

TIP

This lightbulb lets you know that you're reading on-target advice — often little-known insights or recommendations that we've picked up over the years.

WARNING

This icon serves as a warning, telling you to avoid something that's potentially harmful. Take heed!

Beyond the Book

In addition to the material in the print or e-book you're reading right now, this product also comes with some access-anywhere goodies on the web.

Even though these pages are packed with helpful tips and advice for repairing your credit, we've provided even more tools and resources beyond what's in the book. Go to www.dummies.com/go/creditrepairkitfd5e to find useful forms, worksheets, sample letters, and credit-related legislation and laws. The online material also includes a glossary of commonly used credit-industry terms.

Also, be sure to check out the Cheat Sheet for this book. There you can find contact information for the three major credit bureaus, credit score breakdowns, tips for improving your credit score, and advice on handling an overdue mortgage. Just go to www.dummies.com and type **Credit Repair Kit For Dummies Cheat Sheet** in the Search box.

Where to Go from Here

You get to choose what happens next. This book is packed with information to help you repair your credit. You can use the table of contents and index to jump directly to the topics of most interest to you, or you can start at the beginning of the book and take it from there. With the information in *Credit Repair Kit For Dummies,* you can get great credit and keep it great for the long haul. We wish you all the best in achieving your dreams, which increasingly require good credit to realize. You and your family deserve it.

1

Getting Started with Credit Repair

Understand the basic workings of credit, credit repair, and credit scores.

Find out how to rebuild your credit after a crisis.

Fix inaccuracies and add positive data in your credit reports and boost your credit score.

Solve your credit problems on your own or get expert help that really works for free.

Field calls from debt collectors with confidence.

Deal successfully with debt collectors, lawyers, and court actions.

» Dealing with the issues surrounding equity and diversity in credit

» Rebuilding your credit after a crisis such as a foreclosure or bankruptcy

» Safeguarding your credit and your identity

» Discovering how to manage your credit

» Keeping your credit solid in every stage of life

Chapter **1**

Introducing Credit Repair, Credit Scores, and Your Life on Credit

C redit plays a larger role in life than ever, and it looks like its influence will only expand in the years to come. The good life, happiness, and credit are inextricably linked. It's not that more material things make you happier, but bad credit exacts a price from your life, your hopes, and your dreams, as well as your relationships with others. Think of it as your credit/life connection. Whether it is hard or easy, fair or not, you must learn to successfully manage your credit and, by extension, your personal finances if you are to lead a successful and satisfying life in these United States.

Financial products, credit foremost among them, have become much more complex and powerful, while the price for having a bad credit report or no credit at all has never been steeper. Your *credit report* is a financial snapshot of your life in financial terms. For example, a divorce can wreak havoc in your life, and that instability can show up as missed payments or even a bankruptcy on your credit report as well. When you use credit, the information usually gets reported to a data storehouse known as a *credit bureau.* This information ends up on your credit report for at least the next seven years. The good, the bad, and the ugly are all there for anyone you do business with to see and for FICO and VantageScore to summarize in a three-digit number known as your *credit score.*

Bad credit can keep you from finding a job, getting the promotions you deserve at work, being approved for an affordable loan, getting insurance (or paying the lowest price for it), securing an apartment or house, and more.

This chapter is all about getting you started in repairing, rebuilding, or even just starting your credit so you can get that job, promotion, loan, home, and insurance to protect it. We cover the basics and the fine points. If you don't understand credit, you can't fix it, so we discuss how credit works, how to apply that knowledge to get what you want, how to deal with the effects of life's inevitable setbacks on your credit, and how to recover from those setbacks as quickly as possible. Other chapters build on this information, helping to make your credit the best it can be and keep it that way. Why? Because life isn't always fair, but you still need to repair the damage and carry on without being taken advantage of by unscrupulous financial companies or wasting precious years recovering from credit problems that you can avoid or minimize by using the advice in this book.

Repairing Bad Credit

After you've had a rough patch and fallen behind on your payments, you may think that you can never recover. Between the cost of interest and maybe even collection actions, the situation can be overwhelming. But we assure you that you can reverse the cycle. You can not only reestablish good credit but also keep good credit for the rest of your life. Forever is a long time, but if you follow our advice, you can banish the credit blues permanently! It's not magic, and it won't cost you another dime. By realistically assessing your situation, seeing yourself as others see you, knowing where you stand, using free help if you need it, setting goals, planning your spending and savings, and using credit as part of your overall plan, you can quickly rebuild your credit.

Settling debts

You hear the ads all the time: "Settle your debt for pennies on the dollar!" "You have a right to pay less than you owe!" Debt settlement is an often misunderstood option that may work for you, but only if you handle it properly. Many companies that offer debt settlement services help themselves a lot more than they help you. You can avoid huge fees and potential credit damage if you reach a settlement agreement with your lender on your own or if you use your own attorney.

REMEMBER

You are personally responsible for the actions of the debt settlement company you hire, and your credit will be ruined in a protracted and adversarial settlement process. Chapter 6 gives you the information you need to decide whether debt settlement is for you and outlines your best options.

Resetting your goals

Just as you did when you first started establishing credit, we want you to revisit your goals from time to time. When your life changes, your goals should reflect that new reality. Goals that once seemed within easy reach may move from short term to long term. Others may change as you mature. Buying that red sports car may not be as important to you now as it was in your 20s. Take the time to reset your sights, as we explain in Chapter 2.

Begin by envisioning your life as you'd like it to be over the short, medium, and long term. Next, create a spending plan (or update your plan if you already have one) so that you know your current financial resources. Then begin to see how long it will take to fund your goals and determine when using credit may be appropriate. Chapter 18 goes into detail about how to create and maintain a spending plan and how to use credit wisely as a part of that plan.

To ensure that your credit is up to the task of supporting your goals for the future, check your credit reports and dispute any inaccuracies or out-of-date information. To rebuild your credit reports, you need to start with an accurate credit history, not one riddled with errors that may hold you back. After you check your reports, look for opportunities to review them for free as often as you can. Part 4 tells you everything you need to know about credit reporting.

Rebuilding your credit by using it

The best way to rebuild your credit is to exercise it! Using your goals and spending plan as a guide, start making those payments as agreed, on time and for the correct amounts. Every month you do so, you build better credit while your older, bad credit either counts for less or drops off your credit reports altogether.

TIP

Consider opening a *secured credit card* (backed by a bank account deposit) or a *passbook loan* to add a revolving and installment account to fatten your credit history and boost your score. You can find the details in Chapter 10.

Using a cosigner or becoming an authorized user

We normally don't recommend that you cosign for a loan, but in this case, someone else is doing the cosigning! Enlisting a cosigner is a way to get access to credit so that you can begin to rebuild your credit history with the credit bureaus. But you need to keep in mind a few important rules:

>> You have to make all the payments on time.

>> If you can't make a payment when it's due, you have to tell the cosigner in advance so that the cosigner can make the payment and protect his or her credit. You can pay your pal back later.

>> You can't get mad at the cosigner for not being understanding or more helpful while you owe him or her money. Your cosigner is doing you a huge favor at great personal credit risk!

Another way to rebuild your credit is to become an authorized user on someone else's credit card. After you're added to the other person's account, his or her good credit history flows onto your credit record as a positive account and payment stream, beefing up your record and credit score. The person needs to have good credit, though, or his or her bad credit will negatively affect yours. We suggest that you decline getting your own card for the account so that only the other person's charges appear on the account. That way, if he or she has a bad memory (as we do), you're spared monthly calls asking whether this or that charge is yours. Although you won't have access to new credit, your credit score gets a boost.

Finding sources of free help

You can do a lot of things on your own, but sometimes having a pro on your side to give you tips helps. You can find that help in three main places, and it ranges from inexpensive to free. Nonprofit credit counselors, pro bono lawyers, and HUD-approved counseling agencies offer priceless insight, assistance, and advice. The trick is to know to ask for it.

Nonprofit credit counselors work with you to set goals, develop a spending plan, and assess your ability to repay your debts. They can set up a repayment plan in concert with your lenders to lower your payments and interest rates and get positive information back on your credit reports faster than you could on your own. They're funded by creditors but work for you, and we recommend the good ones highly. Discover where to find the good ones in Chapter 4.

Lawyers sometime offer free or pro bono help if you can't afford to pay. Chapter 4 includes a list of resources to help you find one in your area.

A mortgage is a different and sometimes dangerous type of loan. The rules for handling a delinquent mortgage are different from those for regular consumer debts, and the penalty for a mistake can be the loss of your home. So, we strongly recommend that if you have a mortgage problem, you get professional, HUD-certified help. You can find an agency at the HUD website (www.hud.gov).

WARNING

Watch out for bad help. In a nutshell, if someone approaches you and offers to help for a fee, don't do it. The free resources work well. The costly ones too often are just ways to separate you from your money while you're under stress.

Dealing with collectors

Sometimes, you have to take the call. You know it's a debt collector, but you don't know what to say, do, or offer. Chapter 5 spells out how to take control of the collection process. Collectors must follow certain rules, and if you know the rules, you'll feel more confident in dealing with a stressful situation. The Fair Debt Collection Practices Act (FDCPA) regulates what collectors can and can't do. In general, this law protects you from abuse and threats. For example, a collector can't threaten an action that it can't or doesn't intend to take, can't make harassing calls, and can't use abusive language. When you know your rights and insist on being treated fairly, you can negotiate a payment schedule that fits your budget. If you need help coming up with a workable plan, you can always ask a credit counselor for assistance.

Chapter 5 offers solutions that work. From how to handle calls and threatening letters to how to craft a repayment proposal, we walk you through how to keep a small collection annoyance from becoming a major and upsetting life event.

Weathering a Major Crisis

Some credit problems are worse than others. In Chapter 7, we cover four of the big ones: mortgages, medical debt, student loans, and auto repossessions.

Mortgage meltdowns

In our experience, a mortgage crisis is among the most upsetting, expensive, and damaging to your credit and relationships. Your home is your castle. When you are at risk of losing it, you likely feel as though your very existence is under attack. Thinking matters through and coming up with the best solution for you and your family may be difficult. In this section, we preview the major options to help guide you along the best path. Check out Chapter 7 for more mortgage information.

Mortgages are different from other types of debts and credit because of a number of factors, including the size of the debt, the importance the lender attaches to a debt secured by a home, and the fact that the debt is probably packaged in a security that's been resold many times and is subject to inflexible collection rules. Mortgage delinquency can have a significant and long-lasting negative effect on your credit score. For example, being just 30 days late on a mortgage payment can cost you 100+ points on your credit score and take three years to recover from. The upshot is that if you're in danger of falling behind on your mortgage payments or you're already behind, you're better off seeking professional help.

Opting for help

In a mortgage crisis, the sooner you get help, the better. The reason is simple: The stakes are high and the help is free.

WARNING

Most people who have a mortgage payment due on the first of the month know that they have until the 15th to pay it. Do you? If you miss that payment on the 15th, you're 45 days late. Mortgages are paid in arrears, so the bill is already 30 days old when you get it. Miss the due date and the 15-day grace period goes away until you catch up. By the 15th of the next month, you're 15 days away from a foreclosure action. Fast, isn't it? So, we suggest that you don't delay in contacting a HUD-approved counseling agency. These agencies are often housed in credit counseling agencies, so they can address all your debt issues at once.

Doing it on your own

You may insist on working out your mortgage problems on your own. The process is tricky and long, but it can be done. Chapter 7 goes into details on the steps and time frames for action. In addition to acting quickly, you need to keep excellent notes about who you speak with, when you talk, and what is said. You're dealing with a bureaucracy, and bureaucracies love to forget that they ever heard from you and send you all over the place to avoid responsibility for helping. So good notes are essential. Chapter 7 lists key terms and things to ask for so you can sound like you know what you're talking about.

REMEMBER

Just because a bank doesn't want to take your home doesn't mean that it won't.

As in any debt resolution process, you need to do your homework before you call your mortgage servicer. Know what you really need in terms of help to take care of your missed payments, and know what you can offer. You may be able to make additional payments over a six-month period to catch up. Or you may need to ask for a reduced payment amount for a certain amount of time. Whatever you need, you have to be specific. Chapter 7 helps you understand the major options, but they change frequently, so you may have to rely on your mortgage servicer (the bureaucrat) to advise you.

If you can't work out a compromise, there are ways to leave your home that result in less credit damage. Among them are

>> **Deed-in-lieu of foreclosure:** You give the house back, saving the bank foreclosure expenses.

>> **Short sale:** You get the bank to agree to let you try to sell the house for less than the mortgage value.

>> **Friendly foreclosure:** You cooperate with the bank and leave the house in good shape on a timely basis.

Chapter 7 goes into more detail about these options.

Strategic mortgage default

Strategic mortgage default isn't an option that anyone likes. However, a number of people consider walking away from their homes as an alternative to trying to work matters out. Based on how much you owe, you may be very, very unlikely to get back the money you're putting into monthly mortgage payments. Why waste thousands in overpayments? Following that reasoning, some people are mailing the keys to the bank and walking away from their homes.

Credit damage from a strategic default is significant and lasts a long time. You can expect to have really bad credit for seven years and to see a credit score drop of 140 to 160 points. (See Chapter 14 for more on credit scoring.) Plus, Fannie Mae, the government agency that guarantees most mortgages, won't guarantee a new loan for you for the next seven years, which means that to buy another home in the next seven years, you'll pay more for a new mortgage and you'll need expensive mortgage insurance.

Medical debt

Being ill is bad enough. Dealing with medical debt can sometimes seem insurmountable. There are special rules in both credit reporting and credit scoring that can help set your mind at ease. Knowing the rules from Chapter 7 may help lower your blood pressure. We also help you deal with medical insurance issues with a list of your options and resources.

Student loans

Chapter 7 covers how to establish a credit history using student loans. When your payments begin, we cover how to avoid a default and, if that's not possible, where to get help. Did you know you may be able to get your student loans forgiven? We cover the rules and how the CARES Act can help.

Car loans

Missing a payment or two may not be a big deal for a credit card, but it can be a disaster for a car loan. Knowing what counts can help you avoid a repossession along with the expenses and damage to your credit that goes along with it. We cover your options to cure a default, scams to avoid, and what happens if your car is repossessed.

Understanding Diversity in Credit

For most Americans, credit is as American as apple pie. But for some, especially minorities, the poor, and immigrants, credit can appear mysterious, unfair, and part of a system designed to ensure an expensive failure on their part. Chapter 19 tackles these issues and more head on. It recognizes the previously discriminatory history of race in credit while offering a solid understanding of why that's no longer the case. It details how credit reporting, credit scoring, and credit legislation have reset the relationship between lending and minorities. It also debunks credit myths with credit facts and offers tips to make you successful, whether you're applying for a loan or need to access help if you get in trouble.

When it's time to take control of your credit, this new chapter is your ticket to success. Just follow the ten steps detailed in Chapter 19, and you'll have great credit and a high score to match.

Filing Bankruptcy

There are times in life when you just can't cope. For some people, this is also true in credit matters. If you're unable to come to terms with the aftermath of being overextended, bankruptcy may enable you to hit the reset button and start over again. But there is no free lunch.

While you pay a price in terms of future credit, bankruptcy for the right reasons and in the right circumstances may be your best bet. This section gives you a quick look at an often misunderstood and misused tool so that you can decide whether the cure for your debts is worth the damage to your credit. Chapter 8 has more information on the updated bankruptcy process, what it means to you, and what your alternatives are.

If you do opt for bankruptcy, you need to pass a means test to see which type you can file for. Chapter 7 bankruptcy gets rid of some of your debts but not others. If you don't qualify for a Chapter 7, Chapter 13 bankruptcy requires you to pay what you can afford to your creditors over a five-year period. In a nutshell, if you earn too much money, you have to pay your bills in a Chapter 13.

Even worse, from our point of view, is that filing for bankruptcy may not solve your problem. If you're in debt trouble because you spend more than you make — or, to put it another way, because your expenses exceed your income — then bankruptcy won't change the situation. Before long, you may be back in debt, but without the option of refiling. After filing for bankruptcy, you face a waiting period before you can file again. This period can range from two to eight years, depending on the type of bankruptcy you file and the type you want to file next.

REMEMBER

In today's tight credit market, expect a long recovery time from a bankruptcy. Recent FICO research indicates that a Chapter 7 filing can lower a good credit score by up to 240 points and that it takes seven to ten years for the score to recover to its original level. Ouch! That's a long stay in the bad credit hotel. Be sure it's worth it!

Protecting Your Credit and Your Identity

Your credit history is increasingly used for more than just determining the interest rate on your credit card. It affects your ability to compete for a job or a promotion; get affordable insurance; qualify for professional licenses, military service, and security clearances; and even find a decent place to live. At the same time, data breaches have exposed the personal information of millions of people to identity thieves. These thieves can use stolen identities to establish credit in your name without your knowledge and then overuse and default on that credit.

Getting familiar with credit laws

Over the last several years, Congress has passed new laws to give consumers more protections. Knowing about and taking advantage of these safeguards can help you keep your credit safe. If your identity is stolen, knowing your rights is essential to a quick resolution. Among the laws we discuss in Chapter 20 are the

>> **Dodd–Frank Wall Street Reform and Consumer Protection Act,** which created a single consumer watchdog agency and allows consumers free access to their credit scores under certain conditions.

>> **CARD Act,** which restricts lenders from raising rates on existing balances and more.

>> **FACT Act,** which gives you access to free credit reports and identity theft protection and remedies.

>> **Fair Debt Collection Practices Act (FDCPA),** which spells out your rights and the rules that debt collectors must follow.

>> **CARES Act,** which impacts student loan repayment, foreclosure rules, free weekly credit reports, and more.

Receiving free reports and filing disputes

As Chapter 13 explains in more detail, the FACT Act entitles you to a free copy of your credit report annually from each of the three major credit bureaus: Equifax, Experian, and TransUnion. We strongly recommend that you get these reports every chance you can and check them for errors. In addition to the one annual free report, your state may require the bureaus to give you more copies — sometimes many more! In addition, you're entitled to extra free reports, free credit scores, if you've been turned down for credit, didn't get the top rate offered, or had an adverse action (like a reduction in credit limit) on a credit card. All these situations are opportunities to check and clean up your credit reports for free.

Signing up for credit monitoring

Every time we turn around, someone is offering to monitor our credit. Do you need this service, and are you willing to pay for it? Chapter 15 gets into the details of credit monitoring. With a few exceptions, we find that it's an unnecessary expense. With all the opportunities you have for free reports, paying for more may be overkill. As for credit score monitoring, expect your score to change frequently as new data comes into and leaves your credit report. Unless you're planning a big purchase in the near future that requires new credit, like a house, knowing your score every day is like knowing the value of your home when you don't intend to sell it — relatively interesting but ultimately useless information.

If you have a credit card, you may already have good fraud-monitoring in place. Most cards monitor spending patterns to sniff out fraud and identity theft before they cost the cardholder a fortune. One less reason to pay to have your credit monitored.

Setting alarms, alerts, and freezes

If you're still worried about others accessing your credit data, you have the right to limit access to only those you approve. Chapter 15 covers how to limit access, along with the pluses and minuses of doing so. Among your options, you can

>> Set up alerts with your creditors to spot new activity on your account.

>> Place an alert on your credit file so that lenders use more caution before approving any changes.

>> Place an active-duty alert on your files if you're a member of the military.

>> Freeze access to your account so that no new creditors can access your information without your express permission (except if you owe the government money).

Identifying identity theft

Still the number one reported crime at the Federal Trade Commission, identity theft isn't going away. The number of cases reported is small in relation to the huge amount of identity information that hackers collect every time you hear of a database compromise. Your identity may be in jeopardy for years to come as thieves warehouse your data for a future time.

Simple vigilance can help you stop identity theft in its early stages before serious damage is done. Follow these tips from Chapter 21:

>> Protect your information at home. Most identity theft is low-tech and committed by people whom you invite into your home.

>> Shred financial documents that contain account and Social Security numbers.

>> Use electronic bill paying to avoid bill theft from your mailbox.

>> Check your credit report at least once a year to look for unfamiliar credit lines. If you see accounts you don't recognize, take the actions we suggest in Chapter 21.

If the unthinkable happens and you become an identity theft victim, you need to take fast, effective steps as soon as you find out you've been victimized. Chapter 9 walks you through what you need to do and whom you need to contact. It also helps you reestablish your credit afterward.

Maintaining Good Credit Throughout Life

Your credit report presents a financial snapshot of your life . . . so far. As your life changes, your credit report changes, too. If your life is filled with positives like a steady job, a good income, controlled expenses, and maybe even a partner, then your credit report should reflect that stability. If, however, you have a reversal of fortune with a job loss, income interruption, illness, or divorce, expect your credit to reflect the stress of your life.

Establishing credit for the first time

Getting credit doesn't need to be scary. You have easy ways to establish credit for the first time — or the second time around as a newly single person. Knowing what to do and what to avoid makes this process simple and foolproof. Chapter 10 covers the essentials of getting your credit up and running. Using simple techniques like borrowing your own money and using retail store cards and authorized user accounts, you can establish good credit in no time. Your credit score can be figured on a history of just a month or two, and then you're on your way. If you're concerned that credit is unfair to minorities, Chapter 19 gives you the facts and tips you're looking for to be sure you'll be financially successful applying for and using credit.

TIP

Here are a few ways to build credit for the first time:

>> Open a savings account at a bank that reports to all three credit bureaus. Then take out a loan using the account as security and make monthly payments on time.

>> Have a relative add you as an authorized user on his or her credit card. Your relative's history will flow onto your credit report.

>> Apply for a secured credit card with a bank that reports monthly to all three bureaus.

Making credit changes at life's stages

As you move through life, you find new needs for credit and encounter new challenges in keeping your credit strong when life gets bumpy. Chapters 11 and 12 help you negotiate life's often turbulent credit waters without capsizing your boat. Credit plays a strong role in every aspect of life, including getting a job, buying a home or renting an apartment, purchasing a car, insuring your home and car, getting married or divorced, paying medical bills, planning for retirement and end-of-life expenses, and more!

Many people know that because a prospective employer may check your credit in the hiring process, having good credit while job hunting is important. But how can you keep your credit in good shape when you've been laid off and don't have enough income to handle all your bills? Chapter 12 tells you how. It also gives you practical tips for safeguarding your credit before, during, and after a divorce.

Avoiding pitfalls

Whether you're new to credit or you're a credit veteran, you need to be careful of counterproductive actions. Some examples of things we advise you to avoid if at all possible are payday lenders, refund-anticipation loans, check cashers, and credit repair companies.

WARNING

You won't go blind from using a *payday lender* once for an emergency, but the very concept of this type of high-interest loan is flawed. If you have no savings, you're living paycheck to paycheck, and an emergency expense comes up, does getting a payday loan make sense? You have to pay back a short-term (two weeks or so) loan on your next payday. But all that money is already committed, so how can you pay it back? Chances are you'll need more than one loan and end up owing lots of money in interest charges.

Refund-anticipation loans are another potentially counterproductive borrowing product. These loans accelerate an e-filed tax refund by a very short period for a very large fee when calculated as an annual percentage rate (APR). Plus, if your refund is held up or reduced, you owe more money on the loan than you expected.

Check cashers perform a valid but expensive function for people with no bank accounts who need to cash checks. We suggest that you get a bank account so you have a place to begin saving and stop paying for unnecessary check cashing.

Credit repair companies have a horrid reputation. Legislation called the Credit Repair Organizations Act has tried to limit the damage caused by fraudulent actions that some companies advise to rig the credit-reporting system. If you're thinking of credit repair companies, think again.

Debt settlers can put you into an adversarial process in which you can get caught in the middle of a financial and legal tug-of-war with potentially devastating consequences. We cover them in Chapter 4.

Managing Credit in Today's Unforgiving Economy

The concept of credit is easy to understand: You receive something *now* in return for your believable promise to pay for it *later.* Mortgages, student loans, credit cards, auto loans, and other types of credit all fit this definition.

Some people think that credit is a way to increase their income. It's not, although credit can help you *manage* your income. Others see credit as a way to enhance status — we have a platinum card and you don't! These distinctions are just ways to wrap additional products, features, and profits into the same credit instrument.

Credit enables you to conveniently spend money that you've already earned or saved or to spend money today that you'll earn tomorrow. But spending tomorrow's money today gets people in more trouble than they ever dreamed of — trouble that can cost them huge interest payments and fees and shut them out of future opportunities. For those with a combination of poor credit management and bad luck, the trouble can take the form of collections and lawsuits. But not for you! Managing your finances is easy if you know the rules of the game, do some basic and painless planning, and know where you stand.

Planning for success

Behind every successful person or venture is a plan. Whether it's detailed or general, a plan for your money and your credit is one of the basic criteria for success. Why? Because others have a plan for your money, and if you don't have one, their plan will win.

Your financial plan begins with envisioning your future as you'd like it to be. Do you desire a home, an education, vacations, a family? The basis of your plan consists of your personal dreams and vision expressed as goals. Long- and short-term goals form a firm base on which to build a plan, and they give you the incentive to fund your plan with savings and targeted spending. Counting up all your income and making decisions on how much to spend and how much to put toward your goals comes next. Called a *budget* or *spending plan*, this tool becomes your road map to financial success. Chapter 18 provides step-by-step instructions for setting up your goals and plan.

After deciding on your goals and setting up your spending plan, you want to consider how credit can help. Using credit cards for convenience and auto and home loans for big-ticket items helps accomplish your goals. Each has different criteria to access to the best, lowest-priced products. The criteria you bring to the table are found in your credit report and credit score.

Reviewing your credit report

Your credit is increasingly used to predict your future value as a customer, employee, and insurance risk. Why? Because if you have bad credit, you're more likely to file insurance claims and perform less well in your job. Research shows that employees with credit problems are less productive and have more absences than those with good credit. So employers use credit reports during the hiring process to complete their assessments of candidates. In a competitive job market, a bad credit report can make the difference between getting an offer and seeing the employer move on to the next candidate.

Lending decisions used to be based on who you were. A local banker typically would know you personally and could approve or deny your application based on your reputation and his prior experience with you. Today, few borrowers have personal relationships with their lenders. Even if they do, most loans go before a committee that requires more than a personal reference to approve a loan. Using the information in your credit report enables a group of strangers to objectively assess your payback record. Lenders still like to see evidence of character, capacity, and collateral, known as the three Cs of lending. Your credit reports show your *character* (whether you keep your promises) and help measure your *capacity* (how much credit you've handled before). These two factors can impact the amount of *collateral* you need to secure a loan at a given rate.

WARNING

The information in your credit report is essential to your financial life, but what if your file contains mistakes? Your credit report contains personal information, account information, and public legal records about you. After you know what is in your report, you can take simple steps to delete out-of-date or erroneous information and add positive data that polishes your credit image to get you what you want and need.

Knowing your credit score

Your *credit score* is a numerical analysis of the years of credit data contained in your credit report. The organizations that calculate your credit score use a proven algorithm (formula) that can predict the likelihood of you defaulting on your next loan over the next two years. Your score doesn't take into account characteristics like gender, race, nationality, or marital status. The result is a discrimination- and prejudice-free assessment of you as a credit risk (see Chapter 19). Boiling down the decision-making process to a three-digit score also gives you the convenience of a quick approval or denial of your credit application.

Two main scoring models are in use today: FICO and VantageScore. Both scores range from 300 to 850. Several weighted factors make up your score. By understanding these factors, you can avoid surprises when you apply for that mortgage or other loan.

Chapter 13 gives you detailed definitions of each of these scoring factors and tells you how to boost your score with simple credit management techniques, like keeping your card balances below 30 percent of your limit and using your savings account to secure a low-interest-rate loan. The differences in interest payments over a number of years can run from hundreds of dollars on a credit card to tens of thousands for a mortgage.

TIP

All the information used to determine your credit score is contained in one place: your credit report. Well, three places. You have at least three credit reports, from the credit bureaus Equifax, and Experian, and TransUnion. The result is that you probably have at least three different credit scores! How can you be sure that the information in each of your credit reports is accurate and as positive as possible, leading to the highest possible credit scores? Great credit begins by knowing what's in your report and what's not. Part 4 provides more information about monitoring your credit reports and scores.

Considering credit a renewable resource

Some people have a block when it comes to math. That block can carry over into credit, which is based on seemingly endless and confusing numbers. We've helped clients understand credit by relating it to something everyone understands: the environment. Everyone knows that pollution is bad for the environment. Everyone knows that environmental resources can either be overused and diminished or be managed well and renewed. And everyone knows that a balance among all the environment's parts is necessary for the environment to be healthy and sustainable. The same principles apply to credit; we call this credit environment your *credit ecosystem*.

You may find understanding your credit easier if you view it as its own ecosystem. Each credit-scoring component affects the others, and pollution in the form of negative reported behavior hurts your ecosystem. Like the real-world ecosystem, damage from credit pollution takes time to clean up. If the damage is bad enough, it causes severe systemic damage for years before your credit environment can recover.

You manage your credit environment by limiting your use of credit and monitoring your credit's health by being aware of your credit score and the information flowing into your reports. Doing so keeps everything in harmony, and the resulting balance strengthens your credit ecosystem. Overspending and overusing credit deplete your resources faster than you can replace them, much like overfishing or excessive logging. An ever-increasing accumulation of debt from using more credit than you have income to support strains your credit ecosystem, perhaps to the point of collapse.

Defaulting on payments introduces pollution into your credit report. Like an oil spill, this pollution can't be covered up and hidden; you have to clean it up properly and put safeguards in place to prevent it from happening again. Credit pollution, like its environmental counterpart, has effects beyond your credit report. A polluted credit report can hurt your job prospects, place a strain on your finances in the form of larger payments for insurance and loans, and more.

We call credit used wisely, in accordance with your plan to build a positive credit history and score, *green credit.* Chapter 17 gives you more insight into this way of understanding your credit and managing it like a renewable resource. Green credit is part of a balanced spending and income system that's reflected in your spending plan. By using credit judiciously, as you would organic fertilizer, you increase the buying power of your present income in a responsible way and replenish the resources you're using before they run out.

Chapter **2**

Turning Your Credit Around

E verybody makes a wrong turn or gets lost from time to time. Sometimes you misunderstand a road sign, other times you get bad directions, and then there are times when you just don't know how to get where you're going but decide to try anyway and figure it out along the journey. Credit works the same way. The big difference is that a lot of people watch and keep score of how you find your way. If your credit isn't in great shape, you want to get it back on track as quickly as possible.

Like a road trip that takes you where you want to go, building and improving your credit helps you attain your life goals. You're more likely to enjoy your journey if you have specific, self-serving, and enjoyable goals in mind when you begin your trip to get into better credit shape. Give yourself permission to dream. Identifying those goals is your first step. You don't have to lay out your whole future in financial terms, but thinking at least five years ahead is an excellent way to start, and it's easy and fun to boot! Credit, like a car, is a means to an end — a tool and nothing more. Building up your credit for no purpose is dull. Credit with a destination is exciting!

This chapter is dedicated to helping you improve your credit and boost your credit score. Consider it your road map designed to help you prevent those credit negatives (or pesky detours) from adding up. Allow me to serve as your navigator. Time to gas up the car and hit the road!

Understanding How Your Actions Impact Your Credit Score

Every time you use or abuse your credit, it has an effect on your credit score. The impact varies with the type of action. Positive actions, like paying bills on time, raise your score and lower your risk in the eyes of a lender, insurer, or landlord. Negative actions do the opposite and, depending on what the damaging action was, could be a big deal or a minor and temporary inconvenience. What factors impact your credit score? Payment history, credit utilization ratio, age of credit history, your credit mix, and new credit inquiries. For example, items in the "small drop" category in Figure 2-1 are minimal and can be offset quickly with other positive actions or even the passage of time. Think of them as small meteors that harmlessly burn up in the Earth's atmosphere. The major and maximum impact items in Figure 2-1 are more like dinosaur-killer meteors!

IMPACT OF VARIOUS ACTIONS ON CREDIT SCORES

ACTION	LENDER INTERPRETATION	SCORE IMPACT
Pays bill on time	Wisely handling debt	Improvement
Low credit utilization	Sufficient access to credit, unlikely to need additional funds	Improvement
Mature accounts	Experienced credit user	Improvement
Uses diverse range of loan products	Experience with different types of repayment requirements	Improvement
Inquiry about new loan	Why the need for credit — exposure or normal expansion?	Small drop
Opens a new loan	Why the need for credit — exposure or normal expansion?	Small drop
New accounts	Will consumer effectively manage new credit?	Small drop
Maxes out credit card (high utilization)	Tipping point: potential for significant exposure	Drop
Pays late — first time	Tipping point: potential for significant exposure	Drop
Pays multiple loans late	All credit at risk	Larger drop
Misses multiple payments on a loan (3 or more)	All credit at risk	Larger drop
Charge off	Default	Major score drop
Foreclosure	Default	Major score drop
Bankruptcy	Default	Maximum score drop, extended time impact

LOW RISK

FIGURE 2-1: The actions and impacts chart shows the relative impact of positive and negative actions on your credit score.

Courtesy of VantageScore

Figure 2-2 helps illustrate the recovery time for five different impacts to your credit score.

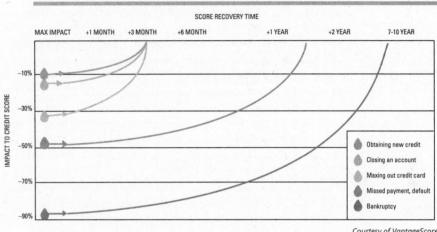

RECOVERING FROM AN ACTION THAT CAUSED YOUR SCORE TO DROP

FIGURE 2-2:
Score recovery
chart.

Courtesy of VantageScore

Using a Cosigner to Raise Your Score

Getting a loan by having someone cosign for you is a triple-edged sword. *Cosigning* means that another party (usually a person with better credit) signs alongside you to guarantee future payments if you default, drop dead, or are abducted by aliens. As long as your lender reports to the bureaus, each time you make a payment on time and for the right amount, you and your cosigner both accumulate more positive items. Also, see Chapter 10 for information on authorized users. As time goes by, this helps offset earlier negative items on your report. Like falling snow, the good stuff covers all the muck underneath.

WARNING

Although a cosigned loan can help get positive info onto your credit report, I call it a triple-edged sword because

>> **You may be borrowing when you shouldn't.** If a professional lender is reluctant to give you a loan, the lender has a good reason. So now the cosigner, who's not a professional and who likely has emotional ties clouding her judgment, decides that guaranteeing your loan is okay.

>> **The cosigner is at risk if you default.** The cosigner is fully responsible for the payment. If it takes 60 days for the cosigner to be informed that you haven't paid on time, his or her credit gets dinged, as does yours.

>> **A default could destroy a relationship.** If your ability to pay off the loan is compromised and you incur late fees or penalties or default on the loan, your cosigner is fully liable, and her credit score may be damaged. This scenario just may mean the end of your relationship, but it does not end the loan obligation.

TIP

My advice: If you ask a friend or relative to cosign a loan, make sure that the loan is for as short a period as possible. The longer the loan is outstanding, the greater the chance a problem will arise or the relationship will become strained. Also, put your agreement in writing to make it official and to ensure that you both under-stand what you're agreeing to.

Turning Small Purchases into Big Credit

Because a lot of your credit score is based on using credit and making payments on time (see Chapter 13), I recommend using small purchases to get back into good standing quickly. Why does making small purchases work so well? Because each item costs less, so more purchases are reported to the credit bureaus faster. My rule is that if it costs more than $10, charge it (and pay it off each month).

Major bank cards certainly report your activity to the credit bureaus. Some store cards may report to only one bureau, or they may not report at all. To find out whether your credit card purchases are being reported and scored, call your card's customer service number and ask.

If your score is less than stellar, don't despair. Practicing good credit habits will raise your score over time. Scoring models look at how much of your limit you use. The more you use above a certain percentage, the higher the risk they believe you to be. To maximize your credit score, spread purchases over more than one card to keep your balance on each card as small a percentage of your maximum limit as possible There is no magic number, but staying under 20 percent to 30 percent of your maximum limit or less is a good goal. Say you have two cards, one with a $10,000 limit and one with a $20,000 limit. Simply charge twice as much on the higher-limit card to maximize your score. When your balance exceeds 20 percent of your limit, you begin to lose points. So, even if you're making lots of small purchases, do your best to either pay off the balance each month or keep it under 20 percent utilization. This is one of the fastest ways to see improvement to your credit score.

Pick up some extra points on your credit score by following a simple plan:

» **Always pay on time.** Your payment history makes up the largest chunk of your credit score.

» **Reduce your debt load.** Only use credit to the extent that you can pay it off every month or keep your total balance below 20 percent of your credit limit.

» **Check your credit report for errors.** You can get free credit reports from the credit bureaus or by requesting it from www.annualcreditreport.com or 877-322-8228. Send a dispute letter to the relevant credit bureau if you find mistakes.

» **Keep your old accounts.** Long credit history indicates stability.

» **Be patient.** It may feel like credit mistakes will haunt you forever, but your payment history from the past two years is more important than your payment history prior to that.

Are you less concerned about your score than about paying down your balances? Some experts suggest that you pay down balances based on the interest rate (that is, pay them in descending order starting with the highest interest rate) to save money on overall payments. Others say that paying off smaller accounts first gives you a feeling of accomplishment, and therefore, you're more likely to achieve your overall goal. My suggestion is that you choose the approach you find more satisfying. Just be sure that *you* make the choice; don't let the first bill that shows up get the extra payment by chance.

CREDITORS THAT DON'T REPORT TO THE CREDIT-REPORTING AGENCIES

Why doesn't every creditor report your history to all three credit bureaus? Because every time your creditors send data on you to a bureau, they have to pay a fee. Some lenders don't think that this step is worth the expense. Others don't see themselves as lenders. They may order a credit report before approving your loan or credit card application, but they want to save as much profit as they can. Typically, these nonreporters include

- **Credit unions:** They look to save money where they can, so some may report to only one bureau and not all three.

- **Utilities:** They don't see themselves as lenders, so they don't use credit reports to hook you up. They also usually don't report unless you pay very late.

- **Tradespeople:** They aren't lenders, but craftsmen and women.

- **Doctors and hospitals:** They don't see themselves as lenders, so they usually don't pay to report unless they send a bill to an outside collector (collectors report you to the bureaus).

- **Local finance companies:** They may not report to a bureau, but they may come visit you if you're late.

- **Landlords:** Most landlords don't report to credit bureaus but may report to a rent bureau (see Chapter 14). However, high-volume landlords (those with a lot of properties) are now able to report rental payments directly to the credit bureaus each month. Trans Union, for example, requires a landlord to have at least 100 accounts before reporting tenant data. Some landlords with 500 or fewer units may report to a rent bureau (such as Experian's RentBureau service).

- **Insurance companies:** They don't report to the bureaus but may report to specialized bureaus like the Medical Information Bureau or C.L.U.E. The impacts of paying late, however, could end up increasing your rates.

If you have a creditor that isn't reporting your activity to all or even one or two of the credit bureaus, you'll get zero to limited benefit from using it responsibly. However, even some prepaid card issuers are offering special offers, cash-back rewards, or mileage for travel.

TIP

Make a list of each credit card, its balance, and its credit limit. Then allocate your payments to reduce your percentage of credit used to 45 percent or less of the limit on as many accounts as possible. Doing so creates some great positive data in your credit report. This approach not only enables you to regain control of your accounts but also helps you maximize your credit score, because accounts that exceed 50 percent of the limit count more heavily against you. When all your cards are at 45 percent of your limit or below, you may want to allocate more money to the highest-interest-rate cards.

If you don't have a major bank credit card, you may want to try a secured card. You can get one without a fee if you shop around. A secured card differs from a regular Visa or MasterCard in that you maintain a balance in a savings account equal to your credit limit (some cards may allow you more credit than you have on deposit) to guarantee your payment. Secured-card activity is reported just as any other credit card activity is reported, and it affects your credit score in the same way, so it can be a great option if you're trying to build credit.

TIP

You can find great card comparisons at www.bankrate.com or www.creditcards.com. The latter has two sections to help you find the right card depending on your circumstance. One section (www.creditcards.com/bad-credit.php) is helpful for those with bad or damaged credit. The other section (www.creditcards.com/no-credit-history.php) is for those who have little or no experience with credit or who need to start a U.S. credit history (credit from overseas doesn't follow you).

Generally, in a typical credit market, if you make all your payments on time for a year you should have enough of a positive payment history to get an unsecured credit card.

Maximizing Your Credit Score with Major Expenditures

Big-ticket creditors — those that specialize in expensive products or services — typically report to the credit bureaus. The reason is simple: They have a lot more to lose if they lend based on inaccurate information, so they want to see as complete and accurate a file as possible.

Examples of big-ticket items that may enhance credit activity are home mortgages, cars, boats, student loans, furniture, and appliances. Major credit purchases may give your credit score a boost for two reasons:

>> **A major purchase is more likely to be in the form of a secured installment loan.** *Secured* means that you pledge collateral on the item you purchase as security for the loan. If you default on the loan, the lender repossesses the security you pledged — in other words, you don't get to keep the item you purchased. Adding secured credit to the other types of credit you use, such as revolving credit (cards), helps raise your credit score.

>> **You make the same payment each month.** When it comes to credit scoring, making set monthly payments enables the people who figure your score to discover more about your creditworthiness. Making a set monthly payment is a measure of your stability. This is different from paying on a credit card, where you can vary your payments depending on your cash flow. Adhering to a regular payment schedule also indicates that you can handle a higher limit than you may have on a store, gas, or credit card account.

Leveraging your mortgage

Owning a home and paying your mortgage can help build your credit in a few different ways. Credit grantors look at your credit report and credit score in order to rate your lendability, but they ultimately rely on you to be responsible for making the payments. Here's where the three Cs of credit really show up: Character, collateral, and capacity are what credit scoring and lending are all about.

REMEMBER

A mortgage on your report tells the reader and the scorer that you have all three of the Cs and that at least one lender was so sure about you that it was willing to lend you a huge amount of money. The report indicates a large installment loan with fixed payments for a long period. All these factors favorably affect your credit score. The opposite is also true: Because of the huge amount of money involved and the seriousness of a long-term commitment, a mortgage default counts for a large negative on your credit history. A foreclosure is an even bigger negative.

A mortgage is secured by the house, so if you default, the lender forecloses and takes the house back to pay off the loan. A foreclosure ends up costing the lender an average of tens of thousands of dollars when all is said and done. But don't feel too bad for the lender: *You're* held responsible in one way or another for any loss on the loan.

Home-equity lines of credit and home-equity loans are a popular subset of traditional mortgages. They're good ways to access money at a low interest rate. They also represent new and additional borrowing on your credit report. For example, you can take out a big mortgage and have only one lender report one loan to the bureaus. If you use a home-equity loan or line of credit in addition to your mortgage, you use the same collateral (your home) and borrow the same amount as you would with a bigger mortgage, but you do so with more than one loan. Thus, more than one item gets reported to the credit bureau each month, building more positive information in the same period. (See the "Lines versus loans" sidebar for more.)

LINES VERSUS LOANS

What's the difference between a home-equity loan and a home-equity line of credit? Here's the scoop: A *home-equity loan* is for a specified lump sum or single cash payment — say, $10,000. When you get the home-equity loan, you get the ten big ones to put down on that car (or whatever else you want to buy), and you have an installment payment due every month, usually at a set interest rate for a set amount of time. In the old days, these loans were called *second mortgages,* and they were a sure sign that you were on the path to ruin. Today, they're called *equity products,* and too many of us seem to have more than one. And yes, they're still a sign that you could be on the road to ruin!

With a *home-equity line of credit,* you get a line of credit, maybe for $10,000 or $20,000, depending on how much you want to have available in case you need it. You don't have to take any money out of the line unless you have a use for it. The money just sits there like a wallflower at a dance, waiting for you to ask it to tango. Generally, you have a set period (called a *draw period*) during which you can access the credit and a set period before which you have to pay it back. So until you use it all, the money is available and just sits there through the remainder of the draw period for free (or sometimes for a small annual fee).

When you do draw money from the line, you generally have the option of paying it off anytime without a prepayment penalty. The loan terms often allow you to pay only the interest and not the principal (an interest-only loan); the principal is due at the end of a period set in the loan agreement. Or you can choose to pay both interest and principal until the debt is paid off. Some loans allow you to decide what you're going to pay on a month-by-month basis, such as paying the principal and interest one month but only the interest the next. Lines of credit are subject to review, and unused portions may be reduced or eliminated if conditions warrant.

WARNING

This scenario has a hitch, however: As you stack more debt on your home or your home decreases in value, you may reach the point where you and your castle are *upside-down* — that is, you owe more on your home than it's worth. I've seen some homes so far upside-down that their owners think they'll never get their money back and question whether continuing to pay good money into a bad investment makes sense. You may think that because you have a 30-year mortgage, you can just wait until prices rise to clear up your debt-to-value problem. But what if your boss offers you the general manager's job in a city too far away to commute to? Or what if the company lays you off and you either have to move to find work or downsize to reduce your mortgage commitment? Or what if your adjustable rate mortgage resets and you can't afford the payment anymore? You'd then be in the position of needing to sell the house, but not at a price that would satisfy the loans attached to your home. If you don't have the money to make up the difference, you could face a potential foreclosure or lost opportunity. (See Chapter 7 for more information about how to avoid a foreclosure.)

Financing your car

Because of the very large price tags on most cars, most of us require some financing in order to purchase one. Such financing typically comes in the form of a two- to five+-year installment loan. Anyone lending you money to buy a car receives and reports credit bureau data. When lenders go on the hook for that much money, they want to be sure that you'll make your payments, even if you get in a cash squeeze. Most car loans are secured by the car.

WARNING

If you're debating using equity in your home to purchase a car, be careful. Using a home-equity loan to buy a car may offer a tax advantage or a low interest rate, but it may increase the risk of a home default and subsequent foreclosure if you can't make the extra payment. If you default on that home-equity loan, your car won't be repossessed; instead, and much worse, your home may be foreclosed on. Plus, any mortgage debt forgiven in a short sale or foreclosure may be subject to income taxes. Although the Mortgage Forgiveness Debt Relief Act eliminates taxes due on forgiven mortgage debts, it excludes non–house-related debt (see Chapter 6).

TIP

Be sure to pay off the loan you used to buy your old car before you buy your next new one! Some people keep old car loans on their home-equity lines long after the cars are gone and keep adding new balances without paying off the old ones. Doing so can lead to an unpleasant surprise when interest rates go up or you need to sell your home.

Weighing the pluses and minuses of leases

Leasing is a popular way to get a car. Please note, I didn't say *buy* a car, because you don't own the car in a lease arrangement. Consider a lease a long-term rental. Leases are popular because they generally require only a small down payment or perhaps none at all. Plus, they're a tax write-off if you're a businessperson. Signing the lease commits you to a stream of payments for an extended period, so this activity is normally reported to the credit bureaus.

WARNING

Leases are difficult and costly to terminate. Unlike with a car loan, you can't sell the car and pay off the loan. With a lease, you owe all the payments, and you can't terminate the lease without making all the payments first.

TIP

An active-duty serviceperson who is called away for military service can break a car lease. Chapter 5 covers this provision in more detail. To read the Servicemembers Civil Relief Act (SCRA) in its entirety, check out www.congress.gov/108/plaws/publ189/PLAW-108publ189.pdf.

Steering clear of upside-down loans

The term sounds as uncomfortable as it is. Basically, in an *upside-down loan*, you owe more than the value of the item securing the loan. Avoid being upside-down in a car loan, or any secured loan (upside-down home mortgages work similarly), if you can help it. A repossession or default is a negative on your credit report and causes your score to fall — hard!

An upside-down loan can hurt you when you want or need to sell the car and stop making payments. Say you owe $10,000 on a car loan, and the value of the car is $7,000. You have to come up with the $3,000 difference or you can't sell the car. If you're in an accident and the car is totaled, the insurance company pays only what the car is worth; you have to pay the upside-down part.

This situation gets worse if your financial situation changes, you can't make the payments on the car, and the creditor repossesses the car. The car is worth $7,000, but that's the retail value. The lender is likely to sell the car at auction, where the creditor gets only $5,000. Among the towing guy, the attorney, and the sales commission to the auctioneer, the fees on the repossession are $2,000. So you are credited with $3,000 against the $10,000 you owe. Now you owe $7,000 in a lump sum to settle your account, you have no car, and you have bad credit.

Paying back student loans

Because of the increasingly unaffordable price tag on higher education, many people have student loans. Student loans make a lot of sense to lenders: Although the person responsible for repayment may have no income at the time of the loan, the lender expects that good income is just around the corner, and the person will soon pay the loan back. But what really makes these loans attractive to lenders is that they can't lose. Almost no student loans are dischargeable in bankruptcy, except in extreme situations, meaning that you have to pay them back sooner or later. Check out www.smartasset.com for a student loan calculator.

TIP

If you have a student loan, chances are that it appears on your credit report. It may be reported more than once. Why? A loan is usually for a semester's or a year's worth of school expenses. Each loan is reported as a separate loan for each enroll-ment period. So four years' worth of student loans may add either four or eight loans to your credit report. Credit reporting agencies may consolidate all the loans into one trade line, but only if they recognize them as part of a single transaction. Making payments and/or filing for benefits on time reflects a positive history on your credit report and adds to your credit score. This can be a lot of good news for your credit report!

WARNING

Conversely, if you end up in default on your student loans, you'll see a lot of negative marks on your credit report from all those individual loan entries, and your credit score will fall. Any missed payments are reported to the bureaus, and you're subject to the full range of collection activity, just like you would be with any other loan.

TIP

If you consolidate your loans after graduation, they'll show up on your report as one loan. *Consolidating* is the process of refinancing all your individual loans into a single loan. The original loans are marked paid in full, and the interest rate for the consolidated loan is often lower and the repayment term typically longer than for the individual loans. The net result is the convenience of a single, lower monthly payment. With a consolidated loan, you typically have a number of different repayment options, including paying the same amount each month, paying less now and more later, and basing your payments on your income.

WARNING

Student loans aren't secured with collateral in the normal sense of the word. When you default on a student loan, you can't defer payment of the loan. In fact, you may have to pay it all at once unless you can come up with an acceptable repayment scheme. Additionally, you're not eligible for further student aid, your school may withhold your transcripts, state and federal income tax refunds may be used to offset the loan amounts, and your wages (when you get that job) may be garnished. Finally, if you don't pay long enough, your Social Security benefits may be garnished.

Understanding How Good Debt Builds Good Credit

No doubt about it: Getting into debt *can* get you into trouble. And if you're reading this book, chances are you've had some experience with debt trouble or you're being proactive and hoping to avert potential credit problems. Although debt certainly has a downside, borrowing money can also do a great deal of good for your credit record. In the following sections, I tell you how.

Achieving goals with the help of credit

Debt enables you to take advantage of those opportunities and experiences that enhance your life and create joy and fulfillment: that dream home with the white picket fence, the around-the-world cruise, the Ivy League education, and more.

When you can train your sights on your life goals and develop a spending plan that allows you to get there in the time frame you set, you've found the secret to the true value of credit.

Sending a message to potential lenders

If you had no debt — ever — then you'd never have used credit, and you wouldn't likely have a credit report or credit score. But let's face it: In today's world, living without credit is hard. Most people need credit to buy those big-ticket items — vehicles, homes, higher education — and they rely on credit for life's emergencies. Creating a positive credit history — a credit reputation, of sorts — says to prospective lenders that you're a good credit risk. Showing that you can handle debt puts you in a position to receive the best rates and terms.

REMEMBER

Using credit wisely not only is good for your lifestyle but also gives prospective creditors the opportunity to show you the respect you deserve based on your past performance. Lenders prefer to loan money to individuals who've borrowed before, who can show that they understand the commitment of credit, and who have a history of prompt payment and reliable follow-through. In fact, given the choice between lending to someone who's *never* borrowed before and someone with a history of debt — even with a couple of blips on the report — my guess is that most creditors would favor the credit veteran over the rookie.

Think of it this way: Say your two 20-year-old nephews ask to borrow your car. One has never driven before, and the other has a four-year driving history, but got a parking ticket last year. Who would you give the keys to?

Giving nonlenders a sense of how you handle responsibility

If you've had no debt and therefore have no credit history, you may find yourself disadvantaged in other ways. Many prospective employers check your credit record as part of the hiring process. If you have no record, they can't confirm their good opinion of you. Plus, they can't use your credit history as a positive factor when deciding whether to hire you. Without that credit record, they lack an additional tool when comparing your application to those of other applicants.

The same holds true when it comes to renting an apartment, applying for insurance, and so on. If you have no track record, you're an untested risk.

Selecting the Best Tools for Building Your Credit

I've learned over time that using the right tools makes any job go faster and gives me better results. The tools for mending your credit are readily available, and I show you how to find and use them in this section. I begin with essential preparation by walking you through a spending plan, and then I discuss how to tweak your credit report. Finally, I tell you how to determine when the job is done by using your credit score.

Spending your way to better credit with a spending plan

Unless you have a trust fund or you make a huge amount of money and just can't seem to spend it all, you need a spending plan. A spending plan, which helps you take care of today's responsibilities and tomorrow's goals, has four components:

>> **Household income:** This includes all the money coming in from salaries, tips, overtime pay, bonuses, royalties, and so on. Be sure to consider your payroll deductions (such as money you put into a retirement plan) as income.

>> **Living expenses:** Your present outlay — from groceries and lunch money to rent or mortgage — makes up your expenses. Also consider those nonessential frivolities that crop up, like your daily dose of designer coffee or the occasional trip to the movies.

>> **Savings for financial goals:** In this category, you account for vacations, college education, retirement, and other important goals.

>> **Emergency fund:** Without an emergency fund to cover unexpected (and usually unpleasant) life events, such as a medical expense or a job loss, you won't succeed. Saving for that unexpected emergency is critical. You need between 6 and 12 months of living expenses; otherwise, when the emergency comes along, you have to get the money from one of two sources: the future (as in spending tomorrow's money today) or your savings for your goals (as in the money you were setting aside for that Ferrari).

Adding up your income

Here's how a spending plan works: You start by identifying all your household income — that's your regular salary or wage, plus overtime pay, bonuses, and predictable windfalls like an IRS refund if you're pretty sure you'll get one. If you're self-employed, I'm talking about your net income from your business or practice here.

REMEMBER

Saving in your company retirement account makes sense, especially if your employer matches your contributions. Plus, saving for retirement probably ties into one of your goals (unless you plan to die at your desk).

Adding up all your expenses

After you have the income part down on paper or in your computer, do the same with your expenses. Make sure to include savings as an expense for each of the financial goals you list. The best way to manage this goal-based savings is to estimate how far in the future the goal is, what the goal costs, and what you have to put aside each month to cover the expense in time.

For example, say you want to take a cruise on your wedding anniversary three years from now. The cost is $3,600 for the two of you. That's 36 months at $100 a month. If you can't afford the $100 a month, postpone the cruise for a year and save $75 a month instead, or take a cheaper cruise and still go in three years. The next time you find yourself standing before the flat-screen TV at the mall, your picture of the future will be in clear focus: the cruise or the TV, but not both.

Paying your existing debts

Don't forget to set aside money to pay your existing debts, such as credit card balances and car loans. You may need to tweak your plan now and then to reconcile the numbers and the time frames for your goals. But you're now more firmly in control of your financial future. From here on, *you* make the decisions about what money goes to which categories — not the marketing guys.

Chapter 18 goes into more detail on budgeting for your future.

Tracking your progress: Paying attention to your credit report and score

Knowing where you and your credit stand is important so that you can gauge your progress and make adjustments if necessary. You don't need to check your credit every day, but you should take advantage of all the opportunities you have for free peeks that come your way. You get a free copy of your credit report annually, another free copy if you apply for credit and don't get the top rate, another when a credit report is used to set your insurance cost, and yet another if you're out of work.

The Fair and Accurate Credit Transactions Act (also known as the FACT Act or FACTA) requires all three major credit-reporting bureaus to provide you with a free copy of your credit report once a year. Some states require that you be given two reports annually. Stagger getting a copy of your report from *each* of the three bureaus, because they often contain different information. (See Chapter 14 for information on how to get your reports.)

When you get your credit reports, read them over and make sure that the information is accurate, complete, and up-to-date. Chapter 14 explains how to scrutinize your credit reports and fix any errors you find.

Generally, negative items stay on your credit report for seven years. The main exceptions are:

>> Overdue tax debts, which stay until they are resolved

>> Child support defaults, which stay posted until they're cleared up

>> Bankruptcy, which remains on your report for up to ten years

Positive account information stays on your credit report for much longer. Some positive trade lines continue to be reported for 10, 20, or even 30 years.

» Verifying the accuracy of your credit reports

» Knowing how credit-related laws can help you

» Disputing and correcting errors on your credit reports

» Ensuring that your reports contain positive information

Chapter **3**

Cleaning Up Your Credit Reports

We live in an information age. Instead of talking, we text, tweet, and TikTok (the mobile app, not the sound of an old clock). When we hear the word *Amazon*, we don't think of the rain forest in Brazil, but of a vast online shopping site where we can buy just about anything from just about anywhere. Today, you can research a new car, apply for a loan, and have the car delivered to your driveway without ever leaving the comfort of your couch. You and your couch may be in an apartment with a lease you applied for online, or in a house you refinanced through the Internet. All these relationships and transactions depend on the flow of vast amounts of information. And your credit report is a critical part of that information, especially in financial transactions. When it goes right, we all benefit. But with billions of pieces of data floating around, errors can and do happen.

You have a say in how you run your financial life and pay your bills, and that payment information should be reported accurately. Mistakes, misreported information, and identity theft or fraud all can affect your credit reports.

More and more financial decisions are being made from long distances by people who know you only from your credit file. In this environment, where your credit reports can make all the difference in whether you get a job, an apartment, or a loan, you should play an active part in ensuring your credit profile is as accurate as possible.

That's why knowing what's in your credit report and polishing it to its highest luster are vitally important. The tools are yours to use; you just need to know what and where they are. That's what this chapter is all about: helping you look your very best by burnishing your credit reports.

It can sound intimidating, but cleaning up your credit reports is not as difficult as you may think. The following sections give you the knowledge you need to make your reports look their best, as quickly as possible. Can you erase the past? No, but you can take steps to ensure all the information is accurate, that it all belongs to you, and that bad stuff that should be removed is removed, including fraudulent information.

Understanding the True Value of Good Credit

Banks and credit unions regularly review your credit profile and use the information largely to decide whether to approve you for a loan or to determine what interest rate to charge you. But banks and credit unions aren't the only ones with a legal right to check your credit report. Employers, landlords, insurance companies, and others are increasingly using the data in your credit reports to make all kinds of decisions, including whether to

>> Extend credit to you and on what terms

>> Rent you an apartment

>> Grant you insurance coverage or set premium prices

>> Hire you for a new job or give you a promotion at work (although it's important to stress that although your credit report may be used for employment decisions, employers never get credit scores)

>> Award you a professional license in your line of work

>> Qualify you for security clearance for your job or in the military

The people who make such decisions know that they're part of an increasingly litigious society. Discrimination on any basis can cost them massive court awards. Consequently, they use independent data — devoid of discrimination, favoritism, or prejudice — to support and validate their decisions. What does this mean to you? If you have negative items on your credit report, you may pay more for an apartment, an insurance policy, or a loan, or you may not qualify at all. That's why having a solid credit report is so important.

The information in your credit report is a good predictor of future financial and nonfinancial behavior in your life. So if you're borrowing, looking for work or a place to live, seeking career advancement, renewing insurance, or getting licensed, you want to make sure that your credit information is accurate, current, and, yes, about you and not someone else.

WARNING

STEERING CLEAR OF CREDIT REPAIR COMPANIES

When you're desperate for a quick credit fix, claims from organizations saying, "We can fix your credit today," sound too good to be true. That's because they are. Predatory "credit repair" companies know that you're looking for any glimmer of hope. What they *really* do is take advantage of your desperation and lack of knowledge to separate you from your hard-earned money, while your credit report goes unchanged. The Federal Trade Commission (FTC) may have said it best: "Credit repair companies can't remove negative information that's accurate and timely from your credit report. Anything a credit repair company can do legally, you can do for yourself at little or no cost. Only time and a personal debt repayment plan will improve your credit."

Here are several other reasons you should avoid credit repair companies that promise a quick fix for a fee:

- **Credit repair services are expensive.** If you're having trouble paying your bills, money is probably already tight. The last thing you can afford is paying someone to do something you can do yourself for free. Some services charge a monthly fee. Just do a quick online search, and you'll find fees starting at $99 per month. That's almost $1,200 per year! We've personally seen instances where the credit repair firm charges $700 to $1,000 per *account* to dispute the information. If you had that much extra cash lying around, you would be better off using it to pay down existing debts and other monthly bills. That would do more for your credit report and credit scores than paying someone to give you false hope. *Remember:* Websites and advertisements for credit repair firms can look very convincing, even to people who are very knowledgeable. They're still charging for services that you can do for free.

(continued)

(continued)

There's no such thing as an easy or quick fix when it comes to credit. And if you're having credit problems, we'd be willing to bet you don't have any money to spare.

- **Credit repair companies have a terrible track record when it comes to delivering what they promise.** For decades the credit repair industry has had a reputation for taking advantage of desperate consumers. The reputation is so bad, in fact, that in 1996 Congress passed a law trying to reign in their unfair practices. The Credit Repair Organizations Act (CROA) spells out what a credit repair company has to do before it takes a penny from you. Know your rights before you agree to anything with an organization that's promising to "fix" your credit. Here are a few of the things CROA says a credit repair company must do:

  - It has to fulfill all the terms of a written contract before receiving any payment. If the credit repair company demands money up front or doesn't provide a written contract, it's breaking the law.

  - It must allow you three days to withdraw from any agreement. If you change your mind in those three days, the company can't take any money or other action against you.

  - It can't ask you to provide false information, such as a name or Social Security number, to alter your credit history. That's fraud. Which brings us to the next important thing to know about predatory credit repair organizations.

- **Credit repair companies can get you into a lot of trouble.** Most credit repair companies use one of two strategies. The first strategy is to challenge, or *dispute,* everything on your credit report, even though they — and you — know the information is accurate. The scheme is to submit so many disputes for the exact same thing that the credit bureau and creditors won't be able to respond to one of the disputes within the legal time frame. As a result, the items not verified will come off your credit report in 30 days. Sounds good, right? Not really. Congress recognized this practice as deceptive and changed the law that governs credit reporting. Now, if a lender doesn't respond in time, the lender can tell the credit bureau to put the information back on your report. The credit bureau has to send you a notice telling you that the information was returned. If the information is accurate, it will eventually come back. And if you're thinking, "Yeah, but I can get a loan while the information is deleted," consider this: When the information comes back on your report, you could be considered to have committed fraud. Ouch!

  The other strategy is to try to establish a new identity for you using an employer identification number (EIN). The idea is that, with your new identification, you'll begin to develop a good credit report and leave all the bad stuff behind. There are several problems with that approach. First, the credit bureaus can recognize numbers that are not valid Social Security numbers, so an EIN would basically be ignored or the credit bureaus may add it as a variation in your identifying information. Either way, you can't duck your existing credit history. The credit bureaus don't just match to the number, they use all your identifying information. Second, by using false identifying information to try to hide from a bad credit history, both the credit repair company and you may be committing fraud, especially after you apply for new credit. Why? Because you've essentially established a false identity and tried to get credit under false pretenses. Not a good idea.

Remember: If you do what a credit repair company tells you to do and any of it turns out to be against the law, you're responsible — and you can be prosecuted!

Reviewing Your Reports for Problems

Learning what's in your credit report really isn't hard, although the things you read and hear can make it sound nearly impossible. But it does take a little time, some patience, and occasionally persistence. You don't need to pay anyone to monitor your credit or send you hourly updates on what's happening in your credit universe. You can do so on your own, and for free in most cases. You should watch for potential problems that could indicate you're a victim of identity theft, that information on your report has been confused with someone else, or in relatively rare instances, that mistakes have been made that could cause your application to be declined or pay higher interest rates. Despite common claims, errors in credit reports that would significantly change your credit scores are pretty unusual. The FTC found that only about 5 percent of credit reports had errors that would result in a drop in credit scores that would affect lending decisions.

REMEMBER

You probably won't find meaningful errors, but it's still very important to check your reports, just in case you do. Your credit history is used to make an increasingly large number of decisions about your future, financial and otherwise, from lending to insurance to employment. You want to keep a close eye on your credit reports to make sure they're in good shape and ready to work for you when you need them.

TIP

To begin, arm yourself with the information in your credit reports (one from each of the three major credit bureaus), as well as your credit score from FICO, VantageScore, a lender, or a credit bureau. (Chapter 14 shows you how to get these reports and your score.) Along with the credit score, make sure you get a list of the "risk factors" that go with it. The risk factors give you specific information about what's having the most impact on your score from your credit report. The risk factors tell you exactly what to look for in your report to work on.

You almost certainly will not able to get the same exact score your lenders use for a number of reasons. Here are just a few:

>> There are hundreds of different credit scores used by lenders, so the one you get probably won't be exactly the same.

>> Lenders have different scores for different types of lending. For example, when you buy a car, the lender uses a score specifically for auto lending, but if you buy a house, they lender will use a score designed to predict the likelihood you'll pay the mortgage on time.

>> You are getting your credit report and score at a different time than the lender. Scores reflect information in your credit report at the moment it's requested, so the numbers probably won't match.

>> Your lender used a credit report from a different credit bureau to calculate the score. Differences in the credit reports can cause the numbers to be different.

Don't get freaked out about not having exactly the same score as the lender. Even though the numbers don't match, what the number represents in terms of risk will be about the same. More important, the risk factors you get with the credit score tend to be very consistent. Address those factors and all your scores will get better. If you can't find out which score is used, any score will do to establish a benchmark of where your credit report ranks and then to track improvement.

As you study your credit reports, you may be surprised by how many accounts you find. Because your report lists negative information for seven years (with the exception of Chapter 7 bankruptcy, which lasts ten years) and positive information for much longer, you could see accounts, referred to as *trade lines*, that you've forgotten about, and perhaps even some that you didn't realize you still had. Some creditors, like retail stores, don't close accounts, even if you haven't used them in years. Your task is to play credit archeologist and sift through the trade lines — current and old, if not ancient — and identify any errors and inaccuracies you find. (For a rundown on all the different sections of your credit reports, turn to Chapter 14.)

Here's what you should look for in particular:

>> **Verify that your name, address, birthdate, and Social Security number are correct.** Variations on your name are okay (for example, Stephen and Steve). With all the data moving through the financial reporting system, however, a Jr. or Sr. can easily be missed, or confusion over a II or III designation may occur.

REMEMBER

The variations you can find listed in your name, Social Security number and addresses are not "mistakes." The credit bureaus list all the variations reported to them to accurately show what your lenders are reporting. If you find variations, the credit bureaus can help you identify the sources and get them corrected.

» **Look to see whether account activity is being reported correctly.** If you see accounts that are familiar but activity that isn't — such as a late-payment notation when you don't recall having been late — report that error to the credit bureau. An account you don't recognize may be a simple misposting of data from someone else's report, or it may be a sign of something more serious, like identity theft. Contact the bureau and find out.

» **Look out for accounts from banks or stores with which you've never done business.** In the most serious cases, accounts you don't recognize could be a sign of identity theft. Or, it could be the result of someone else's account information being added to your credit report because of a misspelled name, a wrong address, or an incorrect Social Security number. Sometimes a merger or account purchase results in a new trade line showing up on your report. Store credit cards are often reported with the name of the bank that actually owns the account rather than the name of the store. Checking the back of your store card for the bank name can often solve a mystery account. Dispute the account using the instructions on your credit report if you aren't sure about it.

» **Identify and verify any accounts that show negative activity.** *Negative activity* can include anything from a missed or late payment to a charge-off (see Chapter 14 for more on delinquencies) or bankruptcy notation. Make sure that this negative information is really yours and is accurate. Also, some negatives are much more serious than others. For example, a 90-day delinquency is more serious than a 30-day delinquency, even though both are negative. Recent negative items are more serious than older ones.

» **Be sure that an account that moved from one source to another is listed as open only once.** Bank and store mergers can result in multiple entries for the same account. Multiple entries can make it look like you have excessive amounts of credit available. Be sure the older account entries are listed as "closed" or have another status indicator that shows they're no longer the active entry.

TIP

If you make a correction to your file, the change may not be reflected in your credit report right away. The dispute process can take up to 30 days, so it could be a while before the updates appear in your credit report. The good news is that most disputes are completed in 10 to 14 business days, and often in just 2 to 3 days. Be sure to allow time for information to be updated if you're planning to apply for new credit. If you're already in the process of applying for a loan, ask whether your lender offers a rapid rescore product for sale. Developed by the three major credit bureaus, *rapid rescore* is essentially an unscheduled update to the information on your credit report. If a recent action (such as paying down a balance or closing a card) helps your credit score, then it can be expedited to the bureau as soon as it's made. The credit bureau can then update your file so that you can get an updated report and score in days, not weeks.

Using the Law to Get Your Credit Record Clean and Keep It That Way

Nowadays, you have expanded rights regarding access to your credit report, granting you more empowerment than perhaps at any other time in the modern history of credit. The Fair Credit Reporting Act (FCRA) and the Fair and Accurate Credit Transactions (FACT) Act both help you get the facts about yourself straight. This legislation can help you with tools to fight the growing crime of identity theft. Additionally, the Dodd–Frank Wall Street Reform and Consumer Protection Act offer new safeguards to consumers.

TIP

To read the Dodd–Frank Wall Street Reform and Consumer Protection Act, go to www.congress.gov/111/plaws/publ203/PLAW-111publ203.pdf. To read the FACT Act, go to www.congress.gov/108/plaws/publ159/PLAW-108publ159.pdf.

In addition to requiring lenders and credit bureaus to play a greater role in protecting you, these laws promote consumer rights by enabling you to

>> **Receive your credit report for little or nothing.** You're entitled to a free copy of each of your credit reports once a year (see Chapter 14 for information on how to get copies of your free annual reports). You can get additional free reports if you believe that your identity has been stolen or if you've had an application declined or did not receive the best terms as a result of information in your credit file. The credit business refers to this as an *adverse action*. Some actions by lenders and some state laws entitle you to multiple free reports each year as well. Check with your state's attorney general's office to find out the laws in your state.

If you've had adverse action taken, the lender has to tell you what credit bureau provided the report and how to get a free copy. Here are the credit bureau websites for requesting a free report if you've been declined or had other adverse action taken with in the last 60 days:

- **Equifax:** https://aa.econsumer.equifax.com

- **Experian:** www.experian.com/reportaccess

- **TransUnion:** www.transunion.com/credit-reports-disclosures/
  free-credit-report

>> **Limit access to your credit report.** Only people and institutions with a need recognized by the FCRA — usually generated by an application with a creditor, insurer, employer, landlord, or other business — may access your credit report.

>> **Require your consent before anyone is provided with your credit reports or specialty reports that contain medical information.** Your employer, prospective employer, creditors, insurers — anyone — needs your permission or an existing business relationship with you before being able to access your private information.

>> **Have access to all the information in your file.** Ask and you shall receive. You must be given the information in your file, as well as a list of everyone who has recently requested access to it. Creditors are required to give you an early-warning notice and a free credit report or score if they place any negative information on your credit report. Your personal credit report includes "soft inquiries" (see Chapter 14) that lenders don't get. So, you actually get more information in your report than lenders do.

>> **Be informed if your report played a part in a negative decision.** People who use information in your credit file as a basis for denying you credit or a job or making an unfavorable rate decision for insurance must tell you that they used the information in your credit report to make the decision. They must also provide the following:

- The name, date, and numerical credit score used in the adverse decision

- The range of possible scores under the model used

- The key factors that adversely affected the credit score

>> **Dispute and have removed any inaccurate or outdated information.** After you file a dispute saying that your report contains inaccurate information, the credit bureau must remove the information and investigate the items — usually within 30 days — and give you a written report of the investigation and a free copy of your credit report with the revisions made if the investigation results in any changes. If the reported information is later found to be valid, it can be reinserted into your report, in which case you must be given written notice of the reinsertion. The notice must include the name, address, and phone number of the information source. As for outdated info, information that is more than seven years old — ten years for some bankruptcies — should be deleted from your credit report.

The seven-year period for late payments starts from the *original delinquency date* (the date the account was first reported late). For charged-off accounts, the seven years starts from the date the account first became late and was never brought back to current. That can be a bit confusing (see Chapter 14 for more information). If the account isn't automatically removed, you may demand that it be dropped.

>> **Place a statement on your report.** You may include a 100-word statement to explain extenuating circumstances or to note your disagreement with items on your report. Including a statement is especially important if you disagree with the results of a dispute. A dispute statement lets you tell your side of the story. For more about this statement, see the section "Adding a 100-word statement" at the end of this chapter.

>> **Exclude your name from lists for unsolicited credit and insurance offers.** Although creditors and insurers may use credit report information as the basis for sending you unsolicited offers of credit or insurance, they must include a toll-free phone number for you to call if you want your name and address removed from those lists. Such offers can be beneficial if you're shopping for credit. They expand opportunities for you from local banks to a national marketplace. You don't have to accept them — the most powerful word in credit is *no.* But if you're certain you don't want them, you can opt out.

You can have your name removed from prescreened offer lists from all three national credit reporting agencies by visiting www.optoutprescreen.com. If you prefer to call, the opt-out toll-free number is 888-567-8688.

>> **Initiate a fraud alert by calling one of the three major credit bureaus.** If you believe that your identity may have been stolen, you just have to make one phone call or visit one credit bureau website (as opposed to contacting each of the three bureaus individually) to initiate an alert. A *fraud alert* warns creditors that you may be a victim of identity theft and requires the creditor to exercise enhanced levels of protection, such as taking additional steps like calling you at the number you provide in the alert, to verify you are who you claim to be.

>> **Freeze access to your credit report.** Freezing your credit report enables you to lock the door on reviews of your credit report if someone uses your identity to apply for new credit, unless you first "thaw" access. A freeze does not prevent identity theft, but it may prevent someone from using your name to falsely apply for a new account after stealing your identity. There is no fee to add, lift, or replace a freeze on your credit report. Just don't forget to lift the freeze before applying or lose your PIN. If you do, your application will be stopped in its tracks.

>> **Receive damages from violators.** If anyone violates the law, you can sue that person in state or federal court. Seek legal advice about whether suing makes

sense. Some cases have resulted in substantial financial awards, into the millions of dollars, but it's usually much less.

>> **Place an active-duty alert to protect your credit as a member of the military.** A business that sees an active-duty alert on your credit report must verify your identity before issuing credit in your name. The business may try to contact you directly, but if you're deployed, doing so may be impossible. Therefore, the law allows you to use a personal representative to place or remove an alert. Active-duty alerts are free, are effective for one year, and may be renewed. When you add the alert, your name is also removed from the nationwide consumer-reporting companies' marketing lists for pre-screened offers of credit and insurance for two years. So, you won't have to worry as much about someone getting credit in your name and running up debt while you're deployed and serving our country.

Identifying and Disputing Inaccurate Information

You can't legally remove accurate and timely info from your credit report, whether it's good or bad. But the law does allow you to request an investigation of any information in your file that you believe is outdated, inaccurate, or incomplete. You're not charged for this investigation, it won't hurt your credit scores, and you can do it yourself at no cost.

REMEMBER

Inaccurate data serves no purpose for anyone in the credit chain. The credit bureaus and lenders want the information in your reports to be accurate, just as you do. Accurate information helps lenders say yes to your application, which is what they really want to do — it's how they make money!

In the following sections, we show you how to file a dispute with the credit bureaus as well as with a particular creditor.

Understanding the dispute process

The process for disputing and correcting inaccurate information is simple. Your role is to check your credit reports at least once a year and before making a major credit purchase. If you see information that looks unfamiliar or wrong, you file a dispute with the credit bureau in question. See the section "Contacting the bureaus," later in this chapter, for details on how to notify them of your dispute.

After you notify a bureau of a disputed item, the bureau contacts the source that placed the data in your report. That source has 30 days to respond. If the source can't verify the data within the time allowed — because the information never existed, the info can't be found, or the dispute processing person doesn't hit the Send button — the bureau must remove the information from your report. If, on the other hand, the information is verified, it stays on your report. In either case, you're notified in writing of any actions or nonactions that occur as a result of your dispute.

If you disagree with the findings, you can contact the company that placed the erroneous information yourself and try to get it changed. Be sure to ask how the investigation was conducted and who was contacted. You also have the right to add a statement to your report or to a specific trade line saying why you disagree. See the section "Adding a 100-word statement" later in this chapter for details on how to write and submit a clear and concise statement.

TIP

If you place a statement on your report, be sure to keep track of the time it's on the report so that it doesn't outlast the negative data it explains and cause you further problems. Today, the bureaus automatically remove statements when negative information falls off, so it should happen without any action on your part. But it never hurts to check!

Correcting all your credit reports

The credit bureaus don't always have exactly the same information in their credit reports. So, if you look at your Experian credit report, see an inaccuracy, follow the dispute process, and have it corrected, you may not be out of the woods. TransUnion or Equifax may have *different* inaccurate information. Therefore, you need to get all three reports to make sure *all* your information is accurate.

If the same error appears on two or all three reports, you need to dispute it only once. If the source of the information makes a change as a result of your dispute, the source of the information has to tell the other bureaus about the change, too. But we recommend double-checking anyway.

Contacting the bureaus

Correcting all three reports is important, because some lenders and businesses purchase the three-in-one report that includes a credit score and credit history information from each of the three bureaus. Each bureau has slightly different procedures for filing disputes, but all three allow you to dispute inaccurate or out-of-date information by phone, by mail, or online:

>> **Equifax:** Call the phone number provided for disputes on your credit report, and be sure to have your ten-digit credit report confirmation number (on your report) available. You can also dispute by mail at Equifax Information Services LLC, P.O. Box 740256, Atlanta, GA 30374 (no confirmation number is required on written correspondence); or online at www.equifax.com/personal/credit-report-services/credit-dispute.

>> **Experian:** You can dispute by phone by using the toll-free number on your credit report; by mail at Experian, P.O. Box 9701, Allen, TX 75013; or online at www.experian.com/dispute.

>> **TransUnion:** You can dispute information by phone at 800-916-8800; by mail at TransUnion Consumer Solutions, P.O. Box 2000, Chester, PA 19022-2000 (be sure to include the completed request for investigation form found on the website); or online at www.transunion.com/credit-disputes/dispute-your-credit.

TIP

Some people recommend that you write to initiate a dispute so that you can maintain a paper trail. Today, when you dispute online, the bureaus provide confirmation throughout the process. Saving or printing the documents along the way also establishes a paper trail for future reference. Either way, be sure to document your interactions.

Disputing online is faster, easier, and more secure than doing it via the mail. Think about sending a letter with all your identification, credit information, and other documents. How many people handle that letter and may be tempted to open it? When you dispute online at Experian, for example, you choose the items you want to dispute with the click of a mouse. You're walked through the process one step at a time. When you've finished, you submit the disputes and any documents you upload to support them. You can print the report, the dispute "shopping cart," your documents, and confirmation to make sure you have that paper trail. And it's all free.

If you choose to dispute items on your credit report via mail, write a letter stating which item(s) you're disputing. Include any facts that explain your case, and include copies (not originals) of documents that support your position. Enclose a copy of your credit report with the items in question circled or highlighted. Be sure to provide your complete name and address and tell the company what your desired action is (correction or deletion). Send your dispute letter by certified mail, return-receipt requested, so you can document the fact that the letter was mailed and received. Keep copies of your dispute letter and enclosures.

REMEMBER

Make sure your dispute is very clear — for example: "I was never late," "The account is not mine," or "The account is fraudulent."

AVOIDING A FRIVOLOUS DISPUTE

A credit bureau must investigate any disputed items in question — usually within 30 days — unless it considers your dispute frivolous, in which case it's required to notify you within five business days. The bureau must tell you why it considers your dispute frivolous and explain what you must do to convert the dispute to one that will launch the dispute process.

So what is frivolous? If you dispute the same thing exactly the same way multiple times, and the source of the information responds the same way each time, the credit bureaus can eventually declare the dispute frivolous. The credit bureaus and the sources of the information keep thorough records of the disputes that have been made and the results, so disputing the same thing over and over won't cause a different result.

TIP

You can find a sample letter to a credit bureau that disputes information on a credit report at www.dummies.com/go/creditrepairkitfd5e.

Following through with creditors and the bureaus

The credit bureau must forward all relevant data you provide to the company that originally reported the information. When the company receives the request for verification from the credit bureau, it must investigate, review all relevant information, and report the results to the bureau.

> **If the information is found to be accurate,** the source notifies the bureau through which you disputed the information that there should be no change.

> **If the company can't verify the accuracy of the information you're disputing,** the information must be deleted from your file. The source of the information must then notify the other credit bureaus to delete the information, too.

> **If the disputed information is incomplete,** the source of the information will tell the credit bureau to update it. For example, if you were once late in making payments but your file doesn't show that you've since caught up, the source of the information will respond to the dispute telling the bureau that the account is now current and to amend your report to show that you're now on time with your payments.

> **If the information is being disputed as fraudulent,** the bureau will dispute it as such with the source, who will then have it deleted. If you have filed a police report or valid identity theft report, the bureaus can proactively "suppress" the fraudulent account and help you work with the source to update their records.

When the investigation is complete, the credit bureau must give you the written results and an explanation of the results or a free copy of your updated credit report if the dispute results in a change of information. (The bureau may refer to your request for an investigation as a *reinvestigation*; they're the same thing.) If an item is changed or removed, the bureau can't put the disputed information back in your report unless the company providing that information subsequently verifies its accuracy and completeness. Then the credit bureau must give you written notice that includes the name, address, and phone number of the company that provided the verification.

You can request that the bureau send notices of corrections to anyone who received your report in the past six months. If you've applied for a job, you can have a corrected copy of your report sent to anyone who received a copy during the past *two years* for employment purposes.

If you aren't satisfied with the results of your dispute, you can dispute the item directly with the creditor (see the section "Contacting the creditor" later in the chapter). In fact, the FACT Act requires creditors to initiate a dispute with the credit bureaus directly if you ask them to. Be sure to provide copies of all the information you have. You also have the right to include a 100-word statement of the dispute in your report and in future reports (see the section "Adding a 100-word statement" later in the chapter). Depending on the bureau's rules, this statement can stay on your report indefinitely, so don't forget about it! When it's no longer relevant, contact the bureau to request that it be removed, if it hasn't been already. Today, such statements are usually deleted automatically, but it never hurts to check.

Knowing the rules on negative information

When negative information in your report is accurate, only the passage of time can assure its removal. Here's how long information remains in your credit report:

>> Open accounts in good standing remain indefinitely.

>> Closed accounts with no negative information remains for ten years. This is good because the positive information remains longer than the negative information, and you won't lose the account history when you close an account.

>> Late payments remain seven years from the date of the delinquency. If you get behind and never catch up, all the late payments and the charged-off account are deleted seven years from the first late payment.

>> Collection accounts are treated like a continuation of the original debt. They're deleted seven years from the first missed payment on the original account. Federal law requires collection agencies to report that date and prohibits them from changing it.

>> Chapter 13 bankruptcy is deleted seven years from the filing date because you repay part of the debt.

>> Chapter 7 bankruptcy remains ten years from the filing date because you don't repay any of the debt.

>> Student loan delinquencies that are brought current (up to date) are reported for seven years from the date of the first delinquency and then reported as current thereafter. If the loan is not brought current for seven years, the entire account is dropped from the credit report, and any subsequent positive information is not reported.

>> *Inquiries* (records that someone requested your report) remain for two years from the date of the inquiry. Don't panic about them, though. If they have any affect at all on your credit scores, it will be very minimal and only for a few months at most.

TIP

If you're unhappy with the results of your dispute or think that you've been treated unfairly, contact the Consumer Financial Protection Bureau (CFPB) at www.consumerfinance.gov/complaint. They have a complaint system that lets you tell them what your issue is. The bureaus work with the CFPB to address those complaints.

WHAT TO DO IF YOU'RE NOT SURE ABOUT YOUR DATA

The law protects the dispute process from abuse, so you don't want to dispute information that you know is accurate or claim that an account listing is the result of identity theft when you know that's not the case. However, you can dispute any information in good faith if you're uncertain of its validity — in other words, if you can't find records that confirm the item, you don't recall the status, or you're simply uncertain that the information has been reported correctly.

Follow the dispute process outlined in this chapter and explain why you believe the item is questionable. Just as you may challenge a word that you aren't familiar with in a game of Scrabble, disputing information that you aren't completely sure about is okay. Disputing information that you know is correct, however, is *not* okay.

Contacting the creditor

Any financial institution that submits negative information about you to a major credit bureau has to tell you so. This heads-up enables you to jump on errors earlier than you could under the old laws.

You have a right to contact the furnisher of the disputed information directly. The contact process varies; it can be as simple as walking into the credit department and explaining the problem, calling the company's toll-free number, or visiting its website (many companies' websites have information on reporting fraud).

After you contact the creditor, it must investigate the dispute and report the results back to you following the same guidelines that the credit bureaus follow (see the preceding section), including responding within the same time frame as the bureaus.

Best of all, the creditor can't continue to report the negative information without noting that the info is in dispute. If the information that's been disputed was reported as the result of a possible identity theft, then it can't be reported at all while the investigation is pending.

WARNING

One bit of caution: Be sure the creditor tells the bureaus to remove the "account is in dispute" notation after your dispute is complete. Sometimes they forget, and the statement can stall things like mortgage loan applications until it's removed.

Again, as with the credit bureaus, the creditor must respond to your request within 30 days. If the creditor doesn't respond, the item in dispute is removed or corrected. If the creditor finds the information to be inaccurate, it must be corrected. If the information is outdated or belongs to someone else, it must be removed. The result must be submitted to each credit bureau with which the creditor has shared the incorrect information. If your dispute isn't found to be valid, you can add a 100-word statement to your report explaining why you dispute the item.

REMEMBER

Be sure to keep good records, including names, dates of contact, and copies of letters and emails. Any company can experience what call *bureaucratic memory loss.* So, if you get a response like, "We can't find this in our records; who were you speaking to?" you'll have the answer handy. Good record keeping on your part can keep delays and irritations to a minimum.

Adding Positive Information to Your Credit Report

Insufficient information on your credit report can also cause trouble. The best way to get positive information inserted into your credit report is to pay your creditors on time and in full every month. Do so for a year or more and you'll make great strides in improving your credit history and your credit score.

TIP

Called a *thin file* in the industry, a file that contains very little information may not be able to be scored. To get around this problem, you may be able to request that a FICO XD score be used. An *XD score* uses information from alternative databases (such as National Consumer Telecom and Utilities Exchange for cellphone landline and cable records along with LexisNexis for public record and property data) to get enough data to form a valid score. Most recently, FICO announced its Ultra-FICO score, which lets you include your checking and savings account history help your traditional credit score. You can learn more at www.fico.com/en/products/ultrafico-score.

The following sections cover ways to add beef up your credit report.

Asking your landlord to report your rent payments

Your landlord can report your positive rent payments to help bolster your credit history. If your landlord doesn't know how to do that, give him information on the following organizations that can work with your landlord to have your rent added to your credit report:

>> **eRentPayment:** www.erentpayment.com

>> **RentTrack:** www.renttrack.com

>> **Zego:** www.gozego.com

Adding your utility and cellphone payments to your report

Utility and cellphone companies don't report positive information, but Experian has introduced a service called Experian Boost, which lets you have your positive cellphone and utility payments added to your Experian credit report. The service is permission based, so if you change your mind, you can ask them to stop. You can learn more about it at www.experian.com/boost.

Experian Boost only reports the utility and cellphone payments on your Experian credit report. They won't show up on the reports from other credit bureaus.

Opening new credit accounts

Another way to get positive information into your data file is to open new credit accounts. Opening types of accounts that aren't already on your credit report is particularly helpful. For example, you may have several credit cards, so you could add an installment account, which can enhance your "type of credit used" profile (see Chapter 14 for more information).

Be careful when using this tactic to improve your credit score. You may do more harm than good if you open an account with a large amount of available credit, which is likely to push your available credit over the limit of what lenders find acceptable. Also, do so well in advance of applying for a loan, because opening a new account may have a short-term negative effect on your score.

Don't get carried away with this strategy. Applying for and opening a lot of new accounts in a short period of time is a sign of risk that can *hurt* your credit score. If you're not sure what to do, get a credit score and read the risk factors that go with it. Those factors will tell you if you need to open a new account or just pay down existing debts.

Adding a 100-word statement

Don't like what others are saying about you? You can add a 100-word statement to explain certain items on your credit report. Although a statement doesn't change your credit score, it may help answer questions that are raised when a lender or employer reviews your report. Yes, the score is important, but so is the analysis by the person looking at your record. Your statement can accomplish several things:

>> **Explain your side of the story for a series of late payments, collections, or charge-offs.** These may be due to a life event such as a job loss, divorce, or illness.

>> **Document your dispute of information that you believe is incorrect but that the source of the information says should not be removed from your credit report.**

>> **Tell your side of a dispute.** For example, you may have ordered a product that wasn't delivered on time or was unsatisfactory and refused to pay for it. Although the situation wasn't resolved in your favor, you may be able to explain it more clearly in your 100-word note.

TIP

You may be able to add more than one statement. Each bureau has its own policy. Experian lets you add several statements: a general statement giving an overview of your credit report woes, as well as individual statements for up to ten items. You may add more, but only after calling Experian. TransUnion lets you file 100 words in dispute and another 100 for a general statement. Equifax allows one 100-word statement.

TIP

You can find a sample 100-word statement at www.dummies.com/go/creditrepairkitfd5e. Just plug in your info!

Do these 100-word statements really help? It depends on who reviews your credit report and what you say. The statement stays on your report for at least as long as the disputed item does, so take time to make your statement clear and concise. You can contact the bureau's customer service department for assistance with your writing if you need it. The online dispute systems also can help craft a strong statement. If you want to write, send your written statement with your credit file number (see the "Contacting the bureaus" information listed earlier in this chapter).

WARNING

If you decide to put a statement on your report, don't forget about it. In a year or two, negative information becomes less of a factor in your score, and eventually it drops off your report. Statements don't affect your score but can highlight past payment problems, especially if the credit report shows no recent delinquencies. Your outdated statement could call attention to situations that no longer apply and thus could hurt more than it helps. To remove an outdated statement from your credit report, reach out to the bureaus (see the "Contacting the bureaus" section earlier in the chapter).

One last bit of advice: Make sure your statement is a "statement of dispute" explaining why you disagree with the results of a dispute and why the information is incorrect. "Statements of excuse" aren't helpful. For example, if your statement says you left for vacation in Tahiti and forgot to mail your check, the lender's response would likely be, "We hope you had a nice vacation, but we still need the payment on time."

Chapter 4

Getting the Best Help for Bad Credit for Free

Where does bad credit come from? The credit fairy? Bad credit karma? No, it comes from overextending your finances and falling behind on your debt payments. Sometimes things happen outside of your control (like a flat tire) that can take you over the edge if you're just making ends meet. Yes, other factors make up a credit score, such as the length of your credit history and whether you've shown that you can handle a variety of types of credit. But nothing whacks your credit score and report like being delinquent on payments or having to file for bankruptcy because your credit is hopelessly overextended.

FICO and VantageScore, the two main producers of credit scores, count late or missed payments as the most damaging factors to your score. And bankruptcy, the logical result of credit or debt gone wild, is the negative on your credit report from which it takes the longest to recover. Once you've fallen behind, lenders are very hesitant to lend money or change loan terms to help you catch up. So the only legitimate way to get rid of bad credit is to get your spending and income in sync and then make all your debt payments on time, as agreed.

Doing so can be easier said than done, so you may need some help. Getting help from someone with lots of experience is a smart thing to do. Getting it for free is even better. Yet many people avoid seeking help for money or credit problems. Why? Because getting the wrong help can just make matters worse. After all, haven't you been taught that when an offer is too good to be true, it usually is?

In this chapter, we help you sort through the conflicting and overblown claims for help that you find in the media. We also include valuable insights to help you decide which problems you can handle on your own, when to turn to others for assistance, and where to get the help you need.

Knowing Whether You Need Help

If you're asking yourself whether you need to get some outside advice or help, you're no doubt feeling some pressure, even if it's only a squeeze. This is a very personal decision with one or two exceptions, which we cover in the following sections.

Gauging your need for outside assistance

To help decide whether outside assistance is right for you, ask yourself — and include your partner if you're not in this alone — a few simple questions:

» **Are you stressed out?** You know you need to get some help when

- You screen your calls to avoid creditors (see Chapter 5).
- You argue with your partner about money or credit.
- Your sleep is interrupted because of financial worries, and you don't look forward to greeting the day in the morning.

» **Are you (or you and your partner) being pulled in multiple directions regarding possible solutions?** You may be unsure about which approach to use:

- Increasing income to support your current bills and future goals (see Chapter 18).
- Decreasing expenses to bring your lifestyle in line with your present income (check out Chapter 16).
- Getting a loan to pay off debt or reduce payments.
- Filing for bankruptcy (see Chapter 8).

» **Are you dealing with multiple creditors or multiple problems?** You probably can use outside help if

- More than two or three collectors or creditors have you on speed dial (check out Chapter 5).

- You have many problems (financial, employment, medical, and/or marital) creating stress in your life at the same time.

» **Are you more than one month late on your mortgage payment?** No matter what else is going on, you need to see a counselor now! A delay or the runaround from your servicer can cost you

- Thousands of dollars.

- Your credit.

- Your home (see Chapter 7 to avoid a foreclosure).

» **Are you thinking that bankruptcy may not be so bad for your credit?** Get professional, nonprofit counseling before you decide; otherwise, you may not know

- Whether bankruptcy will solve your problems or make them worse.

- Whether other alternatives exist that may be less damaging to your credit.

» **Are you new to credit or to the United States and can't seem to break into the financial mainstream, but don't know what to do next?** You'll benefit from help if

- You don't understand how credit works.

- You need to establish credit.

- You want to get started on your own version of the American Dream as soon as possible (see Chapter 10 for more info).

Handling situations on your own

In this section, we outline three credit situations that you can probably resolve without much help.

REMEMBER

To solve any credit/debt problem, you need to

» Identify the cause of the problem and resolve to fix it.

» Know how much money you have to work with.

» Act quickly.

Credit cards

If you can't make this month's credit card payment, or if you've missed a payment already, you need to take action. As long as you know what you can afford and you don't mind explaining your situation over the phone, you can get quick results. Here's what to do: Call the toll-free customer service number and explain who you are, what happened, and how you'd like to handle the situation. If you need a break from making payments, say so. If you can make up the missed payments over the next month or two, make an offer. Just make sure that you can make good on your offer. Be sure to ask the customer service representative not to report your account as late to the bureaus. This decision is up to the credit card company; often, the company is willing to go along with the request as long as you keep your end of the bargain.

If you're polite and proactive and you contact the credit card company before the company contacts you, this approach establishes you as a good customer who needs and deserves special consideration — much better than a customer who is behind in payments, doesn't call, and may be a collection risk.

WARNING

Be careful about asking that a payment be stretched out for more than a month or two. If you need three months to catch up, you may get it — or even qualify for a longer hardship program — but the creditor may close your account, which hurts your credit. Also, don't be surprised if the company asks you to pay more than you think you can. The company doesn't know the details of your situation. Do *not* agree to anything you don't think you can deliver. Saying that something isn't possible and explaining why is much better than caving in but not being able to follow through. Ask to talk to a supervisor — he or she may have more authority to bend the rules.

Mortgages

If you're behind on your mortgage payment, but you're within the grace period allowed in your mortgage loan documents (typically 10 to 15 days from your contractual due date) and you have the money to make up the shortfall, send it in. If you're past the grace period, what you need to do to catch up depends on the state in which you live. Say you haven't yet made your payment of $1,000 from last month. This month you can send in only $500 extra with your $1,000 payment. So you're short $500, right? Wrong. You may be behind the full $2,000 if the bank doesn't accept either payment because you didn't catch up in full. Or the bank may apply the extra $500 to this month's principal payment rather than to last month's deficit. The gist is, if you aren't far behind and you can catch up in one shot, do it. Otherwise, don't delay — see the section "Considering credit counseling" later in this chapter and get help.

WARNING

Mortgage lenders count delinquency occurrences differently than credit card issuers. As soon as you're one day beyond the grace period, mortgage lenders consider you late, back to the original, contractual, non-grace due date. After you're 90 days late from the contractual due date (not the grace period), all the rules change, and you're in serious danger of a foreclosure! (Check out Chapter 7 to find out what a foreclosure can do to your credit and how to avoid it.) Also, be mindful that some banks have shorter grace periods for mortgage holders who don't have bank accounts with them.

Student loans

Getting some breathing room on a student loan isn't difficult if you have a qualifying reason for being unable to pay. Unemployment, a low-paying job, illness, a return to school — any of these reasons may qualify you for a short-term waiver, but only if you give the lender a call before you get into a default situation. Student loan people usually cooperate as long as they think you're playing it straight with them.

REMEMBER

If you don't think that you have enough money to catch up on your payments, you may have an alternative: The money may be hidden in your financial budget clutter. The first step in addressing a financial problem is to maximize your income and minimize your expenses. A spending plan (or budget) helps you with that. Only a real spending plan that accounts for at least 90 percent of your income and expenses will help; rough guesses don't yield the results you need. Turn to Chapter 18 for more on budgeting.

Identifying Help You Can Get for Free

Many sources of financial advice and help, including debt settlement firms, debt reduction companies, debt-erasing lawyers, for-profit credit counselors, credit-monitoring services, and credit repair companies, charge one way or another. And despite the ads that seem to promise better credit and relief from debts, collectors, and even the IRS, only three sources provide truly helpful, truly free assistance for those with credit or debt problems:

>> **HUD-certified mortgage counselors:** Mortgage counselors can obviously help you with mortgage issues. They're experts at helping people decide whether to stay in their homes and then making the decision work in the best way possible. See the next section for help finding a mortgage counselor.

>> **Nonprofit credit counseling agencies:** We're big fans of good credit counselors for a number of reasons: They're free, they take the time to tailor solutions to your situation, they're well trained, and their mission in life is to help, pure and simple. The main things they deal with are goal setting, identifying the sources of problems and solutions, and budgeting (the foundation of everything financial). For tips on locating a good credit counselor, see the section "Finding a great credit counseling agency" later in this chapter.

>> **Pro bono lawyers:** Because credit and collections are governed by laws, and because life isn't always fair, the time may come when you need an attorney. But if you're broke or quickly getting there, paying for an attorney may not be possible. Pro bono lawyers work for little or nothing. See the section "Working with an attorney" later in this chapter for advice on how to find a pro bono lawyer.

WARNING

Celebrity financial gurus may be entertaining and sometimes motivational, but they can't take the time to understand your situation. Plus, you can't get important follow-up advice to fine-tune your options and actions. Magazines offer still more generic help that may give you ideas but rarely solutions.

Getting help with your mortgage

Home mortgage debt is different from all other types of debt and can be very complicated. We strongly urge you to use a professional to make sure that you don't make costly and damaging credit mistakes. Here are a few places to look for professionals:

>> **BALANCE:** Also known as Consumer Credit Counseling Service of San Francisco, BALANCE is a nonprofit credit counseling and financial education agency, serving families nationwide. Since its incorporation in 1969, BALANCE has helped hundreds of thousands of individuals and families overcome their financial challenges and reach their goals. BALANCE is a national HUD-certified housing counseling intermediary agency and accredited by the Council on Accreditation. Its mission is to provide comprehensive financial housing counseling and education programs aimed at helping consumers achieve financial independence through debt reduction, home ownership, and improved money management skills. For assistance, call 888-456-2227 or go to www.balancepro.org.

>> **995Hope:** This organization is an alliance among counselors, mortgage companies, investors, and other players. It helps distressed homeowners work out mortgage problems so that they can stay in their homes. The folks at 995Hope know the ropes, have access to decision makers, and can help you with the necessary paperwork for free. They support the Making Home Affordable Program (www.makinghomeaffordable.gov) by helping you understand your options, prepare your application, and work with your mortgage company. The U.S. Department of the Treasury and the U.S. Department of Housing and Urban Development back this alliance. For help, call 888-995-4673 or go to www.995hope.org.

>> **State housing authorities:** Every state has a housing authority. These organizations offer help to first-time homebuyers and homeowners in crisis,

referrals to counseling, and sometimes funds to cure a delinquency. You can find the housing authority in your state or community at www.ncsha.org/housing-help.

>> **Legal/document review:** One of your last resorts is to have an attorney review your loan documents. Some documents may have been drawn or executed incorrectly and may be challenged in court. A pro bono attorney may be able to help you for free. See the section "Working with an attorney" later in this chapter.

Considering credit counseling

A legitimate, certified credit counselor may offer just the help you need to get a handle on your financial problems. A nonprofit credit counseling agency serves as an objective party to help you see your financial situation without emotion and fear clouding your vision. In addition, a trained and certified counselor may be able to offer you some credit education, personalized budgeting advice, and a custom-tailored plan to get you out of debt — all for nothing or next to nothing.

Recognizing debts credit counseling can help with

Although credit counseling can help in a variety of circumstances, we believe that it's essential in five situations. So if you find yourself dealing with any of the following scenarios, we suggest that you get some outside advice pronto, before matters get further out of hand.

>> **Mortgage default:** The rules are complex, the dates are often inflexible, and the servicers are often paper pushers who waste your time until a foreclosure is imminent. Many credit counselors, but not all, are certified mortgage counselors who can get to the right people faster than you and can lead you through a complex process based on a lot of experience and special access to decision makers.

>> **Multiple bill collectors:** You can handle one or two collectors, but when you get to five, ten, or even more, conflicting demands can be impossible to balance.

>> **Joint credit problems:** Credit problems are exacerbated when you share them with someone who doesn't see things the way you do. An outside, dispassionate point of view can make all the difference.

>> **Debts that are backed by assets:** Loans for cars, houses, and boats are all secured by assets. If you don't or can't pay, the lender can repossess and sell your car, home, or boat. If you don't pay your credit card bill, the lender doesn't have any collateral that it can take, because it has no security beyond

your word and your willingness to pay as agreed. As a general rule, the more security lenders have, the less willing they are to work with you to solve what they see as your problem.

>> **Bankruptcy:** You must get credit counseling before you can file for bankruptcy. Be sure to pick a good agency that does a lot of this stuff. The agency should be fast, efficient, and cost-effective, or you may run into problems and delays later on. (See Chapter 8 for more info.)

In all these situations, you stand to benefit from talking to a professional who can help you with experience, resources, and a clear and unbiased outside view of your situation that you can't get when you're stuck in the middle.

Knowing what a credit counseling agency can offer you

Although no magic wand exists to make all your financial problems disappear, a good, certified credit counselor can offer thoughtful and useful solutions. Expect more than one option for resolving things, including some options you won't like. Your counselor can give you a balanced perspective of what you need to do, how long it will take, and what resources are available to help you along the way. Your counselor will probably discuss bankruptcy as well as other solutions.

GOALS FOR THE FUTURE

A good credit counselor offers solutions with your future goals in focus. A solution that works for you not only deals with current issues but also takes into account how you see your future. For example, if you're planning to buy a house, get a security clearance at work, or send your triplets to college in five years, that future goal affects which courses of action best fit your needs.

IMPROVED COMMUNICATION WITH YOUR FAMILY

For about 70 percent of the more than 2 million people who bare their souls to credit counselors each year, advice and direction are all they need. One unexpected by-product of credit counseling is improved financial and other communication. For many couples and families, the credit counseling session is the first time they openly communicate about goals, spending priorities, and even secrets such as hidden debts.

A PLAN THAT WORKS FOR YOU

Expect to have a customized action plan when you're finished with credit counseling. An action plan has to fit the way you live, or you won't follow it. A comfortable budget designed with your spending and saving style in mind is more likely to be effective.

An often overlooked aspect of using nonprofit credit counseling agencies is that they know a lot about other community resources that may be able to help. Doing due diligence before making referrals to community, legal, and other resources is part of a good agency's service.

REMEMBER

The credit counseling process isn't something you can breeze through in 15 minutes, because the plan you walk away with is tailor-made for you and your financial situation. Many nonprofit credit counseling agencies have the ability to provide a full online or phone credit counseling experience. Be prepared to take the time to go through the details and make sure you follow up with any requests so that you get a comprehensive plan of action.

PERIODIC CHECKUPS

Expect some fine-tuning to adjust to changes down the road. Although your counselor anticipates bumps in the road as much as possible when developing your plan, the counselor can't foresee the future. Murphy's Law applies to financial and credit problems in spades. Not only can things go wrong, but with limited financial resources, every bump in the road feels much worse. Ongoing involvement with your credit counseling agency as you navigate this credit repair journey helps you stay the course. Expect the agency to make it easier for you by giving you the names, email addresses, and phone numbers of people to contact beyond the agency for more help. You should be able to ask your counselor for additional suggestions and referrals as you go along, although most people, when they have a workable plan in hand, are often capable of handling the execution of the plan on their own.

Finding a great credit counseling agency

Here are some things to look for in a quality credit counseling organization:

>> 501(c)(3) tax-exempt status

>> Accreditation by a national independent third-party accrediting organization, especially the Council on Accreditation

>> A willingness to spend at least 45 to 60 minutes with you, and more if needed — and for free

>> A willingness to offer help the way you're most comfortable receiving it — in person, by phone, or via the Internet

Here are a couple of organizations that can help you with your credit counseling needs:

» **The National Foundation for Credit Counseling:** www.nfcc.org; 800-388-2227

» **BALANCE:** www.balancepro.org; 888-777-7526

Deciding on debt management plans

For about 25 percent of those who turn to credit counselors, more than advice is prescribed. In these cases, in addition to an action plan, a debt management plan is recommended. A *debt management plan* (sometimes called a *debt repayment plan*) requires that the agency act as an intermediary, handling both communications and payments on your behalf for a small monthly fee. This plan includes revised payments that

» Are acceptable to all your creditors

» Leave you enough money to handle your living expenses

» Generally get you out of debt in two to five years

THE VALUE OF AN INTERMEDIARY

You may wonder why a credit counseling agency has to serve as an intermediary as part of a debt management plan. Why can't the agency just set up the plan and leave you to follow it on your own, without paying the agency a monthly fee? The answer is twofold:

• **Most people hit a bump or two in the repayment road.** Through its ongoing involvement, your credit counseling agency can explain your situation to the creditor dispassionately and professionally. Many plans would blow up at the first misstep without a trusted intermediary to smooth strained communications.

• **Creditors want the credit counseling agencies involved.** Creditors can easily reach agencies for questions, the agencies' checks don't bounce, and the agencies don't get excited and yell over the phone the way consumers and creditors have been known to do, thereby calming down the whole repayment process. Additionally, they can provide welcome guidance to you during the repayment plan and help coach you to financial wellness.

Debt management plans are an alternative to bankruptcy and often go by other names, such as a *workout plan*, *debt consolidation*, or an *interest-rate-reduction plan*. A debt management plan offers all these benefits and perhaps a lot more. Here's how it works: When creditors realize that you can't meet the original terms of your credit card or other loan agreements, they also realize that they're better off working with you through your credit counselor. Under a debt management plan, your creditors are likely to be open to a number of solutions that are to your advantage, including

>> Stretching out your payments so that the combination of *principal* (the amount you originally borrowed) and interest pays off your balance in 60 months or less

>> Changing your monthly payment to an amount you can afford to pay

>> Reducing your interest rate and/or any fees associated with your loan

>> Refraining from hounding you day and night with collection calls

Why would creditors be willing to do these things for you? Because if they don't, and you really can't make the payments, they'll spend a lot more money on collections than they'd give you in concessions. Plus, if you file for bankruptcy, your creditors may *never* get their money.

REMEMBER

The critical point here is that the creditor has to believe you can't make the payments as agreed. But how does the creditor believe that without staking out your home? The creditor generally takes the word of the nonprofit credit counseling agency you go to for help. Still, being lenders, creditors check your credit report from time to time while you're on a debt management plan to make sure that you haven't opened new lines of credit.

Sounds like a good deal: lower interest rates and smaller payments. Well, a debt management plan isn't a free lunch. The minuses may include

>> A potentially negative impact on your credit report, depending on how your creditors report your credit counseling account (although just being in a debt management plan doesn't affect your credit score)

>> Restricted access to credit during the term of the plan

>> Difficulty changing credit counseling agencies after you begin a debt management plan

STEERING CLEAR OF DEBT SETTLEMENT PLANS

WARNING

Debt settlement isn't the same as credit counseling or a debt management plan. It's sometimes advertised as a way to save money, but it can be one of the most expensive methods of all! In a debt settlement plan, you pay money to a company that holds your money without making any payments until the creditor stops hounding you and supposedly is ready to take less than the face value of the debt.

This course of action *severely* damages your credit for years to come. If that's not enough to scare you off, consider this: Often, if you actually get to a settlement, the amount the creditor forgives actually becomes taxable income to you! You guessed it: The IRS wants you to pay taxes on the forgiven amount, which can add up to thousands of dollars due on April 15 to Uncle Sam. And those agents at the IRS don't go away! Even if you later decide to go the bankruptcy route, the IRS still gets its money.

Debt settlement is an unsavory, confrontational business. Our advice: Don't do it! If you must, use a qualified attorney whom you know to negotiate settlements on your behalf.

REMEMBER

The bottom line is this: If you're in debt crisis or you're concerned that you may be getting close to it, a debt management plan from a good credit counseling agency may be a solution. If you're just shopping for an interest-rate reduction or a consolidation-loan alternative, a debt management plan may *not* be in your best interest.

Working with an attorney

You may be asking yourself if an attorney can possibly be free or low-cost. The answer is yes, if that's what you need. We said *need*, not *want*. If you can't afford an attorney, free or very-low-cost services are available if you know where to find them, and that's what this section is all about.

The phrase *pro bono* comes from the Latin and means "for the public good." Pro bono lawyers exist in most firms; they can be the very same lawyers who charge well-heeled clients hundreds of dollars an hour but will help you for little to nothing. The trick is to find one.

TIP

Here are some suggestions for finding free legal help:

>> **Legal Services Corporation (LSC):** LSC is the largest provider of civil legal aid for those who can't afford it. LSC is a nonprofit corporation that supports

132 legal aid programs through more than 800 offices throughout the United States. It offers a variety of help, including cases involving family law, housing and foreclosure issues, and consumer issues such as protection from lenders, debt management, and bankruptcy. LSC serves consumers who are at or below 125 percent of the poverty level — in 2015, $14,713 for an individual or $30,313 for a family of four. Visit www.lsc.gov or call 202-295-1500.

>> **Local bar association:** Your local bar association can help you find the help you need for what you can afford to pay. The American Bar Association has a consumers' guide to legal help on its website to help you find such resources in your state; see www.americanbar.org/groups/legal_services/flh-home or go directly to www.abafreelegalanswers.org to get your questions answered.

>> **LawHelp:** LawHelp (www.lawhelp.org) helps low- and moderate-income consumers find free legal aid programs in their communities and provides links to other social service agencies.

>> **Pro Bono Lawyers:** This website (www.probonolawyers.org) has referrals covering all 50 states, with contact information for lawyers who may be willing to work for free or for a reduced rate depending on your circumstances.

>> **American Bar Association:** All branches of military personnel, veterans, and their families can find access to ABA resources at www.americanbar.org/groups/legal_services/milvets.

REMEMBER

A qualified attorney can handle anything a mortgage counselor or credit counselor can. The big difference is that most attorneys don't deal with credit situations every day. As a result, they'll probably take longer to get to the same place than someone who deals with hundreds or thousands of these cases every month. So although you can make a versatile tool fit most situations, sometimes you're better off with one designed specifically for the job at hand — especially when it comes to mortgage issues.

» Opening a dialogue with your creditors

» Being proactive with creditors and collectors

» Finding someone who can help you when a collector can't (or won't)

» Controlling your spending and paying your bills

Chapter **5**

Coping with Debt Collection

I f you're reading this chapter, you're probably feeling anxious about your debts. You may be behind on your bills and wondering what to do. You may be getting calls from collectors and wondering how you can possibly meet their demands for payment. If so, you've found the right place to relieve your anxiety, or at least reduce it. Relax, take a calming breath, and read on.

When it comes to coping with bad debt, you have an important ally in the Fair Debt Collection Practices Act (FDCPA). This federal law prohibits abusive practices by debt collectors. That's right, laws exist to protect you from overzealous collectors, who can be stopped and potentially prosecuted if they threaten you, harass you, or lie to you. Knowing that specific rules govern how far a collector may go and that you have rights — legally enforceable rights — should help you feel a little better right away! Knowing your rights under the FDCPA will give you some much-needed confidence when you must communicate with those who attempt to collect from you. We cover your rights and protections in detail in this chapter.

TIP

You can download a copy of the FDCPA at www.ftc.gov/system/files/ documents/plain-language/fair-debt-collection-practices-act.pdf.

We hope that your blood pressure has decreased and you're feeling more comfortable about dealing with your debts. Let's get started!

Handling Those Collection Phone Calls

You couldn't pay some bills, you put off dealing with them, and now you're getting calls from collectors. You may find yourself in the middle of a recurring nightmare of persistent callers who won't go away and who seem to become more determined when you can't give them what they want.

This scenario doesn't have to be the case. The Fair Debt Collection Practices Act (FDCPA) protects debtors from harassment by collectors, particularly harassment via telephone. Armed with your knowledge of the rules and a plan of action, as we describe in this section, you can take control of those calls before they control you.

Knowing what collectors can do

There are a few things a collector absolutely must do when they first contact you. If a collector contacts you about a debt by phone, the collector has five working days to send you a written notification. That notification has to:

- >> State the amount of the debt you owe.

- >> Provide the name of the creditor to whom you owe the debt.

- >> Tell you that this is an attempt to collect a debt and that any information obtained will be used for that purpose.

- >> Inform you that you have 30 days after getting the letter to notify the collector *in writing* (the "in writing" bit is very important) that you dispute that the debt is valid. If you do not respond within that time, they can assume that the debt is valid and they can attempt to collect it.

- >> Include instructions that if you dispute the validity of the debt *in writing* within 30 days, the collector will obtain verification of the debt and mail it to you. If you've been sued, they may send a copy of the court judgment.

- >> Provide you the name and address of the original creditor if you request it within that 30-day period. Your request has to be *in writing*.

The collector clearly has some specific requirements. The one thing you need to do if you don't agree with the debt is write a letter. Under the law, a phone call isn't enough.

Here are the things debt collectors *may* do (meaning, they're allowed to, but they may not do it, depending on how you work with them):

>> **Contact you directly.** However, if you tell the collector not to call you again or to contact your attorney instead, and you give the collector the attorney's contact information, they have to stop. If you give them your attorney's information, the file usually goes straight to a collection attorney. Lawyers like to talk to lawyers.

>> **Contact you by phone between 8 a.m. and 9 p.m., unless you agree to other times.** The collector may contact you outside those hours only if you give your permission to do so.

>> **Call you at work.** However, if you tell the collector that your employer prohibits such contact, the collector must not call you at work.

TIP

Check out www.dummies.com/go/creditrepairkitfd5e for a sample letter you can send to request that the collector not call you at your place of work.

>> **Contact you by mail.** However, the collector can't put information on the outside of the envelope that indicates a collection attempt or send information on a postcard.

>> **Contact others to get information about where you live and work.** The collector can request only contact information. The collector can't say that he or she is calling in regard to an owed debt. The sticky part is that if the collector calls a friend or partner and they ask who the collector is, the collector can state his or her name and the name of his or her employer.

>> **Supersize your statement.** Only charges that you agreed to under the original terms of your loan may be added to your bill. You can find a list of them in the account terms, in the fine print. These charges could include lots of fees, huge interest rate hikes, and the costs of collection. The reality is that the amount being collected probably won't match what you saw on your last statement.

>> **Ask for postdated checks.** Depending on the state in which you live, the collector may be entitled to ask for postdated checks. Look into your state's guidelines. Although your state may permit collectors to ask for postdated checks, providing one is not in your best interest (see the nearby sidebar "Postdated checks: Good for the collector, bad for you"). The law also prohibits collectors from cashing the check before the date on it, if it's postdated.

>> **Tell the credit bureaus that you're behind on your payments.** A delinquency that shows up on your credit report stays there for seven years and lowers your credit score (see Chapter 14).

>> **Hike your interest rate.** However, you may be hit with a penalty rate if the original contract specifies it. You can't pay the current bill, so why would the creditor increase your interest rate to 20 percent or 30 percent? It's because you're a higher risk than the creditor thought, and it could help them recover a bit more of what you owe.

>> **Repossess your purchase.** Repossession is almost always a bad deal for you because the creditor determines the value of the repossessed item and can charge you for costs incurred in reselling it, too. Here's another shocker: You may have to pay income tax on the difference between what they sell the repossessed item for and what you owe. (See Chapter 6 for more details about settled debts.)

>> **Sue you in court.** The collector may ask a judge for a judgment against you in a court of law. Depending on your state's laws, this judgment can be a prelude to garnishing your wages or placing a lien on your home. This kind of civil judgment isn't part of credit reports any more, but it could still pop up to hurt you in other public records and consumer reports reviewed by businesses.

>> **Change the terms of your agreement.** Some collectors may allow you to make up what you owe over time by adding an amount to future payments. Some, to their credit, offer hardship programs, but usually only if you ask. Be sure to get any changes to your agreement *in writing,* particularly if communications are strained. You need documentation to ensure that the agreement is honored.

>> **Accept or offer a debt settlement option for less than the full amount owed.** If a lower amount is agreed on, the collector usually wants the settlement at once and in a single payment. The debt is reported negatively on your credit report as "settled" or "settled, paid for less than originally agreed." Depending on the amount of debt forgiven (usually a $600 threshold), you may get a Form 1099-C from the creditor in the mail at tax time. The IRS considers the forgiven portion of the debt as income and requires you to pay taxes on it. (Check out Chapter 6 for more on settlements.)

TIP

Go to www.dummies.com/go/creditrepairkitfd5e for a sample letter you can send to request a settlement.

Knowing what collectors can't do

Debt collectors are *not* allowed to

>> **Threaten you.** In writing or over the phone, collectors must use businesslike language. Threatening, abusive, or obscene language is not allowed.

>> **Be annoying.** An annoying collector — isn't that redundant? This rule means that collectors aren't allowed to make repetitive or excessively frequent phone calls to annoy or harass you. Yes, any call from a collector is annoying, but the legal definition is a bit more strict.

>> **Be deceptive.** No "trick or treat, smell my feet!" Collectors can't pretend to be anything other than what they are in order to get you on the phone.

>> **Lie about the consequences.** Collectors can't claim that you've committed a crime or that you'll be arrested if you don't send payment. The United States doesn't have debtors' prison.

>> **Make idle threats.** Collectors can't threaten you with illegal actions or actions that they have no intention of carrying out. If they don't intend to take you to court, they can't threaten to do so.

Deciding whether to answer the phone

You may find yourself reluctant to answer the phone for any number of reasons. You may have had a hard day at work, you may be overtired, or you may not be feeling in control of your emotions at the moment. If you've been contacted by the collector and you've already explained that you're doing your best and that's all you can do, having the same conversation again and again may feel frustrating and unproductive, especially if the collector is on the overbearing side. Don't answer the phone if you know that you won't be able to have an effective conversation.

REMEMBER

Keep in mind, however, that although caller ID and voicemail can help you screen calls (and may help save your sanity), they won't help you avoid or solve your debt problems. If collectors can't reach you by phone, they'll try to find another way to contact you. Snail mail still works, and email and texting are also options. You don't have to pick up the phone this time, but you will need to communicate at some point.

Preparing to answer collection calls

When you decide that it's time to bite the bullet and talk to the collector, make sure you're prepared. Write down the key points you want to cover in your conversation with the collector. Having a plan in mind helps you stay on track and in control of the call. It also helps you not to over-promise and under-deliver, to avoid losing your temper, and to know when to hang up if the call gets abusive.

If you start to feel overwhelmed or backed into a corner by the collector, get outside professional help. You can find out about getting help in Chapter 4.

REMEMBER

Even though you may feel nervous, guilty, or angry, you aren't the first or only person to have gone through debt collections. It happens all the time, and you *will* get through it.

If you're late on some bills, expect to get a call from a collector sooner or later — typically when you're 30 to 90 days late or more. If you decide to pick up the phone, here's what you need to do:

>> **Get the caller's name and contact information.** Use the collector's name during your conversation.

>> **Ask for proof of the debt.** Mistakes happen, and crooks call to try to get money from people all the time. (See the section "Asking for proof that the debt is yours," later in this chapter, for more information.)

>> **Explain what happened.** Provide a very short explanation of why you're behind and what, if anything, you're able to do about the debt.

>> **Make a payment offer.** See the section "Negotiating a payback arrangement" later in this chapter.

>> **Don't agree to a payment schedule that you can't keep.** Be realistic, or you may find yourself agreeing to a plan you know you can't follow through on. (See the section "Keeping your promise" later in this chapter.)

>> **Get it in writing.** If you come to an agreement, ask the collector to put it in writing so it's clear to both parties. If the collector won't do so, write the letter yourself (keeping a copy for your records) and send it to the collector by certified mail (return receipt) so you have proof that the collector received it. If the collector provided an email address, make a copy of the letter and send it that way, too. *Remember:* Putting things in writing is important.

Knowing what not to say

WARNING

Saying the wrong thing in a conversation with a collector may be unproductive and can turn the conversation into a hostile confrontation that could end up causing you more harm. No matter how adversarial your caller seems, here are some definite don'ts:

>> Don't let yourself get drawn into a shouting match.

>> Don't make threats. It's illegal for them to threaten you and not helpful for you to threaten them.

- » Don't say that you're getting a lawyer if you don't intend to.

- » Don't say that you're going to file bankruptcy if you don't plan to.

- » Don't lie for sympathy (for example, saying "I got sick and couldn't pay the bill," if you were actually on vacation at the beach). If you're caught stretching the truth, even once, people will have a hard time believing you again. The law prohibits collectors from lying to you. Lying to them will only strengthen their case.

Taking Charge of the Collection Process

The best way to deal with the collection process is to face your debts head on and as quickly as possible. Debts don't improve with age, and they certainly don't go away if you ignore them. In fact, as debts age, they get bigger, uglier, and harder to pay. Unresolved debts also have an uncanny knack for resurfacing when you're least prepared to deal with them.

Accounts that are 30 to 90 days *delinquent* (overdue) are usually handled by people who work for the company from which you bought your product or service, or *inside* collectors. If you're contacted by an outside or third-party collector early in the process, chances are the company hired the collection agency because of its tact and effectiveness rather than its skill at offending people. Outside collectors are covered by the FDCPA and must abide by those rules (see the section "Keeping Collectors in Check" later in the chapter). The creditor and its own internal collection department aren't governed by the FDCPA. The biggest difference between an inside and an outside collector is that an inside collector may want to keep you as a customer in addition to collecting the money due. However, if the company determines that you're unlikely to make your payments, your customer status becomes less and less of a factor in the way the company attempts to work things out with you.

REMEMBER

Calling your creditors before they call you is always better. Contacting them first places you in a much different category than if they're the ones doing the dialing. Good faith is on your side (but even that fades if you don't deliver on your commitments). Plus, when you call first, you can be prepared and ready for business instead of having to respond to an unexpected call.

This section explains what to do to give yourself the greatest chance of success when dealing with collectors.

Asking for proof that the debt is yours

When you get a call or a letter claiming that you have a past-due financial obligation, make sure to verify its accuracy. Even if you're sure that you owe the money, ask for details: which account it pertains to, what the bill was for, how old the debt is, when the statement was mailed to you, and so on. Asking these questions never hurts. Why? Here are two good reasons:

>> **Mistakes happen.** Creditors make mistakes, so asking for a little proof is reasonable. You're not denying that you owe the debt; you're just making sure that you owe this particular debt, making sure the information matches yours, and making sure that the creditor has the right customer and the right account.

>> **Scammers are out there.** These people will call, email, or write and say that you owe money. Maybe you do, but not to them. They may even have proprietary information that persuades you that they must be legitimate. Get the facts in writing through the U.S. mail before you act. Having the information mailed to you opens scammers up to mail fraud charges.

REMEMBER

FDCPA rules say that you have 30 days to respond to a collection attempt, and you're both smart and well within your rights to dispute a debt. Here's how you do it: Send the collector a letter via certified mail with a return receipt. In the letter, ask the collector to provide proof of the debt. Keep copies of everything you send. When you dispute the debt, the collector must stop all activity and provide you with proof of your obligation before reinitiating contact.

Disputing a bill stops collection activity, but it doesn't stop the clock. Your debt continues aging during the process. It's usually in your best interest to try to resolve matters as quickly as possible when you're sure that the debt is yours and the collector is legit.

Knowing when debts fade away: Statutes of limitations

The United States is the land of the present, the here and now. Our culture and our laws enable you to overcome mistakes of the past so you can have a brighter future. This philosophy applies to old debts, too. Every state has a *statute of limitations* (SOL) that limits how long the courts can be used to collect a debt. After a debt is between 2 and 15 years old (depending on your state of residence) without a payment having been made, it disappears as far as the courts are concerned.

To find out exactly what the SOL is for your state, contact your state attorney general's office or check out `https://statelaws.findlaw.com/statutes-of-limitations.html`. Debts that are too old can't be enforced in a court of law. It doesn't stop them from trying, but the statute of limitations severely limits a collector's ability to recover the debt.

REMEMBER

A debt may be too old to collect under the SOL, but if it is less than seven years old, it will stay on your credit report and severely affect your creditworthiness until it drops off.

Here's what to do if you think you may have an old debt that qualifies for SOL treatment:

>> **Verify the last time you made a payment.** Here's another instance where keeping good records works to your advantage. Making a payment can reset the clock on the SOL. Proving that you haven't made a payment can help protect you from unlawful actions by the debt collector. Today's online banking apps can also be your friend. You may have payment records at your fingertips just by logging into your account. If not, call your bank. Depending on your bank, you may be able to access checking-account payments from long ago. You don't want to see any recent payments. Say it has been 6 years and 51 weeks since your last payment, and the SOL for your state is 7 years. If you make a payment, the 7-year period could start all over again. Expect more calls or letters from the collector as the SOL gets closer. They may put on more pressure to get you to send in any amount they can get as the SOL closes in.

>> **Contact your state attorney general's office for your state's age limit for SOL status.** They can tell you exactly what applies where you live to help you decide if it's time for you to see a lawyer if you believe that your debt may qualify.

>> **Get a real legal opinion.** When it comes to the law, we don't trust our friends or cousins, and neither should you. See a lawyer even though it may cost you some cash. This is a legal matter, and they call them *law*yers for a reason. They have their own rules and can help you win that game or tell you it will cost more to play than it's worth. When it comes to courts and the law, it's always in your best interest to get professional guidance. Many lawyers will meet with you the first time for free and can tell you if you have a case.

>> **Have the attorney write a letter.** Lawyers have their own language and can help you get the point across to the collector in legal terms. Just be sure the letter includes documentation of the debt's age, proof that it's over the SOL limit, a statement that you don't intend to pay a penny, and if the attorney is

taking over for you, a note that all future contact must go through the attorney. No collector we know of will bother to try to collect an uncollectible debt from a lawyer who knows better. And collectors can't go around the attorney after you notify them that you have a lawyer, or they can be sued. The last thing the collector wants is to be sued by the person from whom they were previously trying to collect.

Negotiating a payback arrangement

When you and the collector agree that all the particulars of the debt are legitimate, it's time for you to make an offer to resolve the obligation, whether the cause of the delinquency was an unintended error or unfortunate circumstances. You can make an offer to repay the amount over a period of time. Say you owe $1,000. If you offer to pay $50 per pay period for the next 20 weeks, that plan may be acceptable. Or you can offer to pay $25 per pay period until your next raise in three months, at which time you'll pay $75 per pay period. Offering the amount you're able to pay is always better than waiting for the collector to demand a certain amount.

You want to convey your concern and reassure the collector that you're sincere in your commitment to pay. But that doesn't mean you shouldn't try to negotiate some concessions. For example, you may ask the collector to

>> **Keep the matter between the two of you.** If, for example, you're able to pay off your obligation and you're only 30 to 60 days past due, ask the collector not to report your oversight to the credit bureaus. When the collection is still with the creditor's in-house collection division, your chances of it not be reported to the credit bureaus are better. When the debt is so late that it has been sold or transferred to a third-party collector, they'll be less likely to agree not to report it. Taking care of the unpaid debt early is always better if you can.

>> **Lighten the late fees.** It doesn't hurt to ask if they'll waive any late fees. Be sure to tell them that, if they do, you'll be happy to get off the phone so you can run to the post office to mail your check. Most — but not all — will agree if they're getting the balance due without delay.

>> **Reduce your interest rate.** Think it's not the ideal time to try to get a better interest rate? Actually, it is. The collector wants what's called a *promise to pay* from you to resolve your situation. So ask for a break on the interest rate in order to help you pay the debt faster. On a delinquent credit card account, for example, you may be looking at a 30 percent default interest rate. The lender knows that adding this much to a strained budget increases the chance of a longer and more costly default or even a bankruptcy if you feel you have no way out. Lenders are often willing to help if you're sincere.

WARNING

POSTDATED CHECKS: GOOD FOR THE COLLECTOR, BAD FOR YOU

At some point in the collection process, a collector may ask you to send postdated checks. The logic here is that, with the postdated check, you demonstrate a firm intention to honor your payment agreement, and the collector doesn't have to call you to remind you to send in any payments you may have agreed to. This scenario also covers the collector in case you "forget" to send a check at the appointed time.

This practice is akin to putting a piece of bacon on your dog's nose and telling him not to eat it. Giving a collector a postdated check is almost always a bad idea because the collector will likely be tempted to cash the check too early, even though he or she isn't supposed to. If the collector cashes the check early and the money isn't in the account yet, the check will bounce, and the collector will be upset. If the collector cashes the check early and the money is there but the collector gets it sooner than you planned, all your other checks may start to bounce. That can make things even worse for you. You will be responsible for the bounced check. Bouncing a check (called passing an insufficient funds check) has its own set of laws and consequences.

TIP

If you're under extreme financial duress, go a step further and ask if they have a hardship program. You may have to meet some qualifications, but if you do, your interest rate may drop dramatically, perhaps even to zero, and may lower your payments for six months to a year.

If you feel that any repayment plan is unrealistic and may push you over the financial edge, work on a spending plan (see Chapter 18). After you establish your goals, identify your sources of income, and tally up your living expenses, you'll know what you can actually afford for debt service.

TIP

If working out a repayment plan is too intimidating, if you're dealing with multiple collectors, if you just can't seem to communicate on money matters, or if you just want help getting started, a reputable credit counseling agency can help you create a spending plan. See Chapter 4 for help finding an agency.

Keeping your promise

When you've reached payment agreement, it's essential that you keep your end of the bargain. From the collector's perspective, you've already broken your original agreement to make payments. Breaking a second agreement places you squarely in the not-to-be-trusted category.

TIP

To make sure that you and the collector are clear on what you promised, put everything you agree to in writing. Keep copies of the names, addresses, and phone numbers of everyone you talk to and include a written copy of your agreement with the payment. Ask for an email confirming the arrangement. This is a reasonable request. A letter is a little more challenging because the delivery time may cause you to delay acting on your promise while you wait for the mail to be delivered. That can slow things down a week or more. (They don't call it snail mail for nothing.) It's important to the collector that you act quickly, so confirm all agreements in a thorough note with names and times (don't forget to keep your copy) and send it off with your payment — certified mail, return receipt requested, if you want even more documentation.

IF YOU'RE IN THE MILITARY: SPECIAL HELP FOR SPECIAL PEOPLE

In Chapter 10, we discuss the rules of engagement between the financial system and military personnel. Generally speaking, some significant safeguards are built into the Fair and Accurate Credit Transactions Act (also known as the FACT Act or FACTA), the National Defense Authorization Act for Fiscal Year 2007, and a rewrite of the Soldiers' and Sailors' Civil Relief Act (SSCRA), now known as the Servicemembers Civil Relief Act (SCRA). Here's what you need to know about your rights when it comes to debt collection:

- **Delayed court hearings:** If a creditor summons you to court for a hearing, you can request at least a 90-day delay. The judge can grant additional delays as the case warrants.

- **Interest rate reductions:** The interest rates on pre-service loans and obligations can't exceed 6 percent; interest due in excess of 6 percent per year must be forgiven, not just deferred. However, you must ask the lender for the reduction in writing and include a copy of your military orders.

- **Interest rate caps:** Interest rates are capped at 36 percent a year (the military annual percentage rate [MAPR]) for payday loans and refund anticipation loans. This cap includes all fees and charges.

- **Eviction protection:** You can't be evicted from rental property for not paying rent (if the monthly rent is $1,200 or less) without proper court action. The law gives you other special protections if the rent is between $1,200 and $2,400.

- **Lease termination:** You may terminate without penalty a housing lease that you enter into before you start active duty if you're under orders for a permanent change of station or are deployed for at least 90 days. You don't need a military termination clause in your lease.

- **Auto lease cancellations:** You can cancel automobile leases if your orders are for 180 days or more, even if the vehicle is for a family member.

- **Vehicle title loans:** Military personnel can no longer be asked to secure loans with their vehicle titles except as part of receiving an installment loan to purchase a vehicle.

If collectors attempt to contact you to collect debts, let them know your situation and ask for their cooperation in accordance with the SSCRA. If you have a spouse at home, you may have him or her follow up on your behalf; be sure to mention that in your initial letter.

For help, visit the Family Readiness Center on your installation or contact a representative. There are offices on most installations. The centers provide free assistance. Most military units have a financial specialist as well, who may be able to help further. If that fails, contact a lawyer or an accredited credit counseling agency and ask the lawyer or agency to act on your behalf. A lawyer may be expensive but could be worth it. Nonprofit civilian credit counselors are free or low cost, and most try to help you by email or through their websites. (See Chapter 4 to find a credit counselor.)

Identifying Escalation Options That Help

When you're dealing with a debt collector, you may arrive at a sticking point and recognize that the person you're speaking with doesn't have the authority to do what you're asking. Instead of stopping at that frustrating dead end, you're better off tactfully suggesting that you'd like to talk with someone who has greater authority and is empowered to make decisions. This is known as *escalating* the issue. In this section, we show you how to do so, as well as how to contact other people who may be able to help you if the manager can't accommodate you.

Asking to speak to a manager

Collection representatives may have several reasons for not warming to your proposed payment plan. They may

>> Not believe that you're offering your best effort to repay

>> Have a quota to fill, and your offer won't do it

>> Have strict rules regarding permissible payment options

>> Be having a bad day and just don't feel like being helpful

A manager has more flexibility and may have a bigger-picture view that can accommodate your best offer. By asking to speak to a manager, you take the pressure off the little guy and free him to move on to another customer while you and the boss work things out. If you present the situation as though you're helping everyone, you may have an easier time escalating the problem to management.

TIP

You can say something like this:

> I understand that you've done your best to try to resolve this issue satisfactorily. Thank you for helping. But I'd like to speak to someone who has the authority to make exceptions, waive policy, or take my offer to a higher level. It's not fair of me to ask you to go against company policy and take the payment I'm offering, so please let me speak to a manager.

If the collector refuses to let you speak to a manager, say that you'll call back on your own and ask someone else. Thank the collector for trying and say good-bye, nicely. Going over the same ground with the same person quickly wears thin. And being polite can go a long way, especially if the person on the other end of the line isn't.

Approaching the creditor

Stuck with the collection agency and unable to make headway? Taking a step backward may help you move forward. Your original creditor may be willing to cut a deal with you even after sending your bill to an outside collector. Much depends on how you left things with the creditor. If you left with bad feelings or you lost it with a customer service representative, you may not be welcomed back. But if the transition from inside collections to an outside agency was just business for the creditor and not complicated with personal anger or animosity, the creditor may still be willing to talk with you. Just don't wait too long, or you'll find the creditor has moved on.

So, why would you want to approach the creditor directly? If you're not getting anywhere with the debt collector, the creditor may be willing to work something out with you. After all, the creditor just wants the money you owe.

TECHNICAL STUFF

Creditors either place a debt for collection (and pay a commission based on results) or sell the debt outright. The former scenario is more common unless your debt is really old. If your debt has been sold, calling the original creditor won't do any good. The collection agency is then the legal owner of the debt, and you need to work with them. But this bit of bad news has a silver lining. You may well have more room to negotiate in a debt-sale situation because debts aren't sold at full value, so a smaller-than-owed payment may still be very profitable for the collector.

Medical collections are treated a bit differently from other kinds of charged-off accounts. They tend to have less effect on credit scores, and after they're paid, current credit systems ignore them. Although they may still appear in your credit report, if they show paid, they won't hurt your scores, and you could see a big jump. That's something to consider when negotiating.

A number of changes have occurred when it comes to collections for small amounts. Things like parking tickets, library fines, and debts less than $50 or so have been removed from credit reports. If a collector is trying to get you to pay up for a low amount, check your credit history first. You still legally owe the debt, but if it's not in your report, it could help you prioritize its importance in working with collectors.

Fighting harassment

Getting harassed by a collection agency? You're not alone, and you have a couple of options for help from the government. You can file a complaint with the Consumer Financial Protection Bureau (CFPB). The CFPB reported that it received more than 75,000 complaints about debt collections in 2019. It maintains a complaint database and can help you work with the collection agency to resolve your issues. You can also file a complaint with the FTC, which watches over the collection industry and enforces the FDCPA. Some consumers have even taken collectors who violate the law to court, and some of them have won very large settlements. Don't get your hopes up, though. The reality is that winning a big lawsuit is very rare. But you have the right to expect the law to be followed and to be treated fairly and with respect.

TIP

To file a complaint with the CFPB against a collector who is harassing you, visit www.consumerfinance.gov/complaint. They usually follow up with the collector about your complaint. Being contacted by a government agency is almost guaranteed to get the collection agency's attention. To contact the FTC, visit www.ftc.gov or call 877-382-4357. The FTC won't follow up on your specific case, but your complaint helps others by allowing patterns of possible law violations to surface. The CFPB uses its complaint database in the same way. Enough complaints against the same collector and the CFPB or the FTC may act.

Here are some other things you can do about harassment or abuse:

>> **Keep your cool.** Always be professional and as calm as you can manage, and never raise your voice.

>> **Take notes during each call.** Be prepared with facts and dates, and know what you're going to say before you say it. Being prepared can give you an

advantage. The collection agency definitely knows what it's going to say before it calls you!

>> **Get a name.** Always get the name of the person calling you, and ask for full contact information, including the name of the company and the office manager. Do so *before* you get flustered or frustrated and things get out of hand.

>> **Just say no.** If a collector goes too far or breaks a rule (threatens, yells, uses obscene language, and so on), you can tell the collector to stop and call back when he or she can act in a businesslike manner. Keep a record of the call and the behavior. As always, make a note of the interaction. A record of the call with the time, date, name of the individual, and what was said is always in your favor.

>> **Complain to the original creditor.** Even though you aren't in good graces at the moment, a complaint here can result in action. No business wants an abusive collector scaring away past or future customers. The original debt holder may take the debt back and deal with you directly if you make a good case.

TIP

Go to www.dummies.com/go/creditrepairkitfd5e for sample letters you can send to your creditor report harassment from an abusive collector or request no future contact from a collection agency.

>> **Complain to the boss.** Remember, you were smart enough to ask for the manager's name when the collector first contacted you, so use it. Your complaint may be the one that gets the abuser fired. No collection agency wants to be sued because of a bully who can't be professional.

>> **Tell the collector to deal with your lawyer.** This is a double-edged sword. After you tell the collector to contact your attorney, all contact with you ends. Usually, the collection agency sends the debt to its own lawyer.

Communicating with Customer Service Before Being Placed for Collection

Communicating effectively isn't always easy, and many people don't even know where to begin. If you're not sure where to start, keep reading. When dealing with creditors, communication can be even more difficult because of the associated guilt, anger, and other emotions; basically, your emotions can set you up for conflict and communication breakdown.

From your perspective, the situation looks like this: You're a responsible adult who has been a good customer for a long time. A series of unfortunate, unexpected, and undeserved events has descended upon you like a plague. You've tried for months to overcome your payment problems before asking for help. You can't seem to catch up. You're at the end of your rope, dangling at the edge of a cliff. But with some help, you know that you can pull yourself out. The process is similar to the one outlined in the section "Preparing to answer collection calls" but the tone and your options are different.

From the customer service rep's point of view, the scenario looks like this: You made a promise and broke it. Everyone else is required to pay their bills on time, so why shouldn't you? You may be overspending and living beyond your means. You need to catch up on your payments as fast as possible. If you don't come through, the collector's job performance and business will suffer, and if the collector gets fired, he or she will be unable to pay his or her own bills.

REMEMBER

See how two people can see the same scenario so differently? It can be very hard to see things from a different perspective, but we know that you'll be more successful in getting the outcome you want if you're able to see the situation from the other side. For whatever reason, you haven't been able to keep all the promises you made. That doesn't mean you aren't a good person. Always remember: The issue is about money and numbers for the collector; it's not personal. But from a financial perspective, it does indicate that doing business with you may be risky.

So now it's *your* job to explain why the customer service rep should accommodate you. Is resolution possible here? Yes — if you do your homework, offer a solution, and follow through on your promises. Where do you start? What do you say? To minimize negative perceptions, be proactive from the start and follow the steps outlined in this section.

Contacting your creditor promptly

Putting off unpleasant tasks is human nature. However, when it comes to requesting assistance from your creditors, the earlier you make the request, the better. From the creditor's point of view, three types of customers exist:

» Good customers who pay as agreed

» Good customers with temporary problems who are willing to work things out

» Bad customers who won't pay what they owe without being "encouraged," if at all

You'd like to be the first type of customer, but sometimes bad things happen to good people and you slip into the second group. What's really important, however, is not finding yourself lumped into the third group.

TIP

The best time to let your creditors know that you're in trouble is as soon as *you* know and have a solution to offer. Don't wait until you've missed a payment if possible — or one payment at most — on that credit card or auto loan. Don't wait for the phone to ring or a letter to come and *then* give your story. Get in touch *before* the payment is late if you know you aren't going to be able to make it. By taking charge early, you give yourself a much greater chance that negative information won't find its way onto your credit report, where it could haunt you for years! Read on to find out what to say.

Explaining your situation

You may choose to contact customer service by phone, in writing, via email, or through the creditor's website. In some cases, you may even communicate through an intermediary like an attorney or a credit counselor. More about those two options comes later. Whatever method you use, you need to explain your situation as clearly, effectively, and objectively as possible. Do everything you can to take your emotions out of it. Assure the creditor that, despite your temporary difficulties, you intend to get back on financial track as quickly as possible.

But what do you want to say? What can you do to increase your chances of getting the help you need and deserve? Here are some elements to communicate (using a phone conversation as an example):

>> **Introduce yourself and ask for the person's name.** Why? Because doing so adds a human dimension to the dialogue and may help personalize your call. Don't say "you" or "you people." We suggest that you write the name down, because you're probably stressed out and may forget it easily. Plus, when you call again, you'll have a name to refer to.

>> **Begin the conversation on a positive note.** Say something nice about the company and your relationship with it. For example, "I've been a customer for years, and I've always had great products/service from you."

>> **Briefly (in a minute or so) present the facts.** And just the facts. For example, you lost your job, you have no savings, and you have only unemployment insurance for income. Skip the gory details and the emotional commentary.

Offering a solution

After you've succinctly laid out the situation, propose a solution that works for you, *before* you turn control of the conversation over to the customer service representative. Your goal is to make it as easy as possible for the rep to agree to what you need, and the best way is just to ask for what you need! This is a critical and very positive step in the communication process. The customer service rep may actually be pleased that you've come up with a workable plan. Doing so not only increases the chance that you'll get what you want, but may also shorten the call if the rep can agree to your request, thereby making the rep look like a very productive employee. Plus, by keeping more control over the outcome, you have a much better chance of getting a repayment plan that actually works for you. (You may even be able to negotiate a concession or two in your favor; see the section "Negotiating a payback arrangement" earlier in this chapter.)

TIP

Whatever your proposed plan, be sure to cover these bases:

>> **Assure the rep that you're already taking steps to resolve the problem *now*.**

>> **Offer a realistic estimate of how long you need to rectify the situation.** Not "soon" or "I don't know."

>> **Propose a specific payment amount and plan that you can manage.** Don't ask the creditor to suggest an amount. You won't like the answer.

>> **Offer specifics.** Avoid saying, "I can't afford the $300-a-month payment right now. You're going to have to accept less." That's not a plan. Instead, say, "I need to reduce the monthly payment to $150 for the next four months. I could even pay $75 twice a month. Then, in four months, I believe I can return to $300, which only extends the length of the loan by two months." Now *that's* a plan. It shows that you're sensitive to the creditor's situation and that you're making a fair effort to make good.

>> **Don't overpromise.** You may feel intimidated or embarrassed, and it's only natural to want to give the creditor what the creditor wants. Don't be surprised if the creditor pushes back and asks for more. Be firm and don't budge on your offer, if possible. In the end, though, remember that the creditor won't be happy if you promise a certain payment and fail to deliver. If you get stuck, ask to speak to a manager, who may be able to approve your offer.

TIP

If you prefer to handle things in writing, check out the partial payment hardship letter and the offer to return a secured item letter at www.dummies.com/go/creditrepairkitfd5e.

Covering all the bases

After you propose your plan and agree to terms, ask for a letter outlining the new agreement to be mailed or emailed to you so that there's no chance for a misunderstanding. If that doesn't seem to be forthcoming from your contact, or if you don't receive written documentation of the new terms within a few days, follow up yourself, stating the agreement in writing. Always make sure that any agreement you reach with the collection agency is put in writing.

Keeping Collectors in Check

Debt collectors are people, too. Some are thoughtful and considerate, and are just trying to do a tough job that affects people who have fallen on hard times. Other debt collectors see people with debt problems as deadbeats and get a strange satisfaction from bullying them into paying the debts they owe. Many in the collections field see their role as an extension of customer service to customers in trouble. They'll try to work with you. Unfortunately, there are those who get a power trip from their role and use it as an excuse to use unfair and abusive collection practices on people they think are vulnerable. Regardless of which kind of collector you find yourself talking to, being prepared before you get on the phone is key to controlling the conversation.

We cover dealing with the collection process and collectors in the section "Preparing to answer collection calls" earlier in this chapter.

Calling in a credit counselor

On your own, you may be able to get to a customer service manager, but the manager can't get around policy that is set by corporate headquarters. Very often, the top people at a collection agency set a special collection policy that applies only to the legitimate credit counseling agencies with which they've established a working relationship. When professional credit counselors get involved, they may be able to deal with a special department that handles only credit counseling accounts and is much more sympathetic than the line collector or manager you can talk to. So, in one leap, you escalate your account to high-level corporate policymakers.

REMEMBER

Talk to a credit counselor from an independently accredited nonprofit agency. Chapter 4 explains how to pick one from a crowded field. The cost to find out what an agency can do for you is zero, free, nada, and the professional analysis of your financial dilemma and your options can be invaluable. As an intermediary, the credit counselor can deal with your creditors on your behalf and may be able to administer a favorable workout plan (often referred to as a *debt management plan*) while you follow a fairly strict budget.

Fair Isaac's FICO score doesn't take points away for using a credit counseling agency. In some cases, a statement will be added to your credit report that you're repaying a debt through a counseling agency. For some lenders, that's a positive. It tells them you're taking action to get control of your personal finances.

Referring the matter to your lawyer

A good lawyer can work wonders with the more complex legal situations people face from time to time. Like showing up to a gunfight with the second-fastest gun, hiring a so-so lawyer isn't worth the effort. The best attorney for you is one who specializes in debt law. The drawbacks: Lawyers are expensive, and after *you* start down a legal path, so do the collectors.

Get an attorney who specializes in representing debtors. These lawyers know the process, have the right letters on file, and may even know the collection agency or company. Besides sheltering you from having to deal with collectors directly, an attorney helps slow down the freight train of events heading your way. He or she knows what is acceptable to the collector, collection lawyer, and judge (if things get that far). Plus, in today's complex debt sale and resale environment, an attorney can review your loan documents to make sure that your debt is enforceable.

Freeing Up Money to Pay a Collector

It feels like everyone wants a piece of you, or at least a chunk of what little money you have. Where are you going to come up with the money to pay what you owe? In this section, we explore ways to reduce expenses and free up some funds to satisfy those creditors and collectors. We're not going to lie to you: Cutting expenses is no fun! But after you've done it successfully and you have a bit of money to make payments, you'll feel much better. The short-term sacrifice of retooling your spending and changing some old habits will prove to be well worth the effort when you're able to reduce or even eliminate your debt challenge. And establishing new money habits can make the long-term future much brighter.

Utilizing a spending plan

The best way we know to get the most out of every dollar you earn and set yourself on the road to credit recovery is to develop a detailed *spending plan.* A spending plan puts you in control of your finances, allowing you to identify how much money you have to spend on bills and necessities and decide how much money to spend on the stuff you want from what's left. A spending plan tells you just how much available cash you have to meet your obligations and allows you to set some aside to have fun, too. You've probably heard it called a *budget,* but when you look at it as a spending plan, it's less intimidating and actually empowering. More important for this chapter, your spending plan lets you know how much you can afford to offer a collector or creditor to rid yourself of problem debt. For more on developing such a plan, turn to Chapter 18.

Creating a spending plan is technically easy but emotionally challenging. By putting it in writing, you'll make a critical step toward determining what you need to change! If you still feel overwhelmed, Chapter 4 offers advice on choosing a good credit counselor who can help you with this process for free. (Believe it or not, there *are* people who love putting together spending plans.)

Cutting the fat from your monthly spending

The simplest way to cut expenses is much like cutting calories when you're on a diet. When slimming down, you eat the stuff that's lower in calories and skip the cake. When cutting expenses, you do things that cost less (use more coupons at the grocery store and plan meals to match what's on sale) and lay off the expensive stuff (cancel that reservation to the hot new restaurant in town).

TIP

We mention food for a reason. Eating out is one of the biggest entertainment expenses for American families. If you add up your monthly expense for restaurant food, you may be shocked. Even that $4-a-day latte on the way to work adds up to more than $1,000 a year. Instead of eating out, eat in more often, and pack a lunch for work or school. Make eating at home fun by involving the entire family in preparing some of the dishes you'd order at that fancy restaurant. You could see your monthly spending on food shrink by as much as 25 percent to 50 percent.

REMEMBER

You're not giving up doing something you love forever; you're only giving up these things until you resolve your current financial situation.

The important part is to honestly review your monthly expenses and determine whether you can trim back. The hardest part about creating a spending plan can be setting your emotions aside and looking objectively at the numbers.

The savings from cutting back on expenses may seem insignificant at first, but they add up quicker than you realize. And before you believe you can go another day without a triple latte, you'll have reached your goal.

Avoiding Collectors Altogether

If you're reading this chapter, not paying your bills on time may be what got you into a bad-credit situation in the first place. But making on-time payments for the amount agreed every time the bill is due is the most important thing you can do to keep bad credit from getting worse. This section lays out specific ideas to help you pay your bills on time and keep creditors off your back.

Getting organized

Nothing is quite as frustrating as getting hit with a $25 or $35 late-payment fee on your credit card statement when you're trying to cut expenses. The good news is that a late payment doesn't necessarily cost you any more than the fee. Thanks to the Credit Card Accountability, Responsibility, and Disclosure Act of 2009 (CARD Act), you no longer have to worry about whether your interest rate will go up if you're one day late with a payment. Unlike a late fee, which is a one-time expense, a higher interest rate would make you pay more every month going forward. The CARD Act requires a payment to be 60 days past due before the penalty interest rate kicks in. You'll still probably have to pay a late fee, though. Unlike an interest increase, a fee for making a late payment can be charged as soon as it happens. Find out more about how the CARD Act benefits you in Chapter 19.

Getting organized is by far the best way to avoid unnecessary late payments. Here are some options for getting organized:

» **Set up automatic bill payment.** Using online banking tools to make at least the minimum payment due lets you set it and forget it. You don't have to worry about missing a payment — it's automatically deducted from your bank account. The catch is that you have to make sure you have the cash in your bank account before the payment is due on your debt.

» **Pay bills as soon as you receive them.** If you aren't comfortable with automatic payments, make a pact with yourself to get the mail, sit down immediately, and write checks or go online to pay any bills you receive *that day*.

» **Mark a calendar with the due dates for all bills.** Allow at least a week for bills that you mail and a few days for bills that you pay online. Place the calendar where you'll see it every day so you don't miss any due dates. Better yet, set a reminder in your phone calendar so it alerts you when it's time to pay the bills. Technology is your friend when it comes to paying bills! And don't forget to include paying the phone bill in your calendar.

» **Set up a filing system.** Place bills in folders or in due date order, marked with the day of the month that they need to be paid. The trick is remembering to place the bills in the folders or organizer and to check the folders on a daily or weekly basis. You can do it with paper or using a computer with scanned or downloaded documents. Either way, be consistent in gathering and filing the documents every month.

Experiment, find a solution that works for you, and get those bills paid!

Stopping the paycheck-to-paycheck cycle

If you live paycheck to paycheck, you may find it difficult to pay all your bills on time and in full every month because money is so tight, especially when an emergency crops up and you have to pay for it out of money allocated for another bill. Consider these tips:

>> **Start a savings account.** What does starting a savings account have to do with living paycheck to paycheck? Plenty. Without emergency savings, you won't be able to stop living paycheck to paycheck. When you have savings set aside, that unexpected expense is no longer an emergency, and you don't have to take on debt to pay it. Find out more about the importance of savings in Chapter 18.

>> **Ask your creditor to change your due date.** You can request that your due date fall later in the month, or earlier, when you have the money to pay the bill in full and on time.

Check out www.dummies.com/go/creditrepairkitfd5e for a sample letter you can send to make this request.

>> **Look to your job to free up extra cash.** If you want to increase your cash flow and can't get a second (or third) job, you may not have to look far. Here are a couple of things you can do regarding your current job:

● **Check your payroll deductions.** If you get a hefty tax refund each year, see your employer and add withholding allowances on Form W-4 to increase your take-home pay. But if you'll end up writing a check to the IRS, don't do it.

For assistance in figuring out the right number of withholding exemptions you should take, see the IRS Withholding Estimator at www.irs.gov/individuals/tax-withholding-estimator.

● **Free up some money in your retirement plan.** We're not suggesting that you take money out of the plan; doing so would result in some ugly penalties, and a lot less for your retirement in the long run! But you can temporarily reduce or suspend your contributions to help close the gap. Just have a plan to make them up later.

» Settling a debt for less than you owe

» Handling judgments and wage garnishments

» Telling your story in court

» Dealing with undischargeable debts

Chapter **6**

Working with Collectors, Lawyers, and the Courts to Manage Debt Obligations

D ealing with credit is like running a marathon. That's hard enough. But in the credit marathon, you also find obstacles in the way that you have to get over, go around, or move out of the way. Some of the hurdles can be cleared easily. Others can seem like mountains blocking your way. This chapter helps you with some of the biggest credit troubles you'll face: charge-offs, judgments, garnishments, student loans, child support, and IRS debt.

WARNING

Because these debts are so troublesome, they attract hustlers and scam artists who promise to bring you relief for a fraction of what you owe. Claims of settling an IRS debt for pennies or removing valid charge-offs from your credit report are as bogus as those claims made by the endless stream of Nigerian millionaires who ask for your bank account information and promise to share their millions in return — if you'll just send them a few thousand dollars first.

In this chapter, we give you the skinny on charge-offs, judgments, and debts that can't be wiped out, even by a bankruptcy. We tell you how to minimize damage to your credit (yes, you'll still have some if the debts are legitimate) and give you strategies for controlling and even eliminating those sour credit notes before they make your credit score sound flat. So, lace up your sneakers and listen up — the marathon is about to begin.

Getting a Handle on Charge-Offs

During the collections process, you'll come upon some serious hurdles where unresolved matters can trip you up. It's important for you to recognize when you've reached these hurdles, how important they are, and what you need to do to clear them, or at least get around them. In this section, we discuss unpaid charge-offs and paid charge-offs. Understanding how these actions work and what you can do about them may save you credit score points and money in the long run.

So what is a charge-off?

When a collector or creditor has decided that your debt is very unlikely to be collected and they no longer want the debt to remain in their records as an asset, they *charge off* your account. For accounting and tax purposes, the creditor considers your account a loss, and your account is charged off the company's books.

That doesn't happen right away. Usually some time has to pass before they take such a drastic action. Some generalizations about the timeline hold true for many types of unsecured debts like credit cards or personal loans:

» If you pay a bill after its due date, it's technically late.

» Paying up to 30 days late may have some minor consequences, but usually nothing severe.

» When you hit 31 days, the late payment will probably hit your credit report, and your credit scores will get dinged.

» After you get to 60 days late, you may face larger fees and maybe an interest-rate increase. Your credit scores will start to drop substantially and will continue to slide the further past due the payment becomes.

» Being 90 days late can cost you more and often brings on the serious players in the collection department.

» If your account is between 120 and 180 days past due, your debt enters a new phase known as the *charge-off*.

A creditor charging off a debt in no way means that the debt is canceled or that you don't have a legal responsibility to pay it, nor does any interest associated with the account stop accruing. No one is happy about this turn of events, and among those who should be the least happy is you. Why? Because you still owe the bill while fees and interest continue to accrue and the damage to your credit continues to grow.

The rest of this section covers the credit-reporting difference between unpaid and paid charge-offs and explains why paying a charge-off is worthwhile even though it stays on your credit report. We also talk about the role a spending plan plays in getting debts and collectors under control.

Making sense of unpaid charge-offs

A debt charges off when it gets so old (typically 180 days past due) that its value is called into question. If your creditor reports account histories to the credit bureaus, and most do, the charge-off is considered a very serious negative.

When a debt charges off, you still owe it, and the creditor or collector will still attempt to collect it. The charge-off means only that the original creditor no longer counts the debt as an asset. An unpaid charge-off causes more damage to your credit report than a paid one.

If the original creditor or its in-house collection unit is still working with you, until you pay what you owe, the debt is labeled an *unpaid charge-off* on your credit report. When an account first charges off, you may experience a lull in collection attempts. The reason is that the debt is probably changing hands from the in-house collectors who were unsuccessful trying to save the account to third-party collectors who want to save at least some part of it. When the debt goes to a third-party collector, the "charged-off" status for the original debt is final and won't change. You'll probably see a note with the lender's account that says "sold to" or "transferred to" and the name of the collection agency. There will also likely be a new collection account with a note that says "purchased from" or "transferred from" and the name of the lender. That will help you track the history of the debt — and who you should be talking to or paying.

The most experienced collectors typically deal with charge-offs. These collectors have heard it all a thousand times before and have lasted in this business because they're efficient and effective. Make no mistake, collectors will try to collect the money due; however, after they determine that you either can't or won't pay, your account may be sold many times to increasingly aggressive collectors or lawyers whom you really don't want to deal with.

Making charge-off payments

Collectors try to make you promise to pay your debt in full or in a series of agreed-upon payments. They take promises very seriously, so you don't want to make and then break one. We suggest that you know for sure how much you can afford to pay monthly or in a lump-sum amount before you make any promises. The best way to do so is to prepare a spending plan (see Chapter 18) that takes into account all your income and expenses. Using this spending plan (some people call it a budget), you can identify areas to trim so that you can put more money toward paying off your debt. Without a plan, you'll only be guessing, and if you guess wrong it will only hurt you.

TIP

The key steps to making and carrying out a plan (see the household monthly budget plan at www.dummies.com/go/creditrepairkitfd5e for a sample of a spending plan outline) are as follows:

>> List all your income.

>> List all your expenses.

>> Cut out or decrease as many of the expenses as you can.

>> Increase your income if possible.

>> Repeat this process until you have enough money to pay the bill in a reasonable amount of time.

Don't promise more than your plan says you can afford to pay just to get off the phone. Be sincere, explain how you arrived at your payment amount, and request that the collector send you a written agreement for this amount. When you receive the agreement, send the payment, and do so on time, every time. You can ask for a reduction in fees and interest when you negotiate the payment agreement, but a reduction in the amount owed is harder to get (see the next section).

REMEMBER

A delinquent debt that hasn't reached charge-off status and is paid becomes current on your credit report, but a charge-off never does. An unpaid charge-off becomes a paid charge-off if it hasn't been sent to a third-party collector. A paid charge-off is much better for your credit than an unpaid charge-off because it indicates that you had a problem — perhaps a serious one — but that you eventually paid the bill. Hallelujah! Now you can get a little boost on your credit report, and you're on the way to obtaining credit at a more reasonable rate. Why? Simple: You've established that, although you may be a high-risk borrower, you do pay your bills in the end and you're more likely to pay on time in the future.

Coming to a Debt Settlement Agreement

When a creditor allows you to pay off your debt for less than you owe (including principal, interest, and fees), you're *settling a debt.* And because no one likes to lose money, settling a debt is rarely easy. Even if you paid some of the debt, your actions still caused the company to lose money, and you didn't live up to your end of the bargain, which isn't an incentive to do business with you in the future. Settling a debt also has a negative impact on your credit report and credit scores, so you may want to consider what's more important to you, the money or your credit history.

REMEMBER

Having a good credit history can save you a lot of money and a bad one can cost you a lot of money. Don't just think about the short term.

This section focuses on what happens if you agree to a debt settlement.

Considering a debt settlement offer

Some businesses may offer you a debt settlement option if they believe that they may never recover what you owe, continuing collections becomes uneconomical, or they think that they can recover more by settling than by selling the debt to a third-party collection agency. Although a settled debt is considered paid, the settlement appears on your credit report for seven years from the date you missed the first missed payment and never caught up, resulting in the charge off. That date is called the *original delinquency date.* (Remember this date, it will come up again when we discuss credit reports in Chapter 14.) Additionally, you may have a tax liability if the creditor forgives more than $600 of the debt.

REMEMBER

The IRS considers the difference between the amount you owe and the amount you pay as income. It may seem illogical, but the basic reasoning is fairly straightforward. The amount you didn't pay back still went into your bank account and you used it to buy something, just like getting paid. So, from the government's perspective, you could owe income tax. If your settlement amount allows for more than $600 to go unpaid, you're responsible for paying income taxes on that amount. For example, if you owe $5,000 and you work out a settlement where you pay only $3,000, the $2,000 that was forgiven becomes taxable income on your next tax return. As the saying goes, only two things in life are certain — and one of them is taxes!

WARNING

If you decide on debt settlement as a payment resolution, we strongly advise you to get the settlement terms in writing and read them carefully before you send in a penny. You need to be on your guard when you're negotiating a settlement or if you've been offered one. You're dealing with people who know settlements better than you do, and it's easy to make a mistake that is to their advantage and results in paying more than you expect. After you send in the money, you have no leverage with the collector, and any promises that aren't in the written agreement will probably be broken, and there will be nothing you can do about it. Debt settlement can be helpful if done right. It could do more harm than good if you aren't careful.

TIP

Head to www.dummies.com/go/creditrepairkitfd5e for a sample letter confirming your agreement.

Hiring a debt settlement firm

You're likely to see and hear advertisements for debt settlement firms, and you may even be contacted directly if or when they become aware of your debt problems. These companies have come to the attention of the Federal Trade Commission (FTC) and other government agencies like the Consumer Financial Protection Bureau (CFPB) because of their aggressive tactics, questionable claims, often large fees, and tendency to provide limited results for consumers. FTC regulations have curbed some of the abuses, but we still recommend that you try to settle on your own or use an attorney rather than a debt settlement firm. However, if you want to hire a settlement company, keep these points in mind:

>> Make sure that the company is a member of the Association of Settlement Companies (TASC).

>> Don't pay an upfront fee. Companies are required to settle at least one account before charging you anything.

>> Don't sign anything if you feel pressured to do so.

TIP

Consider running any offer by an attorney specializing in financial matters. Doing so will cost you money, but it may save you a lot if you avoid making a mistake or if only a bankruptcy can solve your problem. A consumer debt goes away in a bankruptcy; an IRS debt from a settlement doesn't. Be cautious about attorneys who come to you offering debt settlement. They may provide objective financial advice, or they may be using offers of rapid debt settlement to turn a quick buck. Good legal advice can be invaluable. Poor credit advice can be very expensive.

Reaching expiration dates on debts

Sometimes, procrastination has a silver lining. When a debt reaches a certain age (as defined by the statutes of your state of residence), it's no longer collectible in a court of law. Each state has its own statute of limitations rules. Check out Chapter 5 for more on expired debts and statutes of limitations.

Finding Out about Judgments and What They Mean to You

An unpaid charge-off often makes its way to a lawyer sooner or later. A collection attorney may take your case to court, you may have a judgment entered against you, you'll lose a day to court and incur additional legal expenses, and maybe — if it's just not your day — your wages will be garnished for up to 25 percent of your take-home pay. This is about as much fun as a legal colonoscopy. If you get a court summons for a hearing on a debt issue, answer it! Read on for all the details.

The legal side of the collection process typically begins with a letter. After months of endless phone calls, a simple letter can be easy to ignore, but don't let it set at the bottom of your inbox! The letter is a summons telling you that a court hearing will be held on a certain date in a certain place (see Figure 6-1). We strongly suggest that you show up with a plan and, if possible, an attorney. Courts have their own unique rules. If the collector shows up with their attorney, you should show up with yours. A good plan includes the following:

>> A short explanation of why you haven't paid

>> Any disputes about the bill or collection process so far

>> A plan to repay the debt on terms you can afford

>> Documentation that shows why you can't afford more

REMEMBER

If the debt is valid (not in dispute or belonging to someone else) and hasn't been collected, the court generally issues an order confirming that you owe money and commanding you to pay it. This order is called a *judgment,* and it involves legal fees and dealing with a system that doesn't fool around. There is one bit of good news. The national credit reporting companies no longer include judgments for collections in your credit report. They can still show up in other public record searches, though. Figure 6-2 shows a copy of a typical judgment from a hearing on a debt issue. If you get one of these, you need to wake up and get a repayment plan going. If you *dishonor,* or ignore, a judgment, the next step could be wage garnishment. (Check out the section "Understanding Wage Garnishments" later in this chapter for more info.)

ATTORNEY OR PARTY WITHOUT ATTORNEY (Name, State Bar number, and address):

FOR COURT USE ONLY
(SOLO PARA USO DE LA CORTE)

TELEPHONE NO.:   FAX NO. (Optional):
E-MAIL ADDRESS (Optional):
ATTORNEY FOR (Name):

SUPERIOR COURT OF CALIFORNIA, COUNTY OF
STREET ADDRESS:
MAILING ADDRESS:
CITY AND ZIP CODE:
BRANCH NAME:

PLAINTIFF:
DEFENDANT:

SUMMONS (JOINT DEBTOR) *(CITACIÓN (DEUDOR CONJUNTO))*

CASE NUMBER:
(Número del Caso):

NOTICE! You have been sued. The court may decide against you without your being heard unless you respond within 30 days. Read the information below.

You have 30 CALENDAR DAYS after this summons and legal papers are served on you to file a written response at this court and have a copy served on the plaintiff. A letter or phone call will not protect you. Your written response must be in proper legal form if you want the court to hear your case. There may be a court form that you can use for your response. You can find these court forms and more information at the California Courts Online Self-Help Center (*www.courtinfo.ca.gov/selfhelp*), your county law library, or the courthouse nearest you. If you cannot pay the filing fee, ask the court clerk for a fee waiver form. If you do not file your response on time, you may lose the case by default, and your wages, money, and property may be taken without further warning from the court.

There are other legal requirements. You may want to call an attorney right away. If you do not know an attorney, you may want to call an attorney referral service. If you cannot afford an attorney, you may be eligible for free legal services from a nonprofit legal services program. You can locate these nonprofit groups at the California Legal Services Web site (*www.lawhelpcalifornia.org*), the California Courts Online Self-Help Center (*www.courtinfo.ca.gov/selfhelp*), or by contacting your local court or county bar association. **NOTE:** The court has a statutory lien for waived fees and costs on any settlement or arbitration award of $10,000 or more in a civil case. The court's lien must be paid before the court will dismiss the case.

¡AVISO! Lo han demandado. Si no responde dentro de 30 días, la corte puede decidir en su contra sin escuchar su versión. Lea la información a continuación.

Tiene 30 DÍAS DE CALENDARIO después de que le entreguen esta citación y papeles legales para presentar una respuesta por escrito en esta corte y hacer que se entregue una copia al demandante. Una carta o una llamada telefónica no lo protegen. Su respuesta por escrito tiene que estar en formato legal correcto si desea que procesen su caso en la corte. Es posible que haya un formulario que usted pueda usar para su respuesta. Puede encontrar estos formularios de la corte y más información en el Centro de Ayuda de las Cortes de California (www.sucorte.ca.gov), en la biblioteca de leyes de su condado o en la corte que le quede más cerca. Si no puede pagar la cuota de presentación, pida al secretario de la corte que le dé un formulario de exención de pago de cuotas. Si no presenta su respuesta a tiempo, puede perder el caso por incumplimiento y la corte le podrá quitar su sueldo, dinero y bienes sin más advertencia.

Hay otros requisitos legales. Es recomendable que llame a un abogado inmediatamente. Si no conoce a un abogado, puede llamar a un servicio de remisión a abogados. Si no puede pagar a un abogado, es posible que cumpla con los requisitos para obtener servicios legales gratuitos de un programa de servicios legales sin fines de lucro. Puede encontrar estos grupos sin fines de lucro en el sitio web de California Legal Services, (www.lawhelpcalifornia.org), en el Centro de Ayuda de las Cortes de California, (www.sucorte.ca.gov) o poniéndose en contacto con la corte o el colegio de abogados locales. AVISO: Por ley, la corte tiene derecho a reclamar las cuotas y los costos exentos por imponer un gravamen sobre cualquier recuperación de $10,000 ó más de valor recibida mediante un acuerdo o una concesión de arbitraje en un caso de derecho civil. Tiene que pagar el gravamen de la corte antes de que la corte pueda desechar el caso.

1. TO THE DEFENDANT (name):
    (AL DEMANDADO):
        You are hereby directed to file in this court, within **30** days after this summons is served on you, a written response to the Declaration or Affidavit accompanying this summons, giving any legal reason why you should not be required to pay the unpaid amount of: $ on the judgment rendered by this court on (date):
    against (name each):

Date: Clerk, by   , Deputy
(Fecha)   (Secretario)   (Adjunto)

(For proof of service of this summons, use Proof of Service of Summons (form POS-010).)
(Para prueba de entrega de esta citatión use el formulario Proof of Service of Summons, (POS-010)).

(SEAL)

2. **NOTICE TO THE PERSON SERVED:** You are served
   a. ☐ as an individual defendant.
   b. ☐ as the person sued under the fictitious name of (specify):

   c. ☐ on behalf of (specify):
      under: ☐ CCP 416.10 (corporation)   ☐ CCP 416.60 (minor)
             ☐ CCP 416.20 (defunct corporation) ☐ CCP 416.70 (conservatee)
             ☐ CCP 416.40 (association or partnership) ☐ CCP 416.90 (authorized person)
             ☐ other (specify):
   d. ☐ by personal delivery on (date):

Page 1 of 1

Form Adopted for Mandatory Use
Judicial Council of California
SUM-120 [Rev. July 1, 2009]

SUMMONS (JOINT DEBTOR)

Code of Civil Procedure § 989
www.courtinfo.ca.gov

FIGURE 6-1:
A sample court summons letter.

The judgment itself doesn't force you to pay the debt. It does, however, set you up for execution — not execution as in the electric chair, but a *judgment execution*. If you receive a judgment and you still don't pay, the lender can go back to the judge and get an execution order. Depending on the laws in your state, the order allows the creditor to do the following:

The following is a form image:

```
                                                                              CIV-130
ATTORNEY OR PARTY WITHOUT ATTORNEY (Name, State Bar number, and address):        FOR COURT USE ONLY




       TELEPHONE NO.:              FAX NO. (Optional):
E-MAIL ADDRESS (Optional):
   ATTORNEY FOR (Name):
SUPERIOR COURT OF CALIFORNIA, COUNTY OF
   STREET ADDRESS:
  MAILING ADDRESS:
 CITY AND ZIP CODE:
      BRANCH NAME:

   PLAINTIFF/PETITIONER:
DEFENDANT/RESPONDENT:

         NOTICE OF ENTRY OF JUDGMENT           CASE NUMBER:
                 OR ORDER

   (Check one):   [ ] UNLIMITED CASE    [ ] LIMITED CASE
                      (Amount demanded     (Amount demanded was
                      exceeded $25,000)    $25,000 or less)


TO ALL PARTIES :

1. A judgment, decree, or order was entered in this action on (date):


2. A copy of the judgment, decree, or order is attached to this notice.



Date:
                                                 ▶
_____          _____
(TYPE OR PRINT NAME OF [ ] ATTORNEY [ ] PARTY WITHOUT ATTORNEY)    (SIGNATURE)

                                                              Page 1 of 2
Form Approved for Optional Use                                www.courtinfo.ca.gov
  Judicial Council of California         NOTICE OF ENTRY OF JUDGMENT OR ORDER
CIV-130 [New January 1, 2010]
```

FIGURE 6-2:
A sample court judgment letter.

>> Garnish your wages up to 25 percent. (See the next section for more on wage garnishments.)

>> Place a lien on your home or other property for the amount owed. A lien is like having another mortgage on the property. Before the property can be sold or mortgaged, the lien has to be paid off.

>> Repossess any property involved with the debt you owe (for example, your furniture if it's a furniture loan).

REMEMBER

A judgment is a very serious development in the collection process. At this point, many people seriously consider bankruptcy to wipe out their debts. Unfortunately, for many people who earn above the median income in their states, bankruptcy is no longer an attractive option (see Chapter 8). This is one of the reasons we think consulting a professional early in the game makes a lot of sense. If you don't have the option to file bankruptcy, you want to know as soon as possible.

Understanding Wage Garnishments

If you receive a judgment (see the preceding section) and still won't or can't pay the debt, your employer may be court-ordered to garnish part of your paycheck to pay off your creditor. After the court orders a wage garnishment, certain rules must be followed as defined in the Consumer Credit Protection Act (CCPA). This section focuses on the main points, including how you can avoid wage garnishments. Remember that state law can take precedence over federal law, but only if the amounts allowed for garnishment are lower.

Dodging wage garnishments

Before anyone can garnish your wages, a judgment from a court of law is necessary. You get a summons to appear in court to defend yourself against a suit for payment brought by the owner of your debt. If a judgment is issued and the debt remains unpaid, the creditor can go back to court and execute the judgment to push matters to the next stage, which may include having your wages garnished. You will receive another summons if this happens.

TIP

Each state has its own debt collection laws. Some states permit a creditor to garnish your wages; others don't. Some states exempt large amounts or categories of assets from attachment or seizure by a creditor to pay your debt. Others may force you to sell possessions to satisfy a judgment. The best source for up-to-date information is your state's consumer protection office. You can find a Directory of State and Local Consumer Agencies at www.usa.gov/consumer.

REMEMBER

In many cases, you can avoid wage garnishments by doing the following:

>> **Keep complete records of the collection process.** Be sure to keep a record of names, dates, copies of correspondence, summaries of conversations, and any agreements or disputes.

>> **Show up in court when you're supposed to.** Go to the hearings and speak up! If you have a reasonable story to tell the judge and a reasonable offer to make, you may be surprised at the result. The judge won't be happy that a collector is wasting his valuable time with a case that should have been settled out of court. Bring your own lawyer along if you can. The process can be confusing and intimidating. Having your own legal representation can help take that pressure off.

TIP

State law may set garnishment limits lower than the federal maximum. In that case, the state law supersedes the federal law. The CCPA says that your boss can't fire you for having a garnishment. However, the CCPA doesn't provide this protection for multiple wage garnishments. You can find much more information on wage garnishments by calling the U.S. Department of Labor at 866-487-9243 or by visiting www.dol.gov/agencies/whd/wage-garnishment and clicking on the Garnishment tab.

CCPA protections don't apply to the following types of nondischargeable debts:

>> **Child support and alimony:** The court has little sympathy in matters of delinquent child support payments. The garnishment law allows up to 50 percent of your disposable earnings to be garnished for child support and alimony if you're supporting another spouse or child and up to 60 percent if you're not. An additional 5 percent may be garnished for support payments that are more than 12 weeks in arrears.

>> **Debts owed to the government:** The garnishment restrictions don't apply to certain bankruptcy court orders or to debts related to federal or state taxes.

A consumer debt such as a credit card or personal loan can be garnished up to 15 percent and a student loan up to 10 percent. If you're being garnished for more than one debt, you're subject to a 25 percent maximum. If a state's wage garnishment law differs from the CCPA, the law that results in the smaller garnishment must be observed.

Figuring out how much can be garnished

After your creditor is granted a judgment, you may wonder how much the court can order your employer to garnish from your wages. The court uses *disposable earnings* (the amount left after legally required deductions like taxes, FICA, mandatory retirement withholding, and unemployment insurance) to calculate your garnishment amount.

REMEMBER

Whether you have one or more garnishments, the law sets the maximum amount that your employer may garnish in any workweek or pay period. Exceptions are made for court-ordered support, bankruptcy, or state or federal tax. The amount may not exceed the lesser of two figures: 25 percent of your disposable earnings or the amount by which your disposable earnings are greater than 30 times the federal minimum wage (currently $7.25 an hour). See Table 6-1 for calculations of the latter.

TABLE 6-1 **Maximum Garnishment of Disposable Earnings Under Normal Circumstances* for the $7.25 Federal Minimum Wage**

Weekly	Biweekly	Semimonthly	Monthly
$217.50 or less: none	$435.00 or less: none	$471.25 or less: none	$942.50 or less: none
More than $217.50 but less than $290.00: amount above $217.50	More than $435.00 but less than $580.00: amount above $435.00	More than $471.25 but less than $628.33: amount above $471.25	More than $942.50 but less than $1,256.67: amount above $942.50
$290.00 or more: maximum 25%	$580.00 or more: maximum 25%	$628.33 or more: maximum 25%	$1,256.66 or more: maximum 25%

These restrictions don't apply to garnishments for child and/or spousal support, bankruptcy, or actions to recover state or federal taxes. Source: U.S. Department of Labor www.dol.gov/whd/regs/compliance/whdfs30.pdf.

Stating Your Case in Court

Asking for time off from work to go to court can be intimidating, embarrassing, and expensive. Most creditors count on this and are very happy if you don't show up. Why? Because without you there to object, they'll get just about anything they want from the judge. It's essential that you appear in court at the appointed time if you hope to get any sympathy. Tell the judge your side of the story. Be sure to bring the following:

>> Statements from the account or accounts in question to make sure that the document filed with the court contains no mistakes or unwarranted additions.

>> Records of phone calls and written correspondence — including emails and texts — with the creditor to document that you've been trying to come to an agreement.

>> A budget of your expenses and income to support a payment plan you can afford so the judge can see that your offer is serious. Copies of paychecks or other income sources may help to prove your case about how much you can afford.

REMEMBER

You can represent yourself, but you're at a disadvantage if you do. Trust us: Your creditor is intimately familiar with the ins and outs of the court process. Their attorney or someone trained in the legal process will be at the court hearing. That gives them an advantage over people who don't know the rules of court, no matter how right you may be. If you can afford it, get an attorney. If you can't, you still need to go to court; your presence and your genuine commitment to finding a workable way to repay your debt may be all you need.

Use your records to show the court that you've made a good-faith effort to propose the best settlement you can afford. Show that you've offered a reasonable repayment plan based on your means, but that it was refused. If you went to a credit counselor along the way, mention it; if you can say that the counselor thought your proposed settlement was reasonable, all the better. Of course, none of this reasonable stuff applies to overdue child support; unless your income has changed for the worse, you have to pay what the law requires.

REMEMBER

The following list shows the progression of the process for collections that have gone to an attorney for legal action:

1. **You receive a demand letter from an attorney demanding payment.**

   This letter comes in addition to all the letters you may have received from the creditor or collector. The demand letter gives you one last chance to try to resolve the problem before court action begins.

2. **A suit is filed in court, often within 10 to 30 days of the date of the demand letter.**

   This suit alerts the court to the situation and again demands payment.

3. **You get served with a summons.**

   You get a summons from the court to respond by a certain date and time.

4. **If you don't answer the summons, the attorney can file for a default judgment.**

   If the court enters a default judgment in the matter, the creditor wins. You lose.

5. **If you do file an answer, the discovery process begins, and a trial date is set.**

TIP

When you respond to the suit, be sure to explain any discrepancies in the creditor's claims. If you can't, then be sure to show up in court on the hearing date with all your documentation and your lawyer if possible.

6. **If a judgment is awarded and not paid by the due date, the attorney attempts to locate and verify your assets.**

The attorney initiates court-ordered bank levies, garnishment orders, liens, and so on to satisfy the judgment.

Understanding what happens may help demystify the process and remove one more hurdle that may keep you from reacting until it's too late.

Managing IRS Debts, Student Loans, and Unpaid Child Support

IRS debts, student loans, and unpaid child support are in a special class of debts that aren't dischargeable in a bankruptcy in most cases and must be paid. We cover them in the following sections.

Handling IRS debts

An IRS debt can be one of the easiest debt situations to deal with. First, the IRS knows that *you* know who's in control, so the IRS doesn't need to intimidate you with strong-arm tactics to get your attention. Second, the IRS isn't chasing down its own money — it's chasing down taxpayer money. And third, IRS employees don't get a bonus for collecting a debt. You can probably negotiate a reasonable repayment plan with the IRS that you can manage over time.

TIP

Download IRS Form 9465 at www.irs.gov/pub/irs-pdf/f9465.pdf, fill it out, and send it in. The form isn't hard to complete, so don't wait too long before you act.

If you have an accountant, we suggest that you bring him or her along when you meet with the IRS. Your accountant may be able to calmly explain why you shouldn't owe taxes on some income or why you should get certain deductions. Like lawyers in courts, accountants have their own language and rules. Having a professional with you can give you an advantage.

WARNING

IRS debts just keep growing with age. If you delay too long, the IRS will pull any tax refunds you have coming and direct the money into the Treasury until the debt is paid. As they say, the tax man always gets his money.

REMEMBER

The credit bureaus don't include tax liens anymore — paid or not. However, other companies do collect tax lien information. Businesses check those reports, too. To make sure they don't hurt you in the future, keep good records of payments and discharges, and, if appropriate, the property records at your local town hall. Make sure that the records are updated, or you may not be able to sell your home because it has a big fat lien on it that shouldn't be there.

Educating yourself about student loans

Student loan collections used to be a joke, but no one is laughing anymore. The law doesn't allow you to include student loans in bankruptcy, so lenders can pursue delinquencies forever. The effect on your credit of being in default varies from bad to nuclear meltdown. A lot of people ask us if they owe the money even if they didn't graduate or finish a semester. The answer is yes. You borrowed and spent the money, and you need to repay it. What you did with it is of no interest (no pun intended) to the lender. In fact, if you die while attending school, your estate often still owes the debt. Your parents may have to pay the debt, too, if they cosigned the loans. If so, you not only have a responsibility to the lender, but also to your mom and dad.

TECHNICAL STUFF

The term *default* is defined differently for different types of loans. Check with your lender to determine when your student loan enters into default.

A student loan isn't secured with collateral in the normal sense of the word. When you leave school, whether you graduate or not, certain situations, such as economic hardship or unemployment, may enable you to defer payment for a period of time. See Chapter 23 for details.

However, after your student loan is in default, you lose your opportunity to defer payment. To make matters worse, you may have to pay back the loan all at once unless you come up with an acceptable repayment scheme. You're also unable to receive further student aid, your school may withhold your transcripts, your state and federal income tax refunds may be taken to offset the loan amounts, and your wages (if and when you get a job) may be *attached* or *garnished*. (See the "Understanding Wage Garnishments" section earlier in this chapter.)

FINANCIAL AID: THE ULTIMATE GAMBLE?

It all seems so worthwhile: a college or tech-school education, the promise of a good job, and the great feeling you get from doing the smart thing. But a student loan is a big gamble, and we want you to understand that if anything goes wrong, you lose. Student loans are incredibly high-risk for lenders. Think about it. They're giving you money on the bet that in four years or so you'll graduate with a degree or certification, get a job, and then pay them back. A lot can change in that amount of time. Making student loans is so risky, in fact, that many loans have to be guaranteed by the government, and none of them are dischargeable in a bankruptcy under ordinary circumstances. If you fail to graduate for any reason (even because of illness or some other legitimate problem), if you can't find a job in your chosen profession or need to settle for a lower-paying job, if a pandemic shuts down the economy . . . no matter the reason, you still owe the money, and paying off the loan can take years, and sometimes decades. That's a gamble that millions take every year. Some win and some lose. Look for alternative ways to pay for schooling, or consider community college before taking on the big debt of a big-name school.

Following are some repayment options:

- >> **Normal repayment:** You make principal and interest payments each month.

- >> **Graduated repayment:** You make lower payments at the beginning, and your payments increase at specified intervals for the life of your loan.

- >> **Income-based repayment:** Your monthly payments are based on a percentage of your monthly gross income (for Stafford, PLUS, and Smart loans and federally consolidated loans).

- >> **Extended repayment:** Your repayment term is lengthened.

- >> **Consolidation:** Your federal loans are refinanced into a single, fixed loan with a long payback period.

- >> **Serialization:** You consolidate only the payments into a single payment but retain the original terms and interest rates on all your loans.

See `https://studentaid.gov/h/understand-aid/how-aid-works` for more information.

WARNING

If you can't pay back your loans as originally hoped, use all the options available to you to defer your loans for as long as possible. The goal should be to delay long enough to improve your financial position so you can repay the loan. After you've exhausted your deferments, you'll be in default if you don't agree to a new repayment plan.

TIP

For multiple student loans, consider the Direct Consolidation Loans program. The program provides borrowers who have at least one up-to-date federal student loan the opportunity to consolidate into a single monthly payment. You may also extend the repayment term on a student loan, which can reduce your monthly payment. Eligible loans include the Stafford, PLUS, Perkins, Health Profession, Health Education, and Nursing student loans. You may also be able to consolidate most defaulted education loans if you can make satisfactory repayment arrangements with the current holders or agree to repay the new Direct Consolidation Loan under an Income Contingent Repayment (ICR) plan. For information on the Direct Consolidation Loans program, go to `https://studentaid.gov/manage-loans/consolidation`.

REMEMBER

Delinquent student loans can be a big hiring issue. Getting a job with bad credit is a lot harder if your employer pulls a credit report to see whether you're reliable and stable. This is especially true if the job you're applying for involves managing the company's money in some way. If you have any unpaid loans, explain early in the hiring process why you haven't paid them and that you'll make good on a loan repayment plan as soon as you get a paycheck.

Working with a student loan creditor is essential to moving on with a normal life. Dealing with these folks is very much like dealing with the IRS: You need to get in contact, have a plan, make an offer to repay the loan, and follow through. See Chapter 23 for more information.

Putting your kids first: Child support

Unpaid child support is another category of debt that lives as long as you do. Under the bankruptcy law, child-support obligations can't be discharged. And the courts provide custodial parents the names of collection agencies that specialize in child-support debt, so your ex can easily work with a collection agency to come after you for what you owe.

WARNING

Child-support debt can result in a criminal charge and jail time if you continue not to pay it. The decision whether to seek prosecution in nonsupport cases rests with your state's attorney general. Courts have no sense of humor when it comes to child-support debt. You really don't want that debt hanging over you. Employers also take a dim view of failing to pay child support. Paying child support debt should be your number-one priority.

2

Reducing Credit Damage from Major Setbacks

IN THIS PART . . .

Explore your options before, during, and after a foreclosure, and know where you can get help.

Understand the pros and cons of bankruptcy.

Recognize identity theft when it happens, and take steps to minimize the effects.

IN THIS CHAPTER

» Getting acquainted with the specific rules of mortgages

» Finding help for your delinquent mortgage

» Facing grave mortgage problems, including foreclosure

» Coping with a deficiency balance

» Beefing up your credit before a default

» Adapting to the credit fallout

» Examining options to eliminate medical debts

» Paying off student loans

» Driving around a forthcoming repossession

» Surviving a pandemic and other disasters

Chapter **7**

Reducing Credit Damage in a Crisis

With millennials opting for smaller spaces and generations rooming together, many things have changed about the economics and potential risks of homeownership. What about staying in a home that's worth less than what you paid for it? What are your options if it's worth less than what you owe on the mortgage? And what are the risks to your credit if you have a default? What used to be a no-brainer decision has become more complicated than anyone could have imagined. Millions of people are asking these questions today. This chapter helps you find the answers. Here we cover legal obligations, taxes, credit, and the long arms of credit scores and reports.

This chapter is an important one for everyone, including homeowners who are under financial stress, people challenged with medical debt or student loans, or those struggling with the fallout from natural disasters. Money, credit, self-esteem, and the very roof over your family's head are at stake when a disaster occurs. This chapter provides you with the advice you need to make the best decision for your situation. Getting help and getting it early is critical. Fortunately, help *is* available, and this chapter guides you through the process of getting what you need.

Assessing the Damage from a Mortgage Meltdown

Credit score misinformation is everywhere. What you don't know can and will hurt you if what you don't know is that your credit report and score have been seriously damaged. If you're trying to assess the damage to your score from a mortgage meltdown or even just a mild mortgage sunburn, having the best information available is important. That's what this section is all about.

Today, credit score simulators can provide you some indication of the impacts of negative events on your credit score. Regardless of which credit score is being used (FICO or VantageScore), you can get a fairly accurate picture. The major credit reporting bureaus (Equifax, Experian, and TransUnion), Credit Karma (https://creditkarma.com), and some financial institutions offer credit score simulators as part of your customer experience with no fee associated. All these simulators allow you to use real-life scenarios to gain insight into the impacts certain actions may have on your score. Because they're just a simulation, they don't impact your real score so you can see the positive and negative impacts before you take any actions.

TIP

For an infographic from FICO showing the effects of various types of scenarios and the impacts on your credit score, go to www.dummies.com/go/credit repairkitfd5e. Mortgage defaults, foreclosures, repossessions, and bankruptcy have some of the most significant impacts, underscoring how important it is to resolve any problems as quickly and amicably as possible.

TECHNICAL
STUFF

The terms *default*, *delinquency*, and *negative event* tend to mean the same thing. Strictly speaking, being *delinquent* (late on a payment) leads to a *default* (based on the legal terms in your mortgage documents). Both are negative credit events that you don't want to experience.

REMEMBER

People with great credit who default on a mortgage see a greater credit-score point drop than those whose credit isn't so great. Why? Because a good score has to fall farther in order to end up at the lower point level that indicates serious credit problems. In general, the higher your starting score, the longer it takes for your score to fully recover from the damage.

Delinquencies and some actions that result in your home being taken back by the lender *(deed-in-lieu)* or sold under distress (as in a *short sale*) cost you big points. However, there's no significant difference in credit-score impact between a short sale, a deed-in-lieu, and a settlement. Mega point drops in your credit score tend to occur when the lender loses money in addition to your being in default, such as in the event of a short sale or a foreclosure, both of which cost the bank money. But the worst and longest lasting of all injury to your credit occurs when you file for bankruptcy. Unlike the other, lesser defaults, a bankruptcy can stay on your credit report for up to ten years.

In addition to credit score penalties, you need to take the collateral damage into consideration:

>> Although a score may *begin* to improve sooner, it can take up to seven to ten years to *fully* recover.

>> Fannie Mae (the Federal National Mortgage Association) is the nation's largest mortgage buyer. It buys and then resells mortgages on Wall Street, helping to keep mortgage interest rates low. Fannie excludes borrowers who've gone through a foreclosure from obtaining a Fannie-backed loan for seven years.

>> Fannie Mae won't accept a mortgage from a person who has had a mortgage delinquency in the last 12 months.

>> If you can't get a Fannie Mae loan, you may have to take a nonconforming loan, which may require expensive mortgage insurance premiums and, for those with lower credit scores, higher interest rates and a larger down payment.

Understanding How Mortgages Differ from Other Loans

Mortgages differ from other consumer loans partly because of their size — a lot of money is on the line — and partly because they're backed by what historically has been the gold standard in collateral: your home. With more at risk, the stakes are greater. Furthermore, mortgages are not only underwritten differently from other types of credit but also have a different collection process, generally called the *foreclosure process*. When you default on a mortgage, the lender *forecloses*, or terminates the mortgage, and your house is taken away from you.

From a credit-score and credit-reporting standpoint, mortgage defaults and foreclosures are among the most serious negatives out there, with the exception of bankruptcy.

Obviously, a foreclosure puts a serious hit on your credit score and history. To help you minimize this hit, this section gives you an overview of how mortgages differ from typical credit and how mortgages and credit go hand in hand. Here you can find valuable information to help you understand when a late mortgage payment can quickly cause you problems and what you can do to get help.

Spotting a foreclosure on the horizon

A lender has a lot of money on the line with your mortgage, and the longer you're delinquent, the greater the risk that the lender will lose money on a defaulted loan. The result is that a mortgage lender has a much lower tolerance for delinquency than, say, a credit card issuer. For example, as long as you're less than 180 days past due on a credit card, it's not the end of the world. Generally, you can just pay the minimum due along with a late fee and pick up where you left off. If you're really lucky, you may get the lender to waive the late fee and not report the delinquency. For a mortgage, however, being just 60 days late puts you well on your way to the edge of a cliff, and you may not even be aware of it.

WARNING

The key number to avoid in a mortgage delinquency is 90 days late. After 90 days, unless you get some help or work out an arrangement, the mortgage servicer generally requires the entire amount that is overdue (the *arrearage*) to be paid at once and may not accept partial payments. A 90-day mortgage delinquency on a credit report is very serious. To make matters worse, many people don't understand when the 90 days is up. The time frame isn't as simple as you may think, so we cover it in detail in the next section.

Mortgage servicers don't call you at work or at night, and they don't yell or threaten you over the phone. On the contrary, the tone of their messages (often letters) is concerned, low-key, and polite. If you ignore these messages, you could lose your home. But if you know where to get help, what to ask for, and what to avoid, your situation can change for the better.

Counting to 90

If you're 30 or 60 days late on your mortgage and you make a partial payment, the servicer usually credits your account with the payment. If you cross the 90-day mark and then send in a month or two's worth of overdue payments rather than the entire amount due, however, the servicer may send the money back and let the foreclosure clock keep ticking.

REMEMBER

After you're late on your first payment, your grace period disappears. (Your *grace period* is the period of time specified in your mortgage loan agreement during which a default can't occur, even though the payment is technically past due.) The grace period applies only to loans that are up-to-date, or current. The following example illustrates how this works.

Say your loan agreement states that your due date is March 1. Assuming that you have a typical two-week grace period, your payment actually has to be in by March 15. If you don't submit your payment by March 15, you miss that window of opportunity and lose your grace period. Your April payment is now due April 1. April 15 is no longer an option. In other words, no more grace period in April. If you pay April's payment on or before April 1, you get your grace period back for May and thereafter, as long as you continue making your payments on time.

If you lose your grace period, the counting of the number of days you're late begins on the 1st of the month rather than the 15th. So if you don't send in a payment on March 15, April 1, or May 1, then on May 2, you need to catch up on the payments for March 1, April 1, and May 1, plus any fees and penalties (which can be hundreds of dollars or more), all at once. This sum is a huge amount for someone in financial difficulty. If you don't pay, then the formal foreclosure process can start on May 2, and you may incur fees for collection costs, attorneys, title searches, filings, and more. After the foreclosure process begins (it's up to the mortgage servicer when this process actually begins), the mortgage servicer can *accelerate* the loan, meaning that it can ask for the entire loan balance — not just the late part — to stop the foreclosure.

Knowing Where to Turn for Help

If you're having trouble making your mortgage payments, time is of the essence. Getting your mortgage issue resolved quickly is critical. Remember, the mortgage company doesn't want your house; it just wants to keep your loan *performing/ up-to-date/current* (different terms for the same thing). But also remember that the mortgage company doesn't care whether it has to take your home. If the rules say to foreclose, the mortgage company will foreclose, without hesitation and without remorse.

Following are a few ideas on where to turn for help (along with some tips on who *not* to turn to!). The essential point, however, is not to wait but to take action. You can work directly with your mortgage servicer, but the servicer may offer you only what it thinks is the easiest solution, not the one you need, because the servicer doesn't know your situation in detail.

Finding good help for free

A number of housing counseling agencies are available to help you work out a solution. We strongly recommend that you use a third-party intermediary that's approved by the U.S. Department of Housing and Urban Development (HUD). These intermediaries are cheap, experienced, and knowledgeable and can help guide you through what can seem like an insurmountable problem. They're experts at getting the right information on the right forms and to the right person at the mortgage servicer — no easy task!

TIP

Although the contact information may change over time and new players are continually offering this service, you can look for resources through Fannie Mae's Know Your Options website, www.knowyouroptions.com, or HUD's website, www.hud.gov; contact BALANCE at 888-456-2227 or go to www.balancepro.org; or contact 995Hope at 888-995-4673 or go to https://995hope.org. For the fastest service, call or go online for a virtual visit before you visit an office. You can also get good help by contacting the National Foundation for Credit Counseling at www.nfcc.org/what-we-offer/homeownership-counseling or 866-557-2227. Many credit counselors are also HUD-certified housing counselors. See Chapter 4 for additional sources of help.

Working with your mortgage servicer

If you're unable to make a mortgage payment on time, you can contact your mortgage company for help. If you believe that this may be the beginning of a serious problem that needs serious attention, ask for the *loss mitigation department,* which may be referred to as the *workout department* or the *homeownership retention department.* This department is able to go the extra mile to help you and can deal with complex issues better than the standard collection department, which usually offers only to make catch-up payment arrangements. To find the contact information for these departments, you can look in your mortgage loan documents, on your monthly statement, or in the correspondence you've received from your mortgage servicer. When you call, get names and extension numbers so that you can try to keep a single point of contact and continuity. Doing so may not be possible, but knowing who you talked to, when you talked, and what you agreed on is important in case matters get really serious. Take good notes!

Keeping the call simple is a blessing to everyone concerned, so we suggest that you do some homework before you call and have a written, well-thought-out proposal prepared that meets your needs and helps solve your problem. Be sure to include what concessions you need and for how long. We also suggest that you write down what happened, what changed, and how to contact you or your counselor if you're working with one. Writing down the facts and options before you call helps you keep from drifting during the conversation and keeps everyone focused on the task at hand. When you ask for what you need, be sure to ask what other options may be available beyond the one that's offered.

TIP

If you want some free help on figuring out what specific help you need to ask for, we suggest that you contact a counselor at 995Hope (888-995-4673 or https://995hope.org) or BALANCE (888-456-2227 or www.balancepro.org).

WARNING

If you can't resolve your issue quickly or if you get transferred to multiple people, get expert help quickly. Time is precious, and mortgage servicers can easily pass the buck until you find yourself in a foreclosure situation. See the preceding section for information on where to find free help from experts.

Avoiding help that hurts

Some people make a living, and a good one, on the backs of folks in trouble. People who offer to help you with a mortgage problem for a fee are only trying to help themselves. So proceed with caution and consider the following tips as you evaluate any prospective source of help:

>> Don't decide anything while in a panic.

>> Be sure that you're dealing with a HUD-qualified nonprofit organization. Look them up at www.hud.gov.

>> Don't make payments to anyone other than your mortgage servicer or its designee.

>> Be wary of any organization other than your mortgage servicer that contacts you to offer help. It's fine if you call them, but not if they call you!

>> Never sign a contract under pressure.

>> Never sign away ownership of your property.

>> Beware of any company or person who guarantees that they can stop a foreclosure or get your loan modified.

>> If English isn't your first language and a translator isn't provided, use your own.

>> Get a second opinion from a person or an organization that you know and trust.

WARNING

If you're having trouble paying your mortgage, getting a high-risk, expensive second mortgage won't help. It will only keep you from finding real solutions by wasting critical time and money.

If you receive an offer saying that you've been preapproved for a loan, don't get too excited. It only means that you've been preapproved on a very cursory level and only for the offer, not the actual loan. Don't waste too much time chasing preapproved offers.

Alternatives to Going Down with the Ship

If you're having trouble making your mortgage payments, you may have a host of options to help you avoid the expense and upset of losing your home through a foreclosure. Even if you can't or don't want to keep your house, you can still lessen the damage to yourself, your family, and your credit by taking positive action.

TIP

Before you take any action, assess your situation as dispassionately as you can. If stress and anxiety make that impossible, we suggest that you seek help first from a third-party professional such as a nonprofit HUD counselor (see "Finding good help for free" earlier in this chapter) or an attorney. Your situation may not be as bad as you think it is, or it may be worse. What's important is to know for sure where you stand. You need what's called *loss mitigation counseling*, which is help to develop a solution that enables you to afford to keep your home or lessen the damage caused by a foreclosure.

This section gives you some loss mitigation options to protect your credit.

What to do first

If you already have a plan to resolve your problem, catch up, or at least resume payments in three to six months, consider the following suggestions:

>> **Find a good nonprofit housing counseling agency.** We recommend the Hope Hotline (888-995-4673), 995Hope (888-995-4673 or https://995hope.org), BALANCE (888-456-2227 or www.balancepro.org) or another nonprofit credit counseling agency that has a HUD-approved housing counseling program. Expect an assessment of your overall financial picture and whether you can realistically afford your mortgage payments.

>> **Ask your mortgage servicer about a repayment plan.** The servicer sets up a structured payment plan (sometimes called a *special forbearance plan*) that gets the mortgage back on track in three to six months by making up past-due amounts in addition to your regular payments. Get all the terms in writing so that you're both clear on the terms. The sooner you do so the less damage to your credit report and score.

>> **Check the HUD (**www.hud.gov**) and Fannie Mae (**www.knowyouroptions.com/options-finder**) websites for resources and help.** Both sites have excellent referral resources, information on programs that might be right for you, and warnings to keep you from falling for scams.

>> **Don't wait until it's too late!** Talk to your lender about your need for assistance, and do it soon. Some servicers have programs for those who are not yet delinquent and other programs for borrowers who already are delinquent. For the greatest number of options, get started as soon as you know that you have a problem making your mortgage payments as agreed, and be sure to ask for all the options your servicer may have for you.

What to do for more serious problems

For problems that may take longer than three to six months to remedy, ask for mortgage loan forbearance or loan modifications.

A *forbearance* temporarily modifies or eliminates payments that are made up at the end of the forbearance period. This is where the lender allows you a period of time (usually three to six months), during which time you can make lower or no payments. This option also prevents your credit from being damaged by a string of late payments.

A *repayment plan* is a payment arrangement agreed upon by the lender to accept partial extra payments from you until the delinquent amount is repaid. For example, if the monthly payment is $1,200 and the mortgage is three months delinquent, the lender may allow the borrower to pay $1,800 per month for six months. However, if no agreement is made, lenders will generally reject a partial payment.

A *loan modification* permanently changes one or more terms of the original mortgage in a way that addresses your specific needs. If this option seems intimidating, use a HUD-approved agency to deal with the servicer and offer solutions on your behalf. Clear communication is key here.

Modifications need to be in writing and approved by both the servicer and the borrower. Don't be surprised if the servicer asks for a fee to cover the costs of processing a loan modification.

TIP

To read the Mortgage Forgiveness Debt Relief Act, go to www.govinfo.gov/content/pkg/PLAW-110publ142/pdf/PLAW-110publ142.pdf. To read the Coronavirus Aid, Relief, and Economic Security (CARES) Act, which may allow you to suspend mortgage payments, go to www.congress.gov/116/bills/hr748/BILLS-116hr748enr.pdf.

What to do to end matters

Even when you can't solve your problem or just can't stand it anymore, you're better off staying in control of the process rather than just giving up. Doing so can lessen credit damage and expenses and keep your dignity — and maybe your sanity — intact.

The following are some of the many options available. And don't forget that another reason to use a free professional mortgage counselor is that newer options may be available to you as well. Be sure to check out the resources mentioned in the section "Knowing Where to Turn for Help," earlier in this chapter.

>> **Sell your home:** You may be able to sell your home in a short sale if you have no equity left or a pre-foreclosure sale if the value of the house still exceeds the amount due on the mortgage.

>> **Short sale:** You get your lender to allow you to sell your home for less than the mortgage value. This option is generally cheaper for the bank and less stressing for the homeowner than a foreclosure. Because it is good for the lender, you can negotiate a bit. Ask that the loan deficiency be reported to the credit bureau as a zero balance rather than a charge-off.

TIP

The Mortgage Forgiveness Debt Relief Act of 2007 exempts up to $2 million of forgiven mortgage debt, subject to certain conditions, from federal taxes. (The full text of the act is available at www.govinfo.gov/content/pkg/PLAW-110publ142/pdf/PLAW-110publ142.pdf.) As we wrote this book, the act was due to expire on January 1, 2021. The act initially covered a three-year period through 2010 but was extended five times to 2012, 2014, 2016, 2017, and 2019. It applies to debt that is discharged or forgiven as the result of a written agreement entered into before January 1, 2021, even if the actual discharge occurs later.

The CARES Act directs lenders holding federally backed mortgages to suspend payments for up to a maximum of 360 days if you've experienced financial hardship due to the COVID-19 pandemic. You also won't be charged late fees or reported to the credit bureau. Foreclosures and evictions on eligible loans have been halted until December 31, 2020, as of this writing. If your loan isn't federally backed, check with the lender to see what options are available. (The full text of the act is available at www.congress.gov/116/bills/hr748/BILLS-116hr748enr.pdf.)

>> **Pre-foreclosure sale:** A pre-foreclosure sale arrangement allows you to defer mortgage payments that you can't afford while you sell your house. It also keeps late payments off your credit report.

>> **Deed-in-lieu of foreclosure:** If the home can't be sold, you can sign the title over to the lender and move out. To qualify for this option, you usually can't have a second mortgage, a home equity loan, or another lien on the property.

>> **Stopping payments as part of a plan:** Not our favorite option, but if your plan is to save money for rent or for the larger down payment you'll need for a new place to live, then setting aside the money you would have paid for your mortgage can accrue several months or even years of savings. The price can be high in credit damage and stress, however. See "Strategic default: Stopping payments" later in this section.

Managing a foreclosure

If you're being foreclosed on, you still may have the option to talk to the servicer and try to work things out, buy more time to come up with a solution, or at least make a more dignified exit from your home. But again, timing is very important, so don't wait!

>> **Get a HUD-approved counselor involved and review loss mitigation options with your servicer.** Most want to help. (Check out "Knowing Where to Turn for Help" earlier in this chapter.)

>> **Remain in contact with the servicer's loss mitigation staff until you get a solution you can live with.** If they don't offer workable suggestions, ask to speak to managers and vice presidents or higher. This is not a time to stand on protocol or accept "I'm sorry" for an answer.

>> **See an attorney.** Ask for options. Review all the mortgage and foreclosure documents to be sure they were properly drawn and executed. The technical phrase used here is *truth in lending compliance.* Ask about bankruptcy options and timing so that you know all options available to you.

Strategic default: Stopping payments

A *strategic default* is an intentional mortgage default based on a plan or strategy. Here's an example: A person has a home whose value has fallen so far below what is owed on the mortgage that he will never realistically recover enough equity to break even on the home. Because the house will never be worth what is being paid, the homeowner stops paying the mortgage. This option is more popular in states with *nonrecourse mortgages* (meaning that the house is the sole security for the mortgage loan, and the homeowner isn't responsible for any shortage beyond what the house brings at sale). However, you need to understand some of the possible consequences:

>> **Credit score:** Any defaulted payments (delinquency) and foreclosure will show up on your credit report and lower your credit score. How much your score will be reduced depends on your score *before* the default and other credit activity. A lower score means you may have more difficulty when trying to get approved for credit in the future. If you're able to be approved, you may end up with a higher interest rate.

>> **Housing:** After foreclosure, buying a new home can be difficult. With a foreclosure on a credit report, you may have to wait three years before you can qualify for a Federal Housing Authority (FHA) mortgage (one year on rare occasions) and two to eight years before you can qualify for a *conforming mortgage* (the most common type of non-government loan), depending on the lender.

>> **Deficiency balance:** This is the difference between what the lender sells your home for after foreclosure and what you owe on the mortgage. In some states, called *recourse states,* the lender can sue you for the deficiency balance, which may allow them to garnish your wages or take other collection actions against you. In nonrecourse states, the lender generally cannot sue you for the deficiency balance, although there may be some exceptions. For example, nonrecourse protection may not apply to a refinanced loan or second mortgage.

Other factors to consider include how much longer you would like to stay in the home and how far underwater you are. If you're $25,000 underwater and your home suits your long-term needs, it probably makes sense to just stay put and wait for the market to recover. But if you're $100,000 underwater and your job or family situation requires you to move quickly, you may find strategic default more appealing. At the same time, it may not be your only option. For example, you may be able to rent out your home or get your lender to approve a short sale, where you sell your home for less than what you owe on your mortgage.

Thinking about your goals and the implications of strategic default can help you decide if it's the right choice.

TIP

For a chart that shows each state's timeline for foreclosure based upon the last payment installment in each state, go to `https://singlefamily.fanniemae.com/media/6726/display`.

According to the Federal Reserve strategic default among deeply underwater borrowers (those whose home values are way below what's owed on the mortgage) is less common than originally thought. Unemployment appears to be a bigger cause. Another consideration is that due to some local exemptions, collecting deficiencies is unlikely in some states.

Strategic default is a high-credit-damage strategy, but it may be cost-effective depending on your situation and plans involving loans or credit use in the future.

Strategic default is an unfortunate reality for many of the long-term unemployed. Thousands of homeowners are stopping payments on homes that they can no longer afford or that are deeply underwater. The argument goes: After all, this is business, and businesses routinely stop paying on debts that they can't afford or that are worth less than they owe. You probably have been told that you have to pay your bills, honor your obligations, and keep your promises, but many home buyers are taking a business rather than a personal approach to their homes and finances.

Most mortgages detail what happens if you don't pay. Either you pay or your home is taken away. So the question arises: If you tell the bank to go ahead and take the house, are you meeting your obligations? From the bank's perspective, clearly you're not. From your family's perspective, however, the answer may be different.

Some states require all mortgages to be *nonrecourse,* meaning that the lender has recourse to the defaulted property and nothing else. Also consider that the Mortgage Forgiveness Debt Relief Act prohibits the IRS from taxing as income any *recourse* mortgage debt forgiven up to $1 million ($2 million if filing jointly) from a foreclosure, short sale, or deed-in-lieu action until January 1, 2021.

Staying in a home you can't afford can deprive your family of your precious savings, empty your retirement accounts, and eventually ruin your credit when you finally default. Many people are willing to put up with the price of any shame or guilt in order to ensure a faster recovery with more money in their bank accounts.

Dealing with Deficiencies

When all is said and done, you may still owe some money. If your home sells for less than the amount you still owe on the mortgage, plus fees, then you may have what's called a *deficiency balance.* For example, say you borrow $500,000 to purchase a home, but you fall behind on payments or walk away from the home, and the bank forecloses. The home ultimately sells for $400,000. The $100,000 that the lender loses on the deal is called a *deficiency.* A first mortgage holder may or may not forgive this amount. Second mortgage holders often go after the borrower for deficiencies.

Your lender can get a deficiency judgment lien against your personal property and any other real estate that you own, giving it a security interest in that property. This means that the bank could foreclose on other real estate if you have enough equity for the bank to think that it might get enough money to make the effort worthwhile. However, just because the lender gets a deficiency judgment does not mean that it will try to collect. The lender may opt to write off the debt and issue you an IRS Form 1099-C. If this happens, you might owe taxes on the forgiven amount. See the discussion of the Mortgage Forgiveness Debt Relief Act of 2007 earlier in this chapter.

If a lender comes after you for a large deficiency, consider speaking to an attorney about the benefits of filing for bankruptcy versus trying to work out a payment agreement with the lender. This can help to ensure you're making the best possible decision for your situation.

The most important thing is to realize that your problems may not be over when you leave the home. You may need to deal with the IRS if you don't qualify for mortgage debt forgiveness under its rules.

The following are some potential, and we stress *potential*, situations you may face and what you can do to deal with them:

>> **The lender may ask for a note.** Although this practice isn't current among first mortgage holders, we want you to be aware of it for the future, or if your second mortgage holder loses money on your loan. This note isn't written on monogrammed stationery; it's a promise to pay an unsecured amount to

cover the mortgage deficiency after the sale. Use an attorney if your lender mentions this to you.

» **The lender may send a demand letter.** A mortgage lender may send a demand for payment of any deficiency following the sale of a home. The lender uses a *demand letter* if it doesn't want to give you an unsecured loan for the balance due. In essence, the problem is all yours, and you need to work out a way to pay the balance. Again, if this happens, get an attorney to advise you.

» **The lender may forgive what you owe.** More likely among first mortgage holders, forgiveness isn't required. This gesture is nice as far as it goes, but the IRS counts forgiven debt as income. Forms 1099-A and 1099-C, which are normally used to document unreported income, are also used to report forgiven debt. The amount of the forgiven debt becomes taxable income in most cases, unless you're covered by the Mortgage Forgiveness Debt Relief Act. Remember, the law was extended and provides benefits through January 1, 2021.

Debt reduced through mortgage restructuring, as well as mortgage debt forgiven in connection with a foreclosure, may qualify for this relief. If you spent the forgiven debt money to pay a car loan, credit card bills, or for any non–real estate purpose, it's not covered, and you'll get a tax bill for it. Debt on second homes, rental property, and business property doesn't qualify.

TIP

If you are a foreclosed borrower faced with a sizable 1099-C, you still have hope. If you file IRS Form 982, Reduction of Tax Attributes Due to Discharge of Indebtedness, and you're insolvent at the time of the forgiven debt, the IRS may forgive the liability. (You can find IRS Form 982 at www.irs.gov/pub/irs-pdf/f982.pdf.) Again, see your attorney for the details.

If you receive a Form 1099-C from your mortgage lender for the current tax year, or if you filed a tax return for the prior tax year that included income from mortgage loan forgiveness, this option may be for you. If you meet the requirements of the Qualified Principal Residence Indebtedness (QPRI) exclusion, you don't have to report the forgiven principal as income on your tax return. The QPRI exclusion may allow an exclusion up to $1 million (up to $2 million for married couples) of forgiven debt from their taxable income.

» **The state you live in makes mortgages nonrecourse.** If you live in certain states, you may get a break relating to personal mortgage deficiencies. Some states have passed laws saying that you're not responsible for any mortgage deficiencies.

Preparing for "Credit Winter"

After a foreclosure, your credit will be severely damaged — in some cases and for some purposes, for years to come. Knowing that post-foreclosure credit is hard to come by, you're wise to give some thought to how you'll cope with the credit fallout that may seem like the equivalent of a nuclear winter (see more in Chapter 17).

When you realize that you may be getting in trouble with your mortgage, you can do some things to protect your access to credit in the "credit winter" that often follows a foreclosure. Like the biblical farmer who put aside grain for the lean years to come, you can store up some credit in advance. Here's how:

>> **Review your credit cards to make sure that you have enough credit available.** Open new credit cards before you become delinquent on your mortgage. Doing so ensures that you can lead a more normal credit life while your credit is recovering. Plus, using and paying off multiple cards each month provides new streams of positive data to help repair your damaged credit report.

>> **Establish a personal line of credit at your local bank or credit union that is not secured by your home.**

>> **If you're planning to make a large financed purchase such as a car (purchase or lease), major appliance, or furniture down the road, consider making it before you become delinquent on your mortgage, while your credit is still strong.**

>> **Prepare a short explanation (called a *consumer statement*) of why you defaulted and what you've done to make sure it won't happen again, and have that statement placed in your credit report.** It's like an exit statement that explains why you left your last job in the best possible light. This explanation may be useful if you need to find a new job that checks your credit report, are up for a promotion at work, or are looking for new housing.

Curing Medical Debt

For any health decision, it's always important for you to understand your rights. Whether it's patient privacy, informed consent, or otherwise. State and federal laws provide a variety of protections when it comes to healthcare. However, it's always important to be your own advocate or ensure you assign it to someone who has your best interest.

Receiving a medical bill in the mail doesn't impact your credit score, but if you don't pay it and it goes to a collection agency, it will likely be reported to the bureau. This is when it impacts your score. The challenge is that you may not know when the healthcare provider is sending it to a collection agency because it could be different from provider to provider often from 60 to 180 days or some time in between.

Understanding new reporting and scoring rules

Because of the amount of time it can take even a well person to review and challenge a hospital bill and then to wrangle with an insurer over coding or coverages, the three major credit bureaus standardize medical debt reporting and protect consumers' credit reports from being unduly affected by medical debt. Equifax, Experian, and TransUnion now allow a 180-day waiting period before medical debt appears on your credit report. By taking action within those 180 days, you can prevent medical bills from hurting your credit score.

Medical debt can stay on your credit report for seven years, so an unpaid medical debt on your credit report can weigh heavily on your score if it's sent to a collection agency and is over 180 days old. Curing your medical debt can often be the difference in a change to your score, especially as you deal with the health of you and your family.

Reviewing your options for paying medical bills

Take specific and timely action to negotiate your medical bills, ideally before the treatment or procedure, but you can also contact the provider afterward and discuss options. Consider setting up a repayment plan — many healthcare providers would rather work out a plan with you than refer it to a collection agency. If you don't have healthcare insurance and have to pay out of pocket, you may also find resources to check costs on procedures in your area. Healthcare Bluebook (www.healthcarebluebook.com) and FAIR Health Consumer (www.fairhealth consumer.org) allow you to research average costs of specific procedures in your area. This can also be helpful when negotiating prices for procedures.

Note that state and federal laws have also changed. When a hospital charges you for a particular procedure, it sends the bill to your insurance company. You, of course, then owe the healthcare insurance plan. However, in some cases, when you call your healthcare insurance company, they may even write off your debt, but you have to contact your healthcare plan. Look for an area that says, "If you cannot pay your bill, contact us at this phone number." The major healthcare plans all have community benefits that require them to write off debts.

REMEMBER

If you don't contact and talk to them, they can't help you.

Discovering how insurers get your medical information

In June 1995, the Federal Trade Commission (FTC) announced that it had reached an agreement with the largest insurance provider to provide the same guarantees and protections from unfair treatment in credit and employment investigations for consumers applying for health, disability, and life insurance as they provide to millions of consumers under the Fair Credit Reporting Act (FCRA). See Chapter 4 for more information.

The establishment of the Medical Information Bureau (MIB) effective October 2, 1995, required that all insurance companies that are members of the MIB abide by the FCRA. What does this mean? That you have to be informed when a consumer report (or information included in the MIB) played any part in the insurer's decision to deny coverage or to charge a higher rate. The insurance company must notify you of the name and address of the consumer reporting agency that provided the report, which in this case, would be the MIB. As a result, you're entitled to receive a free copy of your report from the MIB, if requested within 30 days, to verify the information is correct.

Any health, disability, and life insurance provider that is a member of the MIB must give notice to you if they received information from the MIB concerning you, it was used to alert the provider for possible further investigation of your insurability, and the application for the insurance was rated or declined in whole or part because of the information obtained from that investigation.

MIB also provides assistance to finding lost life insurance or unclaimed funds if a loved one has passed away.

To request your consumer report from the MIB, go to www.mib.com.

Monitoring insurance claims for errors

Centralized, comprehensive statistics or reporting regarding errors in medical insurance claims don't exist, but some studies have shed some light on the subject. One audit study from Equifax in 1988 found that 98 percent of hospital bills contained mistakes. The audit of thousands of bills from more than 5,000 public, private, and university hospital bills were reviewed, and an average bill at that time was $39,000, while the average mistake was $1,488. Yikes! Other more recent studies and articles indicate estimates of 30 percent to 80 percent of bills contain errors.

One of our friends found out that her healthcare plan had accidentally created two separate accounts, and she didn't realize she was being charged separately to each account for her healthcare procedures. This resulted in two different bills and doubled the amount she owed — but she didn't realize that the account numbers were different because the procedures were the same! When she sat down with a healthcare administrator, she was able to get the accounts combined and corrected. She even ended up with a $400 refund! You may be one of those people who hate opening medical bills that come in the mail, but this is an area that requires an extra level of diligence. Go through the entire bill and ask questions to make sure you understand the charges.

Dealing with denied medical claims

Be aware of your options if you have denied medical claims. If your medical claim has been denied you may want to consider the following:

>> **Contact your healthcare provider and advise them of your situation.** If you can't pay, you have options. And if you don't have medical insurance, contact the hospital or provider. Most hospitals are required by the IRS to provide benefits back to their communities. Eliminating your debt can certainly qualify as one of those benefits!

>> **If your insurance claim is denied, file an appeal.** This includes writing a letter to your insurance company. The deadline for submitting an appeal is noted in your denial letters. You may have to ask your doctor for assistance if she disagrees with the insurance company or reach out to your insurance regulators for help. For help with filing an appeal, go to www.healthcare.gov/marketplace-appeals/getting-help.

>> **If you cannot be an advocate yourself, find a medical billing advocate who can provide you the help you need.** See resources in Chapter 12 for more professional help or fee-for-service advocate organizations.

Managing Student Loans

Student loans can be a great way to establish a good credit history, as long as you pay them as you agreed. In 2018, the U.S. Department of Education's Office of Federal Student Aid reflected more than 42 million student loan borrowers in the United States totaling more than $1.4 trillion in outstanding debt.

Graduating from college is an exciting time, a time when you can begin a career and potentially move to another location. In many cases, you have a grace period (usually 6 or 9 months, depending upon the type of loan) before you have to begin repayment. Some circumstances — like active-duty military service, loan consolidation, leaving school, or dropping below half-time enrollment — may affect the grace period.

Default timelines

For student loans, the first day after you miss a payment, the loan becomes past due or delinquent, and it remains delinquent until you pay the past-due amount or make other arrangements. If your loan is delinquent for 90 days, your student loan will be reported to the three major national credit bureaus.

TIP

If you feel like you won't be able to make your student loan payment, contact your loan servicer. You may be able to defer your payment based upon the Federal Student Aid definition for discretionary income. If your income is up to 150 percent of the poverty guidelines for your state and family size, deferral may be an option.

If deferral isn't an option, you may want to consider modification of your repayment plan. A graduated repayment plan usually starts with a smaller payment and then graduates to a higher payment for ten years or up to 30 years, if consolidated.

Loan forgiveness programs

In 2018, the U.S. Department of Education initiated a program to allow you to be reconsidered for loan forgiveness under temporary expansion of the Public Service Loan Forgiveness Program. There are specific conditions in which some or all payments can be made on a William D. Ford Federal Direct Loan. It's offered on a first come, first served basis and is only available until the $350 million appropriation has been allocated or other criteria are met. To find out if you qualify for the loan forgiveness program, go to https://studentaid.gov/manage-loans/forgiveness-cancellation/public-service/temporary-expanded-public-service-loan-forgiveness.

If you're a veteran who is totally and permanently disabled, you may qualify to have your loan forgiven. You have 60 days from the date of your notification of eligibility to decline the loan discharge, which you may decide to do because of tax liability in your state or if it makes it more difficult for you to receive future student loans.

Where to get help

We always recommend a discussion with a nonprofit credit counselor, because they're trained to know how to help you create the best plan for your situation. Contact BALANCE (888-456-2227 or www.balancepro.org) or the National Foundation for Credit Counseling (800-388-2227 or www.nfcc.org) to find a nonprofit credit counseling agency near you.

If you need help with managing the repayment of your student loan, go to the Office of the U.S. Department of Education at https://studentaid.gov/manage-loans/repayment#.

If you're a totally and permanently disabled veteran, check out www.disability discharge.com.

The impact of the CARES Act on student loans

The Department of Education has been monitoring the COVID-19 pandemic. Prior to the enactment of the CARES Act, the Secretary of Education gave direction to the Department of Education to provide relief to the Department of Education's federal student loans. It included the suspension of loan payments, cessation of collection activity on defaulted loans, and a reduction of interest to 0 percent for 60 days.

The CARES Act included relief on the Department of Education's federal student loans through September 30, 2020, which has been extended as of this writing to December 31, 2020, and may be extended further. For updates and additional information, go to https://studentaid.gov/announcements-events/coronavirus.

For information regarding student loan repayments, go to https://studentaid.gov/manage-loans/repayment.

Avoiding Car Repossession

When you finance a car or truck, the lender holds certain rights on the property until you make your final loan payment. This means that if you default on the contract by missing payments, they have the right to *repossess* (take back) the vehicle.

If you're having financial trouble, contact your lender immediately. Don't wait until you've missed a payment or two. Depending on the state where you reside, the lender may not need a court order or provide advance warning to repossess the vehicle. In some cases, they may repossess after just one missed payment!

Before the vehicle is repossessed, review your spending plan or contact a non-profit credit counseling agency (see Chapter 4). See if there are any areas of your budget where you can cut back. Maybe you can get a second job or a part-time job to add to your income. If you can't make changes that will enable you to afford the payments, you have a few options:

>> You can contact your lender and ask for assistance.

>> If the vehicle's value is more than you owe on the loan, you may want to consider selling the vehicle.

>> You may decide to give the vehicle back to the lender. This is called a *voluntary repossession.* Not only can a voluntary repossession save you the repossession fee, but the lender may also agree to waive the deficiency balance and not report it as a repossession on your credit report. (Get these promises in writing!)

Don't be afraid to contact your lender. In almost all cases, they don't want the vehicle — they want you to repay the loan. So, the earlier you make this contact, the better. If you wait until after you've missed a payment, it may be too late. If you've looked at your cash flow and know what you have to work with, you can begin to negotiate. Explain your situation — whether it's temporary or permanent, and how much money you have (if any) to go toward the payment. Your options for resolution may include the following:

>> **Making no or reduced payments for a period of time:** When that time is up, you either increase your future payments until you repay the balance due or add the amount you owe to the loan and make extra payments at the end.

>> **Refinancing your loan:** If your credit rating is good and the value of your vehicle is greater than the loan balance, you may be able to refinance the loan with a better interest rate or longer payment term, which would reduce your monthly payments. For example, if you have two years left on your loan, you may be able to get a new loan where you have five years to repay, which will reduce the payment because of the longer time frame.

WARNING

AVOIDING "KICKING THE TRADE" SCAMS

Kicking the trade is one of those shady car salesman tactics that make us cringe. A trade-in where you, as the buyer, trade in your current vehicle as credit toward another vehicle is often critical in the car-buying process. However, a practice known as "kicking the trade" has dealers telling buyers to give their cars back to their lenders (voluntary repossession) while selling them a new one. Don't fall for it! When dealerships "kick the trade," you leave the dealership with two loans and two vehicles for which you're now on the hook. It's hard to say how prevalent this practice is, but it can definitely make for a worse situation than the one you had when you walked into the dealership.

Repossession: What you can do

If you can't make a payment arrangement with your lender and you don't make your payments, eventually the lender can hire someone to repossess the vehicle. If that happens, you have a few options:

» **Reinstating the contract:** Depending on your state and the contract, you may have the right to *reinstate* the contract (pay all past-due installments, including late fees and costs the lender has incurred in repossessing and storing the property).

» **Redeeming the car:** You may be able to *redeem* the car (pay off the whole debt for the car in one lump sum, including late fees and costs the lender has incurred in repossessing and storing the property).

Not all states have these options, nor do all contracts, so check with your lender on what options may be available to you after a repossession.

Dealing with auto loan default deficiencies

If you can't reinstate the contract or redeem the car (see the preceding section), the lender will sell the car at a wholesale auction. Whether you or someone else buys it, you'll be responsible for the deficiency balance if the vehicle sells for less than the loan amount. A *deficiency balance* is the difference between the amount that you owed on the loan and the price the vehicle sold for at auction — plus repossession, storage, and auction costs.

With car repossessions, there is almost always a deficiency balance. Some lenders may sue for this sum, while others may try to work with you to repay it or even forgive it. If the lender does forgive it, the IRS will consider that amount income and will assess taxes due on the forgiven debt.

In some circumstances, the lender may decide that the deficiency balance is uncollectible and "charge off" the loan as an unsecured debt. This generally means that the lender will claim it as a loss to its business. However, you should be aware that the dealer may still sell this "uncollectible" debt to a collection agency, which will then seek you out to collect on the loan.

Coping with So-Called Acts of God and Other Things That Are Not Your Fault

It seems as though, just when you think you can get your finances together, something else comes along beyond your control (for example, a natural disaster, a pandemic, or a terrorist attack).The good news is that, often, when disasters occur (and depending upon significance of the impact), programs are set up to assist those in need.

You're more than likely dealing with many other important things after a disaster, but timely action is key. Missing payments can significantly impact your credit score, even if you were injured, your home was destroyed, or you lost your job. If you're having financial difficulty as a result of the disaster, or you think you'll have trouble keeping up with your financial obligations, don't wait until after you've missed your payment to contact your lenders or creditors. Even the IRS may have access to additional hardship options. These are specific actions that can help put your mind at ease during these difficult times.

Creditors can add information or special codes when they report to the credit bureaus to grant special treatment to victims of natural disasters. In the past, those codes neutralized positive and negative information on your score, which may have resulted in your score being reduced. Recently, the VantageScore was modified so that missed payments for these victims are neutralized so your credit score isn't impacted if you aren't able to pay your bills during this time.

TIP

Monitor your credit reports for fraudulent activity after a natural or declared disaster. After the declaration of the pandemic, the three national credit reporting bureaus made it possible for you to request a free credit report each week through April 2021.

TIP

Check out www.experian.com/blogs/ask-experian/how-does-a-natural-or-declared-disaster-impact-my-credit for helpful links and tips on coping with a disaster.

Chapter **8**

Filing for and Recovering from Bankruptcy

B ankruptcy used to be easy. You decided that you were too far over your head in debt, and you went to see an attorney, who made your debts disappear. The result was a surge in bankruptcy filings, with losses hitting more than $60 billion. Creditors, ever vigilant of their bottom lines, noticed. As a result, in 2005, new and more restrictive bankruptcy laws were enacted to reduce the significant losses and abuse of the old bankruptcy system. Although the bankruptcy laws changed in 2005, the option to file bankruptcy is still available, if needed. What hasn't changed, however, is our opinion that bankruptcy should be your last resort.

Still, bankruptcy can be a cure for over-indebtedness that threatens to deprive you and your family of the hope for a prosperous financial future. A fresh start is the intent of the law, and, when done correctly and for the right reasons, that's exactly what you get. Either way, you have to decide whether the hit to your credit for cleaning up your finances is worth it.

Assessing the role bankruptcy plays in your life for years to come as a result of damaged credit and long waiting periods before you can file again, should give you pause. With credit playing an increasingly important role in most Americans' financial lives, the damage a bankruptcy can do to your future had better be worth it. But how do you know whether bankruptcy is right for your situation? How do you know which type or chapter of bankruptcy you qualify for and which bills you'll still be responsible for after you file?

This chapter gives you an accurate and unbiased picture of how bankruptcy law works, helping you figure out whether bankruptcy makes sense, which type of bankruptcy is best for your situation, and how to minimize a bankruptcy's effects on your credit. Sometimes people go into bankruptcy without a full understanding of the consequences or they file for the wrong reasons; instead of providing them with a fresh start, it places them in situations that impact their lives more and for longer than anticipated. However, this chapter can help you see past the legal fine print and consider what may be the most important financial decision you'll make in the next seven to ten years.

Deciding Whether Bankruptcy Makes Sense for You

Declaring bankruptcy is a big decision that affects your life, your self-esteem, and your confidence for seven to ten years or even longer. It creates a condition that redefines your credit report, lowers your credit score, and may also cause issues for future credit and employment.

Both financial and quality-of-life components may factor into your decision to file for bankruptcy. The benefits gained may outweigh the damage to your credit. If your wages are about to be garnished because of your inability to pay a bill — perhaps a totally unexpected medical bill — do you allow your family to suffer the financial consequences for years, or seemingly forever? More than half of those who file bankruptcy have large uninsured or underinsured medical expenses. In other words, bankruptcy is a major life event, so you want to consider it very seriously. Don't get us wrong — bankruptcy may absolutely just be the best choice if you've suffered some serious financial setbacks. Before rushing into the decision to file, you need to invest time in carefully weighing all your options before you take the plunge.

Deliberating the bankruptcy decision

When facing this decision, you may already be feeling more pressure than you thought you could bear, but it's a great time to take a step back and evaluate your situation. Can you do anything more to help meet your obligations? Is there any hope of finding a solution that's acceptable to both you and your creditors? If you answered no to both questions, we think you're on the right track in considering bankruptcy. Have an objective third-party professional evaluate the situation if you can.

Before you make the final decision, review the following:

» **Be sure that bankruptcy will actually solve your financial crisis.** Getting rid of all your debts and making those annoying collection calls go away may solve your current problems, but if the real problem is too much spending and not enough income, declaring bankruptcy will just be a short-term fix with long-term consequences. Likewise, bankruptcy won't help if you've been using credit to supplement your income for basic living expenses. More significant behavioral changes will be required.

» **Understand the consequences of your decision on your near-term goals.** Ask yourself how this decision will affect your chances of buying a home, getting married or divorced, or getting a job. Think about your goals for the next ten years, and understand the impact that a bankruptcy would have on those goals. Bankruptcy is a big step, and its consequences may affect you for years to come. Don't make the decision based only on immediate events without considering the future impacts, because that would be a mistake.

» **Consider all your options.** Make a list of other ways to deal with your debts. Can you increase your income? Reduce your expenses? Stretch out your payments? Sell some possessions to pay your bills until your situation improves? Find good resources in your community to help you evaluate all your options, such as Legal Aid (www.lsc.gov/what-legal-aid/find-legal-aid), the National Foundation for Credit Counseling (www.nfcc.org), 995Hope (https://995hope.org), and BALANCE (www.balancepro.org).

» **Talk to a good credit counselor.** You'll be required to meet with a credit counselor within six months of filing for bankruptcy even if you've met with one before. Expect this visit to give you options; an analysis of your spending and income, including a written budget; and an action plan. This consultation goes a long way toward answering the question of whether bankruptcy will help you. See Chapter 4 for more on credit counselors.

» **Get a professional legal opinion.** Find a lawyer who has a great deal of experience in bankruptcy law. Find out whether you qualify for bankruptcy and, if so, which chapter. Make sure you understand what bankruptcy can and can't do for you. Ask about alternatives, including settlements and statutes of limitations. Also ask about the pros and cons of filing for bankruptcy on your own. Called *pro se*, the law allows you to represent yourself, and in some courts with sympathetic judges, doing so can be a money-saver. (In other courts, it can be a disaster.) An experienced lawyer is the best person to guide you here.

>> **Talk to your creditors.** Seriously. If you're considering a bankruptcy, let your lenders know and ask if they can offer you a repayment plan. Keep in mind that you have to be able to afford this plan. Don't expect too much, but talking to your creditors is always worth a shot.

>> **Consider the requirements of the current bankruptcy laws.** Here's a brief summary of the most impactful provisions that may help you decide whether a bankruptcy is worth pursuing in your situation:

- **Passing a means test is required to be eligible for Chapter 7.** Except in limited circumstances (check out the "Qualifying for and Filing for Bankruptcy" section later in this chapter to see if you qualify), your net income has to be below the median income in your state of residence to file for liquidation of your debts in a Chapter 7.

- **You're required to get credit counseling from an "approved nonprofit budget and credit counseling agency" before you can file.** The Executive Office of the U.S. Trustee provides a master list of approved agencies from which you may choose. You can find out who's on the list by contacting the clerk of the court where your bankruptcy is to be filed, by going to the U.S. Department of Justice website (www.justice.gov/ust/eo/bapcpa/ccde/cc_approved.htm), or by talking to your attorney. Counseling may be offered by phone, online, or in person.

- **After you file, you must complete a course in financial management before you're discharged from bankruptcy.** You may contact the same provider for this requirement as for the credit counseling requirement, or you can use a different provider. You can find a list of approved providers at www.justice.gov/ust/eo/bapcpa/ccde/de_approved.htm.

- **You're limited in what you can buy immediately before filing.** Having made the decision to file, you're prevented from going out and spending up a storm or taking out cash advances and then not having to pay. Generally, the limits apply to the 90 days preceding your filing.

- **You have to wait a long time after getting a discharge for bankruptcy before you can get another one.** The law requires eight years between Chapter 7 bankruptcy discharges, two years between Chapter 13 bankruptcies, six years between a Chapter 13 and a Chapter 7, and four years between a Chapter 7 and a Chapter 13.

- **Your *homestead exemption* (how much equity in your home you can keep out of your filing and keep for yourself) is limited by state law.** In addition, if you acquired your home less than 40 months before filing, you're allowed a maximum exemption of $170,350, regardless of your state's exemption allowance. Check for updates to this number as it adjusts from time to time.

- **Under Chapter13 bankruptcy, you're allowed to spend only what the IRS guidelines allow.** The rest of your disposable income must be included in the plan, and every year you have to document your income and expenses to see whether you can pay more (or less).

- **Your attorney must certify that what you say in the documents you submit to the court is true.**

- **You still may owe some past and future debts.** These debts include taxes (incurred in the last three years, unfiled, or filed late), domestic support, restitution and fines for drunk-driving injuries and other criminal offenses, and student loans. Courts are extremely reluctant to discharge student loans, and the general policy is not to discharge them. Rarely, some older student loans can be discharged; if an "undue" hardship condition exists, you file a separate motion with the bankruptcy court and then appear before a judge to explain your hardship.

- **Domestic-support obligations are a priority debt that you must pay.** A *priority debt* takes precedence over other debt payments you owe and is paid completely. However, the *bankruptcy trustee* (the person appointed by the court to administer your Chapter 13 plan) gets administrative fees before any money goes to any other creditor or person.

- **You may be evicted if you don't pay your rent after you've filed for bankruptcy.** Bankruptcy creates a time stamp on the debts that you have up to that date. New debts or defaults on new or ongoing credit obligations after filing bankruptcy are not included.

- **You must provide your most recent tax return to your creditors if they ask for it.** Before you can finalize your bankruptcy, you need to give your creditors information about your financial status so they can see that you can't afford to pay what you owe. If you're filing for Chapter 13, you must provide your tax returns for the last four years.

» **Find a small circle of people who care about you.** Although these people may not be professionals, they know you and may offer important perspectives. You don't have to agree with them, but their guidance may be helpful. Avoid visiting with someone who would be personally affected by your choice (such as a person you owe money to, someone who owes you money, or a dependent).

» **Be intentional.** Given your current financial state, will your mindset allow you to use bankruptcy as a fresh start? Consider your goals; weigh the options offered by your creditors, your credit counselor, and your lawyer; and consider the advice of others who care about you. Now you're ready to decide what's best for your future and your peace of mind. Whatever you decide to do, make sure it's the best decision you can make based upon the information that you have. If you don't like what you see, go through the process until you do, and then do what you think is in your best interest. Don't wait too long to make a decision, though. Sometimes the hardest decision may be the best one.

LOCATING A BANKRUPTCY ATTORNEY

A qualified attorney is essential if you're considering filing bankruptcy. We always consider friends, family, or close coworkers who've had a satisfying experience with an attorney as good sources of referrals. Often even one of their attorneys has a connection to a good bankruptcy attorney. We're not suggesting that you shout from the rooftop or blast it on social media, but someone who has already experienced the bankruptcy process may be a good referral source.

Online resources can also be helpful, but make sure you look for good, credible resources. Here are a few that you may want to check out:

- National Association of Consumer Bankruptcy Attorneys (www.nacba.org)
- Lawyers.com (www.lawyers.com)
- American Bankruptcy Institute (www.abiworld.org)

If you've used a lawyer to handle other issues, ask for a referral to someone who specializes in bankruptcy. Don't use your cousin, the real estate lawyer. Get a pro. You have to live with any mistakes made here for years.

Adding up the pluses and minuses

Like anything in life, bankruptcy is neither all good nor all bad. In the following sections, we explain the benefits of bankruptcy, as well as the harsh reality of bankruptcy's consequences.

The silver lining of filing bankruptcy

We're always in favor of hearing the good news first. With bankruptcy, it's no different. Here are some of the positives that bankruptcy can do for you:

>> **You get a fresh start.** The collection activity stops. The fees and penalty rates stop. In fact, in a Chapter 7 bankruptcy, virtually all your debts may go away. Without the ability to put a stop to the madness of credit gone awry, some people would never — and we mean *never* — be able to live a normal life again. Bankruptcy can enable that to happen.

>> **You get credit education.** The bankruptcy law says that anyone who files is required to get some credit education. This is an opportunity to look back at

what happened and reset your financial and credit course going forward. If you take full advantage of this opportunity, you'll walk away with a much better sense of how to manage your financial life, which means that you'll be less likely to end up back where you started.

The darker side of filing bankruptcy

As you can probably guess, filing bankruptcy may create some pretty heavy consequences, too. Here are the major ones:

>> **You may still owe money.** Bankruptcy may not wipe out *all* your debt. Some debts don't go away, even though you'd like them to, and you must pay them in full. The debts that typically don't disappear are

- Federal, state, and local taxes

- Child support

- Alimony

- Student loans (except in very limited circumstances)

- Money owed as a result of drunk driving and other criminal offenses, such as willful injury or damage to people and property

>> **Your credit score will be affected for years.** Bankruptcy is a major negative on your credit report that appears as a public record in your file as well as in your account history for up to ten years. Worse, it causes your credit score to stay depressed longer than a normal delinquency does. Good credit can plunge by 200 points. Declare bankruptcy and you're likely to see your score drop to the lowest 20 percent of all credit scores. Ouch! See Chapter 7 for more info.

>> **Borrowing money becomes more difficult.** When lenders see a score in the lowest percentile, your interest rates and terms escalate. In a tight credit market, lenders may decline to give you credit at any price.

WARNING

Some lenders, however, specialize in loaning to people with bad credit. They're delighted to see you; the fact that you've just gone bankrupt is a big plus in their eyes. Why? Because under the law, you can't file a Chapter 7 bankruptcy again for eight long years. So although lenders get to charge you high interest rates as a risky borrower, you can't avoid repaying them by playing the bankruptcy card. If you fall behind, you can run, but you can't hide. These lenders are very good at collecting overdue accounts. The bottom line: Avoid these lenders at all costs. If you must borrow shortly after a bankruptcy, use a reputable lender.

>> **Renting an apartment may become more complicated.** Many landlords use credit reports to approve tenant applicants. They may refuse to rent to you, require a cosigner, or demand a larger deposit if they see a bankruptcy.

>> **Insurance costs rise.** A bankruptcy may cost you more in insurance premiums, particularly for homeowner's and auto insurance. The insurance mavens and their actuarial elves love credit reports. All those dispassionate numbers lend themselves to justifying rate increases much more than real claims do. So even if you have no claims, expect your premiums to go up. Some states don't allow credit to be a factor in setting rates, but many do.

>> **Employment searches may be more difficult.** There have been some changes in employers utilizing credit reports over the years with recent health and privacy concerns, but many employers still do credit or financial checks on candidates. If you're job hunting, ask questions during the interview to understand the process. As a practical matter, some licenses won't be given to people who've filed for bankruptcy, and security clearances can be denied. See Chapter 11 for more info.

>> **Your self-image and confidence may suffer.** Bankruptcy can take its toll, because like it or not, a great deal of the way many people view themselves is wrapped up in their financial persona. Most people think of themselves as responsible adults, and they've been taught that responsible adults pay their bills and keep their promises. Even though you know that filing for bankruptcy is okay and that you have no choice in the matter, you may find that you have an unexpected internal conflict to deal with.

Considering a debt management plan first

One of the stops you're required to make on the road to getting help from the bankruptcy courts is a credit counseling agency. The court recognizes the value of the work done by these agencies by requiring that a court-approved agency review your financial circumstances (*before* you file). The idea is that you'll get an unbiased assessment of your financial condition and that you may, upon reflection, find other alternatives to handle your debt.

Understanding what a debt management plan is

One of the services provided by the credit counseling industry is the debt management plan. You begin with an individually tailored spending plan that you create with the help of a credit counselor. A *debt management plan* uses the equivalent of your disposable income after actual expenses and reallocates some or all of your income to pay your creditors. Many creditors require that you be able to pay off the balance in 60 months to allow the account to be placed under a debt management plan. The average plan is set up for three to five years but in practice may be completed in about two years. (For more on debt management plans, turn to Chapter 4.)

Seeing how a debt management plan differs from bankruptcy

Under a debt management plan, the money left (if any) after you've paid your living expenses and your creditors is yours to use as you see fit. If you file Chapter 13 bankruptcy, however, all your disposable income goes toward paying off your creditors. The amount you get to use for living expenses with minor adjustments comes from less-than-generous IRS guidelines.

Unlike the terms of a Chapter 7 or a Chapter 13 bankruptcy, a debt management plan is a voluntary arrangement between you and your creditors, using the credit counseling agency as an intermediary. You can walk away from a debt management plan at any time and still file for bankruptcy. Or, if you're on the receiving end of a windfall, you can pay off your creditors and be done with it.

Of course, your creditors don't have to accept the terms of the debt management plan, whereas they *have* to accept a court-ordered repayment plan if you file bankruptcy. That said, most creditors do accept debt management plans because they know that you'll be off to the courthouse to file bankruptcy if they say no. Additionally, if a creditor refuses to negotiate with a credit counselor, the court can order that the uncooperative creditor's debt get a 20-percent haircut.

REMEMBER

Whereas a Chapter 7 bankruptcy liquidates many debts, a Chapter 13 bankruptcy forces creditors to accept a lower payment over a set period that may not cover all that you originally owed. The difference between what you owe and what you pay under Chapter 13 is what the creditors lose. They also can't charge interest or fees under Chapter 13. A debt management plan allows the creditors to collect interest charges, although many creditors reduce the rate to one that's more affordable and reflects your circumstances and your desire to repay the debt.

Perhaps one of the biggest differences between a Chapter 7 or Chapter 13 bankruptcy and a debt management plan is the effect on your credit score. Bankruptcy has a large negative impact on your score, which affects your ability to do lots of the things we mention earlier in this chapter for years after the *end* of your bankruptcy. A debt management plan, on the other hand, doesn't have the same negative impact on your credit score. In fact, many creditors don't report to the credit bureaus that your account is being handled by a credit counseling agency. Those that do report it to the bureaus report it as a description of the account (for example, credit card, real estate mortgage, or credit counseling), not as a payment history item (such as "pays as agreed" or "X days late"). Payment history items are included in calculating your credit score, but account descriptions may not. Further, your credit report shows the credit counseling account description only until you pay off the account or decide to discontinue the plan, at which point the notation is removed.

More good news: Even while you're enrolled in a debt management plan, the FICO scoring system doesn't subtract any points. That's right — your credit score isn't affected. A credit counseling notation on your file is perceived as neutral, not a negative or public-record item.

REMEMBER

If you decide to try the debt management-plan route rather than a Chapter 13 and the debt management plan doesn't work out for you, you can always file for bankruptcy without a waiting period. We suggest that when you get your mandatory counseling on the road to bankruptcy, you explore making a debt management plan work for you. You, your credit, and your score may be glad you did.

Understanding Bankruptcy, Chapter and Verse

Filing for bankruptcy is a very serious decision for which you need to be armed with all the information you can find. Why? Because for all the problems a bankruptcy solves, it can create many more if you make a mistake. As with many laws, bankruptcy laws may seem like a secret code. Besides being long and written in legalese, these laws contain mysterious chapters with numbers — 7, 11, and 13 — rather than names. What do the chapters really mean, and which one is right for you? That's what this section is all about.

In basic terms, the reason for filing bankruptcy is to seek the protection of the court from your creditors. It's that simple. If you can't pay what you owe on your own, now or in the foreseeable future, call in the judge, and the judge will handle your collectors.

The courts allow many different types of bankruptcy, identified as chapters with numbers. The variety of options reflects the variety of solutions needed for different situations. One size doesn't fit all. A farmer's problems and needs differ significantly from a corporation's. A Chapter 12 bankruptcy, for example, allows farmers to reorganize their debt and keep their farms.

Among all the various chapters, two are most commonly used by consumers who find themselves unable to come to agreement with or to meet contractual payments with their creditors:

>> **Chapter 7:** Also known as *liquidation,* this is the most popular form of bankruptcy. It may require you to give up some assets (the liquidation part), but it gets you out of almost all your liabilities.

>> **Chapter 13:** Often referred to as *wage-earner bankruptcy,* this form of bankruptcy allows you to keep most of your assets and pay back what the judge rules you can over a period of time, usually three to five years, under court supervision and protection.

Regardless of which chapter you file, our final advice is to make sure that bankruptcy will truly solve your problems — the problems you have today, the problems you'll have tomorrow, and the complications of dealing with the financial, employment, and insurance systems in the future.

Qualifying for and Filing for Bankruptcy

After reviewing the previous sections, you may determine that bankruptcy is the best or only viable solution for your financial situation. But you still need to see whether you qualify for bankruptcy. Both Chapter 7 and Chapter 13 bankruptcies have eligibility requirements, which we cover in the following sections.

TIP

For a look at the rules, refer to the bankruptcy code filing procedures chart at www. dummies.com/go/creditrepairkitfd5e.

Qualifying for Chapter 7

If qualified, under a Chapter 7, you receive relief from virtually all your debts, with a few exceptions, and you get it fast — like the same day (unlike a Chapter 13, which may take up to five years before you get a discharge).

Passing the means test

The first hurdle in moving forward with Chapter 7 bankruptcy is meeting the *means test.* If you have too many means (that is, too much money), you can't declare Chapter 7. And the courts won't take your word for it; you have to *prove* that your income really is what you say it is. If your income over the last six months is above the applicable median for your state of residence, you can't file for Chapter 7.

TIP

To find out whether your income is above the median in your state of residence, go to the U.S. Census website: www.census.gov/search-results.html?search Type=web&cssp=SERP&q=median income by state. See www.legalconsumer. com/bankruptcy/means-test for a good means-test calculator, which includes the latest revised means tests forms while excluding any CARES Act payments from monthly income.

If your income is above the median, don't give up just yet. Next, you want to determine whether you have excess monthly income of more than $166.66 to pay $10,000 of debt over five years. So what counts as excess income? To find out, you have to use the spending guidelines approved by the IRS. Allowable expenses are shown at https://www.justice.gov/ust/eo/bapcpa/20200501/bci_data/ median_income_table.htm. An updated chart with the allowable expenses for each state can be found under the heading "Median Family Income Based on State/Territory and Family Size." The IRS guidelines may be very tight for you.

Using the IRS allowable expenses as a guide, if you *fail* the means test, the best you can do is to file under Chapter 13.

If you have less excess monthly income than the magic number of $166.66 after IRS expense allowances, you may proceed to the next hurdle: Do you have an extra $100 a month over the next 60 months? And will that $6,000 account for at least 25 percent of your debt? If the answer to both questions is no, you can pass go and file for Chapter 7. If not, you likely go directly to Chapter 13.

TIP

Tithing — giving money to your church — is allowed in both Chapter 7 and Chapter 13 bankruptcies. You may donate up to 15 percent of your gross income and have it count as an expense that may lower your income. Donating to your church may just help you make the numbers work to become eligible for a Chapter 7 rather than a Chapter 13.

Receiving required counseling

At some point during the six months before you file for bankruptcy, you have to receive counseling and get a certificate from a court-approved nonprofit credit counselor.

The Office of the U.S. Trustee has a website (www.justice.gov/ust/credit-counseling-debtor-education-information) that lists approved agencies.

Credit counseling costs are on a sliding fee scale. They are free if your income is below 150 percent of the poverty level for your family size. Otherwise, up to $50 is considered reasonable.

Just because the court has approved the counseling agency doesn't make it the right one for you, so exercise caution when selecting. (See Chapter 4 for guidance in choosing a credit counselor.) You want someone who has a good track record and has electronic-certificate-issuing capability. Why? Because if the counselor makes a mistake or the certificate is delayed in getting to you, you could face costly delays in getting this matter successfully concluded.

Qualifying for Chapter 13

The strict guidelines to qualify for filing a Chapter 7 bankruptcy mean that some people qualify only to file Chapter 13. The requirements for counseling and proof of income are the same for both types of bankruptcy. Although you must take the same means test, the outcome leads to different results.

Chapter 13 differs from Chapter 7 in that, after establishing your income and deducting allowable expenses, you must use the remainder of your excess monthly income to repay your debt. *Excess* is defined by subtracting the IRS allowable expenses from your income (see the earlier "Passing the means test" section).

Just as with Chapter 7, those filing for Chapter 13 bankruptcy must establish that their family income is either below or above the median for their state. If your total income is above the state median, your excess income gets disposed of (paid to your bankruptcy trustee, who forwards it to your creditors) for the next five years, unless you can show that you can pay off 100 percent of the debt in less than 60 months. If your total income is below the state median, your excess income may be paid to your creditors over the next three years. The rest of the debt that you owe to your creditors goes unpaid, and no interest accrues on any of the accounts involved. You also want to understand any tax implications as creditors forgive that debt.

The current bankruptcy law is intended to require those who can afford to make payments toward their debt to do so.

FILING, THEN BACKING OUT

If you decide that bankruptcy isn't for you *after* you file your court papers, you can ask the court to dismiss your case before you get your discharge. For example, say you file a Chapter 7 and then find out that you have to give back that 3-carat diamond ring your sweetie gave you recently. Or in the case of a Chapter 13, maybe you've been making payments and eating peanut butter for a month and can't go on. Or, looking on the bright side, perhaps you get a windfall inheritance from a rich uncle and can pay off the Chapter 13 in one fell swoop.

No matter what the reason, you can call the whole thing off and get a dismissal. Keep in mind, however, that the credit-reporting bureaus pick up the record of your bankruptcy filing and report it, even if you stop the process without getting out of any debts. The bureaus must report that the filing was dismissed, but the record of your filing a bankruptcy stays on your credit report and continues to lower your score for the remainder of the reporting period (up to ten years). Both you and your creditors have the same rights and remedies as you had before you filed your bankruptcy case.

If you ask for a dismissal, you won't be the first to do so. In fact, the law has a specific section that deals with people who not only change their minds but also change them back again. Perhaps after you back out of the bankruptcy to save the diamond ring, your creditors turn up the collection heat to the point where you'd gladly give them the ring and your grandfather's watch if they'd just leave you alone.

Here's how the change works the second time around: In your first filing, after you file the paperwork with the courts, you receive an automatic *stay* (or suspension) of collection activity on the part of your creditors. The length of time for the collection stay can vary depending on the type of debt or action pending, but generally it's in place until you discharge your debts (that is, get rid of them). But if you change your mind, ask for a dismissal, and then change your mind and refile a second time within one year of the original filing, the automatic stay (the stopping of all collection activity) is for only 30 days. So you have to get all your testing, counseling, and paperwork done in the 30-day period or the collectors and foreclosers return in force. If this is your third such filing in a year, you don't get *any* stay unless the court orders it.

In other words, when you file for bankruptcy, do your best to make sure that it's a decision you can live with for the long haul.

When you're confortable that filing bankruptcy is what you want to do, you can stop all collection activity by telling your creditors and/or collectors of your intent. Go to www.dummies.com/go/creditrepairkitfd5e for a sample notification letter declaring your intent to file bankruptcy.

Managing Your Credit After a Bankruptcy

Declaring bankruptcy is more of a hassle than it used to be, and qualifying for relief is definitely harder. But if you take the bankruptcy plunge, don't think that you're out of the woods. You still have to live with the effects of bankruptcy on your credit report and your credit score, as well as the barriers that your new status creates. You're likely to discover that bankruptcy has an impact on your insurance rates and your ability to get hired or licensed. Your bankruptcy status remains on your credit report as the mother of all credit negatives for up to ten years, and that's a long time.

So how do you get a handle on your credit future post-bankruptcy? You rebuild your credit as quickly as possible, and you use credit carefully as you go forward. This section shows you how to do so.

Telling your side of the story

Now that your credit report shows a bankruptcy and will continue to show it for a long time, expect the matter to come up from time to time in a number of life's scenarios. You need to be ready with an explanation of what happened, what you did about it, and why it won't happen again. Work on a short statement that describes your valid reasons for filing for bankruptcy. Businesspeople and potential lenders who have access to your credit report want to know your reasons to help them decide whether to extend you credit or do business with you in general.

Note: This statement *isn't* the 100-word statement we discuss in Chapter 3 that you can attach to your credit report. This is a verbal statement that you make when you're doing anything that requires other parties to review your credit report (applying for a loan, applying for a job, and so on). Be proactive and tell them about your bankruptcy before they see your credit report, but only if you're sure they'll be looking at it. (Why raise the issue if they would never know about it otherwise?)

Like the statement you use to explain why you left your last employer, a tight and targeted statement explaining your bankruptcy may be important. Whatever your circumstances were, your explanation may put a positive spin on the truth. It's short, sweet, and rehearsed. Having it at the ready enables you to convey yourself as confident, professional, and reliable.

BEWARE OF SOLICITATIONS

After you declare bankruptcy, you'll likely face a flurry of solicitations and telemarketing calls from companies that receive notices of your filing. Many businesses use bankruptcy notices as mailing lists for the high-cost credit products or scams that they sell.

Read the fine print on any solicitations, and be suspicious of a company that's eager to give you a new start. You're very vulnerable from both a personal and a financial perspective. This may be a good time to opt out of the credit bureau and direct marketing programs that a lot of solicitors use to send you preapproved offers. If you want your name and address removed from mailing lists obtained from the main consumer credit-reporting agencies, go to www.optoutprescreen.com or call 888-567-8688. The Direct Marketing Association can provide information about opting out of lists produced by companies that subscribe to their mail and telephone preference services. Contact the DMA at the following addresses:

- Direct Marketing Association Mail Preference Service, P.O. Box 643, Carmel, NY 10512

- Direct Marketing Association Telephone Preference Service, P.O. Box 1559, Carmel, NY 10512

You can also contact the DMA at www.dmaconsumers.org/consumerassistance.html. Include the following information with your request:

- The date

- Your first, middle, and last name (including Jr., Sr., III, and so forth)

- Your current address

- Your home phone number (only for the telephone preference service)

Check out the credit bureau sample opt-out letter at www.dummies.com/go/credit repairkitfd5e, which is recommended by the Federal Trade Commission. Be sure to send your letter to all three credit bureaus.

It wouldn't hurt to make sure you're included in the Federal Trade Commission's National Do Not Call Registry as well: www.donotcall.gov.

Although it's rare for one debt to push you over the edge, a single traumatic event such as a divorce, layoff, or illness is easier for a lender, employer, or landlord to accept. Something that's beyond your control is a plus. Your efforts to pay the debts or deal with collectors are only of interest to you. All you need to convey is that you reviewed all other solutions. End the short statement with some words of wisdom, like, "I've learned a lot from this experience" or "I've become better at saving money as a result." Here's an example of a tight little speech that takes less than two minutes to share:

When you look at Steve's credit report, you'll see a bankruptcy there. It's not something he's proud of, but because of an illness, he ended up with $100,000 in medical bills. He felt terrible about having to declare bankruptcy, but he had no choice. He has increased his insurance coverage and savings so that this will never happen again. Steve certainly learned a painful lesson, but that's all behind him now.

Reaffirming some debt

As part of your bankruptcy rights, you can request to keep some of your debt if you can show the court that you can afford to pay it. After all that trouble to relieve yourself of the terrible burden, isn't keeping some of your debt sort of like going through a knock-down divorce and remarrying your spouse? Well, people do both, and here's why.

Believe it or not, keeping some debt (and its associated credit lines) has some benefits. This is technically called *reaffirmation.* For starters, having some ready credit available when you walk out of the courthouse may be a good idea. Also, a chunk of your credit score is based on longevity of accounts. Keeping an old account with a positive credit history may help you rebuild your credit score.

TIP

If you decide to keep some of your debt, make sure that you really *can* afford to pay. And more important, if the debt is in the form of a credit card, be sure that the terms of the card, including your original unused credit limit and interest rate, don't change because of the bankruptcy.

Repairing your credit score

Your credit score is likely to suffer dramatically from a bankruptcy. The better your score originally, the more it drops. If you had terrible credit before, a filing may not cause such a big drop. Either way, you'll likely have a very low credit score for a very long time unless you take positive action to improve it.

In Chapter 13, we cover the factors that influence your credit score. Here's how those factors are influenced by a bankruptcy:

>> **Timeliness of payments:** This category may be heavily affected, especially if yours is among the nearly half of all bankruptcies that happen with no prior

delinquencies. After you get new credit, be sure to make all your payments on time or the full balance, every time.

» **Amount and proportion of credit used:** In a bankruptcy, you or your lenders close most of your accounts. Your available credit drops to $0 in most cases. As you reestablish credit, expect low limits at first. Try not to carry balances over 20 percent of your limit for best results.

» **Length of time you've been using credit:** Here again, your score is damaged, because the history on your open accounts stops at your filing. Negative accounts typically drop off your record in seven years, although the public bankruptcy record may remain listed for up to ten years. Positive accounts are reported for at least ten years and sometimes longer.

» **Variety of accounts:** Chances are you're left with only secured debt such as mortgages, student loans, or car loans. All your revolving and retail accounts may be gone, which means that you don't have the variety of accounts that helps boost your credit score. Consider a secured credit card or a passbook loan to restart your revolving or installment credit history.

» **Number and types of accounts you've opened recently:** After the bankruptcy, you may have more activity here than usual as you attempt to reestablish your credit. And your score will fall. (The more inquiries you create for new accounts or changes, the lower your score.) To minimize damage, don't apply for more accounts than you need.

A helpful tactic is to take steps to improve your credit in each of these five areas. And don't forget that creditors don't necessarily report to all three credit bureaus. Now more than ever, you want to make sure that your good creditor experiences get onto *all* your credit reports. Ask a potential creditor whether it reports all your information to all three bureaus. If it doesn't, try to get credit from another creditor that does.

Follow the tips below to increase your credit score as much as you can in the aftermath of your bankruptcy:

» **Keep one or two of your older and lower-balance cards or lines of credit open by reaffirming them.** See the preceding section for more information.

» **Apply for a secured credit card.** This type of account uses a deposit to secure or guarantee that you will make the payments. Most report to the credit bureaus as any other credit card would, but be sure to ask the issuer whether the card you choose is reported.

» **Open a savings account, and then take out a "credit builder" loan against it to demonstrate that you can make those fixed payments on time every month.** Again, make sure that the lender reports the loan to the credit bureaus.

Establishing new credit

Yes, you can probably get new credit soon after you come out of bankruptcy. In fact, establishing new lines of credit could be the first step in improving your credit score. However, make sure you aren't creating debt you can't handle if you can't pay it off each month. You'll face some challenges as you pursue new credit opportunities. For example, you'll discover that the best loans at the most attractive terms and interest rates may not be available to you. Instead, you may find that you're being pursued by loan-shark types that make Jaws look like a guppy (see the earlier sidebar, "Beware of solicitations").

WARNING

Be extra careful about committing to new lines of credit, especially payday loans (see Chapter 10). Not only are you a target for unscrupulous lenders who specialize in post-bankruptcy loans, but also — now more than ever — you're vulnerable to slipping back into an out-of-control borrowing situation. You don't want to get trapped in debt again. New credit is okay as long as it's part of a plan to rebuild your rating, you're 100 percent confident that you can handle the payments, and it fits into your spending plan.

Moving forward with a game plan

Moving forward with a plan is very different from moving forward *without* one. Although plans may not always work out exactly as you want them to, plans give you the direction, motivation, and tools to achieve your financial ends, and they help you realize when you're drifting.

TIP

Begin by paying close attention in the post-bankruptcy education class you must attend as a springboard for your future. You may feel that this class is a waste of time, but it isn't. Then, if you didn't create a spending plan when you went to the credit counseling agency (as you were required to do before filing for bankruptcy), work with your counselor to develop a detailed spending plan that includes saving for financial goals.

A credit counselor will work with you to craft a spending plan that not only fits your current needs but also enables you to set aside money for emergency savings and savings for those goals you want to achieve in the future. This plan tells you how much money you can comfortably spend each month and helps you make sure that you're spending only on those things that you've consciously decided to spend your money on. No impulse buying for you. That money will be allocated to other choices you make — like a college fund, a vacation fund, or a retirement account.

Chapter 9

Repairing Credit Damage in the Wake of Identity Theft

Recovering from identity theft is almost always more difficult and time-consuming than most people think. If you're a victim of identity theft, you need to act quickly and comprehensively. Don't rely on others to resolve this mess. You have the biggest interest in getting this situation stopped, fixed, and behind you, and you need to assume all responsibility for doing so. This chapter tells you who to contact, what to do, and, most important, how to minimize the damage and move on.

Taking Fast Action When Identity Theft Occurs

If your identity has been stolen or you believe that it has (you don't need a smoking gun, video, or a ransacked room to act), do everything we recommend in the following sections as soon as possible. Most of the places you need to contact are open 24 hours a day, so a late-night call won't bother anyone.

Communicating with the right people

You may read different advice on who to call *first* when you believe your identity has been compromised or stolen. Some sources say to begin by reporting the crime to the police to establish a formal record, others suggest that you call your creditors, and still others say to notify the credit bureaus. Our advice is to begin in one of two places, depending on your circumstances:

>> If your existing bank or credit accounts have been compromised, call your financial institution or creditors first.

>> If you find out about accounts you've never heard of and didn't open, call the credit bureaus first.

Either way, don't wait long between the two calls.

TIP

Before you pick up the phone, do one more thing: Start recording everything that happens from now on. You want dates, times, names, badge numbers, phone numbers, and so on. Documentation is critical because, unfortunately, this situation may go on for a long time and require a lot of calling and writing to resolve. Don't trust your memory or count on people to call you back when they say they will. You'll help yourself out by writing down the facts and promises.

TIP

To report identity theft and create a recovery plan, go to www.identitytheft.gov. The website also includes an area that's helpful if you've been a victim of identity theft on your unemployment benefits. Other helpful information regarding sample letters, dealing with debt collectors, and accessing records may be useful to you, including the following:

>> **Dispute letter for credit card charges:** www.identitytheft.gov/Sample-Letters/dispute-credit-card-charges

>> **Dispute letter for ATM/debit card transactions:** www.identitytheft.gov/Sample-Letters/dispute-debit-card-transactions

>> **Identity theft letter to a credit bureau:** www.identitytheft.gov/Sample-Letters/identity-theft-credit-bureau

>> **Request letter for getting business records related to identity theft:** www.identitytheft.gov/Sample-Letters/request-records-related-identity-theft

>> **Identity theft letter to a debt collector:** www.identitytheft.gov/Sample-Letters/identity-theft-debt-collector

Finally, go to www.ftc.gov/idtheft for prevention tips and free resources.

Canceling your cards

If your credit or debit cards have been compromised, call the card issuers, ask for the fraud department, and have the cards cancelled immediately. You can find the phone number on your monthly statements, in your terms-and-conditions brochure, or on the card issuer's website or mobile app on your phone. If you have the card, look for the toll-free customer service number on the back of the card.

A small comfort: Your liability on stolen credit card accounts is relatively low — just $50 maximum per card, and it may even be $0. However, you need to contact all your creditors as quickly as possible so that the thief doesn't continue to rack up charges in your name or open new accounts.

For ATM and debit cards, your maximum liability is $50 if you report the loss within 48 hours of noticing it, but the liability can be $500 or even the full amount of your accounts (including any overdraft protection) if you delay too long.

Getting in touch with the credit bureaus

If you call just one of the three major credit bureaus (Equifax, Experian, or TransUnion) to report identity theft, a 90-day *fraud alert* is placed on all three of your credit files within 24 hours. A fraud alert often makes it more difficult for a thief to get credit in your name because it alerts creditors to follow certain procedures to protect you. (See the section "Sending out a fraud alert" later in this chapter for more info.)

Fraud alerts aren't foolproof, and compliance by lenders may not be foolproof either. You may prefer to lock a door rather than just close it. So, consider putting a *credit freeze* on your credit reports until you know how severe the identity theft damage is (see Chapter 21 for info on how to place a freeze). A "frozen" credit report means a creditor cannot pull your credit report to issue new credit without your express permission. You can always thaw your accounts later.

You can also add a *victim's statement* to your credit report. This statement informs the people who view your report that the information in your file has a potential problem and that they should be wary of making any decisions based on that information. Most creditors take strong notice of this fact and won't issue new credit in your name.

Adding a victim's statement to your report may motivate creditors to suspend existing accounts that weren't affected until they can determine that you're safe again, which may keep you from using your accounts until you can speak with the creditors.

After you notify the credit bureau of your situation, you'll receive a free credit report from each of the bureaus. Be sure to keep a copy of all reports. (Store them with those copious notes you're taking.)

Contacting the Federal Trade Commission

The Federal Trade Commission (FTC) is the nation's number one consumer protection agency and supports an entire department that handles identity theft issues. The folks in the identity theft clearinghouse don't follow up on individual cases, but they play an important role in looking for patterns and accumulating statistics that help everyone concerned with stopping identity theft.

Call the FTC's Identity Theft Hotline at 877-438-4338 (877-ID-THEFT) or go to www.ftc.gov. You can report and gain access to information to create your recovery plan, obtain sample forms, understand how to deal with debt collectors and browse the steps of the recovery plan for each impacted area (credit cards, student loans, and bankruptcy, if one has been filed in your name).

Notifying the police

If you call the sheriff, will he flip on his blue and red lights and tear around town to find the thief? Not exactly. But a crime has been committed, so you need to call the police and report it. Plus, some of the people you'll be dealing with may require a police report to take action.

The police report is also a way for others in the process to get a straight, consistent story from a third party about what happened and when. You'll have less difficulty convincing a collector if you can send an official police report to bolster your story. Be sure to get a copy of the report as soon as it's available, or at least get the report number for reference.

Here's how the police reporting process works:

1. **Contact your local police station if you suspect that someone is using your identity.**

   You don't need legal proof to prove your claim; it's your identity, and your suspicion is enough to file a police report.

2. **File the report, providing all the facts and circumstances.**

   Supply all account numbers and other relevant information (see the preceding section regarding the FTC Identity Theft Complaint Assistant or Theft Affidavit). No standard form or procedure exists; each police department has its own.

3. **Get the police report number with the date, time, police department, location, and name of the officer writing the report.**

   You'll likely need to provide this info when dealing with insurance claims, credit card companies, or lenders or collectors to clear your account.

4. **Be persistent but polite if the police seem reluctant to take your statement.**

   Most states require police departments to file reports for identity theft victims, but some police departments may not be required to do so. If your local police are reluctant to file a report, you can remind them that, without a police report, credit bureaus may not block fraudulent items on your credit report, and the lack of a formal police report may inadvertently help a crook.

TIP

If your police department still doesn't want to file a report, contact your state's attorney general's office (you can find contact info at www.naag.org) for assistance.

Alerting the post office

Many identity theft cases result from unauthorized and illegal access to information via the U.S. mail. Tampering with the mail is a federal crime. If you're a victim of identity theft and think that your mail may have played a role, contact the U.S. Postal Inspection Service and report your concerns. Call 877-876-2455 or report it by going to www.uspis.gov/report and clicking Identity Theft.

Protecting your identity through the FACT Act

The Fair and Accurate Credit Transactions Act (the FACT Act or FACTA) has numerous provisions for businesses, credit bureaus, and you. An entire book could be written on the topic, but in essence, the FACT Act was designed to bolster the Fair Credit Reporting Act (FCRA) and address issues surrounding incomplete or inaccurate credit reporting, including new safeguards for identity theft. It creates benefits for consumers and requires anyone making credit decisions about you to tell you the information they relied upon when making their decision. This allows you to determine whether there is erroneous information that needs to be disputed or corrected.

TIP

For more information on the FACT Act, refer to Chapter 3 and go to www.congress.gov/108/plaws/publ159/PLAW-108publ159.pdf for a copy of the full act.

The following bulleted list highlights the consumer-oriented, identity theft–related provisions of the act that are most informative or useful:

>> You're entitled to at least one free credit report each year from each of the three credit bureaus. You can often get more than one report if you file a fraud alert (see the next section) or an active-duty alert. Specialty reporting agencies, such as insurance and landlord reporting services, must also give you a free report if you ask. (See Chapter 14 for more info on specialty bureaus.)

>> Information based on an account that you've reported as fraudulent or that you've shown to be inaccurate or incomplete cannot be reported to a bureau.

>> Businesses must cooperate with you to help clear your name in the event of identity theft. They must provide copies of records about goods or services that they provided to the thief. Businesses may require a police report and may take up to 30 days to comply.

>> You may place a 90-day fraud alert, a 7-year extended fraud alert, and a 1-year military active-duty alert on your credit file. For more information on placing fraud alerts on your credit file, check out the following resources:

- **Information on active duty alerts from the FTC:** www.consumer.ftc.gov/articles/0273-active-duty-alerts

- **Seven Things to Know about Fraud Alerts from Equifax:** www.equifax.com/personal/education/identity-theft/7-things-to-know-about-fraud-alerts

- **Fraud and active duty alerts from Equifax:** www.equifax.com/personal/credit-report-services/credit-fraud-alerts

- **Identity theft help from Experian:** www.experian.com/help/identity-theft-victim-assistance.html

- **Fraud alert information from Experian:** www.experian.com/fraud/center.html

- **Fraud alert information from TransUnion:** www.transunion.com/fraud-alerts

>> You may block any fraudulent trade lines on your credit report if you've reported the crime to a police department or law enforcement agency. (See "Blocking fraudulent credit lines" later in this chapter.)

>> You may request that your Social Security number be truncated (shortened) on your credit report and communications in case it falls into the wrong hands. And credit report users can't just throw your used reports into the trash. They have to dispose of the reports in a legally sanctioned manner.

>> Businesses must truncate your credit card number on credit card receipts. In other words, your restaurant receipt shouldn't show your entire credit card number — just the last four or five digits.

Sending out a fraud alert

As we mention earlier in this chapter, contacting the credit bureaus is one of the first steps you should take when you discover an identity theft. When you contact them, you have the opportunity to place a fraud alert and a victim's statement in your file. These two items indicate to those who view your report that the request for credit they received recently may not actually be from you. The creditor should contact you before approving a subsequent request for a new account or a change to an existing account.

REMEMBER

A fraud alert is placed on your account for 90 days. Any new activity, including your own, is researched and reported to you. So if you open new credit lines during this time, you may notice a slower-than-normal approval process. It's worth the extra red tape to ensure that you and your identity are protected.

If you aren't sure whether your identity has been stolen but you know that the information necessary to steal it has been compromised, consider an *extended alert* on your credit report. An extended alert lasts seven years. Why use an extended alert? Say that your hospital's network is hacked, and the hacker gets access to patients' Social Security numbers, birthdates, and credit information. The thief may not sell or use your information right away; he may save it for future use. The extended alert covers a long enough period to prevent the information from being used to open an account, say, next year.

An extended alert can be a bit of a nuisance. After you place an extended alert on your credit file, potential creditors are required to contact you, or meet with you in person, before they issue new credit in your name. Still, an extended alert warns you of any suspicious activity even after you've forgotten about the original event that triggered you to establish the alert in the first place.

TIP

A small silver lining: After you put an extended fraud alert on your file, you're entitled to two more free copies of your credit report from all three bureaus at any time during the next 12 months.

Blocking fraudulent credit lines

"Block that line" may sound like a football cheer, but blocking can be a powerful tool. Be sure to request that the bureaus block any lines of credit that you believe are fraudulent. You'll have to provide information about the account you want blocked and a copy of your valid police report or state-approved identity theft form. The block prevents those accounts from being sold, transferred, or placed for collection. In addition, ask the credit bureaus to remove any inquiries on your record as a result of those fraudulent lines. Those inquiries can hurt your credit score.

Finally, ask the credit bureaus to notify anyone who may have received reports over the last six months with the erroneous information and inquiries on them. Doing so helps alert creditors and other interested parties to the situation — and can save your reputation.

Getting and Using Credit After Identity Theft

As with any theft, break-in, or personal attack, as a victim of identity theft you likely feel traumatized, fearful, and angry. You may want to avoid any experience with credit and borrowing in the future.

But recognize these feelings for what they are — feelings — and not give up altogether. After all, credit — though it certainly can be abused and exploited — is a powerful and sometimes indispensable tool that can help you achieve personal and financial goals that you may not be able to achieve otherwise. We strongly suggest that you adopt a strong offense and move forward with your personal goals. Whether you're planning to buy a house or a car or you're simply taking advantage of a retailer's offer for 10 percent off with a new credit account, don't be afraid to use credit to your advantage. This section outlines some steps that you can take to get your credit going again without putting yourself at renewed risk for identity theft. See Chapter 21 for more ways to protect your identity.

Closing and reopening your accounts

Whether your accounts were broken into, stolen, or just sniffed at, change all your user IDs, passwords, and account numbers. Unfortunately, fraudsters have had success in accessing information like this over the years. In many cases, your account may need to be closed and reopened, and your cards or account numbers may need to be reissued. Doing so may be a hassle, but if you've been a victim of identity theft, you already know the meaning of *hassle.*

Here's a list of which accounts may need to be reissued:

» **Bank accounts:** When your information is compromised, you never know if or when trouble will pop up. Changing the account numbers results in dead ends for a thief. Place alerts on your accounts so that you're informed when transactions occur. This can be helpful so that any transaction that may be created or authorized will trigger an alert to you and you can contact the creditor immediately.

» **Credit card accounts:** When you contact the card companies, they'll ask you for proper identification. (This is good — you *want* them to be suspicious!) They're used to closing accounts and reopening new ones quickly and painlessly. We suggest that you reopen only those accounts that you use. If you haven't used a card in two years, you may begin to wonder why it's taking up space in your wallet or sock drawer.

» **Other accounts:** Contact your Internet service provider, telephone service provider, and utility companies to alert them of the identity theft and to get new account numbers.

Virtually all financial institutions are pretty good at dealing with this issue today and have processes in place to monitor activity with a heightened sensitivity.

Altering your PINs, passwords, and radio transmissions

When you reopen your bank accounts, change your personal identification numbers (PINs), too. And when you access money at ATMs or in public places, make sure that no one can see you enter the PIN. Getting close to the machine may block the sight of someone across the street using binoculars or a camera with a telephoto lens. (Yes, thieves really *do* go that far.)

In the United States, most credit cards have been converted to chip cards, a small square component of technology on the card that increases its security. Some newer credit cards use technology that allows you to make a charge by tapping your card (a contactless transaction) on a reader rather than dipping it or inserting it into the reader. In the wake of COVID-19, there was a significant increase in the use of this technology at the point of sale to eliminate transference of the virus and keep consumers and employees safe. The adoption of mobile wallets, such as Apple Pay and Google Pay, has yielded additional security features. This allows you to keep your accounts on your phone and use the contactless feature of your mobile wallet. See Chapter 21 for more identity-protection measures.

TIP

For online access to bank, credit card, bill-paying, and investment accounts, switch to a *pass phrase* instead of a password. A pass phrase uses a short series of words like "Mauiis#1" instead of a single password. Pass phrases tend to be longer and harder to crack. Include some capital letters, numbers, and non-letter characters for additional strength.

Changing your Social Security number and driver's license number

If you can't seem to shake the damage done by identity theft (because new occurrences keep popping up or collectors keep landing on you like mosquitoes), you may need to take more serious action. Consider contacting the Social Security Administration to inquire about getting a new Social Security number.

WARNING

Getting a new Social Security number is a huge pain for everyone. Imagine all the places you've used your old number. If you go this route, you need to change all your records yourself. For more information, visit the Social Security website at www.socialsecurity.gov or call 800-772-1213 (800-325-0778 TTY for the hearing impaired). They also refer online reports of identity theft to www.identitytheft.gov, which will allow you to report the identity theft and get a recovery plan.

You won't be the first person who had to take this step. Besides the storied federal witness protection program, Social Security numbers are changed for domestic violence victims and others when warranted. But with all the emphasis on national security, changing your number isn't easy.

A few circumstances can prevent you from changing your Social Security number. You can't get a new Social Security number if

>> You've filed for bankruptcy.

>> You intend to avoid the law or your legal responsibility.

>> Your Social Security card is lost or stolen, but there's no evidence that someone else is using your number.

REMEMBER

Be sure to document everything. This dog can have a very long tail. You may need to dig up documentation a year or two after you thought all the dust had settled. Good written records, with names and dates, are a godsend.

While you're at it, go to the Department of Motor Vehicles and get your driver's license number changed, especially if someone is using yours as an ID.

3 Rebuilding Credit, No Matter Where or When You Begin

Create good credit for first-timers, immigrants, students, military service personnel, and couples, and shelter your credit during a divorce.

Maintain your good credit so it won't limit your new job opportunities.

Learn the new credit-reporting rules for small-dollar and medical debts.

- » **Avoiding common mistakes of credit newbies**

- » **Establishing credit when you're first starting out**

- » **Identifying credit issues for immigrants and first-time credit users**

- » **Knowing some special credit rules for students and military members**

Chapter **10**

Starting or Restarting Your Credit in Real Life

redit isn't an American invention. It's been around in one form or another since ancient Roman times. Modern consumer credit, however, is as American as apple pie. Taking off after the GIs returned from World War II, credit has been among the most prolific of financial services. Life without it is almost unimaginable today, but if you're among those starting over or just getting started, getting the credit you need may be easier said than done. Those starting over because of divorce or death can find the process to be a stressful endeavor, while credit newbies such as recent immigrants and high school or college graduates may wonder where to start. You may find yourself feeling like you're looking through a shop window but can't find the door to get in.

This chapter is your point of entry. We help you understand why a good credit history and financial-services relationships are essential to getting the credit you need. Your confidence gets a boost when we show you the size and importance to lenders of the underbanked market (meaning people like you, whose financial needs aren't being met), so you know just where you stand. We also debunk some credit myths that you may have brought with you from another country or may have been taught right here at home by well-meaning but misinformed friends. We include help for young people as well, with sections for students, grads, and military members. Take your seat at the table and help yourself to a big piece of the American dream: credit.

Debunking Misinformation about Banking and Credit

Depending on your culture or what your friends and family may have told you, you may not have an accurate understanding of how credit really works. However, with a few tips, you'll find that using credit can increase your enjoyment of life and all it has to offer. The following list debunks some commonly held misconceptions about banking and credit:

» **Banks aren't safe places to put money because they can fail, causing you to lose all your money.** Not so. All depository institutions (like banks) are insured by the full faith and credit of the U.S. government for up to $250,000 per depositor. No one has ever lost a penny of money that was insured in an FDIC or NCUA federally insured depository account.

» **Bank accounts are unsafe because currency can decrease in value or become worthless overnight.** When you deposit money into a U.S. bank, it's deposited in dollars. The dollar, though subject to fluctuations in value, is the most stable and trusted currency in the world. So it's safe!

» **The government may nationalize your bank and your account.** If the financial crisis taught people anything, it's that the government wants to support, not own, banks.

» **You need to be rich to be treated well at a bank.** Not so. Adding new customers is a top priority for banks, and the size of your account, no matter how small your deposits may be, doesn't determine your value as a customer. Banks know that many big depositors start out small and increase their deposits over time. If a bank doesn't respect you on your terms, take your money to a competing bank.

» **Using cash is safer than using credit or debit cards.** A lost or stolen card is protected against misuse by another person (most have a liability of $50 or less); lost or stolen cash is gone. Plus, purchasing with cash never builds the credit history you need for a credit score.

>> **You can't build a credit history if you have only a consular ID or a green card and not a Social Security number.** Not true. You can establish a credit history and use credit without a Social Security number.

The following sections explain why you need credit and why it's safe. We hope that this information eases any anxiety you may have.

Why you need credit

What's your definition of the good life? A good job, a safe place to live, a car, some financial security, and a good education for your kids? The reality of life in the U.S. is that having good credit is important in accomplishing goals like these.

Let's start with that good job. Chances are that at some point you'll have to compete with others for a good position. Many employers check your credit history to see whether you're reliable or you have distracting financial issues at home before making an offer. People can lie about their experience (ADP Screening and Selection Services says that about half of applicants lie on their resumes), and they can pretend to be nice during an interview, but a good credit history is tough to fake. As one employer put it, "When you think about it, people who have good credit keep their promises and are responsible, so it makes sense that if their credit is good, they may be more honest." So, all other things being equal, the job may go to the candidate with the best credit history.

BUILDING FROM CHECKING TO CREDIT TO A BUSINESS

A solid credit report and a good credit score help you gain employment, borrow money, and get a credit card, a decent apartment, and insurance. They can also form the first building block in starting a new business. With good credit, savings, and the stability that savings bring, you're a prime candidate to step up to that business you may have always wanted.

Good personal credit is essential. If you want to start a business, you can't be financially successful in doing so unless you move from the underbanked to traditional banking. That big piece of the American dream called credit is now yours to enjoy. Be sure to bring the family! For more information about starting your own business, check out *Small Business For Dummies,* 4th Edition, by Eric Tyson and Jim Schell (Wiley).

The same thing happens when you try to rent an apartment, buy insurance, apply for a college loan, or vie for a promotion at work. In all these circumstances, the person making the decision may check your credit history as part of the qualification process. Being underbanked and relying on cash may knock you out of the race. It pays to understand how to build good credit and use the banking and financial system to your advantage.

Why credit is safe

The credit industry didn't become the huge and powerful entity that it is today without addressing the question of safety. The federal government has put many regulations and safeguards in place over the last several years to ensure the safety and fair treatment of credit users. As a result, you have access to one of the fairest and most market-driven credit systems in the world. The following laws play a major role in protecting borrowers in the U.S.:

>> **The Fair and Accurate Credit Transactions Act (FACT Act or FACTA)** gives you lots of rights when it comes to how your credit is reported and what you can do to correct mistakes. It also gives you rights and remedies in the event of identity theft.

>> **The Fair Debt Collection Practices Act (FDCPA)** spells out what third-party bill collectors can and can't do when they try to collect a debt. If they step over the line, you can sue them.

>> **The Equal Credit Opportunity Act (ECOA)** prohibits credit discrimination on the basis of race, color, religion, national origin, sex, marital status, age, and whether you get public assistance. Creditors may collect this information, but they can't use it to decide whether to give you credit or how to set your credit terms.

>> **The Credit Card Accountability, Responsibility, and Disclosure Act (CARD Act)** protects you from unfair credit card billing practices. Major protections spell out notification requirements, grace periods, fees, interest rate changes, restrictions on student cards, and more.

>> **The Dodd-Frank Wall Street Reform and Consumer Protection Act** established an independent consumer financial protection bureau within the Federal Reserve to protect borrowers against abuses in mortgage services, credit card services, payday lending, and credit counseling.

>> **The Truth in Lending laws** ensure that you won't find any hidden surprises when you borrow money. All the costs of borrowing must be spelled out for you before you sign a contract.

» **The Coronavirus Aid, Relief, and Economic Security (CARES) Act** backs up your use of credit to purchase a home mortgage by stopping a lender or loan servicer from foreclosing on most mortgages and allows you to request a six-month to one-year forbearance on payments due to the COVID-19 pandemic. It also requires that a lender has to report your account as current if you were current and received any forbearance, modification, partial payment, or other assistance from that lender. This act took effect on January 31, 2020, and will remain in effect until 120 days after the national emergency declared by the president terminates. See https://crsreports.congress.gov/product/pdf/R/R44125 for more information.

Obtaining Credit: Starting Out on the Right Foot

You're ready to begin building your own credit, but you're not quite sure where to start. They say that a journey begins with a single step, which just goes to show how wrong people can be. The journey actually begins when you have a destination in mind. Then, after packing your lunch and other essentials, you take that first step. You build up a credit history over a period of time. How much time depends on how active you are and which scoring model is used to rate your credit file.

Don't fret, though. This section walks you through the steps to help you begin your credit journey down the right path.

Establishing a credit file without a Social Security number

You don't need a Social Security number to start building your credit report. In fact, a frequent misconception is that to establish a credit history, and thereby a credit score, you need a Social Security number, a driver's license, or a voter registration card. None of these items is required to establish a successful and envious credit record.

REMEMBER

When a credit bureau receives a new data line, the bureau matches the data with the following items, in the order shown:

1. Your name

2. Your birthdate

WHY BANKS WANT TO DO BUSINESS WITH YOU

Why do banks do anything? To make money, of course. With hundreds of millions of dollars in profits at stake from tens of millions of unbanked and underbanked people like you, some of the biggest and best names in the financial-services industry would love to have you as a long-term customer. Why do they like long-term customers? You guessed it: They're more profitable. Why do they like you? Because the Federal Reserve estimates there are about 55 million people who could use but can't currently access banking services and products. Selling something new to someone you know is much easier than selling to a stranger. So banks really do want your business, although at times you may not know it from the way they act.

Now that you know you're a valued and valuable customer in a large market segment that banks want to do business with, you should expect to be treated well, respected, and, yes, maybe even spoiled just a little. Anything less and you can just move on to the next player, who may know better how to treat a valuable customer like you.

3. Your address

4. Your Social Security number

No number? No problem. The bureaus can use plenty of other matching points to get your information into the right file. But being consistent is important! For example, make sure to spell your name exactly the same way every time you apply for or use credit.

Setting goals before you set out

Figuring out what your goals are prior to seeking credit is an important step, especially for the underbanked and those new to credit. Writing down your goals enables you to see what you need to do financially to achieve success.

To begin setting goals, we suggest that you (and your partner, if you have one) follow these steps:

TIP

1. **Set aside some uninterrupted time to dream about the future you want.**

   Allow at least an hour, and set an end point so that you finish before you are exhausted. You can always come back to this step later after some reflection.

2. **Write down some short-term (one year or less), intermediate-term (one to five years), and long-term (more than five years) goals.**

   Typical goals include beginning to save this year, beginning to save next year, getting out of debt in a year, and rebuilding bad credit. Other goals may be to get some financial education on topics such as investing, children's college savings accounts, and retirement accounts.

   Writing down your goals serves two purposes: It clarifies what you're talking about, and it makes your goals seem more real.

3. **Make a list of the actions you need to take to reach each goal.**

   For example, if you want to get a better apartment and a new job, how do you do so? Good credit can help. A smart first step is to get a free copy of your credit report at www.annualcreditreport.com and make sure that it's accurate. Dispute and remove any inaccuracies or out-of-date items to improve your credit. Consider adding utility payment histories and banking information using programs like Experian Boost (www.experian.com/consumer-products/score-boost.html) and UltraFICO (www.fico.com/ultrafico). Then make sure to make your payments on all your accounts on time. It's simple, but it works. Chapter 18 has more suggestions about budgeting and goal setting.

4. Track your progress.

Reviewing your progress toward your goals periodically is not only an incentive to keep up the good work but also an opportunity to celebrate your interim successes.

A REAL-LIFE COUPLE: HOW GOALS CAN HELP

We love using examples to illustrate and clarify concepts. To help us, we invented Roland and Carlotta, two recently engaged young people who are new to credit and want to get a head start on their life together. They begin by spending an hour one evening imagining what they want their futures to look like and then setting goals to make it happen.

Roland and Carlotta want to get married in a year, and they agree that they want a better apartment and eventually a small house for the family they'd like to start as soon as they're able. Roland wants a better job than the hourly one he currently has, and he would really like to buy a better car. Carlotta wants to decorate their new place and buy some new furniture for it. She also wants to establish credit for herself, and Roland needs to repair his credit.

You don't need to be in complete agreement on all the specifics as long as you can agree on the concept. You can make adjustments as you get closer to your goals.

	Roland's Goals	Carlotta's Goals
Short term	Get married	Plan a wedding and get married
	Open savings and checking accounts	Establish credit
Medium term	Get a better apartment	Get a bigger apartment
	Repair credit	Furnish and decorate apartment
	Get a better job	
	Buy a car	
Long term	Buy a big house	Buy a house
	Have six children	Start a family

Establishing a relationship with a financial institution

The saying "That's as good as money in the bank" means that it's as good as it gets. Having money in the bank is a good thing; it is the situation you want to be in. If you don't have a relationship with a bank or credit union, we can't stress enough how important this relationship is to your ultimate success. You want to develop a relationship with a bank by setting up at least a savings or checking account, not just so you have a place to take out a loan or get a titanium credit card to impress your friends, but because you need a place to put the money you earn but don't spend right away. Saving is essential to your success.

WARNING

Spending everything you make or using credit to supplement your income is a recipe for disaster. There's no substitute for savings when life throws you a curveball. Chapter 5 has details on what you can do when times get tough. But without savings, even life's little bumps are enough to hold you back on your journey to financial success.

Why you need to save

Everything is going okay. The money that comes in goes out, and your debt is under control. You may be a little short at the moment and your credit card balances may be building, but you figure that will end as soon as you get that promotion in six months. Then your car muffler falls off and costs $500 to repair, your tooth breaks at lunch and you need $1,200 for a crown, and your roommates tell you that they're moving out and you have to pay the rent on your own. Where does the money come from if you have no savings?

You can use credit if you have any left. But if you do, you may be paying a high interest rate and getting closer to your card limit, your credit score may be dropping, and your minimum payment may now be huge.

Without access to credit or savings, you have fewer choices. You may have to carpool, have the tooth removed rather than crowned, and be forced to move to less-expensive housing. That's why you need savings; credit and good luck are never enough for you to be financially successful.

How to get started saving

Fortunately, starting to save is easy and painless once you get going. The key is not to focus on how you're going to save six months' worth of living expenses, which could test even a saint. (For your information, St. Matthew is the patron saint of money managers.) What we want you to do is start with a small savings program but make it automatic.

TIP

To get started saving, take the following steps:

1. **Go to a nearby bank or credit union and ask about automatic deposit savings and checking accounts.**

   You probably don't have much to put away, at least right now, but that's okay. Limited funds are no excuse for not saving. Tell the bank that you don't want to pay any fees because you'll be using automatic deposit. If the bank charges a fee, go to another bank or credit union. Banks and credit unions usually waive all fees for people who save regularly through payroll deductions.

2. **After you open two accounts, one checking and one savings, go to your human resources or payroll department at work and say that you want your pay automatically deposited into these two accounts.**

   For example, you want all your take-home pay minus $5 (or more if you can) put into checking and the remaining $5 (or more) put into your savings account. At the end of the first pay period, you will have saved $5. Not a huge sum, but you're starting a habit that will grow and add up with time.

TIP

   If direct deposit isn't available through your employer, you can have your bank automatically transfer money monthly from your checking account to your savings account as soon as your paycheck is deposited.

3. **When you get that next raise or promotion, have half the increase automatically deposited into your savings account.**

   Now you're making a smart financial move — increasing your savings by putting away the extra money from your raise before you have an opportunity to spend it! Do the same thing for tax refunds and other windfalls. In no time you'll have a cushion that can get you over life's bumps without stretching your credit or damaging your credit history!

To secure your financial future, stop cashing paychecks and start automatic savings. You owe it to yourself, your family, and your future.

Using prepaid and reloadable cards

While you are building your credit, you may want to consider using prepaid and reloadable cards as alternatives to using cash. They're neither credit cards nor debit cards; rather, they exist somewhere in between. You deposit money onto the cards at locations throughout the nation and then use them as you would a credit or debit card. But they don't build your credit history or score.

REMEMBER

The following list outlines the major advantages of prepaid and reloadable cards:

>> You can use money without getting mugged for the cash in your pocket.

>> You need no credit record or credit check — just your name, address, and phone number and the ability to pay a one-time fulfillment fee. Non-U.S. citizens can provide an alternative form of ID, such as a driver's license, passport, or alien registration. Funds may post to your account within 30 minutes.

>> Prepaid cards offer convenience, easy availability, guaranteed approval, and other features that can make them ideal substitutes for credit cards.

>> You can use prepaid cards online, over the phone, and in many other places, just like a credit card or debit card.

>> Prepaid cards can help with financial discipline and the building of good financial habits.

Fattening up your credit file

If your credit file is underweight, you're not alone. Today, up to 55 million U.S. adults — nearly 25 percent of credit-eligible consumers — come back from credit inquiries to the major bureaus either as no-hits or as *thin files* (files with too little data in them to receive a credit score).

If you fit this category, don't worry. You can take action to build your credit muscle. The following options work well for credit newbies and underbanked individuals:

>> **Continue using your foreign credit card if you have one.** You may be surprised to find out that foreign credit history doesn't carry over and can't be imported into your U.S. credit file. However, you can still use your impeccable overseas credit experience to your advantage. You can either continue to use your foreign credit card or get a letter from a multinational bank extolling your virtues so that the local underwriters will approve you for an American credit card that is reported to the American credit bureaus.

TECHNICAL STUFF

Global scoring is expected in the future; in fact, FICO claims a proven global score that's accurate in every country in the world except France *(quelle surprise!)*. However, while the global score is being used in many countries, it isn't used in the U.S. yet.

>> **Ask that an alternative score (like FICO Score XD) be used to score your application for credit.** FICO Score XD is a one-time snapshot that obtains positive and negative landline, cell phone and cable data from the National

Consumer Telecom and Utilities Exchange (NCTUE), and public record and property data from LexisNexis Risk Solutions to generate a score for those who may have a thin file (very little data) or only stale information in their credit reports. (Check out Chapter 3 for more info.)

» **Take out a passbook loan:** A *passbook loan* is a loan the bank makes to you using your own money. It may sound strange, but if you open a passbook savings account at a bank or credit union and then borrow the money back, the bank gladly charges you interest (low interest, thank heavens) and reports your loan repayment history to the credit bureaus. You use your money in place of credit for the loan until you can build enough credit to get an unsecured loan. Faster than you can say "Super Prime," you're adding positive history to your file and improving your score.

TIP

Check with your bank or credit union to make sure that it reports the loan to at least one, and preferably all three, of the major credit-reporting bureaus. If it doesn't, request that it do so. If the bank is unwilling to report the loan to at least one of the bureaus, take your business elsewhere.

» **Get a secured credit card.** A secured card is a cross between a credit card and a prepaid card. After you establish a savings account and build up the balance, you can ask the bank to give you a credit card backed by your deposit in the bank. You may qualify for a credit line in excess of the amount you have in savings.

Many credit issuers eventually move you to a traditional credit card after a period of successful payment. The best part is that, unlike most prepaid cards, many secured cards are reported to the three major credit bureaus and can help you build a history and a credit score. Shop around for the best terms; many secured credit cards have high interest rates and fees.

Here's how to get and use a secured card:

1. **Contact your bank or credit union to find out whether it offers secured credit cards, or look online for an issuing bank.**

   Watch out for annual processing or maintenance fees. You can get secured credit cards for free — you just have to look around for banks or credit unions that offer them.

2. **Deposit the funds to be used as security for the card.**

   Be sure that the account is FDIC or NCUA insured.

3. **Use the card for purchases, making sure that you can pay the balance each month.**

   You don't need to use the card a lot. Just make a few purchases each month.

4. **Make on-time payments every month.**

Avoiding high interest, fees, and scams

Unfortunately, being new to something leaves you vulnerable to abuse by people who know the rules better than you do. Abuses perpetuated on immigrants and credit newbies have been around forever and aren't about to go away. This section lists several that you're likely to run into, along with some guidelines on how to handle them.

Payday loans

When you have a job but you don't have savings or credit but you have an unexpected expense, what do you do? An entire industry has arisen to answer this question. *Payday lenders* charge a very high interest rate or fee for a short-term loan guaranteed by your next paycheck. The fee is based on the amount of your paycheck, and you must supply the lender with a signed check for the date the loan is due.

It's not unusual for a person seeking such a loan to need additional money after the lender cashes the postdated check. This can start a vicious cycle of high-fee, high-interest loans rolling over or piling up with no practical way to pay them off. Payday lenders don't report your loan experience to the credit bureaus, so you receive no credit history–building benefit. If you must use a payday lender, look for one that's a member of the Community Financial Services Association of America (www.cfsaa.com). Members subscribe to a code of conduct and may offer extended repayment terms if you can't pay back a loan as scheduled.

Refund anticipation loans (RALs)

Refund anticipation loans (RALs) are high-fee loans secured by your tax refund that may, and the operative word here is *may*, get you your refund a week or so earlier than having it direct-deposited after filing your return electronically.

The real downside of these loans is that the person who sells you the loan has an incentive to inflate your tax refund to get you to take out a higher loan.

If your actual refund is less than what you borrow, you owe the difference plus a hefty interest rate. A much better idea is to open a bank account and have any refund direct-deposited. You get it fast, free, and with no surprises.

Check-cashing for a high fee

Going to a check-cashing place instead of a bank or credit union is like shopping at the most expensive store in town in the worst possible neighborhood. Check cashers are often located in places that are rife with crime. Why? Because everyone coming out has a pocket full of cash. A bank or credit union with which you have an account won't charge you to cash your check, and you don't have to take all the cash with you when you leave — you can deposit it in your savings and checking accounts.

Instant credit rating

WARNING

Credit repair companies may offer you a new identity or a repaired credit rating for only a few hundred dollars. Don't spend the money. The new identity is often illegal, and the instant credit repair doesn't exist.

Foreign bank accounts

Occasionally, you may receive a letter or email saying that you've been chosen (lucky you!) to help a rich foreign person get some money into the U.S. and that you'll receive a fat percentage of the amount for your small trouble because you're trustworthy. Most of these communications come from Nigeria, but they can originate anywhere. Don't do it!

Overcoming Credit Fears and Mistakes

Everyone makes mistakes, even lenders and credit bureaus. A mistake needn't be a big deal if you deal with it quickly.

As a person new to credit and maybe even new to the United States, you may be a tad scared of having to deal with credit and the problems that can come along with it. Bill collectors aren't above using threats of deportation or imprisonment if they think that doing so will help them collect a bill. The truth is, they can't legally do either. You won't be deported and you won't go to jail, no matter what they say. How do we know for sure? Well, these companies only get paid for collecting the money due their employers. If they actually deported you or put you in jail, they wouldn't get their money!

TIP

You can find complete copies of the FACT Act at `www.congress.gov/108/plaws/publ159/PLAW-108publ159.pdf`, the CARD Act at `www.ftc.gov/sites/default/files/documents/statutes/credit-card-accountability-responsibility-and-disclosure-act-2009-credit-card-act/credit-card-pub-l-111-24_0.pdf`, and the Fair Debt Collection Practices Act at `www.ftc.gov/system/files/documents/plain-language/fair-debt-collection-practices-act.pdf`.

If you're a credit newbie or have had a problem with your credit (including checking overdrafts), keep these basic tips in mind for dealing with mistakes:

>> **Don't delay.** Credit and debt problems don't improve with age. If you're proactive and make an effort to resolve a problem before you receive a call, you'll get a much better reception and improve your chances of a favorable resolution.

>> **Open your statements when you get them and challenge anything you don't understand or remember.** You can correct errors, but often there are time limits. And what may look like an error may turn out to be the beginning of an identity theft.

TIP

If you overdraw your checking account, be sure to contact the bank as soon as you find out. The objective is to work out a solution before the bank reports the overdraft to one of the specialty credit bureaus (see Chapter 14 for more information on specialty bureaus). Having this kind of a black mark on your report can make it difficult or even impossible to open a checking account for up to several years afterward.

TIP

At `www.dummies.com/go/creditrepairkitfd5e`, you can find a sample letter to send to your creditor when you see an error on a billing statement.

>> **Do everything in writing.** You may resolve simple problems over the phone, but to protect your rights in a dispute, you need to make your case in writing. If you really want a problem fixed, do it in writing and keep good records.

>> **Keep track of contacts.** Keeping notes on who promised what to whom not only keeps you from making more mistakes but also tells the other person that you know what you're doing. So when the manager says that this is the first time you've called, you can say, "You are mistaken; I called on these occasions, and I spoke to these people, who told me these things."

>> **Keep cool and calm.** Nothing can derail your effort to resolve an error faster than raising your voice. After you escalate the volume, you'll be directed to someone who does "loud" professionally, or you'll be politely ignored. Either way, you lose. Call back if you need to, but don't lose control.

>> **Safeguard your identity.** Newbies to credit often come from a culture of sharing. Whether you shared with your family in Mexico or you shared with your roommate at Harvard, the time for sharing information and credit is over. Identity theft is a serious and growing crime that can take years to unravel and cost thousands of dollars to fix. Chapter 9 tells you how to safeguard your identity, but in brief, guard your personal identification, mail, computer passwords, and bank account information. Shred financial mail. If you invite people into your home, be sure to put away your financial statements and checkbook. You wouldn't leave $20 bills all over the floor and furniture. The same applies to financial information.

Chapter 14 has more information on what to do if you run afoul of the credit-reporting system. If you do end up owing more than you can pay and you have to deal with collectors, Chapters 5 and 6 have the advice you need.

Qualifying for First-Time Cards and Lending

This section looks at how credit impacts two major and basic consumer credit instruments that most people need when they get started on life's journey: credit cards and loans. You may think that you know how these instruments work, but things have changed because of regulations like the CARD Act and the 2008 financial meltdown that threatened banks with failure due in large part to lax underwriting standards.

Getting a credit card

Getting credit for the first time used to be easy. All you had to do was drive to your nearest gas station and fill out an application for a gas card and then wait for the mail to arrive with your new plastic. If you were a city dweller who didn't drive, the trip may have been on foot to a department store, which would often grant credit on the spot. Both types of credit were relatively easy to get, and they reported your credit history to the three bureaus so that you built a credit history quickly. More and more department store and gas cards are tightening their standards to reflect credit conditions. You can try for cards issued by banks that use a national transaction network such as Visa. Though these cards are more versatile and powerful than their earlier counterparts, they're also harder to get. Getting that first card now requires a new approach.

To begin with, you need a credit history. But how do you get a credit history without credit? Three of the most popular ways are to use someone else's credit, supply your own data, or use a secured credit card.

Using other people's credit

In most instances, when you use another person's credit, the other person is a family member or a person with whom you have an emotional attachment. Why? Because using someone else's credit can be dangerous to that person if you mess up. Only someone who really likes you is willing to risk helping you get started.

You can piggyback on another person's credit in two ways. The most popular way is to be added to the person's account as an authorized user. The other way is to have the person cosign for you.

BECOMING AN AUTHORIZED USER

Being named an *authorized user* on someone's credit account enables you to have his or her credit history reported on your credit report while you use a card for which the other person is solely financially responsible. The card statement goes to the account owner, he or she pays the credit card company, you pay the card owner, and the card's credit history is reported in both your and the owner's files. Problems with this approach can arise if you overcharge and the account owner has to ask you for more money than you have available, which can cause a rift between you.

COSIGNING

Cosigning on an account is more often than not a recipe for disaster, and we usually don't recommend it. The cosigner's credit history doesn't show up on your credit report. Instead, all that shows up is your own payment history. The statement for a cosigned account doesn't go to the cosigner, so unless you share the information, the cosigner has no idea what's happening to the account. Often, the cosigner first hears of a problem when a collector calls and demands an overdue payment. Unfortunately, if you make late payments, the delinquency history appears on the cosigner's credit report, and negative information stays on the cosigner's credit history for a full seven years.

If you decide to go the cosigning route, we suggest that as the borrower, you commit to paying this bill before almost any other. You also need to have the courage to keep your cosigner informed of any changes in your financial picture, especially if you may be late on a payment.

Supplying your own data

In the past, the only way information could get to your credit report was via a creditor. Using products like Experian Boost (www.experian.com/consumer-products/score-boost.html) and UltraFICO (www.fico.com/ultrafico), you can add your own information drawn from utility payments or banking accounts. See Chapter 14 for more information on adding positive data to your credit reports.

Using secured cards

A secured card looks and works just like a credit card but is backed by a cash deposit at the bank that issues the card. Typically, your deposit qualifies you for a credit card with a limit equal to that deposit amount. As a result, limits on secured cards tend to be low, but the real value here is to establish a credit history so that you can get an unsecured card and reallocate your deposit to a better purpose, like your emergency savings account.

TIP

You can find and compare secured cards on a number of websites. Our favorites include www.bankrate.com and www.creditcards.com. You want to balance services, fees, and interest rates to find the best card for you.

Using savings for credit

Most banks and credit unions are happy to lend you your own money. If you accumulate some savings in a passbook account, you can use the savings to secure an installment loan of the same or a lesser amount. Needless to say, with 100 percent collateral in cash for the loan, the interest rate should be very low. Make sure that the loan is reported to the credit bureaus so that you build your credit as you pay the money back.

EQUITY AND DIVERSITY IN CREDIT

For decades, minorities were disadvantaged in accessing credit fairly. The reality is that, today, most lenders are racially blind when it comes to credit decisions. But stereotypes and prejudices exist on both sides of the lending desk when a person has to apply for a loan in person.

Before applying for a loan, review your credit report for errors or out of date data, and know your credit score and what loan terms you're qualified for. That way, you'll know if you're being fairly treated. See Chapter 19 for more on this topic and how you can get the most out of the credit system regardless of your background.

Considering Credit for Students and Military Members

At first blush, students and military members may not seem similar. However, as a credit grouping, they share some commonalities. For example, both have relatively limited means, a high number of younger members, a susceptibility to scams, and laws designed to protect them. And bankruptcy doesn't work as well for students or military members as it does for the general population.

In this section, we show you the protections offered under the CARD Act and Dodd-Frank legislation, as well as the impact of the Servicemembers Civil Relief Act. We also offer practical advice tuned to the unique needs of students and military members.

Giving credit to students

Most young people entering college or technical school have been brought up using their parents' credit cards. They'd sooner be without their cellphones than do without a credit card. But after they cross that line from authorized son or daughter user to customer, they're exposed to all the pluses and minuses of the credit industry.

Imagine new drivers getting behind the wheel with no driver's education, no insurance, no speed limit, and no police to tell them to slow down. Not a pretty picture, is it? This scenario applies to students and credit, and this section helps you avoid crashing your credit and maybe your immediate future with some insights and suggestions for students and their parents.

Checking out the CARD Act

The Credit Card Accountability, Responsibility, and Disclosure Act of 2009 (CARD Act) aimed to bring about more responsible lending and borrowing and foster more accountability in debt management. The CARD Act set rules to stem the tide of heavily indebted students who often have to drop out of school, work full-time jobs while studying to pay off credit card debts, or enter the job market with damaged credit that can interfere with finding a job. Key provisions include

>> **Proof of income:** Under the law, if you're under the age of 21, you must show proof that you can repay any credit card debt you may incur.

>> **Cosign requirement:** If you don't have sufficient income, you need to find someone who does to cosign on the account.

» **Credit limit regulations:** Card companies can no longer offer a preapproved credit limit just because you're a student. Limits have to be based on your independent ability to repay, or you need a cosigner. And if you have a cosigner, the cosigner must approve limit increases in writing.

» **Fewer sign-up incentives:** Card issuers can't turn your head with sign-up rewards such as free T-shirts, pizza, or electronics. The law also prohibits credit card companies from hitting you up on school property. They must remain a specified distance away from campuses. However, they can set up shop at other locations favored by students.

» **Account management assistance:** Your statement must tell you how long it will take to pay off your balance if you make only the minimum payment. It must also allow you at least 21 days to make a payment and your due date has to be the same day of the month, every month.

Practicing student credit etiquette

No, you don't need white gloves or a tie to practice credit etiquette. But if you're new to having your own credit and being responsible for the consequences, here are some basic rules for keeping your credit neat and tidy, regardless of how messy your roommate is:

» Don't apply for a credit card you don't need. Every time you apply for a card, it counts against your credit score, whether you're approved or not.

» It's okay to leave your socks lying around, but not your credit cards or billing statements. Misuse and identity theft happen to students, too!

» Lend a shirt, your car, or your date to a friend, but never lend your credit card. You're fully responsible for anything your friend does with your card. Anything!

» Decide what you consider to be an emergency worthy of using your credit card before one happens to you. If you can wear it, eat it, or drink it, it isn't an emergency!

» Stick to one low-interest-rate card and charge only what you can afford to pay in full each month. If you must use more than one card, pay off the card with the highest interest rate first, and make at least the minimum payment on the other(s), on time.

» Before you charge an item, reflect on whether you can pay it off at the end of the month. If you know that you would have to carry the balance over, estimate how long you would need to pay it off before swiping. If the answer is more than 90 days, seriously reconsider buying the item!

STUDENT CREDIT LOOPHOLES TO WATCH OUT FOR

Any law has its loopholes, and the CARD Act is no exception when it comes to protecting students from credit card schemes. The CARD Act doesn't allow credit card issuers to market their cards on campus, but they may operate just over the edge of campus. Older students have been buying beer for younger students forever, so cosigning for a student under 21 is nothing new. Students need to show income to get a card, and some applications may allow student loan proceeds to be counted as income. Income verification beyond filling out the application can be spotty for young adults who may not file their own tax returns.

Following military credit rules

America owes a tremendous debt of gratitude to those who volunteer to defend this country and way of life. Not surprisingly, Americans take a dim view of those who take advantage of soldiers and sailors during their term of service. Life is complicated enough in the service without having financial concerns distract you from your mission. This section discusses some of the rules of engagement between the military and the financial-services sector.

Enlisting with credit issues

In addition to meeting rigorous moral character standards, those seeking to join the military undergo a background check that includes a review of their credit history. Uncle Sam doesn't want to give you a loan; he wants to make sure that you don't have existing financial problems, because you're not likely to overcome those difficulties on recently enlisted pay. See Chapter 2 for ways to get your credit under control before you walk into a recruiting station and raise your hand.

Serving with credit issues

Credit problems happen in the military as well as in civilian life. Military personnel have extra protections under the law known as the Servicemembers Civil Relief Act. They're entitled to enhanced protection from eviction, auto lease cancellation penalties, high interest rates, and being summoned to a court hearing while serving. For more information, see Chapter 5.

TIP

A program sponsored by the U.S. Department of Defense, Military OneSource (www.militaryonesource.mil) offers financial counseling if you're having financial difficulties. Military One Source also offers confidential resources and support for service members and their families on a wide range of topics. In-person financial counseling sessions are available at no cost to active-duty, National Guard, and Reserve members and family members, as well as deployed Department of Defense civilians and their families. Financial counseling is available in person in partnership with a vetted nonprofit organization (currently the National Foundation for Credit Counseling, or NFCC). Military OneSource must arrange for you to meet face-to-face with a financial consultant in your community in order for you to receive the service at no cost.

Financial counseling over the phone is provided by the financial management team located within the Military OneSource call centers. This team is made up of highly qualified certified financial counselors.

Counseling includes education and coaching in the areas of

>> Budgeting

>> The creation of a realistic action plan using specific, manageable steps

>> Housing (prepurchase, foreclosure prevention, and reverse mortgage)

>> Credit and active-duty alerts

>> Debt management

>> Debt collections

>> Financial-related deployment issues

>> The Servicemembers Civil Relief Act (SCRA)

>> Payday loans, title loans, and rent-to-own

To reach Military One Source, call 800-342-9647 from inside the U.S., 800-342-6477 from outside the U.S., or 484-530-5747 for an international collect call, or go to www.militaryonesource.com.

» Leveraging your credit with landlords and lenders

» Using your credit to get the best deal on a car

» Knowing credit's role in insurance matters

Chapter **11**

Ending Life's Negative Credit Surprises

In our experience working with consumers since the early 1990s, we've learned that life, happiness, and credit are intertwined. Not to say that better credit or more money makes you happier, but financial failure takes a toll on the rest of your life and your relationships with others. So rather than look at your life in one place and your credit in another, we invite you to look at the two as highly correlated.

You would probably define a successful and fulfilling life as one that includes a job, a place to call home, a car to get you to your job and elsewhere, and, of course, insurance. In all these life scenarios, a good credit record is important. Employers often check credit reports before making job offers. Landlords and mortgage lenders require you to pass a credit review. To get a car, you need both credit and a down payment. And insurance involves a credit check that may determine your premium or eligibility.

Bad credit doesn't just deny you these things. Oh no, it can be much worse. What do you get with bad credit? Job problems, eviction or foreclosure, and debts and collections.

In this chapter, we offer you credit insights into some of what we call life's structural events and give you strategies to help you make the most of these credit-challenging situations. We show you ways to manage your credit for your maximum benefit as you step out in your early years. In Chapter 12, we continue this theme with credit's effects on the more personal areas of your life, such as marriage, divorce, and more.

So how important is good credit to your life? Very! How can you make sure that you have the credit you need as you set up the structure of your life? That's what we show you in this chapter.

Keeping Your Credit from Hurting Your Job Prospects

Most people dislike searching for a job, be it a 1st job or a 15th. We've been through the job-search process more times than we would have liked, and we understand the angst that many suffer as they take stock of their credentials and gear up to enter the job hunt. The role of credit in a job competition is sometimes overlooked, but it can be important and even critical if the competition is stiff enough.

Why? Because as part of the hiring process, employers frequently pull credit reports on candidates before making an offer. Before you get outraged at this possibility, you should know that you've probably given the potential employer permission to review your credit report thanks to some obscure language in the job application. If your report contains disturbing data, the employer can ask you to explain or simply move on to the next candidate. After all, passing on a prospect, if a number of other candidates are available, is safer and less confrontational.

As you can see, keeping your credit clear when you're looking for a new job — and even when you're up for a promotion — can be a big deal. Following are two simple steps you can take to help you keep your credit clear, whether you're new to the job market, looking to make a change, or trying to get back into the workforce:

>> **Get copies of your credit reports from the three major credit bureaus.**
The good news is that you're entitled to one free copy of your report from each of the bureaus (Equifax, Experian, and TransUnion) per year under the FACT Act as well as an additional report if you're unemployed and looking for work. Due to COVID-19, from now until at least April 2021, you can get one every week. Also, because of data breech issues, Equifax is offering an

additional six free credit reports annually. To find out how to order your copies, head to Chapter 14.

>> **Read your reports to make sure that no one else's negative history has been placed on your record by mistake.** Credit bureaus get millions of pieces of data each month that they have to apply to the right files. Sooner or later, one goes to the wrong place because of an address mix-up, a misspelled last name, a dropped suffix, and so on. If you see anything on your report that doesn't look familiar, you need to dispute it immediately; we explain how to do so in Chapter 14.

TIP

Correcting inaccuracies in your reports can take a few months, so be sure to start the process well in advance of when you need your reports looking good for a potential employer's judging eye. If you ask after the errors are fixed, the credit bureau will send a copy of your updated report to any employer who has requested it in the last two years, or to any business that has requested your credit report. That way, those employers and businesses get the most accurate and up-to-date info in your file.

If you're new to the credit game — perhaps you're just entering the workforce or you've immigrated to the United States from another country — flip to Chapter 10 for pointers on creating a personal credit history.

If the negative information in your reports is accurate and not out of date, be sure to see our advice in Chapter 1.

Dealing with Rental Application Checks

Renting an apartment or house used to be a great way to start out on your way to homeownership. Today, however, more people choose renting over homeownership because selling a home can be difficult and the long-term outlook for home prices is uncertain. Others have been foreclosed on and then rent as a result. If you're looking to call an apartment or rented house home sweet home, forever or just for a while, you need to understand how credit plays into the rental process.

REMEMBER

Credit reports figure prominently in a landlord's decision to rent to you. They show how you handle routine payments.

TIP

You can have your rent payments reported to the three major credit bureaus. Just sign up with a rent-reporting service that will report your on-time rent payments to the major credit bureaus and they show up on your credit report.

Landlords also rely on data available through some national, specialty reporting bureaus that focus exclusively on rental information. Rental data, when available, is reflected in your VantageScore credit score, and in the newer versions of your FICO score (FICO 9 and later). (See Chapter 14 for more on credit reports.)

The type of information a specialty rental reporting agency (not one of the three big credit reporting bureaus) may contain includes damages, noise complaints, past due balances, lease skips, unauthorized pets, and other tenant history information from landlords who report their experiences with tenants. Unlike credit reports, specialty bureau reports can pick up evictions without and with monetary judgments; they can even note a pending eviction. They also contain information about when you moved into or out of your rentals and can include landlord reports on lease violations and ratings. The goal of all this data? To help landlords identify good, as well as problem, tenants.

So what happens when you finally find a great apartment, only to hear from the leasing agent that your background check has revealed problems? Is it time to move on? No way! This section offers some effective ways to address credit and background concerns so you can move into the apartment of your dreams.

TIP

If you're trying to rent an apartment after a mortgage foreclosure, you definitely want to be upfront about what happened, because the foreclosure *will* appear on your credit report. If you find yourself hitting a brick wall when dealing with large apartment complexes, which can have less-flexible renting criteria, try a smaller complex, or even a house, condo, townhome, or duplex. Individuals (versus big rental companies) and owners of small complexes may be less likely to run a credit check on you; at the very least, they may be more understanding about your situation if they do run a check.

Knowing what's on your reports

First things first: Pull your credit reports (ideally before you begin searching for an apartment) and look them over carefully. If your reports contain negative data that's out-of-date (over seven years old) or accounts you don't recognize, quickly dispute the inaccurate or out-of-date items with the credit bureau(s). Next, if you find any erroneous negative items, explain to the leasing agent that you're in the process of correcting the errors and ask the agent to repull your report. Disputed items come off your report until they can be checked out further.

REMEMBER

Landlords can still say no to your application; however, if you can explain what happened, what you did about it, and why it won't happen again, many may be willing to work with you.

TIP

To find out what information is contained in the specialty bureaus' databases and whether it's correct, we suggest that you ask the leasing agent or landlord which specialty bureau he or she uses and then get a copy of that bureau's report by using the contact information we provide in Chapter 14. Dispute errors just as you would for a credit report; instructions for doing so come with your free report.

Taking action

If clarifying that certain information on your report is incorrect isn't good enough for the landlord, you may need to take additional action. Here are some suggestions that may help you get past such a sticky credit situation:

>> Write a letter explaining the circumstances from your point of view. Submit this letter *with* your application (not later), and be sure to say why the problematic situation won't happen again.

>> Offer a larger deposit. Remember, you get the money back when you move.

>> Offer more than one month's rent upfront.

>> If you're renting now, get a letter of recommendation from your present landlord saying that you're a good tenant (you pay on time and in full each month and take good care of the apartment).

>> Find a roommate who has good credit or who can help you with a larger deposit. Agree to have a roommate for a year. When you renew the lease, you can go your separate ways if you like.

WARNING

You could get a *cosigner* (essentially, a person who guarantees your performance), but we don't recommend doing so if you can avoid it, largely because it can put a strain on relationships, especially if you run into money problems. If you do decide to go ahead with a cosigner, family members or even friends may be willing to help.

Qualifying for a Mortgage

If you've done your homework and you come out on the buy side of the rent-versus-buy decision, then you're ready to dig into the next phase of the mortgage-qualification process. But first it helps to know what you need in order to be successful in your quest:

>> Steady, reliable income

>> Good credit

>> Documentation to verify savings

>> Savings to get through a temporary setback such as an unexpected loss of income or a home-maintenance emergency, in addition to your down payment and closing costs

WARNING

If you're already having credit or financial difficulties, we strongly suggest that you do what's necessary to resolve these issues before you start the home-buying process.

The subprime mortgage market collapse of 2007 will live on in lenders' memories for the next two decades, and it should! The upshot is that lenders are being more intelligent in their decision making. What does that mean for you? Simply that you need to adopt the same critical approach to your credit. In this section, we help you understand the essentials you want to master *before* you start looking for a home and the mortgage required to purchase it.

Ordering your credit report and score

When you apply for a mortgage, the quantity and quality of the accounts on your credit report are incredibly important. They ultimately affect your *credit score*, the three-digit number that lenders use to figure out what interest rate and other deal terms to offer you. You're entitled to a free copy of your credit report from each of the three major credit bureaus every 12 months (every week until at least April 2021), but you have to fork over some cash to find out your credit score. Of course, if you've already received a copy of your free credit report(s) from each bureau, then you may have to pay for another one as you begin the mortgage application process unless you live in a state that allows you more than one annual free report (you want the most current report). Either way, we explain how to order your report and score in Chapter 14.

Because your credit score makes a big difference in the interest rate you get for your loan — and that interest rate can make a difference of tens of thousands of dollars over the course of the loan — you need to have a solid understanding of the components that make up the two main types of credit scores (FICO and Vantage-Score) so you can try to get the highest score possible. We reveal the breakdown of the components for both types of credit scores in Chapter 13.

TIP

So do you need a perfect credit score to qualify for a mortgage? No way! Although lenders are certainly very hesitant to lend to people with low scores, they also understand that perfect credit is virtually a myth given all the moving parts to your score and reports. What you really need is good enough credit to quality for a mortgage and get the best deal. Because what's considered "good enough credit" changes with the financial markets, we suggest that you check respected sites like www.bankrate.com and www.myfico.com to see the prevailing rates for various credit score tiers.

Your credit score varies with each credit report because each bureau may have different information or errors. Chances are a mortgage lender will check all three reports, so you should too.

Looking at your credit file like a lender

When a lender looks at your loan application, he or she wants to see more than just your credit score. You can expect any lender to look at the following items, all of which determine whether you're a good risk:

>> Your income, employment history, and monthly debt payments

>> Your savings and assets, such as investments and properties that can be sold relatively quickly for cash

Lenders love to see money in the bank, otherwise known as *cash reserves.* The mere fact that you have a cash reserve speaks volumes about how you manage your money and your life.

>> Your credit history

If you believe that you may come up short in any of these areas, be sure to have a plan to address the shortcoming with your lender during the loan origination process. For instance, if you have a short employment history, point out to the lender how stable your company and job are and that you just received a great performance review.

The process called *underwriting* looks at many factors and applies seasoned judgment to what's there. The term itself explains what happens. In earlier times, when a risk was reviewed and approved, the person responsible would write his name below the application — hence, underwriting.

Preparing to Purchase a Car

A car dealer (or any lender, for that matter) wants to know three things about you before deciding whether to make you a loan. They call them the three Cs of credit:

>> **Your character:** To a dealer, your character boils down to whether you'll make the payments as agreed. Sometimes a person can have great income,

low fixed expenses, and a fat down payment but just be too lazy, disorganized, or distracted to pay on time. So the issue here is not *can* you make the payment, but *will* you!

>> **Your capacity:** *Capacity* refers to how large a loan you can handle. Car dealers take into account all your other financial obligations in addition to the monthly car payment relative to your income.

>> **Your collateral:** *Collateral* is something a lender can take away and sell if you default on your loan, such as your car. The more equity you have in your car, the better the dealer will feel about financing your purchase.

Although purchasing a car is a big step, credit doesn't have to be a major consideration if you prepare beforehand. This section details what you should take care of before you set foot onto the lot and offers insight into what you should consider after you pick the car you want.

Arming yourself with information

Unless you plan to pay cash, your credit has a lot of say in what size car payment and maybe even what type of car you end up with. Naturally, you want to follow the process we describe in Chapter 14 to obtain copies of your credit reports from all three major bureaus and pore over those reports to see whether you can spot any errors. If you find any, dispute 'em (Chapter 14 also has advice on correcting inaccuracies).

If you're smart, you'll also look into your credit score, a tool that helps a lender predict how risky your loan is likely to be. In modern America, lenders can't ask your friends or enemies if you're reliable. They can't make decisions based on anything that may be discriminatory, such as how you look or sound or where you live. This is where the credit score shines. Your credit score looks at your credit history plus any consumer-supplied items (see Chapter 14 for Experian Boost and UltraFICO) on your credit report. Using a complex set of formulas, your score predicts the likelihood of your defaulting on your next loan.

REMEMBER

Find out your credit score before you approach a lender or dealer about an auto loan. Most lenders use a score developed by either FICO or VantageScore. If you know in advance if your credit is great or horrible, you'll be prepared to hold out for the best rate you qualify for rather than just accepting an offer that may have a higher interest rate tacked on to see whether you're paying attention.

TIP

If you're considering a specific car dealer for your purchase or a certain bank or credit union for your car loan, we suggest that you find out which credit bureau's report and score the dealer or bank uses to determine eligibility. Then you can go to that site and order just what you need.

TIP

After you know your score, you can check www.bankrate.com to determine what your interest rate will be for a car loan from a traditional bank or credit union. This is good information to have before you ever set foot in a dealer's finance department. Sure, you may still want to use a dealer incentive and opt for a loan through the dealer, but this way you can make a valid comparison.

Reviewing what to consider when you're at the dealership

It's easy to get overexcited when you're finalizing your car deal. The thrill of owning a new car and the prospect of getting a bargain can lead you to miss a fine point or two in your decision-making process. To keep your passion in check, consider the following points before you pick up a pen and sign anything:

>> **Think about dealer financing if your credit score isn't the best.** A dealer may have more flexibility than a bank or credit union when making a loan. Why? Because dealers make money on the cars they sell, so loaning you money is worth more to them than it is to a bank, which profits only from the loan and not the car sale.

>> **Remember that when you sign a lease, your credit will impact your monthly payment and overall cost.** With a lease, you agree to pay the lease monthly, keep the car insured, and take good care of the vehicle for the term of the lease. From a credit perspective, you're essentially taking out a loan for the amount by which the car is expected to depreciate (decline in value) over the lease term. Your credit report and score are big determining factors in what interest rate is applied to the term of the lease and your resulting monthly payment.

KICKING THE TRADE

Trading in your current car has long been a way to reduce the price of a new car. Beware of unscrupulous car dealers who may tell you to just give your car back and have it repossessed to free up cash for a new car payment — in a practice known as *kicking the trade*. This practice can lead to court action, deficiency judgment, and vigorous collection actions. See Chapter 7 for more information on car loans.

>> **Don't fall into the trap of weighing monthly payments more than the overall price.** A common car dealer tactic is to talk to you about a vehicle's cost in terms of what you're willing to pay per month instead of the actual price. Though the monthly payment amount is an important part of your budget, don't lose sight of the total amount you'll pay over the term of the loan. A longer payment period (seven years versus three years) can cost you much more overall than a shorter one.

If you're unhappy with your loan payment or interest rate for your new car purchase, don't despair. Instead, follow our advice in Chapter 3 to polish up your credit. Within six months to a year, your score may have improved enough that you can look into refinancing your balance at a lower interest rate and a lower payment! For a possibly faster fix, try adding positive consumer-supplied information via one of the newer reporting products like Experian Boost or UltraFICO. Leases, however, can't be changed later.

TIP

Another thing you can do to help your credit is to pay off your existing car loan early, provided the loan doesn't have a big prepayment penalty. A credit report with a good payment history and no outstanding car loan scores higher than one with a good payment history and a large balance due.

Unveiling the Relationship between Your Credit and Your Insurance Premiums

Credit plays a significant role when you're looking for car insurance, renter's insurance, or homeowner's insurance. A thin credit file, inaccuracies in your credit reports, or just plain bad credit can hurt your chances for coverage, and insurance will likely cost you a small bundle. Perhaps you already have blemished credit and think that being charged more for insurance before a fender's ever dented or a window's ever broken just adds insult to injury. Well, the Federal Trade Commission (FTC) agreed that this situation might be unfair (or worse, a proxy for discrimination aimed at overcharging policyholders). So it did some investigating and issued a congressionally mandated report examining credit-based insurance scores (www.ftc.gov/opa/2007/07/facta.shtm). The good news and the bad news is that these scores really do predict claim experience and often result in lower prices for people who are better risks — as in people who are smart about their credit. The FTC also found that credit scores have virtually no discriminatory bias.

But just what is a credit-based insurance score? And how can you get your hands on your score? This section not only answers these questions but also reveals what you can do to make sure you get the best insurance rate you can.

Understanding insurance scores

Understanding how your credit history affects your insurance options can be a challenge. When evaluated with other information like your claims history and driving record, your credit-based insurance score (also known simply as an *insurance score*) helps insurance companies determine whether you qualify for coverage based on their underwriting guidelines and what rate you'll pay.

REMEMBER

Your insurance score is a snapshot of your insurance risk at a particular point in time. It's a number based on the information in your credit report that shows whether you're more or less likely to have claims in the near future that result in losses for the insurance company. As with other scores, the higher your insurance score, the better off you are.

TECHNICAL STUFF

Another way to look at this score is to contrast it with your credit score. An insurance score is a credit-based statistical analysis of a consumer's likelihood of filing an insurance claim within a given period in the future. Actuarial elves look at those items on your credit report associated with credit management patterns that statistically correlate with claim risk, such as outstanding debt, length of credit history, late payments, collections and bankruptcies, and new applications for credit. A credit score, on the other hand, is a credit-based statistical analysis of a consumer's likelihood of a credit default within a given period in the future.

Note: Neither your insurance score nor your credit score is adversely affected if you contact several insurance companies for quotes.

Getting a copy of your insurance score and insurance claim report

Fair Isaac Corporation, the provider of FICO credit scores, and ChoicePoint, owned by LexisNexis, are the most well-known developers of insurance scores. Fair Isaac insurance scores range from 300 to 900, and ChoicePoint scores range from 300 to 997. To find out where you stand, you can ask your insurance company for your number. You may find when you ask that your insurance company considers this information to be proprietary, but in the land of the free, you can almost always get someone to sell you your score.

TIP

For a small fee, you can get a copy of your LexisNexis Attract insurance score by going to `https://consumer.risk.lexisnexis.com/consumer`.

While you're on the LexisNexis website, you can get a copy of your C.L.U.E. personal property and auto reports at no charge under the annual disclosure rules of the Fair and Accurate Credit Transactions Act (FACT Act or FACTA; we explain the basics of this act in Chapter 9). If you don't have Internet access, you can order your reports by mail at LexisNexis Solutions Consumer Center, P.O. Box 105108, Atlanta, GA 30348-5108, or by calling toll-free 866-414-4436. LexisNexis also offers what's known as a full file disclosure that covers your insurance, employment, and tenant histories all in one swoop. Get a copy by following the instructions at `personalreports.lexisnexis.com/access_your_personal_information.jsp`.

Figuring out what to do with your newfound knowledge

After you have a copy of your insurance claim report, take the time to check it out. If you believe that any of the information on your report is incorrect or incomplete, you can file a dispute, just like you would with one of the credit-reporting agencies, by following the instructions included with the report. All claims are verified or removed. You can also include an explanation regarding any information that's factually correct but may warrant further discussion. Send disputes to LexisNexis Consumer Center, ATTN: FACT Act Dispute Request, P.O. Box 105295, Atlanta, GA 30348-5295; or call 866-897-8126 or email `consumer.documents@lexisnexis.com`.

TIP

A small but still bright spot in the insurance underwriting process is that if you don't get the best rate available because of information contained in your credit report, you must be told about it, and you can get a free copy of the credit report used (in addition to any free annual credit reports you're automatically entitled to). Be sure to check the report carefully for errors and out-of-date information. Dispute any mistakes you find and then ask your insurer for a premium recalculation.

Taking other factors into account

Be aware that insurers have no responsibility to take into account catastrophic events that may damage your credit score either directly or indirectly. Consider adding a statement to your credit report and contacting your insurer for a rate review if, for example, you were unable to pay bills on time because

>> You were injured or seriously ill and hospitalized.

>> You live in an area hit by a natural disaster such as a hurricane and were unable to pay your bills on time because of the storm's effects.

>> You have been adversely impacted by a pandemic, resulting in a loss of income.

>> Your company closes and you lose your job.

WARNING

Insurers may use more than your own credit history to adjust your rates or deny you coverage. They may order the reports and/or scores of other people living at the same address, even if those people aren't listed on the policy. For example, insurers may consider unnamed persons' driving records at the same address. If you purchased an item or property with a former spouse and that person defaults or pays late, even if the property and debt responsibilities have been reassigned by court order, your credit history and score may be adversely affected, which in turn may affect the cost of your insurance premiums. For more on the credit impacts of divorce, see Chapter 12.

» **Sheltering your credit in a divorce**

» **Maintaining your credit after losing your job**

» **Handling debt incurred because of medical bills or the death of a spouse**

» **Using credit wisely in retirement**

Chapter **12**

Protecting Your Credit During Major Life Challenges

L ife is full of surprises. You may plan to get married, but few of us plan to get divorced. You may plan to get a job but end up unemployed. You may plan time at the gym to be healthy, but you may not plan for illness and subsequent medical debts. And have you planned how to handle your credit when your spouse or partner passes on?

That's what this chapter is all about. Building on Chapter 11, which links your life goals to your credit, here you find what you need to know to survive the surprises that life events bring. No matter what life throws at you, you're better able to cope if you maintain good credit. In marriage or divorce, in employment or unemployment, in sickness or health, knowing how to keep your finances under control makes your recovery faster and stronger.

In this chapter, we offer you credit insights into some of life's personal events and offer strategies to help you make the most of these often credit-challenging situations. We show you ways to manage your credit for your maximum benefit as you journey through your own personal odyssey. Whether you are embarking on the sea of life for the first time or the last, this chapter's for you.

Tying the Knot in Life and in Credit: A Couples' Guide to Building Good Credit

Nothing is more hopeful than deciding to get married. And nothing can be as potentially dangerous to your finances. Keeping your credit in its best shape can be tricky enough when you're making financial decisions on your own. Add another person's emotions and excitement to the mix, and the process can get out of hand unless you're careful. In this section, we offer you our very best hopes for the future, along with advice to match.

Engaging in prenuptial financial discussions

Understanding and communicating with your spouse is critical in all aspects of married life, but especially when it comes to financial issues. We advise all engaged couples to spend significant time discussing and exploring how they plan to handle their finances, what their credit looks like, how they'll pay their bills, and what their long-term financial goals are. After all, new couples want to continue the honeymoon phase as long as possible, and arguing over finances does nothing to achieve that goal. This section helps you begin the communication and budgeting processes.

Identifying and agreeing on your major money issues

If you're soon to be married or partnered (or even if you already are and haven't yet talked money), you need to openly discuss a range of money issues, including your current credit and financial status. If you could live on love, the conversation would be unnecessary, but if you two pool your resources, you need to determine together how your credit and your money plans will affect your lives as a couple.

Here's a list of ten things to do before your "I do" day. If you've already taken the plunge and you haven't yet discussed these issues, do it now!

>> **Show each other your credit reports and credit scores.** Discuss what you see, but don't judge.

>> **Discuss your current annual income and your income hopes for the future.** This is a chance to show support, not to criticize.

LOOKING AHEAD TO "DESSERT"

When Barbara, Steve's wife, and Steve go out to dinner, she always looks at the dessert menu first. In the beginning of their courtship, this behavior baffled him. As a typical linear-thinking man, Steve approached his meal choices in the order he planned to consume them — starter, salad, entrée. In fact, he typically wouldn't even think about dessert until he was sopping up the last of the marinara sauce from his plate.

Finally, Steve got up the nerve to ask his wife about this display of, in his view, backward behavior. She explained that dessert, for her, was the most important part of the meal, and she wanted to plan ahead to accommodate what for her was a priority. If she saw bread pudding (her favorite) on the menu, she'd go for a light entrée or salad and skip the sticky rolls. If the dessert choices were just so-so, she'd order a heartier main course and perhaps take an extra piece of bread.

Although Steve's wife's logic, as always, is different from his own (and usually right), her approach to dining out is a great way to look at household budgeting. Focus on the goal (like traveling to an exotic destination or buying your dream home) instead of zeroing in on all the mundane bills and expenses of everyday life. This approach has served their relationship well.

>> **Determine your financial style — are you a saver or a spender?** Find out the same about your partner.

>> **Talk about your debts and how you plan to handle them.** Will you each pay your own debts? Will you pool them together and split them 50-50? Or will the bigger earner pay more?

>> **Tell each other about any major negative financial events in your past.** These events may include outstanding (or defaulted) student loans; for those in second marriages, the effects of a bankruptcy may be around longer than the kids, and you wouldn't forget to talk about *them.*

>> **Discuss your spending habits (whether you're frugal, indulgent, or don't even know how to budget).** The frugal one may be the better choice to handle your bill paying.

>> **Talk about whether you've cosigned any loans.** Cosigning for an old flame may be forgiven, but hiding it won't.

>> **Discuss your personal approaches to budgeting.** Will you count every penny or go for estimates instead? Yes, you need a budget!

>> **Discuss your financial goals for the next five years.** Make this exercise fun. After all, it is about dreams and hopes. No wet blankets allowed!

>> **Talk about your long-term financial goals and how you'll fund them.** Will you retire at 50? Sail around the world? Give all your worldly possessions to charity?

TIP

I strongly advise that you exchange copies of your credit reports when your relationship turns serious. Credit is a critical relationship factor, and bad credit can be a deal breaker. You may have bared your heart and soul to your sweetie, but until you bare your credit, the job's not done. Flip to Chapter 14 to discover how to get copies of your credit reports.

Building a budget for your new life together

I strongly recommend that you and your partner sit down and make out a budget for your new household. Budgeting is among the most important first steps you can take together to strengthen your relationship and reduce the risk of a split due to financial stress and spending incompatibility.

Explore together and agree on what you want to save for, such as a family, a house, a cat or two, or early retirement. This discussion paves the way for all the saving steps you want to establish in order to reach your goal. You also need to budget for the everyday stuff (utilities, transportation, food, housing, and the like). If you find that you just aren't able to get the numbers to add up, consider a credit counselor. Good credit counselors aren't just for credit, debts, or problems — they can help you plan a budget before disaster strikes. (See Chapter 4 for more on credit counseling.)

TIP

Chapter 18 is all about how to budget.

When working on your budget, always start with the fun part: your future goals. What could be more inspiring than describing all the things you're going to do and the adventures you'll share together over the years? For example, Steve and his wife are planning an extended road trip to look for the perfect piece of blueberry pie.

REMEMBER

By committing to maintaining communication, establishing common goals, and working together for mutual benefit, couples can achieve financial bliss.

Considering joint accounts

If your sweetheart has a less-than-glowing credit history, it begins to affect *you* as soon as you apply for credit together and open joint accounts. Why? Because the bank reviews both of your credit histories. You keep your own history, but your new joint accounts appear on both of your credit reports. So if you're concerned that your spouse may not be as diligent as you are in paying bills on time, paying the bills yourself is a good idea.

WARNING

Many couples decide to merge their accounts because consolidated accounts often make for easier record keeping and enhance that feeling of togetherness. But beware: Both of you are equally responsible for all debt incurred in any joint credit accounts. Regardless of which one of you takes the credit card out for a joy ride, a missed payment on a joint account negatively affects both of your credit records. Also, if you miss a payment on an individual account, that missed payment may affect your ability to open joint accounts because both credit histories are considered.

In states with community-property laws, you may be responsible for your spouse's debts even if you aren't on the account. As long as the debt is incurred during the marriage, you're liable, even if you receive no benefit from it or don't even know about it. Currently, 9¾ states fall into this category: Arizona, California, Idaho, Louisiana, Nevada, New Mexico, Texas, Washington, and Wisconsin. Alaska has an opt-in provision (so we count it as half), and Puerto Rico has community-property laws but isn't a state (so we count it as a quarter).

KEEPING SEPARATE ACCOUNTS

If you have a credit-challenged spouse or partner or if you're merely cautious and want to take the credit sharing slowly, you can always keep separate accounts and allow each other to be authorized users on your accounts. Both of you can charge on the account, both of you get the credit history reported on your credit reports, but only one of you is responsible for the bill.

Although this strategy can safeguard your credit score from a late payment, it also exposes you to the potential of at least one bigger-than-expected bill (if your spouse or partner is a dangerous shopaholic, this setup won't protect you from his or her spending). But if you can trust your sweetheart not to go crazy with the credit card, this method allows him or her to add credit history while you keep responsibility for and control of the account in your hands. (And, of course, if your sweetie gets out of control with the credit card, you can always remove him or her from the account.)

Provided you don't live in a community-property state (see the "Considering joint accounts" section for a list), separate accounts can really make sense, especially if you and your spouse or partner come together later in life and each of you has substantial assets of your own. As long as you both agree, this sort of financial independence can keep you looking attractive to your sweetie long after your personal charms have become less charming. It can also help each of you feel the independence and vigor that only money of your own can provide. For Steve's birthday one year, his wife took him, at her exclusive expense, to Walt Disney World. If they had merged all their finances, she couldn't have done so without spending at least some of Steve's money. Happy birthday to Steve!

Even if you decide to consolidate your accounts with your spouse, always keep at least one credit account in your own name as a safeguard in the event of an emergency. Keeping an individual account can also be a good thing in the event of divorce or the untimely death of a spouse; having your own account can help you reestablish credit on your own.

Managing joint debt

Talking to your creditors is hard, but talking to your sweetie about money may be even more daunting. Dealing with joint debt isn't necessarily twice as difficult as dealing with debt alone — it can be 20 times harder! If you're trying to keep your bad credit from getting worse and you have some joint debt, you may feel as though your situation is out of control. And it may be.

The most helpful tool at your disposal is communication. Here's what you and your partner need to discuss:

>> **Agreeing on goals:** Starting here is important. This conversation is about the future, and setting goals gives you a shared future that you both buy into as the impetus to make some changes. Goals may include saving for college tuition, retirement, or vacations. In the goal-setting process, you don't have to be specific the first time around. After you get through all the steps that follow, go back to the goals and put a price tag and date on each. Then rework the plan to see how many goals you can fit in and what needs to be cut or delayed. Keep in mind that goals change over time. Refer to these shared goals as you continue talking.

>> **Eliminating debt:** You're trying to keep bad credit from getting worse, so determining the best way to eliminate debt is a priority. How much can you allot each month to paying off debt? While paying down debt, agree that neither one of you will add to credit card balances.

>> **Paying bills:** If possible, pay bills together so you both know how much you owe each month and where your money is going. Decisions that need to be made, such as how much to pay on a particular credit card balance, can be made together.

>> **Keeping track of payments:** Make sure that you both record all checking account transactions (including checks you write, electronic checks, and automatic debits) in one place so that you can keep up with your balance. The same goes for using your ATM or debit card; you both need to record expenses. If you have separate accounts, decide who pays what and let each other know how things go with your respective bills.

>> **Saving:** Come to an agreement as to how much you can afford to put aside in savings each month. Early in your financial life, you may save only $5 or $10 a paycheck. But the key is to start a habit; savings *do* add up over time.

With good feelings flowing and a plan in place, make a commitment with your partner to track your progress, communicate regularly about your finances, and avoid making large purchases without discussing them first.

Avoiding money conflicts

The moose on the table. The elephant in the room. These are just a couple euphemisms we've heard to describe those huge, looming issues that couples or families pretend don't exist. But ignoring credit and money conflicts is done at great peril to a marriage. You can pretend it's not there, but it will still wreck your home.

Too often, couples who thought they were in perfect — though unspoken or assumed — agreement find out after the wedding that they're polar opposites when it comes to spending, borrowing, and saving. If you talk with your spouse about finances, you shouldn't run into credit conflicts — certainly none that could destroy your marriage. But money seems to be a taboo topic, even among married couples. Couples often don't discover money conflicts until a bounced check, late payment notice, or mammoth-sized credit card balance shows up, and by then, the discussion may not be pretty.

WARNING

Lack of careful and constant communication about money can lead to irreconcilable differences that result in divorce. When divorce is on the horizon, the fighting can escalate. Here are some of the pitfalls we hope you can avoid:

>> **Not being open with each other about how you see and value savings, money, and credit:** Silence is your enemy. The list in the "Identifying and agreeing on your major money issues" section earlier in the chapter can help you start a money-focused discussion.

>> **Pooling your funds, earnings, and credit:** Keeping some credit in your own name is important. The same goes for money. How much? Enough that you feel comfortable!

>> **Surprising your partner with a big expenditure (a car, boat, home theater system, designer shoes, donation to a cat-rescue fund, and so on):** Spending joint money without consulting your spouse is a big no-no. Determine together a spending limit, such as $100, and agree to discuss beforehand any purchase exceeding that amount.

>> **Criticizing your partner's money style in front of others:** No one wants to be ridiculed in front of others, even in good humor. If you're uncomfortable

with your mate's spending behavior, talk about it when the two of you are alone.

» **Failing to set mutual goals:** Discuss your goals and agree on a plan for achieving them. (Turn to Chapter 18 for budgeting advice.)

» **Not meeting your financial obligations:** If you're unable to pay a bill that's your responsibility, let your partner know as soon as possible.

» **Letting kids set the rules:** Kids know how to play you against each other to get what they want. This time-tested strategy can lead to discipline issues, overspending, and fights between Mom and Dad. If you have a blended household (kids from different marriages), establishing rules and standing together as a united front are especially important.

Protecting Your Finances in a Divorce

Marriage is the ultimate expression of hope for the future. When that hope goes unfulfilled, you may be faced with the prospect of a divorce, which can impact your credit and finances. If your financial life was challenging as a married couple sharing a common future, in divorce it may become even more so. To add to the stress, you may find that some of your expenses increase as you separate into two households; for example, you may have two mortgage or rent payments every month. The financial fallout from a divorce can also include difficulties in opening new accounts and obtaining new loans in your own name. This section outlines the steps you can take to protect and, if need be, restore your good credit in the event of a divorce.

Taking precautions when a split-up looms

TIP

If you suspect that a divorce may be in your future, consider the following. Even if things end up working out, these strategies are still worth considering.

» **Keep good credit in your own name.** A couple different types of accounts — such as revolving (credit card), installment (car loan), and retail (department store card) — should be sufficient.

» **Build your own credit while you're married.** Remember that your credit score is made up mostly of the amount you owe and whether you pay on time. (For the scoop on all the components that make up your credit score, turn to Chapter 13.)

» **Open your own bank account with checking and savings features.**
Overdraft protection can be a plus, especially if it's free.

» **Keep track of your joint credit accounts by checking your credit reports
frequently or by enrolling in a credit monitoring service.** Doing so may
provide you with an early warning that your partner is having some issues.
At a minimum, check one of your three credit reports every four months.
(Chapter 14 explains how to obtain copies of your credit report from the
three major credit bureaus.)

Preparing your credit before heading to court

If the possibility of divorce becomes a reality, you want to ratchet up your credit
protection action. Quickly separating your financial selves to the best of your abil-
ities is important. Here's how:

» **Inform your spouse that you're closing joint accounts, and then send a
letter to each joint creditor asking that the account be closed to any new
activity.** Closing accounts protects you. Telling your spouse in advance allows
him or her to make other plans and is the decent thing to do. Just don't wait
too long to send the letters.

» **Attempt to agree on how joint or community property accounts will be
paid and who'll be responsible for making the payments.** If you can't reach
an agreement, make the minimum payments yourself so that your credit
doesn't deteriorate. You can always recoup the money in a reconciliation or
divorce settlement; just keep track of what you pay.

» **Transfer joint balances to individual accounts if possible.** Also, include a
division of joint debts as a stipulation in your divorce decree, with specific
amounts assigned to each person.

» **Build individual credit as soon as possible.** Start small and build up
gradually if you have to. If your credit is damaged already, start with a credit
card that has a small credit limit — perhaps a card from a local department
store, gas station, or credit union. After paying your bills on time for six
months or so, apply for another card and continue paying bills consistently.
(Check out the section "Getting new credit in your own name" later in the
chapter for more info.)

» **Check your credit more frequently than normal.** Consider subscribing to a
credit monitoring service or freezing your credit to prevent the addition of any
new accounts.

YOUR JOINT CREDIT HISTORY MAY OUTLAST YOUR MARRIAGE

From the time you open your first joint account, you and your mate link your credit futures together. Your personal credit history and credit score are now influenced by the behavior of your partner on any joint debts. A blemish on his or her part is a blemish on yours, too.

How long do you have to suffer from your ex's joint-account misadventures? Negative credit items are reported for seven years in most cases. A Chapter 7 bankruptcy is reported for ten years. Your spouse's debts may be with you for a long, long time after you go your separate ways.

WARNING

Even if your prospective ex is uncooperative, keep paying at least the minimums on all joint bills on time. Don't listen to uninformed but well-meaning friends and relatives who may tell you to stop making payments or run up debts to spite your ex. Missed payments generally stay on your credit reports for seven years, making it hard or more costly to obtain new credit, employment, insurance, and maybe even a new spouse or partner.

REMEMBER

If you change your name, be sure to write to all your creditors and the three major credit bureaus to let them know. Doing so helps keep errors based on name mix-ups from affecting your credit history.

Protecting your credit in a divorce decree and beyond

When the judge rules in your divorce decree, be sure that all joint debts are clearly and specifically assigned and that both you and your ex understand that these debts must be paid on time. Close all remaining joint accounts by the date on which the divorce is granted. In the case of joint real estate that will eventually be sold, the party living on the property has more interest in making sure that the payments are made and should ask the judge to rule that the person in the house will send in the payments, even if the money comes from the other party.

REMEMBER

A divorce decree doesn't end either party's responsibility for joint debts incurred, including individual debts in community-property states (see the section "Considering joint accounts" earlier in the chapter for a list). After all, you both promised the lender that you'd repay the loan. The fact that the judge says only one of you has to make the payments from now on doesn't change your contract with the lender. Each person is fully responsible for the entire balance of joint accounts, from credit cards to car loans to home mortgages.

This section helps you figure out your next steps after your divorce is finalized.

Overcoming your ex's defaults on your joint accounts

Given the stress associated with divorce, the fact that your ex may miss a payment or two is almost understandable. We said *almost.* Although you may be understanding of such a mishap, often creditors are not. Keeping your credit record as clean as possible is critical in rebuilding a positive credit history as a single person.

Because you want to address any missed payments as soon as possible, you need to stay up-to-the-minute on payment status. You may find out about a delinquency in a number of ways: a letter, a phone call, a duplicate billing statement (you can request one), a website visit, or a credit monitoring service. As soon as you know that a payment wasn't made, take action.

>> **If your relationship allows, contact your ex to find out whether the bill has been paid.** If trust is a concern or if your relationship precludes direct communication, let your lawyer handle it. Instruct your attorney to notify your ex's attorney that the court order has been violated, and ask for a response.

>> **If the situation isn't resolved, you can always go back to court.** You can ask the judge to reorder your ex to pay as agreed or face the not-so-pleasant legal consequences of contempt of court, which can include jail time. Returning to court to enforce the paying of assigned accounts is a lengthy and expensive course of action, so consider making the payments yourself if you think the two of you can resolve the issue. Making the payments costs you money, but perhaps less than bad credit (not to mention attorney fees) costs you.

By now you've probably figured out two things: Life isn't fair, and paying a bill yourself may be easier than dealing with your ex and may be beneficial to you in the long run.

Repairing the damages

Credit damage from divorce isn't unusual, but you can take the following steps to lessen the negative impact to your credit report and score:

>> **Pay your bills on time.** Paying on time adds positive credit history on top of any negative history. Over time, your credit score gives a large number

of new, positive reports more weight than older negatives. As your credit report ages, older items count for less, so make the most of new credit going forward.

>> **Add a 100-word statement to your credit report.** Through this statement you can explain circumstances that a prospective lender or employer may not know about when considering your application.

WARNING

Be careful not to leave this statement on your report longer than you need to, because it may draw attention to a past problem that's no longer a factor in your credit score.

>> **Review your credit reports frequently.** Getting copies of your credit reports can help you control unexpected negatives, especially if your ex is still paying off joint or community-property debts. If your ex winds up not paying on a joint account, you'll probably be subject to collection activity and have to pay, or you may end up in a different court. (The rationale here is that creditors shouldn't be made to suffer just because your marriage failed.)

TIP

You can pay for credit monitoring services that alert you to any negative entries as soon as they occur, allowing you to take immediate action to reduce the damage. See Chapter 15 for the scoop on credit monitoring.

Getting new credit in your own name

The first step in getting credit in your own name is to find out where your credit stands. Begin by obtaining your credit report and your FICO score or VantageScore (I tell you how to get both in Chapter 14). The national average score is around 680 based on the VantageScore model and 703 based on the FICO score model. If you're at 780 or above, you're in Super Prime territory!

IF YOU HAVE A GOOD CREDIT SCORE

If your FICO score is 680 to 700 or above, you probably have a good chance of getting new credit in a normal credit environment.

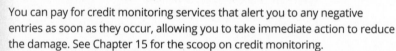

REMEMBER

Credit standards tighten or loosen from time to time. In loose credit periods, a good score gets the job done. In a tight credit environment, a good score may not be enough to get the terms or even the credit you want. We suggest that you apply for the following in your own name; this diversity of credit helps you respond to most financial situations that arise and helps build your credit score with on-time payments:

>> Checking account

>> Savings account

>> Small installment loan (use the savings account for collateral if you must)

>> Retail store credit card

>> Major bank credit card

>> Library card (because it saves you money on books, videos, and more)

IF YOU HAVE A BORDERLINE CREDIT SCORE

If your score is 660 or lower, your journey toward establishing credit in your own name may be a bit slower. Begin with the following:

>> Checking account

>> Savings account

>> Passbook loan (secured by your savings account)

>> Major bank credit card (if you qualify)

>> Secured credit card (if you don't qualify for an unsecured credit card)

A secured card gives you a line of credit based on a savings deposit to secure the credit line. This card shows up on your credit report just like an unsecured card; no one but you and the issuing bank will know!

>> Retail store credit card (you're likely to qualify if you qualify for a bank credit card)

>> Library card (no kidding)

TIP

If you apply for a credit card from your credit union or bank and you aren't sure whether you'll qualify, bring your credit report into a branch and have the bank employee look at it rather than asking the employee to pull your report. Why? If the bank declines you, a credit report inquiry won't show up on your credit report and lower your credit score unnecessarily.

WARNING

If you have a sympathetic parent or relative with decent credit, you may be able to speed up the process of reestablishing credit by having that person cosign for you, but we don't recommend it. Too often this arrangement fails, and relationships are damaged along with credit.

Keeping Credit Strong While Unemployed

The job market fluctuates just as the stock market does. The economy has good years and bad years. During bad years, you may find yourself laid off or downsized. During good years, you may decide that the time is right to change jobs on your own and for good reasons (higher pay, for example).

The reality is that you can expect that your employer will make the decision to say farewell to you at least once in your career. We can tell you from experience that the event will arrive at the least advantageous time possible. In this section, we help you through this almost inevitable fact of modern life — temporary unemployment.

REMEMBER

Employment information isn't regularly reported as part of your credit report. The credit bureaus don't keep track of where you work or what you earn. So any unemployment impact doesn't show up on your credit record unless you fail to make your payments on time, exceed your credit limits, or do something silly, like opening a lot of credit lines just in case you need them.

Preparing your credit for the worst-case scenario

The following suggestions help you protect your credit in case of unemployment:

>> **Start an emergency savings account if you don't have one already.** Fund it regularly so it grows to between six months' and a year's worth of living expenses (not income — your expenses should be less than your income). Six months to a year is how long you're likely to be unemployed if you're caught by surprise.

>> **Keep one or two credit cards or lines of credit open.** Many employers view your credit report when hiring, so you want your report to look its best even if you're unemployed. To do so, continue to pay your bills on time and keep your credit card balance at less than 50 percent of available credit if possible. (See Chapter 14 for more on what you can do to avoid raising any hiring-related red flags on your credit report.)

Using credit when you don't have a job

If you're unemployed, don't beat yourself up. You're in good company. Many people lose their jobs, often more than once. But if you've established savings and you have some available credit, you have two tools to help get you through this time without damaging your credit or your employment prospects. You can put together a new plan that includes finding a new job and a budget that works while you do so. This section tells you how.

WARNING

Stay away from using cash advances on your credit cards! Spending money this way is much more costly than simply using the credit card to pay for items. Cash advances incur an extra fee, usually have a much higher interest rate than purchases, and often have a lower limit than your credit limit.

Looking at credit differently

When you're unemployed, you move from spending resources to *conserving* them, a situation that calls for you to change your credit use priorities and start looking at credit differently. While you were employed and earning a regular income, you may have used credit differently than cash. You also may have used it for larger purchases that you needed some time to pay off.

When you're unemployed, possibly for longer than you anticipate, you don't have those earnings coming in (you may have funds from a severance package or unemployment benefits, but they're only temporary, and they may not last as long as your unemployment does). With little to no funds coming in, you may need to use credit for basic living and job-hunting expenses only. This is just about the opposite of what most people advise, but you'll do it for a limited time and for a specific, worthy purpose. If it helps, think of this approach as borrowing money for a surefire investment: you and your future.

TIP

Preserve your cash for as long as possible by using credit first. You want to keep your cash because you can't replace it after it's gone. This advice may contradict what you've heard in the past. Conventional wisdom says to control expenses by paying cash for as many things as possible. But when you're unemployed, within reason and as part of a plan, the opposite is true. Use credit *for essentials* and save the cash. You can limit your overall spending to just the essentials by closely following a budget.

Refiguring the family budget

With your reduced resources, cutting back your spending to only basic needs is essential. Begin by sitting down with your family and discussing the situation and the need to reduce expenses temporarily. Don't be embarrassed in front of the kids. This situation is an important lesson in reality for them. And you can show them how adults face difficult issues and win.

TIP

For additional budgeting pointers, whether you need to start a budget from scratch or revise a budget that you've already created, turn to Chapter 18.

TIP

If your severance is being paid out over time or you haven't yet received it, ask your employer to raise your tax deductions to the maximum allowed. The IRS wants a report of anyone with more than ten deductions, so you should generally ask for ten (after all, you don't want the IRS looking at you unnecessarily). This strategy results in more cash flowing through to you now, when you need it. Yes, you may owe some taxes on this money in April (though your deductible job-hunting expenses and reduced earnings for the year may offset that). But you want to maximize today's income at the possible expense of tomorrow's demands.

Getting credit counseling to help

If you're overwhelmed and think you can benefit from some professional perspective or guidance, go to an accredited credit counselor. You can get information on credit counselors and where to find them in Chapter 4.

Protecting your credit lines

The downside to using your lines of credit for your basic living expenses while unemployed (a strategy we recommend) is that you *may* do some damage to your credit. Here are some tips for protecting your credit status while you leverage your available credit to help you get through this challenging time:

» **Keep balances at less than 50 percent of your available credit limit.** If it becomes necessary, spread your credit use over several accounts to keep your balance on each card at less than 50 percent. For example, rather than have a $2,000 balance on one card and a zero balance on three other cards, consider spreading the amount over all four cards equally, with each balance at $500.

» **Make all payments on time.** Remember that 35 percent of your credit score has to do with whether you make payments on time. (For the full scoop on the various components of your credit score, see Chapter 13.)

» **Pay the car loan first.** A car can be repossessed in as little as two weeks. Then how will you get to work when you do find a job?

» **Pay your mortgage a very close second.** Not all bills are created equal, and your mortgage is the most unequal of all. Partial payments don't work, and falling behind 90 days begins a very-difficult-to-stop foreclosure process (see Chapter 7).

REMEMBER

Don't contact your creditor unless you *know* you're going to miss a payment. If you just *think* you may miss a payment, it's none of their business. If you *know*, however, telling the creditor before it happens is important. Why? Because you'll have more options if you do.

TIP

If you have any income, ask for a *hardship program* — a special repayment arrangement that may be offered to a good customer in need of some extra help. Such programs tend to last for no more than three to six months. Most creditors have them, but the hardship has to be real and imminent, and you have to ask for it.

TIP

If the hardship program isn't sufficient to bridge the gap between what you can afford to pay and what the creditor insists you pay, send a letter stating that you can't make any payments but that you intend to do so in the future, as soon as you find employment. You can find an example unemployment letter at www.dummies.com/go/creditrepairkitfd5e.

Curing Medical Debt

Little in life can seem more unfair than medical debt. You didn't ask for it, you got no pleasure from it, but you owe it just the same. Medical debt isn't much different from any other type of unsecured debt except that it tends to come unexpectedly and in large amounts. The key to curing medical debt is to be proactive by negotiating discounts before a service is provided or, in the case of overwhelming debt, to cut your losses early.

Medical debts are usually incurred involuntarily and you may be dealing with an insurance company that's dragging its feet, so medical collections have their own unique set of rules. Medical debts won't appear on your credit report until they're six months old. They also tend to have less effect on credit scores, and after the debts are paid, current credit systems ignore them. Although they may still appear in your credit report, if they show paid, they won't hurt your scores, and you could see a big jump in your credit score. That's something to consider when negotiating. See "Negotiating your debt down" later in this chapter.

If you have health insurance coverage, your approach to maintaining your credit is different from the approach you'd take if you didn't have insurance, at least initially. Even if you're insured, dealing with health insurance and how it covers your medical bills can be complicated and stressful. Not to worry, though. This section covers the relevant issues concerning medical debt and your credit.

Reviewing your options for paying medical bills

When faced with a pile of medical bills, you have five main options:

>> You can work with the healthcare provider to pay the bills over time.

>> You can seek assistance from a patient advocate resource.

>> You can seek medical debt consolidation.

>> You can attempt to negotiate your bills down (this works just like when you settle credit card debt — see Chapter 7).

>> You can file for bankruptcy.

TIP

If you know in advance that you'll be incurring uninsured medical expenses and you don't know whether you can afford them, we suggest that you speak to your service providers as soon as possible. Ask if discounts are available for underinsured/uninsured patients. (Note that you may have to provide financial disclosures to qualify for these discounts.) Be sure to get all agreements in writing so there's no misunderstanding.

Applying for medical financial aid

Many hospitals provide charitable or financial aid to patients who qualify. Many clinics and doctors' offices also consider helping those who can prove that they're under unusual financial duress because of escalating medical bills or decreasing incomes. However, if you decide to apply for assistance, you may be better off doing so as soon as possible because many providers have time limits on aid applications (usually 6 to 12 months). Although you have to complete a substantial amount of paperwork and supply a lot of information, you may wipe thousands of dollars off your financial ledger.

Getting professional help

Help is available to consumers in the form of advocates. A number of organizations, some nonprofit, help you negotiate fees and payments or just get through the process of filling out the forms you're likely to encounter in the bill-negotiation process.

Here are some of the advantages to using an intermediary:

>> They know the industry, the laws, and the regulations.

>> They're not emotionally involved.

>> They've done this before, and you may not have.

>> They may help you identify benefits, grants, and entitlements.

>> They may have developed existing relationships that can be helpful in resolving issues more quickly.

TIP

The Patient Advocate Foundation is a national nonprofit organization that has provided mediation and arbitration services since 1996. It offers assistance to patients dealing with the effects of chronic, debilitating, or life-threatening illnesses. Its free services include resolving insurance-access issues, helping patients with employment issues, and assisting with medical-debt crises. Reach the organization at 800-532-5274 or www.patientadvocate.org.

You can find fee-for-service advocate organizations on the Internet but you may want to check out:

>> **Healthcare Advocates, Inc.** (www.healthcareadvocates.com), knows the industry, laws, and regulations to help you get the best healthcare.

>> The **Alliance of Claims Assistance Professionals** (www.claims.org) is a nationally recognized association of independent Claims Assistance Professionals (CAP). It provides medical claims assistance and patient advocacy to individuals and businesses and are fee-based. Each business determines its own scope and cost of services.

Negotiating your debt down

Believe it or not, you can negotiate medical expenses. Most providers have more than one rate for the same service or product — the insured price and the uninsured price. Because they negotiate prices in advance, many insurers get much lower prices than individuals paying out of pocket do. Asking for a discount is nothing new, and asking for insurance company pricing shouldn't cause any heart rates to rise at your provider's office. Explain your financial situation to your health-care provider. Offer to make a partial payment up front if you can afford one in exchange for the remainder of the balance being forgiven or at least a 0 percent interest rate on the balance. If you can't put any money down, ask for a discount on the charges to the Medicare rate.

TIP

If you're not comfortable attempting to negotiate medical charges yourself, try working with a patient advocate group that has experience in this area.

Financing your medical debt

Having one bill to deal with may be easier than keeping track of many service provider payments. Here are the two ways to consolidate your medical debts:

REMEMBER

TIP

>> **Pay with credit cards:** Putting your medical debt on a credit card may seem like a way to make the problem go away, if only for a billing cycle. But what you're really doing is borrowing money from a lender to pay a medical provider. You may be better off making a deal with the provider than with a lender if you have a hardship.

If you opt to use plastic to cover your bills, be sure that you can afford your payments, you know what interest rate your card charges, and you're aware of any possible issues paying with credit may cause, such as affecting your eligibility for Medicaid (check your state rules to be sure medical debt on a credit card qualifies as a medical expense).

Be sure to consider a new card or one that has a balance transfer option with a long, low introductory interest rate to keep payments affordable.

>> **Pay with installment loans:** Another option is to get an installment loan from your bank or credit union. This type of loan has a fixed interest rate, term, and payment. Under the Fair and Accurate Credit Transactions Act (FACT Act or FACTA), lenders can't use your medical condition against you when they decide whether to give you credit and when they establish terms. To help ensure enforcement of this requirement, your copy of your credit report shows the name of the creditor so you can identify the debt. To protect your privacy, others ordering your report see only the generic descriptor "medical payment data."

WHAT TO DO WHEN YOUR INSURANCE COMPANY DENIES PAYMENT

If your insurance covers only a portion of a bill and you can't afford the balance, you have a couple alternatives to letting the bill go to collections, which damages your credit:

- **Ask for a discount.** Big insurance companies ask for discounts all the time, and hospitals grant them. Don't be afraid to ask your provider.

- **Ask the doctor to accept the insurance payment amount as payment in full.** Doctors do this all the time. Doctors in a network get whatever the insurer pays. The doctor agrees to this arrangement upfront in order to become a member of the network and get referrals. You may be able to get the same deal if you ask.

Filing for medical bankruptcy

You may hear the term *medical bankruptcy* touted as though it's different from a regular bankruptcy, but technically the two are the same. Personal bankruptcies are generally either a Chapter 7 or a Chapter 13. A Chapter 7 eliminates many but not all debts, and to qualify you have to pass a means test based on your state's median income. A Chapter 13 bankruptcy allows you to repay what you can from current earnings, typically over a five-year period, and is not income restricted.

A medical bankruptcy is brought on by medical bills that are either so large or owed to such aggressive providers or collectors that they can't be satisfied. No one we know of is happy when forced to consider bankruptcy. However, in the case of overwhelming medical debts, you need to

>> Be realistic in assessing whether you'll ever be able to repay what you owe.

>> Know the full extent of what you owe and to whom you owe it.

TIP

After you know that your bills are insurmountable and providers won't accept reduced payments that you can afford, see an attorney to assess your legal options and plan your best strategy. To ensure that a bankruptcy is in your best interest, use an attorney who specializes in debt problems. A nonspecialist may leave debts out of a filing or expose your assets to claims. Income, recentness of debt acquisition, and homestead exemptions are examples of items that can be overlooked.

REMEMBER

Going without medical treatment isn't an option just because you can't afford to pay for it.

Discovering how insurers get your medical information

Whether you like it or not, insurers have access to your medical records and prescription drug records, thanks to the MIB and the newer prescription drug databases. When we say MIB, we're not referring to the Men in Black but to the even more mysterious Medical Information Bureau, which maintains a database that's home to health-related information on millions of people. Roughly 450 to 500 member insurance companies use and share the MIB's information to supplement their underwriting before pricing their services or issuing life, disability, or individual health insurance products. And that information isn't always accurate.

Not everyone has an MIB file. You need to have applied for life, disability, or individual (not group) insurance from an MIB member company. Information about your health or longevity is sent to the MIB by the member company in an encrypted format. The data identifies medical conditions or tests and a few nonmedical codes. Those codes report potentially hazardous avocations or hobbies or a motor vehicle report showing a poor driving history.

Insurers also rely on prescription drug databases, such as those operated by OptumInsight and Milliman, primarily when you're seeking private health, life, or disability insurance. Prescription drug databases can go back as far as five years, detailing drugs used as well as dosage and refills — and they aren't always error-free, either.

TIP

You're entitled to copies of your records at the MIB and both prescription drug databases. Simply call the organizations (I provide contact information in Chapter 14) and ask how to obtain your free copies. To dispute any inaccurate information, just follow the instructions on your report. Should the dispute not be resolved to your satisfaction, you can submit a statement of dispute, which becomes part of your MIB file. From that point forward, any MIB member that receives your MIB file also receives a copy of your statement of dispute.

Monitoring insurance claims for errors

You may be tempted to ignore the whole medical-payment process and assume that the insurance company and the doctors will handle everything satisfactorily. But you know better — what can go wrong often does. Claims payments and treatment-authorization communication between doctors and insurance companies are coded, and one misplaced digit can make a big difference in what medical care is paid for or allowed. Catching small errors early is important, and you, as the party responsible for the bill, have the most at stake.

Between the insurance companies — which have a better day when they don't pay a lot of claims — and the underpaid staff in medical offices and hospitals who code all the procedures, errors are common, and legitimate claims are sometimes rejected. If your claim is rejected, ask for the bill to be resubmitted and for an explanation of why it was rejected the first time.

TIP

You don't have to be a claims whiz to keep track of the insurance process. Familiarizing yourself with your coverage limits is worth your time. Read through your insurance contracts (sorry, it's not the most scintillating reading). Get a copy of your coverage if you don't already have one. It may be a policy, a booklet, or something called a *summary plan description*. (The insurance policy itself is the best and most complete source.) The health plan description is 20 to 30 pages or more. The devil is in the definitions; terms you want to pay attention to include the following:

>> **Schedule of benefits:** This section explains what the insurance company pays and what you pay — deductibles, percentages, co-pays, and so on.

>> **Covered benefits:** Often separate from the schedule of benefits, this section is a laundry list of what's covered.

>> **Exclusions and limitations:** This section tells you what isn't covered, as well as items that are covered but with limits.

>> **Claims procedures:** This section explains the steps for filing claims and appealing denials. You may want to read all the way through this part, as it usually includes important time limits and details.

TIP

Reviewing these key components should give you a good idea of your coverage. If bills and statements start showing up and you find that keeping track of expenses and reimbursements is just too stressful, consider a *daily money manager (DMM)*. Relatively new on the scene, a DMM is similar to a personal financial advisor — someone who can provide a wide range of services depending on your needs. This individual can also keep track of medical bills and insurance forms. The best way to find a good DMM is through a referral. If no one you know can direct you to a good DMM, contact the American Association of Daily Money Managers (AADMM) at www.aadmm.com or 814-357-9191.

Dealing with denied medical claims

Most doctors and hospitals don't report payment histories to credit bureaus. They don't like to pay the fees, and some of them don't like to think that they're in the credit business. However, if a debt moves from a medical provider to an outside collection agency, odds are it will hit your credit report. The message here is that you have more wiggle room with a medical provider, but be sure to ask whether the provider reports your payment history to one of the credit-reporting agencies.

TIP

Keep in touch with the hospital billing people, who assume that if the insurance company denies a claim, you'll pay the difference. Communicating that you don't consider the claim settled and that you need their help to resubmit or appeal a decision makes them a part of the process and keeps their expectations in line with yours. Just as you take an active role in your care and treatment as a patient, you also have to take an active role in the payment of your medical costs.

If you have a hard time getting your bills covered and you think the insurance company is wrong, take the following steps:

1. Complain.

Insurance carriers, believe it or not, don't like complaints. Here's a list of people to complain to, starting with the lowest one on the totem pole:

- Claims adjuster
- Supervisor
- Unit manager (over several supervisors by line of business)
- Assistant manager (over unit managers, but not in all offices)
- Claims manager or claims vice president (in charge of a local office)
- Regional claims vice president (in charge of several offices in a region)
- Home office claims, senior vice president
- President

REMEMBER

Despite how frustrated you may be feeling, always be polite and direct. Nasty complaints are easily dismissed or sent to a lawyer.

2. Maintain detailed records.

When dealing with insurers, keep records of conversations (times, dates, and what was said), as well as copies of any documents you receive. If you write to an adjuster, copy the supervisor and request a written response within a set time frame.

3. **File a written complaint.**

If you reach an impasse, write to your state insurance regulatory agency. Don't go into great detail; just explain the basic issues that are in dispute. To find your state regulator online, go to www.naic.org. Complaining to your state regulator is likely to motivate the insurer to pay better attention to resolving your claim.

REMEMBER

If you have no insurance, let the doctor or hospital know this fact early in the process. Then ask about discounts and payment plans, but be sure you can afford the payment plan before you agree to it. (You may want to follow the process we recommend in the "Keeping Credit Strong While Unemployed" section earlier in this chapter, which involves resetting your spending priorities until you have the new bills under control.) Being willing to pay a reasonable bill over time is the best course of action to keep collection activity off your credit record. Communicating with your doctor and hospital is the key.

MANAGING EXPENSES TO AVOID CREDIT REPERCUSSIONS

If, when all is said and done, you're left with medical expenses that you're responsible for paying, you have some options:

- **Suggest a reduced repayment amount either in a lump sum (ask the service provider to consider an ease-of-handling discount for cash) or a set payment every month.** Do so before you get billed. When third-party billers get hold of a debt, they're tenacious, and the providers generally don't want to get in the middle. Deal with the provider first if you can.

- **Find out whether your hospital is covered under the federal Hill-Burton Act, which prohibits discrimination in providing services.** In 1975, Congress amended the Hill-Burton program, which established federal grants, loan guarantees, and interest subsidies for certain health facilities to require that they must provide uncompensated services forever. The U.S. Department of Health and Human Services at the Health Resources and Services Administration has information about where to find the 170 facilities covered under Hill-Burton. Check out www.hrsa.gov/get-health-care/affordable/hill-burton/index.html. There are no such facilities in Alaska, Indiana, Minnesota, Nebraska, Nevada, North Dakota, Rhode Island, Utah, or Wyoming, and all the territories except Puerto Rico.

Resolving Credit Issues After the Death of a Spouse or Partner

If you've lost a spouse or partner, you're already going through one of life's most emotionally draining experiences. Unfortunately, in the midst of the often debilitating experience of losing a loved one, numerous financial matters surface, including credit and debt issues.

WARNING

For one thing, thieves may use the deceased's Social Security number and identity to open fraudulent credit accounts. Promptly sending a copy of the death certificate to the credit bureaus can help deter this crime:

>> **Equifax,** P.O. Box 105069, Atlanta, GA 30348

>> **Experian,** P.O. Box 9701, Allen, TX 75013

>> **TransUnion,** P.O. Box 6790, Fullerton, CA 92634

Stabilizing your credit in the event of a death can be difficult, especially if your spouse held all or most of the credit in his or her name. A creditor wants a copy of the death certificate and typically asks the estate to pay the bill. As a rule, you aren't personally responsible for credit held in the deceased's name alone unless the two of you lived in a community-property state.

REMEMBER

In community-property states — Arizona, California, Idaho, Louisiana, Nevada, New Mexico, Texas, Washington, and Wisconsin — credit accounts opened during a marriage are automatically considered joint accounts. That means you're responsible for any debt your deceased spouse incurred during the marriage. This may also be true in Alaska if you opted for community-property status when you moved there. Although Puerto Rico is an American territory and not a state, it has community-property laws, too.

This section tells you how to protect your credit when the debts belong to a deceased spouse.

Understanding what happens to joint credit when you're single again

By law, a creditor can't automatically close a joint account or change the terms because of the death of one spouse. Generally, the creditor asks you, the surviving spouse, to fill out a new credit application in your own name. If your creditor doesn't approach you with this option, close the joint account and open a new individual account in your name alone. The creditor then decides whether to continue to extend credit or alter the credit limit. *Remember:* You don't have to deal with this issue the day after your spouse's death, but sooner is better than later, because a major change to your account has occurred.

Knowing exactly what your liability is

If you're a joint account holder on a credit card, or if you live in one of the community-property states noted earlier, you may owe the debts of the deceased. In a community-property state, as long as the debt was incurred during the marriage, you are liable, even if you received no benefit from it or didn't even know about it.

In non-community-property states, credit card debts and other debts that are solely in the name of the deceased aren't passed on to surviving spouses or children. However, notifying creditors is still a good idea, even if you aren't liable. They generally request that a certified copy of the death certificate be forwarded to them to close the account. If the estate has assets, creditors may try to collect any balance due from the estate's executor. If the estate doesn't have enough cash and has few assets that can be sold, the issue generally ends there.

TIP

Some people feel that they should pay their deceased spouse's debts, whether out of a sense of obligation or honor or just to set the record straight. Paying the debt of your deceased spouse isn't necessary unless you're required to do so by law. Creditors understand risk very well and factor it into their fees and interest rates. In that regard, they've already been paid. If a creditor tries to pressure you into paying a debt that you aren't obligated to pay, we recommend telling the creditor to take a hike.

TERMINATING THE DECEASED'S PREAPPROVED CREDIT OFFERS

Credit bureaus automatically update records with periodic reports from the Social Security Administration. When the update is made, your spouse's credit history is flagged, and his or her name is removed from any preapproved credit offer mailing lists. This reduces the mail you get in your spouse's name. You can speed up this process by notifying the three major credit bureaus (use the information provided earlier in this section).

Building your credit record on your own

If your spouse or partner has died and you shared financial matters, you need to reestablish yourself as an individual. Your first task is to come up with a spending plan that covers your expenses as a single person. This plan helps you understand how your financial situation has changed, for better or worse. We offer pointers on creating a spending plan in Chapter 18. When setting goals, we suggest that you stick to short- and intermediate-term goals until your life has settled down.

When you know where you stand financially, you can begin deciding how you want to use credit. Because your credit score determines what you pay for credit and under what terms it may be available, we suggest that you get your FICO score from www.myfico.com, along with copies of your credit reports (www.annualcreditreport.com). The better your score, the less you have to pay to borrow or use credit. (For guidance on reviewing your reports, flip to Chapter 14.)

REMEMBER

Don't close old accounts with positive credit histories unless you have to. The length of time an account is open counts in your favor for credit scoring purposes. Having a variety of accounts also helps your score. If you have a mortgage or a car payment and you can afford to pay it off, you may want to consider keeping it open for a short while to keep new positive information flowing into your credit file.

Fitting Credit into Retirement

Until a certain point in their lives, most people think of their kids or their home as the most expensive part of their financial environment. Then they hit retirement. Retirement may not last as long as your kids or your home, but it does require more saving and planning. The sooner you begin to plan, save, and invest for your exit from the workforce, the better.

Credit can be a help or a hindrance in retirement. On the positive side, using credit rather than cash can be a great convenience and can add value in your later years if done wisely. But because credit essentially allows you to use tomorrow's income today, you may wind up overusing credit, which can be difficult to rebound from when you stop getting paychecks and raises and find that your income is more or less fixed. To avoid falling into a credit crunch in retirement, make sure that you have a solid budget. You need to know what you're spending and what you have coming in each month. In this section, we present the basics on creating a budget that can set you up well for retirement, and we help you understand how the use of credit changes in this phase of life.

Budgeting on a fixed income

Following are the essential ingredients for successful budgeting. (Chapter 18 goes into detail about constructing a budget that works for you, not against you.)

>> **Set short-term and long-term goals.** Whether you're 55 or 95, you need a reason to get up in the morning. Goals provide this motivation and more. Although they may differ from those you had earlier in life, goals, especially around spending, keep you looking forward to tomorrow. They may include traveling to places you've always wanted to see, making a difference in your community, or just seeing more of family.

   Short-term goals for your stage of life should be in the 6- to 12-month range, while longer-term ones may go out to 5 years.

>> **Know your monthly income and expenses.** After you settle on your goals, you need to fund them. Don't guess; know what you can afford. Make sure that you can cover basic, recurring monthly expenses, and don't forget to keep an emergency fund. You don't need the standard 12 months of expenses because you won't have to fund a period of unemployment. But you will need to meet any unexpected out-of-pocket expenses like home repairs, major car repairs, or insurance deductibles. Know what your exposure is and set funds aside for it.

>> **Protect your cash.** When your cash is gone, it's gone! Be sure to control your urge to spend for items not in your budget. Don't use tax-deferred retirement funds to pay off debt if you have any other choice. Although you may be beyond the age of early-withdrawal penalties, taxes take a big chunk out of withdrawals. Use excess cash flow to pay down debt gradually whenever possible. Home equity loans or reverse mortgages may be sources for interest-deductible or tax-exempt funds if they fit your goals and plan.

>> **Control debt payments.** Any new debt payments must fit into your budget. Try to match the time it takes you to pay off a debt with the time you'll be using an item. For example, the debt you incur by paying for a meal out with a credit card should be paid off at the end of the month. The debt you incur for a car should be paid off over the useful life of the car or before you plan to buy a replacement. The debt you incur in buying a home that you intend to live in for the rest of your life need not be paid off until you die.

Using credit for convenience

Although your income may decrease when you hit retirement, your credit history keeps on growing. Great reasons to use credit rather than cash include reward points and easier tracking of expenses. These conveniences add value to the money you spend.

With some simple caveats, credit can be as big a boon to seniors as it is to the population as a whole. Here are three easy and simple safeguards to consider:

» **Never lend your good credit to someone else.** Adding an authorized user to your account to help a friend with bad credit or cosigning on a loan usually ends in disaster. Giving someone else access to your credit gives that person access to your cash and your future well-being; it's absolutely not worth it.

» **Don't put yourself in a position to become a victim of credit card fraud.** To avoid becoming another statistic, be on guard when you use credit. When shopping online, look for the padlock icon in the address bar or *https* in the web address; both indicate that the connection is secure. And never give your credit card information to anyone who contacts you first.

» **Check one of your free credit reports every four months, more often if allowed, alternating requests among the three credit bureaus.** Staying on top of your credit reports is one of the most effective ways to catch credit card fraud early. Be sure to dispute any accounts you don't recognize. See Chapter 3 for details on disputing credit report errors. They could mean identity theft! For guidance on getting free copies of your credit reports from the three major credit bureaus, head to Chapter 14.

4

Making Sense of Credit Reporting and Scoring

» **Figuring out just what a credit report is**

» **Understanding the impact of negative and positive credit information**

» **Getting the scoop on credit scores**

Chapter **13**

Discovering How Credit Reporting Works

Have you ever looked at your credit report? We ask that question often. Once in a while we're surprised when a person tells us they have. Occasionally, we get a blank stare because it's something that never occurred to them. Most of the time, though, they shake their head and either say they don't want to look because they're afraid, or they just don't care because they don't use credit. That's a huge financial mistake. There are a lot of reasons to care about what's in your credit report and no reason at all to be afraid to check it.

Your credit history doesn't just come into play when you want to borrow money. Landlords, insurers, and even employers review credit reports. They use the information from your credit report to make decisions about whether you get a loan, an apartment, a car, and maybe even a job. A poor credit history can cost you thousands of dollars and cause you to miss opportunities you never even knew you had.

Credit reports sound mysterious and confusing, but they really aren't. Your credit report can be a powerful financial tool. You can know exactly what lenders, landlords, utility companies, and even your cellphone provider will see before you ever apply. Anytime lenders and others use your report to determine your credit risk — and especially in a tight credit market — knowing what they'll see is important.

Your credit report and credit scores, calculated using the information from the report, can make a big difference in whether you qualify for a loan and how much you pay in interest or other terms of the loan. They can also make a difference in how much you pay for your auto and homeowner's/renter's insurance. In this chapter, we help you understand why you need to take ownership of your credit reports and scores, what they really are, and where they come from.

After you're up to speed on credit reports and scores, challenge your friends to the credit score quiz found at www.creditscorequiz.org. Hint: This quiz was co-authored by VantageScore and the Consumer Federation of America!

Grasping the Importance of Your Credit Report

Wondering where all the data in your credit history comes from? Despite what you may have heard, there's nothing nefarious afoot. It may be a shock, but you're the first source of information that goes into your credit report. When you fill out an application with a bank, credit card provider, cellphone company, or landlord, the identifying information you provide is the first thing that goes in your credit report. After that, the lenders and other businesses you have accounts with will report your payments — or lack thereof — to the credit reporting companies. Chances are, they're reporting your financial transactions to all three major credit bureaus (Equifax, Experian, and TransUnion) and potentially other specialty bureaus that store information.

When you pay your car payment, mortgage payment, and credit card bill each month, your creditors report your payment history to the credit bureaus. If you miss a payment, your creditor reports that as well. Creditors review the information in your credit report or other specialty reports to determine the terms they may offer you for a credit card, loan, apartment, or insurance policy. So do utility companies and cellphone providers. A good credit history may result in lower security deposits to the utility company, and it will definitely help you get the coolest new mobile device.

Clearly, what you don't know *can* hurt you. You can't report your own credit history to the bureaus (although that may be changing a bit — see the "Revealing the facts about your financial transactions" section, later in this chapter), but you *can* be knowledgeable about what your credit report says and anticipate how it may influence others as you try to negotiate your way through the financial universe. You *can* head off situations that could cost you thousands of dollars or deny you opportunities. And you *can* catch inaccuracies on your report (a fairly common situation) and correct them.

TIP

You have no excuse for not knowing what's in your credit report because you can get a free copy of your report annually from each of the three credit bureaus. Getting the information is fast and easy. Simply visit www.annualcreditreport.com or call 877-322-8228 to order your reports.

What Is a Credit Report, Exactly?

In its most basic sense, your credit report is your financial life history — as far as debts are concerned. Credit reporting companies collect information about your debts and compile it into a file that they then share (as allowed by the law — see Chapter 14) with your lenders or other businesses. Lenders and other businesses use the information as one part of making a decision about your application. There are three national credit reporting companies:

>> **Equifax:** www.equifax.com; 800-685-1111

>> **Experian:** www.experian.com; 866-200-6020

>> **TransUnion:** www.transunion.com; 800-888-4213

The name of the law that governs them — the Fair Credit Reporting Act (FCRA) — is a bit misleading. In fact, it regulates all consumer reporting agencies in addition to the credit bureaus. In addition to the three national credit bureaus, there are also 20 or more specialty consumer reporting agencies, which collect other kinds of information, like whether you've bounced a check or made insurance claims (see Chapter 14).

You can rest assured that your rights are protected in the reporting process because of the FCRA and the Fair and Accurate Credit Transactions Act (the FACT Act or FACTA) that amended it.

TIP

You can find more details on the FCRA and the FACT Act in Chapter 3. To read the FCRA, go to www.ftc.gov/system/files/documents/statutes/fair-credit-reporting-act/545a_fair-credit-reporting-act-0918.pdf; to read the FACT Act, go to www.congress.gov/108/plaws/publ159/PLAW-108publ159.pdf.

The following sections explain what your credit report reveals about your financial relationships — specifically your debts.

Revealing the facts about your financial transactions

Credit reporting has actually been around since the late 1800s. Back then, a person went from business to business in the town and asked merchants about how their customers managed their credit. It was literally the Wild West. Observations and opinions like, "He won't pay, but his father will," and "I won't give him store credit because he drinks too much," could be in the notes. That's in the far, far distant past.

Today, the information in your credit report is specific, factual, and limited to your financial transactions. Either the bill was paid on time, or it wasn't. That objectivity can empower you if you manage your finances well. Keep making your payments on time and don't take on too much debt, and lenders will flock to you asking for your business. On the other hand, they'll also see any signs of trouble very quickly. If you miss even a single payment, it can feel like they disappeared like a drop of water on the hottest day in August in Death Valley. Poof, they're gone.

In truth, credit reports are really pretty simple. All you have to know is that everything in your credit report is debt related. Here's what you'll see when you get your credit report:

>> **Personal identification information:** This info includes your name, Social Security number, date of birth, addresses (present and past), and a list of employers. There are a couple of things to understand about identification information:

- Any variations of your name, Social Security number, and address reported to the bureaus will also be shown. Those aren't mistakes. They're listed so you have a complete record of what lenders are telling them is in their records. For example, if your name is Robert Smith and you also apply as Bob, you'll see both listed.

  Be sure to check any variations closely. They could indicate you're a fraud victim and help you take action quickly.

- The list of employers is not an employment history. The bureaus list the names of employers included in your credit applications. If you don't apply for new credit for a long time and change jobs several times, you may not see all your employers in the list. That's okay. The list is used as an additional identifier and doesn't affect scores or lending decisions in any way.

REMEMBER

Be consistent with your personal information, especially how you spell your name and address. The credit bureaus maintain credit reports on more than 220 million people, and you aren't the only person with your name. Being consistent is a huge help in ensuring your credit information is matched correctly to you and not someone else. Contrary to common myth, the credit bureaus don't just match your information to your Social Security number. They use all the information reported to them to match your credit report details. Another common myth is that you have to have a Social Security number to have a credit report. In fact, you don't. If a lender opens an account without requiring a Social Security number and reports it, you'll have a credit report the bureaus would match to all the other information the lender provided.

Because the bureaus match to all the identifying information, changing your name won't cause a new report to be created. For example, if you're a woman and you take your husband's name when you get married, your files should be automatically updated when you get a reissued credit card or a loan in your new name.

>> **Public record information:** Here's a bit of good news. All public records, with the exception of bankruptcy, have been removed from credit reports. Civil judgments, tax liens, and other fines have been removed. That doesn't mean they won't be part of other specialty consumer reports (see Chapter 14), but they won't be in your credit report.

>> **Collection activity:** If you've had accounts sent to collection agencies for handling, your credit report contains that info.

>> **Information about each credit account (or *trade line*), whether open or closed:** Your credit report includes details on all your credit accounts, including

- Type of account (such as a mortgage, installment, or revolving account). *Revolving* is a fancy word for credit card. You can carry the balance, or revolve it, from one month to the next.

- Your account association. Whether the account is *individual* (just in your name) or *joint* (shared equally with another person), as well as whether you're a cosigner or authorized user. How you're associated with the account is very important because it's directly related to your responsibility for the debt. If you're an individual, joint account holder, or a cosigner, you're responsible for paying the whole debt, even if the other person doesn't pay his share. Authorized users have permission to use an account, but they aren't responsible for paying any of the debt.

- The principle amount. How much the loan was at first. This applies to installment loans.

- Your credit limit. The maximum amount you can charge on a credit card.

- The remaining balance (for installment loans) or current balance (for credit cards) on the account.

- Your monthly payment. This may be estimated, so it may not match exactly but should be close.

- The account status. This indicates things like the account is open and active, paid in full, settled, or charged off as a loss.

- Who you owe. The account entry will show the name of the creditor or collection agency.

- Your payment history (whether you've paid on time or been late). This is by far the most important information in your credit report.

>> **A list of the companies that have requested your credit file for the purpose of granting you credit:** When your credit report is requested, a record of that request, called an *inquiry*, is added. There are two types of inquiries:

- *Soft inquiries* are made for promotional purposes (for instance, when a credit card issuer wants to send you an offer). They also include getting your own report, reviews by your existing lenders, and reports requested for employment or insurance purposes. These inquiries don't appear on the version of your credit report that lenders see, but they do appear on the copy that you get. Because only you see them, they don't affect credit scores or lending decisions.

- *Hard inquiries* are added in response to your applications for new credit. These inquiries *do* appear on the lender's copy of your credit report. They indicate you may have a new debt that doesn't show on your report yet, so they represent a bit of risk at first. New accounts are added at the end of the first billing cycle (about 30 days after it's opened). At that point, the inquiry will no longer have any meaningful impact on your credit scores.

>> **An optional message or ten from you:** You can add a message of up to 100 words in length that explains any extenuating circumstances for your report overall or for any specific account in your report. One message may be enough, but if you have different explanations for more than one account, you can add individual 100-word messages to specific trade lines. See Chapter 3 for more on adding these messages to your credit report.

>> **Maybe your utility, telecom, and rent payments.** A relatively new development in credit reporting is the ability to have your positive cellphone, utility (natural gas, water, electricity), and rent payments added to your report. Services are emerging that enable you to give permission for credit bureaus to check your bank account or credit card statement monthly for your payment and add it to your credit report. For a number of years, landlords have been

able to report your positive rent payments to credit bureaus if the landlord agrees to do so on your behalf, but you have to ask first. Services like Experian Boost (www.experian.com/boost) are free, but they require you to enroll in a service and give permission to access your accounts. Many people report that their scores get better after enrolling in these programs, so they may help give your scores a step up, or they may not. They also require you to share information. Be sure you're comfortable doing so. If not, or if they don't help your scores, you may not want to use them. It's your choice.

Credit reports are easy to read and are constantly being improved. Each of the three major credit-reporting agencies reports your information in its own unique format. The credit-reporting agencies compete with one another for business, so they have to differentiate their products. (Chapter 14 highlights the differences in each agency's presentation.)

TIP

This may come as a shock, but credit scores are not part of a credit report. They aren't part of your report, you can purchase a credit score and explanation of it when you request your free annual report. You can also get free credit scores from a number of sources. Here are a few things to know when you request your score:

>> **The number won't match the one your lender has, but that's okay.** The score will be different depending on which one is used to calculate the number, the scale of the scoring system (we once saw a score with a scale from 75 to 108, but most are 300 to 850 today), the credit bureau information that was used, and when the score was calculated. Information from each bureau can be a bit different, and if something has changed between the time you got your score and the lender got theirs, the number could change, too. Even if the numbers are very different, they almost certainly mean the same thing in terms of risk, and that's what counts.

>> **Make sure you get a list of the risk factors that affected your score.** Although the numbers can be very different, the risk factors tend to be very consistent. They tell you what information from your personal credit report most affected the calculation. By comparing the factors to your report, you can begin to address the biggest issues that are dragging the number down.

>> **Work on the risk factors, and all your scores will get better.** The number gives you a sense of where you stand. The risk factors give you the information you need to change the number. Work on those factors and all your scores will get better.

REMEMBER

Among the list of items *not* included in your credit report are your lifestyle choices, religion, national origin, political affiliation, sexual preferences, medical history, friends, and relatives. In addition, the three major credit-reporting agencies don't collect or transmit data about your assets, including your income, checking or savings accounts, or brokerage accounts. How much money you have in the bank doesn't mean you'll use it to pay your debts. Credit reports and scores look at whether you pay your debts regardless of the assets you have. Believe it or not, there are many rich deadbeats out there.

Your reports also do not include business accounts (unless you're on record as being personally liable for the debt), bankruptcies that are more than ten years old, charge-offs or debts placed for collection that are more than seven years old, or your credit score. It's worth repeating that although your credit score is generated based on information in your credit report, it's not part of the report itself.

TIP

You can view sample credit reports from each of the three major credit-reporting bureaus at www.dummies.com/go/creditrepairkitfd5e.

Providing insight into your character

Many entities use your credit report to predict your potential behavior in other areas of your life. Whether we like it or not, people are creatures of habit. The decisions you make and actions you take in one part of your life give insight into how you'll act in other parts of your life. It's why the fact that you have a history of making credit card payments late suggests to a prospective landlord that you may be late with your rent, too. A home foreclosure in your file may indicate that you take on more than you can handle or that you're just one unlucky duck.

This financial snapshot, which brings into focus the details of your spending and borrowing, also paints a *bigger* picture of two important factors that are critical to employers, landlords, lenders, and others:

>> **Whether you keep your financial promises:** Your credit history is an indicator of whether you follow through with your financial commitments, a characteristic that's important to most people, whether they're looking for a reliable worker, a responsible nanny, a dependable renter, or even a faithful mate ("What's your score?" may be replacing "What's your sign?" as a pickup line!). Needless to say, a person or company that's considering extending you a loan, apartment lease, insurance policy, or job (although employers don't get scores) wants to know the same.

>> **Whether you fulfill your obligations in a timely manner:** Following through with your obligations in a timely manner is the other half of the credit-reporting equation. Tight lending standards make a history of past failures to pay on time harder to accept for lenders who can't afford any more defaults.

WARNING

In the lending business, the more overdue the payment, the more likely it won't be paid in full — or paid at all. That's why, as you get further behind in your payments, lenders become more anxious about collecting the amount you owe. In fact, if you're sufficiently delinquent, the lender may want you to pay back the entire amount at once rather than as originally scheduled. So the longer you take to do what you promised, the more it costs you and the more damage you do to your credit history and credit score.

The Negatives and Positives of Credit Reporting

Whether you're new to the world of credit or you're an experienced borrower, you may be mesmerized by the amount of information on your credit report. In simplest terms, it all falls into one of two categories: negative (information that indicates you may be a financial risk) and positive (information that makes lenders want to throw money at you, or at least not turn you down for a loan). In the following sections, we zero in on the differences between the two so that you can focus on what matters and let go of what doesn't.

The negatives

This may come as a surprise, but you aren't perfect. And neither is your credit report. The good news is that you don't need a flawless credit report to qualify for financial products and services at competitive rates and terms. Perfection is always a good aspiration, but it's never a goal. When it comes to credit, it just needs to be good enough. Here are the answers to some common questions about the negative data found on the vast majority of Americans' credit reports:

>> **How long do bad marks stick around?** The rule of thumb is seven years, although there are a few exceptions, and when that clock starts depends on the information you're looking at. Late payments remain for seven years from the date of the missed payment. If you never catch up after missing the first payment, the charged-off account and any subsequent collections are deleted seven years from that first payment. It's called the *original delinquency date*, and it's the most important date most people have in their credit report.

Chapter 13 bankruptcy public records also remain for seven years, but from the filing date of the bankruptcy. You get a bit of a break because you pay off part of the debt. Chapter 7 bankruptcy stays ten years from the filing date because you don't repay any of the debt. Even though the negative information is out there for a long time, as the months and years roll by, the information becomes less important to your credit profile. For example, most creditors aren't concerned by the fact that you were late in paying a credit card bill one time three years ago, if everything else has gone well since.

>> **Just how much does one mistake cost you when it comes to your credit report?** That depends on the mistake and on the rest of the items on your report that make up your credit history. One late payment in a long, otherwise clean history will have less impact than one that is among many late accounts. A default on a credit card is less serious than a mortgage default, although both are huge problems.

Lenders use credit scores to analyze the information in your credit report and evaluate the risk of lending to you. A *credit score* is a number that's calculated using the information from your credit report. Credit score formulas are developed by studying the information from millions of past credit reports and identifying patterns that indicate repayment risk. The number is simply a way to objectively indicate to the lender the likelihood a person won't repay as agreed. (Check out the section "Cracking credit score components" later in this chapter for more info on credit scores.)

>> **How do those who view your report interpret bad marks?** Think of it this way: Say you have a new neighbor who comes over and asks to borrow your lawnmower. Because you want to establish a good relationship, you say yes. A week goes by and your grass needs mowed, but he hasn't brought the lawnmower back. So, you call and ask for it. The new neighbor promises to get it back to you in a few days. Another week goes by and no mower, so you go knock on his door and demand it back. When you pull the mower out of his garage, it's broken and you're stuck buying a new one. The next day, your other neighbor calls and says the guy wants to borrow *her* mower now. She knows you lent the guy yours and asks what you think. So, you share your experience for her to consider in her decision.

That's essentially how lenders use credit reports and scores. In business, as in friendship, trust and keeping promises are keys to success. Basically, any delinquencies or charge-offs count against you in a big way when it comes to earning the lender's trust and getting approved. However, a creditor tends to look at your bill payments in the creditor's specific area as most important. A car lender, for example, scrutinizes your car payment history more closely than a credit card issuer does. Other, less important concerns include how much you've used (maxing out your credit cards is second only to missing payments) and how much credit you have available (too much isn't a huge factor, but it can ding you).

WARNING

Some unscrupulous lenders may claim negative information from your distant past as a reason to put you into a higher-cost (and potentially more profitable for them) loan, even though you may qualify for a less-expensive one. The scenario can go something like this: You're looking for a loan for a car or some similar big-ticket item. The lender you contact says they reviewed your credit report and offers you a loan at terms that are "a great deal considering your credit history." Translated, this means that the lender is charging you a higher-than-market rate because of your imperfect credit report, assuming you haven't checked them. Knowing your credit history and score can empower you to call their bluff and save you money.

TIP

This scenario is less likely today because the law requires the lender to tell you if you don't get the best rates or terms. If a lender offers you a loan at less than the best terms or denies you a loan, the lender must provide you with and *adverse action notice*, which must include an explanation of why you were denied or didn't get the best terms. It also must include the credit score the lender used and an explanation of that score, along with how your score compares to other U.S. consumers. You're also entitled to a free copy of your credit report from the credit reporting company that was used to obtain that report.

The positives

Positive information — the good stuff that everyone likes to see — stays on your report for quite a while. In fact, some positive data may remain on your report for 10, 20, or 30 years, maybe even longer depending on each bureau's policy and whether you keep your account open.

The more positive information you have in your credit files, the less effect a single negative item has on your ability to get the credit you need. So, if you're an experienced credit user with a long credit history, one missed payment will cause your score to drop, but you'll probably still be able to qualify if you apply. If, however, you're a young person or a new immigrant with only a few trade lines and a few months of credit history, a situation that's sometimes called a *thin file*, a negative item has a much larger effect because you have fewer positive items to balance things out. For pointers on beefing up (or just plain starting) your credit history, flip to Chapter 10.

Your Credit Report's Numerical Offspring: The Credit Score

Your credit score is typically a three-digit number that plays a vital role in a good portion of your financial life, for better or for worse. But where did this all-important number come from? Starting back in the 1950s, some companies, including FICO (formerly known as Fair Isaac Corporation) and more recently VantageScore, began to model credit data in hopes of predicting payment behavior. (A *model* is a series of formulas based on some basic assumptions to make predictions about future behavior. A weatherperson uses models to predict the weather. Credit scoring companies use models to predict whether a person will pay as agreed. We find that the credit folks are much more accurate because people are naturally far more predictable. If you have a spouse or partner, he probably knows what you're thinking before you start to think it. He's not reading your mind. He's just learned your habits and behaviors over the years. Credit scores predict the likelihood that someone will not meet their obligations in much the same way. They study behavior and identify predictable patterns.)

You only have three credit reports, but there are hundreds of different credit scores. Lenders decide which scores they're going to use to evaluate your credit history. They do that in several ways:

>> They may get your credit report and then calculate a score.

>> They may have a third party get your credit reports, combine it with other information, calculate scores, and then send the results to them.

>> In many cases, many cases, the lender has the credit bureaus route your report through a score they pick as the report is being sent to them. They get the report and score at the same time, which makes it look like the score is part of the report, even though it isn't. In reality, the credit report is provided by the credit bureau. The score is proprietary to the company that developed it.

Today, there are two predominant credit scoring companies, FICO and Vantage-Score. The following sections take a closer look at what goes into the scores from those two companies to help you understand their components and ensure that your credit score is the best it can be. We let you in on the secret: There isn't one. You only have to do two things to have great credit scores: Pay your bills on time every time and keep your balances on your credit cards as low as possible. Everything else builds on those two things no matter what score is use.

If you're obsessed with details, read on.

Cracking credit score components

In order to have a credit score, you need to have at least one account open and reporting. FICO requires at least one account to be open for at least six months and for the account to have been updated in the last six months. In some cases, VantageScore can calculate a score after just one month of activity (they don't say it will be a good score), but it usually requires the account to be open for at least three months. For those who have been out of the credit market for a while, VantageScore can generate a score using data that is up to 24 months old. Most scoring systems are now evolving to include rent, utility, and cellphone history in the calculation, although not all do, yet. You can find out more about both main types of scores in the next sections.

Although having no credit history makes it difficult to get credit initially, building credit for the first time is a lot easier than repairing a bad credit history.

What makes up a FICO score?

FICO scores are the most widely recognized scores. The brand is a bit like saying Kleenex instead of tissue. Its best-known scores have a scale from 300 to 850, but not all of them do. If you're buying a car, for example, the scale for FICO Auto Scores goes to 900. The higher the number, the better the credit rating and the better the terms you get when looking for your next loan or credit card. Your FICO score, and other scores, represent your credit history at the moment it is calculated. A new score is calculated each time your credit report is requested. The scores change over time, reflecting changes in your credit history.

Credit scores, including those from FICO can take into account hundreds of factors when building your score. The importance of each factor is dependent on the other factors, the volume of data, and the length of your history. Your FICO score is made up of five components:

» **Payment history (35 percent):** Payment history is the most significant factor when determining whether you're a good credit risk. This category includes the number and severity of any late payments (30 days, 60 days, 90 days late or more), the amount past due, and whether you eventually repaid the accounts as agreed. The more late payments and the further past due they become, the lower your score.

» **Amounts owed (30 percent):** The amount you owe is the next most important factor in your credit score. This category focuses almost entirely on the balances of your credit cards compared to your credit limit, or your *balance-to-limit ratio*. In the credit industry, that's called the *utilization rate*. The lower your utilization rate, the better your scores will be.

Ideally, you should pay your balances in full each month. Leaving a balance doesn't help your scores. It just means you'll have to pay interest on what's left, which costs you money. To a much lesser degree, this category includes the total amount you owe on all your debts, the amount you owe by account type (such as revolving or installment, which for FICO includes mortgage debt), and the number of accounts on which you're carrying a balance.

>> **Length of credit history (15 percent):** The number of years you've been using credit and the type of accounts you have also influence your score. Accounts that have been open for at least two years help increase your score.

>> **Credit mix (10 percent):** The mix of credit accounts is a part of each of the other factors. Also, a lender is likely to give greater weight to your performance on its type of loan, meaning that a credit card issuer looks at your experience with other cards more closely and a mortgage lender pays closer attention to how you pay mortgages or secured loans. The credit scores they use are often industry specific and predict risk for a certain type of loan or type of lender. An ideal mix has a positive credit history with a variety of different types of credit, such as installment and revolving credit lines. That mix will grow with time — you can't create it overnight.

>> **New credit (10 percent):** When you apply for new credit or ask for a raise in your credit line, the creditor makes an inquiry into your credit report. A high number of inquiries in a short time has a negative effect on your credit score. The reasoning is that if you apply for several accounts at the same time and get approved for them, you may not be able to afford your new debt load.

What makes up a VantageScore?

VantageScore has been around since 2006. It now uses the same score range as traditional FICO scores: 300 to 850. As with FICO scores, the higher the number, the better the score. Your VantageScore is made up of six components. Vantage-Score approaches the factors in their formula a bit differently. Rather than percentage breakdowns for each element they describe how influential each component is.

>> **Total credit usage, balance, and available credit (extremely influential):** This category represents your total utilization rate. To calculate your total utilization rate, add up all your credit card balances and divide the total by the sum of your credit limits. The lower, the better. VantageScore recommends keeping revolving balances under 30 percent of credit limits.

>> **Credit mix and experience (highly influential):** This is about the kinds of credit you use. A history with mixed types of credit (mortgage, car loan, credit cards, retail stores, and so on) is best. The mix of credit you use usually grows over time.

>> **Payment history (moderately influential)** Paying on time (satisfactory), paying late (delinquent), or not paying at all (charge-off) show up here. Paying your bills on time every time builds your credit mix and affects credit usage. Pay your bills on time in order to have good credit scores.

>> **Age of credit history (less influential):** People with higher scores generally have a longer history of open accounts with good payment history. The longer your credit history, the better it is for your credit scores. Patience pays.

>> **New accounts (less influential):** This category includes the number of recently opened credit accounts and all new inquiries. Although it's the least important factor, you still should be careful not to open too many new accounts in a short period of time.

If you're just beginning to build credit, be patient. It'll take time for your scores to improve. To figure out what you need to do to help make things go a bit faster, get your credit report, a score, and the risk factors that are most affecting it. You can use the factors to identify what steps you need to take to make all your scores better. As you can see in these categories, the two most important are paying your bills on time, every time, and keeping your credit card balances as low as possible.

Also, ask your lender if they have other tools they can use if you lack a sufficient traditional credit history. For example, some lenders can apply a FICO Expansion Score, which draws from other data sources to help verify that you're a good credit risk.

For examples of ways to start a credit history, including using a secured card or a passbook loan, check out Chapter 10.

REMEMBER

There is more to a credit decision than score component weightings. Consider the weighting factors as directional indicators rather than a guarantee of great credit rates and terms.

The reasoning behind risk factors

When you see your credit score for the first time, you may say: "They must be wrong; my credit is better than that!" If so, you're not alone. As a result, the two scoring companies, FICO and VantageScore, have developed risk factors and brief statements that accompany them to help you know what went wrong with your credit that resulted in your particular credit score. VantageScore set up an online resource, www.reasoncode.org, that goes into more depth than the simple risk factors and corresponding statements that you get with your score by providing details about what each risk factor means in plain English. Features of Reason-Code.org include

>> A primer on what reason codes are and how they are used

>> Searchable and interactive reason code definitions and explanations

>> A glossary of common reason code terms

See Chapter 14 for additional information about risk factor statements.

TECHNICAL STUFF

Credit scoring companies are constantly studying the economy, market, and consumer behaviors. They regularly introduce updates to their scores to reflect changes in consumer behavior, and to incorporate new information. From time to time, they introduce scores that incorporate new technology that can help lenders better predict risk and help people gain access to lower-cost credit. VantageScore reviews its scoring system annually and adjusts it. The most recent model is VantageScore 4.0. Their scores were the first to include information about utility payments, cellphone payments, and rent payments. In 2019, FICO announced two new credit scores, FICO 10 and FICO 10T. FICO 10 is a normal evolution of its traditional scoring models. FICO 10T introduces something called *trended data.* Unlike other credit scores that are a snapshot of your credit history at a moment in time, FICO 10T will look at your credit history over time. The intent is to identify trends in the way a person manages his debt. For example, a lender may be able to tell that a person has had some problems in the past but has been improving, so he could be a good credit risk. Such a score could result in a person getting approved when an older score would have resulted in denial of his application.

It can take many years for lenders to adopt new scores. Validating that the scores will work for them and incorporating them into their underwriting systems is a complex and expensive process. As a result, you may not see these new scores right away.

ALLOWING FOR ACTS OF GOD

Sometimes things happen to people that are so far beyond their control that even lenders don't want to hold them responsible. We put what we call acts of God in this category. Things like hurricanes, earthquakes, fires, and pandemics affect large portions of the population. When those kinds of things happen, lenders may indicate that an account belongs to a natural disaster victim when reporting account activity to the credit bureaus. Reporting an account with the natural disaster reporting code means that the account will not have a negative effect on your credit scores. In most cases, the lender will also work with you to arrange a special payment accommodation, such as forbearance or deferment. Doing so will let you temporarily stop making payments so you can deal with the aftermath of the disaster. The disaster codes made available by the credit bureaus, along with the payment accommodation by the lender will both appear in your credit report. The credit scoring systems will then either ignore the accounts or treat them differently. No new negative information will be added to your reports while your accounts are in forbearance or deferment. But catching up on late payments, reducing your credit card balances, or making other positive changes will still be shown and can help your credit scores.

» **Investigating specialty credit reporting and data**

» **Reviewing your reports and fixing inaccuracies**

» **Obtaining your credit score and figuring out how it affects you**

Chapter **14**

Understanding Credit Reports and Scores

nformation in your credit report plays an important role in a growing number of financial decisions. Everything from getting a loan or credit card to qualifying for the best insurance rates can involve a credit report. If you've had money problems, it can seem as if the system is being used against you. But at its most basic level, that's what credit reporting is helping lenders do: Identify when someone has a greater chance of not fulfilling his financial obligations and when there is a strong chance he will. When you understand how credit reports work, you can control what lenders and others see in your report. And, in a way, that gives you control over the decisions they make.

Credit information collected about you is contained in your credit reports from the three major credit bureaus. Getting copies of those reports and reviewing the information in them is as easy as it is important, and doing so shows you exactly what most people or programs evaluating your credit see.

In this chapter, we explain how to get your credit report. We walk you through the process of reviewing your credit report from each of the three major credit-reporting bureaus and explain how to make sense of what's in them. We also explain how you can dispute any information you find in your reports that you believe is inaccurate. Of course, the three major credit bureaus aren't the only ones compiling financial information about you. We introduce you to a growing number of specialty reporting agencies in this chapter as well; these specialty bureaus provide details on things other than your debts.

Credit scores are also a part of the credit-reporting picture, although they aren't part of credit reports. We share how to obtain and make sense of your scores. By the time you're done reading this chapter, you'll be armed with the information you need to discover exactly how potential employers, lenders, landlords, and insurance agents see you when viewing you through the lens of your credit history.

Getting Copies of Your Credit Reports

The three main collectors of credit information in the credit industry today are Equifax, Experian, and TransUnion. These major credit bureaus are basically huge databases of information. (We reveal where all that information comes from in Chapter 13.)

Given the enormous amounts of data that flow into and out of the bureaus every month, it's important to know what's there, or isn't, and to be sure it's all correct. Getting copies of your credit reports from the three credit bureaus to make sure that the information in your files is a true representation of your credit use is essential. By reviewing your reports, you'll also know if someone has stolen your identity and used it in an effort to establish fraudulent credit accounts.

REMEMBER

Any incorrect information included in your credit report has the potential to be very costly to you. For example, erroneous info could mean that you don't get the loans or terms you want or that you have to pay a much higher interest rate than you should have to pay. Lenders are not required to report to all three of the credit bureaus, so checking your credit report from just one bureau isn't good enough. The information that Equifax has may be slightly different from the information that Experian has, and the information that Experian has may be slightly different from the information that TransUnion has. Also, you can have a perfectly clean report with one bureau while another report contains some negative items in error.

The good news is that you don't have to do much heavy lifting to get your hands on all your credit reports thanks to the Fair and Accurate Credit Transactions Act (commonly referred to as the FACT Act or FACTA). This act entitles every American to at least one free credit report from each of the three bureaus every 12 months. You're also entitled to an additional free report from each of the bureaus if you:

>> Were denied credit in the last 60 days from the credit bureau used by the lender

>> Are unemployed and planning to seek employment in the next 60 days

>> Are on welfare

>> Are a victim of fraud or identity theft and request an initial security alert, also called a *fraud alert,* be added to your credit reports

REMEMBER

If you are a victim of fraud or identity theft, report it to the police and add a victim statement to your credit report. If you do so, you'll qualify for additional free reports.

Several states also provide for additional free credit reports each year. Check with your state's attorney general to find out if you qualify.

Finally, from time to time, credit card issuers offer free peeks at your credit reports as do the bureaus themselves. During the COVID-19 pandemic, the bureaus allowed free credit reports weekly.

In the following sections, we explain how to get your reports, what kind of information you need to provide, what to watch out for, and when you should check your reports.

Where to get your reports

To obtain your one free credit report from each of the three major credit bureaus each year, simply visit the website www.annualcreditreport.com. Or, if you prefer, you can request copies by phone or mail:

Annual Credit Report Request Service
P.O. Box 105281
Atlanta, GA 30348-5281
877-322-8228

TIP

You need to fill out a request form if you use the mail to get your free copies from the central source. The request credit file form is included at www.dummies.com/go/creditrepairkitfd5e.

WARNING

Many different websites with similar-sounding names have cropped up since the central source for free credit reports was established. These sites advertise free credit reports, but the fine print is that your free report costs you something because you must purchase another product or service to receive it. You shouldn't have to purchase anything to get your free copies. If the site requires you to provide payment information, you're on the wrong site.

Note that your credit score isn't provided with your free annual credit reports when you use www.annualcreditreport.com. You'll be "offered an opportunity" to purchase your score after you get your free report. Credit scores are available free from a number of sources as well.

To request a report directly from the credit bureaus, you can get things started with a phone call, a visit to the bureau's website, or through the mail. Here's the contact information for the three major credit-reporting bureaus:

» **Equifax,** P.O. Box 740241, Atlanta, GA 30374; 800-685-1111; www.equifax.com

» **Experian,** P.O. Box 2104, Allen, TX 75013-2104; 888-397-3742; www.experian.com

» **TransUnion,** 2 Baldwin Place, P.O. Box 1000, Chester, PA 19022; 800-888-4213; www.transunion.com

When you order your credit report, the bureaus will offer to sell you a credit score as well. See the section "Ordering your score," later in this chapter, for more information.

What you need to provide

Whether you contact a credit bureau directly to get a copy of your report or you go through the free central source to get all three at once (see the preceding section), you need to provide information that helps the bureaus verify you are who you claim to be. So be ready to give all the information you've always been told not to give to a stranger over the phone or Internet. In this one case, it's okay. The goal is to protect you from fraud and ensure your credit information isn't sent to the wrong person.

REMEMBER

The information requested can vary a bit from one bureau to the next, but the following is a list of some information you're likely to be asked for:

» Your full name

» Your current and former addresses

» Your birth date

» Your Social Security number

You'll likely also be asked a series of questions to further verify your identity. These questions can include things like what lender your mortgage is with, if you've ever had a car loan with a given company, the name of a previous employer, and other things that only you should know. The questions are typically based on your credit history and other information sources. They're sometimes called "out of wallet" questions, because the answers are not something an identity thief would know by stealing your purse or wallet.

When to get copies of your credit reports

You're entitled to a free copy of your credit report from each of the big-three credit bureaus once a year, and you should review them at least that often.

TIP

If you don't have any issues with fraud or other reasons we discuss in this section, you can get a report from one of the three bureaus every four months, rotating through the bureaus so that you have three separate chances, at evenly spaced intervals, to see whether something unexpected has shown up. To make it easy to remember when to reorder each report, we suggest that you pick three times during the year that stand out and are roughly four months apart. Consider New Year's Day, Fourth of July, and Halloween, for example.

There are several exceptions to the rule, though. You should check your reports more often if:

>> You believe that a problem may be lurking as a result of identity theft.

>> You believe there may be an error in one or more of your reports.

>> You're going to be submitting a major credit application in the next six months or so.

In these cases, get all three reports at once in addition to your normal free annual report rotation.

Get copies of your reports from all three bureaus at the same time when you're planning to:

>> Buy or lease a car

>> Buy or rent a house or an apartment

>> Refinance a mortgage

>> Apply for a job

>> Be up for a promotion

>> Apply for a professional license (such as to sell securities or insurance)

>> Apply for a security clearance

>> Join the military

>> Get married or divorced

>> Switch insurance companies or buy new insurance

WHO ELSE HAS ACCESS TO YOUR REPORT?

Anyone can get a copy of your credit report if the person has a *permissible purpose* as defined under federal law — in other words, a valid business reason to review your report. You don't have to give your permission for a report to be accessed if the business has a permissible purpose, although you almost always provide it when you apply for credit. The permission is often buried in the fine print of a credit card application. The one exception is for employment purposes: If an employer wants to check your credit report, they have to first get your written permission on a separate permission form from your application.

What counts as a permissible purpose under the law? Here are some examples:

- **Getting your own report:** It may go without saying, but we're going to say it anyway. You can get a copy of your own report as often as you like. Doing so will not hurt your credit scores or affect your ability to get credit. Don't be afraid to look at your own credit report. You can't do anything to make it better until you know what's in it.

- **Apartment rental:** It only makes sense that a landlord would want to know whether you're likely to pay your rent on time before giving you the keys to a piece of real estate. For that reason, most rental applications ask for permission to access your credit report. It stands to reason that if you pay your other bills on time, you'll probably pay your rent on time, too. Your credit report is often included in a *tenant screening report* that also includes any tenant history information that may be available from sources other than the credit bureaus. A few examples include Cozy (www.cozy.co), MyRental (www.myrental.com), and RentPrep (www.rentprep.com).

- **Credit approval:** When you apply for credit (whether you're filling out a credit card application or applying for a car loan, student loan, mortgage), creditors and lenders have the right to get a copy of your credit report. They need to know whether you have a history of defaulting on loans or whether you're overextended on credit already and about to miss your next payment.

- **Court order or subpoena:** If a court orders you to appear before the court or subpoenas information about you, the court can also get access to your credit file.

- **Employment:** When you apply for a job, the prospective employer can get a copy of your credit report, if they first get your written permission. Why would they need your credit report? There are two primary reasons. First, you're applying for a position that involves managing or handling the company's money. If you're having difficulties with personal finances, you may have trouble with company money, too, or so the logic goes. The second reason is to verify that you are who you claim to be. Employers match the identifying information in your credit report to what you say in your job application. That can help them prevent job application fraud, and maybe even protect public safety. One example is chemical plants, which check applicants' credit reports because they don't want a dangerous person to have access to something that could harm other people.

  It's also important to note that employers never get credit scores. Despite what you're likely to hear, credit scores do *not* prevent you from getting a job. This is one of the most common credit myths.

- **Insurance:** Depending on the type of insurance you apply for and the state in which you live, the insurer may get a copy of your credit report and use the information in it to help predict the likelihood of your filing a claim. Insurers and their actuaries have shown that a strong relationship exists between past credit performance and future claim experience. So when you apply for car, homeowners, renters, medical, or any other kind of insurance, in most states, your insurance company has the right to get a copy of your credit report.

- **IRS debts:** If you owe the tax man and don't pay on time, the IRS looks in your credit report to find out if you have assets to attach or sell, like real estate, cars, or bank accounts.

- **Professional license:** Licensing authorities take their responsibilities very seriously. Before allowing you to become licensed — in other words, approved to perform a specific job — they want to know all they can about your background and how you've conducted yourself. If you want a license to be a financial planner and deal with someone else's life savings, for instance, it makes sense to see how you handle your own money. Want a gambling license? Same thing applies.

- **Review or collection of an existing account:** If your account is overdue and sent to collections, the collector wants to know who else you owe money to and what kind of payer you are. If you move a lot, the collector uses the information in your credit report to find a current address or phone number. (The industry term for this practice is *skip tracing*.) However, even if you're current in your payments to your credit card issuers, mortgage company, or other creditors, your creditors may look at your account from time to time to determine whether your credit quality is deteriorating or, on the brighter side, whether they should increase your limits.

WARNING

Real estate closings can be delayed, mortgage rates can go up, and job opportunities can be lost if your credit report contains incorrect negative information. So, give yourself time to correct your reports before going forward with your plans. We recommend getting your reports a minimum of three months and up to six months in advance of your plans so that you have time to dispute any errors or fraudulent account information. As you get within a month or two of applying for credit, insurance, or a job, consider getting copies of your reports again to be sure everything is in order.

Tracking Down Specialty Reports: From Apartments to Casinos to Prescriptions

Specialty reporting agencies, as the name implies, gather information for specific industries. They gather information that the big-three credit bureaus do not. The information in your credit report is limited to things that are debt related. Specialty reporting agencies collect details about your relationships in areas such as gambling, checking accounts, medical claims, insurance, and rental and employment history. If you're being checked out because you're applying for a loan, insuring your car, finding a new apartment, or being considered for a promotion at work, the person reviewing your application has the option to request a report from a specialty agency in addition to a traditional credit report from one of the big-three credit bureaus (Equifax, Experian, and TransUnion).

WHO'S REPORTING YOU TO THE SPECIALTY BUREAUS?

Included in the growing list of companies that report on you are those that specialize in your rental history, workers' compensation claims, prescription drug purchase history, and gambling history.

Until recently, use of prescription drug use databases was unheard of. Insurers' use of these databases was first publicized when the Federal Trade Commission sued two owners of drug databases. (See www.ftc.gov/opa/2007/09/ingenixmilliman.shtm.) Like the Medical Information Bureau reports, these reports are used primarily when you're seeking private health, life, or disability insurance. Rx drug databases can go back as far as five years, detailing drugs you've used as well as dosages and refills.

Among the better-known specialty report providers are the following:

>> LexisNexis, which sells its C.L.U.E. products based on your auto and home-owners insurance claims history, as well as information for background employment and rental checks

>> The Medical Information Bureau (MIB), which accumulates and sells your medical-insurance claims history report

>> ChexSystems, SCAN, and TeleCheck, all of which keep records of bounced checks and sell various check-verification products. These organizations are sometimes called *debit bureaus* because they're looking at your bank accounts.

Many people aren't aware of these specialty reporting agencies or the fact that you have the right to request and obtain free copies of your credit reports from these agencies annually, just as you do with the traditional credit bureaus. Some reports contain only negative information, or they may have absolutely no information about you at all. We suggest that you request your free reports from them annually just to make sure that the information in the report is yours and is accurate. You may not be aware that one of these databases is being checked because they aren't as top of mind as the three main credit bureaus.

Table 14-1 provides the contact information for the major specialty bureaus to get you started. Call any bureau you want a report from and ask how to order a free copy. You must contact each of them separately to request your report.

TABLE 14-1 **Specialty Credit-Reporting Bureaus**

Category	Bureau Name	Phone Number
Casinos	Global Cash Access (Central Credit)	888-898-8021
Checking accounts	Certegy	866-543-6315
	ChexSystems	800-428-9623
	Early Warning Services	800-325-7775
	SCAN	800-262-7771
	TeleCheck	800-366-2425

(continued)

TABLE 14-1 *(continued)*

Category	Bureau Name	Phone Number
Employment	Accurate Background	800-784-3911
	American DataBank	800-200-0853
	EmployeeScreenIQ	800-235-3954
	First Advantage	800-321-4473
	GIS	800-265-4917
	HireRight	800-381-0645
	Infocubic	877-360-4636
	Intellicorp	866-202-1436
	LexisNexis	866-312-8075
	Pre-employ.com	800-300-1821
	Trak 1 Technology	918-779-7000
	Verifications Inc.	877-884-1313
	The Work Number	866-604-6570
Identity	ID Analytics	Web only
Insurance	C.L.U.E. Auto History	866-897-8126
	C.L.U.E. Homeowners' History	866-897-8126
	Insurance Information Exchange	866-560-7015
	ISO's A-Plus Auto and Property Databases	800-709-8842
Medical information	Medical Information Bureau (MIB)	866-692-6901
Supplementary credit report	Innovis	800-540-2505
	L2CInc.	866-268-7156
Payday lending	Clarity Services	866-390-3118
Prescription drugs	DataX	Web only
	Factor Trust	866-910-8497
	Microbilt	877-772-2123
	Milliman	877-211-4816
	Teletrack	877-309-5226

Category	Bureau Name	Phone Number
Rental information	Accufax	800-256-8898
	Advantage Tenant	800-894-9047
	American Tenant Screen	800-888-1287
	Contemporary Information Corp.	800-288-4757
	Micobilt	877-772-2123
	Resident History Report	877-448-5732
	Core Logic Safe Rent	888-333-2413
	Leasing Desk	866-934-1124
	LexisNexis Resident History	866-312-8075
	National Tenant Network	800-228-0989
Property tax filings	Tenant Data Services	800-228-1837
	CoreScore Credit Report	877-532-8778
Utilities	National Consumer Telecom and Utilities Exchange	866-343-2821

Perusing Your Credit Reports

You may be hesitant to get your credit reports because you've heard scary stories about trying to interpret the codes and abbreviations in them. Years ago, that may have been true, but the credit bureaus have done a lot to make your personal credit report much easier to read and understand. Still, getting your credit report for the first time can be a bit intimidating. Don't let that stop you. Perhaps the best way to get a handle on the information in your credit report is to take it apart and break it into its various sections.

Credit reports can include information in the following general categories. Yours may not include everything. For example, if you've never declared bankruptcy, you wouldn't see that section in your report.

>> Identifying information

>> Accounts summary

>> Bankruptcy public records

» Account history

» Credit inquiries

» Your 100-word statement(s) (optional; see Chapter 3 for info on writing a 100-word statement)

The following sections cover each of these parts of your report in detail. Bear in mind, though, that the three credit-reporting agencies may use slightly different descriptions for each of these sections.

For samples of Equifax, Experian, and TransUnion credit reports, go to www.dummies.com/go/creditrepairkitfd5e.

Identifying information: It's all about who you are

This section of your credit report may be labeled "Personal Profile" or "Personal Information," depending on which credit bureau issues the report. The credit bureaus maintain files on more than 220 million credit active consumers, so all your identifying information is critical to making sure your credit report is accurate and complete.

Appearing first in the order of credit report elements, your profile section contains the key components that help you verify that the report is actually about *you:* your name (and any of your previous names — for example, if you changed your name because of marriage or divorce, or if you use multiple spellings or nicknames like Steve instead of Stephen), Social Security number, address(es), and current and previous employers.

Be sure to check the personal profile section and verify that all the information is correct. You may see variations of your Social Security number or street address if they're reported to the credit bureaus. Variations are not errors. They're included so you have a complete record of what your lenders are reporting is in their records. Variations you don't recognize could indicate you're a fraud victim, so check your identifying information closely.

Accounts summary: An overview of your financial history

Each of the three bureau reports includes a summary of your credit or accounts that gives you a high-level overview of what's included in your credit report, and things you may want to look at more closely. It includes open and closed accounts, credit limits, total balances of all accounts, payment history, and number of credit inquiries. The summary may also point out information that may be viewed negatively by lenders based on the credit bureaus' experience. If you have a short attention span, the summary provides a one-page snapshot of your credit history. But don't worry: If you're hungry for painstaking detail, you can find it in the Account History section, which we describe later in this chapter.

TIP

A quick review of the summary section lets you know whether you need to scrutinize something in more detail that appears to be inaccurate or isn't related to your account at all. For example, if you don't have a mortgage, finding a mortgage account listed in your summary is an immediate red flag.

Bankruptcy public records: The most serious element in a credit report

Bankruptcy public records may be the most harmful entry in a credit report. They indicate that your debts have gotten so unmanageable that you've gone through a legal process to have them dismissed. Lenders will take a dim view of your creditworthiness if you don't pay them as agreed, and if you've declared bankruptcy, you may not have paid them at all. Bankruptcy public records can be a part of your credit report for up to ten years, depending on the chapter you filed. They'll drag your scores down for the entire time, although less as they get older.

Defaulting on child-support payments may also be included in this section, but it could also be listed as an account by the state agency. Unpaid child support is the only thing that may be worse for your credit than bankruptcy.

In the not-so-distant past, there were other public records in credit reports — things like civil judgments if you were sued and lost, tax liens, and even parking tickets or library fines. The good news is that those have all been removed from credit reports. However, they may be included in a specialty credit report like those discussed earlier in this chapter.

Credit inquiries: Tracking who has been accessing your file

Want to know who has asked for your credit report? This section is where you should look. It includes everyone who has asked for your credit report in the last two years. People who are legally allowed to view your credit information and have requested copies of your report are listed here.

There are two types of inquiries:

TIP

>> **Hard inquiries:** Hard inquiries are the result of your application for credit or other services. They indicate you may have additional debt that doesn't yet show as an account in your credit report, so it represents a bit of risk to lenders. For that reason, they're shared with lenders and can have a small impact on your credit scores until the new account is added. You may see these listed in your report as "Inquiries shared with others."

Although hard inquiries don't have a very large impact on the average credit report, they can have a more serious negative impact on a credit file with a short credit history or few entries. These files are also called *thin files*. They may not cause a greater score decrease in terms of points, but when you already have a limited history and a low score, a few points could affect a lender's decision more than it would for a person with a high score.

>> **Soft inquiries:** Soft inquiries are shown only to you (not anyone else, like a lender) on your personal credit report, and they don't affect credit scores or lending decisions. They include things like preapproved credit offers, your requests of your own credit report, requests by employers to whom you've given your permission, and insurance companies requesting your report. You may see them listed under a heading of "Inquiries shown only to you."

REMEMBER

Inquiries are simply a record that someone with a permissible purpose under the law has asked for your report, such as employers, insurance companies, and lenders, as well as yourself. (For more information on this topic, see the earlier sidebar "Who else has access to your report?")

This section also shows the date of each inquiry and how long the inquiry will remain on your report.

Account history: Think of it as a payment CSI

Your account history section, sometimes titled "Account Information," is the heart of your credit report. It shows all open and closed accounts with near forensic detail about payment history, balances, and account status. How long the information remains on your report depends on the type of information (see "When credit information is deleted" to know when the clock starts and ends). If you see negative items that you don't recognize or that have exceeded the allowed timeframe, dispute them using the instructions included with your report and they'll be removed.

Each credit bureau displays these account details in its own unique way, as outlined in the following sections.

WHEN CREDIT INFORMATION IS DELETED

Here's the good news: Positive information always remains longer than negative information. The bad news is that negative information can remain in your report for up to ten years. Here's a breakdown of how long stuff stays in your report:

- **Open, active accounts with no negative payment history:** These accounts can remain indefinitely. We've seen accounts that have been on reports for more than 30 years!

- **Closed accounts with no negative payment history:** These accounts remain for ten years from the date they're closed. You don't lose the account history when you close it. The positive information will stay longer than any negative information, even after the account is closed.

- **Late payments:** These remain seven years from the date of the delinquency. Simply put, the date you miss the payment starts the seven years. If you miss a payment one month, catch up the next month, and miss the month after that, the first missed payment will be removed seven years from the date it was missed. Then a month will go by, and the second missed payment will be deleted.

- **Charged-off accounts:** These accounts remain seven years from the "original delinquency date" or "date of first delinquency" of the debt. That means that if you miss a payment, never catch up, and the creditor charges off the account, the account will be deleted seven years from that very first missed payment. (See Chapter 6 for more information about charge-offs.)

- **Collection accounts:** These accounts remain seven years from the original delinquency date of the original account. The original account is the one that was charged off. Basically, collection accounts are treated as a continuation of your loan from the original creditor and will be deleted at the same time.

- **Bankruptcy public records:** These records are deleted at different times depending on the chapter you declared. A Chapter 13 bankruptcy is deleted seven years from the filing date because you've repaid part of the debt. A Chapter 7 bankruptcy is deleted ten years from the filing date because you didn't repay any of the debt included in the filing.

- **Inquiries:** These remain for two years. They have very little effect on credit scores, and that impact typically goes away after a couple of months. If there is a new account, it will be the main thing lenders are interested in. If there isn't a new account a couple of months following the entry, the inquiry doesn't represent any risk to the lender because there is no debt associated with it.

Equifax's version

Equifax reports account history by type of account, such as mortgages, installment accounts, and revolving accounts. Under each account type, open accounts are listed first, followed by closed accounts. A short summary at the beginning of each account includes your account status, which indicates whether you have paid as agreed or are late (and if so, how late).

TIP

Go to www.dummies.com/go/creditrepairkitfd5e for a sample Equifax credit report.

Here's a list of all the information Equifax reports for each account in its Account History section:

>> **Account name:** A brief description of the account type and creditor. For example, 123 Mortgage Co., Address, Phone Number.

>> **Account number:** That long, alphanumeric string that's unique to your card or loan. Note, though, that account numbers are shortened for the protection of your account information.

>> **Account owner:** Indicates whether the account is an individual or joint account.

>> **Type:** Here are the account types you may find:

- **Mortgage account:** First mortgage loans, home equity loans, and any other loan secured by real estate.

- **Installment account:** Loans that are for a set amount of money and often for a set period. A car loan is an example of a common installment loan.

- **Revolving account:** An account that has a credit limit and a minimum payment and doesn't have to be paid off in a set amount of time. Credit cards fall into this category.

- **Other account:** Includes those accounts that don't fit into the set categories, such as charge accounts that must be paid in full each month, like some American Express cards.

- **Collections account:** An account that has been sold or turned over to a collection agency, usually when the account is more than 180 days past due.

- **Negative account:** A past-due account that is less than 180 days late, or a debt that was written off because you couldn't pay it and is now a collections account.

>> **Term duration:** The total number of payments you're expected to make (for example, 60 payments for a five-year car loan).

- **Date open:** The date on which you opened the account.

- **Date reported:** The latest report from the lender, whether provided monthly, quarterly, or less frequently.

- **Date of last payment:** The date listed here may be different from the date reported. If you're past due, your last payment may be from September 2013, and the last date reported may be December 2013. If you had no activity on a credit card account for six months, the last payment date may be June 2013, and the last reported date may be December 2013.

- **Scheduled payment amount:** Information that applies only to installment accounts, in which a set amount of money is due at a set time every month.

- **Creditor classification:** The type of creditor.

- **Charge-off amount:** Debt or portion of debt that the creditor wrote off because of nonpayment and inability to get the money from you. For example, if you don't pay your credit card for 180 days, it will be listed as charged off. You want this amount to be *zero*. Any amount — no matter how small — is not a good thing to have on your record.

- **Balloon-payment amount:** The big lump-sum payment at the end of some loans. Your loan may or may not have one.

- **Date closed:** The date you or the lender terminated an active account.

- **Date of first delinquency:** Any late payments recorded during the seven-year reporting period.

- **Comments:** Additional information about the closed account. Some examples are "Account Transferred or Sold," "Paid," "Zero Balance," and "Account Closed at Consumer's Request."

- **Current status:** Whether you've paid or are paying as you said you would. You may see terms such as "Pays," "Paid as Agreed," or "X Days Past Due."

- **High credit:** The highest amount of credit you have used.

- **Credit limit:** Your maximum limit for this account.

- **Term's frequency:** How often your payment is due (weekly, monthly, and so on).

- **Balance:** The amount owed to the creditor.

- **Amount past due:** The amount you owe that should have been paid by now but hasn't been.

- **Actual payment amount:** The amount of your last payment.

- **Date of last activity:** The last time you used the account.

>> **Months reviewed:** How many months are in the payment history section (up to 81).

>> **Activity designator:** A description of account activity, such as "Paid" and "Closed."

>> **Deferred payment start date:** Some accounts have no payment for a year or other promotional terms.

>> **Balloon-payment date:** When that big lump-sum payment at the end of some loans is due. Your loan may or may not have one.

>> **Type of loan:** For example, auto or credit card.

>> **81-month payment history:** Equifax shows each month's status for the last seven years of payment history. Terms used in reporting the status include the following:

- Pays as agreed
- 30 (30 to 59 days past due)
- 60 (60 to 89 days past due)
- 90 (90 to 119 days past due)
- 120 (120 to 149 days past due)
- 150 (150 to 179 days past due)
- 180- (180 or more days past due)
- CA (collection account)
- F (foreclosure)
- VS (voluntary surrender)
- R (repossession)
- CO (charge-off)

Experian's version

On Experian's credit report, potentially negative items are listed first. The remainder of your accounts in the Account History section are listed as accounts in good standing. You of course want all your accounts to be listed as being in good standing.

TIP

You can find a sample Experian credit report at www.dummies.com/go/creditrepairkitfd5e.

Here's a list of the information that Experian reports for each account in its Account History section:

- **Address of creditor and account number**

- **Status:** Open or closed and paid, past due by X days, or settled for less than originally agreed.

- **Date open:** The date you opened the account.

- **Reported since:** First reported date.

- **Date of status:** Last time the status was updated.

- **Last reported:** Last time the update (which may be new or old) was reported.

- **Account type:** Installment account, revolving account, and so on.

- **Terms:** The total number of payments you're expected to make (a 30-year mortgage would be 360 payments, for example).

- **Monthly payment:** The last reported minimum payment you owe(d). This typically applies for installment loans such as auto loans and mortgages, if reported at all.

- **Responsibility:** Individual, joint, authorized user, and so on.

- **Credit limit/Original amount:** The highest credit limit you've ever been approved for.

- **High balance:** The most you've ever owed on the account.

- **Recent balance:** The amount you owe. Sometimes balance information is on the report and sometimes it's not. This isn't because the credit bureau wants to save trees but because some creditors don't want their competition to know what a big spender and great customer you are.

- **Recent payment:** Your most recent payment amount.

- **Account history:** Whether you've paid late, and if so, how often.

- **Your statement:** This is where you tell your side of the story. For example, you may contest an account that shows you haven't paid as agreed if you contend that you didn't receive the services for which you were charged.

- **Account history for collection accounts:** Comments that the creditor may have sent to the bureau, such as when the account was placed for collection.

TransUnion's version

TransUnion reports public records and collection accounts first. The Account History section for all other accounts is listed under Trades.

TIP

You can find a sample TransUnion credit report at www.dummies.com/go/ creditrepairkitfd5e.

Here's a list of the information that TransUnion reports for each account in its Account History section:

>> **Account name:** Name and address of the creditor.

>> **Account number:** Only a partial account number is included.

>> **Account type:** Automobile, credit card, and so on.

>> **Credit limit:** The maximum amount of credit approved by the creditor. The creditor doesn't always report this information if your limit isn't firm (such as with American Express) or if you're allowed to exceed your limit under the terms of your agreement (such as with Visa Signature accounts).

>> **Balance:** The balance owed as of the date of verification or when closed.

>> **Date opened:** The date the account was opened.

>> **Responsibility:** Individual, joint, authorized user, and so on.

>> **High credit:** The highest amount ever owed on the account.

>> **Past due:** Amount past due as of date verified or closed.

- **Terms:** Minimum payment amount.

- **Pay status:** Whether you are paying as agreed.

- **Account type:** Open or closed.

>> **Date paid:** The date the account was last paid.

>> **Remarks:** Explanation of dispute or account credit condition as reported by the creditor. Includes account closed by consumer.

>> **Terms:** Number of payments, payment frequency, and dollar amount agreed upon.

>> **Date closed:** If the account is closed, the date on which it was closed.

>> **Date verified:** The date of the last update on the account.

>> **Loan type:** The type of loan and/or the collateral used for an installment loan. Includes home equity loan, mortgage, and automobile.

>> **Late payments:** A graphical representation of all paid months being reported as agreed or late.

>> **Payment pattern:** A numerical indicator 1–9 indicating paid as agreed (1) to charged off (9).

TIP

Your revolving utilization rate is a key component of your credit scores. *Utilization* is the ratio of your credit card balances compared to your credit limits. It's the second most important factor in credit scores. If you have credit cards charged to the limit, or close to it, pay them down to see a quick increase in credit scores. For more on how your credit score is calculated, see the section "Getting and Understanding Your Credit Scores" later in this chapter.

Your optional 100-word statements: Making sure your voice is heard

You have the right to add statements of up to 100 words to your credit report that can help explain any extenuating circumstances that may have led to negative information being included. You can add an overall statement that covers all your accounts, and you can add a statement for one or more trade lines with which you disagree. For example, a general statement describing a temporary job loss can explain why many of your accounts were 60 days late. A trade line or individual account statement can explain why a particular account is being reported negatively and why you disagree.

If you disagree with the results of a dispute, you should add a statement explaining why. These *statements of dispute* ensure you have an opportunity to explain your side of the situation. Just be sure that it's a reason that lenders would understand and appreciate. If you forgot to mail your payment because you were on vacation, a statement to that effect probably won't help. A lender's response would just be, "I hope you had a great vacation. I still need my payment on time." On the other hand, a statement explaining that your lender misapplied your payment to the wrong account and still reported it as late, even though it was sent to them on time could be very helpful.

The credit bureaus are required to include these statements whenever anyone accesses your credit report. Anyone who requests your report will be alerted that there is a statement on your credit file. On the flip side, lenders may not always pull a full credit report when ordering a score for screening, so keep in mind that your statement may not always be seen.

REMEMBER

Use the 100-word-statement privilege with care, and be sure to circle back to make sure it's deleted when the negative information is removed. It most cases today, that happens automatically, but it's good to be sure. If you don't request that it be removed, your comments could stay on the report and raise unwanted questions from a potential lender.

WHAT'S NOT IN YOUR CREDIT REPORT?

The easiest way to answer this question is that if it's not debt related, it's not part of your credit report. There is nothing in your report about the following:

- **Criminal history:** Things like arrest records and traffic stops aren't collected by credit-reporting companies.

- **Medical information:** There is nothing about the specific illnesses you may have been treated for, who provided the treatment, or other health-related information. Medical collection accounts, however, *can* be part of your credit report; if so, lenders only see "medical collection." Your personal report will include the name of the healthcare provider or medical collection agency, along with contact information because you may need it.

- **What you buy:** Your credit report would not show exactly what you purchase with credit. If, for example, you bought a new, red, Corvette convertible with a black leather interior, the only thing on the credit report would be an auto loan. If you use a credit card to buy green carpet and orange curtains, that wouldn't show either. There would just be an increase in the reported balance.

- **Income or assets:** There is nothing about how much money you make, the balance in your savings or checking accounts, a 401(k), mutual funds, certificates of deposit, individual retirement accounts (IRAs), or any other asset. Credit reports help lenders determine whether a person will repay a debt as agreed, regardless of how much money she has in the bank. Just because you have a lot of cash, doesn't mean you'll use it to pay your bills as agreed. Believe it or not, there are a lot of rich deadbeats out there.

Although your credit report may not include things like medical information or exactly what you buy, lenders and others will consider all the information as a whole, and it may raise concerns you could be asked to address. For example, if your credit report has a lot of addresses, a lender may want to know if you've moved frequently and why. Moving around a lot may suggest your living situation is unstable and could affect your ability to pay your debts.

Managing your credit report and ensuring that it's accurate can help prevent any information from getting on your report that could raise red flags for lenders, employers, or insurance companies reviewing your report.

Correcting Any Errors You Find

Considering how many individual credit histories are maintained and the vast amount of information flowing into and out of the credit bureaus every day, credit reports are highly accurate. But they aren't perfect, and mistakes can happen. The good news is that if you find mistakes, they don't have to remain a part of your credit file.

REMEMBER

Credit-reporting agencies are required to investigate all disputed listings. They must verify the item in question with the creditor *at no cost to you*, the consumer. The law requires the creditor to respond to and verify disputed entries within 30 days, or the information must be removed from your credit report. In most cases, though, disputes are completed within 10 to 14 business days, and often much faster, today. The credit bureau must notify you of the outcome of your disputes. If information in the report is changed or deleted, you can get a *free* copy of the revised report. If a lender makes a change to one credit bureau as a result of your dispute, they must also notify every other consumer reporting agency to which they reported it to make the change, too. It's a good idea to check your other reports after a change just to be sure the update has been made with all three.

You have two options for fixing errors that you find on your credit reports: contact the credit bureau or contact the creditor who reported the incorrect information. We walk you through both processes in the sections that follow.

Contacting the credit bureau

If you notice incorrect information on your credit report, contact the credit bureau that reported the inaccurate information. Each of the three major bureaus allows you to dispute information in your credit report on its website, or you can call the bureau's toll-free number (we provide contact info for the big-three credit bureaus in the earlier section "Where to get your reports"). Having a current personal credit report, not one from a lender, when you dispute online makes the correction process simple. In most cases all you have to do is enter the report number and follow the instructions. Experian will even give you a free report if you don't already have one and need to dispute something. If you opt to call the toll-free number, you're unlikely to get a live person on the other end, but you'll be told what information and documentation you need in order to submit a written request. Either way, after you properly notify the credit bureau, you can count on action.

Contacting the creditor

Another way, and sometimes a better way, to remove inaccurate information from your credit report is outlined under the FACT Act: Deal directly with the creditor who reported the negative information in the first place. Customer service contact information appears on your billing statements from that creditor, and the general address and phone number are on your credit report. After you dispute the information, the creditor must look into the matter and can't continue to report the negative information while it's investigating your dispute. This approach is more direct and eliminates the possibility of your dispute being miscommunicated or delayed as it's passed between you, the bureau, and the lender.

TIP

We recommend that you contact the creditor directly. A call or email may be sufficient. If your relationship is testy, consider submitting your issue in writing and through the mail, requesting a return receipt for every piece of correspondence you send.

For new delinquencies, the FACT Act requires the lender to notify you if negative information is reported to a credit bureau. Be sure you read the fine print carefully. Anyone who extends credit to you must send you a one-time notice either before or not later than 30 days after negative information — including late payments, missed payments, partial payments, or any other form of default — is furnished to a credit bureau. This includes collection agencies, as long as they report to a credit bureau. The notice (known as an *adverse action notice*) may look something like this:

>> **Before negative information is reported:** "We may report information about your account to credit bureaus. Late payments, missed payments, or other defaults on your account may be reflected in your credit report."

>> **After negative information is reported:** "We have told a credit bureau about a late payment, missed payment, or other default on your account. This information may be reflected in your credit report."

REMEMBER

Receiving notification about what a creditor has reported about you to the credit bureaus isn't a substitute for your own close monitoring of your credit reports, bank accounts, and credit card statements.

Getting and Understanding Your Credit Scores

Getting your hands on your credit reports is pretty straightforward. You only have three of them and you can request them all from the same website. Getting copies of your credit scores isn't as straightforward. Your credit score is a tool used in most credit reviews to objectively analyze the information from your credit report.

When a lender orders your credit report, it often also orders a credit score, which helps predict the chances that you won't be able to pay a new loan as agreed.

The two best-known credit scoring companies are FICO and VantageScore. They developed the credit scores most commonly used by lenders today. FICO is the best known name in credit scores. VantageScore is its largest competitor, although less well known. Four of the top five financial institutions, all credit card issuers, and two of the top five auto lenders use VantageScores for lending decisions. The most common scores from both companies range from 300 to 850.

REMEMBER

Don't get hung up on a number. Be as good as you can be, but don't get excited and yell at the cat over a score of 820 instead of 850. The most important thing is to know what your *lenders* know about your credit score and what's in the credit report they look at. On this topic, you want to be on the same page.

The main points to keep in mind regarding credit scores are as follows:

>> Your score is different for each credit bureau report, if only because each bureau has slightly different data about you in its files.

>> Be sure you know which score you're getting: a FICO score, a VantageScore, or a proprietary score from the service providing it.

>> You can only improve your credit score by improving your credit history, not the other way around. Perhaps the most important thing we can share is that if you take care of your credit report, your credit scores will take care of themselves.

>> About 5 percent of credit reports have errors that would result in a score change of 25 points or more according to the Federal Trade Commission. If your report has errors, that can be enough to cause you to be declined or pay higher interest rates. That's why it's important to check your report regularly. Dispute errors and outdated items to ensure your credit score accurately reflects your creditworthiness.

With a grasp of the essentials about credit scores, you're ready to take the plunge and get your score. Of course, once you have it, you can count on us to explain what it means for you and what you can do about it. Read on!

Ordering your score

TIP

The Fair Access to Credit Scores Act that was bundled into the massive Dodd–Frank Wall Street Reform and Consumer Protection Act allows you free access to your credit score if you've been denied credit or if some other "adverse action" (denial of insurance or utilities, for example) was taken as a result of your credit score. In fact, the law requires the lender or business that took adverse action to give you a score it used. You don't have to request your credit score if such an adverse action is taken based on that score; a copy of the score used to make the decision is automatically sent to you.

To get your current score, you need to order a credit report at the same time, because your score is calculated based on the information in your credit report at the time you order the score.

If you want your credit score, you can get it from a number of places today for free:

>> **Your lender:** Your lender may provide a FICO score to you through its online banking app or with your billing statement.

>> **Experian** (www.experian.com): You can get your FICO score for free when you enroll in its basic monitoring service or sign up with its mobile app. You'll get offers for credit cards or other services. Just be prepared to say no.

>> **Equifax** (800-685-1111; www.equifax.com): Enrollment in its service at the time of writing is $19.95 a month.

>> **myFICO.com** (800-319-4433; www.myfico.com): Enrollment in its basic service is $19.95 a month at the time of this writing.

>> **TransUnion:** You can get the VantageScore through its online service, which is $24.95 a month as of this writing.

The credit bureaus worked together in development of the VantageScore (a fierce competitor of FICO). Oh, and all three credit bureaus compete with one another every chance they get.

REMEMBER

The number you get will almost never match the one your lender gets exactly. That's okay. When you get your score, you should also get an explanation of what the number means in terms of risk. If the score you get says you're a good risk, your lender's score will as well. What's important is to know what the number you get means within its scale, not that it matches the score your lender has. You should also get a list of risk factors (also called *reason statements*) that explain what in your credit report most affected the number. Although the numbers may differ, the risk factors tend to be very consistent. Address them, and all your scores will improve. We discuss risk factors and reason statements in detail later in this section.

WARNING

When you're ordering scores, most sites try to get you to sign up for a credit-monitoring service. Be sure you understand what you're agreeing to before you do. You should be able to get your one-time credit report and a score without signing up for a long-term service, but monitoring services may have advantages, too.

Just be sure you read the fine print and know what's in it for you before you sign up. We discuss credit-monitoring services and their benefits and costs in Chapter 15.

Telling a good score from a bad one

There are many scores with different ranges for different kinds of lenders and different kinds of lending. So, how do you know if your score is a good one, or not? The answer is that a good score is one that's good enough to get you what you want at a price you can afford. A really good score will get you the amount you want to borrow at the best interest rates and terms.

An important bit of good news is that if you have a good score on one scoring system, you'll have good scores on the others, too. For purposes of discussion, we're going to use examples from FICO, which produces the most widely used scores in the market.

REMEMBER

As you look at scores, remember that they change to reflect the behavior of the "market," which just means all consumers as a group. When the economy crashed in 2008, average credit scores dropped like lead balloons. As a result, the definition of *good* shifted down the scale somewhat. As the economy recovered, average scores improved and what was defined as a "good" score moved back up the scale. That shift was fairly small. Generally, a "good" score starts somewhere around 700 on the FICO scale. A "really good" score is usually is 750 or higher.

FICO likes to give you a picture of where you stand in comparison to others using an eight-bar graph and an eight-column chart, as shown in Figure 14-1.

Another useful way to understand score dynamics is to look at score distribution over time. Table 14-2 shows how the percentage of people with FICO scores of different tiers fared between April 2005 and April 2019. Although the number of people with low scores decreased over time, it was a gradual change. Moving into higher tiers is difficult. During the 14-year period, the number of people in the lowest tier decreased by only 2.8 percent. In the same time period, the number of people in the highest tier increased by 6.1 percent. It may be hard to move your score, but it's not impossible. What's the best way to do so? With a plan and over time! Anyone who claims that he can turn your credit score around overnight is not telling the truth. But there are tools today that may help you make that jump a bit faster.

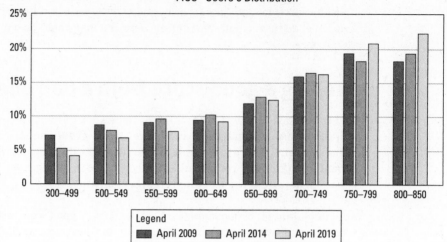

FIGURE 14-1: The distribution of FICO scores nationally over the period April 2009 to April 2019.

FICO® Score 8 Distribution

Legend
■ April 2009   ■ April 2014   ☐ April 2019

Courtesy of FICO

REMEMBER

The difference in loan terms between a score of 750 and a score of 800 (the top two groups) may be small, but those with a score of 650 or lower may not be eligible for credit at all. This tends to be true no matter what the economy is like at the moment. However, not all lenders view risk the same way. One lender may consider a credit score of 650 to be a high risk, while another lender may not consider such a score to be too risky to take a chance and may have a special program to give credit to lower-scoring consumers — just be aware that it may not be the kind of credit you really want. You'll likely be charged high fees and interest, and you could find yourself in a debt trap.

WARNING

A bad credit score and history can make you a target for unscrupulous lenders. If your credit is damaged, read the fine print on any credit agreement carefully and understand all fees, penalties, and interest rates before you act.

So, how high is high enough? In a time of relatively easy credit, the saying often is all you need is a pulse to get a loan. Although this may not be entirely true, getting a loan with a lower score in good times is certainly easier than it is when times are hard. Over time, the standard for lending tends to swing like a pendulum from easy to tight and back again. So keeping your credit as clean as you can is all the more important, because today's record will be there for at least the next seven years, while tomorrow's credit market will surely change.

TABLE 14-2　　　**FICO Score Distribution Over Time, Percent of Population**

	April 2005	April 2006	April 2007	April 2008	April 2009	April 2010	April 2011	April 2012	April 2013	April 2014	April 2015	April 2016	April 2017	April 2018	April 2019
300–499	6.8	6.2	6.3	7.2	7.3	6.9	6.3	5.7	5.6	5.4	4.9	4.6	4.7	4.2	4.3
500–549	8.1	8.0	7.9	8.2	8.7	9.0	8.7	8.5	8.4	8.1	7.6	7.1	6.8	6.8	6.8
550–599	8.7	8.9	8.9	8.7	9.1	9.6	9.9	10.0	9.9	9.6	9.4	9.0	8.5	8.1	7.8
600–649	10.0	10.2	10.1	9.6	9.5	9.5	9.8	10.1	10.1	10.2	10.3	10.3	10.0	9.6	9.3
650–699	13.1	12.8	12.5	12.0	12.0	11.9	12.1	12.2	12.2	12.8	13.0	13.3	13.2	13.0	12.5
700–749	16.5	16.5	16.1	16.0	15.9	15.7	15.5	16.0	16.3	16.4	16.6	16.9	17.1	16.2	16.2
750–799	20.4	20.0	19.9	19.6	19.3	19.5	19.6	19.0	18.9	18.2	18.2	18.5	19.0	20.2	20.7
800–850	16.2	17.4	18.2	18.7	18.2	17.9	18.1	18.5	18.5	19.3	19.9	20.4	20.7	21.8	22.3
Total	100.0	100.0	100.0	100.0	100.0	100.0	100.0	100.0	100.0	100.0	100.0	100.0	100.0	100.0	100.0

Courtesy of FICO

WHAT SHAPE IS YOUR CREDIT IN?

VantageScore recently described the U.S. population according to its scoring scale, with the shocking result that almost 25 percent of Americans are in less than good shape. Using this scale, you can estimate your place in the credit pecking order:

- **Excellent:** The top 26.1 percent of the population is in this category, with scores ranging from 781 to 850.

- **Great:** 18.1 percent of the population. Great scores range from 721 to 780.

- **Good:** 17.8 percent of the population. Good scores range from 661 to 720.

- **Fair:** 13.6 percent of the population. Fair scores range from 601 to 660.

- **Unfavorable:** 19.8 percent of the population. Unfavorable scores range from 500 to 600.

- **Deficient (formerly called High Risk):** 4.6 percent of the population. Deficient scores range from 300 to 499.

Connecting pricing to your credit score

Most lending today is done using something called *risk-based pricing*. Risk-based pricing means that instead of saying "no" to a high-risk customer, a lender would say "yes" and still make money on the risky loan by charging a higher interest rate and fees. This model allows more people with lower scores to get more loans, albeit at a higher cost. That doesn't mean everyone can qualify for a loan. Lenders still have a threshold below which an account is too risky to accept. So, although your credit score may get you a higher or lower interest rate, if it's too weak for the lender's standards, you may get a "no, thank you" instead.

To get the best deals on credit, you need to have a good credit score, which means you have a good credit report. Having a perfect credit score (a FICO or Vantage-Score of 850) is extremely rare and not necessary. Lenders aren't looking for a perfect score. What they want to see is a good enough score to approve the credit for which you're applying. All that takes is common sense and good credit management. When you hit the number for the lender to give you the best rates, you're good to go. That number won't even be close to a "perfect" score. We know, that's easy to say, but not always easy to do.

For a given type of credit — such as revolving (credit cards) or installment (car loans and mortgages) — credit grantors divide customers into different score ranges or buckets and offer them different rates and terms based on where they fall. For example, the rate for a 30-year mortgage may be the same for people with scores between 760 and 850, all other underwriting criteria (such as income and job stability) being equal.

What do credit-score groupings look like in the current market? As an example, say you have a $300,000 30-year fixed-rate mortgage. (Keep in mind that we're using numbers from mid-2020 at a time when interest rates are at historic lows. The rates for loans today may be different.) This example is meant to illustrate the magnitude of difference between scores and rates. The interest rates for each grouping for this particular loan look like this:

FICO Score	Rate	Monthly Payment	Interest Paid
760–850	2.501%	$1,186	$126,787
700–759	2.723%	$1,220	$139,357
680–699	2.9%	$1,249	$149,528
660–679	3.114%	$1,283	$161,999
640–659	3.544%	$1,355	$187,625
620–639	4.09%	$1,448	$221,228

Source: www.bankrate.com/mortgages/how-your-credit-score-affects-your-mortgage-rate

Using this table, a person with a FICO score of 639 and an interest rate of 4.09 percent pays out a total of $521,228 over the term of the $300,000 mortgage, whereas a person with a FICO score of 760 and an interest rate of 2.5 percent pays only $426,787. That's a difference of $94,441! Higher interest rates create even more shocking differences. As you can see, maintaining the highest credit score possible can save you hundreds a month and tens of thousands in mortgage payments over the term of the loan. You can plug in your own mortgage amount and interest rates to see exactly what you'll pay using the calculator at www.myfico.com/credit-education/calculators/loan-savings-calculator.

Although the amount of money you save on smaller loans may not be as high as that associated with a mortgage loan, a high credit score saves you money in interest charges for any amount you plan to borrow. In addition, in a tight credit market, a low credit score may mean that you don't qualify for credit at any price.

Your goal is to get into the best bucket you can by the time you need the type of credit in question. How? By building a plan that gets you to your goal of "good enough" credit. Take some time and include everyone with whom you share your life. List your credit-oriented goals, and then check a resource like www.bankrate.com to find out what credit score will get you into the next-highest tier of borrowers. Unless you're in the top tier, come up with actions to take based on what you find in your credit report.

New tools like having your positive rent payments reported or adding your cell-phone, utility, or video-streaming service payments can also help bump up your scores if you have a limited credit history. Talk with your landlord and consider services like Experian Boost (www.experian.com/boost). Be sure you understand what you're agreeing to before signing up. There is generally little or no fee for these kinds of services, but they'll likely ask for information so they can make other offers for you to purchase. If you can say no to credit card offers or other products, Experian Boost can work to your advantage.

FICO has also introduced a new score called UltraFICO that looks at the information from your bank accounts, like checking and savings. A history of maintaining good balances in your checking and savings accounts is a good sign you'll manage credit well, too, especially if you don't have a very extensive credit history. You have to opt in for your lender to use the UltraFICO score. Learn more at www.fico.com/ultrafico.

You can find details on how a credit score is built in Chapter 13.

Credit scores also are changing the way they look at some kinds of information in a credit report. For example, collection accounts used to do serious harm to your scores the entire time they were in your report. New scores from FICO and VantageScore, though, now exclude paid collections from the calculation or significantly reduce the impact. So, paying off a collection account could help your scores as soon as they show "paid" in your credit report.

You should also check your credit reports regularly and make sure there are no errors or out-of-date information. Disputing any you may find can pump up our scores. Because credit scores normally look back over several years of credit history to develop an accurate picture of your risk profile, overcoming any negative data that may be hurting your score takes time. Removing errors or out-of-date information, however, has an immediate effect on your score.

WARNING

Avoid companies that promise to improve your score by removing accurate negative information from your credit report. They can't do what they claim, and they may get you into even more trouble if, for example, you're approved for a loan based on fraudulently altered credit information. See Chapter 3 for more information about illicit credit repair companies and your rights.

Knowing the reason for reason statements

Along with your credit score, you get up to five reason statements, sometimes called *risk-factor statements,* on your credit-score report. A *reason statement* is a simple explanation of why your score is less than perfect. What's the reason for reason statements? Well, a lender can't make money turning down business, so if a poor score is keeping a lender from approving your application, knowing the reasons your credit scores aren't up to snuff can help identify how to dig out and get those fees and loans flowing again!

Creditors get what's called a *reason code* or *risk-factor code*, and you get the interpreted version of that, which is called a *reason statement*. For example, if a reason code reveals that your lower-than-it-could-have-been score is because your credit cards are maxed out and not because you never pay on time, you can focus on reducing balances and using less of each credit line to raise your score.

There are more than 100 possible reason codes for some scores that give you and your lender specific information about the most important things causing your credit to sag. Although the numbers from credit scores can be different, the reason statements tend to be very consistent. By addressing the reason statements you receive, you'll be able to improve all your credit scores.

Reason statements are generated every time a credit score is calculated. When you get a credit score, you should also get the reason statements along with it. If you get credit scores as a service along with your credit report, you'll typically find the reason statements listed immediately following the credit score. In some cases you may only see the things that are hurting your credit score, called the *negative reason factor* for obvious, well, reasons. Some may list both positive and negative reasons for your score, with tips to help increase your score muscle.

According to FICO, the most frequently used reason statement is, "Proportion of balances to credit limits on bank/national revolving or other revolving accounts is too high." This tells you that you're using more of your limits than the scoring model thinks is safe. A high percentage of usage — say, 50 percent ($10,000 on a $20,000 credit line) — is inherently riskier than 25 percent (or $5,000). The lower the balances on your credit cards, the better for your credit scores.

Ironically, VantageScore's most frequent reason statement is, "Available credit across all open, recently reported accounts is too low." That's just another way of saying the balances on your credit cards is too high, exactly like the FICO example. If you see this reason statement in your credit report or one like it, you need to reduce your credit card balances. It's time to slow your charging and increase your payments.

The bottom line is that you need to focus on the top reason statements you received and that are affecting your scores. They're different for everyone.

To help you decode your reason statements, VantageScore developed a microsite that explains them. See www.reasoncode.org for more info.

Chapter **15**

Monitoring Your Credit Reports and Scores

The next time you get a billing statement from a credit card company, bank, or insurance company, you may find that in addition to asking for your payment, they're offering to check your credit report and credit scores monthly, too. As a perk for customers, or an enticement to be a customer, they may offer a credit monitoring service at no cost, or to help with their profit margin they could ask you to pay for it. The question is, should you sign up? As with almost all things related to credit, the answer is, it depends. Have you had issues with fraud in the past? Are you planning to make a big credit purchase in the near future? Are you just the kind of person who worries a lot about your credit? In this chapter, we lay out what you should think about before signing up for a monitoring service, whether free or for a fee.

REMEMBER

Don't confuse credit monitoring with identity theft protection. Credit fraud can be the result of identity theft, but it can also lead to other kinds of crimes that don't affect your credit report. Credit monitoring won't stop someone from stealing your identity and using your Social Security number in a false job application or to file taxes in your name, but it may enable you to detect a potential problem early and take action to stop it. We deal with identity theft in detail in Chapters 9 and 20.

In this chapter, we discuss how credit monitoring works and what you get when you enroll so that you can decide if it's worth the effort or you should just handle checking your credit reports on your own.

How Credit Monitoring Really Works

Enlisting a company to monitor your credit means that you give the company access to your credit reports so that it can watch them and notify you of any suspicious additions or changes. Basic services are often free, but for more premium services you may have to pay a monthly or annual fee. So, how does credit monitoring happen? It's pretty much exactly what it sounds like. Each service provider has a series of programs that it runs against databases to which it has access. Some, like Experian, have their own credit database but also have access to others and search social media and the dark web, looking for changes, updates, or patterns that indicate something may be amiss in your world.

TECHNICAL STUFF

The *dark web* consists of web pages on the World Wide Web that are not indexed by search engines and are not viewable in a standard web browser like Chrome, Firefox, or Safari. The dark web is where lots of nefarious and illegal activities take place.

Some services monitor only one credit bureau, others monitor all three, and still others monitor some of the many national, specialty, consumer-reporting bureaus (see Chapter 14) for activity or changes to your reports such as

>> The opening of new accounts

>> Larger-than-normal charges

>> Unusual account activity, such as a change in the frequency, location, or type of charges appearing on your credit reports

>> A surge in balances

>> Other changes to your accounts, such as payments, late payment notices, credit inquiries, public records, employment, addresses, and fraud alerts

Some monitoring services also search the Internet, the dark web, social media sites, and other public records for suspicious use of your identifying information. They may produce detailed reports about your credit score and even suggest ways to make it more attractive to lenders and improve your creditworthiness. Most also give you free credit reports and scores (they may be proprietary scores or a FICO or VantageScore; see Chapter 13 for the differences between score types).

Lastly, monitoring services check your data with differing frequency. Some check daily, others weekly, others monthly and others quarterly, depending on their service level. The more they do and the more often you can get updated reports, the more you'll likely have to pay.

Understanding the Types of Monitoring Services Available

A universe of services is available to help you monitor or safeguard your credit.

Before we dive into the details, let us add that in our experience, you can handle most of the monitoring on your own *if you have the time and inclination.* For instance, you're entitled to a free credit report from each of the three major bureaus annually. You get additional free credit reports under certain circumstances, such as if you think you've been the victim of identity theft or if you don't receive the best rates available for a loan or insurance policy based on information in your credit report. In the case of a natural disaster, the credit bureaus may provide more frequent access to your credit reports; for example, during the COVID-19 pandemic, you could request a credit report free once a week until at least April 2021. So, with at least one opportunity to get a free look at your report every four months, you can do a credible job of monitoring your credit at no cost, especially if you don't have anything causing you concern or giving you a reason to check more often. You just have to remember to order your report and then examine it to see what's changed. (For more on monitoring your credit yourself, see the section "Monitoring on your own" later in this chapter.)

If you're interested in having someone else do the monitoring for you, here's a look at each type of service in more detail:

>> **Credit report monitoring:** This service notifies you about changes to your credit report(s). It often provides frequent access to your credit report upon request. Some services monitor only one credit report, while others monitor reports from the three major credit-reporting agencies (Experian, Equifax, and TransUnion) as well as some of the national specialty-reporting bureaus. Credit report monitoring may provide limited help in giving you an early warning about identity theft, but because such services monitor only the data in your credit report, an identity theft that involves noncredit or unreported areas won't be addressed.

>> **Credit score monitoring:** This service may include all or some of the credit report monitoring services, but it also includes checking your credit score or

credit scores. Which score or scores depends on your service provider. For example, Experian's free basic service includes a FICO 8 score. Its premium service will give you up to six more FICO scores, including industry-specific scores, like auto and bankcard scores.

>> **Identity theft monitoring:** This service may include additional monitoring areas beyond credit. It focuses mainly on financial databases and not on criminal or law enforcement data, medical billers that don't report to the credit bureaus, or government data.

>> **Credit freeze or lock products:** These products, offered by the credit bureaus, work by limiting access to your credit report. When your information is used to apply for new credit, you must first give express permission before your report can be accessed. Typically, a lender reviews your credit file before issuing a new loan or credit card. The inability to do so may prevent the issuance of new credit to criminals. For more info, see the section "Setting Alarms, Alerts, and Freezes" later in this chapter. Also, `https://helpcenter.idtheftcenter.org/s/article/Place-a-Credit-Freeze` outlines your legal right to request a freeze and explains how to do so.

>> **ID theft recovery products:** By definition, recovering from identity theft requires a clearing of all fraudulent records and charges created by an identity thief. You can find companies to do all the research and restoration work for you.

>> **Data sweep services:** Data sweep companies monitor the Internet for listings of your personal identifying information that may expose you to identity thieves or use of your information that indicates you're already a victim. They may also monitor specific websites known for questionable activities on the dark web. If your personal data is detected, these services alert you. They may also offer insurance if they fail to perform.

>> **Virtual account numbers:** Superman used Clark Kent, Batman had Bruce Wayne, and you have a virtual credit card number to protect your identity from being discovered and misused by evil forces! These onetime computer-generated surrogate numbers enable you to better limit what personal information of yours — such as billing address, account number, or email address — appears when you're online shopping, paying bills, or registering at websites. It does so by replacing your real information with anonymous data that has a very short life span and is useless after your transaction is completed. It works for almost any type of purchase except for items to be picked up later that may require you to match your credit card number to the receipt. Movie/game tickets fall into this category. If your number is stolen, you have to cancel only that number instead of your main account number. A similar technology is being incorporated by credit card companies using your smartphone. Some credit cards that now reside in your "mobile wallet"

generate a unique transaction code for every purchase, making it harder to steal your card number or identity.

>> **Identity theft insurance:** ID insurance may be a stand-alone policy or an add-on to one of your existing policies. It helps replace out-of-pocket expenses you may incur after your identity is stolen and misused. Note that ID insurance doesn't keep you safe from theft itself. Collecting legal costs used to defend yourself against a crime committed by an ID thief may require an acquittal or a dismissal of charges.

Making a Case for and against Third-Party Credit Monitoring

You really only need your credit score when you're applying for credit — when it has a reason or a purpose. Paying someone to monitor your credit or score without a specific purpose or reason is an equally empty exercise. Before paying for a monitoring service, ask yourself why you need it or want it. If you're trying to improve your credit or get to a certain credit score so that you can make a large purchase like a home or a car, laying out some dough for a professional monitoring service can make sense. Also, if you are a "credit worrier," checking your credit scores daily, and you can't sleep soundly without all the safeguards and early warning bells in place, then a monitoring service may be right for you.

REMEMBER

Your lender's score may well differ from the one you get because it may come from another company (FICO, VantageScore, a credit bureau, and so on), because the information in your report may have changed between the time you received a score and your lender did, or because the lender applies its own algorithms based on proprietary factors that it weights based on its specific business experience.

WARNING

No credit monitoring service can offer you complete protection. If a lender or vendor doesn't report to the credit bureaus, or if it does report but not to the bureau monitored by the service you've chosen, you won't know whether a fraudulent account has been opened in your name until a problem arises down the road and a collector or the authorities call. Furthermore, creditors typically update your account information once a month, so you're likely to experience a delay in catching fraud indicators in your credit report.

REMEMBER

You shouldn't rely on a credit monitoring service alone. Always check your billing statements and watch for other signs that fraud may be occurring, like getting collection notices for accounts that aren't yours.

Monitoring on your own

TIP

You can monitor your credit on your own by taking these simple actions:

>> Get a free copy of your credit report every 12 months from each of the three major credit-reporting agencies (Experian, Equifax, and TransUnion). Stagger the ordering so that you get a different report every four months. Review them and dispute any inaccuracies.

>> Be sure to get a free credit report if you dispute an item on your report. You're entitled to a free report to make sure that the mistake has been removed.

>> Get extra free copies of your credit reports directly from the bureaus (not from www.annualcreditreport.com) if you live in Colorado, Georgia, Maine, Maryland, Massachusetts, New Jersey, or Vermont. These states require that you be allowed an additional free report annually — except you lucky Georgia residents, who get two more free reports a year from each bureau, for a total of three. Puerto Rico, not a state (yet), requires that residents be given free credit reports as well.

>> Get a free report if you're turned down for credit. Anytime you are turned down for credit, you're guaranteed a free report from the credit bureau the lender used.

>> Get a free report if you're unemployed and looking for a new job. Within the first six months of seeking employment, you can have a freebie.

>> If you apply for a mortgage, you're entitled to a copy of the credit report and score the lender uses.

>> Order your free national, specialty consumer reports annually (see Chapter 14). Doing so may give you many more free looks into your cyber files.

>> Need to add a fraud alert or an extended fraud alert to your credit report? You get one or two additional free reports, respectively, over the next 12 months from each bureau.

>> Every time your insurance renews, look at the disclosure language, which is usually in the front of your policy, to see whether your insurance company used a credit report to set your rates. If so (and it's very likely), follow the instructions and get another free credit report if you didn't get the best rates.

>> Monitor your bank and credit card accounts online weekly. If something funny is going on, you'll know about it sooner.

>> Set up free alerts on your accounts that tip you off when certain types of transactions are made or if a dollar limit is exceeded.

>> During natural or declared disasters, you may be able to get additional free reports, too. During the COVID-19 pandemic, the credit bureaus allowed everyone a free report once a week.

When paid monitoring may be worth the time and money

Depending on the depth of your wallet and your degree of credit anxiety, paid monitoring may be for you. Here are some circumstances when paid monitoring makes sense:

>> Your credit is damaged and you've been trying to improve it for some time. Rather than ordering your report frequently at a premium price, a service that gives you more frequent access for a low monthly or annual fee may make sense so that you can make a plan and track your progress.

>> You're planning on making a large purchase that requires your credit score to be in primo condition. You can take your scoring temperature often so you know when the time is right to see the man. Always start checking your report at least three to six months before you plan to apply so you have time to address any issues and make improvements.

>> You've been the victim of identity theft and accounts are being opened in your name. After you add fraud alerts and maybe place a credit freeze (see Chapter 20), monitoring may help you sleep better at night.

>> You're slightly obsessive-compulsive about your identity or credit file. Monitoring may give you a sense of security.

REMEMBER

Credit report or score monitoring isn't done in real time. Information can be days, weeks, or months old. In addition to the fact that monitoring companies report at differing frequencies, not all credit issuers (small credit unions, medical providers, utilities, and so on) report to the credit bureaus. As we point out earlier in this chapter, credit monitoring doesn't prevent someone from stealing your identity. Credit monitoring alerts you only after you have a problem so you can take action.

TIP

If you decide to try a monitoring service, check to see whether it offers a free trial period. Most do, and many services today are entirely free, at least for their basic level. If you do take advantage of a trial period, don't forget to cancel before the trial period ends if you're not going to stay with the service.

Sadly, data breaches are all too common today. In response to a breach, companies often offer a free credit-monitoring subscription. Taking advantage of those offers can be a good idea. Just be sure you understand the terms. Like free trial periods, the no-cost service may expire and you could find yourself stuck with a credit card charge you didn't expect.

Recognizing the protection you have already

You and your credit card are already protected against fraud under federal law. (See Chapter 19 for more on your legal protections.) Unless you fail to notify your credit card company about erroneous or questionable charges on your statements within 60 days, your total liability for fraud is limited to $50 per card. That's not much, but if you have several cards that are affected, it could add up. On a positive note, most credit card companies will wave that liability today if you contact them in good faith, even after the 60 days. If you have homeowners insurance, the $50 charge is probably a covered peril for which you can get reimbursed. Debit card liability also begins at $50 but can escalate after two days have passed from the time you find out about the fraud. Where debit card fraud is concerned, act in haste or you may repent at leisure!

Many of the major creditors have adopted zero-consumer-liability policies to further limit your exposure and increase your confidence in being able to use your cards safely. They've also become much more sophisticated in identifying patterns of card use that could indicate fraud.

Many credit card companies and banks today can adjust the sensitivity of their systems to recognize you are the one making the purchases, even if you're traveling outside of the country.

Still, most lenders appreciate your help in letting them know when you're traveling away from home. Be sure to check on their policies by calling customer service and asking whether you need to notify them.

Check your lender's website to see what it offers in terms of optional alerts that you can set up. One major credit card company will notify you by email or on your mobile phone if:

>> A cash withdrawal is made.

>> A purchase exceeds a limit that you set, is made outside the United States, or is made online or over the phone.

>> Someone tries to reset your password or billing address.

>> They see a questionable transaction.

These types of services are becoming increasingly common.

Getting Your Money's Worth from Monitoring Services

If you decide that monitoring is a good fit for you, you may need some help to cut through the huge volume of providers. We can't analyze each one, but we can provide tips to help you make your decision.

Asking the right questions before you buy a service is important. Here are some questions you should ask before you sign on the dotted line, or sign up online, to be sure you get the most out of the service, even if it's free:

>> **What are the total costs and fees?** Set a limit that you're willing to pay and stick to it. Weigh the possible $20 to $50 a month charge against your odds of suffering a credit card fraud that you'd be liable for. Any liability is likely to be low. Also, banks, insurers, and the big-three credit bureaus all offer products to detect fraud and give you a credit score. Shop around for the best price. You may get a better price from someone you already do other business with.

Free isn't always, free, either. You usually trade something for the service. In most cases, the currency is your information. In return for the free monitoring service, you agree to get offers for things you may want to buy or credit you would qualify for if you choose to apply. Be sure you're comfortable with that exchange. Information today is as valuable as cash. If you can say no, or want to take advantage of opportunities you thing you'll find useful, sharing your information can be a worthwhile price to pay.

>> **What is the monitoring company's reputation and track record?** Like nearly everything else today, you can get reviews of services online. Sites like www.nextadvisor.com and www.fightidentitytheft.com offer user ratings that you can compare.

>> **Exactly what will you get for your money or information?** Know how comprehensive you want the monitoring to be. Be sure that you're getting the type of score you want; some services offer proprietary or bureau scores that lenders don't use. These scores may be okay for reference but won't be as

easy to compare if you're using them to estimate the loan interest rates or deal terms you'll get. Here are some common safeguards you can expect:

- Frequent or unlimited access to your credit report

- Frequent or unlimited access to a credit score of some type

- Monitoring of one or more credit reports

- Alerts when critical changes are made, including address changes

- Alerts if your credit score deteriorates into a lower lending category

- Alerts if personal information like your Social Security number or your credit card number starts showing up on public websites

- Warnings if patterns of credit use change or multiple applications for credit occur within a short time span

- A periodic statement summarizing your credit report changes, score, and alerts

- Assistance in restoring your identity if it's stolen

>> **What is the monitoring company's cancellation and renewal policy?** Avoid automatic renewals unless you're absolutely certain you'll continue to use the service. They require storing your credit card data, so you'll have to remember to end the contract in accordance with their terms of service or you'll face ongoing charges.

>> **Can you get help from a live customer service person when you want?** Be sure to check the hours the service reps are available. If you need help, you don't want to have to wait until Monday morning.

>> **What exactly will the company do to restore your identity if your identity is stolen and misused?** The service should pay for and perform all the tasks needed to restore your identity. The service shouldn't push this time-consuming, expensive, and difficult process off on you.

WARNING

If a company makes unrealistic claims or offers unlimited guarantees, chances are it may not be able to deliver. Be sure to check user reviews and industry ratings.

Setting Alarms, Alerts, and Freezes

We've all seen the spy movies where they put a piece of tape across the door seam to know if there has been an intruder. Although you can't use a piece of tape to warn you of credit or identity intrusions, you do have access to an array of early warning tools that can warn you something is amiss.

Alarms

You can set an alarm to go off with your bank or credit card company by establishing certain parameters for notification. For example, if a charge for more than a certain amount hits your checking account, they can send an email. You can do the same and more for your credit card accounts easily and for free. Check out your card's website and look for options. You can use texts or smartphone messages if email is too slow — or use all three to make sure you get the alert.

Fraud alerts

You can place a fraud alert on your credit file if you think that someone may be trying to compromise your information. Say you're notified that your personal information was accessed in a data breach. You may or may not have anything to worry about, but a fraud alert requires anyone using your report for new accounts or limit changes in the next 12 months to exercise extra caution and make sure that you're actually the one doing the asking. You also get a free credit report from each bureau.

>> **Extended fraud alerts:** These longer-lasting alerts give you seven years for fraud alert protection and two additional free annual credit report reviews. You need to give the credit bureau a copy of the police fraud or identity theft report you filed. See Chapter 9 for details.

>> **Active-duty alerts:** If you're an active-duty military person, there's an alert just for you. An active-duty alert lasts for one year on your credit report.

>> **Widget alerts:** Norton, the antivirus software company, has a free widget tool called the Norton Cybercrime Index that sits on your desktop or phone and warns you about real-time cybercrime so you can take preventative measures. The tool also provides in-depth information on cybercrime trends and patterns. Think of it as a traffic report that alerts you to trouble spots, areas and streets to avoid, and potential hazards on the road. Others are now providing similar services.

Credit freezes

A freeze on your credit report locks your report against applications for new credit in your name. In order to review your report, a lender or other party would need to ask you to unfreeze your account. This request tips you off that your identity is being used to apply for credit right away and prevents new accounts from being opened without your permission. There is no fee to freeze or unfreeze your credit report with the national credit bureaus. Unlike fraud alerts that are shared among the bureaus, you must request a freeze separately from each of them. Before you apply for credit or other services, you also must remember to lift the freeze by providing a PIN or following the instructions for each separate bureau.

REMEMBER

A credit freeze will not prevent identity theft. If someone is using your information to apply for credit, you're already a victim. After placing a credit freeze, you must still be vigilant in protecting your identity and ensuring that it isn't being used in ways that are not credit related. Things like tax fraud, making purchases with your existing credit counts, buy-here-pay-here loans, payday loans, job application fraud, and other crimes could still happen using your stolen identity.

5

Successfully Managing Your Credit for Life

Give your credit score a boost by identifying your credit style and achieving balance with your spending and savings.

Get a new and easy way to understand the role of credit as a renewable resource in your balanced credit ecosystem.

Make a firm foundation to build good credit in today's unforgiving credit environment.

Understand how to deal with systemic injustice and your own prejudices and stereotypes about credit and lending.

Understand your consumer protections in the CARD Act, Dodd–Frank legislation, FACT Act, and Fair Debt Collection Practices Act.

Spot early signs of identity theft, control access to your identity, and keep your personal information safe.

Chapter **16**

Putting Yourself in Control of Your Credit

When Henry Ford decided that you could have any color you wanted for your new Model T Ford, as long as it was black, it wasn't because car buyers liked black. It wasn't even because Henry liked black. It was because drying the paint on cars coming off the assembly line took the longest of all the operations, and black dried the fastest of all the colors. By sticking with black, Ford could ship more cars each day and make more money, faster.

Credit issuers operate pretty similarly; profitability is their top priority. They shovel out credit offers by the truckload based on cursory reviews of your relative creditworthiness. Sure, some of the things they tell you may actually apply to your specific situation (for instance, you may indeed have earned the right to exclusive privileges and benefits), but the only thing you can be sure of is that the offer is designed to enhance lender profitability. Whether you need the credit product in question, or whether it's even remotely advantageous to your life, that's up to you to figure out. Like the black paint on a Model T, what you get may only make sense — *and* money for the lender. Unless, of course, you put yourself in control of your financial and credit future.

This chapter is all about helping you take the control of your credit away from the issuers. We unmask the plans others have for your financial future and introduce you to the tools you need to chart your *own* course to success. We also help you figure out how to perk up your credit score; gauge your credit style; and balance your spending, savings, and credit use.

Determining Your Credit Style

Lenders, particularly banks, divide their credit card customers into two main categories: *transactors* and *revolvers.* The people in these categories need different things from their credit, so identifying your type is important in the process of picking a credit product that fits your lifestyle.

Transactors, also referred to as *convenience users,* are pretty straightforward in their credit use. You fall into this category if you use your credit cards primarily for convenience in place of cash. Doing so reduces your need to carry a wad of bills with you. You pay your balances in full every month and avoid fees and interest charges.

TIP

If you think that you may be a transactor, focus on the incentives that a card offers you for using it, like airline tickets or hotel stays, rather than a low interest rate. No balance means no interest, so who cares if it's 19.8 percent over prime; if you don't carry a balance, the interest rate is irrelevant to you.

Be sure that you use the card enough to benefit from it. For example, if you choose an airline mileage card that requires you to charge $25,000 annually to get a free ticket, and you plan to spend only $10,000 a year on the card, it may not be a good choice. You may want to consider a cash-back card instead. Some cash-back cards have an annual fee. Again, be sure you get more out of the card than you pay into it.

Revolvers frequently carry a balance from month to month. If you're one of these more desirable customers (from a lender's point of view), you consider your credit card a line of credit to use to pay for purchases over time. You make your payments on time, and often pay the minimum or more, but you rarely pay the balance in full. You pay interest every month and may not look too carefully at what the interest costs you over the long haul. Your bank could only love you more if you missed a payment or two and racked up even more interest and penalty charges!

TIP

A revolver's best choice is a card that offers a low interest rate. A low rate does a lot to help keep your balance down because your interest charges are included in the minimum payment you make each month. If your rate is high and you make minimum payments, you carry debt for much longer. Shopping for a zero-percent-interest card makes sense, but expect to change cards more often, as these rates usually apply for limited periods.

Be careful about incurring a 3 to 5 percent fee for transferring the balance from an old card with an expiring rate to a new one. Changing cards often has a negative effect on your credit score (see the list of score components in Chapter 13).

In addition to the usual card user categorizations, we have a few of our own that you may find helpful in identifying yourself:

>> **The quicksand charger:** You qualify as a quicksand charger in our book if you spend on impulse and don't notice that you're slowly sinking into debt. Using credit without knowing how or when you'll be able to pay the bill is a bad habit that usually leads to an unhappy ending.

Use short-term installment loans for expenses that you plan to carry for six months or more. The fixed payment helps you pay off the debt more predictably, and the additional type of credit use can help your credit score. Plus, every time you apply for a new installment loan, you get a free reality check from your lender.

>> **The clueless charger:** If you continue to find unpleasant surprises on your credit card statements (like unexpected balance transfer fees and penalties), you may be a clueless charger. Students and other credit newbies tend to find themselves being taken advantage of because they don't understand how their cards work and lack a plan for using credit.

Read and understand the terms that come with your credit card. Believe that you have to make payments on time as your card agreement says, and not what other clueless chargers may tell you. For example, you can and eventually will be sued in court if you don't make the minimum payment required by the card issuer, even if the lesser payment you're making is all you can afford. Get some financial education from a responsible provider. Lenders and credit counseling agencies can help you make an affordable plan to get out of debt.

>> **The great pretender:** With apologizes to the Platters, who released the hit song "The Great Pretender" in 1955, this category includes millions who extend their income or lack thereof by using credit as if it gave them additional money to spend. A $10,000 credit limit does not mean you can now afford to spend an additional $10,000! This approach may help you make ends meet in the short term, but it is often a disaster in the end.

The tighter your finances, the tighter you need to control your use of credit. Start with a budget, trim your expenses, increase your income, and use credit only when you know that you can pay it off in a reasonable length of time (90 days or less is best). If you can't say when you will be able to pay off a charge, don't charge it. It's better, and cheaper, to cut back now rather than later, when your credit is trashed.

Balancing Spending, Savings, and Credit Use

An orchestra is beautiful to hear. A gourmet meal is a delight to eat. What makes each experience a pleasure is balance. Whether it's the balance of instruments or the balance of ingredients, each component must be in harmony with the others. If the balance is wrong, the outcome can be a disaster.

The same idea of balance applies to your finances. Your spending, savings, and credit use must work together for the most pleasing results. The next sections show you how to take baby steps toward achieving that all-important balance. (For details about crafting your future vision into achievable goals, turn to Chapter 18.)

Spending on your terms

If your spending is under control and you have money for periodic expenses, chances are you've built a strong foundation for your financial house, and your credit will be safe and strong when you need it. Say your car has a mechanical problem; where does the money come from to fix it? If you plan your spending, then you should have a category for periodic auto maintenance and repairs. So the money comes from there and not your available credit on a credit card.

REMEMBER

When you use credit, you use tomorrow's money — money you haven't yet earned and may not earn. Look at it as using tomorrow's money today. When tomorrow comes, how are you going to pay if you've already spent tomorrow's money yesterday? The more you shelter your credit from surprises or overuse by planning where and how to spend your money, the stronger your credit history, credit score, and financial future will be.

Saving for financial emergencies

If a spending plan gives you a firm foundation on which to build, then emergency savings provide the roof for shelter. Saving for emergencies and goals is essential to financial success. Let us say that again. If you don't save, you'll fail, becoming more and more vulnerable to money shortages caused by factors beyond your control. Anything from a car expense to a layoff to an economic shock caused by a pandemic or natural disaster along with the stress they bring is much worse for you and those who depend on you if you don't have a substantial emergency savings stash.

TIP

We're sure you don't *want* to live paycheck to paycheck, but perhaps money is tight and you're wondering how on earth you can possibly save anything, much less, enough. Here are four essential ways to save your hard-earned moola:

>> **Make saving painless.** Use direct deposit to put money from every paycheck into a savings account. Start small with what little you can afford — even $5 a week. The amount doesn't matter.

>> **Make saving a habit.** Automatic deposits build slowly. Your confidence in seeing savings where there were none before will build faster. Soon you'll have enough saved to handle a small emergency or even just a part of one.

>> **Add to savings with money you don't have yet.** Make a commitment to put half of new raises, tax refunds, and other windfalls like birthday money into the account. This is money you never had, never counted on, and won't miss.

>> **Consider joining a savings club or organization.** Groups like America Saves (www.americasaves.org) and the Women's Institute for Financial Education (www.wife.org) offer valuable ideas and support to keep you on track. Local banks or credit unions may offer savings clubs tailored to specific expense categories like Christmas, taxes, and vacations, with incentives. Check them out.

Using credit to enhance your life

With your spending under control and money in the bank for emergencies and expected big-ticket items, you can use your excellent credit to get the best offers. You get the best terms on loans and credit cards thanks to a solid credit history and score. Even better, you free up thousands of dollars for trips, school, and other expenses when you get the lowest interest rates on mortgages, car loans, and more. Great credit also gives you lower insurance rates, access to better housing, and even an edge at work. Hiring and promotional decisions often involve credit report reviews. Your good credit can give you a competitive edge over other applicants or coworkers who have blemished credit.

Remembering the Importance of Planning When It Comes to Your Credit

Imagine a football quarterback saying that he plays the big game based on how he feels that day. If he sets no goals, practices no plays, and doesn't monitor his performance after each practice, would you bet on him leading his team to a win? In the sport known as credit, you need to follow a plan if you want to succeed.

But you don't have any competition, you say? Wrong! Lenders, credit grantors, insurers, landlords, and employers are constantly measuring your credit performance, and the cost of a substandard performance can be higher interest rates and fewer opportunities. These players and others use your credit profile as a gauge of your potential for success or failure, so having a plan and goals for your credit makes real sense.

The following sections reveal the plans that others have for your money and introduce you to the steps you can take to take control of your funds so that you don't fall prey to plans that benefit only credit issuers.

Zeroing in on the plans others have for your money

People constantly try to get you to spend money that you don't really need to spend. Just think of the credit offers you receive. These offers may ebb and flow with the economy and lenders' appetites for new customers, but inevitably they continue to show up from banks, investment companies, and even strangers. Rest assured that the issuers design these offers to be great for them without knowledge or regard for your particular situation. If you answered many (or all!) of the offers you receive, your credit score would take a hit each time your report was reviewed for an offer, and you'd get a further score reduction every time you were approved for new credit. Trust us, the issuers don't care that their plans are winning at the expense of your credit.

If credit issuers' hidden goals seem a bit nebulous to you, consider what happens when you set foot in your local grocery store. The fact that the milk is located on the opposite side of the store from the door is no accident. This setup forces you to walk through the entire store, past an array of tempting products, to get to the one thing you need. The potential for an impulse buy is greatly enhanced, to the delight of the store owner and at your expense.

REMEMBER

The bottom line is that if you have no plan for your finances and others do, you're more likely to fail and they're more likely to win.

Developing your own plans for your future

To avoid being a pawn in some credit issuer's chess game, you need to craft a plan for your finances. Specifically, you need to identify what you want to spend money on (goals), develop a spending and savings plan that reflects your goals, and then determine how credit fits into those plans. Chapter 18 presents the process of developing a spending and savings plan in detail, but the key tasks are as follows:

- » Set and prioritize your financial goals.

- » Take simple steps to create a workable plan.

- » Adjust your plan as you go along.

The same process applies to your credit, but with a few differences. Yes, you need to set credit goals, but they can be simpler. For example, perhaps you want to buy a home in three years. If you had to wait until you saved up, say, $300,000 to purchase your dream house in cash, you might be ready for assisted living before you moved into your first home. Borrowing on future income to move in today makes sense and may well improve the quality of your life for years to come. You need to save for a down payment, and you need to have good credit to get a good mortgage interest rate and terms. This won't happen overnight, so you need to plan to make it happen.

TIP

Setting goals is easy. Just keep these steps in mind:

1. **Do a little prep work.**

   Set aside an evening or a weekend afternoon, sit down alone or with your partner, without distractions, and look into the future. No need to pull out a crystal ball; simply describe what you want your future to look like. Consider the short term (generally from a few months to a year), intermediate term (two to five years), and long term (five years and beyond). Your goals may include such things as getting a car, buying a home, having a family, saving for college or weddings, and going on a fabulous vacation. In no time, you'll be imagining all those things you've always wanted to do.

2. **As you identify goals, write them down.**

   Documenting your dreams is important because doing so makes them seem more real. Better yet, cut out or print out pictures that illustrate your goals — maybe a picture of a cruise ship or a tropical island surrounded by blue waters, or just you relaxing without fiscal worries.

As part of your planning, find out where you stand by obtaining free copies of your credit report and ordering your credit score; we explain how to do both in Chapter 14. Review your report for inaccuracies and then dispute any errors or out-of-date items you find using the pointers in Chapter 14.

After you take care of the inaccuracies, you can use the correct information in your report as a starting point for building the credit you want. Make adjustments to your credit usage based on your credit-score report's four statements about how you can improve your credit, called *reason statements*. They may indicate that you have too many active cards or that you have too much credit available. Both situations can hurt your credit.

VantageScore thinks understanding reason codes is so important that it has devoted an entire site to them. Check out www.reasoncode.org.

Next, use your spending plan to determine which of your goals (say, buying a home or taking a cruise) need to be funded using credit. Then find out the credit criteria for a low-interest mortgage rate and determine what kind of credit card you want to use on your cruise. Consider a card that gives you points toward a cruise as an incentive. Now you're making decisions about which credit offers to accept or turn down instead of just accepting the preapproved offers that show up, whether or not they fit your needs.

When you match your spending goals to a credit or lending need, you take charge of your own finances.

Now that you've taken the critical steps toward creating a successful plan, you've established a powerful reason to save a portion of your income. And you have the motivation to get your credit standing back on track to help you achieve those goals. Believe it or not, achieving your goals is generally not the problem. Knowing where you're going — and, for couples, agreeing on mutual goals — is the trickiest part.

Take the list of goals you made when creating your plan and reference it when things get a little rocky. Doing so can be a big help in getting you through difficult periods (for example, when something *not* on your list of goals is calling your name).

Chapter **17**

Taking a Sustainable Approach to Your Credit

Not everyone is comfortable with numbers. So, for the large number of people who don't see the world through a financial lens, we want to offer another way to understand credit. Steve gave a keynote address on this topic to 200 teachers, and they agreed that their students need a better way to relate to credit that isn't just dollars and cents. Everyone understands the environment, so why not draw a parallel? Well, Steve did. And he calls it the ecology of credit, or green credit.

Not long ago, Americans didn't understand the connection between their actions and their environment. They didn't get that something as seemingly minor as spraying for mosquitoes could upset the ecological balance of nature, or that throwing trash into the ocean could harm sea creatures and endanger whole species. Today, we see the connections, and although we can disagree about whether humankind is experiencing climate change, everyone understands that actions have consequences, sometimes for years to come.

Most people don't see these types of connections in their use of credit, but the reality is that credit decisions can create both negative and positive feedback loops, just like you see in the environment. For example, paying only the minimum payment on a credit card means that you pay more interest, which means that you have less money to deal with emergencies, which may make it more likely that you accumulate more debt as you go along.

In this chapter, we help you better understand credit by drawing parallels between your natural environment and your credit environment. Our "green credit" point of view advocates a sustainable approach to managing your financial resources and the stewardship of your credit ecosystem through self-interested individual behavior. We help you recognize that credit is an integral part of modern life, not just an accessory. So come along with us as we take you on a field trip to the wilds of credit and beyond.

Going Green: Treating Credit as a Renewable Resource

Looking at credit as a renewable resource changes your perspective: You want to better understand how it works so you don't unknowingly harm it. It also makes you responsible for not overusing or abusing this important resource to the point of endangerment or even extinction. To be a good steward of your credit, you need to understand how credit coexists with all the other parts of your financial ecosystem and how it fits into the rest of your life. In this section, we show you how to recognize the parts of your credit environment, their relationships to one another, and ways to keep them all in sync so that they complement one another.

Recognizing your credit environment

You've heard about ecology or ecosystems at one time or another. What is an *ecosystem*, really? It's a unit consisting of a number of factors that function together in an environment. Each participant in an ecosystem depends on the others to survive. Together, they sustain one another in a routine pattern of give and take. The balance can be delicate and easily upset. Major disruptions to the ecosystem can be disastrous to all the participants and can take years to undo. For example, in nature, if too many fish were born, they would use more than their share of water and plants, affecting the delicate balance.

Similarly, your credit ecosystem has a number of parts — lines of credit, emergency savings (to fund unexpected expenses without relying solely on credit), mortgages, credit cards, car loans, a payment history, and so on — that function and interact together. If one part is out of control, it impacts the others. A late payment on a bill can cause a ripple effect throughout your credit ecosystem, as sure as a forest fire damages more than trees. Each factor in your credit ecosystem has an effect on the rest of your life, such as your job, insurance rates, borrowing capabilities, and housing options. Central to the credit ecosystem concept is the idea that your credit, savings, and spending are continually engaged in an interrelated set of relationships with other financial elements that need to be kept in balance to be healthy.

When you take a walk through any environment, you like to know what to look for. If you're at the beach, you look for footprints in the sand that tell you whether seagulls or terns have been there recently. The presence of horseshoe crabs, clam-shells, or broken lobster pots tells you other things about the tide, currents, or passing storms. The same applies in the world of credit. Does your financial beach have excess income? Is your credit score rising or falling, like a barometer indicating a brewing storm? Does your credit report show healthy activity or signs of stress? The signs are there for you to read if you know where to look and what they mean. In the sections that follow, we help you predict tomorrow's financial weather and your long-range forecast.

Taking a closer look at the parts that make up your credit ecosystem

The major components of your credit ecosystem include your net income, your debts, the types of credit you have available, your payment history, and any major financial missteps (toxic spills) that you've made over the last seven to ten years. You may think that some of these items, like your income, aren't strictly credit related. And you're right in a narrow sense, but as in any ecosystem, all the parts influence one another and their environment, both positively and negatively.

On the left, Figure 17-1 shows the interdependencies of a typical financial ecosystem. Beginning with income, this figure visually depicts the relationships among the financial factors that make up your ecosystem. The right side of Figure 17-1 details the credit portion of your ecosystem. If any part of the system is out of whack, the others are compromised, beginning with offers of credit and building to credit scores.

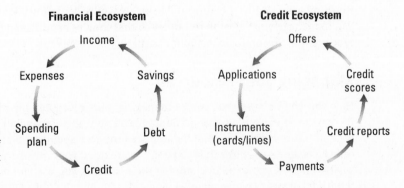

FIGURE 17-1: Your financial environment is made up of interdependent parts.

Counting your income

Income is always our favorite topic, so we want you to start there. Every biosystem needs nourishment in order to support its inhabitants. Krill are a type of small shrimp that form the basis of a food chain. The krill found at the South Pole nourish migrating fish, birds, and mammals. No krill? No chain of life as we know it.

Your credit ecosystem's nourishment is income. Because you have income, you can support spending, debt, and credit. Knowing how much income you have tells you what you have to work with and what you can support. If you don't know what your spendable income is, you can only guess and hope that you don't harm your environment by overspending or overtaxing your resources. Surprisingly, many people don't have a clear picture of how much income they have available or whether they're losing income through leaks in their paychecks. You can find examples of leaks and things you can do to maximize your income in Chapter 18.

But what can you do if your income suddenly disappears or is dramatically reduced? Realize that there is no *if.* Only a *when.* Sometime during your adult life, this will happen to you. It may be a layoff, a new career that doesn't work out, a divorce, a pandemic, or a natural disaster. The only answer is to plan for it with savings (cover at least six months to a year of expenses), a spending plan so you'll know what your essential expenses are and which ones can be reduced, and a solid credit report and credit score.

Balancing your expenses

If income is your fertile resource, then your expenses represent what you take out of your environment. If you're a farmer, you need to balance the types of crops you grow or the types of animals you graze on your fertile land; too much of either and you won't be successful. If you're a fisherman, knowing how many fish you can catch and what kinds you need to leave behind for balance is important for a sustainable ecosystem.

Knowing what you're spending and how fast you're depleting your income enables you to manage your income resources so that they're healthy and productive for a lifetime. For tips on focusing your expenses, see Chapter 18.

Managing your resources

How can you be sure that you're managing your resources for maximum yield? It's easy. You use a plan that accounts for all your income and all your expenses. We call it a *spending plan.* Making and sticking to a spending plan — sometimes called a *budget* — assures that you don't overextend your income resources. Doing so also enables you to be in charge of the resources you use and how fast you use them so that you stay in control of your environment. Just like knowing how many fish a pond can support, you want to know how many expenses you can afford before you commit to them. Failure to plan may result in an ecosystem collapse!

You can find help and tips on creating a spending plan that works for you in Chapter 18.

Introducing credit

Using credit in your environment can be a powerful way to increase yields in the present. Credit can be a great thing as long as you don't overstress your environment to the point of doing long-term damage. A farmer may add fertilizer to the soil and growth hormones to cattle feed. Doing so can enhance growth and yield, but too much of either can damage resources and cause a failure down the road. Knowing the right time to use credit and the right amount to borrow to improve, rather than harm, your credit environment is your goal.

Sustaining Your Credit Ecosystem for Life

In this section, we show you how financial goals and planning help keep your ecosystem in balance. We talk more about goals in Chapter 18, but in brief, you want to set goals for life's major credit-related financial milestones and then create a plan to reach those goals. Among your goals may be paying for college, buying a home, or purchasing a car. Here we take an ecological look at each of these goals.

Funding college

Unless you're fortunate enough to have a trust fund, you and/or your parents may have to take out a student loan to pay for your higher education. For the purposes of this example, we're going to assume that you'll have to make at least some, if not all, of the loan payments in the future. How does this type of loan fit into your overall financial environment and credit ecosystem? Be sure that it fits well, because, like an invasive species, this type of loan can't be eradicated by ordinary means.

Student loans are exempt from most bankruptcy proceedings, so you need to understand what your payments will be and what income stream you can expect from your chosen career field. If this loan is going to eat up too much of your future income — if, say, you're studying to be a modestly paid social worker — you may want to supplement the loan by working part-time. Or you could pass on that expensive Ivy League school in favor of a lower-priced community or state college to lessen the future stress on your income.

Balancing your current spending with your future ability to make payments keeps this loan sustainable. This advice works for parents as well as students. How much would you pay for a mystery item hidden in a box? Not much, we bet. How much would you borrow to fund an education leading to an unknown job with an unknown income?

Home sweet home

In the past, millions of Americans bought a home as soon as they were able. Today, with home value appreciation no longer a certainty, the goal of homeownership warrants a second look to see how it fits into your credit and overall financial landscape. Beyond making sure that you can afford the payments on a mortgage and that your career or job is secure enough to enable you to make a long-term commitment to those payments, consider this: Homeownership isn't a good fit for everyone. Changes to employment and income and opportunities to move or travel can make a long-term commitment less certain today. Owing more than your home is worth (referred to as being *upside down* on a loan) can keep you from relocating for an opportunity. Having your own place is great, but it may not be all roses for your career, finances, or credit. Homeownership complements and fits best into a stable credit environment.

Credit on wheels

You will probably use credit to make a purchase as expensive as a car. Making a down payment that's large enough to keep you from owing more than your car is worth when you drive it off the lot keeps your options open. Unless you have savings to make up the difference between the sale price and what you owe, making a small down payment prevents you from selling your car, which you may want to do if your income drops or you want to spend that money some other way. If you owe more than the car (or any asset) is worth, you're upside down on your loan. You don't want to turn a big part of your credit ecosystem upside down — it's as uncomfortable as it sounds!

Steering Clear of Credit Pollution

Your credit report offers you a graphical representation of your credit ecosystem. Each account listed on your report is like a tree growing in a forest. The older it is, the better it is for you and your credit score because its age indicates strength and stability. As negative items appear on your report, they can spread from one account to another as defaults increase your cost of credit. Late payments can cause damage that weakens your credit and its ability to play its role in supporting your goals. This damage is the equivalent of pollution seeping into your natural ecosystem. Just as too much pollution can create a toxic environment, too many negative items on your credit report can cause major credit problems before you realize what has happened. So how do you recognize this situation, and what can you do to restore your credit to a healthy balance? Read on!

Endangering your payment history

In most cases, credit card or loan payments are reported to one or more of the credit bureaus. A payment that is on time and for the amount due helps your credit report and score grow stronger. Missing a payment or paying too little dumps toxic data into your credit file. The effects can go far downstream in your financial environment. Bad credit can cost you a new job or promotion, licenses in some fields, higher insurance costs, and the opportunity to buy or rent decent housing. After damage is done to your credit forest, regrowth may take from two to seven years — or even ten years, as we explain in the next section.

REMEMBER

Paying off a delinquent account or bringing it to a current status doesn't undo the damage already done, but it does prevent future damage and enables you to begin to rebuild your credit over time.

Your payment history can harm your credit environment in many ways:

» Overspending by using credit means higher payments. Higher payments limit the amount of money you can devote to savings and place a strain on your credit from overuse and lack of replenishment.

» Drying up your savings can cause a damaging cash-flow drought that weakens your ability to respond to new or unexpected challenges.

» Although creditors can no longer raise your interest rates on existing balances if you miss a payment on another loan, you damage your payment history as soon as you're 30 days late, and creditors can raise the rate on new purchases (see Chapter 20 for more information).

» If you miss two payments on a credit card (in other words, you're more than 60 days late), your existing-balance interest rate will explode like a wind-driven wildfire and consume more of your income than you can imagine when you can least afford it.

Clear-cutting your credit in bankruptcy

Among the most damaging things that can happen to a forest is overlogging — clear-cutting all the trees and leaving a wasteland behind. When you're forced to declare bankruptcy, you're clear-cutting your credit. All those credit accounts and lines that had been strong and growing trees on your credit report are chopped down. The resulting wasteland takes years to regrow, just as in nature.

Despite the devastation of a credit clear-cut, you may still owe a lot of money. Bankruptcy may not wipe out *all* your debt, and the debt that remains can be the most tenacious and longest-surviving of all. Like plastic bags and inorganic products that can live on in the environment for years and years, some debts just don't disappear, including

>> Federal, state, and local taxes

>> Child support

>> Alimony

>> Student loans

>> Money owed as a result of drunk driving

Some bankruptcy-resistant debts continue to grow and consume precious resources. For instance, unpaid student loans can result in the seizure of tax refunds or even part of your Social Security payouts until they're satisfied.

WARNING

Some lenders specialize in giving new loans to people with damaged credit. Why? Because they can charge super-high rates, and because, under the law, you can't clear-cut your debt with a second Chapter 7 bankruptcy filing for eight long years. Our experience with these types of bottom-feeding lenders is that they verge on predatory, and you're better off not doing business with them. They make risky loans all the time, so they're ready, willing, and very able to hammer you for any delayed, missed, or short payment.

Living in a post-bankruptcy wasteland has other challenges. See Chapter 8 for more info.

REMEMBER

If you need to wipe out all your debts because you're overwhelmed, be sure that this extreme measure will solve your problems. For example, if your defaults were caused by overuse of credit to supplement your income for basic living expenses, a bankruptcy won't solve your problem unless you're able to lower your expenses below your income.

People tell us it's unfair that they're penalized for the damage they've done by filing for bankruptcy. After all, they had no choice, and the situation genuinely may not have been their fault. Still, the trees are all gone, and it takes time to regrow your credit and convince lenders and others that you'll take better care of your environment next time.

Outlasting a long, cold credit winter

As if the damage you can do to your credit ecosystem isn't enough, we want you to consider one more aspect of your financial environment. You're in an environment that has seen a major shift in climate. No, we're not talking about climate change, but about credit change! Like the dinosaurs, millions of people have had a meteoric meltdown hit their financial lives. Beginning in late 2007, the economy tanked, housing prices dropped, and unemployment gushed like an angry volcano spewing darkness over the sky. The result? A "credit winter." Credit remained frozen in many places for years. And as we're writing this book, a global pandemic has caused widespread unemployment and loan defaults. It may take years before credit flows as it did before this latest crisis.

You can avoid a dinosaur-like fate for your financial dreams by adding new credit only when you need it, by making payments on time and for the full amount due, and by keeping balances low to remain nimble.

Surviving and Reviving After a Credit Catastrophe

Whether your credit has taken a toxic hit from delinquencies or has been wiped out in a clear-cutting due to a bankruptcy, you can minimize ongoing damage and foster a recovery. We have three suggestions to help speed your credit ecosystem's revival and some tips to get you through the rough spots until your credit has healed.

Understanding what happened

The first thing you need to do is to understand what happened and why. For most people, the problems can seem like a blur. But credit problems can usually be traced to two main causes: gradual accumulation of debt by an extended period of overly optimistic overspending, or an event such as an illness or accident.

Planning for your next challenge

You can remedy the slow and easy overspending trap by developing a spending plan that accounts for all your income and expenses. A spending plan helps you make conscious decisions about where you spend your money and keeps you from slowly sinking deeper and deeper into debt. Chapter 18 goes into the nuts and bolts of setting up a spending plan that works for you.

A number of different tsunami-like events can wash out your finances. Illness, even if you're insured, can deluge you with huge amounts of debt. An unexpected and uninsured or underinsured calamity like a house fire or a car accident can make a serious dent in your finances. Global financial meltdowns beyond your control can dry up your income stream. The way to avoid a repeat is to insure for what you can and save for the rest. Be sure that your auto, home, and disability insurance policies are adequate to protect you in the event of a loss. Establish a plan to save between six months and a year of living expenses in an emergency account to last you through income interruptions from a job loss or to fund deductibles and expenses not covered by insurance.

Minimizing the damage as you move forward

You still need to live through the months that follow a credit crisis despite the complications that damaged credit can cause. It's important to recognize and to be proactive about situations where your damaged credit may hurt you when someone checks your credit report. Realize that your credit ecosystem is part of your larger financial environment and that each one affects the other.

Damaged credit can affect you far beyond being unable to get a credit card. Some events trigger a review of your damaged credit report while you're in the process of restoring your financial environment. These events include getting a new job, being considered for a promotion, moving to a new apartment, and buying a car. Here are some details about these events:

>> **Employment/promotions:** Employers commonly pull a credit report as part of the hiring or promotion process. If you're up for a new job or a promotion, be sure to have an explanation of what happened in your credit history and what you've done since to ensure that it won't happen again. Mistakes are common; showing that you learned from them is not.

>> **Moving:** Landlords want to know if you *will* pay your rent, not just if you're able to. Bad credit is cause for concern unless you can explain what happened. You may want to offer a larger security deposit to set your landlord's mind at ease.

>> **Car financing:** A reliable car is an essential part of making a living for many people. If you're buying a car with damaged credit, be prepared to put down more money than usual so that the financing company is protected against a default. Be careful of dealers who charge high interest rates and penalties for prepaying your loan. Establishing a relationship with a credit union can be a good way to get a loan at a reasonable rate, even with blemished credit.

Rebuilding your credit ecosystem

Is rebuilding a damaged credit ecosystem a chicken-or-egg puzzle? Or is it a catch-22 situation, with the catch being that you can't do what you want from where you are? It's neither, although it can sure seem that way.

Following an oil spill or other disaster, environmental experts show up and analyze the damage. They come up with a plan for what needs to be done to restore balance, and they predict how long it will take for the ecosystem to heal. Your credit score indicates the health of your credit ecosystem. A low score means that your credit environment has had some damage that will take time to repair. In times like these, getting new credit to show that you can handle it can be challenging. But if you heed the following simple steps, you'll be growing healthy credit lines and a garden full of blooms in no time.

REMEMBER

When oil was spilled into the Gulf of Mexico, experts predicted that it might take years for the fragile coastal ecosystem to recover. They began working to clean up the damage and built berms to protect against future damaging events. A toxic credit report and score take time to restore as well. Slowly rebuilding your report with fresh accounts that you pay on time and as agreed leads to a thriving credit ecosystem again. Showing that you can handle different types of credit can favorably impact your score, too.

Try the following for diversity and a speedy recovery:

>> **Secured credit card:** Using a secured credit card may help you rebuild your credit and boost your score over time when other products aren't available. No one will know that you have a bank account securing this card. Secured by a cash deposit, many of these cards report every on-time payment to the credit bureaus, just like an unsecured card does. Confirm that the secured account will be reported to the credit bureaus before you open the account.

>> **Passbook loan:** Open a savings account and borrow the amount that you have on deposit. Just make all your payments on time. This personal loan is inexpensive and grows your credit.

>> **Retail store cards:** Usually easier to get than an unsecured bank card, a revolving credit line from a retail store can even get you discounts. But use it only when you're shopping for a need, not when you feel the need to shop.

TIP

Checking your credit report and score periodically can offer you a simple measure of your progress. You can get a free copy of your credit report annually at www. annualcreditreport.com. For measuring growth in your credit saplings, we suggest that you check one report every four months; that way you can have three free looks each year.

» Setting and prioritizing your financial goals

» Taking simple steps to create a workable plan

» Tapping into some financial resources

» Making adjustments to your plan as you age

Chapter **18**

Safeguarding Your Credit with a Spending Plan

magine that you're competing in the Olympics. The other athletes entered in your event have trainers and training plans to keep them focused and on track. You'd be at a severe disadvantage if you just made up your training as you went along instead of following a comprehensive plan that builds on a series of steps, each of which makes your workout more effective. Well, consider this book your trainer and this chapter a training regimen to help you develop spending and savings plan muscles for financial success.

So what does a spending plan have to do with credit? Everything! Your credit is a financial reflection of your life. If your life is out of control, chances are your finances are, too, and your credit isn't far behind. But if you successfully manage your spending and savings, your credit will never get overextended, you'll be able to pay the full balances of all your bills on time every month, and your credit score will be great as a result. Without a plan for your finances, you're destined to fail, but if you make a plan and follow it, you'll succeed big time.

In this chapter, we show you how some simple planning helps focus your spending and credit use to achieve the goals you set for yourself and your family, to protect and build your credit, and to sleep soundly at night. This plan isn't about sacrifices that keep you from doing the things you want to do and can afford. It's a plan that will make your dreams a reality. Plus, it will keep others from diverting your financial future into their pockets. We take you through the process of figuring out how much you're spending and where your money is going now and how you'd like to spend your income in the future. You accomplish this task by allocating your income to spending areas that you choose and by selecting the most advantageous types of credit for your needs. We help you get your plan in shape so you can win the gold in your financial Olympics!

Appreciating the Benefits of a Solid Spending Plan

A *spending plan* (formerly known as a budget) is a powerful tool that lets you decide how to spend your money to your greatest advantage and build your credit at the same time. It's a critical component of your financial ecosystem that keeps your life in balance, allowing you to adopt a sustainable approach to using credit. (See Chapter 17 for more on financial sustainability.) It's your personal road map for spending your income, building up your savings, and using credit to save money and to enhance your credit profile. A spending plan can be as detailed or as general as you want it to be. To create a plan, you need to know your income and expenses and have a general idea of your financial goals. Your plan helps you organize your financial life and attain your goals in the near and long term.

REMEMBER

Many people incorrectly think that a spending plan is restrictive and may cramp their style or their ability to be spontaneous. In many ways, a spending plan is to a budget what planning a balanced, satisfying, and healthy menu is to going on a diet. You get to enjoy *exactly* what *you* want. How is this possible? You discover how to eliminate spending money on things that others (friends, marketers, and so on) want you to buy while focusing your hard-earned money on those things you really want.

As we explain in Chapter 17, credit is a tool. It doesn't give you more money to spend; it simply allows you to spend the money you haven't earned yet. If you borrow to cover emergencies or big-ticket items, you're spending money today that you won't earn until tomorrow.

So what happens when you get to tomorrow and find that you spent all the money that was supposed to be there? Nothing pleasant, we can assure you. You can't use credit to extend your income indefinitely. Sooner or later, overusing credit catches up with you. Why do people keep spending money they don't have? For many reasons, one of which is that they listen to other people's ideas regarding what will make them happy instead of relying on their own plan and goals. But not you. You are going to develop a winning plan that helps you attain all *your* goals!

REMEMBER

Here's a short list of things that a good plan can help you do:

>> **Reach your financial and personal goals:** Your plan is a GPS that keeps you on track, helping you put aside money to reach your goals without getting sidetracked. Whether your goals include an exotic vacation, an addition to your home, or a new car, a plan assures that you get there.

>> **Master your finances:** Deciding in advance where to spend your money helps assure that you spend it on those things that are most important to you. In addition, your plan builds your credit record and score with timely payments for those items you purchase with credit. For everything you need to know about credit reports and credit scores, including how to improve your score, flip to Chapters 13 and 14.

>> **Save more than you thought possible:** You may notice when you begin the planning process that your expenses equal — or, in some cases, exceed — your income. Spending less than you make is a great way to ensure that you don't become overextended, because the money you don't spend can be saved for inevitable unplanned expenses and emergencies.

TIP

One of the best ways to live within your means is to have a plan for what you do with extra money you don't currently have, but expect to have in the future, such as tax refunds, raises, and promotions. When a chunk of cash shows up, save half and spend half. Before you know it, your bank account will be buff!

>> **Uncover extra cash:** The best part of having a spending plan is that you end up with more money to spend on what you want. Eliminating waste puts more money in your pocket every month. Instead of spending money on things you don't really want or need, you can use that cash any way you want, from buying new toys to building savings.

>> **Share common goals:** An effective spending plan pertains to your entire family. For example, your children are much more likely to go along with watching Netflix movies rather than going to the movie theater for several months if they understand that doing so will give them an extra day at Disney World! The same is true of your sweetie: If the two of you agree that an update to your home is your top financial priority, you'll be on the same page when it comes to making the necessary financial adjustments.

Go to www.dummies.com/go/creditrepairkitfd5e for a goal-planning spreadsheet you and your family can complete together.

>> **Be as prepared as an Eagle Scout:** As part of your plan, you set up and grow an emergency savings account. This account covers unexpected expenses such as major car repairs, large appliance replacements, or big medical bills.

>> **Keep debt in its place:** Because planning helps you bring your expenses in line with your income and builds savings, you don't need to use credit unless it's in your best interest to do so.

>> **Manage your credit:** Keeping your debt down improves your credit and builds your credit score. Your score improves with lower amounts owed, fewer accounts with late or over-limit fees, and a smaller proportion of your credit limit being used. For details on your credit score and how to manage it successfully, check out Chapter 14.

>> **Give yourself peace of mind:** Being in control of your money helps you avoid the financial stress that causes sleepless nights, reduced productivity at work, and even physical symptoms like headaches or ulcers. You'll have a smile on your face instead of worry lines.

Deciding on Goals: Imagining Your Future as You Want It to Be

Imagining your future is the fun part of building a spending plan. Many people wander through life without goals, letting events take them where they will. Well, there's a better way, and setting goals is a key first step. The first part of managing your finances and credit is to decide what you want to do and when. Don't worry — this isn't a test, and you can't fail. In fact, you can change your goals as often as you want.

Setting the stage for planning

Set aside an hour or so — more if you can — to envision your future as you'd like to live it. If you're sharing your life with another, be sure to involve that person in the discussion. Heck, make it a date! Over a glass of wine or a cup of tea, get comfortable and dare to dream. Or go to a favorite quiet place — a nearby park, the steps of a monument, a scenic overlook — and let your surroundings inspire you.

At this point, the sky's the limit! Dream as big as you want. Have you always wanted to take a year off and sail around the world? Jot it down. Do you yearn to go back to school or launch a new career? Add it to the list. Buying a home, owning a sports car (or just a reliable one) — this goal-setting stage is your opportunity to indulge in *all* your financial fantasies. Getting them down on paper and discussing, assessing, and prioritizing them is an important part of the process of tailoring your spending plan to meet your personal goals.

Be sure to include some details. For example, you may have written down, "Go to Disney World." But to flesh it out a bit more and bring it alive, be more specific. Will you stay at the Grand Floridian or the Days Inn? Will you go for a weekend or a week or two? Try to be as specific as possible. This level of detail not only gives you a clearer target but also keeps communication about your goals clear.

TIP

Wherever you do your planning, record your goals and put a date next to each one. If you're in the mood, you can have some fun with this step: Get out the scissors (or your mouse) and cut and paste pictures from magazines, calendars, and other sources to illustrate your goals. These images can be powerful motivators. Put them up on your refrigerator or turn them into a screensaver so that you can refer to them as you go along.

Categorizing your goals

We like to say that you eat an elephant one bite at a time. We suggest that you separate your goals into categories to keep from being overwhelmed. Otherwise, you may focus only on short- or long-term goals. For the best results, we recommend that you use four general categories:

>> **Short-term goals** are no longer than one year. They may include taking that vacation to Disney World, starting a retirement plan or an emergency fund, or even repairing your credit.

>> **Intermediate-term goals** require one to five years to accomplish. These may include saving enough money to buy a new car, to begin a family, to purchase new furniture, or to pay off your debts.

>> **Long-term goals** are at least five years down the road. These may include saving for your kids' education, starting your own business, or buying a home or boat.

>> **Life goals** don't have a time frame, because you'll probably never *fully* achieve them. These goals aren't necessarily money-driven but capture the imagination. For example, you may want to have less stress in your life. Imagine what it would take and write it down. Have at least one goal you can pursue that may be unattainable through money alone. Who knows? You won't succeed if you don't try.

Pay attention to how many goals you have in each category. Are all your goals focused on the short term? If so, spend some time thinking a little further into the future. Also, remember that not all goals require money to realize. Adding some nonmonetary goals to your list can help take some of the financial pressure off the ones that do. For example, spending more time doing a shared activity, such as volunteering to assist the elderly or help out at the local library, may offer a non-financial respite — and can be a great exercise in togetherness. Look for other opportunities to work "free" into your future.

Putting your goals in order

After you list all your goals and sort them into categories, the next step is to prioritize them. We suggest that you assign a high priority to short-term goals that you think you can reach easily or that are particularly motivating. That way you can experience the thrill of victory early on and gain momentum for tackling the next goal.

TIP

If you have goals that you know will be difficult to achieve or will require a lot of saving, we suggest that you segment them. By breaking large goals into smaller chunks, you're better able to see your progress. Plus, you'll have more reasons to celebrate.

This process shouldn't be a slog to the finish. You need to have fun along the way. It's important to celebrate every milestone. And don't be afraid to make adjustments as you go. An unexpected bonus can move up a timeline; a layoff or illness can set it back. Adjust your plan accordingly.

Building Your Vision of Your Future

Setting and prioritizing your goals establishes a powerful incentive for turning easy immediate gratification into a plan that puts you, not others, in control of your finances and your life. Now what you need is a tool, or a series of tools, to help you achieve your goals. That's where the spending plan that we discuss in detail in this section comes in.

REMEMBER

You're creating a plan not to *restrict* your spending, but rather to put yourself in charge of directing your money to where you want it to go.

Identifying resources and eliminating waste are great places to begin. Start with your current income and expenses. After all, you can't decide how much money to spend and where to spend it until you know how much you have to go around.

Step 1: Counting up your income

Figuring out how much you earn in a year can be easy or tricky depending on how you're paid. If you earn a regular salary or work a set number of hours per week, the task is easy — just multiply your regular pay by the number of pay periods in a year. On the other hand, if you earn commissions or tips or if you're, say, a fisherman or a landscaper, you need some basis on which to project your income. Perhaps your work is seasonal (you sell ice cream or prepare tax returns, for example) and you bring in more income at certain times of the year, or maybe you work extra hours at inventory time and that affects your income. We suggest that you look at last year's income as a starting point. Your old tax return should have most of the information you need.

Whatever your situation, try to estimate a year's worth of income. If you find it helpful to come up with a monthly average, start with a high-earning month rather than a low-earning one. That way you can save some of that month's extra income to tide you over in a low-income month.

Use Table 18-1 to list all the sources of income you expect each month. Be sure to use your take-home, or *net*, pay rather than your *gross* pay (your salary before taxes and other deductions). For example, if you earn $60,000 a year, your gross income is $5,000 a month — but you probably take home about $3,600 after Social Security, federal and state taxes, and other deductions. You may also want to list the expenses that are deducted from your paycheck. Be sure to consider ways to reduce or eliminate deductions.

TABLE 18-1

Income Worksheet

Source of Income	Planned	Actual	Difference
Salary 1			
Salary 2			
Bonus			
Interest			
Dividends			
Other periodic income			
Child support/alimony			
Rental-property income			
Gifts/tax refunds			
Deduction changes/other			
Total Income	$	$	$

For income items that are uncertain, use the Planned column. Put a value you know you can count on in the Actual column and then record the Difference as you receive payment. If an amount in the Difference column is bigger than you feel comfortable with, you may want to pare down your Planned number. Here's an example: Your current (Actual) take-home pay is $4,000 a month. In a few months, you expect a 10 percent raise, which takes it to $4,400 (Planned). The Difference is $400. If the raise doesn't come to pass, ask yourself if your plan will work without the extra $400 in income.

TIP

You can print out a copy of this worksheet at www.dummies.com/go/credit repairkitfd5e. If you prefer to use computer-based budgeting tools, see the section "Budgeting websites" later in this chapter.

TIP

Many people over-withhold for taxes. If you got a $2,400 tax refund last year, that money was an interest-free loan to the IRS that you could have put to better use. We suggest that you reduce your withholding by half the amount of your refund. For a $2,400 refund, you're overpaying $200 a month in taxes. Reduce your withholding by $100 a month. That still leaves you a cushion with the tax man but adds some extra cash to your budget.

You may have income from other sources besides your regular paycheck. Don't forget to include child support, alimony, overtime pay, bonuses, investment income, royalties, or rental-property income. If you have income from a part-time activity such as playing in a band or selling stuff on eBay, add it to the pile!

After you list all your income sources, come up with an average monthly income. Why monthly? Because you pay most of your major expenses on a monthly basis — mortgage or rent, utilities, phone, and even many charitable contributions are often portioned out in monthly increments.

Step 2: Tallying what you spend

After you know what's coming in, you need to calculate what's going out — and where it's going. Determining your monthly spending isn't difficult, but for some people it requires a little digging. Many of your major expenses — mortgage or rent, credit card bills, utilities, car loans, and so on — hit monthly. If you have an expense that occurs other than monthly, prorate it to a monthly amount. For example, a $2,000 homeowner's insurance bill due once a year is $166.66 a month. For frequent yet varying expenses such as electricity and entertainment, gather several months to a year of history and then determine a monthly average.

Table 18-2 helps you get started. Using your checking and savings account statements, credit card statements, cash receipts for significant purchases, other financial records, and/or a financial planning program such as Quicken, enter and categorize all your expenses to figure out what you spend each month. If you don't have complete financial records, don't worry — just use your best estimates to fill in the blanks.

TABLE 18-2

Expenses Worksheet

Expense	Planned	Actual	Difference
Rent/mortgage			
Property taxes			
Renter's/homeowner's insurance			
Home maintenance			
Water			
Sewer			
Garbage			
Gas/oil for heating			
Electricity			
Telephone			
Car payment			
Car insurance			
Gasoline			
Car repairs/maintenance			
Clothing			
Groceries/household supplies			
Doctor/dentist			
Prescriptions			
Health insurance			
Life/disability insurance			
Childcare			
Tuition/school expenses			

(continued)

TABLE 18-2 *(continued)*

Expense	Planned	Actual	Difference
Child support/alimony			
Personal allowance (small, out-of-pocket expenses)			
Entertainment			
Eating out/vending			
Cigarettes/alcohol			
Newspapers/magazines			
Hobbies/clubs/sports			
Gifts			
Donations			
Work expenses			
Cable/satellite TV/streaming services			
Internet service			
Cellphone			
Student loans			
Pet/veterinary expenses			
Other:			
Other:			
Total Expenses	$	$	$

Here, use the Planned column for your best guesses of expenses that are not fixed, like electricity, and then record the Actual amounts as bills roll in. If an expense is fixed, like rent, put it in the Actual column. Fill in the Difference column as you track your Planned expenses and find out the Actual Amounts.

TIP

You can print out a copy of this worksheet at www.dummies.com/go/creditre pairkitfd5e.

If you're like most people, you'll be able to account for around 80 to 90 percent of where your money is spent. But you're likely to find that a fraction of your income seems to vanish into parts unknown. We call these items "money gobblers" — small cash expenditures that never seem to register in your memory, let alone make it to the checkbook register or any other account ledger. I've assembled a list of some of the more common of these expenses. You may be able to save in some of these areas if you decide that you'd rather consciously reallocate the money or reallocate the expense to personal allowance:

- **Allowances:** Your kids will hate us for this, but you don't have to give them set allowances.

- **Bank fees:** There is no reason to pay fees for a checking account if you take the time to shop around. You may need to have your paycheck direct deposited or have a certain number of transactions each month, but you could save $300 a year. You can save even more by using electronic bill pay rather than ever more expensive postage stamps.

- **Babysitting:** See if you can work out a deal with friends or neighbors to watch their kids one day in exchange for them watching yours the next. Or take shameless advantage of the grandparents — most are only too happy to volunteer their services.

- **Salon:** Instead of going to a high-priced salon, look for a beauty school in your area. You may be able to get your hair done for free (or for a nominal charge), and the attention to detail you get is phenomenal — the students are supervised by teachers, and they're working to impress.

- **Beer, wine, and soda:** For some people, giving up brewskis, a favorite cabernet, or soft drinks may seem like a real hardship. But when you add up how much money you're spending, it may be enough of a motivation to abstain or cut back if you can attain a goal with the proceeds.

- **Fast food and vending machines:** The stuff is bad not only for your body but also for your wallet. Shop at the grocery store instead; use coupons for amazing savings.

- **Books, magazines, newspapers, CDs, and movies:** One of the greatest resources at your disposal is your public library. You can get all the books, magazines, and newspapers you want — free of charge. Most libraries also lend audio books, e-books, music CDs, and movies for free.

- **Car expenses:** You may be able to refinance your car loan at a lower rate if interest rates have dropped, your credit score has risen, or you have more equity in your wheels. Safe driver? Consider raising your deductible if you have some savings cushion. Not using a car for a period of time? Consider dis-insuring it while it sits idle.

- **Car washes:** Now, I'm not suggesting that you never wash your car. I'm just suggesting that, when you need to do it, you do it yourself or toss a sponge, some soap, and the hose at your kids and set them loose. They have fun, your car gets a little cleaner, and you save significant dough.

- **Lottery tickets and other forms of gambling:** A dollar in the bank is much more valuable than a dollar spent gambling. End of story.

- **School fundraisers:** When the neighbor kids come a-knockin', just say no. If you want to help your local school, you can volunteer at the library, coach a sports team, or lead a scouting troop.

- **Entertainment (concerts, movies, sporting events, and so on):** Look for ways to entertain yourself and your family free of charge. Instead of going to a professional baseball game, go to the park and toss a ball around with your kids or your friends. Instead of going to a movie, check out a DVD from the library.

- **Health foods:** Eating healthfully is important, but health foods can be pricey. Shop the produce department of your grocery store, stick to whole grains and lean meats, and you and your spending plan will be fine.

- **Hobbies:** Most hobbies cost money, and although they're fun, so is saving money. Make *that* your new hobby.

- **Eating out:** Even if you're eating at fast-food restaurants, eating out costs a lot. You can save big money by preparing your food at home.

- **Pets:** If you're in financial trouble, getting a new pet isn't a good idea. Even healthy pets cost money, and if your pet gets sick, you're in for more expenses. If you already have pets, stick to the necessities (food, vaccinations, hugs) and avoid store-bought toys. You can make a rope bone out of old T-shirts or throw a tennis ball around in the yard — all your pet cares about is you (and food).

- **Tobacco:** You already know that you shouldn't be smoking. Add up the financial costs, and you can see the damage it's doing *beyond* the damage to your health.

- **Yard sales:** If your idea of a fun Saturday morning is going from one yard sale to the next looking for bargains, wash the car instead. Most people think that they're getting bargains, but they usually end up buying things they don't really need.

REMEMBER

You don't have to cut all these items out of your life. Just be aware that you're spending discretionary money and consider how important each item really is. For example, you may not be willing to scrimp when it comes to Fido's super-premium dog food — if that's the case, just make sure to budget for it every month.

To identify that last 10 to 20 percent of expenses, track your daily expenditures. Record all those cash expenses that are such a part of your routine that you hardly notice them — the morning paper, coffee, snacks, and so on. Again, I'm not saying you shouldn't *have* them — the goal is just to be aware of where your money is going so you can decide whether that's the best use of your funds.

ARE YOU AN AVERAGE SPENDER?

You may be looking for guidelines to tell you whether your spending is in line with that of others. Look no further. The nice people at the Bureau of Labor Statistics (BLS) have been hard at work adding up grocery store receipts and watching how often people fill up at the gas station. Their report is available at www.bls.gov/news.release/cesan.nr0.htm. They have their ways of getting the stats on what Americans are spending. The latest data is a year or so old but is probably fine for your purposes.

To help simplify your spending plan discussions, we summarize some of the main items as percentages of expenditures for a "consumer unit" (sort of like a modern incarnation of a family). See the BLS website for the full details. We're not suggesting that you plan according to these percentages, but you may find them useful as guidelines to see whether your estimates are way out in left field. For example, your family may spend more on housing and less on entertainment, and your neighbor may do the opposite. The key to remember is that *you* get to decide.

Item	All Consumers Units	Married Couples without Children	Married Couples with Children
Housing	32.8	30.2	31.3
Transportation	15.9	15.6	17.1
Food	12.9	12.4	13.2
Personal insurance and pensions	11.9	11.7	14.0
Healthcare	8.1	10.2	7.0
Apparel and services	3.0	2.7	3.2

The really good news about this tracking is that you need to do it for only two months to catch almost everything. After that you'll have a good handle on what's gobbling up your extra cash, and you can either plug the hole or include it as an expense in your budget.

Step 3: Making savings part of your spending plan

How can *savings* be part of a *spending* plan? Easy — consider savings an allocation of your available money. Then it becomes an expense, even though you aren't actually spending it.

Most people don't budget for savings, and that's a huge mistake. To be successful, you need to save money for emergencies beyond your identified goals. Add up what you need to save in a year to reach your prioritized financial goals and divide by 12. That's the monthly amount you need to include in your plan. If you don't have that much to allot to savings, you have a decision to make — spend less in another area(s), increase your income, or rearrange your goals.

The old saying "Pay yourself first" is a wise one indeed. If you save only what drifts to the bottom line, you're shortchanging yourself and losing out on an essential way to protect your credit — an emergency savings cushion.

Taking the direct (deposit) approach

The best way I've found to save is to have money from your paycheck directly deposited into a savings or checking account. After you get into the habit, it will become self-reinforcing. Seeing that balance rise will inspire you to do more when you can. You won't think to spend money if you can't see it. We do this ourselves and have found it to be painless.

TIP

Have your paycheck set up so that the money you need to run your household (your monthly budget minus savings) goes directly into your checking account every pay period. We suggest that half of any pay raise, bonus, or leftover money above that amount be left to go directly into your savings. You never see it and never spend it — unless, of course, you want to. You get half and the savings account gets half. What could be more fair?

Your savings plan is really two-pronged: You're saving to achieve the goals you've set for yourself, and you're saving so that you have money in case of an emergency. We cover both in the following sections.

Saving the easy way: The grown-up version of a piggy bank

Remember when saving consisted of getting change and putting it into a piggy bank? Remember the happiness you experienced as those quarters and dimes clinked into your personal treasure chest? Well, you will have that feeling back and more once you start a savings plan that works for you. Security, confidence, and the sheer potential of a pile of money waiting for you to transform it into your fondest wish make your childhood excitement pale in comparison. All you need is a little encouragement and a tip or two and you'll have savings for emergencies and the good things in life in short order.

A technique that helps Steve make the most of his spare pennies is to roll change. No, he doesn't mean pretending that he's someone else. At the end of the day,

Steve places his loose pocket change into a neat little bank that separates the coins by denomination so he can put them in those cute little tubes you can get (for free) at the bank. Stay away from the machines that change coins into dollars for a fee. For guys, gathering change is easy, because the coins usually fall out onto the floor when they hang up their trousers. Ladies will not only save money, but also save the expense of physical therapy to address the damage caused by purses weighted down with coins. Expect that this exercise will yield about $200 a year per person.

Another way to save is to use your credit cards less. Paying with cash helps reinforce the link between spending, earning, and the cost you're paying. Paying for a $100 item is easy with a swipe of your favorite mileage-accruing credit card. If you have to peel off ten $10 bills, the experience is different. It's real money — and a lot of it! Plus, when your roll of cash is nearly gone, you may find yourself thinking twice about a purchase.

Give yourself a fat raise by bagging your lunch. Going out to lunch every day costs you thousands! Check out the math: With 260 business days in a year, a $10 lunch special becomes $15 per lunch (including tax, tip, and gas/transportation), which equals $3,900 a year. If you pay 25 percent federal income tax, 7 percent state income tax, and 7 percent Social Security, bringing your lunch to work and saving $3,900 after taxes is the equivalent of nearly a $6,400 pre-tax raise ($6,400 – $1,600 [25 percent of $6,400] – $448 [7 percent of $6,400] minus another $448 [7 percent of $6,400] = $3,904 take-home). Think of the goal you can realize with that money! The same math works for breakfast, too.

Finally, buy a Sunday paper and cut coupons. We know, newspapers are dying. So you'll be saving jobs and doing a public service in the process. Or visit a website such as www.coupons.com where you can browse for coupons that you need. If you can put in a half-hour and come up with $20 in savings every week, you've made a great trade. How much? How about the equivalent of a $1,445 raise!

Managing to save for a goal

After you've agreed on your goals, you know your income, and you've tracked your spending, the next task is to break down a goal into bite-sized pieces to make it more easily attainable. If you can do so with *all* your goals, you'll be closer to a plan that works for you.

Take an intermediate-term goal as an example. Say you want to take a trip costing $2,000. If your goal is to go in 18 months, divide the $2,000 by 18 months. The result — $111.11 — is what you must put aside each month to pay for the trip by the time you're waving goodbye to the cats and driving to the airport.

But $111.11 a month isn't chopped liver. So where will the money come from? You need to either increase your income or reduce your expenses. For example, if you can get overtime at, say, $20 an hour, you'll need 100 overtime hours in the next 18 months, or 5.55 hours a month. On the expense side, you're looking to redirect $5.13 per workday ($2,000 ÷ 390 days) or $3.65 per day ($2,000 ÷ 548 days). Maybe your trip really is as easy as passing up that coffee and doughnut on your way to work!

TIP

With some longer-term plans, it's fair to apply income that you're pretty sure will show up but hasn't yet. Say you expect a 4 percent raise in six months. You may want to count that raise in your figuring.

Building an emergency fund

As one of your major long-term goals, you should have between 6 and 12 months of living expenses in an unallocated emergency account for unforeseen financial emergencies. A number that big can seem impossible to achieve. But remember: You only need to cover *expenses.* You don't have to replace your entire annual salary, just the expenses you'd have during, say, a lengthy period when you may not be working. Thanks to your spending plan, you know what your expenses are, so the number is a real one.

WARNING

Some people used to say that a home equity line of credit was as good as an emergency savings fund. They've learned otherwise. Using credit to cover an emergency can leave you much worse off if the emergency (such as a layoff) lasts longer than your credit does. Use up your savings and you're back to square one. Use up your savings and all your credit, and you're at the bottom of a deep hole.

To start, shoot for something — even one month or one *week* of expenses. All you need to do is start building today. Having one week of expenses saved can be a world of difference from having none. Two weeks is divine. And a month — you're ahead of most people. So relax, start small, and keep at it.

Put aside money for emergencies while you're saving for other things. But if you're saving for three things at once, won't it take three times as long? No! Because you'll be more likely to stick with a savings plan if you're saving for three things at once and at least two of them are things that have a personal payoff to you — like a vacation. When you have emergency cash socked away, turn the money that would have gone into savings toward achieving one of your other planned goals.

We mention this strategy earlier, but it bears repeating: Automate your savings plan. Arrange to automatically deposit part of your pay into different savings, checking, or investment accounts. If you never see the money in your paycheck, you won't miss it. As you get raises or bonuses, put at least half into your savings account. Tax refunds get the same treatment. Make it easy and automatic, and your savings will grow faster than you can imagine.

Step 4: Managing your credit to improve your spending plan

Credit and the loans made possible by credit have a place in your plan. Credit is a tool to be used — as long as the tool fits the job. In fact, credit can make things easier. It can enable you to defer a payment to a more convenient time or to make a payment in such a way that it benefits you more than paying cash does. However, you should use credit cards only for spending money you already have or know you'll have soon.

I'm talking about consumer credit here. A number of different incarnations of consumer credit exist, and you can use each type to your advantage:

>> **Noninstallment credit:** With noninstallment credit, you pay the entire balance each month. This type of credit is used by some retail stores, membership clubs, and the like. It is credit in its simplest form, available as a convenience to you — and a benefit to the merchant. You're not deterred from spending simply because you don't have the cash in your pocket. You get what you want, the merchant makes a sale, and everybody's happy — which is the essence of using credit properly.

   You can use this type of credit to handle expenses for local services like trash removal, gardening, or lawn care. An extra benefit is that you get the service first, so if it's faulty, the provider is more likely to fix it.

>> **Installment, closed-end credit:** Frequently used by department and furniture stores, this type of credit involves loaning an amount equal to the amount of a specific purchase to you for repayment in installments.

   Here's an example of how you can use this type of credit: You buy a new bedroom set at a local furniture store, and the store offers you installment credit, giving you 12 months to pay in full. Normally, interest is associated with this type of loan, but the store was having a special sale — no payments for six months, and no interest for the next six. A sweet deal from your perspective, and a sweet sale from theirs.

WARNING

If you use this type of credit, make sure that you pay off the entire amount before the end date, or you may be charged a high rate of interest starting from the original date of purchase.

>> **Revolving, open-end credit:** This is how most credit cards work. You're granted an amount of credit — with a limit, say, of $5,000 — to use any way you want. You choose how much of the limit to use at any point in time. As you use the card, you must make payments on time and for the amount agreed. As you make payments, the amount that goes to principal recharges the line. You can pay off the entire amount, which restores the credit line to its original and full amount, or you can just pay what your spending plan will allow — or even make only the minimum payment. You get to decide.

An example of using this type of credit is to spread the cost of airline tickets. You need to have a set time frame for paying off the purchase (preferably 90 days or fewer) and make sure that the needed monthly amount is available in your spending plan before making the purchase. Don't forget to include the interest charged for carrying a balance when you come up with your monthly payment amount.

REMEMBER

You're supposed to *benefit* from the use of credit, not get taken advantage of. Use credit cards as tools when they fit short-term needs and you can pay them off quickly and with certainty. Remember that bedroom set? You could have used a credit card to finance it, but you would have paid 18 percent interest, and you'd have had to make payments right away. The installment, closed-end type of credit clearly fits the job better.

Step 5: Looking at your insurance options

Insurance is dull — until you need it! It is, however, an essential part of planning for your future. A catastrophic illness, an accident, or a loss of property can crush the best-conceived plans. We don't advocate insurance for every little thing that comes up. The amount of insurance you buy is a personal decision. To a degree, it depends on your resources and willingness to absorb the cost of lower-level exposures in your life, such as car insurance deductibles.

But you should be concerned about the major life events that can dramatically affect your finances at all stages of your life — from the death of a spouse, to a major medical disability that prevents a wage-earner from working, to being responsible for a serious car accident.

Here are a few critical coverage areas to consider as you pull together your plan:

>> **Life insurance:** If someone will miss your income if you die, you need life insurance. *Term life insurance* covers you for a specified time frame, but you can usually renew it at an increasing cost as you age. It has no cash or investment value — your beneficiary gets paid only if you die. Make sure that you have enough coverage to bridge the shortfall that your death would cause to the household budget. And, of course, you want to have appropriate coverage on your partner as well. ***Note:*** A good credit rating can reduce your life insurance costs (see Chapter 14).

>> **Disability insurance:** If you're unable to work for a period of time, disability insurance helps cover your expenses. It's available to cover both long-term and short-term problems. Be good to yourself and your loved ones, and be sure that you get this insurance.

>> **Homeowners insurance:** Your home is one of your biggest assets and one of your biggest liabilities. As an asset, you'd have a tough time replacing it if an uninsured event took away part or all of your home. Keep up with building-code changes that affect your replacement costs, and add insurance to cover the unlikely stuff. If it happens, you'll be glad you did. Examples of the types of insurance you should have include flood insurance, earthquake insurance, and umbrella coverage on top of your limits (to insure you for personal and medical liability if someone falls down your front steps and you become the long-term disability insurer by default). Be sure to deduct the value of your lot from the insured value.

We favor high limits and as high a deductible as you are comfortable with. The best use of insurance is not to reimburse you for everything that may go wrong — just the big things that you can't handle on your own. So if you can handle a $1,500 or even a $3,000 surprise using your emergency fund, you'll eventually save enough in lower premiums to cover the deductible. After that, you get to keep it all.

>> **Car insurance:** Insuring yourself against being sued for running into or over someone, medical payments, and uninsured motorists is actually more important than having coverage to replace or repair your damaged vehicle. Many states require certain levels of insurance to drive. Your insurance agent can help you choose a policy that meets your needs. ***Note:*** In a number of states, bad credit can increase your auto premiums.

For much more information on insurance policies, check out *Insurance For Dummies* by Jack Hungelmann (Wiley).

Step 6: Planning for the IRS

Okay, we understand that planning for the IRS may be like planning for the dentist, but pretax flossing and brushing make this unpleasant subject a lot easier to swallow. Without getting into Novocain-like numbing details, you're better off if you look at this issue as an important component of your spending plan. Why? Because if you owe tax money, if you're counting on your tax refund to fill out your budget, or if you're considering bankruptcy, then drilling down into this subject can save you from a financial toothache.

Typically, you pick a number of deductions and your employer withholds money from your paycheck and sends it to the IRS. The deductions reflect an *estimate* of what you'll owe, but most people end up either owing too much to the government on April 15 or getting too large a tax refund.

TECHNICAL STUFF

Not all income is subject to withholding. Among the exceptions are dividends, interest, income from side businesses or hobbies, tips, investment gains, gambling winnings, money paid to you as an independent contractor, small-business income, forgiven debts, rents, and gifts above a certain dollar amount. But that doesn't mean you don't have to pay taxes on that income! Know what you owe, and prepare yourself for that inevitability.

As you do your planning, you can choose one of three approaches to what we very generally call Goldilocks tax planning:

>> Overpay

>> Underpay

>> Strive to pay just the right amount

You can probably guess which strategy is the right one, but just in case, we cover them all in the following sections.

Overpaying your withholdings

WARNING

Many people tell us, "I don't want to owe any money," or, "I use my refund to pay down my credit cards after holiday shopping," so they deliberately overpay their taxes as a budget-balancing/forced-saving strategy. But overpaying is too hard on your budget. At a minimum, you're giving the IRS an interest-free loan that you could be using to pay down your debt, build up savings, or achieve any of a zillion other good purposes. If you've overpaid all year and an emergency comes along in November, you can't ask the government for an advance of your refund to cover it. But you could use that money if you had it in a savings account, or even under your mattress.

If you're consistently getting a refund check, go over your situation with a qualified tax preparer. You can likely find a better way not to owe on April 15 without overpaying every pay period.

Underpaying your withholdings

A too-soft approach to taxes ends with a nasty surprise. If you under-withhold and owe a big tax bill in April, you may find your credit cards absorbing even more unplanned expenses, including tax penalties, interest, and a fat convenience fee. Ouch! Plus, your cards may well be full already.

Most local, state, and federal taxes usually can't be discharged in a bankruptcy, nor can credit card debt incurred from paying your taxes.

Paying just what you owe

Oh, this feels just right! Adjusting your withholdings so you either give a little or get a little is not as difficult as it may seem.

You may be surprised to discover that you can have more deductions than you have people in your household. It's true. We don't recommend adding the cat as a dependent, but a deductible mortgage payment can count as one or two additional deductions. We suggest that you consult with a tax preparer to get a good forecast of your tax commitments for the year. You may get an early budget bonus if you find that you're over-withholding and can decrease your deductions, which may enable you to fund some of those short-term goals you've been saving for.

On the other hand, if some nasty bears are in your future, you're much better off knowing about them in advance so that you can be prepared and not be caught asleep when they come in the front door.

The right amount isn't a precise number. Until all the figures are in, there's no way to know exactly what you'll owe. We suggest that you pad your estimates of what you'll owe in April by $600 to $1,000. An amount of $50 to $80 a month won't make a big difference to your monthly budget, and as long as your income is relatively stable and your deductions from last year haven't changed a lot, tax time may be a walk in the woods.

Step 7: Planning for retirement

Unless you're one of those people who can't imagine not working, planning for retirement is important stuff. In fact, even if you can't imagine it, pay attention, because the choice of staying or leaving may not be up to you. Health issues (your own or a loved one's), economic contractions, and more can influence when you leave your job. If you're like us, you can't wait!

We suggest that you find either a Certified Financial Planner (CFP), a Chartered Financial Consultant (ChFC), or, if you're in the heavy-duty-investment end of things, a Chartered Financial Analyst (CFA) to help you develop a plan that meets your retirement goals. The spending plan and goals you have developed will make you look like a star when you walk into a planner's office. If you tend to be more of a do-it-yourselfer, you can find good resources to get you started on this topic at both Charles Schwab (www.schwab.com) and Fidelity (www.fidelity.com).

TIP

Whether you're doing your planning face to face or over the Internet, you're better off if you have an idea of what you need to save to fund your retirement plans. Here are some simple tips as you look into the near or distant future:

>> **Estimate your life expectancy.** Chances are it's longer than that of your parents. Just don't guess too conservatively. The Centers for Disease Control (CDC) estimates between ages 76 and 81. You can also find some fun web calculators that can help you with an estimate. One example is www.livingto100.com. If you weren't born yesterday and you're still in reasonably good health, you're looking at more than what the CDC estimates. Check out the good news at www.cdc.gov/nchs/fastats/life-expectancy.htm.

>> **Pick the right retirement date.** The difference between the age at which you want to retire and your last birthday is the time period you need to budget for.

>> **Consider inflation.** After you have a number that you think you'll be comfortable living on in retirement, be sure to increase that number for future inflation — the further out your retirement, the happier you'll be if you increase it. A number of good websites and financial planning programs adjust for inflation and investment experience (how much your investments will earn).

>> **Don't underestimate medical expenses.** The good news is that you've got years to go. The not-so-good news is that medical expenses can be a big part of your future. No one knows for sure how the government's actions to reduce medical costs will work out, so it pays to do some preparing on your own by budgeting for medical expenses and insurance coverage in your retirement planning.

>> **Remember that time is still money.** If you end up with too little money and too much retirement, we recommend three courses of action: Save more for the same amount of time, save the same for longer, or spend less in your retirement budget. You can increase your current savings by earning more or spending less today. You can just keep pushing out the retirement date until the surplus you've accumulated or an increased retirement benefit makes your numbers work. Or you can do with less later. The choice is up to you.

COMPOUNDING INTEREST: INVESTING FOR THE FUTURE

One of the key components of successfully budgeting for your future is having your savings earn as much as possible for your future needs. You've seen the charts loudly proclaiming that if you had only saved XX dollars a year from the time you were 10 years old, you'd have a zillion dollars when you retired.

Well, behind all the smoke and mirrors is a grain of truth. Prudent investing is an important tool. However, you have the right to feel comfortable with the process. If you haven't started, it's never too late. Check out some of the resources in this chapter and start at your own speed and with your own goals in mind.

Whether you do it yourself or use a paid professional doesn't matter. The compounding of interest and tax advantages available today from some types of investments makes investing too great an opportunity to miss.

Using Cool Tools to Help You Build and Stick to a Spending Plan

With computers and smartphones, tools to help you develop — and stick to — a spending plan fill the shelves of most office-supply stores.

REMEMBER

Not all budgeting tools have to be electronic to be cool or even useful. If you want a less technologically based approach to budgeting, here are some suggested tools to add to your budgeting kit:

>> **Pencil:** Lead, not ink, is the tool to use when developing a plan that you'll be adjusting throughout the process.

>> **Sticky notes:** An easy way to supplement your planning ideas, sticky notes can be moved to different places on a planning board or document as you make changes.

>> **Envelopes:** They're handy for keeping money to be spent or receipts for what was spent, by category. Consider using one envelope for tax-deductible receipts, for example. Filing by expense categories or pay periods can be helpful.

>> **Accordion files:** They work similarly to envelopes, but they're more portable — and you're less likely to misplace them.

This section takes a closer look at different tools you can use when keeping good records.

Web-based financial calculators

Web-based financial calculators are cool tools to help you figure out where you stand and what it will take to get you where you want to be. They're great at helping you manage your money because they give you the information you need to make informed choices about what a course of action or purchase will actually cost you and for how long.

You can find calculators to figure out your mortgage payments at different interest rates, calculators to tell you the true cost of a loan and its impact on your budget, and even calculators that tell you how much you need to budget for how long to pay off those credit cards.

If you need a web-based calculator, check out the following:

>> www.choosetosave.org: A nonprofit clearinghouse, this site has a large number of calculators from many different sources, such as the investment regulators at the Financial Industry Regulatory Authority and the American Institute of CPAs.

>> www.myfico.com: Fair Isaac, or FICO, developed the original (FICO) credit score. This website has excellent tools for determining the effects that different credit scores have on loan interest rates and the total costs to you.

>> www.bankrate.com: Bankrate is a trusted financial resource and megasite that has general calculators for many financial functions. Plus, it's the home of yours truly, the Debt Adviser, at www.bankrate.com/search/results.aspx?q=bucci.

Budgeting websites

You can find easy-to-use, basic budgeting and spending advice and tools online. The following are a few of our favorites:

>> www.nfcc.org/resources/planning-tools-and-calculators/monthly-budget-planner/: A good budget planner from the National Foundation for Credit Counseling. You can get live help if you like.

>> www.daveramsey.com/tools/budget-forms/: Not only does Dave look a bit like me when I have a beard, but Dave offers both online and paper budgeting help.

>> www.moaa.org/calculators/: This is a good site for all military personnel, officers or not. The Military Officers Association of America (MOAA) is the United States' largest veterans organization for active-duty, National Guard, Reserve, former, and retired military officers and their surviving spouses. It even has an office in the Pentagon! Although the MOAA focuses a fair amount of its efforts on lobbying, its financial calculators impress us.

Smartphone apps

Every smartphone has a zillion different apps that you can download (some for a price) that can jazz up your spending planning. Apps are so numerous and new ones are coming on the scene so quickly that we suggest you do a search for your phone's financial apps when you're ready to go. User reviews are readily available.

Spending plan assistance

There's no shortage of places you can go to get free help building a spending plan that works for you. But beware of scammers who promise help and just help themselves. Here are three great nonprofit resources where you can get help for free:

>> **The National Foundation for Credit Counseling** (www.debtadvice.org) has good advice and referrals along with a high-level budgeting calculator that plots your spending, based on income, against national averages to let you know whether you're in the ballpark of your peers. Its member-agency network offers budgeting assistance as well as debt management solutions.

>> **Money Management International** (www.moneymanagement.org/establishing-a-budget) is the largest nonprofit financial counseling organization in the United States. Can't sleep at night because of budgeting worries? A budget counselor is available 24/7 at 866-889-9347.

>> **Operation HOPE** (https://operationhope.org/credit-and-money-management/) is a nonprofit organization that helps people restore their financial dignity by helping them solve complex debt and credit issues though programs of individual counseling, education and advocacy aimed at equipping consumers with the financial tools they need to secure a better future. Clients are counseled to transform established financial mindsets and develop customized action plans, raising their credit scores, buying homes, or simply making better decisions with the money they have. You can reach them at 404-491-2919 or 888-388-4673.

Adjusting Your Priorities and Your Plan

Depending on your stage of life, your primary budget needs vary. The basic tools of planning your spending remain the same, but the emphasis of your plan shifts as you move to each new stage:

>> **In your first job:** Chances are you have big ideas and little money. At this stage, just establishing good habits, such as developing a spending plan and beginning a small savings program, is most important. Be sure to keep current on student loan payments, consolidate into a better repayment program, or get deferrals if needed.

>> **As a couple:** Your focus may be paying off old debts, finding out how to communicate about money, agreeing on financial goals and a spending plan, establishing joint and separate credit and savings accounts, setting up a household account, and preparing for a family.

>> **With a growing family:** Adjusting to a stay-at-home spouse or childcare expenses, paying for your kids' sports programs and braces, expanding living expenses, and saving for education and weddings are just some of the issues a family with children faces.

>> **Going solo:** Whether you never marry or you go through a split, you're likely to confront situations such as adjusting to living and saving on one income, taking care of children solo, and perhaps paying off divorce expenses and dealing with alimony and child support.

>> **In an empty nest:** As the kids fly the coop, it's time to confirm your vision for the future and recast your budget for a new lifestyle. This may include enjoying retirement, exploring estate planning, considering Social Security and Medicare issues, and having some fun with your savings.

Credit and financial challenges await you at different times and under differing circumstances. You'll be so much better prepared to weather any turmoil the future may bring and to take advantage of opportunities if you have a plan that enables you to know where your money is going and how to maximize your savings. As your priorities change, a dust-off of your goals, income, and expenses offers all you need to make successful adjustments. A good rule is to revisit your plan whenever one of life's big events occurs.

» **Diving into the financial system**

» **Controlling your own credit**

» **Discovering the rules of the financial system**

» **Paying off debt**

» **Buying your own home**

Chapter **19**

Understanding Equity and Diversity in Credit

I n the past, minorities and other marginalized communities applying for loans were routinely rejected — even if they were more qualified than a white person the loan officer approved two minutes before. It was yet another reason for minorities to feel like the whole system was stacked against them — because it was. As a community, minorities wanted a piece of the American Dream just as much as white people did; they wanted to participate in the system to achieve financial success, but they were usually rejected and left to find other ways to make ends meet.

But we have good news: If you're a person of color in the United States, you do not have to live in those times anymore! The credit application and evaluation process, and the disclosure of information used to make those decisions, are fairer today than they were in the past. Changes to policy and regulation have shifted the credit system so it relies on objective data rather than the subjective nature of that bigoted loan officer from the past.

Creating equity in credit and eliminating bias creates opportunities for diverse populations. The creation and use of a credit score has provided objective quantitative modeling techniques to level the playing field. The same measuring stick and scoring scale are used for everyone, regardless of race, gender, or nationality. In fact, lenders that use models and scores for their credit decisions must do their own due diligence to ensure that it isn't adversely impacting protected classes.

In this chapter, we show you how you can overcome the challenges of the past and build a better future for yourself and your family.

ORIGIN STORY

Melyssa Barrett, one of the authors of this book, drove the writing of this chapter because of her own personal experience. Here's where Melyssa is coming from:

The daughter of an African-American father and immigrant Panamanian mother, born in the Bronx, New York, I began working at the age of 15 as a debt collector. Today, I'm a vice president at Visa. In this position and throughout my career, I've met numerous people struggling with their finances and those who've had a wealth of success. I've seen a difference between people who have misinformation and incorrect perceptions about credit and other people who've utilized the system to create opportunities to achieve financial success.

Accessing credit was a challenge for minorities in the past. My parents and their parents had to go into a bank or lending institution, meet with a loan officer face-to-face, and convince that loan officer that they would pay back the loan on time and with any appropriate interest. My father used to tell me stories of how he had to make sure he was well dressed and wore a tie to make a good first impression. He would be nervous and full of anxiety, but he wanted a better life for his children, so he did it. The meeting with the loan officer was usually very uncomfortable. My father would be subjected to extreme scrutiny, questioning, and evaluation during the loan evaluation process, until the loan officer was satisfied. Quite frankly, there was usually no satisfying the loan officer because the loan officer's own perceptions and biases were not only *incorporated* into the decision-making process, but *relied upon* as part of the "trusted reasoning" when providing credit or loans.

Melyssa brought her family's background to the writing of this chapter, so you can trust, no matter what your background, that she has your back.

Benefitting from Financial Inclusion

Financial inclusion is centered around ensuring individuals and businesses have access to useful and *affordable* financial products and services. Whether it's retail banking products like savings and checking accounts, access to business or consumer credit, or insurance, the key word in the definition centers on affordability.

Government agencies and companies are looking at how to bring those who are *credit invisible* (people who don't have a credit file at one of the big-three credit-reporting agencies) or *unbanked* (people who don't have a bank account) into the mainstream.

You hear about financial inclusion a lot in developing countries, but you also hear about it even in developed countries like the United States because of the benefits financial inclusion has for the overall economy, including lower costs and higher profits for the companies providing access to those financial services.

Financial inclusion is especially relevant to minorities, who are more likely to have insufficient credit histories to generate a credit score. In 2010, approximately 15 percent of African Americans and Latinos were deemed credit invisible, compared to 9 percent of whites and Asian Americans. In 2018, one in five credit-invisible Latinos had no financial footprint, and 24 percent had no bank accounts at all.

REMEMBER

Racism is the systemic oppression of a racial group to the social, economic, and political advantage of another. You cannot discuss equity in credit without discussing racism because financial rules and systems were created to disadvantage and marginalize entire communities of people. Although these systems have largely been dismantled, outdated attitudes still exist today. Credit reporting and credit scoring are racially blind, but some loans that require personal interaction may still be tainted by personal prejudice or unconscious bias.

TIP

Knowing where you stand in terms of credit can give you the confidence to know that you're qualified for the credit you're seeking and alert you to lending bias when your knowledge of what you qualify for is different from what you're being offered. For example, a great credit score entitles you to great interest rates, so if the rate you're offered is high, you can take your business elsewhere or complain to management that you aren't being fairly treated.

WARNING

Conversely, *expecting* to be mistreated financially can become a self-fulfilling prophesy if you fail to prepare, don't have an understanding of how credit works, or see unfair discrimination where it does not exist.

Participating in the Financial System

Learning how to manage your money can offer you keys to generations of economic sustainability for your family. Bolstering your credit standing requires diligence. However, you can't boost a credit score if you aren't participating in the financial system.

Start by establishing a savings and checking account at a local bank or credit union. If you've had a checking account that was closed by the bank, be sure you've straightened the matter out before you try to open a new account, even at another bank (see Chapter 9 for help reopening accounts). Some financial institutions (like Ally, Bank of America, and Chime) allow you to open bank accounts entirely online.

You may also want to apply for a secured credit card to help begin to establish or re-establish credit (see Chapter 10 for more information).

REMEMBER

No matter where you are in your financial journey — whether you're new to credit or you're just trying to push past the pain of credit and financial troubles — it can be challenging. Setting goals is a great first step. (Chapter 18 walks you through the goal-setting process.)

Taking or Retaking Control of Your Credit

REMEMBER

You have the power to make positive changes to your situation. This book gives you tools and tips to be successful in managing and monitoring your credit. Whether you're dealing with a divorce, a chronically ill family member, a child headed to college, or a repossessed car, you *can* improve your credit and financial health.

Knowing and understanding your credit report and how credit scoring affects you is essential in determining how it can be used to your benefit (see Chapter 14 for more information).

Start at least one healthy financial habit today. Here are some examples:

>> **Pay on time.** Your payment history makes up a huge chunk of your credit score.

>> **Reduce your debt load.** Even if you pay on time, a large debt load can lower your score, but an extra payment or a payment of more than the minimum can begin to help you turn things around.

>> **Be patient.** Your payment history from the last two years is more important than your history prior to that.

There are nonprofit resources that can help you get control of your credit, if needed (see Chapter 4).

Educating Yourself on How the System Works

In order for you to not only participate in the financial system but also build wealth within it, you need to understand how the system works, so you can put it to work for you.

As we explain in Chapter 3, the Fair Credit Reporting Act (FCRA), enacted in 1970, provides the rules about the accuracy and privacy of information about consumers that can be used in credit evaluations and for other purposes (like insurance applications and employment applications). The FCRA was enacted to eliminate the subjectivity that was baked into the process in the past — the process that allowed creditors or banks to discriminate against people based on "gut feelings" (which were often based on race). Effectively, the FCRA provides a fair and level playing field for those using information about you to make credit decisions.

The Fair and Accurate Credit Transactions (FACT) Act amended the FCRA in 2003 to improve the accuracy of credit reporting. It also granted every American one "free" credit report from each of the big-three credit bureaus every year (see Chapter 14). Reviewing your credit report allows you to validate, dispute, or update any incorrect information. The FACT Act also allowed consumers to purchase, for a reasonable fee, a credit score, along with information about how the score is calculated. It requires that specific notices are sent to you to disclose pricing, which is set based upon the level of risk determined by your high or low credit score. Creditors must tell consumers why they were denied credit or offered higher interest rates. In addition, the credit bureau that provided information to the creditor that denied you credit must give you a copy of your credit report so you can review it for accuracy. It also included additional enhancements to help reduce identity theft.

These rules create an objective, fact-based store of data about you that's used for credit evaluation purposes. Credit scores are built on the information in your credit reports, which document how you use credit. If you don't have much (or any) experience using credit (if you've never had a credit card, for example), your credit score will be low (or you may not even have one).

HOW CREDIT SCORES ARE CREATED

The credit reporting system uses data and technology to create credit scores, often using machine learning or artificial intelligence, but it needs information on all populations to get the best results. We really do all matter when it comes to data and better credit scoring!

Due to the challenges of the economic downturn in 2008, the Office of the Comptroller of Currency (OCC) modified its guidance to lenders relying on quantitative measures for financial decision making. The goal was to ensure that the information that lenders put into their models (input), how they process that information, and the quantitative score (output) they use to make financial decisions has more rigorous controls and diligence — in other words, that lenders can't discriminate. Typically, lenders use credit scores to help them make lending decisions; in some cases, they may use their own scores to detect fraud, determine credit lines, or determine product eligibility. The two most used models for credit scores are FICO and VantageScore (see Chapter 14).

Whether you start with no credit score, a low credit score, or a credit score somewhere in between, you may feel like it'll take forever to achieve a good credit score, but don't worry! You can raise your credit score — and it doesn't take forever. Chapters 3, 14, and 21 offer more detailed information to help you with your credit report, credits score, and identity theft.

Large financial institutions or lenders often focus on customers with the best credit because they can offer lower interest rates to high-scoring consumers. High credit scores equate to lower risk and, ultimately, higher profits for the lender. They don't have to pay for a large staff of collectors to make phone calls, pay postage for collection notices, or suffer losses that may come after non-payment.

Sub-prime lenders may offer higher interest rates to account for the risks they're taking by lending to consumers with lower credit scores. Sometimes taking on a loan with a higher interest rate can get you back on track to a positive financial future. It all depends on where you are on your financial journey. You have to make the decisions that provide you the benefits you need to achieve your goals. For example, you may take on a loan with high interest. If you pay off your purchases each month, you can be on your way to creating a better credit score. However, because you're paying higher interest, if you don't pay off your account each month, it could end up costing you more and causing you to fall further behind.

DISPELLING THE MYTHS YOU'VE BEEN TAUGHT

We all learn lessons about money from our parents, our environment, and the culture at large. Not surprisingly, most of us are walking around with some false impressions. One of the keys to moving beyond a past full of financial challenges — whether your own or those of your ancestors — is separating fact from fiction. Here are some common myths and the reality to keep in mind:

Myth	Reality
I don't need a spending plan. I have no extra money to spend and circumstances beyond my control take all my money anyway.	If you don't have a spending plan and you don't create one, your situation won't improve. A spending plan will ensure that as much of your money as possible is going toward paying down debts. When you create a spending plan, you'll be surprised how much money you'll find. (Turn to Chapter 18 for more on creating a spending plan.)
If I could only make more money, I could get out of this mess and I'd be fine.	No matter how much money you make, it's about what you *do* with your money, and how you save and spend. Financial empowerment is about creating that peace of mind about your finances that allows you to open yourself up to building wealth and financial freedom.
I'll get myself together, and *then* I'll go see a credit counselor.	Why would you keep trying to get yourself together when a credit counselor can partner with you to help you do so? Credit counselors are specially trained and certified and will provide education that will help empower you. Think of credit counselors like personal trainers — you don't wait until you're fit and in shape before you go to one.
My credit score sucks. I'll never be able to get a good loan.	The best way to improve your credit score is to make your payments on time and reduce the amount of credit you rely on each month. Even small purchases with a small credit line that are paid off at the end of each month will begin to improve your score over time.
I need to pay someone that will write letters and get my credit repaired.	You can and should take control of repairing your own credit. You don't have to spend money to repair your credit. You can take action yourself! All the information you need is in this book.

REMEMBER

The lenders *want* to assist you. Why? Because they can't make any money saying no. This is one reason why you see financial institutions and credit unions providing financial coaching and assistance. Even employers are finding the opportunity to provide financial coaching as part of employee benefit packages. When you, as an employee, feel empowered to manage your finances better, it actually makes you a better employee because you aren't stressed and distracted and you can focus on your work.

TIP

Be sure to follow these tips to maintain a healthy financial history:

>> Review your credit reports and credit score at least once a year, make sure they're accurate, and correct any errors. You can also use free websites like Credit Karma (www.creditkarma.com) to check your score every month. You can access your free credit reports from the big-three credit-reporting bureaus at (www.annualcreditreport.com).

>> Make any loan, utility, rent, or credit card payments on time.

>> Manage your credit utilization. Paying off your credit cards each month is always ideal. However, ensuring you're only using up to 20 percent of your credit limit will help you improve or maintain a better credit score.

>> Don't apply for credit unless you need it. Applications for credit show up as inquiries on your credit report and can negatively impact your credit score. Don't be afraid to apply for a loan when you need one, but don't apply for credit cards every time you get an offer in the mail.

>> Open any letters you receive regarding a denial of credit to find out what information that company relied on for its credit evaluation. The creditor has to give you a free copy of the credit report and score used when you're denied credit.

Tackling Debt

People of color have been disadvantaged by generational wealth disparities. Typically, they rely more heavily on student debt, rely more on payday loans, and are more likely to be contacted by debt collectors. In addition, debtors in bankruptcy who reside in majority African-American areas are twice as likely to have their bankruptcy dismissed (or thrown out) than debtors living in majority white areas. Student loan debt is a part of life for students of color, often leading to higher debt loads, longer payoff periods, and more defaults than their white counterparts. Closing the racial wealth gap is of continued concern, underpinning the disparity in borrower experiences with debt.

Student loans

African Americans tend to have more student loan debt. In fact, 82 percent of black college graduates have college debt as compared to 68 percent of white graduates. The significant divide in wealth between black and white families underpins the disparity in borrower experiences. Learning how to manage credit early is critical for anyone, but especially when you're managing debt as a young adult and even more so for people of color who may be strapped with more debt when they finish college.

Unfortunately, many people graduate from college with little understanding of financial management, and many don't graduate at all but still owe student loans without the benefits and skills of a degree. Whether you're graduating high school or just finished your doctoral degree, financial skills will give you the means to achieve your dreams.

TIP

Before taking on debt for education, think about what you'd like to do for a living and what you can expect to be paid in your chosen field of study. Figure out how much debt you can safely take on while still living a normal life (and not surviving on ramen noodles). Go to www.bls.gov/oes/current/oes_nat.htm to get information on occupational employment statistics and the median wages by major occupational group. Estimate your living expenses and determine your monthly student loan payment so that you know exactly what percentage of your income will go to pay off student loan debt. If you aren't sure that you can get the grades to graduate or you don't have a major in mind, consider a less expensive community college until you know.

Chapter 23 is all about student loan debt.

Payday loans

The payday loan industry was set up to fill the gap for those who didn't have access to savings or credit but had a job. Consumers of payday loans are disproportionately low income and disproportionately African American or Hispanic. Typically, those lenders target minority consumers and communities with high concentrations of African American, Hispanic, and low-income households. A number of studies also note price discrimination against minorities. Often consumers may not understand the terms or risks of prolonged indebtedness with these types of loans. Access to these types of loans may compromise the readiness and performance of military personal, consumers' financial well-being, prioritization of expenses, and overall health. Payday lenders charge high interest rates or fees often using post-dated checks and the guarantee of payment when you receive your next paycheck. Payday lenders don't report your loan or payment experience to the credit bureaus, so if you pay off your loans successfully, you're not helping boost your credit score at all.

Turn to Chapters 10 and 20 for more information about payday loans.

Collections

What do you do when the creditors just won't top calling? Surveys of consumer debt indicate that 48 percent of Latinos reported an issue in the debt collection process, including whether the debt was theirs or the balance was accurate, with 23 percent disputing the debt in collection. This compared to 52 percent who reported an issue and 28 percent disputing the debt in collection for the white population.

REMEMBER

Validate the accuracy and get evidence of the debt. If the amount of debt is inaccurate or it isn't yours, file a dispute with the lender or the credit bureau and make sure the information isn't on your credit report. If the information *is* accurate, work out a payment plan and refer to your rights under the Fair Debt Collection Practices Act (see Chapter 20).

Bankruptcy

Managing bankruptcy operations and working on industry research to understand some of the root causes of bankruptcy, Melyssa had the opportunity to hear from people about their struggles and ultimate decision to file bankruptcy. It's usually a very difficult decision, sometimes coupled with feelings of depression and inadequacy. Bankruptcy is usually one of the last options.

Bankruptcy laws changed in 2005. They now require consumers to receive "debtor education" as they go through the process. You can emerge from the experience and use the resources to build a better future.

If you've filed bankruptcy or you're considering filing bankruptcy, turn to Chapters 8 and 22.

Working Toward the Goal of Homeownership

Today, gaps in homeownership rates between African-American and white families are wider than they were when redlining was legal decades ago (see "Redlining: Understanding the history," later in this chapter, for more on this practice). The gains that were made for nearly 30 years after the 1968 Fair Housing Act were eliminated after 2000 when less informed minorities were disproportionately victims of predatory lending, *subprime loans* (loans with higher interest rates than the prime rate), or unsafe refinance products. Because homeownership remains a principal way most families build wealth in the United States, disentangling the racial homeownership gap requires changes to systemic and structural barriers and a better informed home buyer.

TIP

Check out the U.S. Department of Housing and Urban Development (HUD) website for more information regarding programs in your area at www.hud.gov or find a HUD-approved housing counseling agency at https://apps.hud.gov/offices/hsg/sfh/hcc/hcs.cfm. You can also contact BALANCE, a nonprofit HUD-approved housing counseling agency at 888-456-2237.

Cultural attitudes toward money and credit may perpetuate to drive actions that end up costing you even more. For example, if you're coming from a country in South America, you may be less inclined to put your money in a bank or financial institution. If you're African American, you may have been raised in a family that doesn't talk about money, making it difficult for you to learn how to save money, spend money, and understand how to manage your finances except through trial and error. You have to overcome those biases to begin to chip away at the wealth gap.

Buying a house can be a rewarding experience. U.S. Census Bureau data shows that African Americans have the lowest rate of homeownership compared to other racial groups:

Racial Group	Own Their Own Home
White	76 percent
Asian, Native Hawaiian, and Pacific Islander	61.4 percent
Hispanic American	51.4 percent
African American	47 percent

TIP

Find out if there are home buyer education workshops and pre-purchase mortgage counseling are available in your area by contacting the resources listed in Chapter 7. Attending a workshop offered by your local housing authority may get you a lower interest rate, as well as help prepare you better for home ownership challenges.

REDLINING: UNDERSTANDING THE HISTORY

Beginning less than a hundred years ago, Congress passed the Emergency Relief and Construction Act of 1932. This act created the Reconstruction Finance Corporation (RFC) and authorized loans to private corporations, which in turn provided housing for low-income families. On the heels of the Great Depression, the prospects of improving the financial status of Americans increased, and the National Housing Act of 1934 was passed to relieve unemployment and stimulate the release of private credit in the hands of banks and lending institutions for home repairs and construction. This law also created the Federal Housing Administration, which, through its insurance programs, provided for the mortgage loan amortization with regular monthly payments, the secondary market for home mortgages, and home loans. The Federal National Mortgage Association (or Fannie Mae) was chartered in 1938.

What does this all have to do with equity in credit? Segregation and disenfranchisement, as well as access to credit and home ownership, were areas of inequity in which systemic racism and regulations that were put in place legally discriminated against African-American, Latinx, Jewish, and impoverished white communities, as well as many immigrant populations. With segregation and migration of people to the suburbs, these systems created inequities and marginalized populations of people. The migration of people to the suburbs triggered the creation of maps that would identify where "higher-risk" groups resided. Higher-risk areas would be identified on maps in red and were typically areas where people of color, Jewish people, immigrants, and poor whites lived. Those red areas led to a practice called *redlining*, in which financial services were denied to residents of these red areas based on their race or ethnicity. This was government-sanctioned regulation limiting opportunities for these marginalized communities to access credit and create wealth.

Although, redlining was finally made illegal in 1968, the effects have long-lasting impacts on social, racial, and economic justice. These effects resulted in a myriad of issues and inequities, which affect a range of health and quality-of-life risks and outcomes including conditions in which people are born, grow, work, live, and age, along with a wider set of forces and systems like economic policies, social policies, health and healthcare, and education.

African–American homeowners are more likely than white homeowners to miss or defer their mortgage payments, further impacting a widening gap and disparity in homeownership. Missing a mortgage payment is more serious than missing a credit card payment. Being three months late on a credit card can result in fees and interest expenses, but being three months days late on a mortgage can initiate a foreclosure! If you already have a mortgage, turn to Chapter 7 for ways to recognize, deal with, and possibly avoid a crisis.

» **Demystifying the CARD Act**

» **Realizing the implications of the Dodd–Frank legislation**

» **Knowing your rights under the FACT Act**

» **Using the Fair Debt Collection Practices Act with collectors**

» **Ensuring your protections under the Credit Repair Organizations Act**

Chapter **20**

Knowing Your Rights to Protect Your Credit

Y ou've heard it more than once, and maybe even said it yourself: "I'm never going to use credit again." Whether this statement comes from a perception that credit grantors, bankers, or Wall Street tycoons have fixed the game in their favor or you've been burned with loans that never should have been made, or you've made some bad decisions yourself (we all do), the truth is that you'll continue to have to deal with credit in one form or another. It's an important financial tool when you use it well. Debt is the financial problem counterpart.

Because credit is used for so much more than lending today, you need to understand what protections you have to help ensure it works for you and you aren't taken advantage of by those who would use what you don't know against you. You need to be prepared when making financial decisions, whether applying for a loan, checking your credit, dealing with collections, or seeking help after going through a hard time. Having the right tools in your tool chest can level the playing field and even give you the upper hand. This chapter gives you those tools. Here, we explain your protections and what you have a right to expect from lenders, credit reporters, and collectors, just in case they need to be reminded.

Why You Have the Right to Credit Protections

Americans value fair play. The problem is that when you don't know the rules, others can take advantage of them and you. Most people who lived through the last recession agree that no one fully trusts a lender to be conservative, to offer only loans that people can afford, or to fully disclose all the terms of a deal.

What caused this big change in lending? We could tell you that it was greed, pure and simple, but the situation was more complex than that. In a few words, these lending changes resulted from the decoupling of the ability to make money from being held responsible for results. Lenders were able to originate (make) a loan, earn a commission on it, and then turn around and package and resell the loan (and the risks of default) to someone thousands of miles away. So if your bank can give you a mortgage, package it with others in a security, and sell it on Wall Street to a hedge fund, and that fund sells your mortgage to investors in China, we think you'll agree that you need more protections than you might if your local credit union owned the mortgage on your home! Millions of Americans have been frustrated by credit decisions made in the 2001-to-2007 boom that preceded the recession that began at the end of 2007. That frustration filtered down to Washington and resulted in new regulations and an extension of consumer protections.

The Credit Card Accountability, Responsibility, and Disclosure (CARD) Act of 2009 was designed to curb lending practices that many people perceived as unfair and unfriendly to consumers. The CARD Act was followed by the Dodd–Frank Wall Street Reform and Consumer Protection Act, which established the Consumer Financial Protection Bureau (CFPB). This bureau regulates a wide range of financial products and services, including credit reporting, credit counseling, payday loans, mortgages, credit cards, and other bank products. The Fair Access to Credit Scores Act piggybacked on Dodd-Frank and allows you free access to your credit score in the case of an *adverse action* (denial of insurance or utilities, for example). These new pieces of legislation join older consumer protection laws such as the Fair Credit Reporting Act (FCRA).

Table 20-1 gives you an at-a-glance look at the best and most important consumer protection laws and what they cover. We provide details on most of them in this chapter.

TABLE 20-1

Consumer Protection Laws

Law	Main Areas Covered
CARD Act	Credit cards
Dodd-Frank Act	Wall Street regulation, consumer protection
FACT Act	Identity theft
Fair Access to Credit Scores Act	Adverse actions, credit scores
Fair Credit Reporting Act	Credit reporting
Fair Debt Collection Practices Act	Debt collection
Credit Repair Organizations Act	Credit repair companies

The CARD Act: Shielding You from Credit Card Abuse

The Credit Card Accountability, Responsibility, and Disclosure (CARD) Act of 2009 focuses on your protections from credit card industry practices that have been deemed to be either unfair or just plain tricky. Among the key protections are easier-to-understand terms, fewer retroactive interest rate increases on existing card balances, more time to pay your monthly bills, more notice of changes to your credit card terms, and the right to opt out of many changes in terms on your accounts.

Here's a list of the top protections that consumers are due:

>> **No more bait and switch:** Card issuers can't hike interest rates on existing balances except under certain conditions. Consequently, interest rates on new card charges can't change in the first year, major terms of the agreement can't change overnight, and you get 45 days' advance notice of any big changes.

>> **No more universal default:** You may have heard of people having their rates raised on one card when they have a problem with another one (known as *universal default*). This practice has been severely curtailed. (See Chapter 21 for details.) Card issuers may use universal default only on future credit card balances that exist at the time of the default, and they must give you at least 45 days' notice of the change. You now have time to change cards, get other financing, or pay off the balance.

REMEMBER

» **Limits on interest rate increases:** Card issuers may raise your interest rate on existing balances only if

- The rate was part of a promotional period that ended.

- The index used to set your variable interest rate rises.

- You're at the end of a hardship or special payment agreement.

- You have late payments of 60 days or more.

» **Credit-granting restrictions for young adults:** Creditors can't give credit cards to young adults with no income. People under 21 must show that they have enough income to repay the card debt or have a cosigner who does. Additionally, credit card companies must stay at least 1,000 feet away from colleges if they offer incentives to entice students to apply for credit cards. No more signing up for credit cards to get free pizza and T-shirts your first day on campus!

TIP

Be very careful about cosigning for anyone, including your kids. If one of your kids misses a payment for any reason, that missed payment not only damages his or her credit, but also hurts your credit as well (not to mention your relationship). Instead of cosigning for your kids, add them as authorized users on your account. You don't even have to hand over a credit card or allow them to spend money. This way, you're helping them build positive credit while remaining in control of their credit (and yours!). Alternatively, get your kids prepaid cards (only one per kid) that you can add to as they need funds. If you want to help them build credit and savings, help them set up secured credit card accounts with your bank or credit union — that can help them save money and build credit at the same time. Just be sure they understand that abusing a secured credit card can wipe out their savings and their credit history just as quickly.

» **Graceful grace periods:** Card issuers must give you "a reasonable amount of time" (at least 21 days after the bill is mailed) to pay monthly bills. More time to get your payment in should result in fewer late fees.

» **No tricky due dates or times:** Card issuers can no longer set early-morning deadlines (before the mail is delivered) for payments. Cutoff times must be 5 p.m. or later on the date due, and due dates can't be on a weekend, a holiday, or a day when the card issuer is closed for business.

» **Payments applied fairly:** If you owe money at different rates on the same card (many cards have different rates for regular purchases versus cash advances and balance transfers), payments over the minimum due must go to the balance with the highest interest rate first. Consequently, your payment will reduce more of your balance faster.

» **Easy on the over-limit fees:** Card issuers can't charge you over-limit fees without your permission. If you opt out or say no, transactions exceeding your credit limit are rejected. Opting out of over-limit fees is a good idea. If you decide to opt in, though, no fees can be larger than the amount of the overage. For example, going $10 over your limit can't incur a fee of $39; the limit is $10. Better just to say no to those fees and face the potential embarrassment of having your card declined if you go over the limit.

>> **No double-dealing double-cycle billing:** Interest on outstanding balances must end in the billing month in which you pay off the balance. For example, your statement runs from June 1 to June 30, but the payment is due on July 20. The interest from June 30 to the payment due date of July 20 can no longer be charged if you pay off the balance in full, even though the card issuer didn't get your payment until July 20.

>> **Disclosing how making minimum payments can keep you mired in debt:** Card issuers must indicate how long paying off the entire balance will take if you make only the minimum monthly payment. They must also indicate how much you need to pay each month to pay off a balance in 36 months, including interest. Seeing the high cost of minimum payments enables you to make better-informed decisions about how you pay for the use of credit.

>> **Restricted late fees:** Late fees are limited to $25 unless you're late more than once in a six-month period. Your late payment is not reported to the credit bureau until your account is a full 30 days past due. This restriction results in fewer and lower fees charged to your account and gives you time to resolve issues before they hit your credit report.

>> **Right to opt out of changes:** Card issuers must give you advance notice of changes to the terms of use for your credit cards. You now have the right to reject many significant changes in terms to your credit card accounts.

If you opt out of some changes, you may be required to close your account and pay off any balance under the old terms and conditions.

WARNING

REMEMBER

Although the CARD Act provides a lot of consumer protections, it's not all-encompassing. It doesn't cover business and corporate accounts or interest rates on future purchases. Cards with variable or floating interest rates (which includes most cards) are subject to interest rate increases as the prime rate goes up. And a card issuer can still close your account or lower your limit without warning.

If you believe that a card issuer has violated any of the provisions of the CARD Act, contact customer service and ask for an explanation or a rebate. If you disagree with the answer, you can contact the Federal Trade Commission (FTC; www.ftc.gov), your state's attorney general or consumer protection department, or the Consumer Financial Protection Bureau's Consumer Response Center (www.consumerfinance.gov/complaint).

TIP

For the full text of the CARD Act, go to www.ftc.gov/sites/default/files/documents/statutes/credit-card-accountability-responsibility-and-disclosure-act-2009-credit-card-act/credit-card-pub-l-111-24_0.pdf.

The Consumer Financial Protection Bureau: The New Cop on the Financial Beat

The Consumer Financial Protection Bureau (CFPB) is vested with exclusive rule-making authority over all federal consumer financial law. It was created by the Dodd–Frank Wall Street Reform and Consumer Protection Act. It's a new and powerful agency that has a virtually unlimited budget and very broad regulatory powers. The CFPB has the authority to regulate a wide range of financial products and services, from smaller players like credit counseling agencies and payday lenders to big guys like mortgage originators, underwriters, and servicers; credit card issuers; various bank products; and the credit reporting agencies. This authority extends to new rules to prohibit unfair, deceptive, or abusive acts, practices, and disclosures for financial products and services.

So, who's protected by the CFPB? You, that's who! The CFPB was established to make sure that consumers are treated fairly and are protected when dealing with the U.S. financial system. Through the use of strict regulations, the CFPB seeks to protect you from any person or organization that offers or provides a consumer financial product or service for personal, family, or household purposes. It also has specific authority to crack down on a person or company it identifies as being unlawful, unfair, deceptive, or abusive to any consumer financial product or service transaction.

Think of the CFPB as a tough but consumer-friendly cop on the financial product and services beat that aims to level the playing field so that you know what you're buying. See Chapter 21 for details on the work the CFPB is doing that may affect you in today's financial marketplace.

Safeguarding Your Credit Data through the FACT Act

The Fair Credit Reporting Act (FCRA) and its update, the Fair and Accurate Credit Transactions Act (the FACT Act or FACTA), were put in place to ensure that anytime your record of credit use is reported to a credit bureau or other consumer reporting agency, the record is accurate, timely, fair, and protected from inappropriate access. The FACT Act applies not just to the three big bureaus (Equifax, Experian, and TransUnion), but also to a large number of specialty consumer-reporting agencies (see Chapter 14). Some agencies accumulate and sell information about your check-writing history, medical records, and rental history, among other things.

TIP

So, what are your rights and protections? Here's a summary of the biggies. For the full story, check out the FACT Act at `www.congress.gov/108/plaws/publ159/PLAW-108publ159.pdf`.

>> **You must be notified if anyone takes a negative action based on your credit report.** Anyone using a credit report or specialty-bureau consumer report to deny your application for credit, insurance, or employment — or to take any adverse action against you, like not offering their lowest interest rates — must tell you so and give you access to the information by telling you how you can get a free copy of the report from the credit bureau used to make the decision.

>> **You have the right to know what's in your file.** You can get a copy of all the information about you in the files of a consumer-reporting agency.

>> **You can get a free copy of each of your reports annually at** `www.annualcreditreport.com`. Reviewing your credit reports every 12 months is just what the doctor ordered for good credit health.

WARNING

Beware of imposter websites! When you order your free annual credit reports online, be sure to type in `www.annualcreditreport.com` to avoid being misdirected to other websites that offer supposedly free reports but only with the purchase of other products and services, such as credit monitoring. Also, be aware that after you get your report from the legally mandated free site, you'll be offered additional products or services for a price. You're not required to make a purchase to receive your free annual credit reports.

>> **You can get extra free copies of your credit report if you meet certain other criteria.** For example, if you're the victim of identity theft, you're entitled to a free report. You can also get a free copy if you're on public assistance or if you're unemployed but expect to apply for employment within 60 days. (See Chapter 14 for details.)

>> **You have the right to know your credit score.** Believe it or not, this didn't used to be the case. In the past, credit scores were not provided to consumers by lenders or the credit bureaus. That's changed, and now you have the right to request your score from consumer-reporting agencies for certain real property loans (typically mortgages), but you may have to pay for it. Mortgage lenders are increasingly providing your scores for free. (See Chapter 14 for more info.)

>> **You have the right to dispute incomplete, out-of-date, or inaccurate credit information and have it removed from your reports.** After you report an issue to the consumer-reporting agency, the agency has to investigate (they say

reinvestigate). Unless your dispute is frivolous, the agency must notify the source of the information — usually a lender — of your dispute. The source then has 30 days to respond to the dispute and tell the credit reporting agency to remove the information, update it, or leave it unchanged. You must then be notified of the results. While the dispute is underway, the information will remain in your credit report. If the source of the information fails to respond within 30 days, the credit reporting company must remove the account. However, the lender can notify the agency to restore the information after that deadline has passed. When that happens the credit bureau must send you notice that the information is being returned to your credit report. If you disagree, you should request that a "statement of dispute" be added to your report telling why you disagree and how you believe it should be shown.

>> **You have the right to limit access to your file to only those who have a legally defined purpose for requesting it.** A consumer-reporting agency may sell information in your file only to people with a valid use, called a *permissible purpose* — usually to consider an application with a creditor, insurer, employer, landlord, or other business purpose. They may also sell it to businesses like credit card and insurance companies that want to make a preapproved or prescreened credit offer. You can limit access to your information for unsolicited prescreened offers for credit and insurance.

TIP

You can opt out of such preapproved credit offers with the nationwide credit bureaus at 888-567-8688 or online at www.optoutprescreen.com.

>> **You have the right to collect damages for violations of your rights under the FCRA.** If a credit-reporting agency or user or furnisher of information violates the FCRA, you can sue the party in state or federal court.

>> **You have additional rights if you're an identity theft victim or an active-duty military service person.** For example, you can appoint a personal representative to handle your affairs while you're deployed outside the U.S. Additionally, you may place an active-duty alert on your file, which requires creditors to exercise greater caution and verify your identity before making credit decisions. (For more info, see Chapter 20.)

TIP

Although the FACT Act is a federal law and is enforced by the FTC and the CFPB, states may also enforce the law, and most states have their own consumer-reporting laws. You may have additional rights under your state's laws. To find out what applies in your state, contact your state or local consumer protection agency or your state attorney general. Explain your concerns and ask what your rights are and how you can get help. Be sure to record names, dates, and actions in case you need to follow up.

The FDCPA: Providing Protection Against Debt Collectors

What do you do when a debt collector sends you a letter or calls to say how much he or she misses your payment? Whether you're feeling helpless or angry, knowing the rules that apply is important — specifically, what collectors really can and can't do. The Fair Debt Collection Practices Act (FDCPA) is the key piece of legislation that regulates debt collectors. It prohibits debt collectors — meaning collection agencies, lawyers who collect debts, and companies that buy delinquent debts and try to collect them — from using abusive, unfair, or deceptive practices to attempt to collect from you. This section gets you better acquainted with the FDCPA.

REMEMBER

The FDCPA covers most personal, family, and household debts, such as personal credit card accounts, car loans, medical bills, and mortgages. It doesn't cover debts incurred in running a business.

Controlling the contacts

A collector may contact you at a reasonable time, such as after 8 a.m. or before 9 p.m. If these times don't work, you get to define what a reasonable time is. But you must allow collectors to do their job, so you can't be too restrictive. A collector also may not contact you at work if you tell the collector (orally or in writing) that you're not allowed to get calls there.

TIP

Be sure to follow up any conversations or agreements in writing as soon as possible. Doing so documents what you and the collector have agreed to and helps eliminate miscommunications in a stressful environment.

Have an attorney and want her to take over? Let the collector know. After you do, the collector must contact the attorney and only the attorney, rather than you or anyone else. If you don't have an attorney, a collector has the right to contact others to get your address, home phone number, and place of employment. However, collectors can't tell anyone else why they're calling or that they're debt collectors.

Finding out about the debt

You have the right to receive a validation notice from the collector within five days of contact that tells you how much money you owe. The notice must include the name of the creditor to whom the collector claims you owe the money and procedures to follow if you don't think you owe the money.

If you don't owe the money or an error has been made, send the debt collector a letter (to be sure it gets there and to know they got it, send it certified mail with a return receipt) within 30 days of receiving the validation notice and state that you're disputing the debt. If you're not 100 percent sure whether you owe the money, ask for verification of the debt. The good news is that, until the debt is verified, the law prohibits further collector contacts.

REMEMBER

Collectors can begin contacting you again after they send you written verification of the debt, like a copy of a bill for the amount you owe.

Stopping a collector from contacting you

When a collector first contacts you about a debt, it usually comes as a surprise. If you decide after being contacted by the collector that you don't want to hear from the collector again, you have the right to tell the collector (in writing) to stop contacting you. Here's how.

Send an original copy of your demand by certified mail, and pay for a return receipt so you can document that the collection company received it. Keep copies of everything you send or receive. After the collector receives your letter, the collector may not contact you again, with two exceptions:

>> The collector may contact you to tell you that no further contact will occur. We know, it sounds silly, but that's the law.

>> The collector may let you know that the collector or the creditor intends to take a specific action as a result of your ending the conversation, such as filing a lawsuit, but only if it actually intends to do so.

No idle threats are allowed. For example, if you owe a debt to a hospital, it may hire a collection agency to collect the debt. If the collector knows that the hospital's policy is not to sue a former patient, then the collector can't threaten to sue.

REMEMBER

Sending a letter to a debt collector stopping all contact doesn't get rid of the debt, but it should stop the collector from contacting you. The creditor or the debt collector still can, and often will, sue you to collect the debt. They'll also likely report the debt to the credit reporting agencies, which will make it difficult for you to get credit in the future, or at least the next few years.

Spotting prohibited behavior

Debt collectors aren't allowed to get away with certain behaviors. Here are some highlights, or lowlights, of what a collector may not do:

>> **Harass or threaten you:** Debt collectors may not harass, oppress, or abuse you or any third parties they contact. They may not threaten violence or harm, publish your name as someone who refuses to pay your debts (but they can report you to a credit bureau), use obscene or profane language, or repeatedly call to annoy you.

>> **Lie to you:** Like Pinocchio, debt collectors who lie get in trouble. Their noses may not grow, but they can be sued if they pretend to be attorneys, government representatives, or employees of a credit bureau. They also get in trouble if they claim that you've committed a crime or lie about the amount you owe. They also can't pretend that the papers they send you are legal forms if they aren't or indicate that the papers they send you aren't legal forms if they are.

>> **Be unfair:** Collectors may not engage in unfair practices. So what's not fair play? Trying to collect more than what's due unless the contract that created your debt — or your state law — allows an additional charge; depositing a post-dated check early; or contacting you by postcard to embarrass you with the mail carrier or your family.

If a collector violates any of the provisions of the FDCPA, contact your local consumer protection agency, your state's attorney general, or your lawyer. The first two public resources should be able to stop the abusive or unfair behavior with a phone call or letter. Your attorney may also file suit for damages against the collector/collection agency.

Suing a collector

You (or better, your attorney on your behalf, and not actually you) can sue a collector in a state or federal court within one year if the collector violates the law. If you win, you can be awarded any damages you can prove resulted from the illegal collection practices, like lost wages and medical bills. You also can be reimbursed for your attorney's fees and court costs. In some states, you could also receive punitive damages, which could be big, but don't bet on it — big dollar court rulings are not very common. Consider it a win if the collection is dismissed, you no longer owe the debt, and your credit history is restored.

REMEMBER

If a debt collector violates the FDCPA in trying to collect a debt and you win a lawsuit against that collector, the debt still may not go away if you owe it. Also, if you lose your suit, you may owe more in fees and costs in addition to the debt.

The CROA: Getting What You Pay For

Imagine calling the toll-free number on the "We'll Fix Your Credit!" sign nailed to the telephone pole you passed on the way to work and hearing this: "Need a new big-screen TV for the big game but your credit score is getting in your way? Maxed out your credit cards? No problem! Collection notices stuffing your mailbox? No big deal. Declared bankruptcy last week? Who cares? Just write us a check, and we'll get that stuff off of your report and boost your score by 300 points in the next month!"

Sound too good to be true? That's because it is — and it's illegal, too.

The Credit Repair Organizations Act (CROA) was enacted to protect people from companies that make outrageous, false claims to fleece them of their hard-earned money when they're desperate for help and don't know where to turn. This section explains your rights and protections provided by CROA against illicit credit repair firms.

REMEMBER

The FTC has said there is nothing a credit repair firm can do for you that you can't do yourself for free. You can dispute information in your credit report at no cost. If you need help with your finances, there are excellent nonprofit credit counseling services that can help you gain control of your personal finances, create workable budgets, and help you work with your lenders for little or no cost. Two good sources are the National Foundation for Credit Counseling (www.nfcc.org) and Operation HOPE (https://operationhope.org/credit-and-money-management).

Knowing what credit repair organizations must do

The average cost of for-profit credit repair organizations charging monthly fees is about $100 a month. That's $1,200 a year. CROA clearly defines what a credit repair firm must do before you have to pay a single dime. Knowing what those things are could save you a pretty penny, or possibly thousands of dollars. Here are the key things that they're required to do:

>> Provide a written contract defining exactly what they'll do for you. They also have to fulfill all the terms of that contract before accepting any payment.

>> Allow you three days to withdraw from the contract if you change your mind.

>> Tell you that you can dispute information with the credit bureaus yourself for free.

>> Inform you that you can sue the credit repair company if it violates CROA.

The credit repair company can't bury these notifications in the fine print, either. They have to give them to you on a form separate from the rest of the documentation they may put in front of you.

Understanding what credit repair companies can't do

Understanding what a credit repair firm cannot do is just as important. It could save you a lot of money and maybe keep you out of trouble with the law. Here's what a credit repair company can't do if you choose to work with them:

>> **Take payment up front.** That means they can't ask you for cash, a check, or a credit card number before they do anything for you. They can't take a dime from you until they meet all the terms of the contract you signed.

>> **Promise to remove accurate information from your credit report, positive or negative.** If it's accurate, it's going to stay in your credit report until the timeframes specified in the law for it to be deleted. (See Chapter 13 for more about when information is removed from your credit report.)

>> **Suggest you change identifying information or make false statements to the credit bureaus to dodge bad debt.** If you do so, both you and the credit repair firm may be prosecuted for fraud.

TIP

Make sure you know your rights before hiring a credit repair firm. Having someone repair your credit for you can sound tempting, but there is no quick fix for accurate information in your credit report. A good credit counselor won't sell you a bill of goods. He'll work with you on a plan to get back on track, but it will take time and work on your part. (See Chapter 4 to learn more about credit counseling.)

Exploring Other Protections

People turn to payday lending and debt settlement when they find traditional financing difficult or even impossible to obtain. These industries weren't tightly regulated before the 2007 recession, but nowadays, protections are available if you know where to look. In this section, we take you on a quick tour of these businesses and the protections you have if you decide to use them. We also introduce you to an age-old protection called the statute of limitations that's worth knowing about.

The ins and outs of payday loans

If you think payday loans are small time, think again. A number of state laws have been passed restricting payday lending, so it's not as big as it once was, but the business is still doing very well. As of 2017, there were 14,348 payday lending storefronts in the United States (that's slightly more than the number of McDonald's restaurants at the time).

Astronomical interest rates, predatory lenders, and unsuspecting people forever in debt: That's generally what comes to mind when people think of payday loans. As with most things, the reality isn't so simple. A *payday loan* is a short-term cash loan secured by a personal check. Say you need a short-term loan to cover some unexpected expense. You may not have access to credit lines or cards. Your bank won't give you a short-term loan. So you go to your local payday lender. You write a personal check for the amount you want to borrow, plus a fee, and you receive cash. Your check is held for future deposit or electronic access to your bank account, usually on the date of your next payday, hence the term *payday loan* and the short period of the loan (usually one or two weeks). Payday loans charge extremely high fees: Using a typical $17.50 fee for every $100 borrowed up to a maximum of $300, the interest rates total 911 percent for a one-week loan, 456 percent for a two-week loan, and 212 percent for a one-month loan.

These loans are small in dollars and high in transaction costs. Many banks find them unprofitable and won't make them. The result is the payday loan industry. As expensive as these loans are, they can be less expensive than overdraft charges on your bank account, which are now limited by law but used to be so steep and unfairly applied that payday loans were cheap by comparison.

Payday lenders claim that their loans aren't high-cost if they're used properly. Here's an example of their thinking: You take a taxi for short distances and a plane for long ones. You wouldn't take a taxi from coast to coast, nor would you take a plane to the local grocery store. Just because the taxi's rate per mile is higher than the plane's cost per mile doesn't necessarily mean that the taxi is overcharging for its service. Unless, of course, the taxi takes you from Times Square to Lincoln Center via Los Angeles.

Looking at the rules of payday loans

Lenders are required to quote the cost of a payday loan as both the dollar finance charge and the annual percentage rate (APR). In addition, many states have rules and limits for payday lenders. Find out your state's rules at www.ncsl.org/issues-research/banking/payday-lending-state-statutes.aspx.

Here are the rules for the five largest states:

>> **California** allows loans of 31 days of up to $300. Fees allowed are up to 15 percent of the amount loaned. The APR for a $100 loan for 14 days is 459 percent.

>> **Florida** allows loans of not less than 7 days or more than 31 days of up to $500, exclusive of fees. Fees allowed are up to 10 percent of the loan plus a verification fee. The APR for a 14-day, $100 loan is 419 percent.

>> **Illinois** allows loans of 13 to 120 days of up to the lesser of $1,000 or 25 percent of the borrower's gross monthly income. Fees allowed are $15.50 per $100 loaned. The APR for a 14-day, $100 loan is 403 percent.

>> **New York** prohibits foreign banking corporations from issuing payday loans. It also has a 25 percent interest rate cap on loans. Payday loans are effectively illegal in New York: It is a violation of state law to make payday loans in person, by telephone, or over the Internet. It is also illegal for a debt collector to collect, or attempt to collect, on a payday loan in New York.

>> **Texas** allows loans of 7 days to 31 days without limitation. Fees allowed vary according to a chart contained in state legislation. The effective APR for a 14-day, $100 loan is 309 percent.

On the federal level, the Department of Defense provides protections for men and women in the armed forces and their families. Specifically, lenders may not charge more than 36 percent annual interest, including most fees and charges. Instead of payday loans, military personnel may get financial assistance from military aid societies, such as the Army Emergency Relief, Navy and Marine Corps Relief Society, Air Force Aid Society, or Coast Guard Mutual Aid.

TIP

If you're in the Navy or the Marine Corps, the Navy and Marine Corps Relief Society will pay off your payday loan if you're having trouble repaying it, and then you can pay back the relief organization on better terms.

Getting help if a lender violates the rules

If you think that a payday loan lender has taken advantage of you, you have a couple places to turn:

>> **Your state's lender regulation agency:** Regulators may be able to help you work out a payment arrangement with a lender. And if you live in a state that doesn't allow payday lending, the state regulator can take action against a lender. Go to www.consumerfinance.gov/askcfpb/1637/how-do-i-find-my-states-bank-regulator.html to find a link that helps you find the right agency.

>> **The Community Financial Services Association of America (CFSA):** More than half of payday lenders are members of the CFSA, an organization that requires its members to subscribe to a code of conduct that goes beyond state laws. You may complain to the CFSA (www.cfsaa.com) if you feel you've been treated unfairly or abused. Under its code of conduct, you can request and receive an extended payment plan that allows you to extend your loan for four payday cycles without any additional fees or charges.

WARNING

Many nonmember payday lenders don't offer payment plans. Their idea of a payment plan is a loan rollover until you collapse under the weight of the fees and cumulative interest charges.

The details of debt settlement

Wouldn't it be great if you could go to a lender and say, "Hey, what if I give you part of what I owe you, and we just call it even, and then you take that account off my credit report?" That's the basic premise behind the debt settlement industry. In a nutshell, debt settlers try to get lenders to settle or accept a lower payment than is due to satisfy a debt. Why would a lender accept less? Because less is better than nothing! It sounds great, but like most things that sound too good to be true, debt settlement usually is. Debt settlers expect you to pay everything that's due, or at least most of it — they just expect you to pay a big chunk of it to them and not to the lender.

A debt settler generally collects a monthly amount from you, but instead of paying your creditors, it holds onto the payments for at least three to six months, depending on your circumstances and your creditors. Next, it tries to negotiate with your creditors on your behalf to settle the accounts for less than the full balance. Some creditors will negotiate, and others will not. During this lengthy process, nothing is being paid to your creditors, and all the while they use all the remedies they have to collect the debt from you, including judgments and garnishments.

WARNING

Unless the debt settlement company is able to settle all or most of your debts, the penalties and fees you may incur on the unsettled debts can cost you more than you save. And the settlement process seriously damages your credit whether it's successful or not. In the end, accounts you settled are reported as, well, "settled," or "settled for less than agreed." Settled accounts hammer credit scores because you didn't pay what you actually owed.

The CFPB and the FTC regulate debt settlement. Debt settlers can't charge fees before actually settling a debt. The FTC's debt settlement rules apply to for-profit debt settlement and credit counseling, debt negotiation companies, and companies that falsely claim to have nonprofit status.

Beware of advertisements for "debt consolidation." Debt settlement companies often describe themselves as debt consolidation companies. What that means is you consolidate all your payments into one check that you send to the debt consolidation/debt settlement company instead of making payments to your lender.

There is a different kind of traditional debt consolidation that pays off your smaller debts with one larger loan. A debt consolidation loan from your bank, credit union, or student loan servicer can actually be a good tool to reduce your payments over time and protect your credit report because all the debts are reported as "paid in full, as agreed." Be sure you don't confuse the two.

The new rules don't apply to in-person or Internet-only debt settlers, nor do they limit how much you can be charged for a debt settlement service.

Credit counseling agencies may be a viable alternative to debt settlement, plus they are free or very low cost. See the section "Considering credit counseling" in Chapter 4 for details.

Beware of any company promising to settle your debt if it

>> Charges a fee before settling your debts.

>> Claims that there is a "new government program" to eliminate debts.

>> Guarantees to make your debt go away.

>> Tells you to stop communicating with your creditors.

>> Claims to be able to stop collection calls and legal actions.

Debt settlers must

>> Represent their services accurately.

>> Tell you how long paying off your debt will take, inform you of the conditions under which the settlers will negotiate settlements with creditors, and tell you how much money you must pay before a settlement offer is made.

>> Disclose that debt settlements will trash your credit rating and potentially expose you to lawsuits from creditors.

>> Successfully settle or negotiate at least one of your debts, with at least one payment going to a creditor before you're charged any fees.

>> Provide you with a written contract, debt settlement plan, or oral agreement outlining the payback strategy, as well as details of the potential pitfalls of debt relief services.

A debt settled is a debt forgiven. You may owe taxes on any forgiven portion of debts settled.

If you think that a debt settler has taken advantage of you, you have a couple places to turn. Your state agency that regulates debt settlers may be able to help. Look for the agency in the consumer protection department or the attorney general's office. Also, the CFPB may be able to assist. Here's how the CFPB works: Go to its website (www.consumerfinance.gov/complaint/) and enter your complaint. It forwards your complaint to the company and works to get a response, or it forwards your complaint to another government agency if it thinks that agency can better assist you. The company reviews your complaint, communicates with you as needed, and reports back to the CFPB about the steps that have been taken or that will be taken on the issue you identified in your complaint. Then the CFPB lets you know that response and gives feedback. As a bonus, it shares this data with state and federal law enforcement agencies.

You can also contact the Better Business Bureau, but doing so may not be an effective alternative because it relies on cooperation from the debt settler to help you.

The scoop on the statute of limitations

The *statute of limitations* (SOL) ensures that you can't be held accountable for past mistakes forever, at least with regard to credit. Each state has a law restricting the time that legal proceedings may be brought against you to collect a debt. Those laws set a maximum period for a creditor to file a lawsuit, depending on the type of loan or claim. The period varies by state. Federal statutes set the limitations for suits filed in federal courts. If you're not sued before the statutory deadline, the lender loses its right to sue you. If you're talking to a lawyer, you may hear the term *time barred debt,* which is referring to the SOL and the fact that it "bars" or blocks them from suing after a certain period of time.

For a list of statute of limitation laws for different states, check out www.nolo.com/legal-encyclopedia/statute-of-limitations-state-laws-chart-29941.html.

Statutes of limitations go way back to early Roman law and were designed to prevent fraudulent and stale (really old) claims from arising after all evidence was lost or after the facts became obscured through the passage of time, defective memory, death, or the disappearance of witnesses. We'll leave that last one up to your imagination and the movies.

To use this protection, you must show up before the court and answer the lender's complaint. If you don't, you waive the use of this defense and aren't permitted to use it in any subsequent proceedings.

Here's what you need to keep in mind about the SOL:

>> If your debt is older than allowed under your state's SOL, you can't be sued in court to collect it.

>> The SOL has nothing to do with the time a debt stays on your credit report. A debt can be on your credit report for seven years but prohibited from collections lawsuits after a much shorter period. Likewise, depending on the state law, you could still be sued for collections after the debt has been removed from your credit report.

>> The SOL begins to run from the day the debt — or payment on an open-ended account — was due and not paid.

>> The SOL doesn't eliminate your debt after it expires. It keeps you from being sued in court. A collector can still ask you to repay the debt.

>> Depending on your state's law, making a partial payment may restart the SOL clock and extend the time you may be sued. In that case, SOL could mean something different to you. States that specify that a partial payment doesn't restart the clock, unless there's a new written promise to pay, include Arizona, California, Florida, Iowa, Kansas, Maine, Massachusetts, Michigan, Minnesota, Mississippi, Missouri, Nevada, New York, Texas, Virginia, West Virginia, and Wisconsin.

Chapter **21**

Protecting Your Identity

dentity theft doesn't involve someone dressing like you and copying your hairstyle. It's much simpler than that. The thief simply acquires and uses the myriad numbers associated with your name to become you, electronically and financially. But how does an identity thief get this valuable data about you? Often by stealing your mail, hacking into your computer, breaking into your home, or sifting through receipts and personal information found in your trash can.

It used to be that we were worried about account numbers on our receipts or someone trying to counterfeit our credit cards. Now many fraudsters are more sophisticated. As more people go online, companies and industries are coming together to raise security standards and become more diligent about protecting your privacy. However, sometimes data breaches or unauthorized attacks can hijack your personal information. Being diligent about security — whether you're transacting in person or online — helps. But you need to know what you can do to protect yourself and "fix it" if it happens to you.

Depending on what information the thief steals from you, he can use your favorite credit card or open new credit card accounts in your name. He can buy a car in your name, rent an apartment and leave you to pay the damages, order furniture, and stay a week at the Ritz in Buenos Aires — all while posing as *you*. And, of course, the thief makes no payments on any of the debts. The negative credit activity is reported on your credit report, and if the thief is lucky — and you aren't — you may not discover him living it up and wrecking your credit rating for months (or longer!). You may discover that your identity has been stolen only when you apply for a line of credit and are rejected, or when you receive a flurry of aggressive calls from collection agencies for not paying bills of which you aren't even aware.

After you discover the ID theft, you do get to defend yourself and prove that the fraudulent accounts aren't yours, but the process can be expensive and may take a long time to resolve. Fortunately, as the problem has become worse, the timeframes and investment to correct the issues have become less burdensome and quicker to resolve. The Bureau of Justice reported more than 55 percent of identity-theft victims who resolved associated financial or credit problems did so in one day or less, while other studies reflect an average of 15 hours.

In this chapter, we tell you the important steps you need to take to protect yourself, your identity, and your credit from identity theft. See Chapter 9 for guidance on repairing the damage if it does occur.

Keeping Thieves at Bay

Your identity may be stolen by a stranger. Then again, as often happens, it may be stolen by someone you know and willingly let into your life, such as a friend, relative, or coworker. To reduce your chances of falling victim to identity theft, make sure that you protect your personal information. In short, don't leave financial or confidential documents out in the open, open online, or use passwords that are easy to find, guess, or access.

New solutions, like BreachClarity (www.breachclarity.com), are also being brought to market to help you protect yourself. These services analyze every consumer's unique breach history to prescribe personalized actions that protect your identity and credit. Monitoring your credit activity and signing up for texts when transactions are made are just a few steps that can help. Nearly 50 percent of victims discovered identity theft when they were contacted by the financial institution about suspicious activity. So, sign up for texts when certain transactions occur so you can quickly stop thieves in their tracks!

In the following sections, we walk you through some simple steps you can take to reduce the chances of your identity being stolen.

Getting on the technology train

One of the easiest ways to protect yourself is to simplify bill-paying, information transfers, and financial transactions by performing them all securely and electronically. Having bills and statements delivered to your password-protected computer is much safer than having them delivered to your mailbox outside your home. Statistics say that the more information you send and receive electronically, the lower your chances of identity theft.

Using a computer has other benefits as well: When you receive your information online, as in the case of your bank statement, you can check it anytime you want — no need to wait until the end of the month for a statement to arrive. We recommend that you do a quick once-over of your account activity weekly or have preset dollar-level alerts emailed or texted to you. For example, you can arrange for transactions that exceed $100 to generate an email or text automatically. Virtually every financial institution now offers text messages that can be sent for every purchase over a certain amount. Set your alert level so that it doesn't result in dozens of notices but does catch the transactions you're most concerned about. That way, you can spot a problem early and you won't have to spend a day or two trying to resolve it.

WARNING

Take precautions when conducting business via the web. As long as you use only secure websites and ensure that you're protected by a firewall, you're much better protected than you are with snail mail. (See the next section for info on determining whether a website is secure, and see the section "Safeguarding your computer data" for a few words on firewalls.)

Looking out for phishing scams

Phishing occurs when a stranger pretending to be someone you trust (for example, a Facebook friend, a credit card company, or a representative of your bank) emails you and asks you to confirm critical information about your account — for example, by replying with your password or Social Security number. Phishing can also be perpetrated via a spyware program that you unwittingly download to your computer by clicking a link or opening a file; the program then records your personal information and sends it to the thief.

REMEMBER

Phishing scams are increasing and becoming more sophisticated. Bottom line: Think twice before replying to any unsolicited requests or giving out your personal information over the Internet. As with phone solicitations, don't give out your personal information unless *you* initiate the transaction. You can find out more about preventing Internet fraud, securing your computer, and protecting your personal information by visiting www.onguardonline.gov.

Here are some do's and don'ts that can help keep you and your personal info safe:

- » **Do be suspicious of any email with urgent, exciting, or upsetting requests for personal financial info or money.** The sender is using your emotions to stimulate an immediate, illogical response to the request. Pay special attention to any website addresses or domain names that are included. If it doesn't look right, don't click the link.

- » **Do protect your passwords and consider turning on two-factor authentication (2FA).** Don't share your passwords over the phone, in texts, or by email. Legitimate companies will *never* ask you for your password. Using 2FA requires a password and typically a code that's texted or emailed to you or generated by an authenticator app like Google Authenticator, which you install on your smartphone. If you write down your passwords, keep them locked up on your computer or in a safe and out of plain sight. Consider using a password manager like 1Password (www.1password.com), which allows you to generate very long, random passwords (ones so strong you would never be able to remember them); you can (and should) create a different password for every website you visit, but you only have to remember one master password to access all the passwords you've created.

Why a different password for every site? Because, that way, if one website gets hacked and your password is compromised, the hacker can't use that same password to log in to your email account, your credit card company, your bank, and so on.

- » **Don't give out personal or financial info unless you're certain of the source and you can confirm that the link is secure.** You can tell that you're on a secure website if the site's address begins with `https://` rather than `http://`. A secure site encrypts data as it's being transmitted, which is especially important when you're entering personal information.

Email is almost *never* secure, which means that you should never email your credit card number, Social Security number, or other personal info to anyone, even someone you're sure you can trust. This is particularly important if you're using a general hosting provider (like Gmail or Hotmail, for example). Those emails are stored and backed up in files that you don't want holding your account numbers.

- » **Don't respond to emails that aren't personalized or that have your name misspelled.** If the message has your name wrong or doesn't include your name at all, chances are high that it's a fraud.

- » **Don't click links in email messages to find out what the great offer is unless you know you signed up for that service.** If you click the link, you may end up downloading spyware onto your computer, and your security may be compromised.

- **Don't unsubscribe to emails unless you know that you subscribed in the first place.** Some phishers send you emails hoping that you'll respond or unsubscribe, thereby confirming that your email address is valid.

- **Do be careful of emails pretending to be from companies you do business with.** We periodically get emails that look like they're from banks we use, but the emails lack the detailed logo or look and feel of the real companies, or they ask us to update information that we know the banks already have.

- **If you suspect that you're being phished, do forward the email to the Federal Trade Commission at** spam@uce.gov **and file a complaint with the Internet Crime Complaint Center (IC3) by going to** www.ic3.gov**.** The IC3 is a partnership among the FBI, the National White Collar Crime Center (NW3C), and the Bureau of Justice Assistance (BJA). The IC3 website not only lets you report suspected Internet fraud but also provides disturbing statistics about this growing crime.

Safeguarding your computer data

You need to safeguard your computer so that it doesn't give up its secrets without a fight. Here are some computer-safety rules to consider:

- **Don't leave your laptop, smart phone, or tablet out where it can be picked up.** Whether at home, in a hotel, or at work, when you're not in the same room as your device, put it away out of sight. Would you leave a $100 bill lying around? The same consideration applies here.

- **Don't walk away from your computer and leave files with personal information open, particularly if you're online.** If you're offline, anyone in the room can see your information. If you're online, especially with a broadband connection, your computer can be hacked and your data stolen, or you can be observed for sensitive information like passwords. Lock your computer when you walk away, even if it's in your own house.

- **Come up with a username and personal identification number (PIN) or password that isn't obvious, and set your computer so that this information is required in order to log on.** You can also use a screensaver that has a password so that if you walk away from your desk for a certain period and the screensaver comes on, you need to enter a password to get back to your desktop.

TIP

- **Include at least one number, capital letter, or special character in your password as a minimum precaution.** A good example is Steve@1. Don't use birthdates or Social Security numbers; they're too easy for hackers to guess.

>> **Don't use your kid's or pet's name or birthday as your password.** These things are easy for someone who knows you to guess.

>> **Don't keep a list of your passwords under your keyboard or near the computer.** That's the equivalent of leaving your house key under the mat.

>> **Install a firewall.** A *firewall* is a program or device that filters information before it gets to your computer. If you use a wireless network, make sure that the network and firewall are encrypted. (You can get firewalls for your home computer at most office-supply stores.)

>> **Use antivirus and spyware protection programs to keep key loggers off your computer.** Make sure you keep your antivirus and spyware protection programs up to date. *Key loggers* are programs that send to a crook any information you type while on your computer, including your credit card numbers, usernames, passwords, Social Security number, and so on.

>> **Make sure to delete all personal information on your computer if you decide to get rid of it.** Your best bet is to reformat your hard drive, which wipes it clean and gets rid of everything. You may want to reformat your drive more than once to do a thorough job of permanently erasing data. (Check with your computer manufacturer to find out how to scrub your hard drive.)

Keeping passwords secret

A testament to the trusting nature of Americans is that if you want to know something personal or secret about them, all you have to do is ask. But you'd be wise to keep your computer password secret because it protects you from others — even trusted coworkers — accessing your personal information. To make sure that you don't get taken advantage of, follow these suggestions:

>> **Don't give anyone your password.** If the guy in the next cubicle wants to be helpful, you can enter your password for him.

>> **If you have to give out your password, be sure that you trust the source, and then change your password immediately.** And by immediately, we mean right after you give out your password. Don't wait until the next day or the next week.

REMEMBER

Avoid giving confidential information to friends, acquaintances, or even your kids. They may not be identity thieves, but they sure are great, naive sources of information.

Protecting your mail

The fact that tampering with the U.S. mail is a federal crime doesn't seem to deter identity thieves from helping themselves to the contents of people's mailboxes. And your mail often contains sensitive information. For example, although some credit card issuers don't include your full account number on your monthly statement, others still do. And you don't want a thief to have access to your bank account numbers. Unless you write with a Uni-ball Gel Pen, which uses the only type of ink that thieves can't acid-wash, an enterprising identity thief can also easily convert that check you sent off for the heating bill into ready cash by acid-washing the original recipient off the check and replacing the name.

TIP

Following are some easy ways to reduce your exposure to mail fraud:

>> **Move as much of your financial business online as you can.** Doing so helps you avoid delivering information to the waiting hands of the criminal scouting your unattended mailbox. Mailboxes can be targets of theft, particularly when mailbox stations are shared with other neighbors.

>> **Explore alternatives to your unlocked, end-of-the-driveway mailbox.** Consider using a post office box or a locked mailbox that accepts mail (not unlike the old slot in the door).

>> **Don't mail checks or financial information from your home mailbox.** Use a post office mailbox or bring your mail to work with you. (Don't forget the stamps, or the boss may cancel your work identity.)

>> **Ask your bank to hold new check orders and pick them up at the bank.** Check reorder boxes are easy to spot with a trained eye. You wouldn't send cash through the mail; don't send checks, either.

>> **If you're away for a day or more, have someone pick up your mail or, better yet, have the post office hold it until you return.** Don't let it sit in your mailbox overnight.

Storing financial data in your home

You may believe that your financial information is safe inside the sanctuary of your home, no matter where it's located. Unfortunately, even in your home, securing your documents and personal information by keeping them out of sight is best. Your information is still accessible to anyone who may gain access to your inner sanctum, friend or foe. The following sections describe ways to protect your information and yourself in your home.

Securing confidential documents and information

Keep all confidential, financial, and legal documents and information in a secure place — a strong box, a locked desk drawer, or a locked file cabinet. Doing so ensures that your valuable data is safe from prying eyes and sticky fingers, and you benefit from having all critical information in one place in case you need to access it quickly.

Destroying information

Your mailbox isn't the only place that identity thieves look for useful information. Your garbage can is also ripe with potential. A determined thief doesn't mind sifting through your detritus if it means snagging a credit card number from those statements covered in coffee grounds. A fishing expedition in the backyards and trash cans of suburbia can yield a good return.

TIP

Purchase a good crosscut shredder and shred all financial documents that contain account numbers (including savings, checking, and credit card statements) before you discard them. Don't overlook all those preapproved offers for credit you receive, either; a thief can send them in with a change of address and get new credit that you won't know about until it's too late. Look for a shredder that takes multiple sheets of paper, is easy to use, and can be emptied without making a mess. Why? Because you're more likely to use it if it meets these criteria.

Putting your credit information on ice

Frozen margaritas, frozen yogurt, frozen credit? The option to freeze your credit to keep it from identity thieves is available to everyone. In fact, many financial institutions also offer you the opportunity to "freeze" your card or "lock" your account or card, if needed. This prevents purchases from being made until you want to make a purchase or you locate the card that fell inside the cushion on your couch. If you lock it, though, make sure you remember to unlock it before you make that next purchase. The concept is similar with your credit report: You can freeze, or lock up, your credit information at the major credit bureaus (meaning that your credit report won't be available for new creditors to view) so that anyone who's looking to extend credit has to ask you to thaw (unlock) your file. Freezing your credit information seriously hampers an identity thief from opening credit in your name without your knowledge because few lenders extend credit without a credit report in hand.

REMEMBER

When deciding whether to freeze your credit information, the main consideration is whether you value access to instant credit more than you fear your personal information being compromised. Only you know the answer to that question.

WARNING

Of course, the freeze-your-credit-info strategy isn't foolproof. Thieves can still pirate and abuse existing accounts by using such tactics as swiping your mail, changing your address from Peoria to Las Vegas, and getting replacement cards issued. So a freeze may help protect your *information*, but it may not protect your *money*, although hopefully you'd notice a problem before it got too far out of hand. Given the low personal level of liability on credit cards, your monetary losses shouldn't be significant.

The bottom line of a freeze is as follows:

>> All the bureaus allow you to freeze your credit files regardless of the laws in your state.

>> Freezing doesn't prevent abuse of existing accounts.

>> Thawing an account takes a few days and may keep impulse or sale purchases from happening — which can be a good thing or a bad thing, depending on how you look at it.

TIP

If a freeze seems extreme to you, consider a fraud alert. It's like an account "chill" rather than a hard freeze in that it requires only enhanced verification of identity. To place an alert, contact any of the big three credit bureaus using the information in Chapter 15. The bureau you contact will automatically forward your request to the other two big credit bureaus for action. For details, see the section "Sending out a fraud alert" in Chapter 9.

Shielding your credit card number

One of the easiest ways to safeguard your identity is to ensure that thieves don't have access to your credit card numbers. Luckily, the Fair and Accurate Credit Transactions Act (the FACT Act or FACTA) has made this task a lot easier. Electronically generated receipts for credit card and debit card transactions may not include the card's expiration date or more than the last five digits of the card number. If you receive a receipt that has your full account number on it, bring it to the attention of the business and insist that it get with the program — now! Virtually all credit card issuers print only partial account numbers on statements as well.

TIP

You can find out more about the FACT Act in Chapter 19 and at the Federal Trade Commission website (www.ftc.gov/sites/default/files/documents/reports/40-years-experience-fair-credit-reporting-act-ftc-staff-report-summary-interpretations/110720fcrareport.pdf).

SAFEGUARDING ACTIVE-DUTY MILITARY PERSONNEL

While on duty outside the United States, military personnel — as well as their families at home — may lack the time or means to monitor their credit. After all, calling TransUnion about an error isn't exactly a high priority when defending our freedoms, and families back home can understandably get distracted and let their guard down when a loved one is serving overseas. So it seems only fair that while soldiers are protecting their country, their country should protect them from credit problems. Thanks to the FACT Act, active-duty military personnel can place an *active-duty alert* on their credit reports as a way to notify potential creditors of possible fraud.

If you're in the military and away from your usual base or deployed, place an active-duty alert on your credit report by contacting any of the three major credit-reporting bureaus (don't bother calling all three bureaus, because the one you contact will notify the other two; see Chapter 15 for contact info). You'll be required to provide proof of identity, which may include your Social Security number, name, address, and other personal information.

The active-duty alert stays on your credit report for at least one year. It helps minimize the risk of identity theft by requiring that a business take reasonable care to verify your identity before issuing you credit. However, if you're in a distant land trying to keep the peace, verifying your identity may not be feasible. So before you leave your base or home for active duty, be sure to appoint a personal representative and provide that person's contact information to the credit bureau. If you don't, a creditor only has to "utilize reasonable policies and procedures to form a reasonable belief" before granting credit to someone claiming to be you. This is way too *reasonable* for our comfort level. Be sure to appoint someone you trust!

With an alert in place, lenders have to take further steps before issuing additional credit cards or changing your limits. When you place the alert, you can get an additional free credit report in addition to the annual report you're already entitled to (see Chapters 13 and 14 for more on this). Plus, your name is removed from preapproved offer lists for credit cards, insurance, and loans. To lessen the chances of an identity theft, you can place additional alerts if your deployment is to last longer than a year. (To delete an alert, just contact one of the bureaus; it will notify the others of your desire to deactivate the alert.)

Remember: If your contact information changes before your alert expires, update it or have your representative do so.

You may also want to examine the Servicemembers' Civil Relief Act (SCRA), which is a federal law that provides protections for military members as they enter active duty. The SCRA's benefits and protections include an interest rate cap on financial obligations incurred prior to military service, the ability to stay civil court proceedings, protections in connection with default judgments, protections in connection with residential (apartment) lease terminations, and protections in connection with evictions, mortgage foreclosures, and installment contracts such as car loans. These are benefits that can really assist you so you can focus on more important things. For more information on SCRA, go to www.justice.gov/servicemembers/servicemembers-civil-relief-act-scra.

Catching Identity Thieves in the Act

If your identity is stolen, you may not notice it for days, weeks, or even months. If a thief sets up a phony identity at another address and you don't get the bills, you may not know about the crime until the debts go bad and a collector finds you. Called *skip tracers,* these collectors look for people who don't pay their bills and then move — which is what they'll consider you until you straighten matters out.

The IRS may contact you if your identity is stolen. The IRS uses your Social Security number (SSN) to make sure that your tax filing is copacetic, and that if you are due a refund you get it. A notice or letter from the IRS could alert you that someone else is using your SSN. *Note:* The IRS doesn't initiate contact with tax-payers via email, text, or social media message. If you get an email that claims to be from the IRS, do not reply or click any links it may contain. Instead, forward it to phishing@irs.gov.

By being vigilant, you can spot signs of identity theft. Vigilance can make all the difference between a minor and a major crime. The following sections introduce you to some key indications of identity theft so that you can be on the lookout for them.

Watching for early-warning notices

To help spot identity theft early on, the FACT Act requires creditors to give you what may be called an *early-warning notice* (and it may be the first sign of a problem). When credit is used within 30 days of a missed, late, or partial payment or other type of default, you must be sent a one-time notice letting you know that this information is being sent to the credit bureau(s) to which the creditor reports data. This notice has to be sent by collection agencies, too, as long as they report to a credit bureau.

PREDICTING IDENTITY THEFT

The FACT Act demands that financial institutions establish procedures to attempt to spot identity theft *before* it occurs. Predicting identity theft may seem as farfetched as calling in a psychic on a missing person's case. But like our trusty weather forecasters who look to the skies for clues to tomorrow's weather, financial prognosticators are writing programs to look for specific activity in your financial records that may indicate a problem. In fact, several credit card companies now tout their own programs to fight identity theft. Chapter 15 talks about the efforts American Express, Visa, MasterCard, and other companies are making to spot fraud and theft as quickly as possible. A change in pattern, fraud information, or type of spending may trigger an alert to your phone or email if you have an alert in place. Alerts are free and easy to set up; see Chapter 15 for more information.

Certain events — such as a change of address, a request for a replacement credit card, or efforts to reactivate a dormant credit card account — may trigger a fraud alert. Be patient if you get declined for a purchase. The intent is to protect you from fraud, and a quick phone call can usually set things straight. That said, you can only do so much to protect yourself from identity theft. Even with prevention programs in place, you may not know about the problem until after the fact.

REMEMBER

Do your part by closely monitoring your credit reports, bank account statements, and credit card statements.

An early-warning notice means that something bad is in your account history, and if it's reported to a credit bureau, it has a negative effect on your credit and score. Whether or not it's reported, it's lurking out there. Before negative information is reported, the early-warning notice may look something like this:

> *We may report information about your account to credit bureaus. Late payments, missed payments, or other defaults on your account may be reflected in your credit report.*

After negative information has been reported, the notice may look like this:

> *We have told a credit bureau about a late payment, missed payment, or other default on your account. This information may be reflected in your credit report.*

REMEMBER

The wording makes it sound as though the bad information may not show up. It will, and it probably already has. Make sure you're reviewing your account statements every month so that you can spot and dispute any suspicious transactions. Regular monitoring can eliminate some additional steps and reduce additional fraud activity on your account.

So what do you do if you get a notice? Immediately contact the issuer and find out what's going on. The issuer will be as interested as you are in shutting down a thief, so you can expect cooperation and maybe even a thank-you for acting quickly.

Early warnings from the IRS

What's worse than having your identity stolen? Having it stolen and used to cheat the IRS. If someone uses your Social Security number (SSN) to get a job, her employer will use the stolen identity to report any earned income to the IRS using your SSN. Because you don't know about it, you won't report those earnings, thereby failing to report all your income from the IRS's point of view. You'll receive a notice or letter saying that you failed to report income.

Also, if someone uses your SSN to file for your tax refund before you file, that person may get your refund instead of you.

TIP

If you think that someone used your SSN to get a job or a tax refund — or the IRS sends you a notice or letter indicating a problem — contact the IRS immediately. Specially trained agents will work with you to file your tax return, get you any refund you are due, and protect your IRS account from identity thieves in the future. The IRS will want a copy of your police report or an IRS Form 14039, Identity Theft Affidavit (available at www.irs.gov/pub/irs-pdf/f14039.pdf), as well as proof of your identity, such as a copy of your Social Security card, driver's license, or passport.

Contact the IRS Identity Protection Specialized Unit at 800-908-4490.

In addition, ensure you take these additional steps outside of the IRS:

>> Report incidents of identity theft to the Federal Trade Commission at www.consumer.ftc.gov or to the FTC Identity Theft hot line at 877-438-4338 or TTY 866-653-4261.

>> File a report with your local police.

>> Contact the fraud departments of the three major credit bureaus:

- Equifax: www.equifax.com, 800-525-6285

- Experian: www.experian.com, 888-397-3742

- TransUnion: www.transunion.com, 800-680-7289

>> Close any accounts that have been tampered with or opened fraudulently.

Handling a collections call

If you're the victim of identity theft, you may receive a collections call, likely a demanding and unpleasant one, from a collector insisting on payment for an overdue account — an account that the collector is certain you owe but that you've never heard of. What should you do? The FACT Act, designed to address identity-theft issues, states that you need to tell the collector very clearly that you didn't make the purchase and that you believe your identity may have been stolen.

After you tell the collector that you believe your identity may have been stolen, the collection agency is required by law to inform the creditor. You're also entitled to a copy of all the information the collection agency or creditor has about this debt, including applications, statements, and the like, as though this really were your account or bill. We suggest that you request your copy before the collector gets off the phone or in your written response if the collection activity is in the form of a letter.

The best part is that, under the FACT Act, as soon as you notify the creditor or collector that the debt is the work of an identity thief, the debt can't be placed for collection or sold to another collector.

Detecting unauthorized charges

Are you among the many people who just look at the amount due on your monthly statement and pay it? Or is your credit card bill automatically paid from your bank account and you check the details later? In either case, you may be paying for purchases you didn't make, and more important, you may be missing an opportunity to stop a thief!

Take the time to review your statements to ensure that all the charges are legitimate. Set a reminder to alert you to check your statement in detail on a regular basis. Remember, you have a limited time to dispute an error. Plus, an identity thief is faster than the proverbial speeding bullet! So, don't delay checking your statements, or you may be in for quite a surprise.

TIP

Don't rely on your memory as you review your statement. Keep all credit card receipts in a convenient place, at least until you receive, verify, and pay your bills.

REMEMBER

If you see any unauthorized charges on your statement, call the card issuer's customer service number and get the details. You may have to dispute the charge, but that's no big deal. Also, the representative may see some indication of identity theft. That happened to Steve — he saw a stray charge and called the credit card company, and the customer service rep recognized it as fraud right away. Make the call.

Being denied credit or account access

Rejection is always a painful thing, but it's especially painful when you're rejected because of something you didn't do. If you're rejected for credit, you should always ask why and what information they reviewed to make the decision. Order a copy of your credit report and look for evidence of identity theft (accounts you never opened and/or activity you don't recognize). You can get a free copy of the credit report used to deny your application in addition to the free annual reports you get normally. (We tell you how to order those in Chapter 14.)

WARNING

Another sign of identity theft is receiving a notice that you've been rejected for credit that you never asked for. Take this notice seriously. Someone may be applying for credit in your name.

You may try to access an ATM and get a denial message. If this happens, contact your bank immediately to determine whether it's the result of identity theft.

Noticing missing account statements

Your monthly bank statement is really late. Hmm . . . now that you think of it, you didn't receive a statement last month, either. Yes, we know this was one of your birthday wishes, but the real reason you're not hearing from your creditors may be more sinister. It could mean that an identity thief has changed your address in order to use your bank account, hoping that you won't notice for a few months.

TIP

Create a system to remind yourself when statements are due and bills must be paid. This way, you're more likely to stay on top of your payment schedule and be alerted when something is amiss. Paying bills and getting statements online instead of by snail mail makes it harder on thieves (and easier on you).

6

The Part of Tens

IN THIS PART . . .

Be aware of the consumer protections in place to shield you from shady practices.

Understand your options for repaying your student loans.

Decide whether to stay in your home or leave, and reduce credit damage in the event of a foreclosure.

Chapter **22**

Ten Consumer Protections Everyone Needs to Know

It has been said that a person can't be too good-looking or have too many friends. This has never been truer than in the world of credit — at least the part about friends. The world of credit can be complex, unforgiving, and very expensive! The credit-granting, credit-reporting, and credit-scoring industries have become increasingly complex and powerful to the point where they are used for everything from issuing credit cards to getting jobs. Consumer advocates recognized that we need effective ways to keep errors, both yours and theirs, from seriously complicating your life. The result is a series of laws, protections, and agencies whose purpose is to keep the credit game honest and give consumers a fair opportunity to access the American financial system. These protections may not always work as you'd like, but if they didn't exist, you'd be at the mercy of big business, and that's no place you want to be.

In this chapter, we cover our top ten legal protection resources you have to guide you in dealing with the world of consumer credit.

The Fair Debt Collection Practices Act

Being protected is especially important when a debt collector comes a-calling. The Fair Debt Collection Practices Act (FDCPA) limits debt collectors' activities and spells out your rights. Highlights include

>> Prohibiting collectors from abusing you, being unfair, and trying to trick you into paying.

>> Applying the law to most personal debts, including credit cards, auto loans, medical debts, and debts secured by your home.

>> Defining when and where a debt can be collected — for example, between 8 a.m. and 9 p.m., or not at work.

>> Requiring a validation notice that specifies how much you owe and what you should do if the debt isn't yours or has been paid already.

>> Allowing you to just say no. If you don't want to hear from a collector, you can write to the collection agency and demand that it not contact you again. Doing so doesn't satisfy a legitimate debt, but it ends collector contact. It may, however, begin legal contact to sue you for the debt.

>> Giving you the right to sue for breach of the rules. You have a year to bring action for violations.

The Bankruptcy Abuse Prevention and Consumer Protection Act

The Bankruptcy Abuse Prevention and Consumer Protection Act (BAPCPA) revised the process of getting a fresh start when you are overwhelmed by debt. The major provisions in this law include

>> Mandatory credit counseling before filing

>> Stricter eligibility for Chapter 7 filing to encourage Chapter 13

>> Fewer debts discharged and fewer state exemptions

>> Tax returns and proof of income required for means test

>> Mandatory five-year Chapter 13 plan if over your state's median income

>> Mandatory financial management education after filing

>> Time between Chapter 7 filings increased to eight years

Bankruptcy was designed to give you the ultimate protection of the courts from your creditors. The process can be as effective as it is damaging to your credit, and you should use it with great care, and only if you've already considered less damaging courses of action.

In some states, you can file your own bankruptcy petition (called *pro se*); in others, you need an attorney. Regardless, we recommend that you use an attorney who does this for a living. A poorly thought out or executed bankruptcy can leave you with unresolved debts and deprive you of the opportunity to use this protection again for several years. A good bankruptcy attorney will spend a significant amount of time with you to compare bankruptcy with other possible ways of handling financial problems.

See Chapter 8 for advice on how to determine whether bankruptcy is for you.

Your Lawyer

Lawyers often get a bad rap, but if you want an effective weapon in providing consumer protection, you need look no further. Whether your issue is a debt collector, a retailer who won't step up to resolve a problem, or a contract with unsuspected gotcha clauses, a knowledgeable and persistent attorney is hard to beat. Yes, we know, lawyers are expensive, but there are times when only the best will do. Using a second-rate attorney is like showing up at a gunfight with the second-fastest gunslinger. Better not to show up at all!

Here are some points to consider when looking for a consumer attorney:

» Nothing is better than a referral from a satisfied friend, colleague, or relative. Ask someone in whom you have confidence. You may get a great referral or a solution you hadn't thought of.

» Look for someone who does a lot of what you need. Like picking a heart surgeon, you want lots of experience here.

» If you already have a lawyer, ask for a specialist recommendation.

» Check your local American Bar Association affiliate or attorney association. They often maintain lawyer referral services.

» Look for someone your gut says you can work with. Is the lawyer concerned about you and your problem? Always interview more than one attorney. This situation is important.

>> Don't be deterred by hourly rates. A good attorney who charges more can be a bargain if you get resolution quickly and permanently.

>> Get all agreements in writing to avoid miscommunication. Be sure to read the agreement before you sign it, and ask about anything that's not clear to you.

Coronavirus Aid, Relief, and Economic Security (CARES) Act

In March 2020, Congress passed the Coronavirus Aid, Relief, and Economic Security (CARES) Act to help minimize the impact of the COVID-19 pandemic. The CARES Act provides a number of important financial safeguards intended to last until the crisis is over or for a set period of time afterward. Given Congress's penchant for keeping laws on the books long after originally intended, and because no one at this time can tell when or if the crisis will be resolved, here are some relevant highlights of the CARES Act:

>> **Protections for renters:** If you rent in federally subsidized housing or are renting from an owner who has a federally or government-sponsored enterprise (GSE)–backed mortgage (for example, Federal Housing Administration [FHA], Veterans Affairs [VA], U.S. Department of Agriculture [USDA], Fannie Mae, or Freddie Mac), the CARES Act may provide for a suspension or moratorium on evictions.

>> **Protections for homeowners:** If you have a federally or GSE-backed mortgage and had a hardship caused by COVID-19, you have the right to request and obtain a forbearance extension for up to another 180 days (for a total of up to 360 days), without additional fees, penalties, or additional interest (beyond scheduled amounts). The law prohibits GSE lenders and servicers from beginning or finalizing a judicial or nonjudicial foreclosure or sale against you.

>> **Protections for those with student loans:** You got automatic suspension of principal and interest payments on federally held student loans through September 30, 2020. And what's more, suspended payments count toward any student loan forgiveness program, as long as all other requirements of the loan forgiveness program are met.

Lenders must report any current loans on which they offer forbearance to the credit bureaus as being current as long as the terms of the agreement are observed.

TIP

Although not part of the law, the three main credit bureaus are allowing free weekly credit reports at least through April 2021.

Statute of Limitations Laws

This protection is worthy of Perry Mason: "I object, Your Honor, for this charge is too old." Well, maybe Perry didn't say exactly that, but he'd be happy to see that each state has a law called a *statute of limitations (SOL)* that sets a limit on how long a debt collector can sue you in court, depending on the type of loan you allegedly owe. This is only fair, because after several years, who keeps all those receipts and slips of paper? Either hurry up and sue or forget about it!

This protection isn't automatic; you have to ask for it. What do you need to know and do? Read on.

>> If a debt is past the SOL, the creditor can't successfully sue you in court to collect it. But you must show up and prove that the debt is too old.

>> Credit reports show a delinquency for seven years. This has nothing to do with the time a debt is collectible.

>> The period used to figure how old your debt is starts when you miss a payment and never make another one. A payment may restart the SOL clock, depending on the state in which you live.

Your State Attorney General

Every state has an attorney general. All attorneys general have at least one thing in common: One of their primary responsibilities is to enforce their states' consumer protection laws. Every state has a consumer protection statute prohibiting deceptive acts and practices. These statutes include laws that address specific industries or practices. For example, many FACT Act protections, especially for credit reporting, have stricter state regulations, giving you more rights and a local resource for help.

State attorneys general love to go after abuses and illegalities in the marketplace, including deceptive trade practices, telemarketing and Internet fraud, fake charities, ID theft, and false or misleading advertising. It's good press for them and good protection for you. Generally, these public officials have a low tolerance for financial shenanigans. So if you think you're being abused, taken advantage of, or scammed in a credit or personal finance transaction, this is the office to call.

I've had good luck working with the consumer protection sections of several state attorneys general. If you decide to ask them for help, we suggest that you be organized and to the point, and have the pertinent information at hand. Attorneys general are no-nonsense law enforcement officials who appreciate you calling for their help but not wasting their time.

The Consumer Financial Protection Bureau

Reforming our financial system isn't easy, and the Feds know it, so they formed a new agency — the Consumer Financial Protection Bureau, or CFPB — to carry on the fight of protecting you long after the ink dried on the Dodd–Frank Wall Street Reform and Consumer Protection Act (the legislation that created the CFPB). Not since J. Edgar Hoover headed up the FBI has a federal agency had such far-reaching powers. The CFPB sets rules for payday lenders, credit card issuers, and all the players in between. Here are the major protections this agency delivers:

» Need information? Use the question-and-answer service at www.consumer finance.gov/askcfpb/ for inquiries about mortgages, student loans, debt collections, credit reports, and more.

» Have a complaint? Go to www.consumerfinance.gov/complaint/ and let 'em have it. Bank accounts, credit cards, credit reporting, debt collections, money transfers, mortgages, student loans, and consumer loans are among the topics you can get help with. You complain, and the CFPB forwards your beef to the company and works to get an answer. It reviews the response and shares it with other agencies to identify patterns of abuse and write better regulations. It also sends you email updates and has a secure consumer portal that you can use to track your complaint and give feedback about company responses to help the CFPB prioritize complaints. Just like the *Dragnet* guys: dum-ta-dum dum!

» It requires anyone who issues credit or prepaid cards to give you better, more easily understandable terms-and-cost disclosures.

» If you have to sign it, you should be able to understand it. The CPFB assures that paperwork is understandable.

>> It helps set rules on transaction fees for interchange activity, like on your Visa or MasterCard.

>> It closely regulates consumer credit counseling, debt settlement, and debt collectors to keep you from being victimized.

The Credit Card Accountability, Responsibility, and Disclosure Act

Fed up with tricky terms, excessive penalties, fees, and unfair banking practices, Congress enacted the Credit Card Accountability, Responsibility, and Disclosure Act (CARD Act) to give you a fair playing field in the area of credit cards. Here are your major protections:

>> Credit card companies can't raise card interest rates except under specific circumstances, such as at the end of a promotional rate, or when a variable interest rate index to which your card is tied rises, or if you're 60 days late on a payment. Also, double cycle interest billing, which used your average daily balance for the current and previous billing cycles to charge you more, is no longer allowed.

>> If your rate or terms change, you get 45 days' notice to plan what to do.

>> You can opt out of changes you don't like. Doing so may cause your account to be closed, but you can pay off the debt under the old terms.

>> Card companies can't issue cards to people under 21 who have no income. This sounds like a no-brainer, but for years creditors had been giving students credit despite their having no income to repay their charges.

>> Creditors must give you at least 21 days after a bill is mailed to make your payment. The due date can't be before the mail is delivered or on a weekend, a holiday, or a day when the creditor is closed for business. If you're late, fees are limited to a maximum of $25.

>> All payment amounts above the minimum payment due must be applied to the balance with the highest interest rate, not the lowest.

>> If you exceed your credit limit, the card company must ask you whether you want that transaction to be processed and incur an over-limit fee. Saying "no thank you" results in the purchase being denied but also saves you the over-limit fee. Even if you say yes, the fee can't exceed the amount by which you exceed the credit limit. So if you exceed your limit by $10, the fee can't be more than $10.

The Fair and Accurate Credit Transactions Act

Fairness is something you can hope for in your dealings with the credit bureaus and those other consumer-reporting bureaus that are increasingly in the news. But before the protections afforded in the Fair and Accurate Credit Transactions Act (FACT Act or FACTA) became effective, fairness was strictly in the eye of the beholder. And the beholder wasn't you! Congress acted to end a number of perceived and real abuses.

Congress understood that the nation's banking system was becoming increasingly dependent on credit reporting, that inaccurate reports resulted in unfair and inefficient banking, and that you have a right to privacy. The result is that you now have more control over what's said about you in credit bureau files and who can access your information. You also have the right to dispute errors or out-of-date information and to get a free copy of your credit report from each bureau every year. Not bad for the crowd from Washington, D.C.! Here are your main protections:

>> You must be told about any negative action taken as a result of information contained in your credit report, and you must be given free access to the same information. If the interest rate on your favorite credit card goes up, for example, you get to see a copy of the report that contains the data that led to that increase.

>> You can find out what information is in your personal file. No more secrets! It's your information and your file, so you can look at it.

>> You can get a free copy of your credit report at least every 12 months if you ask for one. You can also get a free report whenever you're the object of identity theft or fraud, you're on public assistance, or you're unemployed but expect to apply for employment within 60 days.

>> You have the right to know your credit score. This score used to be as big a secret as what was in your bureau files. Score watching has become a favorite pastime for many and a profitable business for others.

>> The data in your file must be accurate, verifiable, and current. If data is incorrect or too old, you need only to ask, and it will be verified or removed pronto.

>> Only those who have a legitimate business purpose can see your file, and you can stop everyone from accessing your file without your express permission if you like. Usually only creditors, insurers, employers, landlords, and others with whom you do business get to see what's in your file. You can slam the door on everyone with a credit freeze.

The Federal Trade Commission

The Federal Trade Commission (FTC) is the alter ego of the Bureau of Consumer Protection (BCP). Although it doesn't deal with individual consumer complaints, it does protect consumers by accumulating and analyzing complaints and then taking industry-wide action to address issues that you bring to it. Some examples of BCP protections are your ability to get a free annual credit report, the National Do Not Call Registry to block unwanted telemarketing calls, and appliance disclosure stickers that show the energy costs of home appliances, to name just a few.

The BCP looks out for unfair, deceptive, or fraudulent practices in the marketplace. It investigates and sues companies and people who violate the law. It also develops rules to protect you and requires businesses to give you better disclosure of your costs, rights, and dispute-resolution options. It also collects complaints about consumer fraud and identity theft and makes them available to law enforcement agencies across the country.

Of the bureau's seven divisions, here are the five that you may find useful:

>> **Advertising practices:** Enforces truth-in-advertising laws. If an offer seems too good to be true and it is, complain to the FTC.

>> **Financial practices:** Protects you from deceptive and unfair practices in the financial services industry, including predatory or discriminatory lending practices, deceptive or unfair loan servicing and debt collection, and fraudulent credit counseling and debt settlement companies.

>> **Marketing practices:** Responds to Internet, telecommunications, and direct-mail fraud; spam; fraudulent work-at-home schemes; and violations of the Do Not Call provisions of the Telemarketing Sales Rule.

>> **Privacy and identity protection:** Protects your financial privacy, investigates data breaches, helps consumers whose identities have been stolen, and implements laws and regulations for the credit reporting industry, including the FACT Act.

>> **Enforcement:** Sues to address issues on these practices.

REMEMBER

Your complaint, comment, or inquiry may help identify a pattern of violations requiring law enforcement action, but the FTC doesn't resolve individual consumer disputes.

Chapter **23**

Ten Strategies for Dealing with Student Loans

S tudent loans are hard to live with and, for many, hard to live without! Few question the value of a post-secondary education, whether it be in a technical field, for a skilled trade, or for a four-year (or more) degree. More education frequently yields a better, fuller life as well as more income. But with the cost of education rising fast and the job market always unpredictable, there is a growing disconnect between the cost and the benefit. This is demonstrated by the default rate of student loans, which has been on an upward trend, with a recent two-year default rate of 10 percent. So how do you get the benefits you want and need without the risk of owing more than you can pay? This chapter is just what you're looking for, with our favorite heads-up advice to keep you moving in the right direction.

Differently Than Other Loans

The way that student loans are reported often catches people off guard. What most of us didn't know when we were in school is that, depending on how your education is funded, you may have a new loan every semester. That equates to up to two loans per year, or a total of eight smaller loans hitting your credit report instead of just one big one, even though you may pay them all with one check each month. When you start repaying the loans, each of them will reflect being paid on time (or not).

All this activity can build your credit score, but failing to pay can sink you big-time if you end up defaulting.

Another unique feature of student loans is that they are not normally discharge-able in a Chapter 7 bankruptcy. A student loan is a commitment that follows you until you honor it, regardless of how long it takes.

If you are not yet convinced that student loans are different from garden-variety credit card and auto loans, don't forget that in a Chapter 13 bankruptcy, they can grow even bigger! See the section on bankruptcy later in this chapter.

Dealing with the Collection Process

Now that you know the stakes are high, you'll want to handle any collection process quickly. The key to minimizing damage from a defaulted student loan is to address it right away. Don't procrastinate or ignore the letters and calls. Private student loans may charge off in as few as 120 days rather than the traditional 180 days for normal loans. Early action can enable you to handle loan issues quickly with the servicer rather than a collection agency. Servicers are more likely to work with you to come up with a solution that works for both you and the lender. (For more information on charge-offs, see Chapter 6.)

Federally guaranteed student loans, in particular, may offer alternatives to help you get through a financially challenging period and avoid the prospect of default altogether. Contact your loan servicer at the first sign you may have difficulty and they can discuss alternatives with you. Here are two of those alternatives:

>> **Forbearance:** While in forbearance, your loan payments are temporarily suspended or reduced. However, interest continues to accrue, so be sure you understand the terms of the agreement. During the COVID-19 pandemic,

federal student loans were proactively placed on forbearance to protect student loan borrowers.

>> **Deferment:** When a loan is placed in deferment, your payments are suspended and interest usually does not accrue, although that isn't universal. If interest continues to accrue, you'll need to be prepared to repay it when the deferment period ends.

These tools may help you avoid defaulting or even becoming late with your payments if you act soon enough.

TIP

Before you call or write to the loan servicer (we suggest that you begin with a call and follow up in writing), organize your thoughts. Treat this as a very important job interview. Explain coherently why you weren't able to pay: medical issues, job loss, pay reductions, armed-service call-up, or family emergency. If you're calling to propose a payment alternative, have a number prepared and be able to justify it based on your budget. Call your servicer or the U.S. Department of Education information line at 800-872-5327, but be sure to do it before you miss a payment.

REMEMBER

Collectors are not obligated to offer you the best repayment terms you can get. They just want to get as much money from you as fast as they can. A loan servicer is much more likely to steer you to programs that will keep you out of collections, but you have to act fast.

Quick action also means that any delinquencies will be early, which typically gives you more options to get on top of the situation. The later you are, the fewer options are available to you.

Identifying the Best Repayment Option for Your Situation

A huge number of repayment programs are available, and they change all the time. We suggest that you check out the big sites that deal with them, such as Federal Student Aid (https://studentaid.gov/manage-loans/repayment/plans) and FinAid (www.finaid.org).

TIP

If you qualify for student loan forgiveness, you may have to pay income tax on any amount that is forgiven.

Taking Your Loans to Bankruptcy

Because the value of your education can't be repossessed, a student loan generally can't be wiped out in a bankruptcy. And if you're not careful, you could end up increasing the amount you owe if you choose a Chapter 13 bankruptcy filing. Trying to get rid of student loan debt through a bankruptcy is difficult and perilous, but in some cases it can be done.

Most debtors do not qualify to discharge (eliminate) student loan debt in a Chapter 7. The exception comes when you can prove to the court that repaying your student loans would cause you undue hardship. This provision is known as the *hardship exemption.* One size doesn't fit all, and the criteria can vary by court. Your best chance is if your income is very low or your loans are from a for-profit trade school.

Here are some factors the court may look for:

>> **Poverty:** Based on your current income and expenses, you can't maintain a minimal standard of living for yourself and your dependents if you are forced to repay your loans.

>> **Persistence:** Your current financial situation is likely to continue for a significant part of the repayment period.

>> **Good faith:** You have made a good-faith effort to repay your student loans.

REMEMBER

If you have a Health Education Assistance Loan (HEAL), your loan is more than seven years past due, and repayment would impose an "unconscionable" burden on your life, you may be able to get a discharge. A qualified attorney can advise you on your chances for a discharge.

Dealing with the Prospect of Default

Before you can be late on your loan, you have to have used up your grace period (the length of time you have after leaving school before you have to make your first payment). Determining when you have used up your grace period can be complex. Each type of loan may have a different grace period. For example, if you have a federal Stafford loan, your grace period is six months, while it is nine months for a federal Perkins loan. Federal PLUS loans can be based on when they were issued (see `https://studentaid.gov/app/launchPLUS.action` for more info). Check your loan documents or contact your lender to find out when your grace period runs out.

Additionally, to provide relief during the COVID-19 pandemic, the U.S. Department of Education stopped collection activity on defaulted federally owned student loans and/or grant overpayments. In addition, the Department of Education temporarily set interest to 0 percent on defaulted federally owned student-aid debt between March 13, 2020, and December 31, 2020, so be sure to check https://studentaid.gov/announcements-events/coronavirus to see if any time periods are extended. You can also still make payments if you choose.

Here are some simple steps that may help keep you out of trouble:

>> **Keep in communication with your lender or servicer.** If you move, tell them. Being hard to find isn't a plus. If they send you a letter or an email, read it. Ignoring a potential problem only allows it to grow more serious.

>> **Find out which plans are available to you.** Federal loans are usually based on a ten-year repayment plan. If you can't or don't want to have that big of a bite taken out of your earnings, change your repayment plan. Extending your payments costs you less each month but more over time. You get to decide what's best for you. (See the earlier section "Identifying the Best Repayment Option for Your Situation.")

>> **If you have a private loan, contact your lender for forbearance options.** Private loans are different from federal loans and are not eligible for income-based repayment or other federal plans, deferments, or forgiveness. Your private lender may offer other types of forbearance plans, but expect to pay for them. They may include interest-only payments for a set period.

>> **Look to community banks and credit unions for refinancing options of private student loans.** An example is the cuGrad Private Student Loan Consolidation program (https://consolidation.custudentloans.org). Available from many not-for-profit credit unions, it can be used to refinance and consolidate existing private student loan debt into one payment at a lower monthly rate.

WARNING

Interest accrues on all types of loans during forbearances and on some types of loans during deferment, increasing your total debt.

Gaining Student Loan Forgiveness

In most cases, your loans are yours to have and to hold until you pay them back or expire trying. However, on some occasions student loans may be forgiven, canceled, or discharged. Following is a summary of the types of loan absolution that are available.

Different rules govern Direct Loans, Perkins Loans, and Federal Family Education Loans (FFEL). Be sure to know which rules apply to your loans.

>> **Total and Permanent Disability Discharge:** Like the name says, this discharge is for those who have been permanently disabled by military service or those receiving Social Security Disability. You also qualify if your physician certifies that you couldn't work for the last five years, your impairment can be expected to last for at least five years, or you are expected to die.

>> **Death Discharge:** This one comes into play if you die. No life, no loan.

>> **Discharge in Bankruptcy:** See the section "Taking Your Loans to Bankruptcy" earlier in this chapter.

>> **Closed School Discharge:** Direct Loans and FFEL are forgiven only if your school folds.

>> **False Certification of Student Eligibility, Unauthorized Payment Discharge, Unpaid Refund Discharge:** To qualify for this discharge, your school has to have messed up in a major way, like approving your loan for a degree in law enforcement when you have a felony record disqualifying you as a law enforcement officer or giving money to an identity thief in your name.

>> **Teacher Loan Forgiveness:** This discharge may be yours if you have taught full-time in a low-income elementary or secondary school or educational service agency for five consecutive years. Only $17,500 of your subsidized or unsubsidized loans are forgiven. PLUS loans cannot be included.

>> **Public Service Loan Forgiveness (includes Teacher Loan Forgiveness):** If you work in a specified public service job or nonprofit and make 120 payments on your Direct Loans (beginning after October 1, 2007), the remaining balance that you owe may be forgiven.

>> **Perkins Loan Cancellation and Discharge:** Federal Perkins Loans may be cancelled if you perform certain types of public service or are employed in certain occupations. Generally, each complete year of service gets a percentage of your loan canceled. Occupational categories include volunteers in the Peace Corps or ACTION program (including VISTA), teachers, members of the U.S. armed forces (serving in areas of hostility), nurses and medical technicians, law enforcement and corrections officers, Head Start workers, child and family services workers, and professional providers of early intervention services.

You can find more info at https://studentaid.gov/manage-loans/forgiveness-cancellation.

Lowering Your Bill While You're in School

There is no need to let the bill for your student loans grow while you're in school. Unless you have a subsidized loan, interest accrues and accumulates during the term of your education. Consider these strategies to reduce or eliminate your interest buildup.

TIP

>> **Pay your interest as it accrues.** For students trying to save money on student loan debt, one solution is to make payments of at least the new interest that accrues during the in-school and grace periods. There are no prepayment penalties on federal and private student loans, so you can make interest-only payments. When making a payment, include a note asking for the payment to be applied to interest.

   If you have both subsidized and unsubsidized student loans, specify that the extra payment should be applied to the unsubsidized loans.

   Paying off interest early not only saves you money, but also enables you to get used to working with your student loan servicer and helps you establish a relationship for successful repayment. It also gets you in the habit of making payments. Plus, you may get some tax benefits! As much as $2,500 in interest paid on student loans may be deductible on your federal income tax return. This may result in a refund that you could use to prepay a portion of your loan to lower the cost of your loan even further. Sweet! See IRS Publication 970 (www.irs.gov/publications/p970) for details.

>> **Pay both interest and principal.** Doing so gives you all the benefits listed in the preceding section, plus it reduces your principal, which seriously lowers your future payments. A $5,500 loan might accrue $31 a month in interest. Paying the interest as you go could result in a savings of about $1,500. Paying on the principal will lower the debt even more.

>> **Work a little to save a lot.** You don't need a full-time job to make a big difference in future loan payments. If you can earn only $57 per month (or $13.25 a week, or $1.89 a day), you can pay all the interest that will accrue on a typical $10,000 unsubsidized Stafford loan throughout four years of college and your six-month grace period. This means you can get your diploma owing only $10,000 instead of $13,060 (your principal plus interest). And don't forget, you may get a fat tax deduction as a bonus for deducting the interest you pay on your loans each year.

Keeping Up with Your Loans After You're Out

Remember, federal student loans are real loans, just like car loans or mortgages. You must repay your student loans even if your financial circumstances become difficult. Your student loans cannot be canceled because you didn't get the job you expected or you didn't complete your education (unless you couldn't complete your education because your school closed, as explained in the earlier section "Gaining Student Loan Forgiveness").

You need to make payments to your loan servicer. Each servicer has its own process, so check with your servicer if you aren't sure how or when to make a payment. You are responsible for staying in touch with your servicer and making your payments, even if you do not receive a bill. It's your job to know who services your loan(s).

A lot of repayment plan options are available; see our summary in the "Identifying the Best Repayment Option for Your Situation" section, earlier in this chapter. How much you have to pay and for how long depends on the plan you choose, so it's critical that you understand and act on your options. We strongly suggest that you figure your real repayment amount under each plan before you pick one.

You may be able to consolidate your loans. Understand what consolidating means for you and how it may affect your future payments. You may also want to consider loan forbearance or deferment to temporarily reduce or postpone payments if you go back to school, join the military, or experience a hardship.

You may qualify for discharge, cancellation, or forgiveness in certain circumstances that we cover earlier in this chapter.

WARNING

Although student loans do offer generous terms, the danger here is that many young people just out of school don't have much experience budgeting and living on their own. You may find yourself in a real-live "grown-up" job with a salary that makes you feel like a millionaire, and you may start spending like a millionaire, too. Without tools such as a spending plan, you may quickly lose control of credit and debt responsibility and find negative items being added to your credit report. See Chapter 18 for tips on creating a spending plan so you're sure to have the money to pay your loan installments.

Setting Limits During the Planning and Application Process

Beware of passion and peer pressure. Deciding your financial limits early in the game saves you from the emotions that are sure to surface as you narrow down your choices. Begin by setting a value for the education you're pursuing get in the field you plan to enter. Don't know your career choice yet? Then we strongly suggest that you minimize loans until you do. Consider community colleges. Like buying a house before you know where you'll be working or what you can afford, buying an expensive education without knowing what type of job or salary you're likely to get is a mistake.

TIP

Shop around with different types of lenders, including the government, private nonprofit sources like your state student loan authority, private lenders, banks, and credit unions. Give extra points to those lenders that keep and service the loans they originate. Keep Parent PLUS Loans and cosigning to a minimum.

Getting Help if You're in the Military

The GI Bill (https://benefits.va.gov/gibill) offers substantial benefits to service personnel who have at least 30 days of active duty. More than one program is available, and programs typically offer tuition, books, and housing allowances. Be sure to check your eligibility before you take on any student loan debt. Here are three simple steps to consider:

>> **Reduce your interest rates.** Currently serving active-duty personnel are eligible to have interest rates lowered to 6 percent on *all* student loans taken out prior to active-duty military service under the Servicemembers Civil Relief Act (SCRA; formerly the Soldiers and Sailors Act). The SCRA provides protections for military members as they enter active duty and includes items such as rental agreements, security deposits, prepaid rent, evictions, installment contracts, credit card interest rates, mortgage interest rates, mortgage foreclosures, civil judicial proceedings, automobile leases, life insurance, health insurance, and income tax payments. It also provides benefits to dependents. Ask your loan servicer how to apply.

>> **Opt for Income-Based Repayment (IBR) and Public Service Loan Forgiveness (PSLF).** These are two great options to repay federal student loans. IBR ties the amount of your monthly payment to your income and

family size. PSLF can forgive any remaining balance on federal student loans after you make ten years of on-time qualified payments while working full-time in public service, like active-duty military service or service with the government or certain nonprofit organizations.

Begin IBR as soon as possible so that every payment you make is a qualifying monthly payment. Make 120 qualified monthly payments, and the balance of your loan can be forgiven.

>> **Manage your private loans.** After you've chosen options for your federal loans, remember that private loans don't qualify for IBR or PSLF. Postponing payments on private loans through deferment or forbearance may give you short-term relief if you're having trouble making ends meet. The terms and conditions of these payment plans vary, but for most private student loans interest continues to accrue after you suspend your payments. This means that your debt grows while you wait. You may be better off paying back your private loans if you can afford it. If you can't afford to repay your loans while you're on active duty, ask your servicer about interest-only payments instead of deferment or forbearance. This stops your loan balance from growing while providing you with some relief.

TIP

If you run into trouble keeping up with your payments, contact your Judge Advocate General for assistance.

» **Getting the best help**

» **Preparing your credit and minimizing the damage**

Chapter **24**

Ten Ways to Deal with a Mortgage Meltdown

For most people, a house is more than just a building you live in. It's a place you worked hard to earn, plan a life, grow a family, and make memories. It's a home. Sometimes those dreams don't come true and that mortgage can become unsustainable. But misinformation, stress, and denial can make it hard to accept the writing on the wall when you're in trouble with your mortgage.

Lenders may take a soft approach to early mortgage delinquencies, hoping you can get back on track. Unfortunately, when you can't get back on track, they can take a hard line on foreclosures. If you owe a past-due balance on a credit card, you'll get phone calls and letters that feel like harassment. Mortgage holders aren't nearly as aggressive when you're late on your payments. After all, they have security for their loan: your home. To them, that dwelling you live in is collateral that can be sold to recoup their losses.

This chapter outlines ten things you need to know and do after you realize you aren't going to be able to pay back the mortgage but before you leave or are asked to leave your home.

Knowing When You're in Trouble

You aren't in trouble if you owe more than the value of your home. You aren't in trouble if your roof leaks and you can't afford to fix it (although that may be an early warning sign). You may be in trouble if you can't pay your real estate taxes, but chances are, your unpaid taxes won't result in the bank calling. But you are *definitely in trouble* if you are late on your mortgage payments and have a feeling you're on the edge of a cliff and at any moment could fall off and into the foreclosure abyss.

If you're late on a single payment, you can probably just catch up. There may be a late fee, a hike in interest rate, or a penalty. At that point, it's financially advantageous for your lender to say, "Thank you, but this fee is a reminder to not be late again." On the other hand, if you've fallen several months behind, your mortgage lender might say, "No thank you!" Why would they do that? It's complicated, but basically, here's how it works: Because most mortgages are packaged into securities and sold in bulk to investors, the default terms for all the mortgages in the "package" must be spelled out in great detail and generally be the same. The result is a rigid set of rules that were made up in advance and have very little flexibility when applied.

It's not that your lender is an unfeeling automaton. As people, they do care. But legal agreements and contracts spell out what they must do. If you're more than 90 days late and you try to make a payment or even two, there is an excellent chance that your money will be refused and returned to you. You may need to make up *all your payments at once* to get any payment applied to your mortgage. A day late is indeed a dollar short when it comes to home mortgages. To further complicate matters as only bankers and lawyers can, the 90-day payment cliff does not include your grace period (typically 15 days). See Chapter 7 for more information about crossing the 90-days-late line, and check out `http://portal.hud.gov/hudportal/HUD?src=/topics/avoiding_foreclosure/foreclosureprocess` for more details on the foreclosure process.

REMEMBER

If you're late on your mortgage, it's vital that you open and answer your mail. The notices you receive generally offer good information about your options. The sooner you seek help, the more options you'll have to save your home.

Knowing How Your State's Laws Treat Foreclosures

Every state has its own foreclosure laws. It is important to know how your state's laws work so that you don't inadvertently cross a line or miss an important date. You can find summaries of the laws for all states at www.foreclosurelaw.org. The following sections outline a few critical differences.

Nonrecourse or recourse

If your lender is foreclosing on your mortgage, whether you live in a "recourse" state or a "nonrecourse" state makes a big difference. In general, if you live in a nonrecourse state, you can't be held liable for any deficiency between the amount you owe and the amount your home sells for in the foreclosure. If you live in a recourse state, the lender may get a deficiency judgment against you in court. For example, if you owe $200,000 on your mortgage but your home nets only $150,000 at the foreclosure sale, the deficiency is $50,000. You would then be responsible for paying that "deficiency" of $50,000.

But knowing which states are nonrecourse states isn't enough. Some states define certain loans as nonrecourse if, for example, they were used only to purchase a home but as recourse debts if part of the proceeds of the loan were used for some other purpose, like paying off credit card debt. Other states limit the amount of the deficiency to the fair value of the property versus the sale price. Still other states have a one-action limit. For example, New York makes lenders choose between the acts of foreclosing on the property and suing to collect the debt.

Consult a housing counselor certified by the U.S. Department of Housing and Urban Development (HUD) or an attorney to get definitive information about the rules for your state.

WARNING

State nonrecourse rules don't apply to the IRS. If you lived in your home for less than two years, you may not qualify for the $250,000 individual home sale exclusion, so you may have a capital gain or phantom income from a foreclosure. See your tax professional for advice.

Judicial or nonjudicial

It is important to know whether your state handles foreclosures on a judicial or nonjudicial basis. If you live in a nonjudicial foreclosure state, your lender does not have to go to court in order to foreclose on your home. This means that the foreclosure can proceed more quickly. In judicial states, foreclosures go through a court. These are called *judicial foreclosures* and may take longer to finalize.

The nonjudicial states include Alabama, Alaska, Arizona, Arkansas, California, Colorado, District of Columbia (sometimes), Georgia, Idaho, Maryland, Massachusetts, Michigan, Minnesota, Mississippi, Missouri, Montana, Nebraska, Nevada, New Hampshire, New Mexico (sometimes), North Carolina, Oklahoma (unless the homeowner requests a judicial foreclosure), Oregon, Rhode Island, South Dakota (unless the homeowner requests a judicial foreclosure), Tennessee, Texas, Utah, Virginia, Washington, West Virginia, and Wyoming.

REMEMBER

Time is your enemy in a nonjudicial state. Lenders are required to give very little notice of foreclosure sales, and once the foreclosure process begins, you may have no further options.

Deciding Whether to Stay or Go

This decision used to be a no-brainer. It was a matter of pride. People would do everything they could to keep their house. The stigma of losing the roof over your head was a big one. Today, though, the decision is often less about emotion and more about the math. Faced with seemingly unrecoverable deficits, some home-owners crunch the numbers and decide to save time, money, and stress by letting the foreclosure process run its course. Some move out, and others stay until the home sells to a new owner or the bank forces them to leave. The following sections describe your options.

Walking away

Strategic default is a new term in the language of mortgages. When the housing bubble burst in 2008, some properties went so far *underwater* (more is owed than the home is worth) that it seemed that it would take years or even decades for the home to regain the value of its mortgage — or it never will. Some borrowers choose to stop making payments, even if they can afford to make them, because they see their house as just another investment, and a bad one at that. Walking away is known as a strategic default.

Potential drawbacks to strategic default include deficiency judgments, significant credit score damage, problems buying or renting in the future, the personal impact of a major life failure, and to a much lesser degree these days, stigma in the eyes of others.

Working with the lender to exit

A more lender-friendly version of a strategic default is the deed-in-lieu of foreclosure option. Rather than go through a long and expensive foreclosure process in order to obtain title, the lender agrees to accept the deed to the property. This option may also incur a deficiency judgment for the difference between the fair market value of the property and the total debt owed. You'll still see damage to your credit scores and possibly a "deed-in-lieu" notation on your credit reports.

Another option in this category is a *short sale,* which involves selling your home for less than what you owe. If you choose this option, you may be subject to a deficiency judgment, depending on the terms you work out with your lender and the laws in your state. A short sale will have an equally serious effect on your credit scores, but don't look for the term *short sale* on your credit report. It's an unofficial phrase that was created to more gently describe settling your loan, and your lender will report the mortgage as "settled."

TIP

In March 2013, Fannie Mae and Freddie Mac began letting some borrowers who are current on their payments give up their underwater properties and cancel the debt under their Mortgage Release and Standard Deed-in-Lieu of Foreclosure programs. If this option is of interest to you and you have a Freddie Mac mortgage, go to https://sf.freddiemac.com/content/_assets/resources/pdf/fact-sheet/deed_in_lieu_fact_sheet.pdf for more information. If you have a Fannie Mae mortgage, go to www.knowyouroptions.com/avoid-foreclosure-overview.

Staying the course

If you decide to do all you can to stay in your home, several courses of action are open to you. The major ones include the following:

>> **FHA Short Refinance:** If you owe more than your home is worth and you want to refinance, the lender can reduce the amount you owe on your first mortgage to no more than 97.75 percent of your home's current market value.

>> **Loan modification/refinancing:** The two main types are the Home Affordable Modification Program (HAMP) for Freddie Mac and Fannie Mae mortgages and conventional refinancing for others. A conventional mortgage servicer or lender may modify your loan to make it more affordable, but each one has its own programs and guidelines. Speak to your servicer about HAMP. If your loan is owned or guaranteed by Freddie or Fannie and you are ineligible for conventional refinancing, HAMP can change the type of your loan from adjustable to fixed, to a longer fixed term, or to a lower interest rate and

can add past-due payments to the principal balance to be repaid over the full mortgage term.

>> **HUD Foreclosure Avoidance Counseling:** HUD offers free counseling to anyone who may be faced with foreclosure. They may be able to help you find alternatives to losing your home, or help with special loan programs to modify or refinance your mortgage or reduce your monthly payments to help you keep your house. To find a HUD counselor near you visit https://apps.hud. gov/offices/hsg/sfh/hcc/fc/index.cfm.

>> **Assistance because of a natural or declared disaster:** Hurricanes, fires, earthquakes, tornadoes, volcanoes, and global pandemics can put lots of people in situations beyond their control. During times of disaster, federal and state governments, lenders, and credit reporting agencies may offer special relief programs. If you've been affected by a disaster, check with your lender about payment accommodations, such as forbearance or deferment, to help you maintain your mortgage payments through a period that is beyond your control.

Tightening Your Spending to Stay in Your Home

Whether your financial life has a ding or two or is upside-down, tightening your budget can help you free up sorely needed cash and get back in control of your situation. If you don't have a budget, now is the perfect time to make one. (See Chapter 18 for details on budgeting.)

Making a budget is basic but effective. Begin by listing all your expenses and then list your income. Look carefully at both sides of the equation, make some cuts to expenses, and look for ways to add to your take-home pay (like reducing your tax withholding) or increase your income with a part time job. For example, if the bank forecloses, you'll lose your cable TV anyway. Cutting cable now may give you the extra cash that helps keep you in your home.

Technically it's not a spending cut, but you can also try to sell some stuff to raise cash for a mortgage payment. We've all seen the "Cash for gold!" signs. Selling old and unused gold or jewelry is something you may want to consider. Having a yard or garage sale, downsizing to one car, and selling your violin should also be on your list. You get the idea. Lightening your load of stuff may buy you the time you need to catch up.

Prioritizing Your Spending to Build Cash

No matter what you choose to do in the event of a mortgage crisis, you're going to need some cash. It may be to pay an arrearage. It may be to come up with first and last month's rent and a damage deposit on a new apartment. Either way, you need to tighten your budget (or create one; see the preceding section). Yes, this step is basic, but as with everything in life, you have to start at the beginning. As described in the preceding section, list all your expenses and then list your income. Take a look at both sides of the equation and determine where you can make changes — by cutting expenses and/or increasing income. (See Chapter 18 for details on budgeting.)

REMEMBER

Car repossessions can happen within weeks — not months — of missing a payment. So if you need your car to get to work, keeping up on your car payment is critically important.

If you can't make your mortgage payment, it's important to save as much of the money you're not sending to your lender as possible. If your payment is $1,000 and you can only scrape together $800, don't spend it on something else. Put the money aside to help ease your transition into a new place.

TIP

Want some help with creating a spending plan? Try a nonprofit consumer credit counseling agency member of the National Foundation for Credit Counseling (www.nfcc.org). Organizations like Operation Hope also offer money management programs. There may be a Hope Inside center near you (https://operationhope.org/credit-and-money-management).

Lessening the Damage to Your Credit

In a nutshell, if you stiff your mortgage lender with a loss in the form of a short sale or foreclosure, your credit will take a much bigger hit than if you come to an agreement to repay or forgive any deficiency. See the section "Assessing the Damage from a Mortgage Meltdown" in Chapter 7 for more on what you'll need to negotiate.

For a person with decent credit and a FICO score in the 720 range, the difference in credit score deduction between a short sale with a deficiency and one without can be more than 50 points. See Chapter 7 for details on the damage to your credit and credit score that various mortgage problems can cause.

Knowing Who to Call

You know that you have the right to remain silent, and remaining silent can be wise in some situations, but not when you're facing a mortgage crisis. If you're behind on your payments, your lender will communicate with you by mail. The worst thing you can do is to remain silent, which could leave the bank no other option than to take legal action (see Chapter 7 for details).

The best thing you can do is to open your mail and speak to your mortgage servicer at once. I also strongly recommend that you contact an independent HUD-approved mortgage counselor (www.hud.gov/i_want_to/talk_to_a_housing_counselor) or your state housing agency. Avoid foreclosure-prevention companies like the plague they are. The best help is easy to find and available for free.

Beware of Scams

It's easy to forget a lifetime of wisdom when the pressure is on and you are desperate for a solution. Knowing that you're vulnerable during a mortgage crisis, scammers will try to charge you money or even trick you into signing your deed over to them. Keep in mind that not everyone out there wants to help you; many just want to help themselves.

Here are some quick scam signs to watch out for:

>> Never pay a fee in advance. The best help is free.

>> Never believe someone who guarantees that they can stop your foreclosure.

>> Be wary of anyone who contacts you and offers to help. Always get a second opinion from a person or an organization you trust.

>> Never hand your mortgage money over to anyone other than your mortgage servicer.

Beefing Up Your Credit

As soon as you default on your mortgage, your credit scores will take a nosedive. You likely won't be able to qualify for new accounts for quite a long time. Now is the time to take steps to improve your credit as much as possible so you can be in a position to move forward.

Pay down as much debt as you can, especially on your credit cards. If you're not making the mortgage payments, put the money toward your credit card balances. Lower credit card balances will help you bump up your scores and reduce your debt burden after the foreclosure proceedings have completed.

Try not to take on any more debt. Any purchases you make should be essentials. It's why having a budget it so important. Digging yourself deeper into debt when you can't pay what you already owe will only make things worse.

Take advantage of other new tools that can help bolster your credit scores, as well. Having things like your on-time cellphone, utility and video streaming payments added can help bolster your credit scores. Services like Experian Boost (www.experianboost.com) can be worth looking into. Just be sure you understand what you're signing up for. Although these kinds of services are free from a cash point of view, you'll likely get marketing offers to tempt you to open your wallet. Be prepared to say no thank you. You may sign up for alternative scoring systems like UltraFICO (www.fico.com/ultrafico), that incorporate information not included in credit reports. Lenders may consider that information in addition to the traditional scores to approve your application.

If you lose your house, you may find yourself renting. Studies have shown that doing so almost always helps build your credit. Talk to your landlord about having your positive rent payments reported or sign up with a rent payment service yourself. Here are a few options:

>> **ClearNow:** www.clearnow.com/creditreporting

>> **eRentPayment:** www.erentpayment.com

>> **PayYourRent:** www.payyourrent.com/residents

>> **Rent Track:** www.renttrack.com

You should know that there may be a nominal fee for these services to report your rent payments, so compare their offers to find the one that's right for your situation.

Consulting an Attorney

You have rights and you have legal options. Only an attorney can give you sound legal advice, so before your mortgage crisis gets too far along, spend the money to get a competent assessment of where you stand and what the law can do to help.

For example, a bankruptcy filing can stop a foreclosure in its tracks — probably not forever, but maybe long enough. A Chapter 7 or 13 bankruptcy may be a way to reduce other debt or the amount of your mortgage that exceeds the value of your home. It may be enough to get you back on track with your mortgage payments. Also, not all mortgage documents are properly drawn and executed. Have a lawyer review your files to see if they are unenforceable or flawed in any way.

REMEMBER

Bankruptcy is a last resort. It's the most serious financial decision you can make related to your debts. It's there for a reason, but that reason is that there is no other financial option.

TIP

A good lawyer who does a lot of foreclosure-prevention work can sometimes work minor miracles, maybe even delaying foreclosure for years, which can help you begin to build your savings account to pay for your next move, or maybe even keep your house.

Index

A

AADMM (American Association of Daily Money Managers), 235

ABA (American Bar Association), 75

ABI (American Bankruptcy Institute), 150

account closures, 28, 57, 221–222, 275

accountant, 114

active-duty alerts, 53, 305, 396

active-duty serviceperson. *See* military personnel

Acts of God, 144, 260, 430

adverse action
  discussion, 50–51
  FACTA rules on, 368
  notification of, 255, 284–286, 373

African Americans
  debt and, 362–364
  homeownership by, 364–366
  inclusion of, 356–357

alarms, 19. *See also specific types of alerts*

alimony, 111–112, 151, 323

American Association of Daily Money Managers (AADMM), 235

American Bankruptcy Institute (ABI), 150

American Bar Association (ABA), 75

apartment rental. *See* renting

APR (annual percentage rate), 21, 380

Asian Americans, 357

Association of Settlement Companies (TASC), 106

ATM cards, 166–167

attorneys. *See also pro bono* attorneys; *pro se* representation
  appearing to court with, 107, 111
  bankruptcy advice from, 147
  consulting on SOL with, 85–86
  for dealing with collections, 97
  debt settlements and, 106
  debt-erasing, 67
  discussion, 407–408

  foreclosure-prevention advice from, 433–434
  hardship program advice from, 418
  legal/document review from, 69
  medical debt settlement advice from, 234
  referring collections to, 92
authorized users, 12, 20, 193
automatic bill payment, 99

B

bad credit. *See also* credit damage
  car buying with, 205–208
  causes of
    bankruptcy, 16–17
    car loans, 16
    discrimination, 16
    medical debt, 15
    mortgage problems, 13–15
    overextension, 63
    student loans, 15
  effects of, 9–10, 23, 30
  insurance scores and, 208–211
  marriage and, 215–216
  minimizing effects of
    job opportunities, 200–201
    overview, 199–200, 326
    rental applications, 201–203
  qualifying for mortgage with, 203–205
  repairing, 10–13
  from strategic default, 15, 428
BALANCE counseling agency
  bankruptcy help, 147
  discussion, 68, 72
  financial assessment, 129
  free mortgage resources, 126–127
  local programs, 365
  student loan help, 141

balance transfer fees, 311

bankruptcy. *See also* Chapter 7 bankruptcy; Chapter 13 bankruptcy; credit counseling; medical bankruptcy

attorney advice for, 150, 433–434

bad credit due to, 16–17

borrowing after declaring, 151

CCPA protections not applicable to, 112

on credit report, 42, 252, 273

debt management versus, 73, 152–154

deletion timeframe for, 17, 28, 123, 275

discussion, 2, 63

divorce and, 10, 160

filing for

caution, 145–146

considerations, 146–148

credit counseling, 70

credit effects, 146, 323–324

dismissing filing, 158

income limitations, 109

limited value, 17

mandatory counseling, 148, 152–154

nonprofit credit counselors, 147–148

requirements, 148–149

solicitations/telemarketing, 160, 163

minorities and, 364

pro se filing for, 147, 406

pros and cons of, 150–151

rebuilding credit after, 159–163

social security number and, 174

unavailable for student loans, 115, 149, 151, 323, 418

Bankruptcy Abuse Prevention and Consumer Protection Act (BAPCPA), 405–406

bankruptcy trustee, 149

banks, 44, 136, 173, 178, 339

Barrett, Melyssa, 356

BCP (Bureau of Consumer Protection), 413

big-ticket creditors, 33–34

bill payment prompt, 99

borrowing, 45, 151, 179

bounced checks, 87

budgeting. *See also* spending plan

during marriage, 216, 354

professional counseling, 353

tools, 351–353

when unemployed, 227–229

Bureau of Consumer Protection (BCP), 413

C

CAP (Claims Assistance Professionals), 231

capacity, 23, 34, 206

car buying

with bad credit, 205–208

considerations in, 207–208

discussion, 2, 322

free credit reports and, 265

car insurance, 346

car lease, 89

car loans

bad credit due to, 16

boosting credit via, 36

discussion, 322

free credit reports and, 265

paying off, 208

repossession and, 141–144

specialty agencies and, 268

during unemployment, 228

CARD Act (Credit Card Accountability, Responsibility, and Disclosure Act of 2009)

complete text of, 191, 370

discussion, 18, 99, 180, 411

limitations of, 371

loopholes in, 197

protections offered by, 369–371

purpose of, 368–369

reporting complaints to, 371

student loans and, 195–197

CARES (Coronavirus Aid, Relief, and Economic Security) Act

discussion, 16, 18, 181

mortgage problems and, 130–131

protections offered by, 408–409

student loans and, 141

cash, 178, 343

casinos, 269

CCPA (Consumer Credit Protection Act), 110–112, 368

Certified Financial Planner (CFP), 350

certified mail, 82, 84, 88

CFA (Chartered Financial Analyst), 350

CFPB (Consumer Financial Protection Bureau)
  complaint system, 58, 91, 371
  on debt settlement services, 106
  discussion, 372, 410–411

Chapter 7 bankruptcy
  Chapter 13 versus, 153, 157
  debt liquidation under, 153
  debt management versus, 153
  deletion timeframe for, 48, 58
  discussion, 17, 154–155
  dismissing filing of, 158
  mandatory counseling in, 156–157
  means test, 148
  qualifying for, 155–156
  tithing under, 156

Chapter 11 bankruptcy, 154–155

Chapter 12 bankruptcy, 155

Chapter 13 bankruptcy
  Chapter 7 versus, 153, 157
  debt management versus, 153
  deletion timeframe for, 58, 253–254
  discussion, 17, 154–155
  dismissing filing of, 158
  mandatory counseling in, 157
  qualifying for, 149, 157
  tithing under, 156

character
  car buying and, 205–206
  credit report for judging, 252–253
  loans and, 23, 34

charged-off account
  7-year period start date on, 52
  auto loan default deficiencies and, 143–144
  deletion timeframe for, 275
  discussion, 101–102
  paid, 104
  steps leading to, 102–103
  unpaid, 103

Chartered Financial Analyst (CFA), 350

Chartered Financial Consultant (ChFC), 350

cheat sheet, 5

check cashers, 21

checking account
  for building credit, 224–225
  discussion, 358
  information from, 60
  specialty agencies and, 269

ChFC (Chartered Financial Consultant), 350

child support
  defaulting on, 42
  discussion, 101
  not dischargeable, 111–112, 117, 151, 323

civil unions. See marriage

Claims Assistance Professionals (CAP), 231

closed-end credit. See installment loans

C.L.U.E. reports, 210, 270

Coast Guard Mutual Aid, 381

collateral, 23, 206

collections. See also charged-off account; medical
    collections
  avoiding getting to
    offering solutions, 95
    overview, 92, 98–100
    promptly contacting creditor, 93–94
  court summons and, 107
  on credit report, 249
  credit score and, 2
  debt management preferable to, 73
  deletion timeframe for, 58, 275
  discussion, 13–14, 364
  FDCPA and
    debtor rights, 77–78
    permitted actions, 78–80
    prohibited actions, 80–81
    protections provided, 375–377
    responding to collections, 84
  harassment from, 81
  help from counselors for, 69
  identity theft and, 166, 400
  internal versus outside, 83, 90
  letters from, 107
  loans and, 34

collections *(continued)*

nonprofit counseling agencies and, 97

paying, 97–98

permissible purpose access and, 267

phone calls from, 78, 81–83, 107

process, 113–114

student loans and, 416–417

success when dealing with

asking for proof of debt, 84

attorneys, 97

communication, 92–96

escalation options, 89–92

nonprofit credit counselors, 96–97

overview, 83

payback arrangements, 86–89

preparation, 96

SOL, 84–85

uncollectible debts, 84–86

suing, 377

threats from, 13, 81, 190–191

community college, 116

Community Financial Services Association of America, 189, 382

community-property laws, 217, 221–222, 238–239

complaints, 58, 91, 371, 391

compounding interest, 351

conforming mortgage, 132

consolidated accounts, 216–218

consolidating loans, 38

consular ID, 178

Consumer Credit Counseling Service of San Francisco, 68

Consumer Credit Protection Act (CCPA), 110–112, 368

consumer databases

breaches of, 19

credit bureaus, 54, 262

credit monitoring of, 296

discussion, 1–2

FICO XD score, 60, 91, 187–188

specialty bureau, 203

Consumer Financial Protection Bureau. *See* CFPB

consumer protections. *See also specific consumer protection laws*

CFPB, 372

collections, 375–377

from credit card abuse, 369–371

credit data, 372–374

credit repair companies and, 378–379

debt settlement and, 382–384

discussion, 17–18, 136, 367–368

history of, 368

legislation aimed at, 46, 50, 368–369, 405

payday loans and, 379–382

SOL and, 384–385

contract reinstatement, 143

contractual due dates, 66–67

Coronavirus Aid, Relief, and Economic Security Act. *See* CARES Act

cosigning

discussion, 12

establishing credit via, 193

loans and, 29–30

for rentals, 203

risks in, 29–30

student loans and, 115

Council on Accreditation, 68

coupons, 343

court

appearances, 107, 112–114

permissible purpose access and, 267

summons, 107, 110–111

court-ordered bank levies, 114

COVID-19 pandemic

chip credit cards and, 173

credit score and, 260

discussion, 181

free credit reports during, 200, 263

student loans and, 141, 419

credit. *See also* credit ecosystem; financial inclusion; spending plan

after death of spouse/partner, 238–240, 420

controlling use of

balance, 312–313

balancing spending and, 25

caution with credit issuers, 313–314

determining credit style, 310–311

overview, 309–310, 358–359

discussion, 1, 22, 177–178

effects of late payments on, 322

good habits with, 358–359, 362

importance of, 179–180

misconceptions about, 178–179

online market and, 43–44

from overseas, 33

percentage use of, 31–33

protecting, 17–19

regulation of, 180–181

as renewable resource, 24–25, 317–318

during retirement, 240–241

spending plan and, 22, 332

three Cs of, 23, 34–35, 205–206

credit bureaus

changed surnames and, 222

collections and, 80

consumer databases

dispute process, 54–56

inaccuracies, 31, 51–52

specialty agencies, 262

credit score simulators, 122

discussion, 10, 18, 24, 247

FACTA rules on, 42

identity theft and, 166–168

inaccuracies and, 283

payback arrangements and, 86

sample opt-out letter, 160

Credit Card Accountability, Responsibility, and Disclosure Act of 2009. See CARD Act

credit cards

authorized users on, 12

cash versus, 178

comparing, 33

cosigning for, 12

credit bureaus and, 31

for establishing credit, 20

foreclosure and, 136

good credit and, 179

identity theft and, 166–167, 173

joint accounts and, 216–218, 239

managing, 24

maximum liability on, 302

maxing out, 28

Medicaid and medical bills on, 232

monthly pay-off of, 31

negotiating hardship program with, 66

new users of, 192–194

paying medical bills with, 232

problems with, 65–66

protections on, 369–371

secured credit card versus, 33

wage garnishments and debt from, 111

credit counseling. See also bankruptcy; Chapter 7 bankruptcy; Chapter 13 bankruptcy; nonprofit credit counselors

benefits of, 70–71

debt and, 69–73

sources of, 71–72, 148, 157, 378

during unemployment, 228

credit damage. See also bad credit

from bankruptcy, 17, 28, 123, 275

discussion, 121–122

to good credit more severe, 123, 161

minimizing, 326

from mortgage problems

CARES Act, 130–131

help, 126–130

Mortgage Forgiveness Debt Relief Act, 130–131

overview, 121–123

reducing damage, 431–433

solutions, 130–131

credit ecosystem

components, 319–321

discussion, 24–25, 318–319

pollutants

bankruptcy, 323–324

negative payment history, 323

overview, 322–323

repairing, 327

surviving, 325–326

sustaining, 321–322

credit freeze

discussion, 19, 52, 167

identity theft and, 394–395

monitoring services, 298, 305–306

credit history, 11, 28, 31

credit invisible. See immigrants; underbanked market

Credit Karma, 122, 362

credit monitoring
  alarms/alerts, 304–305
  caution with, 286–287
  determining need for, 299, 301–302
  discussion, 295–297
  freezing credit and, 298, 305–306
  personal, 300–303
  services offered in, 67, 296–297, 302–303
  tips with, 303–304
  types of, 297–299
credit repair companies. *See also* credit counseling
  discussion, 21, 67
  instant credit rating from, 190
  obligations of, 378
  predatory nature of, 46
  prohibited actions, 379
  reasons to avoid, 45–47
Credit Repair Organizations Act (CROA), 21, 46, 369, 378–379
credit report. *See also* 100-word statements; specialty reporting agencies
  analyzing
    account history, 274
    accounts summary, 249–250, 272–273
    bankruptcy records, 42, 158, 252, 273
    collections, 249
    Equifax account history, 276–278
    Experian account history, 278–279
    general categories, 271–272
    inquiries, 250, 273–274
    negative information, 268
    personal identification information, 248–249, 272
    public record information, 249
    time needed for, 268
    TransUnion account history, 279–280
  cleaning up
    free help, 18
    legal remedies, 50–53
    overview, 43–44
    reviewing report, 47–50, 53
  credit score in relation to, 24, 290
  debt management plan and, 73
  decisions influenced by, 44–45
  discussion, 9–10, 261–262
  employer use of, 23, 44
  free copies of
    additional copies, 201, 262–263
    adverse action, 50–51
    Equifax additional copies, 200–201
    FACTA rules, 18, 89, 262–263, 359, 373
    inaccuracies, 283
    information needed, 264–265
    when to order, 265–266
    where to obtain, 247, 263–264
    yearly copy, 18, 31, 42
  function of, 245–247
  inaccuracies in
    contacting credit bureaus, 283
    contacting creditor, 283–284
    correcting, 283–284
    costs of inaccuracies, 262
    dispute letters, 31
    disputing, 11, 292
    overview, 23, 247, 283
  information not tracked in, 107, 181, 251–252, 282
  information tracked in, 23, 43–44
  insurance use of, 44
  judgements not included on, 107
  judging character via, 252–253
  landlord use of, 44
  lender used of, 23
  limiting access to, 51
  medical debt and, 137, 229–230
  most damaging factors to, 63
  negative information deletion from, 253–255, 275
  non-lending use of, 1–2
  passbook loans and, 188
  permissible purpose access to, 266–267
  placing freeze on, 19, 52, 167–168
  positive information in, 60–61, 255, 275
  sample copies of, 252, 272
  small debts and, 91
  statements of dispute in, 281
  tax liens not included in, 115
  time period covered by, 48
  victim statement in, 167–168

credit score
  Acts of God and, 144
  borrowing and, 45
  charge-offs and, 103–104
  common range of, 285
  components of, 256–259
  composed of three digits, 10, 24, 204, 255
  credit report in relation to, 24, 285, 290
  current market groupings of, 291
  debt management plan and, 154
  deciphering, 251, 287–290
  discussion, 9, 262, 285
  effect of bankruptcy on, 17, 151
  effect of debt settlement on, 105
  effect of foreclosure on, 136
  effect of repossession on, 37
  effect of strategic default on, 17, 132
  FACTA and, 359–360, 373
  factors considered in
    amount of credit, 162
    credit history, 258–259
    new credit, 258–259
    number of accounts, 162
    overview, 23–24, 63
    payment history, 257–258
    proportion of credit use, 162, 258, 293
    timely payments, 161–162, 228, 358
    utilization rate, 28, 257–258
    variety of accounts, 162
  fraud alerts on, 170, 221
  history of, 255–256
  impact of various actions on, 27–28
  inquiries and, 274
  joint credit and, 216–218, 221
  major purchases to boost
    car financing, 36–37
    mortgage, 34–36
    overview, 33–34
    student loans, 37–38
  maximizing
    keeping old accounts, 31, 162
    overview, 287
    reducing debt, 31
    reducing percentage use, 31–33, 162
    savings account, 162
    small purchases, 30–31
    timely payments, 31, 161
  medical debt and, 91, 229–230
  monitoring services, 297
  non-lending use of, 1–2
  obtaining, 251, 264, 284–286
  online quiz, 246
  perfect, 290
  protecting, 17
  range of, 24
  reason statements and, 251, 288, 292–293
  regularly checking, 41–42
  repairing, 10–13, 360
  revolving utilization rate in, 281
  risk-based pricing and, 290–292
  trended data in, 260
credit score simulators, 122
credit unions, 32, 44, 136
credit-based insurance scores. *See* insurance scores
credit-life connection, 1, 9
creditors. *See also* collections; lenders
  calls from, 64
  counseling agencies and, 72
  customer service, 92–96
  directly contacting
    communication suggestions, 94
    complaints, 92
    disputing inaccuracies, 58
    offering solutions, 95
    overview, 83, 90–91
    promptness, 93–94
criminal fines, 151, 282, 324
CROA (Credit Repair Organizations Act), 21, 46, 369, 378–379

D

daily money manager (DMM), 235
dark web, 296
data breaches, 17, 200–201, 302
data sweep services, 298
death, 238–240, 420
debit bureaus. *See* specialty reporting agencies

debit cards, 166–167, 178, 302

debt. *See also* collections; community-property laws; joint debt; medical debt; student loans; undischargeable debt

  African Americans and, 362–364

  asking for proof of, 82, 84

  credit counseling and, 69–70

  credit report and small, 91

  credit score and, 2

  DFCPA rights and, 78

  dispute letters and, 79

  forgiveness of, 135

  good forms of, 38–39

  Hispanics and, 362–364

  managing shared, 218–219

  priority, 149

  reducing, 31, 358

  during retirement, 241

  SOL on, 84–85

  spending plan for, 38–39, 332

debt collections. *See* collections

debt management plan

  bankruptcy versus, 73, 152–154

  credit counseling and, 72–73

  credit score under, 154

  debt settlement versus, 74

debt reduction companies, 67

debt settlement agreements, 105–107

debt settlement services

  consumer protections and, 382–384

  debt management versus, 74

  discussion, 10–11, 22, 106

debt-erasing attorneys, 67

debt-sale, 90, 103

deed-in-lieu of foreclosure, 15, 123, 131, 429

default judgment, 113

deferments, 260, 417

deficiency balance, 132, 134–135

deficiency judgment liens, 134

delinquencies

  7-year period start date on, 52

  in credit report, 49

  discussion, 63

  duration of information from, 57

FACTA requirements on new, 284

  on mortgage, 66–67

  original date on, 105, 253

  on student loans, 58, 117

demand letter, 135

Department of Health and Human Services, 237

Department of Housing and Urban Development (HUD), 68, 126, 128, 365

Department of Justice, 148, 157

Department of Labor, 111–112

Department of the Treasury, 68

deportation, 190

Direct Consolidation Loans program, 117

Direct Loans, 420

Direct Marketing Association Mail Preference Service, 160

Direct Marketing Association Telephone Preference Service, 160

Directory of State and Local Consumer Agencies, 111

disability insurance, 138, 234, 346

disabled veterans, 140–141

disaster codes, 260. *See also* Acts of God

dischargeable debts, 84–85, 106–107. *See also* statutes of limitations

discrimination. *See also* redlining

  bad credit and, 16

  credit reports use to avoid, 45, 194

  discussion, 355–357

  of minorities, 362–366

disenfranchisement. *See* discrimination

disposable earnings, 112, 140. *See also* income

dispute process

  avoiding abuse of, 56, 58

  contacting creditors in, 59

  correcting all credit reports, 54–57

  discussion, 49, 53–54

  dispute letters in, 55–56, 62

divorce

  bankruptcy and, 10, 160

  budgeting during, 354

  credit score and, 30

  discussion, 213–214

  free credit reports during, 266

  possible financial effects of, 10

precautions prior to, 220–221

protecting credit during, 222–224

DMM (daily money manager), 235

doctors, 32

documentation

  of collections process, 111

  of debt settlements, 105–106

  discussion, 59, 166, 174

  of letters sent to collections, 84

  of payback arrangements, 82, 88, 96

  when dealing with errors, 190

Dodd-Frank Wall Street Reform and Consumer Protection Act

  credit scores access and, 285–286

  discussion, 18, 50, 180

  protections under, 195

  purpose of, 368–369

draw period, 35

driver's license number, 174

drunk driving, 324

due date, 100

E

Early Warning Services, 269

early-warning notice, 397

ECOA (Equal Credit Opportunity Act), 180

e-filed tax returns, 21

EIN (employer identification number), 46–47

emergency fund

  discussion, 40, 100

  spending plan and, 312–313, 344–345

  unemployment, 226

Emergency Relief and Construction Act of 1932, 366

employer identification number (EIN), 46–47

employment. *See also* job opportunities

  credit reports and, 1–2, 23, 39

  permissible purpose access and, 267

  problems with, 2, 10, 30, 57, 111

  specialty reporting agencies and, 268, 270

entertainment and meals expenses, 98, 339–340

Equal Credit Opportunity Act (ECOA), 180

Equifax

  180-day reporting period, 137

  account history, 276–278

  credit reports from, 262

  credit score from, 286

  credit score simulators, 122

  discussion, 24, 247

  disputing inaccuracies with, 54–55

  education on fraud, 170

  FACTA and, 372–374

  free credit reports, 18, 200–201, 264

  identity theft and, 167

  sample credit report, 276

equity products, 35

escalation, 89–90

eviction, 2, 88, 149

execution order. *See* judgment execution

Executive Office of the U.S. Trustee, 148, 157

expenses. *See also* budgeting; spending plan

  balancing, 312–313, 320

  decreasing, 64

  living, 40

  reducing entertainment, 98, 339–340

  during retirement, 241

  during unemployment, 227–228

Experian

  180-day reporting period, 137

  account history, 278–279

  credit reports from, 262

  credit score from, 286

  credit score simulators, 122

  discussion, 24, 247

  disputing inaccuracies with, 54–55

  FACTA and, 372–374

  free credit report from, 18, 264

  identity theft and, 167, 170

  information on natural disasters, 144

  sample credit report, 278

Experian Boost service, 60, 181, 194, 292, 433

expired debts, 84–85, 106–107

extended fraud alerts, 171, 305

F

FACTA (Fair and Accurate Credit Transactions Act)
  adverse action rules, 358
  C.L.U.E. reports under, 210
  complete text of, 191
  credit bureaus under, 372–374
  credit reports and, 51
  credit score and, 359–360, 373
  creditors under, 57
  discussion, 42, 50, 180, 369, 412
  FCRA and, 247
  identity protection, 169–170
  installment loans and, 232
  military personnel protections, 88
  protections, 374
  purpose of, 372–373
  requirements on new delinquencies, 284
  rules on free credit report, 18, 262–263, 359, 373
Fair Access to Credit Scores Act, 285, 368–369
Fair and Accurate Credit Transactions Act. See FACTA
Fair Credit Reporting Act. See FCRA
Fair Debt Collection Practices Act. See FDCPA
FAIR Health Consumer, 137
Fair Isaac Corporation. See FICO
Fannie Mae
  creation of, 366
  loans from, 123
  mortgage help from, 129
  programs, 429–430
  strategic default and, 15
FCRA (Fair Credit Reporting Act). See also FACTA
  discussion, 50, 247, 368
  leveling effect of, 359
  protections, 373–374
  purpose of, 372–373
FDCPA (Fair Debt Collection Practices Act)
  on collections, 84
  complete text of, 191
  debtor rights under, 77–78
  discussion, 13, 18, 180, 369
  FTC and, 91
  minorities and, 364
  protections, 375–377, 405

FDIC, 178
Federal Family Education Loans (FEEL), 420
Federal Housing Authority (FHA), 366, 132
Federal National Mortgage Association. See Fannie Mae
Federal Student Aid, 417
federal taxes. See taxes
Federal Trade Commission. See FTC
FEEL (Federal Family Education Loans), 420
FHA (Federal Housing Authority), 366, 132
FHA Short Refinance, 429
FICO (Fair Isaac Corporation). See also Ultra-FICO score
  credit score
    access to credit, 189
    credit counseling, 96
    history, 255–256
    impacts infographic, 122
    national distribution, 288
    overview, 10, 24, 285–286
    range, 257
    time distribution, 289
  debt management plan and, 154
  discussion, 210
  on effects of Chapter 7 filings, 17
  trended data, 260
FICO Score XD, 60, 91, 187–188
FinAid, 417
financial aid, 115–116
financial documents
  safe storage of, 393–394
  shredding, 19, 394
financial inclusion, 355–357
financial system
  educating oneself on, 359–360, 362
  misconceptions about, 16, 178–179, 361
  participating in, 358
first-time credit. See new credit
forbearance, 129, 260, 416, 419
foreclosure. See also mortgage problems
  CARES Act and, 181
  credit score and, 2, 136
  discussion, 34, 124, 425

judicial, 427–428

late payments and, 66–67

managing, 131–132

nonjudicial, 428

preparing for, 136

state laws on, 427–428

state timeline chart of, 133

foreign credit cards, 187

Form 982 (Reduction of Tax Attributed Due to Discharge of Indebtedness), 135

Form 1099-A, 135

Form 1099-C, 134

Form 9465, 114

Form 14039 (Identity Theft Affidavit), 399

Form W-4, 100

fraud

after natural disasters, 144

blocking, 171–172

discussion, 43

free credit report in cases of, 263

mail, 393

protection during retirement, 240–241

fraud alerts

after identity theft, 167

discussion, 52, 170, 305

extended, 171, 305

free credit reports and, 263

Freddie Mac, 429–430

freezes. *See* credit freeze

friendly foreclosure, 15

FTC (Federal Trade Commission)

on credit repair companies, 45

on credit report errors, 47

on debt settlement services, 106

discussion, 413

FDCPA and, 91

filing complains with, 91

information on fraud alerts, 170

National Do Not Call Registry, 160

report on insurance scores, 209

reporting complaints to, 371

reporting identity theft to, 19, 168

G

gambling, 268, 340

garnishments. *See* wage garnishments

GI Bill, 423

goals

credit score, 291–292

good debt and, 38–39

long-term, 22–23

reevaluating, 11

for retirement, 241, 349–351

sample spreadsheet for, 332

short-term, 22–23

spending plan

adjustments, 354

categorizing, 333–334

intermediate, 333

long-term, 333

overview, 331–332

planning, 314–316, 332–333

prioritizing, 334

savings account, 312–313

short-term, 333

Step 1: income, 335–336

Step 2: expenses, 336–341

Step 3: savings, 341–345

Step 4: credit and loans, 345–346

Step 5: insurance, 346–347

Step 6: tax withholdings, 348–349

Step 7: retirement, 349–351

tools, 351–353

good credit

borrowing and, 179

establishing, 10, 30–31, 221

maintaining, 20–21, 221

negative events and, 123

rewards of, 1–2, 30, 44–45

spending plan and, 40–42, 329–330

good debt, 38–39

good-enough credit, 30

grace period, 125, 140, 370

graduated repayment plan, 140

green card, 178

green credit, 25, 317–318

GSE-backed mortgages, 408

H

HAMP (Home Affordable Modification Program), 429–430

harassment

  from collections, 78, 81, 91–92

  prohibited by FDCPA, 375–377

hard inquiries, 274

hardship program

  negotiating for, 66, 229

  payback arrangements and, 87

  sample letter requesting, 95

  student loans and, 418, 420

Health Education Assistance Loan (HEAL), 418

Health Education loans, 117

health insurance, 138

Health Profession loans, 117

Health Resources and Services Administration, 237

Healthcare Advocates, Inc., 231

Healthcare Bluebook, 137

high-interest loans, 21

Hill-Burton Act, 237

Hispanics, 357, 362–364, 366

Home Affordable Modification Program (HAMP), 429–430

home buying, 1, 10, 34–36

home rentals. *See* renting

home-equity credit lines, 34–35

home-equity loans, 34–36

homeowners insurance, 346

homeownership, 322, 364–366, 408

homeownership retention department. *See* loss mitigation department

homestead exemption, 148

hospitals, 32

HUD (Department of Housing and Urban Development), 68, 126, 128, 365

HUD Foreclosure Avoidance Counseling, 430

HUD-approved counseling agencies, 12

HUD-certified mortgage counselors, 12–13, 67, 128, 432. *See also* BALANCE counseling agency

Hungelmann, Jack, 346

I

IBR (Income-Based Repayment), 423–424

IC3 (Internet Crime Complaint Center), 391

ICR (Income Contingent Repayment) plan, 117

identity theft

  chip credit cards and, 173

  collections and, 166, 400

  credit bureau help with, 170

  discussion, 3, 19, 43, 165, 387–388

  FACTA and, 169–172, 398

  free credit report in cases of, 50, 263, 265

  laws aimed at, 17–18

  monitoring services, 18–19, 298

  new credit and, 191

  predicting, 398

  preventing

    blocking fraudulent trade lines, 170–172

    cancel credit cards, 167

    computer safety, 391–392

    credit freeze, 394–395

    credit rejection, 401

    initiating fraud alert, 52

    insurance, 299

    limiting credit access, 19

    mail fraud, 393

    missing statements, 401

    modernization, 388–389

    online safety, 242, 390–391

    overview, 19–20, 388

    passwords/PINS, 173, 390

    phishing attempts, 389–390

    during retirement, 240–241

    unauthorized charges, 400

  rebuilding credit after, 172–174, 327

  reporting, 399

  SCRA and, 397

  signs of, 397–399

  skip tracing and, 397

  specialty reporting agencies and, 270

  steps to take in, 165–169

Identity Theft Affidavit (Form 14039), 399

Identity Theft Hotline, 168

illness, 30, 67, 160

immigrants, 1, 16, 65, 355–356. *See also* financial inclusion; underbanked market

income, 40, 64, 282, 319–320. *See also* disposable earnings

Income Contingent Repayment (ICR) plan, 117

Income-Based Repayment (IBR), 423–424

individual insurance, 138, 234

in-house debt collection, 83, 90, 103

inquiries, 51, 58, 250, 274–275

installment account, 11

installment loans, 232, 345–346

insufficient funds check, 87

insurance
 bad credit and, 10
 claims and errors, 138–139, 235
 credit score and, 17
 effect of bankruptcy on, 152
 free credit reports and, 266
 good credit and, 179–180
 medical debt and, 233–236
 permissible purpose access and, 267
 specialty reporting agencies and, 268, 270

insurance companies
 access to medical information, 138
 credit non-reporting by, 32
 credit report use by, 1–2
 discussion, 32
 MIB, 138, 234

Insurance For Dummies (Hungelmann), 346

Insurance Information Exchange, 270

insurance scores, 208–211

interest rate
 collections and, 80
 credit report inaccuracies and, 262
 payback arrangements and, 86
 paying down balances based on, 31–32
 reductions and caps in, 88

interest-rate-reduction plan. *See* debt management plan

Internal Revenue Service. *See* IRS

Internet Crime Complaint Center (IC3), 391

IRS (Internal Revenue Service)
 contact from, 397

 debt with, 101, 114–115
 Form 982 (Reduction of Tax Attributed Due to Discharge of Indebtedness), 135
 Form 1099-A, 135
 Form 1099-C, 134
 Form 9465, 114
 Form 14039 (Identity Theft Affidavit), 399
 Form W-4, 100
 identity theft warning from, 397, 399
 permissible purpose access and, 267
 spending guidelines, 156
 Withholding Estimator, 100

J

Jews, 366

job opportunities
 bad credit and, 200–201
 credit report and, 44–45, 265
 with delinquent student loans, 117
 disputed inaccuracies and, 57
 effect of bankruptcy on, 152
 good credit and, 179

job promotion, 3, 10, 180, 265, 268

joint credit
 after spouse/partner death, 238–239
 closing, 221–222
 on credit report, 249
 help from counselors for, 69
 during marriage, 216–218
 negative information from, 222

joint debt, 218–219, 222–223, 239

judgment execution, 109–111

judgments, 101–102, 107–109

judicial foreclosure, 427–428

K

"kicking the trade" scam, 143, 207

L

landlords, 1–2, 32, 39. *See also* renting

late fees, 86

late payments
    CARD Act and, 99
    in credit report, 49, 322
    discussion, 30, 63, 322
    timeframe for deletion of, 57, 275
Latinos, 357, 362–364, 366
leasing, 36, 88–89
Legal Aid, 147
Legal Service Corporation (LSC), 74–75
legislation, 16–18, 46, 50. *See also* consumer
    protections; *specific laws*
lenders. *See also* creditors
    credit reports and, 1–2
    discrimination by, 16
    discussion, 47, 286
    non-reporting, 32
    that ignore judgments, 110
letters. *See also* sample letters
    for apartment rental, 203
LexisNexis, 60, 269–270
LexisNexis Attract insurance score, 210
LexisNexis Resident History, 271
LexisNexis Risk Solutions, 188
library cards, 225
liens, 109, 114
life expectancy, 350
life insurance, 138, 234, 346. *See also* installment
    loans
liquidation. *See* Chapter 7 bankruptcy
litigation, 52–53
loans
    bad credit and, 10
    credit report and, 23
    forgiveness of, 140–141
    modification of, 130
    mortgages compared to other types of, 124
    to reduce debt payments, 64
    repayment terms, 12–13
    three Cs of, 23
    vehicle title, 89
    wage garnishments and debt from, 111
local finance companies, 32
local taxes. *See* taxes
long-term goals, 22–23, 333

loss mitigation counseling, 128
loss mitigation department, 126–127
low-interest-rate loans, 34–36
LSC (Legal Service Corporation), 74–75

M

Making Home Affordable Program, 68
marriage
    budgeting during, 216, 354
    discussion, 213–214
    discussions prior to, 214–216
    free credit reports and, 266
    future goals and, 214–216
    joint credit in, 216–218
    joint debt in, 218–219
    money conflicts in, 219–220
    separate accounts in, 217
means test, 17, 148, 156
Medicaid, 232
medical bankruptcy, 146, 233
medical claims, 268
medical collections, 91
medical debt
    180-day waiting period and, 137
    bad credit due to, 15
    claims inaccuracies in, 138–139
    discussion, 136, 229–230
    FACTA and, 232
    insurance and, 139, 233–236
    options for paying
        credit cards, 232
        financial aid, 230–231
        installment loans, 232
        negotiating debt down, 232
        overview, 137–138, 230
        professional help, 231
        settling, 234
    timeframe for deletion of, 137
    undischargeable, 237
medical history, 1–2, 282
MIB (Medical Information Bureau), 138, 234,
    269–270
Military OneSource program, 198

military personnel
  credit score and, 17
  discussion, 36
  free credit reports and, 266
  new credit for, 195, 197–198
  protections for
    active-duty alerts, 53, 305, 396
    1-year alert, 170
    overview, 88–89
    SCRA, 397
  student loans and, 423–424
Milliman, 234, 270
minorities
  debt management for, 362–364
  financial inclusion of, 355–357
  homeownership by, 364–366
  lack of access to credit by, 1, 16
  marginalization of, 355–356
  redlining and, 366
misconceptions, 16, 178–179, 361
mobile wallets, 173, 298–299
Money Management International, 353
mortgage. *See also* foreclosure
  boosting credit with, 34–36
  compared to other loans, 124
  credit score and, 2
  defaulting on, 69
  delinquencies on, 14, 66–67
  discussion, 13–14, 322
  foreclosure of, 124–125
  qualifying for, 203–205, 265
  during unemployment, 228
Mortgage Forgiveness Debt Relief Act of 2007, 36,
    130–131, 133–134
mortgage problems. *See also* foreclosure
  bad credit due to, 13–15
  discussion, 65, 121–122, 425
  help with
    avoiding scams, 432
    BALANCE counseling agency, 68,
      126–127, 129
    CARES Act, 130–131
    first steps, 129
    forbearance, 129

    free sources, 68–69, 126–128
    HUD-certified counselors, 432
    loan modification, 130
    Mortgage Forgiveness Debt Relief Act,
      130–131
    mortgage servicers, 126–127
    overview, 126
    repayment plan, 129–130
    seeking help, 14
    self-help, 14–15, 66–67
    things to avoid, 127–128
  recognizing degrees of, 426
  reducing damage from, 431–433
  solutions to
    attorney consultation, 150, 433–434
    deed-in-lieu of foreclosure, 131, 429
    FHA Short Refinance, 429
    HAMP, 429–430
    HUD Counseling, 430
    HUD-certified counselors, 13
    pre-foreclosure sale, 131
    short sale, 130–131, 429
    special relief programs, 430
    spending plan, 430–431
    strategic mortgage default, 15, 131, 428
Mortgage Release and Standard Deed-in-Lieu of
    Foreclosure programs., 429
myths. *See* misconceptions

N

National Consumer Telecom and Utilities Exchange
    (NCTUE), 60, 150, 187–188, 271
National Credit Union Administration (NCUA), 178
National Defense Authorization Act for Fiscal Year
    2007, 88
National Do Not Call Registry, 160
National Foundation for Credit Counseling.
    See NFCC
natural disasters, 144, 260, 430
Navy and Marine Corps Relief Society, 381
NCTUE (National Consumer Telecom and Utilities
    Exchange), 60, 150, 187–188, 271
NCUA (National Credit Union Administration), 178
negative information, 49, 57–59

negative reason factor, 293
new credit
  after divorce, 224–225
  after spousal/partner death, 240
  for building credit, 163
  credit score and, 28, 61, 258–259
  establishing
    credit cards, 192–194
    FICO Score XD, 60, 91, 187–188
    foreign credit cards, 187
    immigrants, 65
    overview, 4, 33, 181–182
    passbook loans, 188
    prepaid/reloadable cards, 186–187
    savings account, 185–186, 194
    secured credit card, 188, 194
    setting goals, 183–184
    without social security number, 182–183
  handling mistakes with, 190–191
  identity protection and, 191
  inquiries and, 28
  for military members, 195, 197–198
  for students, 195–197
  things to avoid with
    high-fee check cashing, 190
    instant credit rating, 190
    payday loans, 189
    RALs, 189–190
    scams, 190
NFCC (National Foundation for Credit Counseling)
  discussion, 72, 198, 378
  help
    bankruptcy, 147
    mortgage problems, 126
    spending plan, 353
    student loans, 141
90-day fraud alert, 170
995Hope organization, 68, 126–127
noninstallment credit, 345
nonjudicial foreclosure, 428
nonprofit credit counselors
  bankruptcy help from, 147–148
  collections help from, 96–97

debt management plans from, 72–74
  discussion, 12, 67, 69
  financial assessment from, 129
  help avoiding car repossession, 142
  Military OneSource program, 198
  mortgage help from, 126
  searching for, 71–72
  situations warranting help from,
    69–71
  spending plan and, 163, 431
nonrecourse loans, 132–133, 427. *See also* strategic
    mortgage default
notes, 134–135

O

OCC (Office of the Comptroller of Currency), 360
Office of Federal Student Aid, 139–140
old accounts, 31
1-year military active-duty alert, 170
100-word statements
  after divorce, 224
  in credit report, 250, 272
  discussion, 52, 54, 57, 61
  Experian policies regarding, 62
  making sure to delete, 281
  sample, 62
  TransUnion policies regarding, 62
open accounts, 57, 275
open-end credit. *See* revolving account
Operation HOPE, 129, 353, 378, 431
original delinquency date, 105, 253

P

paid charge-offs, 104
pandemics, 144, 260, 430
partnering. *See* marriage
passbook loans, 11, 188, 225, 327
passphrase, 173–174
passwords, 173, 390–392
payback arrangements
  documentation of, 82, 88, 96
  negotiating, 86–88

payday lenders
  consumer protections and, 379–382
  discussion, 21, 189, 380
  minorities and, 363–364
  specialty agencies and, 270
payment history, 25, 28. *See also* late payments
payments. *See also* late payments
  credit repair and, 10–12
  defaulting on, 25, 28
  making timely, 31, 34, 358
  SOL and recent, 85
payroll deductions, 100
perfect credit, 30, 290
Perkins loans, 117, 418, 420
permissible purpose, 266–267, 374
personal debt repayment plan, 45
phishing, 389–390
PINS, 173, 391
PLUS loans, 117, 418, 423
police reports, 168–169, 263
postdated checks, 79, 87
preapproved credit offers, 239, 274
pre-foreclosure sale, 131
prepaid cards, 186–187
prescreened offer lists, 52
prescription drug databases, 1–2, 234, 268, 270
priority debts, 149. *See also* alimony; child support
pro bono attorneys
  consulting SOL with, 85–86
  discussion, 12–13, 68
  legal/document review from, 69
  searching for, 74–75
pro se representation, 147, 406
professional licenses
  bankruptcy and, 152
  credit report and, 44–45
  credit score and, 17
  free credit reports and, 265
  permissible purpose and, 267
promise to pay, 86
property data, 60
public record, 23, 60, 249
Public Service Loan Forgiveness (PSLF), 423–424

Q

QPRI (Qualified Principal Residence Indebtedness) exemption, 135

R

racism. *See* discrimination; financial inclusion
RALs (refund anticipation loans), 21, 189–190
rapid rescore, 50
reaffirmation, 161
reason statements, 259–260, 288, 292–293. *See also* risk factors
Reconstruction Finance Corporation (RFC), 366
record-keeping. *See* documentation
recourse loans, 427
redlining, 366
Reduction of Tax Attributed Due to Discharge of Indebtedness (Form 982), 135
refund anticipation loans (RALs), 21, 189–190
reinvestigation, 57, 373–374
reloadable cards, 186–187
rental history
  in credit report, 17, 250–251, 265
  discussion, 39, 44–45
  permissible purpose access and, 266
  positive information from, 292
  specialty agencies and, 201–202, 268, 271
renting
  bad credit and, 10, 201–203
  bankruptcy and, 152
  CARES Act and, 408
  cosigning and, 203
  eviction and, 88
  good credit and, 179–180
  house, 271, 292
  recommendation letters and, 203
repayment plan, 129–130
repossession
  of automobile, 141–144
  collections, 80
  dishonored judgments, 109
  effects on credit score, 37
  help for, 69–70

retail store cards, 31, 48, 225, 327

retirement

  credit during, 240–242

  planning for, 100, 349–351

revolving account, 11, 249, 346

revolving utilization rate, 281

RFC (Reconstruction Finance Corporation), 366

risk factors. *See also* reason statements

  credit score and, 292–293

  discussion, 28, 47–48, 251

  from lender, 286

risk-based pricing, 290

risk-factor code. *See* reason statements

S

sample letters

  for charge dispute, 166

  for credit bureau opt-out, 160

  for debt settlement agreement, 106

  discussion, 4

  for due date change request, 100

  for partial payment request, 95

  for payment agreement, 82

  for reporting identity theft, 166

  for reporting unemployment, 229

  to stop calls to place of employment, 79

savings account

  for building credit, 162, 224

  in credit report, 60

  discussion, 40, 100, 358

  for establishing new credit, 20, 185–186, 194

  low-interest-rate loans and, 24

  in spending plan

    direct deposit, 342

    emergency fund, 344–345

    goals, 343–344

    overview, 312–313, 341–342

    piggy bank, 342–343

scams

  discussion, 190

  Internet, 241

  "kicking the trade," 143, 207

  mortgage, 432

  phishing, 389–390

Schell, Jim, 179

SCRA (Servicemembers Civil Relief Act), 36, 88, 195, 197, 397

second mortgages, 35, 128

secured credit card

  for building credit, 162, 188, 327, 358

  discussion, 11, 33

  for establishing new credit, 194

secured installment loans, 33

security clearances, 17, 44–45, 265

segregation. *See* discrimination; redlining

Servicemembers Civil Relief Act (SCRA), 36, 88, 195, 197, 397

7-year extended fraud alert, 170

short sale, 15, 123, 429

short-term goals, 22, 333

short-term loans, 21

short-term waiver, 67

skip tracing, 267, 397

Small Business For Dummies, 4th Edition (Tyson, Schell), 179

social security number

  bankruptcy and, 174

  building credit without, 179, 182–183

  changing, 174

  in credit report, 48–49, 272

  IRS alerts regarding, 397, 399

  protecting, 19, 171

soft inquiries, 51, 250, 274

SOL (statutes of limitations). *See* statutes of limitations

Soldiers' and Sailors' Civil Relief Act. *See* Servicemembers Civil Relief Act

special forbearance plan, 129

specialty reporting agencies

  discussion, 262, 268–269

  free reports from, 269

  listing of, 269–271

  rental history and, 201–202

spending plan. *See also* budgeting; goals; nonprofit credit counselors

  adjustments to, 354

  after bankruptcy, 163

  to avoid car repossession, 141–142

  balance in, 312–313

  benefits of, 40, 330–331

for charge-off payments, 104
components of, 40–42
discussion, 3, 11, 22, 329–330
for mortgage problems, 430
for paying collections, 97–98
professional counseling and, 353
during retirement, 241, 349–351
role in good credit, 329–330
sample outline of, 104
smartphone apps, 353
tools, 351–353
websites, 352–353
SSCRA. *See* Servicemembers Civil Relief Act
Stafford loans, 117, 418
state attorney general, 85, 409–410
state housing authorities, 68–69
state laws
  on foreclosure, 427–428
  on free credit reports, 42, 50, 263
state taxes. *See* taxes
statements of dispute, 281
statutes of limitations (SOL)
  consumer protections and, 384–385
  discussion, 409
  expired debts and, 84–85, 106–107
stolen identity. *See* identity theft
store cards. *See* retail store cards
strategic mortgage default
  consequences of, 132–133, 428
  considerations in, 133–134
  discussion, 15, 428
structured payment plan. *See* special
    forbearance plan
student loans
  bad credit due to, 15
  calculator for, 37
  CARES Act and, 408
  consolidating, 117
  credit score and, 2
  defaulting on, 38, 418–419
  delinquencies on, 58, 117
  discussion, 16, 101–102, 321–322
  extended repayment on, 117
  good credit and, 180

  help with, 140–141
  high-risk nature of, 116
  income-based repayment of, 117
  managing
    absolutions, 419–420
    collections, 416–417
    COVID-19 pandemic, 419
    default timelines, 140
    grace periods, 140, 418–419
    graduated repayment plan, 140
    hardship program, 418, 420
    loan forgiveness programs, 140
    military personnel, 423–424
    overview, 139–140, 415
    payment options, 421
    repayment plans, 417, 422
    self-help, 67
  minorities and, 363
  not dischargeable, 115, 149, 151, 323, 418
  paying off, 37–38
  payment deferrals on, 115–116
  planning before taking out, 423
  repayment options, 116
  reporting of, 416
  serializing, 117
  wage garnishments and, 38
sub-prime lenders, 360
summary plan description, 235
supplementary credit report, 270

T

TASC (Association of Settlement Companies), 106
taxes
  CCPA not applicable to, 111–112
  on debt settlement agreements, 105
  liens on returns from, 115
  not dischargeable by bankruptcy, 151, 324
  overdue, 42
  property, 271
  RALs and returns from, 21
  withholdings from, 348–349
Teacher Loan Forgiveness, 420
telecommunications payment, 250–251

tenant screening report, 266

term life insurance, 346

thin file, 60, 187, 274

third-party credit monitoring services. *See* credit monitoring

third-party debt collection, 83, 90, 103

third-party intermediary, 126, 231

threats

  from collectors, 13, 81, 190–191

  prohibited by FDCPA, 375–377

time barred debt. *See* statutes of limitations

tithing, 156

trade lines, 48, 170, 249

transcripts, 38, 115

TransUnion

  account history, 279–280

  credit score from, 286

  credit score simulators, 122

  discussion, 24, 247

  disputing inaccuracies with, 54–55

  FACTA and, 372–374

  free credit report from, 18, 262, 264

  180-day reporting period, 137

  reporting identity theft to, 167

  sample credit report, 280

trended data, 260

truth in lending laws, 132, 180

two-factor authentication (2FA), 390

Tyson, Eric, 179

U

Ultra-FICO score, 60, 181, 194, 292, 433

uncollectible debts, 84–86. *See also* statutes of limitations

underbanked market

  discussion, 177–178, 187

  Federal Reserve estimates on, 182

  financial inclusion of, 355–357

underwriting, 205

undischargeable debt. *See* child support; priority debts; student loans

unemployment

  bankruptcy and, 160

  budgeting during, 227–229

  credit counseling during, 226–228

  discussion, 213–214, 226

  free credit reports during, 263

  hardship program during, 229

  letter to creditor, 229

  preparing for possible, 226

  protecting credit during, 228

  strategic mortgage default and, 133

universal default, 369

unpaid charge-offs, 103

upside-down loans, 35–37

U.S. Census website, 156, 365

utility payments, 32, 250–251, 271

utilization rate, 28, 257–258, 281, 362

V

VantageScore

  credit scores

    credit access, 189

    history, 255–256

    overview, 10, 24, 285–286

    score range, 28, 258, 290

  reason statements, 293

vehicle title loans, 89

victim's statement, 167, 168, 263

virtual account numbers, 298–299

voluntary repossession, 142–143

W

wage garnishments

  avoiding, 110–111

  calculations for, 112

  causes of, 38, 109, 115

  CCPA and, 110–111

  court-ordered, 114

  discussion, 80, 101–102

  limits on, 111

  resulting from judgments, 107

wage-earner bankruptcy. *See* Chapter 13 bankruptcy

welfare, 263

William D. Ford Federal Direct Loan, 140

working poor, 1, 16, 366

workout department. *See* loss mitigation department

workout plan. *See* debt management plan

About the Authors

Melyssa Barrett: Melyssa is vice president in data, security, and identity products at Visa, Inc. Her responsibilities include the development and management of identity products detecting and mitigating fraud to reduce identity theft, synthetic identity, and account takeover. Her focus includes product excellence across the life cycle within account origination, authentication, and authorization to meet and maintain appropriate privacy, regulatory, and governance requirements while mitigating applicable risk. In her roles, she has developed and managed bankruptcy, business intelligence, and predictive products while optimizing solution delivery for clients. Melyssa is also the CEO of Advanced Resolution Services, Inc., a subsidiary of Visa, Inc., and a consumer reporting agency. Prior to joining Visa, Melyssa held several positions at Citibank and worked in retail banking at Wells Fargo.

She currently serves on the board of directors for BALANCE and several other local community nonprofit organizations that provide services and advocacy to youth and families. She has served on the board of directors for the American Bankruptcy Institute and the advisory board for the National Foundation for Credit Counseling.

Melyssa holds a bachelor of science degree from University of Phoenix. She lives just outside the San Francisco Bay Area in Tracy, California, where she raised her three children and enjoys spending time with her six grandchildren.

Steve Bucci: Steve has been helping people decode and master personal credit and debt issues for the last 20 years. For more than a decade, he has authored a popular weekly personal finance column for the financial mega-site Bankrate (www.bankrate.com). He also writes a weekly column on credit scoring that appears on CreditCards.com (www.creditcards.com). Steve is also a personal credit coach, speaker, and expert witness.

Steve was formerly president of the Money Management International Financial Education Foundation and the president of the Consumer Credit Counseling Service of Southern New England. He founded the Consumer Credit Counseling Service of Rhode Island and the University of Rhode Island Center for Personal Financial Education.

Steve began his career in counseling at the Yale Psychiatric Institute before switching to business careers in management consulting and then finance, developing and bringing to market both publicly and privately traded investment products. Steve returned to his first love, helping individuals, in 1991, this time using his financial and management experience to launch Rhode Island's first private, nonprofit financial counseling agency.

Steve has served as director of the CDNE Education Foundation, the University of Rhode Island Center for Personal Financial Education, the National Foundation for Credit Counseling, the Better Business Bureau of Rhode Island, and the Investment Commission for the Episcopal Diocese of Rhode Island. He is currently a member of the investment board at South County Health Care Systems. He was named Visiting Executive in Residence at the University of Rhode Island in 2005. Steve received his BA and MA degrees from the University of Rhode Island at Kingston. He and his wife, Barbara, live with their two cats, Peanut Butter and Smokey, at Sand Hill Cove in the seaside community of Narragansett, Rhode Island.

Rod Griffin: Rod is Senior Director of Consumer Education and Advocacy for Experian, where he manages the national consumer education and advocacy program in North America. With more than 20 years of experience in the credit reporting and information services industry, he is an expert on consumer issues, particularly credit reporting, credit scoring, and identity theft. He frequently appears on national television, in print, on radio, in online media, and presents regularly at regional and national financial literacy events.

In his role, Rod supports national financial literacy and financial inclusion partnerships and conducts training programs for clients, Experian employees, and consumer organizations across the United States.

He currently serves on the JumpStart Coalition for Financial Literacy board of directors and is a member of the Business Insider Money Council and the America Saves Week Advisory Committee. Rod previously served as chairman of the National Consumers League–LifeSmarts Corporate Advisory Board. Rod was named 2016 Educator of the Year by the Institute for Financial Literacy.

Prior to joining Experian, Rod was a community newspaper reporter and editor and worked in municipal government communications. He is a graduate of the University of Kansas and has a Fair Credit Reporting Act certification from the Consumer Data Industry Association.

Rod and his wife, Phyllis, live with their two dogs, Bella and Bear, in the Dallas, Texas, area.

Dedication

This book is dedicated to all the good people out there who have bad credit and are committed to improving their credit and their lives.

Authors' Acknowledgments

We want to thank John Wiley & Sons for allowing us to update this book — not only because so much has changed in the world of credit, but also because it represents a vindication of the holistic approach to credit that we have been espousing for the last two decades. Credit can only be repaired from the bottom up, not the top down. That is to say, you can only build and maintain excellent credit by beginning with a strong foundation and then adding on more layers in stages. This method relies on addressing the root causes of your credit problems as a way of building a sound financial base, improved credit, and a better life for you and your family. The two are inseparable!

No successful person works alone. That's why this edition has three authors from different aspects of the credit industry. We sincerely hope that the information contained in this book will make a difference for all who buy it.

Publisher's Acknowledgments

Senior Editorial Assistant: Elizabeth Stilwell

Project Editor: Elizabeth Kuball

Copy Editor: Elizabeth Kuball

Technical Editor: Michael Staten, PhD

Production Editor: Siddique Shaik

Cover Photos: © Song_about_summer/ Shutterstock

Take dummies with you everywhere you go!

Whether you are excited about e-books, want more from the web, must have your mobile apps, or are swept up in social media, dummies makes everything easier.

Find us online!

Leverage the power

Dummies is the global leader in the reference category and one of the most trusted and highly regarded brands in the world. No longer just focused on books, customers now have access to the dummies content they need in the format they want. Together we'll craft a solution that engages your customers, stands out from the competition, and helps you meet your goals.

Advertising & Sponsorships

Connect with an engaged audience on a powerful multimedia site, and position your message alongside expert how-to content. Dummies.com is a one-stop shop for free, online information and know-how curated by a team of experts.

- Targeted ads
- Video
- Email Marketing
- Microsites
- Sweepstakes sponsorship

20 MILLION PAGE VIEWS EVERY SINGLE MONTH

15 MILLION UNIQUE VISITORS PER MONTH

43% OF ALL VISITORS ACCESS THE SITE VIA THEIR MOBILE DEVICES

700,000 NEWSLETTER SUBSCRIPTIONS TO THE INBOXES OF *300,000* UNIQUE INDIVIDUALS EVERY WEEK

PERSONAL ENRICHMENT

Staying Sharp

9781119187790
USA $26.00
CAN $31.99
UK £19.99

Facebook

9781119179030
USA $21.99
CAN $25.99
UK £16.99

Guitar

9781119293354
USA $24.99
CAN $29.99
UK £17.99

Investing

9781119293347
USA $22.99
CAN $27.99
UK £16.99

Beekeeping

9781119310068
USA $22.99
CAN $27.99
UK £16.99

Digital Photography

9781119235606
USA $24.99
CAN $29.99
UK £17.99

Meditation

9781119251163
USA $24.99
CAN $29.99
UK £17.99

Pregnancy

9781119235491
USA $26.99
CAN $31.99
UK £19.99

Samsung Galaxy S7

9781119279952
USA $24.99
CAN $29.99
UK £17.99

iPhone

9781119283133
USA $24.99
CAN $29.99
UK £17.99

Crocheting

9781119287117
USA $24.99
CAN $29.99
UK £16.99

Nutrition

9781119130246
USA $22.99
CAN $27.99
UK £16.99

PROFESSIONAL DEVELOPMENT

Windows 10

9781119311041
USA $24.99
CAN $29.99
UK £17.99

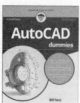

AutoCAD

9781119255796
USA $39.99
CAN $47.99
UK £27.99

Excel 2016

9781119293439
USA $26.99
CAN $31.99
UK £19.99

QuickBooks 2017

9781119281467
USA $26.99
CAN $31.99
UK £19.99

macOS Sierra

9781119280651
USA $29.99
CAN $35.99
UK £21.99

LinkedIn

9781119251132
USA $24.99
CAN $29.99
UK £17.99

Windows 10

9781119310563
USA $34.00
CAN $41.99
UK £24.99

SharePoint 2016

9781119181705
USA $29.99
CAN $35.99
UK £21.99

Fundamental Analysis

9781119263593
USA $26.99
CAN $31.99
UK £19.99

Networking

9781119257769
USA $29.99
CAN $35.99
UK £21.99

Office 2016

9781119293477
USA $26.99
CAN $31.99
UK £19.99

Office 365

9781119265313
USA $24.99
CAN $29.99
UK £17.99

Salesforce.com

9781119239314
USA $29.99
CAN $35.99
UK £21.99

Coding

9781119293323
USA $29.99
CAN $35.99
UK £21.99

dummies.com

dummies®
A Wiley Brand